Psychopathology

Fourth Edition

To those with the courage to share their experience of mental illness and the willingness to help others lead a meaningful life

Sara Miller McCune founded SAGE Publishing in 1965 to support the dissemination of usable knowledge and educate a global community. SAGE publishes more than 1,000 journals and over 600 new books each year, spanning a wide range of subject areas. Our growing selection of library products includes archives, data, case studies, and video. SAGE remains majority owned by our founder and after her lifetime will become owned by a charitable trust that secures the company's continued independence.

Los Angeles | London | New Delhi | Singapore | Washington DC | Melbourne

Psychopathology

Fourth Edition

William J. Ray

Pennsylvania State University

FOR INFORMATION:

2455 Teller Road
Thousand Oaks, California 91320
E-mail: order@sagepub.com

1 Oliver's Yard
55 City Road
London, EC1Y 1SP
United Kingdom

Unit No 323-333, Third Floor, F-Block
International Trade Tower
Nehru Place, New Delhi—110 019
India

18 Cross Street #10-10/11/12
China Square Central
Singapore 048423

Acquisitions Editor: Mary Dudley
Content Development Editor: Sam Held
Project Editor: Veronica Stapleton Hooper
Copy Editor: Colleen Brennan
Typesetter: diacriTech
Cover Designer: Gail Buschman
Marketing Manager: Victoria Velasquez

Copyright © 2025 by Sage.

All rights reserved. Except as permitted by U.S. copyright law, no part of this work may be reproduced or distributed in any form or by any means, or stored in a database or retrieval system, without permission in writing from the publisher.

All third party trademarks referenced or depicted herein are included solely for the purpose of illustration and are the property of their respective owners. Reference to these trademarks in no way indicates any relationship with, or endorsement by, the trademark owner.

Printed in the United States of America

Library of Congress Control Number: 2023920975

Paperback ISBN: 978-1-0718-8636-6

Loose-Leaf ISBN: 978-1-0719-2847-9

This book is printed on acid-free paper.

24 25 26 27 28 10 9 8 7 6 5 4 3 2 1

BRIEF CONTENTS

Preface		xix
Acknowledgments		xxix
About the Author		xxxi
Chapter 1	An Overview of Psychopathology and Changing Conceptualizations of Mental Illness	1
Chapter 2	Neuroscience Approaches to Understanding Psychopathology	45
Chapter 3	Research Methods	93
Chapter 4	Assessment and Classification of Psychological Disorders	133
Chapter 5	Childhood and Adolescent-Onset Disorders	163
Chapter 6	Mood Disorders	211
Chapter 7	Stress, Trauma, and PTSD	261
Chapter 8	Anxiety Disorders and Obsessive-Compulsive Disorders	299
Chapter 9	Dissociative Disorders and Somatic Symptom Disorders	339
Chapter 10	Eating Disorders	367
Chapter 11	Sexual Disorders, Paraphilic Disorders, and Gender Dysphoria	401
Chapter 12	Substance-Related and Addictive Disorders	443
Chapter 13	Schizophrenia	501
Chapter 14	Personality Disorders	545
Chapter 15	Neurocognitive Disorders	589
Chapter 16	The Law and Mental Health	627
Glossary		653
References		665
Author Index		721
Subject Index		749

DETAILED CONTENTS

Preface	xix
Acknowledgments	xxix
About the Author	xxxi

Chapter 1 An Overview of Psychopathology and Changing Conceptualizations of Mental Illness — 1

- Understanding Psychopathology: Definitions and Key Considerations — 3
  - Defining Psychopathology and Understanding Its Components — 3
  - Impact of Mental Disorders — 4
  - Stigma and Mental Disorders — 5
- The Three Major Themes of This Book — 7
  - Levels of Analysis — 8
  - Biopsychosocial Approach — 9
- The Relation of Evolution and Culture to Psychopathology — 10
  - Is Psychopathology Universal? — 14
- Historical Considerations in Understanding Psychopathology — 15
  - Ancient Greek and Roman Influences—Mental Illness Involves the Brain — 15
  - Psychopathology in the Middle Ages — 16
  - From the Renaissance to the 1700s—The Beginning of Modern Science — 16
- Discovering the Function of the Brain in Behavior and Psychopathology — 19
  - The 1700s to the 1900s — 20
  - A Growing Understanding of the Role of Evolution — 24
  - A Search for Organization — 25
- Historical Approaches to Care for Those With Mental Disorders — 26
  - From the Past to the Present — 30
- Biological Approaches to Treating Mental Illness — 31
- Psychological Treatment Perspectives in the 20th and 21st Centuries — 32
  - Psychodynamic Perspectives on Treatment — 33
    - Sigmund Freud — 33
  - Existential-Humanistic Perspectives — 34
  - Behavioral and Cognitive Behavioral Perspectives — 36
- Summary — 40
- Study Resources — 42
- Key Terms — 43

Chapter 2 Neuroscience Approaches to Understanding Psychopathology — 45

- The Growing Importance of Neuroscience, Genetics, and an Evolutionary Perspective — 47
- Brain Anatomy, Neurons, and Neurotransmitters — 49
  - A Quick Review of Brain Anatomy and Function — 49
  - Neurons and Neural Transmission — 51
    - How Does the Neuron Pass Information? — 52
    - Major Neurotransmitters — 53
    - Encoding Information — 53
  - The Brain and the Microbiome — 54

How Do We Observe the Brain at Work?	57
Electroencephalography	57
Evoked Potentials	60
Magnetoencephalography	61
Positron Emission Tomography	62
Functional Magnetic Resonance Imaging	63
Diffusion Tensor Imaging	64
Spatial and Temporal Resolution	66
Neuroethics	70
Networks of the Brain	71
Neurons Connect in a Network	71
What Is the Brain's Default (Intrinsic) Network?	73
Different Networks Are Involved in Different Tasks	73
Genetics and Psychopathology	75
The Historical Study of Genetics	75
What Do Genes Do?	76
DNA	77
How Do Genes Influence Behavior?	78
Epigenetic Processes	79
Mitochondria and Mitochondrial Inheritance	81
What Are Endophenotypes?	81
Current Thinking on Genetics and Psychopathology	82
Evolution and Psychopathology	85
The Themes of Evolution	85
Psychopathology From an Evolutionary Perspective	86
Summary	89
Study Resources	90
Key Terms	91

Chapter 3   Research Methods   93

What Is Science?	94
Nonexperimental Methods of Psychological Research	96
Case Study	96
Naturalistic Observation: Just Looking	98
Correlational Approach: What Goes With What?	100
The Experimental Method: Making It Happen	103
Definitions in the Experimental Method	103
Research Methods in Action: Does Playing Music Change the Brain?	104
Logic and Inference: The Detective Work of Science	106
Validity	106
What Do I Expect to Happen?	107
Designing an Experimental Study	108
Participants in the Study	109
Putting Participants in Groups	109
Designing and Structuring the Experimental Study	110
Is the Dependent Variable Related to the Independent Variable?	111
Null Hypothesis and Inferential Statistics	112
Confound Hypothesis	113
Research Hypothesis	113
Other Types of Experimental Designs and Research Considerations	116
Single-Subject Designs	117
Longitudinal Research	117

Epidemiological Research	119
Research Involving Genetics	120
Behavioral Genetics	121
Clinical and Statistical Significance	122
Replication and Meta-Analysis	123
Ethics and the Scientific Experiment	125
The Experiment as an Ethical Problem	126
Ingredients of the Initial Scientist–Participant Dialogue	127
Voluntary Participation	127
Informed Consent	127
The Rights of the Research Participant and the Responsibilities of the Experimenter	128
What Is Harmful to a Research Participant?	128
The Institutional Review Board	129
The Ethical Relationship	129
Summary	130
Study Resources	131
Key Terms	132

Chapter 4 Assessment and Classification of Psychological Disorders — 133

Initial Assessment and the Mental Status Exam	135
The Clinical Interview	135
The Mental Status Exam	136
Structured Interviews and Assessment Considerations	136
Structured Clinical Interview for DSM Disorders	137
Assessing Cultural Dimensions	137
Reliability and Validity in Relation to Psychopathology	139
Reliability	140
Assessment Validity	141
Models of Assessment	141
Symptom Questionnaires	142
Personality Tests	142
Minnesota Multiphasic Personality Inventory (MMPI)	142
Projective Tests	144
Rorschach Inkblots	144
Thematic Apperception Test (TAT)	146
Neuropsychological Testing	147
Neuropsychological Tests and Mental Illness	149
Using Neuroscience Techniques to Identify Mental Illness	149
Diagnostic Considerations in Psychopathology	150
Categorical Versus Dimensional Approaches	150
Comorbidity and Hierarchical Approaches to Psychopathology	151
Utilizing Neuroscience Methods in Diagnosis and Treatment	152
Classification Systems for Mental Disorders	156
International Statistical Classification of Diseases and Related Health Problems	156
Diagnostic and Statistical Manual of Mental Disorders	157
Origins of the DSM	157
Early Versions of the DSM and the Eventual Focus on Diagnostic Criteria	157
DSM-5 and DSM-5-TR: The Current Version	158
Summary	160
Study Resources	161
Key Terms	162

Chapter 5   Childhood and Adolescent-Onset Disorders   163

- Important Aspects of Normal Childhood Development   166
  - Brain Development   167
  - Theories of Attachment   169
    - Harry Harlow's Experiments With Infant Monkeys   169
    - John Bowlby's Research on Attachment   170
    - Mary Ainsworth's Work and Styles of Attachment   171
    - Long-Term Consequences of Early Attachment Patterns   172
  - Imitation Learning   175
  - Theory of Mind   176
  - Adolescence   177
    - Social Brain in Adolescence   178
    - Risk Taking in Adolescence   178
  - Brain Systems Involved in Social Relations   180
- Attachment Disorders, Conduct Disorder, and Oppositional Defiant Disorder   181
  - Attachment Disorders   181
  - Conduct Disorder   182
  - Oppositional Defiant Disorder   183
  - Treatment for Conduct Disorder and Oppositional Defiant Disorder   183
- Autism Spectrum Disorder   186
  - Characteristics of Autism Spectrum Disorder   186
    - Autism as a Spectrum   186
    - Autism and Intelligence   188
    - Social and Behavioral Patterns in Autism   189
    - Autism and Development   190
    - Prevalence of Autism   191
  - Causes of Autism Spectrum Disorder   191
    - Environmental Contributions to Autism Spectrum Disorder   191
    - Genetic Contributions to Autism Spectrum Disorder   191
    - Brain Contributions to Autism Spectrum Disorder   192
  - Special Talents   193
  - Treatment for Autism Spectrum Disorder   194
- Attention Deficit/Hyperactivity Disorder and Learning Disorders   196
  - ADHD   196
    - Prevalence and Characteristics of ADHD   198
    - Causes of ADHD   200
    - Treatment for ADHD   201
  - Learning Disabilities   202
- Intellectual Developmental Disorder   203
  - Characteristics of Intellectual Developmental Disorder   203
  - Levels of Functioning   203
  - Causes of Intellectual Developmental Disorder   204
    - IDD Related to Chromosomes   204
    - IDD Related to Metabolism   205
    - IDD Related to Gestation   205
  - Treatment for Intellectual Developmental Disorder   205
- Summary   207
- Study Resources   209
- Key Terms   209

Chapter 6   Mood Disorders   211

- Introducing Mood Disorders   212
- Major Depressive Disorder   216

Characteristics of Major Depressive Disorder	216
Causes of Depression	220
Developmental Aspects of Depression	221
Cognitive Model of Depression	221
Are Depression and Inflammation Related?	222
Evidence That Depression Runs in Families	223
Evolutionary Perspectives on Depression	224
Resource Conservation	225
Social Competition	226
Social Risk Hypothesis	226
Treatments for Depression	227
Biological and Neuroscience Treatments for Depression	227
Psychological Treatments for Depression	230
Combination Therapies	234
Efforts to Prevent Depression	235
Bipolar Disorder	**236**
Characteristics of Bipolar Disorder	238
Diagnosis of Bipolar Disorder	239
Bipolar I Disorder	239
Bipolar II Disorder	243
Cyclothymic Disorder	243
Prevalence of Bipolar Disorder	244
Causes of Bipolar Disorder	244
Genetics of Bipolar Disorder	244
Bipolar Disorder and Creativity	245
Brain Imaging and Bipolar Disorder	245
Neurotransmitter Dysregulation	247
Environmental Factors	247
Treatment for Bipolar Disorder	247
Psychological Treatments for Bipolar Disorder	247
Medications for Bipolar Disorder	248
Suicide	**249**
Cultural and Gender Differences in Suicide	250
Suicide Underreporting and Methods Used in Suicide Attempts	252
Endophenotypes and Suicide	252
Long-Term and Short-Term Factors Related to Suicide	252
Suicide in the Military	254
Preventing Suicide	255
Summary	**257**
Study Resources	**259**
Key Terms	**260**

Chapter 7   Stress, Trauma, and PTSD   261

Psychological Stress and Psychopathology	264
Does Trauma Produce Mental Illness?	265
The Physiological Mechanisms Related to Stress and Trauma	265
What Makes You Run From Bears? Stress and the Hypothalamic–Pituitary–Adrenal Axis	266
The Autonomic Nervous System	268
Psychological Stress and the Immune System	270
Trauma Changes Our Genes Through Tagging (Epigenetics)	271
Is Social Pain Like Physical Pain?	273
The Study of Stress	274
Does Fight or Flight Apply Equally to Males and Females?	275
Does Social Stress Produce a Similar Reaction to Physical Stress?	277

Adjustment Disorders, Acute Stress Disorder, and Prolonged Grief Disorder	277
Adjustment Disorders	278
Acute Stress Disorder	278
Prolonged Grief Disorder	281
Post-Traumatic Stress Disorder	281
Causes, Characteristics, and Prevalence of PTSD	283
DSM-5-TR Criteria for PTSD	286
The Physiological Aspects of Post-Traumatic Stress Disorder	290
Treatment for Post-Traumatic Stress Disorder	292
Summary	296
Study Resources	297
Key Terms	298

Chapter 8 Anxiety Disorders and Obsessive-Compulsive Disorders   299

Overview of Anxiety Disorders	300
The Nature of Anxiety and Evolutionary Explanations	301
Cognitive Processes in Anxiety	304
Neurobiology of Anxiety Disorders	306
Developmental Aspects of Anxiety	306
Models of Anxiety Development	309
Anxiety Disorders Around the World	309
Major Types of Anxiety Disorders	312
Generalized Anxiety Disorder	312
Psychological Treatment for Generalized Anxiety Disorder	313
Biological Treatment for Generalized Anxiety Disorder	315
Social Anxiety Disorder	317
Neuroscience Aspects of Social Anxiety	319
Treatment for Social Anxiety Disorder	320
Separation Anxiety Disorder	320
Treatment for Separation Anxiety Disorder	321
Phobias and Panic Disorder	321
Specific Phobia	321
Neuroscience Aspects of Specific Phobias	324
Treatment for Specific Phobias	325
Panic Disorder	326
Neuroscience Aspects of Panic Disorder	327
Treatment for Panic Disorder	327
Agoraphobia	327
Obsessive-Compulsive Disorder	328
Characteristics, Prevalence, and Significant Aspects of OCD	329
Other DSM-5-TR Disorders Categorized With OCD	331
Neuroscience Aspects of OCD	333
Treatment for OCD	334
Summary	335
Study Resources	337
Key Terms	337

Chapter 9 Dissociative Disorders and Somatic Symptom Disorders   339

What Is Dissociation?	340
Dissociative Disorders	343
Depersonalization/Derealization Disorder	343
Dissociative Amnesia	344
Dissociative Identity Disorder	346
Treatment for Dissociative Disorders	351

Somatic Symptom and Related Disorders	352
Somatic Symptom Disorder	354
Illness Anxiety Disorder	354
Conversion Disorder	356
Factitious Disorder	363
Treatment for Somatic Symptom Disorders	364
Summary	365
Study Resources	366
Key Terms	366

Chapter 10 Eating Disorders — 367

Feeding Disorders	369
Pica	369
Rumination Disorder	370
Avoidant/Restrictive Food Intake Disorder	370
Obesity	371
Neuroscience Aspects of Obesity	372
Prevalence of Obesity	374
Body Image and Attitudes Toward Weight	377
Overview of Eating Disorders	379
Anorexia Nervosa	382
Characteristics of Anorexia Nervosa	382
Neuroscience and Anorexia	385
Causes of Anorexia Nervosa	388
Treating Anorexia Nervosa	389
Bulimia Nervosa and Binge Eating Disorder	391
Characteristics and Prevalence of Bulimia Nervosa	391
Causes of Bulimia Nervosa	392
Treating Bulimia Nervosa	394
Binge Eating Disorder	395
Treating Binge Eating	395
Summary	397
Study Resources	398
Key Terms	399

Chapter 11 Sexual Disorders, Paraphilic Disorders, and Gender Dysphoria — 401

Sexuality in Context	402
Historical Perspectives	403
Recent Studies on the Sexual Activities of Americans	404
Sexual Desire, Arousal, and Response	408
Your Brain and Sexual Activity	411
Normal Sexual Functioning	412
Sexual Dysfunction Disorders	416
Erectile Disorder	417
Female Orgasmic Disorder	418
Delayed Ejaculation	419
Early Ejaculation	419
Female Sexual Interest/Arousal Disorder	419
Male Hypoactive Sexual Desire Disorder	419
Genito-Pelvic Pain/Penetration Disorder	419
Treatment Approaches for Sexual Dysfunction Disorders	420
Sex Therapy	420
Medications and Other Treatments	421

Paraphilic Disorders	422
Exhibitionistic Disorder	424
Frotteuristic Disorder	424
Fetishistic Disorder	425
Pedophilic Disorder	426
Sexual Masochism Disorder	427
Sexual Sadism Disorder	428
Transvestic Disorder	428
Voyeuristic Disorder	428
Other Paraphilic Disorders	429
Causes and Treatment Approaches for Paraphilic Disorders	430
Gender Dysphoria	431
Gender Roles, Gender Identity, and Gender Dysphoria	432
Development, Characteristics, and Prevalence of Gender Dysphoria	434
The Brain and Gender Dysphoria	434
Providing Assistance for Individuals With Gender Dysphoria	435
Summary	438
Study Resources	440
Key Terms	441

Chapter 12 Substance-Related and Addictive Disorders — 443

Drug Use in the United States	445
Disordered Substance Use, Dependence, and Addiction	449
Substance Disorders in DSM-5-TR and ICD-11	450
Who Becomes Addicted?	451
Genetic, Environmental, and Evolutionary Influences	452
Pattern of Addiction	453
Can Drugs Change Your Brain?	454
Alcohol	458
Effects of Alcohol on the Human Body	461
Alcohol and Genetics	463
Moderate, Heavy, and Binge Drinking	463
Do People Who Drink More Like It More?	466
DSM-5-TR Alcohol-Related Disorders	466
Cannabis, Hallucinogens, and Opioids	469
Cannabis	469
Cannabis and Psychosis	474
Hallucinogens	475
Opioids	478
Do You Have Opium Receptors in Your Brain?	479
Stimulants: Cocaine, Amphetamines, Caffeine, and Nicotine	480
Cocaine	480
Cocaine, Dopamine, and Your Brain	481
Amphetamines	482
Caffeine	484
Tobacco and Nicotine	485
Gambling	487
Treatment of Substance-Related Disorders	490
Principles of Effective Treatment	491
Psychosocial Therapies and Addiction	494
The 12-Step Program	494

Controlled Drinking Approaches	496
Medications Used to Treat Addiction	497
Summary	497
Study Resources	499
For Further Reading	500
Key Terms	500

Chapter 13 Schizophrenia — 501

Schizophrenia Basics: Prevalence, Course, and Symptoms	502
Prevalence and Course of Schizophrenia	504
Positive and Negative Symptoms	507
Positive Symptoms	507
Negative Symptoms	510
Multilevel Process for Diagnosing Schizophrenia	510
Are There Subtypes of Schizophrenia?	511
Historical and Evolutionary Perspectives on Schizophrenia	515
Historical Perspective	515
Evolutionary Perspective	517
Factors in the Development of Schizophrenia	519
Genetic Factors in Schizophrenia	520
Endophenotypes Associated With Schizophrenia	523
Causes and Effects: Neuroscience Findings About Schizophrenia	525
Schizophrenia and Brain Function	525
Schizophrenia and Brain Structure	527
Gray Matter and White Matter Changes in Individuals With Schizophrenia	527
Ventricle Changes in Individuals With Schizophrenia	530
Schizophrenia and Brain Networks	531
Neurotransmitters Involved in Schizophrenia	532
Schizophrenia and Cognitive Processes	533
Treating Individuals With Schizophrenia	535
Antipsychotic Medications	537
Psychosocial Interventions for Schizophrenia	538
Summary	542
Study Resources	543
Key Terms	544

Chapter 14 Personality Disorders — 545

Personality Disorders and Personality	546
What Is a Personality Disorder?	546
Prevalence of Personality Disorders	548
Comorbidity of Personality Disorders	551
Environmental and Genetic Studies of Personality Disorders	552
Personality Disorders and Typical Personality Traits	553
The Characteristics of a Healthy Self	554
Typical Personality Traits	555
Evolution and Different Personality Characteristics	556
Maladaptive Personality Traits and Personality Disorders	557
Categories and Dimensions	559
Odd, Eccentric Personality Disorders	560
Paranoid Personality Disorder	560
Schizoid Personality Disorder	560
Schizotypal Personality Disorder	561

Dramatic Emotional Personality Disorders	562
Antisocial Personality Disorder and Psychopathy	562
Antisocial Personality Disorder	563
Psychopathy	564
Brain Involvement in Psychopathy	566
Borderline Personality Disorder	567
Brain Studies of Those With Borderline Personality Disorder	570
Trust and Borderline Personality Disorder	571
Histrionic Personality Disorder	574
Narcissistic Personality Disorder	576
Anxious Fearful Personality Disorders	578
Avoidant Personality Disorder	579
Dependent Personality Disorder	579
Obsessive-Compulsive Personality Disorder	579
Treatment of Personality Disorders	580
Dialectical Behavior Therapy	581
Other Proven Therapies for Treating Borderline Personality Disorder	583
Treatments for Other Personality Disorders	584
Summary	586
Study Resources	588
Key Terms	588

Chapter 15 Neurocognitive Disorders — 589

Normal Cognitive Changes Related to Aging	591
Do Cognitive Abilities Change With Age?	595
How the Brain Changes With Age	598
Categories of Neurocognitive Disorders	600
Delirium: Characteristics, Prevalence, and Causes	601
Neurocognitive Disorders: Characteristics, Prevalence, and Diagnosis	602
Neurocognitive Disorder Due to Alzheimer's Disease	605
Characteristics, Prevalence, and Diagnosis of Alzheimer's Disease	605
Brain Changes With Alzheimer's Disease	606
Neurofibrillary Tangles and Neuritic Plaques	606
Microglia	608
Genes and Alzheimer's Disease	609
Neuroimaging of Alzheimer's Disease	610
Other Causes of Neurocognitive Disorder	611
Vascular Neurocognitive Disorder	611
Frontotemporal Neurocognitive Disorder	611
The Development of Frontotemporal Neurocognitive Disorder in a Scientist and Artist	611
Neurocognitive Disorder Due to Traumatic Brain Injury	615
Neurocognitive Disorder Due to Lewy Body Dementia	617
Neurocognitive Disorder Due to Parkinson's Disease	617
Neurocognitive Disorder Due to HIV Infection	618
Substance-Induced Neurocognitive Disorder	618
Neurocognitive Disorder Due to Huntington's Disease	619
Neurocognitive Disorder Due to Prion Disease	619
Prevention, Treatment, and Support	620
Prevention of Neurocognitive Disorders	620
Can an Individual's Activities Be Protective in Brain Changes?	620
Treatment of and Support for Those With Neurocognitive Disorders	621
Summary	624
Study Resources	625
Key Terms	626

Chapter 16 The Law and Mental Health — 627

- The American Legal System and the Insanity Defense — 630
- Legal Competence: Standing Trial and Making Decisions — 634
  - Decision-Making Competence — 636
  - Competence and Mental Health Courts — 637
- Ethical and Legal Issues in Mental Health Treatment — 638
  - Ethical and Legal Aspects of the Initial Contract for Treatment — 639
  - Emergency Commitment — 641
  - Psychiatric Advance Directives — 642
- Sexual Predator Laws — 642
- Neuroscience and Evolutionary Perspectives on the Legal Aspects of Psychopathology — 647
- Summary — 650
- Study Resources — 651
- Key Terms and Concepts — 652

Glossary — 653

References — 665

Author Index — 721

Subject Index — 749

PREFACE

Abnormal psychology books from the mid-20th century largely contained descriptions of particular disorders but not much about the experiences of having a mental disorder. Since that time, society has a new conceptualization of what it means to have a mental disorder. There is also a greater awareness of how many people with a mental illness are able to live full lives and have productive occupations. In this text, I want to introduce some of these individuals and describe their experiences.

Also, in a textbook from the last century, there would not be much written about research studies. The research included would be focused exclusively on studies related directly to abnormal psychology. It would not be connected with the larger human condition and how mental illness is part of our evolutionary history and related to human cognition, emotion, and motor processes. In many ways, the field of abnormal psychology at that time remained disconnected from other areas of psychology as well as the life sciences.

Jumping ahead to the beginning of the 2000s, abnormal psychology textbooks included more research. However, the amount of research related to the neurosciences was limited. There was little in the way of brain imaging and the manner in which different disorders are related to one another on an underlying level. However, there was a realization that mental illness is a complex process and cannot be explained on a single level such as the possibility of mental illness being produced by a single gene or by one type of environmental experience.

Using this broader perspective, the dichotomous positions of nature versus nurture or innate versus learned fuse into the larger question of how aspects of each lead to an understanding of behavior and experience and their relationship to mental illness. Understanding that human behavior and experience take place on a number of different levels replaces the strict dichotomous approach pitting one level against another. On a molecular level, for example, we now know that genes must be turned on and off. What this means is that many significant human processes are directed by the environment. That is, environmental factors are able to influence which genes turn on and off. On a higher level, the "genetics versus culture" debate may be of limited value without understanding the manner in which humans both live within a culture and are influenced by historical environments.

In this book, I use the terms *psychopathology, mental disorders*, or *mental illness* to refer to those disorders traditionally described in scientific and professional research and practice. *Psychopathology* is the word commonly used in the neurosciences and the one you would want to use when performing literature searches in research and clinical journals. *Abnormal psychology* as a research area has a long tradition in psychology, and this tradition will be noted by that term. To reflect the strong scientific tradition currently seen in the study of psychopathology, the name of *The Journal of Abnormal Psychology* was changed in 2022 to *Journal of Psychopathology and Clinical Science* (Patalay & MacDonald, 2022). Likewise, the current edition of this text now uses the title *Psychopathology*.

DEVELOPMENT OF BRAIN IMAGING

As we entered the 21st century, questions of importance to psychology were being embraced by the neurosciences. This allowed for both richness and an integration of scientific information concerning important psychological questions. In the past 30 years, we have seen a shift in focus that has included the "Decade of the Brain" of the 1990s as well as a real emergence of the cognitive and affective neurosciences. A number of scientists have also begun to ask how neuroscience approaches can influence psychopathology and inform the diagnosis of different types of mental disorders.

Recent developments in brain imaging have provided important perspectives on psychopathological processes. These developments include functional magnetic resonance imaging (fMRI), electroencephalography (EEG), and magnetoencephalography (MEG), and their basics should be understood by students seeking an overview of psychopathology. The perspectives based on these brain imaging techniques are beginning to emphasize the manner in which underlying cortical networks may reflect particular changes in psychopathological conditions and give us a better understanding of the manner in which normal social and emotional processes may become dysfunctional. For example, we know that there are a variety of basic networks in the brain, some of which are involved in internal processes such as mind wandering when there is no external stimulation and others that become activated when interaction with the external world is required. A number of researchers have sought to articulate how these so-called default networks as well as other networks are associated with psychopathology. Other researchers have focused on emotional circuits that are either under- or overactivated in particular psychopathologies. One aspect of this emotional expression is the role it has played in our survival, mating, and social relationships from throughout our history. This brings us to the value of an evolutionary perspective.

DEVELOPMENT OF AN EVOLUTIONARY PERSPECTIVE

An evolutionary perspective examines the close interaction of organisms with their environment. In this close connection, the organism seeks ways to solve the fundamental problems or challenges of its existence. In many cases of mental illness, this close connection is no longer functioning in an optimal manner. The environment for humans includes not only nature but also culture. Throughout their evolutionary history, humans have always lived in groups with other people. The manner in which cultures understand and solve problems related to mental illness is one crucial question I will explore in this book. An evolutionary perspective also can give us insight into why some disorders such as schizophrenia are seen in similar proportions around the world, whereas other disorders vary by geographical location.

IMPLICATIONS FOR TREATMENT

An integration of research from the neurosciences with traditional psychological research helps clarify the efficacy and mechanisms of psychological treatments. For example, recent brain imaging research concerning treatment suggests that the type of treatment used determines the brain response. On the one hand, research concerning treatment of depression shows that psychotropic medications work from a bottom-up perspective by influencing the limbic areas that, in turn, influence higher cortical networks. On the other hand, cognitive therapies work in a top-down manner by influencing the prefrontal cortex (PFC), which, in turn, has an inhibitory effect on the lower brain processes. Even within traditional psychotherapy outcome research, there is a new sense of integration of traditionally dichotomous positions. This includes a search for specifying empirically supported procedures, such as the successful relationship between client and therapist, which determine treatment outcomes. In terms of prevention, there has been a recent increase in neuroscience research that shows the manner in which enriched environments, as well as exercise, can influence brain development and play an important role in the prevention of both pathophysiology and psychopathology.

NEW PERSPECTIVES IN PSYCHOPATHOLOGY

In the same way that psychology offers important insights in terms of human behavior and experience, the science of psychopathology must also consider these perspectives. This includes not only the signs and symptoms seen in particular disorders but also the abilities of individuals with these disorders to live productive lives. From this perspective, you will read stories of people with even serious mental disorders who have made important contributions in their professional and personal lives.

Behavior and experience take place on a number of levels, and it is imperative that abnormal psychology texts begin to offer such an integrative perspective. For example, recent thinking in social neuroscience suggests that it is not productive to teach brain anatomy or emotionality in one chapter of a textbook and social relationships, influence, and perception in another. Within the community of abnormal psychology researchers, there is an increasing understanding of the manner in which various disorders reflect impairments in social processes and the brain functions associated with them. With such an integrated approach, students can come to understand the nature of impaired relationships on a variety of levels, including cognitive, affective, and motor processes.

THIS TEXT

The purpose of this text is to bring together current perspectives in understanding mental disorders. In addition to the traditional psychological literature, additional information from the cognitive and affective neurosciences, ethology, evolution, and genetics will be discussed. The focus is on a unification and integration of these understandings within a broader consideration.

THIS FOURTH EDITION

Based on feedback from numerous faculty and researchers in the field, some changes were undertaken in this fourth edition. Throughout the text, chapter organization has been streamlined, with learning objectives connected to each major section to facilitate assessment and student comprehension. All diagnostic criteria and discussions have been updated to reflect changes in the *Diagnostic and Statistical Manual of Mental Disorders, Fifth Edition, Text Revision* (*DSM-5-TR*), published in 2022. Particular care has been paid to language and coverage of eating disorders in Chapter 10 and sexual disorders, paraphilic disorders, and gender dysphoria in Chapter 11 to reflect the evolving scientific and social understandings of the topics in these chapters. New insights related to emerging findings from genome-wide association studies (GWASs) have been added in many chapters. The photo program throughout the book has been updated. Also, all web links have been updated and new references have been included in the For Further Reading section at the end of the chapters. Specific chapter changes are described below.

Chapter 1

- The chapter's first section elaborates further on the use of the word *psychopathology* in the field and discusses language considerations such as person-first language and the stigma associated with slang words often used to describe mental illness.
- Data in the text and figures on the impact and prevalence of mental disorders have been updated.
- The chapter's discussion of 21st-century treatment approaches now considers the importance of diversity and cultural competency within the context of evidence-based care.
- A new paragraph and new citations have been added on the unified treatment model/unified protocol, also known as transdiagnostic therapy.

Chapter 2

- A new paragraph and new citations have been added on evolving understandings of the function of passive and active dendrites.
- The chapter now better clarifies the distinctions between biochemical substances considered neurotransmitters and those considered hormones.
- A new extended section discusses the relationship between the brain and the microbiome with reference to a number of studies conducted in the past 5 years.
- New study citations are included on cortical networks.

- The section Genetics and Psychopathology has been reorganized to consolidate discussions of epigenetics and GWASs. The discussion of GWASs has been updated and expanded to include recent research reflecting current approaches to these studies and new findings in the field that have emerged from these studies.

Chapter 3

- New study citations have been added on endophenotypes as they relate to schizophrenia.
- The chapter now notes the increasing feasibility of GWASs; study citations have been added on the benefits of GWASs for understanding schizophrenia.
- An example has been added discussing a meta-analysis considering the efficacy of telehealth services during the COVID-19 pandemic.

Chapter 4

- New information has been added on the newly released *DSM-5-TR*.
- The discussion of the cultural formulation interview has been updated to reflect updates in the *DSM-5-TR*, particularly related to consideration of cultural identity in migrants.
- The discussion of the Minnesota Multiphasic Personality Inventory (MMPI) has been updated to reflect the 2020 release of MMPI-3.
- New study citations have been added on linking the Rorschach test to its neuroscience principles.
- The section Comorbidity and Hierarchical Approaches to Psychopathology has been extensively revised, including new study citations, to consider recent work on the p factor and the emergence of the Hierarchical Taxonomy of Psychopathology (HiTOP).
- A new figure has been added illustrating the HiTOP model.
- The box LENS: Assessment, Classification, and Clinical Practice: The RDoC Alternative to the *DSM* has been thoroughly updated, including new citations and a new figure illustrating elements of the RDoC framework.
- The section Classification Systems for Mental Disorders now elaborates on the goal of reliability of diagnosis.
- The section on *DSM-5-TR* has been updated to reflect the latest changes and the effort to make the *DSM-5* and *ICD-11* more similar with each new edition.

Chapter 5

- New study citations have been added on the effects of genetic malfunctions and early environmental experiences on brain development.
- Discussion of early life stress has been expanded with updated data from child protective services, considering the unequal distribution of these data by race and ethnicity. This section also includes recent study citations on early life adversity's effect on the developing brain structure.
- The box Cultural LENS: Romania Adoption Study has been updated to cite a follow-up study published in 2020.
- New study citations have been added on mirror neurons and imitation learning.
- A new study citation has been added on gender differences in the rate of brain development.
- The section Conduct Disorder includes a new consideration of the etiology and brain processes underlying the disorder.

Preface **xxiii**

- New subheadings have been added throughout the section Characteristics of Autism Spectrum Disorder to facilitate easier reading.
- Table 5.3 has been updated with the *DSM-5-TR* criteria for autism spectrum disorder.
- New subheadings have been added throughout the section Causes of Autism Spectrum Disorder to facilitate easier reading.
- New study citations have been added on genetic contributions to autism spectrum disorder.
- Table 5.4 has been updated with the *DSM-5-TR* criteria for attention deficit/hyperactivity disorder.
- The section Intellectual Development Disorder has been updated to reflect the *ICD-11*'s move away from the term *mental retardation*.
- A new study citation has been added on the relationship between Down syndrome and Alzheimer's disease.

Chapter 6

- The name of this chapter has been changed to "Mood Disorders."
- Figure 6.1 has been updated with more recent data on disability-adjusted life years (DALYs) lost due to depression in countries around the world.
- In the section Characteristics of Major Depressive Disorder, prevalence data have been updated and new studies have been cited related to increases in depression in college students during the COVID-19 pandemic and the likelihood of recurrent depressive episodes.
- Table 6.3 has been updated with the *DSM-5-TR* criteria for major depressive disorder.
- The box Understanding Changes in *DSM-5* and *DSM-5-TR* has been updated to discuss the diagnostic category of prolonged grief disorder, new to the *DSM-5-TR*.
- In the section Causes of Depression, new study citations have been added on models developed to map the pathway from stress to depression.
- A new study citation has been added on the genetic connection between inflammation and symptoms of depression.
- A new discussion and citations have been added on the potential of psilocybin to treat depression.
- A new study citation has been added on vagal nerve stimulation treating depression by reducing inflammation.
- The section Characteristics of Bipolar Disorder has been reorganized to facilitate easier reading and consolidate the discussions of bipolar I, bipolar II, and cyclothymic disorder.
- Table 6.5 has been updated with the *DSM-5-TR* criteria for bipolar I disorder.
- The section Causes of Bipolar Disorder includes new discussion and study citations on recent findings from GWAS research. This section also now discusses the correlation of bipolar I with schizophrenia and of bipolar II with major depressive disorder.
- A study citation has been added on the efficacy of psychosocial family-based treatments for children and adolescents with bipolar disorder.
- A new study citation has been added on the interpersonal-psychological theory of suicide.
- Figure 6.10, Map of Suicide Rates Worldwide per 100,000 people, has been updated with 2019 data.

- A new discussion and study citation have been added on gender differences in suicide attempts, including rates of mood disorders and suicide attempts among gender minorities.
- Data in the box LENS: Suicide Among College Students have been updated.
- The section Preventing Suicide has been updated with the new nationwide suicide hotline in the United States and a new discussion/study citation on the efficacy of machine learning in predicting who is at risk for suicide.

Chapter 7

- The title of this chapter has been changed to "Stress, Trauma, and PTSD."
- New study citations have been added on the relationships between childhood stress and trauma and the later development of physical and mental health problems.
- New study citations have been added on the relationships among the immune system, inflammation, the gut microbiome, trauma, and psychopathology.
- New study citations have been added on physiological reactions to stress and trauma.
- A new study citation has been added on the nature of epigenetics as related to stress.
- Table 7.1 has been updated with updated with the *DSM-5-TR* criteria for acute stress disorder.
- In the section Acute Stress Disorder, prevalence data have been updated.
- A new section, Prolonged Grief Disorder, explains this new diagnostic category in *DSM-5-TR*.
- The section Post-Traumatic Stress Disorder has been elevated to a major section in the chapter. This section has been reorganized to facilitate easier reading.
- In the section Causes, Characteristics, and Prevalence of PTSD, new studies are cited on the development of PTSD among health care workers during the COVID-19 pandemic as well as the role of genetics in the development of PTSD. Prevalence data have also been updated.
- Table 7.3 has been updated with the *DSM-5-TR* criteria for post-traumatic stress disorder.
- A new study citation has been added on examining the hippocampus in individuals with PTSD.
- The section Treatment for Post-Traumatic Stress Disorder includes new study citations on cognitive and behavioral therapies and exposure therapy for people with PTSD.

Chapter 8

- A new study citation has been added on the brain networks underlying anxiety.
- New study citations have been added on temperament research among infants and models of anxiety development.
- Table 8.5 has been updated with the *DSM-5-TR* criteria for generalized anxiety disorder (GAD).
- New study citations have been added on the most effective treatments for GAD.
- The box LENS: Anxiety and the Prescribing of Benzodiazepines has been updated with new data.
- Table 8.6 has been updated with the *DSM-5-TR* criteria for social anxiety Disorder.
- New study citations have been added on the brain networks and regions underlying social anxiety, particularly research related to the amygdala.
- The chapter's discussion of phobias and panic disorder has been elevated to a major section.

- Table 8.9 has been updated with updated with the *DSM-5-TR* criteria for specific phobia.
- Table 8.10 has been updated with updated with the *DSM-5-TR* criteria for panic disorder.
- Table 8.11 has been updated with the *DSM-5-TR* criteria for obsessive-compulsive disorder (OCD).
- A new study citation has been added on the relationship between OCD and autoimmune disorders.
- In the section Neuroscience Aspects of OCD, new study citations have been added related to the genetic components of OCD.

Chapter 9

- The heading structure and learning objectives in this chapter have been streamlined and realigned to facilitate easier reading.
- A new study citation has been added on the origins of dissociative symptoms.
- A new study citation has been added on depersonalization as the result of difficulty integrating external stimuli with internal experiences.
- Prevalence rates of depersonalization have been updated.
- Table 9.3 has been updated with the *DSM-5-TR* criteria for dissociative identity disorder.
- A new study citation has been added on neurofunctional biomarkers of pathological dissociation.

Chapter 10

- The heading structure and learning objectives in this chapter have been streamlined and realigned to facilitate easier reading.
- The section Obesity has been retitled, and it begins with a new paragraph both clarifying that obesity is not a mental disorder and explaining why it is considered alongside feeding and eating disorders. The section includes a revised framing of the causes of obesity and discussion of different connections between genetics, physiological processes, and the foods we eat.
- Prevalence data on obesity and data on caloric intake worldwide have been updated.
- The discussion of body mass index (BMI) has been nuanced to reflect current thinking about its utility in discussions of obesity and health.
- A new study citation has been added on weight perception among transgender and nonbinary young adults.
- Prevalence data for eating disorders have been updated.
- A new study citation has been added on the association between childhood experiences and eating disorders.
- Table 10.3 has been updated with the *DSM-5-TR* criteria for anorexia nervosa.
- A new study citation has been added on brain networks as they relate to anorexia nervosa.
- A new study citation has been added on cardiovascular measures in adult women who were treated for anorexia as adolescents.
- A new study citation has been added on GWAS research into eating disorders.
- Table 10.5 has been updated with the *DSM-5-TR* criteria for bulimia nervosa.

Chapter 11

- Data on sexual orientation and behaviors of Americans have been updated.
- The section Normal Sexual Functioning includes a new discussion of intersex individuals.
- The section Pedophilic Disorder has been nuanced to clarify the distinction between the mental disorder pedophilia and the criminal behavior that results from acting on these urges.
- The section Transvestic Disorder has been nuanced to better distinguish among people with transvestic disorder, transgender individuals, and individuals who engage in drag performance.
- A new study citation has been added on the efficacy of Lupron as a treatment for paraphilic disorders.
- Language throughout the section Gender Dysphoria has been revisited and revised to align with GLAAD guidelines for language use.
- The box Understanding Changes in *DSM-5* and *DSM-5-TR:* Sexual and Gender-Related Experiences has been updated in relation to new culturally sensitive language use in *DSM-5-TR*.

Chapter 12

- Data on drug use and substance use disorder prevalence have been thoroughly updated throughout this chapter based on the most recent available data from the Substance Abuse and Mental Health Services Administration and the United Nations.
- The section Disordered Substance Use, Dependence, and Addiction has been retitled.
- New study citations have been added on the risk of brain changes in adolescents associated with drug use and on the epigenetic factors involved in the association between teenage alcohol consumption and later-life alcohol use disorder and anxiety.
- New study citations have been added on what GWAS approaches reveal about the heritability of addiction.
- New study citations have been added on the neural networks involved in the reward experiences of taking drugs.
- The section Alcohol has been reorganized to discuss culturally accepted uses before clinically disordered uses.
- New study citations have been added on how alcohol influences the brain through changes in gene expression and epigenetic processes.
- Table 12.5 has been updated with the *DSM-5-TR* criteria for alcohol use disorder.
- Table 12.6 has been updated with the *DSM-5-TR* criteria for alcohol intoxication.
- Table 12.7 has been updated with the *DSM-5-TR* criteria for alcohol withdrawal.
- The section Cannabis, Hallucinogens, and Opioids has been retitled.
- Table 12.8 has been updated through 2022 with developments related to the legalization of cannabis in the United States.
- A new study citation has been added on the effects of cannabis on the developing brain.
- A new figure and study citation have been added on changes in the brain related to cannabis use disorder.

- The box LENS: The Legalization of Cannabis has been updated to reflect the legal status of cannabis use by states.
- A new study citation has been added on psilocybin as a potential treatment for major depressive disorder.

Chapter 13

- A new study citation has been added on a narrative study that examined the nature of the delusions experienced by people with schizophrenia.
- Table 13.2 has been updated with the *DSM-5-TR* diagnostic criteria for schizophrenia.
- The chapter now discusses the AMP-SCZ initiative.
- New study citations have been added on the relationship between the gut microbiome and schizophrenia.
- New study citations have been added on GWAS research related to schizophrenia.
- A new study citation has been added on the genetics of schizophrenia.
- A new study citation has been added on work by the ENIGMA Working Group that used data from over 3,000 individuals to compare the brain structure of individuals at high risk for developing psychosis and a control group.
- A new study citation has been added on network models of schizophrenia.
- New study citations have been added on the neurotransmitters involved in schizophrenia.

Chapter 14

- Table 14.1 has been updated with the *DSM-5-TR* diagnostic criteria for general personality disorder.
- New study citations have been added on comorbidities among personality disorders as seen in both clinic-based studies and large-scale studies of the general population.
- New study citations have been added on the neurobiological processes that underlie borderline personality disorder.
- New prevalence data have been added for obsessive-compulsive personality disorder.

Chapter 15

- The heading structure and learning objectives in this chapter have been streamlined and realigned to facilitate easier reading.
- Data on aging populations worldwide have been updated based on the most recent available data from the U.S. Census Bureau.
- A new study citation has been added on genes that can change during aging and how these relate to neurocognitive disorders.
- Table 15.1 has been updated with the *DSM-5-TR* criteria for mild neurocognitive disorder.
- Table 15.2 has been updated with the *DSM-5-TR* criteria for major neurocognitive disorder.
- New study citations have been added on neurocognitive disorder due to Alzheimer's disease.
- Prevalence data for Alzheimer's disease have been updated.

- Table 15.3 has been updated with the *DSM-5-TR* criteria for neurocognitive disorder due to Alzheimer's disease.
- Coverage of recent research related to microglia has been added, noting the importance of microglia in the development of Alzheimer's disease.
- New study citations have been added on the association of Alzheimer's disease with the APOE gene and the *TREM2* gene as well as GWAS approaches that are searching for risk locations of additional genes.

Chapter 16

- Discussions of mass shootings in the United States have been updated to account for recent events.
- The section Competency to Stand Trial has been reframed with new subheadings added to facilitate easier reading.

ACKNOWLEDGMENTS

I appreciate the many individuals who have contributed to this book. Ken Levy, Sandy Testa, Mike Wolff, and Cliff Evans discussed their clinical work with me and contributed case studies seen throughout this book. I also appreciate the students in my senior seminar on abnormal psychology from a neuroscience perspective who over the years gave me insight into how to present the information seen throughout this book as well as finding new information and perspectives. Faculty from across the country were extremely helpful in their reviews of this book and suggestions. They include the following individuals:

Glen M. Adams, *Harding University*
Chinenye S. S. Asobiereonwu, *Northcentral University*
Jamie Bodenlos, *Hobart and William Smith Colleges*
Andrea Bonior, *Georgetown University*
Cameo F. Borntrager, *University of Montana*
Sharon Boyd-Jackson, *Kean University*
Julie Boydston, *Washburn University*
Amy Badura Brack, *Creighton University*
Jennifer A. Bradley, *Northampton Community College*
Adam Brown, *Hunter College, City University of New York*
Lynne Carroll, *University of North Florida*
Isabelle Chang, *Temple University*
Elysia V. Clemens, *University of Northern Colorado*
Jessamy Comer, *Rochester Institute of Technology*
Deborah G. Conway, *Community College of Allegheny County*
Michael E. Cox, *Southern New Hampshire University*
GiGi Crawford, *Rowan University*
Amanda di Bartolomeo, *University of California, Los Angeles*
Mitch Earlywine, *University at Albany, SUNY*
Fred Ernst, *University of Texas–Pan American*
Donald D. Evans, *Simpson College*
David M. Feldman, *Barry University*
Brian Fisak, *University of North Florida*
Sarah Fischer, *The University of Georgia*
Nathan Fox, *University of Maryland*
David E. Gard, *San Francisco State University*
Brian K. Gehl, *Coe College*
Henry J. Grubb, *University of Dubuque*
Rob Hoff, *Mercyhurst University*
Lisa R. Jackson, *Schoolcraft College*
Bruno M. Kappes, *University of Alaska Anchorage*
Andreas Keil, *University of Florida*
Lynne M. Kemen, *Hunter College, CUNY*
William Kimberlin, *Lorain County Community College*
Paul Kochmanski, *Erie Community College*
Lee Kooler, *Modesto Junior College*
Jürgen Werner Kremer, *Santa Rosa Junior College*

Rebecca M. Langley, *Henderson State University*
Jason M. Lavender, *University at Albany, SUNY*
Martha Low, *Winston-Salem State University*
Aaron M. Luebbe, *Miami University*
Richard Martielli, *Washington University in St. Louis*
Ryan A. McKelley, *University of Wisconsin–La Crosse*
Jan Mendoza, *Golden West College*
Courtney K. Mozo, *Old Dominion University*
Kimberly Renk, *University of Central Florida*
Anne Richards, *Seattle Central College*
Brigitte Rockstroh, *Universität Konstanz, Germany*
Ashley M. Rolnik, *Loyola University Chicago*
H. Russell Searight, *Lake Superior State University*
Fran Sessa, *Penn State Abington*
Gemma Dolorosa Skillman, *The University of South Dakota*
Steven J. Snowden, *University of Florida*
Kim Stark, *University of Central Missouri*
Wayne S. Stein, *Brevard Community College*
Don Tucker, *CEO, Egi.com and University of Oregon*
Naomi Wagner, *San Jose State University, Palo Alto University*
Nancy Wilson-Soga, *Warren County Community College*
Philip Yanos, *John Jay College*

I also appreciate the staff at Sage. Mary Dudley is an organized editor who has moved this project through to its completion. Sam Held handled project management, and Isabel Saraiva efficiently handled permissions. Veronica Stapleton Hooper is excellent as a production editor who carefully brought everything together as a quality book. In addition, Judy Ray has supplied important insights and new perspectives to this project.

ABOUT THE AUTHOR

William J. Ray is an emeritus professor of psychology at Pennsylvania State University. He received his PhD from Vanderbilt University and was a fellow in medical psychology at the University of California Medical Center in San Francisco. He received his undergraduate degree from Eckerd College, where he learned about the value of primary sources and the need to integrate information from a number of perspectives. As part of his clinical training, he has worked in a number of mental hospitals and clinics across the country, where he developed an appreciation of the experiences of those with mental disorders. In his career, he has served as a visiting professor and researcher at the University of Hawaii, Münster University, University of Rome, Tübingen University, and Konstanz University. At Penn State, he was the director of the SCAN (Specialization in Cognitive and Affective Neuroscience) program and was previously the director of the Clinical Psychology Program. His research has focused on approaching clinical questions from a neuroscience perspective. He has used psychophysiological and brain imaging techniques such as EEG, MEG, DTI, and fMRI to study emotionality, psychopathology, and individual differences. These studies can be found in his numerous articles, book chapters, and books. His work has been published in such journals as *Science, Proceedings of the National Academy of Sciences, Journal of Neuroscience, Psychophysiology, Physiological Reviews, Journal of Personality and Social Psychology, Developmental Psychology, Journal of Abnormal Psychology, Cognitive Brain Research, Biological Psychology, NeuroImage,* and *Clinical Neurophysiology.* This work has been funded by both national and international agencies, including NIH, NIMH, NASA, NATO, and the DAAD. In addition to research, teaching has been an important part of his career. His textbooks include *Abnormal Psychology now Psychopathology, Research Methods for Psychological Science, Psychophysiological Methods* (with Robert Stern & Karen Quigley), *Evolutionary Psychology: Neuroscience Perspectives Concerning Human Behavior and Experience, Fundamentals of Brain and Behavior: An introduction to Human Neuroscience,* and *Introduction to Psychological Science.*

iStock.com/Rawpixel

1 AN OVERVIEW OF PSYCHOPATHOLOGY AND CHANGING CONCEPTUALIZATIONS OF MENTAL ILLNESS

LEARNING OBJECTIVES

1.1 Describe the components of and key considerations of psychopathology.

1.2 Discuss the major themes of this book.

1.3 Explain how evolution and culture are relevant to psychopathology.

1.4 Summarize the historical influences on modern conceptions of mental disorders.

1.5 Explain how discoveries about the brain contributed to an understanding of psychopathology.

1.6 Discuss historical methods of care for those with mental disorders.

1.7 Discuss the origin and evolution of biological treatments for mental illness.

1.8 Examine the psychological perspectives that guide present-day treatment of mental disorders.

The biography *A Beautiful Mind* describes the fascinating life and experiences of mathematician John Nash (Nasar, 1998). The powerful story was made into a major Hollywood film that won the Academy Award for Best Picture in 2001. John Nash was a remarkable figure who received a PhD in mathematics from Princeton University and taught at both MIT and Princeton. In 1994, Nash won the Nobel Prize in Economics for his work on game theory. From what you just read, you would probably assume that John Nash had a very productive career, and in many ways he did.

However, there was another aspect to John Nash's life that caused considerable distress to himself and puzzlement for others. One day at work, when he was 30 years old, he walked into a room full of others in his department, held up a copy of the *New York Times*, and said to no one in particular that the story in the upper-left corner contained an encrypted message. Not only was it a message in code, he claimed, but it had also been put there by inhabitants of another galaxy, and he knew how to decode it (Nasar, 1998, p. 16).

From that day on, there were times Nash was productive, but there were also times when he had disordered thoughts, mumbled to himself without thought of those around him, and experienced delusions of situations that did not exist. He felt there were individuals around him who put him in danger. He even wrote letters to officials in the U.S. government to suggest these individuals were setting up alternative governments. John Nash suffered from schizophrenia.

In Terri Cheney's memoir *Manic* (2008), the author, who rose to success as an entertainment attorney in Beverly Hills, told of her experience of exceptional energy. She described one time she was in Santa Fe, New Mexico:

> The mania came in four-day spurts. Four days of not eating, not sleeping, barely sitting in one place for more than a few minutes at a time. Four days of constant shopping—and Canyon Road is all about commerce, however artsy its façade.

Terri Cheney
Suzanne Allison

She further described her experiences:

> Mostly, however, I talked to men. Canyon Road has a number of extremely lively, extremely friendly bars and clubs, all of which were in walking distance of my hacienda. It wasn't hard for a redhead with a ready smile and a feverish glow in her eyes to strike up a conversation and then continue that conversation well into the early-morning hours, his place or mine. (pp. 6–7)

Many individuals experience feelings of high energy or sexuality that would not be considered a mental disorder. However, as you will see in Chapter 6 on mood disorders, those with bipolar disorder often experience high levels of energy for long periods of time and an intense desire to engage in sexual activity, gambling, or shopping. Our task is to understand which types of activities would be considered psychopathology or mental illness.

UNDERSTANDING PSYCHOPATHOLOGY: DEFINITIONS AND KEY CONSIDERATIONS

At one time in our history, health professionals distinguished between physical disorders and mental disorders: Physical disorders involved the body, and mental disorders involved the mind. For example, addiction was at one time seen as a lack of will, with little to do with physiology. Today, we see the close connection of the brain with what were previously considered mental processes. Mental disorders are brain disorders. Further, those physiological processes involved in physical disorders, such as the immune system, the bacteria in your gut, the turning on and off of genes, and the chemical processes of the body, are equally involved in mental disorders.

In this book, the terms *psychopathology*, *mental disorders*, or *mental illness* refer to those disorders traditionally described in scientific and professional research and practice. *Psychopathology* is the word commonly used in the neurosciences and the one you would want to use when performing literature searches in research and clinical journals. *Abnormal psychology* as a research area has a long tradition in psychology, and this tradition will be noted by that term. In the middle of the 20th century, a textbook such as this one would have focused more on the description of particular disorders than on scientific research. With the advent of the neurosciences, mental disorders and their relationship to the brain have become an important focus of research. Overall, this was referred to by the term *psychopathological research*. To reflect the strong scientific tradition currently seen in the study of psychopathology, the name of the *Journal of Abnormal Psychology* was changed in 2022 to the *Journal of Psychopathology and Clinical Science* (Patalay & MacDonald, 2022).

Defining Psychopathology and Understanding Its Components

Mental disorders are part of our human condition. We have many names for these conditions. We speak of people with *mental illness*. For over a century, psychologists have studied these conditions in terms of **abnormal psychology**, which is the study of abnormal behavior. Others have used the term **psychopathology**. This is in contrast with *pathophysiology*, or pathology of our physiology. Slang words such as *crazy* or *nuts* have been around for hundreds of years. However, many of these terms stigmatize those who experience a mental disorder. To avoid stigmatizing of groups of people, person-first language, such as "an individual who experiences schizophrenia," or "a person who experiences depression," is more widely used today. However, some terms referring to psychopathology have endured in our legal system. For example, one of the oldest legal terms is *insanity*, or *insane*, which comes from the Latin meaning "not healthy."

Mental disorders have been with us throughout our human history. Since the time that written language became a part of our experience, humans have described mental disorders. We find such descriptions in Egyptian, Greek, Chinese, Indian, and other texts throughout world history. Today, our films, novels, plays, and television programs often portray problems experienced by those with mental disorders.

The experiences of the individuals described in the chapter opening give us insights into the nature of mental illness. Terri Cheney told how she experienced great energy, which lasted for 4 days. She described the experience of mental illness as something happening *to* her. In this sense, Terri Cheney and John Nash did not feel they had an alternative way of acting. Thus, one important characteristic of mental illness is the lack of control over one's experience. This can also be described as a loss of freedom or an inability to consider alternative ways of thinking, feeling, or doing. Some individuals show this loss mainly in terms of emotional experiences, as in the case of Terri Cheney with bipolar disorder. Others show the loss in terms of cognitive processes, such as the experiences of John Nash. At the beginning of many of the chapters of this book, you will read first-person accounts from individuals with particular disorders. In this way, you can discover how people with a mental disorder experience their world.

Another common theme seen in psychopathology is the loss of genuine personal contact. Individuals with depression or schizophrenia often find it difficult to have social interactions as experienced by other people. Just having a simple conversation or talking to clerks in stores may seem impossible. Mental illness not only affects individuals' interpersonal relationships but also their relationship with themselves, their *intrapersonal* relationship. When individuals with schizophrenia or depression talk to themselves, they often think negative thoughts about who they are and what will happen in the future.

In many cases, the experience of a mental disorder results in personal distress. Not being able to get out of bed, or feeling that a voice in your head is telling you that you are evil, or worrying that a rice cake or an apple will make you fat all represent different degrees of distress.

Thus, we can consider four important personal components in psychopathology (Table 1.1). These are a loss of freedom or ability to consider alternatives, a loss of genuine personal contact, a loss of connection with one's self and the ability to live in a productive manner, and personal distress. As you will see with the disorders presented in this book, personal distress over time is one of the criteria required for a diagnosis to be made. There is also a global component in which the person's behavior and experiences are considered to be deviant in terms of cultural and statistical norms.

Impact of Mental Disorders

Today, the National Institute of Mental Health (NIMH) estimates that 22.8% of the U.S. population experiences a mental disorder during a given year (see For Further Reading at the end of this chapter). This represents roughly 57.8 million people in the United States (Figure 1.1).

Having a mental disorder results in lost productivity, lost personal enjoyment, and potentially even premature death. The World Health Organization (WHO) estimated that in the United States and Canada, mental disorders cause a greater loss in what they refer to as disability-adjusted life years (DALYs) than cardiovascular disease or cancer. DALYs represent the total number of years lost due to illness, disability, or premature death (see For Further Reading).

With mental illness being so common, you might think that we as humans would have a complete understanding of the factors involved. However, this is not the case. We are not even sure how to refer to individuals with mental disorders. Are they abnormal? How you answer this question may be related to your experiences, including your cultural perspective.

Depending on your perspective, one can be normal or abnormal. Many famous artists such as the Impressionists of the 19th century had their work initially rejected because it did not fit into the standards of what was considered "good art" at the time. However, today we appreciate that these artists showed us another way of viewing the world. Likewise, many movies and online media today would be rejected at a previous time as not representing mainstream values. Being part of the LGBTQ community was considered a mental disorder at one time. Further, what would be acceptable in one culture might be seen as completely "crazy" in another.

TABLE 1.1 ■ Four Key Personal Components of Psychopathology
1. Loss of freedom and ability to consider alternatives
2. Loss of genuine personal contact
3. Loss of connection with one's self and the ability to live in a productive manner
4. Personal distress

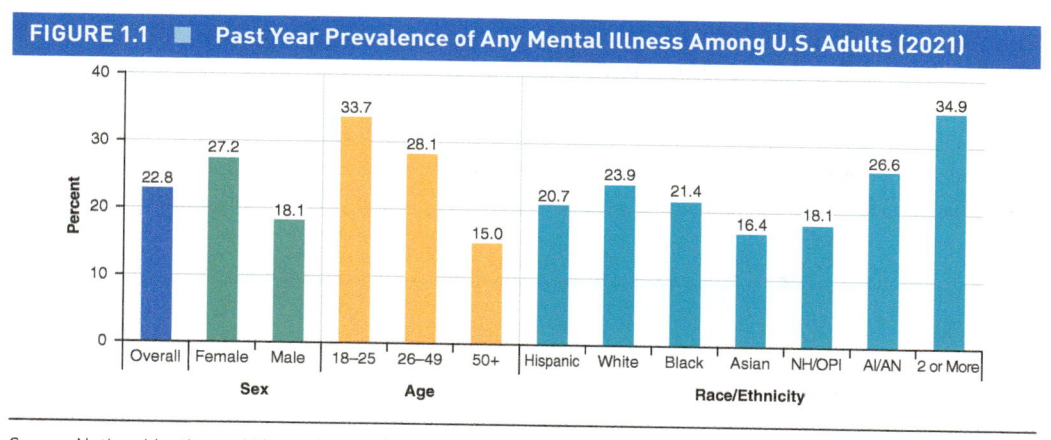

FIGURE 1.1 ■ Past Year Prevalence of Any Mental Illness Among U.S. Adults (2021)

Category	Group	Percent
	Overall	22.8
Sex	Female	27.2
Sex	Male	18.1
Age	18–25	33.7
Age	26–49	28.1
Age	50+	15.0
Race/Ethnicity	Hispanic	20.7
Race/Ethnicity	White	23.9
Race/Ethnicity	Black	21.4
Race/Ethnicity	Asian	16.4
Race/Ethnicity	NH/OPI	18.1
Race/Ethnicity	AI/AN	26.6
Race/Ethnicity	2 or More	34.9

Source: National Institute of Mental Health. (2023, March). *Mental illness.* http://www.nimh.nih.gov/health/statistics/prevalence/any-mental-illness-ami-among-us-adults.shtml

Persons of Hispanic origin may be of any race; all other racial/ethnic groups are non-Hispanic. NH/OPI = Native Hawaiian/Other Pacific Islander. AI/AN = American Indian/Alaskan Native.

Stigma and Mental Disorders

As you will see throughout this book, experiencing a mental illness does not mean that one has to live a limited life. Individuals like John Nash and Terri Cheney not only have had productive careers, but they also have enjoyed successful personal relationships. However, many children, adolescents, and young adults with a mental illness report being told they could never perform in a high-level profession or have the types of relationships that others have. Mental disorders are seen throughout the U.S. population regardless of gender, age, and race/ethnicity (see Figure 1.1).

There is often a stigma experienced by those with a mental disorder. Historically, stigma has been defined as a mark of disgrace associated with a particular person. In psychological terms, stigma involves negative attitudes and beliefs that cause the general public to avoid certain people, including those with mental illness. Throughout the world, those with mental illness experience stigma. In many cultures, they are seen as different. When they are thus stigmatized, they are no longer treated as individual people, but only as part of a group who is different. It becomes an "us versus them" way of thinking.

Part of the stigma comes from inaccurate information about those with mental illness. For example, many people think that anyone with a mental illness is violent. In 2012, a mass shooting killed 20 children and 6 teachers at the Sandy Hook Elementary School in Newtown, Connecticut. Immediately after, it was suggested that the killer had a mental illness. Officials of the National Rifle Association claimed that this crime could not have been committed by a sane person. However, the data do not support a strong relationship between mental disorders and violence.

The MacArthur Foundation followed hospitalized individuals with mental illness after their release and found that only 2% to 3% became involved with violence with a gun. As a general rule, individuals with mental illness do not show more violent tendencies than is seen in the general population. However, particular disorders such as antisocial personality disorder (psychopathy) are associated with serial killers and other violent criminals. Also, substance abuse can increase violence in some individuals. With these exceptions, however, having a mental illness has not been found to increase violence toward others.

Stigma can be seen on a number of levels. If a society believes that mental illness is the fault of the person, and that individuals can change themselves by willpower, then it is less likely to spend the money necessary to set up clinics and train professionals. For similar reasons, society may also be less likely to set up school-based programs to help adolescents contend with bullying or handle thoughts of self-harm or suicide. As well, companies may not be willing to include mental health treatment in their insurance coverage, or they may place limits on benefits for treatment of these disorders.

As a society, Americans demonstrate a number of different values when considering those with mental illness. On the one hand, we may want to help those who experience distress. On the other hard, we may feel it is the responsibility of these individuals to take care of themselves. *LENS: American Attitudes Toward Mental Illness* portrays some of these differing values.

In the United States, attitudes are moving toward less stigma. In 1996, for example, 54% of the U.S. population viewed depression as related to neurobiological causes. During the following 10 years, this increased to 67%. With a better understanding of the disorders presented throughout this book, it is possible to have a more compassionate as well as intellectual understanding of those with mental disorders.

LENS
AMERICAN ATTITUDES TOWARD MENTAL ILLNESS

Throughout American history, a number of traditions and themes have developed in relation to U.S. society. At times, these themes create a dynamic tension. For example, there is often a call for the federal government to tax less. However, in times of disaster, we expect the government to spend money to help our community. Such desires create a dynamic tension between different ideas and values.

iStock.com/Rich Legg. Stock photo. Posed by model.

There is also such a dynamic tension in relation to individuals with mental illness. This partly comes from a desire to take care of those who are not able to take care of themselves. Historically, in many countries from which Americans originally came, the king, queen, or government took care of those who could not care for themselves. However, there is also a tradition in America represented by the pioneer or cowboy spirit in which we support the individual's right to do what they want and to live the type of life desired.

In the United States, we have contradictory attitudes toward mental illness. In terms of treatment, 94% of Americans believe it can help people with mental illness lead normal lives. This might suggest that society would encourage treatment of mental illness and reduce any stigma around seeking help. However, it is estimated that only about 20% of those with a mental disorder actually sought help in the prior year. This may have resulted from embarrassment or an attempt to hide the condition from others. This leads to less treatment and may, in turn, affect work and life opportunities. The attempt to hide mental problems may also reflect a reality, as only around 60% of Americans believe that people are generally caring and sympathetic to people with mental illness.

The picture becomes more complicated when we realize that in any given year, about one fourth of all adult Americans have a mental disorder, including anxiety, depression, and substance abuse. Emotional problems and psychological distress are also experienced by those with chronic physical conditions such as arthritis, cancer, diabetes, and cardiovascular problems. Given the large number of individuals experiencing different types of emotional problems and psychological distress, you might expect that these conditions would be more accepted. However, stigma and negative attitudes toward mental illness are common in the United States. Some people even see having a disorder as being the person's fault and believe that they could change if they wanted to.

The dynamic tension between taking care of others and being independent becomes clear when we see individuals with mental illness who have difficulty securing permanent housing. This raises a number of questions. Can we take these individuals off the street if they don't want to be taken to a shelter? If they do not want to take medication, can we force them to take it if this would help them function better in our community? Should it be the police or health care workers who work with these individuals? In the final chapter of this book, which focuses on legal and ethical issues and mental health, a number of these questions will be considered.

Thought Question

Who do you believe should take care of people with mental illness in American society?

Note: Data presented above are taken from Centers for Disease Control and Prevention (CDC) (2012).

CONCEPT CHECK

- What are the four key components of psychopathology? Give an example of each.
- How does reading about the experiences of individuals with mental illness inform our understanding of the nature of psychopathology?
- What are the impacts of mental illness in the United States in any given year?
- Describe the dynamic tension in American attitudes toward mental illness.

THE THREE MAJOR THEMES OF THIS BOOK

In this book, three major themes will be explored. The first theme takes a behavioral and experiential perspective on psychopathology. Here, current ways of classifying and describing abnormal behavior are discussed. You will also consider the experience of having a psychological disorder, and this book will present first-person reports from individuals with particular disorders. It is also important to examine the role of one's social groups and culture.

We will also discuss symptoms and signs. Traditionally, *symptoms*, such as feeling sad, are seen as subjective, and may be reported by the individual to a professional, whereas *signs*, such as having a fever, are objective processes that can be measured and would be apparent to a professional. An important aspect of this perspective is the degree to which the symptoms and signs of a particular disorder are seen in a similar manner throughout the world. The universality of mental disorders has been an important consideration for scientists. It is also important to note the role culture plays in the manifestations of behaviors and experiences related to psychopathology.

The second theme examines what we know about particular psychopathological experience from a neuroscience perspective. In particular, the structure and function of the brain as it relates to psychopathology is discussed. With neuroscience techniques such as brain imaging, it is becoming clear that mental disorders are also brain disorders. In fact, with every disorder we will consider in this book, it is possible to examine how the structure and function of the brain is changed. The neuroscience perspective will also help us to consider how certain disorders share a similarity in underlying brain processes. For example, knowing that the same brain networks involved in physical pain are also involved in social rejection helps us understand the experience of each and how they are similar.

The third theme asks much broader scientific questions and examines psychological disorders from an evolutionary perspective. In adopting this perspective, we can think about how certain ways of

Culture: How are we a part of culture, and what is its influence?
iStock.com/Vikram Raghuvanshi

seeing or being in the world might be adaptive. Being afraid of heights, for example, keeps us from taking unnecessary risks. We can ask if there is any advantage to behaving and feeling in certain ways that others consider abnormal. We can also ask if the disordered behavior is secondary to another process that is beneficial. This could include an attempt by our body to protect itself.

In the same way that we know that having a fever is protective and beneficial to recovering from sickness, we can look for similarities in psychological disorders. We can also ask questions about why particular disorders continue to exist. Individuals with schizophrenia, for example, generally have fewer children than those without the disorder. Thus, you might expect that schizophrenia would have gradually disappeared over our evolutionary history through the production of fewer children with the genetics related to the disorder. However, this is not the case, and in fact, schizophrenia occurs in approximately the same percentage (1% of the population) throughout the world in both developed and developing countries. As will be discussed in more detail later in this book, this suggests that schizophrenia is an old disorder that has existed since humans migrated out of Africa around 100,000 years ago (Benton et al., 2021), and it is not related to stresses unique to developed countries. It also suggests that the multiple genes associated with schizophrenia may be associated with more positive human traits such as creativity.

Levels of Analysis

As we explore together the themes of behavior and experience, neuroscience contributions, and evolutionary perspectives as they relate to psychopathology, you will see that we will move across a variety of **levels of analysis** ranging from culture to genetics. You can group these levels into three domains. The highest-level domain examines the individual in relationship with others. This includes our culture and society as well as our social relationships. From there, we can look at an individual domain, which includes our actions and our experiences. This is typically how we experience ourselves every day. Included in this are our sensory, motor, emotional, and cognitive processes. We can examine both of these levels as they influence our behavior and experience.

The final domain focuses on the physiological processes that make up our central and peripheral nervous systems. This will take us to the cortical network level, and you will see how neurons and their connections form the basis of information transfer and processing. The most basic level you will be introduced to in this book is the genetic level, which in turn will require us to understand how environmental conditions influence genetic processes. You will also learn about a related process, *epigenetics*,

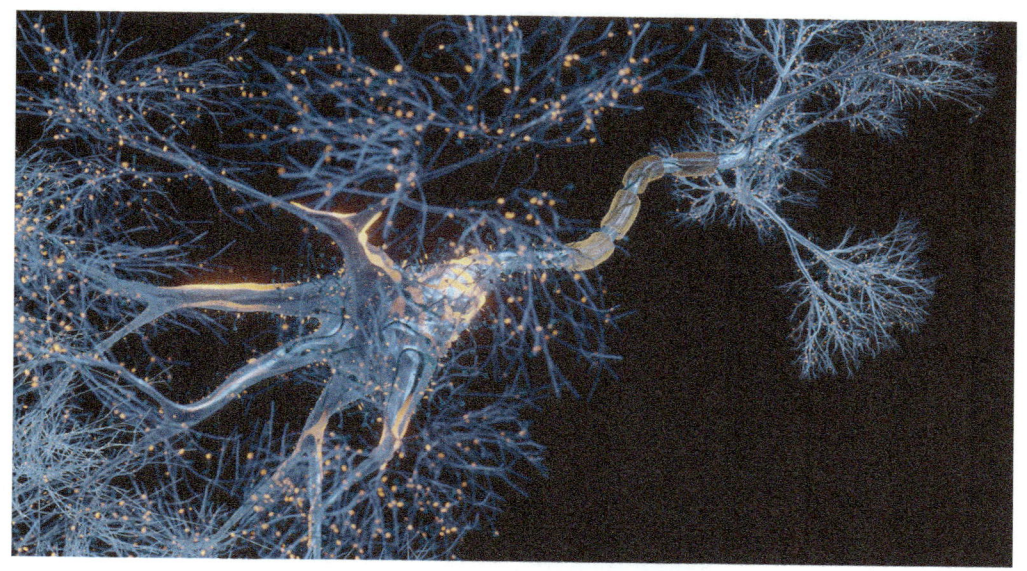

How do our neurons form networks?
iStock.com/koto_feja

in which genes can be turned on or off by the environment, and these mechanisms can be passed on to future generations without actually changing the basic genetic structure.

As you will read throughout this book, since the 1970s researchers have come a long way in understanding how various levels ranging from genetics to culture interact with each other in a complex manner. In the next section of this chapter, we will turn to a consideration of culture through the ages that will take us to an understanding of behavior and experience on a number of levels. In later chapters, you will be introduced to additional levels of analysis.

To help focus their work, scientists often concentrate primarily on one of these levels of analysis. However, in this book a more integrative approach that draws on a number of these levels will be used. You should not take any one of these levels of analysis as being more important or truer than another. A similar plea was made by George Engel in 1977 when he helped to develop the biopsychosocial approach to understanding mental illness.

Biopsychosocial Approach

In his 1977 paper in the journal *Science*, George Engel introduced the term *biopsychosocial*. He suggested that individuals with mental illness or another medical disorder should be understood from more than just a biological perspective. Type 2 diabetes, for example, is a disorder, but it is also related to how the person eats and exercises. Likewise, depression and anxiety can be influenced by social and emotional factors. Thus, it is necessary to see the signs and symptoms of the disorder in a larger context. Otherwise, one has a limited perspective that ignores the social, psychological, and behavioral dimensions of any disorder. Therefore, as a mental health professional, you would want to know more about an individual than just the symptoms that the person describes, as represented in Figure 1.2. This could be their family life, work conditions, and cultural practices as well as eating habits and how the person exercises.

CONCEPT CHECK

- Identify the three major themes this book takes in regard to psychopathology.
- What does *level of analysis* mean? Identify three domains presented for studying psychopathology. Which is the most important?
- How is the biopsychosocial model related to the broader levels of analysis approach?

FIGURE 1.2 ■ The Biopsychosocial Model

Individuals with mental illness should be understood from an integrative perspective that includes psychological, social, and biological variables.

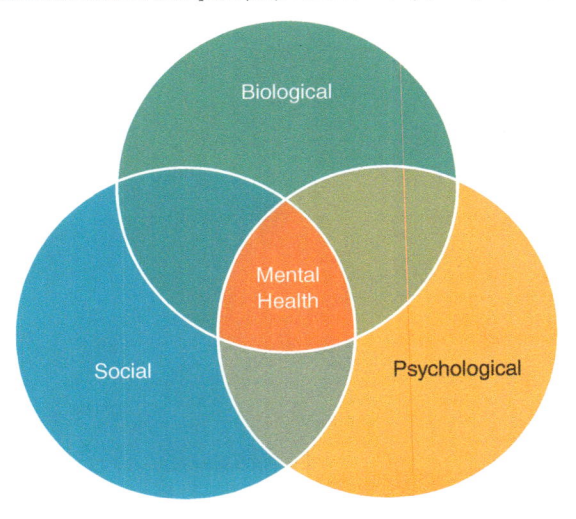

THE RELATION OF EVOLUTION AND CULTURE TO PSYCHOPATHOLOGY

Considering psychopathology from evolutionary and cultural perspectives goes beyond the traditional psychological and physiological considerations (Ray, 2013). These perspectives make us realize that for at least the last 100,000 years, humans have been social beings who have lived within the context of a group in which there were interactions related to gathering and preparing food, having sexual relations, and being part of a community. Cultures developed from this.

The **cultural perspective** emphasizes the social world in which a person lives (Krendl & Pescosolido, 2020; López & Guarnaccia, 2000). In this sense, culture can be viewed as "information capable of affecting individuals' behavior that they acquire from other members of

In many countries, informal networks of families, friends, and other community members are utilized to care for those with mental illness.

iStock.com/Igor Alecsander

their species through teaching, imitation, and other forms of social transmission" (Richerson & Boyd, 2005, p. 5). From this perspective, culture can be seen as a system of inheritance. Humans learn a variety of things from others in their culture, including skills, values, beliefs, and attitudes. Historically, parents and others taught children how to perform particular tasks such as farming, toolmaking, and hunting. In addition, human culture has formalized learning in the form of schools and apprenticeships. Cultures also differ in their level of economic development and the amount of resources they devote to mental health. In *Cultural LENS: Global Mental Health: Available Treatment*, the availability of mental health professionals across the world is described.

CULTURAL LENS
GLOBAL MENTAL HEALTH: AVAILABLE TREATMENT

Mental health services are available worldwide. However, they differ by country in terms of how available they are and the nature of the services offered. In countries in which individuals have a higher income, such as the United States, Canada, England, Germany, France, Japan, and Australia, there are many more mental health care workers, such as psychologists and psychiatrists, than there are in countries with lower incomes on average, such as India, China, and many countries in Africa. Figure 1.3 shows the number of psychologists throughout the world in 2019. This map illustrates the number of psychologists per 100,000 people in the country.

High-income countries have the greatest number of mental health professionals, and low-income countries the least. Figure 1.4 shows the number of psychiatrists, psychologists, nurses, and social workers by income level. The governments of about one third of all countries do not have a specific budget for mental health. In many countries, informal networks of families, friends, and other community members are utilized to care for those with mental illness. These data are updated regularly on the World Health Organization (WHO) website.

FIGURE 1.3 ■ Where Are There Psychologists Available for Those With Mental Illness?

Human resources for mental health care (psychiatrists, psychologists, nurses, and social workers) vary by country. This figure shows the number of psychologists available by country for every 100,000 people in that country.

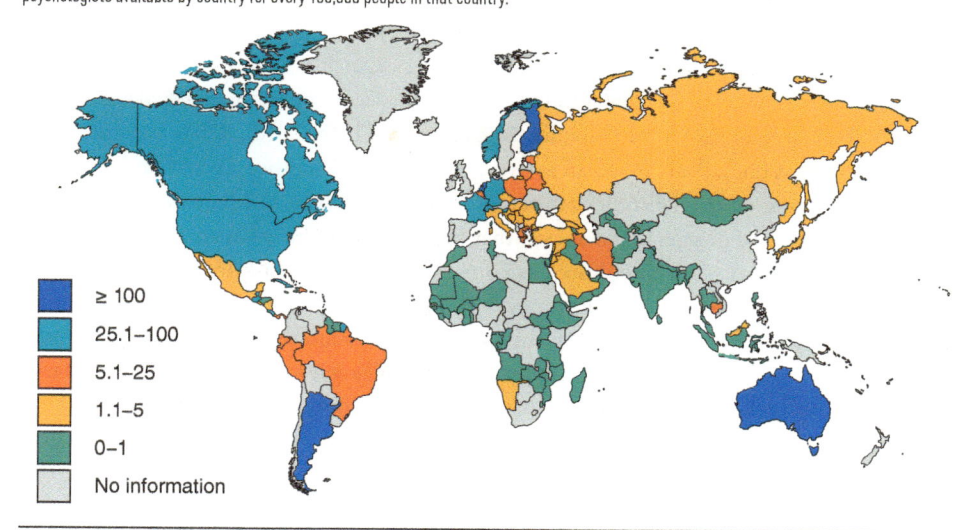

Legend:
- ≥ 100
- 25.1–100
- 5.1–25
- 1.1–5
- 0–1
- No information

Credit: World Health Organization. (n.d.) *Psychologists working in mental health sector (per 100,000).* https://www.who.int/data/gho/data/indicators/indicator-details/GHO/psychologists-working-in-mental-health-sector-(per-100-000)

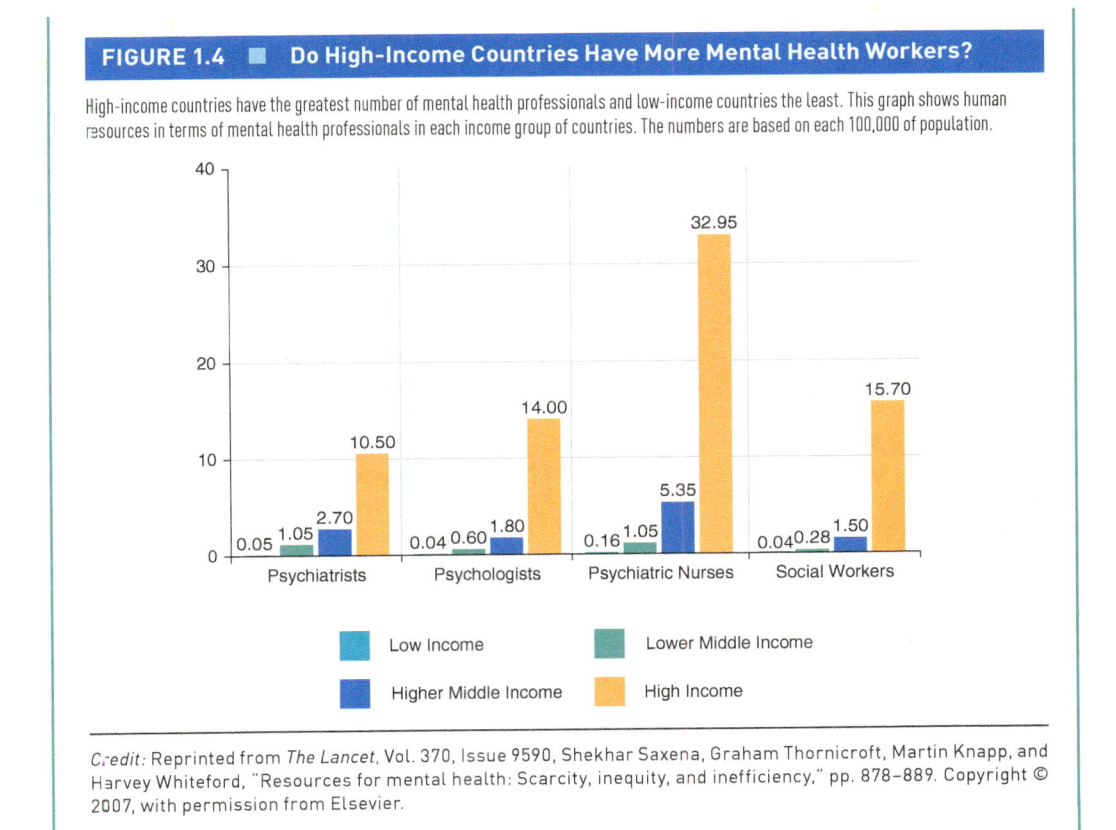

FIGURE 1.4 ■ Do High-Income Countries Have More Mental Health Workers?

High-income countries have the greatest number of mental health professionals and low-income countries the least. This graph shows human resources in terms of mental health professionals in each income group of countries. The numbers are based on each 100,000 of population.

	Low Income	Lower Middle Income	Higher Middle Income	High Income
Psychiatrists	0.05	1.05	2.70	10.50
Psychologists	0.04	0.60	1.80	14.00
Psychiatric Nurses	0.16	1.05	5.35	32.95
Social Workers	0.04	0.28	1.50	15.70

Credit: Reprinted from *The Lancet*, Vol. 370, Issue 9590, Shekhar Saxena, Graham Thornicroft, Martin Knapp, and Harvey Whiteford, "Resources for mental health: Scarcity, inequity, and inefficiency," pp. 878–889. Copyright © 2007, with permission from Elsevier.

Thought Question

What are some ways mental health care professionals in both higher- and lower-income countries can work together to increase the availability and quality of mental health resources in the countries with the fewest resources?

For a more complete understanding of psychopathology, it is important to understand the particular rules a culture has for expressing both internal experiences and external behaviors (Marsella & Yamada, 2000). One simple way to distinguish cultures is whether they emphasize the importance of individual achievement, such as those cultures seen in the United States and Europe, or whether they emphasize collective values and working together, as seen in Asian cultures, such as those of China and Japan. This in turn can influence the type of psychological distress experienced. For example, social anxiety is more common in collective as compared to individualistic cultures (Hong, 2018). What may be a common stress-free experience in one culture may lead to stress and anxiety in another. Even what individuals tell themselves about having a mental disorder can vary from culture to culture. Likewise, artistic and spiritual experiences considered normal in one society may be considered "crazy" in another.

Historically, a simplistic view of culture has emphasized how each culture is locally determined, without reference to universal psychological processes. When universal ways of behaving, feeling, or thinking are suggested, this view assumes that this information is acquired by social learning. Although this is an important aspect of culture, such an emphasis will quickly lead you into the outdated nature–nurture debate, which lacks the insights of modern evolutionary and neuroscience perspectives. For example, consider the question of why foods with milk are found in European diets and not in Asian diets. One answer could be cultural preferences. However, a more complete answer includes the fact that Northern Europeans have a gene that allows them to continue digesting milk products after the traditional time of weaning.

This gene would have conferred an advantage to those who carried it since dairy products are a high-quality food source, and over time—probably less than 10,000 years—that advantage would have allowed these genes to be passed on to almost all of the European population. Today, 98% of all individuals in Sweden have this gene. In the United States, with its large European migration, 88% of white Americans are lactose tolerant, meaning they can digest milk products. Native Americans, on the other hand, are lactose intolerant. Overall, this suggests a close connection between cultural and evolutionary perspectives.

The picture becomes even more complicated in terms of psychological processes. There is a particular form of a gene (5-HTT) related to the neurotransmitter serotonin that is associated with being prone to developing higher levels of anxiety and depression. When its occurrence is examined cross-culturally, studies have shown that 70% to 80% of Japanese individuals carry this gene, whereas only 40% to 45% of Europeans carry it (see Ambady & Bharucha, 2009). Likewise, brain imaging studies have shown that cultural values can influence which areas of the brain are active during self-evaluation (Chiao, 2011; Knyazev et al., 2021).

The larger question raised by these studies is whether this genetic variation influences the manner in which cultural structures formalize social interactions and how this might be related to what is considered mental illness. That is, a society that has more individuals who are prone to anxiety may develop different forms of social interaction than one that does not. Not only can the environment influence genetics, but genetics can also influence culture. This work is just beginning to be applied to viewing psychopathology from a cultural standpoint.

Considering how a condition such as lactose tolerance is found in some groups of individuals around the world and not in others gives us additional insights into when this condition may have developed. Since lactose tolerance is not found throughout the world but is limited to particular groups, one would assume that it was not part of the human condition when humans migrated out of Africa some 100,000 years ago. We can ask similar questions in terms of psychopathology. One question might be how long, in terms of our human history, a particular psychopathology has existed.

Let's take schizophrenia as an example. A WHO study examined the presence of schizophrenia in a number of countries with very different racial and cultural backgrounds (Sartorius et al., 1986). If schizophrenia had an important environmental component, then you would expect to see different manifestations of the disorder in different cultures. Higher-income countries would show different rates from those of lower-income countries. Areas with different climates might also show differences, as is the case with multiple sclerosis. What these authors found was that, despite the different cultural and racial backgrounds surveyed, the experience of schizophrenia was remarkably similar across countries. Likewise, the risk of developing schizophrenia was similar in terms of total population presence—about 1%. Further, the disorder had a similar time course in its occurrence, with its characteristics first being seen in young adults.

The evolutionary and cultural perspectives help us ask questions such as what function a disorder might serve, as well as how it came about. For example, humans fear animals they have little contact with but do not fear more likely causes of danger such as automobile accidents. Unlike other species, humans live in environments that are different in many respects from those that shaped our early evolutionary history. We have developed large cities and the technological abilities to communicate instantly around the planet. We have also developed ways to mitigate conditions such as the weather experienced in our personal environment that would have played a greater role in our lives thousands of years ago. Compared with other species, humans live less in nature and more in culture. However, it is important in considering psychopathology to remember the environment in which humans as a species developed.

In thinking about our evolutionary history, we can consider how one basic human process developed in relation to an earlier one. For example, in the same way that pain can be seen as a warning system to the body to protect it from tissue damage, anxiety may have evolved to protect the individual from other types of potential threats. In fact, an evolutionary perspective has led to neuroscience research findings that social processes such as feeling rejected use similar brain circuits as those processes involved in physical pain. Further, many of the outward expressions of social anxiety parallel what is seen in dominance interactions in primates. Submissive monkeys avoid contact with more dominant ones, just as humans experiencing social anxiety avoid more dominant individuals. Thus, one hypothesis would be that anxiety may have its evolutionary origins in dominance structures. If this were true, we might expect to see some relationship to sexual instinctual processes, as is the case with dominance. Indeed, social anxiety begins to show just prior to the onset of puberty—around 8 years of age. Of course, this merely shows how evolution may be related to anxiety. The evolutionary perspective can help us think about the roots of psychopathology as well, and it will be a recurring theme of this text.

Is Psychopathology Universal?

If psychopathology is part of our human makeup, then we would expect to see similar manifestations of it worldwide. One classic study was performed by Jane Murphy (1976) of Harvard University. It dates from the 1970s when mental illness was considered to be related to learning and the social construction of norms. In fact, some suggested that mental illness was just a myth developed by Western societies. In this perspective, neither the individual nor their acts are abnormal in an objective sense. One important implication of this view was that what would be seen as mental illness in a Western industrial culture might be very different from what was seen as mental illness in a less developed rural culture. That is to say, mental illness in this perspective was viewed as a social construction of the society. The alternative to this perspective is more similar to other human processes such as emotionality, in which humans throughout the world recognize similar expressions of the basic emotions. If mental illness is part of our human history, as evolutionary psychologists suggest, then we would expect to find similar manifestations across a variety of cultures.

Murphy first studied two geographically separate and distinct non-Western groups: the Inuit of northwest Alaska and the Yoruba of rural tropical Nigeria. Although many researchers of that time would have expected to find the conceptions of normality and abnormality to be very different in the two cultures, this is not what Murphy found. She found that these cultures were well acquainted with disturbed thought and behavior processes in which a person was said to be "out of his or her mind." This included the person doing strange things as well as hearing voices. Murphy concluded that processes of disturbed thought and behavior similar to schizophrenia are found in most cultures and that most cultures have a distinct name in their language for these processes.

In addition, Murphy reported that these cultures had a variety of words for what traditionally is referred to as neurosis, although today we would call it anxiety or depression. Mood disorders include feeling anxious, tense, and fearful of being with others as well as being troubled and not able to sleep. One Inuit term was translated as "worrying too much until it makes the person sick." Thus, it appears that most cultures have a word for what has been called neurosis, what has been called psychosis, and what has been called normalcy. What is also interesting is that many cultures also have words for people who are "out of their mind" but not "crazy": witch doctors, shamans, and artists.

To add evidence to her argument that psychopathology is indeed part of our human nature, Murphy also reviewed a large variety of studies conducted by others that looked at how common mental illness was in different cultures. The implication here is that if its prevalence is similar in cultures across the world, then it is more likely to be part of the human condition rather than culturally derived. What these studies suggest is that many forms of mental illness such as schizophrenia are found at similar rates around the world. Overall, this research established that mental illness was not a created concept by a given culture, but rather part of the human condition in both its recognition and its prevalence. However, one's culture plays a role in how mental illness is manifested in a specific society.

CONCEPT CHECK

- What evidence would you cite to characterize the relationships among genetics, culture, and evolution in human development?
- Is psychopathology universal? What kinds of evidence show that it is? What evidence is there for cultural differences in psychopathology?

HISTORICAL CONSIDERATIONS IN UNDERSTANDING PSYCHOPATHOLOGY

Humans have gone from a worldview in which magic, including the idea that you could be possessed by spirits or demons, produced mental illness to a time in which our scientific understanding describes a complex set of processes on many levels that contribute to mental illness. As you have seen, these levels go from society and culture to research from the neurosciences, including the role of genes and neurons.

Today, we see those with mental illness as whole people with both abilities and deficits. In terms of the future, there is a growing movement to empower people with mental disorders to have a greater say in their treatment. A person's high functioning and ability to make decisions are not completely taken away by having a mental disorder. The person is still able to describe their experiences and, in the best of conditions, to ask others for help. However, this is getting ahead of ourselves.

Psychology seeks to describe and understand human behavior and experience. In fact, as humans, we have a long history of trying to understand ourselves. In this section, you will see some of the historical conceptions that have influenced psychology (see Finger, 2000, or the classic Boring, 1950, for more information). One of these conceptions is the role of the body and its involvement in our mental processes. Some of the ideas we will examine date back thousands of years yet still influence our views today.

Ancient Greek and Roman Influences—Mental Illness Involves the Brain

Beginning with Pythagoras in the 6th century BCE, whom we know for his theorem concerning the sides of a right triangle, there was an emphasis on identifying the underlying scientific principles that may account for all forms of behavior. Pythagoras not only coined the term *philosophy*, which can be translated as love of meaning or wisdom, but also began to set the stage for understanding human behavior and experience as related to internal processes and natural causes. This was in contrast to the prevailing view that human behavior and related disorders reflected the actions of the gods, such as the belief that mental illness was a divine punishment. Pythagoras was one of the first to see the brain as the structure involved in human intellect as well as in mental disorders.

In the next century, Hippocrates, often seen as the father of modern medicine, moved this concept to the next level with his emphasis on careful observation and a continued articulation of the idea that all disorders, both mental and physical, should be sought within the patient. His view of the brain suggests it is the brain that produces "joys, delights, laughter and sports, and sorrows, griefs, despondency, and lamentations." He further notes that "we become mad and delirious, and fears and terrors assail us, some by night, and some by day, and dreams and untimely wanderings, and cares that are not suitable, and ignorance of present circumstances, desuetude, and unskillfulness. All these things we endure from the brain" (Hippocrates, 400 BCE/n.d.).

Galen (130–200 CE) was a physician in the Roman Empire who influenced Western and Islamic thought until the Renaissance. Some see him as a representation of the beginning of experimentation in medicine because he used dissection to better describe the structure and function of physiological structures. His work as a physician to the gladiators would have also given him firsthand knowledge of the consequences of trauma and its treatment.

During his lifetime, Galen wrote hundreds of treatises on science, medicine, and philosophy. He was largely a champion of *empiricism*, which stresses the use of direct observation as a means of gaining information. Writing in his treatise *On Medical Experience*, Galen (ca. 165–175 CE/1944) stated, "I am a man who attends only to what can be perceived by the senses."

From chance encounters with human accidents and trauma and his anatomical work using a variety of animals, Galen carefully described the brain; the cranial nerves that are involved in sight, smell, movement, and other functions; and the nerves of the sympathetic nervous system involved in fight-or-flight reactions, among others. From his experiments with animals, Galen knew that blood was transported throughout the body. He had an early theory of how blood was changed by the organs based on the idea of *spirits*. Galen believed that blood was made in the liver, which gave it *natural spirits*. It then went to the heart where it developed *vital spirits* and then, with the introduction of air to the blood on the way to the brain, it was transformed into *animal spirits*. These animal spirits could be stored in the

New doctors take the Hippocratic Oath, so named after the Greek physician Hippocrates.
Pat Greenhouse/The Boston Globe/via Getty Images

ventricles of the brain until they were needed. Today, we think in terms of hormones rather than spirits. Galen's works became the encyclopedia of medicine for the next 1,500 years.

Psychopathology in the Middle Ages

Although the Greek and Roman periods included individuals who attempted to understand psychopathology in a more humane way, this perspective disappeared as these civilizations declined. During the Middle Ages in Europe, disease and especially mental illness was seen from a religious perspective, with the devil being a major player. That is, when someone was observed to act in strange and bizarre ways, it was assumed that the person was a witch or possessed by the devil. As such, mental illness did not exist. What existed was the devil working through individuals. This view continued in Europe until the 1800s, especially among people with less education.

One of the classic books in this genre was the *Malleus Maleficarum* (The Hammer of the Witches), published in the 1480s. This book was written by two German priests and approved by the pope. It went through a number of editions and became the handbook of the Inquisition. It explained how witches existed and flew through the air as well as how they should be tortured if they did not confess. In a "catch-22," the captured witches were tied to a device and lowered into cold water. If they floated, they were thought to be possessed by the devil and most likely were then killed by hanging or fire. If they sank to the bottom and drowned, then they were innocent. During the interrogations, witches were not to be left alone or given clothes, since the devil would visit them or hide in their clothing. Although the writers of the time did not understand the nature of psychopathology, they did describe in some detail particular characteristics of different disorders including bipolar disorder, depression, and such psychotic processes as hallucinations and delusions.

From the Renaissance to the 1700s—The Beginning of Modern Science

Between the time of Galen and the Renaissance, Western science and medicine remained fairly stagnant, with little new knowledge being added. One problem during this period was that authority, which was often the Church, determined what was true or not. Since authority was able to use its own standard of truth, it was difficult to argue another position. For example, the Church was able to say that the earth was the center of the universe, and that was that.

During the Middle Ages, mental illness was perceived as the work of the devil, and individuals were accused of witchcraft.

iStock.com/Nastasic

Beginning in the 14th century, however, a new spirit began to emerge in Europe. It influenced art, literature, politics, and science. In art, there was a desire for a sense of realism, which led artists such as Leonardo da Vinci to carefully study the human body. He performed dissections on animals and human cadavers to carefully reveal the structure of organs. Figure 1.5 shows one of da Vinci's drawings.

With the detailed drawings of human anatomy created by da Vinci and other artists of the time, there was now the possibility for the scientists of the 1600s to consider function. One important focus was the manner in which the nervous system allows us to perform both involuntary and voluntary functions. How physiological processes are involved in remembering, moving, feeling, and thinking became topics of consideration. Mechanical models emerged, as illustrated by the writings of French philosopher René Descartes (1596–1650).

Descartes was intrigued by mechanical machines such as the large clocks in Europe with moving figures or water displays in large fountains. By analogy, he assumed that reflexes or involuntary actions of organisms were based on similar principles. Thus, moving your hand quickly from a hot stove or even digesting food was seen as a mechanical operation. For Descartes, all animal behavior could be explained by mechanical principles, as could human involuntary actions. In Figure 1.6 from Descartes' work, you can see the mechanical means by which a hot fire would cause an involuntary or reflexive movement.

The important distinction that continues today is that behavior can be categorized as either involuntary or voluntary. Voluntary actions such as thinking or consciously performing an act were different in that they required a mind, and humans were the only organism to have a mind, according to Descartes. By thinking, humans can know with certainty that they exist—thus, the famous philosophical statement of Descartes, "I think, therefore I am."

Given his understanding that the bodies of animals are totally mechanical and that humans have both a body and a mind, Descartes created a mind–body distinction that science has had to face in its explanations. The problem is, how can a material body including the brain be influenced by an immaterial process such as the mind? How can a thought influence a cell in the brain?

FIGURE 1.5 ■ Leonardo da Vinci Drawing of the Structure of Human Organs

Before Leonardo da Vinci, there were few drawings of actual human organs. Beginning in the 14th century, da Vinci performed dissections on animals and human cadavers. He was then able to draw the structure of organs.

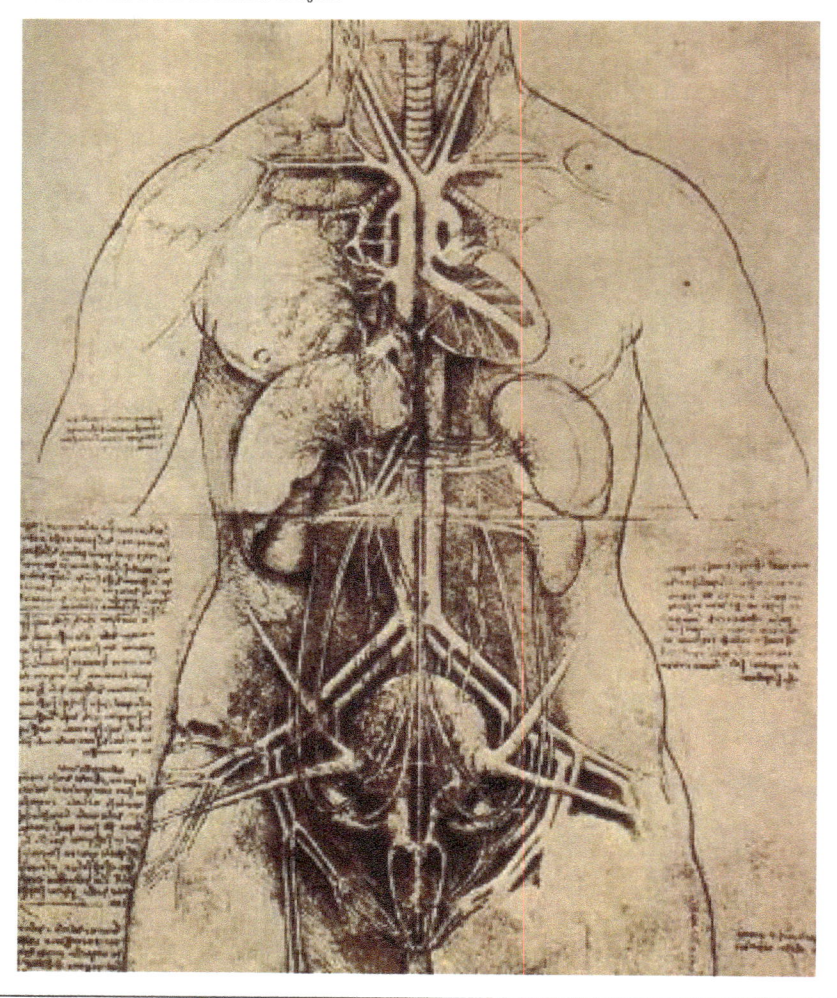

Credit: The Picture Art Collection/Alamy Stock Photo

Although today we generally talk about the mind–body problem, the metaphysics of Descartes' era would often make the distinction between body and soul. Descartes answered this problem by suggesting that the rational soul was able to control the mechanical body by having both functions come together in one particular organ of the brain, the pineal gland. It is in the pineal gland, Descartes claimed, that the mind not only controls the body but also senses the nature and flow of the mechanical nervous system.

Today, most neuroscientists see the mind as resulting directly from the brain and believe that the mind–body problem is not actually a problem to be solved. However, the question of whether particular behaviors seen in individuals with mental illness represent involuntary processes performed without the benefit of a conscious mind has plagued our legal understanding of mental illness.

In the 1600s, science as a way of knowing about the world began to emerge. At the beginning of this period, prior authorities such as Aristotle or the Church determined the worldview. In this century, Galileo led a movement that would eventually replace authority with experimentation. This movement toward experimentation was greatly aided by Galileo's own inventions, such as the telescope, the thermometer, an improved microscope, and a pendulum-type timing device. Each of these instruments allowed people to experiment and answer for themselves the questions of nature. With Galileo's work, a new science based on observation and experimentation was beginning. Galileo was part of a revolution that was to challenge authority. In the 1680s, Isaac Newton's classic work *Principia* was published

FIGURE 1.6 ■ Involuntary or Reflexive Movement

In this drawing by Descartes from the 1600s, the person is shown touching the fire with his foot, which results in an impulse being sent to the brain.

Source: Descartes, R. (1664). *L'homme et la formation du foetus.* J. Le Gras, p. 27.

(Newton, 1687/1969). Designated by science historian Gerald Holton (1952) as "probably the greatest single book in the history of science," this work describes Newton's theories of time, space, and motion as well as his rules of reasoning for science.

> **CONCEPT CHECK**
>
> - Concepts in understanding psychopathology date back thousands of years yet still influence our views today. What important contributions did the ancient Greeks and Romans—particularly Pythagoras, Hippocrates, and Galen—make to current views of psychopathology?
> - Describe the shift from authority to science as a way of knowing that happened during the Renaissance. Specifically, what did Leonardo da Vinci, René Descartes, Galileo, and Isaac Newton contribute during this period that led to this shift?

DISCOVERING THE FUNCTION OF THE BRAIN IN BEHAVIOR AND PSYCHOPATHOLOGY

The developing spirit of science during the 1600s set the stage for a new breed of scientist to emerge. One of these scientists was an English doctor, Thomas Willis (1621–1675). He was interested in neurology and in fact coined that term along with a number of anatomical terms, such as *lobe, hemisphere,* and *corpus striatum*. He may also have been the first person to use the word *psychology* in English.

Willis sought to combine the study of brain structure and function. He suggested that lower-brain structures were responsible for more basic functions of life and that these structures could be found across a variety of vertebrates. On the other hand, those structures located higher in the brain must be involved in more advanced processes seen in higher organisms such as humans. Implicit in this idea is a break with Descartes' suggestion that animals are only machines.

By the end of the 1700s, the nervous system had been completely dissected and the major parts described in detail. The brain was seen to be composed of gray matter and white matter, terms we continue to use today (Figure 1.7). White matter was involved in moving information to and from the gray matter. Today, we have a fuller understanding of brain structure, with the thin outer shell of the brain consisting of cells, which appear to be a darker color and are thus called *gray matter*. Underlying this are the axons, which transfer information throughout the brain. Their myelin sheaths are lighter in color, and thus these areas are referred to as *white matter*. Myelin is made up of fats and proteins and wraps around axons like insulation does around electrical cables, resulting in an increased speed of information transmissions.

Also by the 1700s, scientists knew that there was a general pattern in all human brains in how the brain was structured in terms of surface structures or bumps, which were called *gyri*, and the grooves between them, referred to then and now as *sulci* and *fissures*. The present-day terms used to describe parts of the brain also come from Latin, so the lobes of the brain are the *frontal lobe, parietal lobe, temporal lobe*, and *occipital lobe*. This can be seen in Figure 1.8.

Scientists of the 1700s also determined that the nervous system had a central division consisting of the brain and spinal cord and a peripheral division consisting of nerves throughout the body (Figure 1.9).

The 1700s to the 1900s

With the basic structure of the nervous system known, scientists of the 1700s began a quest to understand how the system developed and how it worked. One of the contributions of this quest was the realization that the body created and used electrical activity in its basic processes. Today, this electrical activity shows differences in various types of mental illness.

Scientists such as Luigi Galvani and Emil du Bois-Reymond were able to show that electrical stimulation causes a frog's leg to twitch. With this demonstration, nerves began to be thought of as wires through which electricity passes. Further, it was determined that the brain could itself produce electrical activity. The greater impact of this discovery was that electricity was also something that could be

FIGURE 1.7 ■ Gray Matter and White Matter in the Brain

The outer level of the brain contains cells that appear darker in color and thus are called *gray matter*. Axons transfer information throughout the brain. Their myelin sheaths are lighter in color and thus are called *white matter*.

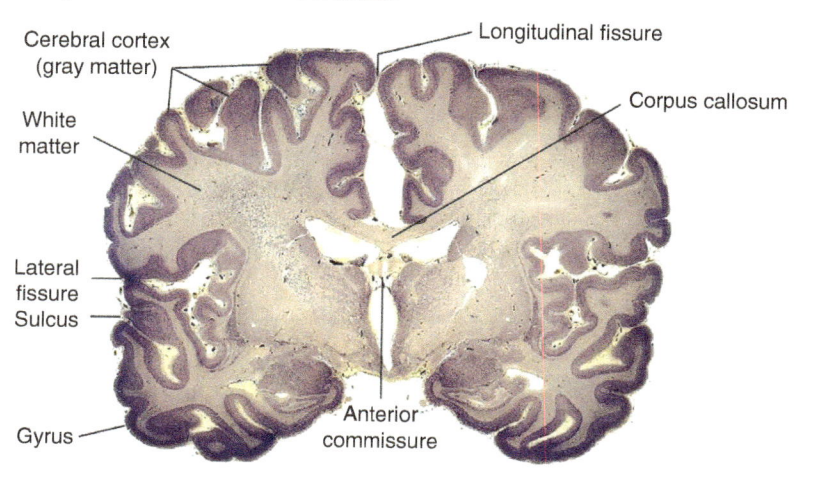

Credit: Reproduced (or adapted) with permission from Caution-Caution-Caution-http://brainmuseum.org, Specimens used for this publication are from the Defense Health Agency Neuroanatomical Collections Division of the National Museum of Health and Medicine, the University of Wisconsin and Michigan State Comparative Mammalian Brain Collections supported by the U.S. National Science Foundation.

FIGURE 1.8 ■ The Lobes of the Brain

The present-day terms used to describe parts of the brain come from Latin, so the lobes of the brain are called the *frontal lobe, parietal lobe, temporal lobe,* and *occipital lobe.*

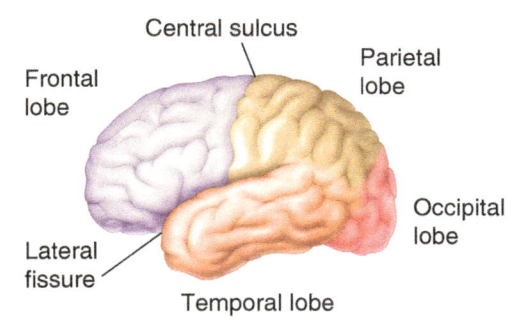

FIGURE 1.9 ■ Distribution of the Nervous System

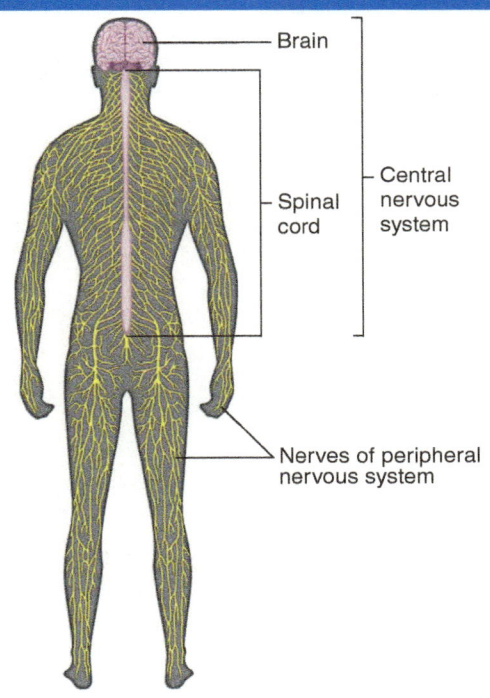

measured, thus setting the stage for the following centuries in which experimentation in the electrical activity of the brain and body would play a significant role in physiology and psychology.

One discovery during the early part of the 1800s was that there is a system for sending information to the muscle, which results in muscle movement, and another system for bringing sensory information back to the brain. When you hold a glass, for example, the sensory or *affector* system relays information on what the object you are touching feels like, whereas the muscular or *effector* system tells the muscles how to hold and pick up the glass. Thus, in many nerves there are connections for both receiving and sending information (Figure 1.9). These pathways are called *fiber tracts.*

At the level of the spinal cord, these fiber tracts split, with the sensory information being conveyed by the dorsal root and the action or motor information involving the ventral root. By the 1850s, Hermann von Helmholtz had measured the speed of the nerve impulse and found it to be around 90 feet a second, which is a little more than a mile a minute. This is much slower than the speed of electricity in a copper wire, which approximates the speed of light (186,000 miles per second). However, the advantage of the nerve impulse—as shown in later research—is that it is not diminished over the length of its travels.

One important realization of the 1700s was that particular functions could be localized to different parts of the brain. One person often cited today is Joseph Gall. Although Gall was correct in suggesting that the frontal part of the brain involved higher cognitive processes and social determinations, he was wrong in assuming that somehow brain function would be reflected in the shape of (and bumps on) the skull. If an individual were good at a particular ability, Gall assumed that their skull would look different from another person's skull who was not as talented. To support this idea, he examined the skulls of people at the extremes, such as great writers, statesmen, and mathematicians, as well as criminals, people with mental illness, and individuals with particular pathologies. Overall, he defined 19 processes that he thought humans and animals both performed and another 8 that were unique to humans (Figure 1.10).

Gall and his followers never scientifically tested their ideas, and research by others did not support their claims about the structure of the head. What Gall did that *was* supported was to suggest viewing the brain as capable of performing a variety of functions and that these functions could be localized in different parts of the brain.

Abilities related to understanding and producing language greatly aided specific discoveries related to cerebral localization of function. Physicians began to collect considerable information on patients

FIGURE 1.10 ■ Gall's Structure of the Head

Gall's depiction of functional localization in the brain. Each area of the brain was thought to be related to a particular ability, such as art, humor, curiosity, and even the ability to murder another person.

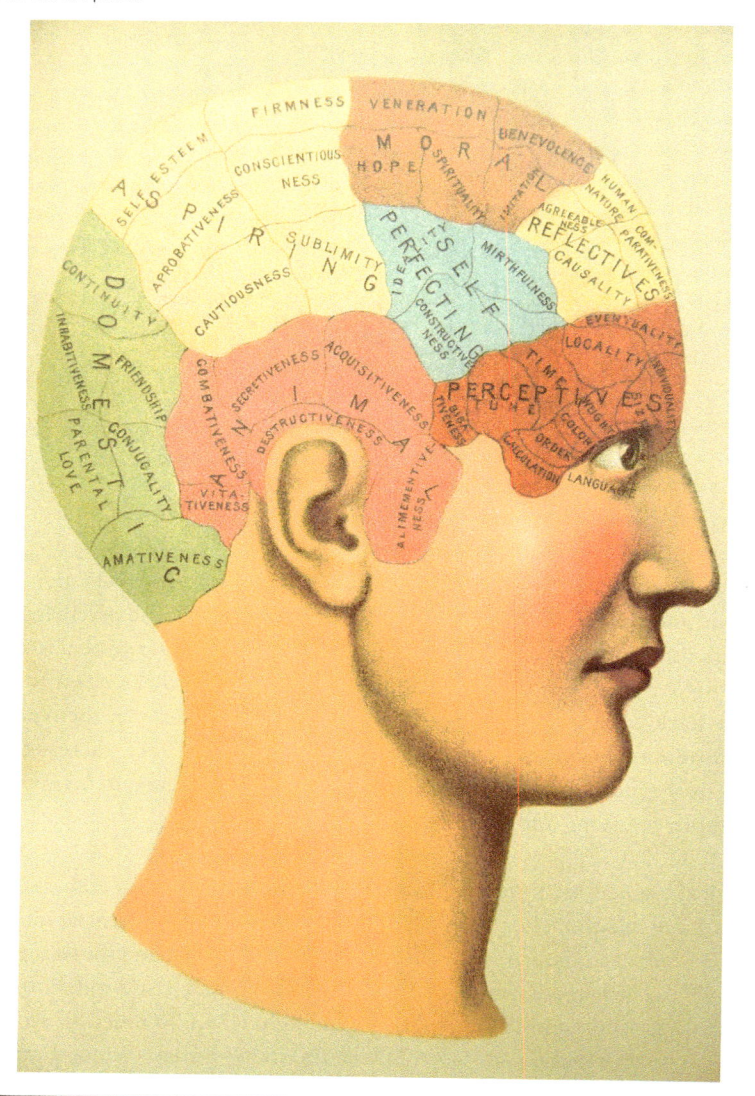

Credit: iStock.com/Mark Strozier

who had a variety of difficulties with language. Some patients could understand language but could not produce speech. Others had trouble remembering words. Still others could not understand language.

In 1861, a major turning point occurred when physician Paul Broca examined a patient who could understand language but could not speak. This patient was sent to Broca because of a much more serious medical condition and died shortly thereafter. Broca then performed an autopsy and reported an abnormality in an area on the left side of the frontal lobe. Based on a variety of cases, Broca was able to show that language is a left hemispheric process and that damage to the frontal areas of the left hemisphere results in problems in higher executive functions such as judgment, the ability to reflect on a situation, and the ability to understand things in an abstract manner (Finger, 2000). Today, the area related to language production in the left hemisphere is called *Broca's area* (Figure 1.11).

In 1874, Carl Wernicke published a paper that suggested that language understanding was related to the left temporal lobe. He studied patients who were unable to comprehend what they heard. At the same time, they were able to produce fluent speech, although it was incomprehensible and included nonexistent words. The specific place in the brain identified by Wernicke is now called *Wernicke's area* (see Figure 1.11). The discoveries of Broca and Wernicke helped the scientific community understand that language was made up of different processes, including the ability to understand and to produce language.

Throughout his career, British neurologist John Hughlings Jackson examined the brain from a developmental and evolutionary perspective (see Williamson & Allman, 2011). Hughlings Jackson saw the brain as composed of three levels. The earliest part of the brain to evolve was the spinal cord and brain stem, which controlled the vegetative functions such as breathing, sleep, and temperature control. The next level to evolve included the basal ganglia, which is connected to various other parts of the brain and is involved in movement. The third level to evolve included areas involved in higher cortical functions, including thought. It is the task of the higher level to keep the person aware of changes in the environment.

Within this framework, Hughlings Jackson suggested principles based partly on evolutionary analysis. One important principle is **hierarchical integration** through inhibitory control. By this, he meant that the various levels of the brain, such as the brain stem, the limbic system, and the neocortex, are able to interact with each other. Further, the type of interaction from the higher levels restricts or inhibits the lower levels.

In terms of mental illness, Hughlings Jackson (1894) suggested that symptoms such as illusions, hallucinations, and delusions are not in themselves the result of disease. Rather, it is when higher-level processes no longer inhibit the earlier evolved processes of the brain that these symptoms appear.

FIGURE 1.11 ■ Language Is Shown to Be Related to Different Parts of the Brain

Broca's area is a part of the temporal lobe that is involved in speaking a language. Wernicke's area is involved in understanding language.

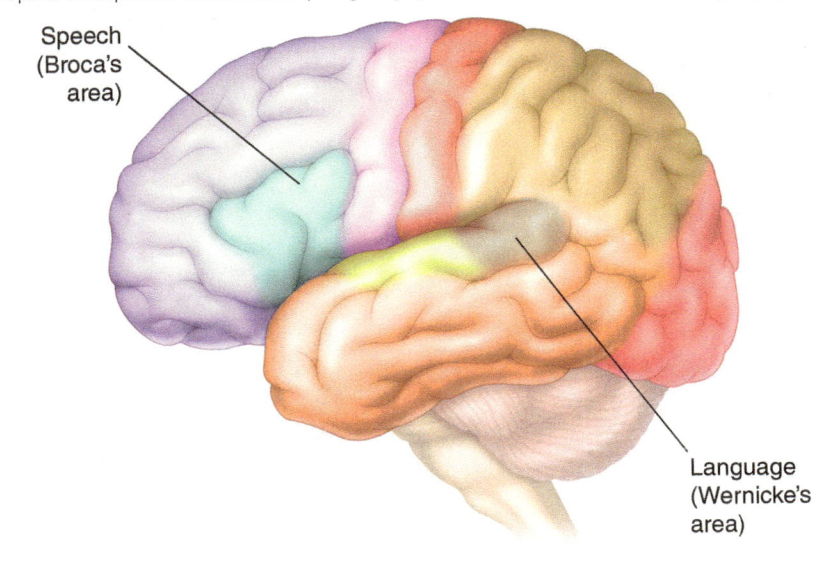

Speech (Broca's area)

Language (Wernicke's area)

Highlings Jackson referred to this process as *dissolutions*. Dissolutions are the reversal of the normal process of evolution. Thus, the primitive experiences seen in psychosis, for example, represent the primitive parts of the brain working normally. What is missing is the relationship of these primitive areas with higher mental processes.

A Growing Understanding of the Role of Evolution

Another big idea that emerged in the 1800s was that all of nature is in constant flow and that things, including organisms, change. This idea focused on the evolution of species and is most often associated with the work of Charles Darwin (1809–1882). **Variation** was to become one of the major components of Darwin's thinking concerning evolution. In fact, he began his thinking with the assumption that heritable variations can and do occur in nature. Darwin then presented the important realization that not all plants or animals that come into existence survive. Many organisms such as sea stars, for example, produce millions of eggs of which only a limited number survive. Depending on climate conditions, food supply, predator population, and a host of other factors including disease, only a limited number of those born survive to maturity.

Consequently, Darwin (1859) suggested, "There is a frequently recurring struggle for existence." Who is to survive in this struggle? Darwin suggested that if an individual has even a slight variation that helps it to compete successfully for survival, then over time the species will be made up more and more of members with these characteristics and less and less of individuals lacking these features. This process is referred to as **natural selection**. Darwin described this process in his 1859 book, *On the Origin of Species by Means of Natural Selection*.

Darwin later extended the theory of natural selection to include **sexual selection,** or the manner in which males and females choose a mate. This work is described in his 1871 book, *The Descent of Man*. Darwin noted that males and females differ not only in terms of organs of sexual reproduction but also in secondary sexual characteristics such as mammary glands for the nourishment of infants in females or facial hair in males. According to Darwin, sexual selection depends on the success of certain individuals over others of the same sex. Darwin also saw that besides same-sex competition, there is also competition to attract members of the opposite sex. There has been continuous debate and research concerning what attraction means for males and females of all species.

Charles Darwin

Julia Margaret Cameron; archived in Library of Congress Web Archives at https://www.loc.gov/pictures/item/2004674431/

Darwin began the *Origin* work with the question of natural selection especially as it related to animals. In *The Descent of Man*, he expanded these ideas to humans and also examined the question of sexual selection. In other works, such as his notebooks, he extended his research to cognitive and emotional processes. The broad question is that of how psychological functions have evolved. One answer he gives is that living in social groups produces an increase in cognitive ability. Darwin also presents notes on memory and habit, imagination, language, aesthetic feelings, emotion, motivation, animal intelligence, psychopathology, and dreaming (Gruber, 1974). One important question is the manner in which self-preservation, sexual selection, and social processes are reflected in psychopathology.

Overall, Darwin helped us understand the close connection between the environment and genetic processes, although Darwin did not know about genes at that time. Today, we know that this close connection makes such questions as what is responsible for our behavior, nature in terms of genes **or** nurture in terms of experiences, meaningless. As you will see later, genes influence our environment and our environment influences which genes are activated or not. It is this close connection that allows for change. Humans are born less fully developed at birth than many other species and thus are sensitive to changes in their environment as they continue to develop. Unlike animals that live within nature, humans largely live within the backdrop of our culture. Another part of the complexity with humans is our ability to reflect on ourselves and our world. In this way, a layer of thought, including expectation and imagination, is injected between the person and the environment.

A Search for Organization

One of the themes of the sciences of the 1800s was the search for organization. In understanding psychopathology, an important person associated with this search was the Paris physician Jean-Martin Charcot (1825–1893). Charcot sought to bring organization to an understanding of neurological disorders through a variety of methods such as careful observation. This observation was of both what the patient said, which we refer to today as symptoms, as well as what the clinician observed, or what we refer to as signs. The overall search was for which signs and symptoms go together to form a syndrome. An additional technique—autopsy, or examination of the body after death—further allowed for the connection of syndromes with underlying anatomy. Autopsies allowed for the determination of which tissue showed signs of pathology. Using this method, Charcot was able to confirm the correctness of Hughlings Jackson's thoughts on neurological organization. Overall, Charcot showed that the human motor cortex is organized similarly to that of other animals, with the left hemisphere controlling the right side of the body and vice versa.

Charcot is best known for initially describing brain disorder relationships for a number of motor-related disorders, including Parkinson's disease and multiple sclerosis. Charcot also established Tourette's syndrome as a separate disease when he asked his assistant Gilles de la Tourette to help him. De la Tourette wrote of cases that included a teenage boy who would show involuntary movements and scream swear words.

Charcot was also able to show that *conversion reactions,* in which the person shows outward signs of trouble hearing or seeing, or being unable to experience pain in the hand, were without any underlying pathology. During Charcot's time, conversion reactions were referred to as "hysteria." A young Sigmund Freud heard Charcot's lectures on hysteria, including the observation that psychological trauma could trigger these reactions. This became the initial basis of Freud's psychoanalytic work.

Charcot helped to integrate symptoms of a disorder with both psychological and brain processes. He also emphasized that, as in the case of hysteria, much of what had been seen as possession by demons could be viewed as resulting from natural causes. Thus, there was no need for faith healers or church rituals to remove evil spirits. This also encouraged society to view an individual with hysteria or another mental affliction as someone with a disorder rather than as an evil person. Much of Charcot's work took place at the Salpêtrière Hospital for the poor in Paris. These hospitals served as both research centers and places where treatments were developed for mental illness.

Charcot demonstrates a case of hysteria (painting by André Brouillet).
GL Archive/Alamy Stock Photo

HISTORICAL APPROACHES TO CARE FOR THOSE WITH MENTAL DISORDERS

In 1330, a convent of the order of St. Mary of Bethlehem became the first institution for people with mental illness in England. The institution eventually received a royal charter and, over the years, the word *Bethlehem* became *Bedlam*, and the institution was referred to as "Old Bedlam." The English word *bedlam* comes from this institution. Various reports suggested that the inmates were often chained, treated cruelly, and not given proper food or clothing. As depicted in novels of the day, people in the 1700s would go to Bedlam to see the inmates as an outing in much the same way that today we might go to a zoo. In 1814, some 96,000 people visited the asylum.

In the 1800s, there was a campaign in England to change the conditions for the patients, which led to the establishment of the Committee on Madhouses in 1815. This ushered in a period of concern for the patients rather than seeing them as objects of curiosity as in the previous century. Treatment for patients during the 1800s brought new practices, including the therapeutic value of work.

During this period, there was a spirit throughout the world to adopt a "moral treatment of the insane." Three important individuals in this movement were Benjamin Rush (1745–1813) in the United States, Philippe Pinel (1745–1826) in France, and Vincenzo Chiarugi (1759–1820) in Italy (Gerard, 1997). In the United States, Rush, who had signed the Declaration of Independence, later established a wing at the Pennsylvania Hospital in Philadelphia for the treatment of mental illness. He is often considered the father of American psychiatry and saw mental illness as a problem of the mind. However, he continued to practice bloodletting as the best treatment for mental illness. Rush developed a tranquilizing chair that he believed would change the flow of blood. Professionals tend to view this invention as neither helpful nor hurtful to the patient. He also wrote the first psychiatric textbook published in America.

In France, Pinel sought to change the way that people with mental illness were treated. He believed that mental illness could be studied using the methods of the natural sciences. In 1793, Pinel became the director of the Bicêtre asylum in Paris. As director, he reviewed the commitment papers of the patients, toured the building, and met with each patient individually. The building was in bad shape, and the patients were chained to walls. As Pinel (1806) himself described the institution, "everything presented to me the appearance of chaos and confusion" (pp. 1–2). Pinel petitioned the government and received permission to remove the chains, and he also abandoned the practice of bloodletting.

THE RAKE'S PROGRESS.
PLATE 8.
SCENE IN BEDLAM.
From the Original Picture by Hogarth

The English word *bedlam* comes from the name of the first institution for people with mental illness in 14th-century England.

iStock.com/duncan1890

In France, Pinel sought to change the way individuals with mental illness were treated. Here, he removes the chains from a patient.

iStock.com/duncan1890

Pinel began to carefully observe patients and also talk with them. In these discussions, he attempted to create a detailed case history and to better understand the development of the disorder. This led to a classification system he published in 1789, which sorted mental diseases into five categories: melancholia, mania without delirium, mania with delirium, dementia, and idiocy. In 1795, Pinel became the chief physician at the Salpêtrière (which was then a hospice for poor women), where he remained for the rest of his life. Pinel is known as the father of scientific psychiatry.

Vincenzo Chiarugi was not well known outside of Italy until a paper published in the middle of the last century, which brought his name to the attention of Americans (Mora, 1959). Some 8 years earlier than Pinel, Chiarugi began removing chains from his patients. Early in his career, Chiarugi became the director of a large hospital in Florence that included special facilities for people with mental illness. The institution had been established with the passage of a law in 1774 in Italy that allowed these individuals to be hospitalized. As director of the hospital, Chiarugi created guidelines concerning how patients were to be treated. One of his rules specified that patients were to be treated with respect. He also directed that if restraints were required, they should be applied in a manner to protect the patient from sores and be made of leather rather than chains. He also used psychopharmacological agents such as opium for treatment.

In addition to mental health professionals, a number of other individuals promoted the humane care of people with mental illness. William Tuke (1732–1822) was a successful English merchant and a Quaker philanthropist. Some friends had told him of being turned away from an asylum in York, England, when they had tried to visit a fellow Quaker who had been confined there. Within a few days, the patient was reported dead. Tuke visited the asylum and found the conditions deplorable. Having retired, he decided to devote his life to creating alternative places where "the unhappy might find refuge" (Tuke, 1813).

In 1796, near the town of York, Tuke created the Retreat for Persons Afflicted With Disorders of the Mind. This Quaker retreat, as it was called, carried with it the idea that the individuals who were there should be given respect as well as good food and exercise. There were to be no chains or manacles. The model for the retreat was a farm, and the patients performed farm duties as part of their treatment. Others visited to learn of its operation. In 1813, the Quakers of Philadelphia founded the Friends' Asylum for the Use of Persons Deprived of the Use of Their Reason, which was the first private psychiatric hospital in the United States. Both the retreat in York and the Friends' Hospital of Philadelphia continue to function today as places for mental health treatment.

Another individual who contributed to the American mental health movement was Dorothea Dix (1802–1887). While teaching women at the East Cambridge House of Correction in

Dorothea Dix

S. J. Prentiss; archived in Library of Congress Web Archives at https://www.loc.gov/pictures/item/2019630777/

Massachusetts, Dix had her eyes opened to the terrible conditions these women faced. Dix also realized that a number of these women had some type of mental illness. She fought against the idea that those with mental illness could not improve or be helped. From this experience, she devoted her life to crusading for the improved treatment of people with mental illness. As part of this crusade, she visited every state east of the Mississippi River and testified before local and national legislatures. It is estimated that her work led to the establishment of some 40 mental hospitals in the United States and Europe.

By the 1950s, a number of hospital facilities existed in the United States for those with mental illness. These were administered by both state governments and private organizations. This changed in the 1950s as described in *LENS: Closing Mental Hospitals in America*. This was the result of both the development of psychiatric medications and a movement to switch to a more community-centered idea of mental health care.

LENS

CLOSING MENTAL HOSPITALS IN AMERICA

During the first half of the 20th century, state mental hospitals were the main source of treatment and care for those with serious mental disorders in the United States (see W. Fisher et al., 2009; Torrey, 1997). By the 1950s, there were more than a half million individuals in these hospitals. However, during the 1950s and 1960s, a number of events occurred that changed the way individuals with mental disorders were treated in the United States.

A closed hospital

iStock.com/Steven_Kriemadis

One significant event was the introduction of antipsychotic medication. Prior to this, individuals with serious mental disorders such as schizophrenia needed a high level of care and protection. With the introduction of medications that would help treat the disorder, it was possible for some of these individuals to live outside the hospital.

The Community Mental Health Act of 1963, signed into law by President John F. Kennedy, reflected the growing understanding that all but a small portion of those in mental hospitals could

FIGURE 1.12 ■ When Did the Number of Individuals in Mental Hospitals in the United States Decrease?

Beginning in the 1960s, the number of individuals in mental hospitals began to decline.

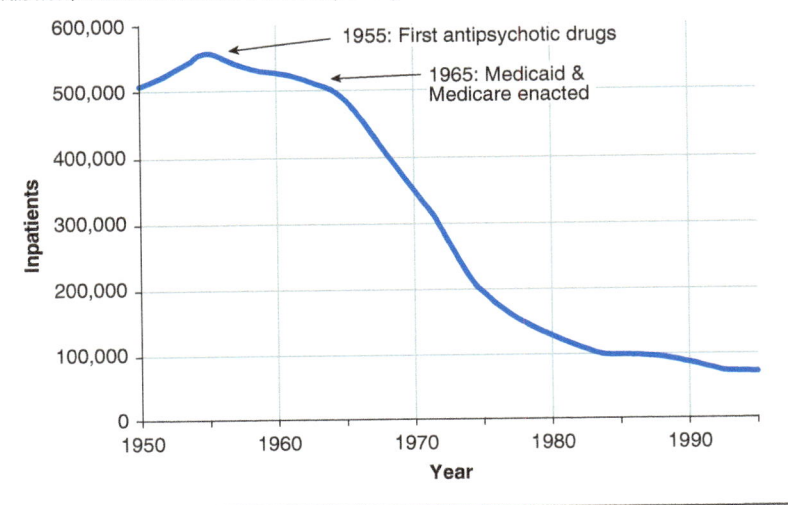

[Line graph showing Inpatients (y-axis, 0 to 600,000) vs. Year (x-axis, 1950 to 1990). The line peaks around 1955 at ~560,000, with annotations "1955: First antipsychotic drugs" and "1965: Medicaid & Medicare enacted", then declines sharply through the 1970s to around 90,000 by the 1990s.]

Credit: Torrey, E. F. (1997). *Out of the shadows: Confronting America's mental illness.* Wiley.

be treated in the community. The basic idea was that community mental health centers would offer a variety of programs to help those with mental illness.

Although the population of the United States increased by 100 million between 1955 and 1994, the number of individuals in mental hospitals decreased from 550,239 to 71,619 (Torrey, 1997). The process of moving individuals from mental hospitals to the community was known as *deinstitutionalization*. Figure 1.12 shows this drastic change. Figure 1.12

Patients with mental illness who were placed in a hospital in the 1950s would have found their quality of life much worse than what is available today. However, for many individuals, the ideals of the community mental health movement were never fulfilled. The community facilities for those with mental illness were never fully funded or were not even built. This left many individuals without the type of treatment they needed. Some have found themselves homeless. Others who were disruptive or who concerned the community found themselves in jails and prisons with little mental health treatment and care. Similar deinstitutionalization occurred in the United Kingdom and other developed countries.

Thought Question

Our history has shown us that neither institutionalizing nor deinstitutionalizing all individuals with serious mental disorders has been effective. What do you think are some characteristics of a workable solution?

From the Past to the Present

In light of the history discussed thus far, mental illness has been considered from two perspectives. The first perspective involves spirituality, often invoking the devil or supernatural forces. This was seen in the worldview of many early humans and was also the perspective of the Christian Church, especially in the Middle Ages. Rituals were performed to remove the demon from the person, which rarely benefited the individual. Today, some churches offer forms of exorcism.

The second perspective is that of psychology and physiology in a broad sense. This perspective uses research and the sciences to understand what mechanisms lead to mental disorders. Treatment involves the manipulation of these mechanisms through psychotropic medications and psychotherapy. The discovery of psychotropic medications greatly changed treatment of mental illness around the world. As noted in the previous *LENS*, these drugs allowed for individuals to live in a more independent manner. Throughout this book, you will learn about the medications used to treat the major mental disorders.

> **CONCEPT CHECK**
>
> - What major advances in our knowledge of the brain and nervous system were made during the 1600s and 1700s?
> - The research of John Hughlings Jackson has contributed much to our understanding of the brain. Describe his concepts of localization of function, three levels of the brain, and hierarchical integration through inhibitory control.
> - What are the primary aspects of Charles Darwin's theory of evolution? How might those processes be reflected in psychopathology?
> - What did Jean-Martin Charcot mean by the terms *symptoms*, *signs*, and *syndromes*? How did they help bring organization to an understanding of neurological disorders that is still used today?
> - Indicate whether you agree or disagree with the following: Large institutions for treating people with mental illness should be closed and all treatment given in the community. Choose one side of the debate, and present evidence for your position.

BIOLOGICAL APPROACHES TO TREATING MENTAL ILLNESS

Throughout our history as humans, we have used natural substances to treat illness. Often, treatment was a hit-or-miss procedure as people learned which substances were more effective than others. With the development of better chemical methods in the past hundred years, scientists began to modify the substances and create them as drugs. Today, we refer to these substances, when used to address mental illness, as *psychotropic medications*. The overall category of psychotropic medications can be broken into categories based on what they were designed to accomplish. These categories include mood stabilizers, antianxiety drugs, antidepressant drugs, and antipsychotic drugs.

During the U.S. Civil War, a textbook by Union Army Surgeon General William Hammond suggested that lithium bromide be used to treat manic patients (see Perlis & Ostacher, 2016). However, it was not until 1949 that the Australian John Cade reported that lithium had a calming effect on animals and humans with mania. As you will see, lithium is still used to treat mania, which we refer to as bipolar disorder today. Drugs that came to be called *antidepressants* for the treatment of depression, such as monoamine oxidase inhibitors (MAOIs) and the tricyclic antidepressants (TCAs), were discovered through serendipity in the 1950s (Fava & Papakostas, 2016). SSRIs (selective serotonin reuptake inhibitors) such as Prozac were developed later. You will learn about these substances in the chapter on mood disorders. Benzodiazepines such as Valium have been used for the treatment of anxiety for at least 50 years.

One significant event came in 1952 when a French naval surgeon was attempting to find medications to give to reduce stress before an operation (Freudenreich et al., 2016). He discovered that an antihistamine substance called chlorpromazine left individuals feeling indifferent about their operation. Noticing its calming effect, he suggested that this might be useful in the treatment of mental disorders. In particular, it was discovered that chlorpromazine (trade name Thorazine) helped to reduce the symptoms of schizophrenia and initially became an important antipsychotic medication. This, in turn, led to the reduction in the number of patients in mental hospitals (as noted in the previous *LENS*). Some of the early antipsychotic medications had problematic side effects. Newer drugs used today have fewer of these side effects.

Other treatment approaches seek to influence the individual's brain by changing the underlying electrical activity. Some of these treatments are considered *noninvasive* (Camprodon et al., 2016); that is, there is no requirement that electrodes or other devices be placed inside the brain itself. The oldest of these techniques is *electroconvulsive therapy* (ECT) in which electrical activity is used to disrupt normal brain activity and produce convulsions (Welch, 2016). ECT has improved over the years with a reduction in motor convulsions and a reduction in the number of brain areas affected. It is seen as an effective treatment for those with severe depression that does not respond to other types of medication or psychotherapy. An alternative to ECT, referred to as *transcranial magnetic stimulation* (TMS), disrupts brain activity using magnetic stimulation to treat mental disorders, including depression.

More invasive treatments require that electrodes be placed in the brain that change the existing brain networks. The technique has been referred to as *deep brain stimulation* (DBS) and has been used for the treatment of motor disorders such as Parkinson's disease, as well as obsessive compulsive disorder (OCD) and depression. Stimulating electrodes are placed deep in the brain, and these are connected to a pulse generator that is placed under the person's skin, typically below the neck. Today's devices allow health care professionals to adjust the stimulation from wireless devices outside the skin.

The most invasive procedures are surgeries in which different areas of the brain are removed or their connections disrupted. Severe epilepsy, in which a person has numerous seizures and cannot work or function normally, has been treated in this manner. Today, surgical procedures of the brain are limited to very small areas. In fact, gamma rays rather than a knife are used to make the small cuts. Such small cuts in the brain are used with individuals who show no improvement in epilepsy, depression, or anxiety using standard treatments.

Not all of the biological treatments have been successful. In the first half of the 1900s, as a treatment for mental illness, the frontal areas of the brain were disconnected from the rest of the brain. This procedure, called a *frontal lobotomy*, was used until the 1950s and then discontinued. It left the person with limited emotional and cognitive abilities. Even during its time, there were serious debates as to its ethics and effectiveness.

As you will see throughout this book, biological approaches play an important role in the treatment of mental disorders. Determining effective treatment is not an either/or question of psychological and biological approaches but an attempt to combine treatments that work together in an effective way. For example, research from 2015 shows that the combination of psychotherapy and lower levels of psychotropic medication is very effective for treating schizophrenia (Insel, 2015; Kane et al., 2016). As you will also learn, psychotherapy and biological approaches work through different brain mechanisms and at different levels of the brain. Throughout the chapters of this book, particular biological approaches will be described in terms of each disorder.

The next section will examine psychological factors involved in developing, maintaining, and treating mental disorders. What people learn through interacting with others and with their environment is crucial. In addition, what individuals tell themselves or how they experience significant others in their lives is an important aspect of this perspective.

PSYCHOLOGICAL TREATMENT PERSPECTIVES IN THE 20TH AND 21ST CENTURIES

Before the middle of the 20th century, very little formal research had been performed to see how effective psychological interventions were. This was also true of traditional medical procedures. Beginning in the 1950s and 1960s, a movement started to determine the effectiveness of both medical and psychological treatments in a scientific manner. In medicine, this came to be known as *evidence-based medicine*. In psychology, the terms *empirically based treatments* and *empirically based principles* refer to treatments and their aspects for which there is scientific evidence of effectiveness (Clark, 2018; David et al., 2018). During the 21st century, there has also been a focus on the importance of understanding diversity and cultural competency within the context of evidence-based care (Huey et al., 2014). Treatment effectiveness is now considered worldwide with diverse populations (e.g., Ravitz et al., 2019). Also, researchers have sought to discover any general factors such as empathy and positive regard on the part of the therapist (Elliott et al., 2018; Farber et al., 2018; Norcross & Lambert, 2018). This research suggests that relationship factors are important to successful treatment regardless of the therapeutic approach used.

As researchers and clinicians began to focus more on approaches and principles for which there was scientific evidence that they were effective, there began a movement to develop effective treatments for particular disorders. There has been more willingness to integrate techniques from the three different approaches as well as from other perspectives. For example, in the chapter on personality disorders, you will see that one of the most researched treatments—dialectical behavior therapy (DBT)—is based on techniques from each of the three approaches described in this chapter. This effective treatment uses aspects of cognitive behavioral, dynamic, and humanistic-existential techniques.

Psychodynamic Perspectives on Treatment

The **psychodynamic perspective** is based on the idea that psychological problems are manifestations of inner mental conflicts and that conscious awareness of those conflicts is key to recovery. Historically, Sigmund Freud laid the foundation for this perspective.

By the beginning of the 20th century, there was an understanding that psychological processes were an important source of information about mental illness. Freud had worked with Charcot in Paris and observed individuals with hysteria. In this disorder, the experience, such as not feeling pain in a limb or difficulty hearing, did not match the underlying physiology. Witnessing this type of disordered behavior led Freud to seek psychological explanations for the cause and treatment of mental disorders.

Sigmund Freud

Freud was initially trained as a zoologist before he completed medical school. The nature of the neuron was just being discovered, and Freud based his early theories on the neuroscience of his day. He was an enthusiastic reader of Darwin and credited his interest in science to an early reading of his work. A number of Freud's ideas can be seen as coming from Darwin (Ellenberger, 1970; Sulloway, 1979), although Freud emphasized sexual selection over natural selection. According to Freud, the sexual instinct (libido) is the major driving force for human life and interaction. Freud was also influenced by the suggestion of the neurologist Hughlings Jackson that in our brains we find more primitive areas underlying more advanced ones. Thus, it is quite possible for the psyche to be in conflict with itself or at least to have different layers representing different processes.

For Freud, higher cortical processes could inhibit the experience of lower ones, a process that would come to be called *repression*. Anxiety is the result of society and culture having inconsistent rules for the expression of sexuality and aggression. This anxiety and our inability to acknowledge these instinctual experiences lead to defense mechanisms and neurosis. Freud believed that the brain was basically a blank slate upon which experiences become connected with one another driven by instinctual processes of sexuality and self-preservation. The human psyche for Freud becomes the real-life laboratory in which nature and nurture struggle.

Sigmund Freud

Photo 12/Alamy Stock Photo

Hans Strupp was one of the first researchers to empirically examine change with psychodynamic treatment.

Courtesy of Vanderbilt University

Freud's concept of treatment was based on the search for ideas and emotions that are in conflict and the manner in which the person has relationships with other people. His specific treatment came to be called *psychoanalysis*. One basic procedure was *free association*, in which an individual lay on a couch with the therapist behind them and said whatever came to mind. It was the therapist's job to help the client connect ideas and feelings that they were not aware of. One thing Freud was searching for was connections within the person's psyche when external stimulation was reduced. Dreams were also analyzed in this way, since they are produced outside of daily life.

Other aspects of psychoanalysis included examining *resistance*, or what the client is unwilling to say or experience, and *transference*, or the manner in which a person imagined how another person thought about or sought a certain kind of relationship with them. Freud has greatly influenced therapies based on insight. *Insight therapy*, which has been used to treat disorders such as anxiety and depression, is based on the principle of bringing patterns of behavior, feelings, and thoughts into awareness. In order to do this, it is necessary to discuss past patterns and relationships to determine how they are being replayed or are influencing the present.

A number of dynamically orientated therapies have been shown to be effective (Barber et al., 2021; Fonagy, 2015). One empirically supported therapy based on dynamic principles was developed by Hans Strupp and his colleagues. Strupp embodied the dynamic principles in a therapy of a few months' duration (Strupp & Binder, 1984). The focus of this therapy is the relationship between the client and other individuals in the client's life. It is assumed that the client's problems are based on disturbed relationships. The therapeutic relationship between the client and the therapist offers an opportunity to see disturbed relationships in a safe environment. Transference is an important mechanism in which the client tends to see the therapist in terms of significant others in their life. As the client talks with the therapist, they will replay prior conflicts and enact maladaptive patterns.

The role of the therapist in this approach is mainly to listen. As the therapist, you listen to your clients, seeking to understand what they are saying and how they feel as they describe their world. You would note to yourself when they find talking to you difficult or experience distress as they talk about their life. On a larger level, the therapist is looking for themes and patterns that come from their clients' pasts. In a relaxed, nonjudgmental manner, it is the task of the therapist to help the client understand the patterns and to see how they interfere with living and having rewarding relationships with others. Different versions of dynamic psychotherapy have been shown to be effective for a number of disorders, especially the personality disorders.

Existential-Humanistic Perspectives

The *existential-humanistic perspective* begins by asking: What is the nature of human existence? This includes both the positive experiences of intimacy and the negative experiences of loss. Historically, two clinicians influenced by Freud—Carl Jung and Karen Horney—helped to set the stage for the existential-humanistic movement in that they emphasized the value of internal experience.

As the existential-humanistic movement grew, a number of themes became critical. The first is an emphasis on human growth and the need for a positive psychology that moves beyond the discussion of stress and neurosis seen in the psychodynamic approaches. A second emphasis is the idea that psychological health is more than just the absence of pathology. Not having a problem is not the same as finding meaning in one's life. The third theme stresses the importance of considering not only the external world and a person's relationship to it, but also the internal world. In the humanistic-existential perspective, the internal world of a person and their experiences are valued. With the emphasis on experience, you will also see the therapies that developed from this approach referred to as humanistic-experiential therapies.

Carl Rogers brought the humanistic movement to the forefront by creating **client-centered therapy,** also referred to as *person-centered therapy*. Rogers considered psychotherapy to be a releasing of an already existing capacity in a potentially competent individual. In fact, Rogers emphasized the relationship between the therapist and client as a critical key to effective therapy.

There are three key characteristics of the client-centered approach. The first is empathic understanding. As the therapist reflects back what the client says, the client begins to experience their own innermost thoughts and feelings. The second is what Rogers referred to as unconditional positive regard. That is, the therapist accepts what the client says without trying to change the client. For some individuals who have experienced significant others in their lives as critical of them, to be accepted by the therapist is a new experience. The third characteristic is for the therapist to show genuineness and congruence (agreement). In this way, the therapist models what interactions between two real people could be like.

A number of humanistic-experiential–orientated therapies have been shown to be effective (Elliott et al., 2013, 2021). One of these empirically supported therapies based on humanistic principles was developed by Leslie Greenberg and his colleagues. This approach is known as **emotion-focused therapy** or *process-experiential therapy*

Karen Horney
Bettmann/Contributor/via Getty Images

Carl Rogers
Bettmann/Contributor/via Getty Images

(Greenberg, 2002). In this therapy, emotion is viewed as centrally important in the experience of self. Emotion can be either adaptive or maladaptive. However, in either case, emotion is the crucial element that brings about change. In therapy, clients are helped to identify and explore their emotions. The aim is to both manage and transform emotional experiences.

Emotion-focused therapy can be thought of in three phases (Greenberg & Watson, 2006). The first phase is one of bonding and awareness in which it is the job of the therapist to create a safe environment for emotional experience to take place. Empathy and positive regard are part of the way the client is helped to feel safe. In the early part of therapy, the client is helped not only to experience an emotion but also to put words to it.

The second phase is evocation and exploration. At this point, emotions are evoked and even intensified. The therapist also helps the client to understand how they might be interfering with their own experience of emotion. Such examples of interference would include changing the subject and beginning to talk about the emotion in a cognitive manner as a way to distance oneself from the experience. The third phase is transformation and generation of alternatives. It is at this point that the therapist helps the client construct alternative ways of thinking, feeling, and doing that are more consistent with their real self. Empirical studies have shown that emotion-focused therapy is effective with depression and emotional trauma (Greenberg & Watson, 2006).

Another therapeutic technique that has gained popularity and been empirically shown to be effective is **mindfulness** (Creswell, 2017; Ong et al., 2020). Mindfulness techniques were originally meditation techniques developed in Theravada Buddhism. These techniques involve an increased, focused, purposeful awareness of the present moment. The idea is to relate to one's thoughts and experiences in an open, nonjudgmental, and accepting manner (Kabat-Zinn, 1990). The basic technique is for the individual to observe thoughts without reacting to them in the present. This increases sensitivity to important features of the environment and one's internal reactions, leading to better self-management and awareness as an alternative to ruminating about the past or worrying about the future. This in turn reduces self-criticism.

Nonjudgmental observing allows for a reduction in stress, reduction in reactivity, and more time for interaction with others and the world. Also, feelings of compassion for another person become possible. This broadens attention and alternatives. Meta-analysis performed by Hofmann, Sawyer, Witt, and colleagues (2010) examined 39 studies of mindfulness. They found significant reductions in anxiety and depression following mindfulness techniques. Grossman and his colleagues (Grossman et al., 2004; see also Hofmann et al., 2011) examined 20 studies and found overall positive changes following mindfulness approaches. Empirical evidence using mindfulness techniques has shown positive change with a number of disorders, including anxiety, depression, chronic pain, and stress (Wielgosz et al., 2019). Mindfulness is also a component of DBT, which is an effective treatment for borderline personality disorder.

Overall, the existential-humanistic perspective emphasizes the emotional level. There is also an emphasis on the value of internal processes and the manner in which the exploration and experiencing of these internal processes can lead to changes in behavior and experience.

Behavioral and Cognitive Behavioral Perspectives

The **behavioral perspective**, as the name implies, has focused on the level of actions and behaviors. Most histories of behaviorism begin with a discussion of Ivan Pavlov, the Russian physiologist who won the Nobel Prize in 1904 for his work on the physiology of digestion. Pavlov noted in his Nobel Prize speech that the sight of tasty food makes the mouth of a hungry man water. However, what became of interest to behavioral psychologists was not the salivary reflex itself but the fact that other objects associated with the presentation of food could also produce salivation. For example, in Pavlov's work with dogs, it was shown that any sensory process, such as sound, that was paired with the food would produce salivation. After a number of pairings, the sound alone without the food could produce this reflex. This came to be known as *classical conditioning*.

Classical conditioning occurs when an unconditioned stimulus, such as food, results in an unconditioned response, such as salivation. If this unconditioned stimulus is paired with a neutral stimulus

In Pavlov's work with dogs, it was shown that any sensory process, such as sound, that was paired with the food would produce salivation.

Pictorial Press Ltd/Alamy Stock Photo

a number of times, then the neutral stimulus will produce the response. After a period of time, the "conditioned stimulus" such as sound, when presented alone, will no longer produce the response. This process is referred to as **extinction**. Behaviorists saw classical conditioning as one mechanism underlying the development of mental illness.

John Watson is often described as America's first behaviorist. His work set psychology on the course of emphasizing environmental explanations for behavior and rejecting the theoretical value of internal concepts. This called into question the value of studying such topics as consciousness and other internal processes. Watson set the course of only studying observable behavior with his 1913 paper *Psychology as the Behaviorist Views It*. Watson suggested that the proper study of psychology was to focus on behavior and not the mind. Further, Watson saw the goal of psychology as identifying environmental conditions that direct behavior. Under no circumstances should the theory make reference to consciousness, mind, or other internal unobservable events. Watson created a psychology based on observable behaviors alone, which helped promote the development of a strong stimulus–response psychology. Watson's statement emphasizing the role of the environment in development is well known.

> Give me a dozen healthy infants, well-formed, and my own specified world to bring them up in and I'll guarantee to take any one at random and train him to become any type of specialist I might select—doctor, lawyer, artist, merchant-chief, and yes, even beggar-man and thief, regardless of his talents, penchants, tendencies, abilities, vocations, and race of his ancestors. (Watson, 1924, p. 82)

As the quote implies, Watson assumed that there existed "talents, penchants, tendencies, abilities" that were part of an individual but that these could be overridden by environmental factors. In fact, Watson demonstrated that an 11-month-old infant named Little Albert could be conditioned to fear an animal such as a lab rat that the infant had previously enjoyed playing with (Watson & Rayner, 1920). The procedure (which would be considered unacceptable and unethical today) was to create a loud noise when the infant was observing the animal. A loud noise will produce a startle response. In a classical conditioning manner, the pairing of the aversive noise and the animal led to conditioned fear. Behaviorists used classical conditioning as a mechanism for understanding phobias and other processes seen in mental illness.

B. F. Skinner became the 20th century's most vocal proponent of behaviorism. Beginning with his 1938 book, *The Behavior of Organisms*, Skinner played a significant role in experimental psychology until his death in 1990. His experimental procedure was to demonstrate that an animal, generally a laboratory rat or pigeon, could be taught to make specific responses if, after the occurrence of the desired response, the animal was given a reward, generally food. This procedure came to be known as **operant conditioning**. The basic idea was that behavior could be elicited or shaped if **reinforcement** followed its occurrence. Consequently, if these behaviors ceased to be rewarded, the occurrence would decrease. Thus, the emphasis was on behaviors and the rewards that follow them as opposed to the environmental stimuli evoking them.

Skinner suggested that freedom, will, dignity, and other concepts referring to the mind or internal states have no explanatory value. Psychologists should only be interested in the relationship between behavior and consequences, according to Skinner. Even processes such as language learning were seen as the result of words being reinforced and learned one at a time. In this manner, any type of complex behavior was seen as the result of learning simple behaviors, which were then chained together. The larger implication was that humans came into the world ready to be influenced by the reinforcement contingencies of the environment to determine their development and actions in the world. Watson and Skinner ushered in an era in psychology that strongly emphasized the environment and largely ignored any discussion of internal processes or mechanisms for understanding life.

In the mid-20th century, a number of psychologists began to see the limitation of strict behaviorism in that it ignored internal processes. Simple demonstrations, such as offering a 6-year-old a candy bar if he would do a particular task, showed that the idea of a reward was enough to motivate behavior. Also, behaviorally oriented psychologists such as Albert Bandura showed that humans would imitate the behaviors of others even without reinforcement. This type of learning was called **observational learning**, or *modeling*. One classic set of studies involved children hitting a Bobo doll after seeing cartoon characters being aggressive. In another study, children watched an adult interact with the Bobo doll in an aggressive or nonaggressive manner. Those children who watched the aggressive adult later showed more aggression than those who watched a nonaggressive adult.

Nonclinical areas of research in psychology, such as the study of cognitive processes and social processes, were demonstrating that humans often make quick decisions based on information that is outside of normal awareness. Humans make these decisions without actually realizing there are alternative ways of thinking. Further, evolutionary thinking was showing how humans come into the world with an evolutionary history such that they develop fears of some objects such as snakes or spiders more

B F. Skinner was the 20th century's most vocal proponent of behaviorism.
Science History Images/Alamy Stock Photo

readily than fears of a toy truck or a flower. Arne Öhman at the Karolinska Institute sought to determine the basis of fear learning and how it relates to psychopathology (see, e.g., Öhman, 1986). Others emphasized the fact that humans talk to themselves and pay attention to their own thoughts, which can influence behavior. All of these developments moved many in the psychology discipline away from Skinner's more rigid behaviorism.

The **cognitive behavioral perspective** suggests that dysfunctional thinking is common to all psychological disturbances. By learning in therapy how to understand one's thinking, it is possible to change the way one thinks as well as one's emotional state and behaviors. One basic feature of our thinking is that it is automatic. Ideas just pop into our mind, such as "I can't solve this" or "It is all my fault." A number of therapies based on cognitive principles along with behavioral interventions have been shown to be effective (Hollon & Beck, 2013; Newman et al., 2021).

Aaron Beck (1967; see also Beck, 2019, for an overview and update) developed a cognitive therapy for depression in the early 1960s. The model is described in terms of a cognitive triad related to depression (Figure 1.13).

The first component of the triad is the individual's negative view of self. This is when the individual attributes unpleasant experiences to his own mental, physical, and moral defects. When something negative happens, the person says it is his fault. In therapy, the client can become aware of the content of his thinking. The second component is the individual's tendency to interpret experiences in a negative manner. That is, the person tailors the facts to fit negative conclusions. The basic idea is that thinking influences emotion and behavior. The third component is that the person regards the future in a negative way. He envisions a life of only hardships and anticipates failure in all tasks. In therapy, the basic idea is that the individual can modify his cognitive and behavioral responses. Overall, the therapy is directed at the automatic thoughts in relation to *catastrophizing*—believing that nothing will work out; *personalization*—believing that everything relates to you; *overgeneralization*—believing that one event is how it always is; and *dichotomous thinking*—believing that things are either good or bad.

In the history of **cognitive behavioral therapy (CBT)** research, most therapies were directed at treating particular disorders such as anxiety, depression, phobias, and so forth. However, it was noted that negative affect is present in a number of different disorders (Barlow, Allen, & Choate, 2016). This led to the development of a treatment approach directed at the common underlying mechanisms of these different disorders. Overall, the approach seeks to help the individual understand emotional experiences and their cognitive appraisal. This approach has been referred to as the unified treatment model or unified protocol and also transdiagnostic therapy (Norton & Roberge, 2017). Research

FIGURE 1.13 ■ How Do Individuals With Depression See the World?

According to Aaron Beck's cognitive triad, those with depression have negative views about the world, about the future, and about themselves.

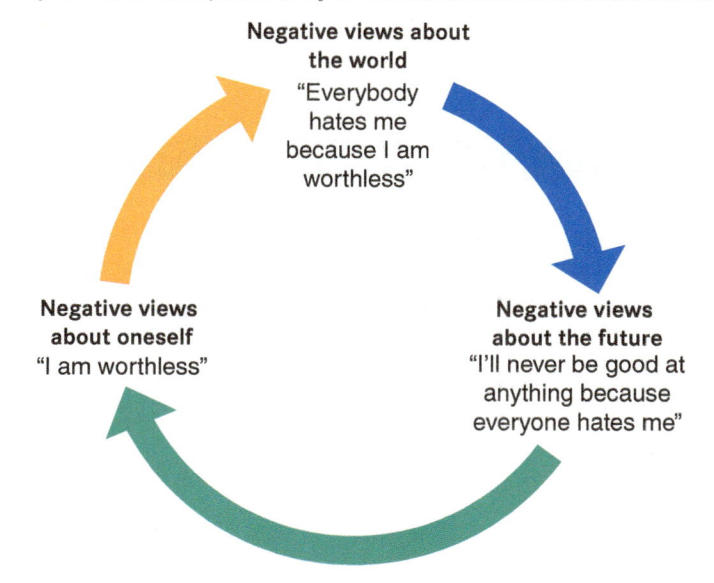

Negative views about the world
"Everybody hates me because I am worthless"

Negative views about the future
"I'll never be good at anything because everyone hates me"

Negative views about oneself
"I am worthless"

Aaron Beck
Courtesy of the Beck Institute for Cognitive Behavior Therapy; www.beckinstitute.org

studies have shown this treatment to be effective in disorders such as anxiety and depression (Carlucci et al., 2021; Sakiris & Berle, 2019).

Overall, the CBT movement sought to understand how cognitions were disordered or disrupted in mental disorders. Whereas humanistic therapies emphasized emotional processing, cognitive behavioral approaches emphasized thoughts. This includes the manner in which a person conceptualizes their life and experiences, including internal emotional experiences. The basic idea is that psychological disturbances often involve errors in thinking. One real value of many cognitive behavioral approaches is that they have been tested empirically and are presented in books and manuals that describe the steps involved in therapy.

As with other perspectives, cognitive behavioral approaches have been expanded to include several other techniques. Some of these are mindfulness approaches and dialectical behavior therapy, as discussed previously, as well as acceptance and commitment therapy (ACT) and acceptance-based behavioral therapy (ABBT). ACT and ABBT combine mindfulness with an emphasis on accepting inner experiences without judgment, along with awareness and resilience.

These approaches have been called the *new way* or *third wave of CBT* (Hayes & Hofmann, 2017; Hofmann, Sawyer, & Fang, 2010; Perkins et al., 2023). One common theme in these approaches is the role of acceptance. In each approach, clients are encouraged to not react to negative thoughts and feelings. Throughout this book, you will be introduced to the way in which these and other therapies have been used to treat specific disorders.

CONCEPT CHECK

- What does *empirically based treatment* mean? Why is it important, and what impacts has the concept had on treatment for psychopathology?
- Describe the basic principles underlying each of these perspectives on psychological treatment: psychodynamic perspective, existential-humanistic perspective, behavioral perspective, and cognitive behavioral perspective. Identify the scientists associated with them, and give an example of an empirically based treatment related to each.

SUMMARY

Three major themes—behavior and experience, neuroscience, and the evolutionary perspective—give us important perspectives for thinking about psychopathology. In addition, an integrative perspective ranging across a number of different levels of analysis provides a greater understanding of psychopathological processes. These levels range from the highest levels of environment, culture, and society to social relationships to individual behavior and experience to our sensory, motor, emotional, and cognitive systems to the physiological processes that make up our central and peripheral nervous systems to the cortical network level to the most basic level of genetics and epigenetics. The genetic level in turn takes us back up to the highest level to understand how environmental conditions influence genetic processes.

Four ideas are critical to the concept of psychopathology. First, there is a loss of freedom and ability to consider alternatives. Second, there is a loss of genuine personal contact. Third, there is a loss of connection with one's self and the ability to live in a productive manner. Fourth, there is person distress.

Considering psychopathology from evolutionary and cultural perspectives goes beyond the traditional psychological and physiological considerations. Culture can be seen as a system of inheritance: Humans learn a variety of things from others in their culture, including skills, values, beliefs, and attitudes. For a more complete understanding of psychopathology, it is important to understand the particular rules a culture has for expressing both internal experiences and external behaviors. Overall, research suggests a close connection between cultural and evolutionary perspectives. Not only can the environment influence genetics, but genetics can also in turn influence culture. The evolutionary and cultural perspectives help us ask questions such as these: (1) Can genetic variation influence the manner in which cultural structures formalize social interactions, and how this might be related to what is considered mental illness? (2) How long, in terms of our human history, has a particular psychopathology existed? (3) What function might a disorder serve, and how did it come about? (4) How can a basic human process (e.g., the pain of social rejection) develop in relation to an earlier one (e.g., the brain circuits involved in physical pain)?

One of the main themes of the study of evolution is the manner in which organisms are in close connection with their environment. It is this close connection that allows for change, including the turning on and off of genetic processes, to take place. Humans are born less fully developed at birth than many other species and thus are sensitive to changes in their environment as they continue to develop. Unlike animals that live within nature, humans largely live within the backdrop of our culture. Another part of the complexity with humans is our ability to reflect on ourselves and our world. In this way, a layer of thought, including expectation and imagination, is injected between the person and the environment.

Mental disorders have been with us throughout our human history. Since the time that written language became a part of our experience, humans have described mental disorders. Examples of historical conceptions of psychopathology include those of Pythagoras and Hippocrates in ancient Greece and Galen from the period of the Roman Empire; advances in anatomy by da Vinci in art and Descartes in science from the Renaissance; advances in understanding the brain and nervous system in the 1700 to 1900 period; and Darwin's description of the theory of evolution and Charcot's classification of psychological and brain disorders in the 1800s. Historically, the care and treatment of individuals with mental illness also advanced, as did our understanding of the experience of these disorders. Although the Greeks already saw mental illness as a disorder involving the brain, it is only within the past 125 years that scientific support began to clarify this position.

Biological treatment for psychological disorders usually involves psychotropic medications, which have been expanded and improved over the past 60 years. Where medications have not been effective, other techniques are sometimes used, including ECT, TMS, and DBS.

There are currently three broad perspectives for the psychological treatment of mental disorders: the psychodynamic perspective, the existential-humanistic perspective, and the cognitive behavioral perspective. They were developed somewhat independently and often in opposition to one another. Beginning in the 1950s and 1960s, however, there was a movement to determine the effectiveness of psychological treatments in a scientific manner. Researchers and clinicians began to focus more on approaches and principles for which there was scientific evidence of effectiveness. This led to developing effective treatments for particular disorders and greater integration of techniques from the three different approaches as well as from other perspectives.

STUDY RESOURCES

Review Questions

1. Why do stigmas arise in regard to mental illness? What impacts do stigmas have on individuals with psychopathology as well as their families, communities, and society as a whole?

2. Three major themes—behavior and experience, neuroscience, and the evolutionary perspective—are presented as giving us important perspectives for thinking about psychopathology. What are some of the ideas each of these perspectives offers?

3. What levels of analysis are important to consider in understanding psychopathology? What are the advantages of considering multiple levels and taking an integrated approach?

4. This chapter states that "considering psychopathology from evolutionary and cultural perspectives goes beyond the traditional psychological and physiological considerations." What arguments does the author put forth to explain the importance of these two perspectives in asking critical questions that need to be answered? Do you agree?

5. What are the four critical characteristics to be included in answering the following question: What is psychopathology?

6. How does reading about the experiences of individuals with mental illness inform our understanding of the nature of psychopathology?

7. Describe how mental illness was understood in each of the following historical periods and how that understanding was advanced: ancient Greece and Rome, the Renaissance, and the 1700s to 1900s. Give examples of the individuals and ideas critical to each period.

8. How were individuals with mental illness treated during different historical eras? Who were some of the people who played a critical role in advancing treatment?

9. Descartes created a mind–body distinction that science since that time has had to address: How can a material body including the brain be influenced by an immaterial process such as the mind? How can a thought influence a cell in the brain? How would you handle the mind–body problem?

10. What we now know about the structure and function of the human brain and nervous system has developed throughout history. What is your model of how the brain is involved in mental illness?

11. Describe the contributions of the following individuals from different perspectives to the field of psychological treatment as a whole: Sigmund Freud, Hans Strupp, Carl Rogers, Leslie Greenberg, B. F. Skinner, Albert Bandura, and Aaron Beck.

For Further Reading

Andreasen, N. (2001). *Brave new brain*. Oxford University Press.

Beck, A. (1967). *Depression: Clinical, experimental, and theoretical aspects*. Harper & Row.

Beck, J. (2011). *Cognitive behavioral therapy* (2nd ed.). Guilford Press.

Cheney, T. (2008). *Manic*. William Morrow.

Darwin, C. (1859). *On the origin of species by means of natural selection*. John Murray.

Freud, S. (1966). *Project for a scientific psychology* (Standard edition, Vol. 1, pp. 281–397). , . (Original work published 1895)

Harrington, A. (2019). *Mind fixers: Psychiatry's troubled search for the biology of mental illness*. Norton.

Kandel, E. (2005). *Psychiatry, psychoanalysis, and the new biology of mind*. American Psychiatric Association.

Kandel, E. (2012). *The age of insight: The quest to understand the unconscious in art, mind, and brain, from Vienna 1900 to the present*. Random House.

Kottler, J. (2006). *Divine madness: Ten stories of creative struggle*. Jossey-Bass.

Nasar, S. (1998). *A beautiful mind*. Simon & Schuster.

National Institute of Mental Health. (2023, March). *Mental illness*. U.S. Department of Health and Human Services. http://www.nimh.nih.gov/health/statistics/prevalence/any-mental-illness-ami-among-us-adults.shtml

Pribram, K., & Gill, M. (1976). *Freud's "project" re-assessed*. Basic Books.

Skinner, B. F. (1974). *About behaviorism*. Random House.

Strupp, H., & Binder, J. (1984). *Psychotherapy in a new key*. Basic Books.

World Health Organization. (n.d.). *Disability-adjusted life years (DALYs)*. https://www.who.int/data/gho/indicator-metadata-registry/imr-details/158

KEY TERMS

- abnormal psychology
- behavioral and experiential perspective
- behavioral perspective
- classical conditioning
- client-centered therapy
- cognitive behavioral perspective
- cognitive behavioral therapy (CBT)
- cultural perspective
- emotion-focused therapy
- evolutionary perspective
- existential-humanistic perspective
- extinction
- hierarchical integration
- levels of analysis
- mindfulness
- natural selection
- neuroscience perspective
- observational learning
- operant conditioning
- psychoanalysis
- psychodynamic perspective
- psychopathology
- reinforcement
- sexual selection
- signs
- stigma
- symptoms
- syndrome
- variation

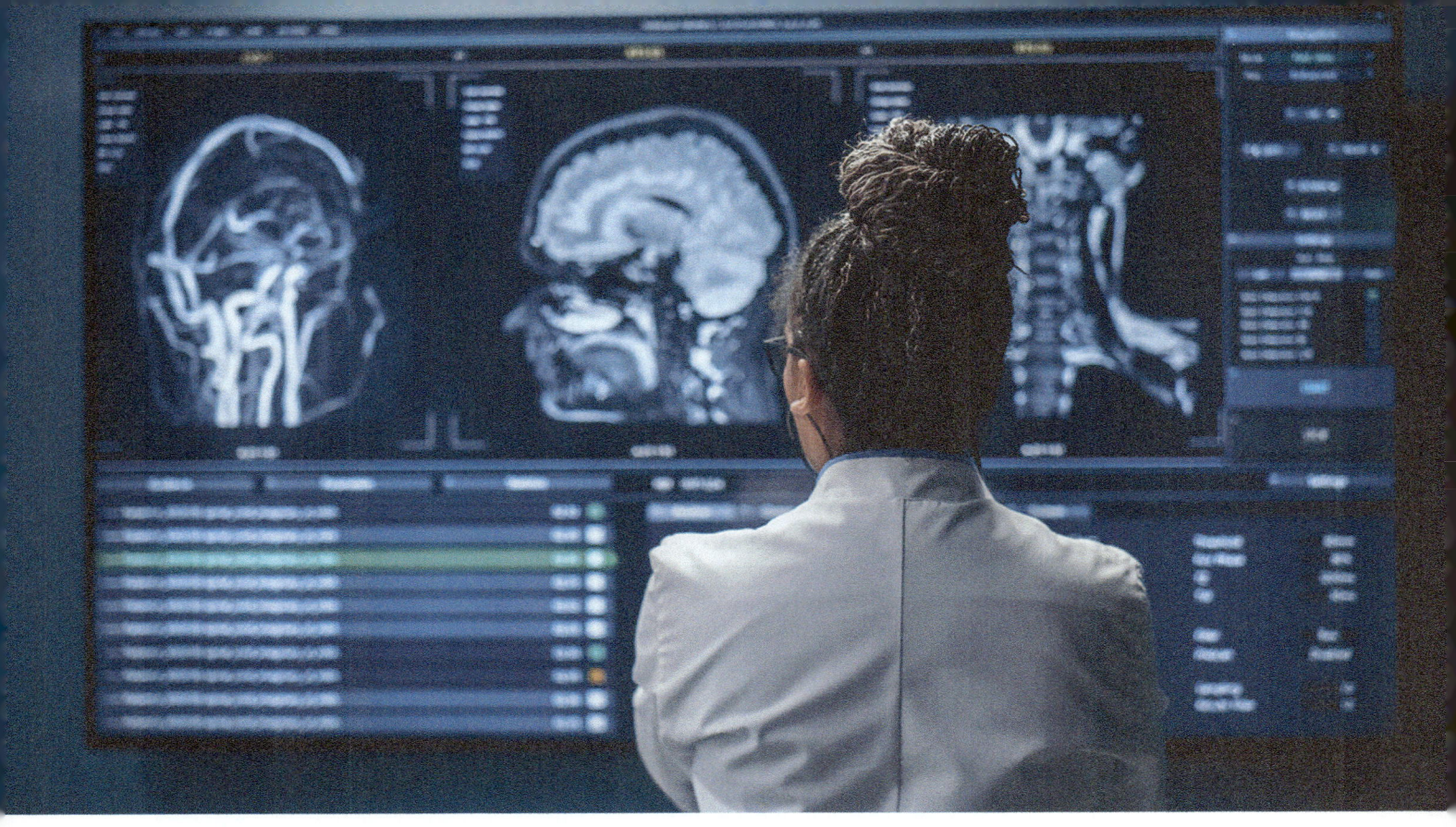

iStock.com/gorodenkoff

2 NEUROSCIENCE APPROACHES TO UNDERSTANDING PSYCHOPATHOLOGY

LEARNING OBJECTIVES

2.1 Explain why neuroscience, genetics, and an evolutionary perspective are increasingly important in understanding psychopathology.

2.2 Describe how information is communicated within the human brain.

2.3 Describe the major techniques used to view the human brain at work, and their related ethical implications.

2.4 Explain what brain networks are and how they influence human behavior.

2.5 Explain the function of genes, epigenetics, and endophenotypes.

2.6 Ask critical questions about psychopathology from an evolutionary perspective.

The neuroscientist V. S. Ramachandran (1998) told about an individual, David, who came to see him at the medical center in San Diego, California. David appeared completely normal. He had no problems with memory, engaged easily in conversation, expressed emotions, and otherwise appeared as anyone you might meet any day. However, he did one very puzzling thing. When he saw his mother in any context, he would say, "That woman looks exactly like my mother, but she is not my mother!"

As a clinician, how might you understand this? You might ask if this was some type of psychosis in which David had the delusion that his mother was not his mother. However, David showed no other signs of disorganization or problems with functioning. You might also ask if David had any type of emotional conflict with his mother. The answer was no. After more information gathering, it was discovered that David, at times, also thought his father was not his real father. Additional information revealed that David did indeed experience his parents as his parents when talking to them on the phone.

The formal name for this condition is *Capgras syndrome*, named after the physician who first described the symptoms in the 1920s. However, the mechanisms involved are still not clear today. Since David had previously had a motorcycle accident, it was possible that normal brain processes were not functioning correctly. In order to understand David, Ramachandran asked himself what was missing in David's experience of his mother. His answer was that there was no emotional response.

The normal emotional response to seeing someone like our parents occurs as follows: Our visual system gives us the experience of seeing the person. In humans, one particular part of the temporal lobe is sensitive to seeing faces (Figure 2.1).

FIGURE 2.1 ■ The Fusiform Face Area in the Brain, Activated When Humans Look at Faces

The fusiform face area is part of the human visual system located in the temporal and occipital lobes. If this area is damaged, individuals cannot recognize faces. They see the parts but cannot put them together into a whole face.

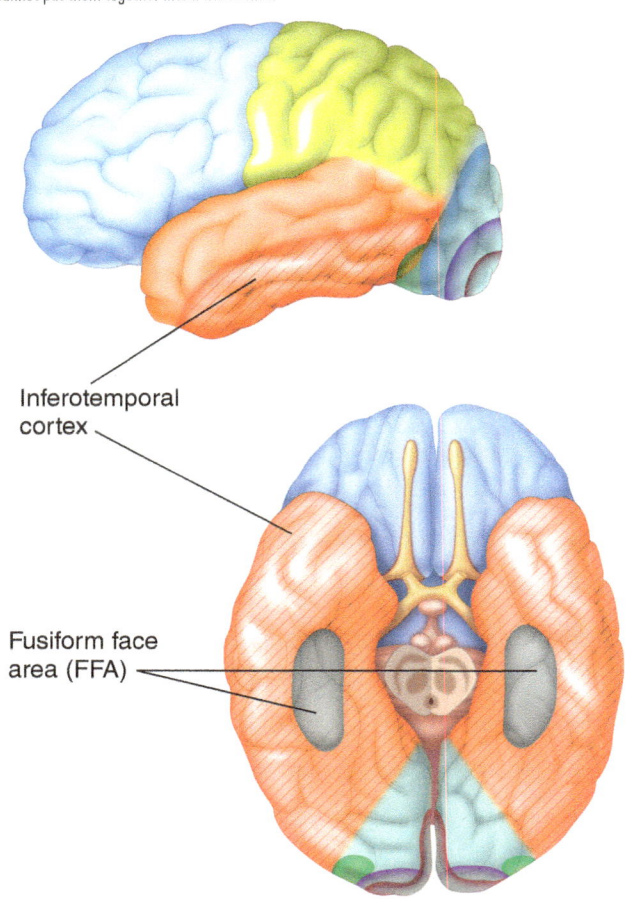

Inferotemporal cortex

Fusiform face area (FFA)

FIGURE 2.2 ■ Amygdala and Other Areas of the Brain Associated With Emotion

The amygdala is an almond-shaped structure on each side of the brain connected to other structures in the limbic system. These areas are involved in the processing of emotions such as fear.

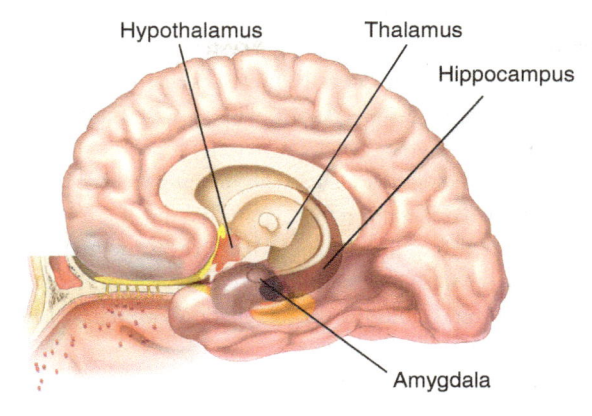

In turn, this information goes to a variety of areas, including the limbic system, which is involved in emotional processing. One particular structure, the amygdala, is involved in perceptions that are emotionally important to us (Figure 2.2). The amygdala has rich connections with other cortical areas, which together give us the experience of emotion.

If David had no emotional response to seeing a face, how might this be tested? Emotion is processed not only in the brain but also in the *autonomic nervous system (ANS)*, which prepares the body for dangerous situations. If we see a bear and run away, it is the *sympathetic* part of the ANS that makes us feel excited and moves blood to our muscles for a quick getaway. One easy way to measure the sympathetic nervous system is to pass a small electrical current along the skin, usually between the palm and the finger, to assess *electrodermal activity (EDA)*. If we are excited, then our skin sweats slightly. This, in turn, makes it easier for the electrical current to pass between the two electrodes. Whenever we have an emotional response to what we see, we get changes in the EDA. David did not show any EDA differences when viewing pictures of those close to him. This suggested to Ramachandran that there was a disconnection between his visual face perception areas and the emotional centers of the brain. Since the auditory system is wired differently, that would also explain why David did not have the same experience when talking with his parents on the phone. The point of David's story, as strange as it may seem, is to suggest that one important way to understand our mental processes is through their underlying mechanisms.

We can discuss David on different levels. We can consider his actual behavior of saying his mother was not his mother. We can also ask David to tell us what he experiences when he sees his parents. In this case, David said that he sees them as nice people but that he does not expect from them what he expects from his parents. We can discuss how this affects other people, such as his parents, to be told they are not his parents. We can also look at the interaction between him and his parents. From another standpoint, we can consider cognitive and emotional mechanisms involved, such as the memory of his mother and his emotional feeling for her. In other chapters of this book, discussions of mental illness from the levels just described will be discussed. The present chapter will focus on current neuroscience approaches to understanding mental illness with an emphasis on brain imaging, genetics, and evolutionary perspectives.

THE GROWING IMPORTANCE OF NEUROSCIENCE, GENETICS, AND AN EVOLUTIONARY PERSPECTIVE

The historical considerations of psychopathology emphasized careful observation and interaction with the afflicted individuals as important methods for understanding the nature of the disorder. However, with progress in the neurosciences, brain imaging, and genetics, other levels of analysis have become possible. The new levels offer different perspectives for the field of mental illness, but because many of these discoveries are so new, it is not surprising that our understanding of the field of mental illness is currently in flux. Neuroscience research has been used to find more objective markers in the diagnosis and treatment of mental disorders. It has also helped describe cognitive, emotional, and motor processes in both health and illness. This has resulted in a better articulation of what underlies these processes, such as problems in setting goals, having relationships with others, thinking, and feeling, as well as deficits in the memory system and the reward system.

The past 40 years have brought forth new technologies that allow us to study human behavior and experience in ways not previously possible. As you will see with many of the techniques described in this chapter, sampling brain processes or genetic material is basically simple and painless for the people involved. In terms of psychopathology, by using brain imaging techniques it is possible to see how individuals with a particular mental disorder perform cognitive and emotional tasks differently from those without the disorder. We can also examine genetic differences between those with a certain disorder and those who do not show the signs and symptoms of the disorder. Further, to understand the brain and genetic levels, it is important to consider the role that evolution has played. These three approaches will be emphasized in this chapter.

One word of warning before we continue: Currently, we have no neuroscience technique that can definitively diagnose a given individual in terms of mental disorders. What we can say is that a group of individuals with a particular disorder appear to differ on certain measures compared to a group of individuals without the disorder. Even those with the same disorder may show differences in how the disorder is manifested.

To understand mental illness as a brain disease, we need methods for showing how the brain is involved in psychopathology (Andreasen, 2001). Within the past five decades, a variety of research techniques have been developed or significantly improved that allow us to better specify the nature of mental disorders from the standpoint of the brain. In this quest, there has been a strong emphasis on brain imaging, genetics, and an evolutionary perspective. In general, these approaches have allowed researchers to study individuals with mental disorders on a number of levels simultaneously.

Historically, what we now consider to be neuroscience approaches to psychopathology were limited. For example, Paul Broca in the 1800s needed to wait until his patients died before he could study the nature of their brains. In the early part of the 20th century, work with animals was the major way of understanding how the various structures of the brain influenced behavior. Some scholars such as Carl Jung added EDA to reaction time research. Jung used the word association test developed by Wilhelm Wundt to better understand psychopathology and how individuals with different disorders process

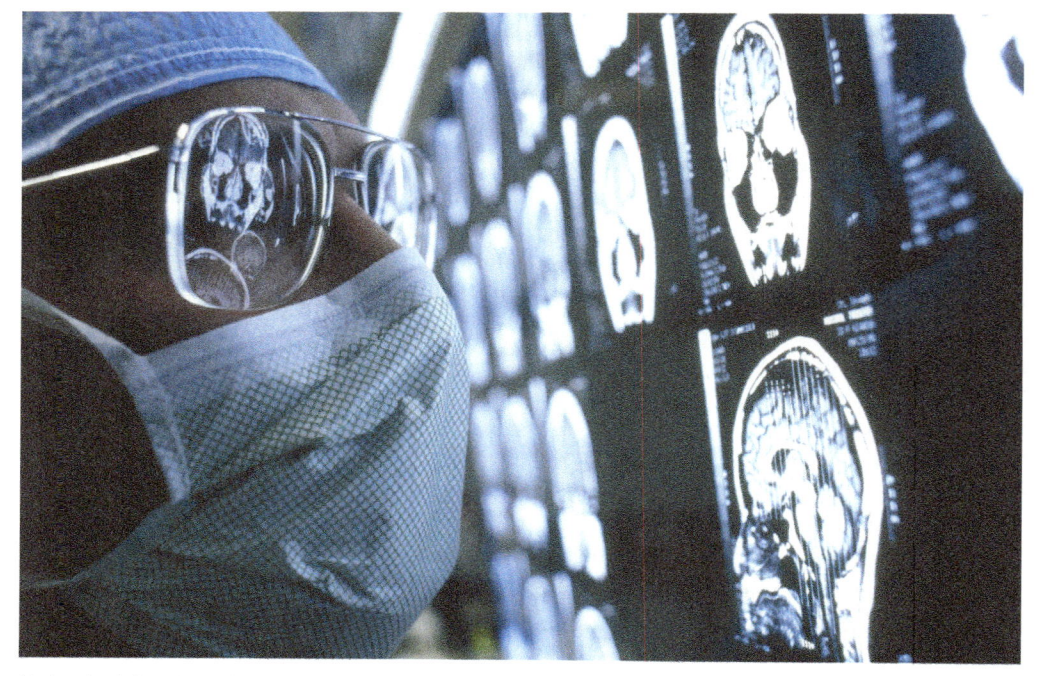

Modern brain imaging techniques help researchers discover how mental disorders appear in the brain.
iStock.com/undefined undefined

cognitive and emotional information. The second part of the 20th century expanded a tradition that used psychophysiological measures such as *electroencephalography (EEG)* and EDA to study psychopathology. In this century, a variety of noninvasive techniques have allowed researchers and clinicians to obtain a better view of how the brain and other physiological systems function in psychopathology (see Raichle, 2011, 2015a for overviews). These will be reviewed in this chapter.

One common conviction of neuroscientists is that there is something unusual about the human brain, both in complexity and in ability, that leads to humans' abilities to perform a variety of tasks (Northcutt & Kaas, 1995; Preuss & Kaas, 1999). The human brain has been estimated to contain 86 billion neurons and more than 100,000 kilometers of interconnections (Hofman, 2001; Goldstone, Pestilli, & Börner, 2015). Estimates in mammals suggest that a given neuron would directly connect to at least 500 other neurons and probably more. This, in turn, would suggest there are 50 trillion different connections in the human brain!

Regardless of how exact this estimate may be, the conclusion is that the human brain has an extremely complex set of networks. Neurons created before birth follow chemical or other pathways in the brain to create the necessary connections to allow for vision, hearing, and other processes. In addition, we know that neurons are also created in humans after birth. A 1-year-old infant has more neurons than they will have throughout their life. After that, neurons are gained and lost depending on use. The genetic and brain mechanisms that create and remove neurons from the developing brain play an important role in the development of mental disorders. Let us now turn to the brain itself.

BRAIN ANATOMY, NEURONS, AND NEUROTRANSMITTERS

In this section, you will be introduced to the basic mechanism of the brain, the neuron. Over millions and even billions of years of evolution, the neuron has served as the basic building block of many organisms ranging from jellyfish to humans. First, let's briefly review brain anatomy.

A Quick Review of Brain Anatomy and Function

Let's begin with some simple terms. Structures closer to the front of the brain are referred to as *anterior*, whereas those closer to the back are called *posterior*. You will also see the terms *dorsal*, which is toward the back side, and ventral, which is toward the belly side. The brain appears symmetrical from the top with *left* and *right hemispheres*. Structures closer to the midline dividing the left and right hemispheres are referred to as *medial*, whereas those farther away from the midline are called *lateral* (Figure 2.3).

FIGURE 2.3 ■ Terms Used to Describe Location of Brain Areas

Traditionally, Latin terms are used to describe orientation in the brain, such as above (*superior*) and below (*inferior*) as well as front (*anterior*) and back (*posterior*).

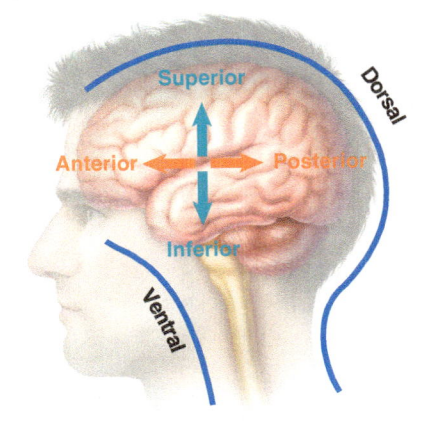

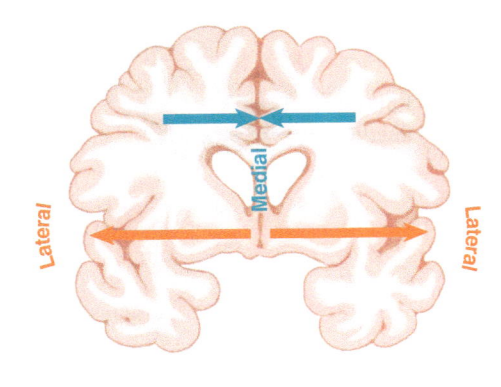

Brain areas can be described both in terms of location and function. Looking at the left hemisphere from the side, we can describe four lobes of the brain (Figure 2.4). The *frontal lobe* is located at the front of the cortex and is involved in planning, higher-order cognitive processes such as thinking and problem solving, as well as moral and social judgments.

There is a cavity referred to as the *central sulcus* that separates the frontal lobe from the parietal lobe. The brain area behind the central sulcus receives sensory information from our body, including the experience of touch. The area in front of the central sulcus allows the muscles of our bodies to make movements such as picking up a glass. The *parietal lobe*, which is toward the back and at the top of the cortex, is involved in spatial processes such as knowing where you are in space and performing spatial problems. The *occipital lobe* is located near the back of the brain and toward the bottom. The occipital lobe is involved with the processing of visual information and receives information from our eyes. Below the frontal and parietal lobes is the *temporal lobe*. Looking at the brain, you can see that the frontal and temporal lobes are separated by a deep groove, which is called the *lateral fissure*. The temporal lobe receives information from our ears and is involved in hearing as well as aspects of language. Other parts of the temporal lobe are involved in the naming of objects from visual information processed in the occipital lobes. The areas of the brain that are associated with different functions are shown in Figure 2.5. Let us now turn to the manner in which information moves throughout the brain, with an emphasis on the neuron.

FIGURE 2.4 ■ The Left Hemisphere of the Brain From the Left Side Noting the Major Anatomical Structures

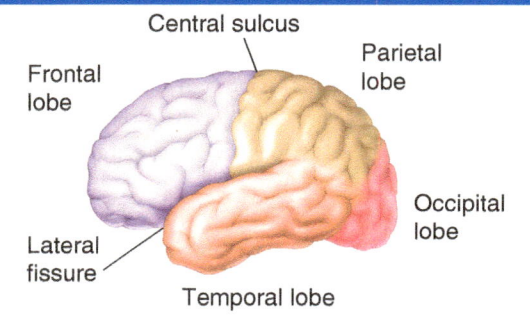

FIGURE 2.5 ■ The Brain in Terms of Structural and Functional Anatomy

Neurons and Neural Transmission

The brain's function involves one basic element, the *neuron*. Although neurons come in a variety of sizes and shapes, there are some basic characteristics (as shown in Figure 2.6):

1. The cell body contains a nucleus, which includes *deoxyribonucleic acid (DNA)* and other elements including mitochondria, which are involved in supplying energy.
2. The axon is a slender nerve that conducts electrical impulses away from the cell body. Axons can be fairly short, as found in the human brain, or 4 or 5 feet in length, such as those that go from the spinal cord to the arms and legs.
3. The dendrites receive information from other cells.

The dendrites receive information from other neurons, which connect at different locations on the dendrites. Although illustrations in textbooks usually show only a few connections between neurons, there are generally thousands of these connections. Recent research has helped to change the view of the function of dendrites (Chavlis & Poirazi, 2021). Dendrites influence how neurons process information. What are called *passive dendrites* filter the information traveling to the cell body. This allows neurons to infer the distance of incoming signals. *Active dendrites* can produce signals of their own, referred to as dendritic spikes. These dendritic features amount to different types of nonlinear integration and allow individual neurons to perform complex computations. That is, they function in ways that are more complex than simply adding and subtracting the number of signals present.

The terminal branches from other neurons do not actually touch the dendrites of a given neuron; they instead make a biochemical connection through a small gap filled with fluid, which is referred to as a synapse. These biochemical connections can release molecules (ions) with an electrical charge.

As more of these electrical charges add together, it increases the size of the electrical potential. At a critical point, an action potential is produced at a location near the cell body, which travels quickly down the axon in one direction. An action potential is referred to as an "all or none" signal, since above the critical value an action potential is produced, whereas below the critical value, no electrical activity is sent down the axon.

FIGURE 2.6 ■ Basic Characteristics of a Neuron

Input from other neurons comes through the dendrites to the cell body. Signals move down the axon, with output to other neurons.

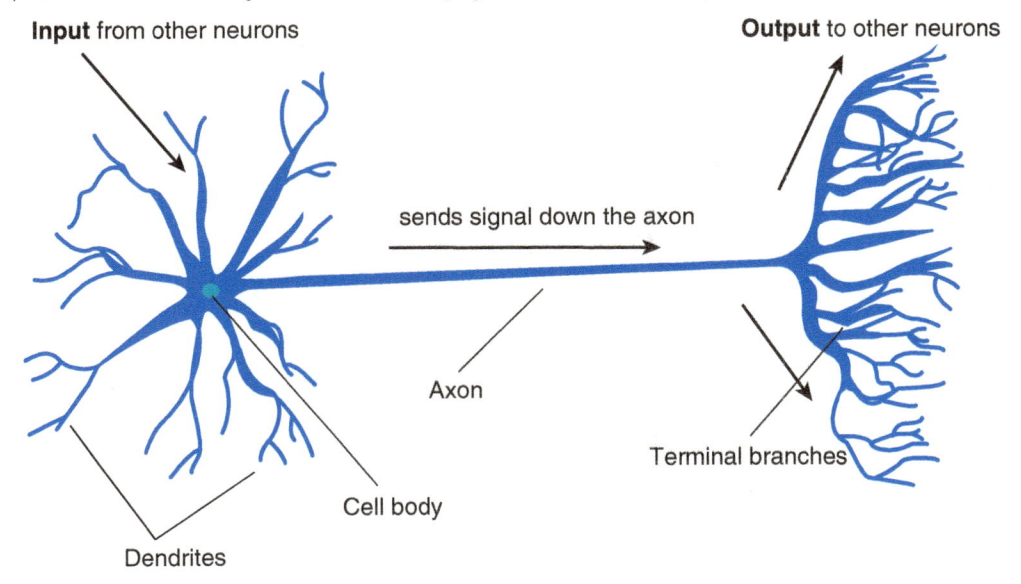

FIGURE 2.7 ■ Depiction of the Structures and Processes of Synapses

Presynaptic neuron

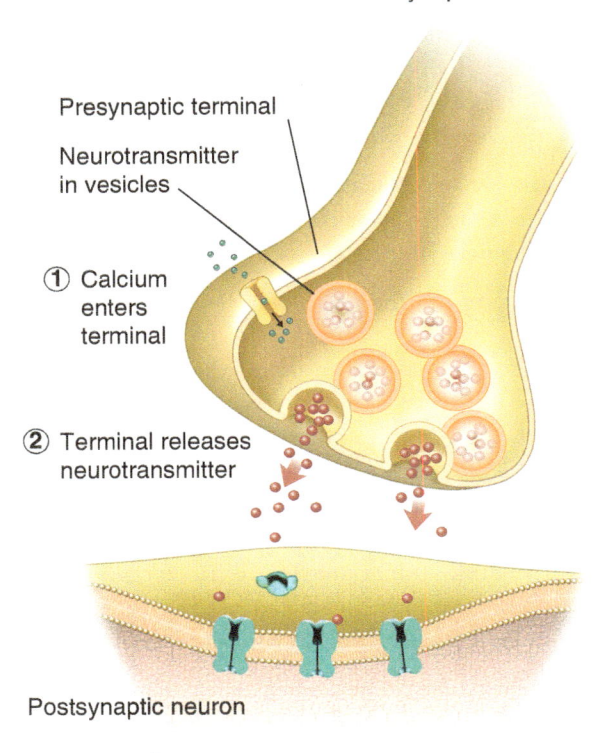

Presynaptic terminal

Neurotransmitter in vesicles

① Calcium enters terminal

② Terminal releases neurotransmitter

Postsynaptic neuron

③ Neurotransmitter interacts with receptors, opening ion channels

The speed at which the action potential travels down the axon depends on two factors. The first is the width of the axon. For example, action potentials travel faster in larger diameter axons. The second factor relates to whether the axon is covered with an insulating material called the *myelin sheath*. Myelin is made up of fats and proteins. It wraps around axons like insulation does around electrical cables and results in an increased speed in information transmissions. Action potentials travel faster in axons surrounded by myelin. Thus, an axon with a larger diameter and wrapped in myelin would have the fastest conduction times. People with disorders such as multiple sclerosis and autism show deficits in axonal connections.

It should be noted that there are two major types of synapses. One type, referred to as a chemical synapse, involves secretion from the previous neuron of various types of neurotransmitters (Figure 2.7). These neurotransmitters create a current flow. This changes the physiological state of the next (postsynaptic) neuron such that it is more likely (excitatory) or less likely (inhibitory) to create an action potential. The second type of synapse is electrical in nature. Current flows through special channels that connect the gap between the two neurons.

How Does the Neuron Pass Information?

Passing information from one neuron to another involves a number of steps:

1. Neurotransmitters need to be created and stored.
2. An action potential travels down the axon to the terminal.
3. Through a variety of processes, a neurotransmitter is released into the gap between the two neurons.
4. The neurotransmitter then binds with specific proteins in the next neuron.

5. This either increases (excitatory) or decreases (inhibitory) the possibility that the next neuron will create an action potential.

6. The gap between the two neurons must be made neutral at this point by any of a number of mechanisms, including making the neurotransmitter inactive, having the neurotransmitter taken up by the first neuron (referred to as reuptake), and removing the neurotransmitter from the gap between the two neurons.

It is these neurotransmitters that lead to anxiety processes in some cases but depression in others. Most medications used for treating mental illness influence the neurotransmitters at the synapses. It is also true that going to psychotherapy and learning new skills can also influence the structure and function of synaptic processes. In terms of disorders, Alzheimer's disease, which results in memory loss, is caused by destruction of individual neurons throughout the brain (Nath et al., 2012). Most addictive drugs increase the amount of dopamine in the gap between the neurons. Thus, having an understanding of the role of neurotransmitters is important.

Major Neurotransmitters

In the chemical synapse, neurotransmitters play a critical role. Neurotransmitters transmit signals from one neuron to another. It is also the case that psychotropic medications largely have their influence at the site of the synapse. To date, more than 100 different neurotransmitters have been identified. Neurotransmitters have been classified both in terms of structure and in terms of function. Most neurons utilize more than one type of neurotransmitter for their functioning.

Regarding their structure, neurotransmitters can be classified in terms of size (Purves et al., 2013). This results in two broad categories. The first type is small molecule neurotransmitters such as *glutamate*, which is excitatory, and *GABA* (gamma-aminobutyric acid), which is inhibitory. They are often composed of single amino acids. These small molecule neurotransmitters tend to be involved in rapid synaptic functions.

Glutamate is considered to be the most important neurotransmitter in terms of normal brain function. In abnormal conditions, the firing of rapid glutamate neurons can lead to seizures in a number of areas of the brain. GABA is inhibitory, and drugs that increase the amount of GABA available are used to treat such disorders as anxiety.

The second type of neurotransmitter in terms of size is larger protein molecules referred to as *neuropeptides*. These can be made up of 3 to 36 amino acids. Neuropeptides tend to be involved in slower, ongoing synaptic functions.

In terms of function, neurotransmitters can also be categorized into three broad groups (Nadeau, 2004). The first group includes those neurotransmitters that mediate communication between neurons, such as glutamate and GABA. The second group includes those neurotransmitters that influence the communication of information, such as opioid peptides in the pain system. The third group includes those neurotransmitters that influence the activity of large populations of neurons, such as dopamine, adrenaline, noradrenaline, and serotonin. For example, cocaine blocks the ability of a neuron to remove the neurotransmitter dopamine from the synapse, which increases the experience of addiction. (See Table 2.1 for a description of various neurotransmitters.)

It should be noted that the same biochemical substance can be either a neurotransmitter or a hormone. If the substance is released into the gap between neurons in the brain, it is referred to as a neurotransmitter. Overall, neurotransmitters are fast acting, as they facilitate or inhibit the action potential and thus process information in the brain. If the biochemical substance is released into the blood supply, it is referred to as a hormone. In general, hormones take longer to produce effects. Changes produced by hormones are in the time frame of seconds to days, depending on the particular hormone involved.

Encoding Information

Information is encoded by means of action potentials in terms of frequency. That is, a loud sound would be encoded by a series of action potentials from the cells sensitive to sound intensity. A soft

TABLE 2.1 ■ Some Representative Neurotransmitters

Neurotransmitter	Function
Acetylcholine	Transmitter at muscles; in brain, involved in learning, etc.
Monoamines	
Serotonin	Involved in mood, sleep and arousal, aggression, depression, obsessive-compulsive disorder, and alcoholism.
Dopamine	Contributes to movement control and promotes reinforcing effects of food, sex, and abused drugs; involved in schizophrenia and Parkinson's disease.
Norepinephrine	A hormone released during stress. Functions as a neurotransmitter in the brain to increase arousal and attentiveness to events in the environment; involved in depression.
Epinephrine	A stress hormone related to norepinephrine; plays a minor role as a neurotransmitter in the brain.
Amino Acids	
Glutamate	The principal excitatory neurotransmitter in the brain and spinal cord. Vitally involved in learning and implicated in schizophrenia.
Gamma-aminobutyric acid (GABA)	The predominant inhibitory neurotransmitter. Its receptors respond to alcohol and the class of tranquilizers called benzodiazepines. Deficiency in GABA or receptors is one cause of epilepsy.
Glycine	Inhibitory transmitter in the spinal cord and lower brain. The poison strychnine causes convulsions and death by affecting glycine activity.
Neuropeptides	
Endorphins	Neuromodulators that reduce pain and enhance reinforcement.
Substance P	Transmitter in neurons sensitive to pain.
Neuropeptide Y	Initiates eating and produces metabolic shifts.
Gas	
Nitric oxide	One of two known gaseous transmitters, along with carbon monoxide. Can serve as a retrograde transmitter, influencing the presynaptic neuron's release of neurotransmitters. Viagra enhances male erections by increasing nitric oxide's ability to relax blood vessels and produce penile engorgement.

sound would result in fewer action potentials being fired. When observed in relation to a stimulus, action potentials are also referred to as spikes, and a number of spikes over time are referred to as *spike trains*. Figure 2.8 shows different levels of firing. Understanding the nature of spikes and how they relate to information in the brain has been an important question since the beginning of the 20th century when they were first recorded (Rieke et al., 1999).

The Brain and the Microbiome

In discussing the brain, we want to induce you to a system of communication that is gaining more relevance in neuroscience. Traditionally, the brain and the gastrointestinal system have been studied separately. However, this is changing with a new understanding of how they are connected—in particular, through bacteria.

In our bodies there are around 10 trillion microorganisms, referred to as the microbiome (P. Kelly et al., 2022; Smith & Wissel, 2019). These organisms include fungi, archaea, viruses, and bacteria. It is the bacteria that have been the focus of much study. It is estimated that 500 to 1000 species of bacteria are found in our bodies, including the gut (J. A. Gilbert et al., 2018). Besides the gut, these organisms are also found on the skin and in the mouth, nose, lungs, and genital tract. Each of these strains of

FIGURE 2.8 ■ Spike Trains Produced by Different Levels of Firing of Neurons

Neurons fire in relation to the intensity of the signal. A loud noise, for example, would produce a larger number of spike trains than a soft noise. Each of the spikes in the figure represents a single neuron firing.

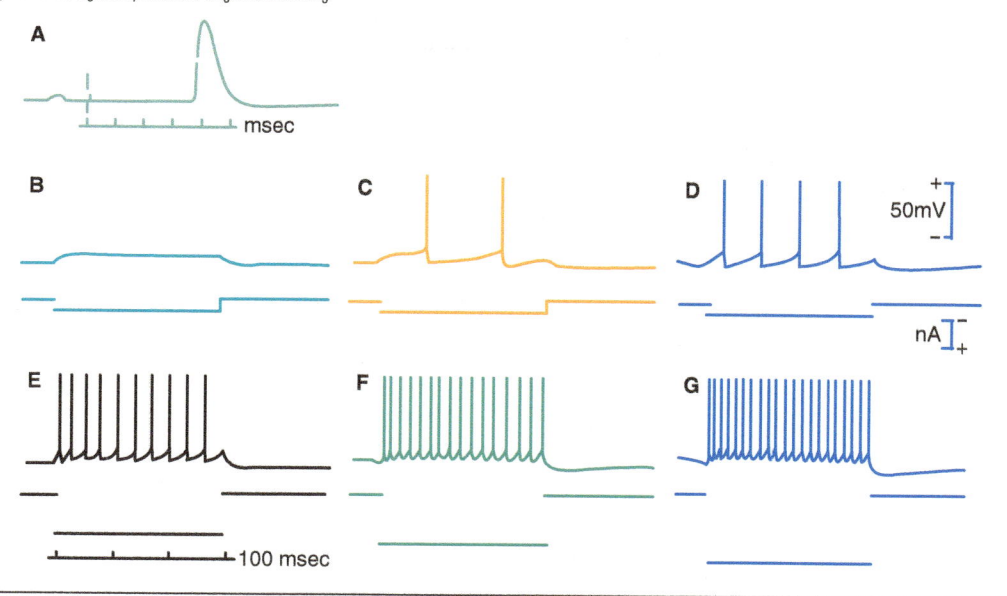

Credit: Spencer, W. (2011). The physiology of supraspinal neurons in mammals. In *Supplement 1: Handbook of physiology, the nervous system, cellular biology of neurons* (pp. 969–1021). American Physiological Society.

bacteria has a genome of its own that contains thousands of genes. In fact, these bacteria have more genetic diversity and thus more flexibility than the human genome.

Although many people think of bacteria as harmful, they can also play an important positive role in our lives (Tuganbaev et al., 2022). Scientists are beginning to understand the role of the gut in human health, disease, and mental disorders. These bacteria in the gut (referred to as the gut biome or gut microbiome) are correlated with a wide variety of conditions. On the positive side, growing evidence is suggesting that the gut microbiome can play a role in cognition, especially executive function and verbal memory (Mayneris-Perxachs et al., 2022). On the negative side, disorders associated with the gut biome include autism spectrum disorder, depression, inflammatory bowel disease, and even cancer and Parkinson's disease (Brown & Goldman, 2020).

Although there are specific species of bacteria, how they influence behavior and experience is complex. Some are associated with the production of such biochemical substances as GABA, while others are related to serotonin production. These chemical substances can then influence other organs, including the brain, through a number of mechanisms, including the blood system and the vagus nerve. One important player connecting the gut to the spinal cord and brain and vice versa is the vagus nerve (Needham et al., 2020). It should be noted that the gut contains the second most neurons in your body after your brain.

What is interesting is that different individuals have very different collections of these bacteria. In fact, studies have shown a relationship between the composition and diversity of microbiome in the gut and human personality traits (Johnson, 2020). Those who work on farms have a different microbiome than those who work in a big city. Surprisingly, the biome of identical twins can vary.

The composition of the human gut is influenced by actions of the immune system as well as a number of other factors. It is assumed that during and shortly after birth, the mother and other environmental factors help to establish the composition of the biome in the gut. After weaning, the human gut biome becomes fairly established and remains stable in healthy individuals. It is known that malnutrition can influence early brain development. Recent work has shown an important role for the gut microbiome in the development and function of the nervous system (Coley & Hsiao, 2021; Foster, 2022).

There is some suggestion that antibiotics taken early in life may affect the gut biome in a manner that can lead to specific disorders (Brodin, 2022; Lu & Stappenback, 2022). Later in life, major changes in diet can also influence the biome. If the person were to resume their original diet, then the original biome would reappear. However, the microbiome also changes with aging (Bana & Cabreiro, 2019), and sleep deprivation and stress can influence the gut biome in a negative manner that increases inflammation. Other lifestyle changes such as exercise appear to influence the structure of the biome by reducing inflammation, thus improving health. Gut bacteria in childhood is also associated with asthma and allergic reaction in later life.

Current research has also examined weight and the biome. The gut biome is associated with whether the person is lean or obese (Walters et al., 2014). Other studies have shown how the brain and gastrointestinal system communicate in order to regulate energy homeostasis (Clemmensen et al., 2017; Cryan & Mazmanian, 2022). New research is examining ways to influence this communication through the gut biome as a potential treatment for obesity. The modulation of the gut biome can also offer treatment for certain psychological states. One study showed differences in brain activity related to social stress in participants who received a particular probiotic that contained a live beneficial bacteria for 4 weeks versus those who received a placebo (H. Wang et al., 2019). Another similar study gave medical students probiotics for 12 weeks leading up to their qualifying exams and showed reductions in stress-related symptoms (Nishida et al., 2017). We will describe specific psychopathological disorders and their relation to the microbiome in separate chapters in this book.

Let us now move from the consideration of neurons and neurotransmission to an overview of some of the specific neuroscience techniques that are used to understand psychopathological processes. Following an examination of these neuroscience techniques, we will move to a discussion of the networks of the brain.

CONCEPT CHECK

- What are the four major lobes of the brain, and what is the primary role of each?
- "The brain's function involves one basic element, the neuron." What are the different parts that form the structure of the neuron, and what roles do they play?
- How does the neuron pass information on to other neurons, and how is that information encoded?

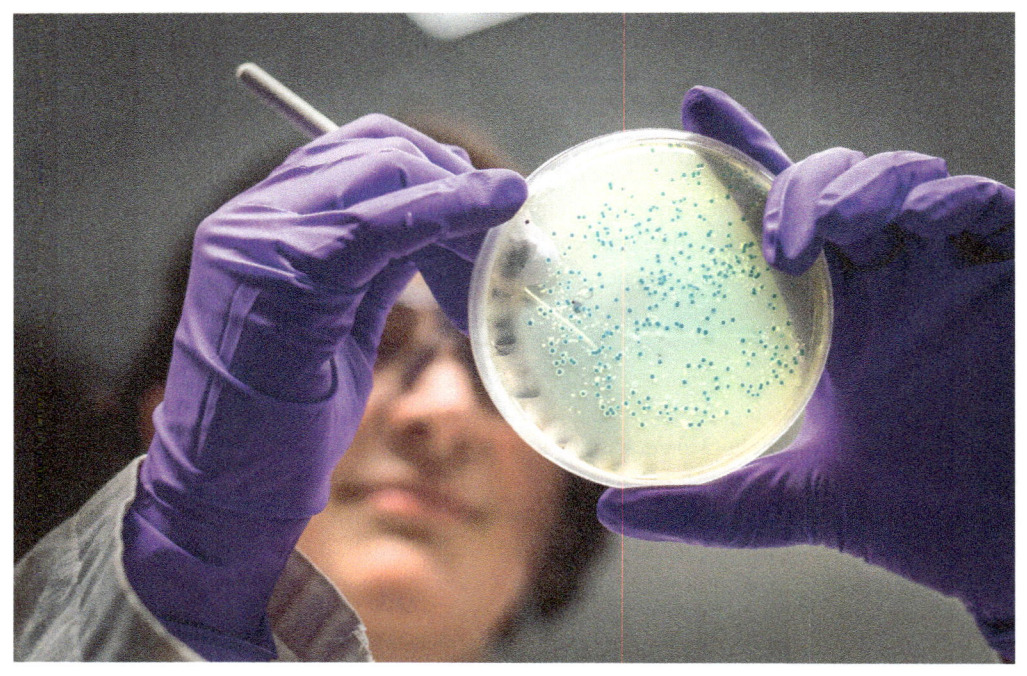

Research into the human gut biome is revealing how these bacteria can affect behavior and experience.
iStock.com/manjurul

HOW DO WE OBSERVE THE BRAIN AT WORK?

With 86 billion neurons and 50 to 200 trillion connections between neurons in the human brain, understanding these connections on a neuronal level would be an impossible task. However, scientists have been able to use the manner in which neurons work as a window into their function. A variety of techniques for observing activity in the brain have been developed.

Currently, the major types of brain imaging techniques are *electroencephalography* (EEG), *magnetoencephalography (MEG), positron emission tomography (PET)*, and *functional magnetic resonance imaging (fMRI)*. EEG is a technique for recording electrical activity from the scalp related to cortical activity. MEG measures the small magnetic field gradients exiting and entering the surface of the head that are produced when neurons are active. PET is a measure related to blood flow in the brain, which reflects cognitive processing. fMRI is based on the fact that blood flow increases in active areas of the cortex. It is also possible to use the magnetic resonance imaging (MRI) magnet to measure cortical connections in the brain, which is referred to as *diffusion tensor imaging (DTI)*. Let's take a look at each of these techniques, and consider the strengths and weaknesses of each type.

Electroencephalography

Electroencephalography (EEG) is a technique for recording electrical activity from the scalp related to cortical activity. It reflects the electrical activity of the brain at the level of the synapse (Nunez & Srinivasan, 2006). It records the product of the changing excitatory and inhibitory currents. Action potentials contribute very little to the EEG. However, since changes at the synapse do influence the production of action potentials, there is an association of EEG with spike trains (Whittingstall & Logothetis, 2009).

The EEG was first demonstrated in humans by Hans Berger in 1924, and results were published 5 years later (Berger, 1929/1969). Since the neurons of the brain and their connections are constantly active, EEG can be measured during both waking hours and sleep. In fact, EEG serves as an objective measure of depth of sleep (Figure 2.9).

FIGURE 2.9 ■ Electroencephalogram as an Objective Measure of Sleep Stages

EEG can be used to determine the stage of sleep that is present. Being awake reflects low-amplitude, faster EEG activity. During the night, the EEG becomes of a lower frequency as the person goes into deeper sleep. People generally goes through three or four cycles of sleep during the night, in which they move from Stage 1 to Stage 4 and back again.

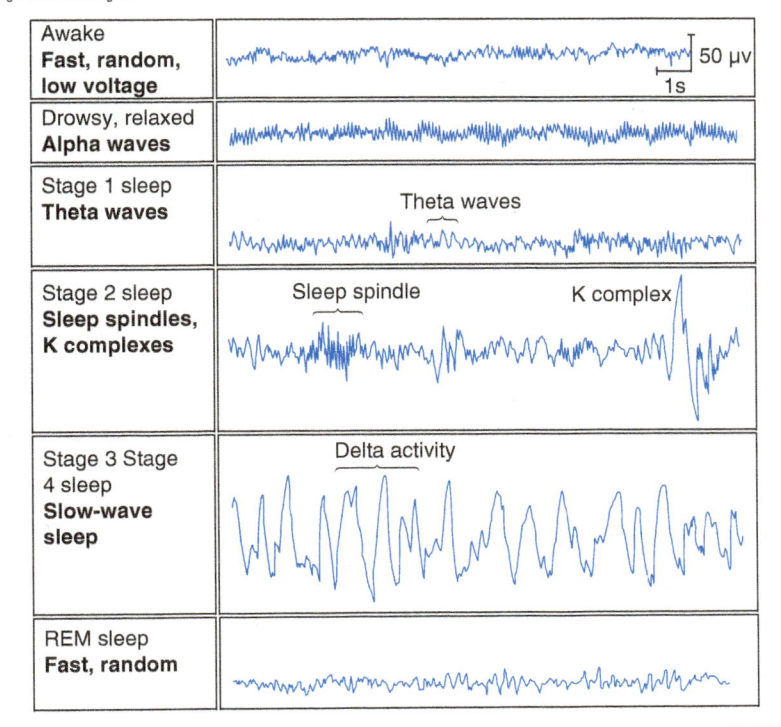

Credit: Hauri, P. (1982). *Current concepts: The sleep disorders*. Upjohn.

EEG can be measured with only two electrodes or as a high-density array of more than 200 electrodes. EEG activity has been used to infer brain processing. The actual measure of EEG is the difference between the signals at any two electrodes. Traditionally, the second or reference electrode was placed at a location not considered to produce electrical signals, for example, the ear lobe. Today, a common practice is to average the signals in all of the electrodes available and compare that with each specific electrode.

Some aspects of the EEG signal may appear almost random, while other fluctuations appear periodic. Using signal processing techniques, it is possible to determine the major frequency and

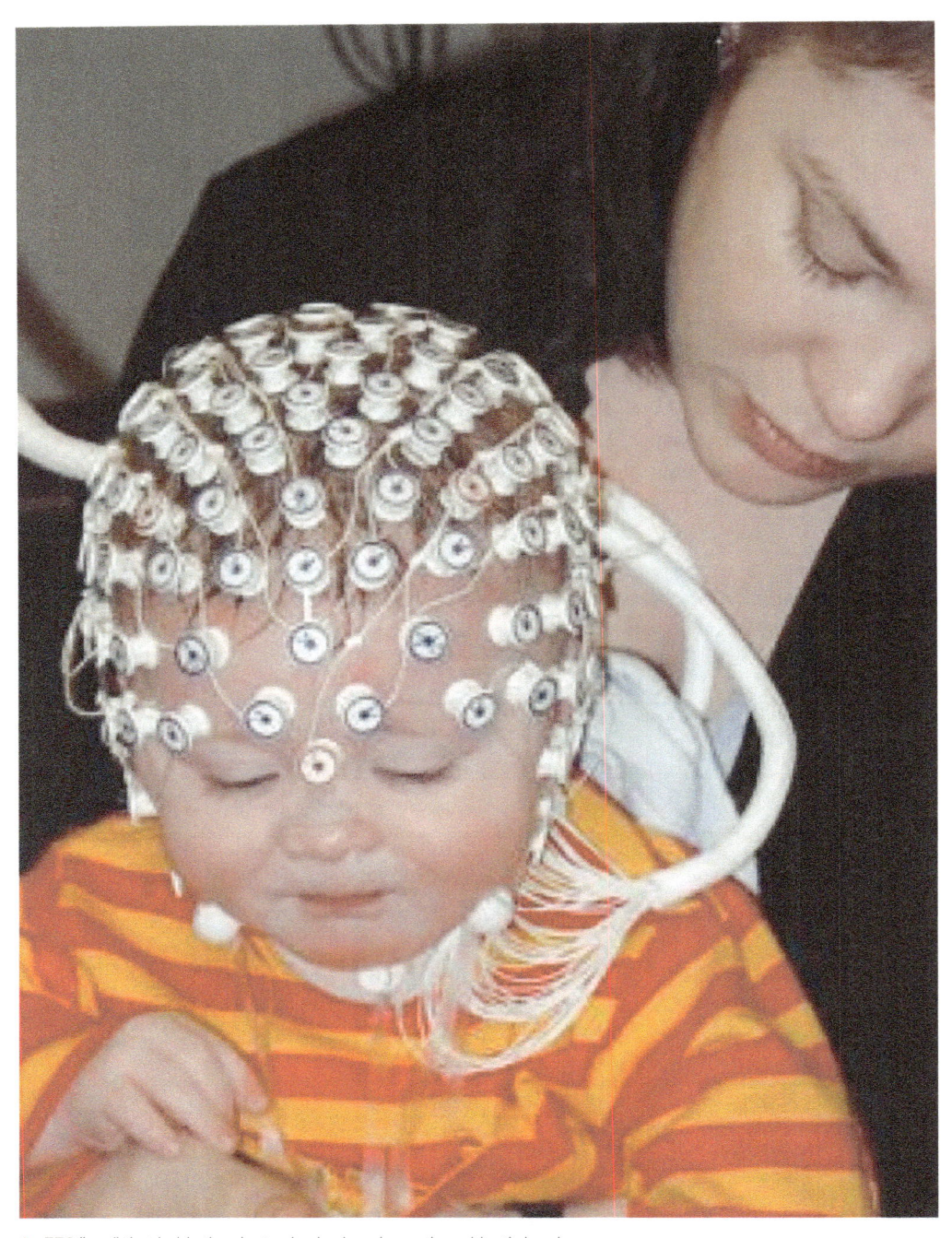

An EEG "cap" that holds the electrodes is placed over the subject's head.
Don Tucker

amplitude seen in the signal. Amplitude refers to how large the signal is, and frequency refers to how fast the signal cycles, measured in cycles per second, or Hertz (Hz). Over the years, researchers have noticed that specific patterns of EEG activity were associated with a variety of psychological states (Figure 2.10). When an individual is relaxed with their eyes closed, high-amplitude regular activity is seen in the EEG at a frequency of 8 to 12 Hz. Alpha activity in the 8- to 12-Hz range was the first pattern of EEG activity Berger noted. If the person begins to perform some mental activity such as mental arithmetic, lower-amplitude EEG is seen at a higher frequency, above 20 Hz, and is referred to as beta activity.

EEG oscillations are one way in which information is transferred in the brain (Knyazev, 2007). For example, theta oscillations are associated with memory performance (Liebe et al., 2012). Theta is also involved in coordinating emotional information between the limbic areas and the frontal areas of the brain. Delta oscillations are seen in sleep and motivational processes such as drug use. Drugs such as cocaine produce changes in a number of EEG frequency bands. Alpha oscillations, on the other hand, are involved in inhibiting the activity of various brain areas.

In recent years, researchers have become interested in the processing of a percept (Singer, 2009; Singer & Gray, 1995; Tallon-Baudry & Bertrand, 1999). For example, when one sees a black and white spotted Dalmatian dog against a black and white background, there is usually a subjective experience of having the image "pop out." Associated with this perception is a burst of EEG gamma activity. Figure 2.11 compares the amount of EEG gamma activity in those individuals trained to see the Dalmatian as compared with those who were not trained.

FIGURE 2.10 ■ Depiction of Specific Patterns of Electroencephalography Activity

EEG activity is named in terms of its frequency and amplitude. Delta (0–4 Hz) is seen in deep sleep, theta (4–8 Hz) is seen as one goes to sleep, alpha (8–13 Hz) is seen during periods of relaxation, beta (13–30 Hz) is seen when a person is actively thinking, and gamma (about 30 Hz) is seen in perceptual processes.

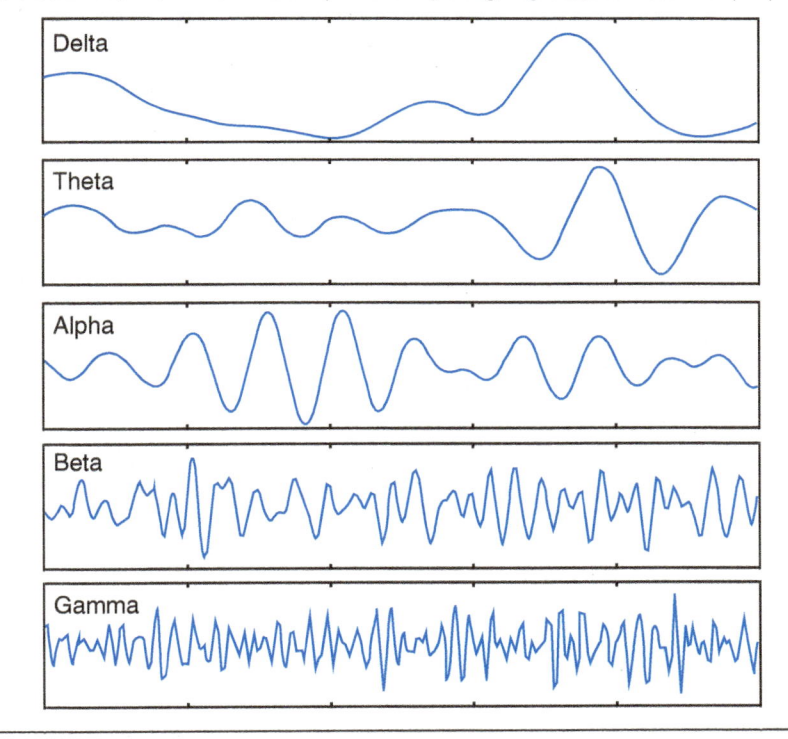

Source: Gamboa, H. (2005). https://commons.wikimedia.org/wiki/User:Hgamboa, licensed under CC BY-SA 3.0 https://creativecommons.org/licenses/by-sa/3.0/.

FIGURE 2.11 ■ Wavelet Analysis Associated With Seeing the Dalmatian Dog

When the person recognizes that there is a dog in the picture, there is a burst of EEG gamma activity (yellow in the graph), as seen in the right wavelet analysis in panel B.

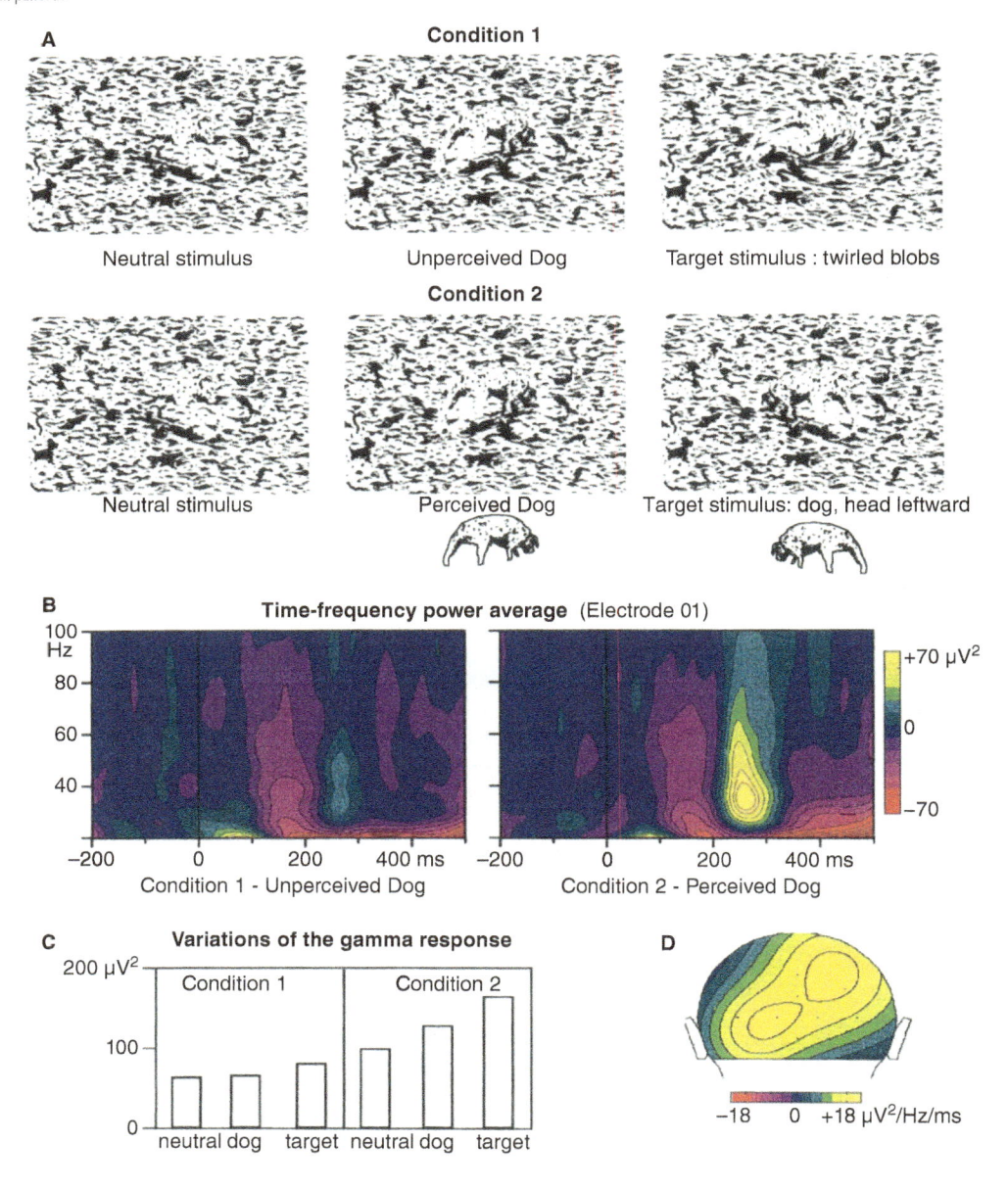

Credit: Reprinted from *Trends in Cognitive Sciences*, Vol. 3, Catherine Tallon-Baudry & Olivier Bertrand, "Oscillatory gamma activity in humans and its role in object representation," pp. 151–162, Copyright 1999, with permission from Elsevier.

Evoked Potentials

Event-related potentials (ERPs), also known as **evoked potentials (EPs)**, show EEG activity in relation to a particular event. Imagine taking a continuous EEG signal during which a picture or tone is presented to an individual a number of times. If we were to take the EEG in the half-second following the stimulus presentation and average these together, we would have the brain response to the stimulus (Figure 2.12).

The waveform of the ERP is described in terms of positive and negative peaks and the time elapsed from the stimulus presentation. Thus, a P300 waveform is a peak in the ERP in the positive direction occurring 300 milliseconds (ms) after the stimulus presentation. Likewise, N100 would

FIGURE 2.12 ■ Evoked Potentials Are Created by Averaging Periods of EEG

(A) Ongoing EEG. (B) Responses to a stimulus are then averaged together to create the evoked potential. Event-related potential waveforms come from the ongoing electroencephalography.

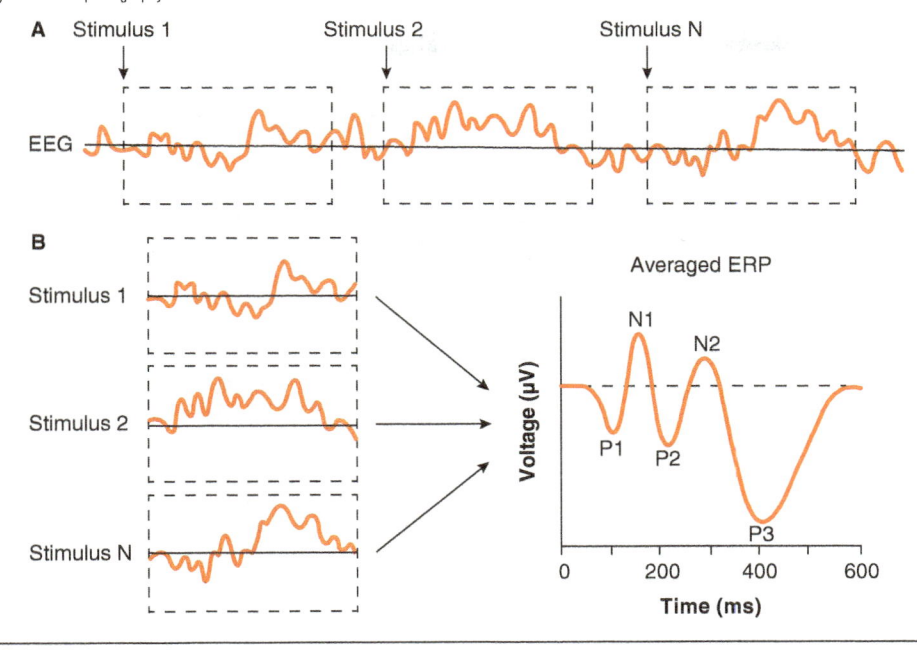

Credit: Reprinted from *Trends in Cognitive Sciences*, Vol. 4, Steven J. Luck, Geoffrey F. Woodman, & Edward K. Vogel, "Event-related potential studies of attention," pp. 432–440, Copyright 2000, with permission from Elsevier.

be a peak in the negative direction 100 ms after the stimulus presentation. Based on early recording equipment characteristics, positive peaks are often shown pointing downward and negative peaks upward. For simplicity, P300 is sometimes referred to as P3, since it represents the third positive peak following a stimulus presentation. Thus, one may see both N1 or P3 as well as N100 or P300 used in the literature.

Evoked potentials offer a view of cognitive and emotional processing that takes place in the brain outside of awareness. They are also useful in groups such as infants who cannot respond verbally. In one study, evoked potentials were recorded from 7-month-old infants as they saw faces with emotional expressions. A stronger reaction was seen at around 400 ms when they saw a fearful face as opposed to a happy face (Taylor-Colls & Pasco Fearon, 2015). A common use of evoked potential research in terms of mental disorders has been to show how cognitive and emotional processing differs for those with a disorder and those without. Evoked potentials have also been used to distinguish those with schizophrenia from those without (Laton et al., 2014). In addition, evoked potentials have shown that children with ADHD (attention deficit/hyperactivity disorder) show different types of evoked potential components from those with autism spectrum disorder (Tye et al., 2014).

Magnetoencephalography

Magnetoencephalography (MEG) measures the small magnetic field gradients exiting and entering the surface of the head that are produced when neurons are active. It uses a SQUID (superconducting quantum interference device) to detect small magnetic activity that results from the activity of neurons. As shown in the photo, the person simply puts their head in a device that contains magnetic sensors.

MEG signals are similar to EEG signals but have one important advantage that stems from the fact that magnetic fields are not distorted when they pass through the cortex and the skull. This makes it possible to be more accurate in terms of spatial location of the signal with MEG. For example, youth with bipolar disorder show greater activation in the frontal gyrus and less in the insula following negative feedback than do control participants (Rich et al., 2011).

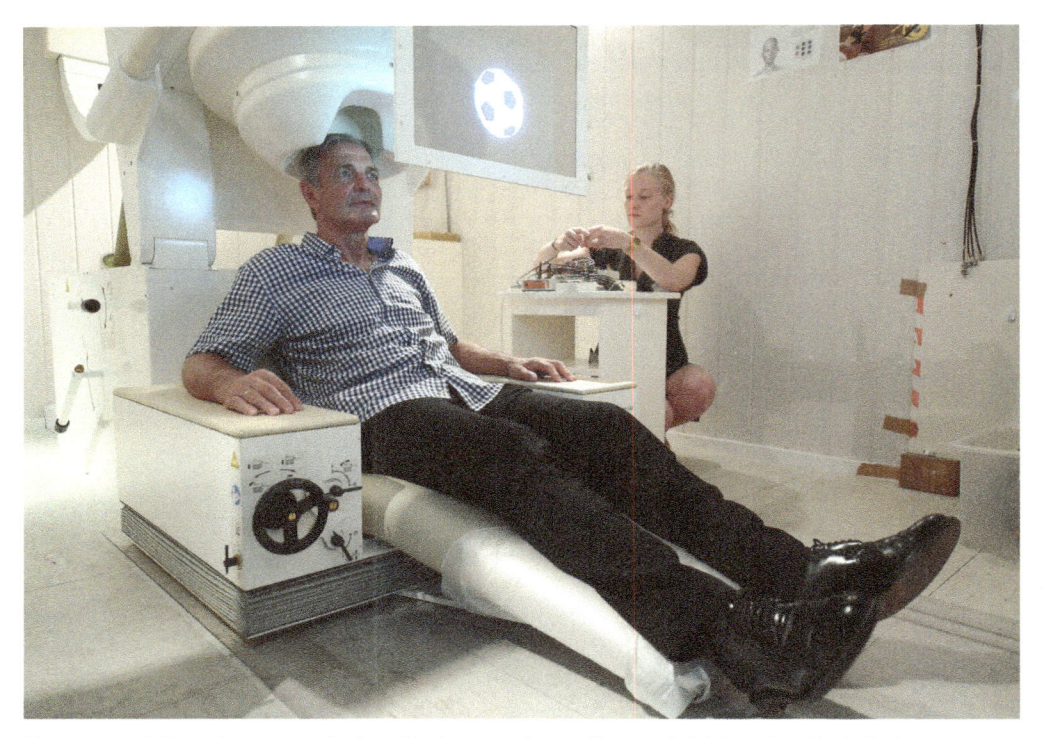

Magnetoencephalography measures brain activity by measuring small magnetic fields produced in the brain.

dpa picture alliance/Alamy Stock Photo

Positron Emission Tomography

Positron emission tomography (PET) measures variations in cerebral blood flow that are correlated with brain activity. It is through blood flow that the brain obtains the oxygen and glucose from which it gets its energy. By measuring changes in blood flow in different brain areas, it is possible to infer which areas of the brain are more or less active during particular tasks. Blood flow using PET is measured after participants inhale, or are injected with, a tracer (a radioactive isotope) that travels in the bloodstream and is recorded by the PET scanner (a gamma ray detector). Figure 2.13 depicts a PET scan in which individuals with schizophrenia show less metabolism in the frontal lobes as compared with healthy controls (Buchsbaum & Haier, 1987).

The general procedure is to make a measurement during a control task that is subtracted from the reading taken during an experimental task. Although it takes some time to make a PET reading,

FIGURE 2.13 ■ Comparing Positron Emission Tomography Scans

Control subjects show more activity (brighter colors) than individuals with schizophrenia.

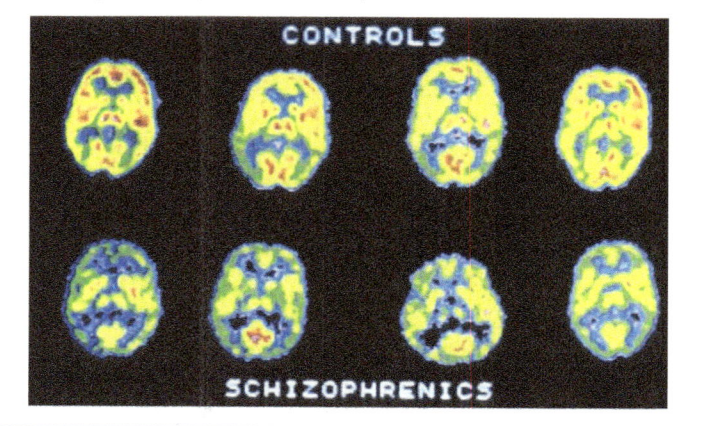

Credit: Buchsbaum, M. S., & Haier, R. J. (1987). Functional and anatomical brain imaging: Impact on schizophrenia research. *Schizophrenia Bulletin, 13*(1), 115–132.

which reduces its value in terms of temporal resolution, it is possible to determine specific areas of the brain active during different types of processing. Since PET can measure almost any molecule that can be radioactively labeled, it can be used to answer specific questions about perfusion, metabolism, and neurotransmitter turnover.

Some of PET's main disadvantages include expense; the need for a cyclotron to create radioactive agents; the injection of radioactive tracers, which limit the number of experimental sessions that can be run for a given individual; and limited temporal resolution. Due to risks associated with exposure to the radioactive tracer elements in a PET study, participants typically do not participate in more than one study per year, which limits the degree to which short-term treatment efficacy can be studied. With the development of fMRI, PET is no longer the technique of choice for research studies in psychopathology.

However, PET does offer an advantage for studying specific receptors such as dopamine receptors in the brain, which are particularly active in those with an addiction or inactive in those with Parkinson's disease. Another study used PET to examine serotonin in those with social anxiety disorder (Frick et al., 2015). An overactive serotonin system was found at the synaptic level in those with social anxiety disorder as compared to matched controls.

Functional Magnetic Resonance Imaging

Functional magnetic resonance imaging (fMRI) is based on the fact that blood flow increases in active areas of the cortex. Specifically, hemoglobin, which carries oxygen in the bloodstream, has different magnetic properties before and after oxygen is absorbed. Thus, by measuring the ratio of hemoglobin with and without oxygen, the fMRI is able to map changes in cortical blood and infer neuronal activity. Measurements using fMRI are made by having a person lie on their back inside a large magnet and radio frequency device, which measures changes in blood oxygen levels.

In contrast to an fMRI, an MRI creates only a structural image MRI, like an X-ray, that shows the *anatomy* of the brain but does not reflect *activity* (Figure 2.14). It is possible to measure brain areas with an MRI in terms of size. Often, measures of those with a disorder are compared to those without the disorder. For example, reduction in brain volume is seen in a variety of disorders, including schizophrenia. These measures can be determined from the MRI.

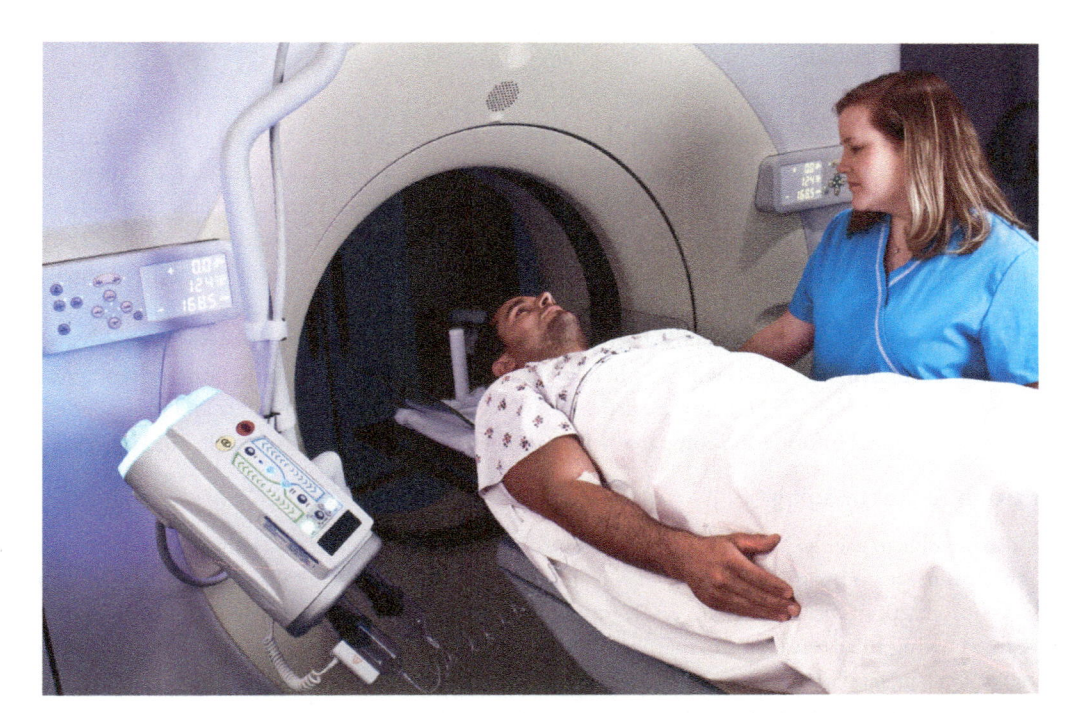

Blood flow measurements in the brain using fMRI are made by having a person lie on his back inside a large magnet and radio frequency device.

iStock.com/Mark Kostich

FIGURE 2.14 ■ Magnetic Resonance Imaging (MRI) Shows the Anatomy of the Brain

Unlike fMRI, MRI does not reflect brain activity but only the structure of the brain.

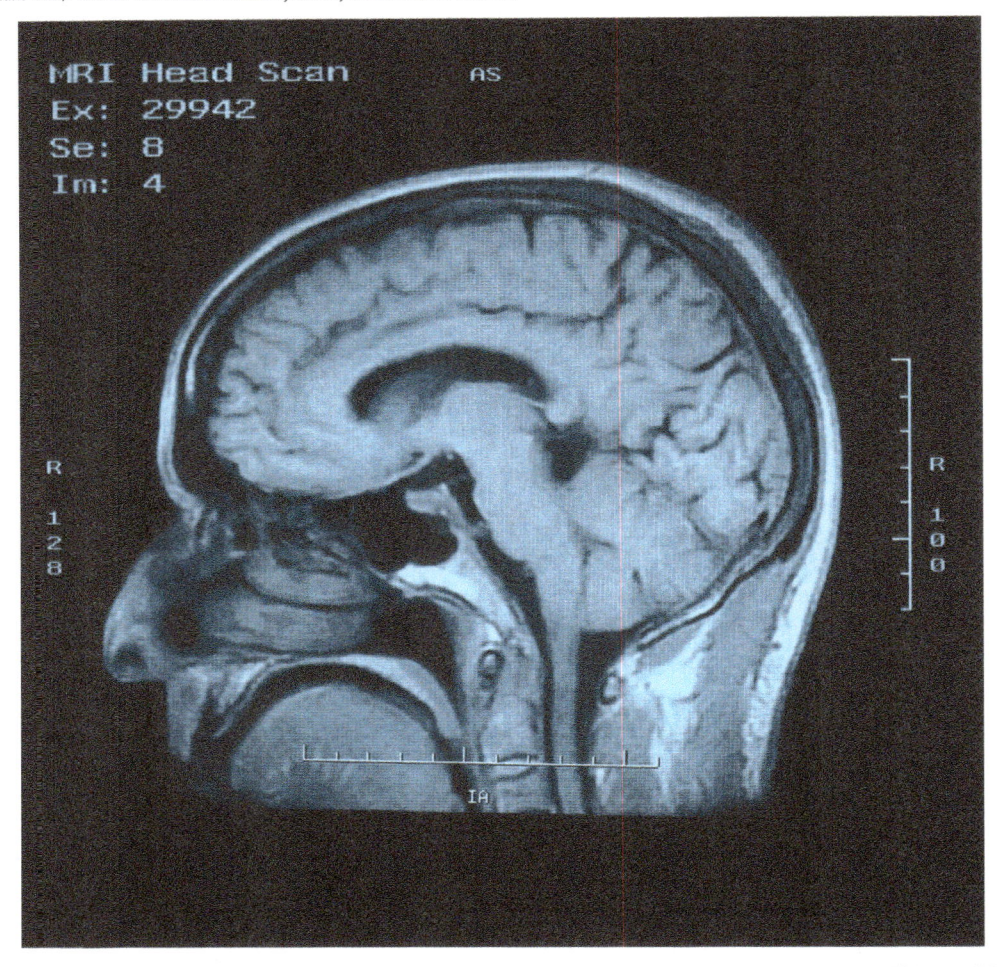

Credit: iStock.com/CGinspiration

Brain activity can be determined with the fMRI, or functional MRI. A common procedure for showing brain activity is to take a baseline in which the patient just relaxes. Following this baseline period, the patient performs specific tasks. The fMRI response recorded during the task is subtracted from that during the baseline period. This shows which specific areas of the brain are involved in performing a task. This information is then placed on the structural MRI image of the brain as shown in Figure 2.15. The color used reflects the amount of activity seen in a particular brain area. As you will see throughout this book, fMRI has been used with almost every disorder discussed. You can also compare one group of individuals with another. For example, Figure 2.16 shows that women with posttraumatic stress disorder (PTSD) activate different areas of the brain (the amygdala and insula) when processing emotional information compared with women without PTSD (Bruce et al., 2013).

Diffusion Tensor Imaging

It is also possible to use the MRI magnet to measure cortical connections in the brain, which is referred to as **diffusion tensor imaging (DTI)**. DTI is available with most MRI imaging systems (see Thomason & Thompson, 2011; Waszczuk et al., 2021, for overviews of DTI and psychopathology). It is a procedure for showing fiber tracts (white matter) in the brain. This information can then be visualized by color coding it as shown in Figures 2.17 and 2.18. This allows one to map the white matter connections in the brain. In these figures, the connections between different parts of the brain can be seen.

FIGURE 2.15 ■ Functional Magnetic Resonance Imaging (fMRI)

In these fMRI scans, the amount of color reflects the amount of activity seen in a particular brain area. The activity is related to the energy demands needed to perform a particular task.

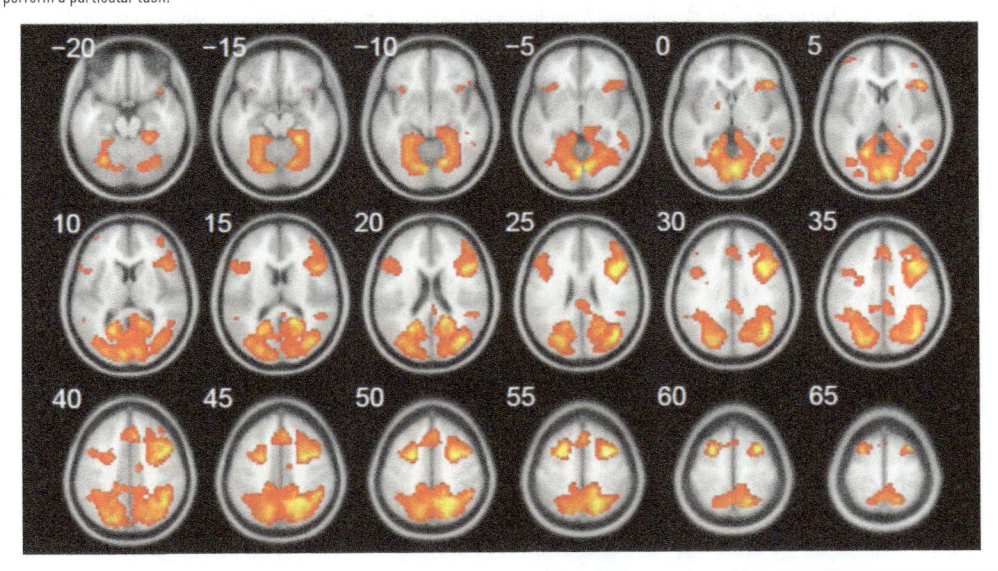

Credit: Zhang, K., Johnson, B., Pennell, D., Ray, W., Sebastianelli, W., & Slobounov, S. (2010). Are functional deficits in concussed individuals consistent with white matter structural alterations: Combined FMRI & DTI study. *Experimental Brain Research, 204*, 57–70, Figure 3B.

FIGURE 2.16 ■ Brain Activation Differences in the Amygdala and Insula

This figure shows the fMRI scans of the brain at two different levels along the z-axis. Women with post-traumatic stress disorder (PTSD) activate the amygdala and insula more when processing emotional information compared with women without PTSD.

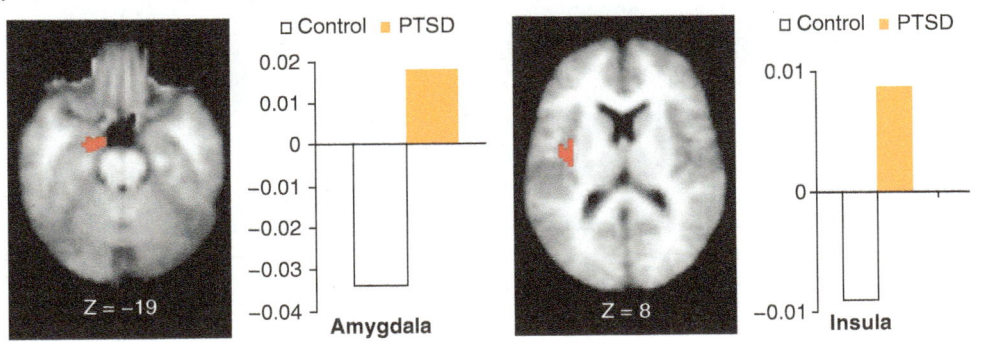

Credit: Reprinted from *NeuroImage: Clinical*, Vol. 2, Steven E. Bruce, Katherine R. Buchholz, Wilson J. Brown, Laura Yan, Anthony Durbin, & Yvette I. Sheline, "Altered emotional interference processing in the amygdala and insula in women with post-traumatic stress disorder," pp. 43–49, Copyright 2013, with permission from Elsevier.

Developmentally, after-infancy measures of white matter suggest a linear development until a person is in their 30s. Following a plateau, these gradually decline with age. Using DTI, it is possible to map the mild cognitive impairment seen in dementia and the more severe impairment seen in Alzheimer's disease. Disconnections are seen between the major areas involved in memory, such as the hippocampus and the temporal lobes (Stebbins & Murphy, 2009). As would be expected, this loss of connectivity is greater in Alzheimer's than in mild cognitive impairment. Individuals with schizophrenia also exhibit problems with cortical connections (Phillips et al., 2011). It is also possible to compare the structure of pathways in the brain between humans and other primate species (Wedeen et al., 2012). DTI and other brain imaging techniques have also given us a better understanding of cultural differences as described in *Cultural LENS: Using Brain Imaging to Understand Culture*.

FIGURE 2.17 ■ Mapping White Matter Connections in the Brain Using Color Coding

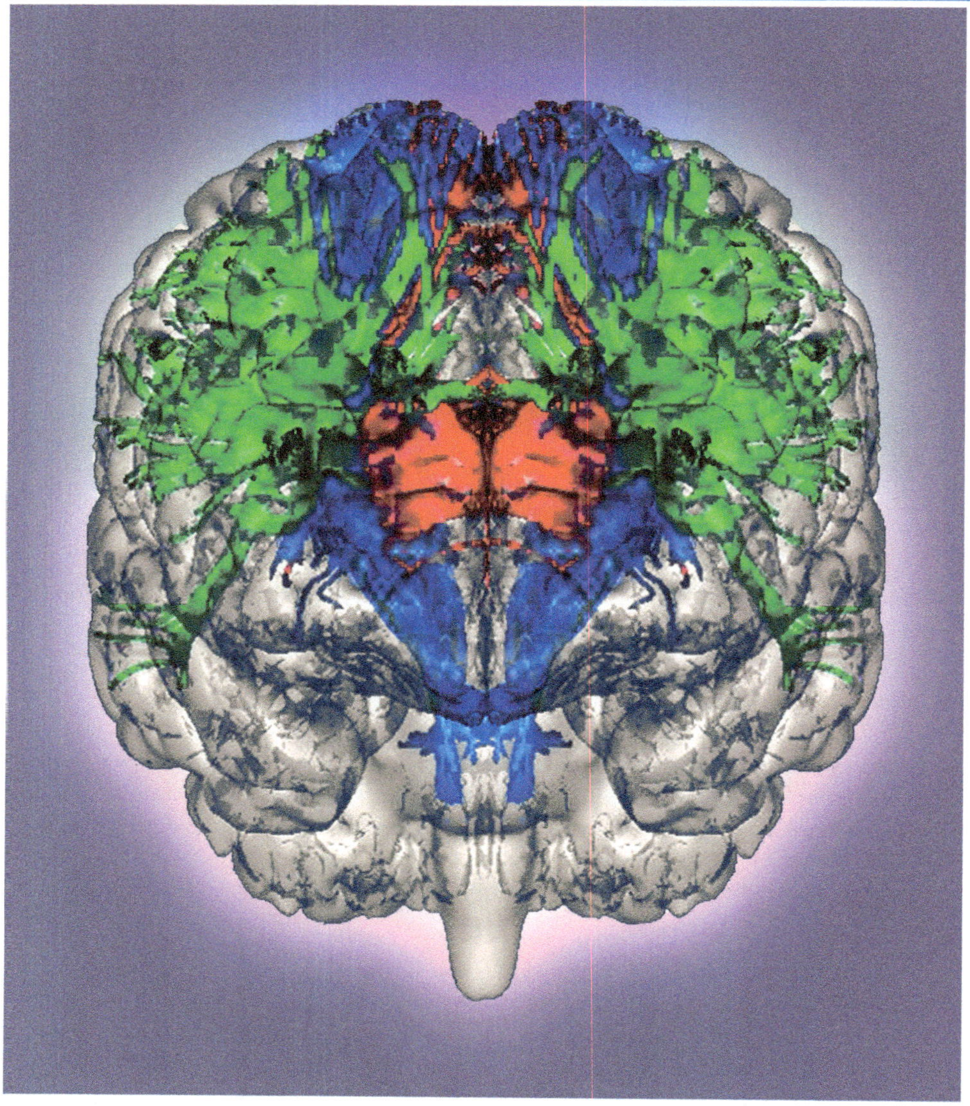

Credit: © Zephyr/Science Source.

Spatial and Temporal Resolution

There are a number of trade-offs that researchers must consider when choosing a brain imaging technique (see Table 2.2 for pros and cons of using the different techniques). It begins with the research question one is asking. If you wanted to know if the areas of the brain associated with memory, such as the hippocampus, are larger or smaller in individuals with PTSD, then you would want a measure of structure. If you wanted to know if those with autism quickly viewed different emotional faces in a different way, then you would want a measure that reflects changes in brain processes.

One important question is how fast a particular technique can measure change. This is referred to as *temporal resolution*. EEG and MEG, for example, can measure quick changes in the brain on the millisecond level. PET, on the other hand, can only record changes that take place in a period of a few minutes or more. Another consideration is spatial resolution, that is, what size of brain area a technique can measure. PET and fMRI are better able to pinpoint the location of activity in the brain, whereas with EEG it is less possible to know specifically where in the brain activity came from. The relationship between spatial and temporal resolution is shown in Figure 2.19.

FIGURE 2.18 ■ Mapping White Matter Connections in the Brain Measured With Diffusion Tensor Imaging (DTI)

DTI reflects fiber tracts in the brain. This information can then be visualized by color coding the size of the tract.

Source: Schultz, T. (2006). https://commons.wikimedia.org/wiki/File: DTI-sagittal-fibers.jpg, licensed under CC BY-SA 3.0 https://creativecommons.org/licenses/by-sa/3.0/.

TABLE 2.2 ■ Pros and Cons of Different Neuroscience Techniques

Technique	Pros	Cons
EEG	Reflects quick changes in the brain, inexpensive, not invasive, safe, little discomfort	Difficult to know which brain areas produced the EEG
MEG	Reflects quick changes in the brain, not invasive, safe, no discomfort	Basic equipment is expensive
MRI and fMRI	More exact location of structure and activity, safe, little discomfort	Basic equipment is expensive, cannot be used with people who have any metal in their body (heart pacemaker or metal pins), fMRI not able to measure short-term changes in the brain
PET	Able to measure specific neurotransmitters	Basic equipment is expensive, injection of radioactive tracers limits number of scans per year, not able to measure short-term changes in the brain

FIGURE 2.19 ■ Spatial and Temporal Resolution of Imaging Techniques

EEG and MEG have temporal resolution of less than a second. Using these techniques, it is possible to measure quick changes in the brain. PET takes a longer time to complete a measurement. Although MRI measurements are slower than EEG, the ability to image specific areas of the brain is better.

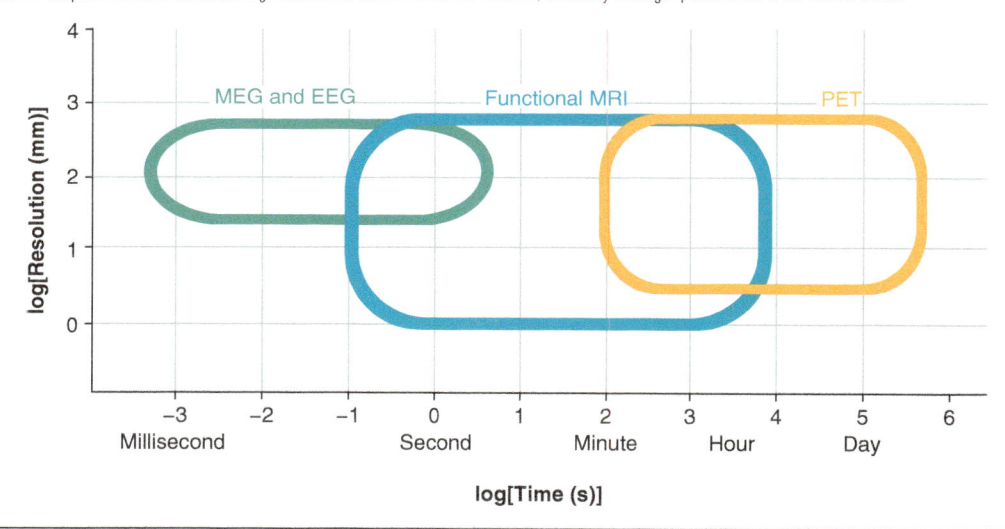

Credit: Meyer-Linderberg, A. (2010). From maps to mechanisms through neuroimaging of schizophrenia. *Nature, 468,* 194-202. https://doi.org/10.1038/nature09569

CULTURAL LENS
USING BRAIN IMAGING TO UNDERSTAND CULTURE

Historically, those interested in psychopathology and neuroscience research have focused more on the universality of human processing rather than the diversity found in different cultures. This is beginning to change with an integration of human diversity and neuroscience perspectives on human behavior and experience (see Chiao, 2009, 2011; Henderson et al., 2016; Kitayama & Cohen, 2007).

People around the world have various understandings of mental illness and appropriate treatment.

iStock.com/Edwin Tan

In terms of assessment and *classification* of mental disorders, it is critical when working with individuals from different cultures to understand the rules of expression as well as the labeling of mental disorders. This is especially true if the rules for expression of distress and emotion differ greatly from the interviewer's culture. It is also important to understand what would be considered a mental disorder in another culture. For example, in some cultures such as the Shona of Zimbabwe, there is a disorder referred to as thinking too much (*Kufungisisa*). Thinking too much is seen to cause anxiety and depression as well as headaches and dizziness. A common theme in Latin America is to speak of nerves (*nervios*) as a common idiom for psychological distress. People may say that they cannot function because of nerves. In Japan, there is a broad concept of social concern when interacting with others (*taijin kyofusho*). This can include concern that one is making too much or too little eye contact, has an unpleasant body odor, or is making inappropriate body movements (see Mezzich & Ruiperez, 2015, for an overview). Cultural displays of emotional expression vary. Individuals from different cultures may display their emotions differently even though the underlying experience of the emotion may be similar.

Neuroscience research has shown that human reactions are also culturally sensitive. We know that the amygdala shows increased activity in response to emotional reactions, especially fear. Japanese people and white Americans show greater amygdala responses to fear expressions of those of their own culture. To put it another way, a person shows less response when viewing an emotional expression of someone who is not part of their own culture (Figure 2.20).

FIGURE 2.20 ■ Cultural Specificity in Bilateral Amygdala Response to Fear Faces

Do we respond differently to those in our culture? In terms of fear faces, people show more amygdala responses to the expression of such fear faces by those in one's own culture. Less response is seen to fear faces of those from cultures other than one's own. In the various panels in this figure, (A) portrays fear expressions on a Japanese person and a white American, and (B) shows an illustration of bilateral amygdala response to fear faces. As shown in the graphs, participants show greater left (C) and right (D) amygdala response to fear expressed by members of their own cultural group.

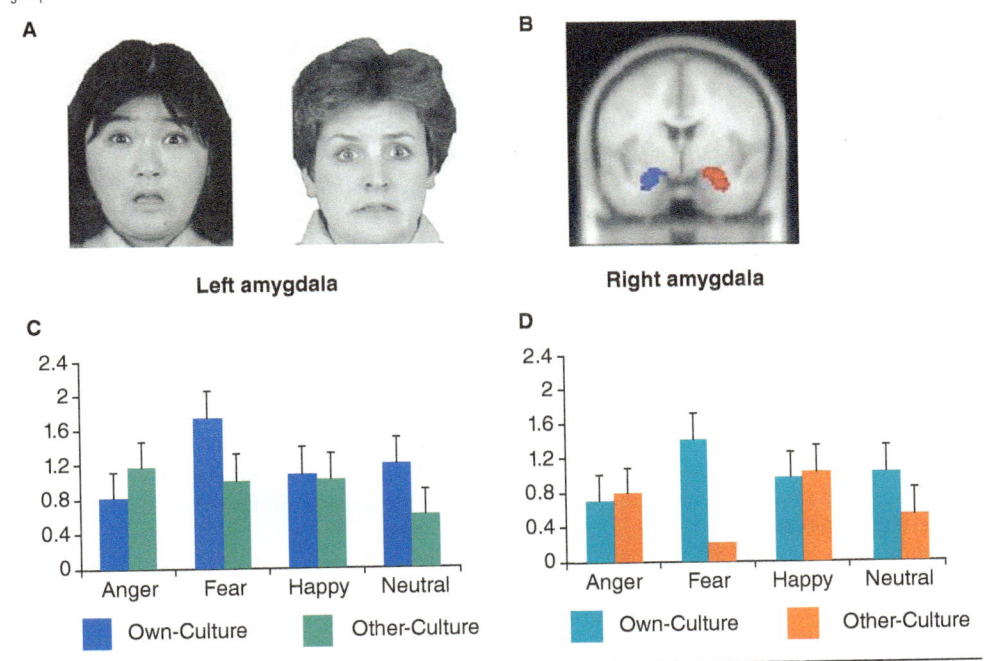

Credit: Reprinted from *Progress in Brain Research*, Vol. 178, Joan Y. Chiao, "Cultural neuroscience: A once and future discipline," pp. 287–304, Copyright 2009, with permission from Elsevier.

Thought Question

What cultural factors need to be considered in the assessment and classification of mental disorders? How could the failure to notice cultural differences lead to an incorrect assessment?

Neuroethics

When we read in the news about discoveries in the neurosciences, they are often presented in an optimistic manner. We are told they will help us treat medical disorders or learn more about how we think and feel. This is true. However, traditionally, societies have based codes of conduct and the law on observable behaviors. An important question currently being asked is who should have access to data and scans of your internal processes. *LENS: Neuroethics: Ethical Considerations When Using Neuroscience Techniques* examines the field of inquiry that is asking these questions. It is referred to as **neuroethics**.

LENS
NEUROETHICS: ETHICAL CONSIDERATIONS WHEN USING NEUROSCIENCE TECHNIQUES

Through genetics, brain imaging, and other neuroscience procedures, it is now possible to know not only about one's behaviors but also about one's internal processes. For example, predictions can be made from genetics about certain types of medical and psychological disorders that are more likely to develop in one's future. This raises ethical questions concerning who should have access to this information and how this information may be used by a society.

In the first half of the 20th century, certain Western societies attempted to make changes in future populations. This was referred to as *eugenics*. The basic idea was that it was possible to improve the human race by discouraging reproduction among those considered to be inferior and encouraging reproduction among those who were considered to be healthy or otherwise preferable. Individuals with mental disorders and mental disabilities were among those sterilized. The eugenics movement impacted policies in the United States, Britain, and elsewhere, then reached its extreme in Nazi Germany during World War II.

Although today eugenics is thought of as a disreputable crusade of the past, ethical issues in terms of one's own genetic information raise important questions. Should people who want to have children be told about the possible characteristics, including potential disorders such as autism, of their future child? Should an insurance company know whether you might have the potential to experience schizophrenia or depression in your lifetime? Should companies be able to patent human genes that could prevent disease? Should people be told early in their life which disorders they might develop 40 or 50 years in the future? These are just a few of the complex questions to be considered.

There are also a number of questions related to brain imaging techniques. For example, with millions of MRI scans being performed for research, scientists may discover what are referred to as *incidental findings*. Should an individual be told that they have a non-normal brain if a neurologist does not consider the findings relevant to the person's physical health?

At this point in time, brain imaging techniques cannot absolutely determine if one individual has a mental disorder or not. What neuroscientists *can* say is that a group of individuals with a particular disorder will show different patterns of brain activity than another group of individuals who do not have the disorder.

Neuroethics takes us beyond the questions of traditional research ethics and focuses on the ethical, legal, and social policy implications of neuroscience (Illes & Bird, 2006; Young et al., 2021). Because of this, a number of scientific neuroscience groups and governmental agencies have sought to understand the ethical problems that neuroscience will bring our society (Ramos et al., 2019).

Thought Question

Neuroethics focuses on the ethical, legal, and social policy implications of neuroscience and asks complex questions. Choose a position on one of the questions presented in this *LENS*, and present evidence to support your position.

> **CONCEPT CHECK**
>
> - Describe four major types of brain imaging techniques currently being used, and identify a psychological disorder for which each is especially valuable.
> - What are some of the trade-offs that researchers and clinicians must consider when choosing a brain imaging technique? What questions help inform their decision?

NETWORKS OF THE BRAIN

Given that the human brain has some 86 billion neurons with some 5,000 synapses, each resulting in trillions of synaptic connections, it is clear that a higher-level analysis of brain function is necessary (Goldstone et al., 2015; Herbet & Duffau, 2020). A variety of brain imaging techniques have allowed for a network analysis that describes which areas of the brain are involved in specific tasks. The first step has been to describe the normal processing of networks such as those involved in rewards or fear. The next step is to understand how these networks become involved in more psychopathological states such as addiction and anxiety. The goal now is to better understand how the basic network becomes involved in psychopathological processes. Is it a lack of connections between brain areas, or is there a reorganization of normal processes that underlies specific psychopathologies? This is one question scientists are asking.

Following the discovery of brain areas involved in particular functions, such as Broca's area, in the 1800s, researchers searched for specific areas involved in particular cognitive, emotional, and motor processes. With the increased sophistication of brain imaging technologies came a greater ability to view the manner in which certain parts of the brain work together as well as large-scale turning off and on of various areas. Some processes involve a pathway using only a few neurons. Being startled by a loud noise or touching a hot stove are examples of processes that have short neuronal pathways. Other processes use a more complex series of connections. More voluntary and complex processes use a much larger series of neuronal connections referred to as networks.

Researchers examine how specific brain areas work together as networks. This search has also extended to psychopathology. Psychopathology can be seen in terms of problems involving either particular brain areas or the connections between areas that make up the network.

We all experience the brain organizing itself in terms of various networks throughout our day. One of the most familiar is sleep. Another is waiting for a lecture to start, when we just let our mind wander. Both of these cases are not responses to external stimuli but are self-organizing processes that occur. These types of processes are controlled by a large number of neurons working together in the form of a network.

Networks allow our brains to process information efficiently (Khona & Fiete, 2022; Laughlin & Sejnowski, 2003; Sporns, 2011, 2022). Overall, cortical networks are influenced by experience and designed to be efficient in terms of connections between neurons in the network. This efficiency allows for less use of energy. One way energy is conserved is through not having every neuron connect with every other neuron.

Neurons Connect in a Network

How are neurons connected in a network? The answer may seem strange. Neurons are neither totally random in their connections with other neurons nor totally patterned. It appears that neurons are connected to one another in the same way that all humans on this planet are socially connected.

In the 1960s, the social psychologist Stanley Milgram (Travers & Milgram, 1969) asked the question, "What is the probability that any two people randomly selected from a large population of individuals such as the United States would know each other?" He answered this question by giving an individual a letter addressed to another person somewhere in the United States. This individual was to send the letter to someone they knew who might know the other person. In turn, this person was to send the letter to someone they knew who might know the person. Surprisingly, it only required five or six different people for the letter to go from the first individual to the final individual. This phenomenon has been referred to as the small world problem; more recently, the phrase *six degrees of separation* has been used.

Various studies have shown that the neurons in the brain can also be considered within a **small world framework** (Sporns, 2011). Neurons have numerous short-distance local connections, which, taken together, can be considered as a hub or module. From these hubs extend more long-distance connections to other hubs.

Local hubs can be made up of neurons that connect with each other over very short distances. Such connections are seen in gray matter. Underlying this are the axons, which transfer information throughout the brain. Their myelin sheaths are lighter in color, and thus, these areas are referred to as white matter. About 44% of the human brain is white matter. White matter generally represents longer connections between neurons. This allows for cortical networks over larger areas of the brain. Knowing this, it is possible to examine the network connections in individuals with a particular disorder and their matched controls. For example, individuals with schizophrenia have been shown to have disrupted global networks of the brain (O. Wang et al., 2012) as have those with depression (Li et al., 2018).

Networks have been studied in terms of a variety of cognitive and emotional tasks (Bressler & Menon, 2010; Raichle, 2015a). These include separate networks involved in the processing of visual or auditory information, sensorimotor processes, attentional processes, executive control, salience, and default mode (Figure 2.21).

Three of these networks have been examined in terms of psychopathology (Menon, 2011). These are the **default or intrinsic network**, the **central executive network**, and the **salience network**. The default network is active when an individual is not performing a particular task, such as when one's

FIGURE 2.21 ■ Major Networks of the Brain

When someone is doing a task, it is possible to determine which areas of the brain are connected to each other. This figure shows those areas of the brain that work together when performing certain types of tasks.

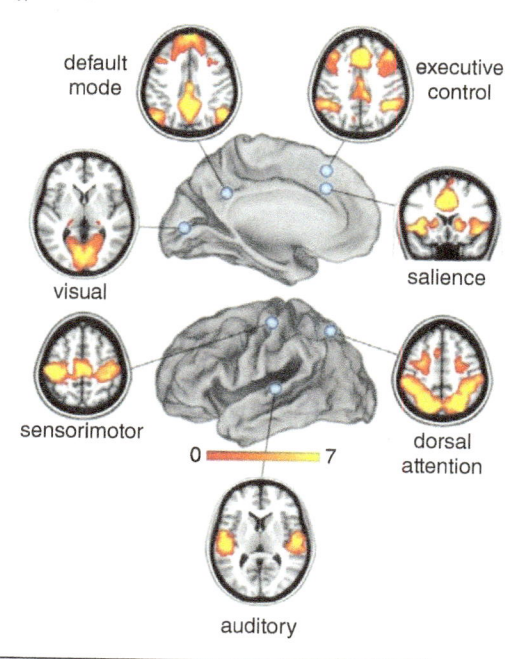

Credit: Raichle, M. E. (2015b). The restless brain: How intrinsic activity organizes brain function. *Philosophical Transactions of the Royal Society B, 370,* Article 20140172. https://doi.org/10.1098/rstb.2014.0172, licensed under CC BY 4.0 https://creativecommons.org/licenses/by/4.0/.

mind wanders or is processing internal information. The central executive network is involved in higher-order cognitive and attentional tasks. The salience network is important for monitoring critical external events as well as internal states. As will be described throughout this text, psychopathological disorders such as schizophrenia, depression, anxiety, dementia, and autism have been shown to involve problems in turning networks on or off as well as problems in the connections within the network itself.

What Is the Brain's Default (Intrinsic) Network?

What does your brain do when you are just sitting and waiting or daydreaming or talking to yourself? This is a question that is just now beginning to be explored. In psychology, most of the research you read about involves a person doing something. Reacting to emotional pictures or solving cognitive problems are common examples. In these cases, one's attention is focused on a task in the external world.

In the same way that the brain is organized to process spatial and verbal material differently and involve different cortical networks, it also appears that different circuits are involved with internal versus external information. A variety of studies have examined brain imaging procedures in which individuals performed internal tasks versus external tasks (e.g., Ray & Cole, 1985).

However, we all know that even without an external task to do, our mind is constantly working. It jumps from one thought to another. The psychologist William James called this process the *stream of consciousness*. Recent researchers have referred to this process as mind wandering.

Those neural networks that are active during internal processing have come to be referred to as the brain's *default or intrinsic network* (Buckner et al., 2008; Buckner & DiNicola, 2019; Raichle, 2011; Raichle & Snyder, 2007). It has been suggested that *intrinsic* is a better term than *default*, since a variety of internal tasks use this network (C. Kelly et al., 2012). The default network is separate from, but it can be understood as similar to other networks, such as those involved in visual perception or motor activities. It is made up of a set of interacting brain regions. Those areas involved represent periods of brain imaging when individuals are not engaged in any active task.

Overall, the default network is involved during internal or private considerations that do not require processing external sensory information. In fact, it appears as if there is a negative correlation between activities in the default network versus networks associated with processing information from the environment. That is, when someone begins some cognitive activity, then new networks associated with that task become active and the default network becomes less active. This suggests that separate brain mechanisms evolved for dealing with information involving the external environment as opposed to considerations internal to the person. A variety of psychopathology disorders show problems with the default network in terms of being able to turn it off and engage in a more active external task. People with schizophrenia, ADHD, and autism are groups that have difficulty turning off the default network and moving to an active task that uses a different network.

Different Networks Are Involved in Different Tasks

The central executive network is involved in performing such tasks as planning, goal setting, directing attention, performing, inhibiting the management of actions, and coding representations in working memory (Eisenberg & Berman, 2010). These are sometimes referred to as frontal lobe tasks, since damage to the frontal areas of the brain compromises performance of these tasks. These tasks are also referred to as **executive functions**, because they assist in planning, understanding new situations, and having cognitive flexibility. The salience network, as the name implies, is involved in monitoring and noting important (i.e., salient) changes in biological and cognitive systems.

Figure 2.22 shows those areas of the brain that Menon (2011) found to be associated with each of these networks. The figure shows an MRI structural image of the brain in black and white. The areas that are activated during the task are displayed in color. The brain is shown in terms of a three-dimensional image along an *x*-, *y*-, and *z*-axis. The *x*-axis shows the brain from the side, the *y*-axis from the back, and the *z*-axis from above. The numbers below the image represent the location along each axis. Using these three numbers, brain imaging programs can identify the areas in relation to traditional anatomical structures.

FIGURE 2.22 ■ Structural Image of Three Brain Networks

In this figure using MRI technology, the executive network is shown in blue, the salience network in yellow, and the default network in red. Note that the *x*-, *y*-, and *z*-axis for each is different. That is, the three networks show different parts of the brain.

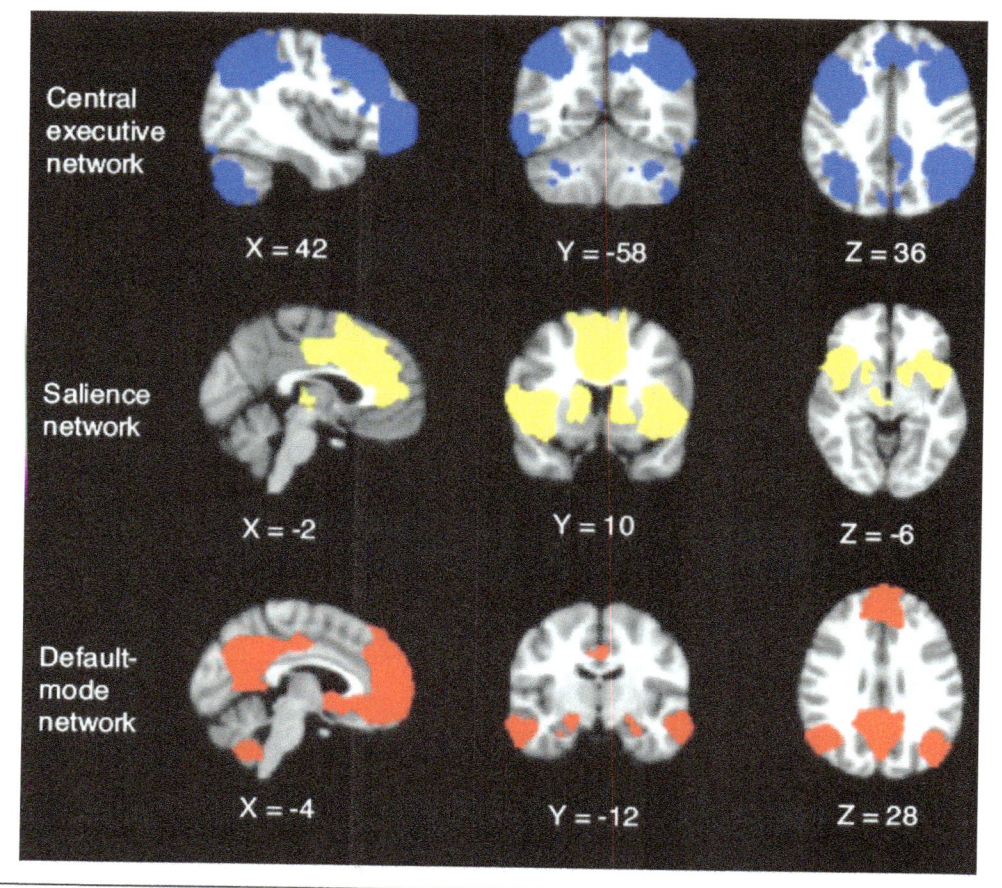

Credit: Reprinted from *Trends in Cognitive Sciences*, Vol. 15, Vinod Menon, "Large scale brain networks and psychopathology: A unifying triple network model," pp. 483–506, Copyright 2011, with permission from Elsevier.

In Figure 2.22, the central executive network, which is involved in higher-order cognitive and attentional demands, including planning for the future and remembering concepts, is shown in blue. The salience network, which is important for monitoring critical external events and internal states, is shown in yellow. The default network, which is active during mind wandering and when the person is not engaged in active problem solving, is shown in red.

Let's take a moment to understand how researchers describe brain function in terms of networks. One important concept is **modularity**. Modularity describes how specific areas of the brain are dedicated to certain types of processing. For example, as discussed early in the chapter, we know that a particular part of the temporal lobe, the fusiform face area, is involved in processing responses to the human face. fMRI measures, for example, would show greater brain activation in this area when observing the human face as opposed to nonhuman faces.

Another important concept is **connectivity**. This asks how different areas of the brain work together in specific conditions. To determine connectivity, researchers examine fMRI or EEG measures from a large number of locations throughout the brain. It is assumed that those areas whose activity is correlated are in some way working together.

The three networks—default, executive, and salience—show deficits in individuals with specific psychopathologies. Menon (2011; Menon et al., 2023) has reviewed the research literature and suggests that these networks play a prominent role in schizophrenia, depression, anxiety, dementia, and autism. As you will see throughout this book, the role of these networks may be dysfunctional in the network itself or in the ability to activate or deactivate specific networks in changing situations.

> **CONCEPT CHECK**
>
> - How does the brain operate as a "small world framework," and why is this significant?
> - How is the brain's default or intrinsic network different from the central executive and salience networks?
> - Researchers are concerned with modularity and connectivity in terms of neural networks. What are modularity and connectivity, and how are they important in thinking about psychopathology?

GENETICS AND PSYCHOPATHOLOGY

In this section, we consider the genetic level of analysis. This discussion includes a historical understanding of the study of genes as well as their structure. You will then learn about the role of DNA, genes' influence on behavior, epigenetics, mitochondria, and endophenotypes.

Genes form the blueprint that determines what an organism is to become. Specific sets of genes have been associated with a variety of disorders, as will be described throughout this book. It was initially assumed that one day genes would be able to explain the development of psychopathology, especially schizophrenia. However, after decades of research, it is clear that simple genetic explanations are not forthcoming. Psychological disorders are related to many genetic differences, each having a small effect (Plomin, 2018). Many of the genes that are related to problems of mental illness are also involved in normal development. What has become apparent is that there is a complex interaction of genetic and environmental factors involved in mental illness.

The Historical Study of Genetics

The study of genetics begins with the work of Gregor Mendel (1822–1884). Being curious as to how plants obtain atypical characteristics, Mendel performed a series of experiments with the garden pea plant. Peas are a self-fertilizing plant, which means that the male and female aspects needed for reproduction develop in different parts of the same flower. Therefore, successive generations of peas are similar to their parents in terms of particular traits, such as their height or the color of their flowers.

Mendel found that when combining peas that have white flowers with those with purple flowers, the next generation had all purple flowers. Allowing this generation to self-fertilize brought forth plants that had purple flowers but also some that had white flowers. Mendel explained these findings by suggesting that a plant inherits information from each parent, the male and female aspects. Mendel was hypothesizing that information must be conveyed. He further suggested that one unit of information could be dominant in comparison to the other, which we now call a recessive trait. In this case, the unit of information that coded for purple would be dominant.

Mendel did not know about genes but hypothesized the existence of a specific structure he called elements. From his experiments, he determined the basic principle that there are two elements of heredity for each trait (e.g., color in the previous example). Mendel also assumed that one of these elements can dominate the other and if the dominant element is present, then the trait will also be present. In addition, Mendel suggested that these elements can be nondominant, or recessive. For the trait to appear, both of these nondominant elements must be present. These ideas are referred to as **Mendel's first law or the law of segregation**.

Put in today's language, Mendel suggested that variants of a specific gene exist, which account for variations in inherited characteristics, and that an organism receives one of these from each parent. Further, one of these can be dominant or recessive, which determines which characteristics are expressed. Mendel also realized that the inheritance of the gene of one trait is not affected by the inheritance of the gene for another trait. In the previous example illustrating the inheritance of color and height, those factors influencing color do not affect height, and vice versa. That is, the probability for each occurs separately. This is known as **Mendel's second law or the law of independent assortment**.

Since Mendel's time, we have learned a great deal about the process of inheritance. What he referred to as elements or units of information, we now call *genes* (Figure 2.23). We also know that genes can have alternative forms, which we call alleles. Independent researchers, Walter Sutton and Theodore Boveri, in 1903 put forth a theory we now accept as fact, that genes are carried on **chromosomes**. We now know that each of the approximately 20,000 human genes occurs at a specific site, called a locus, on one of our 23 different pairs of chromosomes. As genetics progressed in the 20th century, it was necessary to go beyond the two laws suggested by Mendel to a more complex understanding of how traits are passed from generation to generation. For example, if two genes are located close to one another on the same chromosome, then the result is different from that predicted by Mendel's second law.

What Do Genes Do?

Genes form the blueprint to describe what an organism is to become. Over our evolutionary history, a majority of human genes reflect little variation. In fact, you are the same as every other human being in over 99% of your genes (Plomin, 2018). This is why all humans have two eyes and one nose and one mouth. However, perhaps one fourth of all genes allow for variation. What makes things interesting is that the two genes of these pairs are usually slightly different. The technical name for the unique molecular form of the same gene is an **allele**. It has been estimated that of our approximately 20,000 to 21,000 genes, some 6,000 exist in different versions or alleles (Zimmer, 2001). Current research suggests that the high heritability of mental disorders is related to many genetic differences, each having a small effect (Plomin, 2018).

FIGURE 2.23 ■ Genetic Components Found in a Drop of Blood

A drop of blood contains red and white blood cells. From this, one can determine the person's DNA. The DNA is contained in 23 pairs of chromosomes in humans. Located at specific sites on those chromosomes are some 20,000 genes in each human. One part of the cell nucleus related to energy production is mtDNA (discussed later) and is passed on from the mother.

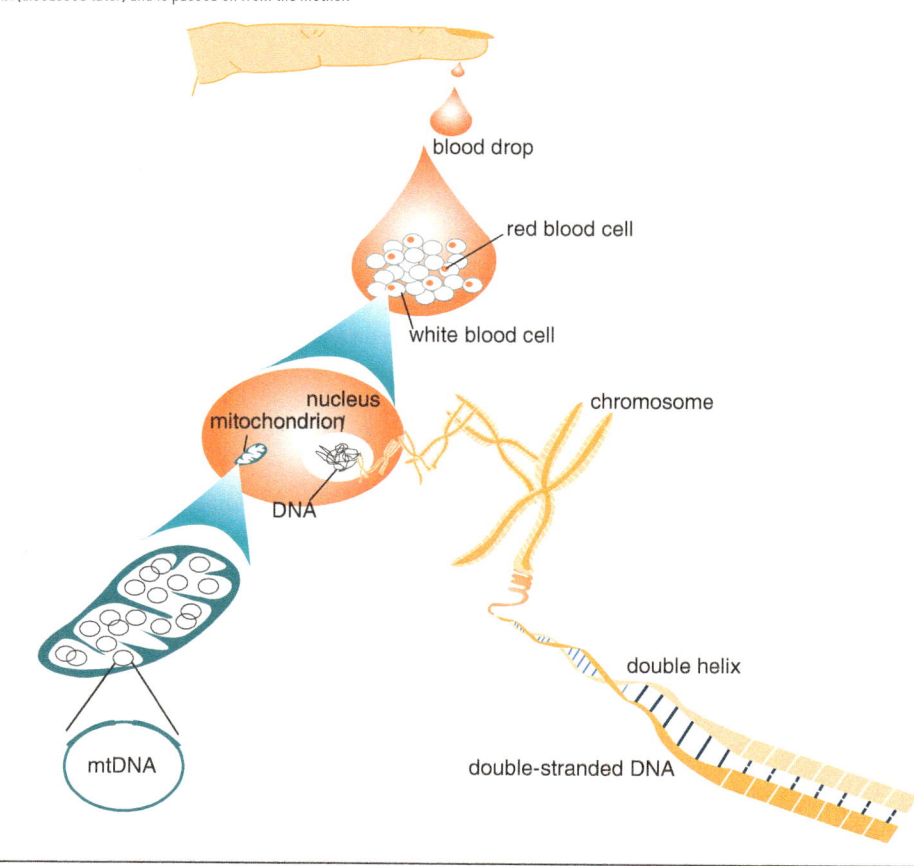

Courtesy: National Human Genome Research Institute, https://www.genome.gov.

When a person has two copies of the same allele, they are said to be **homozygotes or homozygous** for that allele. If, on the other hand, they have two different alleles for a particular gene, they are said to be **heterozygotes or heterozygous** for those alleles. Given that the alleles that come from your mother may not result in exactly the same characteristics as those from your father, variation is possible. It is these variations that allow for the process of natural selection to have its effect.

The job of a gene is to lay out the process by which a particular protein is made. That is, each gene is able to **encode** a protein, influencing its production. **Proteins**, which do the work of the body, are involved in a variety of processes. Functionally, proteins in the form of enzymes are able to make metabolic events speed up, whereas structural proteins are involved in building body parts. Proteins are diverse and complex and are found in the foods we eat as well as made by our cells from some 20 amino acids. Proteins serve as signals for changes in cell activity as illustrated by hormones. Proteins are also involved in health and disease as well as in development and aging.

Although the cells in the body carry the full set of genetic information, only a limited amount is expressed at any one time related to the function of the cell. That is to say, although a large variety of proteins could be produced at any one time, there is selectivity as to what is produced relative to internal and external conditions. Further, the location of the genes makes a difference in that cells in the brain produce different proteins from those in the muscles, or liver, or heart.

A gene is turned on (produces the protein) or turned off (does not produce the protein) relative to specific events. Just because a person has a specific gene does not mean that it will necessarily be expressed. The environment in which a person develops and lives plays an important role in gene expression. Even identical twins with the same *genotype* can display different *phenotypes* (defined in the next paragraph) if their environmental conditions differ during their development. For example, if one was to grow up in a high mountain range and the other in a desert below sea level, important physiological differences such as lung capacity and function would be apparent. There are few factors other than blood type in terms of human processes that can be explained totally by genetic factors alone. It is equally true that few human processes can be explained totally by the environment.

DNA

With the discovery of the structure of DNA by James Watson and Francis Crick in 1953, specifying the method by which genetic material was copied became possible. **Deoxyribonucleic acid (DNA)** provides information necessary to produce proteins. Proteins can be viewed as a link between the **genotype** (complete genetic composition of an organism) and the **phenotype** (an organism's observable characteristics). Moving the genotype to the phenotype initially begins in two steps. First, the information in DNA is encoded in **ribonucleic acid (RNA)**. Second, this information in RNA determines the sequence of amino acids, which are the building blocks of proteins. Technically, the DNA synthesis of RNA is called transcription, whereas the step from RNA to protein is called translation. RNA is like DNA except its structure is a single strand, whereas DNA has a double strand. Once encoded, the RNA goes to a part of the cell capable of producing proteins. Proteins are produced by putting together amino acids.

To be more specific, DNA represents the chemical building blocks, or nucleotides, that store information. There are only four types of bases for this coding. DNA molecules are composed of two strands that twist together in a spiral manner. The strands consist of a sugar phosphate backbone to which the bases are attached. Each strand consists of four types of nucleotides that are the same except for one component, a nitrogen-containing base. The four bases are adenine, guanine, thymine, and cytosine. These are generally referred to as A, G, T, and C. To give you some sense of size, each full twist of the DNA double helix is 3.4 nanometers (i.e., one billionth of a meter). Said in other terms, if we took the DNA in the 46 chromosomes of a single human cell and stretched it out, it would be around 6 feet long. This measurement gives you some idea of the thinness of DNA.

DNA, which is the information storage molecule, transfers information to RNA, which is the information transfer molecule, to produce a particular protein. Further, change in the rate at which RNA is transcribed controls the rate at which genes produce proteins. The expression rate of different genes in the same genome may vary from 0 to approximately 100,000 proteins per second. Thus, not only do genes produce proteins, but they do so at different rates. The crucial question becomes what causes a gene to turn on or off.

Genome is the name given to the complete set of genes in a given cell. The Human Genome Project was started in 1990 by the United States with the goal of mapping all the genes of the human body. It was an international project that was declared complete in 2003. The estimation at that time was that there are approximately 20,500 genes in a human cell.

How Do Genes Influence Behavior?

In terms of behavior and experience, the production of proteins can be transitory. For example, touching a cat's whiskers causes changes in gene expression in the cells of the sensory cortex of the brain (Mack & Mack, 1992). This is just a momentary change. Changes can also be long term. Turning on one set of genes may have lasting influence on the ability of other genes to produce specific proteins. For example, when a songbird first hears the specific song of its species, a particular set of genes comes into play, which, once set, determine the song produced by that bird for its entire life. This process has been mapped by a number of researchers (see, e.g., Mello et al., 1992; Ribeiro & Mello, 2000). Likewise, raising mice in an enriched environment—that is, one with lots of toys and stimulation—will cause increased gene expression in genes that are associated with learning and memory (Rampon et al., 2000).

How do we know which genes are involved? In the Rampon et al. (2000) study, the genes of mice in enriched environments were compared with those of control mice who did not have this experience. Another way to know which genes are involved in a process is to actually change the genes in a particular organism. So-called "knockout" mice are genetically engineered to have particular genes turned off by breeding them in specific ways. Research shows that simple genetic changes made experimentally in animals can result in protein changes that influence social behavior. Some examples of such behaviors are increased fear and anxiety, increased grooming, hyperactivity, and even increased alcohol consumption when stressed.

As researchers studied how genes turn on and off and what factors influence this, the story became even more complicated: The processes that determine which genes turn on and off could themselves be

When a songbird first hears the specific song of its species, a particular set of genes comes into play, which, once set, determine the song produced by that bird for its entire life.

iStock.com/Paul Tessier

passed on to the next generation. Of course, which factors turn the genes on and off are largely influenced by the environment of the organism. Thus, although the genes themselves could not be influenced by the environment, it was possible for the environment to influence future generations through its changes to those processes that turn genes on and off. This is referred to as **epigenetics**.

Epigenetic Processes

One basic idea from Mendelian genetics was that genes are not changed by experience. What is passed on, except in the case of damage to the gene, is exactly the same gene that was received by the organism from its parents. This came to be called the central dogma of molecular biology as described by Crick. He basically stated that information flow was one-directional. That is, it went from the gene to the protein. What came to be called reverse translation was seen as impossible. Thus, the gene could not be influenced or changed by changes in proteins. This was the basic view from the 1950s until very recently.

As researchers became interested in how genes turn on and off and what factors influence this, it became apparent that the story was more complicated. It was discovered that the processes that determine which genes turn on and off could themselves be passed on to the next generation. Of course, which factors turn the genes on and off are largely influenced by the environment of the organism. Thus, although DNA itself could not be influenced by the environment, it was possible for the environment to influence future generations through its changes to those processes that turn genes on and off.

This possibility of another form of inheritance came to be called **epigenetic inheritance** (Cavalli & Heard, 2019; Hallgrímsson & Hall, 2011; Nestler, 2011; Ospelt, 2022). Instead of actually changing the gene itself, epigenetic modifications mark a gene. This alters how it is turned on and off. Briefly, DNA is wrapped around clusters of proteins called histones. These are further bundled into structures called chromosomes. Being tightly packed keeps genes in an inactive state by preventing access to processes that turn genes on. When action is needed, a section of DNA unfurls and the gene turns on. Whether a segment is relaxed and able to be activated or condensed, resulting in no action, is influenced by **epigenetic marks or tags** (Figure 2.24). As a tag, histone acetylation tends to promote gene activity and is called a *writer*. Histone methylation and DNA methylation tend to inhibit it and are called *erasers*.

FIGURE 2.24 ■ Epigenetic Changes Alter Gene Activity

Genes can be turned on or turned off. Being tightly packed keeps genes in an inactive state by preventing access to processes that turn genes on. When action is needed, a section of DNA unfurls and the gene turns on. Whether a segment is relaxed and able to be activated or condensed, resulting in no action, is influenced by epigenetic marks or tags.

Courtesy: National Human Genome Research Institute, https://www.genome.gov.

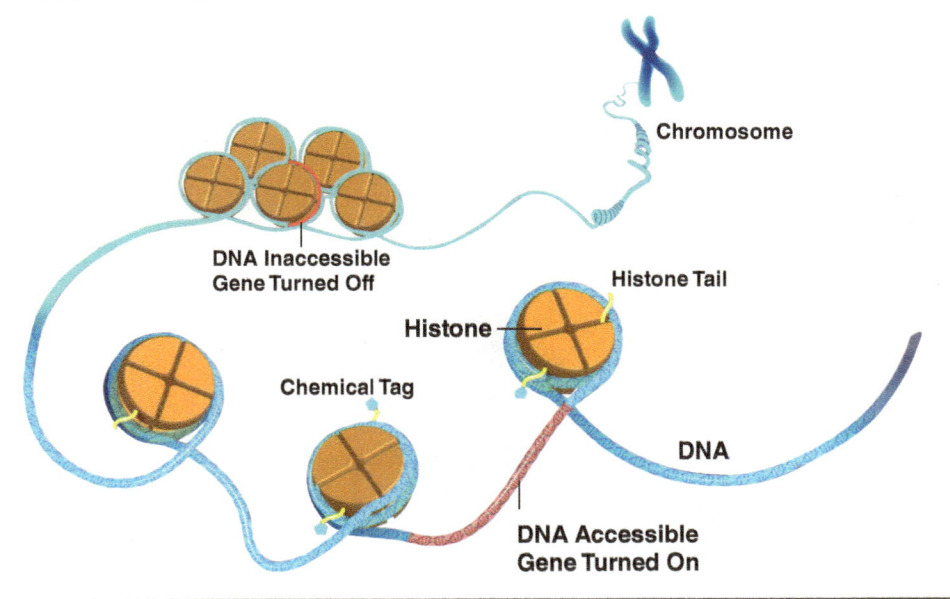

The environment can influence these writer and eraser tags. Tags help an organism respond to a changing environment. Some tags last a short time, whereas others can last a lifetime. In a now classic study, researchers observed that some rat mothers displayed high levels of nurturing behavior, licking and grooming their pups, while others were less diligent (Weaver et al., 2004). Behaviorally, the offspring of the more active mothers were less anxious and produced less stress hormone when disturbed than pups cared for by more passive mothers. Further, the females raised by nurturing mothers became nurturing mothers themselves.

The intriguing part of this study is that the offspring of the rat mothers who showed more licking and grooming differed in epigenetic factors. Pups raised by passive mothers showed more DNA methylation than aggressively groomed pups in the regulatory sequences of a gene encoding the glucocorticoid receptor, which is a protein present in most cells in the body that mediates an animal's response to the stress hormone cortisol. This excessive methylation was detected in the hippocampus, a brain region involved in learning and memory, and this causes nerve cells to make less of the receptor. Activation of the glucocorticoid receptor in the hippocampus actually signals the body to slow production of cortisol. The epigenetic reduction in receptor number exacerbated the stress response in the animals. This made the animals more anxious and fearful. Further, these traits persisted throughout their lifetime. Overall, attentive mothers cause the methyl marks to be removed. Inattentive mothers, on the other hand, cause methyl marks to be added. Thus, rats inherit certain behaviors based on experience. The genes had not changed, but the tags had.

At this point, a variety of studies have shown other examples of epigenetic mechanisms at work. For example, the diet of a mouse mother before conception can influence the hair color of her infants and even her infants' infants (e.g., Cropley et al., 2006). One interesting aspect of this research is the suggestion that a mother's diet can influence future generations, independent of later changes in diet.

Fathers can also influence their offspring. It has been shown that a mouse will develop a diabetes-like disease if its father's diet before the mouse's conception was high in fat (Skinner, 2010). Also, if a mouse father is overweight, then gene activity in the pancreas of the father's offspring will be abnormal (Ng et al., 2010). Since the pancreas makes insulin, which regulates blood sugar, this may set up the possibility of future diabetes. The opposite is also the case. If the father's diet

In a classic study, rat pups raised by actively nurturing mothers versus more passive mothers differed in epigenetic factors.
iStock com/slomotiongli

results in an underweight condition, then genes in the liver associated with fat and cholesterol synthesis are more active in the father's offspring (Carone et al., 2010). Another study suggested that whether a human father smoked early in life was associated with his sons being heavier in weight at age 9 (Pembrey et al., 2006).

Overall, this type of research implies that behavior and environmental experiences at critical periods could later influence characteristics for future generations (Keverne, 2015. Current health research related to such disorders as diabetes and cancer, as well as types of psychopathology, is suggestive of such a relationship (see Katsnelson, 2010; O'Donnell & Meaney, 2020; van Os, 2010, for overviews). Both addiction and depression have been shown to have an epigenetic component (Nestler, 2011). Likewise, schizophrenia and bipolar disorder can be influenced by epigenetic processes (Jeremian et al., 2022; Varela et al., 2022). Thus, epigenetic inheritance, which involves tags or marks that determine when genes are turned off or on, offers a parallel track to traditional Mendelian inheritance for influencing phenotypes. Further, a new area of research uses identical twins to study specific epigenetic mechanisms with the goal of determining how genetic and environmental factors influence epigenetics (e.g., Bell & Spector, 2011; Tan, 2019). This approach may offer better insight into the expression of complex traits as seen in normal and psychopathological processes.

Mitochondria and Mitochondrial Inheritance

Mitochondria are structures within a cell that are involved in the production of energy. It is assumed that mitochondria descended from bacteria that began to live inside single-celled organisms more than a billion years ago. As such, mitochondria have their own DNA (see next paragraph), which contains 13 coding genes with about 16,000 base pairs. Thus, a given cell in your body contains both the nuclear DNA and mitochondria and their DNA.

What is interesting is that generally **mitochondrial DNA (mtDNA)** is inherited only from the mother, clearly a violation of Mendelian inheritance. Because mtDNA does not recombine sections of DNA from the mother and father, it is very stable and mutates slowly. This gives mtDNA a special application in the study of evolution. It has helped researchers to discover the genetic link in certain disorders that show maternal or **mitochondrial inheritance** patterns, such as Leber's hereditary optic neuropathy, a disorder that results in rapid loss of vision beginning in adolescence.

Evidence is also accumulating that mitochondrial dysfunction is involved in specific mental disorders (Fanibunda & Vaidya, 2021; Regenold et al., 2009; Rossignol & Frye, 2012). This is referred to as the *mitochondrial dysfunction hypothesis*. Mitochondrial dysfunction has been identified using a number of different techniques. One technique is to identify structural changes in mitochondria. A second is to examine the manner in which the mitochondrially related genes produce proteins. A third is the use of metabolic studies. Since mitochondria are involved with energy production, it is possible to measure glucose concentration in cerebrospinal fluid. These studies have shown differences in mitochondrial functioning in individuals with bipolar disorder, schizophrenia, and autism spectrum disorders as compared to healthy controls.

What Are Endophenotypes?

In a move to go beyond using only the signs and symptoms of psychopathology, there has been a search for stable internal physiological or psychological markers that underlie a disorder (Bigdeli & Harvey, 2021; Correa-Ghisays et al., 2022; Gottesman & Hanson, 2005; Gottesman & Shields, 1972; Insel & Cuthbert, 2009; Miller & Rockstroh, 2013). Such markers have been called *endophenotypes*. **Endophenotypes** are patterns of processes that lie between the gene (the genotype) and the manifestations of the gene in the external environment (the phenotype). Unlike symptoms that can be observed, endophenotypes cannot be seen except with special equipment and computational analysis, such as brain imaging procedures or patterns of performance on neuropsychological tests. For example, individuals with a given disorder may show certain types of electroencephalogram (EEG) responses to particular stimuli or a certain pattern of brain activity that is different from that seen in healthy individuals. Those with autism have been shown to have fewer connections between brain areas than siblings or controls, and this is seen as an endophenotype (Moseley et al., 2015).

Like genes, the presence of the endophenotype does not necessarily mean that the disorder itself will be present. For example, a specific endophenotype may be seen in both a person with schizophrenia and their first-degree relatives, although the relatives themselves do not have schizophrenia. As such, an endophenotype can help to identify the systems involved in a particular disorder as well as note which genes are influenced by environmental and other internal factors related to a disorder. The potential of endophenotypes is their ability to better articulate the relationship between genetic and environmental factors in the development of psychopathology and to clarify which processes are influenced. In Chapter 4, you will learn about a National Institute of Mental Health (NIMH)–supported diagnostic approach based on endophenotypes, the Research Domain Criteria (RDoC).

Current Thinking on Genetics and Psychopathology

As our understanding of the genetic and environmental factors that contribute to mental illness has become more complex, research has begun to target particular processes related to psychopathology. For example, there exists a gene (SERT) that is involved in the removal of the neurotransmitter serotonin from the synapse. A variant of the SERT gene has been associated with depression, alcoholism, eating disorders, ADHD, and autism (Serretti et al., 2006). Likewise, a variant of the gene DßH, which is associated with the synthesis of norepinephrine from dopamine, is associated with schizophrenia, cocaine-induced paranoia, depression, ADHD, and alcoholism (Cubells & Zabetian, 2004). It is suggested that the lower level of the proteins produced by the DßH gene is associated with a vulnerability to psychotic symptoms.

As researchers discover genes related to specific forms of mental illness, there may be a need to reorganize how we view mental illness. One study analyzed the genes from 33,332 individuals with a mental disorder in comparison with 27,888 without a disorder (Cross-Disorder Group of the Psychiatric Genomics Consortium et al., 2013). This research suggests that similar genetic risk factors involved in calcium channel signaling exist for what we have considered to be five separate disorders: autism spectrum disorder, schizophrenia, bipolar disorder, major depressive disorder, and ADHD. This study implies that a particular genetic makeup may put some individuals at higher risk for developing a variety of disorders. There is also research that suggests that having certain mental disorders, such as schizophrenia, may actually protect these individuals from getting certain types of cancer (Tabarés-Seisdedos & Rubenstein, 2013).

More recently, as the cost of performing genotyping has been reduced, it has become possible to obtain a more complete analysis of an individual's genome (Friedman et al., 2021; Plomin, 2018). Studies based on this rich data are referred to as genome-wide association studies (GWASs). These studies typically use the genetic data from a large number of individuals to statistically determine genetic differences associated with a particular trait, such as personality factors, or a particular mental disorder, such as depression, eating disorders, PTSD, addiction, and so forth. Some studies use data from as many as 100,000 individuals. Currently, over 800 researchers from 40 countries share genomic data from over 400,000 individuals (see For Further Reading for a description of this work).

One interesting GWAS showed that mental disorders show less genetic variation across disorders, whereas neurological disorders such as Parkinson's disease, epilepsy, Alzheimer's disease, and multiple sclerosis show a unique set of genes associated with each disorder (The Brainstorm Consortium, 2018). We will refer to GWASs when appropriate throughout this book. GWASs also offer an alternative to the traditional twin studies (Friedman et al., 2021).

In GWASs that examine the effects of many genes on psychological processes (Breen et al., 2016; Giangrande et al., 2022), researchers go through hundreds or thousands of changes in DNA called single-nucleotide polymorphisms (SNPs, pronounced "snip"). Each of us has about 4 million SNPs, but we all do not have the same 4 million. As shown in Figure 2.25, the task is to find similar SNPs in those with a particular disorder as compared to a control group. These studies have been applied to psychological disorders and involve a number of researchers from over 40 countries (Breen et al., 2016; Sullivan et al., 2018).

The logic of performing a GWAS is to begin with the trait or disorder that one wants to study. The focus is then on the genetic structure related to a specific trait or disorder. Genetic differences seen

FIGURE 2.25 ■ SNP Analysis in a Genome-Wide Association Study

In this type of study, the genome of those with a disorder (left side of the figure) is compared to a group of individuals without the disorder (right side of the figure).

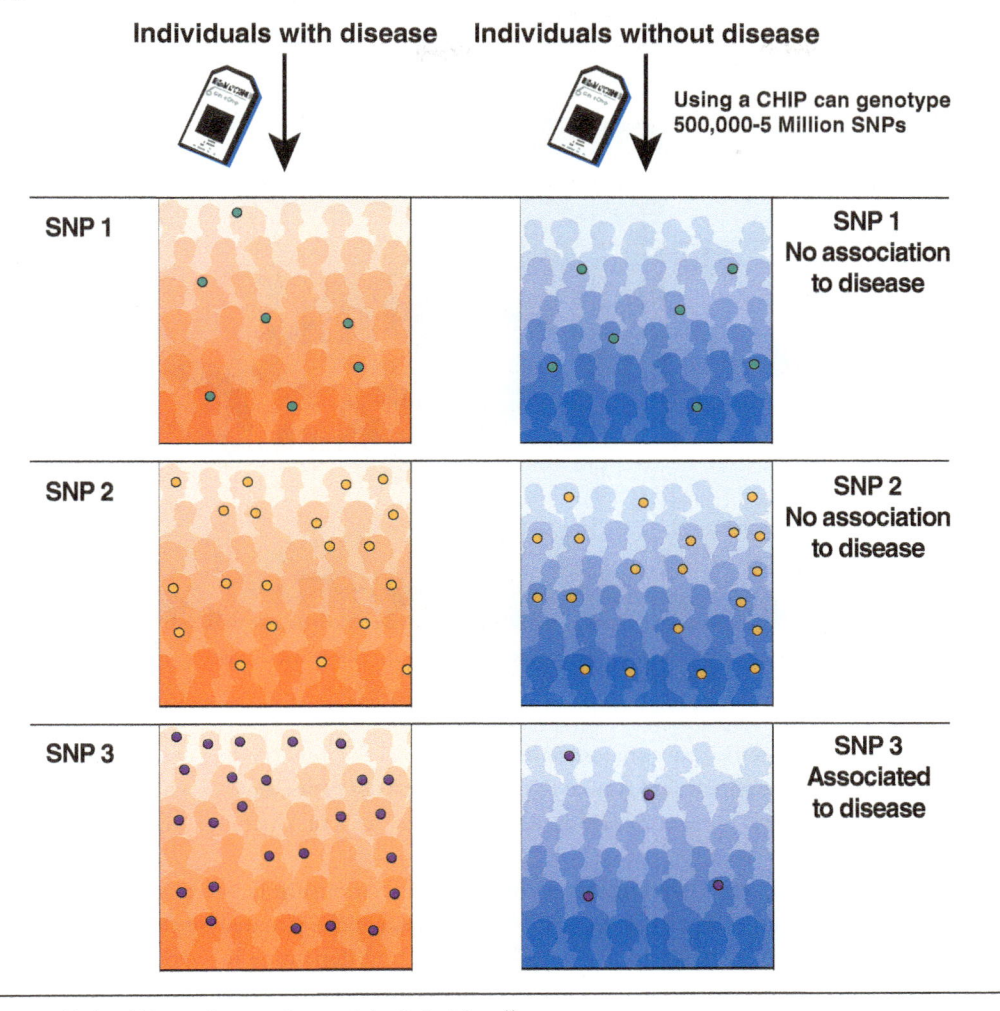

Courtesy: National Human Genome Research Institute, https://www.genome.gov.

in even a large number of individuals can be very small. Thus, what one needs to do is to statistically determine which genetic properties are correlated with the trait under study from the large number of individuals. The result of this type of correlation procedure is referred to as a polygenic score. The actual procedure is more complicated than this and uses a structural equation model. However, the basic idea is to determine how well a polygenic score derived from a GWAS is able to predict individual differences (Friedman et al., 2021; Plomin, 2018).

There are multiple current approaches to GWASs. One approach is to examine specific networks of the brain, such as executive, default, and salience networks, in terms of common genetic variants influencing these processes (Zhao et al., 2022). Further research studies have begun to examine networks of genes in the brain as reflected in their co-expression (Hartl et al., 2021; Yates, 2021). Gene co-expression analysis is a data analysis technique that helps identify groups of genes with similar expression patterns across several different conditions (Montenegro, 2022). Mental disorders disrupt a variety of cognitive, emotional, and motor processes that develop over a person's lifetime and are guided by thousands of genes (see Plomin, 2018, for an overview).

In addition, research has also shown rare variants of a small number of genes that can have a large effect (Gibson, 2012; Singh et al., 2022). For example, one study showed that 10 rare variants of some genes are associated with substantial risk for schizophrenia (Singh et al., 2022). Likewise,

There is a complex interaction of genetic and environmental factors involved in mental illness.
iStock.com/Cavan Images

very rare variants of specific genes are associated with bipolar disorder (Palmer et al., 2022). Overall, disorders such as schizophrenia are related to both hundreds of genes, each of which has a common influence, and to a small number of rare variants of a gene, each of which has a large effect (Iyegbe & O'Reilly, 2022).

Traditional genetic research suggests a complicated relationship between genetic conditions and environmental factors. For example, the MAOA gene, which is located on the X chromosome, makes the neurotransmitters serotonin, norepinephrine, and dopamine inactive and is associated with aggression in mice and humans. Caspi and his colleagues (2002) performed a longitudinal study and found that mistreatment as a child influenced some boys differently from others later in adulthood. Those boys who were mistreated in childhood and had a particular form of the MAOA gene were more likely to be violent and engage in a variety of antisocial behaviors as adults, as well as have problems with law enforcement officials. Those without this particular form of the gene did not display antisocial behaviors, even if they had been mistreated as children. Thus, environmental influences in terms of maltreatment modulate the expression of specific genetic structures but not the expression of others.

CONCEPT CHECK

- What are the two important principles of Mendelian genetics? What evidence led Mendel to their discovery?
- What do genes do, and how and where do they do it? What are the roles of DNA and RNA in that process?
- How do we know that genes change behavior? What are GWASs, and how do they work?
- What is epigenetic inheritance? How does it work?
- What is an endophenotype, and how does it relate to psychopathology?

EVOLUTION AND PSYCHOPATHOLOGY

Thus far, we have considered brain changes and genes turning off and on. These events are typically short term and can change quickly. Moving to the evolutionary perspective, we will look at a longer time frame in which environmental factors influence the genes that are passed on to the next generation. Let's begin with the major themes of evolution and then consider psychopathology from an evolutionary perspective.

The Themes of Evolution

One of the main themes of evolution is the manner in which organisms are in close connection with their environment. It is this close connection that allows for change to take place, including the turning on and off of genetic processes. In humans, there is another layer of complexity involved in the process. Part of this complexity comes from the fact that humans are born less fully developed at birth than many other species and thus are sensitive to changes in their environment as they continue to develop. This includes our relationships with our family and others with whom we initially come in contact. As humans, we also develop societal and cultural perspectives. These perspectives become the backdrop of our environment. Unlike animals that live within nature, we as humans largely live within the backdrop of our culture. Thus, we are influenced by our culture and pay close attention to it.

Another part of our complexity as humans is our ability to reflect on ourselves and our world. In this way, a layer of thought can be injected between the person and the environment. This allows for expectation and imagination to play a role in human behavior and experience. Some have even suggested that humans may be the only species to imagine the world and themselves differently from how they appear. In this sense, our inner world of thoughts and feelings becomes another environment in which we live. For example, you can tell yourself you are wonderful or you are stupid, and there is no one inside you to dispute this. One positive aspect of this is that your inner world allows you to plan future actions and reflect on past ones, but it can also be experienced as distress when your internal thoughts reflect such states as anxiety or hopelessness. Our internal thoughts at times may lead to interpretations of the environment or ourselves that may not be productive. This adaptive human ability to

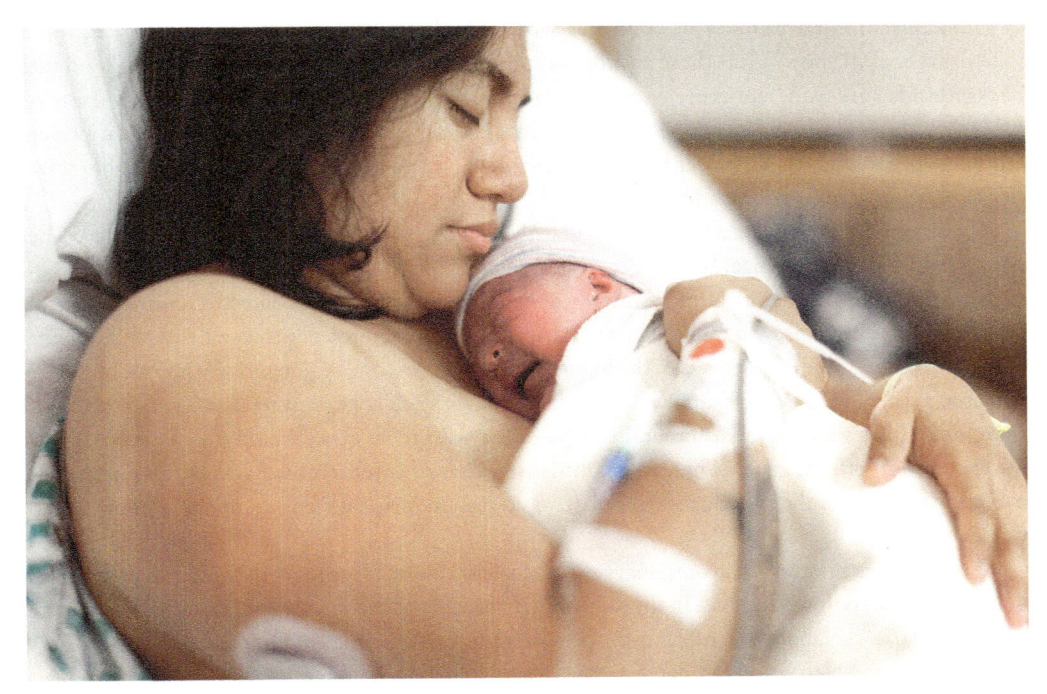

Human infants are helpless at birth.

iStock.com/timnewman

reflect, which should lead to successful survival, sexuality, and social relations, sometimes leads instead to interactions that reduce the close connection between the individual and their internal and external environment. As we will see, this lack of connectedness lies at the heart of psychopathology.

As noted in Chapter 1, humans not only consider themselves but also consider others. A positive side of this is the ability to understand the internal experiences of another. This allows us to experience empathy. We can also consider how we appear to others and other questions of self-image. One aspect of this is related to sexual processes. That is, we can say or do things that make us more attractive to a potential mate. In terms of self-preservation, humans also have a personal history that allows each individual to learn from the past and develop strategies for living. These strategies tend to protect us and may even have saved our lives in exceptional cases. However, it is also possible for the strategies that work in one environmental situation not to work in another. When a person loses contact with the current environment and applies strategies that worked perhaps in an earlier time, then unsuccessful adaptation is the result.

This lack of connectedness to our environment may take place on both an external and an internal level. On an external level, the person finds herself different from the group or even seeks to be separate from others. This is not our historical experience, since individual humans have never lived in isolation. As a species, we have always lived in close contact with other humans, which has led to the development of societies and cultures. In fact, many of the specific abilities of humans are geared to social interactions on a variety of levels. When they no longer have the connection with the group, many individuals experience a sense of loss. This loss typically carries with it the experience of negative affect and depression and often a need to withdraw from contact with others and even themselves. On an internal level, humans frequently have the need to explain to themselves the events that have just occurred, which may include anger, distorted perceptions, or a genuine plan for recovery. The extreme cases we refer to as psychopathology.

Psychopathology From an Evolutionary Perspective

Psychopathology from an evolutionary perspective goes beyond the traditional psychological and physiological considerations. Considering the evolutionary perspective, we ask additional questions. One question might be, how long in terms of our human history has a particular psychopathological disorder existed? As noted in Chapter 1, a WHO study examined the presence of schizophrenia in a number of countries with very different racial and cultural backgrounds (Sartorius et al., 1986). What these authors found was that despite the different cultural and racial backgrounds surveyed, the experience of schizophrenia was remarkably similar across countries. Likewise, the risk of developing schizophrenia was similar in terms of total population presence (about 1%). Further, the disorder had a similar time course in its occurrence, with its characteristics first being seen in young adults.

If you put these facts together, they suggest that schizophrenia is a disorder that has always been part of the human experience. Because it is found throughout the world in strikingly similar ways, this suggests that it existed before humans migrated out of Africa. The genes related to schizophrenia were carried by early humans who migrated from Africa, and thus, its presence is equally likely throughout the world. Given these estimates as to the history of the disorder, one might ask why schizophrenia continues to exist. We know, for example, that individuals with schizophrenia tend to have fewer children than individuals without the disorder. Fewer children with these genes would over time lead to even fewer children with the genes. Thus, we might assume that schizophrenia would have disappeared over evolutionary time in that it reduces reproductive success and has a genetic component. However, this is not the case.

This creates a mystery for evolutionary psychologists to solve. To answer this question, we can draw on many considerations. Perhaps, in the same way that sickle-cell anemia is associated with a protection against malaria, schizophrenia protects the person from another disorder. Or, perhaps like the reaction of rats to stress, which results in depression-like symptoms, the symptoms seen in schizophrenia are the result of a long chain of stressful events in which the organism breaks down in its ability to function. Psychopathology could even go in a more positive direction and be associated with creative and nontraditional views of the world. For example, there are a number of accounts that have noted greater creativity in families of individuals with schizophrenia.

The evolutionary perspective helps us ask such questions as what function a disorder might serve as well as how it came about. In the same way that pain can be seen as a warning system to the body to protect it from tissue damage, anxiety may have evolved to protect the person from other types of potential threats. For example, many of the outward expressions of social anxiety parallel what is seen in dominance interactions in primates. Submissive monkeys avoid contact with most dominant ones in much the way that human individuals experiencing social anxiety avoid dominant members of their group. This suggests the possibility that anxiety may have its evolutionary origins in dominance structures. If this were the case, then we might expect to see some relationship to sexual instinctual processes, as is the case with dominance. The evolutionary perspective also helps us think about what might be solutions to how psychopathology should be treated. As touched on in Chapter 1, these are some of the questions that will be discussed in this book.

One perspective of the evolutionary approach has been to redirect psychology back to the basic processes of human existence such as survival, sexual processes, and social behavior. We can then ask what types of disorders are found within each broad category. We can also consider the developmental and social processes and ask how these processes may be involved in psychopathology. Thinking in these terms, we may come to discover that disorders that have very similar end states may have developed from distinct beginning conditions. Depression, for example, can result from extreme stress that brings forth self-preservation instincts. Depression can also result from the loss of significant people in one's life. Further, loss of social status is also associated with depression. Thus, what appear to be similar symptoms may have been produced by separate and distinct trajectories.

Another psychopathology that has been approached from an evolutionary perspective is the category of personality disorders. Personality disorders reflect a rigid approach to dealing with social relationships. Two commonly discussed personality disorders are antisocial personal disorder (also known as psychopathic personality) and histrionic personality disorder. Psychopaths are described as manipulative, callous, dishonest, and self-centered. They are antisocial in the sense that they display no need

Submissive monkeys avoid contact with dominant ones, just as humans experiencing social anxiety avoid dominant members of their group.

iStock.com/DavidCallan

to follow the traditional rules of a society and little remorse or guilt for their actions. For example, they would contract and collect money for a job they had no intention of doing. They would clearly qualify as those whom evolutionary psychologists refer to as cheaters. On the other hand, individuals with a histrionic personality disorder overly seek the attention of others and are very emotional in their reactions. They can be manipulative in their interpersonal relationships.

Harpending and Sobus (1987) suggested that the psychopathic and the histrionic personality styles represent different adaptive strategies in relation to sexuality. Both of these personality types were viewed by Harpending and Sobus as cheaters. Given that it is more common to see men with antisocial personality disorder and women with histrionic personality disorder, these researchers suggest that this results from different reproductive strategies. A man cheating in a sexual relationship should be able to persuade a woman to copulate with him while deceiving her about his commitment to her and his willingness to offer resources for the offspring. A cheating woman, on the other hand, would exaggerate her need for the man and make herself appear helpless and in need so that he would give her additional attention and resources. She would also be willing to put her own needs ahead of those of her offspring even to the extent of abandoning them. The work of Harpending and Sobus shows how evolutionary thinking can help to explain possible motivational factors of a particular disorder as well as the demonstrated gender differences.

Let's look at another well-studied process—sleep—as a model for thinking about psychopathology. Since sleep disturbance is often associated with a variety of psychopathological disorders, this will let us consider how normal processes may be influenced to appear pathological. Most people would like to go to sleep when they want to and not be awakened during the night. However, evolution is not always about what makes us feel good. The critical question from an evolutionary perspective is what function sleep plays. In considering this question, we can look at sleep as a model for how we might approach other basic psychological processes.

One initial question to ask is this: Has sleep been shaped by natural selection? Some researchers answer yes to this question (Nesse & Williams, 1994). They offer at least five reasons for why this is so. First, sleep is found in a variety of organisms and is perhaps universal among vertebrates. However, not all animals sleep in the same way. Elephants and cows spend most of their sleep time standing up. Dolphins sleep with one half of their brain, while the other half remains awake. Second, all vertebrates share similar mechanisms that control sleep and dreaming. These mechanisms are found in the more primitive areas of the brain. Third, the pattern of sleep seen in mammals with periods of rapid eye movement and faster EEG activity within the sleep period is also seen in birds. Since the evolution of birds went down a different pathway before the time of dinosaurs, this suggests that sleep is a very primitive and basic mechanism. Fourth, in examining the sleep patterns across species, there appears to be support for the idea that these patterns adapted to match the ecological niche of that particular animal. Fifth and finally, all animals show deficits in response to a lack of sleep. Currently, a variety of researchers are seeking to determine the function of sleep. The best evidence suggests that it allows for restoration of certain physiological processes. There is also evidence that sleep consolidates information learned during waking hours. One conceptual idea is that, given the light–dark cycle produced by the earth's rotation around the sun, sleep developed as a protective mechanism since it is more dangerous to be out alone at night.

In summary, we can ask critical questions concerning psychopathology that relate to other evolutionary processes:

1. We can ask if the experience of mental illness is universal. If it were not universal, then it would be difficult to argue that we should study psychopathology from an evolutionary perspective. If it is a universal process such as emotionality or language, then we can begin to ask about the nature of mental illness and how its existence fits into our history as humans.

2. We can ask if there is an adaptive value to the behaviors and experiences displayed in psychopathology. It is easy to see that there is a value in not trusting what someone tells you some of the time, but is there any adaptive value in not trusting what anyone tells you all of the time or to think that everyone is always out to get you?

3. We can look for evidence of psychopathology across human history. This includes the question of whether we see signs of psychopathology in nonhuman species.

4. We can seek to understand the nature of psychopathology. That is to say, should we consider psychopathology to be qualitatively different from normal functioning, or is it the situation in which normal processes have been taken to the extreme? We know, for example, that allergic reactions are situations in which our immune system is overreactive. We also know that fever is the process by which body temperature is raised to fight infection. However, the fever uses energy and can damage the body.

5. We can ask if it is protective in some manner. Like carrying the trait for sickle-cell anemia, does having schizophrenia or depression, for example, make you less likely to experience another disorder?

6. We can ask if psychopathology is a recent process. That is, should we consider psychopathology as the result of a mental system that evolved millennia ago and is interacting with a high-paced modern environment? For example, aggression in teenagers involved in gangs may reflect behaviors that were adaptive in previous times but are no longer adaptive for society today.

These questions are not mutually exclusive. As you will see, they also represent some of the ways scientists and others have sought to understand psychopathology. From an evolutionary perspective, the study of psychopathology begins with the three instincts of survival, sexuality, and socialness. From this perspective, psychopathology becomes a disturbance of these instinctual processes. Throughout this text, considerations of how certain evolutionary processes might contribute to psychological disorders will be discussed.

CONCEPT CHECK

- One of the main themes of evolution is the manner in which organisms are in close connection with their environment. Animals live in nature, but for humans there is another layer of complexity. Describe three uniquely human characteristics that impact our connectedness to our environment. What role do they play in psychopathology?
- What are the six critical questions an evolutionary perspective asks concerning psychopathology?

SUMMARY

The basic element of the brain is the neuron that is connected to other neurons. Since the human brain has been estimated to contain 86 billion neurons and more than 100,000 kilometers of interconnections, scientists have analyzed them in the context of networks. Three specific networks have been examined relating to psychopathology—the default network (also called the intrinsic network), the central executive network, and the salience network. Psychopathological disorders have been shown to have problems in turning networks on or off as well as problems in the connections within the network itself.

Scientists have been able to use the manner in which neurons work as a window into their function. A variety of techniques for observing activity in the brain have been developed. Currently, the major types of brain imaging techniques are EEG, MEG, PET, and fMRI. There are a number of trade-offs that researchers and clinicians must consider when choosing a brain imaging technique. It begins with the research or clinical question one is asking, which determines whether the appropriate measure is one of structure (spatial resolution) or how fast a process can be measured (temporal resolution). With the opening of this window into individuals' internal processes, the new field of neuroethics has started asking questions concerning who should have access to that information.

Genes form the blueprint that determines what an organism is to become. They are found on chromosomes in every cell of the body. Within each gene, DNA (the information storage molecule) transfers information to RNA (the information transfer molecule) to produce a particular protein. The location of the genes in the body makes a difference in that cells in the brain produce different proteins from those in the muscles, or liver, or heart. A gene is turned on (produces the protein) or turned off (does not produce the protein) relative to specific events.

The basis of evolution is genetic variations that occur in response to the environment and that can be inherited and passed on to future generations. The study of genetics began in the 1800s with the work of Gregor Mendel, who established the initial principles of genetic inheritance. Subsequent research has added complexity to that initial conceptualization. Mitochondrial inheritance, for example, has been found to involve the mtDNA that generally is inherited only from the mother. Epigenetic inheritance is based on the fact that the processes that determine which genes turn on and off can be passed on to the next generation. Thus, although DNA itself cannot be influenced by the environment, it is possible for the environment to influence future generations through its changes to those processes that turn genes on and off. Given this complexity, it is no wonder the original hope of finding a few genes that were involved in particular mental disorders has not panned out. Currently, one promising focus of research has been to identify endophenotypes—patterns of processes lying between the gene (the genotype) and the manifestations of the gene in the external environment (the phenotype)—for particular psychological disorders.

One of the main themes of evolution is the manner in which organisms are in close connection with their environment. It is this close connection that allows for change to take place, including the turning on and off of genetic processes. In humans, there is another layer of complexity involved in the process. Part of this complexity comes from the fact that humans are born less fully developed at birth than many other species and thus are sensitive to changes in their environment as they continue to develop. Unlike animals that live within nature, we as humans largely live within the backdrop of our culture. Another part of our complexity as humans is our ability to reflect on ourselves and our world. In this way, a layer of thought can be injected between the person and the environment. This allows for expectation and imagination to play a role in human behavior and experience. This lack of connectedness to our environment may take place on both an external and an internal level.

From an evolutionary perspective, the study of psychopathology begins with the three instincts of survival, sexuality, and socialness. From this perspective, psychopathology becomes a disturbance of these instinctual processes. The evolutionary perspective goes beyond the traditional psychological and physiological considerations and asks some critical questions concerning psychopathology. First, is the experience of mental illness universal? Second, is there an adaptive value to the behaviors and experiences displayed in psychopathology? Third, can we see evidence of psychopathology across human history as well as in nonhuman species? Fourth, what is the nature of psychopathology—is it qualitatively different from normal functioning, or have normal processes been taken to the extreme? Fifth, is psychopathology protective in some manner? Sixth, is psychopathology a recent process—a result of a mental system designed in prehistory interacting with a thoroughly modern environment?

STUDY RESOURCES

Review Questions

1. What are genotypes, phenotypes, and endophenotypes? How are these three concepts used in understanding the development of psychopathology?

2. This chapter states that there is a complicated relationship between genetic conditions and environmental factors. How are these two concepts involved in the development and maintenance of psychopathology? How is it made even more complex by epigenetic processes?

3. How have the discoveries of epigenetic inheritance and mitochondrial inheritance enriched our understanding and added to the complexity of Mendel's initial theory of genetic inheritance?

4. How does the small world framework from social science help us understand how neurons are connected in a network? What implications does this have for the transmission of information within a network and across networks?

5. Historically, those interested in neuroscience research have focused more on the universality of human processing than on the diversity found in different cultures. What evidence can you present to show that culture creates diversity in human psychological processing?

For Further Reading

Ananthaswamy, A. (2015). *The man who wasn't there.* Dutton.

Andreasen, N. (2001). *Brave new brain: Conquering mental illness in the era of the genome.* Oxford University Press.

Eagleman, D. (2011). *Incognito: The secret lives of the brain.* Pantheon.

European Bioinformatics Institute. (n.d.). *GWAS catalog.* https://www.ebi.ac.uk/gwas/

Nesse, R. (2019). *Good reasons for bad feelings.* Dutton.

Plomin, R. (2018). *Blueprint: how DNA makes us who we are.* MIT Press.

Psychiatric Genomics Consortium. (n.d.). https://pgc.unc.edu/

Ramachandran, V. S. (1998). Consciousness and body image: Lesions from phantom limbs, Capgras syndrome and pain asymbolia. *Philosophical Transactions of the Royal Society of London B, 353,* 1851–1859.

Ramachandran, V. S., & Blakeslee, S. (1998). *Phantoms in the brain.* William Morrow.

Seung, S. (2012). *Connectome: How the brain's wiring makes us who we are.* Houghton Mifflin Harcourt.

KEY TERMS

- allele
- central executive network
- chromosomes
- connectivity
- default or intrinsic network
- deoxyribonucleic acid (DNA)
- diffusion tensor imaging (DTI)
- electroencephalography (EEG)
- encode
- endophenotypes
- epigenetic inheritance
- epigenetic marks or tags
- epigenetics
- event-related potentials (ERPs)
- evoked potentials (EPs)
- executive functions
- functional magnetic resonance imaging (fMRI)
- genes
- genotype
- heterozygotes or heterozygous
- homozygotes or homozygous
- magnetoencephalography (MEG)
- Mendel's first law or the law of segregation
- Mendel's second law or the law of independent assortment
- mitochondrial DNA (mtDNA)
- mitochondrial inheritance
- modularity
- neuroethics
- neurotransmitters
- phenotype
- positron emission tomography (PET)
- proteins
- ribonucleic acid (RNA)
- salience network
- small world framework

3 RESEARCH METHODS

LEARNING OBJECTIVES

- **3.1** Describe the characteristics of the scientific approach.
- **3.2** Describe the characteristics of the nonexperimental methods of psychological research.
- **3.3** Explain why the experimental research method is generally considered more reliable than nonexperimental methods.
- **3.4** Identify the steps in designing an experimental study.
- **3.5** Identify other types of research and considerations in studying psychopathology.
- **3.6** Discuss the ethical considerations that must be observed in performing psychological research.

Let us begin with a story that took place in Central Europe over 150 years ago, in 1847 to be exact. At the Vienna General Hospital, a physician named Ignaz Semmelweis faced a serious problem when he noticed that previously healthy women who had just given birth to healthy children were dying. The women died of a condition that included fever, chills, and seizures. As you can imagine, numerous theories were offered. Some thought the deaths were related to the diet of the women. Perhaps they drank bad water. Maybe the flowers that were brought to their rooms were the problem.

Observing the overall conditions in the hospital, Semmelweis saw that other women in the same hospital who ate the same food, drank the same water, and smelled the same flowers did not die. Consequently, he reasoned, it was not the food, water, or flowers that caused the deaths. Yet the fact remained that women who had just given birth died of the mysterious condition. Semmelweis became aware of a crucial clue when he learned that a hospital assistant who had accidentally cut his hand during an autopsy later died. Further, this assistant had displayed the same symptoms as the mothers. What was the connection between the death of the assistant and the deaths of the mothers? Was there any connection at all?

One of the first questions Semmelweis asked was where the assistant worked. Perhaps the autopsy laboratory might be the cause of the mysterious deaths. To evaluate this notion, he traveled to other hospitals and recorded what physicians did just before delivering babies. From these observations, he learned that some physicians gave pathology lectures to the interns in the hospital as part of their daily duties. He also noted that when the physicians who delivered the babies came directly from a pathology lecture in which they handled diseased tissue or performed an autopsy, the death rate was highest.

Semmelweis suggested that it was the physicians who were transferring the diseases from the pathological tissue to the healthy mothers, just as the assistant had accidentally infected himself with the knife cut. The physicians of the day were outraged at the suggestion that they were the cause of the women's deaths. Semmelweis found further evidence by demonstrating that in hospitals where some births were assisted by midwives rather than physicians, those mothers survived at a much higher rate.

In a rather striking, though not totally controlled, experiment, Semmelweis is said to have placed himself at the door to the delivery ward and forced all physicians who entered to wash their hands first. The number of deaths decreased dramatically. Although not everyone accepted Semmelweis's findings, these data spoke for themselves, and modern medical practice has been shaped by this event (Glasser, 1976).

WHAT IS SCIENCE?

In many ways, those who study psychopathology, including both researchers and those who consume the research, are faced with dilemmas similar to those that faced Semmelweis. We can observe and describe various disorders. However, researchers are still trying to determine which are the most important factors that likely cause psychological disorders and which factors they can rule out. Informed consumers want to know how to understand the research and factors that are important for their own lives and relationships. Both researchers and informed consumers seek to evaluate the information. The best method for doing this is a scientific approach, which will be described in this chapter. What are some of the characteristics of the scientific approach?

First, science involves *detective work*. An important aspect of both science and good detective work is careful observation. In his case, Semmelweis observed how doctors in different hospitals went about their day and what experiences preceded other experiences. In addition, he observed others such as midwives who were also involved with births. Thus, careful observation is an important first step.

Second, science involves valid *logic*. In this case, Semmelweis reasoned that if food, water, or flowers were involved, then they should have affected *all* of the mothers. However, since there were other mothers who did not get sick and ate the same food and water and were around the same flowers as the mothers who did get sick, it was possible for Semmelweis to conclude this assumption was not supported.

Third, *luck* often plays a role in science. In this case, the bit of luck was the fact that the assistant cut his hand during an autopsy and had similar symptoms as the mothers who died. Although this was unlucky for the assistant, his death gave Semmelweis an important clue as to which variables were involved.

Fourth, science involves **hypothesis** testing. Semmelweis had the hypothesis that the disease was carried on the hands of the physicians. To test this hypothesis, he had the physicians wash their hands, and then he determined how this influenced the wellness of the mothers. If washing the hands of the physicians did not make a difference, then this hypothesis could be determined false. However, washing did make a difference, which allowed for further experimentation as well as establishing techniques for the prevention of the disease.

You may find it surprising that the physicians at first did not believe Semmelweis. Although we do not know if they did not believe that a doctor could be responsible for a patient's death, one key ingredient in psychological research is the need to understand how other people see themselves and their world.

In designing research in psychopathology, we need to take human nature into account. One important aspect of the human experience is that we tend to think and recall things in a psychological way rather than a logical way. For example, most of us tend to remember good times better than bad times. However, in terms of mental illness, some individuals, such as those with depression, tend to remember the bad times more often. We also remember events that put us in a good light rather than in a bad one. Sometimes we remember things differently from the way they may have happened or perform differently if we know we are being observed. Thus, psychological researchers look for a variety of techniques for obtaining information, including self-report, direct observations, and reports of mental health workers, as well as indirect measures such as neuroscience techniques.

In general, there is no single scientific method, yet there is a general process called science. This process consists of experiencing the world and then drawing general conclusions (called **facts**) from observations. Sometimes these conclusions or facts are descriptive and can be represented by numbers. For example, we say that the moon is 238,000 miles from the earth or that the average human heart rate is 72 beats per minute. Other times, these facts are more general and can describe a relationship or a process. For example, we say that it is more difficult to learn a second language after puberty than before puberty or that as we age we can hear fewer high-frequency sounds. Whatever the topic, the known facts about a particular subject are called **scientific knowledge** (see Ray, 2022, for more on this).

There is another aspect to science that many people do not think about. This is the aspect of **doubt**. In science, we use doubt to question our ideas and our research and ask whether factors other than the ones that we originally considered might have influenced our results. Likewise, when we consume

Careful observation is an important aspect of both science and good detective work.
iStock.com/SrdjanPav

information, we still want to know how to question what we are being told. In science we use doubt to question our research and ask whether factors other than the ones that we originally considered might have influenced our results. As an informed consumer, we also want to know how to evaluate what we are being told. By doing this we come to see that science is a combination of interaction with the world and logic.

The logic of science leads us to the realization that one of the real strengths of science is showing us when we are wrong. If someone says that all swans are white, for example, seeing a white swan—or seeing 500 swans, all of which are white—does not actually prove this to be the case. However, seeing just one black swan would clearly show that the statement was wrong. In this spirit, Einstein is reported to have said, "No amount of experimentation can ever prove me right; a single experiment can prove me wrong." The philosopher of science Sir Karl Popper referred to this approach as **falsification**. Thus, one important aspect of doing science is to ask yourself, how would I know if I was wrong?

The methods of science closely parallel our ways of learning about the world. We can think about these in terms of three stages.

First, scientists begin with an idea or expectation. A formally stated expectation is called a hypothesis. The scientist says, "I expect this to happen under these conditions," and thus states the hypothesis.

Second, scientists look to experience to evaluate the accuracy of their ideas and expectations about the world. That is, they try to find or create the situation that will allow them to observe what they are interested in studying. Through observation and experimentation, scientists can begin to evaluate their ideas and expectations. Learning about the world through observation and experimentation is an example of **empiricism**.

Third, on the basis of their observations and experiments, scientists seek to draw conclusions or inferences about their ideas and expectations. They reorganize their ideas and consider the impact of the new information on their theoretical conceptualizations.

Overall, science is a way of determining what we can infer about the world. In its simplest form, the scientific method consists of asking a question about the world and then experiencing the world to determine the answer. When we begin an inquiry, what we already know about our topic leaves us in one of a number of positions. In some cases, we know little about our topic, or our topic may be very complex. Consequently, our ideas and questions are general. For example, how does our memory work? What causes mental illness? What factors make a fruitful marriage? How can we model the brain? Can experience change our brain?

This chapter will focus on the methods of psychological science. It will begin with case study, observational, and correlational approaches and then move to more formal experimental approaches. The chapter ends with a consideration of ethics as applied to research.

NONEXPERIMENTAL METHODS OF PSYCHOLOGICAL RESEARCH

As you first set out to learn about a phenomenon, you seek to observe it and describe it as it occurs. At times, you may be unable to perform an experiment. In this section, three of these nonexperimental research methods will be described. They are the case study, naturalistic observation, and the correlational approach. Each of these has played an important role in the study of psychopathology.

Case Study

The **case study** is one of the most widely used methods for studying individual participants. It is based on the logic of describing, analyzing, interpreting, and evaluating a set of events and relationships within a framework or theory (Bromley, 1986; Yin, 2017). The typical descriptive case study focuses on either problematic or exceptional behaviors of one individual. Indeed, for years the case study approach has been the primary method for studying phenomena in clinical medicine, clinical psychology, and the neurosciences. It has a particularly important history in the study of mental disorders.

The case study method has a rich tradition in studying unique situations that do not lend themselves to traditional experimental procedures. Much of our initial understanding of brain function came from careful study of individuals who had had accidents or experienced war injuries. With psychopathology, the case study offers a means of examining in some depth the manner in which a person understands and experiences their disorder. Further, the case study offers a means of helping researchers develop new questions to be asked concerning a disorder in terms of how it developed and might be treated.

In psychopathology research, the advantage of the case study is its ability to present the clinical implications of a particular disorder. One classic example that Freud discussed is the case study of Anna O., which will be introduced in Chapter 9. Another example is described in Morton Prince's book *The Dissociation of a Personality* (1913). Prince described a case of multiple personality (now called dissociative identity disorder) at a time when the existence of that diagnostic category was in question.

An advantage of such extended discussions in a case study is the ability to describe processes not easily reduced to a single variable. For example, Luria (1972) described in great detail the attempt of one man to overcome a neuropsychological deficit that left him with "a shattered world." This is a story about a brilliant young Russian scientist, Zasetsky, who became a soldier in World War II and was shot in the head. Zasetsky's wound was such that areas of the brain that help one move in space or understand complex language were damaged, whereas areas that allow one to reflect on one's condition were not. Luria's intriguing work describes both his and the patient's own experiences over a 25-year period. Initial case studies from battlefield experiences also helped to clarify the nature of post-traumatic stress disorder (PTSD), which will be discussed in Chapter 7.

Another famous case study in the history of neuropsychology is that of Phineas Gage. In 1848, Phineas Gage was a railroad construction supervisor in Vermont. Part of his job was to prepare the charges to blast rocks so that the railroad tracks could be laid. To do this, a hole was drilled in the rock and then gunpowder was placed in the hole followed by sand. This was then tamped down with a long iron rod. On September 13, 1848, Gage did not realize that the sand had not been added and began to drop the iron rod into the hole. As the rod went into the rock, a spark ignited the gunpowder and the 13-pound iron rod shot out and through Gage's brain and landed some 30 feet away (Damasio et al., 1994).

Amazingly, after being momentarily stunned, Gage regained full consciousness and was able to talk and to walk with help. He was taken back to his boardinghouse and seen by a local doctor.

Phineas Gage after the accident.
ART Collection/Alamy Stock Photo

What was surprising was that, over time, Phineas Gage was able to recover from his physical injuries. He continued to be able to speak and perform the everyday motor processes required. His intelligence and ability to learn new information remained as before the accident. However, his personality showed such a drastic change that his coworkers said he was "no longer Gage." Whereas he had been a mild-mannered person before the accident, afterward he was prone to angry outbursts. Gage also lacked a sense of social conventions after the accident and frequently used profanity. The accident had influenced his emotional processing. This case study, as described by his physician, Dr. Harlow, has helped scientists understand the manner in which brain damage can influence social and emotional processes seen in other types of mental disorder. This helped later scientists consider which areas of the brain might be involved in mental disorders that show deficits in social and emotional processing. The iron rod and Gage's skull have been retained in a museum at Harvard University.

Modern researchers have returned to the case of Phineas Gage to ask new questions. They sought to use the case to illustrate types of brain damage. Hanna Damasio and her colleagues (1994), using photographs and X-rays of the skull, created a three-dimensional reconstruction, including the entry and exit points of the iron rod. From this, they described the suggested damage to the left and right prefrontal cortex, which would include a lack of inhibition as shown by Gage's angry outbursts, a lack of planning, memory problems, and deficits in social cognition. Peter Ratiu and his colleagues (2004) performed computerized axial tomography (CAT) scans on the skull of Phineas Gage to determine the manner in which the rod was projected through his skull. Using these same CAT scans, John Van Horn and his colleagues (2012) sought to model damage to the white and gray matter of the brain. In order to estimate the damage to Gage's brain, these researchers examined the white matter connections of 110 healthy male individuals 25 to 36 years of age using brain imaging techniques. They suggested that Gage suffered from damage to the left frontal cortex and that impairment to network connectedness between the left frontal area and other brain areas would have been considerable. This modeling is shown in Figure 3.1.

The basis of every case study is the clinical notes of the professionals. Diagnosis and treatment notes are kept for each individual these professionals see. The case study offers an opportunity for an in-depth examination of an individual's manifestation and experience of psychopathology. It is particularly important for the description of rarer conditions in which the salient factors are not yet well understood. However, it is difficult to know from a case study whether the relationships described were unique to that individual or could be generalized to others with the disorder. As such, it is perhaps most useful for directing future research concerning the critical variables involved in the disorder.

Naturalistic Observation: Just Looking

If little is known about a particular phenomenon, it often is useful simply to watch the phenomenon occur naturally and get a general idea of what is involved in the process. Initially, this is accomplished by observing and describing what occurs. This scientific technique is called **naturalistic observation**. A classic example of this approach is Charles Darwin's observation of animals in the Galápagos Islands. He carefully noted their appearance and environment, and these observations formed the basis of his theory of evolution. Psychologists have used naturalistic observation techniques to study children and adults, as well as the interactions of those in a mental hospital. New technologies such as video and audio capture have allowed for even greater possibilities.

Using a naturalistic observation study, Rachel Tomko and her colleagues (2012) collected data from individuals with borderline personality disorder (BPD) and other individuals with depression. These researchers wanted to better understand the social and emotional interactions of individuals with these disorders. As you will read in later chapters, individuals with BPD may show emotional instability, such as angry outbursts. Those with depression do not. The researchers used a device that periodically recorded 50-second snippets of audio. What these researchers reported was that individuals with depression were more likely to spend time alone if they had previously been angry. Individuals with BPD did not display withdrawal from others after anger and at times showed the opposite.

FIGURE 3.1 ■ Three-Dimensional Reconstruction of the Rod

Hanna Damasio and her colleagues (1994), using photographs and X-rays of the skull, created a three-dimensional reconstruction of the rod in Gage's brain, including the entry and exit points. Panel A shows the skull itself, which can be seen at the Warren Anatomical Museum at Harvard Medical School. Panel B shows a CAT image in which volumes were reconstructed and spatially aligned. Panel C is a rendering of the Gage skull with the best-fit rod trajectory and provides an example of the fiber pathways in the left hemisphere intersected by the rod. Panel D is a simulation view of the interior of the Gage skull showing the extent of fiber pathways intersected by the tamping iron.

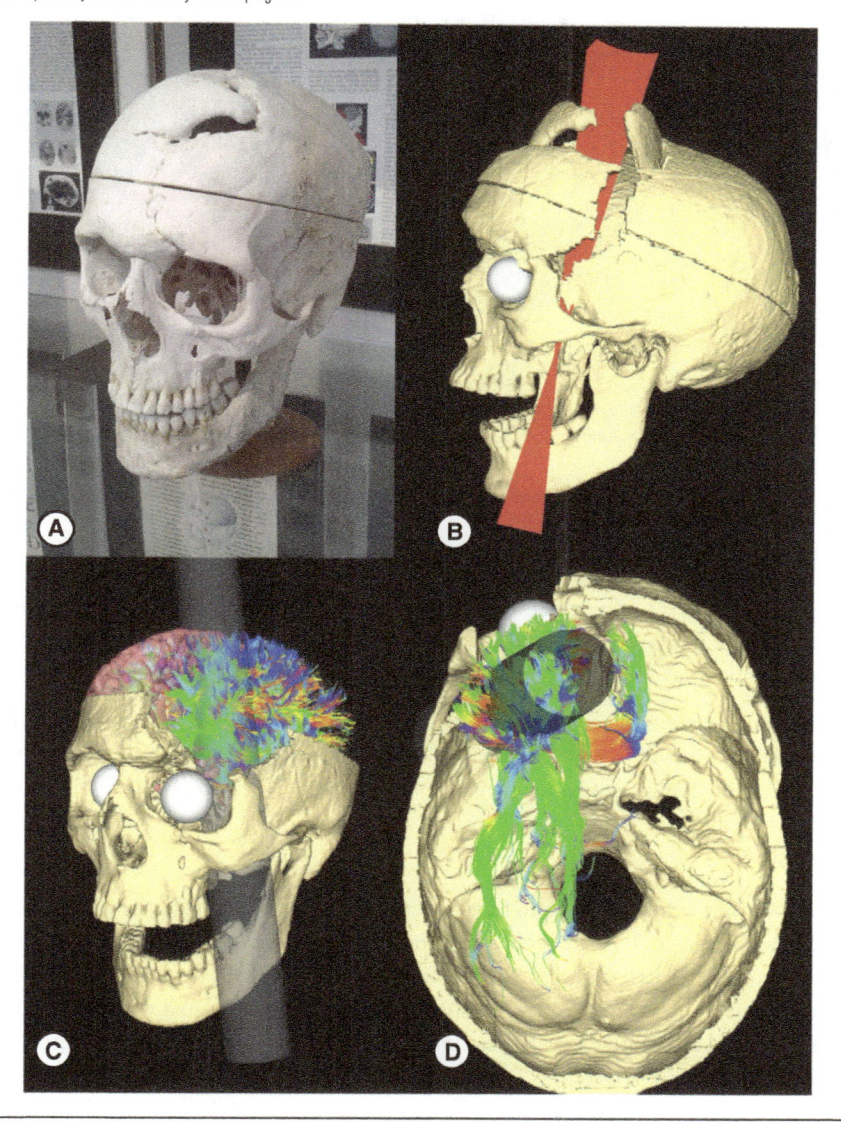

Credit: Van Horn, J. D., Irimia, A., Torgerson, C. M., Chambers, M. C., Kikinis, R., & Toga, A. W. (2012). Mapping connectivity damage in the case of Phineas Gage. *PLOS ONE, 7*(5), Article e37454. https://doi.org/10.1371/journal.pone.0037454; licensed under CC BY 4.0 https://creativecommons.org/licenses/by/4.0/.

The naturalistic observation method has four characteristics:

1. Noninterference is of prime importance. Scientists using this method must not disrupt the process or flow of events. In this way, they can see things as they really are, without influencing the ongoing phenomenon.

2. This method emphasizes the invariants or patterns that exist in the world. For example, if you could observe yourself in a noninterfering manner, you might conclude that your moods vary with the time of day, particular weather patterns, or even particular thoughts.

DARWIN TESTING THE SPEED OF AN ELEPHANT TORTOISE (GALAPAGOS ISLANDS).

In the Galápagos Islands, Charles Darwin used naturalistic observation techniques by carefully observing and describing animals in their natural habitat.

Chris Madden/Alamy Stock Photo

3. This method is most useful when we know little about the subject of our investigation. It is most useful for understanding the "big picture" by observing a series of events rather than isolated happenings.

4. The naturalistic method may not shed light on the factors that directly influence the behavior observed. The method provides a description of a phenomenon; it does not answer the question of why it happened.

Correlational Approach: What Goes With What?

The **correlational approach** is designed to help us understand how specific factors are associated with one another. As with much of human behavior, there are complex relationships between psychological variables and factors associated with them. The correlational approach helps us see what factors are related to one another. For example, you can ask if having friends is associated with better physical and psychological health or if negative experiences in one's past are associated with becoming depressed. Thus, we ask if one aspect of a system is associated with another aspect. It should be noted that both the statistical methods used to determine the degree of association and the research designs used to research the relationship between variables use the same term: *correlational*.

How would you go about answering these questions? Let's begin with the relationship between friends and health. You would first need to determine how you know how many friends someone has. One way is simply to ask them. Or, you could ask how many friends they have texted in the past week. What about health? One approach is to determine the number of times the person went to the health center in the past year. If you did this with a number of individuals, you would have two numbers for each person—their number of friends and their number of health center visits.

What would you do with these data? One helpful technique is to create a *scatterplot*. A scatterplot is a graph on which the data from each person are plotted. In this way, we would use the *y*-axis to display the number of friends someone has (e.g., 0–150) and the *x*-axis to display the number of visits to the health center during the past year (e.g., 0–20). We could then look at these measures for each person and plot that point on the graph. It is now possible to look at the graph and visually determine if there is a relationship.

Although humans are good at determining patterns, a statistical technique would allow for better precision. Such a technique is the **correlation coefficient**. The correlation coefficient gives both the strength of the relationship and its direction. If the number of friends was associated with more health center visits, then this relationship would be called a **positive correlation**. However, if fewer friends were associated with more visits, then this relationship would be called a **negative correlation**.

In the real world, few relationships are perfectly related to one another. Thus, the correlation coefficient is also able to reflect the *degree* of an association between two variables. Technically, the degree of relationship determined by the correlation coefficient is denoted by the letter r. Whether the relationship between the variables is positive or negative is denoted by the + and − signs. The correlation coefficient can range from −1 to +1. A perfect positive relationship would be $r = +1$, and a perfect negative relationship would be $r = -1$. If there was no relationship, it would be $r = 0$. Figure 3.2 shows a variety of relationships that differ in degree and direction; Figure 3.3 shows a variety of relationships and their corresponding r values.

What are the basic ideas of correlational studies? In correlational studies, researchers are interested in asking whether there is an association between two variables, but they do not attempt to establish how one variable influences the other, only that a relationship exists. Establishing that such an association exists may be the first step in dealing with a complex problem.

My colleagues and I used a correlational technique to understand whether being tortured influenced the brain differently if one had dissociative experiences, in which one feels detached from reality (Ray et al., 2006). Although not much is known concerning neuroscience measurements of individuals who have been tortured in their native country, there has been some suggestion that torture leads to different types of psychopathological disorders. There is also some evidence to suggest that torture victims adopt psychological mechanisms to escape the experience of the situation. Dissociation is one such mechanism in which individuals are able to distance themselves from such extreme negative experiences as torture or rape. We developed a dissociative scale that asked individuals about dissociative experiences they had experienced. Since some other neuroscience work had shown that non-normal MEG (magnetoencephalography) activity was seen in different areas of the brain in disorders such as schizophrenia, depression, and PTSD (e.g., Rockstroh et al., 2007), we used MEG as the variable to correlate with dissociative experiences. We found a positive correlation of .60 between our measure of MEG activity and the dissociation scale for the left hemisphere as a whole and a negative correlation

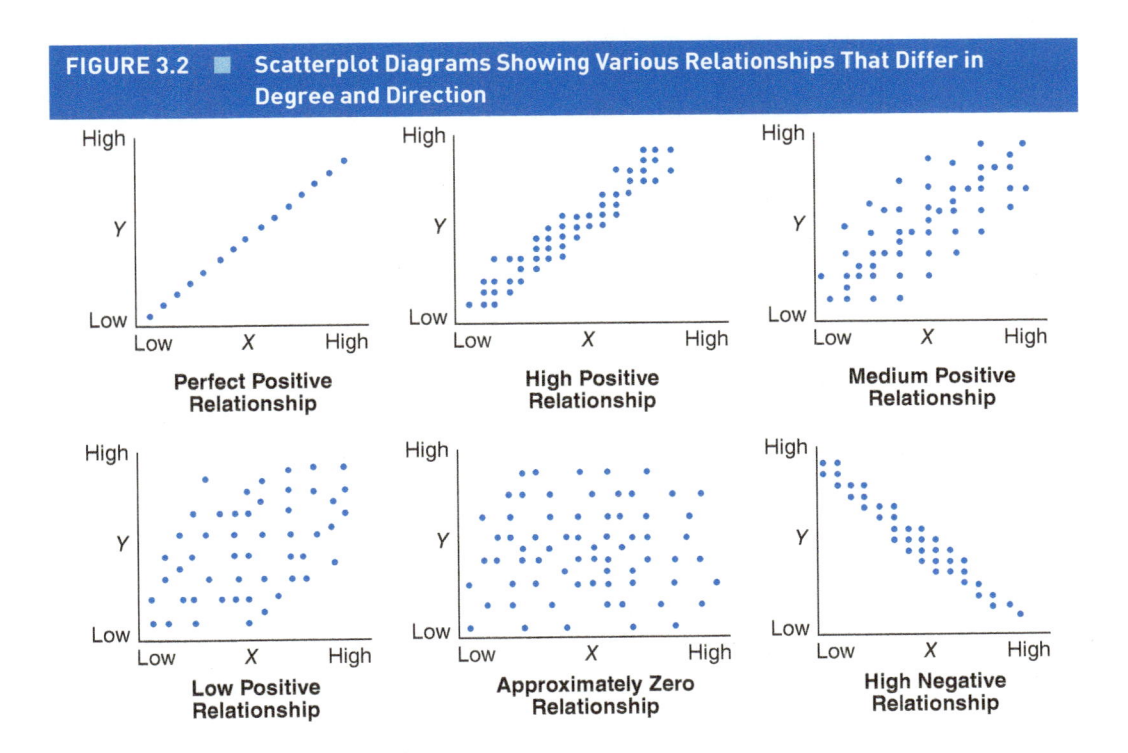

FIGURE 3.2 ■ Scatterplot Diagrams Showing Various Relationships That Differ in Degree and Direction

Perfect Positive Relationship

High Positive Relationship

Medium Positive Relationship

Low Positive Relationship

Approximately Zero Relationship

High Negative Relationship

FIGURE 3.3 ■ Scatterplot Diagrams of Different Relationships and Their Corresponding *r* Values

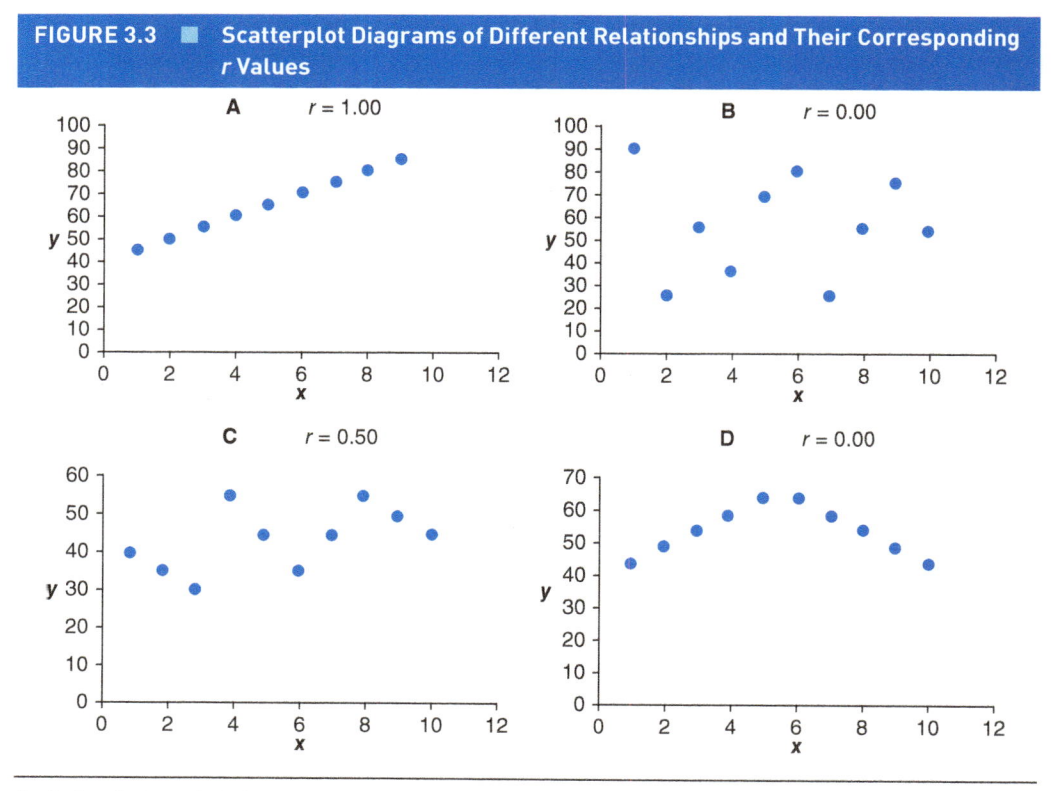

Credit: Landis, R. S. (2007). Measures of association/correlation coefficient. In S. G. Rogelberg (Ed.), *Encyclopedia of industrial and organizational psychology* (pp. 471–474, Figure 1). Sage.

of −.61 for the right hemisphere as a whole. More precise analysis showed the involvement of the left ventral region of the anterior cortical areas.

What we cannot know from correlational research is whether either variable influences the other directly. There are a variety of ways that one can see a high correlation. It might be that there is a direct relationship. That is, having lots of friends might make you feel better and make you less susceptible to disease. However, it might also be true that if you went to the health center often, you might not have time for friends or not feel like being with others. In our torture study, one might logically assume that the torture influenced the brain. However, it might have been the case that those individuals who had particular types of MEG activity would be those that later developed dissociative experiences.

It is also possible that a third unspecified variable actually may have influenced the two variables in a correlational study. For example, there is a strong correlation between eating ice cream and wearing bathing suits. However, in this case it is a third variable, the warm weather, which produces the relationship. In the case of health and friends, it could be genetic makeup or having a job, both of which could influence the time one had for friends as well as for health. Thus, the nature of a correlational study is to describe the relationships but not to suggest which variable influences which other variable.

It is often said that correlation does not imply causality. For example, a researcher might want to know whether a relationship exists between the type of food a child eats and the likelihood of the child having a particular mental disorder such as hyperactivity. One approach would be to examine the diets of children who show hyperactivity and those who do not. What if there was a high association between eating foods with sugar, for example, and hyperactivity? You could conclude little other than that there was an association or correlation between the two variables. There are at least three ways to understand this relationship. (1) It might be that sugar is associated with hyperactivity. (2) It might also be that those who are hyperactive seek sugar. (3) A third variable such as a specific gene or neurotransmitter or sleep pattern might lead to both eating foods with sugar and showing hyperactivity.

The association of two factors does not in itself imply that one influences the other. However, if there is a *low* correlation between the events, you can infer that one event does *not* cause the other. A high degree of association is always necessary for establishing that one variable influences another;

a correlational study is often the first step to providing the needed support for later experimental research, especially in complex areas.

> ## CONCEPT CHECK
>
> - What are four characteristics of the scientific approach? What are two additional key ingredients in psychological research?
> - What are the three stages of the scientific process?
> - Why has the case study been particularly valuable in psychopathology research?
> - What are the four characteristics of the naturalistic observation method?
> - If a research study reports that two variables are correlated, what do you know about their relationship? What don't you know about their relationship?

THE EXPERIMENTAL METHOD: MAKING IT HAPPEN

Just finding that a relationship exists between two events does not allow us to determine exactly what that relationship is, much less that one event actually caused the other to happen. If we want to state that one event produced another event, we need to develop a much stronger case for our position.

To do this, we could see how some single event over which we have control affects the phenomenon we are studying. In this way, we begin to interact with the phenomenon. We structure our question in this form: If I do this, what will happen? Numerous questions can be asked in this way, such as, Will people with depression learn words better in a foreign language if each word is of the same class (e.g., negative emotional words) than if they are from a variety of different classes (some emotional, some objects, some neutral words)?

As our knowledge grows, we may even get to the point of formulating specific predictions. In particular, our questions are structured in this form: If I do this, I expect this will happen. Sometimes our predictions are more global, and we predict that one factor will be stronger than another. We might predict that more people are likely to help a stranger if they perceive the environment to be safe than if they think it is dangerous. At other times, however, we may know enough about an area to make a more precise prediction or point prediction. For example, we might predict that 3 months of exercise will lead to a drop in self-reported depression on a standard scale. These approaches, in which we interact directly with the phenomenon we are studying, are examples of the experimental method.

Definitions in the Experimental Method

What if we want to know if exercise affects depression? The hypothesis, or idea being tested, is that exercising would influence depression. To test the hypothesis, we could have one group exercise and another not exercise. The group that performs the exercise is called the experimental group. The group that does not is called the control group. A control group is one that is treated exactly like the experimental group except for the factor being studied. In this case, the factor being studied is exercise and its influence on depression.

Depression can be viewed on a number of different levels, so we need to have a definition of what depression means in our study. These representations of psychological events in the physical world are called *operational definitions*. An operational definition defines events in terms of the operations required to measure them and thus gives our idea a concrete meaning. Depression could be defined as the score received on a measure of depression such as the Beck Depression Inventory (BDI).

The idea that watching violence on television or playing video games with violent content increases aggression is certainly a reasonable and potentially important notion. The popular press has often tried to link violent video games with those who carry out school shootings. Yet before we can test this idea, we must define exactly what is meant by violence on television or in video games. Is a program with an unseen murder more violent than an exciting boxing match? Should violence be rated by how many minutes it appears on the screen, by the particular type of act, by how much blood is shown, or by a

To test a hypothesis that exercise affects depression, we could have one group exercise and another not exercise.
iStock.com/Dean Mitchell

combination of all three? Likewise, to perform this research we need to devise some measure of aggression. We would have to adopt operational definitions.

An operational definition takes a general concept, such as depression or aggression or effectiveness, and places it within a given context. That is, it redefines the concept in terms of clearly observable operations that anyone can see and repeat. For example, we might define *aggression* as the number of times a child hits a toy after watching a violent video.

In an experimental study, we want to know how one variable that we manipulate affects another variable. Think of a study in which you want to know if drinking coffee improves your memory. Whether or not someone drank coffee is the manipulated variable. This is also called the **independent variable (IV)**. Memory in this example is the variable influenced by the coffee and is called the **dependent variable (DV)**. That is, it depends on or is influenced by the IV.

What other factors could influence a memory test? If we suspect that some unintended factor may also be operating, then the truth or **validity** of the experiment is seriously threatened. Thus, the conclusion that the IV influenced the DV could be questioned. In the memory experiment, if the control group was run in the morning and the experimental group in the afternoon, then time of day could have an effect. Whenever two or more IVs are operating, the unintended IVs (those not chosen by the experimenter) are called **confounding variables**.

Other confounding variables may **covary** with the IV and be more difficult to notice. For example, assume that a researcher compared a new medication against a problem-solving approach for the treatment of anxiety. If the researcher found that the problem-solving approach led to a greater reduction in anxiety, could they conclude that problem solving produced the reduction? Although that is one possibility, it also may have been the case that spending time with a professional produced the reduction in anxiety. That is, because giving medications requires less time with a patient than discussing problem-solving techniques, the results found may not have been due to the IV as planned in the study but rather to a confounding variable of time with the patient.

Research Methods in Action: Does Playing Music Change the Brain?

Let's examine a specific study in which both experimental and correlational procedures were used. Thomas Elbert and his colleagues (Elbert et al., 1995) began with the idea that experience could change the manner in which connections in the brain were established. What these researchers needed to do was find a task that would allow them to measure change and make logical inferences. Since they were interested in long-term changes, they sought to find a skill that people learn in childhood. They decided on an experiment that involved playing a musical instrument.

What musical instrument would you choose for such an experiment—piano, saxophone, violin, or another instrument? They chose the violin. Here is where logic and experimental design came in. By choosing the violin, these researchers were able to compare the differences between the violinists' left and right hands and their representation in the brain. Right-handed violinists use their left hand to continuously finger the strings. The right hand moves the bow back and forth and does not require the same fine motor skills. If playing a violin for 20 years would affect the brain, then it should affect those areas involved with the left hand in a different manner from those involved with the right. This is exactly what the research team found.

To measure neuronal activity in the brain, the researchers used a brain imaging device, the MEG. They found that neuronal activity in the brain was different between the areas of the brain related to the left and right fingers of musicians. Further, they found that the brain areas of the musicians' right hands were not different from those of the control group who did not play a musical instrument. Thus, the experimental comparison was between individuals who had played a musical instrument since childhood and the control group, those who had not. There was also a comparison between the brain areas involved with the left and right fingers of the musicians. Further, these researchers examined the correlation between neuronal activity and the length of time an individual had played an instrument. Figure 3.4 shows this relationship. As you can see, this is a negative correlation in that the earlier one began to play an instrument (with early age being a lower number), the stronger the neuronal activity was. The experimental and correlational aspects of this research helped the researchers logically conclude that previous experience can influence brain organization. The major point here is that prior experience can influence the brain, which will be an important consideration in fully understanding the development of mental illness and its treatment. For example, therapy for depression changes the flexibility of the brain connections, whereas stress restricts flexibility (Castrén & Hen, 2013).

FIGURE 3.4 ■ How Playing Music Affects the Brain

This graph shows the relationship between neuronal activity (dipole strength) and the length of time an individual had played an instrument. Those who started playing an instrument at a later age or stopped playing an instrument early showed fewer changes than those who started early and continued to play. Those who never played an instrument showed the least amount of change in the brain.

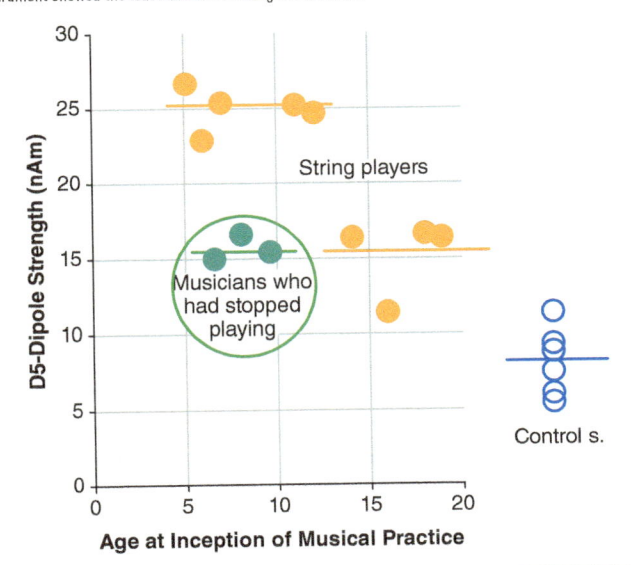

Credit: Elbert, T., Pantev, C., Wienbruch, C., Rockstroh, B., & Taub, E. (1995). Increased cortical representation of the fingers of the left hand in string players. *Science, 270*(5234), 305–307.

Logic and Inference: The Detective Work of Science

Perhaps you have heard the story of the man from Boston who got up every morning, went outside his house, walked around in a circle three times, and yelled at the top of his voice. His neighbor, being somewhat curious after days of this ritual, asked him for the purpose behind his strange behavior. The man answered that the purpose was to keep away tigers. "But," the neighbor replied, "there are no tigers within thousands of miles of here." To this, our friend responded, "Works quite well, doesn't it?"

How could we demonstrate to our friend that his yelling is not causally related to the absence of tigers? One strategy might be to point out that the absence of tigers might have come about for other reasons, including the fact that there are no tigers roaming in the greater Boston area. Our friend's reasoning was incorrect because it overlooked many other plausible explanations for the obvious absence of tigers. Although our friend sought to infer a relationship between his yelling and the absence of tigers, his *inference* was weak.

Logic is particularly important in science as an aid to answering this question: What question should my experimental study answer to test my ideas about the world? That is, logic can help us to answer questions of inference. **Inference** is the process by which we look at the evidence available to us and then use our powers of reasoning to reach a conclusion. Like Sherlock Holmes engaged in solving a mystery, we attempt to solve a problem based on the available evidence. Did the butler do it? No, the butler could not have done it because there was blond hair on the knife and the butler had black hair. But perhaps the butler left the blond hair there to fool us. Like a detective, scientists try to determine other factors that may be responsible for the outcome of their experiments or to piece together available information and draw general conclusions about the world. Also like the detective, the scientist is constantly asking, "Given these clues, what inference can I make, and is the inference valid?" Logic is one method for answering these questions.

One example of using logic to help solve a question in psychopathology involved the relationship between giving a child the MMR (measles, mumps, and rubella) vaccine and the development of autism. In the late 1990s, based on one published study (which was later discredited by the journal in which it appeared), it was suggested in the media that the MMR vaccine led to the development of autism. The MMR vaccine is given to a child around 12 to 15 months of age. The first signs of autism appear around 15 to 18 months of age. Thus, it was argued that the vaccine led to the development of autism. What type of evidence would you need to show this was not the case? You might first ask if everyone who receives the vaccine develops autism. Since many who receive the vaccine do not develop autism, then if the relationship exists, it is not a simple one. More important from a logical standpoint, you might ask if there exists a child who did not receive the vaccine but did develop autism. This would help to rule out vaccination being the single cause of autism. As you will see in Chapter 5, a critical finding is that there are signs of autism in children before the age of vaccinations. Thus, logically, researchers were able to rule out vaccines as the single cause of autism.

Validity

Logical procedures are also important for helping us understand the accuracy or validity of our ideas and research. *Valid* means true and capable of being supported. In studying mental illness, one important way to show that our ideas can be supported is to *replicate* them with different individuals in different locations. If we hypothesized that a certain type of stress led to depression, for example, then we would need to show that this is the case not only in our research clinic but also in other clinics.

Historically, we have discussed various types of validity in psychology, which arise from differing contexts. These contexts range from developing types of tests to running experiments. The overall question is this: Does a certain procedure, whether it is a test of mental illness or an experiment, do what it was intended to do? There are two general types of validity (Campbell & Stanley, 1963).

The first is **internal validity**. The word *internal* refers to the experiment itself. Internal validity asks the following question: Is there another reason that might explain the outcome of our experimental procedures? Students are particularly sensitive to questions of internal validity, for example, when it is time for final exams; they can make a number of alternative suggestions about what the exam actually measures and why it does not measure their knowledge of a particular subject. Like students, scientists look

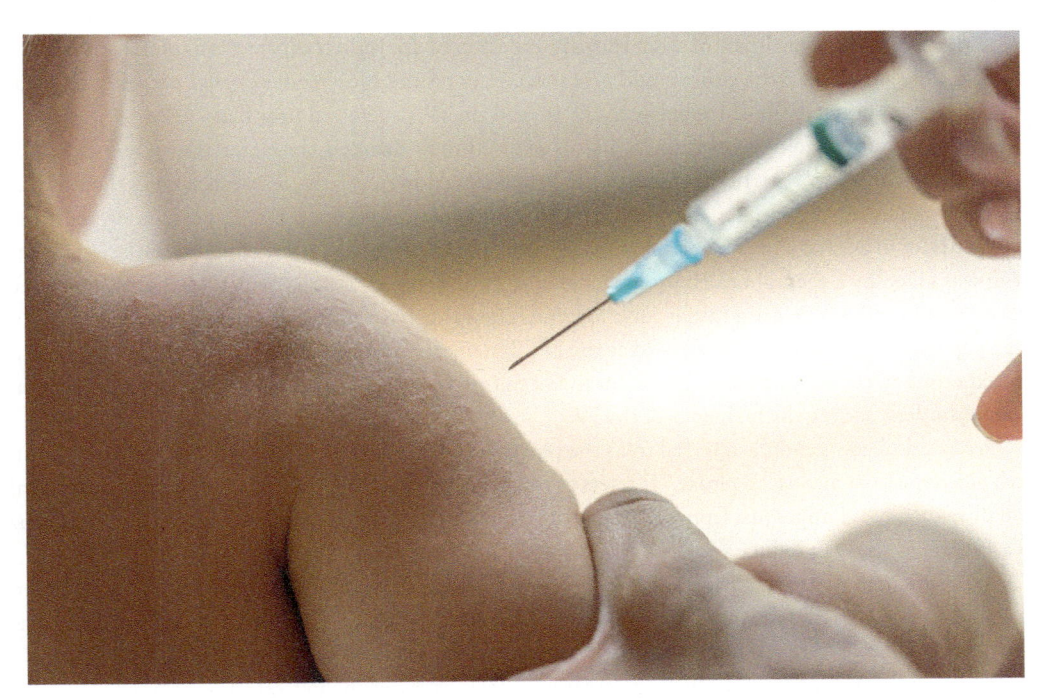

What type of evidence would you need to show that a vaccine did not lead to the development of autism?
iStock.com/Gajus

for reasons (threats to internal validity) that a particular piece of research may not measure what it claims to measure. In the case of our friend from Boston, the absence of tigers near his house could have reflected a long-standing absence of tigers in his part of the world rather than the effectiveness of his yelling.

The second type of validity is **external validity**. The word *external* refers to the world outside the setting in which the experiment was performed. External validity often is called **generalizability**. Remember the story of Semmelweis. His finding that the deaths of the mothers who had just given birth were the result of physicians touching them after handling diseased tissue was true not only for his hospital but also for all other hospitals. Thus, in addressing the question of external validity of Semmelweis's work, we would infer that his answers could be generalized to other hospitals with other women and not just to his own original setting. External validity, therefore, refers to the possibility of applying the results from an internally valid experiment to other situations and other research participants.

Research is logically designed to rule out as many alternative interpretations of our findings as possible and to have any new facts be applicable to as wide a variety of other situations as possible. In many real-life situations in which external validity is high, however, it is impossible to rule out alternative interpretations of our findings. In a similar way, in laboratory settings in which internal validity is high, the setting is often artificial, and in many cases our findings cannot be generalized beyond the laboratory. Consequently, designing and conducting research is always a trade-off between internal and external validity. Which one we emphasize depends on the particular research questions being asked.

Before continuing, let's clear up one misconception. It is the idea of designing "the one perfect study." Although we strive to design good research, there are always alternative explanations and conditions not included in any single study. It is for this reason that Donald Campbell, who introduced scientists to the idea of internal and external validity, also emphasized the importance of replicating studies. If the same study is performed a number of times with similar results, then we can have more assurance that the results were valid. Even better, if the study is performed in a variety of settings around the world, we have even more confidence in our results. The topic of replication will be discussed later in the chapter.

What Do I Expect to Happen?

One characteristic of human beings is that we seek to determine what will happen next. When we are talking with someone, we anticipate the next word they will say. The same is true in psychological experiments. Participants imagine what they are expected to do. If their expectation interferes with the influence of the IV, then the study could give inaccurate results. Any tendency that prevents an accurate reflection of the relationships between the IV and the DV is referred to as bias.

In research terminology, one type of bias is referred to as **demand characteristics**. Demand characteristics occur when a participant's response is influenced more by the research setting than by the IV. For example, a study might examine the effects of a drug as compared with exercise on reducing hyperactivity in adults. Many participants might believe the drug to be most effective, especially if the drug was given by a mental health professional and the exercise by a non–mental health professional. Those who received the drug might look for signs the drug was reducing hyperactivity. They might then pay more attention to the task used as the DV. If demand characteristics play an important role in the experiment, then they pose a significant threat to internal validity and offer an alternative explanation for understanding the influence of the IV.

A related phenomenon is referred to as the **placebo effect**. The term *placebo* comes from the Latin verb *placere*, which means "to please." It refers to the phenomenon that some people show psychological and physiological changes just from the suggestion that a change will take place. How might this occur in a treatment study to reduce anxiety?

Experimenters also have expectations. For example, knowing that one set of subjects has been assigned to one condition rather than another could result in those participants being treated differently. Such situations are referred to as **experimenter effects**.

To control for the placebo effect in research as well as experimenter effects, various procedures have been used. One is to use a control group that receives either no treatment or a treatment previously shown to be ineffective for the particular disorder under study. In medical research, it is common to give a "sugar pill" that looks exactly like the medicine with the active ingredient. In psychotherapy research, a control group could be given relaxation training, which has been shown not to be effective on its own for mental disorders.

A more powerful control is to use a **double-blind experiment** in which the experimental group is divided into two groups. One group is given the actual treatment, and the other is given a treatment exactly like the experimental treatment but without the active ingredient. Neither the placebo group nor the experimental group would know which treatment they are receiving, and in this way, these research participants are said to be **blind controls**. The term *double blind* indicates that the experimenters giving the medication also do not know which treatment is experimental and which is a placebo.

Types of bias can be found in many experiments. In order to sort through the results of our experiments, we must be like detectives who constantly ask if there is another way to understand what was found. Our way of doing that is through research, logic, and doubt. We use research to design a study to consider alternative possibilities. We use logic to consider if our conclusions follow from the results. We use doubt to ask if there is a way to know if we are wrong.

CONCEPT CHECK

- What is the difference between the experimental group and the control group? Why is the control group important?
- What is an operational definition? How does it help advance scientific knowledge?
- How are the IV, the DV, and confounding variables related?
- What is a double-blind experiment, and what are we trying to control for by using that design?

DESIGNING AN EXPERIMENTAL STUDY

One goal of experimental research is to determine the relationship between the IV and the DV. Less bias in terms of demand characteristics related to both the participant and the experimenter aids in creating a logical relationship between the IV and DV.

FIGURE 3.5 ■ How Do You Perform an Experiment?

There are four conceptual steps in experimentation. The first is to select the participants to be part of the study. The second is to assign the participants to a group. The third is to administer the IV to each group as required. The fourth step is to compare the results and interpret the reason for the differences.

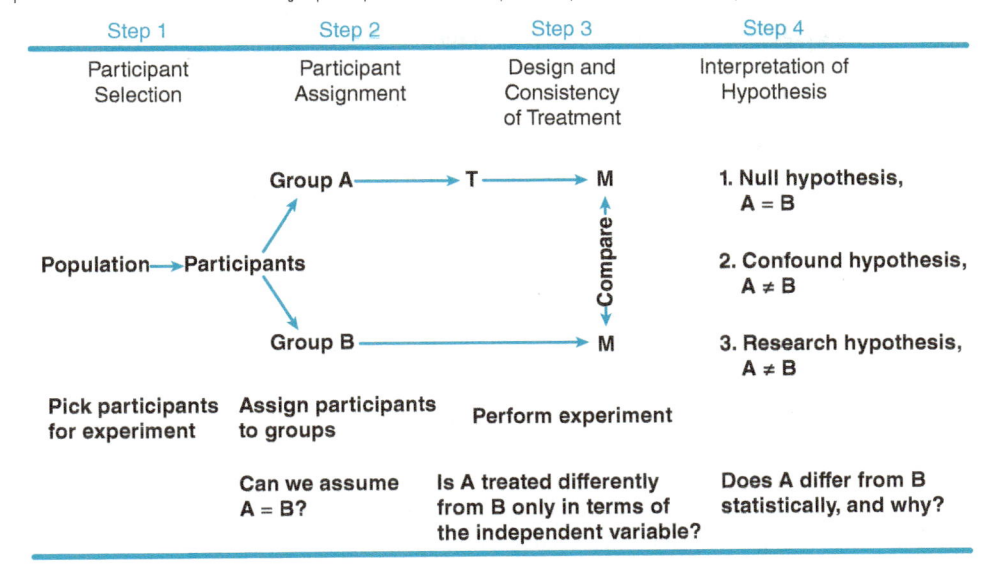

Step 1	Step 2	Step 3	Step 4
Participant Selection	Participant Assignment	Design and Consistency of Treatment	Interpretation of Hypothesis

Population → Participants → Group A → T → M
Population → Participants → Group B → M
(Compare M to M)

1. Null hypothesis, A = B
2. Confound hypothesis, A ≠ B
3. Research hypothesis, A ≠ B

Pick participants for experiment | **Assign participants to groups** | **Perform experiment** |

Can we assume A = B? | Is A treated differently from B only in terms of the independent variable? | Does A differ from B statistically, and why?

There are an additional four factors that are critical to sound inference (Figure 3.5). These are as follows:

1. Participant selection
2. Participant assignment
3. Design and consistency of experiment
4. Interpretation of relationship of IV to DV

Participants in the Study

It may seem simple to select subjects for an experiment. However, this is often a greater problem than it appears. The individuals selected for the study should be directly related to the hypothesis being tested. If you want to know if individuals with schizophrenia perform better on a memory test after drinking coffee, then of course you select individuals with schizophrenia. If you want to be able to apply the results to the **population** of all adults, then it is necessary for adults of all ages, genders, and ethnic backgrounds to be included in the study.

Researchers use a variety of means for selecting participants. The best is some form of random sampling. You might choose every tenth person in the college directory, or every fourth person admitted to the ward for treatment of schizophrenia, for example. When the selection is not random—that is, every person is not equally likely to be chosen—then bias can appear.

Putting Participants in Groups

After the participants have been randomly selected from the larger population under study, they can then be randomly assigned to experimental and control groups. This ensures that the groups are equal before the experiment begins. **Randomization** controls for both known and unknown potentially confounding variables. Randomization leaves the assignment of participants to a group to chance. In this way, any differences—even unknown or unsuspected differences—will also be nullified by being randomly distributed between the two groups.

In medical and psychological treatment research, the gold standard is considered to be the **randomized controlled trial (RCT)**. RCTs assign individuals randomly to the treatments being studied. For example, in a recent study of the effectiveness of certain stress reduction strategies, Melissa Polusny and her colleagues (2015) randomly assigned veterans at the Minneapolis Veterans Affairs Medical Center to one of two treatments. The first was a mindfulness-based stress reduction procedure. The comparison treatment centered on having the therapy focus on the current problems in the person's life. In this study, mindfulness resulted in a greater reduction in the PTSD symptoms compared with the current problems procedure.

Much of the early research involving clinical disorders was based on observation and interviews. With the advent of psychological testing and more advanced neuroscience techniques, greater insight has been gained in the structures and mechanisms involved in mental health and illness. Since mental illness cannot be studied in a traditional experimental manner, new methodologies and statistical techniques for comparing genetic, physiological, cognitive, emotional, gender, and stress factors are being developed.

One important design type in psychopathology research is a **match subjects design**. The closer a scientist can match individuals in the experimental and control groups, the stronger the logic of the design. A researcher cannot randomly assign individuals to control and experimental groups if the experimental group is composed of individuals with a specific disorder and the control group is composed of individuals without that disorder. Therefore, an alternative method other than random assignment must be used to ensure that the two groups are similar on characteristics not under study. Some important variables include education level, socioeconomic status (SES), general health, types of medications used, age, gender, and others related to the specific question being asked in the research. Thus, the general task is to ensure that the participants in the study are like one another except for having a mental illness. For example, when Tom Borkovec and his colleagues (Borkovec & Ruscio, 2001) sought to determine if cognitive behavioral therapy was effective in treating generalized anxiety disorder (GAD) as compared with other treatments, it was important that those with anxiety were matched in terms of age, gender, income, education level, and other such variables in terms of the experimental conditions.

The strongest version of matching is to use identical twins. The situation in which one twin has a particular disorder and the other does not helps researchers focus on the critical variables. One classic study involving twins was performed by E. Fuller Torrey (1994) and his colleagues in the 1990s. They studied individuals who developed schizophrenia or bipolar disorder (manic depression). Twins who lived together were matched in terms of such factors as genetics, family history, SES, and a number of others. However, twins are not always available, and thus researchers need to match those with a disorder and those without. The use of twins in psychological research will be discussed at greater length in the Behavioral Genetics section later in this chapter.

Designing and Structuring the Experimental Study

Science is a way of asking questions about the world. The quality of the answers we receive is influenced by several factors, one of the most important being the experimental design that we use. Somewhat like a blueprint, the experimental design directs the procedures and gives form to the experiment. In essence, an experimental design is a plan for how a study is to be structured.

In an outline form, a design tells us what will be done to whom and when. To be evaluated favorably, a design must perform two related functions. First, it must provide a logical structure that enables us to pinpoint the effects of the IV on the DV and thus answer our research questions. Second, it must help us rule out confounds as an alternative explanation for our findings.

Imagine a study in which a clinical psychologist was interested in determining if teaching children with autism to look at a person's face would increase their interaction with others. Thus, the question asked would be whether looking at a face (IV) results in the participant interacting more with others (DV). After the subject was taught to look at a face, they could be placed in situations in which other individuals were present. The researcher could measure the number of interactions in which the child engaged.

If we were to diagram the design of this study, it would be as follows:

Select the group → Teach facial focus → Measure number of interactions

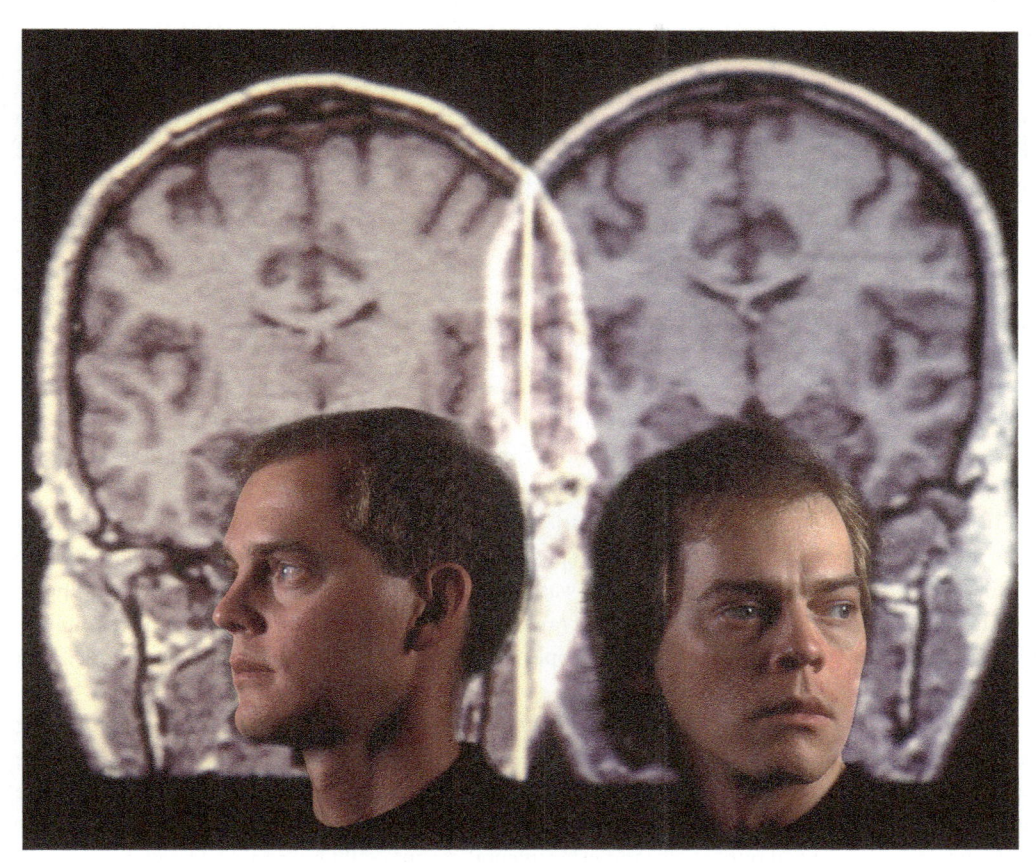

In 1995, identical twin brothers David (left) and Steven (right) Elmore took part in E. Fuller Torrey's classic study. David is mentally healthy, and Steven has schizophrenia. The study found that Steven's brain has less tissue and larger ventricles than David's.

Joe McNally/Hulton Archive/via Getty Images

If we performed the experiment with just a single group, what could we conclude? We could determine if our participants had a certain number of interactions. However, this would not help us determine if this was related to the facial focus procedure. Such a design would not be much help in pinpointing the effect of the IV on the DV, nor would it rule out confounds.

A stronger design would use a control group. This design would appear as follows:

Experimental group → Teach facial focus → Measure number of interactions

Control group → No treatment → Measure number of interactions

Since the control group had not received the treatment, we would have stronger evidence that the treatment was related to differences in number of interactions.

Is the Dependent Variable Related to the Independent Variable?

Once we have collected our data, we want to know how to interpret the experimental results. We do this by considering three separate hypotheses:

1. **Null hypothesis**—This is a statistical hypothesis that is tested to determine if there are differences between the experimental and control groups. Part of this statistical procedure is to ask the question of whether our results could have happened by chance.

2. **Confound hypothesis**—This is a conceptual question that asks if our results could be the result of a factor other than the IV.

3. **Research hypothesis**—This asks the question of whether our results are related to the IV.

Null Hypothesis and Inferential Statistics

We usually perform research with a limited number of individuals so that we can infer the behavior of all individuals related to the group we studied. For example, we might study how a group of individuals with depression responded to mindfulness meditation in terms of measures of distress.

What are the odds that the individuals with depression in our group are like all those with depression everywhere? To determine this **probability**, we use **inferential statistics**. Technically, we refer to all individuals with depression as the population and the particular participants in our study as the **sample**. *Inferential statistics* concerns the relationship between the statistical characteristics of the population and those of the sample.

One way of viewing the inferential process conceptually is to assume that the same experiment was run an infinite number of times, each time with a different sample of individuals chosen from the entire population. If we were to plot the statistics from each experiment, the population of estimates would then represent all the possible outcomes of the experiment.

In more technical language, inferential statistics is used to infer from a given sample of scores on some measure, the parameters for the set of all possible scores. All possible scores would be that of the population from which our particular sample was drawn. Implicit in this statement is the assumption that the sample we are discussing is the result of random sampling or some systematic form of sampling. That is, each person in the population of all people is equally likely to be included in the sample, with some known probability.

The important thing to remember is that inferential statistics constitutes a set of tools for inferring from a particular sample to larger populations. One way of viewing this conceptually is to ask how the statistics of our sample (i.e., the mean and the standard deviation) match what we expect to be the same measures in the larger population.

Conceptually, we ask if our control and experimental groups could be considered equal before any treatment (IV) was introduced. That is, would we expect them to be drawn equally from the larger population? One way in which we seek to make our experimental and control groups equal is through random assignment to the groups. A critical question that is asked in terms of empirically supported treatments is whether the participants were randomly assigned to the treatment condition. If so, then we take the support for a particular treatment as being more valid.

Inferential statistics might be used to study how a group of individuals with depression respond to mindfulness meditation.
iStock.com/Goodboy Picture Company

Given a group of potential subjects, we could expect some of them to be motivated to be part of the experiment, others to be tired, some to be more intelligent, some to have faster reaction times than others, and so forth. By randomly assigning these individuals to groups, we would expect to make the two groups equal.

Another part of the statistical treatment of the null hypothesis is related to probability. If you were to toss a coin a large number of times, you would expect to have an equal number of heads and tails. The idea of no differences forms the basis of the null hypothesis, which was developed by Sir Ronald Fisher (1935). He sought to determine whether a set of results differed from what would be expected.

What we need, of course, is a technique for determining if a set of results is different from what would be expected. One of the common statistical techniques used for this is called the t test. It was actually developed near the beginning of the 20th century by William Gosset, who worked for the Guinness Brewery in Dublin. Gosset wanted a way of knowing if all the batches of beer were the same. In this case, he actually wanted the null hypothesis to be true. Fisher developed the F test, which is conceptually similar to the t test. In fact, mathematically, $t^2 = F$.

In our experiment, we can think of the t test or F test, asking the question of what is the difference in reaction time between the experimental and control groups. The larger the difference, the more certain we can be that the IV had an effect. In the end, we are never fully certain that our results are or are not due to chance. Instead, we use statistics to help us to make a best guess by assigning a probability to the statement that our results are not due to chance alone. That is, we may say that results from our study could have happened by chance less than 1 time out of every 100. Said in other words, if we ran the same study 100 times, each with a different set of subjects drawn from the total population, what are the odds we would not obtain the same results?

Confound Hypothesis

The second question asked is whether our results are due to a **confound** rather than the IV. What is a confound? Almost anything can be a confound. A confound is something that systematically biases the results of our research.

It may be the fact that women are more likely to go to their mental health provider than men. Thus, a study that looks at rates of a particular disorder based on provider reports may be biased in terms of a gender difference. Since the amount of sunlight can influence the experience of depression, a confound may be introduced into a depression experiment if one group is studied in the winter when there is less light and another group is studied in the summer when there is more sunshine. A confound may also be introduced when one group is made up of more men than women if the disorder under study shows gender differences. In one treatment study, the control group was instructed by young, inexperienced technicians, whereas the experimental group was instructed by an older, more experienced professional. This difference may have produced a confound in the results.

Some confounds can be prevented or controlled. However, other factors can never be controlled. You cannot control world events, but you can ask whether there is any reason to believe that a particular event that took place inside or outside of the laboratory could have influenced one group more than another and thus introduced a confound.

Research Hypothesis

After ruling out the null hypothesis and the confound hypothesis, we can assume that the results reflect the action of the IV. Our next step is to consider what this means. We begin to generalize from our set of data and consider both the implications of our results for other groups of people and the theoretical implications of the data. Sometimes we are led to new ideas, which in turn generate new research hypotheses, which can be investigated with additional experiments.

Figure 3.6 presents a simplified outline of this procedure, which reflects the evolutionary nature of science. The steps include (1) the development of the hypothesis, (2) the translation of this hypothesis into a research design, (3) the running of the experiment, and (4) the interpretation of the results. You will notice that there is also an arrow from Step 4 back to Step 1. Researchers take the results and interpretations of their studies and create new research studies that refine the previous hypotheses.

In psychological research, we have some powerful techniques to help us achieve this goal. Unlike the detective who must always reconstruct events after the fact, the researcher has the advantage of being able

FIGURE 3.6 ■ Four Major Steps in the Experimentation Process

Experiments begin with a hypothesis. One then designs the experiment. Next, the experiment is performed and the results are interpreted.

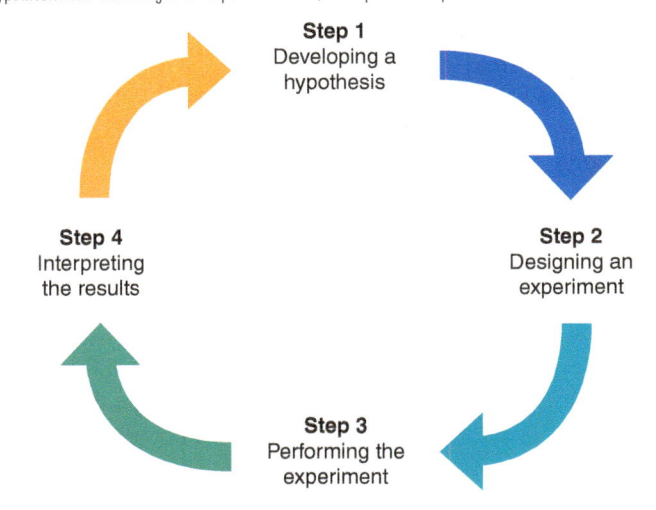

- Step 1: Developing a hypothesis
- Step 2: Designing an experiment
- Step 3: Performing the experiment
- Step 4: Interpreting the results

to create a new situation in which to test ideas, such as the study looking at coffee and memory. This is comparable to a homicide detective's being able to bring a dead man back to life and place him in the presence of each suspect until the murder is reenacted. Such a reenactment might lack suspense and not make it in prime time, but it would increase the certainty of knowing who committed the murder.

Increased certainty is a large part of the experimental process. Scientists increase certainty by creating an artificial situation—the experiment—in which important factors can be controlled and manipulated. Through control and manipulation, participant variables may be examined in detail, and the influence of one variable on another may be determined with certainty. This chapter's *Cultural LENS* describes RCTs, examining treatments for mental illness in low- and middle-income countries.

CULTURAL LENS
RANDOMIZED CONTROLLED TRIALS OF GLOBAL MENTAL HEALTH TREATMENTS IN LOW- AND MIDDLE-INCOME COUNTRIES

There is a large difference in mental health treatment in high-income countries like the United States, England, Germany, France, Japan, and Australia as compared with low- and middle-income countries such as India, Pakistan, China, Chile, Mexico, and many countries in Africa. In high-income countries, there are a larger number of professionals who can deliver mental health services. Treatment procedures such as medications and psychological therapies have also been developed and tested in these higher-income countries. In contrast, there are fewer mental health professionals in low- and middle-income countries. Thus, family members and nonprofessionals are often involved in the treatment of mental disorders. It is critical that low-income countries use treatments that are both effective and available at low costs.

Treatment research suggests that local communities can offer effective treatment for depression and schizophrenia. In low- and middle-income countries, these disorders often go untreated. This *LENS* focuses on depression, although similar positive results have been shown for schizophrenia, particularly in China. Depression is a common disorder throughout the world, so having effective treatments for depression worldwide is critical. Effective treatments are available for depression in terms of both psychotherapy and antidepressant medication. Both of these approaches can be delivered in a relatively inexpensive manner in low-income countries by community members with training in that one procedure. These trained individuals also have the advantage of understanding the culture in which their clients live. Not only does the treatment improve the lives of individuals who have the disorder and their community, but it also has a positive effect on the economy by reducing days lost from work.

A number of researchers have begun to evaluate the treatment of depression in low- and middle-income countries (Dias et al., 2019; Patel et al., 2007). Some examples of this research are shown in Table 3.1. To achieve the greatest scientific benefit, it is important that the participants in

TABLE 3.1 Randomized Controlled Trials for Treatment of Depression in Low-Income and Middle-Income Countries Since 2001

Country	Setting	Study Design	Sample	Intervention	Comparison Group	Main Results
Uganda	Villages	Cluster RCT	248 villagers of both sexes with depression	Group interpersonal psychotherapy	Villages without intervention groups	93.5% recovered with intervention vs. 45.3% in comparison group at the end of treatment, and 88.3% vs. 45.1% at 6 months ($p < 0.001$)
India	General medical outpatients at a district hospital	RCT	450 adults with common mental disorders	Fluoxetine or individual problem-solving treatment	Placebo	70% of antidepressant group recovered at 2 months compared with 54% of placebo group ($p = 0.01$); no difference between psychotherapy and placebo
Chile	Primary care	RCT	240 depressed women living in deprived urban areas	Multi-component stepped-care program including psychoeducational groups for all and antidepressants for more severe only	Usual care	70% recovered with intervention vs. 30% in usual care at 6 months ($p < 0.001$)
Pakistan Karachi	Urban community	RCT	366 lower-middle-class women with depression or anxiety	Eight individual counseling sessions at home by minimally trained counselors	No intervention	Reduction in mean symptom scores ($p < 0.001$) at the end of intervention (8 weeks)
Mexico	Community mental-health centers in Mexico City	RCT	135 female patients with depressive symptoms	Six psycho-educational group sessions	One session of information	Both groups improved but no differences between groups at 4 months and deterioration at 2 years (only 39 women included in final analysis)

RCT = Randomized controlled trial.

Credit: Reprinted from *The Lancet*, Vol. 370, Vikram Patel, Ricardo Araya, Sudipto Chatterjee, Dan Chisholm, Alex Cohen, Mary De Silva, Clemens Hosman, Hugh McGuire, Graciela Rojas, and Mark van Ommeren, "Treatment and prevention of mental disorders in low-income and middle-income countries," pp. 991–1005, Copyright 2007, with permission from Elsevier.

A group therapy session in Mexico.

iStock.com/Marcos Elihu Castillo Ramirez

the experiment be assigned to groups using an RCT design. That is, the participants in the study must be randomly assigned to the treatment group.

Thus, if the person's family and community can be involved in the treatment, the results are more positive. Performing treatment studies in low- and middle-income countries not only benefits the community but also helps the researchers establish the generalizability of the treatment worldwide. Similar research with medical disorders in Africa by the Gates Foundation also suggests that successful interventions developed in low-income countries can be applied to low-income areas of the United States.

Thought Question

What are the challenges and benefits involved in delivering and researching mental health treatment in low- and middle-income countries?

CONCEPT CHECK

- What are four factors critical to enabling sound inference in determining the relation between the IV and the DV in an experiment?
- Why is randomization important to selecting participants and assigning them to groups in an experimental study?
- What is a match subjects design? When would you use this design instead of a randomized study?
- What roles do the following hypotheses play in interpreting experimental results?
- Null hypothesis
- Confound hypothesis
- Research hypothesis

OTHER TYPES OF EXPERIMENTAL DESIGNS AND RESEARCH CONSIDERATIONS

Let's look at a few additional types of research that are used in the study of psychopathology. These include the study of a single person in an experimental manner, research that follows a number of individuals over a period of time, research that seeks to determine how frequently a disorder is present in a population, and research involving genetics. This section will conclude with a discussion of clinical and statistical significance and the importance of replication.

Single-Subject Designs

A single-subject design, also referred to as a small-*N* design, uses the data from one individual participant without averaging it as part of a group of participants. It is assumed that the topic under study is accurately reflected in the single individual and can be controlled appropriately. With this approach, statistical tests are typically replaced with graphical changes. For example, if you wanted to know if a child with autism would respond to a particular type of praise, you could determine this by having a condition in which you give praise and a baseline condition in which you do not. A stronger design, referred to as ABAB, would have a baseline condition (A) followed by the treatment condition (B). This is referred to as a reversal design. Such a design would appear as in Figure 3.7.

Hersen and Bellack (1976) used a multiple-baseline design to demonstrate the effects of a treatment program for a patient with schizophrenia. The patient made little contact with others, rarely engaged in conversation, and was compliant even to unreasonable requests. The treatment consisted of training in the development of assertiveness skills and skills for making contact with others. The measures taken over the baseline and treatment sessions were the amount of eye contact while talking, the amount of speaking without prolonged pauses, the number of requests made of another person, and the number of unreasonable requests not complied with. This design requires that baselines be taken for the four measures and that treatments be introduced at different sessions for each of the behaviors to be changed, while measurements of all behaviors are continued. This type of design helps us to determine whether the treatment was specific to a particular behavior such as eye contact, giving compliments, and so forth (Figure 3.8). Notice that the treatment was introduced at a different time (dotted vertical line) for each of the four targeted behaviors.

Longitudinal Research

A longitudinal design allows the researcher to follow a specific group of individuals across a period of time to document any changes that take place during that period. For example, one study followed children diagnosed with attention deficit/hyperactivity disorder (ADHD) for 9 years and noted

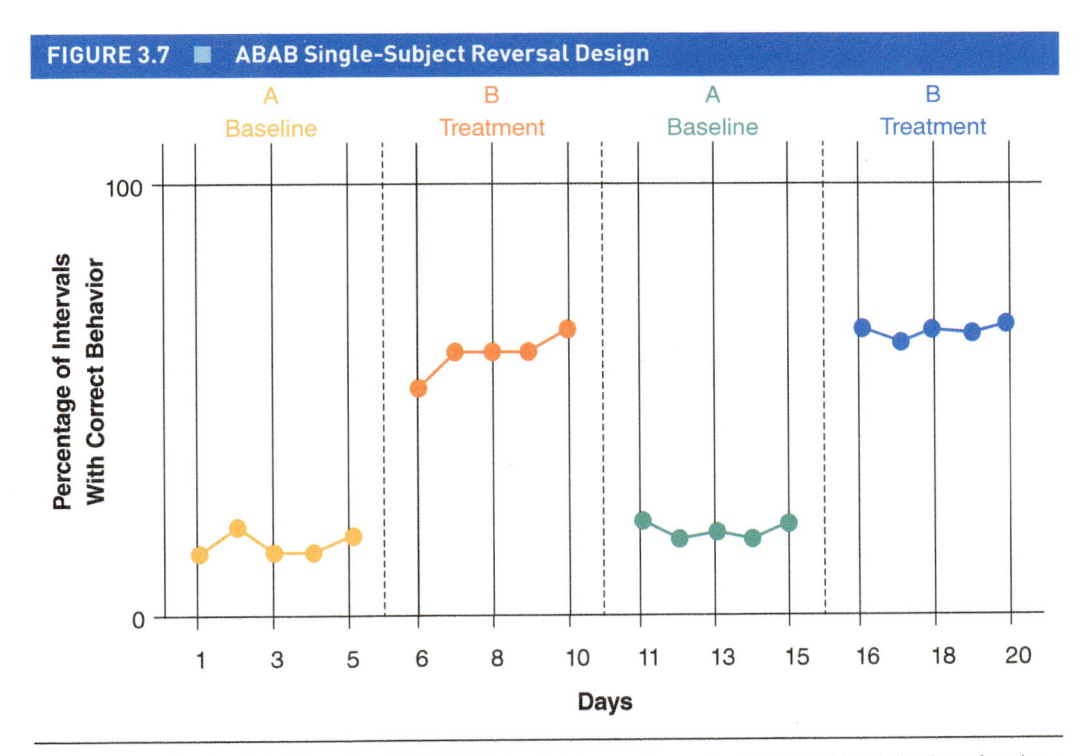

FIGURE 3.7 ABAB Single-Subject Reversal Design

Credit: Dyer, K., Dunlap, G., & Winterling, V. (1990). Effects of choice making on the serious problem behaviors of students with severe handicaps. *Journal of Applied Behavior Analysis, 23*(4), 515–524. https://doi.org/10.1901/jaba.1990.23-515

FIGURE 3.8 ■ Probe Sessions During Baseline, Treatment, and Follow-Ups for Subject 1

Data are presented in blocks of eight scenes. This design requires that baselines be taken for the four measures and that treatments be introduced at different sessions for each of the behaviors to be changed, while measurements of all behaviors are continued.

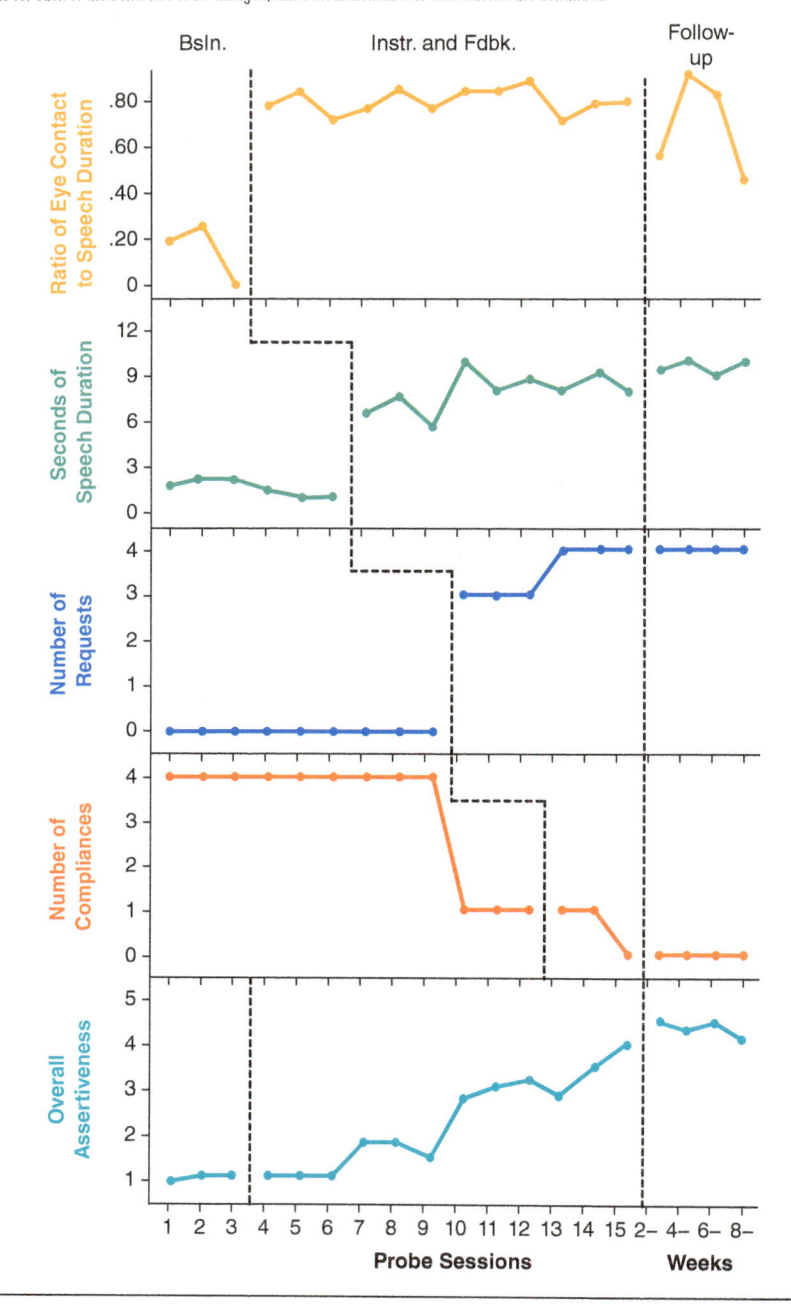

Credit: Hersen, M., & Bellack, A. S. (1976). A multiple-baseline analysis of social-skills training in chronic schizophrenics. *Journal of Applied Behavior Analysis, 9*(3), 239–245. https://doi.org/10.1901/jaba.1976.9-239

changes in specific symptoms (Lahey & Willcutt, 2010). By comparing the children with ADHD to children without the disorder, it was possible to determine normal developmental changes as opposed to changes related to ADHD itself. These researchers were also interested in knowing if ADHD symptoms in Year 1 were predictive of symptoms and teacher ratings in later years, which they were. Another study asked if living in difficult neighborhoods and being maltreated as a child would predict drug use in middle adulthood, which it did (Chauhan & Widom, 2012).

There are a number of advantages to using a longitudinal design. First, it allows us to study the natural history of the development of a mental disorder in one group compared to a similar group without the disorder.

In a longitudinal study on children with ADHD, a researcher may observe the same group of individuals for a period of years in order to detect changes over time.

iStock.com/KatarzynaBialasiewicz

Second, we can note when and in what manner the changes in the disorder take place. Some disorders, such as schizophrenia and bipolar disorder, tend to have an abrupt onset. Third, longitudinal designs are particularly useful for studying prevention or treatment programs regarding longer-term changes. Of course, the disadvantage of these designs is that they require a significant period of time to complete the study.

Epidemiological Research

Epidemiology is the study of the distribution and determinants of the frequency of a disorder in humans (see Tsuang et al., 2011; Olshan et al., 2019, for overviews). Within psychopathology, epidemiological approaches have been used to determine how frequently a particular disorder is present in men or women and if a particular disorder is related to other factors such as income or level of industrialization of a country.

Epidemiological research is particularly helpful in determining the nature, etiology, and prognosis of a given disorder. From this type of research, we know that autism begins early in life and continues throughout one's lifetime. Anxiety disorders, on the other hand, can begin in adolescence, but by early adulthood, a number of individuals who experienced one or more of these in adolescence will no longer experience the disorder. We also know that schizophrenia is seen in similar percentages throughout the world.

There are a variety of measures used in epidemiological research to describe the statistical profile of psychological disorders. One common measure is **prevalence**, which is the proportion of individuals who have a particular disorder at a particular time period. If you go to the National Institute of Mental Health (NIMH) website (see For Further Reading) you can see the prevalence rates for the major disorders from the *Diagnostic and Statistical Manual of Mental Disorders (DSM)*. For example, you will see that the 12-month prevalence for general anxiety disorder (GAD) in adults is 3.1%. What this means is that 3.1% of the U.S. population during a 12-month period had the disorder. Another type of prevalence is referred to as **lifetime prevalence**. This is the percentage of a specific population that had the disorder at some point in their life, even if they no longer show symptoms of the disorder currently. As would be expected, lifetime prevalence is always larger than the number of individuals who have the disorder during a given 12-month period. In the case of GAD, lifetime prevalence is 5.7%. Further types of epidemiology data can include prevalence rates of the disorder in terms of specific factors such as gender, age, or average age at onset of the disorder. These data are shown for GAD in Figure 3.9.

FIGURE 3.9 ■ How Many People in the United States Experience Anxiety?

The graph on the left shows the percentage of the U.S. population that has experienced clinically significant anxiety sometime in their life, those who have experienced it in the last 12 months, and those who have experienced severe anxiety in the last 12 months. The graph on the right shows lifetime prevalence of clinical anxiety in terms of age. These data were published in 2005.

Prevalence

- 12-month Prevalence: 3.1% of U.S. adult population
- Severe: 32.3% of these cases (e.g., 1.0% of U.S. adult population) are classified as "severe"

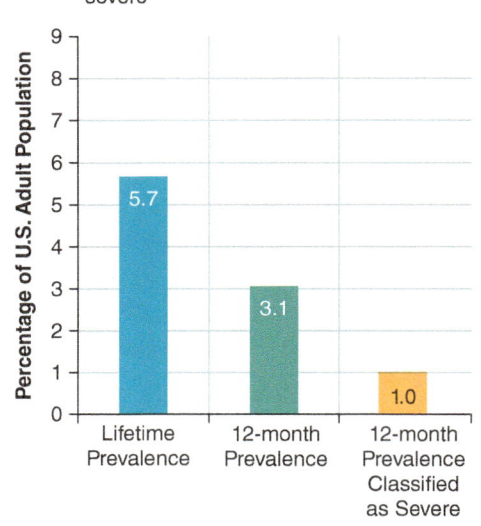

Lifetime Prevalence: 5.7
12-month Prevalence: 3.1
12-month Prevalence Classified as Severe: 1.0

Demographics (for lifetime prevalence)

- Sex: Not Reported
- Race: Not Reported
- Age:

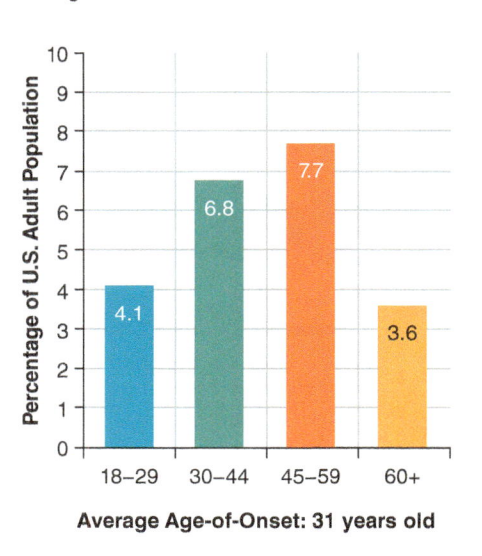

18–29: 4.1
30–44: 6.8
45–59: 7.7
60+: 3.6

Average Age-of-Onset: 31 years old

Credit: National Institute of Mental Health. (2005). Generalized anxiety disorder. U.S. Department of Health and Human Services. http://www.nimh.nih.gov/health/statistics/prevalence/generalized-anxiety-disorder-among-adults.shtml

Epidemiological studies also allow us to look at particular populations. For example, we could ask what percentage of individuals in prison have a mental disorder. These data were collected in 2002 and 2004 and are shown in Figure 3.10. From this graph, it can be seen that there are higher rates of inmates with mental disorders in local as compared with federal prisons. Although not shown in the graph, in the United States, there are now more than 3 times more seriously mentally ill individuals in jails and prisons than in hospitals (Torrey et al., 2010).

Another epidemiological measure is **incidence**, which refers to the number of new cases of a disorder that develop during a certain period of time. Another way of thinking about incidence is to describe it as **risk**. That is, what is the risk of someone in a specific population developing the disorder in a given time period?

Risk is also considered in a statistical manner in terms of correlation or association. For example, you can ask if there is a relationship between environmental variables such as abuse in childhood and development of a particular disorder such as depression. Subject variables such as gender are also used in this way. For example, 1 in 4 females and 1 in 10 males will have depression in their lifetime. Thus, there is a greater risk factor for females as compared with males in terms of developing depression. As with all measures of association, the presence of a relationship does not imply causation.

Research Involving Genetics

Traditional genetics studies have sought to determine which aspects of a person's behavior can be attributed to genetic factors and which can be said to be related to environmental factors. Early research sought to find the single gene or genes involved in psychological disorders such as schizophrenia. However, with continued progress in understanding the approximately 20,000 genes of humans and

FIGURE 3.10 What Percentage of Inmates Have Mental Health Problems?

These epidemiology data show the percentage of inmates with mental health problems in state prisons, federal prisons, and local jails.

Inmates With 12-Month Mental Health Problem

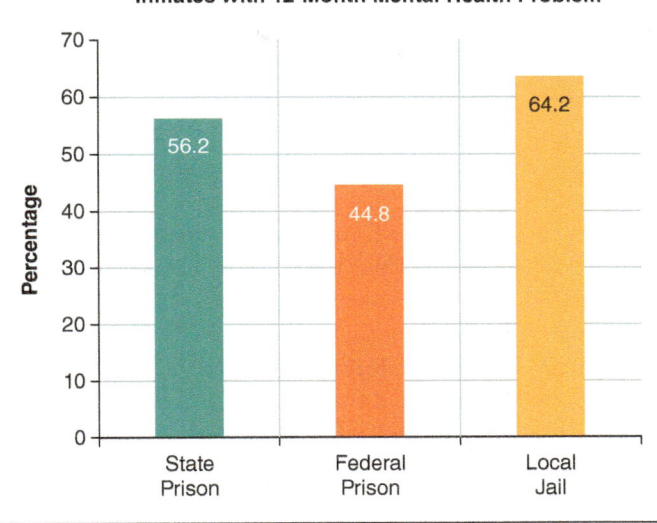

Facility	Percentage
State Prison	56.2
Federal Prison	44.8
Local Jail	64.2

Source: Data from James, D. J., & Glaze, L. E. (2006, September). *Mental health problems of prison and jail inmates* (Report No. NCJ 213600). Bureau of Justice Statistics, U.S. Department of Justice. https://bjs.ojp.gov/content/pub/pdf/mhppji.pdf

the role of epigenetic factors in turning genes on and off, the picture has become much more complicated than previously thought.

This has led scientists to search for endophenotypes (see Chapter 2), which lie between the genotype and the phenotype. For example, when we think about schizophrenia, we most often think in terms of the phenotypes, including hearing voices and having delusions. However, endophenotypes involving cognitive and memory problems are an important part of schizophrenia (Barch & Ceaser, 2012; Donati et al., 2020; Galinska-Skok & Waszkiewicz, 2022) and are found in both individuals with schizophrenia and, often in nonclinical manifestations, their first-degree relatives. Both cognitive and emotional-related endophenotypes are seen in other disorders.

Behavioral Genetics

One type of genetics research involving psychopathology is **behavioral genetics**, which is the study of genetic and environmental contributions to organisms' behavior (see Carey, 2003; DiLalla, 2004; Kendler et al., 2011; Knopik et al., 2017; and Plomin, 2018, for overviews). One large question is the manner in which genes and the environment work together to shape behavior. Researchers use a variety of behavioral genetic approaches to quantify the amount of variance, which can be attributed to genetic and environmental influences.

One traditional distinction has been between *gene by environment interaction* as opposed to *gene by environment correlation* (Plomin et al., 1977; Plomin, 2018). **Gene by environment interactions** refer to the possibility that individuals with different genotypes may respond to the same environment in different ways. For example, some children respond to stress differently from others based on their genotype. As noted, mistreatment as a child influenced some boys differently from others later in adulthood (Caspi et al., 2002). Those boys who were mistreated in childhood and had a particular form of the MAOA gene were more likely to be violent and engage in a variety of antisocial behaviors as adults.

A **gene by environment correlation** concerns how certain genotypes and certain environments occur together. For example, sensation seeking as a personality trait has been shown to be inherited. Those individuals who are sensation seekers are more likely than others to put themselves in high-risk environments such as mountain climbing or auto racing. In this example, it is more difficult to determine the amount of variance attributed to genetic influences and environmental influences as separate factors. Thus, it is possible for genetic and environmental factors to influence each other in subtle ways.

One major paradigm of behavioral genetics involves **twin studies**. Twins offer an occurrence in nature that allows for understanding critical factors related to genetic influences. This is largely based on the fact that there are two types of twins. **Monozygotic (MZ) twins** are identical twins resulting from the zygote (fertilized egg) dividing during the first 2 weeks of gestation. Because they both come from the same egg, their genes are identical. MZ twins help us to understand how an environment can influence how genes function. NASA in 2019 released results of an astronaut who spent a year in space while his twin brother remained on earth (see For Further Reading). Spending time in space changed the way specific genes turned on and off (Garrett-Bakelman et al., 2019). Although the twin who spent time in space retained the basic genetic structure as the one who remained home, about 7% of his genes turned on and off in different ways.

Dizygotic (DZ) twins, on the other hand, arise from the situation in which two different eggs are fertilized by two different spermatozoa. These are called fraternal twins, since they share approximately 50% of their genes—the same as that between any two siblings. DZ twins can be either same sex or opposite sex, whereas MZ twins must always be the same sex. By comparing the psychological traits of MZ and DZ twins, it is possible to obtain an estimate of heritability.

A classic research design is to compare the responses of MZ twins with DZ twins on particular behavioral traits, such as intelligence or personality characteristics. Since it is assumed that both DZ and MZ twins would have similar environmental influences in their family, any differences between MZ and DZ twins would be seen to be the result of genetic influences. For example, Gottesman (1991) has studied schizophrenia with this design. In these studies, a particular MZ twin was more likely (.50) to have schizophrenia if the other twin also did. In DZ twins, this was not the case.

Statistically, researchers examine the degree to which twins are identical to each other as a function of genetic influences and environmental influences. To answer this question, researchers create correlation coefficients for MZ twins and DZ twins. This correlation reflects how similar each type of twin is on a particular trait. From this, it is possible to determine the percentage of contribution to the trait that comes from environmental influences and the percentage of contribution that comes from genetic influences. For example, personality factors such as extraversion have been shown to have a 50% contribution of genetic factors and a 50% contribution of environmental factors.

Another important type of behavioral genetics research is the **adoption study**. This is the situation where DZ and MZ twins have been raised apart. In the United States since 1979, a series of twins who were separated in infancy and reared apart have been studied by researchers at the University of Minnesota (Bouchard et al., 1990).

In work with identical twins, researchers studying over 100 pairs of twins found that about 70% of the variance in IQ could be associated with genetic factors (Bouchard et al., 1990). Later studies have supported the role of genetics in intelligence (Savage et al., 2018). However, if the child's family lived in poverty, the degree of association dropped drastically. Although it is not surprising to find IQ or temperament to have genetic associations, it is intriguing to see that the leisure time interests (e.g., sporting activities, hobbies, reading preferences, etc.) of each twin in the pair were similar whether the twins were reared together or apart.

As noted in Chapter 2, with the reduction in the cost of sequencing a person's full genome, the field has moved to more genome-wide association studies (GWASs) that examine a large number of individuals in terms of genetic processes. In terms of psychopathology, schizophrenia has benefited from this approach (Singh et al., 2022; Trubetskosky et al., 2022). GWASs will be discussed throughout this book.

Clinical and Statistical Significance

When performing research studies, we use inferential statistics to determine whether the IV influences the DV. By using statistics, we ask, if we performed the same experiment 100 times, what is the probability we would obtain the results seen in the present study? Actually, with statistics, the convention is to ask the question in the other direction. That is, how many times would we expect the results *not* to be the same? If the answer is less than 5 in 100 times ($p < .05$), we say that the results of the study are **statistically significant**.

When considering medical or psychological disorders, we also want to know if the results of the study are **clinically significant**. For example, if you did a study related to dieting and everyone in the experimental group lost .5 pounds, while everyone in the control group gained 2 pounds, the results would be statistically significant. However, clinically, you would not recommend a treatment that only resulted in weight loss of half a pound.

Consider a study in which a researcher wants to determine whether exercising will reduce depression. In this study, the experimental group would receive the exercise training for 2 months and the control group would not. Assume that the exercise did indeed reduce the depression score on a particular measure of depression from 21 to 20, whereas the control group's depression did not change. Statistics might show a significant relationship between the two sets of data. However, clinically, it would not be worth the effort of having participants exercise for 2 months to have depression change by only 1 unit. Thus, a distinction is often made in clinical work between results that are statistically significant and those that are also *clinically* significant.

One way to measure the magnitude of effect that a treatment has on the DV is referred to as **effect size**. Effect size measures are important to clinical researchers for two reasons. First, they describe in quantitative terms the influence of the treatment, and second, they aid a researcher in knowing how many participants need to be included in a research study to determine an effect. Effect size is an important measure of the effects of a treatment on a mental disorder. One could compare two different types of psychotherapy, for example, or even a psychotherapy combined with a particular medication.

Replication and Meta-Analysis

Although researchers seek to design studies to rule out alternative hypotheses, they cannot consider every possibility. When a study is performed in different laboratories with different participants, a process referred to as **replication**, we can have more certainty that the results found reflect the true nature of what we are studying (Tackett et al., 2019). Thus, scientists seek to find a number of different studies from different laboratories that answer the same research question. For example, various studies from around the world have shown structural brain differences in individuals with schizophrenia, including enlarged ventricles in the brain (Faludi & Mirnics, 2011). A number of journals, such as *Clinical Psychology Review* and *Psychological Bulletin*, are designed to publish reviews of research in the field.

Once the literature in a particular area has been reviewed, it is possible to examine statistically the results of all the studies taken together. This technique is referred to as **meta-analysis**. Meta-analysis is a statistical technique for combining a number of studies to improve the reliability of the results. For example, a large number of studies have examined depression and how it can be treated with cognitive behavioral therapy (Butler et al., 2006). With a meta-analysis, we could ask: What if we consider all of these studies to be one study? Then we could calculate the common effect size of all of the available studies. A meta-analysis along these lines was performed to examine the effectiveness of psychotherapy in treating depression among youth 13 years after their initial treatment (Eckshtain et al., 2020).

Another recent meta-analysis considered the efficacy of telehealth services. In-person psychotherapy became more difficult once the COVID-19 pandemic began in 2019. Health care professionals began to use teletherapy to offer treatment in a safe manner. However, it was unknown if remote therapy was as effective as in-person treatment. A meta-analysis of randomized clinical trials of teletherapy versus in-person studies was conducted (Lin et al., 2022). This study found no difference in the treatment outcomes of those who were treated via teletherapy versus in-person therapy.

Although the use of meta-analysis is often invaluable, *LENS: Treatment and Clinical Perspectives* points to a potentially complicating factor when undertaking such a review of previously published studies.

LENS

TREATMENT AND CLINICAL PERSPECTIVES: FAILURE TO PUBLISH THE RESULTS OF ALL CLINICAL TRIALS IS HURTING MEDICAL SCIENCE

Imagine that you have just set up a new program for treating an eating disorder. How do you know the new treatment you developed works? The gold standard is to perform a randomized controlled trial involving the treatment. In this case, you would randomly select individuals with a particular eating disorder who would either receive your treatment or an alternative, usually a placebo. Once the study is complete and your treatment works, what do you do next?

If you are like most scientists, you write up the results and publish them. However, if your treatment did not show a significant difference in comparison to the alternative, what do you do then? The ideal response is to publish the results so that the world knows not only what works but also what does not work. However, publication of negative results does not always happen. Sometimes, scientists move on to more productive projects. This failure to publish negative results has come to be called the *file drawer problem*. This phenomenon is a significant complication if you do a literature search. Typically, your literature search shows you the treatment studies in which the treatment made changes in the disorder. However, what you do not see are those studies that did not find a significant change, as they remain unpublished in the researcher's file drawer or computer.

Why would so many studies go unpublished? Researchers, based on their own treatment preferences, might not like the results of a study that didn't verify certain treatment effectiveness. Large drug companies encourage the publication of studies whose results support their own interests. Journals choose to publish articles of research that found positive results. All of these factors contribute to the so-called file drawer problem.

To help deal with this problem, in 2007 the U.S. government passed an amendment to the Food and Drug Administration Act. It requires clinical trials of drugs, medical devices, or biologics to be registered at the website ClinicalTrials.gov. Further, a basic summary of the results is required to be submitted through the website within 1 year following the completion of the data collection. This was considered to be an ethical obligation to human participants to present results in an understandable fashion.

In order to determine the rate of compliance with the law, Monique Anderson and her colleagues (2015) examined 13,327 studies that ended during the period from 2008 to 2012. Of these, over 77%

Why do so many clinical studies go unpublished?
iStock.com/triloks

were drug trials. Of all the trials, only 13.4% reported summary results within 1 year of completing the research. When using a 5-year time frame, 38.9% reported summary results.

A British physician, Ben Goldarce, is part of an international campaign called AllTrials, which seeks to require researchers worldwide to publish their results. He noted that an antidepressant he had prescribed for his patients showed positive results in the published literature. Whereas the published literature showed this antidepressant to be as effective as any other antidepressant drug, *unpublished* data involving 3 times as many people as the published data did not find the same results. A similar situation happened for another type of antidepressant drug, referred to as SSRIs (selective serotonin reuptake inhibitors). Prozac is one example of this class of drugs. Although these were introduced in the 1980s, it was not until 2006 that data submitted to the FDA showed a relationship between the drug and suicidal ideation in adolescents. Further, only 51% of the studies submitted to the FDA showed that use of SSRIs led to a positive result, whereas 94% of *published* studies showed positive results.

Thought Question

What role should the U.S. federal government play in ensuring treatment data from all clinical trials are available to the public?

Source: Adapted from *The Economist.* (2015, July 25). Spilling the beans: Failure to publish the results of all clinical trials is skewing medical science. https://www.economist.com/science-and-technology/2015/07/25/spilling-the-beans

CONCEPT CHECK

- What kinds of research questions could you explore using each of the following research designs? What are the advantages and disadvantages of each?
  - Single-subject design
  - Longitudinal research
  - Epidemiological research
- What is the overall goal of behavioral genetics research? What are the three primary types of research designs used in behavioral genetics research?
- Which is more important, statistical significance or clinical significance? Why?
- If a research study has already been conducted and its results have been communicated, why should it be replicated?

ETHICS AND THE SCIENTIFIC EXPERIMENT

Ethics is the study of proper action. Ethics examines relationships between human beings and provides principles regarding how we should treat each other. The ultimate decision in ethical questions resides in judgments of value. Ethical considerations of psychological experimentation have at their heart the idea that people participating in research should not be harmed (see Ray, 2012). Specifically, at the end of an experiment, participants should not be affected in a way that would result in a lower level of human functioning. This includes emotional distress.

In most cases, the scientist has a question that they want to ask and that the participant is willing to help answer. In some cases, the participants learn something about themselves from the experience and they are glad to have participated. In brain imaging studies, for example, participants often report that they enjoy seeing their brain activity (e.g., functional magnetic resonance imaging [fMRI], electroencephalography [EEG]) displayed. Thus, they are willing to participate in research in exchange for these types of experiences.

If these experiences were always pleasant and any changes in the participant always positive, participants would participate gladly in experiments, and scientists would face few ethical questions. However, at times the scientist may want to answer a question that requires that the participant experience psychological or physiological discomfort. In terms of psychopathology, we need to be especially certain that the individual with a particular disorder understands what is being asked of them and can freely respond. These situations raise a number of questions:

1. What are the responsibilities of the scientist toward the participant?
2. What are the rights of the participant?
3. Are there guidelines for reconciling conflicts between the rights of the participant to pursue happiness and the rights of the scientist to pursue knowledge?
4. What type of relationship or dialogue would be most productive for helping the scientist and participant to fulfill their needs and desires?

Since the 1950s, the American Psychological Association (APA) has published a set of guidelines. This is available online (see For Further Reading). In 1974, the National Research Act was signed into law in the United States. This law sought to protect human research participants. In response to the law, the Department of Health, Education, and Welfare held a conference in 1976 and produced a report. This is referred to as the Belmont Report (see For Further Reading). The Belmont Report identifies three basic ethical principles—respect for persons, beneficence, and justice.

1. *Respect for persons* includes the idea that people can choose on their own whether to participate. Further, people with diminished autonomy are entitled to protection. This suggests that all individuals with mental disorders must be protected in research. An important consideration is to determine if individuals can speak for themselves and are able to agree to be part of an experiment.
2. *Beneficence* is to be understood as meaning that researchers should do no harm as well as maximize possible benefits and minimize potential negative experiences.
3. The third ethical principle of *justice* is a statement that research participation should be available to all people and not just to special classes or groups. This principle is operative in at least two different ways: first, that researchers use more than an easily accessible or compromised sample such as people in a mental hospital and second, that groups of individuals not be excluded. For example, during the mid-20th century, little was known about the manner in which different types of treatments for mental disorders were influenced by cultural factors. Part of the problem was that individuals from some ethnic origins were not recruited into research studies. Another problem was that clinicians tended not to offer Black Americans the same choice of treatment alternatives offered to white Americans.

The Experiment as an Ethical Problem

Let's begin with an extreme case of conflictual experimentation: the Nazi medical experiments during World War II. In several concentration camps, such as Ravensbrück, Dachau, and Buchenwald, prisoners were injected with a virus or bacterium and then received drugs to determine the drugs' effectiveness against the injections. Although medical knowledge was gained from these experiments, the world judged the experiments to be unethical and criminal.

During the trials of the Nazi scientist-physicians held in Nuremberg, Germany, it was determined that they were guilty of war crimes. Seven of them were later hanged, and eight received long prison sentences. As a result of these trials, a code of ethics for medical experimentation with human participants (called the Nuremberg Code) was adopted as a guideline for future research. What was unethical about the experiments at the Nazi concentration camps was not that human beings were given a virus. Almost all of our current procedures of preventive medicine (the polio vaccine as a historical example) required that the procedure be tested on human beings. What was deemed unethical was that these Nazi physicians had conducted experiments *without the consent of their participants.*

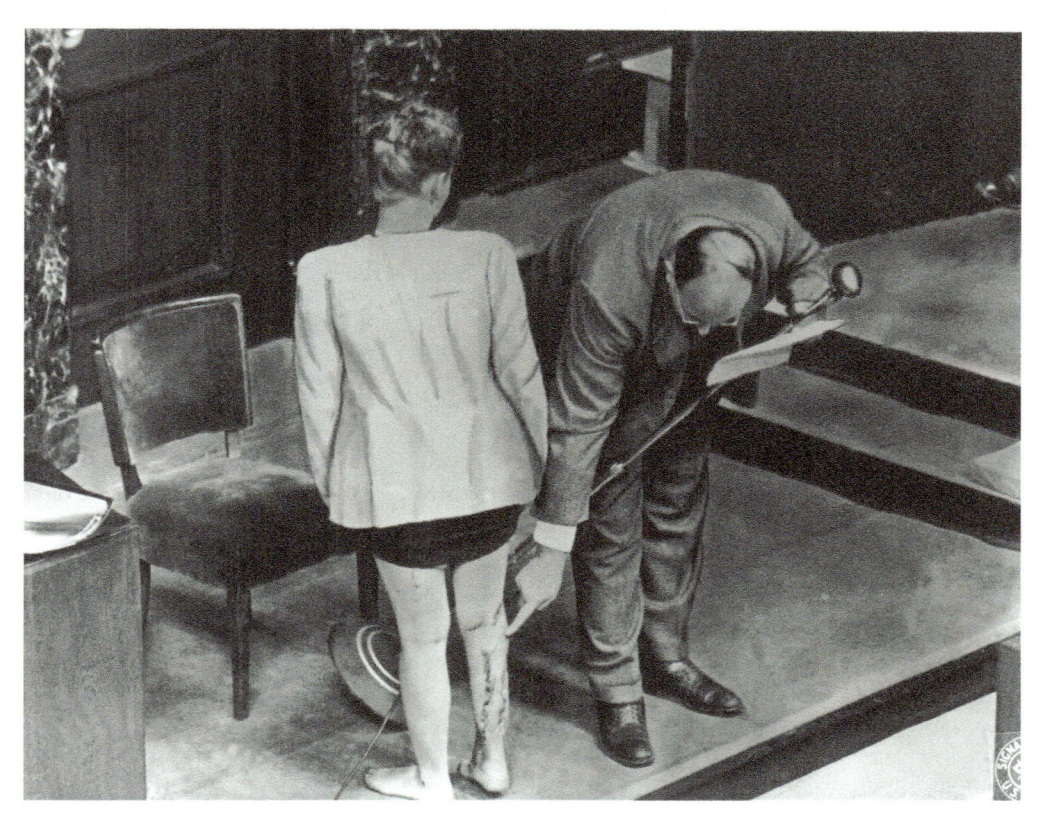

A Polish survivor displays scars she endured at a concentration camp during World War II. After the war, the Nuremberg trials focused on how the German Nazi government treated people under their control, including subjecting thousands of prisoners to medical experiments. These trials helped establish ethical considerations in research.

dpa picture alliance/Alamy Stock Photo

Ingredients of the Initial Scientist–Participant Dialogue

One of the first principles of research is that the participants must consent to being part of an experiment. Furthermore, they must also be informed of the experiment's purpose and its potential risks. Thus, major ingredients in the dialogue between the scientist and the research participant are voluntary participation and informed consent.

Voluntary Participation

In the initial dialogue between the scientist and the prospective participant, the scientist must ask the participant to be a part of the experiment. This is the principle of **voluntary participation**. In essence, the voluntary participation principle requires that a person should participate in an experiment only by free choice. In addition, this principle states that a participant should be free to leave an experiment at any time, whether or not the experiment has been completed.

As you think about voluntary participation, you will become entangled in the question of whether anyone can ever make a free decision and, if so, under what circumstances. As you might have realized already, this question becomes even more complicated for someone interested in developmental psychology, which requires research with children, or for someone interested in psychopathology, which requires research with clients or patients who are mentally impaired. In terms of ethical concerns involving research with children, a number of recommendations have been put forward by the National Academies of Sciences, including how to obtain informed consent and ensure voluntary participation in research (Field & Behrman, 2004).

Informed Consent

Assuming for a moment that someone can agree freely to participate in research, the scientist in the initial dialogue should inform the prospective participant about what will be required of them during the study. The scientist must also inform the prospective participant about any potential harm that may come from participation. Thus, the prospective participant must be given complete information on which to base a decision. This is the principle of **informed consent**. As you can imagine, the principle of informed consent raises the issue of how much information about an experiment is enough, and that is sometimes a gray area.

From the principles of voluntary participation and informed consent, one can see that it is the initial task of the scientist to fully discuss the experimental procedure with prospective participants and to remind them that they are human beings who do not give away their rights just because they are taking part in a psychological experiment.

The Rights of the Research Participant and the Responsibilities of the Experimenter

In our society, research participants have the same rights during an experiment that they have outside the experimental situation. One major one is the **right to privacy**. Most of us at first think of the right to privacy as the right to spend time by oneself or with others of one's choosing, without being disturbed. This is the external manifestation of the right to privacy. But there is also an internal or intrapersonal manifestation of this right (Raebhausen & Brim, 1967). This is the right to have private thoughts or, as it is sometimes called, a **private personality**. This means that the thoughts and feelings of a participant should not be made public without the participant's consent. It also means that a conversation between a participant and a scientist should be considered a private event, not a public one. This is an important consideration when studying those with mental disorders, as private events are often the focus of the research.

Given the research participant's right to privacy and a private personality, you may wonder how the scientist can ever report their findings. There are two considerations that are part of the scientist's responsibility to the participant: *confidentiality* and *anonymity*.

The principle of **confidentiality (for research participants)** requires that the scientist not release data of a personal nature to other scientists or groups without the participant's consent. Even during the experiment, researchers keep any personal data in a secure location and often destroy personal information once the experiment is completed.

The principle of **anonymity** requires that the personal identity of a given participant be kept separate from their data. The easiest way to accomplish this is to avoid requesting names in the first place; however, there are times when this may be impossible. Another alternative is to use code numbers that protect the identities of the participants and to destroy the list of participants' names once the data analysis has been completed.

What Is Harmful to a Research Participant?

As stated earlier, it is the right of a research participant not to be harmed. In most psychological research, physical pain and harm present no problems, either because they are absent completely or because the participant is fully informed of the particular procedure that will be used, such as making a loud noise or placing the participant's hand in cold water to measure physiological responsiveness.

However, the question of psychological harm presents a much larger issue—one that will continue to be debated for years to come. This may be especially true when working with those with a psychopathology. Is it harmful to show participants something true but negative about themselves? Is it harmful to create situations in which participants feel negative emotions such as fear or anger? Is it harmful to make participants feel like failures in order to determine how this affects their performance? These are the types of questions that are being debated currently.

As a scientist, where do you go for help? There are two major sources: the APA's guidelines on ethics and the institutional review board, also known as the human subjects committee or office of research compliance, at the institution where you study or work. In addition, many specialty organizations have adopted guidelines for specific populations. For example, the Society for Research in Child Development has established ethical standards for research with children.

The Institutional Review Board

The U.S. Department of Health and Human Services requires that each scientist whose institution receives federal funds must seek a review of the ethical considerations of research with human participants, whether or not there is a deviation from the APA guidelines. Known as an **institutional review board (IRB)**, this type of review committee is required to judge the appropriateness not only of proposed psychological research but also of any type of research with human participants. The committee that reviews the research is to be made up of people who work at the same university, hospital, school, or other institution as the scientist and to also include members of the community where the institution is located.

The main task of the IRB is to determine whether the participants are adequately protected in terms of both welfare and rights. One major question that the committee asks is the following: Are there any risks—physical, psychological, or social—associated with participating in a given piece of research? Almost everything we do each day involves varying degrees of risk, so the committee attempts to determine when a risk is unreasonable.

The committee also considers the potential long-term effects of a particular treatment on a person. For example, asking a participant to run a mile, to give a small sample of blood, to have their heart rate measured, or to discuss their sexual behavior or childhood involves some risks in the way the term is used by most internal review committees. However, the IRB may decide that, in light of the information that would be gained, these risks are not sufficient to prevent the study from being performed. Thus, a second major question that a review committee asks is the following: Are the risks to the participants outweighed by the potential benefits to them or by the estimated importance to society of the knowledge to be gained? If the committee determines that the answer to this question is yes, a third question is asked: Has the experimenter allowed the prospective participants to determine freely whether they will participate in the experiment? Finally, the committee asks the following: Will the experimenter obtain the participants' informed consent?

The Ethical Relationship

As we conclude these considerations, let's remind ourselves that ethical questions have at their base issues of relationships and traditions. As scientists, we ask what *is* and what *ought to be* our relationship with our participants and our society with regard to research. To answer these questions, we stress that part of our ethical responsibility is to consult with others about our research. In this context, we described the manner in which internal review committees evaluate the ethics of research and the

Institutional review boards review the ethical considerations of research with human participants.
iStock.com/kali9

> **CONCEPT CHECK**
>
> - "Ethical considerations of psychological experimentation have at their heart the idea that people participating in research should not be harmed." What four questions does every scientist need to consider in designing a research study?
> - Which four sources of ethical and legal guidelines help the scientist in designing and conducting psychopathology research?
> - What do *voluntary participation* and *informed consent* mean in the context of scientific research? What are some of the specific issues they raise in terms of psychopathology research?
> - How do confidentiality and anonymity figure into the experimenter's responsibility to protect the research participant's right to privacy?
> - What are the questions an IRB asks in regard to the risks of a psychopathology research study?

SUMMARY

In general, there is no single scientific method, yet there is a general process called science. This process consists of experiencing the world and then drawing general conclusions (called *facts*) from observations. In science, we use doubt to question our ideas and our research and ask whether factors other than the ones that we originally considered might have influenced our results. By doing this, we come to see that science is a combination of interaction with the world and logic. There are three stages to the scientific method: (1) Develop an idea or expectation (hypothesis), (2) evaluate the ideas and expectations about the world through observation and experimentation, and (3) draw conclusions or inferences about the ideas and expectations and consider the impact of the new information on theoretical conceptualizations.

There are many research designs, and determining which one to select begins with the question the scientist wants to answer. Some of the research designs used to study psychopathology include case study, naturalistic observation, correlational approaches, experimental method, single-subject design, longitudinal research, epidemiological research, and behavioral genetics designs. Logic can help us answer questions of inference, which is the process by which we look at the evidence available to us and then use our powers of reasoning to reach a conclusion. Logical procedures are also important for helping us understand the accuracy or validity of our ideas and research.

Increased certainty is a large part of the experimental process. Scientists increase certainty by creating an artificial situation—the experiment—in which important factors can be controlled and manipulated. Through control and manipulation, participant variables may be examined in detail, and the influence of one variable on another may be determined with certainty. There are four steps to the experimental process, which reflect the evolutionary nature of science: (1) the development of the hypothesis, (2) the translation of this hypothesis into a research design, (3) the running of the experiment, and (4) the interpretation of the results. Researchers take the results and interpretations of their studies and create new research studies that refine the previous hypotheses, and the cycle begins anew.

One goal of experimental research is to determine the relation between the IV and the DV. It is the task of the experiment to reduce extraneous factors not related to the IV that can influence the DV. Additional factors critical to sound inference are participant selection and assignment, the design of the experiment, and the interpretation of the relationship of the IV to the DV. The experimenter considers three hypotheses in interpreting whether the DV is related to the IV: the null hypothesis, confound hypothesis, and research hypothesis. Both statistical significance and clinical significance are important in interpreting research results. Replication of studies in different locations with different participants increases the certainty that the results found reflect the true nature of what is being studied. Meta-analysis is a statistical technique for combining a number of studies to improve the reliability of the results. Of course, if the data from relevant studies have not been published—the so-called "file drawer problem"—the meta-analysis would be biased.

Ethical considerations of psychological experimentation have at their heart the idea that people participating in research should not be harmed. In addition, research participants have a right to privacy, including the right to a private personality. To protect those rights, participants must be informed of the experiment's purpose and its potential risks (informed consent) and then voluntarily agree to participate in the experiment (voluntary participation). Confidentiality and anonymity are two additional considerations that are part of the scientist's responsibility to the participant. Guidelines for reconciling conflicts between the rights of the participant to pursue happiness and the rights of the scientist to pursue knowledge are provided by such resources as the APA, the U.S. National Research Act, the Belmont Report, and IRBs.

STUDY RESOURCES

Review Questions

1. What does the author mean by "science is a combination of interaction with the world and logic"? What key role does doubt play in the process of science?

2. Why can't you design "the one perfect study"? What trade-offs do you need to consider in designing an experimental study in the real world? What can you do to improve the quality of your study?

3. Your research group has been asked by the World Health Organization (WHO) to develop a research program to study anxiety in children around the world using multiple research methodologies. Taking into consideration the characteristics of each of the following methods, what is a research question you could study using each approach?
   - Case study
   - Naturalistic observation
   - Correlational approach
   - Experimental approach
   - Single-subject design
   - Longitudinal research
   - Epidemiological research
   - Twin study

4. How is a scientist conducting psychopathology research like a detective solving a mystery? How are they different?

5. If we think about psychopathology research as an ethical problem, what are the rights of the research participant, and what are the responsibilities of the experimenter in ensuring the protection of those rights? What legal and ethical resources are available to guide this effort?

For Further Reading

American Psychological Association. (2023, April). *APA ethics office*. https://www.apa.org/ethics/

Kandel, E. (2006). *In search of memory: The emergence of a new science of mind*. Norton.

Kuhn, T. (1970). *The structure of scientific revolutions* (2nd ed.). University of Chicago Press.

National Aeronautics and Space Administration. (2021, March 22). *Human research program*,

National Institute of Mental Health. (n.d.). *Statistics*. U.S. Department of Health and Human Services. https://www.nimh.nih.gov/health/statistics

Sacks, O. (1985). *The man who mistook his wife for a hat and other clinical tales.* Summit Books.

Thomas, L. (1979). *The Medusa and the snail: More notes of a biology watcher.* Viking.

Office for Human Research Protections. (2022, October 17). *The Belmont Report.* U.S. Department of Health and Human Services. https://www.hhs.gov/ohrp/regulations-and-policy/belmont-report/index.html

KEY TERMS

adoption study
anonymity
behavioral genetics
blind controls
case study
clinically significant
confidentiality (for research participants)
confound
confound hypothesis
confounding variables
control group
correlation coefficient
correlational approach
covary
demand characteristics
dependent variable (DV)
dizygotic (DZ) twins
double-blind experiment
doubt
effect size
empiricism
epidemiology
ethics
experimenter effects
experimental group
experimental method
external validity
facts
falsification
gene by environment correlations
gene by environment interaction
generalizability
hypothesis
incidence
independent variable (IV)
inference
inferential statistics
informed consent
institutional review board (IRB)
internal validity
lifetime prevalence
longitudinal design
match subjects design
meta-analysis
monozygotic (MZ) twins
naturalistic observation
negative correlation
null hypothesis
operational definition
placebo effect
population
positive correlation
prevalence
private personality
probability
randomization
randomized controlled trial (RCT)
replication
research hypothesis
right to privacy
risk
sample
science
scientific knowledge
single-subject design
statistically significant
twin studies
validity
voluntary participation

iStock.com/Bulat Silvia

4 ASSESSMENT AND CLASSIFICATION OF PSYCHOLOGICAL DISORDERS

LEARNING OBJECTIVES

4.1 Explain what the mental status exam is and how it is used.

4.2 Identify cultural and other considerations used in the assessment of psychological disorders.

4.3 Identify the tests and techniques used in assessing mental illness.

4.4 Discuss diagnostic considerations in approaching psychopathology.

4.5 Explain the significance of the *DSM-5-TR* and RDoC in the classification of mental disorders.

Elyn Saks told of her time as a graduate student at Oxford University after graduating from Vanderbilt University. As a student at Oxford, she began to have a hard time concentrating on academic work and lectures. She turned in papers that her tutor did not understand. A friend of hers who was a nurse asked her fiancé, who was a physician who specialized in neurology, to talk with Elyn. Saks (2007) remembers the conversation as follows:

"Jean and I are very concerned about you," he said quietly. "We think you may be quite sick. Would you mind if I asked you some questions?"

"I'm not sick," I responded. "I'm just not smart enough. But questions, yes. Ask me questions."

"Are you feeling down?"

"Yes."

"Loss of pleasure in daily activities?"

"Yes."

"Difficulty sleeping?"

"Yes."

"Loss of appetite?"

"Yes."

"How much weight have you lost in the last month?"

"About fifteen pounds."

"Do you feel like a bad person?"

"Yes."

"Tell me about it."

"Nothing to tell. I'm just a piece of shit."

Elyn Saks

John D. and Catherine T. MacArthur Foundation, used with permission; licensed under CC BY 4.0 https://creativecommons.org/licenses/by/4.0

"Are you thinking of hurting yourself?"

I waited a moment before answering, "Yes."

After a number of other questions, Saks was referred to a mental health professional to diagnose her distress and formulate a treatment plan. In this chapter, you will be introduced to the ways in which mental health professionals clarify the type of problems a person is describing. This will include methods of assessment that have been developed to maximize reliability and validity. Following will be a discussion of the major classification systems used throughout the world.

INITIAL ASSESSMENT AND THE MENTAL STATUS EXAM

If you are a clinician, people come to see you in a variety of ways. Some people set up an appointment and tell you about how they are feeling distressed. They may tell you about feeling anxious or sad. If you work in a hospital, people may be brought to you by others who are concerned by the behaviors these patients display or the experiences they describe. As a clinician, your job is to make sense of the information you are given. The first task is that of *assessment*.

Psychological assessment is simply the process of gathering information about a person so that you can make a clinical decision about that person's symptoms. In the process, you may create a variety of hypotheses about the possible causes of the symptoms. Had the person taken drugs that were causing the behavior? Did the person suffer a negative experience such as being robbed or raped? Is the behavior part of an underlying physical or mental disorder? Part of the task of the clinical assessment is to gather data necessary to rule out or support the possible causes of the symptoms.

The Clinical Interview

Most mental health professionals use a clinical interview to initially gather information concerning the status of an individual with whom they are working. Since the interview is also an interaction between two people, it is a chance for the professional to establish rapport, which will lead to more complete information. The information gained from this interview includes not only the individual's present symptoms but also the social and cultural context in which these symptoms appear. This context includes the individual's social support, family relationships, and connections within their community. It is also important to assess the individual's attitudes, emotions, and experiences of others in their world. The clinical interview further offers the opportunity to assess the individual's current ability to maintain their own health and well-being.

During the clinical interview, mental health professionals gather information about the status of an individual they are working with.

iStock.com/Kobus Louw. Stock photo. Posed by model.

Overall, the major areas of consideration in a clinical interview are (a) the current areas of distress and their history; (b) any past mental health problems; (c) social history, including social support; (d) the manner in which cultural factors may influence the current condition; and (e5) any way in which previous family, medical, or psychological factors may influence the current situation.

The Mental Status Exam

Throughout the world, the clinical interview has been organized into major categories and is referred to as the **mental status exam**. This exam is often given quickly to gain initial information of both an objective and a subjective nature.

The first major category of the exam is the individual's appearance and behavior. In the report, the mental health professional would note such factors as the individual's clothing, grooming, and posture. Motor activity, such as slow movements, may be part of a later diagnosis of depression, whereas quick, abrupt movements may be associated with mania.

The second major category of the exam is mood and affect. *Affect* refers to the emotions that the individual is expressing during the interview. The person might seem happy or sad. The professional might note that the person laughs or cries in describing situations, where other individuals would not laugh or cry. Such affect would be described as inappropriate. It should also be noted if the individual shows no affect when describing situations where others would be happy or sad, such as receiving a large raise in pay or losing a friend. Such affect is said to be flat. Mood, as compared with present affect, is more long term. To assess this, the professional notes how the individual has been feeling recently. For example, has the individual been feeling blue or angry?

The next category is speech quality. Here, the professional notes the manner in which an individual speaks. Is the person speaking quickly or very slowly? Does the person's manner of speaking feel pressured? Does the person speak very quietly or with great volume? These are the types of speech characteristics the professional can observe and record.

The next major category is thought processes. In describing thought processes, the professional can note if the individual answers the questions that are asked and adds more information when appropriate. On the other hand, some individuals will produce responses that are not related to the question asked or tell a narrative in which each sentence is not related to the one that came before it. This is referred to as a **flight of ideas**. The content of the individual's thought is also important. Is there a theme to the thoughts, such as that the CIA is out to get the individual? This would be referred to as **delusional thinking**. Does the individual keep repeating a certain theme? For example, some individuals express constant concern that they will have a heart attack or that their spouse is cheating on them. This is referred to as **obsessional thinking**. The professional should also take particular note if the person is talking about suicide or homicide. This may require an intervention.

Another major category is perceptions and a general awareness of one's surroundings. Distorted perceptions can include hallucinations, in which the individual perceives experiences without external stimulation. Individuals with a psychotic disorder may hear a radio program talking to them directly or respond to voices in their head. General awareness of one's surroundings includes the question of whether the person knows who and where they are and the present date and time.

The final categories describe intellectual functioning and insight. Intellectual functioning is generally noted in terms of current vocabulary used in the interview as well as previous academic achievement. The professional can also note if the person has an abstract understanding of the information they are reporting. Insight refers to the individual's awareness of their own self and the factors related to their current situation and distress.

STRUCTURED INTERVIEWS AND ASSESSMENT CONSIDERATIONS

A **structured interview** is an evaluation technique that is tightly systematized in terms of the questions asked. The idea is that by asking clients the same set of questions, it is possible to have better consistency across interviewers. Likewise, because every client receives the same questions, it is assumed that there will be more consistency across clients.

Structured Clinical Interview for *DSM* Disorders

The current classification manual used by most clinicians in North America is the *Diagnostic and Statistical Manual of Mental Disorders* (5th ed., text rev.; *DSM-5-TR*) (American Psychiatric Association [APA], 2022). The *DSM* will be discussed in some detail later in this chapter. Based on the *DSM-5-TR*, with its specific criteria for each category of psychological disorder, it is possible to ask questions in an interview that directly probe for the existence of these criteria. The **Structured Clinical Interview for *DSM* Disorders (SCID)** sets forth these questions along with a decision tree for directing follow-up questions. For example, if you want to determine if a person displays an obsessive–compulsive disorder, you would begin with a general question concerning whether the individual experiences thoughts that keep recurring. If the person says yes, you would then ask what those thoughts were. The decision tree would help you to determine if the individual conceived of these thoughts as something produced in their own mind or imposed on the person by an outside agent. Thoughts experienced as not from oneself would be more characteristic of a psychotic disorder, whereas those recognized as coming from one's own mind might indicate a possible obsessive–compulsive disorder. Individuals with anxiety may also experience worries as thoughts coming into their mind, and the SCID would help to determine whether the person experiences obsessive–compulsive disorder or anxiety. The next set of questions would help the professional determine whether compulsions were also present. The SCID would instruct the interviewer to ask if there is anything the person has to do over and over again, such as constant hand washing or checking a door lock several times.

Assessing Cultural Dimensions

Over the past 40 years, mental health professionals have become increasingly aware that mental illness takes place within the context of a particular culture (Henderson et al., 2016; Marsella & Yamada, 2007). Initially, there was a realization that specific disorders, such as depression, schizophrenia, and stress-related disorders, are understood differently in different cultures (Draguns, 1973; Draguns & Tanaka-Matsumi, 2003). That is to say, a fuller understanding of mental illness requires an understanding of cultural context. Although every culture has words for severe mental illness (e.g., psychosis) and mood disorders (e.g., depression and anxiety), cultures vary in what they commonly consider normal and deviant. *Cultural LENS: Empirically Supported Research Approaches and Cultural Competence* notes that culture not only informs how individuals view their own distress but also influences how that distress is expressed.

With *DSM-5*, a **Cultural Formulation Interview (CFI)** has been developed to help mental health professionals obtain information concerning the person's culture. (This has been updated in *DSM-5-TR*.) In general, the CFI focuses on five domains:

Cultural identity of the individual—This domain in *DSM-5-TR* describes how the individual sees themself in terms of ethnic, racial, or cultural identity. It can also include how connected the person is with their culture of origin. For migrants, this includes the individual's connections to both their place of origin and their new home.

Cultural conceptualizations of distress—This domain refers to how the person's culture would influence their experience of the disorder. For example, different types of symptoms might be more acceptable in one culture than another. Also, some individuals may be less willing to seek help and unwilling to describe the experiences they are having in certain aspects of their lives.

Psychosocial stressors and cultural features of vulnerability—Psychological concerns, as noted in *Cultural LENS: Empirically Supported Research Approaches and Cultural Competence*, vary by culture. Likewise, the amount of support offered by the family and community also vary. In conducting an interview, the mental health professional needs to obtain an overall picture of the individual's social environment, including religion, family, and social networks. An emphasis on how cultural elements affect the presentation of a particular distress or disorder must be considered.

Cultural features of the relationship between the individual and the clinician—This domain emphasizes how the relationship between an individual and a mental health professional can be influenced by cultural factors. If a person has experienced negative situations with authority figures in the world outside of the interview, this could influence how the person relates to the mental health professional. Likewise, if the culture places a high regard on health professionals, then the person may not correct or interrupt with additional information during the interview. This domain would also include how the person expects to be treated by the mental health professional and expectations for future treatment.

Overall cultural assessment—This domain represents an overall assessment and implications of what was identified in the previous domains. Treatment preferences can be described that may be incorporated into the treatment plan.

Understanding the cultural context of a disorder helps increase the validity of the assessment and diagnosis procedure. The CFI asks 16 questions related to culture indirectly. For example, the mental health professional would ask the person how their family, friends, or community view what is causing the problems. In this manner, people can describe their understanding of their problems with a direct or indirect reference to their culture.

CULTURAL LENS
EMPIRICALLY SUPPORTED RESEARCH APPROACHES AND CULTURAL COMPETENCE

Beginning in the 1950s and 1960s, there was a movement among researchers and clinicians to evaluate the effectiveness of both medical and psychological assessment and treatment in a scientific manner. In medicine, this came to be known as *evidence-based medicine*. In psychology, the terms *empirically based treatments* and *empirically based principles* refer to assessment and treatments and their aspects for which there is scientific evidence that the procedure is effective.

There is a movement in the training of mental health professionals to emphasize cultural competence.
iStock.com/fstop123

Recently, a movement in the training of mental health professionals has begun to emphasize *cultural competence* (Good & Hannah, 2015). In this approach, the focus of interventions begins with the person who is being served. That is, a clinician should consider and understand the worldview of the individual being treated. This includes the client's willingness to describe internal thoughts and feelings, the client's understanding of how a particular disorder affects them, what the client expects from treatment, as well as the client's relationships with significant others. For example, in one study, Latinos with depression were less likely to take antidepressants since they had cultural concerns about addiction or dependence (Vargas et al., 2015).

The existence of these two movements has led to a debate concerning the degree to which a particular psychological disorder should be considered from a more universal standpoint (represented by empirically based principles) as opposed to a manifestation of cultural processes (represented by cultural competence). This debate is of particular concern in countries such as the United States, where immigration from different cultures has led to an increasingly diverse population. At the same time, increasing numbers of women and individuals from a variety of cultures becoming mental health professionals have led to significant changes in the diversity of those offering health and mental health services.

Some researchers see a dynamic tension between cultural considerations, with an emphasis on the individual client and their way of expressing and experiencing mental illness, and empirically based principles that emphasize treating all clients in a consistent manner (Good & Hannah, 2015). That is, there is a tension between flexibility and consistency. Other researchers suggest this dynamic tension can be overcome by beginning with particular cultural groups and developing an intervention based on the cultural factors found in that particular group (Weisner & Hay, 2015).

One alternative is to classify treatments in terms of culture (Evans & Jackson, 2009). *Transcultural* concepts and treatments would be appropriate to individuals in all cultures. *Multicultural* concepts and treatments would be appropriate for individuals from groups that have similar worldviews, practices, and traditions. *Culturally adapted* and *culture-specific* concepts and treatments would be designed for individuals from a specific group. At this point, however, there has been limited research that fully integrates cultural factors with empirically supported approaches to treatment (Helms, 2015; Jackson, 2015).

Thought Question

What are some particular benefits that each of these two approaches—empirically based principles and cultural competence—bring to psychological treatment? If you were a mental health professional, how would you bring the benefits of the two approaches to your clients?

Reliability and Validity in Relation to Psychopathology

Concerns about the accuracy of assessment and classification of psychopathology require us to consider two very different questions. The first has to do with the person who is being interviewed. We need to know if the person is giving us accurate information. Sometimes, individuals will "fake bad" if there is some advantage, such as receiving a larger disability payout. Other times, individuals will "fake good" and deny there are any problems.

The second question is which assessment instruments to use. An assessment instrument can be an interview, an inventory, a mood scale, or other type. In considering instruments, we think about measurement. Measurement considerations help to define the variety of instruments that we use and the theoretical variables that these reflect.

Traditionally, the two key measurement issues are *reliability* and *validity*. That is, does an instrument measure the construct consistently (reliability) and accurately (validity)? The measurement of temperature, for example, is based on the kinetic theory of heat, which helped define the type of devices used. With psychopathology, however, we lack formal definitions that tell us exactly how to make measurements. In fact, we are both trying to learn about disorders and creating techniques for making diagnoses. This makes reliability and validity considerations both more difficult and more important.

Reliability

Reliability asks the question of whether the instrument is consistent. We would expect, for example, that the odometer in our car would reflect that we drove a mile each time we drove 5,280 feet. We would also expect our bathroom scale to show the same reading each time we step on it if our weight had not changed. Researchers interested in questions of measurement discuss a number of types of reliability:

Internal reliability—Internal reliability assesses whether different questions on an instrument relate to one another. If we were seeking a general measure of depression, for example, we would want to use questions that relate to one another. Questions related to feeling sad, not having energy, and wanting to stay in bed would be expected to show internal reliability.

Test–retest reliability—Test–retest reliability determines whether two measurement opportunities result in similar scores. A key consideration with test–retest reliability is the nature of the underlying construct. Constructs seen as stable, such as intelligence or hypnotizability, would be expected to show similar scores if the same instrument was given on more than one occasion. In psychopathological research, measures of long-term depression or trait anxiety would be expected to show a higher index of test–retest reliability than measures that reflect momentary feelings of mood.

Alternate-form reliability—As the name implies, alternate-form reliability asks whether different forms of an instrument give similar results. If you were giving an IQ test, for example, you would not want to ask the same questions each time, since the individual could learn the answers from taking the test. Thus, it would be important to create alternate forms that reflect the same underlying construct.

Inter-rater reliability—Inter-rater reliability asks how similar two or more individuals are when they observe and rate specific behaviors. Psychopathology researchers often rate the emotional responses of children as they engage in various activities. An index of inter-rater reliability would measure how consistent different observers are in rating the same situation. Historically, one of the motivating factors for developing the *DSM* classification system was the discovery that different clinicians in different locations watched a film of a person with a mental health disorder and diagnosed it in different ways.

We expect our bathroom scale to show the same reading if our weight has not changed. Likewise, researchers are concerned with the reliability, or consistency of measurement, of assessment instruments.
iStock.com/tetmc

Assessment Validity

Validity, as described in Chapter 3, asks whether the instrument we are using is accurate. A clock, for example, could be reliable if it was always 5 minutes fast, but it would not be accurate. Unlike time, for which there is a definition in terms of atomic clocks, psychopathological disorders lack exact unchanging definitions. Although measures such as neuropsychological tests, brain images, and molecular and genetic changes suggest possible variables to be considered, there is currently no exact measure by which to diagnose psychopathology. This makes validity an important but complex concept. Partly for this reason, we consider a number of types of validity.

Content validity—the degree to which an instrument measures all aspects of the phenomenon. If a final exam only had questions from 1 week of the course, it would not be representative of what the students had learned. A variety of psychopathological disorders, such as depression, for example, have cognitive, emotional, and motor components. A measure that just asks if a person felt negative about the future would be seen as a less useful measure of depression than one that also asks about feeling sad and thoughts about suicide and self-worth.

Predictive validity—the degree to which an instrument can predict cognitions, emotions, or actions that a person will experience in the future. If an IQ test in high school predicted college performance, then it would be seen to have predictive validity. Many medical tests such as cholesterol measurements are designed to predict who is at risk for later medical conditions such as cardiovascular problems.

Concurrent validity—the ability of an instrument to show similar results to other established measures of the construct.

Construct validity—the extent that an instrument measures what it was designed to measure (Cronbach & Meehl, 1955). If a test was designed to measure what students learned in a course, then it would be a problem if the test was also sensitive to other factors such as intelligence or the ability to understand test questions asked in terms of double negatives.

Ecological validity—the manner in which data collected have been considered beyond the local context. For example, considering which cultural factors could be influencing the information obtained would improve the ecological validity of the data. This would also hold true in research studies involving mental illness in different cultures. That is, the meaning of a concept in one culture may be different from that in another.

CONCEPT CHECK

- What are five critical areas mental health professionals cover in an initial clinical interview?
- Why is it important for mental health professionals to understand the cultural context of an individual's mental disorder? What kinds of information does the CFI help mental health professionals obtain?
- In terms of assessment, what are four types of reliability you should be concerned with, and why?
- In terms of assessment, what are five types of validity you should be concerned with, and why?

MODELS OF ASSESSMENT

This section considers different ways of assessing signs and symbols. These range from simply asking a person about their symptoms to comparing the person to others who have a similar disorder. Specifically, symptom and mood subtests such as the Beck Depression Inventory, personality inventories that are based on psychometric formulations such as the Minnesota Multiphasic Personality Inventory, projective techniques such as the Rorschach inkblot test and the Thematic Apperception

Test, neuropsychological approaches such as intelligence tests, and neuroscience approaches demonstrate the variety of assessment measures.

Symptom Questionnaires

At times, it is important to know what a person's symptoms are and how that person may compare with others in terms of reporting these symptoms. A variety of questionnaires have been developed that focus on particular sets of symptoms such as those associated with pain, sleep disorders, anxiety, and depression.

The Beck Depression Inventory (BDI) has been used in both clinical and research settings to assess symptoms associated with the experience of depression (Beck & Beck, 1972). The BDI has 21 items, each of which is presented in a four-choice format where the individual is asked to indicate which choice best fits their current experience. Here is an example:

I am not particularly discouraged about the future.

I feel discouraged about the future.

I feel I have nothing to look forward to.

I feel the future is hopeless and that things cannot improve.

A questionnaire such as the BDI is useful for determining the level of depressive symptoms that a person is reporting. Given that the measure has been in use for more than 40 years, there is considerable clinical and research data available in terms of level of depressive severity. The measure is also useful for noting changes in depression level during various types of treatment. During psychotherapy, for example, the measure could be given weekly to document changes in depressive experiences. A newer version of the scale (BDI-II) was developed in 1996 in response to the publication of *DSM-IV*, which changed a number of the diagnostic criteria for depression.

Personality Tests

For at least the past 2,000 years, there has been an understanding that individuals have particular styles for relating to the world and others. At the beginning of the 20th century, the personality styles of introversion and extraversion were studied. There was also an effort to examine the relationship between personality styles and psychopathology. A number of questionnaires have been developed to this end. One of the best known of these questionnaires is the Minnesota Multiphasic Personality Inventory (MMPI).

Minnesota Multiphasic Personality Inventory (MMPI)

The Minnesota Multiphasic Personality Inventory (MMPI) is an assessment measurement of personality traits that is composed of items of a true–false nature. The person taking the test simply indicates yes or no to statements such as "I have trouble falling asleep." The test was developed in an interesting manner. The authors, S. R. Hathaway and J. C. McKinley, began with a large pool of items and then reduced these to 504 items that were determined to be independent of one another. They then gave these items to psychiatric inpatients at the University of Minnesota Hospital. These inpatients were further divided by diagnosis, and the responses of each group were compared with non-patients who had come to the hospital as visitors or relatives. The idea was to develop a scoring scheme that would differentiate those with mental disorders from those without. In this sense, the content of the item was less important than its ability to discriminate between those individuals with a specific disorder and those without the disorder, as well as between disorders.

The clinical scales in the original MMPI used the following categories:

- *Hypochondriasis (Hs)*—Individuals who endorse these items show an excessive concern with bodily symptoms.

- *Depression (D)*—Individuals who endorse these items display characteristics of depression, such as trouble sleeping, loss of appetite, feeling sad, suicidal thoughts, and loss of interest in positive events.

- *Hysteria (Hy)*—Individuals who endorse these items tend to view and experience the world in an emotional manner. They may overdramatize their situation. They may also experience emotional difficulties through bodily symptoms such as headaches or upset stomach when in a difficult psychological situation.

- *Psychopathic deviate (Pd)*—Individuals who endorse these items display antisocial tendencies and experience conflicts with their environment. They may also exploit others without remorse.

- *Masculinity–femininity (Mf)*—These items reflect the degree to which an individual endorses the traditional gender roles of men or women.

- *Paranoia (Pa)*—Individuals who endorse these items display suspiciousness of others. They also view the world in terms of "who is out to get them."

- *Psychasthenia (Pt)*—Individuals who endorse these items display excessive anxiety and obsessive behavior.

- *Schizophrenia (Sc)*—Individuals who endorse these items display bizarre disorganized thoughts along with a lack of normal contact with reality, including social aloofness. Various sensory problems such as hallucinations may be present.

- *Hypomania (Ma)*—Individuals who endorse these items experience high-energy states associated with poor judgment and impulse control.

- *Social introversion (Si)*—These items reflect the extent to which an individual's answers indicate social introversion and extraversion.[1]

By placing an individual's responses to questions in each of the categories on a normal distribution graph, it is possible to see which categories deviate from responses seen in the general population. In addition to the clinical scales, the MMPI also contains validity scales. These scales were designed to determine whether the person is trying to skew the results by either "faking good" or "faking bad." One type of item included in these scales is one that most healthy individuals would not agree to, such as "I have never told a lie." This last item would be found on the lie or L scale. The infrequency or F scale is composed of items that are infrequently endorsed by the general population. Endorsing these items could come about because the person wanted to look as if they had psychological problems ("faking bad"). It could also be the case that the individual was confused or could not read or understand the items. The defensiveness, or K, scale seeks to identify individuals who deny having any psychological problems ("faking good"). The number of times the person responds with "can't say" can be noted to help determine the validity of the MMPI. Further, as might be expected after more than 70 years of use, a variety of additional scales have been developed that have been used for both clinical and research purposes.

In 1989, a new version of the MMPI, the MMPI-2, was released, which improved the generalizability of the test. This was followed by the MMPI-2-RC, where RC stands for restructured clinical scales (Ben-Porath, 2012). The 10 scales of the original MMPI plus the validity scales were expanded into 51 scales based on psychometric and research considerations based on 433 items.

In 2020, MMPI-3 was released (Hall et al., 2022). Like the MMPI-2, the MMPI-3 was "normed" on a better representation of the general population in terms of race, age, sexual orientation, occupational level, income, and geographic location. The MMPI-3 has 355 items that are used to construct 10 validity and 42 descriptive scales. These scales are presented as a hierarchy. The three broad scales at the top are Emotional/Internalizing Dysfunction (EID), Thought Dysfunction (THD), and Behavioral/Externalizing Dysfunction (BXD). These are followed by eight clinical scales: Demoralization, Somatic Complaints, Low Positive Emotions, Antisocial

---

[1] MMPI®-2 (Minnesota Multiphasic Personality Inventory®-2) Manual for Administration, Scoring, and Interpretation, Revised Edition. Copyright © 2001 by the Regents of the University of Minnesota. Used by permission of the University of Minnesota Press. All rights reserved. "MMPI" and "Minnesota Multiphasic Personality Inventory" are trademarks owned by the Regents of the University of Minnesota.

Behavior, Ideas of Persecution, Dysfunctional Negative Emotions, Aberrant Experiences, and Hypomanic Activation. The final 26 specific problem scales include such problems as anxiety-related experience, stress/worry scale, suicidal/death ideation, helplessness/hopelessness, self-doubt, anger proneness, behavioral restricting fears, family problems, social avoidance, self-importance, and others' problems.

Projective Tests

Projective instruments are assessment tests composed of ambiguous stimuli. They can range from seemingly random patterns such as an inkblot to ambiguous drawings of individuals or objects. The individual is asked to describe what the patterns look like, what they bring to mind, or what is being depicted in the drawing.

The basic idea of projective testing is based on the theoretical ideas of Sigmund Freud and others who sought to understand the dynamics of the mind. One important distinction Freud made was between types of thinking (Erdelyi, 1985; Westen et al., 2008). Primary process thought, which is seen in dreams or letting your mind wander, is not organized logically but in terms of associations between thoughts and feelings. Secondary process thought, on the other hand, is logically organized. Freud suggested that it was possible to understand the cognitive and emotional connections of a person's mind in terms of primary process. Freud's technique for exploring these connections was free association and dream analysis.

The basic technique of free association is to have a person lie on a couch and say whatever comes into their mind. Since the therapist sits behind the client, there is little in the environment for the client to react to. It is the therapist's job to notice how a person's thoughts and emotions are connected. During free association over a period of months, it is assumed that patterns of responding will emerge. It could be, for example, that whenever a client talks about their pet, they feel sad, or whenever a client begins to describe a certain event, they change the topic.

Projective techniques were formally introduced in the first half of the 1900s as a means of detecting primary process types of thinking and feeling, including instinctual and motivational processes. Since there were few techniques for understanding the connections in one's mind at this time, professionals saw projective techniques as having potential for understanding how thoughts and feelings formed a cognitive network. It was assumed that projective techniques would give a window into the thought processes of those with mental disorders and how they differ from the thought processes of healthy individuals.

Two of the most well-known projective techniques are the Rorschach inkblots and the Thematic Apperception Test (TAT). Both of these tests have a long history of use, although various researchers have been critical of the Rorschach and other projective techniques and suggest clinical situations in which these types of techniques are not useful (Garb et al., 2005).

Rorschach Inkblots

During the early part of the 1900s, Herman Rorschach, a Swiss psychiatrist, experimented with using inkblots. The **Rorschach inkblots** were made by simply dripping ink on a piece of paper and then folding it in half to create a symmetrical design. Some of the inkblots were in black and white (Figure 4.1), and others were in color (Figure 4.2). He initially gave his inkblots to a large number of schoolchildren (Ellenberger, 1970). Rorschach was interested in the sensory processing of these images, which he connected with Carl Jung's idea of introversion and extraversion.

Rorschach saw introversion as focusing on the inner world of kinesthetic images and creative activity. Extraversion, on the other hand, was a focus on color, emotion, and adjustment to reality. For Rorschach, the content of what was seen in the inkblot was less the focus of the interpretation than the elements used, such as whether the person saw whole images or focused on small details of the blot. Viewing the image as containing movement and the use of the colors was also seen as important. A limited number of 10 plates were selected, and Rorschach published a book on the subject in German, *Psychodiagnostics*, in 1921. He died some months later at age 37. His book was translated into English in 1942.

FIGURE 4.1 When You Look at This, What Do You See?

Example of a Rorschach inkblot in black and white.

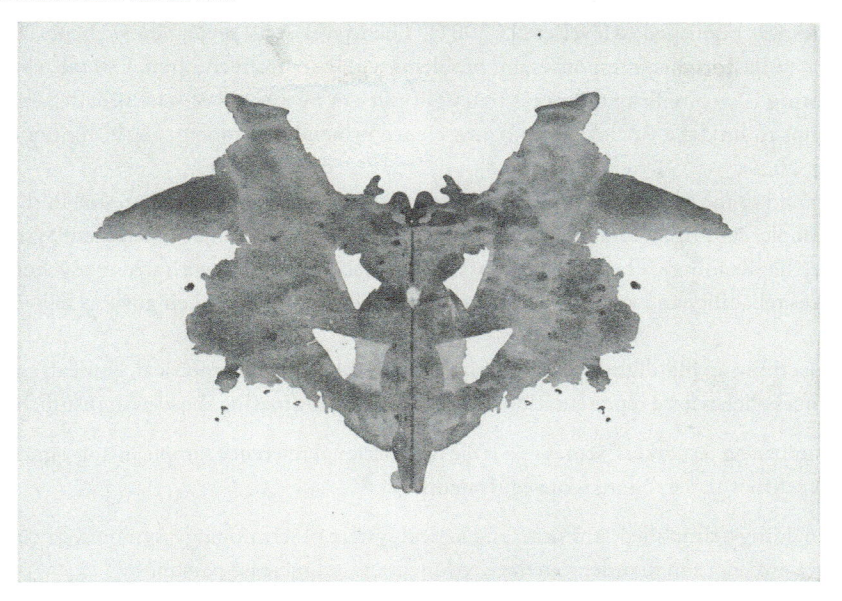

Credit: iStock.com/zmeel

FIGURE 4.2 When You Look at This, What Do You See?

An example of a color Rorschach inkblot.

Credit: iStock.com/zmeel

Following Rorschach's death, various clinicians used the inkblot test in their clinical practice. For a number of years, there was little scientific data concerning the reliability and validity of the measure. Since the late 20th century, there has been a movement to standardize the presentation of the test and the manner in which it is scored. Exner (1986, 2003) offered one such system. Various studies have examined the reliability and validity of the measure with specific diagnostic groups and theoretical constructs (Hunsley & Mash, 2007; Meyer, 2001; Meyer & Archer, 2001; Mihura et al., 2019).

In 2001, a special issue of the journal *Psychological Assessment* was devoted to clarifying the utility of the Rorschach along with its problems from an evidence-based position. To address questions of reliability and validity, a series of norms using the Exner system based on more than 5,800 people from 17 countries was published (Meyer et al., 2007). The Meyer et al. review showed consistency across samples for adult Rorschach responses but problems with data from children. Overall, the Rorschach and its scoring is a complicated process that continues to be a focus of scientific debate. One focus is an attempt to link the Rorschach to neuroscience principles (Erdberg, 2019; Jimura et al., 2021; van Graan, 2021).

To respond to the problems of the Exner scoring system, professionals interested in the Rorschach created a simpler scoring system referred to as the Rorschach Performance Assessment System (R-PAS) (see For Further Reading). The basic idea was to create a scoring system with strong psychometric properties such as reliability and validity. The developers of the R-PAS state their goals as follows:

1. Selecting and highlighting those variables with the strongest empirical, clinical, and response process/behavioral representational support while eliminating those with insufficient support

2. Comparing test takers' scores to a large international reference sample, using a graphic array of percentiles and standard score equivalents

3. Providing a simplified, uniform, and logical system of terminology, symbols, calculations, and data presentation in order to reduce redundancy and increase parsimony

4. Describing the empirical basis and psychological rationale for each score that is to be interpreted

5. Providing a statistical procedure to adjust for the overall complexity of the record and a graphical illustration of its impact on each variable

6. Optimizing the number of responses given to the task in order to ensure an interpretable and meaningful protocol, while drastically reducing both the number of times the task needs to be readministered because of too few responses and the likelihood of inordinately long and taxing administrations because of too many responses

7. Developing new and revised indices by applying contemporary statistical and computational approaches

8. Offering access to a scoring program on a secure, encrypted web platform from any device that can interface with the Internet (e.g., PC, laptop, smartphone, tablet)

The R-PAS system was developed around 2006 and continues to be tested worldwide. An initial review and meta-analysis article was published in *Psychological Bulletin*, which described Rorschach variables with research support and those with little or no support (Mihura et al., 2013). Current research related to R-PAS can be found online (see For Further Reading).

Other researchers have begun to use neuroscience techniques such as brain imaging and electrophysiology to understand physiological processes underlying Rorschach responses. For example, Giromini and his colleagues (2010) examined movement responses on the Rorschach and how these were reflected in the EEG.

Thematic Apperception Test (TAT)

The Thematic Apperception Test (TAT) is composed of 30 black-and-white drawings of various scenes and people (Figure 4.3). The instrument was developed by Christiana Morgan and Henry Murray in the 1930s. Typically, an individual is shown 20 of the cards, one at a time, and asked to create a story about what is being depicted on the card. The basic idea is that by noting the content and emotionality of the individual's responses, it is possible to gain insight into their thoughts, emotions, and motivations, including areas of conflict. For example, if an individual described many of the cards in terms of someone leaving another person, the clinician might ask if abandonment was an

FIGURE 4.3 ■ What Is Happening in This Picture?

Example of a TAT drawing. The person being evaluated is asked to create a story about the picture.

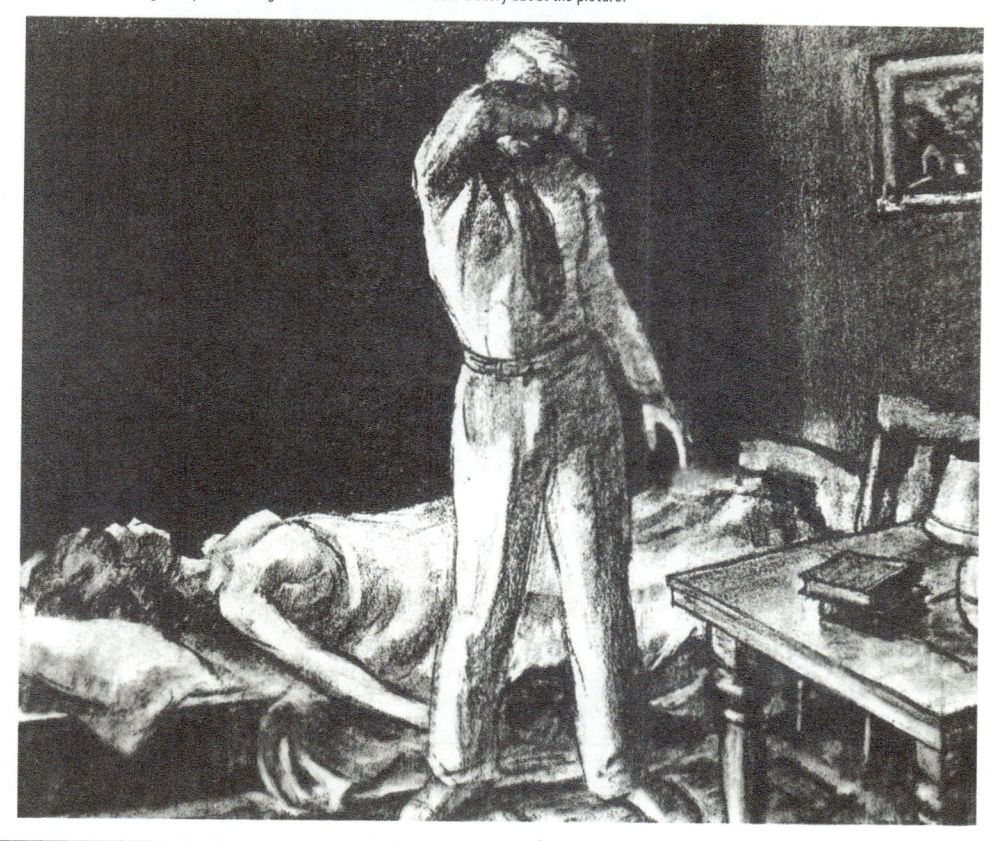

Credit: Science History Images/Alamy Stock Photo

important issue for the person. Although the TAT technique may be useful to gain additional information concerning a person (e.g., suicidal thoughts), it lacks scientific evidence to make it useful in obtaining a formal diagnosis. Similar problems of reliability and validity exist with the TAT as with the Rorschach.

Overall, projective techniques have been the subject of great debate and controversy. Frick and colleagues (2010) presented some of the major pros and cons concerning the use of projective techniques (Table 4.1). Some professionals see their value not in terms of giving exact diagnoses but in their ability to allow a professional to see how an individual responds to ambiguous stimuli, especially in terms of suicidal ideation as well as disorganized thought processes. This may lead to further discussions of areas that a professional would not normally discuss. The major disadvantage of projective techniques centers on questions of validity in terms of both the test's ability to identify specific disorders and the reliance of the test interpretation on a specific population, such as children.

Neuropsychological Testing

Neuropsychological tests have been developed to help mental health professionals assess a person's general level of cognitive functioning. Intelligence tests, for example, are able to compare a given individual with their peers to determine their level of functioning. The common intelligence tests, such as the Wechsler Adult Intelligence Scale (WAIS), have a number of subscales designed to measure verbal and performance tasks. The verbal tasks include measurements of acquired knowledge, verbal reasoning, and comprehension of verbal information. The performance tasks include nonverbal reasoning, spatial processing skills, attention to detail, and visuomotor integration.

TABLE 4.1 ■ Pros and Cons of Projective Tests

Pro	Con
Less structured format allows clinician greater flexibility in administration and interpretation and places fewer demand characteristics that would prompt socially desirable responses from an informant.	The reliability of many techniques is questionable. As a result, the interpretations are more related to characteristics of the clinician than to characteristics of the person being tested.
Allows for the assessment of drives, motivations, desires, and conflicts that can affect a person's perceptual experiences but are often unconscious.	Even some techniques that have good reliability have questionable validity, especially in making diagnoses and predicting overt behavior.
Provides a deeper understanding of a person than would be obtained by simply describing behavioral patterns.	Although we can at times predict things we cannot understand, it is rarely the case that understanding does not enhance prediction (Gittelman-Klein, 1986).
Adds to an overall assessment picture.	Adding an unreliable piece of information to an assessment battery simply decreases the overall reliability of the battery.
Helps to generate hypotheses regarding a person's functioning.	Leads one to pursue erroneous avenues in testing or to place undue confidence in a particular finding.
Nonthreatening and good for rapport building.	Detracts from the time an assessor could better spend collecting more detailed, objective information.
Many projective techniques have a long and rich clinical tradition.	Assessment techniques are based on an evolving knowledge base and must continually evolve to reflect this knowledge.

Credit: Frick, P. J., Barry, C. T., & Kamphaus, R. W. (2010). *Clinical assessment of child and adolescent personality and behavior* (p. 226). Springer. https://doi.org/10.1007/978-1-4419-0641-0_10; reproduced with kind permission from Springer Science+Business Media.

Other neuropsychological tests have been designed to assess specific types of brain functioning as well as brain damage. These include memory, attention, reasoning, emotional processing, and motor processes, including inhibition of action. One advantage of traditional neuropsychological tests is that they have been given to a large number of people so that norms could be established. Thus, it is possible to know whether a 70-year-old individual is showing a normal memory decline in certain areas or if there might be the beginning of a neurocognitive disorder, such as Alzheimer's disease.

Although neuropsychological testing was initially developed to assess brain damage resulting from accidents, strokes, or war, it is now finding a use in delineating deficits in those with mental illness. Today, there is a coming together of neuropsychological tests, measures of cognitive processes in normal individuals, and brain imaging techniques. For example, the Wisconsin Card Sorting Test (WCST) requires that an individual sort cards into four piles. Each card has a specific shape on it, such as a circle or square, and a specific number of these shapes. Each card is also printed in a specific color. Thus, you could sort the cards by shape, by number, or by color. The person administering the test makes note of whether the individual is sorting each card correctly or not. After a number of sorts, the administrator changes the correct sort category. Individuals with frontal lobe damage have difficulty responding to changing demands. Individuals with schizophrenia also have difficulty responding to changing task requirements.

Another test that is commonly used in psychopathology research and assessment is the Continuous Performance Test (CPT), which measures attentional characteristics. In one version of the test, participants are shown a series of letters and must respond whenever a particular letter is displayed. The test then requires that the person respond when one particular letter followed by another letter is displayed. Children with ADHD have problems with this task. Thus, neuropsychological tests are also being used to understand brain processes in those with mental illness.

Neuropsychological Tests and Mental Illness

Neuropsychological tests can help identify cognitive changes associated with a particular disorder. For example, there is a rare occurrence of four sisters who all developed schizophrenia in their 20s. The Genain sisters were monozygotic quadruplets born in the United States in the early 1930s. These sisters were studied throughout their lives in terms of genetic makeup as well as cognitive functioning. When the sisters were 66 years of age, Allan Mirsky and his colleagues (2000) readministered a number of neuropsychological tests including the WAIS, the CPT, and the WCST. The scores for each sister at age 66 were compared with their performance at ages 27 and 51. By showing that the test scores of the sisters over their lifetime had not changed, these researchers were able to show that cognitive decline is not part of schizophrenia.

Using Neuroscience Techniques to Identify Mental Illness

As more and more researchers and clinicians have come to see mental illness as representing problems with the brain, there have been a variety of projects to utilize neuroscience approaches to describe psychopathology (Andreasen, 2001). These have ranged from identifying the presence of certain genes and the manner in which they turn on and off in psychopathology to structural and functional descriptions of brain processes and psychophysiological changes measured throughout the body. The potential for using neuroscience approaches to classify mental illness and inform its treatment is an important one (see Clark et al., 2017; Cuthbert & Insel, 2010, 2013; Glannon, 2015; Halligan & David, 2001; Hyman, 2007, 2010; Insel, 2009; Miller, 2010; Sumner et al., 2015).

Traditionally, psychopathology has been defined in terms of signs and symptoms. The experiences of the client and what is observed by the professional are one level of analysis. In general, the mental health professional identifies symptoms that group together and the time of their appearance. Neuroscience techniques offer another level of analysis. From a research standpoint, scientists have sought to identify underlying markers associated with specific mental disorders. Using various brain imaging techniques described in Chapter 2, such as magnetic resonance imaging (MRI), functional magnetic resonance imaging (fMRI), electroencephalography (EEG), and magnetoencephalography (MEG), there has been a search for structural and functional changes associated with psychopathology.

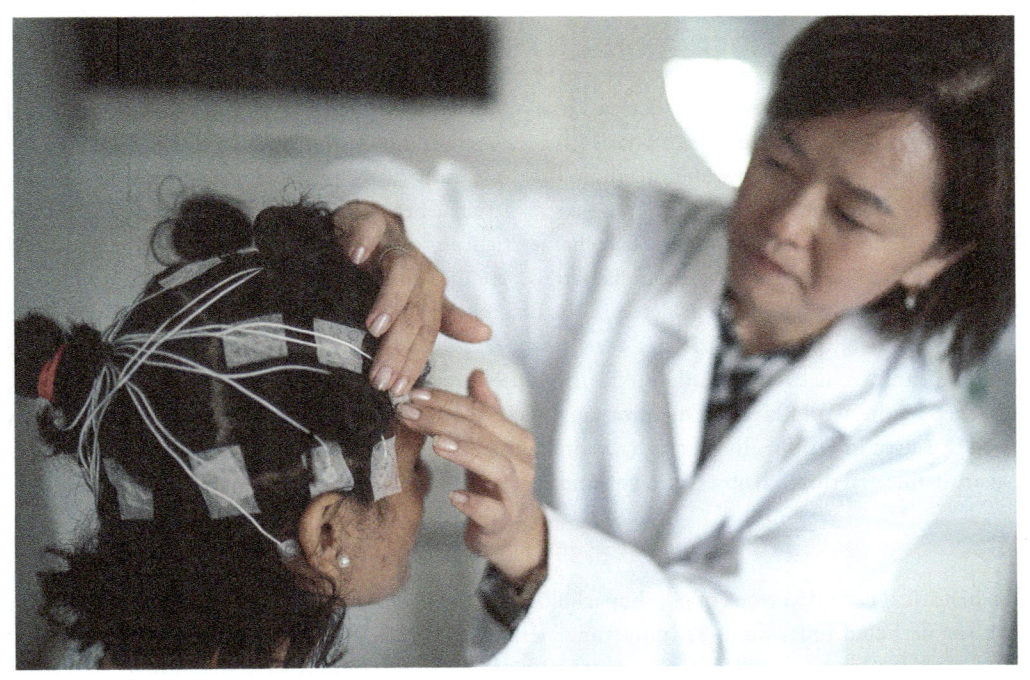

The potential for using neuroscience approaches to classify mental illness and inform its treatment is an important one.
iStock.com/FG Trade

For example, researchers have been able to distinguish individuals with autism (Ecker et al., 2010) and with bipolar disorder (Rocha-Rego et al., 2013) from those without the disorder based on fMRI data.

Part of the potential for using neuroscience markers is related to the fact that not every individual with schizophrenia, for example, reports the same symptoms. Some individuals describe auditory hallucinations, whereas others describe visual hallucinations. What now is considered as a single disorder may be better represented as separate disorders based on underlying mechanisms. Further, certain mental disorders also show gender differences. For example, females tend to develop schizophrenia later than males, but both males and females show similar rates of the disorder. However, females do show higher rates of mood and anxiety disorders.

Overall, neuroscience methods may lead to better diagnostic procedures as well as understanding the mechanisms of the disorder. For example, genetic research suggests similarities between schizophrenia and bipolar disorder in terms of the genes involved. It is also possible to use neuroscience techniques to follow the course of a disorder over time. One study (Raj et al., 2012) based on brain imaging methods suggests that neurocognitive disorders follow specific pathways in the brain. Another potential for neuroscience methods is that by knowing the underlying brain and genetic processes involved in a particular disorder for a particular person, it would be possible to create a treatment that is designed specifically for that individual.

CONCEPT CHECK

- For each of the following types of assessment, what kinds of information can you obtain from it and what is one example of it?
  - Symptom questionnaire
  - Personality test
  - Projective test
  - Neuropsychological test
  - Neuroscience technique

DIAGNOSTIC CONSIDERATIONS IN PSYCHOPATHOLOGY

Over the past 100 years, there have been a variety of debates on how to diagnose and classify mental disorders. In the past 50 years, the emphasis has been on reliability of diagnosis such that mental health professionals in one location would diagnose the same individual in the same manner as professionals in another location. As part of this emphasis, there has been a push for observable characteristics that would define a specific disorder. Such characteristics as depressed mood over the day, diminished interest in activities, weight loss, insomnia, fatigue, feelings of worthlessness, difficulty thinking, and thoughts of suicide would be considered in the diagnosis of depression. These types of criteria make up the structure of the *Diagnostic and Statistical Manual of Mental Disorders (DSM)*, published by the American Psychiatric Association (APA), and the *International Classification of Diseases (ICD)*, published by the World Health Organization (WHO). The *DSM* is used in North America, whereas the *ICD* is used in Europe. In general, the criteria used in the *DSM* and *ICD* are signs and symptoms that are delineated through observation of, and conversation with, the individual.

Categorical Versus Dimensional Approaches

The historical considerations of psychopathology emphasized careful observation and interaction with the afflicted individuals as important methods for understanding the nature of the disorder. Based on these observations of symptoms and signs, individuals were diagnosed and classified as falling into discrete categories of disorders. This is an important level of analysis and one emphasized throughout this book. However, there are other levels of analysis for understanding psychopathology.

With progress in the neurosciences in general and in brain imaging and genetics in particular, other levels of analysis have become possible. These new levels of analysis offer different perspectives for the field of mental illness. What seemed like discrete categories of psychopathology previously are now seen to cluster in new and different ways when considered from the standpoint of genetics. Additional groupings have emerged as scientists have considered the neural networks involved in particular manifestations of psychopathology. This has led to the realization that mental disorders can be described in both a categorical and a dimensional manner.

As shown in the physical sciences, there are times in which a phenomenon can be described both categorically and dimensionally. For example, when water is heated, the rise in temperature can be described in a dimensional manner in terms of a certain number of degrees. However, at a critical point, the water turns to steam, which is a categorically different state from water. Likewise, a reduction in temperature changes water into a different categorical state—ice. The question for the study of psychopathological disorders is to determine the underlying dimensional changes that are associated with categorical-like transformations leading to a disordered state. Further, different underlying processes may actually allow for the presence of more than one disordered state at the same time.

Comorbidity and Hierarchical Approaches to Psychopathology

Technically, when an individual is seen to have more than one disorder at the same time, the disorders are referred to as comorbid. In the National Comorbidity Survey, a large number of individuals with one disorder were found to have one or more additional diagnoses (Kessler et al., 1994). For example, individuals with generalized anxiety disorder will often also show symptoms of depression. Further, these two disorders have overlapping genetic and environmental risk factors (Kendler et al., 1992). The number of diagnoses found in the National Comorbidity Survey was associated with the severity of the symptoms. This has suggested to researchers that there exists a general underlying vulnerability to psychopathology that may be independent of the particular symptoms expressed (Forbes et al., 2021; Lahey et al., 2017; Marshall, 2020; Pittenger & Etkin, 2008; Smith et al., 2020; Widiger, 2021). This general factor of psychopathology, also called the p factor, reflects a number of overlapping considerations, including brain and genetic ones (Hong et al., 2023; Sprooten et al., 2022; Zald & Lahey, 2017).

Historically, researchers sought to determine which disorders tend to co-occur with one another. Initially, two clusters were found. The first is referred to as internalizing disorders. The focus of these disorders, which include anxiety and depression, is the inner world of the person. The second cluster is referred to as externalizing disorders; the behavioral focus of these disorders is the external environment of the person. Externalizing disorders include conduct disorder, oppositional defiant disorder, antisocial personality disorder, substance use disorder, and, in some studies, attention deficit/hyperactivity disorder (ADHD). Studies of comorbidity clusters have led scientists to search for common factors, such as genetics, brain processes, and environmental risk profiles, that might be associated with each cluster. Overall, research has supported the idea that mental disorders can be clustered and that it is possible to identify underlying risk factors (Kendler et al., 2011; Scott et al., 2020).

It is not surprising that with new scientific discoveries the field of psychopathology is experiencing changing perspectives. One of these is the Hierarchical Taxonomy of Psychopathology (HiTOP). Later in the chapter we will also examine the RDoC approach developed by the U.S. National Institute of Mental Health.

The HiTOP consortium was formed in 2015 as a grassroots effort to articulate a fully research-based classification of psychopathology (see For Further Reading). The consortium's resulting HiTOP model (Figure 4.4) is a system for classifying signs and symptoms of psychopathology (Conway et al., 2022; DeYoung et al., 2022; Kotov et al., 2021; Michelini et al., 2021). Three fundamental findings have shaped HiTOP. First, psychopathology is best characterized by dimensions rather than categories. Second, signs and symbols are best examined in terms of how they occur together. And third, psychopathology can be

FIGURE 4.4 ■ The HiTOP Approach

This HiTOP model shows the hierarchical classification of psychopathology. This is in comparison to the DSM approach (see the base of the figure), which presents disorders as discrete.

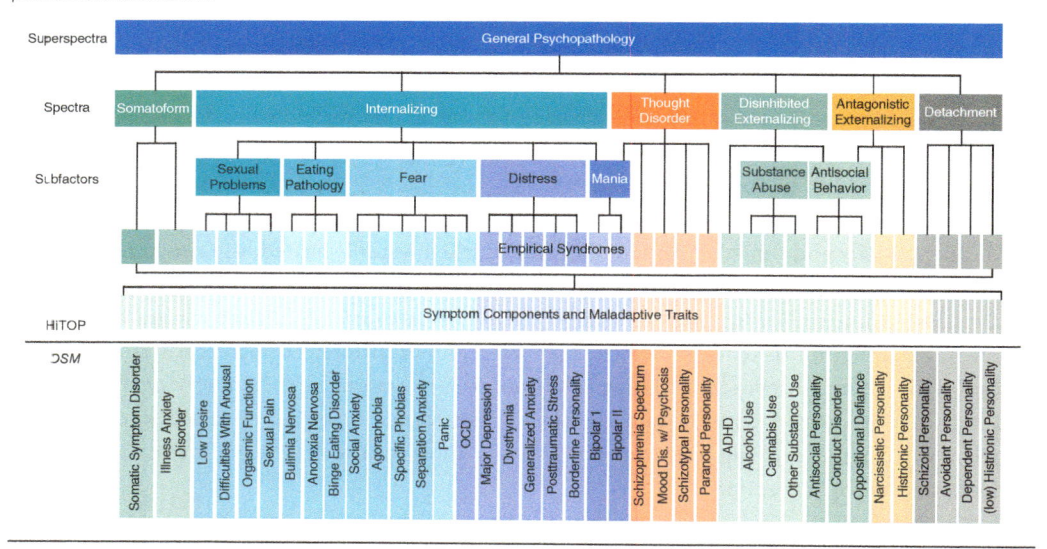

Credit: Conway, C. C., Forbes, M. K., South, S. C., & the HiTOP Consortium. (2022). A hierarchical taxonomy of psychopathology (HiTOP) primer for mental health researchers. *Clinical Psychological Science, 10*(2), 236–258. https://doi.org/10.1177/21677026211017834

organized hierarchically from narrow to broad dimensions. This is consistent with research suggesting a general underlying vulnerability to psychopathology that may be independent of any particular symptoms expressed. There are also efforts to link the RDoC and HiTOP approaches (Michelini et al., 2021).

Utilizing Neuroscience Methods in Diagnosis and Treatment

As noted, there has been a push to find more objective markers that can be used in the diagnosis and treatment of mental disorders using neuroscience research. With the advent of the various levels of analysis available to neuroscientists, including brain imaging, genetics, biochemical and electrophysiological processes, brain networks, behavior, and experience, a variety of researchers have sought to describe cognitive, emotional, and motor processes in both health and illness. This has resulted in a better articulation of what underlies these processes.

One such process is memory. It is possible to describe its underlying mechanism through study of specific brain areas such as the hippocampus, the brain networks involving memory, and the biochemical and structural changes among neurons as new information is retained. With this knowledge, it is also possible to explore psychopathological conditions such as amnesia or delusions that involve the memory system.

Another example is the reward system. Humans seek rewards from a variety of sources, including food, sex, power, acclaim, and affiliation, as well as drugs. A number of studies show that particular brain structures, especially the nucleus accumbens part of the ventral striatum, are influenced by an increase in dopamine during a reward (Figure 4.5). In fact, all addictive drugs result in dopamine release in the nucleus accumbens (Pittenger & Etkin, 2008). Individuals with alcoholism show greater activation to alcohol-related cues in the nucleus accumbens and the anterior thalamus. The activation of the nucleus accumbens also correlates with the degree of craving. One approach involving the reward system is to note its involvement in active reward processes, such as those seen in addiction or mania, as well as those disorders in which reward is reduced, such as depression or schizophrenia (Russo & Nestler, 2013).

Since the beginning of the 21st century, a number of researchers and clinicians have asked whether it would be possible to use neuroscience approaches to classify mental illness and inform its treatment (Cuthbert, 2022; Cuthbert & Insel, 2010; Halligan & David, 2001; Hyman, 2007, 2010; Insel, 2009; Miller, 2010; Sanislow et al., 2010). Part of this desire stems from the fact that not all individuals with

FIGURE 4.5 ■ Reward System of the Brain

Dopamine is an important part of the reward system. A number of studies show that particular brain structures, especially the nucleus accumbens part of the ventral striatum, are influenced by an increase in dopamine during a reward.

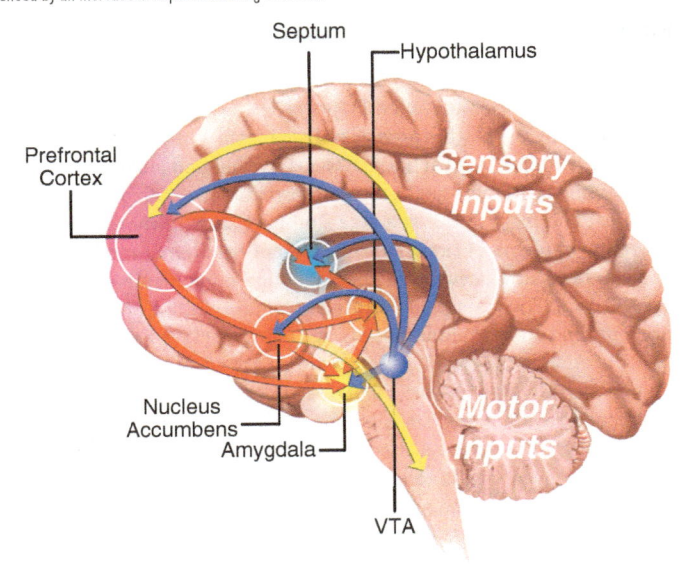

depression, for example, report the same symptoms. This suggests to some researchers that there might be different underlying brain processes involved in what appears as a single disorder. By knowing the underlying processes involved in a particular disorder, it would be possible to create a treatment that was specific to a given individual.

Neuroscience perspectives can also help validate theoretical constructs used in a variety of theoretical orientations. For example, Carhart-Harris and Friston (2010) examined the relationship between brain network processes and Freudian constructs. Likewise, DeRubeis and colleagues (2008) examined the different pathways of treatment for depression found in cognitive therapy versus medication. These researchers suggested that cognitive therapy works through a top-down approach by increasing higher cortical functioning associated with the frontal lobes, whereas medication works in a more bottom-up approach by decreasing excessive emotional responsiveness associated with the amygdala.

One large organization emphasizing the utilization of neuroscience information to understand mental illness is the **National Institute of Mental Health (NIMH)** in the United States (Insel, 2009). Through its research mission, NIMH developed four major objectives:

> The plan calls for research that will (1) define the pathophysiology of disorders from genes to behavior, (2) map the trajectory of illness to determine when, where, and how to intervene to preempt disability, (3) develop new interventions based on a personalized approach to the diverse needs and circumstances of people with mental illnesses, and (4) strengthen the public health impact of NIMH-supported research by focusing on dissemination [of] science and disparities in care. (Insel, 2009, p. 128)

These objectives are designed to identify the manner in which brain processes are involved in a specific disorder. The goal is to better describe the course of a mental disorder, including when the first signs appear (even if abnormal processes are not yet seen), so as to use this knowledge to create a treatment related to a given individual and to make these treatments available to all members of society. Thus, traditional neuroscience perspectives that reflect action on the level of genetics, the neuron, and neural networks are integrated with research perspectives related to more system-level cognitive, emotional, and behavioral processes. See *LENS: Assessment, Classification, and Clinical Practice: The RDoC Alternative to the* DSM for a discussion of the Research Domain Criteria (RDoC) approach that is being explored by NIMH.

LENS

ASSESSMENT, CLASSIFICATION, AND CLINICAL PRACTICE: THE RDOC ALTERNATIVE TO THE *DSM*

Classification of mental disorders in the United States relies on the *Diagnostic and Statistical Manual of Mental Disorders (DSM)*, published by the American Psychiatric Association. The current version is *DSM-5*, published in 2013, with the text revision *DSM-5-TR* published in 2022. *DSM-5* uses very specific psychological signs and symptoms as the main determination for diagnosing a mental disorder.

As noted by Cuthbert and Insel (2013; see also Cuthbert, 2022), whereas significant advances have been made recently in terms of reducing the rates of traditional medical problems such as cardiovascular disease, the same prevention and reduction outcomes have not been achieved in relation to mental disorders. The National Institute of Mental Health (NIMH) has begun a program to better study, prevent, and treat mental disorders. One important aspect of this program is to develop a new way of classifying mental disorders, referred to as **Research Domain Criteria (RDoC)**. Current information on the RDoC framework can be found online (see For Further Reading).

To create a classification system, the NIMH emphasized four steps. The first was to identify fundamental behavioral components, such as affect regulation or executive functions, that cut across a number of disorders. The second was to identify the full range of human functioning. By doing this, variations in normal functioning can be used to identify psychopathology. The third step was to identify reliable and valid measures that could be used in research and treatment. The fourth step was to bring together components from a number of levels, including genetics, brain functioning, behavioral aspects, and environmental aspects, to describe the mental disorder. The RDoC can be illustrated as seen in Figure 4.6.

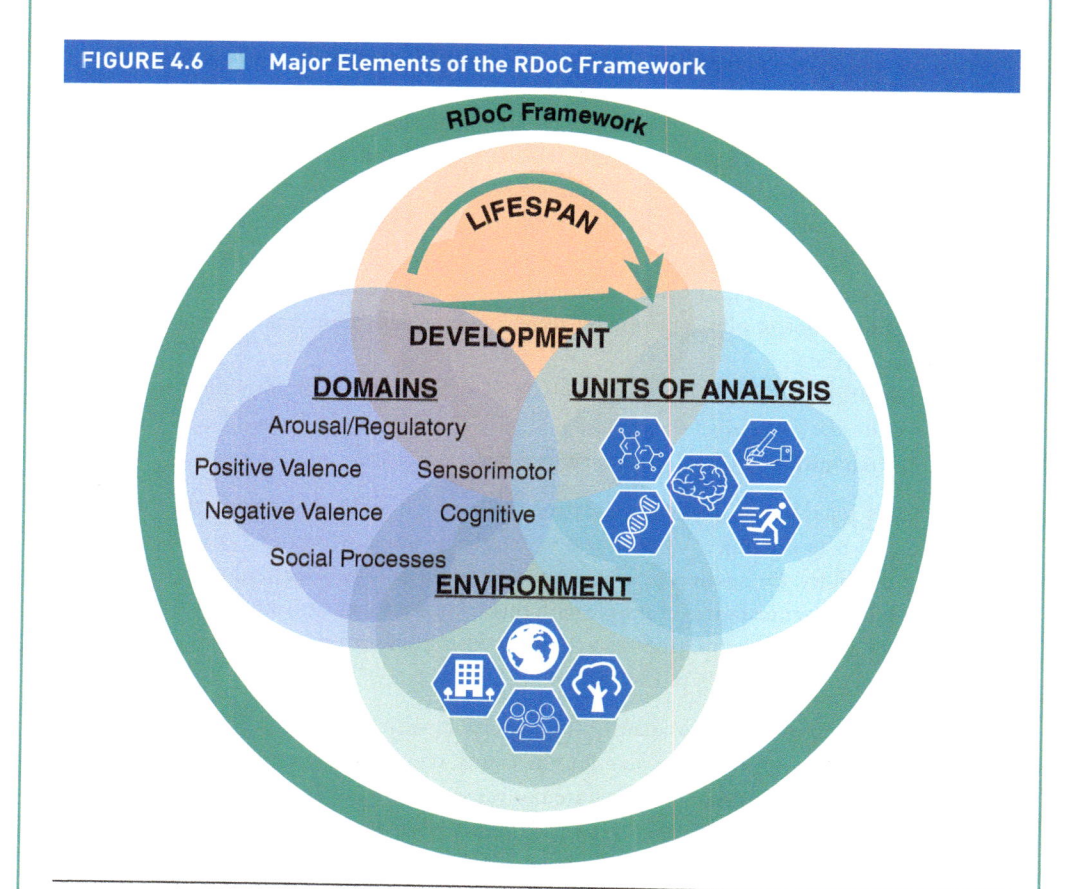

FIGURE 4.6 ■ Major Elements of the RDoC Framework

Source: National Institute of Mental Health. (n.d.). *About RDoC*. U.S. Department of Health and Human Services. https://www.nimh.nih.gov/research/research-funded-by-nimh/rdoc/about-rdoc

In Figure 4.6, you can see the major elements of the RDoC approach. The major domains, such as positive and negative valence, suggest areas of focus that a research design could include. In turn, you can ask how these domains are reflected on different levels, such as the genetic one, one emphasizing brain circuits, one focusing on behavior, and so forth. Overall, it is a lifespan approach that seeks to include both environmental factors, including cultural factors, and neurodevelopmental factors.

In contrasting the NIMH RDoC approach to that of the *DSM*, Bruce Cuthbert and Tom Insel (2013) suggest there are seven significant differences.

1. Rather than beginning with a symptom-based definition as in the *DSM*, RDoC begins with the function of normal human processes. By examining the normal, it is possible to determine what variation from the normal range of functioning would be considered a mental disorder. Also, by starting with normal functioning with its long history of research, it will be easier to identify underlying mechanisms seen when normal functions are no longer present.
2. Since RDoC emphasizes the full range of human functioning across a number of levels, mental disorders will be described in terms of dimensional components. In general, the *DSM* emphasizes categories such as major mood disorder, personality disorder, PTSD, or generalized anxiety disorder. *DSM-5* has begun to consider dimensional aspects such as autism spectrum disorder, but a number of disorders remain categorical; you either have the disorder or you do not.
3. The third point emphasizes the reliability and validity of measures of human functioning. By using a dimensional approach, research can better note changes along the entire range of human functioning. In medicine, presenting blood pressure measurements along a continuum has allowed for advancements in the field in terms of who needs to be treated and at what level. For example, research suggests that those over the age of 60 may experience a higher blood pressure before treatment is needed than those who are younger (James et al., 2014). Looking at levels of anxiety and depression by studying their underlying components on a continuum would better identify who needs treatment and at what age.
4. The fourth point is related to how the *DSM-5* and RDoC dictate the type of research design that is used. *DSM* research typically uses the diagnosis category as the independent variable. For example, individuals with anxiety according to the *DSM* are compared with a control group of individuals without anxiety. RDoC does not allow this type of approach. RDoC begins with a selection procedure. You might begin by looking at everyone who presented themselves at a Veterans Affairs clinic focusing on the treatment of PTSD. Another approach would be to study those who had experienced a trauma in the past month. You would then choose one or more independent variables that fit your research hypothesis. It could be distress, sleep, brain imaging, or something else.
5. The fifth point relates to a search for an integrated understanding of behavioral and brain processes. This is understood in the RDoC approach to mean that both the behavioral measure and the brain measure or other physiological measure would be valid in themselves as a component of a particular disorder. The *DSM*, on the other hand, emphasizes signs and symptoms, without using specific neuroscience measurement techniques.
6. The sixth point reflects the different development trajectories of the *DSM* and RDoC. RDoC began with a focus on those disorders with solid research. Although the *DSM* seeks to be informed by research, the disorders included began with historical precedence.
7. Since RDoC is an experimental approach to understanding mental disorders, it can change as new information is obtained. This has less of an effect on society in terms of insurance payments, legal considerations, and the collection of prevalence rates. That is, every time diagnostic criteria for a *DSM* disorder change, older studies of a disorder with different criteria must be reconsidered.

At this point, a large number of research studies have been designed using the RDoC perspective. Both psychological and pharmacological treatments have been developed. Rather than targeting the treatment of a particular disorder, they focus on aspects of the major domains such as cognitive control or reduction of negative affect (Cuthbert, 2022).

Thought Question

What are the advantages and disadvantages of *DSM-5* and RDoC?

> **CONCEPT CHECK**
>
> - Why is the reliability of diagnosis an important aspect of psychological treatment?
> - What does it mean that mental disorders can be described in both a categorical and a dimensional manner?
> - Why is comorbidity of psychological disorders an important consideration? Discuss some of the advantages of including underlying processes in the study of psychopathology.
> - Identify three specific ways in which neuroscience approaches have been utilized to classify mental illness and inform its treatment.

CLASSIFICATION SYSTEMS FOR MENTAL DISORDERS

Classification is a way to name, organize, and categorize the diversity of symptoms seen in mental disorders. Blashfield and Draguns (1976; see also Blashfield et al., 2010) suggest five different purposes of classification:

1. As a *nomenclature*—The purpose here, in giving a name to a disorder, is to present a way for mental health professionals to describe and discuss the clients they see.

2. As a *basis of information retrieval*—Classifying disorders allows for individuals who may not be professionals to search for information concerning mental disorders.

3. As a *descriptive system*—The name of the disorder summarizes the behaviors, thoughts, and emotions of individuals with the disorder.

4. As a *predictive system*—In this case, the classification allows one to know the course of the disorder if untreated and particular treatments that may be effective.

5. As a *basis for a theory of psychopathology*—The focus in this case is to use classification to understand the disorder.

Over the past 200 years, numerous systems have been developed concerning the diagnosis and classification of mental disorders. In the past 50 years, the emphasis has been on reliability of diagnosis such that mental health professionals in one location would diagnose the same individual in the same manner as professionals in another location. As part of this emphasis, there has been a push for observable characteristics that would define a specific disorder. These types of criteria make up the structure of the *DSM* and the *ICD*. In general, the criteria used in the *DSM* and *ICD* are signs and symptoms that are delineated through observation of and conversation with the individual. Since *ICD* codes are used by many health facilities in the United States, the similarities and differences in *ICD* and *DSM* criteria of mental disorders will be noted throughout this book.

International Statistical Classification of Diseases and Related Health Problems

The *ICD*, currently used in over 100 countries worldwide to classify disorders, has an interesting history. It began with the intent of identifying causes of death.

Based on earlier attempts, a system for recording the cause of death was developed by the French statistician Jacques Bertillon in the late 1800s. This came to be known as the International List of Causes of Death. In 1898, the American Public Health Association suggested that the United States, Canada, and Mexico use this system and support its revision every 10 years. In 1948, the WHO, which collected health-related data worldwide, took over the *ICD*. The sixth edition of the *ICD*, published in 1949, included a section related to mental disorders. Currently, the *ICD* includes two sections, one for medical disorders and the other for mental and behavioral disorders. Because of the *ICD*'s inclusion of medical disorders, it is used for Health Insurance Portability and Accountability Act (HIPAA) purposes such as insurance in the United States.

ICD-11 is the current version, which was updated in 2018 (see For Further Reading). Mental disorders in the *ICD-11* are described as short narratives rather than with specific criteria as seen in the *DSM-5-TR*.

Diagnostic and Statistical Manual of Mental Disorders

The *DSM* was created by a group of psychiatrists in the 1940s, who had been involved in directing mental hospitals and mental health services for the U.S. Army and Navy during World War II, and others who were part of the American Psychiatric Association. The first version of the *DSM* (*DSM-I*) was published in 1952 (see Grob, 1991).

Origins of the *DSM*

A number of factors helped to create the initial *DSM*. One was the search for consistency in diagnosis across clinicians throughout the country. In this sense, the *DSM-I* sought to bring together and standardize the classifications used in state and private mental hospitals, those classifications developed during World War II, and those used by professionals in private practice. Another factor that gained emphasis during World War II was the realization that environmental stress associated with combat was related to the expression of mental disorders. A related understanding was that these disorders could be treated without prolonged institutionalization. In addition, treatment worked best if begun early in the course of the disorder. This required that professionals be able to differentiate those who could be treated and sent back to battle from those who needed long-term care.

Early Versions of the *DSM* and the Eventual Focus on Diagnostic Criteria

The classification system used by *DSM-I* divided disorders into two broad categories. The first category encompassed disorders such as Huntington's chorea or neurocognitive disorders (then called dementias) resulting from brain pathophysiologies. These were disorders that resulted from hereditary origins, infections, long-term drug addictions, tumors of the brain, and other such factors. The

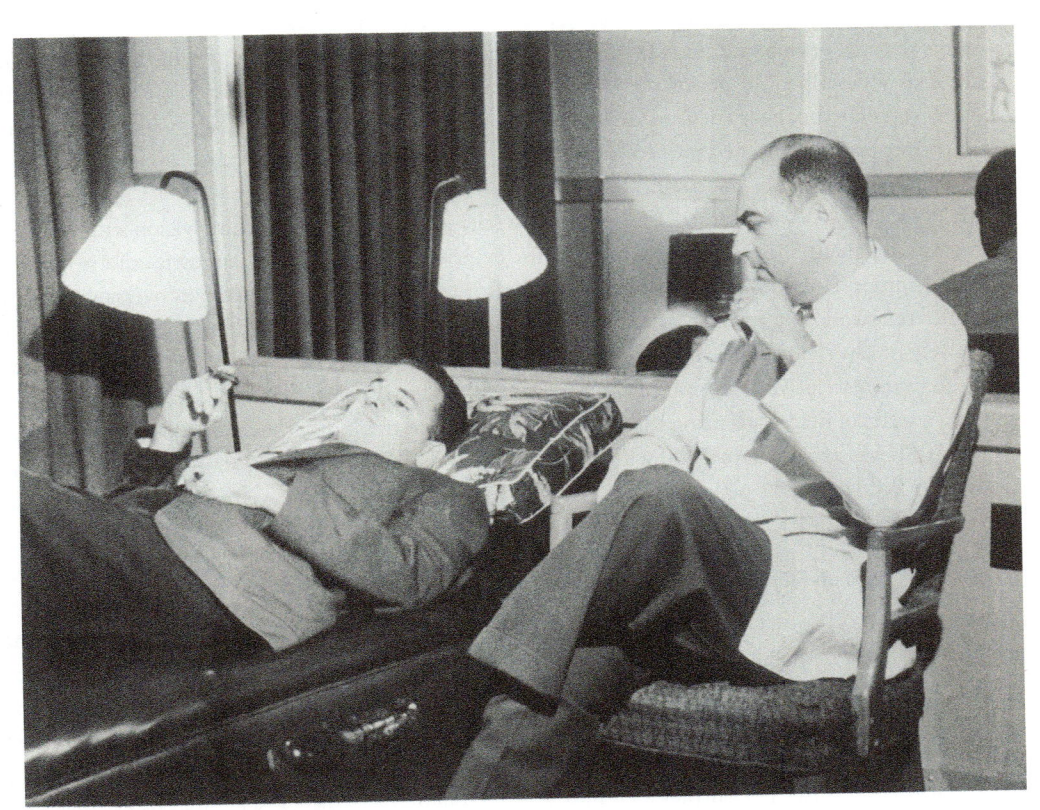

In the early days of psychological evaluation, every clinician had their own system of classification.
Bettmann/Contributor/Getty Images

second category comprised those disorders that included an environmental component in which the individual found it difficult to cope with their world. This second category was further divided into three different types of disorders. The first was psychosis, including schizophrenia and other psychotic disorders. The second was neurosis, such as anxiety disorders. The third was referred to as character disorders, such as psychopathy, which were involved in forensic decisions. As you will see later, those individuals who demonstrate psychopathic tendencies often find themselves accused of crimes, such as cheating others. In general, it was assumed that the neurotic disorders would be more amenable to psychological treatment.

DSM-II was released in 1968. Although it did not differ greatly from *DSM-I*, it did offer an opportunity for the mental disorder categories of *ICD-8* and *DSM-II* to be almost identical. This allowed for a worldwide classification system, which increased the ability to collect statistics on particular mental disorders. One difference was that the *ICD* manual just listed the disorders, whereas the *DSM* included brief definitions.

During the 1970s, there were a variety of changes in issues of importance to both the scientific and the larger lay community that influenced the next version of the *DSM*. In the scientific study of psychopathology, there was an increased emphasis on greater precision in describing the signs and symptoms associated with a particular psychopathology. In addition, there was an emphasis on differentiating one disorder from another as well as on using experimental research to inform these definitions. There was also an understanding that some individuals manifest a particular disorder in different ways. For example, as noted earlier in this chapter, some individuals with schizophrenia will hear voices, whereas others will have visual hallucinations.

When *DSM-III* was released in 1980, it included a number of major changes from *DSM-I* and *DSM-II* (see Blashfield et al., 2010). One was that it sought to rely on observable evidence to create a scientific system rather than just focusing on the interpretations of experts in the field. Another change was that *DSM-III* described disorders in terms of specific criteria rather than the more general descriptions of a disorder seen in *DSM-I* and *DSM-II*. *DSM-III* also introduced a five-level system of axes to give a more complete picture of the person. Axis I described the individual's psychopathological symptoms. Axis II described the person's personality or intellectual disability. Axis III described any medical disorders that the person had. Axis IV described significant environmental factors in the person's life. Lastly, Axis V described the person's level of functioning and any significant role impairment. Overall, *DSM-III* sought to be theory neutral and to use only observable terms. *DSM-III* was adopted in a number of countries and translated into 16 languages. In 1987, *DSM-III* was revised in terms of diagnostic criteria and referred to as *DSM-III-R*.

In 1994, *DSM-IV* was released. One goal of this release was to coordinate this revision with *ICD-10*. There was also an attempt to increase the scientific evidence underlying the diagnostic criteria for each specific disorder. To achieve this goal, a steering committee composed of 27 members oversaw the work of 13 different work groups. The task of the work groups was a three-step process. The first step was to extensively review the scientific literature related to a particular disorder. The second step was to utilize and reanalyze descriptive data from researchers who studied particular disorders. The third step was to conduct a series of field trials using the diagnostic criteria and to modify the criteria based on these trials. *DSM-IV* was expanded in 2000 with the publication of *DSM-IV-TR* (*TR* stands for text revision). *DSM-IV-TR* did not make major changes to the diagnostic criteria but did expand the text information describing each disorder.

DSM-5 and *DSM-5-TR*: The Current Version

DSM-5 was released in May 2013 and *DSM-5-TR* in 2022. The rationale for the changes beginning in *DSM-5* can be viewed online (see For Further Reading). The "TR" in *DSM-5-TR* stands for text revision. *DSM-5-TR* includes revised text and new references, clarifications to diagnostic criteria, and updates to ICD-10-CM codes since *DSM-5* was published in 2013. You may note that *DSM* went from using Roman numerals in previous editions to Arabic numerals for this edition. According to the *DSM-5* development website (see For Further Reading), *DSM-5* sought to expand the scientific basis of diagnosis begun in *DSM-III* by working with the NIMH. An initial conference was held in 1999. Participants developed a series of reports that sought to examine a variety of broad topics beyond diagnosis itself. These topics included developmental issues, gaps in the current system, disability and impairment, neuroscience, nomenclature, and cross-cultural issues. In later papers, age and gender issues were also considered. Further, international organizations such as the WHO, which produced the ICD-11, offered input into the composition of *DSM-5* and *DSM-5-TR*, and a number of conferences were held. There has been an effort to make the *DSM* and the *ICD* more similar with each new edition published.

This fifth edition of *DSM* presents the initial usage of dimensional assessments. As noted earlier, dimensional assessment is designed to determine the severity of a particular symptom on a continuum, or range, rather than just acknowledging its presence or absence. In addition, what were once considered to be separate disorders are now viewed as part of a spectrum. For example, although individuals with autism, childhood disintegrative disorder, pervasive developmental disorder, and Asperger's syndrome may vary in their symptoms and abilities, there are similarities to the disorders. Thus, it would be more accurate to describe autism as a spectrum ranging from mild to severe. In *DSM-5* and *DSM-5-TR*, the term *Asperger's* has thus been replaced with the term *autism spectrum disorder*. Another example is bipolar disorder. Someone diagnosed with bipolar disorder may have a number of severe mood episodes involving mania and depression, or they may have just a few. Dimensional analysis allows for more accurate representation of the disorder by reflecting the severity of these conditions. However, as you will see throughout this book, *DSM-5-TR* still describes a number of disorders that use a categorical definition. That is, if the person meets the criteria, the person has the disorder, and if they do not meet the criteria, they would not be considered to have the disorder. The following table shows the diagnostic criteria for diagnosing a specific phobia, for example. As you can see in Table 4.2,

TABLE 4.2 ■ *DSM-5-TR* Diagnostic Criteria for Specific Phobia

A. Marked fear or anxiety about a specific object or situation (e.g., flying, heights, animals, receiving an injection, seeing blood).
Note: In children, the fear or anxiety may be expressed by crying, tantrums, freezing, or clinging.

B. The phobic object or situation almost always provokes immediate fear or anxiety.

C. The phobic object or situation is actively avoided or endured with intense fear or anxiety.

D. The fear or anxiety is out of proportion to the actual danger posed by the specific object or situation and to the sociocultural context.

E. The fear, anxiety, or avoidance is persistent, typically lasting for 6 months or more.

F. The fear, anxiety, or avoidance causes clinically significant distress or impairment in social, occupational, or other important areas of functioning.

G. The disturbance is not better explained by the symptoms of another mental disorder, including fear, anxiety, and avoidance of situations associated with panic-like symptoms or other incapacitating symptoms (as in agoraphobia); objects or situations related to obsessions (as in obsessive–compulsive disorder); reminders of traumatic events (as in posttraumatic stress disorder); separation from home or attachment figures (as in separation anxiety disorder); or social situations (as in social anxiety disorder).

Specify if:

Code based on the phobic stimulus:

F40.218 Animal (e.g., spiders, insects, dogs).

F40.228 Natural environment (e.g., heights, storms, water).

F40.23x Blood-injection-injury (e.g., needles, invasive medical procedures).

Coding note: Select specific ICD-10-CM code as follows: **F40.230** fear of blood; **F40.231** fear of injections and transfusions; **F40.232** fear of other medical care; or **F40.233** fear of injury.

F40.248 Situational (e.g., airplanes, elevators, enclosed places).

F40.298 Other (e.g., situations that may lead to choking or vomiting; in children, e.g., loud sounds or costumed characters).

Coding note: When more than one phobic stimulus is present, code all ICD-10-CM codes that apply (e.g., for fear of snakes and flying, F40.218 specific phobia, animal, and F40.248 specific phobia, situational).

Credit: Reprinted with permission from the *Diagnostic and Statistical Manual of Mental Disorders, fifth edition, text revision*, DSM-V-TR, pp. 224–225 (Copyright © 2022). American Psychiatric Association. All Rights Reserved.

DSM-5-TR lists a number of different criteria, including duration and intensity, for the clinical diagnosis to be made.

The *DSM-5-TR* suggests that every case must begin with a careful clinical history as well as an understanding of the social, psychological, and biological factors that have contributed to the development of the disorder. It is important to understand the nature of the distress that the person is experiencing, since distress is a critical component of a *DSM* disorder. It is also important to understand if the distress and the individual's behavior should be considered as part of a mental disorder or simply as deviant from the individual's cultural, religious, or other significant groups. Thus, *DSM-5-TR* is more than just a list of symptoms to be checked off by the mental health professional. It is seen as a manual for organizing types of symptoms, which can suggest treatment approaches. However, *DSM-5-TR* does not specify any particular treatment.

Although *DSM-5-TR* suggests that the person be considered within a larger context, it dropped the multiaxial system seen in *DSM-III* and *DSM-IV*. A clinician may continue to note cultural, environmental, and other conditions related to a given disorder, but Axes III, IV, and V are now eliminated. Further, personality disorders are no longer described on a separate axis (Axis II).

Another change from previous versions is in *DSM-5-TR*'s organization. The placement of disorders is based on underlying vulnerabilities as well as symptom characteristics. The chapters are organized by general categories such as neurodevelopmental, emotional, and somatic to reflect how a variety of disorders may have common underlying similarities. Recent advances in brain imaging, genetics, and the neurosciences have suggested similarities not understood previously. For example, genetic research has suggested a closer connection between schizophrenia and bipolar disorder than was previously assumed. However, these still remain as separate disorders in *DSM-5-TR*. A detailed list of changes from *DSM-IV* to *DSM-5* and *DSM-5-TR* can be found online (see For Further Reading).

Since *DSM-5-TR* is used in a variety of settings, it carries with it a number of difficulties (Frances & Widiger, 2012). *DSM-5-TR* is used by mental health professionals to assess individuals. It has also traditionally been used by researchers to study psychopathology. Further, our legal system uses it in court trials in which the outcomes can depend on whether the person is experiencing a mental disorder. All of these usages carry with them different types of demands. The researcher seeks to understand underlying processes of a disorder, whereas the clinician seeks to know how to use the diagnosis to define treatment and induce change. As you will see in later chapters, cultural considerations also play a role. For example, in earlier editions of the *DSM*, "homosexuality" was considered a disorder that could be treated. In later chapters of this text, feature boxes that highlight changes to and criticisms of *DSM-5* and *DSM-5-TR* in relation to specific disorders will be presented.

CONCEPT CHECK

- What are some of the reasons for setting up a classification system for mental illness, such as the *ICD* or the *DSM*?
- How are the *ICD* and the *DSM* similar? How are they different?
- What are two major changes in the way disorders are classified in the most recent edition, *DSM-5-TR*, compared with its predecessor, *DSM-IV*?

SUMMARY

Psychological assessment is the process of gathering information about a person in order to make a clinical decision about that person's symptoms. Most mental health professionals use a clinical interview to initially gather information concerning the status of an individual with whom they are working. Worldwide, the clinical interview, referred to as the mental status exam, has been organized into major assessment categories, including the person's appearance and behavior, mood and affect, speech quality, thought processes, perceptions and general awareness of surroundings, and intellectual functioning and insight. With the most recent edition of the *DSM (DSM-5-TR)*, the SCID has been developed to set forth specific assessment questions in a structured approach along with a decision tree for directing follow-up questions. Over the past 40 years, there has been an increasing awareness that mental illness takes place within the context of a particular culture, and a fuller understanding of psychopathology requires an understanding of this context. With *DSM-5-TR*, the Cultural Formulation Interview (CFI) has been developed to help mental health professionals obtain information concerning the person's culture.

Concerns about the accuracy of assessment and classification of psychopathology require us to consider questions of reliability and validity: (a) whether the person being assessed is giving us accurate information and (b) whether the assessment instrument measures the construct consistently (reliability) and accurately (validity). In terms of assessment, there are a number of types of reliability: internal reliability, test–retest reliability, alternate-form reliability, and inter-rater reliability. Although measures such as neuropsychological tests, brain images, and molecular and genetic changes suggest possible variables to be considered, there is currently no exact measure by which to diagnose psychopathology. This makes validity an important but complex concept. In terms of assessment, there are a number of types of validity: content validity, predictive validity, concurrent validity, and construct validity.

There are several models of assessment that represent different ways of assessing signs and symbols. These include symptom questionnaires, personality tests, projective tests, and neuropsychological testing. Neuroscience techniques offer an additional level of analysis to the models of assessment that focus on signs and symbols. Scientists have sought to identify underlying markers associated with specific mental disorders. Using various brain imaging techniques such as MRI, fMRI, EEG, and MEG, there has been a search for structural and functional changes associated with psychopathology. There might be different underlying brain processes involved in what appears as a single disorder. Thus, neuroscience methods may lead to better diagnostic procedures. It is also possible to use these techniques to follow the course of a disorder over time. Another potential for neuroscience methods is that by knowing the underlying brain and genetic processes involved in a particular disorder for a particular person, it would be possible to create a treatment particular to a given individual.

Classification is a way to organize the diversity seen in mental disorders. Over the past 200 years, numerous systems have been developed; however, in the past 50 years, the emphasis has been on reliability of diagnosis. There has been a push for observable characteristics that would define a specific disorder—signs and symptoms delineated through observation of, and conversation with, the individual. In general, these types of criteria make up the structure of the *DSM*, published by the APA and used in North America, and the *ICD*, published by the WHO and used in Europe. One overall change in *DSM-5* and *DSM-5-TR* is the use of dimensional assessments and spectrum-related disorders. Another change is in the placement of disorders based on underlying vulnerabilities as well as symptom characteristics to reflect how a variety of disorders may have some common underlying similarities. The National Institute of Mental Health (NIMH) has begun a program to better study, prevent, and treat mental disorders, which includes developing a new way to classify mental disorders, referred to as Research Domain Criteria (RDoC).

STUDY RESOURCES

Review Questions

1. What are some of the advantages of conducting a structured interview for an initial mental health assessment? In addition, what specific advantages do the mental status exam and the SCID offer?

2. How do reliability and validity relate to the assessment and classification of psychopathology?

3. How can neuropsychological testing help us understand mental illness?

4. What important areas of potential do neuroscience techniques offer in the assessment and classification of mental illness?

5. "Classification is a way to organize the diversity seen in mental disorders." From what you have read about *ICD* and *DSM*, the advantages of classification are clear, but are there any disadvantages or things that are overlooked?

For Further Reading

American Psychiatric Association. (n.d.). *Diagnostic and statistical manual of mental disorders.* (5th ed., text rev.) https://www.psychiatry.org/dsm5

Frances, A. (2013). *Saving normal: An insider's revolt against out-of-control psychiatric diagnosis, DSM-5, big pharma, and the medicalization of ordinary life.* HarperCollins.

Kitayama, S., & Cohen, D. (2007). *The handbook of cultural psychology.* Guilford Press.

Meehl, P. E. (1954). *Clinical versus statistical prediction.* University of Minnesota Press.

Meyer, G. J., Viglione, D. J., Mihura, J. L., Erard, R. E., & Erdberg, P. (2011). Introduction. R-PAS. *Rorschach Performance Assessment System™* (pp. 1–4). https://r-pas.org/Docs/Manual_Chapter_1.pdf

National Institute of Mental Health. (n.d.). *About RDoC.* U.S. Department of Health and Human Services. https://www.nimh.nih.gov/research/research-funded-by-nimh/rdoc/about-rdoc

R-PAS. (n.d.). https://r-pas.org/

Stony Brook University, Renaissance School of Medicine. (n.d.). *The Hierarchical Taxonomy of Psychopathology (HiTOP).* https://renaissance.stonybrookmedicine.edu/HITOP

World Health Organization. (n.d). *ICD-11 for mortality and morbidity statistics* (11th ed.). https://icd.who.int/browse11/1-m/en

KEY TERMS

Beck Depression Inventory (BDI)
categorical
classification
comorbid
Continuous Performance Test (CPT)
Cultural Formulation Interview (CFI)
delusional thinking
Diagnostic and Statistical Manual of Mental Disorders (DSM)
dimensional
externalizing disorders
flight of ideas
internalizing disorders
International Classification of Diseases (ICD)
mental status exam
Minnesota Multiphasic Personality Inventory (MMPI)
National Institute of Mental Health (NIMH)
obsessional thinking
projective instruments
psychological assessment
reliability
Research Domain Criteria (RDoC)
reward system
Rorschach inkblots
Structured Clinical Interview for DSM Disorders (SCID)
structured interview
Thematic Apperception Test (TAT)
Wechsler Adult Intelligence Scale (WAIS)
Wisconsin Card Sorting Test (WCST)

iStock.com/FG Trade. Stock photo. Posed by model.

5 CHILDHOOD AND ADOLESCENT-ONSET DISORDERS

LEARNING OBJECTIVES

5.1 Summarize the major brain and developmental changes in childhood and adolescence.

5.2 Distinguish among the attachment disorders, conduct disorder, and oppositional defiant disorder and treatments.

5.3 Describe the characteristics of autism spectrum disorder, its causes, and treatment.

5.4 Define ADHD and learning disabilities and discuss their prevalence, causes, and treatment.

5.5 Describe the characteristics of intellectual developmental disorder, its causes, and treatment.

Everyone's childhood is different. Some have a relatively stress-free time, while others experience significant difficulties, including a lack of basic needs or the loss of parents. Some of us find ourselves easily valuing the experiences of our culture, while others feel left out and different. John Robison and Temple Grandin, whose words follow below, both describe themselves as not understanding how others experienced life. In clinical terms, their experiences indicate evidence of autism spectrum disorder.

"Look me in the eye, young man!"

I cannot tell you how many times I heard that shrill, whining refrain. It started about the time I got to first grade. I heard it from parents, relatives, teachers, principals, and all manner of other people. I heard it so often I began to expect to hear it.

To this day, when I speak, I find visual input to be distracting. When I was younger, if I saw something interesting I might begin to watch it and stop speaking entirely. As a grown-up, I don't usually come to a complete stop, but I may still pause if something catches my eye. That's why I usually look somewhere neutral—at the ground or off into the distance—when I'm talking to someone. Because speaking while watching things has always been difficult for me, learning to drive a car and talk at the same time was a tough one, but I mastered it.

And now I know it is perfectly natural for me not to look at someone when I talk. Those of us with Asperger's are just not comfortable doing it. In fact, I don't really understand why it's considered normal to stare at someone's eyeballs.

Excerpt from Look Me in the Eye: My Life With Asperger's, *by John Elder Robison (2007).*

I was my mother's first child, and I was like a little wild animal. I struggled to get away when held, but if I was left alone in the big baby carriage I seldom fussed. Mother first realized that something was dreadfully wrong when I failed to start talking like the little girl next door, and it seemed that I might be deaf. Between nonstop tantrums and a penchant for smearing feces, I was a terrible two-year-old.

I can remember the frustration of not being able to talk at age three. This caused me to throw many a tantrum. I could understand what people said to me, but I could not get my words out. It was like a big stutter, and starting words was difficult. . . . Tantrums also occurred when I became tired or stressed by too much noise, such as horns going off at a birthday party. My behavior was like a tripping circuit breaker. One minute I was fine, and the next minute I was on the floor kicking and screaming like a crazed wildcat.

Excerpt from Thinking in Pictures and Other Reports From My Life With Autism, *by Temple Grandin (2010, pp. 43–44).*

My mind is similar to an Internet search engine that searches for photographs. I use language to narrate the photo-realistic pictures that pop up in my imagination. When I design equipment for the cattle industry, I can test run it in my imagination similar to a virtual reality computer program. All my thinking is associative and not linear. To form concepts, I sort pictures into categories similar to computer files. To form the concept of orange, I see many different orange objects, such as oranges, pumpkins, orange juice and marmalade.

Excerpt from "How Does Visual Thinking Work in the Mind of a Person With Autism? A Personal Account," by Temple Grandin (2009, pp. 1437–1442).

This chapter will focus on disorders that are associated with, or first diagnosed in, childhood, although they are sometimes lifelong in duration. In order to better understand these disorders associated with development, we will begin by describing the process of normal development. In fact, from a *developmental psychopathology perspective*, it is critical to view typical and nontypical development as being influenced by the same factors (Lewis & Rudolph, 2014). These factors include cultural, social, relationship (as between the caregiver and infant), environmental, and genetic factors. As you will see,

Temple Grandin

Helen H. Richardson/Denver Post/via Getty Images

TABLE 5.1 Categories in *DSM-5-TR* in Which Selective Childhood Disorders Are Described

Trauma- and Stressor-Related Disorders

- Reactive Attachment Disorder
- Disinhibited Social Engagement Disorder

Neurodevelopmental Disorders

- Autism Spectrum Disorder
- Attention Deficit/Hyperactivity Disorder (ADHD)
- Disorders of Learning
- Motor Disorders (e.g., Tic Disorder, Tourette's Disorder)

Disruptive, Impulse Control, and Conduct Disorders

- Conduct Disorder
- Oppositional Defiant Disorder

as we develop, we continue to make sense of our environment and learn how to interact with it. There are particularly significant times in normal development in which environmental factors interact with personal factors. This can stress the individual and, in turn, lead to increased manifestations of psychological disorders.

DSM-5-TR describes disorders of childhood in a number of separate categories (Table 5.1). This chapter, to different degrees, will emphasize three of these. The first grouping is **trauma- and stressor-related disorders**. It is in this group that disorders of attachment are included. The second grouping is under the rubric of **neurodevelopmental disorders**. *Autism spectrum disorder* and *attention deficit/hyperactivity disorder (ADHD)* are included here. This group also includes disorders of learning, intelligence, and communication. Motor disorders such as tics and Tourette's disorder are also included in this group. The third grouping is **disruptive, impulse control, and conduct disorders**.

IMPORTANT ASPECTS OF NORMAL CHILDHOOD DEVELOPMENT

What is a normal development process, and what types of events or influences can disrupt this process? Disruptions can be caused by a number of factors, including family and social relationships, one's culture, and one's genetic makeup. These factors can interact with developmental changes at different ages. Thus, it is important to understand normal development processes and how they can be involved in psychological disorders. Social and emotional processes are particularly important. Using brain imaging and other modern investigative techniques, our understanding of social relationships and their contribution to psychopathology has increased greatly.

Although each human is unique, it is also the case that there are universal situations during human development. Unlike some other species, humans are born in an undeveloped state into a world in which they cannot survive alone. Consider that a 200-pound female gorilla gives birth to a 4-pound baby, while a human female of half to two-thirds that weight gives birth to a 6- to 9-pound baby. The implications of this are that mechanisms are needed to ensure the survival of the mother as well as the protection and development of the infant. Historically, it is the group, the family, and the mother who have given this support.

From an evolutionary perspective, human infants display an amazing ability to form connections with their caregivers and maintain a close connection with others. We learn language quickly, know how to understand nonverbal expressions, and later grow to be part of a larger social community. Every infant learns to talk and walk at a different rate and express emotions at a different rate. Mental health professionals have a difficult task in determining what might just be delayed development in certain skills and what represents a developmental disorder. Even with discrete disorders such as autism spectrum disorder, treatment can greatly influence the course of an individual's development. In general, the criteria for diagnosis of a developmental disorder have to do with severity, duration, pervasiveness, and degree of impairment.

There are a number of sensitive developmental periods in which social disruptions can lead to long-term effects. For example, what happens when events such as war or natural disasters interrupt normal caregiving patterns? British psychiatrist John Bowlby (1951) sought to determine what would happen if a young child had their physical needs, such as food and housing, satisfied but did not experience a close emotional connection. His early work examined children who became orphans during World War II, who were physically cared for but lacked the same level of emotional attention typically provided by a caregiver, such as a mother caring for her own infant. Bowlby's and later research has shown that these infants display patterns of interpersonal behavior that have been associated with psychological problems. As we will discuss later in the chapter, he referred to the infant–mother relationship as *attachment*.

Other sensitive developmental periods are directly related to the brain and to the turning on and off of genes. If genetic or other malfunctions happen at these times, psychopathologies or other developmental problems may develop later in the child's life (Miguel et al., 2019).

Thanks to the brain's plasticity early in life, experiences can also influence brain development. This can be positive, as seen in the study presented in Chapter 3 that shows that early experience with music changes how certain brain areas develop. And as you will see, treatment can significantly improve a number of developmental disorders. The effects of experience on the brain can also be negative. Trauma can influence brain structures as well as epigenetic processes in which the environment influences how genes turn on and off. However, as noted by Caspi and others (Byrd & Manuck, 2014; Caspi et al., 2002; Caspi et al., 2010; Nilsson et al., 2018), variations in genetic makeup make some individuals more sensitive to maltreatment and stress than others, which in turn can lead to psychological disorders. Overall, early environmental experiences have been shown to influence brain development, neurotransmitter functioning, and neuroendocrine function, which in turn can influence psychopathological behaviors (Burnette & Cicchetti, 2012; Pollok et al., 2022).

Human infants display an amazing ability to form connections with their caregivers.
iStock.com/SelectStock

Brain Development

There are two critical periods in terms of brain development. The first is during gestation and the early years of life when the brain is establishing its cortical connections. Within this period, children develop the ability to process sensory information, language, and cognitive skills (Figure 5.1). These skills develop in a particular order, and there is some suggestion that disorders such as autism may be related to a mistiming of this development that results in atypical connections in the brain (Bardin, 2012; Chen et al., 2018). Brain connections remain stable until about 12 years of age. During adolescence, there is another critical period when the brain rewires itself in a different manner. At both of these times, external or internal events including genetic processes can occur, which may lead to physical or mental disorders.

As you can well imagine, birth itself represents a major change for the infant (Ben-Ari, 2015; Lagercrantz & Slotkin, 1986). Four critical events occur. First, the infant goes from an environment in which it is surrounded by fluid to one in which it is surrounded by air and must acquire oxygen in a different manner. Second, there is a reduction in temperature. Third, a change occurs in the availability of nutrients in that feeding is not continuous after birth. Fourth and finally, there is a change from a sterile environment to one with pathogens, which in turn help the immune system develop. With these environmental changes come some profound biochemical changes that help to create an alert infant shortly after birth. However, the changes can also trigger the possibility of certain disorders developing. In particular, the neurotransmitter GABA and the hormone oxytocin, which relate to EEG activity in the infant brain, may under certain conditions lead to autism spectrum disorders (Ben-Ari, 2015).

Before a child is born, the brain begins to form the connections necessary to perform basic sensory and motor functions (see Konrad & Eickhoff, 2010, for an overview of connectivity in the brain). Overall, the first areas to develop in an infant are involved in movement and vision. After that, the brain develops from back to front. The last area to develop is the frontal lobes, which continue to develop into early adulthood.

Normal brain development is commonly interrupted by early life stress, defined as a situation in which a child is unable to cope given the demands that they experience (McLaughlin et al., 2012; Pechtel & Pizzagalli, 2011). These situations range from natural disasters to the death of a parent to child mistreatment. Such stress early in a child's life can influence their risk for developing mental disorders that appear before age 5 (Figure 5.2). One way of quantifying the

FIGURE 5.1 ■ What Comes First in Development?

This figure shows that the senses develop first, followed by languages and then higher cognitive functions.

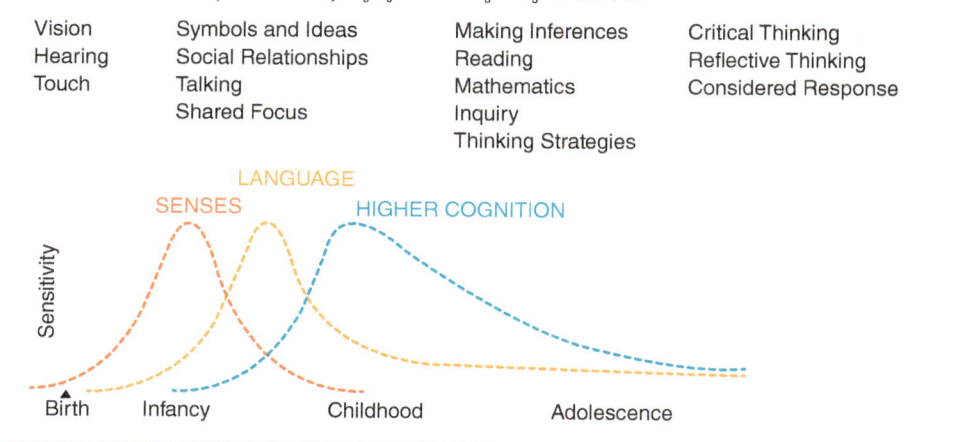

Vision	Symbols and Ideas	Making Inferences	Critical Thinking
Hearing	Social Relationships	Reading	Reflective Thinking
Touch	Talking	Mathematics	Considered Response
	Shared Focus	Inquiry	
		Thinking Strategies	

Credit: Bardin, J. (2012). Neurodevelopment: Unlocking the brain. *Nature, 487,* 24–26. https://doi.org/10.1038/487024a

FIGURE 5.2 ■ When Is a Child at Risk for Developing Mental Disorders?

During childhood, attachment disorders develop prior to autism spectrum disorders. After age 3, oppositional disorders can be seen. School phobia can appear as the child begins kindergarten or primary school.

Development of Psychopathology
Intervals Represent Periods of Greatest Risk for Onset of Illness

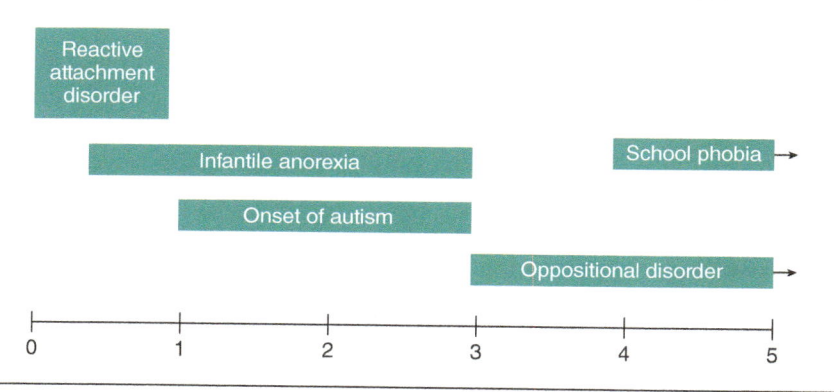

Credit: Tasman, A., Kay, J., Lieberman, J. A., First, M. B., & Maj, M. (Eds.). (2008). *Psychiatry* (3rd ed.). Wiley, p. 107.

numbers of children who experience early life stress is by examining data from child protective services (CPS). In 2009, about 22.5% of all children in the United States came to the attention of CPS. More recent data from the 20 largest U.S. counties suggest that 1 in 3 children will have a CPS investigation, 1 in 8 will experience maltreatment, 1 in 17 will be placed in foster care, and 1 in 100 will have the rights of their parents terminated (Edwards et al., 2021). However, these data are unequally distributed by race and ethnicity; overall, the rate of CPS investigations was highest for Black children and lowest for Asian children. Some 58% of all adolescents reported experiencing some type of adversity during their lifetime, with over half reporting multiple experiences. In terms of *DSM* disorders, these experiences increased the risk for a behavioral disorder by 40% and a fear disorder (e.g., panic disorder, social phobia, and other phobias) by 15% (McLaughlin et al., 2012).

Since brain changes in childhood and adolescence show different patterns for gray and white matter in different areas of the brain, stress and adversity can have a greater impact at this time than later in adulthood (Miguel et al., 2019). Overall, exposure to early life adversity is associated with modifications in volume, microstructure, and connectivity in specific brain regions, including the amygdala and the hippocampus. These differences affect socioemotional outcomes in childhood and the risk for psychopathology later in life. As you will see in later chapters, stress and adversity bring forth changes in hormones and neurotransmitters that in turn influence developmental processes. For example, a common finding is that those who experience extreme stress in childhood show smaller brain structures such as the hippocampus, which is involved in learning and memory (Pollok et al., 2022). Likewise, stress-related processes may influence the amygdala and its role in emotional processing.

Theories of Attachment

John Bowlby developed a theoretical understanding of interpersonal relationships based on the interactions of children with their parents. This type of bonding has great survival value for helpless human infants, who cannot take care of themselves. Along with a number of other instincts, such as the *rooting reflex* in which an infant begins sucking when the cheek or mouth is touched, **attachment** is seen as the basis of early emotional relationships between a mother (or other primary caregiver) and her child. It initially begins with nursing, as the mother and her child learn how to respond to one another. Both internal and external processes and their constant interplay lead to mother–infant bonding. Bowlby (1969) named this process *attachment* rather than the traditional term used in psychoanalysis, which was *object relations*. As you will see throughout this book, lack of successful attachment patterns has been associated with anxiety, depression, dissociation, and personality disorders, as well as disorders of attachment, which are discussed in this chapter.

Bowlby considered the process of attachment to be a social–emotional behavior equally as important as mating behavior and parental behavior. He saw attachment as a multifaceted process involving a variety of developmental mechanisms over the first year of life. Attachment for Bowlby was a process in which the mother was able to reduce fear in her child through direct contact. The mother would also come to provide support, called a secure base, that would allow for the infant's later exploratory behaviors. Bowlby suggested that there were five universal attachment behaviors in human infants: sucking, clinging, crying, following, and smiling. Bowlby assumed that the relative immaturity of the human infant, compared to other primates, resulted in attachment being a slower process in humans. We'll return to Bowlby's work shortly.

Harry Harlow's Experiments With Infant Monkeys

In a classic series of experiments in the 1950s, Harry Harlow initially examined the mechanisms of attachment with primates. Harlow had seen the effects of infant monkeys being raised, like human infants in orphanages of the time, with ample food but little mothering. In Harlow's case, it was because of an infection problem in the lab that required the primate infants to be separated (Blum, 2002). Although healthy, these primate infants showed anxious and withdrawing behaviors. However, Harlow needed a formal experiment to clarify these observations.

To better understand the nature of attachment in monkey infants, Harlow (1958) separated infant rhesus monkeys from their mothers after birth and placed them in isolated cages. In the infant's cage were two surrogate mothers—one made of wire and the other made of terry cloth. The wire surrogates had bare bodies of welded wire, whereas the cloth surrogates were covered by soft, resilient terry cloth. Both surrogates had long bodies that could be easily clasped by the infant monkey.

For half of the infants, a nipple by which they could feed themselves was attached only to the wire mother, and for the other half, the nipple was attached only to the terry cloth mother. In either surrogate mother, the infants had the nutrition that they needed. If attachment was totally learned through reinforcement, then the infant monkeys should go to the mother from which they were fed. What do you think happened? What happened was a finding completely contrary to the learning theory interpretation. As the infants who fed on the wire mother grew, they showed decreasing responsiveness to her and increasing responsiveness to the cloth mother, even though this mother had no food to offer (Figure 5.3). From this, Harlow concluded that it is the contact comfort and not the feeding per se that binds the infant to the mother.

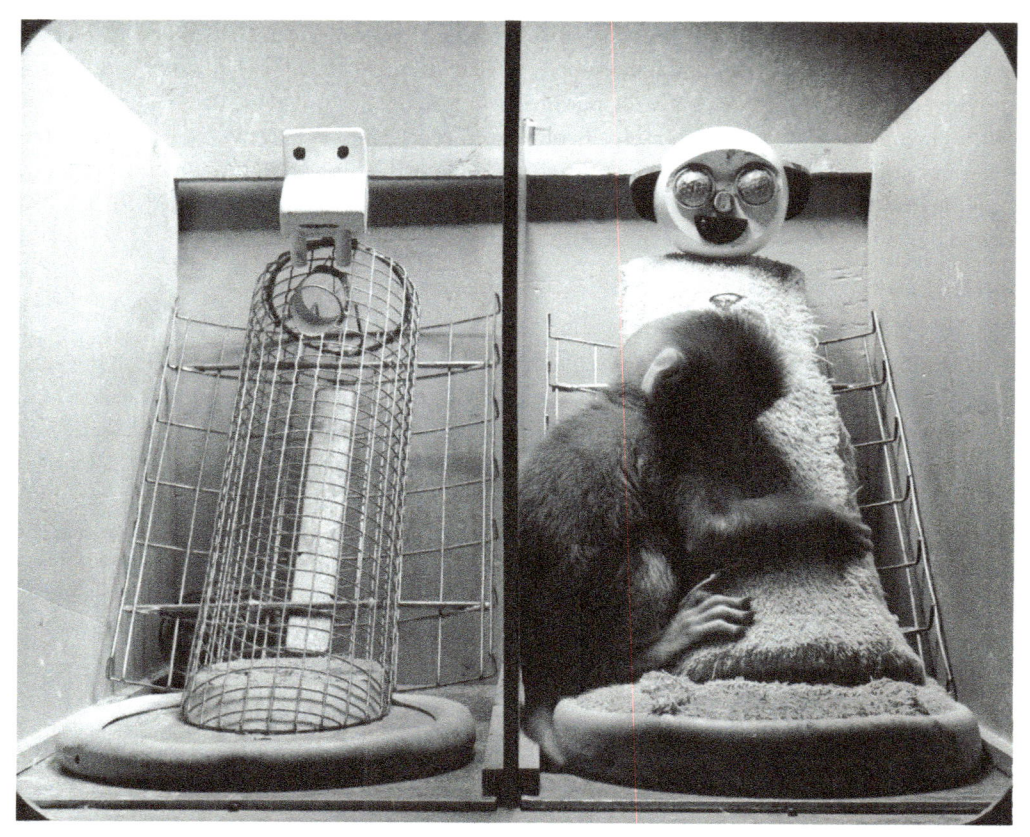

The wire and cloth surrogate mothers. In Harlow's experiment, food was compared with comfort.

Science History Images/Alamy Stock Photo

FIGURE 5.3 ■ Which Mother Gives the Most Comfort?

Based on the number of hours spent with the cloth surrogate, the primate infants liked the cloth mother best, even if food was available on the wire mother. Harlow concluded that it was the contact comfort from the soft terry cloth that made the difference.

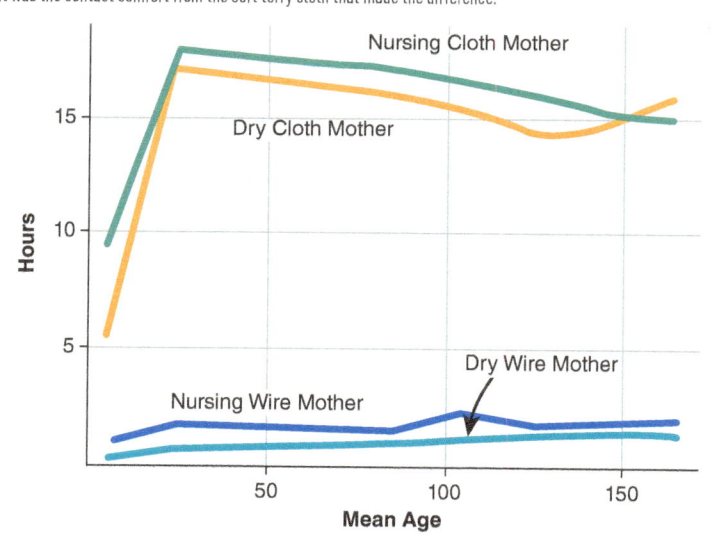

Source: Harlow, H., McGaugh, J., & Thompson, R. (1971). *Psychology.* Albion Publishing, p. 59.

John Bowlby's Research on Attachment

Bowlby's original interest in attachment came from observations of children in orphanages following World War II. As part of a World Health Organization (WHO) project, Bowlby concluded that children deprived of their mothers were at risk for physical and mental illness. In particular, he concluded that separation from emotional caregivers could lead to severe anxiety and psychopathic personality (Bowlby, 1951). Bowlby carefully observed children and recorded his observations in a series of books and articles focused on secure attachment as well as loss and separation anxiety (Bowlby, 1961, 1982, 1988).

In terms of the general characteristics of attachment, Bowlby reported that children who develop a secure bond, or attachment, with a caregiver or parent, who is usually their mother, display patterns of activity that are especially strong from the end of the first year of life until about 3 years of age in relation to that caregiver. First, the infant shows distress when the caregiver leaves. Second, the infant smiles, makes noises, or shows other signs of pleasure when the caregiver returns. Third, the infant shows distress when approached by a stranger, unless the caregiver encourages the interaction. Fourth and finally, the infant shows more exploratory behaviors in an unfamiliar situation when the caregiver is present.

Mary Ainsworth's Work and Styles of Attachment

Based on infants' reactions to their caregiver, Mary Ainsworth (Ainsworth et al., 1978) developed a scenario known as the *strange situation* to research attachment patterns experimentally. The basic procedure is to bring the infant and their mother into an unfamiliar room with toys. With the infant and mother alone, the infant is allowed to explore without the mother being involved. At this point, a stranger enters and talks with the mother and then approaches the infant. During this time, the mother leaves inconspicuously. The stranger reacts to the infant as appropriate. The mother then returns and greets and comforts the infant. Following this, the mother leaves the infant alone in the room, and the stranger returns. The mother then returns again and greets and picks up the infant while the stranger leaves. During this procedure, the researchers observe the infant's reaction to the return of the mother.

Initially, Ainsworth described three patterns of attachment styles (Ainsworth et al., 1978). The first, called the **secure attachment pattern**, is characterized by the infant (a) engaging in active exploration, (b) getting upset when the mother leaves, and (c) showing positive emotions when the mother returns. The second pattern is the **avoidant attachment pattern**. In the avoidant style, the infant shows more interest in the toys than the mother and shows less distress when the mother leaves and less positive emotion when she returns. The third pattern is referred to as the **anxious/ambivalent attachment pattern**. In this pattern, the infant appears preoccupied with having access to the mother and shows protest on her separation. When she returns, the infant may show anger or ambivalence toward her. This attachment pattern is associated with developing anxiety disorders later in life.

Later, other researchers suggested that a fourth pattern of attachment may exist that is characterized as the **disorganized/controlling attachment pattern**. This attachment category was added when it was observed that some infants show disruptions in processing during the strange situation (Main & Solomon, 1990). That is, when their parent is

John Bowlby
Courtesy the University of Cambridge

Mary Ainsworth (center)
JHU Sheridan Libraries/Gado/Archive Photos/via Getty Images

present, these infants show disorganized behavior patterns or disorientation. Children with this attachment style tend to have problems dealing with psychological stress and a tendency to develop dissociative disorders later in life.

Of course, infants do not grow up in a vacuum, so it is also important to characterize the mothering style of the caregiver. With infants displaying secure attachment patterns, the style of the mother is consistent and responsive to her infant's signals. On the other hand, mothers of infants showing avoidant patterns tend to be more rejecting and rigid and, in general, insensitive to the infants' signals, including requests for bodily contact. Anxious or ambivalent patterns tend to be associated with inconsistent mothers who may be intrusive. Disorganized or controlling patterns tend to be associated with parents who show unpredictable abusive behavior or other behaviors that are frightening to the child. Mothers of these children are also more likely to experience depression (O'Connor et al., 2011). The complexity of the situation is highlighted by the fact that some infants are easier to care for than others. That is to say, some infants appear to be temperamentally more irritable than others and thus could be more difficult for a caregiver to approach positively. For example, infants with colic will cry and fuss, making parenting more difficult (Leung & Lemay, 2004).

Long-Term Consequences of Early Attachment Patterns

Attachment patterns can be seen as an internal road map or schema through which the person interprets their own experiences. As such, they are part of a larger overall developmental sequence that can be considered in the development of psychopathology. An attachment pattern gives insight into how a person deals with psychological stress and loss. Is the person able to regulate their reaction to a stressful situation? A secure attachment pattern is protective and associated with successful regulation. On the other hand, insecure attachment patterns reflect one aspect of the complex process that leads to psychological disorders. Since attachment patterns tend to be stable, their effects can be cumulative. They may include the types of statements that people make to themselves, such as negative evaluations of themselves and their abilities, as are often seen in depression. They may also include the manner in which a person deals with emotional regulation, whether in an overreaction, as seen with personality disorders, or not experiencing emotion, as seen in dissociative disorders.

Research has shown children with insecure patterns of attachment to be at risk for several forms of childhood psychopathology (DeKlyen & Greenberg, 2008; Mikulincer & Shaver, 2012; Spalletta et al., 2020). Specifically, the avoidant attachment style is associated with aggressiveness in middle childhood, and the anxious or ambivalent attachment style is associated with passive withdrawal. The disorganized or controlling pattern of attachment has been associated with personality disorders and dissociative disorders. The anxious or ambivalent pattern of attachment has also been associated with mood disorders later in life, such as anxiety and depression (Dozier et al., 2008). *Cultural LENS: Romania Adoption Study* provides a closer look at attachment issues and other challenges faced by children who grew up in Romanian orphanages.

CULTURAL LENS
ROMANIA ADOPTION STUDY

Nicolae Ceaușescu was the head of state of Romania from 1967 to 1989. By the end of his rule, he had become brutal and repressive. Not only was he a ruthless dictator who enforced his rule with the use of the secret police, but he also instituted strict policies requiring Romanians to have more children. He sought to increase the low birth rate in Romania by making divorce difficult and contraception and abortion illegal. He also dictated that women should have at least five children. To this end, Ceaușescu established the menstrual police. These were state gynecologists who conducted monthly checks of women of childbearing age who had not borne at least five children. To encourage additional children, families received a stipend for having more than two children but were also taxed for having fewer than five children. The number of new births did increase, although a number of these children were abandoned since their families could not afford to provide for them. The state encouraged placing these children in state orphanages.

After the fall of the Ceaușescu regime in 1989, it became clear that some 170,000 children had been placed in state institutions. The international media described these children as being "warehoused." Initially, some of these children were adopted internationally, but this practice was later banned by Romania. Ministers in the government after Ceaușescu sought solutions to the problem of institutionalized infants and children and asked U.S. investigators to set up a study examining the efficacy of foster care as an alternative to institutionalization.

Infants in a Romanian orphanage in Bucharest, circa 1995.

Emanuel Tanjala/Alamy Stock Photo

This set in motion a study in which the effects of foster care on attachment relationships and future cognitive, emotional, and physiological development could be assessed and better understood. The Bucharest Early Intervention Project assessed infants and young children then living in institutions in Bucharest, selected families who were willing to foster these infants and children, and set up an intervention to gauge the effectiveness of foster care to remediate the effects of early deprivation. Some infants and children were randomly assigned to families, and others would continue to receive the usual care in orphanages. A control group of children from the Bucharest community, who were neither institutionalized nor raised in foster care, was also identified and provided an important point of comparison.

A team of researchers was able to follow a subset of these children over a number of years. Initially, measurements were taken (a baseline assessment) of the children who were assigned to a foster family as well as those who remained in the institution. These measurements allowed the researchers to know if the intervention was a success and if the age at which infants were removed from the institution and placed into foster homes was a determiner of that success. The baseline measurements were followed by a comprehensive follow-up at 30, 42, and 54 months and at 8 and 12 years. An initial study showed that those children in the institution displayed less attachment to a caregiver than those who had never been in the orphanages and lived in the community (Table 5.2). When assessed at 42 months, more children in foster care showed a secure attachment style, whereas those who received care as usual at the orphanage showed more of the other insecure styles (Figure 5.4).

TABLE 5.2 ■ What Effects Does an Institution Have on Attachment?

Community	Institution
74% secure	18.9% secure
4.0% avoidant	3.2% avoidant
0.0% resistant	0.0% resistant
22.0% disorganized	65.3% disorganized
0.0% unclassifiable	12.6% unclassifiable

Children raised in the community (the control group in this study) showed more secure attachment to a caregiver than those children raised in an orphanage.

Source: Zeanah, C. H., Smyke, A. T., Koga, S. F., Carlson, E., & The Bucharest Early Intervention Project Core Group. (2005). Attachment in institutionalized and community children in Romania. *Child Development, 76*(5), 1015–1028, Table 2.

FIGURE 5.4 ■ Does Foster Care Increase Secure Attachment?

At 42 months, children in foster care showed more secure attachment than those children who remained in the institution.

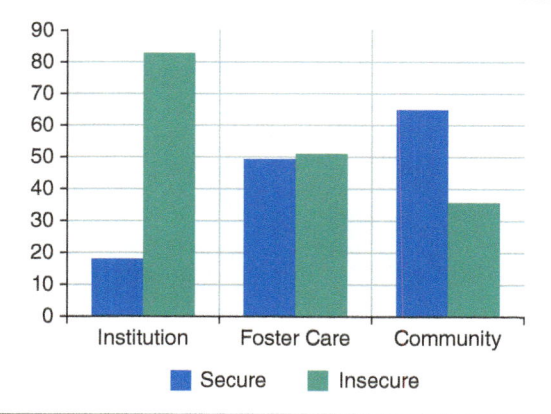

Source: Based on Nelson, C. A., Fox, N. A., & Zeanah, C. H. (2014). *Romania's abandoned children: Deprivation, brain development, and the struggle for recovery.* Harvard University Press.

In addition to attachment, cognitive development (as measured in terms of IQ) was higher the earlier the child was placed in foster care. Physiological measures, including stress responses, EEG, and brain volume, were also shown to be influenced by type of caregiving situation. Those children reared in the institutional setting showed disruptions in their physiological responses to stress (McLaughlin et al., 2015). In terms of the brain, there was less of both gray and white matter in those children who grew up in the institution as compared with children who had never been institutionalized (Sheridan et al., 2012). Likewise, white matter connections were weaker in those who experienced neglect (Bick et al., 2015). Further, the institutionally reared children had more symptoms of anxiety, depression, ADHD, and disruptive behaviors (Slopen et al., 2012). Overall, the majority (53%) of 4½-year-olds who had been reared in the institution had a diagnosable mental disorder, whereas only 22% of those reared in the community had such a disorder. A follow-up study of the original children at age 16 showed that institutionalized children had higher rates of meeting criteria for any psychiatric disorder and higher symptom counts of internalizing, externalizing, attention deficit/hyperactivity, and substance use disorders compared to a community control group that had never been institutionalized (Humphreys et al., 2020).

Although we have known for over 50 years that institutional care is associated with cognitive and emotional problems, the Romanian study with its randomized design allowed for greater validity in the results. Children come into the world seeking interactions with others. This interaction helps with cognitive, emotional, language, and motor development. (See For Further Reading.)

Thought Question

There are many situations in the world where orphanages are the only good alternative for caring for children. From what you've read so far, what three principles do you think are most important in designing and running an orphanage that results in psychologically healthy children?

Source: Based on Nelson, C. A., Fox, N. A., & Zeanah, C. H. (2014). *Romania's abandoned children: Deprivation, brain development, and the struggle for recovery.* Harvard University Press.

Imitation Learning

What happens in your brain when you see someone wave or clap their hands? One intriguing answer to this question comes from research that suggests the neurons in your brain fire as if you had performed the same actions as the person you are seeing. These are called **mirror neurons**, and they were first discovered in monkeys. Mirror neurons were shown to fire not only when the monkey performed a particular action but also when it just observed another monkey, or even a human, performing that action. These mirror neurons were initially found in an area of the brain referred to as F5, which is a part of the premotor cortex. Some researchers suggest that this brain process may lie at the basis of **imitation learning**, as well as other human social phenomena, including language and empathy (Heyes & Catmur, 2022; Rizzolatti & Craighero, 2004; Sinigaglia & Rizzolatti, 2011). A number of studies have suggested a link between mirror neurons, empathy, and psychopathologies such as autism and psychopathy (Gonzalez-Liencres et al., 2013; Minichino & Cadenhead, 2017). Imitation learning occurs throughout one's life, and it is a critical concept in normal human development.

The basic idea for imitation learning is as follows:

- Each time an individual sees an action done by another, the neurons that would be involved in that action are activated.
- This, in turn, creates a motor representation of the observed action.
- That is, we see an action and consider how we might make it ourselves, although we don't do this consciously.
- In essence, the observer's brain turns a visual image into a motor plan.

This process can explain one aspect of how imitation learning can take place. That is, by seeing something, I also come to know how I can do it. Since the same neurons fire in my brain as I watch another person do a task, my brain is able to create an action pattern when I wish to produce the motor response. Even more important for Sinigaglia and Rizzolatti (2011) is that such a network puts the organism at an advantage. This is because this network helps the organism understand not only "what" others are doing but also "why" they are doing it. By having my brain work similarly to another's brain, I have some understanding of what they are experiencing. Although the initial study of mirror neurons emphasized motor behaviors and action, more recent research suggests that the overall system also includes emotion, cognition, and social processing (Bonini et al., 2022).

Mirror neurons lead not only to an understanding of another's actions but also to empathy (Iacoboni, 2009). That is to say, through connections between the mirror neuron system and the limbic system and insula, it would be possible to recognize emotions and thus feel empathy. In a series of studies, it was shown that the more someone imitates your actions, the more you like that person and report that you care about them (Chartrand & Bargh, 1999). Thus, imitation, liking, and caring go together.

Overall, the mirror neuron system offers a basis of imitation and understanding of another's actions. In the same way that individual neurons in the visual system fire in response to specific features of a stimulus, and these, in turn, become integrated into a larger perception, the mirror neuron system can be seen as part of a larger cortical network involving the insula and limbic system, which relates to person perception and feelings toward another. This, in turn, could form the basis of interpersonal relationships and more complex social interactions. Over the past two decades, research has focused on the manner in which the mirror neuron system is involved in autism spectrum disorder (Dapretto et al., 2006; Heyes & Catmur, 2022; Rizzolatti & Fabbri-Destro, 2010; Williams et al., 2001).

Theory of Mind

Theory of mind is the ability to understand one's own or another person's mental state. As you will see later, delays in the development of theory of mind are seen in children with autism spectrum disorder. A number of tasks have been used to study the concept of theory of mind. One common task involves a cereal box. If I show you a box of cereal and ask you what is in it, you would probably say cereal. However, if I opened it and pulled out ribbons, you would no longer say it contained cereal. What if I asked you what friends of yours would say? You would, of course, say cereal, because your friends would not have seen the ribbons being pulled out of the box.

However, young children, as well as individuals with autism, would not give this answer. They would say ribbons because they are unable to understand that what someone else knows could be different from what they know. This ability to take another's perspective is referred to as theory of mind or mind reading. It is an ability that develops over the preschool years, generally between 3 and 5 years of age. Theory of mind has also been seen as a prerequisite for the ability to engage in pretend play and the ability to lie. Some theories of autism suggest that part of the disorder is a deficit in theory of mind (Baron-Cohen, 2009; Baron-Cohen & Belmonte, 2005).

CONCEPT CHECK

- Why is it important to understand the normal course of human development when learning about the psychological disorders of childhood?
- Every human learns to talk and walk at a different rate and express emotions at a different rate. What implications do these individual differences have for the definition, diagnosis, and treatment of childhood disorders?

- What are the two critical periods of brain development in humans? What changes are taking place in the brain during those periods?
- What neurological evidence can you cite to show that experiencing stress and adversity in childhood and adolescence has a greater impact than experiencing it later as an adult?
- What are the general characteristics of attachment? What three problematic styles of attachment have been described, and what implications do these styles have for future psychopathology?
- What brain processes are involved in imitation learning? How is imitation learning related to the development of empathy?

Adolescence

Adolescence is a time of great change, in both the brain and the body, as well as in culture. It is a time of change to one's body and the awakening of new interests and desires associated with brain changes (Blackmore, 2019; Ernst et al., 2014; Sturman & Moghaddam, 2011; Whitaker et al., 2016). An increase in risk taking also leads to various types of accidents, unprotected sex, and use of drugs. This risk taking or impulsivity involves distinct brain networks related to the ability to inhibit one's own actions that may form an endophenotype (see Chapter 2) related to psychopathology (Whelan et al., 2012). As such, adolescence marks the peak onset of many psychopathologies (Paus et al., 2008). These psychopathologies include anxiety and mood disorders, eating disorders, personality disorders, substance abuse, and psychosis. All of these disorders will be discussed in future chapters. Some of these disorders, such as anxiety, may not continue into adulthood, whereas other disorders, such as schizophrenia do.

Specifically, data from the National Comorbidity Survey replication study show impulse control disorders, phobias, and separation disorders begin in childhood around the age of 5, whereas panic, generalized anxiety disorder, post-traumatic stress disorder (PTSD), substance abuse, mood disorder, and schizophrenia most commonly begin around adolescence (Figure 5.5). It is assumed that these later disorders develop as the result of anomalies or exaggerations of typical adolescent maturation processes. These processes include hormonal changes during puberty, adolescent social relationships, and impulsivity, which increase the abuse of certain drugs.

FIGURE 5.5 ■ Which Types of Psychopathology Develop in Adolescence?

This figure shows the onset of psychopathology from age 6 through age 20. Signs of school phobia and ADHD are seen before other types of psychopathology. Schizophrenia and bipolar disorder are seen later in adolescence.

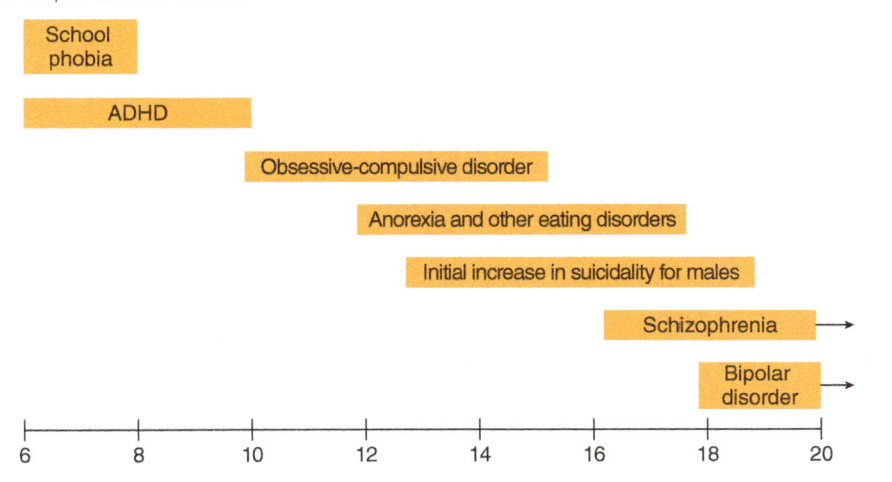

Credit: Tasman, A., Kay, J., Lieberman, J. A., First, M. B., & Maj, M. (Eds.). (2008). *Psychiatry* (3rd ed.). Wiley, p. 107.

Hormonal changes during puberty are thought to be related to the findings that there is an equal number of males and females experiencing anxiety and depression prior to puberty, which changes to a 2:1 female-to-male ratio after puberty. These differences can also be amplified by the increased emotional reactivity to social situations, including peer influence, during adolescence. Further, recreational drugs influence the trajectory of adolescent brain development.

When brain development is examined, it becomes clear that each area has its own time course (Tau & Peterson, 2010). Overall, subcortical areas mature earlier than cortical areas. One implication of this is that those areas related to higher cognitive processes are the last to mature. This in turn can lead to substance abuse (Ernst et al., 2014). Further, there are gender differences in the rate of development, and this is related to later psychopathology (Kaczkurkin et al., 2019).

In considering psychopathology, individuals with ADHD show delays in cortical development that are no longer apparent by adulthood. Schizophrenia, on the other hand, is associated with an earlier pruning of neurons as compared with normal development.

In terms of responses to particular tasks, research suggests that from childhood to adulthood, the brain goes from a largely undifferentiated system to one composed of specialized neural networks. It is also the case that there is a reduction of brain energy requirements from childhood to adulthood. In one study (Jolles et al., 2011), functional connectivity in adolescents (11–13 years of age) was compared with that of young adults (19–25 years of age). These researchers found that similar networks occurred in both groups, although the size and strength of connectivity in the network were greater in adults. Mood and anxiety disorders, which increase dramatically during adolescence, have been associated with the dysfunction of the network involved in social processing (E. Nelson et al., 2005).

Social Brain in Adolescence

Adolescence has been characterized as a time in which an individual moves from a more family-oriented frame of reference to one of peer relations. Peer relationships at this time involve meeting and understanding new individuals as well as determining the types of relationships available. Sexuality and romantic interests develop during this period. As these social and emotional changes take place, there are also large changes in the brain (Lamblin et al., 2017). These brain changes also appear to allow for an increase in psychological disorders, especially mood and anxiety disorders. Anxiety disorders, for example, are seen as an abnormal regulation of fear (Hyman & Cohen, 2013). Overall, adolescents show more of a sensitivity to both positive and negative rewards than do either adults or younger children (Galván, 2013).

Risk Taking in Adolescence

Risk taking can play both direct and indirect roles in adolescence in relation to psychopathology. The direct role can lead to abuse of illegal drugs and other substances. The indirect role combines taking risks with a psychological disorder, potentially resulting in suicide. Abused children also show an increase in risk taking. Basic research has begun to examine risk taking in relation to brain activation.

One of the hallmarks of adolescence is that risky decisions are more likely to occur in the presence of one's peers (Chein et al., 2011). One of the risky behaviors seen in adolescents is related to driving. Using a stoplight driving game and a functional magnetic resonance imaging (fMRI) scanner, Jason Chein and his colleagues compared the results of adolescents (14–18 years of age), young adults (19–22 years of age), and adults (24–29 years of age). The goal of the stoplight game is to drive through 20 intersections as fast as possible. At each intersection, the driver can either stop for the light and experience a short delay or take a risk and go through the red light without any delay. However, running the red light could result in a crash. All participants were also asked to bring a friend of their same age with them. Compared with young adults and adults, adolescents showed more risky decisions and experienced more crashes when they were observed by a friend (Figure 5.6).

The fMRI results showed differences in the left prefrontal cortex (LPFC) by age (Figure 5.7). There were also differences in the right ventral striatum (VS) and the left orbitofrontal cortex (OFC)

FIGURE 5.6 ■ Do You Drive Better Alone or With Friends?

Using a driving game in which participants are to go through 20 intersections as fast as possible, adolescents showed more risky decisions in driving when with their friends. Young adults and adults do not show this characteristic to this degree.

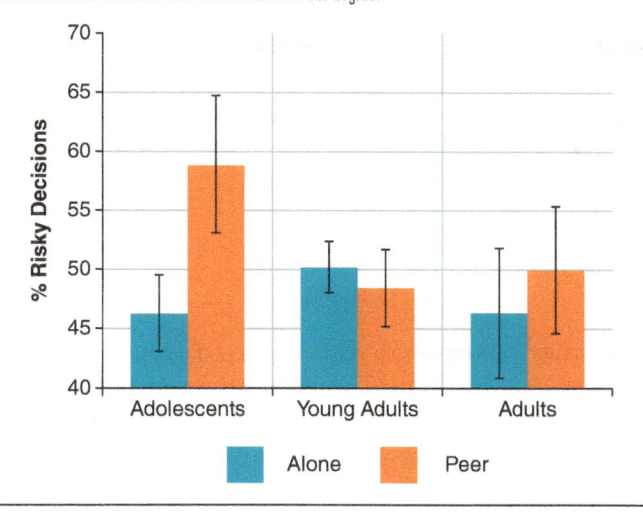

Credit: Chein, J., Albert, D., O'Brien, L., Uckert, K., & Steinberg, L. (2011). Peers increase adolescent risk taking by enhancing activity in the brain's reward circuitry. *Developmental Science, 14*, F1–F10.

FIGURE 5.7 ■ Is Your Brain Different When Driving Alone or With Friends?

Adults show activation of the prefrontal areas when driving, whereas adolescents show activation in areas that are associated with making a decision in a social context. The greater activation of these areas suggests that adolescents see risk taking as more rewarding in the presence of friends. The brain image in (a) shows left prefrontal cortex (LPFC) differences in terms of age group. The brain image in (b) shows the areas affected in terms of age and peer presence. The graphs in (c) show the signal strength changes by group and peer presence.

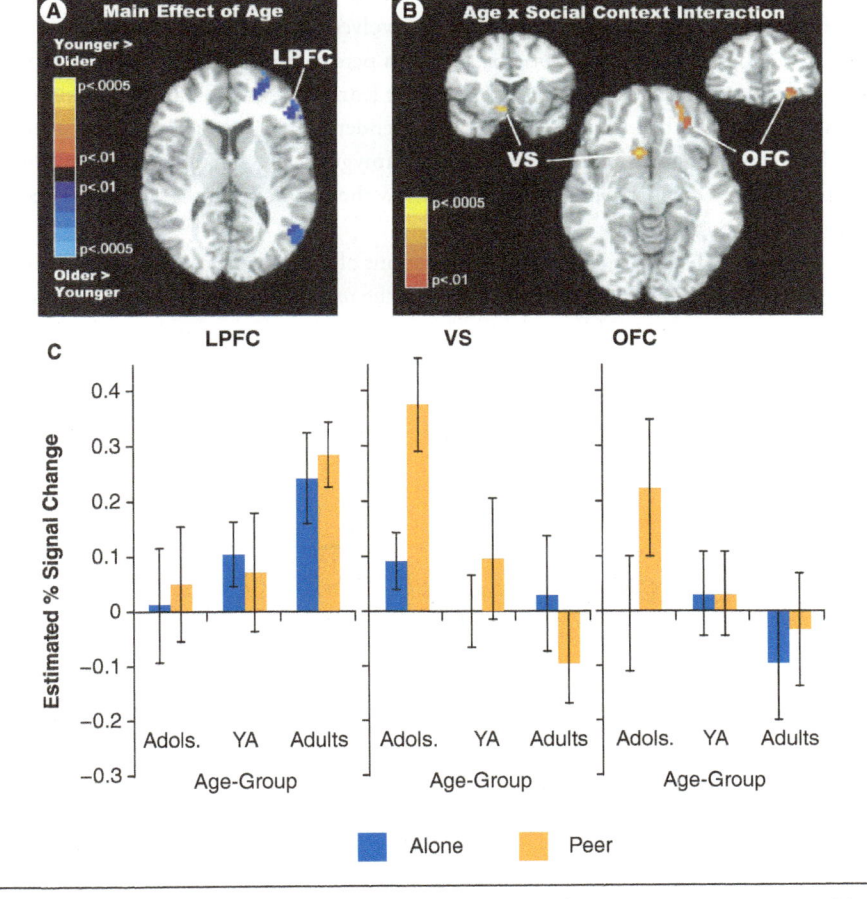

Credit: Chein, J., Albert, D., O'Brien, L., Uckert, K., & Steinberg, L. (2011). Peers increase adolescent risk taking by enhancing activity in the brain's reward circuitry. *Developmental Science, 14*, F1–F10.

in terms of age and whether a friend was present. These areas are associated with making a decision in a social context. The greater activation of these areas suggests that adolescents saw risk taking as more rewarding in the presence of a friend. Overall, this research shows that peer presence makes a greater difference in promoting risk taking, which is also seen in brain processes in adolescents compared with those beyond adolescence.

Peer influences in terms of the use of alcohol and other drugs are also seen in adolescence (Logue et al., 2014). Adolescents rarely drink alone, even in Mediterranean countries where teenagers often drink with their families. Also, adolescents rarely drink for the first time alone. They are much more likely to have their first drink with peers. Peer influence plays a critical role in alcohol use with adolescents.

Brain Systems Involved in Social Relations

Our present-day emotionality has largely evolved within a social context. In terms of brain structure, many of the structures involved in the processing of emotion are also important for social behavior. As you will learn later in this chapter, individuals with autism spectrum disorder show different types of social relationships and even scan the faces of others in a different manner.

Brain structures involved in social interactions can be organized in terms of three processes (Adolphs, 2003; Brothers, 1990; E. Nelson et al., 2005). The first process involves higher-level neocortical regions in the processing of sensory information. This is how we know who we experience through vision, hearing, touch, and other sensory processes. Research suggests that when we look at a face, we process broad categorizations related to gender and to the emotion expressed before we complete the detailed construction of the entire face and determine who we are seeing.

Second, our affective (emotional) system will help us predict what people will do socially. As we see a social interaction, what happens on the level of the brain? What happens first involves the amygdala, striatum, and orbitofrontal cortex. The amygdala is involved in processing the emotional significance of an event. This includes positive emotions, such as a person you care about smiling at you, as well as negative emotions, such as seeing someone angry or fearful. Activation also takes place if a person looks untrustworthy. This determination occurs independent of gender, race, eye gaze, or emotionality expressed. Through its connections to other areas, the amygdala also can influence memory, attention, and decision making. Overall, these areas help us know the emotional context of our perceptions and what we need to do about them.

The third process involves the higher cortical regions of the neocortex. These regions are involved in cognitive understanding and regulation. These are the regions that let us construct an inner model of our social world. Included in this model would be some social understanding of others, their relationship with us, and the meaning of our actions for the social group. It is these areas that are most likely associated with theory of mind, that is, our ability to attribute mental states to other people. Indeed, damage to the orbitofrontal cortex does reduce our ability to detect a faux pas in a given situation.

CONCEPT CHECK

- What characteristics of adolescence contribute to the fact that that period marks the peak onset of many psychopathologies? Does this mean that adolescence "causes" psychopathology? Why or why not?
- What evidence can you cite to show the importance of the social context to risk taking among adolescents?
- The brain structures involved in social interactions can be organized into three processes. What are these processes, what specifically do they do, and how are they represented in the brain?

ATTACHMENT DISORDERS, CONDUCT DISORDER, AND OPPOSITIONAL DEFIANT DISORDER

In the first part of this chapter, you learned about typical developmental processes. However, there are times in which a child appears on a social, emotional, motor, or intellectual level to be different from other children of the same age. Typically, parents or teachers refer a child to you as a mental health professional in these situations. At that point, you need to assess the child. The second part of this chapter will focus on some of the psychopathologies seen in children.

Before discussing those disorders that *DSM-5-TR* classifies as neurodevelopmental, let us consider three disorders that are not in that category. The first is attachment disorder, which *DSM-5-TR* includes as a trauma- and stress-related disorder. The next two disorders, conduct disorder (CD) and oppositional defiant disorder (ODD), *DSM-5-TR* includes in a separate category. It should be noted that once an individual becomes 18 years of age, their behavior would be described in terms of a personality disorder rather than CD or ODD. As you consider the disorders in this chapter, think about the signs and symptoms that these children show and how they might interact with family and peers.

Attachment Disorders

An attachment disorder referred to as a **reactive attachment disorder (RAD)** was introduced in *DSM-III* (Zeanah & Gleason, 2010, 2015). The disorder is the result of inadequate caregiving, which may include caregiving in residential institutional settings. The prevalence of RAD is not known, however, since it is rarely seen in a health care setting. Most often it is the result of young children being exposed to neglect before being placed in foster care or an institution. Much of the research with this disorder has focused on children raised in institutions.

Two clinical patterns can be present. The first is the emotionally withdrawn or inhibited type, and the second is the indiscriminately social or disinhibited type. The question for a clinician to answer is whether attachment is the primary clinical problem that impairs the child beyond interactions with the attachment figure, which would then qualify as RAD. An alternative is that there is another type of psychopathology present that interferes with a number of developmental processes including attachment. Autism would be such an example.

DSM-5-TR describes a child with RAD as one who does not seek comfort or support from a traditional attachment figure when distressed. Further, this child will not accept comfort when offered. Overall, there is a lack of emotional responsiveness and positive affect. There may also be negative emotions seen in interactions with adults that are not related to the nature of the interaction. For a diagnosis of RAD, it is also required that the child was not well cared for. If a child is worried about losing a significant attachment figure, this is referred to as separation anxiety disorder, which is categorized as an anxiety disorder in *DSM-5-TR*.

The second clinical pattern described in *DSM-IV*, disinhibition, has been classified as a separate disorder in *DSM-5* and *DSM-5-TR*, where it is called **disinhibited social engagement disorder**. This is a disorder in which the child is willing to accept strangers who are not attachment figures. This may include going off with strangers and being overly familiar. As with RAD, it is also required that the child was not well cared for. However, if the neglect begins after age 2, there is no evidence that this disorder will be manifested. Since these children are not seen in traditional health care settings, there is little information on the prevalence of the disorder, although it is assumed to be rare.

RAD and disinhibited social engagement disorder have not been studied empirically in terms of treatment procedures. Typically, treatment procedures have focused on helping the child develop a relationship with a caregiver. The goal is for the child to develop an emotional relationship that leads to a more secure attachment. If the child was moved from an institution to a foster family, then the mental health professional would work with the family to develop a new attachment relationship. This treatment would seek to develop a more productive internal schema in the child. In addition, behavioral techniques can be used to modify nonproductive specific behaviors such as those used with aggressive behaviors in children with conduct disorder (CD). Since maltreatment also results in developmental delays in areas such as language and speech, specific treatments for these deficits are also used.

Conduct Disorder

Although all children and adolescents seek to assert their independence, children and adolescents with **conduct disorder (CD)** display more extreme behaviors that reflect little regard for those around them. They actively violate the rights of others. These violations can include bullying or threatening others. These threats may involve a weapon or object that could do serious physical harm. They may also be cruel and begin physical fights and take things from other people. Children and adolescents with CD also violate the rules of their society. Such violations can include destroying property, stealing, and conning others. Their relationships in school and family situations also show a lack of connectedness; they may skip school or run away from home. As these children get older, violations of a sexual nature can also be seen. The behaviors associated with CD also lead to problems in other areas of development. These children are often left behind in academic achievement and have difficulties with interpersonal relationships. They often come from homes with marital discord and high stress levels in terms of neighborhood, financial difficulties, and inconsistent parenting.

The underlying etiology of CD is complex, and both genetic and environmental factors have been seen to play a role (Fairchild et al., 2019). In terms of brain processes, CD is associated with smaller gray matter volume in limbic regions such as the amygdala, insula, and orbitofrontal cortex and functional abnormalities in overlapping brain circuits responsible for emotion processing, emotion regulation, and reinforcement-based decision making. Lower reaction to stress has also been reported.

In terms of environmental factors, a consistent relationship has been found between harsh and ineffective parental discipline and aggression problems in children. It is estimated that 5% to 10% of children and adolescents in developed countries have significant persistent oppositional, disruptive, or aggressive behavior problems (Moffitt & Scott, 2008). Some of these children and adolescents will no longer show these behavior problems as they mature into young adulthood, while others will continue disruptive behaviors and qualify for an antisocial personality disorder at age 18, which will be discussed in Chapter 14.

The *DSM-5* and *DSM-5-TR* criteria for a CD require that the youth show a persistent and repetitive pattern of behavior. This pattern of behavior includes violating the rights of others and the rules of society during the past 12 months. Some of these violations can include aggression toward people and animals, such as bullying or engaging in physical fights or cruelty. Other types of violations include destruction of property, including setting fires. Theft and lying are other forms of violation of society's rules. Finally, *DSM-5* and *DSM-5-TR* include in the violations such examples as running away from home or being truant from school before the age of 13. For a clinical diagnosis of CD, a youth will demonstrate three of these criteria over the past year, and these behaviors will lead to significant impairment in the person's life.

In the journal *Psychological Review* in the 1990s, it was suggested that early-onset CD is a neurodevelopmental disorder involving the brain, whereas onset in adolescence involves social mimicry (Moffitt, 1993). However, with the advent of brain imaging studies, it has been shown that both early- and late-onset CD showed abnormal activation of the amygdala when viewing emotional human faces (Passamonti et al., 2010). Of course, these brain changes can also be influenced by environmental factors and stress.

In a study comparing individuals with early-onset CD, late-onset CD, and matched controls, the researchers found reduced amygdala volume in both early- and late-onset individuals in comparison with controls (Fairchild et al., 2011). For the individuals with CD, a negative correlation was found between the number of CD symptoms and insula volume. Since the insula is involved in awareness of one's own self, including affective (emotional) states, a reduction in volume may be related to deficits in empathy associated with CD.

CASE OF ROBERT
CONDUCT DISORDER

Prior to the initial diagnostic evaluation, Robert had been suspended from school on four occasions due to behavioral misconduct and had been caught stealing an expensive portable compact disc player from his grandmother. Although this specific incident of theft prompted Ms. Johnson to seek mental health treatment for her grandson, she had observed over the prior months that Robert had begun to lie to her frequently and to display a negative, callous, and "hard" attitude toward others. Robert acknowledged the validity of his grandmother's concerns and, during the individual interview portion of the evaluation, reported a more elaborated recent history of engagement in aggressive and antisocial behavior, including unprovoked aggression (i.e., "jumping" peers on the street with his currently incarcerated older brother, Jake) and shoplifting (also with his older brother). The persistence and intensity of Robert's conduct problems, and the extent to which he expressed a fondness for and identification with his delinquent older brother, were of serious concern. Along with the primary diagnosis of CD, Robert carried a preexisting diagnosis of ADHD for which he had been receiving pharmacotherapy through his pediatrician. Robert had experienced a fairly extensive social history of family conflict, traumatic loss, and early deprivation. He was removed from his mother's custody at 18 months due to neglectful conditions accruing from his mother's substance abuse and had endured the murders of his father and uncle. At age 5, Robert was exhibiting very high levels of verbal and physical aggression in his kindergarten classroom, in addition to hyperactive behaviors, and consequently during that year was seen for 20 sessions of psychotherapy and psychiatric consultation in our clinic. Unchecked, it was quite likely that Robert's behavior would progress to far more serious manifestations, with significantly more deleterious consequences.

Source: Based on Boxer, P., & Flick, P. (2008). Treating conduct problems, aggression, and antisocial behavior in children and adolescents: An integrated view. In R. Steele, T. D. Elkin, & M. C. Roberts (Eds.), *Handbook of evidence-based therapies for children and adolescents*. Springer.

Oppositional Defiant Disorder

Children who mainly show anger and defiance but do not act aggressively toward other people or animals or destroy property are described as having **oppositional defiant disorder (ODD)**. These children lose their temper easily and often argue with adults. They may do things to annoy others, blame others for their problems, and be vindictive. The prevalence of the disorder is around 3.3%, with slightly more boys than girls showing the disorder (APA, 2022).

The *DSM-5* and *DSM-5-TR* criteria for ODD require that the youth engage in four of eight behavioral characteristics. These are grouped into three categories. The first is that of an angry or irritable mood, which includes losing one's temper, being easily annoyed, and often being resentful and angry. The second category of behaviors is that of being argumentative and defiant. These behaviors would include arguing with authority figures or refusing to do what they say as well as deliberately annoying others and blaming others. The third category is that of being vindictive. Overall, these behaviors interfere with the youth's social and educational development.

The criteria for both CD and ODD are based on observed behaviors rather than internal processes. As researchers have sought to understand whether there are underlying processes common across childhood disorders, particular groupings have been discovered. For example, a number of studies (as noted in Chapter 4) suggest that disorders including ODD, CD, hyperactivity, impulsivity, and substance use tend to cluster together (Lahey et al., 2008; Lahey & Waldman, 2012). Inattention was not part of this grouping. This dimension is referred to as the *externalizing or disinhibition dimension*. This dimension also seems to share substantial genetic influences (Lahey et al., 2011; Markon & Krueger, 2005). Other studies have shown that anxiety and depressive disorders cluster into an *internalizing or emotional dimension* (Lahey et al., 2008).

Treatment for Conduct Disorder and Oppositional Defiant Disorder

Similar treatments have been developed for CD and ODD. Unlike ADHD, in which the treatment is centered on the individual's relationships with the family, the school, and the clinic, the child or adolescent with oppositional behavior patterns may also be involved with the law enforcement community and juvenile justice facilities. By the very nature of the disorders, children and adolescents with CD or ODD often have an adversarial relationship with those who offer treatment. In addition, a given individual with these disorders may show a number of other conditions that make a single treatment approach difficult.

Empirically supported interventions and treatment for young children with oppositional behavior patterns are largely family based (Brinkmeyer & Eyberg, 2003; McMahon & Kotler, 2008).

In essence, the parents are taught to use behavioral techniques to alter the oppositional behaviors. One of these programs, *parent–child interaction therapy (PCIT)*, has an underlying attachment perspective. Thus, the initial part of the therapy is based on the interaction between the parent and child with the goal of helping the child to develop a secure attachment pattern with the parent. In this approach, this is referred to as PRIDE: *praising* the child's behavior, *reflecting* the child's statements, and *imitating* and *describing* the child's play using *enthusiasm*. This is followed by teaching the parent behavioral management techniques based on social learning theory. In particular, this phase is designed to guide the parent to replace critical comments and commands with positive strategies. Part of this is helping the parent learn how to talk to the child in a direct and specific manner in a way that the child can understand.

Treatment approaches with older children and adolescents may also be conducted in clinic, inpatient, or correctional facilities (Boxer & Frick, 2008; Kazdin, 2005, 2018). As the child grows older, more opportunities become available for the child to engage in property destruction, vandalism, theft, and verbal and physical assault. One empirically supported approach is referred to as *multisystemic therapy (MST)*. As the name implies, this approach seeks to involve the family and other agencies that the youth would be involved with, such as schools, youth agencies, probation offices, and other such facilities. The overall treatment seeks to have those involved with the youth present a consistent message and a set of skills in terms of family interaction, problem-solving skills, and interpersonal relationships. A therapist is needed to monitor the youth in terms of these different facilities.

Other empirically supported treatments for older children are presented in therapy sessions. One of these is *problem-solving skills training (PSST)*. This is a cognitive therapy designed to help the youth determine what they are supposed to do in a given situation, examine possibilities, concentrate on and evaluate the situation, make a choice, and then evaluate the choice. This basic approach can be applied to a school situation, a family situation, or other life situations.

Cultural LENS: School Shootings Around the World asks the question of how society should deal with one horrific problem seen in adolescence: school shootings. Are these events symptomatic of a mental health problem, a statement of alienation and revenge, or a combination of both? Of course, at this point, society does not know the answer to these questions but can consider if prevention is possible.

The elementary school shooting in Uvalde, Texas, in 2022 raised questions both about gun control and about the mental health of the perpetrator.

UPI/Alamy Stock Photo

CULTURAL LENS
SCHOOL SHOOTINGS AROUND THE WORLD

School shootings have been recorded in the United States for at least the past 150 years, although the number has increased in the past 20 years. The mass shootings at Robb Elementary School in Uvalde, Texas, in 2022, which resulted in 22 deaths; Marjory Stoneman Douglas High School in Parkland, Florida, in 2018, which resulted in 17 deaths; Sandy Hook Elementary in Newtown, Connecticut, in 2012, which resulted in 26 deaths; and Virginia Tech University, in 2007, which resulted in 33 deaths, brought to the forefront the need to understand why individuals perform such acts. Quick answers such as the side effects of drugs or violent video games have been part of the discussion.

Others have considered how mental illness plays a role in these cases. Both Adam Lanza, the perpetrator of the Sandy Hook shooting, and Seung-Hui Cho, perpetrator of the Virginia Tech shooting, had showed difficulties in previous situations. In a number of press articles, various psychopathologies have been suggested. However, blaming horrific situations such as these school shootings on mental disorders does not serve society well. Experiencing a mental disorder does not lead directly to violence, although society tends to believe that individuals with mental disorders are more prone to violence. In general, data do not support this generalization.

Overall, these terrible situations offer society an opportunity to consider how to recognize those with difficulties and offer them the necessary help. This requires considerations on a number of levels. Teachers and other professionals need to be trained to recognize individuals with mental health problems. As a society, we need to consider ways to fund mental health services so that individuals without money are not left on their own. We also need to consider laws that recognize when individuals need to be treated. Although stigma appears to be part of the human condition, allowing bullying or making fun of those who are unusual does not strengthen the fabric of society.

This map shows where school shootings have occurred between 1996 and 2012. Although there are examples of shootings worldwide—and these types of incidents have continued to happen—the majority have happened in the United States. The occurrence of such violence is a critical topic to understand.

School Shootings Around the World, 1996–2012

Created by Virender Ajmani, using Google Maps and Source Information Please® Database, Copyright 2012 Pearson Education.

> **Thought Question**
>
> Since school shootings seem to be more of a problem in the United States than elsewhere in the world, what kinds of questions can we ask at different levels of analysis, such as community or culture, to help identify possible solutions?

CONCEPT CHECK

- What are the two attachment disorders described in *DSM-5*? How are they differentiated in terms of diagnostic criteria, and what treatments are available for them?
- What are the primary *DSM-5* diagnostic criteria for CD and ODD? What is the difference between them?
- What effective treatments are available for individuals with CD and ODD? What is the role for parents in these treatments?

AUTISM SPECTRUM DISORDER

Autism spectrum disorder (ASD) is the *DSM-5* diagnosis for a neurodevelopmental disorder in which an individual has difficulty in three separate areas: (1) social interactions, (2) communication, and (3) behavioral processes (Coleman & Gillberg, 2012; Geschwind, 2009; Hodges et al., 2020; Newschaffer et al., 2007; Sigman et al., 2006; South et al., 2008; Tincani & Bondy, 2014). Autism was initially described by Leo Kanner (1943) as an innate disorder in which children do not show normal development in emotional contact with others. Autism spectrum disorder has achieved a significant place in clinical and research programs, which will be discussed later in this chapter.

Characteristics of Autism Spectrum Disorder

As noted in the previous paragraph, individuals with ASD have difficulty in three separate areas. The first is social interactions. Children with autism do not connect with other children or adults in the manner that other children do. They do not look others in the eye or may appear to ignore others while being more interested in other aspects of their environment. The second area is communication. The communication patterns of those with autism spectrum disorder do not usually show the give-and-take of most conversations. The third area is behavioral processes. Individuals with autism spectrum disorder often display stereotypical behaviors and the desire to engage in the same behavior in a repetitive manner (Baron-Cohen & Belmonte, 2005; Kamio et al., 2011). About 30% of children with ASD may also show additional complications such as seizure disorders, intellectual disabilities of various kinds, and gastrointestinal problems.

Autism as a Spectrum

DSM-5 and *DSM-5-TR* use ASD as the new single-disorder "umbrella" term for what were previously separate disorders—autistic disorder, Asperger's disorder, and a general pervasive developmental disorder—to be evaluated and specified on a continuum (spectrum). In *DSM-5*, the term *Asperger's syndrome*, which was added to the *DSM* in 1994, is no longer used. Historically, *Asperger's disorder* was the diagnostic term for a milder form of autism in which developmental language delays may not be present. Also, compared with many others with autism, individuals identified with Asperger's are more adept in social processes and show average to above-average cognitive skills. General pervasive developmental disorder was characterized in *DSM-IV* as a disorder in which the full criteria for autism were not met, and the individuals exhibited a much lower level of ability across domains. Some researchers suggest that autism spectrum disorder offers us a way to study brain development that takes a non-normal route (Wicker & Gomot, 2011) and acknowledges a sharp gradation of ability among those with the disorder. *ICD-11* in 2019 adopted a similar autism spectrum dimension as *DSM-5*.

> # UNDERSTANDING CHANGES IN *DSM-5* AND *DSM-5-TR*
> ## AUTISM SPECTRUM DISORDER
>
> One controversial change in *DSM-5* was the new diagnostic label of autism spectrum disorder (Hodges et al., 2020). Prior to *DSM-5*, these developmental disorders were listed as separate, including autistic disorder, Asperger's disorder (a milder form of autism), and pervasive developmental disorder (a more profound disorder). With the publication of *DSM-5*, these disorders were eliminated. Proponents of this change argued that having separate categories was not based on scientific and clinical evidence (Lord & Bishop, 2015). Further, it was suggested that diagnostic reliability was difficult given the number of factors such as language ability, social reactions, communication styles, and behaviors that needed to be considered in making a diagnosis. So, *DSM-5* now recognizes a new continuum called autism spectrum disorder.
>
> Part of the controversy was that the new category reduced the number of ways to be diagnosed with autism (Barker & Galardi, 2015; Jabr, 2012). In fact, it has been estimated that there were over 2,000 different symptom combinations in *DSM-IV*, but only 11 are in *DSM-5*. The concern is that some individuals who were previously diagnosed with one of the autism-related disorders would no longer meet the criteria for autism spectrum disorder. In fact, using the new criteria in *DSM-5* has led to fewer children being identified as having autism spectrum disorder than would be if other traditional rating scales were used (Mayes et al., 2014).
>
> In addition, as described by Temple Grandin and others, many individuals who were described as having Asperger's disorder realized that they experienced the world and others differently. Many of these individuals valued the distinct way they experienced life and work, even referring to themselves as "Aspies." In Temple Grandin's case, she was able to design structures that allowed farm animals not to experience fear. Some corporations, such as those involved in computer programming, also value the ability of these individuals to focus with unusual intensity on particular aspects of their work. Thus, the loss of the term *Asperger's* was seen as a negative rather than a positive by many for whom experiencing the world differently from others is part of their identity.

An example of a person who would have been diagnosed with Asperger's syndrome is Temple Grandin. At the beginning of this chapter, Temple Grandin described her experiences of being a person who experienced an autism spectrum disorder (Grandin, 2009, 2010). She described how, at age 2½, she did not speak and performed actions in a repetitive manner. She was also very sensitive to certain sounds and would respond to these by rocking or staring at sand dribbling through her fingers. Later as a child, she had no understanding of how people relate to each other. She would watch others, trying to understand how she should behave.

Grandin (2009) described herself as thinking totally in pictures. In fact, she described her mind as an Internet search engine set to locate photos. She stated this as follows:

> My mind is associative and does not think in a linear manner. If you say the word "butterfly," the first picture I see is butterflies in my childhood backyard. The next image is metal decorative butterflies that people decorate the outside of their houses with and the third image is some butterflies I painted on a piece of plywood when I was in graduate school. Then my mind gets off the subject and I see a butterfly cut of chicken that was served at a fancy restaurant approximately 3 days ago. (p. 1437)

Grandin (2010) has used the ability to think in images to help design humane animal livestock facilities.

> I credit my visualization abilities with helping me understand the animals I work with. Early in my career I used a camera to help give me the animals' perspective as they walked through a chute for their veterinary treatment. I would kneel down and take pictures through the chute from the cow's eye level. Using the photos, I was able to figure out which things scared the cattle, such as shadows and bright spots of sunlight. Back then I used black-and-white film, because twenty years ago scientists believed that cattle lacked color vision. Today, research has

shown that cattle can see colors, but the photos provided the unique advantage of seeing the world through a cow's viewpoint. They helped me figure out why the animals refused to go in one chute but willingly walked through another. (p. 4)

Temple Grandin is clearly a person who has been very productive in that she earned her PhD and is a professor of animal sciences at Colorado State University. She has consulted with many companies concerning how to design environments that treat livestock in a humane manner. Grandin (2009) describes individuals with autism as *specialized thinkers*. For her, they are specialized in one of three types of thinking. The first is *visual thinking*, which allows one to view the world and even words in terms of images. The second is *pattern thinking*, in which the thinking is in terms of patterns such as those seen in music and mathematics. The third is *word and fact thinking*, in which the individual displays an ability to know a large number of facts such as baseball scores or the titles of films and who their stars were. More formal research articles have also shown that hypersensitivity to sensory information along with strong logical reasoning ability may be at the basis of talent seen in individuals with autism spectrum disorder (Baron-Cohen et al., 2008). An exception to sensory sensitivity is found with odors. Children with autism spectrum disorder show little reaction to strong unpleasant odors such as sour milk or rotten fish (Rozenkrantz et al., 2015).

Autism and Intelligence

Individuals with autism have often been reported to show a lower IQ than matched control children or adults using traditional IQ tests. Traditional IQ tests have both verbal and spatial components on which children without autism tend to show similar scores. Similar scores to traditional IQ tests are also seen on measures of fluid intelligence such as the Raven's Progressive Matrices test, for those without autism. Figure 5.8 shows an example of a problem from this test.

When adults and children with autism were given the Raven's Progressive Matrices test, they showed scores much higher than they obtained on traditional IQ tests. Their scores on the Raven's were more similar to matched controls (M. Dawson et al., 2007). These researchers concluded that intelligence may have been underestimated in those with autism. Others have suggested that many geniuses such as Isaac Newton, Albert Einstein, George Orwell, and H. G. Wells showed traits associated with Asperger's syndrome (Wicker & Gomot, 2011). The show *Atypical* on Netflix pictures the life of an 18-year-old who has an autism spectrum disorder.

FIGURE 5.8 ■ Example of a Problem From the Raven's Progressive Matrices Test

The task is to determine which of the eight patterns at the bottom complete the puzzle above. NOTE: Eight is the correct answer.

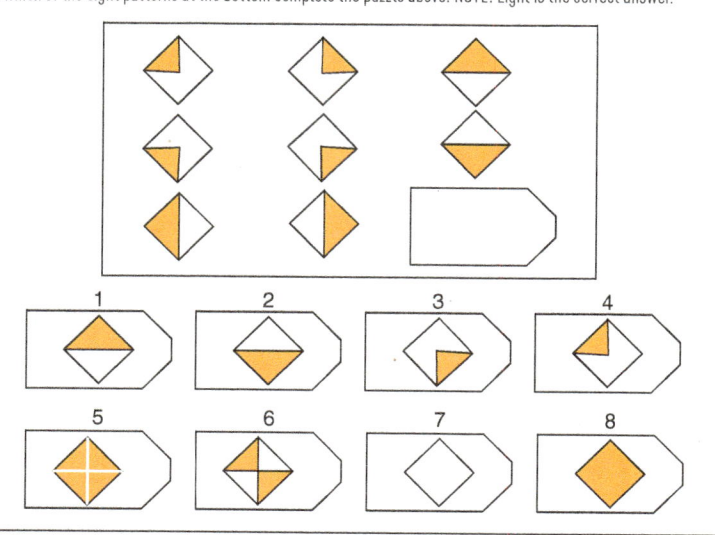

Credit: Reprinted from *Intelligence*, Volume 33, Issue 1, Clancy Blair, David Gamson, Steven Thorne, and David Baker, "Rising mean IQ: Cognitive demand of mathematics education for young children, population exposure to formal schooling, and the neurobiology of the prefrontal cortex," pp. 93–106, Copyright 2005, with permission from Elsevier.

Social and Behavioral Patterns in Autism

DSM-5 and *DSM-5-TR* also describe autism spectrum disorder as characterized by problems in the social realm that begin in childhood, exemplified in terms of interacting and talking with others. Individuals with an autism spectrum disorder have a difficult time holding typical everyday back-and-forth conversations, especially emotional interchanges. They also lack eye contact and a normal understanding of body language. These problems in social processes tend to leave individuals with autism spectrum disorder with fewer emotionally connected relationships and difficulties in changing social contexts.

The interests and behavior patterns of individuals with autism spectrum disorder are more repetitive and fixed. An individual with autism, for example, may watch the same TV show over and over. These individuals also tend to inflexibly follow routines. In addition, they may show sensitivity to normal sensory input such as sound or light. Adults with autism tend to choose occupations that have fewer interpersonal interactions and more focus on manipulating objects. Thus, you would see these individuals designing car engines or programming computers rather than being salespeople. The *DSM-5* and *DSM-5-TR* criteria for autism spectrum disorder are shown in Table 5.3.

TABLE 5.3 ■ *DSM–5–TR* Diagnostic Criteria for Autism Spectrum Disorder

A. Persistent deficits in social communication and social interaction across multiple contexts, as manifested by all of the following, currently or by history (examples are illustrative, not exhaustive; see text).
1. Deficits in social-emotional reciprocity, ranging, for example, from abnormal social approach and failure of normal back-and-forth conversation; to reduced sharing of interests, emotions, or affect; to failure to initiate or respond to social interactions.
2. Deficits in nonverbal communicative behaviors used for social interaction, ranging, for example, from poorly integrated verbal and nonverbal communication; to abnormalities in eye contact and body language or deficits in understanding and use of gestures; to a total lack of facial expressions and nonverbal communication.
3. Deficits in developing, maintaining, and understanding relationships, ranging, for example, from difficulties adjusting behavior to suit various social contexts; to difficulties in sharing imaginative play or in making friends; to absence of interest in peers.

B. Restricted, repetitive patterns of behavior, interests, or activities, as manifested by at least two of the following, currently or by history (examples are illustrative, not exhaustive; see text):
1. Stereotyped or repetitive motor movements, use of objects, or speech (e.g., simple motor stereotypies, lining up toys or flipping objects, echolalia, idiosyncratic phrases).
2. Insistence on sameness, inflexible adherence to routines, or ritualized patterns of verbal or nonverbal behavior (e.g., extreme distress at small changes, difficulties with transitions, rigid thinking patterns, greeting rituals, need to take same route or eat same food every day).
3. Highly restricted, fixated interests that are abnormal in intensity or focus (e.g., strong attachment to or preoccupation with unusual objects, excessively circumscribed or perseverative interests).
4. Hyper- or hyporeactivity to sensory input or unusual interest in sensory aspects of the environment (e.g., apparent indifference to pain/temperature, adverse response to specific sounds or textures, excessive smelling or touching of objects, visual fascination with lights or movement).

C. Symptoms must be present in the early developmental period (but may not become fully manifest until social demands exceed limited capacities, or may be masked by learned strategies in later life).

D. Symptoms cause clinically significant impairment in social, occupational, or other important areas of current functioning.

E. These disturbances are not better explained by intellectual developmental disorder (intellectual disability) or global developmental delay. Intellectual developmental disorder and autism spectrum disorder frequently co-occur; to make comorbid diagnoses of autism spectrum disorder and intellectual developmental disorder, social communication should be below that expected for general developmental level.

Note: Individuals with a well-established DSM-IV diagnosis of autistic disorder, Asperger's disorder, or pervasive developmental disorder not otherwise specified should be given the diagnosis of autism spectrum disorder. Individuals who have marked deficits in social communication, but whose symptoms do not otherwise meet criteria for autism spectrum disorder, should be evaluated for social (pragmatic) communication disorder.

(Continued)

TABLE 5.3 ■ *DSM–5-TR* Diagnostic Criteria for Autism Spectrum Disorder (*Continued*)

Specify current severity based on social communication impairments and restricted, repetitive patterns of behavior (see Table 2):

- **Requiring very substantial support**
- **Requiring substantial support**
- **Requiring support**

Specify if:

- **With or without accompanying intellectual impairment**
- **With or without accompanying language impairment**

Specify if:

- **Associated with a known genetic or other medical condition or environmental factor** (**Coding note:** Use additional code to identify the associated genetic or other medical condition.)
- **Associated with a neurodevelopmental, mental, or behavioral problem**

Specify if:

- **With catatonia** (refer to the criteria for catatonia associated with another mental disorder, p. 135, for definition) (**Coding note:** Use additional code F06.1 catatonia associated with autism spectrum disorder to indicate the presence of the comorbid catatonia.)

Credit: Reprinted with permission from the *Diagnostic and Statistical Manual of Mental Disorders, fifth edition, text revision* (*DSM-V-TR*), pp. 56–57. (Copyright © 2022). American Psychiatric Association. All Rights Reserved.

Autism and Development

Developmentally, symptoms of autism are generally not seen until 8 to 12 months of age (G. Dawson et al., 2009). By the toddler–preschool stage, the traditional symptoms such as social impairment, imitation, responses to emotions, and face processing become apparent. Along with these impairments in social relationships, language delays and repetitive behaviors may also be present, although not all individuals with autism spectrum disorder show language delays (Lord & Bishop, 2015).

Infants with autism show a non-normal pattern of growth of the head (Sacco et al., 2015). At birth, these infants show a small to normal head size. This is followed by an accelerating pattern of growth at about 4 months of age, which results in a larger head size around 1 year of age. Magnetic resonance imaging (MRI) studies suggest that 2- to 4-year-old children with autism have larger total cerebral volume compared with healthy controls. Current prospective studies that have sought to identify changes in the development patterns in those infants who will later develop autism spectrum disorder suggest that some changes can be seen as early as 2 to 6 months of age (Jones et al., 2014).

RESEARCH TERMS TO KNOW

PROSPECTIVE STUDY

A *prospective study* is one in which a group of individuals is followed for a period of time to help clarify the factors involved in the development of a process. For autism spectrum disorder, prospective studies generally choose infants whose relatives show signs of autism, although they themselves have not yet been diagnosed with the disorder.

Behaviorally, individuals with autism display problems in three areas (Baron-Cohen & Belmonte, 2005). These areas are social functions, communications, and restrictions in behaviors and interests. Those previously described by the term *Asperger's syndrome* show social impairments and restricted behaviors but fewer problems in terms of language and communication. One current theory of autism centers on problems related to empathy. In particular, it is suggested that individuals with autism fail to develop a theory of mind. As you remember, theory of mind refers to one's ability to infer the mental states of others in relation to their actions or situations. In a variety of studies, individuals with autism were able to describe what was going on in someone else's behavior on the perceptual level but showed difficulties when asked to describe the social–emotional processes that would be expected to accompany the behaviors. This appears to be a general lack of ability, since these individuals also have problems reflecting on these aspects of their own behavior. Another characteristic of autism is the desire to have a stable set of routines and problems in shifting their attention. Overall, individuals with autism show a variety of characteristics, including differences in brain size, emotional recognition, ability to understand perspective in others, and knowledge of self (Lombardo et al., 2010).

Prevalence of Autism

Although autism spectrum disorder was initially considered to be rare, with greater awareness, estimates have increased over the years. Current CDC estimates suggest that around 1 in every 36 children have the disorder. ASD is more common in boys as compared with girls. Depending on the study, the exact gender ratio varies from 2:1 to 5:1. The ratio of males to females is about 8:1 in cases in which there is no intellectual disability (Frith et al., 2013). More than half of the cases of autism show intellectual disabilities.

The exact number of individuals with autism spectrum disorder is related to how broadly or narrowly the diagnostic criteria were specified in a particular study. One difficulty with diagnosis is that it relies on observations of social interactions of toddlers. Further, different children may show different profiles as well as have varying intellectual abilities. An interesting approach to diagnosis is to examine home videos for early symptoms of the disorder (Costanzo et al., 2015). Trained researchers would code the home videos for the child's interaction with others and attachment behaviors as well as the achievement of developmental milestones.

Professional support and special education programs can produce marked improvement. Some children who show the characteristics of autism before the age of 5 show few of the signs some 10 years later (Coleman & Gillberg, 2012). However, social situations still prove difficult for individuals with autism spectrum disorder.

Causes of Autism Spectrum Disorder

Environmental Contributions to Autism Spectrum Disorder

Autism was initially thought to be largely influenced by environmental factors. In the 1960s and 1970s, individuals with autism were considered to have a form of psychosis similar to childhood schizophrenia. Consistent with the historical view at that time, environmental factors such as bad parenting were suggested to be a cause of the disorder, although today, parenting or social factors are seen to play little role at all. Another study suggested that measles, mumps, and rubella (MMR) vaccinations produced changes in infants that led to autism (Wakefield et al., 1998). Not only has this been shown to be false, but it was also discovered that the original research was fraudulent (Hodgson, 2004).

Genetic Contributions to Autism Spectrum Disorder

Autism has been shown to have a strong genetic component (Chang et al., 2015; G. Dawson et al., 2009). Concordance rates for autism from numerous studies of twins show a range from 69% to 95% for monozygotic (MZ) twins and 0% to 24% for dizygotic (DZ) twins. Also, relatives of those with autism show higher rates of autism-like symptoms. The farther a relative is from the person with autism, the fewer symptoms are seen. This suggests that autism involves a genetic pathway affected by a number of genes in a complex manner. In fact, hundreds of genetic differences have been associated with autism, but each of these represents a small percentage of cases (Chang et al., 2015; Klin et al., 2014; Warrier et al., 2022).

There is also some suggestion that autism spectrum disorder shares common genetic processes with schizophrenia (Chisholm et al., 2015). There is also a connection with ADHD (Lord & Bishop, 2015). A large-scale study of more than 10,000 twin pairs in Sweden reported that an MZ twin with autism spectrum disorder had a 44% chance of also being diagnosed with ADHD, whereas a DZ twin had only a 15% chance (Lichtenstein et al., 2010).

In addition, genetic factors show a complex relationship involving environmental factors such as the age of the mother (Waterhouse, 2012). Younger mothers have the lowest risk for having children with ASD and older mothers the highest risk. There is also some suggestion that the mother's health during pregnancy is associated with ASD, although the exact factors remain ambiguous. Fathers over 50 years of age have 4 times the risk of having a child with autism. Whether this is related to the older males having a different quality of sperm is not known.

A developing area of research related to autism spectrum disorder involves gut bacteria (Vuong & Hsiao, 2016). All humans have bacteria in their gut which play an important role in health and behavior (see Chapter 2). In fact, you have many more bacteria in your gut than cells in your body. Current research shows that those with autism spectrum disorder have different types of gut bacteria than those without (Kushak & Winter, 2018; Sharon et al., 2019). This raises the possibility that it would be possible to use food bioactive compounds to reduce the appearance of traits associated with autism spectrum disorder (Serra et al., 2019; Yang et al., 2018). Modifying gut bacteria would in turn influence processes in the brain through a pathway from the gut to the brain.

Brain Contributions to Autism Spectrum Disorder

In terms of the brain, it is suggested that ASD reflects dysfunction in areas associated with the social brain (Minshew & Williams, 2007; Müller & Fishman, 2018). Briefly, these are the amygdala, specific areas of the frontal lobes, and areas of the temporal lobe. Further, those with autism were shown to have less activity in the mirror neuron system when viewing emotional expressions of faces (Dapretto et al., 2006); there was a negative correlation between cortical activity during this task and the degree of support needs in the social domain. Another characteristic of autism is the desire to have a stable set of routines, which results in problems shifting attention.

Adolescents with ASD showed fewer whole-brain connections than a control group (Moseley et al., 2015). This was particularly true in networks involved in visual processing and the default network. However, those with ASD showed more connections between the primary sensory areas and subcortical areas such as the thalamus and basal ganglia (Cerliani et al., 2015). This helps to explain why those with ASD focus more on sensory stimuli than on social processes.

Current neuroscience studies show that by the time of full brain development, a person with ASD shows deficits in the areas that make up the social brain. For example, whereas individuals without autism tend to scan the eyes when looking at another person, those with autism focus on the mouth (Pelphrey & Carter, 2008). The photos in Figure 5.9 show the focus of eye movements on the faces of adults with and without ASD. Since various features of the eyes give both emotional and social information, those with ASD do not register this information.

Coupled with the inability to empathize is the superior ability to *systemize* in autism. Systemizing is the ability to analyze objects or events in terms of their structure and future behavior. This involves understanding the rules that govern the object. These rules could be a timetable of trains and planes, how animals are classified, the pattern of tides in the ocean, or how things such as automobile engines work. These deficits and abilities make up the empathizing-systemizing theory of autism (Baron-Cohen, 2009; Baron-Cohen & Belmonte, 2005).

There is some suggestion that those with ASD switch their focus of attention to the mouth between 6 and 12 months of age. This implies to some researchers that brain changes in terms of facial focus may serve as a marker to predict who will develop autism (Pelphrey & McPartland, 2012; Walsh et al., 2011). In one study, Mayada Elsabbagh and her colleagues (2012) measured electroencephalogram (EEG) components evoked in response to viewing faces in infants 6 to 10 months of age. These researchers found that the event-related potential (ERP) components were associated with being diagnosed with ASD at 36 months of age.

It appears that the higher-order frontal lobe functions required to adapt to life do not fully develop in individuals with ASD. Physically, infants who were to develop autism were shown to have an increase in head circumference by the end of the first year of life. MRI studies during the second to fourth year of life showed increases in total brain volume in children with autism. This was seen in both total white and gray matter. It also has been noted that this cortical overgrowth coincided with the onset of the signs and symptoms of ASD.

FIGURE 5.9 ■ Do Those on the Autism Spectrum Look at Other People Differently?

Sample scan paths from an eye-tracking study of high-functioning adults with autism *(left column)* and IQ, gender, and age-matched, typically developing comparison subjects *(right column)*.

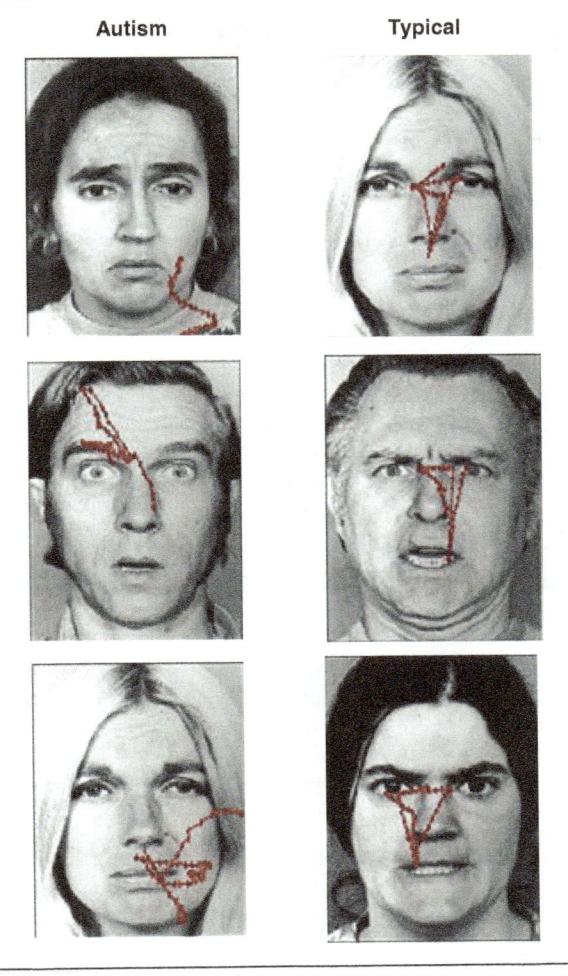

Credit: Pelphrey, K. A., Sasson, J. J., Reznick, J. S., Paul, G., Goldman, B., & Piven, J. (2002). Visual scanning of faces in autism. *Journal of Autism and Developmental Disorders, 32*(4), 249–261.

Although infants who later develop ASD have similar size heads to other babies at birth, they do show larger heads during the first year of life. Enlargement of the brain by 3% to 10% is one of the most consistently reported observations (South et al., 2008). The overgrowth of cortical tissue takes place more in the frontal and temporal lobes than other areas of the brain. It is these areas that are involved in social and language functions as well as facial processing. Although overgrowth has been shown, there is also a consistent finding of less activity in those cortical areas related to facial processing. This overgrowth and reduced activity may lie at the basis of later social problems.

To summarize, the cortical areas involved in individuals with ASD display differential responses on brain imaging measures. Amaral and his colleagues (2008) have described the neuroanatomy of autism. In particular, they depict the cortical structures involved in the three major characteristics of autism. As noted earlier, these are problems in social interactions, problems in communication, and the use of repetitive behaviors, as shown in Figure 5.10.

Special Talents

It is estimated that about 10% of individuals with autism spectrum disorder have special abilities in terms of music, art, calculation, or memory (Treffert, 2009). There are more males than females with these abilities. This has been called the *savant syndrome* and was portrayed in the 1988 movie *Rain Man*

FIGURE 5.10 ■ The Neuroanatomy of Autism

This figure illustrates the areas of the brain involved in social impairment, communication deficits, and repetitive behaviors.

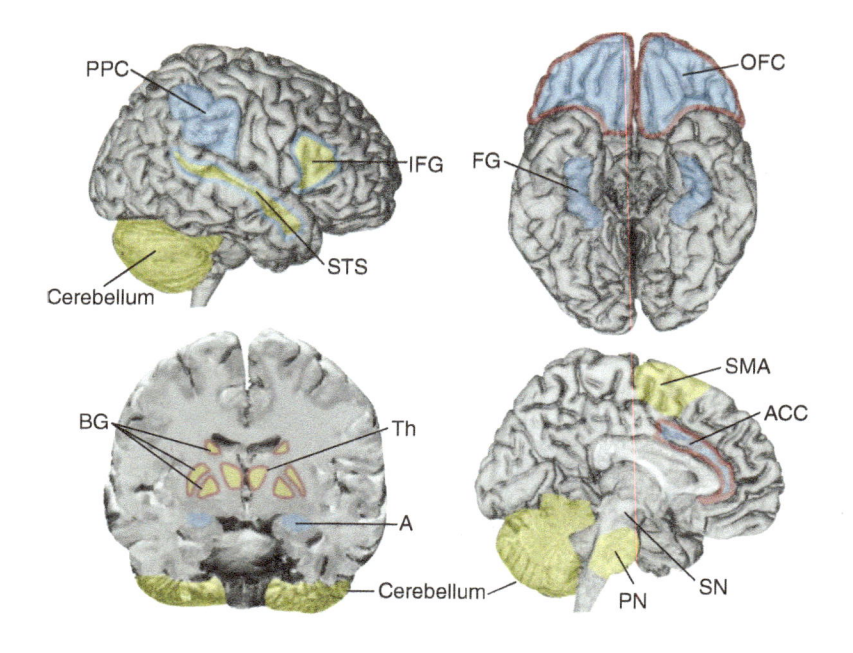

Social impairment	Communication deficits	Repetitive behaviors
OFC-Orbitofrontal cortex	IFG-Inferior frontal gyrus (Broca's area)	OFC-Orbitofrontal cortex
ACC-Anterior cingulate cortex	STS-Superior temporal sulcus	ACC-Anterior cingulate cortex
FG-Fusiform gyrus	SMA-Supplementary motor area	BG-Basal gangila
STS-Superior temporal sulcus	BG-Basal ganglia	Th-Thalamus
A-Amygdala mirror neuron regions	SN-Substantia nigra	
IFG-Interior frontal gyrus	Th-Thalamus	
PPC-Posterior parietal cortex	PN-Pontine nuclei cerebellum	

Credit: Reprinted from *Trends in Neurosciences*, Volume 31, Issue 3, David G. Amaral, Cynthia Mills Schumann, Christine Wu Nordahl, "Neuroanatomy of autism," pp. 137–145, Copyright 2008, with permission from Elsevier.

by the actor Dustin Hoffman. The real-life person on whose story the movie was based could name all U.S. zip codes, had memorized maps, and could tell you how to go from one city to another in the United States as well as move about a city in terms of street names. In addition, he had memorized more than 6,000 books and could repeat facts from a variety of areas. He could also tell you on which day of the week a certain date would occur in any year. Another savant artist was Nadia, who at age 5 drew the horse in Figure 5.11. At this point, there is no single theory that can explain savants. However, it appears that sensory and perceptual areas of the brain are overrepresented in terms of cortical processing. This results in an emphasis on detail and a lack of emotional and social processing.

Treatment for Autism Spectrum Disorder

Since autism spectrum disorder appears early in a child's life, parents turn to a number of different professionals for support. Depending on the levels and differential types of development noted, these professionals can include kindergarten teachers, special education teachers, speech pathologists, child clinical psychologists and psychiatrists, and pediatricians.

Maxwell and colleagues (2018) recently reviewed the empirically supported treatment for autism spectrum disorder. They found that the approaches with the strongest empirical support are the UCLA program originally developed by Lovaas (described next) and approaches that use applied behavioral

FIGURE 5.11 ■ Drawing by Nadia at Age 5

Credit: Selfe, L. (2011). *Nadia revisited.* Psychology Press, p. 32.

analysis. It should also be noted that the National Autism Center at the May Institute (see For Further Reading), which is a treatment center, also seeks to describe empirically supported approaches based on scientific research. These reports are available on their website, along with information for parents of children with autism spectrum disorder.

The first empirically supported treatments were developed by Lovaas and his colleagues in the 1960s (Lovaas & Smith, 2003). This approach, which was based on behavioral principles, was referred to as the UCLA Young Autism Project. This project has reported around 50% "recovery" rates for young children with autism, and these principles have been supported in other studies (Rogers & Vismara, 2008). Besides the success with individual children, this approach helped the field to understand that children with autism can learn important new skills and thus there is plasticity to their brain processes.

The UCLA Project accepts children with autism under 4 years of age with the average age being 2 years 10 months. These children need not show major medical problems such as hearing or vision loss. The children in treatment receive 40 hours a week of one-to-one interventions. This treatment lasts for about 3 years, depending on the individual child. Based on behavioral principles, the treatment was designed to maximize positive outcomes and reduce failure experiences. This includes giving the child short and clear instructions and immediate reinforcement for each correct response. Parents are also an important part of the process.

There are five major stages in the Lovaas treatment program. The first is establishing a teaching relationship, which lasts from 2 to 4 weeks. Since many of these children have previously avoided certain situations through tantrums and other means, the therapist works with the child in following simple directions. The second stage, which lasts from 1 to 4 months, involves teaching foundational skills related to following directions, imitating behaviors, and identifying objects. The third stage lasts for around 6 months and focuses on beginning communication. This includes initial speech processes and identifying objects and actions. The fourth stage, which lasts for about a year, continues communication processes such as labeling colors and shapes and developing the basic concepts of language. The fifth stage, which also lasts about a year, is designed to continue communication processes and help the child adjust to school situations, including peer interactions. The program ends as the child becomes part of a school situation.

Rogers and Vismara (2008) reviewed the treatment literature for autism spectrum disorder in terms of empirically supported treatments. They found a number of child characteristics were associated with successful treatment outcomes. One characteristic was the age at which treatment was begun. Those children who began treatment before the age of 4 had better outcomes than those who started at age 5 or older. Also, higher IQ was associated with better outcomes. Overall, it appears that early intervention in language skills, communication, and peer relationships, along with a reduction in negative behaviors, allows many children with ASD to successfully move through a normal school sequence. However, at this point, it is difficult to estimate the percentage of children that are successfully treated.

In addition to psychosocial treatment approaches, medications have been used to address specific disruptive behaviors seen in ASD. These behaviors include hyperactivity, inattention, repetitive thoughts and behaviors, and aggressive behaviors against others and the self. Medications include antidepressants, stimulants, and antipsychotic medications. These medications are typically given to older rather than younger children with ASD. Those randomized control trials that do exist suggest improvement in irritability and hyperactivity resulting from a number of different medications (Friedman et al., 2015).

> **CONCEPT CHECK**
>
> - Individuals with autism spectrum disorder have difficulty in three separate areas. What are those areas, and what specific types of challenges do these individuals encounter in each area?
> - Is autism associated with a lower IQ? What evidence can you cite to support your answer?
> - What are the primary developmental, genetic, and environmental factors related to autism?
> - What is the savant syndrome, and what are its defining characteristics?
> - What are the five major stages of treatment for autism spectrum disorder in the Lovaas treatment program?
> - What are three characteristics associated with successful treatment outcomes for autism spectrum disorder?

ATTENTION DEFICIT/HYPERACTIVITY DISORDER AND LEARNING DISORDERS

This section will describe disorders classified in *DSM-5* and *DSM-5-TR* as neurodevelopmental disorders. These are attention deficit/hyperactivity disorder (ADHD) and learning disorders. ADHD focuses on problems in attention and inhibiting behavior. Learning disorders are seen when a child is functioning at a level lower than their peers.

ADHD

Attention deficit/hyperactivity disorder (ADHD) is a disorder of childhood that tends to develop before the age of 12 and is seen worldwide (Hinshaw, 2018). Although the conceptualization of ADHD has changed over the years, it currently includes two major dimensions (Adler et al., 2015; Frick & Nigg, 2012). The first dimension is *inattention*. Children and adults with inattention problems tend to exhibit these in a cognitive realm such as letting their mind wander or not paying attention. As shown with the *DSM-5* and *DSM-5-TR* inattention diagnostic criteria (Table 5.4), these individuals may have

TABLE 5.4 ■ *DSM-5-TR* Diagnostic Criteria for Attention Deficit/Hyperactivity Disorder

A. A persistent pattern of inattention and/or hyperactivity-impulsivity that interferes with functioning or development, as characterized by (1) and/or (2):

1. **Inattention:** Six (or more) of the following symptoms have persisted for at least 6 months to a degree that is inconsistent with developmental level and that negatively impacts directly on social and academic/occupational activities:

   a. Often fails to give close attention to details or makes careless mistakes in schoolwork, at work, or during other activities (e.g., overlooks or misses details, work is inaccurate).
   b. Often has difficulty sustaining attention in tasks or play activities (e.g., has difficulty remaining focused during lectures, conversations, or lengthy reading).
   c. Often does not seem to listen when spoken to directly (e.g., mind seems elsewhere, even in the absence of any obvious distraction).
   d. Often does not follow through on instructions and fails to finish schoolwork, chores, or duties in the workplace (e.g., starts tasks but quickly loses focus and is easily sidetracked).
   e. Often has difficulty organizing tasks and activities (e.g., difficulty managing sequential tasks; difficulty keeping materials and belongings in order; messy, disorganized work; has poor time management; fails to meet deadlines).
   f. Often avoids, dislikes, or is reluctant to engage in tasks that require sustained mental effort (e.g., schoolwork or homework; for older adolescents and adults, preparing reports, completing forms, reviewing lengthy papers).
   g. Often loses things necessary for tasks or activities (e.g., school materials, pencils, books, tools, wallets, keys, paperwork, eyeglasses, mobile telephones).
   h. Is often easily distracted by extraneous stimuli (for older adolescents and adults, may include unrelated thoughts).
   i. Is often forgetful in daily activities (e.g., doing chores, running errands; for older adolescents and adults, returning calls, paying bills, keeping appointments).

Note: The symptoms are not solely a manifestation of oppositional behavior, defiance, hostility, or failure to understand tasks or instructions. For older adolescents and adults (age 17 and older), at least five symptoms are required.

2. **Hyperactivity and impulsivity:** Six (or more) of the following symptoms have persisted for at least 6 months to a degree that is inconsistent with developmental level and that negatively impacts directly on social and academic/occupational activities:

   a. Often fidgets with or taps hands or feet or squirms in seat.
   b. Often leaves seat in situations when remaining seated is expected (e.g., leaves his or her place in the classroom, in the office or other workplace, or in other situations that require remaining in place).
   c. Often runs about or climbs in situations where it is inappropriate. (Note: In adolescents or adults, may be limited to feeling restless).
   d. Often unable to play or engage in leisure activities quietly.
   e. Is often "on the go," acting as if "driven by a motor" (e.g., is unable to be or uncomfortable being still for extended time, as in restaurants, meetings; may be experienced by others as being restless or difficult to keep up with).
   f. Often talks excessively.
   g. Often blurts out an answer before a question has been completed (e.g., completes people's sentences; cannot wait for turn in conversation).
   h. Often has difficulty waiting his or her turn (e.g., while waiting in line).
   i. Often interrupts or intrudes on others (e.g., butts into conversations, games, or activities; may start using other people's things without asking or receiving permission; for adolescents or adults, may intrude into or take over what others are doing).

Note: The symptoms are not solely a manifestation of oppositional behavior, defiance, hostility, or a failure to understand tasks or instructions. For older adolescents and adults (age 17 and older), at least five symptoms are required.

B. Several inattentive or hyperactive-impulsive symptoms were present prior to age 12 years.

C. Several inattentive or hyperactive-impulsive symptoms are present in two or more settings (e.g., at home, school, or work; with friends or relatives; in other activities).

(Continued)

TABLE 5.4 ■ **DSM-5-TR Diagnostic Criteria for Attention Deficit/Hyperactivity Disorder** (*Continued*)

D. There is clear evidence that the symptoms interfere with, or reduce the quality of, social, academic, or occupational functioning.

E. The symptoms do not occur exclusively during the course of schizophrenia or another psychotic disorder and are not better explained by another mental disorder (e.g., mood disorder, anxiety disorder, dissociative disorder, personality disorder, substance intoxication or withdrawal).

Specify whether:

F90.2 Combined presentation: If both Criterion A1 (inattention) and Criterion A2 (hyperactivity-impulsivity) are met for the past 6 months.

F90.0 Predominantly inattentive presentation: If Criterion A1 (inattention) is met but Criterion A2 (hyperactivity-impulsivity) is not met for the past 6 months.

F90.1 Predominantly hyperactive/impulsive presentation: If Criterion A2 (hyperactivity-impulsivity) is met and Criterion A1 (inattention) is not met for the past 6 months.

Specify if:

In partial remission: When full criteria were previously met, fewer than the full criteria have been met for the past 6 months, and the symptoms still result in impairment in social, academic, or occupational functioning.

Specify current severity:

Mild: Few, if any, symptoms in excess of those required to make the diagnosis are present, and symptoms result in no more than minor impairments in social or occupational functioning.

Moderate: Symptoms or functional impairment between "mild" and "severe" are present.

Severe: Many symptoms in excess of those required to make the diagnosis, or several symptoms that are particularly severe, are present, or the symptoms result in marked impairment in social or occupational functioning.

Credit: Reprinted with permission from the *Diagnostic and Statistical Manual of Mental Disorders, fifth edition, text revision* (*DSM-V-TR*), pp. 68–70. (Copyright © 2022). American Psychiatric Association. All Rights Reserved.

difficulty paying close attention to details or focusing on activities such as schoolwork or lectures, may appear disorganized, be unwilling to engage in activities that require mental effort, and be easily distracted. Individuals with this type of ADHD may also show learning problems.

The second dimension is *hyperactivity and impulsivity*. Children with hyperactivity and impulsivity tend to show these symptoms in a behavioral or motor realm. As shown in the hyperactivity and impulsivity diagnostic criteria (see Table 5.4), these individuals may have difficulty waiting their turn, waiting to respond, keeping still, and remaining in their seat. Children with this type of ADHD may also show conduct problems. There is some suggestion that hyperactivity problems may lessen as a child grows older, whereas attentional problems may worsen, resulting in increasing difficulty with schoolwork. It is also possible that individuals with ADHD show characteristics of both inattention and hyperactivity.

Prevalence and Characteristics of ADHD

ADHD is reported to be the most common emotional–behavioral disorder treated in youth (Wilens et al., 2002). Epidemiological studies suggest a prevalence rate of 4% to 5% in children in the United States, New Zealand, Australia, Germany, and Brazil. Of those with ADHD, some 20% to 30% have the inattentive subtype, less than 15% have the hyperactive-impulsive subtype, and 50% to 75% have a combination of both. Although long-term studies show different rates, it is assumed that over 50% of the children with ADHD will show continued symptoms into adolescence. A smaller proportion will show ADHD symptoms in adulthood.

The *LENS: Do Adults With ADHD Have a Different Disorder From That Seen in Children?* will discuss adult ADHD. Adults with ADHD show more symptoms related to inattention as compared with hyperactivity and impulsivity (Kessler et al., 2010). Specifically, almost half (45.7%) of the individuals studied who had childhood ADHD continued to meet full *DSM-IV* criteria for current adult ADHD, with 94.9% of these cases having attention deficit disorder and 34.6% hyperactivity disorder.

According to the Centers for Disease Control and Prevention (CDC), boys are more likely (13.2%) than girls (5.6%) to be diagnosed with ADHD. Data from 2016 show similar rates across years in the United States (see For Further Reading). One note of caution is that younger children may be more likely to be diagnosed with ADHD when compared to older children in the same grade (Layton et al., 2018). Since many school districts have cutoff dates of September 1, there can be almost a year of additional development in those born in August before the cutoff date and those born in September, who would need to wait a year to begin school.

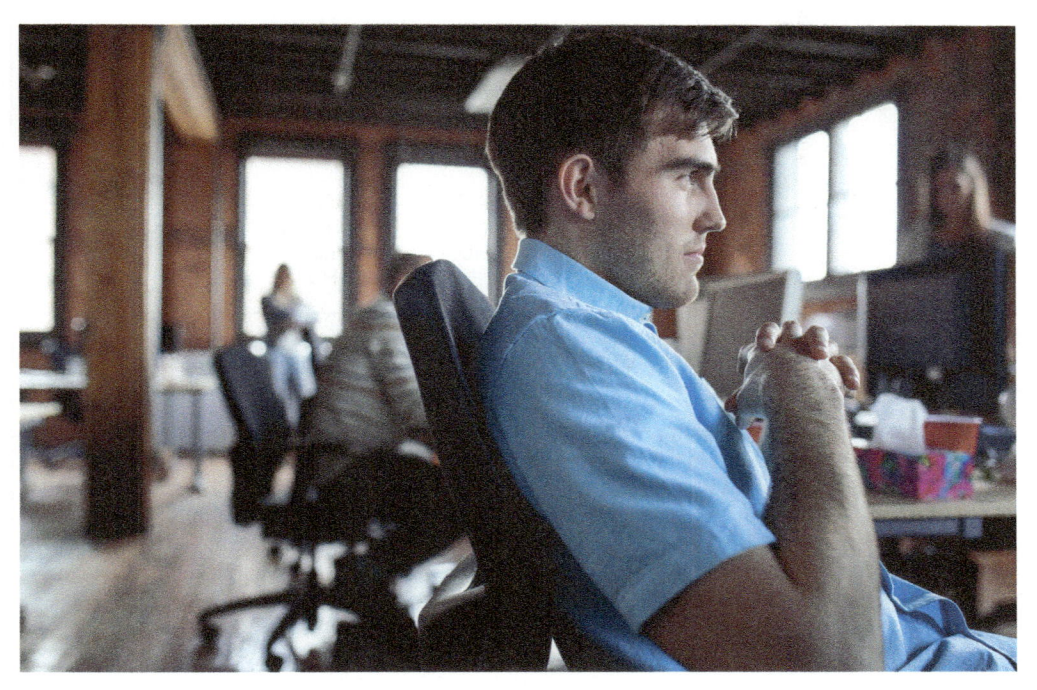

Although ADHD is more common in children, adults may have the disorder, too.
iStock.com/Hero Images. Stock photo. Posed by model.

LENS

DO ADULTS WITH ADHD HAVE A DIFFERENT DISORDER FROM THAT SEEN IN CHILDREN?

DSM-5 and *DSM-5-TR* focus on ADHD in childhood, but about half of those children with ADHD show similar symptoms in adulthood. *DSM-5* and *DSM-5-TR* suggest that ADHD begins in childhood. In fact, in *DSM-5*, both adult and childhood ADHD are seen as neurodevelopmental disorders that begin in childhood. However, until recently, few studies have asked if this is the case. One way to examine this question is to ask if adults who currently show symptoms of ADHD also had the same symptoms in childhood. Terrie Moffitt and her colleagues (2015) asked this question in a prospective design. By using a prospective design, the researchers did not need to rely on the participants' memory of their childhood experiences.

These researchers studied 1,037 individuals who were born between April 1972 and March 1973 in Dunedin, New Zealand. Given that that number represented 91% of all births during that period, this gave the researchers a comprehensive sample that included all levels of socioeconomic factors and health status. Assessments of various types were first performed at birth and then every 2 years from age 3 to 15. Following this, assessments were carried out at ages 18, 21, 26, 32, and 38. Included in these assessments were measures of ADHD. Overall, 6% of the children met criteria for ADHD, and 3% of the adults at age 38 met criteria. What surprised the researchers was that different individuals met criteria in childhood and adulthood. In fact, only 3 of the 61 children who had ADHD symptoms in childhood continued to have the symptoms in adulthood. On the other hand, an additional 28 individuals showed ADHD symptoms at age 38 but did not have them in childhood. These data are shown in Figure 5.12.

> **FIGURE 5.12 ■ Is ADHD in Childhood Associated With ADHD in Adulthood?**
>
> Those with adult ADHD at age 38 and childhood ADHD. Different individuals met criteria for ADHD in childhood from those who met criteria in adulthood.
>
> *Credit:* Reprinted with permission from the *American Journal of Psychiatry*, Volume 172, Issue 10, "Is Adult ADHD a Childhood-Onset Neurodevelopmental Disorder? Evidence From a Four-Decade Longitudinal Cohort Study," Moffitt et al. (Copyright © 2015). American Psychiatric Association. All Rights Reserved.
>
> These data raise the question of whether adult ADHD is a totally separate disorder from the ADHD seen in children. If this is the case, it is important to understand how it develops. It is also important to know if it is associated with other psychological issues such as substance abuse, trauma, or anxiety. There is not a clear answer to this question, since over half of those individuals with adult ADHD in the New Zealand study showed no mental health diagnoses at age 38. Further, one would want to know how to treat adult ADHD because there may be very different mechanisms involved compared to childhood ADHD.
>
> ### Thought Question
>
> What research would you propose to better understand adult ADHD?

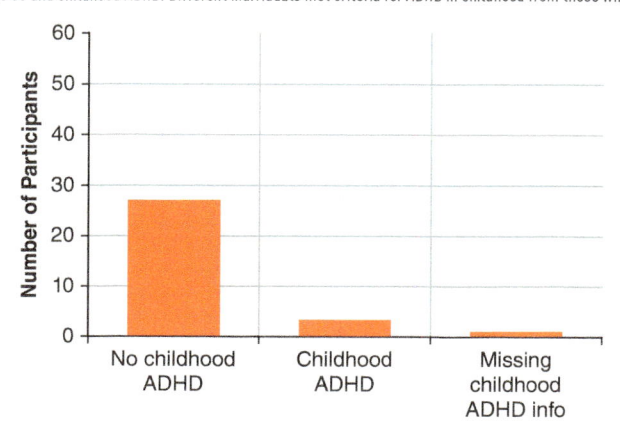

Epidemiological studies have also shown a comorbidity of ADHD with a variety of other disorders (Aguiar et al., 2010; Takeda et al., 2012). Often, childhood disorders are referred to as either externalizing disorders, such as CD and ODD, or internalizing disorders, such as anxiety and mood disorders. Externalizing disorders are those that are manifested in the child's external behaviors that negatively influence the external environment. Internalizing disorders reflect such behaviors as withdrawing, inhibiting, or being anxious. These relate to the child's internal psychological world rather than directly influencing the external environment. In youth, the comorbidity of ADHD and ODD was greater than 32%. Anxiety disorders were found to be comorbid with ADHD at greater than 22% with a higher proportion of girls compared with boys showing the disorder. CD was comorbid with ADHD at greater than 7%.

Causes of ADHD

Researchers who examined neuropsychological functions through a meta-analysis found that children and adolescents with ADHD showed problems in a variety of cognitive processes (Aguiar et al., 2010). These include verbal working memory, spatial working memory, response inhibition in which the individual must inhibit a response, cognitive flexibility, and planning. Vigilance was also shown to be a problem. Those with ADHD have difficulty paying attention and inhibiting their responses.

In terms of brain function related to ADHD, it is suggested that dysfunctions exist in networks involving the frontal, striatal, and cerebellar regions (see Hart et al., 2013; van Ewijk et al., 2011, for overviews and meta-analysis). These networks are related to executive function, which is seen to be dysfunctional in ADHD.

Various studies have also found differences in gray matter and white matter in those with ADHD (Duan et al., 2018). Overall, children with ADHD showed a 7% decrease in total cerebral volume and 8% decrease in total cortical volume in all four major lobes of the brain compared with controls (Wolosin et al., 2009). DTI (diffusion tensor imaging) studies also showed disturbed white matter connections in children, adolescents, and adults with ADHD (Bouziane et al., 2018).

Neurons in the brain are known to be connected in an efficient and economical manner. These connections have been described in terms of small-world properties (Sporns, 2011). Children with ADHD have been shown to have different network properties from children without ADHD (Wang et al., 2009). Although children both with and without ADHD had economical small-world network properties, their networks differed in terms of long-distance and short-distance neural connections. Brain imaging shows that children with ADHD exhibit more efficient short-distance connections as compared with long-distance ones.

Overall, a variety of studies have shown dysfunctional connectivity during both rest and cognitive tasks in the brains of children with ADHD (Castellanos & Proal, 2012; Konrad & Eickhoff, 2010). Cognitive tasks such as having a child inhibit a motor response are associated with less cortical activity in the circuits involving the frontal, striatal, and cerebellar networks in children with ADHD. One common hypothesis directing fMRI research is the idea that individuals with ADHD have a more difficult time switching from resting state conditions to those of active task management.

There is evidence to suggest that ADHD is influenced by genetic components (Hinshaw, 2018; Sharp et al., 2009). The disorder is more prevalent in identical as compared with fraternal twins. Adoption studies also point to a genetic component, especially in first-degree relatives. More than 20 research studies suggest a heritability rate of 76%. Further, at least 25% of parents with a history of hyperactivity have biological children who show hyperactivity. Genes related to dopamine regulation appear to be involved with ADHD. Overall, genetic studies with ADHD show little influence from the family environment. However, preschool cognitive stimulation in terms of reading, singing, and playing is associated with less risk for ADHD, whereas exposure to fast-paced television programs during the first 3 years of life increases the risk of ADHD (Christakis, 2016; Zimmerman & Christakis, 2007).

Treatment for ADHD

The major treatment for ADHD is medications that are stimulants. The benefit of stimulants for this purpose was found by accident in the 20th century. Although initially given to children as a treatment for headaches following an invasive brain X-ray technique, the stimulant amphetamine was also shown to help the children in the hospital to be calmer and more organized in their thinking (Adler et al., 2015). Although it may seem paradoxical to give a stimulant to a person who is hyperactive, these medications have been shown to be effective (Bidwell et al., 2011; Fredriksen et al., 2013). Stimulants appear to improve functioning by changing neurotransmitters in the brain.

The most common drugs used in ADHD treatment are methylphenidates, which include the trade name Ritalin; and amphetamines, including dextroamphetamine, which includes the brand names Adderall and Dexedrine. These drugs reduce the symptoms of ADHD, such as disruptive and noncompliant behavior. They also increase the ability to focus attention. These medications may also improve physical coordination. It has been estimated that 70% of children with ADHD will show symptom reduction with stimulant medications.

Psychosocial methods are also used for the treatment of ADHD. These are often used in combination with medication, and the best treatment results are seen with this combination (Hoza et al., 2008; Newcorn et al., 2015). Reviews of the treatment literature show that psychosocial interventions can have a positive impact beyond that of the medication alone (Watson et al., 2015). With older adolescents and adults, psychological therapies may be useful in allowing the person to talk about the experience of having ADHD and to create cognitive and behavioral strategies for managing their environment. For example, reducing distraction allows the person to function more effectively.

Since EEG can reflect the attentional state of a person, researchers have asked if ADHD symptoms could be modified by having a person change their EEG. This has been referred to as *biofeedback* or *neurofeedback*. The basic procedure involves the individual child or adult being given visual or other feedback concerning the frequencies seen in the EEG. Through this feedback, the individual can learn after a time to produce those frequencies of EEG related to attention and reduce those related to inattention (Monastra et al., 2005). Meta-analyses of neurofeedback treatments suggest that neurofeedback serves as a better treatment for inattention and impulsivity than for hyperactivity (Arns et al., 2009; Holtmann et al., 2014).

Involving parents in the treatment of their child's ADHD has been shown to be empirically effective (Anastopoulos & Farley, 2003). This cognitive behavioral training approach for parents involves 10 components. These are as follows:

1. Get an overview of the characteristics of ADHD and clarification of the parents' understanding of the disorder.
2. Review behavioral management techniques and the problems associated with escalating negative interactions with the child.
3. Increase positive attention to the child's desired behaviors as well as develop skills to allow the parents to ignore certain behaviors that compromise relationships.
4. Learn how to help the child to comply with simple requests, and present requests clearly.
5. Set up a home reward system.
6. Add costs for minor rule violations to the home reward system.
7. Use time-out periods for serious rule violations.
8. Learn how to manage behavior in public.
9. Consider potential problems in the future and the removal of the home reward system.
10. Have a booster session to review progress and troubleshoot situations.

The basic idea is to create a situation in which the parents and the child are not arguing with each other, which only leads to escalating negative interactions. Rather, using behavioral principles, the goal is to increase positive interactions and to help the child be less impulsive. This also allows the parents to communicate more effectively with school personnel such that the child receives a consistent message in their life. Other similar programs have been developed for classroom management, which have been shown to be empirically supported. It has also been shown that involving other children without ADHD in the classroom can be effective.

Learning Disabilities

Learning disabilities are diagnosed when a child's achievement is lower than what is expected from their scores on achievement or intelligence tests (Martínez & Nellis, 2020). The term *learning disability* was first used in the 1960s and replaced the term *minimal brain dysfunction* in federal regulations in the United States. The U.S. Department of Education (DOE) has defined the services required to be provided to students with learning disabilities through the Individuals with Disabilities Education Act (IDEA). Various states and local school districts have also set up regulations related to learning disabilities. For each of the years 1990 through 2015, the DOE reported that 5% of all children had a specific learning disability and 3% had a speech or language impairment (National Center for Education Statistics, 2022).

DSM-5 and *DSM-5-TR* formally categorize learning disabilities as specific learning disorder. A child who has specific learning disorder would show problems in one of the major school tasks or avoidance of them. The tasks include reading aloud, understanding what is read, spelling, writing, remembering number facts, doing arithmetic calculations, reasoning in a mathematical manner. Although there is no precise definition of what constitutes a difficulty, comparisons are made in terms of the child's age, intelligence level, cultural group, gender, and grade. Cultural factors are critical, since various cultural groups worldwide emphasize learning processes differently in their children.

> **CONCEPT CHECK**
>
> - What are the two primary dimensions of ADHD, and what is their prevalence?
> - What are the typical medical and psychosocial treatments for ADHD?
> - What are learning disabilities?
> - What particular school-related problems are examples of a specific learning disorder?

INTELLECTUAL DEVELOPMENTAL DISORDER

Prior to *DSM-5* and *ICD-11*, the term *mental retardation* was used to refer to intellectual disabilities. *Intellectual disabilities* is the term widely used in schools throughout the world. They are estimated to affect between 1% and 2% of the population in Western countries. In *DSM-5* and *DSM-5-TR*, those with intellectual disabilities are said to have an **intellectual developmental disorder (IDD)**.

Characteristics of Intellectual Developmental Disorder

An IDD is defined by three aspects. The first criterion is a deficit in mental abilities such as reasoning, problem solving, planning, abstract thinking, judgment, and ability to learn in both academic and practical settings. The second criterion is a lack of adaptive functioning in relation to one's age and sociocultural background. Adaptive functioning refers to how an individual copes with the problems of everyday life. These are described in terms of conceptual, social, and practical domains. This would include problems in social communication, being part of a group, school and work functioning, and ability to be independent in an age-appropriate manner. The third criterion is that the onset of the disabilities took place prior to adolescence.

Unlike those with learning disabilities in which a child's achievement is lower than that expected from their scores on achievement or intelligence tests, individuals with IDD would be performing consistently with their scores on such tests. They also tend to show more global deficits rather than difficulties with a specific area of functioning, such as mathematical reasoning. Problems are generally seen in cognitive abilities, adaptive processes, social interactions, and understanding proper behavior in the context of situational and cultural norms.

Levels of Functioning

Problems with intellectual development are considered to occur on a continuum described in terms of mild, moderate, and severe levels of disability. Unlike previous *DSM* definitions, an actual IQ score is no longer specified. Previously, only those individuals who scored below 70 on an IQ test would be diagnosed as "mentally retarded" (which today we refer to intellectually disabled). However, it is assumed that intelligence testing will be part of the overall assessment that would describe the person in terms of cultural, social, economic, and other factors.

Those with a mild level of functional disability would show some problems in the conceptual domain. This would include difficulties with academic skills such as math, writing, and reading. Older students and adults with an IDD may show a more concrete approach to problems and solutions in comparison with peers. In the social domain, these individuals may have more difficulty reading social cues and expressing their emotions. In the practical domain, these individuals may need help in tasks such as grocery shopping, taking buses, and matters involving money such as banking and bill paying. Support would also be needed for making medical and legal decisions and raising a family.

The moderate level of functioning would show an adult who conceptually is functioning more like an elementary school student than a high school student. Younger individuals would lag in comparison with their peers. In the social domain, the person may show less complex relationships while still seeking relationships with family and peers. Social cues would be more difficult to interpret. In the practical domain, the person would need support from others. With this support, various types of jobs that have limited conceptual requirements are possible.

The severe level of functioning would require caregivers to help with concepts involving time and money. Written language may be difficult. Social domains remain on a very concrete level. The relationship is less of a give-and-take nature and more of a simple attachment. Practical tasks generally require a caregiver for most activities of daily living, including meals and basic bodily tasks.

Causes of Intellectual Developmental Disorder

Most types of IDD can be traced to biological causes (Mefford et al., 2012). However, the variation is huge. Examining genetic, chromosomal, and metabolic abnormalities has led researchers to identify more than 1,000 forms of impairment (Dykens & Hodapp, 2001). It has been suggested that mild disorders are more related to environmental influences and more severe forms are more related to biological factors (Shapiro & Batshaw, 2011). One way to organize these disorders is in terms of those directly related to chromosomes, those related to metabolism, and those related to events that take place in the womb, such as malnutrition or the mother taking drugs such as alcohol or crack cocaine.

IDD Related to Chromosomes

The most common form of IDD is **Down syndrome**, which was described by the British physician Langdon Down in 1866. The disorder results in both physical and intellectual problems. The IQ is generally around 50 or below but can vary. There is a characteristic appearance of individuals with Down syndrome that includes a flat face with an upward slant of the eyes and smaller hands and feet. Cardiovascular problems are common in these individuals. It is not uncommon for individuals with Down syndrome to develop changes associated with Alzheimer's disease by age 40 (Hickman et al., 2022). A number of projects help individuals with Down syndrome find work, and the Special Olympics offers opportunities for these individuals to compete in sports.

The disorder occurs during pregnancy with cell division, which results in an extra copy of chromosome 21 (Figure 5.13). The CDC estimates that 1 out of every 691 babies born in the United States has Down syndrome, which results in approximately 6,000 births per year (see For Further Reading). This number is lower for young mothers and higher for women over age 35. It is possible to identify a fetus with Down syndrome through a procedure referred to as amniocentesis. The procedure looks for

FIGURE 5.13 ■ Karyotype From a Female With Down Syndrome

Humans have 23 pairs of chromosomes. In those with Down syndrome, there is an extra (third) copy of chromosome 21. Karyotyping is the process of pairing and ordering all the chromosomes of an organism.

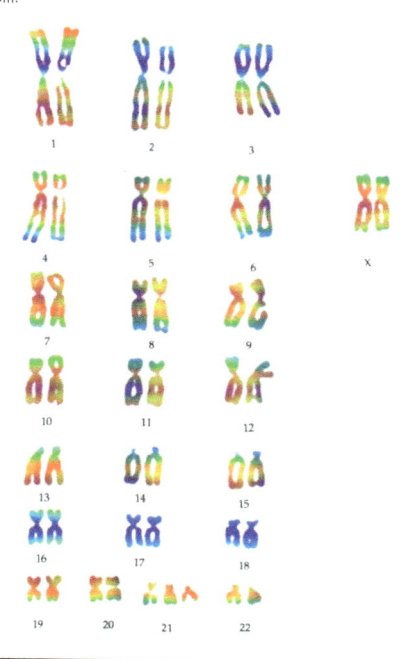

Credit: © Leonard Lessin/Science Source

an extra chromosome 21, which is seen in Down syndrome. Additional tests examine DNA material and are referred to as noninvasive prenatal testing. Brand names of this test include Harmony Prenatal Test and MaterniT21 PLUS. These tests are recommended in the United States and parts of Europe for pregnant women over the age of 35.

Another chromosome disorder that results in IDD is called **fragile X syndrome**. This is caused by a particular gene, FMR1, producing too little of a protein needed for brain development. As the name implies, this takes place on a fragile area of the X chromosome. Since males have only one X chromosome, they show more severe problems than females with the disorder. The symptoms include problems in intellectual development, emotional outbursts, and delays in motor development. Current estimates by the CDC are that about 1 in 4,000 males and 1 in 6,000 to 8,000 females have the disorder.

IDD Related to Metabolism

Phenylketonuria (PKU) is a medical condition in which a particular liver enzyme does not function correctly. This, in turn, can lead to IDD by preventing myelination of the neurons in the brain. The disorder can be treated through diet by restricting foods such as milk and eggs that contain phenylalanine. In the United States, blood testing for PKU at birth is legally required for all infants. The disorder appears to be carried by a recessive gene. Thus, both parents must have the gene for the disorder to appear.

IDD Related to Gestation

The gestational period from conception to birth is a critical one for fetal development. Some researchers see morning sickness as a natural way in which the fetus is protected. That is, this period in which a pregnant woman is sensitive to a variety of foods and feels nauseous and vomits reduces potential danger to the fetus. However, it is possible for the mother to engage in substance abuse, experience malnutrition, or have an infection that can lead to a number of disorders, including IDD. Prevention is designed to reduce environmental risk factors in pregnant women.

The extent to which there are intellectual, emotional, or motor deficits is largely related to the degree of exposure the fetus experiences. Greater exposure may lead to a miscarriage or stillbirth. Less exposure may lead to fewer developmental problems. Maternal malnutrition, such as iron, zinc, or iodine deficiency, will lead to slower developmental processes. Iodine deficiency results in a disorder known as cretinism. Children with this disorder show slower development, including cognitive processes. This disorder is less common today with the addition of iodine to table salt. Substance abuse on the part of the mother can also influence the child's developmental processes. Alcohol, for example, will enter the fetus's bloodstream. Heavy use of alcohol will result in fetal alcohol syndrome (FAS), which includes low birth weight, lower intellectual functioning, and problems with cognitive processes such as attention and memory. Likewise, the use of cocaine leads to a phenomenon known as "crack babies" in which children have problems with language and other cognitive processes. Finally, a variety of infections put the fetus at risk for later developmental problems.

Treatment for Intellectual Developmental Disorder

Treatment for individuals with IDD takes place on a number of levels and varies by age. In the mid-20th century, it was not uncommon for the child to be placed in a state school for the "mentally retarded." This was a residential institution in which children would spend most of their lives. Today, most of these state institutions have been closed. In the 1970s, laws were passed that gave people with IDD the right to receive their treatment in the least restrictive setting.

Alternatives to institutionalization exist that depend on the level of function of the child. Some communities have residential programs run by nonprofit agencies designed to help individuals who have difficulty performing daily tasks. Often, behavioral techniques are used to teach the child to learn to use a spoon and fork, to eat, or to get dressed. The settings of these residential programs look more like houses with rooms than the large institutional settings of the past century.

Children who are able to function at a higher level typically live at home with their parents or in a foster setting. A number of treatment programs have been set up to help the caregiver learn techniques for educating and managing a child with IDD. For example, some children show angry outbursts

A young boy with Down syndrome and his father.
iStock.com/recep-bg. Stock photo. Posed by model.

that must be managed. As the child becomes older, the school system becomes involved in the child's education. Schools in the United States have special education programs designed to help children with developmental disorders. Some school systems place higher-functioning individuals into regular classrooms, a process referred to as mainstreaming. As the child becomes older, some school systems teach the child not only traditional educational material but also life skills. Such skills could include how to buy a carton of milk or toothpaste in a store or how to ride a bus. Programs such as the Special Olympics also involve such life skill techniques as practicing for an event, competing, and learning to be with others.

Young adults with IDD are often helped to learn how to be part of a workplace either through specially designed workplaces for those with disabilities or through jobs in the community. It is estimated that about a third of all adults with IDD are employed. These individuals are covered by the Americans with Disabilities Act (see For Further Reading). Some communities have created apartments with a live-in coach to help these individuals practice life skills and learn to perform successfully at work. This can include helping the person learn how to buy food, deposit their payroll check, use an ATM, and get to work on time.

Although medications are not generally given to children and adults with IDD, there are exceptions. If the child is aggressive or engages in self-harm, then neuroleptic medications may be used. If the child shows patterns of seizure, then epileptic medications are appropriate. There are also new medications being developed to modify the lack of protein production with fragile X syndrome. Other positive biochemical changes are produced by modifying the diet of those with PKU.

CONCEPT CHECK

- What three criteria define an IDD?
- What are the three primary causal categories into which IDD is organized, and what is an example of each?
- What are the typical treatments offered for individuals with IDD?

SUMMARY

Unlike some other species, humans are born into a world in which they cannot survive alone. In fact, human infants are born in an undeveloped state. Every infant learns to talk and walk and express emotions at a slightly different rate. There are a number of sensitive periods in which disruptions can lead to long-term effects. Current research has shown detrimental effects on both physical and mental health in relation to physical and sexual abuse, neglect, and exposure to domestic violence, as well as having a parent who is depressed.

Attachment patterns are part of a larger overall developmental sequence that can be considered in the development of psychopathology. Since attachment patterns tend to be stable, the effects they portray can be cumulative. Research has shown children with insecure patterns of attachment to be at risk for several forms of childhood psychopathology. Three problematic attachment patterns have been identified in addition to the normal secure attachment pattern: (1) avoidant, (2) anxious or ambivalent, and (3) disorganized or controlling. In terms of *DSM* disorders, early life stress increases the risk for a behavioral disorder by 40% and a fear disorder by 15%.

Although brain changes can take place at any point in development, there are two critical periods in which the brain is more sensitive to external and internal factors: (1) the period during gestation and infancy, when the cortical connections are initially being organized, and (2) adolescence, when the brain reorganizes itself. Understanding when brain changes take place in development or whether specific genetic factors prevent normal pathways from being developed is crucial to understanding the nature of developmental psychopathologies. Mental health professionals have a difficult task in determining what might just be delayed development in certain skills and what represents a developmental disorder. Treatment can influence greatly the course of development of the individual. In general, the criteria for diagnosis of a developmental disorder are based on severity, duration, pervasiveness, and degree of impairment.

The brain's mirror neuron system offers a basis of imitation learning and understanding of another's actions. It has been suggested that the mirror neurons lead not only to an understanding of another's actions but also to empathy. The mirror neuron system can be seen as part of a larger cortical network that relates to person perception and feelings toward another. This, in turn, could form the basis of interpersonal relationships and more complex social interactions. Theory of mind is the study of one's ability to understand one's own or another person's mental state. Delays in the development of theory of mind are seen in children with autism spectrum disorder.

Adolescence is a time of great change. It also marks the peak onset of many psychopathologies, including anxiety and mood disorders, eating disorders, personality disorders, substance abuse, and psychosis. Research suggests that from childhood to adulthood, the brain goes from a largely undifferentiated system to one composed of specialized neural networks. Adolescence has been characterized as a time in which an individual moves from a more family-oriented frame of reference to one of peer relations. Risk taking can play both direct and indirect roles in adolescence in relation to psychopathology. In addition, one of the hallmarks of adolescent risk is that it is more likely to occur in the presence of peers.

DSM-5 describes disorders of childhood in a number of separate categories. This chapter emphasizes three: (1) trauma- and stressor-related disorders, including disorders of attachment; (2) neurodevelopmental disorders, including autism spectrum disorder, ADHD, disorders of learning, intelligence, and communication, as well as motor disorders such as tics and Tourette's disorder; and (3) disruptive, impulse control, and conduct disorders. There are two attachment disorders: (1) RAD, in which the child does not seek comfort or support from a traditional attachment figure when distressed and will not accept comfort when offered; and (2) disinhibited social engagement disorder, in which the child is willing to accept strangers who are not attachment figures. These two disorders have not been studied empirically in terms of treatment procedures, which typically have focused on helping the child develop a relationship with a caregiver.

Children and adolescents with conduct disorder (CD) display extreme behaviors that reflect little regard for those around them and violate the rules of society. The behaviors associated with CD also lead to problems in other areas, such as academic achievement and interpersonal relationships. Children who mainly show anger and defiance but do not act aggressively toward other people or animals or destroy property are described as having oppositional defiant disorder (ODD). The *DSM-5* diagnostic criteria for both CD and ODD are based on observed behaviors rather than internal processes. Similar treatments have been developed for the treatment of CD and ODD. Empirically supported interventions and treatment for young children with oppositional behavior patterns are largely family based; one approach is PRIDE. Treatment approaches with older children and adolescents may also be conducted in clinic, inpatient, or correctional facilities. Empirically supported approaches include MST and PSST.

Autism spectrum disorder (ASD) is the new *DSM-5* diagnosis for a neurodevelopmental disorder in which individuals have difficulty in three separate areas: (1) social interactions, (2) communication, and (3) behavioral processes. *DSM-5* includes what were previously separate disorders—autistic disorder, Asperger's disorder, and a general pervasive developmental disorder—as variations on a continuum of ASD. Individuals with Asperger's syndrome tend to be more intelligent and display higher functioning in terms of social processes than those diagnosed with autism. Developmentally, symptoms of ASD are generally not seen until 8 to 12 months of age. Infants with ASD show a nonnormal pattern of growth of the head. ASD has been shown to have a strong genetic component. Environmental factors such as the age of the mother and father show a complex relationship to ASD. Neuroscience studies indicate that by the time of full brain development, a person with ASD shows deficits in the areas that make up the social brain. Current estimates suggest that around 1 in 36 children have ASD with it being more common in boys than in girls. It is estimated that about 10% of individuals with ASD have special abilities in music, art, calculation, or memory, called the savant syndrome. An empirically supported treatment for ASD, first developed by Lovaas and his colleagues at UCLA, has five stages of treatment lasting for a total of about 3 years: (1) establishing a teaching relationship, (2) teaching foundational skills, (3) focusing on beginning communication, (4) continuing communication processes, and (5) helping the child adjust to school situations. In addition to psychosocial treatment approaches, medications have been used to address specific disruptive behaviors seen in ASD, but typically only in older children.

ADHD is a disorder of childhood that includes two major dimensions: (1) inattention and (2) hyperactivity and impulsivity. Individuals with ADHD can also show characteristics of both inattention and hyperactivity. ADHD is reported to be the most common emotional–behavioral disorder treated in youth. Epidemiological studies have also shown a comorbidity of ADHD with a variety of other disorders. Children and adolescents with ADHD show problems in various cognitive processes, including verbal working memory, spatial working memory, response inhibition, cognitive flexibility, vigilance, and planning. There is evidence to suggest that ADHD is influenced by genetic components. The major treatment for ADHD is stimulant medications. Psychosocial treatments, particularly involving parents, are often used in combination with medication with the best treatment results seen with a combination of both.

Learning disabilities (called specific learning disorder in *DSM-5*) refer to the situation in which a child's achievement in specific academic skills is lower than that expected from their scores on achievement or intelligence tests.

An intellectual developmental disorder (IDD) is defined by three aspects: (1) a deficit in mental abilities, (2) a lack of adaptive functioning in relation to one's age and sociocultural background, and (3) onset of the disabilities prior to adolescence. Problems with intellectual development are considered to occur on a continuum described in terms of mild, moderate, and severe levels of disability. Most types of IDD can be traced to biological causes, although the variation is large. One way to organize these disorders is in terms of those directly related to chromosomes, those related to metabolism, and those related to gestation. The most common form of IDD is Down syndrome, which occurs during pregnancy as a result of a chromosomal abnormality. Treatment for individuals with IDD takes place on a number of levels and varies by age and level of functioning.

STUDY RESOURCES

Review Questions

1. Unlike some other species, humans are born into a world in which they cannot survive alone. What implications does this have for normal psychological development as well as for the impact of early disruptions in the developmental process?

2. Given that adolescence marks the peak onset of many psychopathologies, what specific education or treatment programs would you recommend to target adolescent audiences?

3. What is the significance of "spectrum" in the term *autism spectrum disorder?* Why did *DSM-5* group previously separate disorders under this one characterization? How does it help us better understand the disorders in terms of causes, diagnostic criteria, and treatments? What are the disadvantages of grouping the disorders as a spectrum?

4. Childhood disorders have been grouped into externalizing and internalizing disorders. What characterizes these two groupings, and how does that help us understand the disorders presented in this chapter?

5. What are the primary differences between specific learning disorders and IDDs in terms of causes, diagnostic criteria, and treatments?

For Further Reading

Bucharest Early Intervention Project. (n.d.). https://www.bucharestearlyinterventionproject.org/

Centers for Disease Control and Prevention. (2022, August 9). *Data and statistics about ADHD*. U.S. Department of Health and Human Services. https://www.cdc.gov/ncbddd/adhd/data.html

Centers for Disease Control and Prevention. (2023, May 9). *Facts about Down syndrome*. U.S. Department of Health and Human Services. https://www.cdc.gov/ncbddd/birthdefects/DownSyndrome.html

Grandin, T. (2002, May 6). Myself. *Time, 159*(18), 56.

Grandin, T. (2009). How does visual thinking work in the mind of a person with autism? A personal account. *Philosophical Transactions of the Royal Society B, 364*, 1437–1442.

Grandin, T. (2010). *Thinking in pictures: My life with autism* (Expanded ed.). Vintage.

National Autism Center. (n.d.). http://www.nationalautismcenter.org/

Robison, J. (2007). *Look me in the eye: My life with Asperger's*. Crown Publishers.

U.S. Equal Employment Opportunity Commission. (2013, May 15). *Persons with intellectual disabilities in the workplace and the ADA*. https://www.eeoc.gov/laws/types/intellectual_disabilities.cfm

KEY TERMS

anxious/ambivalent attachment pattern
attachment
attention deficit/hyperactivity disorder (ADHD)
autism spectrum disorder (ASD)
avoidant attachment pattern
conduct disorder (CD)
disinhibited social engagement disorder
disorganized/controlling attachment pattern
disruptive, impulse control, and conduct disorders
Down syndrome
empathizing-systemizing theory of autism
fragile X syndrome
imitation learning
Individuals with Disabilities Education Act (IDEA)
intellectual developmental disorder (IDD)
learning disabilities
mirror neurons
neurodevelopmental disorders
oppositional defiant disorder (ODD)
reactive attachment disorder (RAD)
secure attachment pattern
specific learning disorder
theory of mind
trauma- and stressor-related disorders

iStock.com/shironosov

6 MOOD DISORDERS

LEARNING OBJECTIVES

6.1 Discuss the prevalence of mood disorders worldwide.

6.2 Define major depressive disorder and discuss its characteristics, causes, and treatment.

6.3 Identify the types of bipolar disorder and discuss their characteristics, causes, and treatment.

6.4 Discuss the risk factors for suicide, its prevention, and its connection with mental illness.

My path has not been easy. I was a young 23-year-old girl who had the world ahead of me. One day, without even realizing it, everything changed. I moved from Victoria, my home for six years, to escape an abusive relationship to Tasmania, where I was born and bred. My mum started to notice changes in me; I was no longer the happy girl that I was in Victoria. My energy dropped, I was spending longer in bed and my mood was low.

Excerpt from Bec Morrison. (2008). Depression: Disease, Loneliness, Social Isolation, Suicide, Negative Thoughts. Social Alternative, 27, 312–328.

My life came to a standstill. I could breathe, eat, drink, and sleep, and I could not help doing these things; but there was no life, for there were no wishes the fulfillment of which I could consider reasonable. If I desired anything, I knew in advance that whether I satisfied my desire or not, nothing would come of it. Had a fairy come and offered to fulfill my desires I should not have known what to ask. If in moments of intoxication I felt something which, though not a wish, was a habit left by former wishes, in sober moments I knew this to be a delusion and that there was really nothing to wish for. I could not even wish to know the truth, for I guessed of what it consisted. The truth was that life is meaningless. I had as it were lived, lived, and walked, walked, till I had come to a precipice and saw clearly that there was nothing ahead of me but destruction. It was impossible to stop, impossible to go back, and impossible to close my eyes or avoid seeing that there was nothing ahead but suffering and real death—complete annihilation.

Excerpt from My Confession: My Life Had Come to a Sudden Stop, by Leo Tolstoy (1882).

INTRODUCING MOOD DISORDERS

Emotional experiences and moods are an important part of our world as humans. Sometimes we feel happy; other times we feel sad. We have all experienced ourselves as having different moods. Our thoughts are often consistent with our moods, such as when we feel sad and think we are not doing things well. Likewise, our behaviors match our moods. Wanting to stay in bed in the morning or not wanting to be with others is often the outcome of feeling blue. Other times we go in the opposite direction and feel full of energy. Our thoughts when we are in a positive mood influence what activities we can engage in or what accomplishments we can achieve. Behaviorally, we tend to seek social interactions and start new projects.

Neither positive nor negative moods as most of us experience them interfere with our daily life or separate us from ourselves or others. However, the mood disorders discussed in this chapter do. Not only do these disorders separate us, but they also last for a long time. In some cases, they are experienced throughout one's life.

The first part of the chapter will focus on depression, particularly *major depressive disorder (MDD)*. Similar to the vignettes at the beginning of the chapter, those who experience depression describe both psychological and physical symptoms. They feel sad much of the time and may even be close to tears for no apparent reason. If you talk with these individuals, they will tell you that they feel worthless. Not only will you notice their negative affect, but you may also notice a lack of any positive affect. They may even say that they just do not feel like being involved in activities or being with others. They may also think of dying. In terms of physical symptoms, you might notice that these individuals have had weight changes. They will also describe problems with sleeping almost every night. They will report a loss of energy and feeling tired. This loss of energy may also be associated with an inability to concentrate. These symptoms will be described when discussing specific *DSM-5-TR* criteria later in the chapter.

The second part of the chapter will discuss those who experience both depression and mania, previously referred to as **manic depression**. Mania is the experience of tremendous energy and euphoria. When in this state, individuals may speak rapidly and tell you of their ability to accomplish all sorts of things. In the manic state, everything is wonderful and they are full of energy. They stay very active and may require little sleep.

Those who experience depression describe both psychological and physical symptoms.
iStock.com/LaylaBird. Stock photo. Posed by model.

Today we call these alternating periods of depression and mania **bipolar disorder**. This is in contrast to **unipolar depression**, which is the experience of depression without mania. Following this coverage of depression and bipolar disorder, the chapter concludes with a section on *suicide*, which is often tied to underlying mood disorders.

Both depression and mania have been described for more than 2,000 years. The ancient Greek writers Hippocrates, Aretaeus, and Galen each described a condition they referred to as **melancholia**, which today we call depression. Melancholia was described in terms of despondency, dissatisfaction with life, problems sleeping, restlessness, irritability, difficulties in decision making, and a desire to die. Mania, on the other hand, was described in terms of euphoria, excitement, cheerfulness, grandiosity, and at times anger. There was also a realization that mania and melancholia could exist in the same person.

Depression is characterized by depressed mood in which one feels sad or empty without any sense of pleasure in one's activities. All individuals experience depressed mood for brief periods, which is usually accompanied by feelings of sadness, loss of energy, social withdrawal, and often negative thoughts about oneself. With a depressive disorder, the individual may also experience sleep problems and weight changes. Included with the disorder is a sense of worthlessness and self-blame. Clinical depression is present when the majority of these symptoms last for at least 2 weeks.

Depression has been related to a variety of physiological, psychological, family, and social components. It is also estimated to be one of the most economically costly mental disorders worldwide. MDD has been shown to take individuals out of their normal roles or jobs for a number of days equal to days lost due to physical medical disorders. In fact, MDD is second only to chronic back or neck pain in terms of days lost. This is partly related to the fact that only one third of those with depression seek help in the first year of onset. The median delay for seeking treatment among those who did not seek treatment in the first year is 5 years. Even with treatment, the chance of another episode of depression is high. Most patients experience a recurrence within 5 years (Boland & Keller, 2009). Historical figures such as President Abraham Lincoln have described their own experiences of mood disorders.

A number of performers have spoken of their personal struggles with depression. Brian Wilson of the band the Beach Boys said that he would go for long periods without being able to do anything. The actor and singer Ashley Judd describes herself as depressed and isolated. The singer Sheryl Crow has also documented her own experiences of depression and said there were periods she thought about

Abraham Lincoln, famous for his "melancholy," suffered from what we now call clinical depression.
Alexander Gardner; archived in Library of Congress Web Archives at https://www.loc.gov/item/2015645458/

suicide every day. For completeness, it should be noted that many performers and artists have consulted with mental health professionals and reflect this experience in their statements. However, some may say in interviews or profiles, "That sounds like me, so I must have this or that disorder," which may not clinically be the case.

In *Cultural LENS: Mood Disorders Around the World*, you can see lifetime and prevalence data for mood disorders by country. Although rates vary, the data show that mood disorders are common worldwide.

CULTURAL LENS
MOOD DISORDERS AROUND THE WORLD

In 2018, the World Health Organization (WHO) ranked depression as the leading cause of disability worldwide, with women affected by depression more than men (see For Further Reading). The WHO, as part of its mission, has collected data on mental health from countries around the world. Face-to-face household surveys were undertaken with community adult respondents in low- to middle-income countries and high-income countries. Prevalence was assessed with the WHO Composite International Diagnostic Interview. Lifetime and 12-month prevalence data in relation to mood disorders have been compiled (see Tables 6.1 and 6.2).

These data show that mood disorders are common throughout the world. Although not shown here, Kessler et al. (2009) reported additional data that suggest only a small number of those individuals with a mood disorder receive treatment, and even fewer receive high-quality treatment. This, in turn, results in impaired functioning, which has real costs to a society in terms of productivity, financial resources, and quality of life. Figure 6.1 shows how countries rank in terms of disability-adjusted life years (DALYs), a measure developed to reflect the magnitude of nonfatal diseases. DALY measures are seen on a continuum from perfect health to death. Thus, the more severe the disorder is, the larger the DALY measure is.

TABLE 6.1 ■ Lifetime Prevalence for Mood Disorders Worldwide

ANY MOOD DISORDER			ANY MOOD DISORDER		
I. High Income	%	(SE)	II. Low to Middle Income	%	(SE)
Belgium	14.1	(1.0)	Brazil (São Paulo)	18.4	(.08)
France	21.0	(1.1)	Colombia	13.3	(0.6)
Germany	9.9	(0.6)	India	9.0	(0.5)
Israel	10.1	(.05)	Lebanon	10.9	(0.9)
Italy	9.9	(0.5)	Mexico	8.0	(0.5)
Japan	6.6	(0.5)	PRC (Shenzhen)	6.5	(0.4)
Netherlands	17.9	(1.0)	South Africa	9.8	(0.7)
New Zealand	17.8	(1.0)	Ukraine	14.6	(0.7)
Spain	10.6	(0.5)	TOTAL OF ALL COUNTRIES	11.1	(0.2)
United States	19.2	(0.5)			

Note: SE = standard error.

Credit: Kessler, R. C., & Bromet, E. J. (2013). The epidemiology of depression across cultures. *Annual Review of Public Health, 34*, 119–138. Reprinted with permission from *Annual Reviews*.

TABLE 6.2 ■ Twelve-Month Prevalence for Mood Disorders Worldwide

ANY MOOD DISORDER			ANY MOOD DISORDER		
I. High Income	%	(SE)	II. Low to Middle Income	%	(SE)
Belgium	5.0	(0.5)	Brazil (São Paulo)	10.4	(0.6)
France	5.9	(0.6)	Colombia	6.2	(0.4)
Germany	3.0	(0.3)	India	4.5	(0.4)
Israel	6.1	(0.4)	Lebanon	5.5	(0.7)
Italy	3.0	(0.2)	Mexico	4.0	(0.3)
Japan	2.2	(0.4)	PRC (Shenzhen)	3.8	(0.3)
Netherlands	4.9	(0.5)	South Africa	4.9	(0.4)
New Zealand	6.6	(0.3)	Ukraine	8.4	(0.6)
Spain	10.6	(0.5)	TOTAL	5.9	(0.2)
United States	8.3	(0.3)			
TOTAL	5.5	(0.1)			

Note: SE = standard error.

Credit: Kessler, R. C., & Bromet, E. J. (2013). The epidemiology of depression across cultures. *Annual Review of Public Health, 34*, 119–138. Reprinted with permission from *Annual Reviews*.

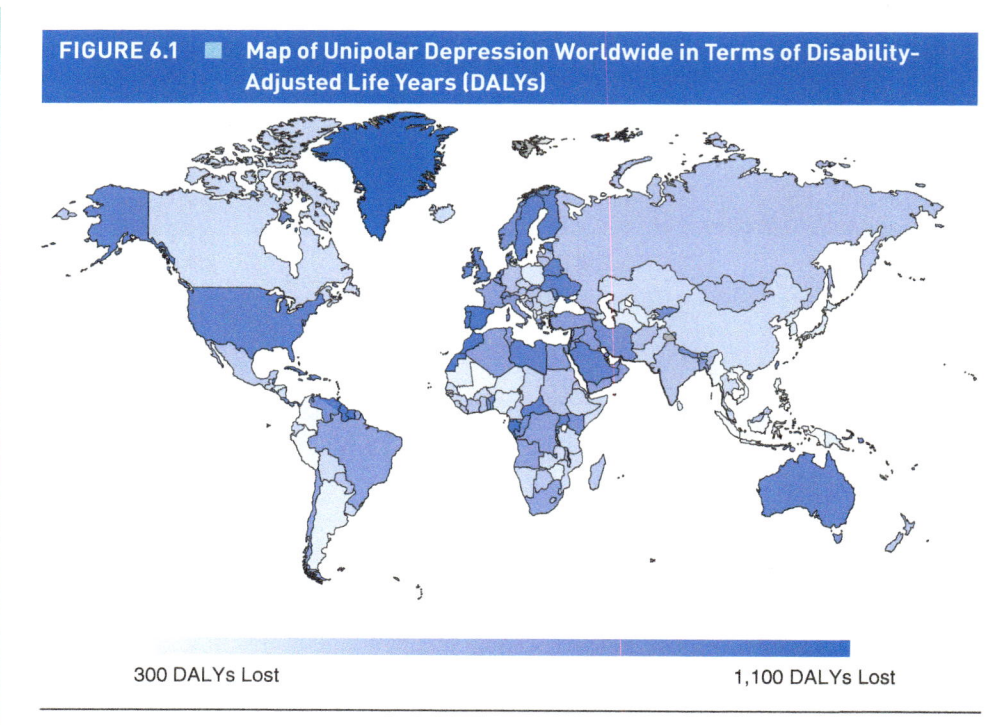

FIGURE 6.1 ■ Map of Unipolar Depression Worldwide in Terms of Disability-Adjusted Life Years (DALYs)

300 DALYs Lost — 1,100 DALYs Lost

Credit: Institute for Health Metrics Evaluation. Used with permission. All rights reserved.

Thought Question

What surprises you about the effects of depression on the quality of life around the world as shown in the map in Figure 6.1? Why do you think the United States has more DALYs than much of the rest of the world?

RESEARCH TERMS TO KNOW
STANDARD ERROR

Standard error is similar to the standard deviation. The standard deviation is an estimate of variability of the estimated population from which a particular sample would have come. The standard error reflects the variability around the mean of the sample used in the study. In studies of prevalence such as that seen in the *Cultural LENS* box, the standard error helps us to know how variable the mean is.

MAJOR DEPRESSIVE DISORDER

With **major depressive disorder (MDD),** a person feels sad and empty and maybe displays an irritable mood. These feelings may include hopelessness and be experienced over a number of days. Physical experiences such as difficulty sleeping and eating are also common. As noted in the quote from the Russian writer Leo Tolstoy at the beginning of this chapter, Tolstoy experienced his depression as though his life was coming to a standstill and felt that everything he undertook would fail.

Characteristics of Major Depressive Disorder

Today, MDD is one of the most commonly diagnosed mental disorders among adults. According to the National Institute of Mental Health, in 2020 it was estimated that 8.4% of U.S. adults, some

21 million people, had had at least one major depressive episode. Worldwide, the number of cases of depression has increased almost 50% over the past 30 years, resulting in more than 264 million people affected (Q. Liu et al., 2020). One meta-analysis showed an increase in depression among college students following the COVID-19 pandemic (J. J. Chang et al., 2021). The likelihood of an additional depressive episode occurring after an initial episode has been estimated to be between 75% and 90% (American Psychiatric Association, 2022; Gotlib et al., 2020). However, some suggest these recurrence estimates are too high (Monroe & Harkness, 2022).

> **RESEARCH TERMS TO KNOW**
> **META-ANALYSIS**
>
> *Meta-analysis* is the process by which a number of independent research studies are considered together as if they were one large study. By combining the results of a number of studies, a more accurate determination of the experimental variable can be determined. It is also possible to determine the magnitude of the experimental results, referred to as *effect size*. If the independent variable has a strong effect, the participants who receive that experimental procedure will show less variance in their results than if the procedure has a weak effect. This is also the major way in which empirically supported treatments are determined.

DSM-5 and *DSM-5-TR* distinguish between a single depressive episode and MDD, in which there are recurrent depressive episodes interspersed with at least 2-month periods without depression. The *DSM-5-TR* criteria for the major depressive episode itself are the same as those for MDD. These criteria note that significant losses such as bereavement, financial ruin, and natural disaster may trigger symptoms that resemble a depressive episode, including feelings of intense sadness, rumination about the loss, insomnia, poor appetite, and weight loss. However, these do not represent MDD. For a diagnosis of MDD, the *DSM-5-TR* criteria require five or more symptoms with a precise duration (Table 6.3). See the "Understanding Changes in *DSM-5* and *DSM-5-TR*" feature in this chapter to learn more about the controversial change to the manual regarding the so-called "grief exception" to the diagnosis of depression.

TABLE 6.3 ■ *DSM-5-TR* **Diagnostic Criteria for Major Depressive Disorder**

A. Five (or more) of the following symptoms have been present during the same 2-week period and represent a change from previous functioning; at least one of the symptoms is either (1) depressed mood or (2) loss of interest or pleasure.
Note: Do not include symptoms that are clearly attributable to another medical condition.
  1. Depressed mood most of the day, nearly every day, as indicated by either subjective report (e.g., feels sad, empty, hopeless) or observation made by others (e.g., appears tearful). (**Note:** In children and adolescents, can be irritable mood.)
  2. Markedly diminished interest or pleasure in all, or almost all, activities most of the day, nearly every day (as indicated by either subjective account or observation).
  3. Significant weight loss when not dieting or weight gain (e.g., a change of more than 5% of body weight in a month), or decrease or increase in appetite nearly every day. (**Note:** In children, consider failure to make expected weight gain.)
  4. Insomnia or hypersomnia nearly every day.
  5. Psychomotor agitation or retardation nearly every day (observable by others, not merely subjective feelings of restlessness or being slowed down).
  6. Fatigue or loss of energy nearly every day.
  7. Feelings of worthlessness or excessive or inappropriate guilt (which may be delusional) nearly every day (not merely self-reproach or guilt about being sick).
  8. Diminished ability to think or concentrate, or indecisiveness, nearly every day (either by subjective account or as observed by others).
  9. Recurrent thoughts of death (not just fear of dying), recurrent suicidal ideation without a specific plan; a specific suicide plan; or a suicide attempt.

(Continued)

TABLE 6.3 ■ *DSM-5-TR* Diagnostic Criteria for Major Depressive Disorder (*Continued*)

B. The symptoms cause clinically significant distress or impairment in social, occupational, or other important areas of functioning.

C. The episode is not attributable to the direct physiological effects of a substance or another medical condition.
Note: Criteria A–C represent a major depressive episode.
Note: Responses to a significant loss (e.g., bereavement, financial ruin, losses from a natural disaster, a serious medical illness or disability) may include the feelings of intense sadness, rumination about the loss, insomnia, poor appetite, and weight loss noted in Criterion A, which may resemble a depressive episode. Although such symptoms may be understandable or considered appropriate to the loss, the presence of a major depressive episode in addition to the normal response to a significant loss should also be carefully considered. This decision inevitably requires the exercise of clinical judgment based on the individual's history and the cultural norms for the expression of distress in the context of loss.

D. At least one major depressive episode is not better explained by schizoaffective disorder and is not superimposed on schizophrenia, schizophreniform disorder, delusional disorder, or other specified or unspecified schizophrenia spectrum and other psychotic disorders.

E. There has never been a manic episode or a hypomanic episode.
Note: This exclusion does not apply if all of the manic-like or hypomanic-like episodes are substance-induced or are attributable to the physiological effects of another medical condition.

Coding and Recording Procedures

The diagnostic code for major depressive disorder is based on whether this is a single or recurrent episode, current severity, presence of psychotic features, and remission status. Current severity and psychotic features are only indicated if full criteria are currently met for a major depressive episode. Remission specifiers are only indicated if the full criteria are not currently met for a major depressive episode. Codes are as follows:

Severity/course specifier	Single episode	Recurrent episode*
Mild (p. 214)	F32.0	F33.0
Moderate (p. 214)	F32.1	F33.1
Severe (p. 214)	F32.2	F33.2
With psychotic features** (pp. 212–213)	F32.3	F33.3
In partial remission (p. 214)	F32.4	F33.41
In full remission (p. 214)	F32.5	F33.42
Unspecified	F32.9	F33.9

*For an episode to be considered recurrent, there must be an interval of at least 2 consecutive months between separate episodes in which criteria are not met for a major depressive episode. The definitions of specifiers are found on the indicated pages.

**If psychotic features are present, code the "with psychotic features" specifier irrespective of episode severity.
In recording the name of a diagnosis, terms should be listed in the following order: major depressive disorder, single or recurrent episode, severity/psychotic/remission specifiers, followed by as many of the following specifiers without codes that apply to the current episode (or the most recent episode if the major depressive disorder is in partial or full remission). **Note:** The specifier "with seasonal pattern" describes the pattern of recurrent major depressive episodes. *Specify* if:

    With anxious distress (pp. 210–211)

    With mixed features (p. 211)

    With melancholic features (pp. 211–212)

    With atypical features (p. 212)

    With mood-congruent psychotic features (p. 213)

    With mood-incongruent psychotic features (p. 213)

    With catatonia (p. 213). **Coding note:** Use additional code F06.1.

    With peripartum onset (p. 213)

    With seasonal pattern (applies to pattern of recurrent major depressive episodes) (p. 214)

Credit: Reprinted with permission from the *Diagnostic and Statistical Manual of Mental Disorders, fifth edition, text revision,* DSM-V-TR, pp. 183–185 (Copyright © 2022). American Psychiatric Association. All Rights Reserved.

Lifetime estimates for MDD indicate that it affects approximately 33 million Americans at some point in their lives. For all Americans over the age of 13, the lifetime prevalence for a major depressive episode is 20.6%, and 10.4% for a 12-month prevalence (Hasin et al., 2018). Lifetime and 12-month prevalence is lower in men than women; over the course of a lifetime, about 1 in 4 females and 1 in 10 males experiences a major depressive episode (Rutter, 2006; see also Hyde & Mezulis, 2020; Ryba & Hopko, 2012). Prevalence is also lower in Hispanic Americans, African Americans, and Asian/Pacific Islanders but higher in Native Americans as compared to white Americans (Hasin et al., 2019). It should be noted that three fourths of those with MDD would also meet criteria for an additional *DSM-5-TR* disorder. Anxiety disorder (59%), obsessive–compulsive disorder (OCD) (31.9%), and substance abuse (24%) are all frequently comorbid with MDD.

Genetic studies suggest that depression is equally influenced by genetic and environmental factors (Rutter, 2006). In one set of studies, monkeys with a genetic risk for depression were raised by either highly responsive or less responsive foster mothers (Suomi, 2016). In this situation, the mothers influenced the outcome, with more responsive mothers having less depressed infants. A more thorough consideration of the underlying causes of depression will be discussed shortly. Meta-analyses have also shown an increased risk for disorders such heart disease, stroke, diabetes, and obesity in those with MDD (Hasin et al., 2019; Otte et al., 2016).

UNDERSTANDING CHANGES IN *DSM-5* AND *DSM-5-TR*
GRIEF AND THE GRIEF EXCEPTION

Humans show grief when they lose something or someone important to them. The way one feels when experiencing grief is not unlike how someone with depression feels. But are grief and depression the same? Before *DSM-5*, if an individual had lost a loved one and showed signs of depression, they would not be diagnosed with major depressive disorder. This came to be known as the grief exception or bereavement exclusion.

This exception was removed in *DSM-5*. Depression, whether the direct result of grief or some other cause, can be diagnosed as a clinical case as long as certain criteria are met (Uher et al., 2014). Professionals who support this change argue that previously, a person suffering from severe depression symptoms a month or two after a loss might not have gotten the treatment that they needed. Further, it was suggested that not treating grief might miss those individuals who have thoughts of suicide.

Those who did not support the change argue that, although both may look the same, grief-related stress is different from depression. Further, grief is a normal human response to loss and not seen only in humans. Based on descriptions by Darwin and others, grief or sadness as the result of loss has been seen in a number of different species. As such, the experience of grief should not be seen as a mental disorder (Wakefield, 2016). Different cultures also illustrate different roles and time frames for those experiencing grief, especially with the death of a parent, partner, or child.

In *DSM-5-TR*, a new diagnostic category, prolonged grief disorder, was added to the trauma and stress-related disorders section (Prigerson et al., 2021). A similar category is also found in *ICD-11*, although it differs in certain ways (Rosner et al., 2021). This disorder represents a prolonged maladaptive grief reaction, and it can be diagnosed only after at least 12 months have elapsed since the death of someone with whom the person had a close relationship. Characteristics of the disorder include intense yearning or longing for the deceased person and/or preoccupation with thoughts and memories of the deceased person. Specific symptoms can also include disbelief about the death, intense emotional pain, intense loneliness, feeling that life is meaningless without the person, and other such factors.

Overall, grief is a common human experience that can be felt and expressed by different individuals in different ways. Some people want others to support and interact with them during periods of grief. Other people withdraw into themselves and avoid interactions with other people. Further, the types of narratives that people tell themselves after a loss may be different from those seen in depression (Tekin, 2015). For example, people experiencing grief may reexperience significant memories of the person who was lost, which gives them comfort, whereas those with depression may see a negative future or tell themselves they are bad. These differences also have implications for the type of treatment that would be more effective for someone seeking help with their grief versus depression. If, indeed, grief and depression represent different underlying processes, then the lack of this distinction would also result in confused research findings in the two areas.

Causes of Depression

Depression is a debilitating disorder. Although research suggests both genetic and environmental factors are involved in developing depression, the genetic component is estimated to be around 35% (Otte et al., 2016). Using the Virginia Twin Registry, researchers have shown that the initial episode of depression has a stronger relationship with environmental factors than later episodes do (Kendler et al., 2000).

Major environmental life stresses such as the loss of a close relationship are highly associated with the development of depression. Individuals with depression are 2.5 to 10 times more likely to have experienced a recent major life event than are individuals without depression (Slavich et al., 2010). Further, studies from around the world show early life stress such as emotional abuse to be associated with later depressive episodes (Martins-Monteverde et al., 2019).

Models have been developed to map the pathway from stress to depression, which results from an overload of energy resources (Arnaldo et al., 2022). A distinction is made between short-term, brief stress that has a motivational effect and long-term, chronic stress that leads to depression (Lemos et al., 2012). (Stress and trauma are discussed in greater detail in Chapter 7.) The pathway from chronic stress to depression includes a reduction in size of the brain regions that regulate mood and cognition, such as the prefrontal cortex (PFC) and the hippocampus (Haukvik et al., 2020; Schmaal et al., 2015), as well as reduced connections between major brain networks (B.-J. Li et al., 2018). A large meta-analysis involving over 800,000 individuals has shown the importance of prefrontal regions to depression (Howard et al., 2019). This study also suggested a complex genetic relationship involving 102 variants of some 269 genes.

Animals under chronic stress also show fewer synapses in prefrontal regions of the brain (Duman & Aghajanian, 2012). Figure 6.2 shows the effects of chronic stress over 7 days on dendrite length and branching. Notice the difference between the neurons of the animal that was not stressed and the one that was. Other studies suggest that chronic stress acts like a switch that changes positive motivational responses to aversive ones in the nucleus accumbens. This switch from active coping to lack of motivation may lie at the basis of the development of depression (Lemos et al., 2012).

An intriguing question is whether genetic factors make some individuals more reactive to environmental stresses. Environmental stress leads the brain to produce and release **cortisol**, a glucocorticoid hormone, in the adrenal cortex. Those with depressive disorders produce more cortisol in response to stress. In fact, some individuals with depression show elevated levels of cortisol throughout the day, even without acute stress. Further, a link has been established between gene coding for these stress responses and depression (Z. Liu et al., 2006).

Epigenetic factors (described in Chapter 2) such as DNA methylation may also be part of a pathway from stress to depression. One study examined Finnish nurses who had worked in a high-stress or low-stress ward for the past 3 years (Alasaari et al., 2012). The nurses who worked on a high-stress ward had Beck Depression Inventory scores that were twice that of those on the low-stress wards. They also showed lower methylation levels at a location that would reduce synaptic serotonin. This, in turn, would result in depressed mood.

FIGURE 6.2 ■ Can Stress Affect How the Brain Grows?

The figure shows shorter dendrite length and less branching in the neurons of mice who were restrained (~30 minutes per day, 7 days) compared to those who were not.

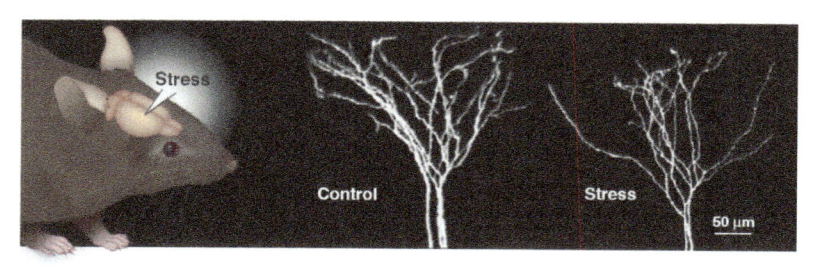

Credit: Duman, R. S., & Aghajanian, G. K. (2012). Synaptic dysfunction in depression: Potential therapeutic targets. *Science, 338*(6103), 68–72. https://doi.org/10.1126/science.1222939. Reprinted with permission from AAAS.

Further studies that show the complex nature of the development of depression deal with the **intergenerational transmission of depression** (see Hammen, 2009, for an overview). These studies focus on the manner in which having one or more parents who are depressed leads to a child becoming depressed. If one's parent was depressed, it would change the nature of the emotional and social interactions during childhood. In general, studies have shown that individuals with a depressive parent experience depression 2 to 3 times more frequently by age 15 or 20 than those without a depressive parent. When these individuals develop depression, it is also more severe and recurrent.

Developmental Aspects of Depression

Adolescence is a period of life when drastic, critical social, emotional, hormonal, and brain changes take place. Mood disorders related to anxiety and depression are common, and research is still attempting to articulate a clear picture of the nature of depression in adolescents (Pine, 2009; Rudolf, 2009). It is estimated that clinical depression occurs in around 3% to 5% of the population of adolescents. Prior to this age, the rates are 1% to 2%. Gender differences in depression emerge by age 13 or 14. By age 18, women show a 2 to 1 prevalence that remains stable throughout adulthood.

Although diagnostic symptoms for adolescents are similar to those for adults, depressed children are more likely to describe physical symptoms such as headache or stomach pains, whereas adults describe hopelessness, helplessness, and suicidal thinking. The rates of depression are very low prior to puberty, with equal numbers of boys and girls experiencing symptoms. After puberty, the rates of depression increase, and more young women than young men are affected. There is some suggestion that females of this age cognitively process social stress differently from males, which places them at risk for depression (Pine, 2009). Currently, there is a lack of systematic nationwide data examining the mental health of transgender and nonbinary youth.

Environmental factors appear to be critical in the development of depression. One study reported that over 90% of depressive episodes were related to stressful events. These events included negative experiences with parents such as marital discord, neglect, and abuse, as well as having a parent with a mental disorder (Goodyer, 2001). Attachment relationships have also been linked to a cognitive vulnerability to depression (Morley & Moran, 2011). If there is a positive relationship with a parent, even in children who have been maltreated, there is less depression (Kaufman et al., 2006).

Adolescence is a time of great change on a number of levels. These include the importance of social relationships and the influence of peers, changes in brain development, and the hormonal changes associated with puberty. All of these have been seen to influence the development of depression in adolescence. One literature review and meta-analysis of brain imaging studies suggested that the prefrontal cortex, anterior cingulate, and amygdala are the areas in which differences are seen in adolescent depression (Kerestes et al., 2014). These are areas involved in the interface of cognition and emotion. One aspect of this is that adolescents who develop MDD may expect social rewards that do not materialize, which in turn decreases the activity of brain areas related to social rewards. Similar results were also found in young adults (ages 19–25) with major depressive disorder.

Cognitive Model of Depression

The **cognitive model of depression** was developed by Aaron Beck (1967, 2019) to describe the manner in which individuals with depression maintain the disorder. It also became the basis for a therapeutic approach that has been studied in a variety of empirical treatment studies (see J. Beck, 2011). The basic model suggests that individuals with depression display a bias in the way they search for and process information. These biases take place out of awareness and represent internal schemas that influence what these individuals see, how they organize information, and what they remember related to their life. These biases generally result in individuals with depression seeing themselves as worthless in a world with little support. If asked to remember their past, unlike healthy individuals, they tend to remember more negative than positive events (Dillon & Pizzagalli, 2018). Research with emotional stimuli also suggests that it is difficult for those with depression to disengage from negative stimuli. In addition, negative rumination, in which the individual thinks repetitively about how a negative event came about, is also characteristic of depression.

The cognitive model is basically a learning theory model that suggests adverse events that occur early in life can lead to the development of depressive schemas. These depressive schemas are characterized by negative self-referential beliefs. Further, when a new stressor appears, it can activate the prior negative schemas. These negative schemas involve three aspects: the self, the personal world, and the future. This is referred to as the **negative cognitive triad**. In terms of the self, the individual with depression will attribute unpleasant experiences encountered in the world to their own mental, physical, and moral defects. The second component involves the person's tendency to tailor the facts to fit the negative schema. The third component involves the person seeing the future as containing only hardship and failure.

Since the original cognitive model of depression was developed over 50 years ago, brain imaging techniques have progressed greatly. Researchers now suggest that the underlying neural mechanisms for the cognitive model of depression can be described (A. Beck & Bredemeier, 2016; Disner et al., 2011). The neural model begins with the observation that attention in healthy individuals involves a number of brain areas, including the prefrontal cortex (PFC). The ability to switch attention is a top-down process that includes three different processes. The first involves choosing what to pay attention to (the ventrolateral prefrontal cortex [VLPFC]). The second is executive control (the dorsolateral prefrontal cortex [DLPFC]). The third involves moving the eyes (the superior parietal cortex).

Attention requires effort when you are focusing on information that does not normally attract you. When individuals without depression are asked not to focus on positive information, the anterior cingulate cortex (ACC) shows activity, whereas in individuals with depression, ACC activity occurs when they are asked to divert attention from negative stimuli. This suggests that healthy and depressed individuals require cognitive effort to accomplish emotional switching in opposite directions. Further, in a bottom-up process, amygdala reactivity to negative stimuli in individuals with depression is more intense and lasts longer than that seen in healthy individuals. Figure 6.3 summarizes the cognitive model from a cortical perspective.

Are Depression and Inflammation Related?

Researchers have recently begun to determine a relationship between depression and inflammation (Alen, 2022; Dantzer, 2012; Dantzer et al., 2008; Dooley et al., 2018; Hodes et al., 2015). In particular, studies suggest that environmental and social stress produces an elevation in inflammation (Slavich & Irwin, 2014), which may in turn be related to the development of depression in both young adults and elderly people (Bell et al., 2017). One longitudinal study measured inflammation markers at age 9 and again at age 18 (Khandaker et al., 2014). Those participants who showed higher levels of inflammation markers at age 9 were more likely to experience depression at age 18 compared with those with low levels of the markers. Research has also shown a genetic connection between inflammation and symptoms of depression (Kappelmann et al., 2021).

Research has noted the similarity between the symptoms of physical sickness involving the immune system and depression. In physical sickness involving pathogens, immune system cytokines influence local and systemic responses. It is these cytokines that act on the brain to produce the experience of sickness. In both depression and responses to pathogens, there is a withdrawal from the physical and social environment, which can be accompanied by pain. There is also a general malaise and decreased interest in activities that produce positive rewards. One difference, however, is that once the pathogens have been removed, the sickness experience is eliminated, which does not happen with depression. This has led some to suggest that the malfunctioning of cytokines may be involved in depression. That is, depression is related to inflammation in the brain. This was initially called the **macrophage theory of depression** (Smith, 1991).

Research supporting this idea shows that individuals with depression have increased blood concentration of inflammatory biomarkers (Bullmore, 2019). Several meta-analyses have shown an association between depression and biomarkers of inflammation (Dowlati et al., 2010). These studies noted that individuals with depression were physically healthy, and thus, the presence of the biomarkers was not the result of underlying pathology. However, the relationship between depression and inflammation may help to clarify the relation between depression and the later development of physical disorders such as heart disease and type 2 diabetes.

FIGURE 6.3 ■ Summary of an Integrated Cognitive Neurobiological Model of Depression

The brain regions in this flowchart are divided into two groups. The first group is associated with top-down influences through cognitive control (shown by green boxes), and the second is associated with bottom-up limbic influences (shown by blue boxes).

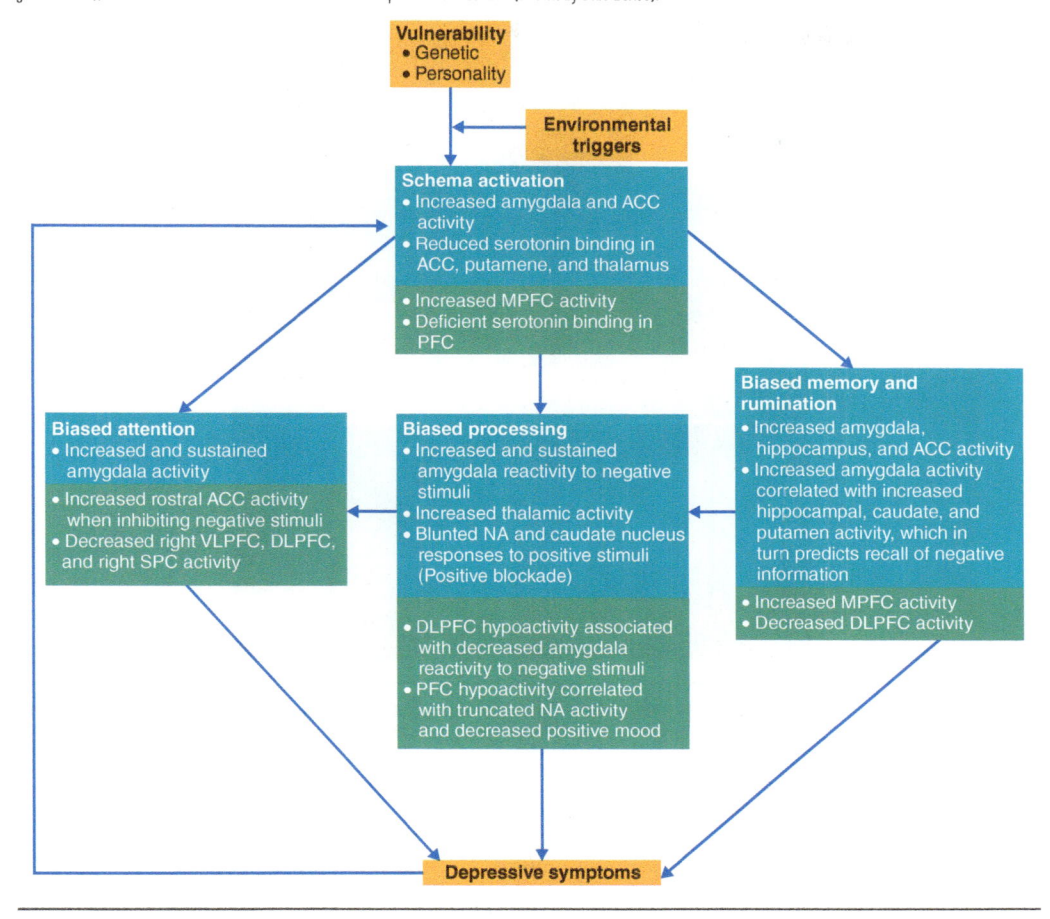

Vulnerability
- Genetic
- Personality

Environmental triggers

Schema activation
- Increased amygdala and ACC activity
- Reduced serotonin binding in ACC, putamene, and thalamus
- Increased MPFC activity
- Deficient serotonin binding in PFC

Biased attention
- Increased and sustained amygdala activity
- Increased rostral ACC activity when inhibiting negative stimuli
- Decreased right VLPFC, DLPFC, and right SPC activity

Biased processing
- Increased and sustained amygdala reactivity to negative stimuli
- Increased thalamic activity
- Blunted NA and caudate nucleus responses to positive stimuli (Positive blockade)
- DLPFC hypoactivity associated with decreased amygdala reactivity to negative stimuli
- PFC hypoactivity correlated with truncated NA activity and decreased positive mood

Biased memory and rumination
- Increased amygdala, hippocampus, and ACC activity
- Increased amygdala activity correlated with increased hippocampal, caudate, and putamen activity, which in turn predicts recall of negative information
- Increased MPFC activity
- Decreased DLPFC activity

Depressive symptoms

Credit: Disner, S. G., Beevers, C. G., Haigh, E. A. P., & Beck, A. T. (2011). Neural mechanisms of the cognitive model of depression. *Nature Reviews Neuroscience, 12*, 467–477. https://doi.org/10.1038/nrn3027

Evidence That Depression Runs in Families

A variety of studies have shown that chronic severe depression is familial (Peterson & Weissman, 2011). Offspring of individuals with MDD have a threefold to fivefold increased risk of developing MDD themselves. From longitudinal studies over three generations, individuals initially show elevated anxiety disorders before puberty, which then become MDD in mid to late adolescence. Further, familial MDD tends to have an earlier onset and to be more severe, more recurrent, and less responsive to treatment than is nonfamilial MDD.

One brain imaging study compared individuals at high risk for developing MDD in the second and third generations of a longitudinal MDD study (Peterson & Weissman, 2011). These high-risk individuals were compared with the children of the study's original control group of individuals without depression. What these researchers found is that individuals with MDD as well as their unaffected family members showed cortical thinning of the lateral aspect of the right hemisphere and the medial aspect of the left hemisphere along with the bilateral hypoplasia of the frontal and parietal white matter. The unaffected family members also showed signs of inattention and poor visual memory for social stimuli. Further, there was a direct relationship between the deficits and the magnitude of cortical thinning and white matter hypoplasia. Likewise, symptom severity also correlated inversely with cortical thickness and with white matter measures (Figure 6.4).

FIGURE 6.4 ■ Does Depression Influence the Thickness of Brain Areas?

In the figure, the top and bottom images show that the less the cortical thickness or volume is (purple is less, red is more), the greater will be the symptoms of major depressive disorder.

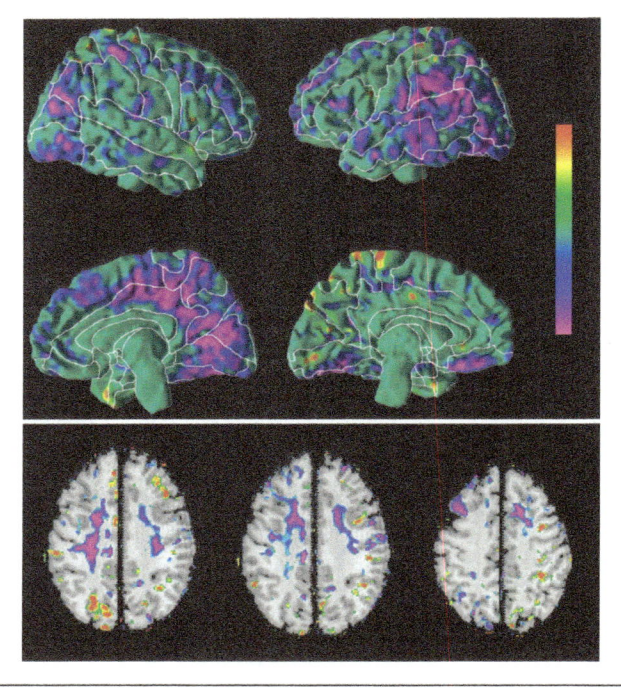

Credit: Bradley S. Peterson and Myrna M. Weissman, "A Brain-Based Endophenotype for Major Depressive Disorder." *Annual Reviews Med.* 2011 February 18; 62: 461–474. Reprinted with permission from *Annual Reviews*.

Evolutionary Perspectives on Depression

Andrews (2007) suggested that there are only a limited number of evolutionary hypotheses that might explain the existence of depression. One hypothesis views depression as resulting from a mismatch between the current demands of our society and our brain and nervous system, which evolved in terms of different demands. Thus, depression results from a novel reaction of the nervous system to the modern environment. This hypothesis suggests that our environment has changed quickly, whereas our nervous system has not. However, Andrews rejected this hypothesis, since depression is seen in a variety of animals such as rats, cats, and primates whose environment has not changed drastically in recent times. Another hypothesis views depression as a process that evolved because it was connected to another trait that was extremely adaptive. This connection has yet to be found.

Paul Gilbert (2005) asked if depression might have evolved because it serves a useful function. Such an advantage would be found in situations in which positive affect and drive should be toned down. One simple answer is that a reduction of positive affect could make one more sensitive to threats. Gilbert then took this question a step further and asked at what point the increase in depressive mood would be adaptive. Sickness or hurt would be one such example. Withdrawing from active life would give the body time to recover health and strength. Likewise, stress, which can result in a variety of depression-like symptoms, including reduction of positive affect, activity, and motivational factors such as hunger, may be reduced with removal from the stressful situation.

Allen and Badcock (2003) considered the role of depressed mood in our social evolutionary history. They saw depressed mood as having evolved in relation to social processes. As with other researchers, they suggested that a depressed state represents a risk management strategy in response to a situation that has a low probability of success and high probability of risk. The emphasis is on social situations in which an individual would be at risk for being excluded from groups or a relationship with another individual. Basically, they saw depressed mood as the result of a computational problem on the part of the organism. That is to say, on some level, the organism evaluates the situation. In a situation in which there is high risk of being excluded, this evaluation leads to depressed mood. Intrinsic to this way of thinking is the assumption that depressed mood was adaptive in our evolutionary history. In other words, feeling depressed would help the organism solve a problem faced by humans from the earliest times.

Overall, there are three questions that need to be approached from an evolutionary perspective in relation to depression (Nesse, 1990):

1. What are the situations that occur over and over again in our environment of evolutionary adaptiveness (EEA) responsible for depressive states?

2. What are the selection pressures in these situations? Said in other terms, what reproductive goals would have been threatened?

3. What are the characteristics of depressed mood that would have enabled the organism to cope with these threats?

These questions have been answered by evolutionary psychologists in terms of three broad models. These are (1) **depression in terms of resource conservation**, (2) **depression in terms of social competition**, and (3) **depression in terms of attachment**. Attachment has been discussed previously and would relate to depression in terms of the experience of loss.

Resource Conservation

Theories of resource conservation suggest that depressive mood protects the organism by conserving energy. Aaron Beck and Keith Bredemeier (2016) have expanded the cognitive theory of depression to suggest that depression can be viewed as an adaptation to conserve energy after the perceived loss of an investment in a vital resource such as a relationship, group identity, or personal asset. By reducing energy expenditure, the organism can both protect itself in the present situation and conserve energy that can be used in future productive situations. Stress and especially uncontrollable events can affect the organism and produce a depression-like state. Clinical depression in these theories results when an individual does not move on to the next situation but rather continues in a situation in which there are few positive payoffs. One way to conserve energy is to spend less time in groups, as described in *LENS: Everyday Social Behavior During a Major Depressive Episode*.

LENS
EVERYDAY SOCIAL BEHAVIOR DURING A MAJOR DEPRESSIVE EPISODE

As you can see in the *DSM-5-TR* criteria for major depressive disorder, symptoms include reductions in enjoyable social contacts, less satisfying social lives, and poor social functioning. However, this information is generally learned from self-reports. There are few empirical studies that have tracked the nature of actual social interactions of those with major depressive disorder. Jenna Baddeley and associates (2012) conducted such a study.

These researchers had individuals with MDD and a control group wear an electronically activated recorder for 3 or 4 days. The device recorded 90-second sound clips from the person's immediate environment every 12 minutes, although the participants were unaware of when the recordings were taking place. These clips were then transcribed. The average age of participants was in the 30s.

Looking at the results of real-life interactions, those with MDD and the controls did not differ significantly in the amount of time they spent with others, the amount of time they talked, and the amount of time they were with one other person. However, there was a difference in the amount of time those with MDD spent in groups or with friends. Those with MDD spent less time in groups. In terms of the recordings' content, those with MDD expressed more negative emotions and spent less time laughing. The negative emotions expressed by those with MDD referred more to themselves

Do those with major depressive disorder spend less time socializing?
iStock.com/U.Ozel.Images. Stock photo. Posed by model.

(e.g., "I feel guilty" or "Sorry"), whereas the negative comments of those in the control group tended to be general statements, such as "That is a stupid idea" or "Damn it."

Overall, this study demonstrates a novel way to study the everyday life of people with depression. The study shows that those with MDD and controls spend similar amounts of time talking and interacting with other people. However, those with MDD spend less time in groups and express more negative emotions, especially with their romantic partners.

Thought Question

How would you design a study to look at everyday social behavior by using social media? What would be your research hypothesis? What would be your independent and dependent variables?

Based on Baddeley, J. L., Pennebaker, J. W., & Beevers, C. G. (2012). Everyday social behavior during a major depressive episode. Social Psychological and Personality Science, 4(4), 445–452. http://doi.org/10.1177/1948550612461654

Social Competition

In discussing dominance hierarchies across species, it has been noted that the most powerful individual has a greater chance of mating and passing on its genes. Typically, two males fight to determine which will be higher in power. It has also been observed that when one of the animals loses the competition, this animal begins to make submissive gestures. David Buss (2005) has extended this type of thinking to humans and suggested that there exists a powerful motivation to acquire rank and status, especially among human males. Price (1996) suggested that there is a connection between depressive mood and losing a fight for status and resources. In particular, he suggested that the losing organism adopts a strategy in which he signals a desire to withdraw and not continue the competition. The winner, on the other hand, tends to escalate the competition and increasingly displays threatening behaviors. Depression from this viewpoint is seen as an involuntary de-escalating strategy that signals to the other individual that he has won.

Social Risk Hypothesis

Allen and Badcock (2003) began to integrate evolutionary psychologists' three broad models of depression with the social risk hypothesis. This hypothesis suggests that when significant interpersonal relationships are disrupted, such as in situations of social humiliation or defeat, depressed mood is the outcome. In this sense, depression is a protective mechanism that prevents further critical losses. It is protective in two ways. First, depressed mood reduces the desire of the individual to immediately enter a social relationship in which there could be an adverse outcome. Second, the outward signs of depressed mood, including changes in voice tone, reaction time, eye contact, and facial expression, signal submission and helplessness to others.

> **CONCEPT CHECK**
>
> - What is the impact of depression from the following perspectives?
>   - Worldwide prevalence
>   - Lifetime prevalence
>   - Gender prevalence
>   - Costs to economy, society, family, and the individual
>   - Other psychological disorders
> - What are some of the factors related to depression in adolescents? How are they the same or different in children?
> - What is the "negative cognitive triad"? What is its role in the cognitive model of depression?
> - What evidence would you cite to answer the question of whether depression runs in families?
> - What three questions need to be addressed by any theory that takes an evolutionary perspective to explain the existence of depression?

Treatments for Depression

Many forms of treatment are available for reducing the problems associated with mood disorders. First, there are techniques for direct manipulation of brain activity through electrical or magnetic stimulation of the brain itself. A second technique is to use psychotropic medications to influence neurotransmitters, which in turn may inhibit or facilitate brain processes. Third, the brain may be influenced indirectly through cognitive, emotional, or behavioral changes. Traditional psychotherapy allows individuals to explore how they interpret their world through thoughts or react to it through emotions and to consider alternative ways of experiencing the world. Other treatment techniques that involve exercise or meditation are also designed with the goal of learning alternative ways to modify internal processes (Gordon et al., 2018). Given that certain treatments work better for some people than for others, an alternative approach seeks to match individuals with the treatment that works best for them (Cohen & DeRubeis, 2018).

Biological and Neuroscience Treatments for Depression

In this section, you will be introduced to techniques used to treat depression that directly modify the brain and its networks (Marwaha et al., 2023). By far the most common treatment is the prescription of medications that are designed to directly modify action at the level of the neuron and its synapses. Other techniques, such as electroconvulsive therapy (ECT), are designed to disrupt the electrical networks of the brain. Another technique directly stimulates the vagal nerve. The final technique described induces a magnetic field in the brain and can influence the experience of depression. In the following section, we will consider psychological treatments for depression.

Medications for Depression The first effective medications for depression were introduced in the 1950s and 1960s (see Gitlin, 2009, for an overview). Two of these were imipramine, a tricyclic antidepressant, and iproniazid, a monoamine oxidase (MAO) inhibitor. The term *tricyclic* refers to the three-ring chemical structure of the drug. *MAO inhibitor* refers to the focus of action at the synapse. One problem with these initial medications was side effects such as weight gain, sleep problems, and irregular cardiovascular functioning. In addition, MAO inhibitors can interact with certain foods that contain the amino acid tyramine, such as cheese, to increase blood pressure to dangerous levels.

In the late 1980s, a second generation of medications was released with fewer side effects. One of the best known was Prozac (fluoxetine). Prozac became an instant hit and was given to a large number of individuals worldwide, although the popular press suggested it was overprescribed. One problem with Prozac is that it is connected with thoughts of suicide in those under 18 years of age. It has also been associated with less sexual desire and symptoms such as headache and joint pain. Prozac is one of a number of drugs referred to as selective serotonin reuptake inhibitors (SSRIs) because of their effects at the synapse. SSRIs prevent the presynaptic reuptake of serotonin, which in turn increases the level of serotonin at the synapse. Newer antidepressant medications alter the central nervous system by influencing serotonin or norepinephrine or both. These are referred to as serotonin and norepinephrine reuptake inhibitors (SNRIs). Cymbalta and Effexor are trade names for two of the SNRIs. In general, it takes more than 4 weeks for antidepressant medications to have an effect.

One faster acting medication for depression that is being researched is ketamine (Andrade, 2017; Hirota & Lambert, 2018; Nemeroff, 2018; Riggs & Gould, 2021). It is generally administered as a slow intravenous infusion. In 2019, a nasal spray related to ketamine was approved by the FDA, which also must be administered in a medical setting. With ketamine, changes in depression are seen within hours but decrease after 3 to 12 days. Ketamine has also been shown to reduce suicidal tendencies in individuals with major depressive disorder. Ketamine was originally used as an anesthetic for animals during operations. In the 1990s, it was compared with fentanyl as a way of treating postoperative pain in humans. It is unclear if ketamine could become a drug of abuse as fentanyl has. At this point, the short-term nature of ketamine's positive results, along with the potential for abuse, has made health care professionals cautious in using it (Newport et al., 2015).

An alternative medication being considered as a potential treatment for depression is the psychedelic psilocybin (Marwaha et al., 2023; Pearson et al., 2022). Although the exact effects of psilocybin are still under study, it does influence brain networks (Daws et al., 2022). In one study, fMRI measures were taken at baseline and again 3 weeks after a second psilocybin administration. In the group that received the treatment, networks of the brain showed more global integration, and symptoms of depression were reduced. In comparison with traditional antidepressant medications, psilocybin worked quickly (Daws & Carhart, 2022). Psilocybin has also been shown to reduce rumination (Barba et al., 2022).

Overall, antidepressant medication has been found to be about 50% effective in clinical trials with adults (Fava, 2003). There have been a number of concerns about antidepressant medication used with children and adolescents. In particular, some studies have suggested, as noted earlier, a risk for increased suicide among adolescents taking these medications (Bridge et al., 2007). In children, antidepressants may interact with normal processes such as exercise, leading to problems. However, for millions of Americans, a range of antidepressant medications have provided significant relief from depression.

Electroconvulsive Therapy **Electroconvulsive therapy (ECT)** is a procedure in which electrical current is passed through the brain for a brief period (Holtzheimer et al., 2012). This electrical activity triggers a brief seizure of less than a minute, which most likely influences changes in brain chemistry and specific networks of the cortex. A series of these treatments has been shown to be effective in treating depression, especially in those individuals for whom other treatments do not work. This is referred to as *treatment-resistant depression*. Typically, ECT is only recommended for those individuals with depression who have not shown improvement with antidepressant medication or psychotherapy treatment (Ross et al., 2018). However, those who have had long depressive episodes and were especially unresponsive to medication have also shown poorer responses to ECT (Haq et al., 2015).

ECT was introduced in the beginning of the 20th century as a potential treatment for schizophrenia. Although it was not shown to be effective for schizophrenia, it was shown to have an influence on depression. Because of the initial techniques used as well as ECT's portrayal in the popular press and movies, it was seen as a barbaric and dangerous procedure. Discomfort, broken bones, and severe memory loss were not uncommon side effects. Today, an individual receiving ECT is given anesthesia as well as muscle-relaxing drugs to prevent discomfort and the possibility of broken bones during the seizure itself. Further, the electrical current is often introduced on only one side of the brain, which is thought to reduce memory loss. The current typical treatment procedure is to give ECT 2 or 3 times a week for a total of 6 to 12 treatments. One advantage of ECT is that symptoms can be reduced more rapidly than with medications. This is beneficial in cases of severe *suicidal ideation*, which will be described later in the chapter.

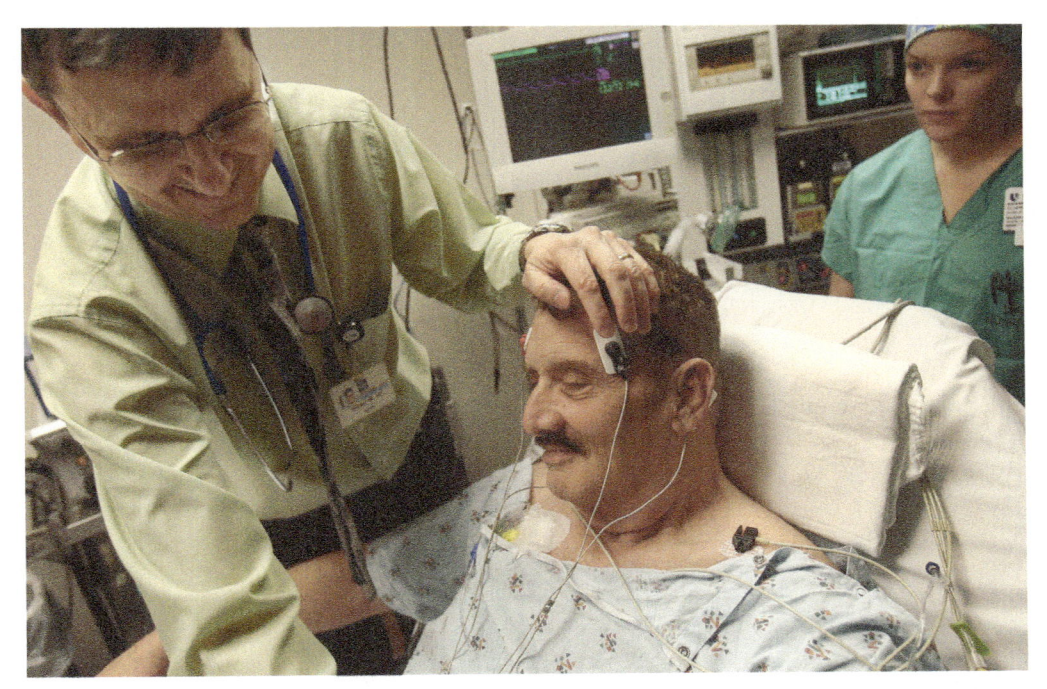

Electroconvulsive therapy is much safer today than in the previous century and can quickly reverse symptoms of some illnesses.

Ethan Hyman/Raleigh News & Observer/Tribune News Service/via Getty Images

With the advent of brain imaging techniques, it is possible to better describe the effects of ECT on the brain (Petrican et al., 2019). As noted previously, different types of connections are seen in the brain between the frontal and the limbic areas—especially the ACC—in individuals with depression as compared with healthy controls. Likewise, those taking antidepressant medication have reduced connectivity between the frontal areas and the amygdala compared with those on a placebo. This has led to a hypothesis that suggests those with depression show more connectivity between the frontal and limbic areas of the brain. Jennifer Perrin and her colleagues (2012) examined the effects of ECT on these frontal limbic connections. What they found was that connections were reduced after ECT. This decrease in functional connectivity was also associated with a decrease in depressive symptoms.

Vagal Nerve Stimulation The vagus nerve is a major cranial nerve that conveys information concerning the organs of the body to the brain. It is also involved in parasympathetic regulation of the heart and the intestines. With **vagal nerve stimulation (VNS)** treatments, an electrical stimulator is surgically implanted next to the vagus. This stimulator is connected to a pulse generator in the person's chest. Like a pacemaker in the heart, the pulse generator can be programmed to deliver electrical pulses at desirable frequencies and currents. In 1997, VNS was approved by the Food and Drug Administration (FDA) to treat epilepsy. VNS was also found to improve moods in treated individuals. This led to the treatment of depression in individuals without epilepsy, which was approved in 2005. A variety of studies have suggested that for individuals whose depression does not respond to antidepressant medication, VNS is a relatively safe alternative (Holtzheimer et al., 2012). However, the effectiveness of the treatment has ranged from 31% to no effect in treating depression. One suggestion is that VNS has its effect by reducing inflammation (Alen, 2022).

Transcranial Magnetic Stimulation It has been known for a long time that electromagnetic activity can induce electrical changes in various materials. In **transcranial magnetic stimulation (TMS)**, an electromagnetic coil is placed on the scalp (Holtzheimer et al., 2012). From the coil, a magnetic field induces a small electrical current in the first few centimeters of the brain, which depolarizes the neurons. One advantage is that TMS is a noninvasive method for stimulating cortical cells in fully awake and responsive individuals.

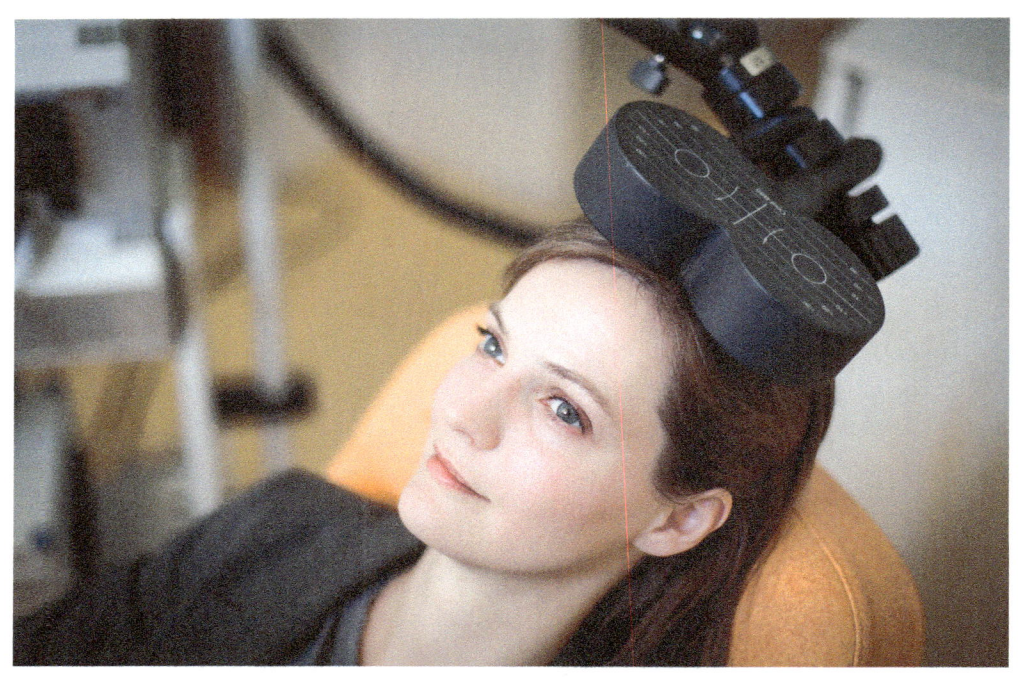

Transcranial Magnetic Stimulation (TMS)
Phanie/Alamy Stock Photo

Initial research used single-pulse TMS to study underlying motor processes by placing the TMS coil above the motor cortex. One of these studies showed a relationship between motor responses and a measure of depression (Oathes & Ray, 2006). More recently, it was found that repetitive TMS (rTMS), where multiple pulses are generated in rapid succession, is effective in the treatment of depression (Loo & Mitchell, 2005). A study from 42 different locations in the United States with 307 outpatients showed significant changes in depression scores following rTMS treatment (Carpenter et al., 2012). Treatment for depression generally places the coil above the DLPFC, an area of the brain shown to be involved in depression. Animal studies have shown rTMS to have similar effects to ECT. In humans who do not respond to antidepressant medication, rTMS has also shown similar results to ECT. The advantage of rTMS in comparison with ECT is that no anesthetic is required and no side effects such as memory loss have been reported. Like ECT, rTMS is recommended for those who do not show changes in depression from medication.

Deep Brain Stimulation Deep brain stimulation (DBS) involves placing electrodes in the brain (Blumberger et al., 2013). A pulse generator and battery are implanted in the person's chest and connected through wires to the brain electrodes. DBS was initially used as a treatment for disorders of movement. More recently, it has been used with those who do not respond to any other treatment for depression. Brain imaging studies have shown that one area of the brain, Brodmann area 25, which is located below the corpus callosum, shows differences in activity between those who respond to treatment for depression and those who do not. In DBS for depression, the electrode is placed in this area. Current research suggests that 18% to 60% of individuals with treatment-resistant depression show improvement with DBS (Blumberger et al., 2013). One of the first double-blind studies found that 10 of 25 individuals with depression displayed a significant decrease of depressive symptoms (Bergfeld et al., 2016). At this point, research in the use of DBS for depression is just beginning in terms of empirical validation.

Psychological Treatments for Depression

All of the three major psychological therapy approaches described in Chapter 1—dynamic, cognitive behavioral, and existential-humanistic—have empirically supported therapies for the treatment of depression (see For Further Reading). Emotion-focused therapy for depression, which is

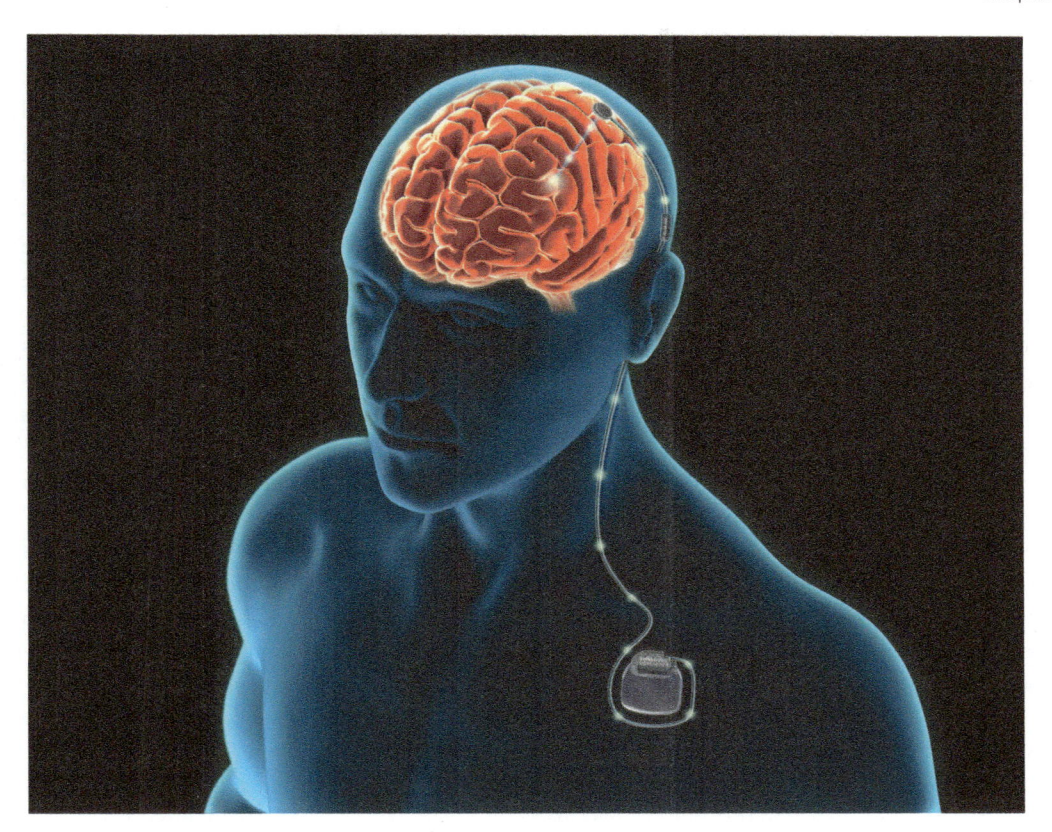

Deep Brain Stimulation (DBS)
Science History Images/Alamy Stock Photo

based on existential-humanistic techniques, has been shown to be useful for individuals with mild to moderate depression (Greenberg & Watson, 2006). As noted previously, whereas the dynamic approach focuses on insight, the cognitive behavioral approach emphasizes the importance of action. That is to say, in dynamic approaches, interpersonal difficulties are examined, with some focus on the origins of thoughts and behaviors that did not work in the past. This often leads to discussion of early and significant relationships. Cognitive behavioral approaches, on the other hand, spend less time on past relationships and more on how to deal effectively with events in the future. The session itself is more of an educational process in which the client is helped to consider alternative explanations and learn how to cope. In cognitive behavioral therapy (CBT), there is little discussion of the relationship between the therapist and the client, as there would be in dynamic approaches. Both approaches examine the manner in which individuals with depression distort and misperceive events in their lives. A number of studies have shown similar changes in depressive symptoms with either a dynamic or CBT approach (Goldfried et al., 1997; Shapiro et al., 1994).

Cognitive Therapy Aaron Beck created a cognitive therapy for depression in the early 1960s (Beck, 1967, 2019; Beck & Alford, 2009; Hollon & Beck, 2013; see also J. Beck, 2011, for an overview and update). The cognitive therapy model suggests that dysfunctional thinking and negative information processing maintain depression. Cognitive therapy for depression is structured and problem focused. By learning in therapy how to understand one's thinking, it is possible to change the way one thinks as well as one's emotional state and behaviors. Thus, the therapy process helps the individual with depression evaluate the validity and utility of their thoughts. For example, if a person says, "It is all my fault" or "No one will ever hire me," the therapist would help the client consider ways to test these ideas empirically. Having a person fill out a log of their activities would help someone who says "I never do anything" determine the validity of that statement. The client might also be assigned homework to move beyond inertia and create potentially positive experiences.

As discussed earlier in the chapter, Beck's cognitive model is described in terms of a cognitive triad related to depression. The first component of the triad is the individual's negative view of self. This is when the individual attributes unpleasant experiences to their own mental, physical, and moral defects. When something negative happens, the person says, "This is my fault." In therapy, clients can become aware of the content of their thinking. The second component is the individual's tendency to interpret experiences in a negative manner. That is, the person tailors the facts to fit negative conclusions. The basic idea is that thinking influences emotion and behavior. The third component is that the person regards the future in a negative way. They envision a life of only hardships and anticipate failure in all tasks. The therapeutic approach to this cognitive triad encourages individuals to modify their cognitive and behavioral responses. Overall, the therapy is directed at the automatic thoughts in relation to catastrophizing—believing that nothing will work out; personalization—believing that everything relates to you; overgeneralization—believing that one event is how it always is; and dichotomous thinking—believing that things are either good or bad.

A number of researchers and clinicians have further developed the classic approaches of Aaron Beck and others. These cognitive behavioral treatments are referred to as "new wave" or "third wave" approaches (Cristea et al., 2013; Hayes, 2004). These approaches focus less on changing the contents of a person's thoughts and more on the person's relationship to their thoughts and how they influence the person's functioning. The goals of these therapies include creating flexibility and a willingness to experience one's thoughts and emotions rather than avoiding them. It is assumed that this experiential avoidance lies at the heart of psychological difficulties. Some examples of these new wave treatment approaches are *acceptance and commitment therapy (ACT)* and *mindfulness-based cognitive therapy (MBCT)*, which have been shown to be effective for the treatment of depression (Kuyken et al., 2016). Several procedures have also been developed to help maintain treatment gains (Table 6.4). In other studies, it has been suggested that mindfulness meditation works through the default mode network to help regulate emotional reactions (Barnhofer et al., 2016).

Another consideration for treating depression using CBT is a cultural one (E. Chang et al., 2018). For example, Asian and Asian American individuals tend to express somatic symptoms in relation to depression, such as headaches, stomach aches, shortness of breath, muscle weakness, and bodily pains, more than white Americans do (Hwang et al., 2018). Likewise, those within Latino cultures may see psychological distress as a problem of their "nerves" (*ataque de nervios*). Although CBT appears to work well with Latino populations, special adaptations are being considered (Ngo & Miranda, 2018). CBT

TABLE 6.4 ■ Empirically Supported Resources Designed to Maintain Treatment Gains

The Society of Clinical Psychology describes a number of empirically supported resources that apply a cognitive approach to depression. Maintenance of treatment gains is enhanced by booster sessions during the first year after termination. Several variants of cognitive therapy have been developed as more structured relapse prevention programs.

- *Cognitive therapy–continuation* (Jarrett & Kraft, 1997) provides 8 to 10 monthly sessions. Patients learn to use emotional distress and depressive symptoms to practice the coping and other skills learned in the acute phase of therapy and to enhance generalization of these skills.

- *Well-being therapy* (Fava & Riuni, 2003) provides 8 to 12 sessions designed to facilitate well-being after recovery from depression and reduce the risk of relapse. This therapy is not symptom-focused but rather focuses on building the components of mental health in Ryff's (1989) model: autonomy, personal growth, environmental mastery, purpose, positive relations, and self-acceptance. Cognitive restructuring, activity scheduling, assertiveness training, and problem-solving skills are used.

- *Mindfulness-based cognitive therapy* (MBCT; Segal, Williams, & Teasdale, 2001) is an 8-session relapse prevention program that combines mindfulness meditation with cognitive therapy techniques. Patients learn to recognize the negative thought processes associated with depression and to change their relationship with these thoughts. By unhooking from these thoughts and recognizing their transient nature, patients can learn to prevent the downward spiral from negative mood to rumination to depression. MBCT is especially helpful to reduce the risk of relapse in those with chronic depression.

Credit: From the Society of Clinical Psychology. (n.d.). *TREATMENT TARGET: Depression.* https://www.div12.0rg/diagnosis/depression/

has been modified for Black populations, especially lower-income individuals. One such modification that includes relationship, spiritual, and family issues has been shown to be more effective than traditional CBT (see Neblett et al., 2018, for an overview). Likewise, traditional and spiritual adaptations have been included in Native American versions of CBT (McDonald et al., 2018).

Emotion-Focused Therapy Emotion-focused therapy (EFT) for depression is an empirically supported therapy developed by Leslie Greenberg and his colleagues (see, e.g., Greenberg & Watson, 2006). As described in Chapter 1, EFT promotes the individual experiencing and processing emotional aspects of their experience. This may involve bringing past emotional experiences and memories into the present. As part of therapy, the client is able to identify their maladaptive emotions and understand their emotional needs in the present. This, in turn, allows the person to discover new ways of satisfying their current needs.

In terms of depression, the treatment begins with the person experiencing the weak or bad sense of self, which lies at the core of depression. Often a sense of shame and fear is associated with this maladaptive sense of self. In EFT, the client must do more than just name the maladaptive sense of self. They must fully experience it so change can take place. The role of the therapist is to empathetically be with the person and help the person regulate these negative emotional states without the fear of being overwhelmed. Thus, EFT works on the level of emotionality rather than the cognitive level as seen in CBT, although both emphasize the meaning a client gives to their experiences. Like dynamic therapy, EFT would also consider the relationship between the therapist and the client on an emotional level. Further, where CBT may be seen as helping the person develop a logic and intelligence for dealing with their thoughts, EFT seeks to develop *emotional intelligence.*

In their empirical research to study the efficacy of EFT, Greenberg and Watson (2006) found that this therapy worked best in individuals with depression who were not completely immobile—those who were able to parent, work, or go to school, although all of these individuals reported difficulty and found little satisfaction in their activities. EFT emphasizes tailoring the therapy to the client, since depression can manifest on a number of levels. Although all of the clients in the study were diagnosed with depression according to the *DSM*, their depression symptoms differed. Some were highly critical and felt like failures, while others had lost relationships and felt abandoned and sad. Still others felt

The therapeutic relationship between the client and the therapist offers an opportunity for the client to see previously disturbed relationships in their life in a safe environment.

iStock.com/ljubaphoto. Stock photo. Posed by model.

empty, confused, and aimless. Their interpersonal relationships with the therapist also differed greatly. In testing the effects of EFT against itself and other therapies, EFT was shown to be effective in reducing the symptoms of depression.

Psychodynamic Therapy One important aspect of dynamic therapy is the search for insight. One focus would be an understanding of how one's depressive symptoms developed. Do they relate to the experience of losses in one's life? Do they relate to previous negative relationships, including critical parents who leave the child with little ability to accomplish life's goals? Do they relate to confusion concerning one's role in a job or relationship? Most short-term psychodynamic therapy would then focus on the theme that's uncovered.

In addition to past experiences, another focus would be on current relationships, including the relationship with the therapist. Like the Strupp and Binder (1984) approach described in Chapter 1, most psychodynamic approaches to depression would begin with an understanding of the client's behavior and relationships and how these contribute to the continuation of the depressive symptoms. Some common themes with depression include feelings of helplessness and dependence, an overdeveloped sense of responsibility, and a feeling of anger for one's situation that becomes internalized.

The therapeutic relationship between the client and the therapist offers an opportunity for the client to see previous disturbed relationships in a safe environment. *Transference* is an important mechanism in which the client tends to see the therapist in terms of significant others in the client's life. As the client talks with the therapist, the client will replay prior conflicts and enact maladaptive patterns. For example, if a parent was very critical of the client's ideas as a child, then the client may initially find it difficult to tell the therapist feelings or thoughts that are very personally important or related to the client's self-image. Another situation would be one in which a parent never allowed the client to engage in tasks they could fail at or the parent would save the client whenever they encountered problems. These past situations would leave the client with unrealistic expectations as to what to expect from the world and from others. In these situations, the person has never really learned what the world is like. They may act like a child, expecting protection from others, and thus miss out on new experiences and learning. By understanding one's life, it is possible to gain insight into avoiding old, unhealthy patterns in new situations, which would maintain depressive symptoms.

Combination Therapies

One problem in the treatment of depression is that even in situations in which symptoms are reduced, individuals are at risk for relapse. For this reason, professionals have searched for a combination of treatments that might help to prevent relapse by involving more than one underlying depressive mechanism. For example, antidepressant medication and a form of psychotherapy such as CBT have been shown to each be effective separately in comparison to a placebo treatment, as well as in combination (DeRubeis et al., 2008). In Figure 6.5, you can see that both CBT and an antidepressant medication show greater progress in reducing symptoms of depression at 8 weeks of therapy as compared with a placebo pill. After 16 weeks of treatment, CBT and medication show equal effectiveness. Other studies have shown the value of combining psychosocial treatment with medication (e.g., Hollon et al., 2005). It should also be noted that giving individuals with depression a placebo that is described as fast acting will itself cause brain changes associated with a reduction in depression (Peciña et al., 2015).

With CBT and an antidepressant medication being equally effective, what do you think would happen if both were discontinued in individuals receiving the treatments? What happened was that in both groups, symptoms of depression began to reappear. However, individuals showed fewer symptoms of depression in the CBT condition than in the drug condition. Thus, what the individuals learned in CBT could continue to be effective although the therapy itself had been stopped. The medication, on the other hand, showed no lingering positive effects once it was no longer given. Other studies have shown that the combination of CBT with an antidepressant medication is more effective than either treatment is alone (Hollon et al., 2005).

FIGURE 6.5 Do Medication and CBT Show Similar Treatment Results With Depression?

Cognitive behavioral therapy (CBT) and antidepressant medication (ADM) have comparable short-term effects.

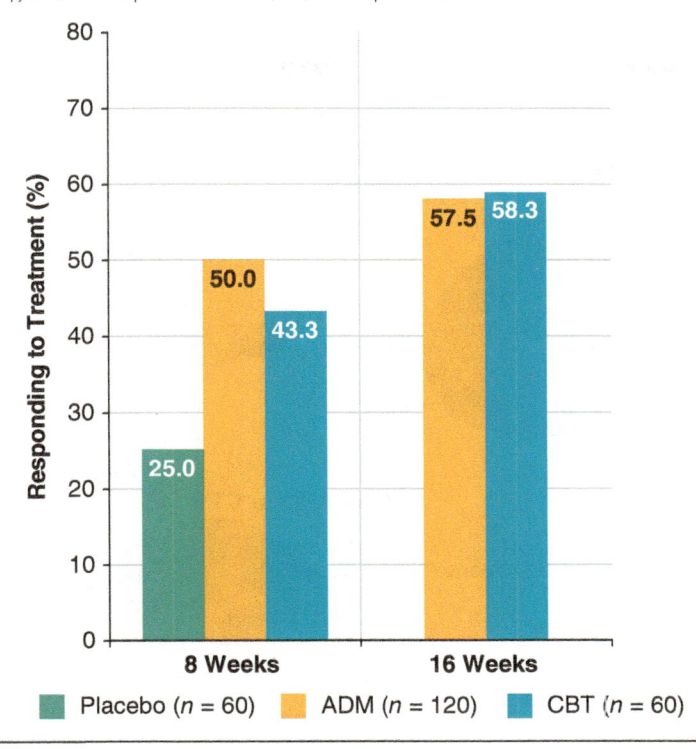

	8 Weeks	16 Weeks
Placebo (n = 60)	25.0	—
ADM (n = 120)	50.0	57.5
CBT (n = 60)	43.3	58.3

Responding to Treatment (%)

Credit: DeRubeis, R. J., Siegle, G. J., & Hollon, S. D. (2008). Cognitive therapy versus medication for depression: Treatment outcomes and neural mechanisms. *Nature Reviews Neuroscience, 9,* 788–796. https://doi.org/10.1038/nrn2345

One explanation for these results is that cognitive therapy and medication work through different pathways in the brain (DeRubeis et al., 2008). As noted previously, brain imaging studies show greater amygdala activity and less PFC activity in those with depression compared with healthy controls. After treatment, amygdala activity is decreased and prefrontal activity increases. DeRubeis and his colleagues suggested that cognitive therapy, with its focus on cognitive processing, may increase prefrontal activity, which in turn is able to inhibit amygdala activity. Antidepressant medication, on the other hand, decreases amygdala activation directly. Thus, neuroscience techniques and findings may help to explain the mechanisms of action as well as the value of utilizing more than one treatment approach (Figure 6.6). Further, additional meta-analyses have shown that SSRI medications and electroconvulsive therapy (ECT) influence different brain areas (Chau et al., 2018).

Efforts to Prevent Depression

Given that the WHO identifies depression as the leading cause of disability in the world, movements worldwide have attempted to develop depression prevention programs (Muñoz et al., 2008). Another aspect of focusing on prevention is that members of certain groups often do not seek treatment for depression and thus could be targeted for prevention programs. For example, Black and Latino adults are less likely than white adults in the United States to use mental health outpatient services. At this point, prevention programs have been directed at adults, at children during their school years, and at mothers during the period following childbirth. These programs typically follow a cognitive behavioral approach emphasizing skills training in mood regulation and interpersonal relationships. Although not every study showed a reduction in MDDs, taken together, the results appear promising.

FIGURE 6.6 ■ How Might Cognitive Therapy and Medication Influence the Brain During Successful Treatment?

Hypothetical time course of the changes to the amygdala and prefrontal function that are associated with antidepressant medication and cognitive therapy. Cognitive therapy (CT), with its focus on cognitive processing, may increase prefrontal activity, which in turn would inhibit amygdala activity. Antidepressant medication (ADM), on the other hand, decreases amygdala activation directly.

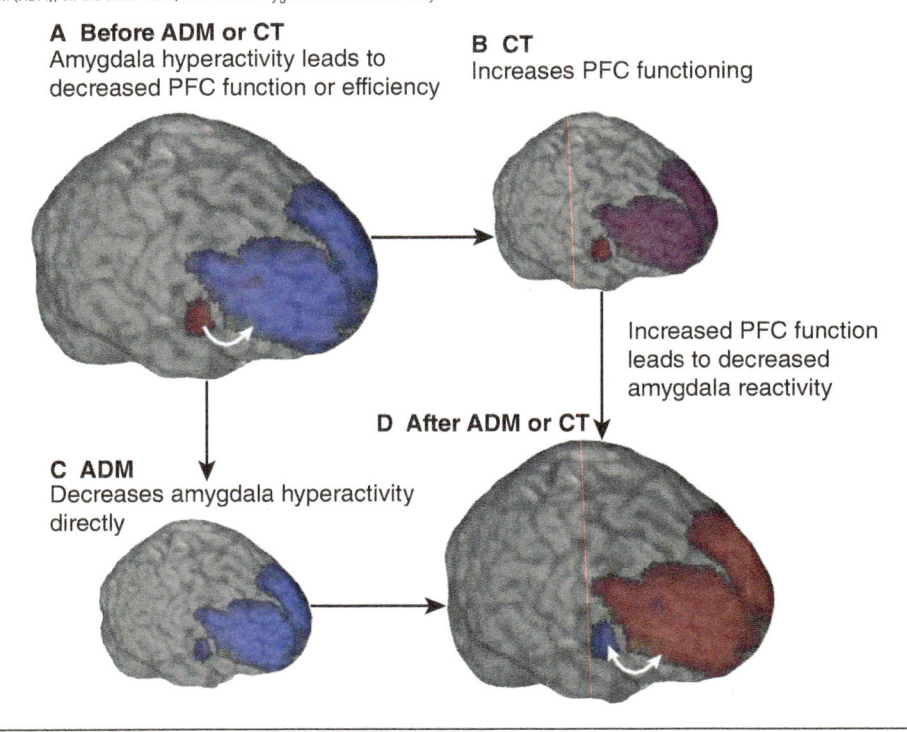

A Before ADM or CT
Amygdala hyperactivity leads to decreased PFC function or efficiency

B CT
Increases PFC functioning

Increased PFC function leads to decreased amygdala reactivity

C ADM
Decreases amygdala hyperactivity directly

D After ADM or CT

Credit: DeRubeis, R. J., Siegle, G. J., & Hollon, S. D. (2008). Cognitive therapy versus medication for depression: Treatment outcomes and neural mechanisms. *Nature Reviews Neuroscience, 9*, 788–796. https://doi.org/10.1038/nrn2345

CONCEPT CHECK

- Currently, what are the primary classes of antidepressant medications? How does each work? What are the advantages and disadvantages of each?
- In what situations is each of the following techniques most effective in treating depression? What are the advantages and disadvantages of each?
  - ECT
  - VNS
  - TMS
- All of the three psychological therapy approaches—dynamic, cognitive behavioral, and existential-humanistic—described previously have empirically supported therapies for the treatment of depression. Considering each of these approaches, what is the primary focus of the therapy in regard to depression, and what course does the therapy typically follow in providing an effective treatment?
- Relapse of symptoms is a serious problem in the treatment of individuals with depression. What are three specific approaches that have been taken to try to reduce the risk of relapse?

BIPOLAR DISORDER

The mania came in four-day spurts. Four days of not eating, not sleeping, barely sitting in one place for more than a few minutes at a time. Four days of constant shopping. . . . And four days of indiscriminate, nonstop talking: first to everyone I knew on the West Coast, then to anyone

Terri Cheney was once a successful entertainment attorney representing the likes of Michael Jackson and Quincy Jones. She now focuses on the cause of mental illness. She is on the boards of directors of several mental health organizations. She also facilitates a weekly community support group at UCLA's Neuropsychiatric Institute. She has chronicled her lifelong battle with bipolar disorder in the *New York Times* bestseller *Manic: A Memoir*, *The Dark Side of Innocence: Growing Up Bipolar*, and *Modern Madness: An Owner's Manual*. Her story has been adapted in the new *Modern Love* television series on Amazon Prime Video.

Suzanne Allison

still awake on the East Coast, then to Santa Fe itself, whoever would listen. The truth was, I didn't just need to talk. I was afraid to be alone. There were things hovering in the air around me that didn't want to be remembered: the expression on my father's face when I told him it was stage IV cancer, already metastasized; the bewildered look in his eyes when I couldn't take away the pain; and the way those eyes kept watching me at the end, trailing my every move, fixed on me, begging for the comfort I wasn't able to give. I never thought I could be haunted by anything so familiar, so beloved, as my father's eyes.

Mostly, however, I talked to men. Canyon Road [in Santa Fe] has a number of extremely lively, extremely friendly bars and clubs, all of which were in walking distance of my hacienda. It wasn't hard for a redhead with a ready smile and a feverish glow in her eyes to strike up a conversation and then continue that conversation well into the early-morning hours, his place or mine. The only word I couldn't seem to say was "no." I eased my conscience by reminding myself that manic sex isn't really intercourse. It's discourse, just another way to ease the insatiable need for contact and communication. In place of words, I simply spoke with my skin.

Excerpt from Manic, *by Terri Cheney (2009).*

I was a senior in high school when I had my first attack of manic-depressive illness; once the siege began, I lost my mind rather rapidly. At first, everything seemed so easy. I raced about like a crazed weasel, bubbling with plans and enthusiasms, immersed in sports, and staying up all night, night after night, out with friends, reading everything that wasn't nailed down, filling manuscript books with poems and fragments of plays, and making expansive, completely unrealistic, plans for my future. The world was filled with pleasure and promise; I felt great. Not just great, I felt really great. I felt I could do anything, that no task was too difficult.

Kay Jamison received her PhD in clinical psychology from UCLA and is a professor of psychiatry at Johns Hopkins University. She has written significant books describing the scientific and clinical aspects of bipolar disorders (e.g., Goodwin & Jamison, 2007) as well as her own experiences in *An Unquiet Mind* (Jamison, 1995). She has also written *Night Falls Fast: Understanding Suicide* (1999; translated into 25 languages), *Exuberance: The Passion for Life* (2004), *Nothing Was the Same: A Memoir* (2009), and *Setting the River on Fire: A Study of Genius, Mania, and Character* (2017).

Leonardo Cendamo/Hulton Archive/via Getty Images

Every day I awoke deeply tired, a feeling as foreign to my natural self as being bored or indifferent to life. Those were next. Then a gray, bleak preoccupation with death, dying, decaying, that everything was born but to die, best to die now and save the pain while waiting. I dragged exhausted mind and body around a local cemetery, ruminating about how long each of its inhabitants had lived before the final moment. I sat on the graves writing long dreary, morbid poems, convinced that my brain and body were rotting, that everyone knew and no one would say. Laced into the exhaustion were periods of frenetic and horrible restlessness; no amount of running brought relief. For several weeks, I drank vodka in my orange juice before setting off for school in the mornings, and I thought obsessively about killing myself.

Excerpt from An Unquiet Mind, *by Kay Redfield Jamison (1995).*

Characteristics of Bipolar Disorder

Bipolar disorder was previously called manic-depressive disorder. In reading the first-person accounts of Terri Cheney and Kay Jamison, we quickly see both the mania and the depression. Changes in mood are an important aspect of bipolar disorders. These include the intense sense of well-being and high energy seen in mania along with its opposite seen in depression. Changes in cognition and perception also accompany these states. In mania, thoughts seem to flow easily, and many individuals find themselves being very productive. Perceptions and sensations may also be heightened. However, mania can also increase a feeling of pressure with racing thoughts and ideas that do not make sense. Sometimes, this includes a feeling of "I can do anything" and the sense that everything will work out. Individuals in a manic state may buy expensive items they cannot afford, place large bets, and engage in all types of risky sexual behavior. It is as if there is nothing to worry about. Depressive episodes show the opposite, with the person experiencing a bleak outlook, low energy in a world of black and white, and a wish to do little. One characteristic experienced by many individuals in both mania and depression is a sense of irritability.

Descriptions of mania and depression have been with us for more than 2,000 years. Hippocrates (460–377 BCE) described both mania and melancholia. He saw these disorders as separate, produced by underlying conditions related to an imbalance in the four humors (blood, phlegm, yellow bile, and black bile). Today, we might refer to this as a hormonal imbalance. In 150 CE, Aretaeus of Cappadocia linked mania and melancholia as one disorder. He described individuals who, after displaying melancholia, show fits of mania and vice versa. From that time until the present, mania and depression were considered as different parts of one disorder. For example, in 1854, French psychiatrist Jean-Pierre Falret described a circular disorder (*la folie circulaire*) and psychiatrist Jules Baillarger described "double insanity" (*la folie à double forme*) to denote the manner in which depressive and mania episodes are part of one disorder. German psychiatrist Emil Kraepelin, in the late 1800s and early 1900s, established in his textbooks the idea that manic depression and schizophrenia are two separate disorders, a perspective that has continued to this day. Further, in 1957, German psychiatrist Karl Leonhard made a distinction between unipolar and bipolar disorders, and this was adopted in the *DSM* in 1980. As noted earlier in this chapter, *unipolar* indicates depression without mania, whereas *bipolar* encompasses both (see Goodwin & Jamison, 2007, for both historical and current perspectives).

The Scream by Edvard Munch (1893). Munch suffered from bipolar disorder.

Nasjonalmuseet/Høstland, Børre. https://www.nasjonalmuseet.no/en/collection/object/NG.M.00939; licensed under CC BY-SA 4.0 https://creativecommons.org/licenses/by/4.0/.

Diagnosis of Bipolar Disorder

DSM-5 classifies bipolar disorder in terms of the manic and the depressive symptoms (see Table 6.5). In moving away from the term *manic depression*, specifying two types of bipolar disorder allows for better description of the condition.

Bipolar I Disorder

For a diagnosis of bipolar I, an individual needs to display three of the following seven characteristics:

1. Inflated self-esteem or grandiosity
2. Decreased need for sleep (e.g., feels rested after only 3 hours of sleep)
3. More talkative than usual or pressure to keep talking
4. Flight of ideas or subjective experience that thoughts are racing
5. Distractibility (i.e., attention too easily drawn to unimportant or irrelevant external stimuli), as reported or observed
6. Increase in goal-directed activity (either socially, at work or school, or sexually) or psychomotor agitation (i.e., purposeless non–goal-directed activity)
7. Excessive involvement in activities that have a high potential for painful consequences (e.g., engaging in unrestrained buying sprees, sexual indiscretions, or foolish business investments)

In Bipolar I, these characteristics manifest in one or more manic episodes. In this classification, the mania needs to last a week unless medication was given.

TABLE 6.5 ■ *DSM-5-TR* Diagnostic Criteria for Bipolar I Disorder

For a diagnosis of bipolar I disorder, it is necessary to meet the following criteria for a manic episode. The manic episode may have been preceded by and may be followed by hypomanic or major depressive episodes.

Manic Episode

A. A distinct period of abnormally and persistently elevated, expansive, or irritable mood and abnormally and persistently increased activity or energy, lasting at least 1 week and present most of the day, nearly every day (or any duration if hospitalization is necessary).

B. During the period of mood disturbance and increased energy or activity, three (or more) of the following symptoms (four if the mood is only irritable) are present to a significant degree, and represent a noticeable change from usual behavior:
   1. Inflated self-esteem or grandiosity.
   2. Decreased need for sleep (e.g., feels rested after only 3 hours of sleep).
   3. More talkative than usual or pressure to keep talking.
   4. Flight of ideas or subjective experience that thoughts are racing.
   5. Distractibility (i.e., attention too easily drawn to unimportant or irrelevant external stimuli), as reported or observed.
   6. Increase in goal-directed activity (either socially, at work or school, or sexually) or psychomotor agitation (i.e., purposeless non–goal-directed activity).
   7. Excessive involvement in activities that have a high potential for painful consequences (e.g., engaging in unrestrained buying sprees, sexual indiscretions, or foolish business investments).

C. The mood disturbance is sufficiently severe to cause marked impairment in social or occupational functioning or to necessitate hospitalization to prevent harm to self or others, or there are psychotic features.

D. The episode is not attributable to the physiological effects of a substance (e.g., a drug of abuse, a medication, other treatment) or another medical condition.
   Note: A full manic episode that emerges during antidepressant treatment (e.g., medication, electroconvulsive therapy) but persists at a fully syndromal level beyond the physiological effect of that treatment is sufficient evidence for a manic episode and, therefore, a bipolar I diagnosis.

Note: Criteria A–D constitute a manic episode. At least one lifetime manic episode is required for the diagnosis of bipolar I disorder.

Hypomanic Episode

A. A distinct period of abnormally and persistently elevated, expansive, or irritable mood and abnormally and persistently increased activity or energy, lasting at least 4 consecutive days and present most of the day, nearly every day.

B. During the period of mood disturbance and increased energy and activity, three (or more) of the following symptoms (four if the mood is only irritable) have persisted, represent a noticeable change from usual behavior, and have been present to a significant degree:
   1. Inflated self-esteem or grandiosity.
   2. Decreased need for sleep (e.g., feels rested after only 3 hours of sleep).
   3. More talkative than usual or pressure to keep talking.
   4. Flight of ideas or subjective experience that thoughts are racing.
   5. Distractibility (i.e., attention too easily drawn to unimportant or irrelevant external stimuli), as reported or observed.
   6. Increase in goal-directed activity (either socially, at work or school, or sexually) or psychomotor agitation.
   7. Excessive involvement in pleasurable activities that have a high potential for painful consequences (e.g., engaging in unrestrained buying sprees, sexual indiscretions, or foolish business investments).

C. The episode is associated with an unequivocal change in functioning that is uncharacteristic of the individual when not symptomatic.

D. The disturbance in mood and the change in functioning are observable by others.

E. The episode is not severe enough to cause marked impairment in social or occupational functioning, or to necessitate hospitalization. If there are psychotic features, the episode is, by definition, manic.

F. The episode is not attributable to the physiological effects of a substance (e.g., a drug of abuse, a medication, other treatment) or another medical condition.
Note: A full hypomanic episode that emerges during antidepressant treatment (e.g., medication, electroconvulsive therapy, etc.) but persists at a fully syndromal level beyond the physiological effect of that treatment is sufficient evidence for a hypomanic episode diagnosis. However, caution is indicated so that one or two symptoms (particularly increased irritability, edginess or agitation following antidepressant use) are not taken as sufficient for diagnosis of a hypomanic episode, nor necessarily indicative of a bipolar diathesis.

Note: Criteria A–F constitute a hypomanic episode. Hypomanic episodes are common in bipolar I disorder but are not required for the diagnosis of bipolar I disorder.

Major Depressive Episode

A. Five (or more) of the following symptoms have been present during the same 2-week period and represent a change from previous functioning, at least one of the symptoms is either (1) depressed mood or (2) loss of interest or pleasure.
Note: Do not include symptoms that are clearly attributable to another medical condition.
  1. Depressed mood most of the day, nearly every day, as indicated by either subjective report (e.g., feels sad, empty, or hopeless) or observation made by others (e.g., appears tearful). (**Note:** In children and adolescents, can be irritable mood.)
  2. Markedly diminished interest or pleasure in all, or almost all, activities most of the day, nearly every day (as indicated by either subjective account or observation).
  3. Significant weight loss when not dieting or weight gain (e.g., a change of more than 5% of body weight in a month), or decrease or increase in appetite nearly every day. (**Note:** In children, consider failure to make expected weight gain.)
  4. Insomnia or hypersomnia nearly every day.
  5. Psychomotor agitation or retardation nearly every day (observable by others; not merely subjective feelings of restlessness or being slowed down).
  6. Fatigue or loss of energy nearly every day.
  7. Feelings of worthlessness or excessive or inappropriate guilt (which may be delusional) nearly every day (not merely self-reproach or guilt about being sick).
  8. Diminished ability to think or concentrate, or indecisiveness, nearly every day (either by subjective account or as observed by others).
  9. Recurrent thoughts of death (not just fear of dying); recurrent suicidal ideation without a specific plan; a specific suicide plan; or a suicide attempt.

B. The symptoms cause clinically significant distress or impairment in social, occupational, or other important areas of functioning.

C. The episode is not attributable to the physiological effects of a substance or another medical condition.

Note: Criteria A–C constitute a major depressive episode. Major depressive episodes are common in bipolar I disorder but are not required for the diagnosis of bipolar I disorder.
Note: Responses to a significant loss (e.g., bereavement, financial ruin, losses from a natural disaster, a serious medical illness or disability) may include the feelings of intense sadness, rumination about the loss, insomnia, poor appetite, and weight loss noted in Criterion A, which may resemble a depressive episode. Although such symptoms may be understandable or considered appropriate to the loss, the presence of a major depressive episode in addition to the normal response to a significant loss should also be carefully considered. This decision inevitably requires the exercise of clinical judgment based on the individual's history and the cultural norms for the expression of distress in the context of loss.

Bipolar I Disorder

A. Criteria have been met for at least one manic episode (Criteria A–D under "manic episode" above).

B. At least one manic episode is not better explained by schizoaffective disorder and is not superimposed on schizophrenia, schizophreniform disorder, delusional disorder, or other specified or unspecified schizophrenia spectrum and other psychotic disorder.

(Continued)

TABLE 6.5 ■ DSM-5-TR Diagnostic Criteria for Bipolar I Disorder *(Continued)*

Coding and Recording Procedures

The diagnostic code for bipolar I disorder is based on type of current or most recent episode and its status with respect to current severity, presence of psychotic features, and remission status. Current severity and psychotic features are only indicated if full criteria are currently met for a manic or major depressive episode. Remission specifiers are only indicated if the full criteria are not currently met for a manic, hypomanic, or major depressive episode. Codes are as follows:

Bipolar I disorder	Current or most recent episode manic	Current or most recent episode hypomanic*	Current or most recent episode depressed	Current or most recent episode unspecified**
Mild (p. 175)	F31.11	NA	F31.31	NA
Moderate (p. 175)	F31.12	NA	F31.32	NA
Severe (p. 175)	F31.13	NA	F31.4	NA
With psychotic features*** (p. 173)	F31.2	NA	F31.5	NA
In partial remission (p. 175)	F31.73	F31.71	F31.75	NA
In full remission (p. 175)	F31.74	F31.72	F31.76	NA
Unspecified	F31.9	F31.9	F31.9	NA

*Severity and psychotic specifiers do not apply; code F31.0 for cases not in remission.

**Severity, psychotic, and remission specifiers do not apply. Code F31.9.

***If psychotic features are present, code the "with psychotic features" specifier irrespective of episode severity. In recording the name of a diagnosis, terms should be listed in the following order: bipolar I disorder, type of current episode (or most recent episode if bipolar I disorder is in partial or full remission), severity/psychotic/remission specifiers, followed by as many of the following specifiers without codes as apply to the current episode (or the most recent episode if bipolar I disorder is in partial or full remission). **Note:** The specifiers "with rapid cycling" and "with seasonal pattern" describe the pattern of mood episodes.
Specify if:

- **With anxious distress** (pp. 169–170)
- **With mixed features** (pp. 170–171)
- **With rapid cycling** (p. 171)
- **With melancholic features** (pp. 171–172)
- **With atypical features** (pp. 172–173)
- **With mood-congruent psychotic features** (p. 173; *applies to manic episode and/or major depressive episode*)
- **With mood-incongruent psychotic features** (p. 173; *applies to manic episode and/or major depressive episode*)
- **With catatonia** (p. 173). **Coding note:** Use additional code F06.1.
- **With peripartum onset** (pp. 173–174)
- **With seasonal pattern** (pp. 174–175)

Credit: Reprinted with permission from the *Diagnostic and Statistical Manual of Mental Disorders, fifth edition text revision,* DSM-V-TR, pp. 139–143 (Copyright © 2022). American Psychiatric Association. All Rights Reserved.

As you read the personal descriptions of Terri Cheney and Kay Jamison, you could see examples of some of these seven characteristics—especially the greatly increased energy and a reduced need for sleep. There were also examples of high-paced discussions and a willingness to enter into high-risk activities such as promiscuous sex. It is often the sense of "I can do anything" that leads individuals with mania to enter into all sorts of activities without thinking. Other reports describe situations in which people think they will never fail, so they place large bets or buy expensive products.

During a manic episode, individuals may gamble and think they will always win.
iStock.com/DavorLovincic

Bipolar I does not require any depressive symptoms for the diagnosis. In fact, some individuals with bipolar disorder never report depression (Johnson et al., 2009). However, the majority of individuals with bipolar disorder do experience depression during their lifetime.

Although only one manic episode is required for a diagnosis of bipolar disorder, almost all individuals with bipolar disorder show recurring experiences (Miklowitz & Johnson, 2006). For example, approximately 20% of individuals who enter outpatient treatment have had four or more mania and depression episodes the preceding year. Examining bipolar I individuals, 37% showed recurrences of mania or depression. This increased to 60% when examined for 2 years and 73% for 5 years. Overall, the depressive symptoms last longer than the ones involving mania.

Bipolar II Disorder

The major distinctions in *DSM-5-TR* between bipolar I and bipolar II are related to the severity and duration of the manic phase. A diagnosis of bipolar II requires at least one *hypomanic* episode. The observable symptoms of hypomania and mania are the same, though in hypomania, the elevated mood is more than that seen in normal mood swings but less than that of bipolar I. Hypomania does not cause as much impairment in social and occupational functioning as mania does, and hypomanic episodes last for 4 days rather than 1 week. Further, individuals with bipolar II disorder are less likely to be hospitalized for the disorder than those with bipolar I.

Bipolar II disorder also includes the presence of a major depressive episode as required for the diagnosis of depression. In fact, individuals with bipolar II, compared with bipolar I, show a greater propensity toward depressive episodes. Only 11% of those with bipolar II develop bipolar I over the following 10 years (Coryell et al., 1995). Empirical support has been found for seeing bipolar I and bipolar II as separate categories (Parker et al., 2021).

Cyclothymic Disorder

An additional diagnostic category is *cyclothymia*, which shows emotional shifts over time that are less severe than bipolar I or bipolar II. **Cyclothymic disorder** is characterized by mood changes that are not as severe as would be required in the criteria for manic or depressive episodes. That is, symptoms of mania are neither as severe nor of the same number or duration as would be required for a diagnosis of mania. Also, the depressive symptoms are neither as severe nor of the same number or duration for a diagnosis of major depressive disorder. Further, there must be no evidence of a major manic episode or major depressive episode during the first 2 years that the person shows the characteristics of cyclothymic disorder.

Prevalence of Bipolar Disorder

A number of epidemiological studies have examined the 1-year and lifetime prevalence of bipolar disorder (see Goodwin & Jamison, 2007, for an overview). Overall, the lifetime prevalence for bipolar I is about 1% and not that different from those with the disorder in the last year. Further, the gender differences are not large. Similar prevalence rates have been found around the world with no major differences in terms of race, ethnicity, or culture. Overall, lifetime prevalence estimates for bipolar I are 1%, bipolar II 1.1%, and cyclothymia 2.4% (Kessler et al., 2007). Using statistical models, it is suggested that the occurrence of bipolar I can be grouped as early, intermediate, or late onset (Bellivier et al., 2003). When the spectrum of bipolar disorders is included, the lifetime prevalence increases to between 3% and 8.3%.

Researchers have been interested in the factors associated with the number of mood episodes that an individual has in a year. Kupka and his colleagues (2005) followed more than 500 individuals with bipolar disorder for a year. The majority of individuals showed only a few episodes during the year, although a subgroup had 10 or more episodes. In the subgroup with four or more episodes a year, which they referred to as rapid cycling, there were more females (62.6%) than in the group with fewer episodes (52%). Further, 40% of the individuals with more episodes reported a history of physical or sexual abuse versus 24.1% in the fewer episodes group.

Causes of Bipolar Disorder

Bipolar disorder can be considered on a number of levels. In this section, initial factors that may be related to the development of bipolar disorder are discussed. These range from genetic factors to brain factors to environmental factors as well as the manner in which these factors interact with each other.

Genetics of Bipolar Disorder

Research over the past 40 years suggests a genetic predisposition for bipolar disorder (Craddock & Sklar, 2009; Goodwin & Jamison, 2007; Harrison et al., 2018; Stahl et al., 2019). Genome-wide association studies (GWAS; see Chapter 2) show a number of genes to be involved with bipolar disorder (Gordovez & McMahon, 2020; H.-J. Li et al., 2021; Stahl et al., 2019). Gordovez and McMahon (2020) suggest three overall findings from GWAS research. First, bipolar disorder is a heterogeneous set of illnesses united by the core clinical feature of cyclic elevation in mood and activity, with substantial individual variation in depressive and psychotic symptoms. Second, there is strong sharing of weak, common genetic risk factors with schizophrenia and major depression. And third, high-risk alleles also exist, but they are rare and nonspecific, and there is so far no evidence for monogenic forms of bipolar disorder.

One traditional test of a genetic predisposition is to see if the disorder runs in families. For bipolar disorders, heritability is about 5% to 10% for first-degree relatives and 40% to 70% for monozygotic (MZ) twins compared with only 14% for fraternal twins. That is to say, a first-degree relative of someone with bipolar disorder has approximately 10 times the risk of having the disorder compared with a random person. This is much higher than chance that a first-degree relative of a person with depression will also have depression, which is about 3 times the risk. Further, relatives of individuals with MDD do not appear to be at risk for mania, whereas relatives of those with bipolar disorder are at risk for depression.

Recent research has shown a partial overlap between the genes involved in bipolar disorder and schizophrenia (Palmer et al., 2022; Smeland et al., 2020). In an MZ twin with schizophrenia, there is an increased risk for both schizophrenia (40.8%) and mania (8.2%) in the other twin. In an MZ twin with mania, there is an increased risk for mania (36.4%) and schizophrenia (13.6%) in the other twin. (Craddock & Owens, 2010; Craddock & Sklar, 2013). Bipolar I disorder is strongly genetically correlated with schizophrenia, driven by psychosis, whereas bipolar II disorder is more strongly correlated with major depressive disorder (Stahl et al., 2019). Mitochondrial functioning has also been shown to be different in individuals with bipolar disorder (as noted in Chapter 2, mitochondria are structures within a cell that are involved in the production of energy; Regenold et al., 2009).

Bipolar Disorder and Creativity

Since at least the time of Plato and Aristotle, *divine madness*, as the ancient Greeks referred to it, has been associated with creativity. Aristotle asked why people who excel in philosophy, poetry, or the arts are melancholic. Numerous writers, poets, and artists, such as Ernest Hemingway, Virginia Woolf, Sergei Rachmaninoff, Peter Tchaikovsky, Sylvia Plath, Jackson Pollock, and Mark Rothko, are all known to have experienced bipolar disorder. This has resulted in speculation about a link between creativity and bipolar disorder, especially the mania aspect. However, most of this attempt to make such a link has been of an anecdotal nature.

Sheri Johnson and her colleagues (2012) sought to determine if there existed a scientific basis for the association between creativity and bipolar disorder. One line that supports this is that above-average accomplishments are seen among the family members of those with the disorder (Johnson, 2005). However, Johnson and her colleagues concluded that at this point, a direct relationship between creativity and bipolar disorder is difficult to make. Likewise, Frederick Goodwin and Kay Jamison (2007) reviewed a number of studies examining the relationship between bipolar disorders and creativity. They concluded that most individuals with bipolar disorders are not unusually creative. However, asking if creative individuals have a mood disorder may produce different results than asking if those with a mood disorder are creative (Taylor, 2017). Thus, there are examples of individuals in whom extremes of mood have contributed to their artistic insights and productivity. Thus, a variety of underlying personality and mood traits that would lead one into creative occupations may be similar to those found in bipolar disorders.

Jackson Pollock, a mid-20th-century American abstract expressionist painter, has been described as having had bipolar disorder.

Science History Images/Alamy Stock Photo

Brain Imaging and Bipolar Disorder

Differences in activation have been found in fMRI studies between the depression phase of bipolar disorder and the mania phase (Ballmaier et al., 2004). During the depression phase, there are decreases in prefrontal activation. During the mania phase, there are increases in activation in the ACC and the anterior limbic network, which includes the striatum, thalamus, and amygdala (see Figure 6.7).

Overall, a variety of studies have suggested that the brain processes underlying the symptoms seen in bipolar disorder involve the anterior limbic brain networks (Li et al., 2021; Marchand & Yurgelun-Todd, 2011; Savitz & Drevets, 2009; Strakowski, 2011). The first network includes the ventral prefrontal network and its connections to the thalamus, globus pallidus, striatum, and their modification by the amygdala and ACC. This system is seen to be responsible for three important aspects. These are (1) the perception of emotional stimuli, (2) the generation of an emotional state, and (3) the production of autonomic responses associated with the emotional state. A second network involving the DLPFC, medial PFC, dorsal ACC, and hippocampus is seen to regulate the affective state. It has been speculated that mood dysregulation in bipolar disorder may involve either or both of these systems.

FIGURE 6.7 ■ What Brain Areas Are Involved in Bipolar Disorder?

During the depression phase, there are decreases in prefrontal activation. During the mania phase, there are increases in activation in the ACC and the anterior limbic network, which includes the striatum, thalamus, and amygdala.

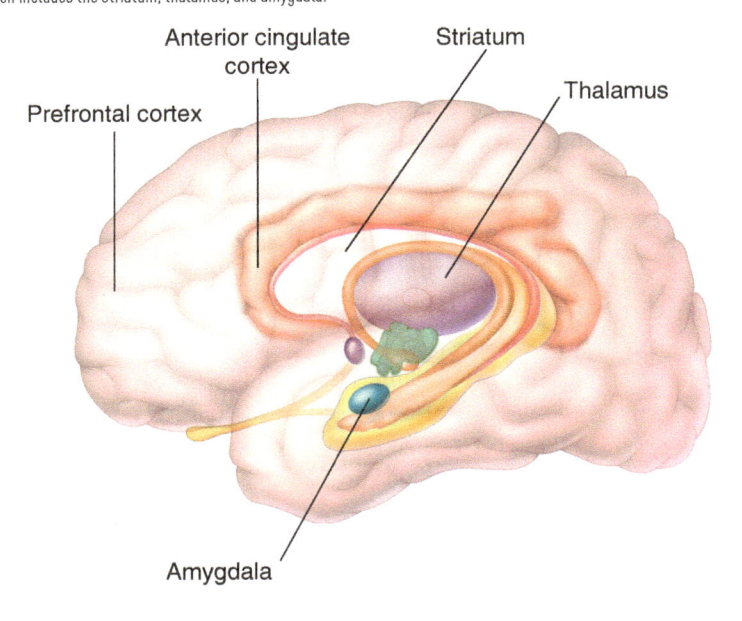

Researchers have also examined brain differences when bipolar episodes are not present. In one study, unmedicated individuals with bipolar disorder and matched controls performed a cognitive task while in the fMRI scanner (Strakowski et al., 2004). Although both groups performed the task equally well, they displayed different patterns of brain activation. The bipolar group showed more activation in the limbic, paralimbic, and ventrolateral prefrontal areas as well as visual association areas. The healthy control group showed greater activation in the fusiform gyrus and medial PFC. These researchers

Winston Churchill described his experience of bipolar-like symptoms as his "black dog."
Underwood & Underwood; archived in Library of Congress Web Archives at https://www.loc.gov/item/2002697673

suggested that individuals with bipolar disorder process cognitive tasks in a manner more consistent with processing emotional tasks, whereas healthy controls show inhibition of emotion networks in the brain while they perform cognitive tasks.

Neurotransmitter Dysregulation

The three neurotransmitters that have been studied in relation to bipolar disorder are norepinephrine, dopamine, and serotonin (Miklowitz & Johnson, 2006). Original perspectives have taken a simple formulation that mania was associated with high levels of norepinephrine and dopamine and depression with low levels. However, a variety of studies suggest that rather than the level of neurotransmitters, it is the sensitivity at the postsynaptic receptor site that plays the important role. In particular, it has been noted that organisms exposed to repeated doses of stimulants become more responsive to their effects (Sax & Strakowski, 2001).

Environmental Factors

The environment in which one lives plays an important role in the course of bipolar disorders. Ellicott and colleagues (1990) studied the stressful events in the lives of individuals with a bipolar disorder. Individuals who experienced more stressful events were at a 4.5 times greater risk for relapse within a 2-year period than those who did not. Miklowitz and his colleagues (1988) found that if an individual with a bipolar disorder returned from a hospitalization to a family situation in which criticism, hostility, or emotional overinvolvement were present, they were more likely to have a relapse. Specifically, 94% of those in a negative emotional environment showed relapse within 9 months compared with 17% of those without a negative emotional family situation.

Treatment for Bipolar Disorder

Until the mid-20th century, there was no effective treatment for bipolar disorder. Even today, it remains a complex disorder to treat. The main treatment goals are to optimize function, minimize symptoms, and establish mood stability. There is no accepted treatment for bipolar disorder that does not involve some form of medication. Because its symptoms may vary from depression to mania and this occurs in an irregular manner, there are fewer medications available for bipolar disorder. Further, a large number of individuals with bipolar disorder report a history of being misdiagnosed. This is partly because it is difficult to diagnose bipolar disorder without a clear picture of its course. Young adults who first show the symptoms in college, for example, may experience the symptoms as part of their lifestyle. It is often during a treatment for a depressive episode when mania appears, and it is realized that bipolar disorder is the correct diagnosis.

Even with treatment, as just noted, individuals with bipolar disorder who live in a negative emotional environment are more likely to relapse. Further, some people with bipolar disorder will discontinue their medication on their own, which leads to relapse. They may discontinue the medication because they miss the "highs" they experienced during mania, or they want a wider range of emotional experience. Some individuals also fail to notice changes in their moods. Thus, most professionals recommend a combination of medication and psychotherapy and other types of support, including family involvement, for those with bipolar disorder. The nature of the disorder and the various psychosocial factors experienced by the person with bipolar disorder make performing research on a single medication or psychotherapy difficult.

Psychological Treatments for Bipolar Disorder

Most psychological therapies that have been used with bipolar disorders focus on both an educational and a psychological perspective (Szentágotai-Tătar & David, 2018). Specifically, techniques related to stress reduction and ways to reduce negative interactions with others are emphasized. In addition, the client is taught about bipolar disorder, its symptoms, the manner in which it may occur over time, and the importance of the use of medication. Family members and significant others in the client's life may also be involved in the education and stress reduction aspects of therapy. These psychosocial family-based treatments have also been shown to be effective for children and adolescents (Brickman & Fristad, 2022).

The American musician and actress Selena Gomez has openly discussed her experience of bipolar disorder.
Kathy Hutchins/Alamy Stock Photo

Monica Basco and John Rush (2005) have developed a 20-session CBT for use with individuals with bipolar disorder. The initial therapy sessions focus on the symptoms of bipolar disorder and the medications that are used to treat them. The next sessions focus on the client's particular symptoms, how to systematically monitor them, and factors related to treatment compliance. Following this, sessions are devoted to understanding one's cognitions, including biased thinking and acting in both mania and depression. The final sessions emphasize an understanding of social relationships and ways to problem-solve and resolve difficult situations.

Medications for Bipolar Disorder

It is important to keep in mind that there are different stages of treatment that require different processes (Goodwin & Jamison, 2007). These can be described as acute treatment, continuation treatment, and maintenance treatment. Acute treatment refers to the period from the beginning of a manic or depressive episode to remission of the symptoms. This period usually lasts from 6 to 12 weeks. Continuation treatment is the period from the remission of the symptoms to the time that they would not be expected to recur. This time has been determined from noting spontaneous recovery times in individuals who have not been treated. This period is around 6 months for a depressive episode and 4 months for a manic episode. Maintenance treatment is designed to prevent or reduce future episodes of mania and depression.

Psychopharmacological treatments for bipolar disorder involve a treatment for episodes of depression, a treatment for episodes of mania, and drugs to reduce relapse (Thase & Denko, 2008). Lithium, a salt found in nature, is the most common treatment for bipolar disorder. It was first used in the 1800s to treat mental disorders, although real interest in its use for the treatment of bipolar disorder began in the 1950s (Malhi, 2009). Lithium is more effective for the mania aspect of bipolar than the depressive aspects, and it works as a mood stabilizer. Although lithium has been used for a number of years, a major review concluded it is not as effective as commonly believed (Geddes et al., 2004). However, this review suggests its use is warranted in those individuals who respond to the drug. One group of individuals who do not respond to lithium are those who show rapid cycling.

Because lithium is not useful with certain groups, drugs referred to as anticonvulsants have been tried, and these have seemed to be effective. Two of these anticonvulsants are sodium valproate and carbamazepine. Other classes of drugs such as antipsychotics discussed in the chapter on schizophrenia have also been used in the treatment of bipolar disorder. One might think that antidepressants would work, but in some individuals these cause a switch to mania and rapid cycling.

> **CONCEPT CHECK**
>
> - Changes in mood are an important aspect of bipolar disorder. How would you describe these changes?
> - What are the important diagnostic criteria for bipolar I, bipolar II, and cyclothymic disorder?
> - What evidence can you cite for the role that the following factors play in the development of bipolar disorder?
>   - Genetic factors
>   - Brain processes
>   - Neurotransmitter dysregulation
>   - Environmental factors
> - As is true with most disorders, a combination of psychological therapy and medication is recommended for treating bipolar disorder. Specifically, what is recommended in terms of
>   - Psychological therapy?
>   - Medication?

SUICIDE

The term suicide first appeared in 1642 in a work called *Religio Medici*, by Sir Thomas Browne. It comes from the Latin word meaning to kill oneself. Suicidal behaviors can be seen as existing on a continuum ranging from thinking about suicide to attempting suicide to an act that leads to death. However, some individuals think often about suicide—referred to as suicidal ideation—without actually attempting to harm themselves. The *DSM-5-TR* does not list suicide as a disorder but describes it presence in other psychological disorders such as bipolar disorder, depression, and personality disorders.

In the United States the rate of suicide attempts did not change between 1950 and 1990. Beginning in 1990 the actual number of suicides declined by 15% and then began to increase in 2000 and then more rapidly from 2006 to 2017 (Twenge et al., 2019). As you can see from Figure 6.8, the overall rate has been stable with some variation over the long term. However, if you look closely at the graph, you will see an increase from 2000 to 2009. According to the Center for Behavioral Health Statistics and Quality, this increase in suicide rate has continued through 2018 and then shows a decrease into 2020 (see For Further Reading).

Suicidal ideation begins around the time of puberty (Nock et al., 2013). Also, having a plan for attempting suicide is associated with actually doing so for the adolescent age group.

One theory related to suicide is the interpersonal-psychological theory (ITPS) (Joiner, 2005; Wolford-Clevenger et al., 2020). This theory suggests there are two important components for an individual to engage in suicidal behaviors. The first is a suicidal desire to die. According to the theory, part of this involves the sense that the person experiences themself as a burden to others and the feeling that they are isolated from and not important to others. The second important component is the capability to attempt suicide. This is also associated with a lowered fear of death. Studies based on this theory have shown that factors such as feelings of being a burden are associated with greater suicidal ideation as well as attempts.

Mental illness has a strong connection with suicide (Goldsmith, 2001). Of those who attempt suicide that leads to death, it is estimated that 90% of adults and 67% of youth would meet diagnostic criteria for a mental disorder. The most common disorders associated with suicide are depression, bipolar disorder, substance use disorders, personality disorders, and schizophrenia, in that order. In bipolar and personality disorders, suicide is often associated with impulsiveness. With schizophrenia, it is more associated with active manifestation of the disorder. In older adults, mental disorders are often comorbid with physical disorders; however, a physical disorder alone is not highly associated with suicide. In older adults, hopelessness along with depression is associated with suicidal ideation.

To put suicide in perspective, more people die annually from suicide than from homicide and even war. In 2014, there were 804,000 people around the world who died from suicide (WHO, 2014). This represents a 1-year prevalence rate of 11.4 per 100,000. This makes suicide the 13th leading cause of death worldwide. It becomes the second leading cause of death among those 15 to 29 years of age. In all age groups, worldwide suicide rates increase with age (Figure 6.9). The graph in Figure 6.9 also shows that males die by suicide more often than females do.

FIGURE 6.8 ■ U.S. Suicide Rates per 100,000 Population by Gender

In 2009, more Americans died from suicide than from traffic-related accidents (Surgeon General Report, 2012). In 2016, suicide was reported to be the 10th leading cause of death in the United States. The first nine causes are medical conditions such as heart disease and cancer. As you will see later in this section, the suicide rate increases with age.

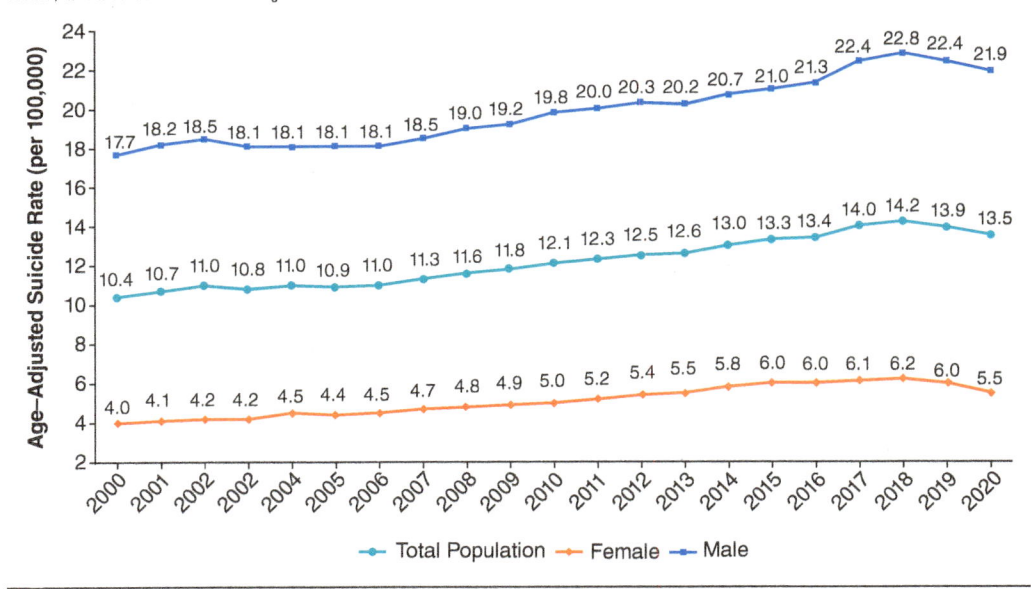

Source: National Institute of Mental Health. (2023, May). *Suicide.* https://www.nimh.nih.gov/health/statistics/suicide

FIGURE 6.9 ■ How Do Suicide Rates Differ Worldwide in Terms of Gender and Age?

Worldwide, suicides increase with age. More men than women die by suicide throughout the life span.

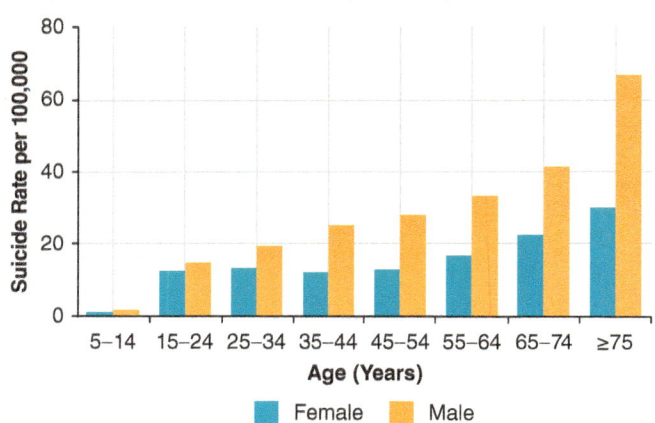

Credit: World Health Organization. (2002). *World report on violence and health.* https://www.who.int/publications/i/item/9241545615, p. 188.

Cultural and Gender Differences in Suicide

As shown in Figure 6.10, there are cultural differences in rates of suicide. In 2021, Korea had the highest national suicide rate (25.7 per 100,000 people) in the world among developed countries. South Korea is second followed by Lithuania (20.3), Slovenia (15.7), Japan (14.6) and the United States (14.1). The lowest rates are found in the Bahamas, Grenada, Barbados, and Antigua, each having less than 2 suicides per 100,000. In the 20 years between 2000 and 2019, suicide rates decreased worldwide by 36%, whereas the suicide rate increased in the United States.

There are also psychological differences related to suicide worldwide. In the United States and Europe, suicide is associated with depression and alcohol abuse, whereas in Asia, impulsiveness plays

FIGURE 6.10 ■ Map of Suicide Rates Worldwide per 100,000 People for 2019

Suicide rate (per 100,000 population): <5.0 | 5.0–9.9 | 10.0–14.9 | ≥15.0 | Data not available

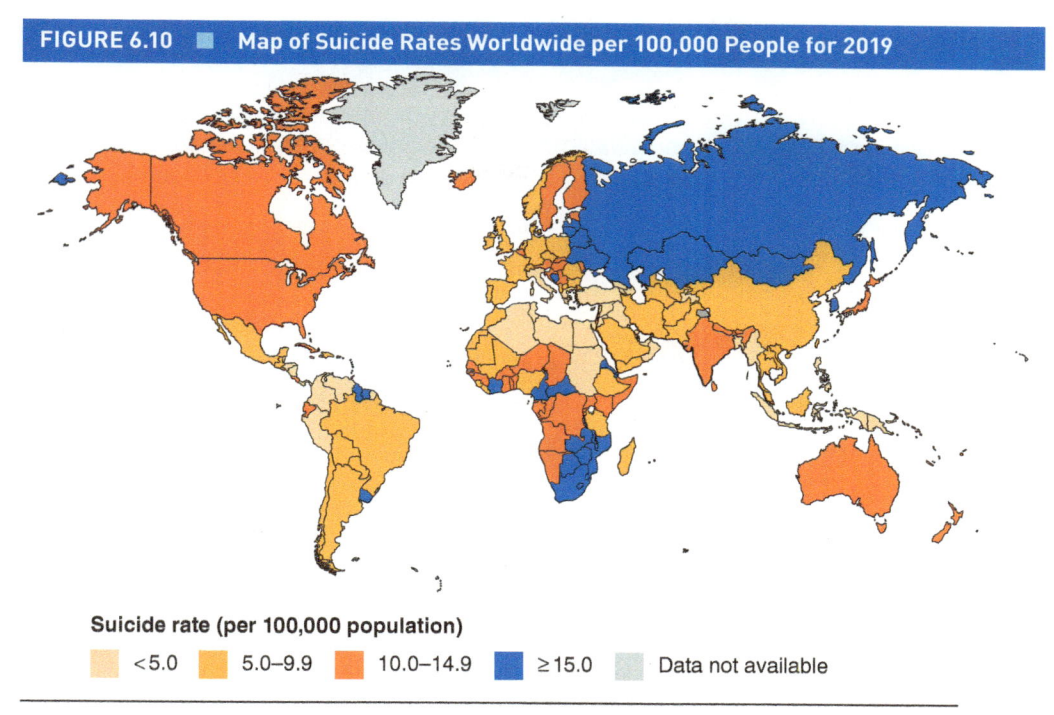

Credit: World Health Organization. (2021). *Suicide worldwide in 2019: Global health estimates.* https://www.who.int/publications/i/item/9789240026643

an important role. There are also cultural differences in gender ratios. The rate is more similar between men and women in Asia but higher for men in Chile and Puerto Rico. Further, the suicide rate among white populations is approximately twice that observed in other races. Countries with low rates of suicide such as Mexico tend to be predominantly Catholic or Muslim, have strong family ties, and have a younger population.

In the United States, the suicide rate is about in the middle of all countries (Miller et al., 2012). The U.S. rate is about 15.3 people per 100,000. However, for children under 15 years of age, the suicide rate is higher than in other industrialized countries, and firearm-related suicide for those under age 15 is some 11 times higher. A strong risk factor for attempting suicide is the presence of a mental illness or substance use disorder. Data suggest that more than 8 million Americans report having serious thoughts of suicide, 2.5 million report making a suicide plan, and 1.1 million report a suicide attempt (Substance Abuse and Mental Health Services Administration, 2011).

Worldwide, religion plays a protective role in preventing suicide. However, in a recent meta-analysis, the protective aspect of religion was stronger in some cultures than others (Wu et al., 2015). The authors of this meta-analysis suggest that the end of life is culturally understood differently in countries of Africa and South America as compared to those of South Asia and Southeast Asia. Overall, Eastern cultures have historically viewed suicide as an act of nobility and selflessness, whereas Western values have typically associated it with shame and cowardice. Religious practices in all cultures have a strong social support aspect, which has been associated with less stress and depression.

As noted, gender differences are also seen in suicide attempts. More recent research also suggests that students of gender minorities (i.e., transgender, genderqueer/nonbinary) had significantly higher rates of depression, suicidal ideation, and suicide attempts than their peers (Horwitz et al., 2020). Although females attempt suicide more often than males, males are 3 to 4 times more likely to die because the methods they use are more lethal (Miller et al., 2012). For example, men are more likely to use firearms or hanging as opposed to drug overdose. Among men, firearms account for about 62% of all suicide deaths. As seen in Table 6.6, firearms and hanging are more likely to lead to death than overdose or cutting oneself.

TABLE 6.6	Suicide Statistics by Type of Attempt as Measured by Emergency Room Visits			
Method	Fatal	Nonfatal	Total	Case Fatality Ratio
Firearm	16,869	2,980	19,849	85
Suffocation/hanging	6,198	2,761	8,959	69
Poisoning/overdose	5,191	215,814	221,005	2
Fall	651	1,434	2,085	31
Cut/Pierce	458	62,817	63,275	1
Other	1,109	35,089	36,198	3
Unspecified	146	2,097	2,243	7
Total	30,622	322,992	353,614	9

Credit. Miller, M., Azrael, D., & Barber, C. (2012). Suicide mortality in the United States: The importance of attending to method in understanding population-level disparities in the burden of suicide. *Annual Review of Public Health, 33,* 393–408. https://doi.org/10.1146/annurev-publhealth-031811-124636 Reprinted with permission from *Annual Reviews.*

Suicide Underreporting and Methods Used in Suicide Attempts

Suicide attempts and rates may be underestimated, since not all attempts result in a hospital visit. Likewise, not all actual suicides are reported. In some cultures, religious or other attitudes condemn suicide, which may prevent the family from reporting the event. There is some suggestion that individuals may use automobile accidents or other accidents as a means of dying by suicide without it being apparent. Police report provocative situations in which an individual causes the police to use force, which may be attempts to be killed by another, known as "suicide by cop." Also, there are very few data on those who attempt suicide but do not succeed. What data there are suggests that more suicide attempts lead to death in old age than in those under the age of 25.

Endophenotypes and Suicide

Traits associated with suicide might serve as endophenotypes (Boldrini & Mann, 2023; Courtet et al., 2011). That is, there may be characteristics related to one's genetics that increase the probability of suicidal ideation and attempts. Two of these traits are aggression and impulsivity. These two factors have been found to be associated with suicidal behaviors. An additional factor found in studies of those who have engaged in suicidal behavior is making disadvantageous choices in tasks unrelated to suicide. This is consistent with the suggestion that frontal lobe dysfunction is associated with suicidal behaviors. Researchers are currently attempting to describe the complicated interaction between genes, neurotransmitters, and environmental conditions. For example, in those who consider suicide, the serotonin system in the PFC may not function normally. Further, hopelessness has been shown to be influenced by the TPH2 gene variants (Lazary et al., 2012). Finally, two HPA axis genes (CRHBP and FKBP5) have also been shown to interact with childhood trauma and increase suicidal behavior (Roy et al., 2012). An intriguing new approach uses machine learning to classify brain responses to stimuli that differentiate those at risk for suicide from those who are not (Just et al., 2017).

Long-Term and Short-Term Factors Related to Suicide

There are both long-term and short-term factors related to suicide (Boldrini & Mann, 2023; Turecki et al., 2012). The long-term factors include a family history of suicide. This suggests that genetics may play a role. This is seen to be separate from mental disorders that run in families. Personality traits as described in terms of endophenotypes also play a role. Children who received negative feedback or abuse are also more likely to engage in suicidal behaviors. If the abuse was performed by a family member, this has been shown to be associated with greater risk of suicidal behaviors. This suggests that it is the trauma related to a family member rather than the actual abuse that is important. This trauma may be involved in epigenetic change, which influences the stress response. Short-term factors include recent life events, current mental illness, and feelings of hopelessness. Also, prior suicidal behavior and substance abuse are predictive of future suicidal behavior. Suicide among college students is described in the following *LENS*.

LENS
SUICIDE AMONG COLLEGE STUDENTS

Each year, hundreds of thousands of new students begin their undergraduate education at colleges around the United States. For most, their lifestyle changes in many ways. They often meet people who are different from their high school peers. Competition increases. Those who made perfect grades or were editors of their school newspapers discover that they are no longer unique. Most students find themselves working harder. Some believe that they are the only ones who feel stressed and are working constantly. For a number of these students, every setback is experienced as an extreme failure. Social comparisons leave them feeling inadequate. Some think of suicide.

In response to concern over suicide, many colleges and universities set up programs to help identify and treat those at risk. Collecting data from mental health centers at over 140 colleges and universities around the United States gives us a picture of who is seeking help. Data from over 90,000 students who went to their local mental health center for all types of distress in 2020 shows that anxiety, stress, and depression are the most common presenting problems. Over 30% of all students in this sample have considered suicide (Table 6.7). However, less than 10% of this group actually attempted suicide (Table 6.8).

TABLE 6.7 ■ Students Who Visited Campus Mental Health Center Who Had Seriously Considered Attempting Suicide (How Many Times)

Number of Suicide Attempt Considerations	Overall (%) $n = 96,839$
Never	67.0%
1 time	11.6%
2–3 times	12.4%
4–5 times	2.5%
More than 5 times	6.4%

Credit: Center for Collegiate Mental Health. (2022, January). *2021 Annual report* (Publication No. STA 22–132). Penn State University. https://files.eric.ed.gov/fulltext/ED617358.pdf

TABLE 6.8 ■ Students Who Visited Campus Mental Health Center Who Made a Suicide Attempt (How Many Times)

Number of Suicide Attempts	Overall (%) $n = 96,599$
Never	90.6
1 time	6.0
2–3 times	2.7
4–5 times	0.3
More than 5 times	0.4

Credit: Center for Collegiate Mental Health. (2022, January). *2021 Annual report* (Publication No. STA 22–132). Penn State University. https://files.eric.ed.gov/fulltext/ED617358.pdf

> In 2020, suicide was the second leading cause of death of Americans in the 10- to 14-year age group and third in 15- to 24-year age group. Unintentional injury, such as that arising from an auto accident, was the first. Data from the Centers for Disease Control and Prevention (2023) show an increase in suicide among those in the 15- to 24-year age group from 2000 to 2021.
>
> ### Thought Question
>
> What is being done on your campus to identify those with suicidal ideation?

Suicide in the Military

Historically, active-duty U.S. Army soldiers had a lower rate of suicide than comparable civilians (Curry, 2015). However, with two decades of war in Iraq and Afghanistan, this has changed. Since 2008, the suicide rate for soldiers has increased, while that of civilians has remained consistent. This led the U.S. Army and NIMH to study this problem. One question asked was what were the characteristics associated with suicide attempts (Ursano et al., 2015). This study examined almost 1,000,000 soldiers who were on active duty between 2004 and 2009. Almost all (98.6%) suicide attempts were among enlisted soldiers and happened early in their time in service. Women and those with less than a high school education also showed higher rates of suicide attempts. Another study showed that suicide attempts were higher in military units that had a history of suicide attempts (Ursano et al., 2017).

Another question asked was whether being sent to the front, such as in Iraq, was associated with increased risk of suicide (Reger et al., 2015). Researchers found that deployment itself was not associated with the rate of suicide, although the rate may be elevated shortly after deployment for some subgroups (Reger et al., 2018). This was surprising, since many people assumed that going to war zones would increase the suicide rate, but this was not the case. However, higher rates of suicide were associated with leaving the military with less than 4 years of service, whether the soldiers went to the front or not. There were also higher rates of suicide for those who left without an honorable discharge.

It has been estimated that every 18 hours, a member of the U.S. armed forces takes their own life.
Gina Kelly/Alamy Stock Photo

Based on the interpersonal-psychological theory of suicide (IPTS) discussed previously, a group of researchers sought to determine the role of capability for suicide (Bryan et al., 2016). These researchers conducted a prospective study of 168 military personnel deployed to Iraq. Specifically, they wanted to know if capability for suicide was acquired over time as suggested by the theory. That is, would the continued exposure to combat and painful experiences lead to greater capability for suicide? However, in this study, the capability for suicide remained constant from pre-deployment to the end of deployment. These researchers suggest it is not the military experience per se but rather a stable individual difference that leads one to suicide. Thus, certain individuals may be more vulnerable than others.

In terms of the treatment of military personnel who express suicide ideation or who attempt suicide, current reviews suggest that CBT, dialectical behavior therapy (DBT), and cognitive therapy offer the most promise. One of these studies compared traditional treatment with an addition of CBT (Rudd et al., 2015). This was a randomized control trial in which 152 soldiers were randomly assigned to either the treatment as usual, which was a general psychotherapy approach, or the treatment as usual plus CBT. This study included assessment at 3, 6, 12, 18, and 24 months following the initial baseline assessment. The researchers found that 18 participants in the traditional therapy group and 8 participants in the CBT group made at least one suicide attempt. This suggests that the CBT group was 60% less likely to make a suicide attempt during treatment. At this point, psychological intervention such as CBT and DBT are the only interventions shown to be effective, with stronger evidence for DBT in reducing suicide attempts (Linehan, 2008; Linehan et al., 2015). No medications have been shown to be effective. In Chapter 14 on personality disorders, dialectical behavior therapy will be described in greater detail.

Preventing Suicide

Suicide prevention programs seek to reduce the factors that increase the risk for suicidal thoughts and behaviors. These programs seek to work on at least four levels: the individual, the individual's relationships, the community, and the society. This can be diagramed as seen in Figure 6.11. Suicide prevention began in the United States in the 1950s and has continued through to the present day. Many communities have hotlines for people to call 24 hours a day. There is also a nationwide suicide hotline in the United States that can be reached by calling or texting 988, which connects to the National Suicide Prevention Lifeline. There has also been a national focus on groups that are at higher risk for suicide, including Native Americans, members of the armed forces, and veterans.

Friends and relatives of individuals who show the signs listed in Table 6.9 should help them find a mental health professional or suicide prevention center in their community. Interestingly, those who attempt suicide but survive the attempt tend to feel relieved. This makes it possible for those individuals to receive help.

In addition to the suicide warning signs discussed, additional research has begun to focus of patterns of linguistic presentation as related to suicide (Ophir et al., 2022). This research asks if machine learning can be used to predict who is at risk for suicide by the way in which they present their thoughts in the same way that computers, text messages, and telephone voice services attempt to predict what you desire to say. Of course, there would be ethical issues associated with monitoring everyone's social media presentation, but in certain situations, this technology may offer additional information to health service professionals to help ensure the safety of certain clients.

The popular Netflix series *13 Reasons Why* was met with significant controversy from mental health professionals due to what was considered a dangerous depiction of suicide. A disclaimer was eventually added, but was that enough to solve the problem?
PictureLux/The Hollywood Archive/Alamy Stock Photo

FIGURE 6.11 ■ What Are the Protective Factors and Risk Factors for Suicide?

Examples of protective factors and risk factors across the four levels of society, community, relationship, and individual.

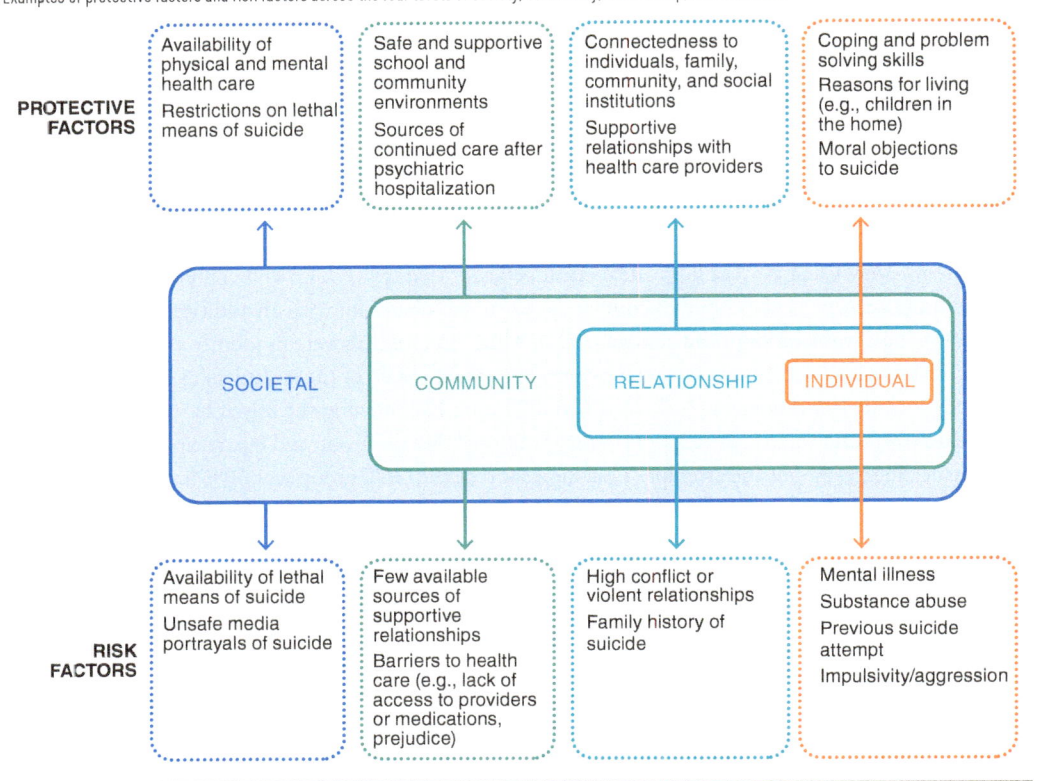

PROTECTIVE FACTORS

- Availability of physical and mental health care
- Restrictions on lethal means of suicide

- Safe and supportive school and community environments
- Sources of continued care after psychiatric hospitalization

- Connectedness to individuals, family, community, and social institutions
- Supportive relationships with health care providers

- Coping and problem solving skills
- Reasons for living (e.g., children in the home)
- Moral objections to suicide

SOCIETAL | COMMUNITY | RELATIONSHIP | INDIVIDUAL

RISK FACTORS

- Availability of lethal means of suicide
- Unsafe media portrayals of suicide

- Few available sources of supportive relationships
- Barriers to health care (e.g., lack of access to providers or medications, prejudice)

- High conflict or violent relationships
- Family history of suicide

- Mental illness
- Substance abuse
- Previous suicide attempt
- Impulsivity/aggression

Source: Office of the U.S. Surgeon General & National Action Alliance for Suicide Prevention. (2012). *2012 national strategy for suicide prevention: Goals and objectives for action. A report of the U.S. Surgeon General and of the National Action Alliance for Suicide Prevention.* U.S. Department of Health and Human Services. https://www.ncbi.nlm.nih.gov/books/NBK109917/

TABLE 6.9 ■ The Warning Signs of Suicide

- Talking about wanting to die
- Looking for a way to kill oneself
- Talking about feeling hopeless or having no purpose
- Talking about feeling trapped or being in unbearable pain
- Talking about being a burden to others
- Increasing the use of alcohol or drugs
- Acting anxious, agitated, or reckless
- Sleeping too little or too much
- Withdrawing or feeling isolated
- Showing rage or talking about seeking revenge
- Displaying extreme mood swings

Source: Office of the U.S. Surgeon General & National Action Alliance for Suicide Prevention. (2012). *2012 national strategy for suicide prevention: Goals and objectives for action. A report of the U.S. Surgeon General and of the National Action Alliance for Suicide Prevention.* U.S. Department of Health and Human Services. https://www.ncbi.nlm.nih.gov/books/NBK109917/

Follow-up studies of suicide prevention programs suggest they are effective. One such study examined youth suicide prevention programs across 46 states and 12 tribal communities in the United States (Garraza et al., 2015). These programs included education and mental health awareness, screening activities, gatekeeper training events, improved community partnerships and linkages to services, programs for suicide survivors, and crisis hotlines. Some 57,000 youth ages 16 to 23 were involved in the suicide prevention programs. These individuals were compared with some 84,000 youth who were not involved in the prevention programs. In the year following the program, there were 4.9 fewer suicide attempts per 1,000 youth in the treatment group compared to the control group. This suggests that thousands of suicide attempts can be averted by such prevention programs.

> ## CONCEPT CHECK
>
> - What evidence would you cite to show that mental illness is related to suicide?
> - What cultural differences are associated with suicide?
> - What gender differences are associated with suicide?
> - What genetic traits and endophenotypes have been suggested as markers for suicide?
> - What short-term and long-term factors are related to the risk of suicide?
> - What are some of the important recent research findings about suicide in the military?
> - What warning signs would you look for in a friend if you were concerned about suicide?
> - What kinds of programs are available to help an individual at risk for suicide?

SUMMARY

Depression has been described for more than 2,000 years. It is characterized by depressed mood in which one feels sad or empty without any sense of pleasure in one's activities. With a depressive disorder, the individual may also experience sleep problems and weight changes, as well as a sense of worthlessness and self-blame. Clinical depression is seen when the majority of these symptoms last for an extended period of time. There is a gender difference in that over the course of a lifetime, about 1 in 4 females and 1 in 10 males experience a major depressive episode. Genetic studies suggest that depression is equally influenced by genetic and environmental factors. Today, major depressive disorder (MDD) is one of the most commonly diagnosed mental disorders among adults and is estimated to be found in about 13 million adult Americans during the preceding 12 months. Lifetime estimates are approximately 33 million Americans. Three fourths of those with MDD would also meet criteria for an additional *DSM* disorder.

Depression has been related to a variety of physiological, psychological, family, and social components. It is also estimated to be one of the most economically costly mental disorders worldwide. Research suggests that the initial episode of depression has a strong environmental component, whereas later episodes are thought to be related to internal physiological changes. Major life stress such as loss of a close relationship is highly associated with the development of depression. Although diagnostic symptoms for adolescents are similar to those for adults, depressed children are more likely to describe physical symptoms. The rates of depression are very low prior to puberty with equal numbers of boys and girls. After puberty, the rates of depression increase, and more females than males are affected.

The cognitive model of depression was developed by Aaron Beck to describe the manner in which individuals with depression maintain the disorder. It also became the basis for a therapeutic approach. It is basically a learning theory model that suggests adverse events that occur early in life can lead to the development of depressive schemas involving three aspects referred to as the negative cognitive triad: the self, the personal world, and the future. Researchers now suggest that the underlying neural mechanisms for the cognitive model of depression can be described. Explaining the existence of depression from an evolutionary perspective includes the assumption that depressed mood was adaptive in our evolutionary history—that feeling depressed would help the individual solve a problem faced by humans from the earliest times (Badcock et al., 2017). Researchers suggest that a depressed state represents a risk management strategy in response to a situation that has a low probability of success and high probability of risk. The social risk hypothesis was developed by Allen and Badcock as an integration of three previous broad models of depression: (1) depression in terms of resource conservation, (2) depression in terms of social competition, and (3) depression in terms of attachment.

This hypothesis suggests that when significant interpersonal relationships are disrupted—including by social humiliation or defeat—depressed mood is the outcome.

Given that the WHO identifies depression as the leading cause of disability in the world, there have been worldwide movements to develop programs directed toward prevention. Many forms of treatment are available for reducing the problems associated with mood disorders. First, there are techniques for direct manipulation of brain activity. This can be accomplished by electrical or magnetic stimulation of the brain itself through techniques such as ECT, VNS, and TMS. A second, far more widely used technique is to use psychotropic medications to influence neurotransmitters, which in turn may inhibit or facilitate brain processes. Third, the brain may be influenced indirectly through cognitive, emotional, or motor changes. Traditional psychotherapy—from the dynamic, cognitive behavioral, and existential-humanistic perspectives—allows a person to explore how she interprets her world through thoughts or reacts to it through emotions and to consider alternative ways of experiencing her world. Other techniques, such as exercise or meditation, are also designed with the goal of learning alternative ways of modifying internal processes. One problem in the treatment of depression is that even in situations in which symptoms are reduced, individuals are at risk for a relapse. For this reason, professionals have searched for a combination of treatments that might help to prevent relapse by involving more than one underlying depressive mechanism—for example, antidepressant medication and a form of psychotherapy such as CBT.

Descriptions of individuals showing evidence of both mania and depression have been with us for more than 2,000 years. From this time to the present, mania and depression were considered as different parts of one disorder. Changes in mood are an important aspect of bipolar disorders. These include the intense sense of well-being along with high energy seen in mania and its opposite seen in depression. Changes in cognition and perception also accompany these states. *DSM-5* classifies the disorder in terms of the manic and the depressive symptoms. The major distinctions in *DSM-5* between bipolar I and bipolar II are related to the severity and duration of the manic phase. An additional diagnostic category is cyclothymia, which shows an affective temperament less severe than bipolar I and bipolar II. Overall, across the spectrum of bipolar disorders, the lifetime prevalence is estimated to be between 3% and 8.3%. Gender differences are not large, and similar prevalence rates have been found around the world. Research over the past 40 years suggests a genetic predisposition for bipolar disorder, since it has been found to run in families. Other genetic research has shown a partial overlap between the genes involved in bipolar disorder and schizophrenia. A variety of brain imaging studies have suggested that individuals with bipolar disorder show differences in brain processes, as well as a complex pattern of neurotransmitter dysregulation. Environmental factors, particularly stress, play an important role in the course of bipolar disorders.

Suicidal behaviors can be seen as existing on a continuum ranging from thinking about suicide (ideation) to attempting suicide to an act that leads to death. Mental illness—particularly depression, bipolar disorder, substance use disorders, personality disorders, and schizophrenia—has a strong connection with suicide. More people die from suicide than from homicide and even war, making it the 13th leading cause of death worldwide. There are cultural, psychological, and gender differences related to suicide worldwide. Although females attempt suicide more often than males, males are 3 to 4 times more likely to die because the methods they use are more lethal. There are both long-term and short-term factors related to suicide. Long-term factors include personality traits, particularly aggressiveness and impulsivity; a family history of suicide suggesting that genetics may play a role; and children who received negative feedback or abuse that may induce epigenetic change, which influences the stress response. Short-term factors include recent life events, current mental illness, and the feeling of hopelessness. Prior suicidal behavior and substance abuse is also predictive of future suicidal behavior. Suicide prevention programs seek to reduce the factors that increase the risk for suicidal thoughts and behaviors and work on at least four levels: the individual, the individual's relationships, the community, and the society. Knowing the warning signs of suicide can help friends and relatives of individuals who show these signs find a mental health professional or suicide prevention center in their community to seek help.

STUDY RESOURCES

Review Questions

1. How would each of the following perspectives answer the question of why depression exists from an evolutionary perspective?
   a. Depression in terms of resource conservation
   b. Depression in terms of social competition
   c. Depression in terms of attachment
   d. Social risk hypothesis
   e. Your theory of why depression exists from an evolutionary perspective

2. The WHO identifies depression as the leading cause of disability in the world. We know that cost-effectiveness is a critical factor in designing programs for developing countries. Given that, what proposal would you offer for a comprehensive program for the reduction of depression in developing countries that addresses the following aspects?
   a. Prevention
   b. Psychotropic medications
   c. Techniques for direct manipulation of brain activity
   d. Psychological therapy
   e. Relapse of symptoms

3. Bipolar disorder is complex. How has that complexity impacted the following aspects of bipolar disorder?
   a. Definition and the development of diagnostic criteria
   b. An individual's experience with bipolar disorder
   c. Research on biomarkers and the development of endophenotypes for bipolar disorder
   d. Treatment of bipolar disorder

4. Mental illness has a strong connection with suicide. This is especially true of depression and bipolar disorder. With what you've learned in this chapter, design a suicide prevention program that targets a specific population of individuals with depression or bipolar disorder.
   a. What cultural, gender, and age factors would you consider?
   b. How would your program focus on the following levels: the individual, the individual's relationships, the community, and the society?
   c. How would your program incorporate the recommended treatment approaches for the disorder you're focusing on?

For Further Reading

Bullmore, E. (2019). *The inflamed mind: A radical new approach to depression*. Picador.

Jamison, K. R. (1993). *Touched with fire: Manic–depressive illness and the artistic temperament*. Free Press.

Jamison, K. R. (1995). *An unquiet mind*. Knopf.

Society of Clinical Psychology. (2022). *Treatment target: Depression*. https://www.div12.0rg/diagnosis/depression/

Solomon, A. (2003). *The noonday demon: An atlas of depression*. Simon & Schuster.

Substance Abuse and Mental Health Services Administration. (2023). *2021 National Survey on Drug Use and Health annual national report*. https://www.samhsa.gov/data/report/2021-nsduh-annual-national-report

World Health Organization. (2023). *Depressive disorder (depression)*. https://www.who.int/news-room/fact-sheets/detail/depression

KEY TERMS

- bipolar disorder
- cognitive model of depression
- cortisol
- cyclothymic disorder
- deep brain stimulation (DBS)
- depression in terms of attachment
- depression in terms of resource conservation
- depression in terms of social competition
- electroconvulsive therapy (ECT)
- intergenerational transmission of depression
- macrophage theory of depression
- major depressive disorder (MDD)
- manic depression
- melancholia
- negative cognitive triad
- suicidal ideation
- suicide
- transcranial magnetic stimulation (TMS)
- unipolar depression
- vagal nerve stimulation (VNS)

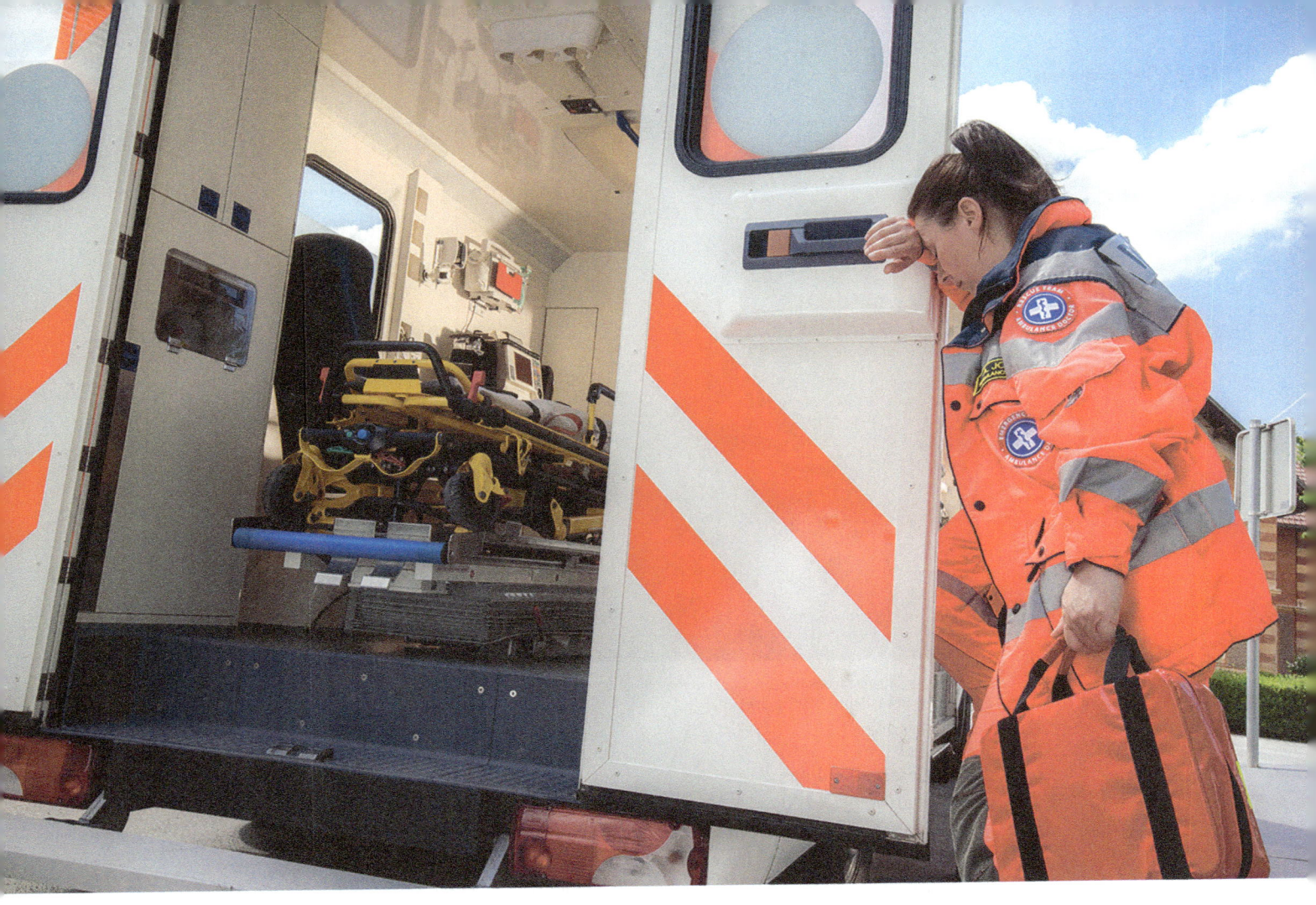

7 STRESS, TRAUMA, AND PTSD

LEARNING OBJECTIVES

- **7.1** Explain how stress and trauma are related to health and psychopathology.
- **7.2** Identify the physiological mechanisms involved in stress.
- **7.3** Discuss major findings about fight or flight and social versus physical stress.
- **7.4** Describe the characteristics of adjustment disorders, acute stress disorder, and prolonged grief disorder.
- **7.5** Define post-traumatic stress disorder and discuss its characteristics, causes, and treatment.

Hurricane Katrina struck the Gulf Coast of the United States in 2005, causing many hundreds of deaths and much devastation in the lives of thousands more.

iStock.com/PattieS

As a journalist, I am used to writing about death and destruction. Natural disasters that rip through homes and lives, leaving tattered and torn pieces of towns in their paths. The tsunami, floods in California, earthquakes in Japan. I have become accustomed, even calloused to these horrors as I write about them and survey the video from a distance. I will never do that again. Hurricane Katrina brought all of us down from our ivory towers. It opened our eyes to the frailty of human life, and man-made structures. We are so small compared to Mother Nature.

My TV station sits about four blocks from the beach, just behind the railroad tracks. I guess we thought we were invincible, because no one there evacuated. As the storm got closer I started to get nervous. Not because of the warnings we were giving to the community, or the projections on the Weather Channel, but because I could hear the fear in our own meteorologists' voices. Professionals who have lived through hundreds of storms were shaking.

As Katrina hit land, the wind sounded like the ocean was in pain, and angry. In awe, we stepped out into our courtyard. I watched as the rain that was falling in sideways circles ripped the roof off of our newsroom. I ran back inside, only to see a hole above my desk and rain pouring onto my computer. In a frantic rush we grabbed equipment, mainly weather computers, and raced to the other, "safer," side of the building. Pieces of insulation began falling, and metal shards flew past, it felt like a combat zone with enemy fire coming from all directions.

The lights in our studio began pulsating, threatening to become hundred pound projectiles. We rushed to the cinder block section of the building which had been dubbed "hurricane proof" and set up makeshift operations, only to hear a crash above us. A piece of concrete had slammed through the roof and into the second floor. Water began seeping in the front and back doors. Then one of the transmitting towers, weighing hundreds of pounds, collapsed. It looked like a twist tie that had been hastily discarded just inches from where we were huddled. If the storm had been any stronger, or lasted even an hour more, I don't know that we would have made it.

As scary as it was at the station, that wasn't the part that frightened me most. As we were rushing out of our crumbling newsroom the phones were still ringing, with frantic viewers on the other end of the line. The sound of the phone crying made my heart ache. I had talked to dozens of people who were stranded, trapped, and scared just minutes before. I still wonder what happened to the woman who called sobbing, climbing to her attic with her baby. There was a man stuck in his house, trying to punch his way to the roof. One of my coworkers called as she jumped out her bedroom window, and her house was sucked into the murky waters. I can only imagine the horror of seeing a 30 foot wave coming towards you and making what might be your last phone call.

Shilo Groover is a graduate of George Washington University's School of Media and Public Affairs (BA, 2003). She now works as a television producer at WLOX (ABC 13) in Biloxi, Mississippi.

From Shilo Groover. (2005, October 19). The Storm: A First-Hand Account of Katrina [Letter to the editor]. By George! www.gwu.edu/~bygeorge/oct1905/letter.html

I came home from Iraq in March 2004, yet I'm still fighting a war, a war here at home. It's a war of shadows, one that no one seems to really understand. A war of anger and anxiety, fought in the recesses of my mind. Just like in the two wars I fought in Iraq and Afghanistan, I don't know who the enemy is. There, insurgents take potshots at you, then go back into hiding. Combating post-traumatic stress disorder, PTSD, is the same. Some days I feel as if I have the enemy on the run; other days it has me pinned down.

I am a former military policeman. I was among the first soldiers to move into Afghanistan after the Sept. 11 attacks. For nine months, my company provided support for Rangers and special operations forces. We returned home in September 2002. Four months later, in January 2003, we were in Kuwait preparing for another war.

I remember the day we moved into Iraq. It was about a week after D-Day [the initial U.S.-led invasion in March 2003]. As soon as we crossed the border, we saw cratered highways, dead bodies and burning vehicles. For the next year, my company provided security for main supply routes and patrolled the streets of Mosul. There was never a firefight, just constant, low-level violence. Sniper fire, RPGs, IEDs and mortar attacks kept us on edge at every moment. We were hypervigilant. We couldn't shut it off. It reached the point when we thought that anything could be a bomb, that anything on the road could blow up.

Many veterans of the wars in Iraq and Afghanistan suffer from PTSD.

Stocktrek Images, Inc./Alamy Stock Photo

Now, the war is on my home front. I often ask myself, why am I still fighting? I'm safe now, aren't I? But PTSD, like an insurgency, is elusive. It attacks from all angles, almost invisibly. The enemy is out there, but you don't know when or from where an attack will come. As a soldier, I saw things no one ever should. I once responded to a call from a field artillery unit that had shot an Iraqi who tried to flee a checkpoint. Have you ever seen what a .50-caliber round does to a person's head? Imagine a large wooden mallet smashing a watermelon. The .50-cal. does the same. Brain matter was splattered all over the inside of the Iraqi's truck. At the time, I didn't feel anything. I felt numb. It was as if nothing had happened. No emotion at all.

Once I came home, once my mind wasn't racing at 100 miles an hour, I had time to think and to detox from the military. And as I processed my memories, I wondered if something was wrong with me. In truth, my family and my wife knew before I did.

Before I deployed, I was very laid-back, an easygoing guy. I joked around a lot. When I returned from Iraq, I was edgy and short-tempered. The smallest thing could trigger an outburst. I viewed everything from a life-or-death perspective. I would get ticked off if my wife and I left five minutes late for an appointment. On a mission, "five minutes late" can get someone killed. You can't be "five minutes late" to a firefight.

I couldn't get out of The Zone.

In Iraq and Afghanistan, I was constantly telling soldiers what to do to stay alive. I did the same at home. In the evening, when my wife would tell me what she did or where she went that day, I might bark at her. "What the hell's wrong with you? You could have gotten hurt."

I couldn't focus on any one particular task. I had to juggle several jobs at once to relax. That's why I thrived in the chaos at my workplace, at a job I hated. I had trouble sticking to a conversation, and I had no patience. I couldn't sit still for more than five or 10 minutes before I had to walk around the house. I couldn't sit through a movie with my wife unless it was full of action. I played war-based video games to put me in my comfort zone. They soothed me.

At my Vet Center, the staff told me what benefits I was eligible for and walked me through enrollment. They helped me with my job hunt. They gave me their personal phone numbers and told me to call if I needed anything.

And they got me the help I needed. A Vet Center counselor had me tested for traumatic brain injury and PTSD, and got me into group and individual therapy. It's still a struggle, but I'm taking back control of my life and my feelings. Each day I'm one step closer.

The author deployed to Afghanistan from January to September 2002 and to Iraq from March 2003 to March 2004. He is now studying sociology at a college in Northern California and plans to pursue a career assisting fellow vets.

From Jeremy P. (2010, February 21). Fighting the war at home. New America Media. Retrieved from newamericamedia.org/2010/02/fighting-the-war-at-home.php

PSYCHOLOGICAL STRESS AND PSYCHOPATHOLOGY

Psychological stress is experienced when something we do not expect and cannot control happens to us. It can be a building we are in catching on fire. It can be another person robbing us at gunpoint. Stress can even come from trying to help someone but finding ourselves in a situation we did not expect. The stories that begin this chapter show people doing their job when a hurricane hit and confronting the horrors of war and life-and-death decisions. At times, these experiences lead to strong emotional reactions and at other times to psychological disorders such as post-traumatic stress disorder (PTSD). Further, as we saw in Chapter 6, the first episode of depression is often connected to a psychologically stressful event happening in someone's life.

Understanding the manner in which stress and trauma are related to health and psychopathology is complicated. Research is beginning to uncover the roles that these factors play in psychopathology. Some disorders have a clear relationship with stress and trauma. PTSD, by definition, is clearly the result of traumatic experiences. Likewise, individuals with depression are 2.5 to 10 times more likely to have experienced a recent, negative, stressful major life event than individuals without depression (Slavich et al., 2010). Further, severe stress and trauma from childhood abuse and neglect are associated with depression, alcohol abuse, and criminal behavior (Cruz-Pereira et al., 2020; Finlay et al., 2022). In disorders such as schizophrenia and bipolar disorder, stress can increase the symptoms.

Overall, early life stress is associated with later mental and physical health problems (Finlay et al., 2022; O'Connor et al., 2021; Taylor, 2011; Tost et al., 2015). Early stressful experiences change both psychological and physiological reactions to future stressful experiences. These changes can be related to psychological factors, developmental changes in the brain, genetic factors, epigenetic modifications, endocrine factors, and economic and social factors.

Does Trauma Produce Mental Illness?

Trauma can produce psychological disorders, especially PTSD. However, although various types of trauma show a relationship to psychopathology, this relationship is not found for every individual (Finlay et al., 2022; Horn & Feder, 2018; Nikulina et al., 2012). Further, these differences involve the immune system and mechanisms related to inflammation (Hori & Kim, 2019).

What researchers have articulated is that children show differential responses to environmental influences, such as maltreatment, which are modulated by genetic factors. Specifically, the monoamine oxidase A (MAOA) gene located on the X chromosome makes certain neurotransmitters inactive and has been associated with aggression in mice and humans. This gene encodes the brain enzyme MAO-A and makes such neurotransmitters as serotonin, norepinephrine, and dopamine inactive.

Following a large number of boys over a long term, Caspi and his colleagues (2002) found that mistreatment as children influenced some boys differently from others later in adulthood. Those boys who were mistreated in childhood and had a particular form of the MAOA gene were more likely to be violent and engage in a variety of antisocial behaviors as adults, as well as have problems with law enforcement officials. Those without this particular form of the gene did not display antisocial behaviors, even if they had been mistreated as children. Thus, environmental influences in terms of maltreatment would be modulated by the presence of certain genetic structures.

Research from a different perspective supports the idea that children show differential responses to not only negative but also positive parental influences. Jay Belsky (2005) has reviewed a variety of these studies. What he determined is that the infants who are most inhibited and fearful and who display negative emotions are the ones most affected by positive parenting. Thus, positive interventions can also influence later outcomes for the better.

CONCEPT CHECK

- What evidence can you cite to show that stress experienced early in life is associated with later mental and physical health problems?
- Although various types of trauma show a relationship to psychopathology, what factors can affect that relationship?

THE PHYSIOLOGICAL MECHANISMS RELATED TO STRESS AND TRAUMA

Our physiological reactions to stress and trauma occur on a variety of levels (Murphy & Heller, 2022; O'Connor et al., 2021; Zefferino et al., 2020). These include the endocrine system involving the hypothalamic–pituitary–adrenal (HPA) axis, the autonomic nervous system (ANS), changes in cortical processes, the reaction of the immune system, and the tagging of genes (epigenetics).

What Makes You Run From Bears? Stress and the Hypothalamic–Pituitary–Adrenal Axis

The evolutionary logic of survival is one of the easiest to comprehend. If an organism is not able to successfully respond to threat, it can be hurt or killed. If it is killed, its genes can no longer be passed on. If it is hurt, this may make it a less appealing mate or not allow it to seek mates. Thus, it is expected that organisms will have evolved sophisticated mechanisms that benefit survival. The basic mechanisms include the ANS; a network of hypothalamic, pituitary, and adrenal responses; the cardiovascular system; metabolism; and the immune system. These mechanisms are particularly sensitive to changes in the environment, and repeated stressful events can modify their functioning.

The basic function of these pathways is to prepare the body for action. If you see a bear, you will need energy to run. It actually does not need to be a bear. Almost all stressors use the same physiological systems to save your life. These pathways move physiological energy resources to the necessary organs and muscles. They create an overall shift from storing energy to using energy. This is like pressing on the accelerator of your car to quickly leave a dangerous situation. Temporally, priorities of the body move from flexibility, including past and future considerations, to focus on immediate circumstances. Your body no longer stores energy, pays attention to sexual matters, or has your immune system worry about long-term disease. Cognitively and emotionally, threat-relevant cues and memories become critical as they relate to the current situation. As you know, your brain plays an important role in deciding what is stressful, whether it is taking an exam or responding to a loud noise. The brain has two major pathways with which it influences peripheral physiology.

The first pathway is the *autonomic nervous system*, which innervates a variety of organs, including the adrenal medulla, resulting in the release of catecholamines (norepinephrine and epinephrine) from the terminal of sympathetic nerves (Figure 7.1). Norepinephrine and epinephrine are fast acting, so you are ready to respond within seconds. If these substances are released at the synapse, they are referred to as neurotransmitters. If they are released into the bloodstream, they are referred to as hormones.

The second pathway involves cells in the hypothalamus that are released into the bloodstream and go to the pituitary gland. This causes the pituitary to release hormones that influence other hormones, which in turn influence peripheral organs such as the adrenals as well as cells in the immune system. These hormones are referred to as glucocorticoids. Simply said, this system helps to convert stored fats and carbohydrates into energy sources that can be used immediately. Historically, given that survival

What happens when faced with a potential threat? According to Cannon (1932), the body prepares you either to fight or to leave the scene.

iStock.com/JNevitt

processes that would have activated this system would have involved conflict and fights, it was important that the immune system also be activated to protect the organism from wounds. This protective pathway is known as the **hypothalamic–pituitary–adrenal (HPA) axis**. In psychology and physiology, these mechanisms have been studied under the rubric of psychological stress. Further, underactivity or overactivity in the HPA axis is seen in a number of psychopathologies, including schizophrenia, autism, and depression (Roggers et al., 2013; Wesarg et al., 2020).

The stress response is accomplished by a variety of interacting brain systems, which include the amygdala, hippocampus, and prefrontal cortex (Figure 7.2). It is these areas that show distinct structural and functional changes in individuals with stress disorders (Chattarji et al., 2015). In particular,

FIGURE 7.1 ■ The HPA Pathway Involved in Physiological Responses to Psychological Stress

In response to stress, the autonomic nervous system (ANS) innervates a variety of organs, including the adrenal medulla, which results in the release of catecholamines. The HPA axis and sympathetic system have largely complementary actions throughout the body, including energy mobilization and maintenance of blood pressure during stress.

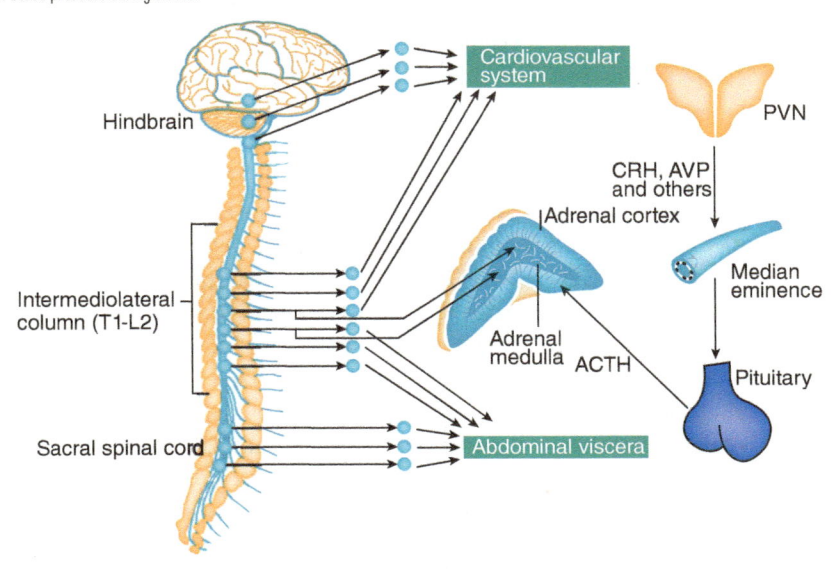

Credit: Ulrich-Lai, Y., & Herman, J. (2009). Neural regulation of endocrine and autonomic stress responses. *Nature Reviews Neuroscience, 10*, 397–409.

FIGURE 7.2 ■ Which Brain Structures Influence the HPA?

The hypothalamic–pituitary–adrenal axis is under excitatory control of the amygdala and inhibitory control of the hippocampus.

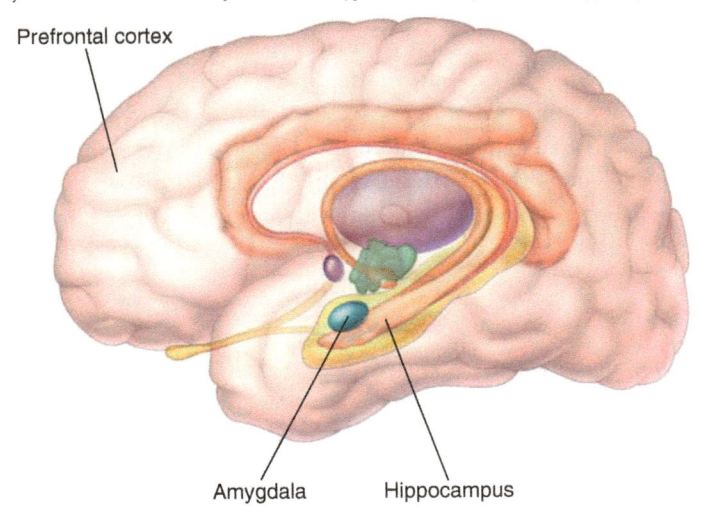

the prefrontal cortex and hippocampus show a reduction in volume and activity in stress. The amygdala shows an increase in activity. These brain areas regulate both short-term and long-term responses to stress (Hariri & Holmes, 2015; McEwen et al., 2015), and these responses result in the hypothalamus activating the sympathetic nervous system and the HPA axis.

Basically, the hypothalamus in the brain produces a substance referred to as *corticotropin-releasing hormone (CRH)* (also called corticotropin-releasing factor [CRF]), which then produces *adrenocorticotropic hormone (ACTH)* in the pituitary. ACTH in the blood results in the adrenal glands producing glucocorticoids, which in turn increases blood sugar levels and thus increases the energy available to our bodies during stress. HPA is under excitatory control of the amygdala and inhibitory control of the hippocampus. The hippocampus releases CRH, which is transported to the adrenal cortex where *cortisol* is released.

Research studies will often measure participants' cortisol levels to assess the perceived stressfulness of the situation. Daily cortisol levels are also higher in individuals with depression. Further, variants in the gene related to CRH can influence the individual's reactivity to stress. Research suggests that this variation influences brain processes before childhood trauma takes place and leaves the individual at risk for greater negative effects from childhood trauma (Rogers et al., 2013). Stress can actually influence brain processes by reducing the connections of one neuron with another, especially in the hippocampus and the frontal areas of the brain (Sapolsky, 2015). Stress shows the opposite effect in the amygdala with the increase of neuron connections. This in turn leaves the person with more connections when responding to fearful situations.

The stress response was initially described by Walter Cannon in 1932 as a bodily response to danger. Although Cannon originally studied animals, research since his time has shown the basic stress response also applies to humans. The overall stress reaction has been referred to as the **fight-or-flight response** (Cannon, 1932). What happens when faced with a potential threat? According to Cannon, the body prepares you either to fight or to leave the scene. It has also been noted that some animals also "freeze" or "play dead" when faced with an attack. Cannon's work emphasized the sympathetic nervous system and the role of epinephrine and norepinephrine in the stress response.

The stress response is accomplished by a variety of interacting systems that include the amygdala and other cortical systems, which results in the hypothalamus activating the sympathetic nervous system and the HPA axis. In general, stress reduces our ability to think and plan while increasing our emotional responses.

In terms of psychopathology, the HPA axis has been linked to anxiety and depression (Lamers et al., 2013). HPA axis overactivity has been seen in individuals with more severe forms of depression. As shown in Figure 7.3, the response to short-term stress results in the production of cortisol and the secretion of CRH and ACTH. Short-term stress also suppresses the immune system and makes energy available. With depression, the mechanisms involved in the HPA axis are disrupted and the normal stress response is not present.

The HPA axis has also been associated with the development of psychosis in adolescence (Walker et al., 2005). Elaine Walker and colleagues noted that four lines of research exist showing that HPA dysregulation is involved in vulnerability for psychosis. First, behavioral studies have shown that clinical symptoms can be exacerbated by exposure to stress. Second, medical disorders such as Cushing's, which involves elevated levels of cortisol, are associated with increased risk for psychosis. Third, unmedicated patients with psychosis show abnormalities in the HPA axis and a positive correlation between cortisol levels and symptoms. Fourth and finally, the hippocampus, which plays a role in regulating the HPA axis, is shown to be smaller in patients with psychosis. Reduced hippocampal volume is seen early in the development of psychosis.

The Autonomic Nervous System

The function of the **autonomic nervous system (ANS)** is threefold. The first task is to maintain homeostatic conditions within the body. This keeps the processing of internal functions, such as heart rate and blood pressure, in balance. The second task is to coordinate the body's response to exercise and

FIGURE 7.3 ■ The Hypothalamus-Pituitary-Adrenal Axis

The amygdala signals a stressful condition to the hypothalamus (1), which stimulates the adrenal medulla (2), which then releases epinephrine and norepinephrine into the bloodstream (3), enabling the fight-or-flight response. The hypothalamus activates the hypothalamus–pituitary–adrenal axis by secreting CRH (corticotropin-releasing hormone) via the portal to the pituitary gland (4), causing the pituitary to release ACTH (adrenocorticotropic hormone) into the bloodstream (5). The adrenal cortex releases cortisol into the bloodstream, producing physiological stress responses (6). Cortisol also provides negative feedback, moderating the stress response (7).

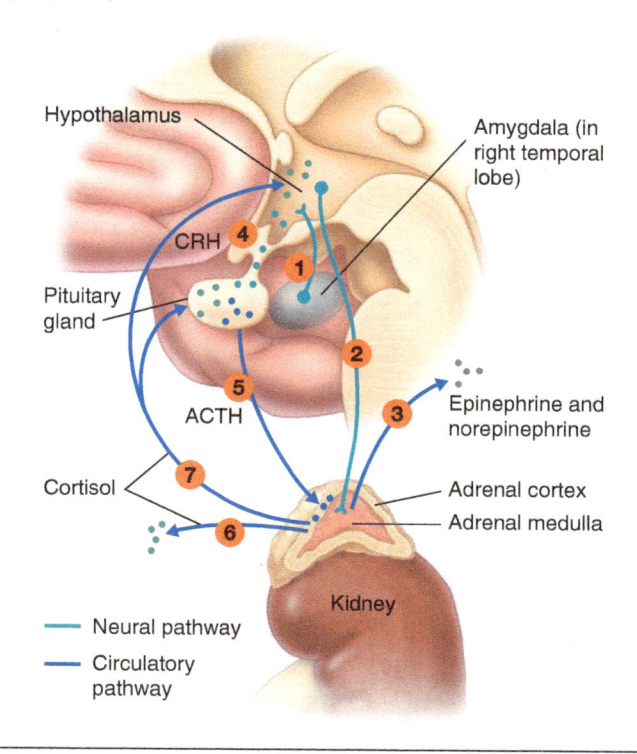

Carolina Hrejsa/Body Scientific Intl.

stress, which is the function that will be emphasized in this chapter. The third task involves helping the endocrine system regulate reproduction.

The ANS is generally discussed in terms of the **sympathetic division** and the **parasympathetic division**. As can be seen in Figure 7.4, the sympathetic division connects with its target organs through the middle part of the spinal cord. The sympathetic division is responsible for the fight-or-flight response. This emergency response produces resources for the body to energize. As such, its connections are *adrenergic*, as they produce the adrenaline reaction of energizing the body. In general, the sympathetic system produces a continuous influence on the organ it innervates. This is referred to as sympathetic tone.

The parasympathetic system, on the other hand, is involved in the restoration of bodily reserves and the elimination of bodily waste. It connects through the upper and lower parts of the spinal cord. Its connections are *cholinergic*, which involves acetylcholine. These reactions are generally a reduction of activity and a process of bringing the body back to a state of *homeostasis*. It should be noted that although the sympathetic and parasympathetic systems are often seen to function in an opposite manner, the actual relationship between the two is much more complicated (Berntson et al., 1991, 1993).

What we have seen thus far are the various systems that have evolved to help the body manage changes within the environment. Humans make predictions about what to expect. When we see something we did not expect, such as a bear in the woods, our body through these systems prepares us to protect ourselves by leaving the situation or staying and fighting. If the unexpected continues to occur, we experience it as psychological stress. This can result in negative reactions in these systems that can lead to psychological disorders. The next section will describe some of the ways that psychological stress has been studied and move the discussion to the level of the person.

FIGURE 7.4 ■ How Do the Sympathetic and Parasympathetic Aspects of the ANS Influence Our Body?

The sympathetic and parasympathetic branches of the autonomic nervous system (ANS) influence internal organs in complementary ways.

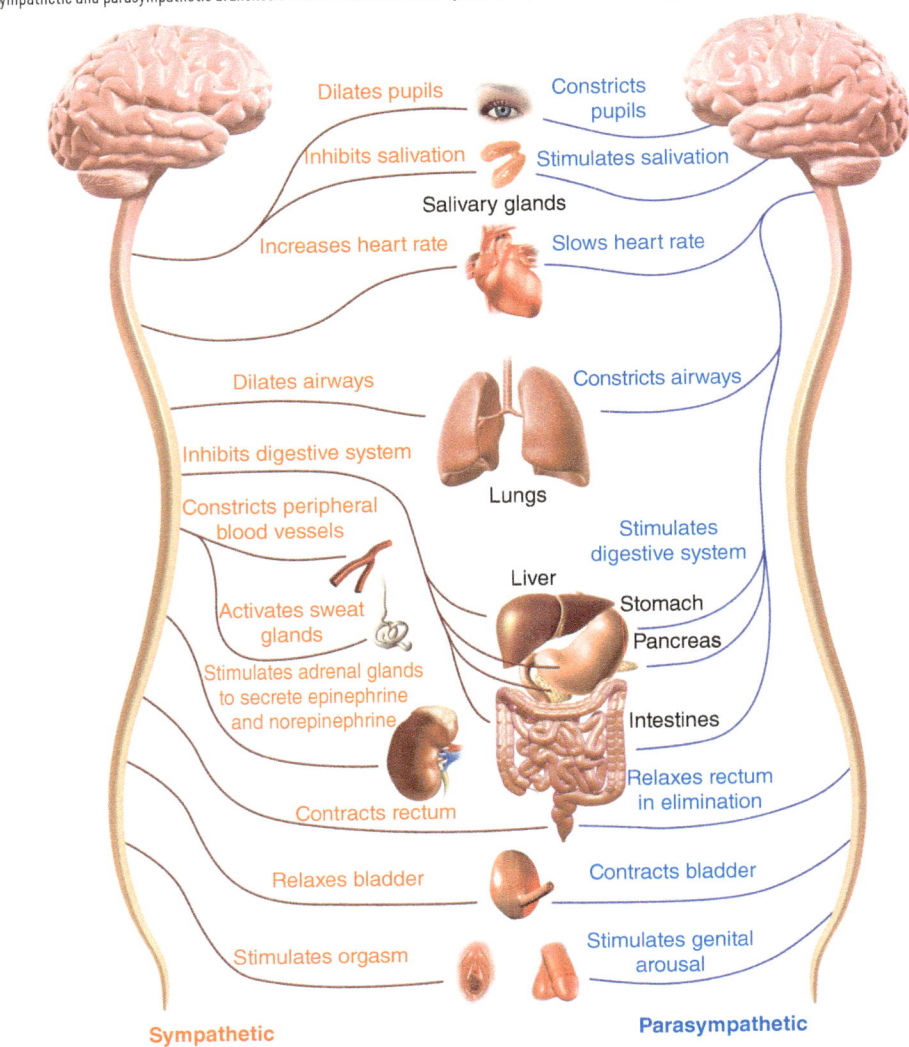

Sympathetic	Parasympathetic
Dilates pupils	Constricts pupils
Inhibits salivation	Stimulates salivation
Increases heart rate	Slows heart rate
Dilates airways	Constricts airways
Inhibits digestive system	Stimulates digestive system
Constricts peripheral blood vessels	
Activates sweat glands	
Stimulates adrenal glands to secrete epinephrine and norepinephrine	
Contracts rectum	Relaxes rectum in elimination
Relaxes bladder	Contracts bladder
Stimulates orgasm	Stimulates genital arousal

Psychological Stress and the Immune System

Imagine that you are ending your first year in medical school, and it is time to take a series of final exams. Clearly, this is a stressor for most students. How do you think taking exams will affect your **immune system** and your experience of psychological distress? To answer this question, Janice Kiecolt-Glaser and her colleagues (1984) took blood samples and gave psychological inventories a month before the exams and on the day of the exams. What they found was that compared with the previous month, the immune system was more suppressed on the day of the exam. This is consistent with the finding that students often get sick or have mouth or lip sores at the end of the term. They also found that the students reported more anxiety, depression, and bodily concerns on the day of the exam. Overall, this suggests that even relatively mild stress in the form of exams can change immune function and cause psychological distress. Since this classic study was performed, we have learned much more about the immune system.

The immune system evolved to help organisms protect themselves from pathogens. The protective mechanisms involved in immune function appear to be some of the earliest to have evolved. Basic reflexes such as sneezing, coughing, and crying are additional mechanisms for removing pathogens before they can enter the body. If pathogens do enter the body, then there are a number of layers of immune function to deal with them.

One important task of the immune system is to determine what is foreign and what cells are part of the self. Foreign substances include bacteria, viruses, and parasites that enter our system and are detected by the immune system. Antibodies that are produced by our immune system can detect literally millions of different foreign substances and engage in a process that hopefully leads to their destruction. Our immune system has evolved to recognize a variety of pathogens. It is also capable of learning the characteristics of new pathogens and attacking them upon later exposure. This, of course, is the basic mechanism through which immunizations work.

The immune system comes into play both in terms of specific pathogens such as viruses and also in terms of stress. At one time, the immune system was viewed as a separate system that functioned independently. However, since the 1970s a variety of studies have demonstrated that the immune system is influenced by the brain and vice versa (Villani et al., 2018; Zefferino et al., 2020) and that the immune system is also influenced by the biome in the gut (Yu et al., 2022). In particular, it has been shown that psychological stress can influence the immune system such that the organism is more likely to become ill. Robert Ader (2007) was also able to show that the immune system could be classically conditioned. These types of studies helped to create the field of *psychoneuroimmunology* (Kemeny & Schedlowski, 2007).

Psychoneuroimmunology is the study of how psychological factors can influence the immune system. One meta-analysis of more than 300 studies showed that stress in the form of loss or trauma suppresses the immune system (Segerstrom & Miller, 2004). Other research suggests that negative emotions can change immune responses and delay healing (Kiecolt-Glaser et al., 2002). Some of the psychological factors that can influence the immune system include loneliness, poor social support, negative mood, disruption of marital relationships, bereavement, and natural disasters (Cohen & Herbert, 1996). Factors such as close friendships, which reduce negative emotions, enhance immune system functioning (Kiecolt-Glaser et al., 2010). It has also become apparent that not only does experience influence the immune system, but the immune system can also influence the brain and thus behavior.

A relatively recent finding is that the immune system can be involved in mental illness (Flux & Lowry, 2023). We all know that infections can leave us feeling sick and experiencing low energy levels. One type of cell involved in this process is a protein called a cytokine. What is striking to some scientists is that the symptoms associated with sickness and those associated with depression are similar. With both sickness and depression, the person withdraws from interactions with others and does not actively seek new experiences. These individuals also do not respond to positive experiences or rewards.

There is now evidence that cytokines can lead certain individuals to develop certain types of depression (Dantzer, 2012; Dantzer et al., 2008; Himmerich et al., 2019). What makes this relationship complicated is that in some studies, the inflammation precedes depression, whereas in others, the opposite is the case. That is, individuals with clinical depression show inflammatory biomarkers in their bloodstream. Other studies have shown that immune cells in the brains of individuals with autism are more active, resulting in increased inflammation (Pardo et al., 2005). Inflammation has also been associated with schizophrenia (Khandaker et al., 2015). Clearly, researchers who study psychopathology now must also consider the immune system. Current research is indeed beginning to focus on stress, the immune system, and psychopathology.

Trauma Changes Our Genes Through Tagging (Epigenetics)

Let's briefly review the nature of epigenetics as related to stress (Murphy & Heller, 2022). Instead of actually changing the gene itself, epigenetic modifications tag a gene. This alters how the gene is turned on and off. As you may recall from Chapter 2, deoxyribonucleic acid (DNA) is wrapped around clusters of proteins called histones. These are further bundled into structures called chromosomes. Being tightly packed keeps genes in an inactive state by preventing access to processes that turn genes on. When action is needed, a section of DNA unfurls and the gene turns on. Whether a segment is relaxed, therefore able to be activated, or condensed, which results in no action, is influenced by epigenetic marks. As a tag, histone acetylation tends to promote gene activity and is called a writer. Histone methylation and DNA methylation tend to inhibit it and are called erasers.

The environment can influence these writer and eraser tags. Tags help an organism respond to a changing environment. Some tags last a short time, whereas others can last a lifetime. In studies, researchers observed that some rat mothers display high levels of nurturing behavior, licking and grooming their pups, whereas others are less diligent (Miller, 2010; Weaver et al., 2004). Behaviorally, the offspring of the more active mothers were less anxious and produced less stress hormone when disturbed than pups cared for by more passive mothers. Further, the females raised by nurturing mothers became nurturing mothers themselves.

In terms of stress, those rat pups raised by less nurturing mothers became more sensitive to stress throughout their lives. When confined to a Plexiglas tube that restricted their movement, they produced more of the stress hormone cortisol. If the mouse mother lacks access to basic needs, then she shows difficulty making nests and spends less time with the young (Roth & Sweatt, 2011). This, in turn, is related to the methylation of the genes, which is passed on to the next generation. Other research found that mice raised by multiple mothers, which is the norm for mice in the wild, show better social adjustment as adults. These mothers also spend more time with their own daughters, and this shows an association with oxytocin receptors (Curley et al., 2009).

There are suggestions that similar mechanisms may be at work in terms of human stress (Murphy & Heiler, 2022). In one of the first studies to examine the effects on offspring of intimate partner violence during pregnancy, Radtke and associates (2011) found changes in epigenetic factors. Examining human mothers and their children 10 to 19 years after birth, DNA methylation of the gene associated with the stress hormone cortisol was seen in the children whose mothers had experienced partner violence during pregnancy. Children whose mothers did not experience partner violence or those whose mothers experienced partner violence before or after pregnancy did not show the effect. Overall, this suggests that mothers' experiences during pregnancy can have long-term epigenetic effects on their children. Although the epigenetic mechanisms were previously unknown, a number of earlier studies showed that children of mothers who experienced psychological stress during pregnancy were more likely to experience anxiety and depression in their life (Huizink et al., 2004).

Another study examined the brains of individuals who had died by suicide (McGowan et al., 2009). These researchers were interested in the question of whether the brains of those who had been abused differed in epigenetic factors from those who had not. What they found was that those individuals who had experienced childhood abuse showed more methyl groups on the stress gene receptor involved with cortisol. This was not the case with individuals who died by suicide but were not abused or a control

Like other species, affection in humans may lead to less stress in adulthood.
iStock.com/Bartosz Hadyniak

group who did not attempt suicide. Overall, initial evidence suggests that childhood abuse can have a long-term epigenetic effect. This illustrates the manner in which action on one level—in this case, the behavioral level—can result in changes in other levels, such as the molecular one.

A variety of recent studies have considered the possibility that epigenetic changes such as DNA methylation and histone modification are involved in mental illness (Iwamoto & Kato, 2009; Murphy & Heller, 2022). At this point, the strongest evidence for epigenetic mechanisms relates to schizophrenia and bipolar disorder, although the mental disorder research suggests anxiety, depression, and addiction can also be related. However, there is still much research to be performed to describe the pathways from psychological stress to psychopathology (Albert, 2010).

Is Social Pain Like Physical Pain?

Over evolutionary time, our physiological and psychological systems have evolved to protect us in a variety of situations as well as to offer mechanisms for sexual and social encounters. One of the most important of these protections is the pain system, which alerts individuals to tissue or nerve damage or times in which our physiological systems are not functioning normally. Muscle pains and headaches are clear examples of these situations.

What about social pain? Rejection and loss of loved ones, for example, are some of the most painful experiences for humans. What is interesting is that over evolutionary time, the processing of social pain appears to have co-opted the basic brain structures involved in physical pain (Eisenberger & Lieberman, 2004; Panksepp, 1998). Linguistically, to refer to emotional pain we use some of the same phrases as with physical pain. We say we have a broken heart or that our feelings are hurt. The impetus for a system to detect and prevent social separation would have developed in childhood to keep the infant close to their mother.

Pain research suggests that there are two separate components to the experience of pain. The first is the sensory experience itself, and the second is the felt unpleasantness (Price, 2000). The sensory experience involves the somatosensory cortex and the posterior insula. The experienced unpleasantness is associated with the anterior cingulate cortex (ACC). It is the second system that appears to be altered in psychopathology and is most sensitive to psychological factors.

Research has shown that in both physical and social pain, the ACC plays a critical role (Eisenberger & Lieberman, 2004). An intact ACC is required for young animals to emit distress sounds when separated from their caregivers. It is also the case that an intact ACC is required for caregivers to show affiliative behaviors. With humans, playing a video game in which the person felt exclusion was associated with ACC activity. Further, the magnitude of the ACC activity correlated with the self-report of social distress. Those with borderline personality disorder, as will be described in Chapter 14, experience this rejection more acutely than other individuals. Additional evidence for the relationship between physical pain and social pain is that an increase in one type of pain also produces an increased sensitivity to the other type of pain. Comforting experiences such as social support will also reduce sensitivity to physical pain. This has implications for the treatment of psychological disorders.

CONCEPT CHECK

- Our physiological reactions to stress and trauma occur on a variety of levels. What are five important levels?
- There is evidence that the immune system is influenced by the brain and vice versa. What is an example where the brain influences the immune system? What is an example where the immune system influences the brain?
- What are the two pathways of the stress response that we have evolved to save us from threats such as bears? What are some of the effects of the stress response for psychopathology?
- What are the functions and structure of the ANS?
- Describe an example of how trauma can lead to epigenetic changes.
- In what respects is social pain like physical pain?

THE STUDY OF STRESS

One of the major figures in stress research was the Hungarian endocrinologist Hans Selye, who worked at the University of Montreal. It was actually Selye who coined the term *stress* in 1936, borrowing the word from physics. In physics, stress refers to the strain placed on a material. Selye used the term as a way of organizing physiological responses to a variety of challenges, including heat, cold, pain, noise, hard work, and so forth. One of Selye's early findings was that the body reacts similarly to a variety of these different stressors. Selye called this response the general adaptation syndrome (GAS). The GAS was seen to involve three stages. The first was the alarm stage. The alarm stage was an initial reaction to the stress that involved an increase in adrenal activity as well as sympathetic nervous system reactions such as increased heart rate. The second stage was the resistance stage. This stage represents an adjustment to the stress that includes the availability of additional energy resources and mechanisms for fighting infection and tissue damage. The third stage was the exhaustion stage in which bodily resources are depleted. One of the paradoxes that Selye recognized was that the physiological stress responses that protect and restore the body can also damage it. However, Selye also reported that repeated exposure to a particular stress situation could also increase the organism's ability to withstand that same stress in greater amounts.

More recently, Bruce McEwen has begun to address the paradoxical nature of the stress response (McEwen, 2010; McEwen et al., 2015). He began by suggesting part of the problem in understanding stress is the ambiguous meaning of the term *stress*. He suggested that the term be replaced with the term *allostasis*. Allostasis refers to the body's ability to achieve stability through change. That is, the brain perceives and adapts to stressful situations. In doing so, the brain determines what is threatening, remembers these situations, and produces stress reactions. This can be either physical or social stress. Brain processes can achieve stability in a number of different ways. A complex set of interactions in our bodies occurs in response to stress; these interactions use the autonomic nervous system, cortisol, our metabolic system, and our immune system to attempt to achieve stability.

Allostatic systems are thus systems designed to adapt to change. Change traditionally related to stress for humans takes on a broad range of possibilities, including dangerous situations, being in crowded and unpleasant environments, getting an infection, and performing in front of others. Some researchers even suggest that stress may be greater for humans than other animals, since we are also able to use our cognitive abilities to increase the experience of stress through imagination.

The overall stress response involves two tasks for the body. The first is to turn on the allostatic response that initiates a complex adaptive pathway. Some examples of this are the *fight-or-flight response* and the *tend-and-befriend response*, which will be described shortly. Once the danger has passed, the second task needs to be initiated—turning off these responses. A variety of research suggests that prolonged exposure to stress may not allow these two mechanisms to function correctly and in turn leads to a variety of physiological problems. This cumulative wear and tear on the body by responding to stressful conditions is called allostatic load.

Allostatic load has been discussed by McEwen (1998) in terms of four particular situations. The first situation reflects the fact that allostatic load can be increased by frequent exposure to stressors. These stressors can be both physical and psychological in nature. A variety of psychological studies have shown an association between worry, daily hassles, and negative health outcomes. One of the most studied areas is cardiovascular risk factors, with stress showing a strong association with heart attacks and the development of atherosclerosis.

The second condition for the increase in allostatic load is where an individual does not adapt or habituate to the repeated occurrence of a particular stressor. Some people, for example, continue to show major physiological responses to everyday situations like driving a long distance or taking an airline flight, even though the data suggest there is limited risk in these situations. Asking individuals to talk before a group also induces stress-like responses in many individuals.

The third situation reflects the fact that not all individuals respond the same to changing situations. In particular, some individuals show a slower return to a non-challenge physiological condition once the initial threat is removed. These individuals appear to be more at risk for developing health-related conditions. Some researchers suggest that high blood pressure is associated with a normal stress response not being turned off.

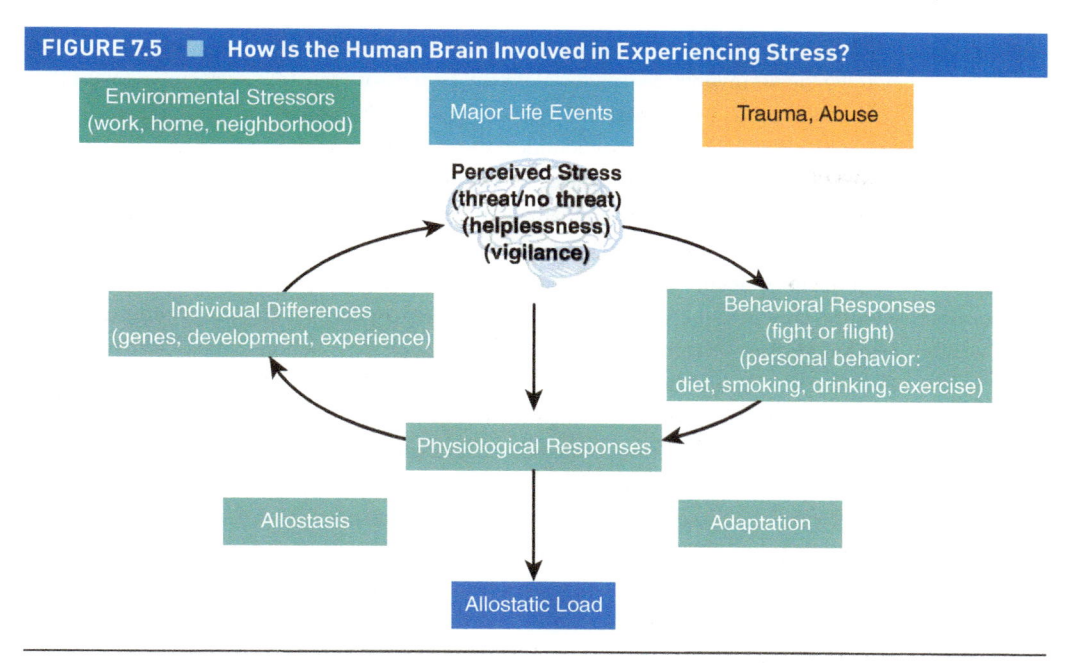

FIGURE 7.5 ■ How Is the Human Brain Involved in Experiencing Stress?

- Environmental Stressors (work, home, neighborhood)
- Major Life Events
- Trauma, Abuse

→ Perceived Stress (threat/no threat) (helplessness) (vigilance)

- Individual Differences (genes, development, experience)
- Behavioral Responses (fight or flight) (personal behavior: diet, smoking, drinking, exercise)
- Physiological Responses
- Allostasis
- Adaptation
- Allostatic Load

Source: Bruce McEwen, The Rockefeller University Laboratory of Neuroendocrinology.

The fourth and final condition discussed by McEwen reflects the situation in which a nonresponse to stress produces an overreaction in another system. That is, if one system does not respond adequately to stress, then activation of another system would be required to provide the necessary counterregulation and return the system to homeostasis. Overall, McEwen emphasized the important question of individual differences and the variety of ways in which perceived stress can influence future health (McEwen, 2013; McEwen et al., 2015). His graphic depiction of the allostatic system is seen in Figure 7.5.

What is less well known is that stressful events activate the same immune and brain circuits as do infections (L. R. Watkins & Maier, 2002). Why is this so? What Watkins and Maier suggested is that the immune system first evolved to be sensitive to pathogens, such as those associated with disease or the common cold. In evolutionary time, the immune system is seen to have evolved before such responses as fight or flight, since all organisms have mechanisms for dealing with pathogens.

Does Fight or Flight Apply Equally to Males and Females?

The fight-or-flight response is seen as a critical mechanism for responding to stress. The problem for current-day humans is that many of the stressors we face do not require a fighting or fleeing response. For example, imagine that you are working in a large company where there are rumors that a number of people are being laid off. Your manager calls you into the office. Your initial response is probably to feel stress, as you could be the next to be fired. As you go in, you can feel your heart pounding. At this point, your manager says, "You have been doing a great job, and I want to ask your opinion on another project." The threat is gone, but your body is still reacting. This fight-or-flight reaction has been critical throughout our evolutionary history, but today, in our different social structure, it may lead to stress-related disorders.

In many ways, males and females have had different evolutionary pressures on them, influencing the manner in which they respond to various challenges. After examining a variety of studies, Shelley Taylor and her colleagues (2000) suggested that the fight-or-flight response better describes a human male's response to stress rather than a female's. For females, they suggested a better descriptor is the tend-and-befriend response. What did they mean by this? First, they noted that, over evolutionary time, females have evolved behaviors that maximize the survival of both themselves and their offspring. Second, when stressed, females respond by nurturing offspring as well as displaying behaviors that protect them from harm. These tending behaviors have also been shown to reduce the presence of stress hormones in infants. Third, like fight or flight, these behaviors are associated with particular neuroendocrine responses, although different hormones are involved. These responses make up the *tending response.* The tending response activated by stress is seen as part of the larger attachment process. The *befriending response* involves a large social group. Females under stress seek contact with their social group, which is also protective in survival terms.

What is intriguing is that the basic neuroendocrine responses to stress appear to be similar in males and females (Taylor et al., 2002). It is initially a sympathetic response, as described previously. However, what is different is that these hormones affect males and females differently. Human males show the sympathetic response of activation and increased arousal, which can lead to aggression—the fight part of fight or flight. The male brain appears to be organized to give aggressive responses in the presence of substances such as testosterone that are less present in the female brain. What is present in the female brain is the hormone *oxytocin*, which is released in larger amounts in females compared with males. Oxytocin has been found in a variety of animal studies to reduce anxiety and calm the organism. According to Taylor and her colleagues, oxytocin leads females to quiet and calm down offspring in response to stress. Thus, whereas males are seen to produce more sympathetic-like responses to stress, females show more parasympathetic-like responses. Oxytocin is seen to lie at the basis of these responses for females—the tend-and-befriend response.

Additional support for the presence of gender differences in response to stress has come from the work of Repetti (1989). She examined the behaviors of fathers and mothers following a stressful workday. Whereas fathers tended to isolate themselves at home following stress, mothers tended to be more nurturing and caring toward their children. Further, similar differences are found in larger social networks, where stressed females tend to seek out other women for comfort and support. Compared with females, males seek support from same-sex friends less often. A variety of anthropological studies suggest that males and females form groups for different purposes. Male groups tend to be larger and directed at well-defined tasks such as defense. Female groups tend to be smaller and carry with them social and emotional connections to a greater degree.

Why did researchers initially not see differences in male and female responses to stress? The answer is simple. During most of the 20th century, females were not studied in this research. Even the animal studies typically used males. Once females were studied more intensely, these differences emerged. If you think about it, you can see that these stress response differences are consistent with mating differences and investment in the care of offspring. That is to say, given that the female typically has a greater role in caring for offspring, her response to stress should not jeopardize herself or her offspring as might be the case with fleeing or fighting.

Females under stress seek contact with their social group, which is also protective in survival terms.

iStock.com/ljubaphoto

What we now know is that gender differences in the stress response can be found at all stages of life (Bale & Epperson, 2015). During pregnancy, males in the womb are at greater risk for maternal and environmental stress. During childhood, negative events increase the risk in women for later affective disorders such as anxiety and depression. Different experiences of stress are also seen in females in different phases of their menstrual cycle. In aging, women also show greater cortisol responses to stress-related stimuli than men do. However, after menopause, the rate of affective disorders is similar for males and females.

Does Social Stress Produce a Similar Reaction to Physical Stress?

Not only does our stress system respond when we are faced with threatening situations from our environment, but it also responds to challenges in our social world (Flinn, 2008). Just being asked to stand up and talk in front of a group of people will produce characteristic stress responses along with the experience of anxiety. Given the social nature of human beings, it is not unreasonable to assume threats to our social system would be important.

However, the evolutionary link that connects social challenges with the stress system for life-and-death situations is less well understood. One would assume that as with many other evolutionary processes, nature used systems already available. Flinn (2008) reviews the idea that the adaptive value of the social stress response begins in childhood. Studies across a variety of species have shown that early exposure to stress will modify how the stress response is expressed in later life. Typically, childhood stress is associated with poorer health outcomes in adulthood (Finlay et al., 2022). It appears that children who experience trauma in the form of abuse, the death of a parent, or divorce show larger stress responses to social stress later in life. Depression is one disorder whose presence can be increased by these prior experiences. PTSD and dissociative disorders result from a more direct pathway with psychological stress and trauma. It is not the case, however, that early physical stress such as experiencing hurricanes or political upheaval in one's country results in a differential stress response. In the next section, stress-related disorders will be described.

CONCEPT CHECK

- According to McEwen, the overall stress response involves two tasks for the body. What are they? What are the impacts of prolonged stress on these mechanisms?
- How is the tend-and-befriend response different from the fight-or-flight response?
- Does social stress produce a similar reaction to physical stress? What factors would you cite in support of your answer?

ADJUSTMENT DISORDERS, ACUTE STRESS DISORDER, AND PROLONGED GRIEF DISORDER

There are several disorders in *DSM-5-TR* that result from the experience of stress. The three most significant of these are **adjustment disorders, acute stress disorder**, and **post-traumatic stress disorder (PTSD)**. We will discuss the first two disorders along with prolonged grief disorder, a disorder newly categorized in the *DSM-5-TR*, in this section of the chapter. The next section is devoted to PTSD.

The severity of the stressor is the least in adjustment disorder and the greatest in PTSD. In fact, an adjustment disorder does not require the experience of a traumatic event but only an event experienced as distressing. An acute stress disorder was originally conceived as a shorter-term reaction to stress, and the stress may be non-traumatic in nature. In PTSD, symptoms must exist for more than a month, whereas an adjustment disorder or acute stress disorder can be diagnosed immediately following a distressing experience. An adjustment disorder does not require specific symptoms but more global distress within 3 months after a stressful event. The requirement for an adjustment disorder is that the reaction to the event is out of proportion to the severity of the stressor. Acute stress disorder and PTSD do require specific symptoms.

Although the stress-related disorders other than PTSD have not been studied extensively in terms of treatment, data suggest that psychotherapy presented early can reduce the development of PTSD (Bryant et al., 2011). One difficult question is how to distinguish a normal stress reaction from an acute stress disorder. It should be noted that a stress reaction should be treated only in those asking for treatment. In studies looking at trauma, requiring workers to be part of a treatment session actually made matters worse (Ehlers & Clark, 2003). This suggests that the timing of when the treatment begins after the trauma is important.

Adjustment Disorders

Everyone reacts when things do not go as expected, like the loss of a job, a breakup with a significant other, or losing money in a business relationship. Natural disasters such as a tree falling on your house or your basement flooding from strong rains create an emotional reaction. Emotional reactions can also be associated with long-term conditions, such as living in a difficult neighborhood or living with a physical disability. These are examples that are upsetting. However, when individuals' reactions to such events are out of proportion to the severity of the event, it can be considered an adjustment disorder. The reaction to the event may also interfere with social functioning and job performance. A diagnosis of adjustment disorder requires that the reaction to the stressful event happen within 3 months of the event's occurrence and that the reaction not last for longer than 6 months.

Although formal epidemiological studies for adjustment disorders are rarer than for other disorders such as anxiety or depression, these disorders are thought to be common within the mental health system. They are estimated to represent up to 20% of those seeking mental health treatment and about 7.1% for inpatients (Jones et al., 2002). Rates of these disorders are slightly higher in women than men (approximately 60% to 40%, respectively). Adjustment disorders are fairly prevalent, but there is little research concerning empirically supported therapies. In general, the same treatments used for anxiety as well as PTSD are used with adjustment disorders. These include both psychosocial therapy and antianxiety medications. These will be described in more depth in the section concerning PTSD in this chapter and in Chapter 8, which focuses on anxiety.

Acute Stress Disorder

Acute stress disorder is a short-term reaction to traumatic events that lasts from 3 days to 1 month. If the clinical symptoms continue past this period, the disorder would be described as PTSD. Like PTSD, the trauma can include events such as war experiences; physical attack; muggings; terrorist attacks; torture; physical and sexual abuse; transportation accidents; and natural disasters, such as hurricanes, fires, and earthquakes. Acute stress disorder can also occur from watching traumatic events happen to another person.

Clinical symptoms following the trauma are described in terms of five categories. The first category, intrusion, can include such symptoms as involuntary distressing memories, distressing dreams, and flashbacks. The second category, negative mood, includes the inability to experience happiness. The third category is dissociative symptoms, such as feeling in a fog or being unable to remember important aspects of the trauma. The fourth category is avoidance symptoms. These symptoms include avoiding situations, people, and places that remind one of the trauma. The fifth category is arousal symptoms. These include sleep disturbance, angry outbursts, showing extreme vigilance, problems with concentration, and a sensitivity to events that cause a startle. A given individual may show symptoms in a limited number or all of these five categories. These specific symptoms are shown in Table 7.1.

The prevalence of acute stress disorder varies in terms of type of trauma (APA, 2013, 2022). The highest rates (19%–50%) are seen with interpersonal traumatic events such as personally experiencing assault, rape, or a mass shooting. Prevalence rates are lower for those events that do not involve interpersonal assault. These include being part of a motor vehicle accident (13%–21%), being burned severely (10%), being part of an assault (19%), and being involved in an industrial accident (6%–12%). Overall, the prevalence is higher for women than men. On an individual level, a number of factors, including negative appraisals of the trauma, high trait anxiety, showing signs of depression, suicide risk, and not being married or employed, have been associated with greater severity of acute stress symptoms.

TABLE 7.1 ■ *DSM-5-TR* Diagnostic Criteria for Acute Stress Disorder

A. Exposure to actual or threatened death, serious injury, or sexual violence in one (or more) of the following ways:
   1. Directly experiencing the traumatic event(s).
   2. Witnessing, in person, the event(s) as it occurred to others.
   3. Learning that the event(s) occurred to a close family member or close friend. **Note:** In cases of actual or threatened death of a family member or friend, the event(s) must have been violent or accidental.
   4. Experiencing repeated or extreme exposure to aversive details of the traumatic event(s) (e.g., first responders collecting human remains, police officers repeatedly exposed to details of child abuse).

   Note: This does not apply to exposure through electronic media, television, movies, or pictures, unless this exposure is work related.

B. Presence of nine (or more) of the following symptoms from any of the five categories of intrusion, negative mood, dissociation, avoidance, and arousal, beginning or worsening after the traumatic events occurred:

Intrusion Symptoms

1. Recurrent, involuntary, and intrusive distressing memories of the traumatic event(s). **Note:** In children, repetitive play may occur in which themes or aspects of the traumatic event(s) are expressed.
2. Recurrent distressing dreams in which the content and/or affect of the dream are related to the event(s). **Note:** In children, there may be frightening dreams without recognizable content.
3. Dissociative reactions (e.g., flashbacks) in which the individual feels or acts as if the traumatic event(s) were recurring. (Such reactions may occur on a continuum, with the most extreme expression being a complete loss of awareness of present surroundings.) **Note:** In children, trauma-specific reenactment may occur in play.
4. Intense or prolonged psychological distress or marked physiological reactions in response to internal or external cues that symbolize or resemble an aspect of the traumatic event(s).

Negative Mood

5. Persistent inability to experience positive emotions (e.g., inability to experience happiness, satisfaction, or loving feelings).

Dissociative Symptoms

6. An altered sense of the reality of one's surroundings or oneself (e.g., seeing oneself from another's perspective, being in a daze, time slowing).
7. Inability to remember an important aspect of the traumatic event(s) (typically due to dissociative amnesia and not to other factors such as head injury, alcohol, or drugs).

Avoidance Symptoms

8. Efforts to avoid distressing memories, thoughts, or feelings about or closely associated with the traumatic event(s).
9. Efforts to avoid external reminders (people, places, conversations, activities, objects, situations) that arouse distressing memories, thoughts, or feelings about or closely associated with the traumatic event(s).

Arousal Symptoms

10. Sleep disturbance (e.g., difficulty falling or staying asleep, restless sleep).
11. Irritable behavior and angry outbursts (with little or no provocation), typically expressed as verbal or physical aggression toward people or objects.
12. Hypervigilance.
13. Problems with concentration.
14. Exaggerated startle response.

C. Duration of the disturbance (symptoms in Criterion B) is 3 days to 1 month after trauma exposure.
   Note: Symptoms typically begin immediately after the trauma, but persistence for at least 3 days and up to a month is needed to meet disorder criteria.

D. The disturbance causes clinically significant distress or impairment in social, occupational, or other important areas of functioning.

E. The disturbance is not attributable to the physiological effects of a substance (e.g., medication or alcohol) or another medical condition (e.g., mild traumatic brain injury) and is not better explained by brief psychotic disorder.

Credit: Reprinted with permission from the *Diagnostic and Statistical Manual of Mental Disorders, fifth edition, text revision*, DSM-V-TR, pp. 313–315. (Copyright © 2022). American Psychiatric Association. All Rights Reserved.

Heavy rains can flood streets in an unexpected manner, causing stress and potentially leading to trauma.
iStock.com/danikancil

However, when these are considered using regression analysis, only high trait anxiety, suicide risk, and trauma appraisal significantly predicted severity of symptoms (Suliman et al., 2013).

The acute stress disorder diagnosis was introduced in *DSM-IV*. This diagnosis helped to identify individuals who showed stress reactions in a short time after an experience of trauma. It was also seen as a set of criteria that would help to identify those who go on to develop PTSD. Changes were made in the *DSM-5* criteria and continued with *DSM-5-TR* for acute stress disorder, and these have been shown to identify those who will later develop PTSD (Bryant et al., 2015). As you will see in *LENS: Does Debriefing Help Prevent PTSD?* one important line of research has involved the search for ways to prevent PTSD from developing in people who experience stress and trauma.

LENS

DOES DEBRIEFING HELP PREVENT PTSD?

Our common sense tells us that the quicker we can intervene with someone who experiences trauma, the better the results will be. After the terrorist attacks on the World Trade Center on September 11, 2001, more than 9,000 counselors went to New York City (McNally et al., 2003). These mental health professionals assumed that those who experienced the attack, including rescue workers, would be at high risk for developing PTSD. Although sites for mental health counseling were set up around the city, few people actually sought help. In fact, only around 650,000 individuals sought help, whereas counselors expected to treat 2.5 million. Some professionals said that New Yorkers were in denial. Others said that there would be a delayed reaction and PTSD would come later. One survey followed up on a sample of New Yorkers at 1 month, 4 months, and 6 months following 9/11 (Galea et al., 2003). This study found the relative prevalence of PTSD to be 7.5% at 1 month, 1.7% at 4 months, and .06% at 6 months. This suggests a rapid recovery in terms of PTSD following 9/11. Other studies have also shown a steep decline in PTSD symptoms after a traumatic event or serving in a war zone around a year later (North et al., 1999).

This raised the question of whether psychological interventions directed at everyone following a traumatic event are necessary. Since the 1980s, one common form of intervention was a *critical incident stress debriefing* (Mitchell, 1983). Initially introduced as a single-session technique to help rescue workers, this strategy has since been used throughout the world. The basic procedure was to discuss the rescue worker's psychological, cognitive, and emotional reactions to the event. This session was conducted within a few days of the exposure. Although well received by most workers, the overall evidence suggests that the intervention is not effective in reducing the incidence of future PTSD (Rose et al., 2002). Thus, many international organizations such as the Red Cross no longer require debriefing for all workers. However, they offer services for those who seek them.

The current approach is to offer information and coping skills to those rescue workers who seek help. The emphasis is on helping the person to cope rather than reexperience the situation. However, services are offered to those who show signs of trauma-related disorders. Those in distress are treated by professional mental health workers. We will explore their experience in the treatment section of this chapter.

Thought Question

What services are offered at your college for students who have experienced trauma?

Prolonged Grief Disorder

As discussed in Chapter 6, *DSM-5-TR* added a category of **prolonged grief disorder** (Prigerson, Kakarala, et al., 2021). It is also present in *ICD-11*. This disorder represents a prolonged maladaptive grief reaction. Characteristics of the disorder include intense yearning or longing for the deceased person. Preoccupation with thoughts and memories of the deceased person can also be present. Specific symptoms can also include disbelief about the death, intense emotional pain, intense loneliness, feeling that life is meaningless without the person, and other such factors. It is diagnosed after at least 12 months have elapsed since the death of someone with whom the person had a close relationship. The presence of prolonged grief disorder is stable over time and different from PTSD, major depressive disorder, and generalized anxiety disorder (Prigerson, Boelen, et al., 2021).

The prevalence of prolonged grief disorder was 1.2% using *DSM-5-TR* criteria and 1.5% using *ICD-11* criteria in the general population (Rosner et al., 2021). It was higher in bereaved persons, with a prevalence of 3.3%. This study found a very high agreement when using *DSM-5-TR* and *ICD-11* criteria. Difficulty accepting the loss was the most frequent single symptom (14%–25%), and grief-related impairment was common (10%–16%).

CONCEPT CHECK

- When a negative event occurs to an individual, what criteria would you use to distinguish between a normal emotional reaction and an adjustment disorder?
- What are the five categories of clinical symptoms that describe acute stress disorder?

POST-TRAUMATIC STRESS DISORDER

I am a middle-aged woman, married with two children. I was diagnosed with posttraumatic stress disorder (PTSD) at age 25. I am grateful to say that I have had tremendous support, terrific professional help, a strong will to recover, and a resolve to do whatever work necessary to overcome all of my trauma. Other miraculous help has been my spiritual beliefs and practices.

As a child I suffered numerous traumatic events that began when I was just two years old. I was physically abused, sexually abused, emotionally abused, and spiritually abused. I was terrorized, tortured, neglected, and abandoned. Unfortunately, there were multiple perpetrators; that has made the healing and confusion about what pieces of the puzzle fit together tiresome at times.

The good news is that it's gotten better! One tremendous step in the right direction was putting myself in therapy at age 21 years. Another was quitting drinking alcohol with the help of Alcoholics Anonymous [AA]. I abused alcohol to escape reality. I am grateful to say I have been sober for almost two decades.

It was just after my first AA anniversary that I began having persistent, terrifying flashbacks that came in many forms, including flashes of images in my mind (like a movie, only skipping some parts), body memories, and loss of time due to dissociation. I admitted myself into a psychiatric hospital, and the journey to recovery began. It was while there I was diagnosed with PTSD.

I'd like to say I no longer suffer from flashbacks, but even at the time of this writing, I am in the middle of recovering another memory from my childhood. This has become routine after all these years, but unfortunately it does include horrible flashbacks—and that is the frustrating part. I have learned they won't kill me or make my head explode, which is something I used to believe.

From K. Waheed. (n.d.). Honoring the person I am. *Retrieved from the Anxiety and Depression Association of America website, www.adaa.org/living-with-anxiety/personal-stories/honoring-person-i-am*

Since at least the American Civil War, there have been studies of long-term health problems related to combat (Levy & Sidel, 2009). It seems that each war has created a new name for what we now call PTSD. In World War I, "shell shock" was a commonly used term. As the name implies, it was thought that the exploding shells caused a psychological and physical reaction, including the feeling of helplessness. During World War II and the Korean War, psychological terms such as neuroasthenia, psychoneurosis, and "battle fatigue" were used. During the Vietnam War, many in American society ascribed the previously described "battle fatigue" to drug abuse or a stress response. There was political debate

iStock.com/kieferpix

over whether PTSD even existed and whether Vietnam soldiers should be treated in government centers for a somewhat vague condition (Hoge et al., 2014). However, a growing acknowledgment of the reality of the disorder led to the first definition of PTSD.

Causes, Characteristics, and Prevalence of PTSD

PTSD results from an experienced threat that produces intense fear, helplessness, or horror (Friedman et al., 2014; Shalev et al., 2017; Vermetten & Lanius, 2012). In addition to war, these experiences can involve family and social violence, rape and assaults, forest fires, and accidents (Table 7.2). During the COVID-19 pandemic, some health care workers were shown to develop PTSD and other disorders (Scott et al., 2023). The highest risk for PTSD is assaultive violence. Cumulative stress also can lead to PTSD. Whereas acute stress disorder is a short-term reaction to trauma, PTSD is present when the reaction lasts more than 1 month. Although environmental factors are important with PTSD, it should be noted that genetics play a role (Gelernter et al., 2019; Ressler, et al., 2022; Seah et al., 2022). It is estimated that 30% to 40% of the risk is heritable.

It has been estimated that 60% of all men and 50% of all women will experience a serious threat to their life or to the life of someone close to them during their lifetime. Of these, 8.7% will develop PTSD during their lifetime. Twelve-month prevalence is 3.5% in the United States (APA, 2013, 2022). The occurrence of PTSD is twice as common in women as men. Women also experience PTSD for longer periods than men do. Although PTSD is found in a variety of cultures, its prevalence is higher in the United States than it is in Europe, Asia, Africa, and Latin America. In these cultures, it is estimated to be around 1%, although New Zealand shows a rate of 6.1% (WHO, 2005). In addition, *DSM-5-TR* reflects the possibility that PTSD can develop in childhood, as illustrated by the first-person account at the beginning of this section.

PTSD has been an important focus of the U.S. Department of Veterans Affairs in that PTSD shows in greater numbers in the military than in the general population. Part of this results from the nature of current military actions in war in which small groups of soldiers go out from the base and cannot predict when there will be an attack. In this situation, there is not a traditional front line. Further, roadside bombs and suicide bombers present additional dangers. Thus, soldiers find their lives under constant threat. Among Vietnam veterans, lifetime prevalence of PTSD is estimated to be 30.9% for men and 26.9% for women (see For Further Reading). For Gulf War (1991) veterans, the lifetime

TABLE 7.2	Stressors Related to Developing Post-Traumatic Stress Disorder
Type of Stressor	**Examples**
Serious accident	Car, plane, boating, or industrial accident
Natural disaster	Tornado, hurricane, flood, or earthquake
Criminal assault	Being physically attacked, mugged, shot, stabbed, or held at gunpoint
Military	Serving in an active combat theater
Sexual assault	Rape or attempted rape
Child sexual abuse	Incest, rape, or sexual contact with an adult or much older child
Child physical abuse or severe neglect	Beating, burning, restraints, starvation
Hostage/imprisonment/torture	Being kidnapped or taken hostage, terrorist attack, torture, incarceration as a prisoner of war or in a concentration camp, displacement as a refugee
Witnessing or learning about traumatic events	Witnessing a shooting or devastating accident, sudden unexpected death of a loved one

Credit: Vermetten, E., & Lanius, R. A. (2012). Biological and clinical framework for posttraumatic stress disorder. *Handbook of Clinical Neurology, 106*, 291–342, p. 293, with permission from Elsevier.

prevalence was lower and estimated to be around 10% to 12%. The Iraq War estimates are around 13.8%. Soldiers who were in recent war zones have experienced not only PTSD but also mild traumatic brain injuries (TBIs), usually in the form of concussions.

During the 1980s, a U.S. government research investigation, the National Vietnam Veterans Readjustment Study (NVVRS), led to the establishment of a 17-symptom definition of PTSD, which remained part of the *DSM* for the next 25 years. The study itself concluded that 30% of Vietnam veterans met the criteria for PTSD at some point in their life, and some 15% still showed the symptoms. In 2006, a reanalysis of the original data with more specific definitions of the criteria resulted in the original estimates being reduced from 30% to 19% (Dohrenwend et al., 2006). It was also suggested that 9% of the veterans still showed PTSD symptoms. Further, it was shown that symptoms were directly related to combat experience and that those with more combat experience exhibited more symptoms.

A 2015 study followed up on the Vietnam veterans nearly 40 years after the end of the war (Marmar et al., 2015). This study found lifetime PTSD experiences to be 17% for men and 15.2% for women. Rates for those who still showed signs of PTSD were 4.5% for men and 6.1% for women. Similar data have been found for veterans of the Iraq and Afghanistan wars (Kok et al., 2012).

At this point, you might also think being part of a war, including being in the general population in a war zone, would increase your chances of experiencing PTSD, and you would be correct (Nandi et al., 2015). This is especially true of those who were abducted to be child soldiers, as described in the *Cultural LENS: Child Soldiers in Africa*.

Those who took part as soldiers in civil wars were also found to suffer from mental health problems, including PTSD. However, in battles in the Democratic Republic of the Congo in Africa, there was a difference for those who volunteered versus those who were forcibly recruited (Hecker et al., 2013). Those who were forcibly recruited were the ones who showed the signs of PTSD.

Further, in a study in Burundi in Africa in which 95% were volunteer soldiers, self-perpetrated violence such as killing did not lead to trauma-related disorders such as PTSD (Nandi et al., 2015). As part of this research, it was determined that some individuals seek to commit violent acts and do not experience distress with these actions. Rather, they find these behaviors appealing, fascinating, and exciting (Elbert et al., 2010). This is referred to as *appetitive aggression* (Elbert et al., 2018).

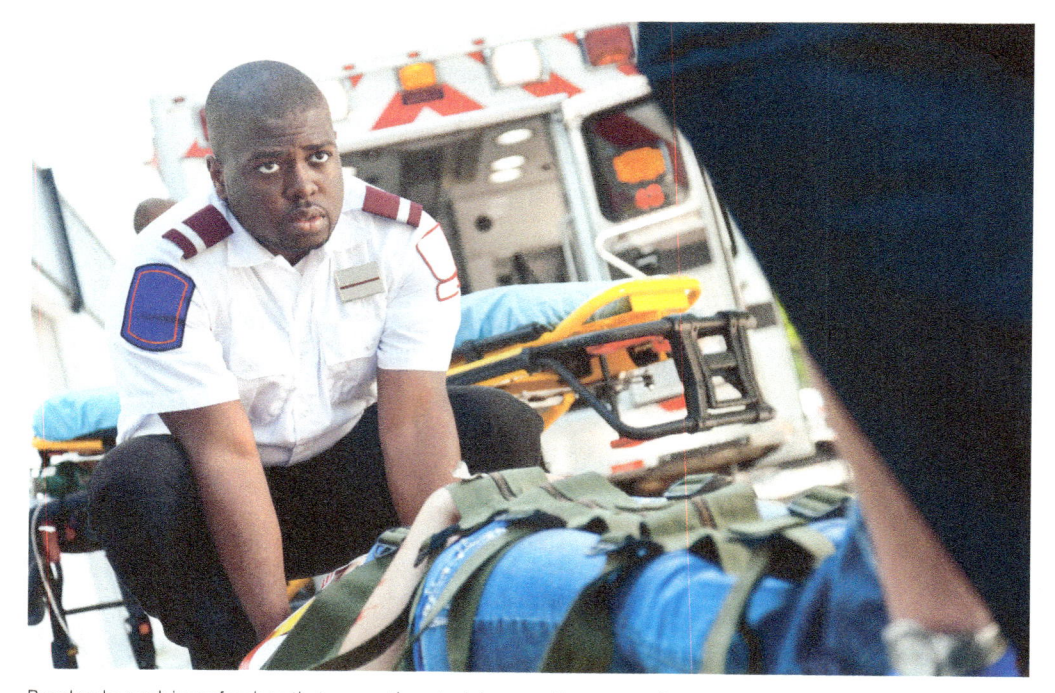

People who work in professions that expose them to violence and trauma, such as paramedics and other health care workers, can also experience stress and PTSD.

iStock.com/SDI Productions

CULTURAL LENS
CHILD SOLDIERS IN AFRICA

There is another group of individuals whose involvement in armed conflict and wars has been associated with psychological disorders. These are children who have been forced to be part of armed forces in Africa. Since the early 2000s, a number of African countries, including Angola, Burundi, the Central African Republic, Chad, Cote d'Ivoire, the Democratic Republic of Congo, Guinea, Liberia, Rwanda, Sierra Leone, Somalia, and northern Uganda, have experienced armed conflict that involved child soldiers (Betancourt et al., 2010; Schauer & Elbert, 2010). In fact, it has been estimated by the United Nations that 250,000 boys and girls have been involved in armed conflict at any given time over the past two decades.

Children involved in armed conflict may develop PTSD as adolescents or adults.

lynn hilton/Alamy Stock Photo

These child soldiers experience a world around them that includes severe violence, which they may be a part of. During the critical preteen and teen developmental periods, they can be experiencing social isolation at a time during which most children and adolescents are developmentally making friends and joining peer groups. In addition, they may also be committing cruelties and atrocities of the worst kind. This exposure to traumatic stress and isolation as they are developing can result in mental and physical disorders, including PTSD.

One 16-year-old described his experience as follows:

> When you would not follow the commander's rule, he could get very angry. People would get beaten terribly for disobedience or if they were trying to escape. When their wounds were open and bleeding, salt was rubbed inside their wound. In that the commander was merciless. You had to follow the rules or you would lose the "protection." When people did something really wrong, they got killed as a punishment. (Schauer & Elbert, 2010, p. 318)

These experiences suggest that child soldiers suffer from both experiencing violence and perpetrating violence on others during armed conflict. Overall, a child soldier would have experienced abduction and traumatic exposure of various types, disruptions of normal developmental stages that in turn are associated with maladjustment. A number of studies show that psychological problems, including PTSD, are common among former child soldiers (Elbert et al., 2018; Ertl et al., 2014).

> **Thought Question**
>
> Sometimes thinking about extreme situations can lead to insights, or at least new questions to ask, in other contexts. How might the example of child soldiers lead us to new questions on the experience of a child growing up in a violent community? Or on the experience of an adult soldier in war?

DSM-5-TR Criteria for PTSD

The *DSM-5-TR* diagnostic criteria for PTSD (shown in Table 7.3) include a variety of traumatic experiences followed by negative reactions. First, the individual is exposed to aversive experiences involving the potential for injury or assault. Repeated exposures of first responders collecting body parts or police investigating child abuse are also included in the definition. Second, following the exposure, the individual experiences intrusions related to the exposure. These intrusions can include flashbacks in which the individual relives the experiences, dream content related to the experience, distressing memories of the event, and distress or physiological reactions to reminders of the event. Third, the individual avoids stimuli involved with the traumatic event. These stimuli could include people, places, or things associated with the event as well as internal thoughts or feelings. Fourth, the individual experiences changes in cognitive processes such as an inability to remember important aspects of the event, negative attributions about one's self, blame of others, negative emotions, detachment, lack of interests, and inability to experience positive emotions. Fifth, the individual experiences increased arousal and reactivity, including sleep disturbances, irritability, and problems with concentration.

TABLE 7.3 ■ *DSM-5-TR* Diagnostic Criteria for Post-Traumatic Stress Disorder

Posttraumatic Stress Disorder in Individuals Older Than 6 Years

Note: The following criteria apply to adults, adolescents, and children older than 6 years. For children 6 years and younger, see corresponding criteria below.

A. Exposure to actual or threatened death, serious injury, or sexual violence in one (or more) of the following ways:
  1. Directly experiencing the traumatic event(s).
  2. Witnessing, in person, the event(s) as it occurred to others.
  3. Learning that the traumatic event(s) occurred to a close family member or close friend. In cases of actual or threatened death of a family member or friend, the event(s) must have been violent or accidental.
  4. Experiencing repeated or extreme exposure to aversive details of the traumatic event(s) (e.g., first responders collecting human remains; police officers repeatedly exposed to details of child abuse).

  Note: Criterion A4 does not apply to exposure through electronic media, television, movies, or pictures, unless this exposure is work related.

B. Presence of one (or more) of the following intrusion symptoms associated with the traumatic event(s), beginning after the traumatic event(s) occurred.
  1. Recurrent, involuntary, and intrusive distressing memories of the traumatic event(s).

  Note: In children older than 6 years, repetitive play may occur in which themes or aspects of the traumatic event(s) are expressed.

  2. Recurrent distressing dreams in which the content and/or affect of the dream are related to the traumatic event(s).

  Note: In children, there may be frightening dreams without recognizable content.

  3. Dissociative reactions (e.g., flashbacks) in which the individual feels or acts as if the traumatic event(s) were recurring. (Such reactions may occur on a continuum, with the most extreme expression being a complete loss of awareness of present surroundings.)

  Note: In children, trauma-specific reenactment may occur in play.

  4. Intense or prolonged psychological distress at exposure to internal or external cues that symbolize or resemble an aspect of the traumatic event(s).
  5. Marked physiological reactions to internal or external cues that symbolize or resemble an aspect of the traumatic event(s).

Posttraumatic Stress Disorder in Individuals Older Than 6 Years

C. Persistent avoidance of stimuli associated with the traumatic event(s), beginning after the traumatic event(s) occurred, as evidenced by one or both of the following:
   1. Avoidance of or efforts to avoid distressing memories, thoughts, or feelings about or closely associated with the traumatic event(s).
   2. Avoidance of or efforts to avoid external reminders (people, places, conversations, activities, objects, situations) that arouse distressing memories, thoughts, or feelings about or closely associated with the traumatic event(s).

D. Negative alterations in cognitions and mood associated with the traumatic event(s), beginning or worsening after the traumatic event(s) occurred, as evidenced by two (or more) of the following:
   1. Inability to remember an important aspect of the traumatic event(s) (typically due to dissociative amnesia and not to other factors such as head injury, alcohol, or drugs).
   2. Persistent and exaggerated negative beliefs or expectations about oneself, others, or the world (e.g., "I am bad," "No one can be trusted," "The world is completely dangerous," "My whole nervous system is permanently ruined").
   3. Persistent distorted cognitions about the cause or consequences of the traumatic event(s) that lead the individual to blame himself/herself or others.
   4. Persistent negative emotional state (e.g., fear, horror, anger, guilt, or shame).
   5. Markedly diminished interest or participation in significant activities.
   6. Feelings of detachment or estrangement from others.
   7. Persistent inability to experience positive emotions (e.g., inability to experience happiness, satisfaction, or loving feelings).

E. Marked alterations in arousal and reactivity associated with the traumatic event(s), beginning or worsening after the traumatic event(s) occurred, as evidenced by two (or more) of the following:
   1. Irritable behavior and angry outbursts (with little or no provocation) typically expressed as verbal or physical aggression toward people or objects.
   2. Reckless or self-destructive behavior.
   3. Hypervigilance.
   4. Exaggerated startle response.
   5. Problems with concentration.
   6. Sleep disturbance (e.g., difficulty falling or staying asleep or restless sleep).

F. Duration of the disturbance (Criteria B, C, D and E) is more than 1 month.

G. The disturbance causes clinically significant distress or impairment in social, occupational, or other important areas of functioning.

H. The disturbance is not attributable to the physiological effects of a substance (e.g., medication, alcohol) or another medical condition.

Specify whether:

With dissociative symptoms: The individual's symptoms meet the criteria for posttraumatic stress disorder, and in addition, in response to the stressor, the individual experiences persistent or recurrent symptoms of either of the following:
   1. Depersonalization: Persistent or recurrent experiences of feeling detached from, and as if one were an outside observer of, one's mental processes or body (e.g., feeling as though one were in a dream; feeling a sense of unreality of self or body or of time moving slowly).
   2. Derealization: Persistent or recurrent experiences of unreality of surroundings (e.g., the world around the individual is experienced as unreal, dreamlike, distant, or distorted).

Note: To use this subtype, the dissociative symptoms must not be attributable to the physiological effects of a substance (e.g., blackouts, behavior during alcohol intoxication) or another medical condition (e.g., complex partial seizures).

Specify if:

With delayed expression: If the full diagnostic criteria are not met until at least 6 months after the event (although the onset and expression of some symptoms may be immediate).

(Continued)

TABLE 7.3 ■ *DSM-5-TR* Diagnostic Criteria for Post-Traumatic Stress Disorder (*Continued*)

Posttraumatic Stress Disorder in Children 6 Years and Younger

A. In children 6 years and younger, exposure to actual or threatened death, serious injury, or sexual violence in one (or more) of the following ways:
   1. Directly experiencing the traumatic event(s).
   2. Witnessing, in person, the event(s) as it occurred to others, especially primary caregivers.
   3. Learning that the traumatic event(s) occurred to a parent or caregiving figure.

B. Presence of one (or more) of the following intrusion symptoms associated with the traumatic event(s), beginning after the traumatic event(s) occurred:
   1. Recurrent, involuntary, and intrusive distressing memories of the traumatic event(s).
   Note: Spontaneous and intrusive memories may not necessarily appear distressing and may be expressed as play reenactment.
   2. Recurrent distressing dreams in which the content and/or affect of the dream are related to the traumatic event(s).
   Note: It may not be possible to ascertain that the frightening content is related to the traumatic event.
   3. Dissociative reactions (e.g., flashbacks) in which the child feels or acts as if the traumatic event(s) were recurring. (Such reactions may occur on a continuum, with the most extreme expression being a complete loss of awareness of present surroundings.) Such trauma-specific reenactment may occur in play.
   4. Intense or prolonged psychological distress at exposure to internal or external cues that symbolize or resemble an aspect of the traumatic event(s).
   5. Marked physiological reactions to reminders of the traumatic event(s).

C. One (or more) of the following symptoms, representing either persistent avoidance of stimuli associated with the traumatic event(s) or negative alterations in cognitions and mood associated with the traumatic event(s), must be present, beginning after the event(s) or worsening after the event(s):

Persistent Avoidance of Stimuli

1. Avoidance of or efforts to avoid activities, places, or physical reminders that arouse recollections of the traumatic event(s).
2. Avoidance of or efforts to avoid people, conversations, or interpersonal situations that arouse recollections of the traumatic event(s).

Negative Alterations in Cognitions

3. Substantially increased frequency of negative emotional states (e.g., fear, guilt, sadness, shame, confusion).
4. Markedly diminished interest or participation in significant activities, including constriction of play.
5. Socially withdrawn behavior.
6. Persistent reduction in expression of positive emotions.

D. Alterations in arousal and reactivity associated with the traumatic event(s), beginning or worsening after the traumatic event(s) occurred, as evidenced by two (or more) of the following:
   1. Irritable behavior and angry outbursts (with little or no provocation) typically expressed as verbal or physical aggression toward people or objects (including extreme temper tantrums).
   2. Hypervigilance.
   3. Exaggerated startle response.
   4. Problems with concentration.
   5. Sleep disturbance (e.g., difficulty falling or staying asleep or restless sleep).

E. The duration of the disturbance is more than 1 month.

F. The disturbance causes clinically significant distress or impairment in relationships with parents, siblings, peers, or other caregivers or with school behavior.

G. The disturbance is not attributable to the physiological effects of a substance (e.g., medication or alcohol) or another medical condition.

> **Posttraumatic Stress Disorder in Children 6 Years and Younger**
>
> *Specify* whether:
>
> **With dissociative symptoms:** The individual's symptoms meet the criteria for posttraumatic stress disorder, and the individual experiences persistent or recurrent symptoms of either of the following:
>
> 1. Depersonalization: Persistent or recurrent experiences of feeling detached from, and as if one were an outside observer of, one's mental processes or body (e.g., feeling as though one were in a dream; feeling a sense of unreality of self or body or of time moving slowly).
>
> 2. Derealization: Persistent or recurrent experiences of unreality of surroundings (e.g., the world around the individual is experienced as unreal, dreamlike, distant, or distorted).
>
> **Note:** To use this subtype, the dissociative symptoms must not be attributable to the physiological effects of a substance (e.g., blackouts) or another medical condition (e.g., complex partial seizures).
>
> *Specify* if:
>
> **With delayed expression:** If the full diagnostic criteria are not met until at least 6 months after the event (although the onset and expression of some symptoms may be immediate).

Credit: Reprinted with permission from the *Diagnostic and Statistical Manual of Mental Disorders, fifth edition, text revision*, DSM-V-TR, pp. 301–304 (Copyright © 2022). American Psychiatric Association. All Rights Reserved.

Overall, symptoms should have lasted for more than 1 month and produced clinically significant distress. The following case of Victoria English (not her real name) illustrates these symptoms in a person who experienced a bomb attack at the World Trade Center in New York City (in 1993, several years before the 9/11 terrorist attacks brought the buildings down).

> ## CASE OF VICTORIA ENGLISH
> ### POST-TRAUMATIC STRESS DISORDER
>
> Victoria English is a single woman in her early 30s. She occupied a position of significant authority in a large corporation. She sees herself as efficient and independent and has never sought mental health services in the past. On February 25, 1993, she was working in her office at the World Trade Center when a bomb exploded. In the initial interview, she showed little emotion when she described being blown into the air and landing on her arm. This resulted in her having a broken arm. During the interview, Ms. English became more tearful and frightened as she described the bombing and how it affected her life. Specifically, she is currently feeling vulnerable and reported difficulties with the demands of her job. When she returned to work 2 weeks after the bombing, she reported being anxious on the subway. She began to work from home. The company physician, after consulting with her, suggested that she obtain a temporary disability and discontinue working.
>
> During Ms. English's assessment, she was administered a Structured Clinical Interview for *DSM* Disorders (SCID) and met criteria for PTSD. Her symptoms included nightmares and intrusive daytime recollections. These could bring her to tears. She also had intrusive fantasies of catastrophic events, such as buildings falling on people, as she went about her daily life. Ms. English also avoided situations such as riding the subway or going to the World Trade Center, which would make her feel vulnerable or remind her of the bombing. She also found herself cut off from others even when they reached out to her. She began cognitive processing therapy with cognitive behavioral components. By the end of therapy, her level of functioning had greatly improved. At the 1-year follow-up, she reported that she was doing well and had moved to a new city and become romantically involved with someone who would become her husband. She also reconsidered her priorities and, according to her, began to live a more balanced life. At the 2.5-year follow-up, she no longer met criteria for PTSD although she reported minor types of psychological distress.
>
> *Credit:* From Difede, J., & Eskra, D. (2002). Cognitive processing therapy for PTSD in a survivor of the World Trade Center bombing: A case study. *Journal of Trauma Practice, 1*, 155–165. Reprinted by permission of Taylor & Francis Ltd, http://www.tandf.co.uk/journals.

The Physiological Aspects of Post-Traumatic Stress Disorder

Researchers who study PTSD may try to create stress in animals. They may expose animals to inescapable stress or repeated stressors. Similar stress responses as seen in humans are reported that include the CRH (corticotropin-releasing hormone), which activates the HPA axis to cause release of ACTH and other chemical substances, as described previously. This generally results in a lessened stress response to additional stimuli and an avoidance of novel situations.

In terms of brain structures, animal models of stress and trauma have shown that exposure to severe and chronic stress can damage hippocampal formation. This is seen to be mediated by elevated corticosteroids, which are thought to damage cells, diminish neuronal regeneration, and reduce dendritic branching. This has resulted in a variety of human studies examining the hippocampus in individuals with PTSD (Gilbertson, 2011; Joshi, Duval, Kubat, & Liberzon, 2020 Lambert & McLaughlin, 2019; Shin et al., 2011).

In addition, an improved understanding of the cortical networks involved in the acquisition and extinction of fear have pinpointed specific brain regions connected with PTSD. These include the hippocampus, the amygdala, and the medial prefrontal cortex (PFC) as well as the default and salience networks (Yuan et al., 2018). The hippocampus is important because of its role in the encoding of memories, including emotional ones. The amygdala is involved in the assessment of threat and plays a role in fear conditioning. The medial PFC, including the ACC, is involved in the inhibition of emotional information during task performance. These are the same brain areas involved in anxiety and fear processes. The brain areas involved in PTSD are shown in Figure 7.6.

In general, there is clear support for the idea that individuals with PTSD have smaller hippocampal volume than those without PTSD. In one meta-analysis (Smith, 2005), individuals with PTSD had, on average, a 6.9% smaller left hippocampus and a 6.6% smaller right hippocampus by volume. An intriguing idea is that stress limits the normal regeneration of new neurons in the hippocampus

FIGURE 7.6 ■ What Are the Major Areas of the Brain Related to Psychological Stress and Trauma?

Brain areas thought to be involved in PTSD. (A) Hypoactivity in the prefrontal cortex (medial, dorsolateral, and ventromedial) may account for the reduced ability to regulate emotions and impaired executive functioning. (B) Hyperactivity in the ACC, insula, and amygdala may account for exaggerated responses to potential threats. (C) Hypoactivity in a circuit that includes the hippocampus, medial prefrontal cortex, thalamus, and locus coeruleus may account for impaired contextual processing. (D) Hyperactivity in the amygdala may account for exaggerated fear reactions.

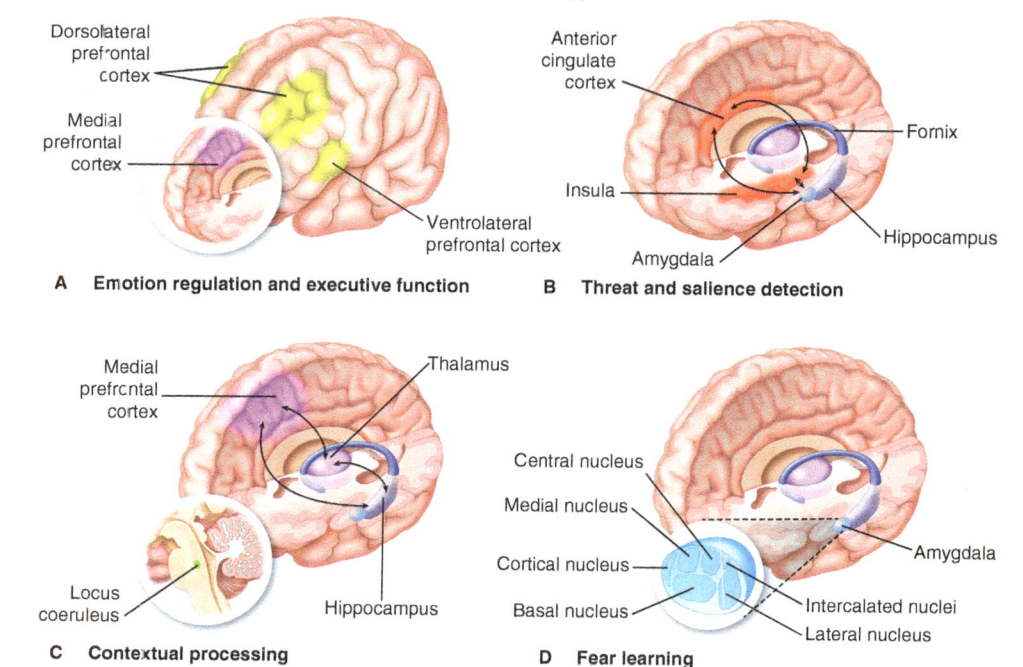

A Emotion regulation and executive function
B Threat and salience detection
C Contextual processing
D Fear learning

Carolina Hrejsa/Body Scientific Intl.

(Lucassen et al., 2013). ACC differences have also been noted in PTSD as well as reduced connectivity between the ACC and the amygdala. Although the amygdala is an important part of the fear network, consistent reductions have not been observed there.

It is suggested that the hyperresponsiveness of the amygdala is related to the exaggerated fear response (Rauch et al., 2006). This may result from a lack of inhibition from the frontal areas to the amygdala. This would also be associated with the inability to inhibit or extinguish fear-related stimuli. The emotional opposite has also been found. That is, those with PTSD show less limbic response to happy facial expressions, which may be related to emotional numbing (Felmingham et al., 2014). As you can read in the feature *Understanding Changes in the* DSM-5 *and* DSM-5-TR, DSM-5 describes emotional numbing as inability to experience positive emotions.

UNDERSTANDING CHANGES IN THE *DSM-5* AND *DSM-5-TR*

PTSD DEFINITIONS IN *DSM-IV* AND *DSM-5*

With the publication of *DSM-5*, there were changes to the criteria for PTSD. PTSD was moved from the section of the *DSM* on anxiety disorders to a new section on trauma- and stressor-related disorders. Eight of the original 17 PTSD symptoms, which had not been changed for 25 years, were changed and reworded. Three additional symptoms were added. In addition, avoidance symptoms have been separated from numbing. That is, avoiding stimuli is differentiated from not reacting to the stimuli. For a diagnosis of PTSD in *DSM-5*, both effortful avoidance and changes in negative mood and cognition must be present. Whereas *DSM-IV* characterized numbing as a restricted range of affect and reduced ability to feel emotions, *DSM-5* changed that to an inability to feel positive emotions.

Charles Hoge and his colleagues (2014) compared the different criteria with veterans from Iraq and Afghanistan. They found that the new criteria did not affect the soldiers' willingness to report symptoms. However, they found that the new criteria did not have greater clinical utility. That is, using the new criteria did not influence how the soldiers' PTSD was treated. Further, 30% of the soldiers who met the PTSD criteria under *DSM-IV* did not meet the criteria under *DSM-5*. This has implications for both research and treatment of PTSD. Also, an equal number of individuals only met the PTSD criteria under *DSM-5*.

Further, in a study of traumatized refugees to Switzerland, different rates in PTSD diagnosis were found to be related to whether the clinician used *DSM-IV* or *DSM-5* (Schnyder et al., 2015). Using *DSM-IV*, 60.4% of the traumatized refugees were diagnosed with PTSD, whereas only 49.3% were diagnosed when the *DSM-5* was used. Differences in diagnosis were also found with a sample of fighters in the Democratic Republic of the Congo (Schaal et al., 2015). Thus, those diagnosed with *DSM-IV* PTSD will be different from those diagnosed with *DSM-5* PTSD.

These differences are troubling to many (McFarlane, 2014). PTSD diagnoses are used in legal jurisdictions and for determining pensions. Further, research would also be different between those with *DSM-IV* criteria and those with *DSM-5* criteria. For example, neuroimaging studies show two different patterns of emotional reactivity. One of these is underreactivity and the other is emotional overreaction. However, neither of these patterns involves only positive affect, as required by *DSM-5*. Overall, all aspects of society, from legal professionals to mental health professionals to researchers, need to be aware of how following the criteria in *DSM-IV* or *DSM-5* determines the diagnosis of PTSD.

One way to think about the physiological changes associated with trauma is to consider the networks involved on both an associative and a cortical level. On an associative level, it has been suggested that some associations become more potent or "hot" than others that remain "cold" (Rockstroh & Elbert, 2010). It has been shown that repeated experiences of trauma will make it more difficult to integrate the experiences into less emotional or "cold" autobiographical memories. Figure 7.7 illustrates such a network, in which being on a dark street results in a cognitive proposition such as "there is no way out" or "something bad is going to happen to me." These thoughts would be followed by emotional and physiological responses related to stress. One goal of therapy is to help the individual move the hot trauma associations to a more cold, or nonreactive, memory process.

FIGURE 7.7 ■ Sensory, Cognitive, Emotional, and Physiological Processes Involved in Experiencing Stress

This figure shows a schematic outline of an exemplary network of propositions implemented as a "trauma network." In PTSD, the border between "hot" and "cold" memory elements (the thick black line) is firm and prevents the integration of emotional and autobiographical memories. Additional experiences add to the "hot" elements but not to the context, thereby strengthening the separation of the two memories.

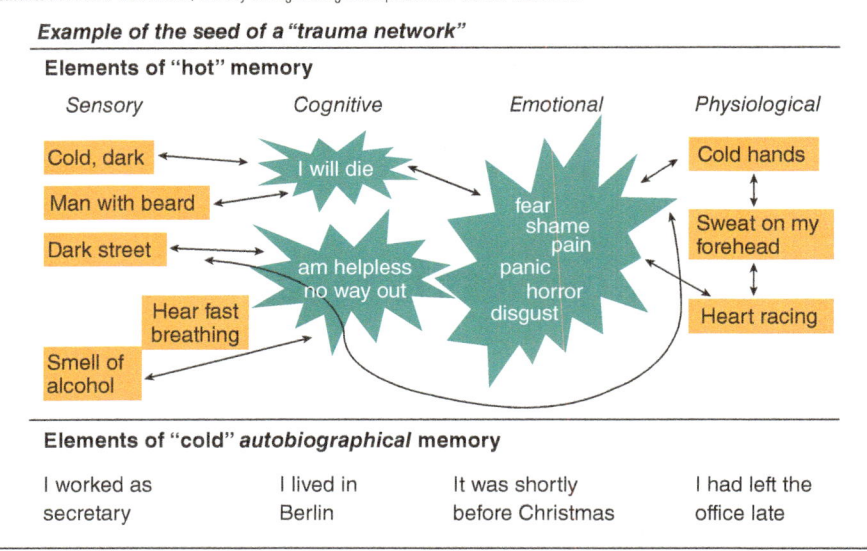

Example of the seed of a "trauma network"

Elements of "hot" memory

Sensory	Cognitive	Emotional	Physiological
Cold, dark	I will die	fear	Cold hands
Man with beard		shame	Sweat on my forehead
Dark street		pain	
	I am helpless no way out	panic	Heart racing
Hear fast breathing		horror	
Smell of alcohol		disgust	

Elements of "cold" autobiographical memory

| I worked as secretary | I lived in Berlin | It was shortly before Christmas | I had left the office late |

Credit: Rockstroh, B., & Elbert, T. (2010). Traces of fear in the neural web—Magnetoencephalographic responding to arousing pictorial stimuli. *International Journal of Psychophysiology, 78*, 14–19, p. 15, with permission from Elsevier.

Treatment for Post-Traumatic Stress Disorder

PTSD is frequently comorbid with other disorders, including depression, substance abuse, and anxiety disorders such as obsessive–compulsive disorder (OCD), panic disorder, agoraphobia, and social anxiety. For example, the National Vietnam Veterans Readjustment Study showed that 98% of individuals with combat-related PTSD had a comorbid lifetime mental disorder (Kulka et al., 1990). They also reported more physical health problems. This suggests that the treatment of PTSD requires more than a single strategy.

Given the plethora of symptoms seen in PTSD, pharmacological treatments have been varied and have included antidepressants, anxiolytics, adrenergic inhibitors, mood stabilizers, and anticonvulsants. Overall, drug treatments were shown to be superior to placebos in reducing symptoms of PTSD (Friedman & Davidson, 2014). New drugs are also being tested that influence the ability to remember traumatic events. For example, animal work has shown that the dopamine D_1 receptor is involved in processing emotional information in the PFC. If these receptors are manipulated, it is possible to block the experiencing of emotional memories (Lauzon et al., 2013).

At present, the most effective therapies for PTSD are cognitive and behavioral therapies (Bisson & Andrew 2007; Bradley et al., 2005; Frueh et al., 2018; McLean et al., 2022; Ursano et al., 2008; L. E. Watkins et al., 2018). In fact, PTSD is one of the *DSM* disorders that is mainly treated by psychotherapy. The most studied therapies include **exposure therapy for PTSD**, cognitive behavioral therapy (CBT) and cognitive restructuring, and eye movement desensitization and reprocessing (EMDR). One key ingredient of most therapies is a controlled reexperiencing of the original trauma. Psychodynamic therapies refer to this as *catharsis*. The task is for the client to reexperience the original trauma in a safe and controlled environment such that its negative emotional effect is reduced. Reviews have shown that therapies that focus on the trauma that the individual encountered are more effective than those that do not (Bisson & Andrew, 2007). *LENS: Treating PTSD and Other Invisible Wounds in Military Veterans* examines stress-related disorders and suicide in the military.

LENS

TREATING PTSD AND OTHER INVISIBLE WOUNDS IN MILITARY VETERANS

As noted in the chapter on mood disorders, there is currently a higher rate of PTSD and depression in the U.S. military than in the general population. The rate of suicide is also higher in the military, a finding that has not been seen since the war in Vietnam. This has resulted in concerns by the military, government officials, and mental health professionals. A number of studies have been conducted to understand these troubling statistics.

The U.S. Department of Defense is using virtual reality techniques as a means of treating post-traumatic stress disorder for those who served in Iraq, Afghanistan, and other combat locations.

John J. Kruzel/US Department of Defense, https://flic.kr/p/5q70Li, licensed under CC BY-SA 2.0 https://creativecommons.org/licenses/by/2.0/.

In 2008, the RAND Corporation published a report on the psychological consequences of military deployment over the previous decade, *Invisible Wounds of War* (Tanielian & Jaycox, 2008). Since 2001, more than a million and a half U.S. troops have been deployed in Iraq and Afghanistan. These troops have been deployed for longer periods and faced combat in smaller groups than troops in previous wars. Given the advances in body armor and medical technology, fewer deaths have resulted compared with the wars in Vietnam and Korea. However, what has become apparent is that these individuals have experienced mental health issues and brain trauma not initially apparent; these are referred to as *invisible wounds*. It is estimated that one third of all soldiers involved in combat in Afghanistan have such an invisible condition, including PTSD, depression, or TBI (traumatic brain injury). Further, 5% of these individuals display symptoms of all three. Given that this is a higher rate of PTSD and depression than that seen in the general population, it is surprising and disturbing that these military personnel only sought help from mental health professionals at about the same rate as the general population. Roughly half of those who met the criteria for PTSD, depression, or TBI had sought help in the year preceding the RAND study. An important reason given for not seeking help was that the soldiers were concerned that the information would not be kept confidential and would hurt future job searches or military advancement.

Not seeking help for a mental condition not only has consequences for the affected individual but also for society in general. Often individuals with stress-related disorders show other problems such as substance abuse, as well as problems in their marriages and social relationships. For society, these conditions can lead to missed days at work, lower productivity, and even homelessness and suicide. However, there is potential to deal with these problems. The RAND report estimates that evidence-based treatments for depression and PTSD would pay for themselves within 2 years and save the country as much as $1.7 billion in lost productivity annually. For both the individual and society, there is great value in not having the person become homeless or attempt suicide. There is also increased quality of life for the individual that results from effective treatments of these disorders.

Based on their research, the RAND Corporation made four recommendations:

1. Increase the cadre of providers who are trained and certified to deliver proven (evidence-based) care, so that capacity is adequate for current and future needs.
2. Change policies to encourage active duty personnel and veterans to seek needed care.
3. Deliver proven, evidence-based care to service members and veterans whenever and wherever services are provided.
4. Invest in research to close information gaps and plan effectively.

Thought Question

What are some ways to ensure that our society treats the "invisible wounds" of war as seriously as the more visible physical wounds our military personnel experience?

Exposure therapy for PTSD is designed to have the individual with PTSD reexperience the original trauma (Foa et al., 2013; McLean et al., 2022). In this way, the person confronts their fears and expectations such that they are reduced. One common procedure for doing this is through *imagery*. The therapist helps the person remember and imagine the details of the experience, including the factors that led up to the event. In some situations such as a car accident, the therapist and the client may actually go to the location of the event so the client can reexperience in detail the situation. One goal of the therapy is to have the person develop a sense of mastery over the situation.

Another approach has used narrative exposure therapy (NET) to treat those with trauma (Schauer et al., 2011). This approach begins with the idea that a fear/trauma network in the brain builds up memories of very stressful, traumatic, and frightening experiences (as previously illustrated in Figure 7.7). Since this information is often stored without a sense of time, when recalled it can flood into a person's experience as if it is happening in the present. The goal of NET is to break up this network. The procedure begins with the child, adolescent, or adult being asked to see their experiences as being along a rope representing the person's life in terms of positive and negative emotions. In the following sessions, the individual reports the most arousing experiences beginning at birth. As the person reexperiences the event, they are able to place it in a particular context rather than experiencing a global reaction. The therapist helps the person describe specific details such as the weather that day, the color of the house, and so on. One outcome is that the individual learns to have greater control over the fear and terror memories. This approach has been shown to be effective for treating trauma in a number of groups, including Burundian children who formerly lived in the streets of the country's capital, Bujumbura (Crombach & Elbert, 2015).

Written exposure therapy (WET) is a five-session trauma-focused intervention in which individuals are asked to write about their traumatic experience following scripted instruction (Sloan et al., 2013). The first session includes psychoeducation about PTSD along with a treatment rationale, followed by 30 minutes of writing. At the beginning of each subsequent session, therapists provide feedback to individuals about the degree to which they followed the writing instructions during the prior session and offer suggestions for adhering to the treatment protocol. After this feedback, individuals write for 30 minutes without interruption. There are no assignments between sessions. WET has been shown to be an effective therapy (Sloan et al., 2018).

EMDR is a form of therapy in which a person imagines the traumatic situation while moving their eyes (Shapiro, 2001, 2013). The basic idea is that PTSD is related to unprocessed memories in the brain. The purpose of therapy is to reactivate these stored memories through direct processing. The person is told to keep their head still and follow the therapist's finger (or a light panel) with their eyes while imagining the trauma. The procedure is repeated until the person no longer experiences distress. Although the procedure has been shown to be effective with PTSD, neuroscience perspectives are just beginning to be articulated (Calancie et al., 2018). However, EMDR remains controversial (Russell, 2008).

Cognitive behavioral approaches seek to modify dysfunctional thoughts and train the individual with PTSD to consider new ways to interpret the situation. One important focus is to help the person restructure their way of thinking and feeling. One way of doing this is to have the person identify the thoughts, such as "I am going to be hurt," that precede the negative emotions experienced in PTSD. Likewise, a woman who has been raped might blame herself for being in the situation and say, "It is all my fault." The therapist would help this person to reconsider this belief and replace it with the truth, that is, that the rape was not her fault. Overall, the CBT process is one of identifying dysfunctional thoughts, evaluating their validity, and replacing them with more productive ones.

An approach used to treat the co-occurrence of PTSD and substance abuse is referred to as *seeking safety* (Najavits, 2002). Seeking safety has been empirically supported by research and consists of five central ideas. The first is safety as the priority of treatment. *Safety* is an umbrella term that includes discontinuing substance abuse, reducing suicidality, reducing self-harm, and letting go of bad relationships such as those that involve the use of drugs. The second idea is that of an integrated treatment that addresses PTSD and substance abuse together. The third idea is a focus on ideals such as the meaning of one's life that are typically lost in the experience of PTSD and substance abuse. The fourth idea incorporates CBT with its emphasis on cognitive, behavioral, interpersonal, and action domains. The fifth idea emphasizes the relationship between the individual and the mental health professional (see For Further Reading). Two processes seen in other therapies for PTSD are not included in seeking safety. The first is the exploration of past trauma. There is a lack of evidence that exploring past trauma with those with substance abuse is beneficial. The second is the use of interpretive statements such as those seen in dynamic therapy. Although useful in some types of therapy, these are seen as potentially upsetting in the initial treatment of PTSD and substance abuse.

Additional new and improved treatment approaches are being developed within the context of modern technology and more sophisticated treatment research. Because many types of trauma-related disorders are largely environmentally determined, prevention programs can be offered. One aspect of prevention includes bringing the psychological situation that led to trauma to light. Currently, sexual

Actress Gabrielle Union has publicly discussed her experience of PTSD stemming from an experience of rape as a teenager.
Image Press Agency/Alamy Stock Photo

assault in the military is one example in which prevention programs have been developed. Another aspect of prevention is helping those who have experienced trauma to recognize the signs and symptoms of psychological distress and learn how to seek help. Assaults against children have also been focused on by many communities and states with the goal of prevention and treatment.

> **CONCEPT CHECK**
>
> - PTSD results from an experienced threat. What are some of the common traumatic stressors?
> - How are specific areas of the brain involved in PTSD?
>
> - What are the most effective therapies for PTSD? Give three examples, and explain the focus of each for treating PTSD.

SUMMARY

Psychological stress is experienced when something we do not expect and cannot control happens to us. At times, these experiences lead to strong emotional reactions and at other times to psychological disorders such as PTSD. The manner in which stress and trauma are related to health and psychopathology is a complicated topic. Overall, early stress has been associated with both later mental and physical health problems, due to the fact that stressful experiences change psychological and physiological reactions to future stressful experiences. Our physiological reactions to stress and trauma occur on a variety of levels, including the tagging of genes (epigenetics), the reaction of the immune system, the endocrine system involving the HPA axis, the ANS, and changes in cortical processes. Over evolutionary time, the processing of social pain appears to have co-opted the basic brain structures involved in physical pain. Pain research suggests that there are two separate components to the experience of pain: (1) the sensory experience itself and (2) the felt unpleasantness. It is the experience of unpleasantness that appears to be altered in psychopathology and is most sensitive to psychological factors.

Our immune system has evolved to recognize a variety of pathogens. It comes into play in terms of specific pathogens such as viruses and also in terms of stress. The immune system is influenced by the brain and vice versa. Organisms have evolved sophisticated mechanisms, which benefit survival. The basic mechanism is to prepare the body for action through two pathways: (1) the ANS and (2) the HPA axis. The overall stress reaction has been referred to as the fight-or-flight response. This reaction has been critical throughout our evolutionary history, but today, in our different social structure, it may lead to stress-related disorders. Given the different evolutionary pressures on males and females, it has been suggested that the fight-or-flight response better describes a human male's response to stress, while the tend-and-befriend response better describes the female's response. However, the basic neuroendocrine responses to stress appear to be similar in both males and females.

Early stress research by Selye found that the body reacts similarly to a variety of different stressors. Selye called this response the general adaptation syndrome (GAS). One of the paradoxes is that the physiological stress responses that protect and restore the body can also damage it. However, repeated exposure to a particular stress situation can also increase the organism's ability to withstand that same stress in greater amounts. McEwen suggested that the term *stress* be replaced with the term *allostasis*, which refers to the body's ability to achieve stability through change. The stress response involves two tasks for the body: (1) turning on the allostatic response that initiates a complex adaptive pathway (e.g., the fight-or-flight or tend-and-befriend response) and (2) turning off these responses once the danger has passed. Research suggests that prolonged exposure to stress may not allow these two mechanisms to function correctly and in turn leads to a variety of physiological problems. Overall, McEwen emphasized the important question of individual differences and the variety of ways in which perceived stress can influence future health.

There are several disorders described in *DSM-5* that result from the experience of stress. The most significant are adjustment disorders, acute stress disorder, and PTSD. The severity of the stressor is the least in an adjustment disorder and the greatest in PTSD. Diagnosis of an adjustment disorder does not require specific symptoms but more global distress, whereas acute stress disorder and PTSD do require specific symptoms. Whereas acute stress disorder is a short-term reaction to trauma, PTSD is present when the reaction lasts more than 1 month. PTSD is frequently comorbid with other disorders such as depression; substance abuse; and anxiety disorders, such as OCD, panic disorder, agoraphobia, and social anxiety. This suggests that the treatment of PTSD requires more than a single strategy. Drug treatments reduce symptoms of PTSD; however, at present, the most effective therapies for PTSD are cognitive and behavioral therapies. The most studied therapies include exposure therapy, CBT and cognitive restructuring, and EMDR. One key ingredient of most therapies is a controlled reexperiencing of the original trauma, referred to as catharsis. New programs related to prevention are also being developed by both communities and the military.

STUDY RESOURCES

Review Questions

1. What are specific examples of how past stressful experiences change both our psychological and physiological reactions to future stressful situations in relation to
   a. Psychological factors?
   b. Developmental changes in the brain?
   c. Genetic factors?
   d. Epigenetic modifications?
   e. Endocrine factors?
   f. Economic and social factors?

2. In the study of stress, researchers Selye and McEwen both referred to the paradox that the same physiological stress responses that protect and restore the body can also damage it. In terms of that paradox, please answer the following questions:
   a. How did our stress responses evolve, and what led to the paradox?
   b. How do our stress responses protect and restore our body and mind?
   c. How can our stress responses damage our body and mind?

3. *DSM-5* includes three psychological disorders that result from the experience of stress—adjustment disorder, acute stress disorder, and PTSD. For each disorder, please answer the following questions:
   a. What are examples of triggering events and common symptoms?
   b. What are the diagnostic criteria?
   c. What is the prevalence?
   d. What are effective treatments?

For Further Reading

Barlow, D., Rapee, R., & Perini, S. (2014). *10 steps to mastering stress* (updated ed.). Oxford University Press.

Foa, E., Keane, T., Friedman, M., & Cohen, J. (2009). *Effective treatments for PTSD* (2nd ed.). Guilford Press.

Friedman, M., Keane, T., & Resick, P. (2014). *Handbook of PTSD* (2nd ed.). Guilford Press.

Johnston, E., & Olson, L. (2015). *The feeling brain: The biology and psychology of emotions*. Norton.

Sapolsky, R. (2004). *Why zebras don't get ulcers* (3rd ed.). St. Martin's Griffin.

Schnurr, P. P. (2023). *Epidemiology and impact of PTSD*. U.S. Department of Veterans Affairs. https://www.ptsd.va.gov/professional/treat/essentials/epidemiology.asp

Treatment Innovations. (2020). *The model: Seeking safety*. http://www.treatment-innovations.org/seeking-safety.html

KEY TERMS

- acute stress disorder
- adjustment disorders
- allostasis
- allostatic load
- autonomic nervous system (ANS)
- exposure therapy for PTSD
- fight-or-flight response
- general adaptation syndrome (GAS)
- hypothalamic–pituitary–adrenal (HPA) axis
- immune system
- parasympathetic division
- post-traumatic stress disorder (PTSD)
- prolonged grief disorder
- psychological stress
- psychoneuroimmunology
- sympathetic division
- tend-and-befriend response

BSIP SA/Alamy Stock Photo

8 ANXIETY DISORDERS AND OBSESSIVE-COMPULSIVE DISORDERS

LEARNING OBJECTIVES

8.1 Discuss the cognitive, neurobiological, and developmental aspects of anxiety.

8.2 Distinguish among the major anxiety disorders, their causes, and treatment.

8.3 Distinguish among agoraphobia, specific phobia, and panic disorder, and describe their causes and treatment.

8.4 Describe the characteristics of obsessive-compulsive disorder, its causes, and treatment.

British superstar Adele has revealed in media interviews that she suffers from stage anxiety and panic attacks.
PA Images/Alamy Stock Photo

The British performer Adele has been at the top of the Billboard 200 (top 200 albums chart); she was also the first female performer to have three singles in the top 10 at the same time on the Billboard charts. She recently revealed that she suffers from stage anxiety and panic attacks.

She told the British magazine *Q*, "I have anxiety attacks, constant panicking on stage, my heart feels like it's going to explode because I never feel like I'm going to deliver, ever. I will not do festivals. The thought of an audience that big frightens the life out of me. I don't think the music would work either. It's all too slow. I'd hate to book a festival and have a ******* anxiety attack and then not go on stage" (Dray, n.d.).

In *Rolling Stone*, she said, "I'm scared of audiences. . . . One show in Amsterdam I was so nervous, I escaped out the fire exit. I've thrown up a couple of times. Once in Brussels, I projectile vomited on someone. I just gotta bear it. But I don't like touring. I have anxiety attacks a lot" (*Rolling Stone*, 2011).

Daniela Grazia (2010) details her life of living with social anxiety as follows:

I felt incredibly awkward and out of place. It seemed everyone's eyes were on me and that they could see how uncomfortable I was. While my brother and the neighborhood kids talked and carried on with the others, I sat there rigid, looking straight ahead and not saying a word—immobilized. I did not fit in here. I did not belong here. I felt like an alien. My throat and chest tightened and my mouth went dry.

OVERVIEW OF ANXIETY DISORDERS

We all feel anxious at times. We worry that things may not work out the way we want them to. Sometimes, we have bodily symptoms such as a dry mouth or gastrointestinal (GI) problems consistent with the stress responses described in Chapter 7. We may have problems sleeping. At times, our anxiety may have the positive effect of alerting us to something that we need to pay attention to. This helps us be more vigilant. The experience of anxiety in itself is part of the human situation. However, when this experience becomes chronic, creates distress, and interferes with our life, we see it as an anxiety disorder. Anxiety disorders influence 19.1% of adults in the United States (see For Further Reading). A number of pop stars, such as Ariana Grande, have discussed their experience of anxiety (Kreps, 2018).

TABLE 8.1 Anxiety Disorders in *DSM-5-TR*
Separation Anxiety Disorder
Panic Disorder
Agoraphobia
Specific Phobia
Social Anxiety Disorder (Social Phobia)
Generalized Anxiety Disorder
Substance/Medication Induced Anxiety Disorder
Anxiety Disorder Attributable to Another Medical Condition
Anxiety Disorder Not Elsewhere Classified

As you will see in this chapter, a number of different conditions (listed in Table 8.1) are classified as anxiety disorders (Calkins et al., 2016). As such, anxiety disorders in *DSM-5-TR* represent discrete categories. One of the most common is referred to as **generalized anxiety disorder (GAD)**, in which the person worries about something that could happen in the future, such as losing a job or a partner. Overall, the person is unable to control their worry. With GAD, there are both physiological and psychological symptoms. The physiological symptoms may include problems sleeping, muscle tension, and feeling fatigued. The psychological symptoms may include feeling on edge, irritability, and difficulty in concentration as well as decision making (Bishop & Gagne, 2018).

For other people, specific situations may bring forth anxiety, such as giving a speech in public or being with others. This is referred to as a **social anxiety disorder (SAD)**. With social anxiety, the person is afraid they will be embarrassed and rejected by others. Although many of us may feel anxiety about certain public events, individuals with social anxiety disorder show fear and anxiety reactions that are out of proportion to the situation.

There are also phobias of specific objects, such as snakes or spiders, or situations, such as being in a high place or swimming in the ocean. Since the actual events result in immediate fear or anxiety, the person with the phobia typically avoids the object or situation. Another anxiety disorder is *panic disorder*. A **panic attack** comes quickly and carries with it an intense feeling of apprehension, anxiety, or fear. It usually happens without an actual situation that would suggest danger. Symptoms may include increased heart rate, sweating, chest pains, feeling dizzy or nauseous, and a sense of loss of control, such as feeling that one is losing their mind or will die.

In *DSM-5* and *DSM-5-TR* (APA, 2022), *separation anxiety disorder* has been moved from the childhood disorders section and is now included as one of the anxiety disorders. Also, *obsessive-compulsive disorder (OCD)* is considered separately from anxiety disorders in *DSM-5* and *DSM-5-TR*. It has been placed in its own section along with related disorders. OCD will be covered at the end of this chapter.

The Nature of Anxiety and Evolutionary Explanations

Anxiety is the fear of what might happen. What if I don't do well when I give a presentation to a room full of important people? Will I get the job I want? What if a snake bites me when I am in the woods? What if the plane I am on crashes? What if I get germs on my hands when I go into a public restroom? What if others do not like me? In this sense, anxiety is about the future, whereas fear typically has a stimulus in the present. With fear, we see a snake and become apprehensive. We look down from a tall building and feel unease. With anxiety, there is often no stimulus in front of us. Instead, the stimulus is in our mind. However, our cognitive and emotional consideration of a negative possibility does not make it any less real. Our body, mind, and emotions experience our ideas as real possibilities. In anxiety, we increase the probability in our mind that an undesirable event will happen.

Some fear and anxiety reactions appear to be innate. Most individuals feel apprehensive when looking down from a high building. Infants of about 9 months of age cry when a stranger takes them from their mothers. Other fears appear to be learned in a complex set of processes. But overall, our understanding of what constitutes the fear and anxiety system is not clearly worked out. Various anxiety disorders all involve the default network and the salience network, as described in Chapter 2, but in different ways (Andreescu et al., 2015; Li et al., 2023). There is some suggestion that a common brain

Some fear reactions appear to be built into our system; for example, infants of about 9 months of age will cry if a stranger takes them from their mothers.
iStock.com/Lisa5201

network underlies all forms of anxiety (Takagi et al., 2018). Yet post-traumatic stress disorder (PTSD), for example, which was discussed in Chapter 7, is thought to use different cortical networks than anxiety. Further, panic attacks, which will be discussed in this chapter, may also be governed by a different set of cortical processes than general feelings of anxiety.

What we do know is that fear and anxiety involve high-level as well as more primitive brain processes (Asok et al., 2019). Cognitively, we can make ourselves feel more anxious by thinking of all the terrible things that can happen in a given situation. We get on an airplane feeling somewhat anxious. We then hear a sound from the engine that we interpret to be a problem. This, in turn, results in our being even more vigilant and listening for every sound. The plane begins to move down the runway, and we tell ourselves it is not going to make it. This allows for emotional reactions to increase that our body normally keeps in check, and we feel anxious.

Limbic system processes, as you learned about in Chapter 7, can also respond to stimuli on their own. For example, our amygdala can respond to an angry face in a manner that begins an autonomic nervous system reaction. In research with rats, Joseph LeDoux (2000, 2003) has shown that there are two pathways for the processing of fear (see Figure 8.1). The higher pathway goes through the cerebral cortex and has high spatial resolution. The lower pathway goes more directly through the amygdala and is very fast but with less conscious experience. This suggests that the organism has a way to respond quickly to potential danger—even if its initial reaction is not correct. Simultaneously, the slow pathway is able to make a conscious appraisal of the situation. Thus, there is both a cortical and a subcortical pathway to respond to dangerous situations. As such, there is great survival value in being wrong in responding to a stick as if it is a snake, when a snake could be dangerous.

From an evolutionary perspective, to be fearful in the presence of dangerous situations would be adaptive. However, extreme anxiety can hurt our performance. Thus, anxiety can both help us and hurt us, depending on the situation and the extent of the anxiety. One scientific aspect of this is the question of how fixed or plastic these anxieties and fears are. From research, we know that certain phobias run in families, suggesting a genetic component. However, not everyone has exactly the same fears, suggesting that fears can be learned during development.

One classic study in fear development is that of Susan Mineka and her colleagues (see Öhman & Mineka, 2001, for an overview). It had been observed that primates in the wild show a fear of

FIGURE 8.1 ■ What Happens When You See a Snake in the Woods?

The LeDoux fear response is made up of two pathways for the processing of fear. One pathway is fast and outside of awareness, while the other is slower and has a conscious component. Visual stimuli are first processed by the thalamus, which passes rough, almost archetypal information directly to the amygdala (red). This quick transmission allows the brain to respond to the possible danger (blue). Meanwhile the visual cortex also receives information from the thalamus and, with more perceptual sophistication and more time, determines that there is a snake on the path (green). This information is relayed to the amygdala, causing heart rate and blood pressure to increase and muscles to contract. If, however, the cortex determines that the object is not a snake, the message to the amygdala will quell the fear response.

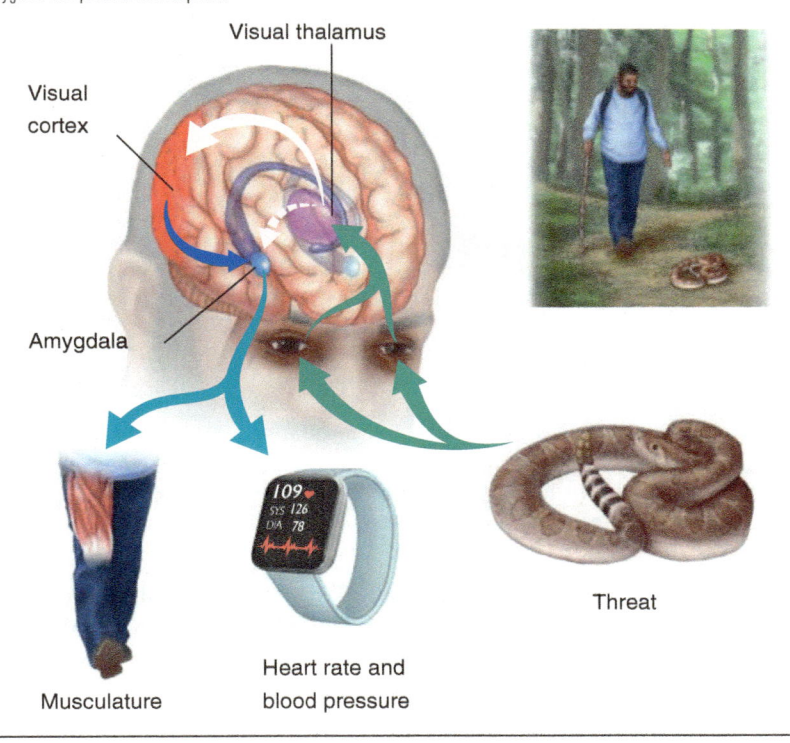

Source: Adapted from LeDoux, J. (1994, June). Emotion, memory, and the brain. *Scientific American*, pp. 62–71. Illustration by Monica Wierzbicki/Body Scientific Intl.

snakes. Since a similar fear was seen in lab monkeys, it was assumed that the fear was somehow innate. However, Mineka asked the question of whether early experience could influence this. In particular, she wanted to know if observational learning could play a role.

What she and her colleagues did was to compare wild-reared rhesus monkeys with those that had been reared in the lab. The wild-reared monkeys that had been brought to the lab some 24 years earlier showed a fear of snakes. This fear existed even though they would have had no experience with snakes during their time in the lab. The lab-reared monkeys, on the other hand, did not show any fear of snakes. In fact, they would reach over the snake to grab food.

How did monkeys develop the fear of snakes? What Mineka did next was to pair a wild-reared monkey with a young lab-reared one. A snake was then presented, and a wild-reared monkey showed fear. The young lab-reared monkey was able to observe this. After this, the lab-reared monkey also showed fear. Clearly, the lab-reared monkey had the ability to quickly acquire the fear but required an experience in which another monkey showed fear for it to happen.

The next question Mineka and her colleagues asked was about the importance of the feared object itself. In a very clever study, she showed some of the young monkeys a videotape of a wild monkey showing fear toward a snake. As expected, they acquired the fear of snakes. However, with another group of young monkeys, she edited the tape so what the young monkey saw was the original fear reaction of the older monkey but this time to a flower. If fear was acquired by a simple associative learning situation in which the stimulus did not matter, then you would expect the young monkeys to acquire a fear of flowers. This was not the case. From this and a variety of other studies, it appears that fear can be learned through observation, but only fear of evolutionarily important objects.

Anxiety affects everyone as they become concerned about the future. However, when that anxiety is unusually strong, recurrent, and interferes with your life, it may be evidence of an anxiety disorder.

iStock.com/FG Trade Latin. Stock photo. Posed by model.

Jaak Panksepp (2004) suggested that fear can be evoked in at least four different ways. The first is by painful stimuli. Research studies have used the experience of shock as a way to induce fear. The second way to induce fear is to pair cues with aversive stimuli. In this way, the cue alone will produce fear. The third way is to present evolutionarily important cues that have survival value for the species. For example, the smell of a cat will produce fear reactions in rats. The fourth way is to create a frustrating situation. For example, if an organism is expecting a reward that is delayed, fear and apprehension will result. This model suggests that anxiety can be produced by expectations that either negative events will happen or that positive events will not happen.

Thus, the brain predicts the future. Part of the way we predict the future is based on past information. As noted in Chapter 5, if a child does not experience their world as safe and secure, then anxiety can become part of the attachment pattern. Globally, these children expect the world not to take care of them. As humans, we also make predictions based on specific situations. As we listen to a person speak or as we drive down the road, we are constantly predicting what will happen next. This prediction is demonstrated by research indicating that if something happens that is different from what we expect, we show electroencephalogram (EEG) changes in the brain. Generally, we predict that our drive down the road will be fine. However, individuals with anxiety disorders see negative alternatives and worry that things will not work out.

Cognitive Processes in Anxiety

It has been suggested that fear mechanisms evolved in humans to aid our ability to disengage from a task at hand so as to pay better attention to threats or potential danger (Öhman & Mineka, 2001). An unexpected loud noise will cause us to jump and focus our attention in its direction. Although this process occurs with all individuals, it is becoming apparent that individuals with anxiety are even more sensitive than others to the possibility of potential threat (Bishop, 2007; MacLeod et al., 2019; MacLeod & Mathews, 2012). What is interesting is that in lab studies, images that are threat-related or seen as emotionally negative will attract the attention of those with anxiety disorders even if presented very quickly. People with depression, on the other hand, require a presentation of over half a second before the image captures their attention (Huys, Daw, & Dayan, 2015). This sensitivity is referred to as **cognitive bias**.

Cognitive bias has been studied in a number of ways. One is to use a modified **Stroop test**. The traditional Stroop test has color names displayed in different colors. That is, the word *green* would be shown in red. When asked to name the color of the words, individuals are slower when the color name and actual color do not match as compared with when the actual color and color name are the same (Figure 8.2). When using a "threat" Stroop, the name of the color is replaced by a threat word (Figure 8.3). Another research procedure is to use a dot-probe task. One version of the task asks individuals to focus on an X in the middle of the computer screen. On each side of the X are words. The person is to press a computer key whenever a word is replaced by a dot. In anxiety studies, both words can be neutral, they can represent different types of threat, or they can consist of one neutral and one threat word.

The basic question is as follows: Does an individual who is anxious show differential reaction times when threat or negative emotional words are present? Overall, the answer is yes. Individuals with anxiety disorders show a selective attentional bias toward threat-related words. When a threat-related word is present, individuals with anxiety show slower reaction times and increased error rates. Even if stimuli are presented in a manner that the individual cannot detect, anxious individuals will display this cognitive bias. This suggests that attention to threat involves more primitive brain processes such as the amygdala rather than just being under higher cortical control (MacLeod & Mathews, 2012).

Individuals with anxiety disorders show a tendency to focus on information that is negative and to expect more negative things to actually happen. They also interpret ambiguous information in a

FIGURE 8.2 ■ The Stroop Effect

Read out loud the color of the words in this figure. This is the Stroop effect: Individuals are slower when asked to name the color of the words.

BLUE GREEN YELLOW

PINK RED ORANGE

GRAY BLACK PURPLE

TAN WHITE BROWN

FIGURE 8.3 ■ The Stroop Effect Using Threat Words

Name the color of the words in this figure. This is an example of the Stroop test using threat words. Neutral words would also be added to compare differences in reaction time.

FAILURE

REJECTION

INFERIOR

USELESS

negative manner. Overall, anxious individuals have a difficult time not paying attention to potential threats in their environment. This, in turn, supports the experience of negative internal emotional states. This type of cognitive bias leads to both the development and maintenance of the condition of anxiety.

Neurobiology of Anxiety Disorders

Although fear and anxiety are often studied together, research suggests that different brain areas are involved. Specifically, those areas involved in anxiety are not those directly responsible for the expression of fear. Rather, anxiety is related to those areas of the brain that regulate the fear system. These include the prefrontal cortex (PFC), the amygdala, and the hippocampus. These are systems involved in cognitions, emotional reactivity, and memory—all important components in the social and cognitive aspects of anxiety. In humans, these systems are also involved in increased vigilance and attention to threat (Robinson et al., 2014). The amygdala also plays a role in fear conditioning.

One of the major neurotransmitters involved in anxiety is **gamma-aminobutyric acid (GABA)** (Millan, 2003; Schmidt-Wilcke, 2018). GABA is the major inhibitory neurotransmitter in the brain. Although GABA is involved in a variety of processes, it is thought to play a major role in anxiety. The basic idea is that individuals with anxiety have reduced GABA activity, which in turn results in less inhibition of those brain structures that are involved in threat responses. It should also be noted that GABA receptors are located densely in the PFC, the amygdala, and the hippocampus. Benzodiazepines, which are common drugs used in the treatment of anxiety disorders, influence the GABA system, which in turn increases its inhibitory effects. Further, animal models of anxiety have shown increased GABA activity in the amygdala and a reduction of fear with the introduction of serotonin in the hippocampus and amygdala. An adult rat that was nurtured and licked as an infant will have greater expression of GABA activity in the amygdala with fewer signs of fearfulness and stress responses (Fries et al., 2004).

In reviewing studies with both humans and other animals, Gross and Hen (2004) suggested that anxiety should be seen as a developmental problem involving both environmental and genetic factors. From twin studies, it is apparent that the genetic contribution to anxiety is moderate (30%–40%). Genetic studies of individuals with anxiety disorders show the highest concordance for monozygotic (MZ) versus dizygotic (DZ) twin pairs as would be expected if there were a genetic component. Panic disorder was associated with a heritability of 48% (Hettema et al., 2001). Similar heritability numbers were found for specific phobias, such as animal (47%), blood injury (59%), and situational (46%). Social phobia was found to be 51%. In studies examining twins with generalized anxiety disorder (GAD), modest relationships ranging from 15% to 30% have been reported (Kendler & Baker, 2007). Family interviews also suggest the presence of GAD in first-degree relatives. Overall, this strongly suggests genetic contributions to the development of anxiety disorders.

With the discovery of functional networks in the brain, psychopathology can be mapped in terms of which cortical networks differ from normal functioning. Chad Sylvester and his colleagues (2012) have performed this analysis in relation to anxiety. They described anxiety disorders in relation to four functional networks (Figure 8.4). The first is the salience or cingulo-opercular network, which is seen to be important in detecting errors or conflicts. Error detection would result in the need for changes in cognitive control. The second network is the executive control or frontoparietal network. This is the network that implements increased cognitive control. The third network is the ventral attentional network and is involved in detecting new stimuli rather than the task at hand. The fourth network is the default network, which is involved in internal processing, including self-inspection, future planning, and emotional regulation. Overall, these researchers suggest that anxiety disorders display a particular pattern of action in the four networks. This pattern includes overactivity in the salience network and underactivity in the executive and default networks. This is consistent with individuals with anxiety disorders having an oversensitivity to threat.

Developmental Aspects of Anxiety

The development of anxiety and fear follows a trajectory that is part of the human condition. Children and adolescents show similar profiles of anxiety and fear across cultures; however, cultures that favor

FIGURE 8.4 ■ Four Networks Involved in Anxiety

These four networks are error detection, executive control, new stimuli detection, and internal processing.

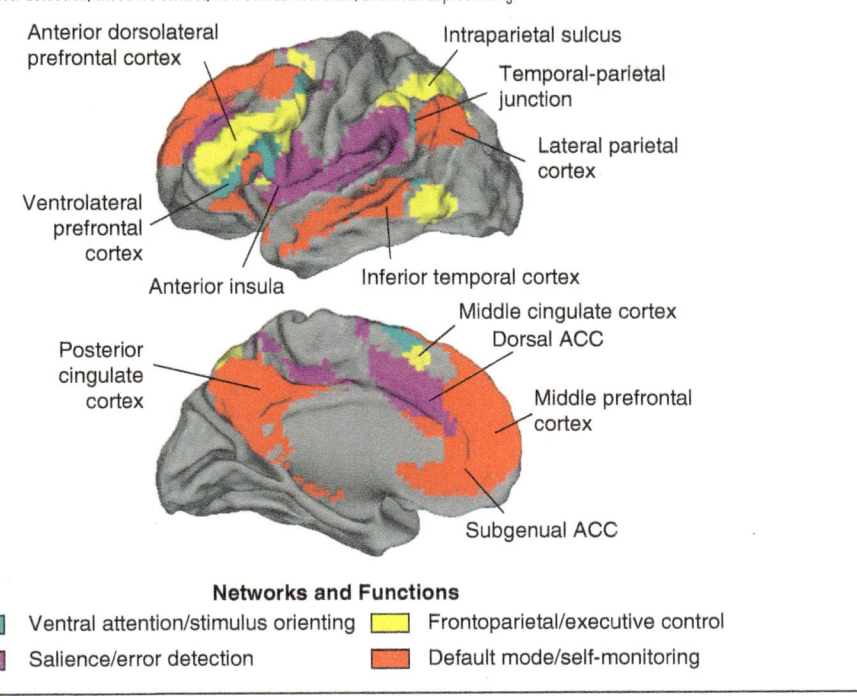

Networks and Functions
- Ventral attention/stimulus orienting
- Salience/error detection
- Frontoparietal/executive control
- Default mode/self-monitoring

Credit: Sylvester, C., Corbetta, M., Raichle, M., Rodebaugh, T., Schlaggar, B., Sheline, Y., Zorumski, C., & Lenze, E. (2012). Functional network dysfunction in anxiety and anxiety disorders. *Trends in Neuroscience, 35*(9), 527–535. With permission from Elsevier.

inhibition, compliance, and obedience also show increased levels of fear (Ollendick et al., 1996). Fears are traditionally seen in relation to immediate experiences. Young children during their first year of life, usually around 9 months, will react fearfully to strangers. After that, they will react to separation. Infants of other species, too, show distress vocalizations when separated from their mothers. Human infants also begin to display distress to specific stimuli, such as insects or flying bees, or animals. By adolescence, the fear turns to anxiety in that the person may display distress when the object of concern is not present. Social anxiety about future situations is common among adolescents. The normal expression of fear and anxiety only becomes pathological when it interferes with the child's or adolescent's ability to function or causes distress.

A number of epidemiology studies have shown that 2.5% to 5% of children and adolescents meet criteria for anxiety disorders at any one time (Rapee et al., 2009). The earliest anxiety disorder to develop is separation anxiety disorder. The next is specific phobias, which begin in early to middle childhood. Next comes social phobia, which begins in early to middle adolescence. Panic disorder appears in early adulthood. Given the nature of adolescence, anxiety disorders at this time have an influence on popularity and social competence. They are also associated with victimization.

The National Comorbidity Replication Adolescent Supplement is a U.S. survey of 10,148 adolescents 13 to 17 years of age. One of its advantages is that it is based on interviews with adolescents. Table 8.2 shows the lifetime prevalence rates for anxiety disorders by age and gender based on *DSM-IV-TR* criteria. As shown in the table, specific phobias and social phobia are the most common anxiety disorders among adolescents. Anxiety disorders in this survey were more prevalent in adolescents than were mood disorders, behavior disorders, or substance abuse.

It is not always the case that if a person has an anxiety disorder in childhood, it will continue into adulthood. This is especially true for specific phobias. As with adolescence, in adulthood, rates for anxiety disorders are higher than the rates for mood disorders. One anxiety disorder that shows increased prevalence is GAD.

TABLE 8.2 ■ Lifetime Prevalence of DSM-IV-TR/CIDI Anxiety Disorders by Age and Gender in the National Comorbidity Survey Replication (NCS-R) and Adolescent Supplement (NCS-A)

Anxiety Disorder	Ages 13–17			Ages 18–64			Ages 65+			Total (Ages 13+)[a]		
	Female	Male	Total	Female	Male	Total	Female	Male	Total	Female	Male	Total
	% (SE)	% (SE)	% (SE)	% (SE)	% (SE)	% (SE)	% (SE)	% (SE)	% (SE)	% (SE)	% (SE)	% (SE)
Panic disorder[b]	2.5 (0.3)	2.1 (0.4)	2.3 (0.3)	7.0* (0.4)	3.3 (0.4)	5.2 (0.3)	2.5 (0.7)	1.6 (0.6)	2.1 (0.5)	4.8* (0.3)	2.7 (0.3)	3.8 (0.2)
Generalized anxiety disorder	2.8 (0.5)	1.6 (0.4)	2.2 (0.3)	7.7* (0.4)	4.6 (0.5)	6.2 (0.3)	4.8* (0.6)	1.3 (0.5)	3.3 (0.4)	5.5* (0.3)	3.1 (0.3)	4.3 (0.2)
Agoraphobia[c]	3.7* (0.6)	1.7 (0.4)	2.7 (0.4)	3.2* (0.3)	2.0 (0.3)	2.6 (0.2)	1.5 (0.5)	0.7 (0.4)	1.2 (0.3)	3.2* (0.3)	1.8 (0.2)	2.5 (0.2)
Social phobia	11.2* (1.1)	6.2 (0.7)	8.6 (0.6)	14.2* (0.7)	11.8 (0.6)	13.0 (0.5)	7.1 (0.9)	5.1 (1.2)	6.3 (0.7)	12.3* (0.6)	8.9 (0.5)	10.7 (0.4)
Specific phobia	23.0* (1.3)	17.1 (0.6)	20.0 (1.0)	17.5* (0.6)	9.9 (0.6)	13.8 (0.4)	9.1* (1.2)	3.6 (0.7)	6.8 (0.7)	18.7* (0.6)	12.3 (0.6)	15.6 (0.5)
Separation anxiety disorder	9.5* (0.9)	5.9 (1.0)	7.7 (0.5)	8.2* (0.6)	4.7 (0.5)	6.6 (0.4)	1.9 (0.4)	1.3 (0.8)	1.6 (0.5)	8.3* (0.5)	5.2 (0.4)	6.7 (0.3)
Post-traumatic stress disorder	6.9* (0.8)	2.3 (1.2)	4.5 (0.4)	11.7* (0.8)	4.0 (0.3)	8.0 (0.5)	2.5* (0.6)	0.4 (0.2)	1.6 (0.3)	8.5* (0.6)	2.8 (0.3)	5.7 (0.3)
Obsessive-compulsive disorder	—[d]	—[d]	—[d]	3.6* (0.6)	1.8 (0.4)	2.7 (0.4)	0.6 (0.5)	0.3 (0.3)	0.5 (0.4)	3.0 (0.5)	1.6 (0.3)	2.3 (0.3)
Any anxiety disorder	38.3 (1.6)	26.8 (1.0)	32.4 (1.0)	40.4 (1.1)	26.4 (1.1)	33.7 (0.9)	17.7 (1.4)	11.1 (1.6)	14.9 (1.3)	37.3 (0.9)	25.6 (0.8)	31.6 (0.7)
(n)	(3219)	(3024)	(6243)	(2978)	(2245)	(5223)	(446)	(263)	(709)	(6643)	(5532)	(12175)

Credit: Kessler, R. C., Petukhova, M., Sampson, N. A., Zaslavsky, A. M., & Wittchen, H.-U. (2012). Twelve-month and lifetime prevalence and lifetime morbid risk of anxiety and mood disorders in the United States. *International Journal of Methods in Psychiatric Research*, 21(3), 169–184, Table 1. https://doi.org/10.1002/mpr.1359

[a] The NCS-A (ages 13–17) and NCS-R (ages 18+) samples were combined without weighting to adjust for the higher probability of selection of adolescents than adults in the two surveys.
[b] With or without agoraphobia.
[c] With or without a history of panic disorder.
[d] Obsessive-compulsive disorder was not assessed among adolescents.
*Significant gender difference within the subsample.

Models of Anxiety Development

At this point, you have read about the development of anxiety on a number of levels. You have learned that children show an anxiety or fear of strangers at about 9 months of age. In previous chapters, you learned that those infants who fail to develop a secure attachment pattern may experience the world as unsafe and experience anxiety in relationships. Other studies have shown a relationship between attachment and the development of anxiety and mood disorders (Simonelli et al., 2004). We also know from temperament research that some infants and children show more outgoing patterns, whereas others show more inhibited patterns (Filippi et al., 2022; Kagan, 2003; Troller-Renfree et al., 2019). Genetics and epigenetics also play a role in this.

As children grow up, they learn from their family and culture. If your father or mother was afraid of being in the woods, or seeing certain animals, you might adopt the same belief. In addition, your family's avoidance of such situations would make it difficult for you to learn that these fears were not supported. Sometimes, as with Susan Mineka's monkeys, just seeing someone else show fear may lead you to do the same through modeling.

In an attempt to integrate the various factors that can lead to anxiety, a number of researchers have come up with models of anxiety development. Two of these are David Barlow with his triple vulnerability perspective (Barlow, 2000) and Susan Mineka with her learning/evolutionary perspective (Mineka & Zinbarg, 2006; Mineka & Oehlberg, 2008; Zinbarg et al., 2022).

Barlow's model of the triple vulnerability perspective suggests that there are three critical components involved in the development of anxiety-related disorders. The first is a generalized biological vulnerability. Temperament would be one example. However, temperament alone does not make one anxious. The second vulnerability is a generalized psychological vulnerability. This would include such psychological factors as believing the world is not safe. You may also come to believe that you will not be able to cope with the problems you experience in life. The third vulnerability is a specific psychological vulnerability. This is where you learn from early experience, including what you are taught, that specific situations or objects are dangerous. When in a difficult stressful situation, we are less likely to be able to correctly assess the situation, and then these three vulnerabilities may come together to lead to the experience of anxiety.

The Mineka model of learning in relation to anxiety disorders goes beyond the simple learning approaches developed by individuals such as John Watson and Little Albert (described later in this chapter) in the early part of the 20th century. For example, Mineka's work with the learning of snake phobias in lab monkeys demonstrated that short-term experiences through modeling can have long-term effects. Likewise, watching a friend give a speech and be criticized can influence one's own sense of social anxiety. Cultural norms also teach us about the social concerns each culture displays. Standing out in an Eastern culture is very different from standing out in a Western one. However, not every human who has had a traumatic experience with a particular object or situation develops anxiety. This suggests that each individual requires a series of background conditions for the anxiety-related disorder to develop. Mineka's overall model suggests that biological vulnerabilities, such as genetics and temperament, combine with prior learning vulnerabilities, such as social and cultural factors. Included in this second vulnerability is the person's experience of a situation as controllable or not. Following this is the experience of a stressful situation, which in turn brings forth emotional processing that can be experienced as anxiety or panic. Further, on a larger level, our evolutionary history as humans influences the types of objects and situations in which a person learns to fear. For example, humans as well as monkeys learn the fear of snakes more easily than fear of most other stimuli (Öhman & Mineka, 2001).

Anxiety Disorders Around the World

In *Cultural LENS: Global Mental Health*, you can see lifetime and 12-month prevalence data for any anxiety disorder by country. Rates may vary by country, but the overall data show that anxiety disorders are common throughout the world. Kessler et al. (2009) reported additional data to suggest that only a small number of those individuals with a mental disorder receive treatment, and even fewer receive high-quality treatment. This, in turn, results in impaired functioning, which has real costs to a society in terms of productivity, financial resources, and quality of life.

CULTURAL LENS
GLOBAL MENTAL HEALTH: ANXIETY DISORDERS

The World Health Organization (WHO), as part of its mission, has collected data on mental health from countries around the world. Face-to-face household surveys were undertaken with community adult respondents in low-income or middle-income countries (Colombia, Lebanon, Mexico, Nigeria, China, South Africa, Ukraine) and high-income countries (Belgium, France, Germany, Israel, Italy, Japan, the Netherlands, New Zealand, Spain, the United States). Prevalence data were assessed with the WHO Composite International Diagnostic Interview.

Lifetime and 12-month prevalence data in relation to anxiety disorders has been compiled (Tables 8.3 and 8.4).

TABLE 8.3 ■ Lifetime Prevalence in Terms of Percentage and Standard Error (SE)

	Any Anxiety Disorder	
	%	(SE)
I. WHO Region: Pan American Health		
Colombia	25.3	(1.4)
Mexico	14.3	(0.9)
United States	31.0	(1.0)
II. WHO Region: African Regional Office		
Nigeria	6.5	(0.9)
South Africa	15.8	(0.8)
III. WHO Region: Eastern Mediterranean		
Lebanon	16.7	(1.6)
IV. WHO Region: European Regional		
Belgium	13.1	(1.9)
France	22.3	(1.4)
Germany	14.6	(1.5)
Israel	5.2	(0.3)
Italy	11.0	(0.9)
Netherlands	15.9	(1.1)
Spain	9.9	(1.1)
Ukraine	10.9	(0.8)
V. WHO Region: Western Pacific Region		
PRC	4.8	(0.7)
Japan	6.9	(0.6)
New Zealand	24.6	(0.7)

Credit: Kessler, R. C., Aguilar-Gaxiola, S., Alonso, J., Chatterji, S., Lee, S., Ormel, J., Ustün, T. B., & Wang, P. S. (2009). The global burden of mental disorders: An update from the WHO World Mental Health (WMH) surveys. *Epidemiology and Psychiatric Sciences*, *18*(1), 23–33. © Cambridge University Press, reproduced with permission.

TABLE 8.4 ■ Twelve-Month Prevalence for Anxiety Disorders Worldwide

	Any Anxiety Disorder		Any Mood Disorder	
	%	(SE)	%	(SE)
I. WHO Region: Pan American Health Organization (PAHO)				
Colombia	14.4	(1.0)	7.0	(0.5)
Mexico	8.4	(0.6)	4.7	(0.3)
United States	19.0	(0.7)	9.7	(0.4)
II. WHO Region: African Regional Office (AFRO)				
Nigeria	4.2	(0.5)	1.1	(0.2)
South Africa	8.2	(0.6)	4.9	(0.4)
III. WHO Region: Eastern Mediterranean Regional Office (EMRO)				
Lebanon	12.2	(1.2)	6.8	(0.7)
IV. WHO Region: European Regional Office (EURO)				
Belgium	8.4	(1.4)	5.4	(0.5)
France	13.7	(1.1)	6.5	(0.6)
Germany	8.3	(1.1)	3.3	(0.3)
Israel	3.6	(0.3)	6.4	(0.4)
Italy	6.5	(0.6)	3.4	(0.3)
Netherlands	8.9	(1.0)	5.1	(0.5)
Spain	6.6	(0.9)	4.4	(0.3)
Ukraine	6.8	(0.7)	9.0	(0.6)
V. WHO Region: Western Pacific Regional Office (WPRO)				
PRC	3.0	(0.5)	1.9	(0.3)
Japan	4.2	(0.6)	2.5	(0.4)
New Zealand	15.0	(0.5)	8.0	(0.4)

Credit: Kessler, R. C., Aguilar-Gaxiola, S., Alonso, J., Chatterji, S., Lee, S., Ormel, J., Ustün, T. B., & Wang, P. S. (2009). The global burden of mental disorders: An update from the WHO World Mental Health (WMH) surveys. *Epidemiology and Psychiatric Sciences, 18*(1), 23–33. © Cambridge University Press, reproduced with permission.

Note: SE: standard error.

Thought Question

What do we know about the prevalence rates of anxiety disorders across the life span and around the world?

CONCEPT CHECK

- What are the two pathways in the brain for processing fear, and how do they work? From an evolutionary perspective, what is the advantage of the two pathways?
- What are some of the ways cognitive bias leads to both development and maintenance of anxiety?

- How is the brain involved in anxiety in terms of brain areas, neurotransmitters, and networks?
- How does the developmental trajectory of anxiety and fear map onto normal human developmental stages?

MAJOR TYPES OF ANXIETY DISORDERS

This section will introduce you to the major anxiety disorders. These include separation anxiety disorder, generalized anxiety disorder (GAD), social anxiety disorder (SAD), and separation anxiety disorder.

Generalized Anxiety Disorder

In *DSM-5-TR*, GAD is characterized by excessive anxiety and worry that have been present for more than 6 months (Table 8.5). Bodily symptoms such as feeling on edge and muscle tension must also accompany the worry. In fact, one of the more consistent physiological patterns seen in GAD is high muscle tension. Finally, the anxiety must lead to one or more of the following four behaviors. These are (1) avoiding activities that can have negative outcomes, (2) overpreparation for activities that can have negative outcomes, (3) marked procrastination in behaviors due to worries, and (4) repeatedly seeking reassurance due to worries.

GAD, along with depression, is the most frequently diagnosed mental disorder in the United States. GAD prevalence rates are 3.1% for a given year, with lifetime rates being 5.7% for those over 18 years of age (Kessler et al., 2005). However, these rates have changed over the years with changing *DSM* criteria. Prevalence rates are twice as high for women as compared with men. GAD occurrence peaks in middle age and declines after that. Most individuals (86%) with GAD also meet criteria for another disorder, mainly major depressive disorder, social phobia, or panic disorder (Brown et al., 2001). In those with both GAD and a major depressive disorder, the GAD was seen in individuals some 7 years

---

TABLE 8.5 ■ *DSM-5-TR* Diagnostic Criteria for Generalized Anxiety Disorder

A. Excessive anxiety and worry (apprehensive expectation) occurring more days than not for at least 6 months, about a number of events or activities (such as work or school performance).

B. The individual finds it difficult to control the worry.

C. The anxiety and worry are associated with three (or more) of the following six symptoms (with at least some symptoms having been present for more days than not for the past 6 months):
   Note: Only one item is required in children.
   1. Restlessness or feeling keyed up or on edge.
   2. Being easily fatigued.
   3. Difficulty concentrating or mind going blank.
   4. Irritability.
   5. Muscle tension.
   6. Sleep disturbance (difficulty falling or staying asleep, or restless, unsatisfying sleep).

D. The anxiety, worry, or physical symptoms cause clinically significant distress or impairment in social, occupational, or other important areas of functioning.

E. The disturbance is not attributable to the physiological effects of a substance (e.g., a drug of abuse, a medication) or another medical condition (e.g., hyperthyroidism).

F. The disturbance is not better explained by another mental disorder (e.g., anxiety or worry about having panic attacks in panic disorder, negative evaluation in social anxiety disorder, contamination or other obsessions in obsessive-compulsive disorder, separation from attachment figures in separation anxiety disorder, reminders of traumatic events in posttraumatic stress disorder, gaining weight in anorexia nervosa, physical complaints in somatic symptom disorder, perceived appearance flaws in body dysmorphic disorder, having a serious illness in illness anxiety disorder, or the content of delusional beliefs in schizophrenia or delusional disorder).

Credit: Reprinted with permission from the *Diagnostic and Statistical Manual of Mental Disorders, fifth edition, text revision*, DSM-V-TR, pp. 250–251 (Copyright © 2022). American Psychiatric Association. All Rights Reserved.

before the onset of depression. This has suggested to some that a period of significant worry may lead to the onset of depression.

Research has analyzed worry in terms of both content and one's ability to control it. In one study comparing a group of people with GAD and a control group of individuals without anxiety, those in the control group reported they were able to control their worrying to a greater degree than those with GAD. Whereas 100% of those with GAD reported problems reducing the impact of their worries, only 5.6% of controls reported such a difficulty (Abel & Borkovec, 1995). There is also some suggestion that those with GAD are not able to move from a process of worry to active problem solving or coping. In addition, in a study by Barlow (2002), 100% of those with GAD reported that they worry about minor things, whereas 50% of those with other types of anxiety disorders reported this. In terms of frequency, those with GAD reported that they worry a larger percentage of each day and tend to have a larger set of domains (e.g., family, money, and friends) that they worry about than those without GAD.

What is the role of worry? One answer is that worry is the manner in which an individual with GAD attempts to reduce the negative emotional experiences associated with GAD (Borkovec, 1994). This is referred to as the cognitive avoidance model of GAD (Borkovec et al., 2004). Worry, in this case, serves two functions. The first function is to use worry as a way to prepare for bad events or even to prevent them from occurring. The second function is to use worry as a way to reduce the person's emotional response. Although a consistent physiological picture of worry has yet to appear, research suggests that worry does produce short-term relief from physiological responses to stress.

Many individuals who report anxiety to their psychologists, psychiatrists, and even their family physicians are prescribed medications such as benzodiazepines or offered one of the types of psychotherapy described in Chapter 1. Studies using psychodynamic, existential-humanistic, and cognitive behavioral approaches have all reported reductions in anxiety. At this point, both medications and psychological treatments show similar reductions in GAD in the short term. However, only about 40% to 60% of those treated with either medication or psychological treatments show full improvement. This is in comparison with other anxiety disorders such as phobias, which show higher rates of improvement after treatment.

Psychological Treatment for Generalized Anxiety Disorder

The best-studied psychological interventions with GAD have involved cognitive behavioral approaches and behavioral approaches (McCabe-Bennett et al., 2018). Dynamic approaches have also been shown to be effective (Barber et al., 2013; Leichsenring & Steinert, 2018). The behavioral approaches include relaxation training and other such techniques. The cognitive behavioral techniques focus on automatic thinking. Typical approaches train clients to detect internal and external anxiety cues and to apply new coping skills that focus on both psychic and somatic symptoms (Borkovec & Ruscio, 2001). Initially, clients are asked to pay close attention to factors in their daily life that trigger anxiety responses. They are also asked to pay attention to physiological and cognitive responses experienced as anxiety develops. In the therapy itself, the client is asked to imagine a situation that would increase stress or anxiety or choose a topic that they would worry about and notice the associated thoughts, feelings, and images. Overall, the major cognitive behavioral approaches are designed to be offered for a specific period of time. These techniques help the client learn how to reduce anxiety and worry, which is a major component of GAD.

Some important components of a cognitive behavioral therapy (CBT) approach are as follows:

1. Identifying the anxiety-associated thoughts, images, beliefs, etc.
2. Discussing these to bring out their causal role
3. Leading clients to question the validity of thoughts or beliefs and to search for evidence
4. Helping clients develop alternative, less anxiety-arousing assumptions or interpretations
5. Testing alternative viewpoints in homework assignments or experiments
6. Teaching the above methods as self-helping coping devices to be used in real life

These components were developed by Tom Borkovec and his colleagues, who tested the effectiveness of therapy components in a variety of outcome studies. In addition, Borkovec and Ruscio (2001) reviewed outcome research from 13 randomized controlled GAD studies that involved a CBT component. As a whole, these CBT studies showed decreases in anxiety and depression following treatment, which was maintained in a 6- to 12-month follow-up. This suggests that CBT is effective not only for GAD but also for some comorbid conditions. Successful treatment was also associated with psychophysiological changes such as in EEG gamma activity (Oathes et al., 2008). Overall, meta-analyses have shown larger effect sizes for psychotherapy (.76) than for medication (.38) for the treatment of GAD (Carl et al., 2020). That is, while both psychotherapy and medication have been shown to reduce anxiety symptoms, effect size, which shows the strength of the relationship between the treatment and the changes in symptoms, suggests psychotherapy is more effective.

Another effective treatment for GAD is mindfulness (Hoge et al., 2013, 2023). Mindfulness-based treatments have the person with GAD focus on the present moment. This attention to the present is performed with openness and in a nonjudgmental manner. This allows for better emotional regulation and reduction of anxiety symptoms. In randomized control trials for the treatment of GAD, mindfulness-based treatment has been shown to be more effective than treatment involving stress reduction techniques (Hoge et al., 2013). Further, functional magnetic resonance imaging (fMRI) changes were seen following mindfulness training in those with GAD in the amygdala and the connections between the frontal areas and the amygdala (Hölzel et al., 2013). These cortical changes were also associated with symptom reduction.

Mindfulness approaches have also been integrated into traditional CBT. One of these is acceptance and commitment therapy (ACT) (Hayes, 2004; Hayes et al., 2011). This approach suggests that those with GAD attempt to control their internal experiences, which often does not work. Based on this failure to control such thoughts and feelings, these individuals avoid internal processes. ACT uses acceptance and mindfulness to regain connections with one's internal processes, including thoughts, feelings, memories, and physical sensations.

Another therapy that has integrated mindfulness with CBT is referred to as acceptance-based behavioral therapy (ABBT) (e.g., Hayes-Skelton et al., 2013; Roemer & Orsillo, 2002; Roemer et al., 2008). This treatment involves educating the individual with GAD about their relationship with internal

Behavioral approaches to treating generalized anxiety disorder include relaxation training and other such techniques.
iStock.com/Luza studios

experiences, especially negative reactions to these. The second part of the treatment includes mindfulness exercises. A third component emphasizes behavioral changes rather than reacting to internal processes. ABBT has been shown to be an empirically supported approach to GAD (Roemer et al., 2008).

The following case study of Adam Caldwell (not his real name) describes the role of therapy in the treatment of an individual with GAD.

CASE OF ADAM CALDWELL
GENERALIZED ANXIETY DISORDER

Adam Caldwell is a 50-year-old European American. He came to the clinic to seek treatment to address his GAD symptoms. At the onset of therapy, he was also experiencing marital difficulties and stress at work. He had previously been divorced and was remarried, living with his second wife at the time of treatment. He had several children from his first marriage as well as several stepchildren. He had a doctoral degree and was employed in an applied science field.

Adam Caldwell defined himself as a man with integrity (trustworthy, honest) and deep commitment to his religion and the contract of marriage. In terms of coping style, he revealed himself to be a logical and analytical thinker, frequently providing detailed and intellectual responses and at first rarely expressing emotions even when directly prompted. His problem-solving style was such that in stressful situations he reportedly tended to deny ("stuff away") his painful feelings and act in a manner that was impulsive and hostile.

At the beginning of therapy, Adam reported a high level of GAD symptoms. These symptoms included worry and somatic distress across a broad range of situations. He reported that he was also experiencing stress at work and was having marital conflict.

Adam reported a difficult interpersonal history. His father was authoritarian, distant, and physically abusive. His mother was kind but submissive to his father and did not protect him from the father's abuse. He reported being a rebellious child who had no close friends. His divorce from his first wife was traumatic, and his children were removed from his care.

Early in treatment, Adam had difficulty implementing and benefiting from techniques prescribed in the cognitive behavioral therapy (CBT) protocol in response to the stressful events. At the end of a guided relaxation exercise in Session 4, however, the client reported a substantial reduction in anxiety and stated to the therapist, "That's the impact you have on me." In Session 5, Adam reported having experienced a shift in his average mood from anxious to relaxed. He also stated that he was able to make this shift by monitoring his anxiety during the day and challenging the associated thoughts. As therapy progressed, Adam appeared to become confident, forthright, active, and even happy.

Source: Based on Castonguay, L., Nelson, D., Boswell, J., Nordberg, S., McAleavey, A., Newman, M., & Borkovec, T. (2012). Corrective experiences in cognitive behavior and interpersonal–emotional processing therapies: A qualitative analysis of a single case. In L. Castonguay & C. Hill (Eds.), *Transformation in psychotherapy: Corrective experiences across cognitive behavioral, humanistic, and psychodynamic approaches* (pp. 245–279). American Psychological Association.

Biological Treatment for Generalized Anxiety Disorder

Since the 1970s, benzodiazepines have been used to treat anxiety (see *LENS: Anxiety and the Prescribing of Benzodiazepines*). Benzodiazepines, such as Valium and Xanax, are thought to influence GABA activity (Nasir et al., 2020). Individuals with anxiety have reduced GABA activity, which in turn results in less inhibition of those brain structures that are involved in threat responses. Unlike antidepressant medications, benzodiazepines show their effect within a week. A large number of studies have shown anxiety reductions in approximately 65% to 70% of GAD clients when given benzodiazepines (Roemer et al., 2002). A smaller percentage shows a full remission of anxiety symptoms. However, when a person discontinues benzodiazepines, GAD symptoms will reappear.

LENS

ANXIETY AND THE PRESCRIBING OF BENZODIAZEPINES

Anxiety is complex. We experience it negatively as something we seek to reduce or eliminate. As human beings, we want to do this quickly and in a simple way. Taking a pill seems easy. We are supported in this decision by advertisements that show people who seem happy thanks to various kinds of psychotropic medications. Many of these ads contain phrases such as "ask your doctor," which further promotes their use. However, the use of these medications may carry negative consequences, such as addiction and overdose.

In 2020, the FDA warned of the risk from all benzodiazepines. This has resulted in a reduced number of prescriptions for benzodiazepines.

iStock.com/Juanmonino

Benzodiazepines are drugs that are commonly used to treat anxiety and sleep problems (Olfson et al., 2015). These psychotropic medications are among the most commonly prescribed drugs in Western countries, including the United States and Canada. It was estimated that over 8% of the population of Canada used a benzodiazepine in 2006. During that same time, over 5.2% of U.S. adults (11 million) filled a prescription for a benzodiazepine. By 2016, this had increased to 12.6% (Maust et al., 2019).

As can be seen from Figure 8.5, benzodiazepine use in the United States increases with age and is more common among women than among men. These gender differences are also seen in Europe and Canada. The increased use with age seems strange to researchers, since anxiety disorders show a decline in the population with age. In older adults, long-term benzodiazepine use has been associated with impaired cognitive functioning, reduced mobility and driving skills, and increased risks of falls.

Although benzodiazepines have been shown to be effective in the treatment of anxiety, in 2011 there were 426,000 visits to emergency rooms related to the use of benzodiazepines. This is up from 272,000 visits in 2008. Often this was associated with the use of alcohol along with benzodiazepines. According to the National Institute on Drug Abuse, in 2021 nearly 14% of overdose deaths involving opioids also involved benzodiazepines.

The United States in 2008 had a population of around 304 million people. That same year, around 75 million benzodiazepine prescriptions were written. This includes multiple prescriptions to the same person in a year. Usually, these are prescribed by primary care physicians rather than psychiatrists. Typically, primary care physicians have not been trained in diagnosing specific anxiety

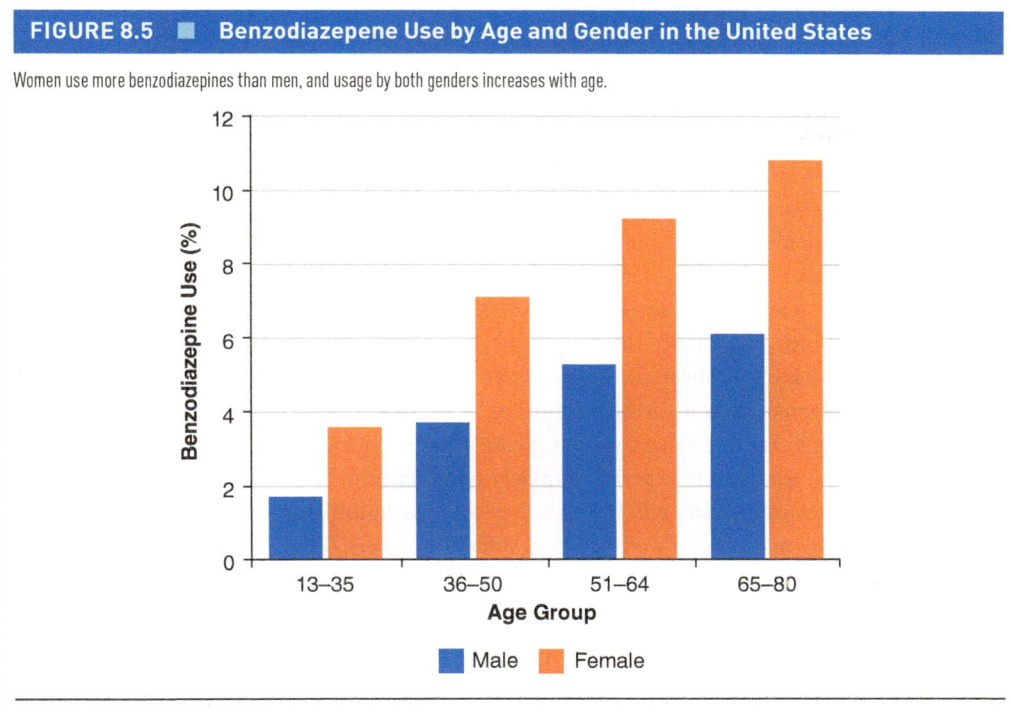

FIGURE 8.5 ■ Benzodiazepene Use by Age and Gender in the United States

Women use more benzodiazepines than men, and usage by both genders increases with age.

Source: U.S. Department of Veterans Affairs. (2016, August). *Re-evaluating the use of benzodiazepenes: A focus on high-risk populations.* https://www.pbm.va.gov/PBM/AcademicDetailingService/Documents/Benzodiazepine_Provider_AD_Educational_Guide.pdf

disorders or in their non–drug-related treatments and may be overprescribing benzodiazepines. In 2016, the U.S. Food and Drug Administration (FDA) issued a warning about prescribing benzodiazepines and opioids together. In 2020, the FDA warned of the risk from all benzodiazepines. This has resulted in a reduced number of prescriptions for benzodiazepines.

Anxiety both protects us when it alerts us to potential threat and impairs us when it interferes with functioning. However, not everyone who experiences anxiety, even though it may be unpleasant, has an anxiety disorder. As a society, we need to consider how we wish to educate the public and other non–mental health professionals about the nature of anxiety and its treatment, including the prescribing of benzodiazepines.

Thought Questions

How would you teach youth about the nature of anxiety? Should drug companies be allowed to market directly to the public?

A second class of medication referred to as azapirones was introduced in the 1990s. Buspirone (brand name Buspar) is a common azapirone that influences serotonin receptors in the brain. This drug influences more of the cognitive components of GAD and has fewer side effects than benzodiazepines. A third class of drugs for GAD is antidepressants. Both tricyclic antidepressants, such as imipramine, and serotonin reuptake inhibitors (SSRIs), such as paroxetine (brand name Paxil), have been shown to be effective in individuals with GAD. A large meta-analysis of 25,441 individuals with GAD showed a number of different medications to be effective in the treatment of GAD as compared to a placebo treatment (Slee et al., 2019).

Social Anxiety Disorder

Most individuals can think of a time when they were concerned about meeting someone or about giving a talk in front of a group. *Perhaps I will say the wrong thing. Perhaps others will think I am foolish.*

Perhaps I will spill my food on my shirt when I am eating. These are all common reactions and are part of our human condition. However, when these feelings are severe and last for more than 6 months, it would be considered a social anxiety disorder (SAD). The *DSM-5-TR* criteria for SAD are shown in Table 8.6. SAD is characterized by marked fear or anxiety about one or more social situations in which the individual is exposed to possible scrutiny by others. Approximately 8% of people in the United States will experience a social anxiety disorder during their lifetime (Kessler et al., 2010). It tends to run in families. It is seen to be more common in women than men. The disorder is also associated with later mood disorders and substance abuse. The singer Sia Furler has described her own experiences with SAD and alcohol abuse.

SAD, which was referred to as social phobia in *DSM-IV*, is characterized by persistent and severe fear of social situations, particularly three social settings that involve evaluation. The first is social interactions, such as having a conversation with others. The second type of situation is one in which the person could be observed, such as eating or drinking. The third type of situation is one in which the person is performing in front of others, such as giving a talk to a group. When in these situations, the individual with social anxiety will experience anxiety symptoms similar to those seen with GAD.

Individuals with social anxiety will fear that they could be humiliated, embarrassed, or rejected in these situations. They may also be worried about offending others. They imagine that the outcomes of social encounters will be negative, and they try to prevent the experience of anxiety by not putting themselves in social situations. In turn, these individuals live a less-than-full life with discomfort and distress.

Previous experiences appear to be more important in individuals with social anxiety as compared with other anxiety disorders. Some 92% of adults with social anxiety report having experienced negative social events in childhood prior to becoming socially anxious (McCabe et al., 2003). This is in comparison with 35% of those with panic disorder and 50% of those with OCD.

TABLE 8.6 ■ *DSM-5-TR* Diagnostic Criteria for Social Anxiety Disorder

A. Marked fear or anxiety about one or more social situations in which the individual is exposed to possible scrutiny by others. Examples include social interactions (e.g., having a conversation, meeting unfamiliar people), being observed (e.g., eating or drinking), and performing in front of others (e.g., giving a speech).
Note: In children, the anxiety must occur in peer settings and not just during interactions with adults.

B. The individual fears that he or she will act in a way or show anxiety symptoms that will be negatively evaluated (i.e., will be humiliating or embarrassing: will lead to rejection or offend others).

C. The social situations almost always provoke fear or anxiety.
Note: In children, the fear or anxiety may be expressed by crying, tantrums, freezing, clinging, shrinking, or failing to speak in social situations.

D. The social situations are avoided or endured with intense fear or anxiety.

E. The fear or anxiety is out of proportion to the actual threat posed by the social situation and to the sociocultural context.

F. The fear, anxiety, or avoidance is persistent, typically lasting for 6 months or more.

G. The fear, anxiety, or avoidance causes clinically significant distress or impairment in social, occupational, or other important areas of functioning.

H. The fear, anxiety, or avoidance is not attributable to the physiological effects of a substance (e.g., a drug of abuse, a medication) or another medical condition.

I. The fear, anxiety, or avoidance is not better explained by the symptoms of another mental disorder, such as panic disorder, body dysmorphic disorder, or autism spectrum disorder.

J. If another medical condition (e.g., Parkinson's disease, obesity, disfigurement from burns or injury) is present, the fear, anxiety, or avoidance is clearly unrelated or is excessive.

Specify if

Performance only: If the fear is restricted to speaking or performing in public.

Credit: Reprinted with permission from the *Diagnostic and Statistical Manual of Mental Disorders, fifth edition, text revision*, DSM-V-TR, pp. 229–230. (Copyright © 2022). American Psychiatric Association. All Rights Reserved.

Neuroscience Aspects of Social Anxiety

In Chapter 5, you learned about the concept of the social brain, which involves such areas of the brain as the prefrontal cortex (PFC), the amygdala, the anterior cingulate cortex (ACC), and the insula. These regions are particularly important in social and emotional processing in both normal and anxiety processing (Hahn et al., 2011; Mizzi et al., 2022). The amygdala is involved in the initial processing of emotional memory and arousal, fast evaluation of novel stimuli, and threat perception. Electrical stimulation of the amygdala will elicit fear, anxiety, and social withdrawal.

The social brain regions are also involved in social anxiety, especially the amygdala and insula areas (Arcaro et al., 2019; Feng et al., 2021; Grill-Spector et al., 2017; Miskovic & Schmidt, 2012; Porcelli et al., 2019). It may be the case that the insula as part of the salience network is overactive. This, in turn, would lead to neutral signals prompting excessive reactivity in which the person with social anxiety pays more attention than should be required. Likewise, higher cognitive processes may not inhibit amygdala responses in those with social anxiety, which would result in greater emotional responses than would be required by the situation. In one study examining brain activation during public versus private speaking, exaggerated amygdala activation was found in individuals with social anxiety compared with individuals without social anxiety (Tillfors et al., 2001). Overall, dysfunctions in the amygdala are associated with social anxiety disorder and predict treatment outcomes (Klumpp & Fitzgerald, 2018). In particular, greater pretreatment amygdala activity in response to threat cues predicts better response to treatment.

Theoretically, it has been suggested that individuals with social anxiety process social situations with evolutionarily older alarm systems such as the amygdala, whereas individuals without social anxiety process the same situations with newer cognitive-analytic processes that use the PFC. It has also been suggested that social anxiety can be seen as part of the larger dominant and submissive system seen across primate species (Öhman, 1986, 2009). This view is supported by research revealing that individuals with social anxiety showed enhanced amygdala activation in response to images of hostile faces. Larger amygdala reactions to faces with a social-evaluative meaning were seen in individuals with SAD (Bas-Hoogendam et al., 2020). To create the social meaning of a face, neutral faces were paired with neutral statements such as "She says you were born in London" or a negative statement such as "She says you are stupid."

Both CBT-type therapies and medication have been shown to be effective with people who have social anxiety disorder.
iStock.com/SDI Productions. Stock photo. Posed by model.

Further, the degree of amygdala activity is positively correlated with the severity of social anxiety but not general anxiety (Phan et al., 2006). Another similar study using faces also found greater activation of the amygdala as well as fewer connections between the frontal areas and the ACC (Hahn et al., 2011). Measures of brain networks of individuals with SAD and their family members from two generations suggest that the attentional network and the frontoparietal network were involved (Bas-Hoogendam et al., 2021). These findings suggest that direct brain stimulation techniques such as TMS could be effective if applied to these networks.

Treatment for Social Anxiety Disorder

A number of psychological therapies have been developed for treating SAD (Hofmann & Barlow, 2002; Rodebaugh et al., 2004; Weiss et al., 2010). These therapies include CBT, exposure therapy, social skills training, and group CBT. These different approaches may also be combined in different ways. Both CBT-type therapies and medication have been shown to be effective with individuals who have SAD. CBT-type therapies show larger changes and fewer side effects compared with medications (Mayo-Wilson et al., 2014). Medications appear to show a faster reduction in anxiety initially. However, following treatment, when no additional medication or psychotherapy is offered, there is a greater relapse with medication treatment than with CBT therapy.

CBT, as described previously, assumes that social anxiety is produced by the person's automatic thoughts in the social situation or the expectation of the social situation. The task is to help the person detect and restructure these thoughts and expectations. In the treatment of social anxiety, it has been offered in both individual and group therapy. Further, CBT has been shown to be effective with different cultural groups (Chang et al., 2018).

Exposure therapy places a client in a feared situation despite the experience of distress. One technique is for clients to create a hierarchy of situations that they would fear or avoid. They can rank this hierarchy in terms of the level of anxiety they would expect to experience. These situations can then be used in therapy. Typically, the person begins with the least anxiety-producing situation, such as talking to the staff at the coffee shop. The person then moves to more anxiety-provoking situations, such as talking to someone the individual wants to impress. At the top of the hierarchy would be the most anxiety-producing situation, such as giving a talk to an audience evaluating the person. The situation can be experienced by either role playing or actually being in the feared environment. Although the underlying mechanisms leading to change have not been determined precisely, exposure therapy has been shown to reduce anxiety in social situations for individuals with SAD (Abramowitz et al., 2011).

Social skills training is based on the idea that individuals with social anxiety have inadequate social interaction skills. It teaches the individual practical social skills through modeling, corrective feedback, reinforcement, and other such techniques. Since this type of training involves trying out new behaviors, it is difficult to separate it completely from exposure therapy in outcome studies.

Psychopharmacological approaches have been shown to be useful in the treatment of social anxiety. One of the earliest drugs used was a monoamine oxidase (MAO) inhibitor, phenelzine sulfate, which was seen as the drug of choice. More recent medications have included the SSRIs paroxetine and sertraline. The norepinephrine SSRI venlafaxine has also been used. The choice of medication is often left with the individual health professional based on a specific person's experience of drug side effects.

Separation Anxiety Disorder

Human infants, as well as the infants of most other mammal species, show distress when separated from their caregivers. Human infants will generally cry. As the infants develop and learn that their caregivers are available even when they cannot see them, the distress is reduced. You can watch children at times checking to see if their parents are around as they play on a playground, for example. You may notice that some preschool children are hesitant to go to a birthday party or other event. However, once they are with other children, they usually forget the initial hesitation and enjoy themselves. These are all normal developmental processes as children develop independence and the ability to function on their own.

Some children—even as they develop normally in various domains—do not show this sense of independence and continue to feel distress when not with their caregivers. These children may not want to go to school and may even follow their caregivers around. They become concerned that something could happen to their caregivers and worry about the caregiver's health. They may have nightmares involving fears of separation. They will not want to leave the house unless their caregiver is with them. This sense of concern and distress can continue into elementary school years, adolescence, and even adulthood. Such children, adolescents, and adults would be diagnosed with separation anxiety disorder.

Separation anxiety disorder in *DSM-5-TR* requires that the symptoms last for at least 4 weeks in children and adolescents and 6 months or more in adults. Further, three of eight different types of symptoms must be present. The first category of symptoms involves the person experiencing distress when they are not at home or with major attachment figures. The second describes a person worrying about the well-being of the attachment figure. The third has the person worrying that an event such as being kidnapped or getting lost could happen. The fourth is an unwillingness to leave home for fear of separation. The fifth is a fear of being alone. The sixth is an unwillingness to sleep alone or outside the house. The seventh is having nightmares related to separation. And the eighth is to have complaints of physical symptoms such as headaches or stomachaches.

Separation anxiety disorder is the most prevalent anxiety disorder for those under 12 years of age. The 12-month prevalence of this disorder is approximately 4% in children and drops to 1.6% in adolescents (*DSM-5*). In adults, the 12-month prevalence is between 0.9% and 1.9%. In community samples, it is more commonly seen in girls than boys.

Treatment for Separation Anxiety Disorder

Treatment for separation anxiety disorder in children includes many CBT principles. In particular, a child is taught to recognize their anxious feelings when they occur. Children then learn ways of coping with these feelings. Often, parents are involved in the child's treatment. However, not all CBT treatment is effective. One study showed less successful results with children who were not motivated, came from lower social status, and had parents who internalized symptoms (Wergeland et al., 2016). That is, children whose parents had anxiety symptoms showed less progress in therapy. Another study showed better results when the CBT treatment was delivered through the Internet (Vigerland et al., 2016).

CONCEPT CHECK

- What evidence would you cite to show that GAD has a significant impact on the U.S. population?
- What medications and psychological therapies are recommended for treating GAD? What aspects of GAD does each type of treatment target?
- What characteristics might make an individual more at risk for developing SAD?
- How is the social brain involved in SAD?
- What are the eight different categories of diagnostic symptoms describing separation anxiety disorder? How many must be present before an individual receives a diagnosis of separation anxiety disorder?

PHOBIAS AND PANIC DISORDER

Two other anxiety disorders described in *DSM-5-TR* are phobias and panic disorder. Phobias are seen when a person has fear or anxiety about an object or situation. Panic disorder occurs when a person has an unexpected abrupt surge of intense fear or discomfort.

Specific Phobia

A specific phobia is an anxiety disorder in which an individual experiences fear of or anxiety about a particular situation or object. Common phobias include fears of snakes, spiders, flying, heights, blood, injections, and the dark. Although almost all individuals have experiences such as driving in bad weather in which they feel concern from time to time, these fears tend not to be long lasting or to result in major lifestyle changes. To be diagnosed with a specific phobia (Table 8.7), the individual must actively avoid the condition or object, and the fear or anxiety must have lasted for 6 months or more. Further, the fear or anxiety causes distress and is out of proportion to the actual danger posed by the situation.

As a background for classifying specific phobias in *DSM-5*, a review of the literature was conducted (LeBeau et al., 2010). These researchers found that prevalence rates in the United States differed by type of phobia (Table 8.8). Animal phobias were a common phobia and showed a lifetime prevalence of 3.3% to 7%. Natural phobias, such as fear of heights, storms, or water, show lifetime prevalence rates of 8.9% to 11.6%, collectively. Of the natural phobias, height phobia is the most common with a 3.1% to 5.3% prevalence rate. Situational phobias, such as fear of flying, enclosed places, or driving, show prevalence rates of 5.2% to 8.4%. Except for height phobia, large gender differences have been found, with more women than men displaying phobias. These include 91% of individuals with animal phobias being women, as well as 87% to 90% of those with situational phobias. Among those with height phobia, only 60% were women. Further, over 50% of people with one phobia were found to also have three or more additional phobias during their lifetime. European rates for specific phobias were similar to those in the United States, while rates in Latin America, Africa, and Asia were lower (APA, 2022).

Table 8.9 summarizes the clinical features of four types of phobias. In terms of focus of fear, individuals were asked, "What are you most concerned will happen?" For the natural environment and situational phobias, the concern was around danger. For the animal phobias, such as spiders or snakes,

TABLE 8.7 ■ *DSM-5-TR* Diagnostic Criteria for Specific Phobia

A. Marked fear or anxiety about a specific object or situation (e.g., flying, heights, animals, receiving an injection, seeing blood).
Note: In children, the fear or anxiety may be expressed by crying, tantrums, freezing, or clinging.

B. The phobic object or situation almost always provokes immediate fear or anxiety.

C. The phobic object or situation is actively avoided or endured with intense fear or anxiety.

D. The fear or anxiety is out of proportion to the actual danger posed by the specific object or situation and to the sociocultural context.

E. The fear, anxiety, or avoidance is persistent, typically lasting for 6 months or more.

F. The fear, anxiety, or avoidance causes clinically significant distress or impairment in social, occupational, or other important areas of functioning.

G. The disturbance is not better explained by the symptoms of another mental disorder, including fear, anxiety, and avoidance of situations associated with panic-like symptoms or other incapacitating symptoms (as in agoraphobia); objects or situations related to obsessions (as in obsessive-compulsive disorder); reminders of traumatic events (as in posttraumatic stress disorder); separation from home or attachment figures (as in separation anxiety disorder); or social situations (as in social anxiety disorder).

Specify if:

Code based on the phobic stimulus:
F40.218 Animal (e.g., spiders, insects, dogs).
F40.228 Natural environment (e.g., heights, storms, water).
F40.23x Blood-injection-injury (e.g., needles, invasive medical procedures).
  Coding note: Select specific ICD-10-CM code as follows: **F40.230** fear of blood; F40.231 fear of injections and transfusions; F40.232 fear of other medical care; or F40.233 fear of injury.
F40.248 Situational (e.g., airplanes, elevators, enclosed places).
F40.298 Other (e.g., situations that may lead to choking or vomiting; in children, e.g., loud sounds or costumed characters).
Coding note: When more than one phobic stimulus is present, code all ICD-10-CM codes that apply (e.g., for fear of snakes and flying, F40.218 specific phobia, animal, and F40.248 specific phobia, situational).

Credit: Reprinted with permission from the *Diagnostic and Statistical Manual of Mental Disorders, fifth edition, text revision*, DSM-V-TR, pp. 224–225 (Copyright © 2022). American Psychiatric Association. All Rights Reserved.

TABLE 8.8 ■ Lifetime Prevalence and Standard Error (SE) of Specific Fears

Specific Fear	Lifetime Fears*		Lifetime Phobia Given Fear†		Lifetime Phobia With Specific Fear in Total Sample††	
	%	(SE)	%	(SE)	%	(SE)
Height	20.4	0.7	26.2	1.8	5.3	0.5
Flying	13.2	0.7	26.9	2.4	3.5	0.3
Closed spaces	11.9	0.6	35.1	2.5	4.2	0.4
Being alone	7.3	0.6	40.7	3.3	3.1	0.4
Storms	8.7	0.5	33.1	3.4	2.9	0.4
Animals	22.2	1.1	25.8	1.2	5.7	0.4
Blood	13.9	0.7	32.8	2.1	4.5	0.3
Water	9.4	0.6	35.8	2.8	3.4	0.3
Any	49.5	1.2	22.7	1.1	11.3	0.6

*Prevalence of lifetime fears in the total sample.

†Probability of specific phobia diagnosis in people endorsing each fear.

††Percentage of people in total sample with specific phobia and each lifetime fear (i.e., 5.3% of total sample have lifetime-specific phobia and a height fear).

Credit: Curtis, G. C., Magee, W. J., Eaton, W. W., Wittchen, H.-U., & Kessler, R. C. (1998). Specific fears and phobias: Epidemiology and classification. *British Journal of Psychiatry, 173*, 212–217. https://doi.org/10.1192/bjp.173.3.212. Reproduced with permission from The Royal College of Psychiatrists.

TABLE 8.9 ■ Clinical Features of Specific Phobia Types

Phobia Features	Animal Phobia	Natural Environment	Situation Phobia	B-I-I Phobia
Prevalence	3.3%–5.7%	4.9%–11.6%	5.2%–8.4%	3.2%–4.5%
Onset	6.3–9.2 years	6.5–13.6 years	13.4–21.8 years	5.5–9.4 years
Gender ratio	Women > men	Women > men, most common type among men	Women > men	Mixed findings
Impairment			Seeking professional help, medication, interference with daily and social life	
Focus of fear	Disgust, revulsion	Danger of harm	Danger of harm	Physical symptoms (fainting), disgust, revulsion
Physiological fear response	Activation of dorsal anterior cingulated cortex, anterior insula			Vasovagal fainting, activation of bilateral occipito-parietal cortex and thalamus
Comorbidity	Depression	Depression, heights phobia in women→anxiety disorders	Affective disorders, childhood-onset disorders, substance use disorders, panic attacks	Marijuana abuse, depression, panic disorder, OCD, agoraphobia, SAD, among diabetics→peripheral vascular disease, cardiovascular disease
Risk factors	Experiential, genetic			Women, low education

Credit: LeBeau, R., Glenn, D., Liao, B., Wittchen, H., Beesdo-Baum, K., Ollendick, T., & Craske, M. (2010). Specific phobia: A review of *DSM*-IV specific phobia and preliminary recommendations for DSM-V. *Depression and Anxiety, 27*, 148–167, p. 151.

Note: B-I-I = blood–injection–injury.

the concern was one of disgust or revulsion. For the blood, injection, or injury phobias, the concern was fainting or disgust but not physical harm. Animal and natural environment phobias are seen earlier in life than situational phobias. The physiological pattern of individuals with blood–injection–injury (B-I-I) phobias was different from those with the other types. It involved an initial heart rate acceleration followed by a deceleration that increased the likelihood of fainting. All other phobias showed heart rate acceleration alone. Although the research is limited, individuals with spider phobia showed a different pattern of brain activation than those with B-I-I phobias.

Neuroscience Aspects of Specific Phobias

A variety of mechanisms have been associated with developing a phobia. As with lab-reared monkeys, seeing another individual being afraid of an object or condition could lead to the development of the phobia through observational learning. Consistent with the observational learning perspective is the finding that individuals with animal phobias were likely to have relatives with an animal phobia. Likewise, those with situational phobias or B-I-I phobias were likely to have relatives who had similar phobias. Although this could also suggest a genetic factor, the genetic relationship has not been shown to be that strong.

Other types of traditional conditioning could also be possible. In the classic 1930s case study of Little Albert, John Watson showed that animals a child had previously played with happily could, through classical conditioning, come to be feared. In this case, a loud sound was made when the animal, such as a rabbit or white rat, was with the child, Little Albert. Although initially the child would play with the animal, after the pairing with a loud sound, the child would withdraw. As a result, the child was conditioned to show fear when in the presence of these animals. Watson's demonstrations with Little Albert appear in many introductory textbooks. However, what is left out is the finding that fear conditioning worked better with evolutionarily relevant objects such as animals but less so with a bag of wool or with person-made objects such as a wooden toy (see, e.g., English, 1929; Watson & Rayner, 1920). In short, humans are biologically "primed" to learn to fear animals or situations that could truly threaten us and not primed to be conditioned to fear inanimate objects.

In reviewing the literature related to fear conditioning in humans, the brain areas involved relate to social brain processes. These include the ACC, the insula, the medial PFC, the OFC, and the thalamus (Sehlmeyer et al., 2009). When fear objects such as snakes or spiders are shown to individuals with phobias, exaggerated activity is seen in the amygdala, the insula, and the cingulate cortex (Etkin & Wager, 2007). Jan Schweckendiek and his colleagues (2011) studied individuals with spider phobia in an fMRI scanner. In this study, the researchers paired neutral pictures with three types of pictures—pictures of spiders, pictures of aversive scenes (e.g., mutilations), or other neutral pictures. In comparison with a

Fear of heights is a common phobia.
iStock.com/deimagine

non-phobia group, those with spider phobias showed enhanced brain activity within the fear network (medial PFC, ACC, amygdala, insula, and thalamus) in response to the phobia-related conditioned stimulus. Further, spider-phobic subjects displayed higher amygdala activation in response to the phobia-related conditioned stimulus than to the non–phobia-related conditioned stimulus. This supports the idea that once a phobia is developed, those conditions or objects that evoke it are associated with greater brain activity in the network of structures associated with fear.

Treatment for Specific Phobias

It is commonly accepted that phobias are best treated by exposure to the feared object (Antony & Barlow, 2002). Lars Öst (1989, 1996) has shown in a number of studies that a phobia such as fear of snakes or spiders can be significantly reduced after a single 3-hour session, although similar results are found in a larger number of shorter sessions. The one-session procedure also works for children (Davis et al., 2019). The basic procedure would be for the client to describe their fears as well as catastrophic expectations and the situations that evoke these in a session with a therapist. This would be followed by the therapist slowly introducing the feared object, such as a snake, from a distance. The therapist checks with the client as this is happening to determine the magnitude of fear. In general, it is the client who directs the speed of the introduction of the feared object. During the session, the therapist would bring the feared object closer to the person until they were able to touch it with reduced fear.

Using Öst's rapid gradual exposure techniques, Thomas Straube and his colleagues (2006) measured brain changes prior to and following therapy. They studied a group of individuals with spider phobia. These individuals received two sessions of therapy with a duration of 4 to 5 hours for each session. Gradual exposure started with the presentation of spider pictures. Then, the individuals were shown the skin of a tarantula, followed by an actual tarantula. Once the actual tarantula was introduced, the goals of the therapy were fourfold. These were (1) to hold a living tarantula for about 10 minutes, (2) to catch moving and nonmoving spiders at least 10 times with a glass at different locations within the therapy room, (3) to catch any species of spider in the basement of the institute at least three times, and (4) to touch a rapidly moving house spider. By the completion of the therapy, all of the individuals with spider phobia were able to fulfill the four treatment goals without strong feelings of anxiety.

An fMRI session was conducted prior to the beginning of any therapy in which the individuals with spider phobia and a control group were shown pictures of spiders as well as neutral pictures. As expected, individuals with spider phobia showed greater activation in the insula and ACC, which is part of the fear network (Figure 8.6). Following therapy, this activation was reduced.

FIGURE 8.6 ■ What Happens in the Brains of People With Spider Phobia When They See a Spider?

Individuals with spider phobia show increased activation in the anterior cingulate cortex and insula in response to images of spiders versus neutral images compared with control individuals.

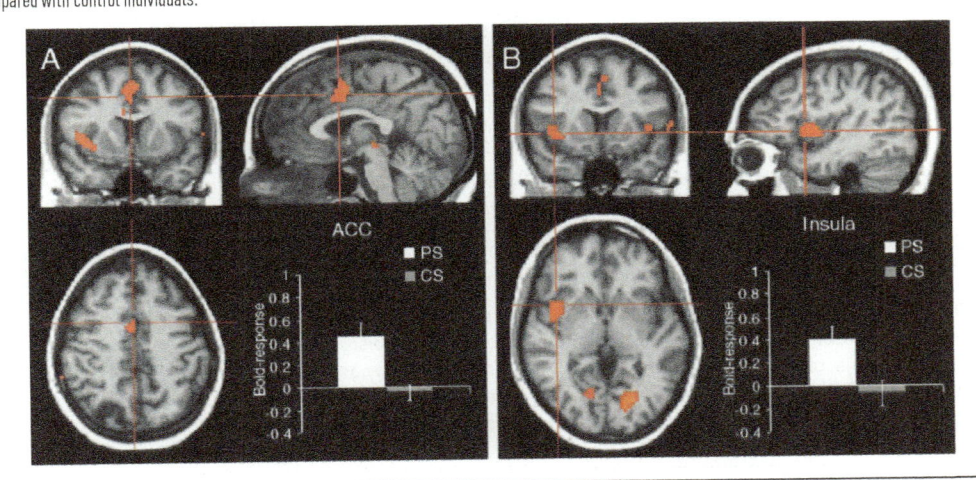

Credit: Straube, T., Glauer, M., Dilger, S., Mentzel, H., & Miltner, W. (2006). Effects of cognitive-behavioral therapy on brain activation in specific phobia. *NeuroImage, 29*, 125–135, p. 129, with permission from Elsevier.

Panic Disorder

A panic attack comes quickly and carries with it an intense feeling of apprehension, anxiety, or fear (Craske et al., 2010; Fava & Morton, 2009). It happens without an actual situation that would suggest danger. Physiological symptoms can include shortness of breath, trembling, heart palpitations, dizziness, faintness, and hot or cold flashes. The person can also experience the world as if it were not real and be concerned about dying. The symptoms usually peak within the first 10 minutes of the attack. The experience of one's heart pounding (97%) and dizziness (96%) are reported by almost all individuals who experience panic attacks. Panic attacks are a frequent cause of individuals going to a hospital emergency room. There is some suggestion that panic is more common during periods of stress. Although many individuals experience an episode of panic-like symptoms at some point in their lives, these symptoms must be recurrent and followed by a month of concern or change in lifestyle for an individual to be diagnosed with a **panic disorder** (Table 8.10).

Once individuals experience a panic attack, they often become concerned about having another attack. They may also try to change their behavior as a way to prevent panic attacks. For example, some individuals will not exercise or do other tasks that would raise their heart rates. Although presented as a separate anxiety disorder, panic attacks can occur within the context of any of the other anxiety disorders. Panic disorder is often seen comorbid with agoraphobia. Lifetime prevalence rates are 4.7% for panic disorder (Kessler et al., 2006). The modal (most frequent) age of onset for panic disorder is between 21 and 23 years of age, although children and adolescents may experience panic attacks along with other anxiety disorders. Studies have shown that twice as many women as men have panic disorder.

TABLE 8.10 ■ *DSM-5-TR* Diagnostic Criteria for Panic Disorder

A. Recurrent unexpected panic attacks. A panic attack is an abrupt surge of intense fear or intense discomfort that reaches a peak within minutes, and during which time four (or more) of the following symptoms occur:
   Note: The abrupt surge can occur from a calm state or an anxious state.
   1. Palpitations, pounding heart, or accelerated heart rate.
   2. Sweating.
   3. Trembling or shaking.
   4. Sensations of shortness of breath or smothering.
   5. Feelings of choking.
   6. Chest pain or discomfort.
   7. Nausea or abdominal distress.
   8. Feeling dizzy, unsteady, light-headed, or faint.
   9. Chills or heat sensations.
   10. Paresthesias (numbness or tingling sensations).
   11. Derealization (feelings of unreality) or depersonalization (being detached from oneself).
   12. Fear of losing control or "going crazy."
   13. Fear of dying.
   Note: Culture-specific symptoms (e.g., tinnitus, neck soreness, headache, uncontrollable screaming or crying) may be seen. Such symptoms should not count as one of the four required symptoms.

B. At least one of the attacks has been followed by 1 month (or more) of one or both of the following:
   1. Persistent concern or worry about additional panic attacks or their consequences (e.g., losing control, having a heart attack, "going crazy").
   2. A significant maladaptive change in behavior related to the attacks (e.g., behaviors designed to avoid having panic attacks, such as avoidance of exercise or unfamiliar situations).

C. The disturbance is not attributable to the physiological effects of a substance (e.g., a drug of abuse, a medication) or another medical condition (e.g., hyperthyroidism, cardiopulmonary disorders).

D. The disturbance is not better explained by another mental disorder (e.g., the panic attacks do not occur only in response to feared social situations, as in social anxiety disorder; in response to circumscribed phobic objects or situations, as in specific phobia; in response to obsessions, as in obsessive-compulsive disorder; in response to reminders of traumatic events, as in posttraumatic stress disorder; or in response to separation from attachment figures, as in separation anxiety disorder).

Credit: Reprinted with permission from the *Diagnostic and Statistical Manual of Mental Disorders, fifth edition, text revision*, DSM-V-TR, pp. 235–236 (Copyright © 2022). American Psychiatric Association. All Rights Reserved.

Neuroscience Aspects of Panic Disorder

It is suggested that panic and anxiety involve different areas of the brain (Graeff & Del-Ben, 2008). Anxiety is integrated in the forebrain, whereas panic is organized in the midbrain, especially the basal ganglia and limbic structures. Decreased gray matter in individuals with panic disorder has also been reported in these areas (Lai, 2011). The idea of different areas for anxiety and panic is consistent with the suggestion that there are two defense systems in the brain (Gray & McNaughton, 2000; McNaughton & Corr, 2004). The basic model suggests that fear and anxiety are involved in different approach-and-avoidance systems that utilize distinct brain networks.

As described in Chapter 7, the stress response involves the hypothalamic–pituitary–adrenal (HPA) axis and the hormone cortisol. HPA is under excitatory control of the amygdala and inhibitory control of the hippocampus. The hippocampus releases corticotropin-releasing factor (CRF), which is transported to the adrenal cortex that releases cortisol. When individuals confront situations that evoke anticipatory or generalized anxiety, cortisol is released. However, cortisol is not released during panic attacks. Overall, this suggests that anxiety and panic reflect different brain and hormonal processes. Specifically, anxiety involves limbic forebrain structures such as the PFC, the amygdala, and the hippocampus (Ghasemi et al., 2022). Panic attacks, on the other hand, involve more primitive structures of the hindbrain such as the hypothalamus and periaqueductal gray (PAG). It has been shown that electrical stimulation of the PAG in surgical patients results in panic-like symptoms (Nashold et al., 1974). It also suggests that a panic attack does not involve the traditional stress reaction in the same way that generalized anxiety does.

Treatment for Panic Disorder

The currently preferred medication treatments for panic disorder are SSRIs, which have been shown to be more effective than placebo treatments. Benzodiazepines have also been shown to be effective. The best-studied psychological treatment for panic disorder is CBT, which has been shown to be effective. In general, CBT approaches educate the individual about the nature of panic symptoms and reduce misconceptions. Internal exposure techniques can also be employed. For example, the person could be asked to exercise to increase their heart rate or spin around in a chair to feel dizzy. In this way, the person is exposed to the internal situation associated with a panic attack. More global aspects of CBT, such as cognitive restructuring in terms of distortions in thinking, are also used. This helps to reduce catastrophic expectations such as thinking that one is going to die when one's heart rate increases. Meta-analyses have shown that combining CBT and antidepressant medication is more effective than either one alone (Mitte, 2005; Watanabe et al., 2009).

Agoraphobia

Agoraphobia is the condition in which a person experiences fear or anxiety when in public. These situations can involve public transportation, open spaces such as parking lots or marketplaces, places with many individuals such as theaters or shops, as well as crowded places or just places outside the home. One characteristic of agoraphobia is that the person is concerned that escape from the situation would be difficult. Prior to *DSM-5*, agoraphobia was diagnosed in relation to panic disorder (Wittchen et al., 2010). In some individuals, panic disorder and agoraphobia go together and in others they do not. Age of onset in both agoraphobia and panic disorder is around 21 to 23 years of age. Agoraphobia is seen more frequently in women than men. Some studies have shown that negative experiences in childhood, such as the death of a parent, are associated with both agoraphobia and panic disorder. With *DSM-5*, agoraphobia is considered a separate disorder, although it

The titular character on *Ted Lasso*, played by Jason Sudeikis, experiences panic attacks stemming from childhood trauma.

UNIVERSAL TELEVISION/Album/Alamy Stock Photo

> **CONCEPT CHECK**
>
> - What are examples of specific phobias? Are the prevalence rates the same for different kinds of phobias? If not, how are they different?
> - What do we know about how specific phobias are developed, as well as how they are treated?
> - What is the common thread between development (initiation) and treatment (extinction)?
> - What are the characteristics of a panic attack? How is it different from a panic disorder?
> - What characteristics would you expect to read in a case study of an individual with agoraphobia in terms of symptoms, prior history, and treatment protocols?

OBSESSIVE-COMPULSIVE DISORDER

I like to make stars in my head, or trace them with my finger. Just like you doodle with a pencil on the side of a piece of paper. Someone will be talking to me and I look like I'm listening, but really all I'm doing is drawing one line of the star for every one word that person says. Our conversation has to end on a multiple of 5, a complete star. My husband might say to me, "What do you want for dinner?" I'm looking him straight in the eyes so I guess he believes I'm deciding, but in fact I'm drawing and thinking 1 and 1/5 stars. He says, "How about pizza?" I still just stare at him, but think 1 and 4/5 stars. He continues, "Do you have any idea?" 2 and 4/5. Finally he'll conclude, "Why don't we just make pasta?" 4 stars.

From Emily Colas, Just Checking: Scenes From the Life of an Obsessive Compulsive (1998).

Obsessive-compulsive disorder (OCD) is characterized by repetitive thoughts and feelings, usually followed by behaviors in response to them. The thoughts are usually perceived as unpleasant and not wanted. A distinction is made between *obsessions* and *compulsions*.

Obsessions are generally unwelcome thoughts that come into one's head. *Will I get sick from using a public toilet? I feel I want to hit that person. Did I put my campfire out? Thinking of touching another person sexually. That picture frame is crooked.* In studies examining these thoughts in patients with OCD, they involve a limited number of categories. The main categories are avoiding contamination, aggressive impulses, sexual content, somatic concerns, religious concerns, and the need for order.

Obsessions can also be defined in terms of how they are experienced by the person who has them (Abramowitz & Jacoby, 2015). These two classes are autogenous obsessions and reactive obsessions. *Autogenous obsessions* are thoughts or images that come into a person's mind. They are generally expressed as distressing and may appear without any stimulus in the environment. Some examples would include urges to perform unacceptable acts of an aggressive, sexual, or immoral nature. *Reactive obsessions*, on the other hand, are evoked by an actual environmental situation. These types of obsessions could result from seeing a dirty bathroom, being touched by a stranger, or seeing a crooked picture. This type of obsession may lead to an action such as making the crooked picture straight.

Compulsions are the behaviors that one uses to respond to these thoughts. Overall, these behaviors are performed in order to reduce anxiety, gain control, or resist unwanted thoughts. Some behaviors, like cleaning or placing objects in order, reflect a desire to respond to the obsessions. Other compulsions, such as hand washing, are more avoidant in nature and stem from fear of what one might say, do, or experience in a particular situation. Often, individuals with OCD will constantly check to see if they performed a particular behavior, such as turning off the stove or unplugging an iron. Interestingly, individuals with OCD may be aware that their thoughts and actions seem bizarre to others, but they cannot dismiss the thoughts or the need to perform the action. For example, one person checked his window locks every 30 minutes even though each time he found them locked.

Characteristics, Prevalence, and Significant Aspects of OCD

OCD is characterized by the two types of symptoms discussed above: obsessions and compulsions (Franklin & Foa, 2008, 2011; Stewart et al., 2016). The comedian and game show host Howie Mandel has described his OCD and fear of germs (Mandel, 2010. See Table 8.11 for the specific symptoms of OCD in *DSM-5-TR*.

OCD has traditionally been considered an anxiety disorder in *DSM* history. Compulsions have been seen as a mechanism for reducing the anxiety or distress caused by the obsession. Not being allowed to engage in these behaviors results in distress and anxiety. Over 90% of those with OCD show both obsessions and behavioral rituals. Some experts have suggested this is not the best way to view OCD. Beginning in *DSM-5*, OCD is now considered in a different chapter from anxiety disorders (see *Understanding Changes in the* DSM-5 *and* DSM-5-TR: *Obsessive Compulsive and Related Disorders;* Abramowitz & Jacoby, 2015; Leckman et al., 2010). One way to inform the question of whether OCD is a type of anxiety disorder is to examine individuals with OCD and determine which other disorders are seen in these individuals and their first-degree relatives as compared with individuals without

TABLE 8.11 ■ *DSM-5-TR* **Diagnostic Criteria for Obsessive-Compulsive Disorder**

A. Presence of obsessions, compulsions, or both:

Obsessions are defined by (1) and (2):

1. Recurrent and persistent thoughts, urges, or images that are experienced, at some time during the disturbance, as intrusive and unwanted, and that in most individuals cause marked anxiety or distress.
2. The individual attempts to ignore or suppress such thoughts, urges, or images, or to neutralize them with some other thought or action (i.e., by performing a compulsion).

Compulsions are defined by (1) and (2):

1. Repetitive behaviors (e.g., hand washing, ordering, checking) or mental acts (e.g., praying, counting, repeating words silently) that the individual feels driven to perform in response to an obsession or according to rules that must be applied rigidly.
2. The behaviors or mental acts are aimed at preventing or reducing anxiety or distress, or preventing some dreaded event or situation; however, these behaviors or mental acts are not connected in a realistic way with what they are designed to neutralize or prevent, or are clearly excessive.

Note: Young children may not be able to articulate the aims of these behaviors or mental acts.

B. The obsessions or compulsions are time-consuming (e.g., take more than 1 hour per day) or cause clinically significant distress or impairment in social, occupational, or other important areas of functioning.

C. The obsessive-compulsive symptoms are not attributable to the physiological effects of a substance (e.g., a drug of abuse, a medication) or another medical condition.

D. The disturbance is not better explained by the symptoms of another mental disorder (e.g., excessive worries, as in generalized anxiety disorder; preoccupation with appearance, as in body dysmorphic disorder; difficulty discarding or parting with possessions, as in hoarding disorder; hair pulling, as in trichotillomania [hair-pulling disorder]; skin picking, as in excoriation [skin-picking] disorder; stereotypies, as in stereotypic movement disorder; ritualized eating behavior, as in eating disorders; preoccupation with substances or gambling, as in substance-related and addictive disorders; preoccupation with having an illness, as in illness anxiety disorder; sexual urges or fantasies, as in paraphilic disorders; impulses, as in disruptive, impulse-control, and conduct disorders; guilty ruminations, as in major depressive disorder; thought insertion or delusional preoccupations, as in schizophrenia spectrum and other psychotic disorders; or repetitive patterns of behavior, as in autism spectrum disorder).

Specify if:

- **With good or fair insight:** The individual recognizes that obsessive-compulsive disorder beliefs are definitely or probably not true or that they may or may not be true.
- **With poor insight:** The individual thinks obsessive-compulsive disorder beliefs are probably true.
- **With absent insight/delusional beliefs:** The individual is completely convinced that obsessive-compulsive disorder beliefs are true.

Specify if:

- **Tic-related:** The individual has a current or past history of a tic disorder.

Credit: Reprinted with permission from the *Diagnostic and Statistical Manual of Mental Disorders, fifth edition, text revision,* DSM-V-TR, pp. 265–266 (Copyright © 2022). American Psychiatric Association. All Rights Reserved.

OCD. In one large-scale study, OCD was found to have a relationship with anxiety disorders such as GAD and agoraphobia as well as depression, grooming disorders (e.g., skin picking), and hypochondriasis (Bienvenu et al., 2012). However, individuals with OCD did show differences from individuals without the disorder in terms of eating disorders, impulse control, and substance abuse. An emerging research literature shows that OCD is associated with autoimmune disorders as well as suicide (Fernández de la Cruz et al., 2022). The relationship between OCD and health is still being examined.

> ## UNDERSTANDING CHANGES IN THE *DSM-5* AND *DSM-5-TR*
> ### OBSESSIVE-COMPULSIVE AND RELATED DISORDERS
>
> In *DSM-5*, OCD was removed from the Anxiety Disorders section and placed in a separate section, Obsessive-Compulsive and Related Disorders. As a result, *DSM-5* changed the conception of OCD from less emotion and anxiety related to more behaviorally oriented. Part of the rationale for this is that anxiety is not used to define OCD. Although some individuals with OCD may reflect fears of becoming sick and so forth, other individuals with OCD who seek symmetry may show little anxiety. The *DSM-5* change views anxiety as potentially part of a number of disorders, OCD being one. But by itself, OCD is not considered an anxiety disorder.
>
> There is also a difference in brain processes involved in OCD and anxiety. Processes associated with OCD suggest involvement of the dorsolateral prefrontal cortex (DLPFC), insula, the temporal and parietal lobes, and the cerebellum. Anxiety is related to those areas of the brain that regulate the fear system. These include the PFC, the amygdala, and the hippocampus. Typically, different medications are used to treat OCD and anxiety, suggesting different pathways for each.
>
> Although behavioral and brain processes are different in OCD and anxiety, the removal of OCD from the Anxiety Disorders section surprised some mental health professionals since there had been few problems related to OCD diagnosis over the past 20 years. Likewise, patient support groups and other disorder-related groups did not seek the move. Further, there were a number of debates as to whether the change should be made (Phillips et al., 2010; Stein et al., 2010).

OCD has an adulthood prevalence of 2% to 3% and a child and adolescence prevalence of 1% to 2%. Approximately 40% of those with childhood OCD report continuing symptoms into adulthood. There is not a gender difference in rates (Stewart et al., 2016).

There is clearly a parallel between the themes found in OCD and concerns expressed by those without the disorder. Most individuals naturally avoid contamination or express concern when they experience unusual bodily sensations. On a society level, there are often rituals concerned with health and success in the world. Historically, cultures have performed rituals to dispel evil spirits or bring in the good ones. Most modern societies have a variety of rituals, including not walking under a ladder, not stepping on sidewalk cracks, or not partaking in other behaviors as ways of avoiding bad luck. Sports teams also have rituals for how to prepare for important games. Not performing any of these rituals may result in a feeling of anxiety for many individuals.

A variety of studies have suggested that OCD is found throughout the world at similar rates (Feygin et al., 2006). Feygin and colleagues suggested that OCD results from the exaggeration of normal traits that can be mapped onto a developmental trajectory. In particular, they discussed obsessive-compulsive responses to stress in terms of four themes. The first theme is loss, similar to that felt by someone with anxious attachment disorder. The obsession is that someone such as a loved one could be lost to the person. There are a large variety of situations in which this could happen. A friend, lover, or child could be killed in an accident, for example. To prevent this, the compulsion is to check on the loved one to make sure that they are still okay or to prevent the loved one from entering risky situations.

The second theme is physical security in one's own environment. A common manifestation is the person checking to make sure everything is in its place. The third theme is environmental cleanliness, which has to do with the fear that one's self or objects in one's environment are dirty and that this will result in disease or other negative events. The behavior of course is to clean obsessively. The fourth theme is that the person will be deprived of personally important resources or objects. A person who experiences these obsessions will either hoard objects or resources or try to prevent any situation in which the person could experience a loss. Each of these themes could be tied to a normal development stage in which fear or threatening situations were overemphasized.

Other research has found consistent groupings in the types of thoughts specified by those with OCD (Leckman et al., 2010). The first grouping includes thoughts and images concerning aggressive, sexual, and religious content and related checking compulsions. This factor may be experienced as forbidden thoughts that an individual would not want to share with another person. The second grouping concerns symmetry and ordering, such as placing objects in a regular pattern or making sure pictures are straight. The third grouping centers on contamination and cleaning. The fourth grouping relates to hoarding. Meta-analyses including individuals from non–English-speaking countries show similar groupings, which suggests a universal nature to these groupings across cultures (Bloch et al., 2008).

Other studies have sought to determine if these four groups are related to different comorbid disorders (Leckman et al., 2010). The answer is yes. Those with OCD centered on aggressive, sexual, and religious content were more likely to also have anxiety or depressive disorders. Individuals with OCD centered on symmetry and ordering were more likely to also have tic disorders, bipolar disorder, panic disorder, or agoraphobia. A contamination and cleaning focus was associated with comorbid eating disorders. The fourth grouping of hoarding was associated with comorbid personality disorders. Figure 8.7 shows the compulsions seen in one group of individuals as they were initially evaluated (referred to as admission).

Other *DSM-5-TR* Disorders Categorized With OCD

In *DSM-5*, a new category was introduced: Obsessive-Compulsive and Related Disorders (OCRD). This category brought together a number of disorders from other sections of previous *DSM* versions. Specifically, besides OCD itself, this category includes hoarding disorder, body dysmorphic disorder, trichotillomania (hair pulling disorder), and excoriation (skin picking disorder).

Historically, hoarding has been seen as a specific type of OCD. However, in *DSM-5* and *DSM-5-TR*, hoarding disorder is considered a separate disorder. It is defined in terms of an excessive

FIGURE 8.7 ■ Common Compulsions in OCD

This graph shows the typical compulsive symptoms found in an initial evaluation of 555 patients. Checking was the most common compulsion.

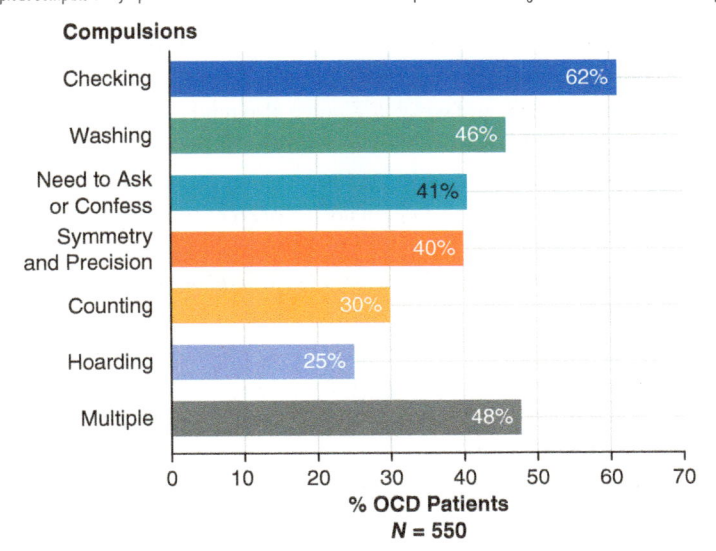

Compulsions

- Checking: 62%
- Washing: 46%
- Need to Ask or Confess: 41%
- Symmetry and Precision: 40%
- Counting: 30%
- Hoarding: 25%
- Multiple: 48%

% OCD Patients
N = 550

Credit: Pato, M., Fanous, A., Eisen, J., & Phillips, K. (2008). Obsessive-compulsive disorder. In A. Tasman, J. Kay, J. Lieberman, M. First, & M. Maj (Eds.), *Psychiatry* (3rd ed.). Wiley, p. 1445.

The cluttered and overcrowded home of a patient with hoarding disorder.
James Hackland/Alamy Stock Photo

acquisition of objects and an inability to discard these objects. Cognitive deficits, including difficulties in making decisions about possessions and avoidance of such decisions, are seen in individuals with hoarding disorder. These individuals also show resistance to family members and others who try to intervene in their behavior. Prevalence rates vary between 2% and 5% in the United States and Europe. It is seen more frequently in older adults (ages 55–95) than younger ones. Overall, it is suggested that areas of the brain related to executive decision and control, such as the frontal lobes and the ACC, are involved in the disorder.

An additional disorder included in the OCRD category of *DSM-5-TR* is **body dysmorphic disorder**. This disorder is characterized by a preoccupation with a perceived flaw in one's physical appearance (Fang & Wilhelm, 2015). These are flaws that are not perceived by others or appear to be just a slight problem. The person feels that they are unattractive or even hideous to others. Any specific body area can be of concern to someone with this disorder, although hair, skin, and the nose are commonly seen as a problem. There are gender differences in terms of which body parts are of concern. Men are more concerned about their genitals, body build, and thinning hair. Women are more concerned with their skin, stomach, and weight. Women also tend to be preoccupied with more areas in comparison with men. Individuals with body dysmorphic disorder may spend 3 to 8 hours a day with these preoccupations. Prevalence is estimated to be about 2.5% of U.S. adult women and 2.2% of U.S. adult men (APA, 2013). Shame and stigma often prevent individuals with this disorder from seeking treatment.

Another disorder included in the OCRD category is *trichotillomania (hair pulling disorder)*. A person with this disorder pulls out their hair frequently. It may be one long episode or short brief periods in which hair pulling occurs. It usually involves the scalp, eyebrows, and eyelids but can occur on any part of one's body. It can be triggered by anxiety, tension, or boredom. The hair pulling is usually done in private. Prevalence is about 1% to 2%. There is a 10-to-1 ratio of women to men who engage in hair pulling.

A similar disorder is *excoriation* or *skin picking*. This is a disorder in which one picks at one's own face, arms, hands, and other body sites. The person may pick at healthy skin as well as pimples or scabs. The *DSM* criterion requires that this picking result in a skin lesion. Most individuals pick with their fingernails but may also use other objects such as tweezers. Skin picking can be triggered by similar emotional states as noted with hair pulling. Lifetime prevalence is around 1.4%.

OCD and OCRD are similar in that the person performs repetitive behaviors and has intrusive thoughts about their body or related to actions and other thoughts. The underlying processes appear to be part of the human condition. For example, it is estimated that 50% of the general population engage in some type of ritualized behaviors and that 80% of all people experience intrusive, unpleasant, or unwanted thoughts (Stewart et al., 2016). However, in most people, these experiences do not occupy the same amount of time or cause the distress required of an OCD/OCRD disorder. Because there is less evidence associated with brain processes and OCRD, the next section will focus on brain processes related to OCD.

Neuroscience Aspects of OCD

Researchers have asked what the problems of thinking are that are found in those with OCD. Individuals with OCD have problems in shifting from one idea to another. They also have difficulty not thinking about a certain idea. Overall, specific cognitive dysfunction associated with OCD, such as response inhibition and difficulties associated with shifting between different tasks, working memory, and planning, suggest involvement of the dorsolateral prefrontal cortex (DLPFC), the insula, the temporal and parietal lobes, and the cerebellum (Gilbert et al., 2011; Gu et al., 2011; Menzies et al., 2008). In addition to cognitive dysfunction, motor responses have been related to networks connecting the basal ganglia with the orbitofrontal cortex (OFC). Individuals with OCD show less volume in the OFC than normal controls. This is also true of ACC, basal ganglia, and the thalamus. Imaging studies suggest overactivation of these circuits in individuals with OCD, which is related to motivational aspects of behavior and the inhibition of unnecessary responses.

A number of studies have shown OCD to have a genetic component (see Goodman et al., 2021 for an overview). OCD appears to run in families, with first-degree relatives of a person with OCD having an eightfold chance of developing OCD themselves. Twin studies also show a role for genetics (Pauls et al., 2014). One large-scale study of Swedish individuals found that the risk for OCD varied with degree of relatedness. That is, MZ twins showed the largest heritability of about 48%, followed by DZ twins and then relatives. However, genome-wide association studies have yet to identify genetic patterns as have single gene studies.

An additional finding is that the rate of OCD among relatives is higher in families of children with OCD than in families of adults with OCD. This suggests that growing up around others who perform OCD-type behaviors may be an influence. Thus, OCD could be transmitted within families in terms of a shared environment. Further research may show whether childhood OCD is different from adult OCD.

In one study, individuals with OCD, their first-degree relatives without OCD, and a matched control group were given a task that required the individual to reverse what they had learned previously (Chamberlain et al., 2008). On each side of a screen, the participant was shown a face superimposed on top of a building. One of the images was considered the target. The faces and buildings were different, and the person had to guess which image was considered correct. After each guess, feedback was given as to whether the person was correct or not. Thus, after a few trials the person could learn the "correct" image. Once an individual was correct on six trials, either the "correct" image was changed or a new set of images was presented. Either way, new learning was required. Using brain imaging techniques (fMRI), it was shown that individuals with OCD and their unaffected relatives had similar patterns of brain activation as compared with controls. In particular, controls showed greater brain activation in the OFC than the OCD individuals and their relatives did. Other studies have shown this area of the frontal cortex to be related to reversal learning and flexibility.

Brain imaging research on OCD involves searching for underlying similarities in brain processing that is associated with the disorder. There is similarity in brain areas across a number of studies (Pauls et al., 2014; Stewart et al., 2016). Overall, research suggests that OCD is associated with increased activation of the OFC, ACC, basal ganglia, and thalamic brain structures. Differences in the pathway from the OFC to subcortical structures can lead to an exaggerated concern about danger or harm on the part of those with OCD. In another study, OCD patients and unaffected first-degree relatives of OCD patients showed overlapping alterations in resting state functional connectivity between the salience network and default network brain regions and between prefrontal regions and the thalamus (Tomiyama et al., 2022).

Using fMRI techniques, David Tolin and his colleagues (2012) compared individuals with hoarding disorder, individuals with OCD, and a control group with neither disorder. These individuals were requested to bring 50 unsorted items, such as junk mail and newspapers, to the scanner. The researchers also had a second set of similar items that did not belong to the participants. When the individuals were at the scanner, they performed a practice trial in which they were asked to determine whether the item shown to them should be discarded or not. If they said discard, they saw it placed in a shredder. During the actual scanning section, the participants were shown pictures of either the items they brought or those from the researchers. They were allowed 6 seconds to make a decision. If no decision was made, the next item was shown.

The behavioral data showed that those with hoarding disorder discarded fewer of their own items (29) versus the controls (40) and those with OCD (37). All three groups were equally willing to discard items from the researchers (over 40). There were also differences in self-reported anxiety ratings between those with hoarding disorder (35), OCD (20), and controls (10). The individuals with hoarding behavior also reported "not feeling right" during the task. In terms of brain imaging, differences were found in the ACC, which is involved in error detection, and the insula, which reflects internal processes including a sense of self and self-feeling. When dealing with items that belonged to the researchers, there was less activity in these two areas. However, when deciding about their own possessions, those with a hoarding disorder showed greater activity than the other groups. It may be that this overactivity reflects an experience that things are not right, and they may make a mistake that, in turn, interferes with the cognitive task of making a decision.

Treatment for OCD

Both psychopharmacological and behavioral therapies have been shown to be effective for OCD (Collins et al., 2018). The most common medications are SSRIs and the tricyclic antidepressant clomipramine. Meta-analysis of randomized control trials (RCTs) show SSRIs to be effective compared with placebos (Abramowitz & Jacoby, 2015). Changes with CBT have been shown to be greater when CBT is compared with SSRIs. However, both together show the best effects (Pauls et al., 2014).

An effective psychosocial treatment for OCD is exposure and response prevention, including discussions with the client concerning beliefs related to the outcome of feared behaviors.

iStock.com/Fat Camera. Stock photo. Posed by model.

These have been shown to be effective for about 60% of people with the disorder. OCRDs have been less well studied with RCTs in terms of psychotropic medications. For those disorders, CBT is considered the treatment of choice at this point.

The psychosocial treatment that has the best empirical support is exposure and response prevention (EX/RP), which is largely based on the work of Foa and Kozak (1986; see also Franklin & Foa, 2008, 2011). One component includes discussions with the client concerning beliefs related to the outcome of feared behaviors. For example, the client may think that they would get germs from being in public bathrooms. Discussions can also be focused on what the person needs to do to prevent the expected negative outcome. Another component of this approach includes prolonged exposure to obsessional cues. For example, if the person finds it distressing to go into public restrooms, then they would be exposed to that actual situation. By prolonged exposure, rituals can be blocked.

In addition to the actual situation, imagery can be used to repeat the situation without the ritual until the anxiety is lessened. Thus, the initial inability to conduct rituals produces the distress. The basic idea with treatment, according to Foa and Kozak (1986), is that repeated, prolonged exposure to feared thoughts and situations will provide information to the person concerning their mistaken beliefs and in turn allow for habituation.

In February 2009, the U.S. Food and Drug Administration (FDA) approved the use of a device for deep brain stimulation to treat OCD. As with deep brain stimulation for severe depression, an electrode is implanted in the brain along with a generator and battery placed under the person's skin. Currently, there are a number of clinical trials examining this treatment (Karas et al., 2019). One study showed that deep brain stimulation disrupts the maladaptive pathways in OCD between the frontal areas of the brain and subcortical structures and thereby restores normal function (Figee et al., 2013).

CONCEPT CHECK

- What are obsessions? What are compulsions? What is their relationship in OCD?
- How is hoarding disorder different from OCD in terms of both observable behaviors and brain processing?
- If a friend or family member asked you for a recommendation of the best treatment for OCD, what would you include in your answer and why?

SUMMARY

The experience of anxiety is part of the human situation. However, when this experience becomes chronic, creates distress, and interferes with our life, we see it as an anxiety disorder. Anxiety is the fear of what might happen. With anxiety, there is often no stimulus in front of us; rather, the stimulus is in our mind. However, our cognitive and emotional consideration of a negative possibility does not make it any less real. Our body, mind, and emotions experience our ideas as real possibilities.

In anxiety, we increase the probability in our mind that an event will happen. Some of these reactions appear to be built into our system. We know that fear and anxiety involve high-level as well as more primitive brain processes. From an evolutionary perspective, to be fearful in the presence of dangerous situations would be adaptive. And, in fact, it appears that fear can be learned through observation only to evolutionarily important objects. In our evolutionary history, it has been suggested that fear mechanisms evolved to aid our ability to disengage from the task at hand so as to pay attention to threats or potential danger. One model suggests that anxiety can be produced by expectations that either negative events will happen or that positive events will not happen. Individuals with anxiety are even more sensitive than others to the possibility of potential threat. This sensitivity is referred to as cognitive bias.

Although fear and anxiety are often studied together, research suggests that different brain areas are involved. Specifically, those areas involved in anxiety are not those directly responsible for the expression of fear but for the regulation of the fear system. Research suggests that anxiety should be seen as a developmental problem involving both environmental and genetic factors. The development of anxiety and fear follows a trajectory that is part of the human condition. Children and adolescents show similar profiles of anxiety and fear across cultures, although cultures that favor inhibition, compliance, and obedience also show increased levels of fear.

In *DSM-5-TR*, generalized anxiety disorder (GAD) is characterized by excessive anxiety and worry that lead to one or more of the following: (1) avoiding activities that can have negative outcomes, (2) overpreparation for activities that can have negative outcomes, (3) marked procrastination in behaviors due to worries, and (4) repeatedly seeking reassurance due to worries. GAD, along with depression, is the most frequently diagnosed mental disorder in the United States. Although a consistent physiological picture of worry has yet to be discovered, research does suggest that worry produces short-term relief from physiological responses to stress. Both medications and psychological treatments show similar reductions in GAD in the short term. However, only about 40% to 60% of those treated with either medication or psychological treatments show full improvement.

Social anxiety disorder (SAD) is characterized by a persistent and severe fear or anxiety about one or more social situations in which the individual is exposed to possible scrutiny by others. Previous experiences appear to be more important in individuals with SAD as compared with other anxiety disorders. It has been suggested that individuals with SAD process social situations with evolutionarily older alarm systems such as the amygdala, whereas non-anxious individuals process the same situation with newer cognitive-analytic processes using the PFC. Both CBT-type therapies and medication have been shown to be effective with SAD. Therapies including CBT, exposure therapy, social skills training, and group CBT may also be combined in different ways to provide treatment.

Human infants, as well as the infants of most other mammal species, show distress when separated from their caregivers. However, when this persists and negatively impacts daily activities, individuals would be diagnosed with separation anxiety disorder. *DSM-5-TR* describes eight different categories of symptoms, of which three must be present for an individual diagnosis of the disorder. Separation anxiety disorder is the most prevalent anxiety disorder for those under 12 years of age and is more commonly seen in girls than boys.

Agoraphobia is the condition in which a person experiences fear or anxiety when in public. In *DSM-5-TR*, agoraphobia is considered a separate disorder, although it may occur with any other disorder, especially the anxiety disorders. Both CBT approaches and antidepressants are effective in treating agoraphobia.

A specific phobia is the condition in which an individual experiences fear of or anxiety about a particular condition or object, and the fear or anxiety causes distress and is out of proportion to the actual danger posed by the situation. It is commonly accepted that phobias are best treated by methods involving exposure to the feared object.

A panic attack comes quickly and carries with it an intense feeling of apprehension, anxiety, or fear, and it happens without an actual situation that would suggest danger. It is necessary for one's symptoms to be recurrent and followed by a month of concern or change in lifestyle to be diagnosed with a panic disorder. Although presented as a separate anxiety disorder, panic attacks can occur within the context of any of the other anxiety disorders. On a brain level, it is suggested that panic and anxiety reflect different brain and hormonal processes. The currently preferred medication treatments for panic disorder are SSRIs. The best studied psychological treatment for panic disorder is CBT, which has been shown to be effective. Combining CBT and antidepressant medication is more effective than either one alone.

In obsessive-compulsive disorder (OCD), a distinction is made between obsessions and compulsions: Obsessions are generally unwelcome thoughts that come into one's head, and compulsions are the behaviors one uses to respond to these thoughts. Research suggests that OCD results from the exaggeration of normal traits that can be mapped onto a developmental trajectory. In looking at the types of thoughts specified by those with OCD, consistent groupings have been found that are related to different comorbid disorders.

In *DSM-5*, a new category called Obsessive-Compulsive and Related Disorders (OCRD) was introduced. This category brought together a number of disorders from other sections of previous *DSM* versions. Specifically, besides OCD itself, this category includes hoarding disorder, body dysmorphic disorder, trichotillomania (hair pulling disorder), and excoriation (skin picking disorder).

Hoarding disorder is defined in terms of an excessive acquisition of objects and an inability to discard these objects. Body dysmorphic disorder is characterized by a preoccupation with a perceived flaw in one's physical appearance. These are flaws that are not perceived by others or appear to be just a slight problem. People with this disorder feel that they are unattractive or even hideous to others. Any specific body area can be of concern to someone with this disorder, although hair, skin, and the nose are commonly seen as a problem.

Specific cognitive dysfunction associated with OCD includes response inhibition, set shifting, working memory, and planning, which suggests involvement of the DLPFC, the insula, the temporal and parietal lobes, and the cerebellum. OCD appears to run in families; however, the existence of a genetic relationship has been difficult to demonstrate. Both psychopharmacological and behavioral therapies have been shown to be effective for OCD. The most common medications are SSRIs and the tricyclic antidepressant clomipramine. The psychosocial treatment that has the best empirical support is EX/RP.

STUDY RESOURCES

Review Questions

1. How are anxiety and fear related? When is our experience of anxiety and fear a normal part of the human condition? What turns it into a psychopathology?

2. How are GAD and worry related?

3. In what ways are agoraphobia, specific phobias, and panic disorder similar in terms of their causes, symptoms, treatment, and prevalence? How are they different?

4. How would you show graphically the relationships in OCD among stressors, developmental stages, symptoms, and comorbid disorders?

For Further Reading

Barlow, D. (2004). *Anxiety and its disorders* (2nd ed.). Guilford Press.

Craske, M., & Barlow, D. (2006). *Mastery of your anxiety and worry* (2nd ed.). Oxford University Press.

Grazia, D. (2010). *On the outside looking in: My life with social anxiety disorder.* BookLocker.

Hazlett-Stevens, H. (2005). *Women who worry too much: How to stop worry and anxiety from ruining relationships, work, and fun.* New Harbinger.

LeDoux, J. (2015). *Anxiety: Using the brain to understand and treat fear and anxiety.* Viking.

National Institute of Mental Health. (2024). *Any anxiety disorder.* https://www.nimh.nih.gov/health/statistics/any-anxiety-disorder

Orsillo, S., & Roemer, L. (2016). *Worry less, live more: The mindful way through anxiety.* Guilford Press.

KEY TERMS

agoraphobia
body dysmorphic disorder
cognitive avoidance model
cognitive bias
compulsions
gamma-aminobutyric acid (GABA)
generalized anxiety disorder (GAD)
hoarding disorder

obsessions
obsessive-compulsive disorder (OCD)
panic attack
panic disorder
separation anxiety disorder
social anxiety disorder (SAD)
specific phobia
Stroop test

9 DISSOCIATIVE DISORDERS AND SOMATIC SYMPTOM DISORDERS

LEARNING OBJECTIVES

9.1 Define dissociation and explain the prevalence of dissociation in normal populations.

9.2 Describe the characteristics of depersonalization/derealization disorder, dissociative amnesia, and dissociative identity disorder, and identify treatments available to individuals with these disorders.

9.3 Describe the characteristics of somatic symptom disorder, illness anxiety disorder, conversion disorder, and factitious disorder, and identify treatments available to individuals with these disorders.

Describing her experience when the Federal Building in Oklahoma City was blown up by a bomb in 1995, a 28-year-old woman offered the following account:

> I felt that what was happening around me was like a scene from a war movie. I was observing it, but I wasn't participating in it. It all seemed so strange and unreal. I saw my burns and the blood pouring out from a deep gash on my arm, but I didn't feel any pain. I was numb, and everything around me was a blur—the noise, the screaming, the smoke. My thoughts started moving a mile a minute, thoughts like where was the nearest exit, how could I get there, how much time did I have before the whole building collapsed. I felt myself moving automatically, almost like a robot walking through a fog, and the next thing I knew, I was outside. (Steinberg & Schnall, 2000, p. 9)

Most of us have had the experience of sitting in a lecture and realizing that we have not been listening for a period of time. Most of us also have had the experience of driving down a highway and all of a sudden realizing that 30 minutes had passed with no awareness of what we had been doing. Sometimes while watching a movie, people become so absorbed in the film that they forget they are in a theater. These are common experiences of dissociation, or "spacing out," shared by most people. However, these dissociative experiences would not constitute a disorder. Overall, dissociation is a situation in which there is a disruption in our normal ability to integrate information from our sensory and psychological processes such as memory and awareness.

The first half of this chapter will focus on what are categorized as dissociative disorders in the *DSM*. Following that discussion, we will cover somatic symptom and related disorders, which are in a separate category within the *DSM*.

WHAT IS DISSOCIATION?

The term **dissociation** (*désaggregation* in French) was introduced by French psychologist Pierre Janet in 1889 to describe symptoms such as repetitive behaviors triggered by distressful memory, presentation of incongruous personality characteristics (e.g., shy, flirtatious) after a triggering event, and limb paralysis under hypnosis. Janet saw these as representing amnesic processes (memory loss from shock or trauma) in which patients "forgot" the ability to receive external stimulation, their own personality, and the ability to move limbs. The common thread in these experiences, according to Janet, was a traumatic event. That is, a traumatic event or talk of a traumatic event preceded the dissociative experiences. For Janet, dissociation resulted from a weak ego that could not tolerate the overwhelming trauma. Freud, on the other hand, saw dissociation resulting from a strong ego that sought to wall off the experience of trauma as something separate and not part of the self.

Many researchers see dissociation as a normal experience in response to a difficult situation. In times of stress, it is a mechanism that protects the individual and allows them to survive (Steinberg & Schnall, 2000). The description presented at the beginning of the chapter of the woman who was working when a bomb went off at the Federal Building in Oklahoma City is one such example. One current perspective suggests that the origins of dissociative symptoms extend well beyond trauma and views dissociative experiences and symptoms in terms of failures of multiple adaptive systems and processes that steer cognitions, emotions, and behaviors in everyday life (Lynn et al., 2022).

In an early study using a community sample of 1,055 individuals from Winnipeg, Canada, it was suggested that over 25% of the individuals reported dissociative experiences, and some 5% showed symptoms consistent with a clinical diagnosis (Ross et al., 1990). Overall, Ross and colleagues concluded that dissociative experiences are common in the general population; do not differ in terms of socioeconomic status, gender, education, or religion of the respondent; and are reported less by older respondents.

Pathological dissociative symptoms are generally experienced as involuntary disruption of the normal integration of consciousness, memory, identity, or perception. These can range from not having a sense of who one is or not remembering large parts of one's past to having no memory of one's personal history or experiencing a lack of a developmental self. *DSM-5-TR* describes four dissociative disorders (Table 9.1). These are *depersonalization/derealization disorder, dissociative amnesia, dissociative identity*

Pathological dissociative symptoms are generally experienced as involuntary disruption of the normal integration of consciousness, memory, identity, or perception.

iStock.com/pixelfit. Stock photo. Posed by model.

TABLE 9.1 ■ Dissociative Disorders in *DSM-5-TR*
Depersonalization/Derealization Disorder
Dissociative Amnesia
Dissociative Identity Disorder
Other Specified Dissociative Disorders

disorder (DID), and *other specified dissociative disorders*. *DSM-5-TR* combines depersonalization and derealization, which *DSM-IV* did not.

A study published in 2006 assessed the prevalence of dissociative disorders among 658 individuals, at age 33, in a longitudinal community sample in upstate New York (Johnson et al., 2006). In this nonclinical sample, 9.1% of the individuals had a dissociative disorder. As can be seen in Table 9.2, depersonalization disorder was seen in less than 1% of the sample, dissociative amnesia in less than 2%, and dissociative identity disorder in 1.5%. This study did not find gender differences. However, other studies have found that women seek help for dissociative disorders more often than men. Further, Johnson and his colleagues found that dissociative disorders co-occurred with anxiety, mood, and personality disorders among the adults in this New York sample.

To better understand dissociative experiences as seen in normal populations, Lukens and Ray (1995) interviewed college students who scored high on a common measure of dissociation. These young adults reported a variety of dissociative experiences. Three of these are presented here:

- One person reported that she would walk through town, and the next moment she would "wake up" standing in line at a store's cash register with unfamiliar store items in her hands. She also reported feeling embarrassed at having no explanation for her actions.

- Another individual reported, "While I was sitting in my room, I zoned out, and then as a third person or camera, I watched myself, my body, leave the room to visit a friend. I then returned to my room whereupon I snapped out of it. An hour had passed."

- Another person said, "I have episodes where I see everything differently, everything starts blending . . . things look more fluid. I snap out of it on purpose because it is a disturbing experience. I can't tell what is real and what is not."

TABLE 9.2 ■ Prevalence of Dissociative Disorders at Mean Age			
	Prevalence of Disorder in the Past Year		
Dissociative Disorder	Males ($N = 309$) N (%)	Females ($N = 349$) N (%)	Total sample ($N = 658$) N (%)
Depersonalization disorder[a]	2 (0.6)	3 (0.9)	5 (0.8)
Dissociative amnesia	3 (1.0)	9 (2.6)	12 (1.8)
Dissociative identity disorder (DID)	5 (1.6)	5 (1.4)	10 (1.5)
Dissociative disorder not otherwise specified (DDNOS)	21 (6.8)	15 (4.3)	36 (5.5)
Any dissociative disorder	30 (9.7)	30 (8.6)	60 (9.1)

[a]One individual met the diagnostic criteria for both depersonalization disorder and dissociative amnesia. Two individuals met the criteria for both depersonalization disorder and DID.

Note: Differences in the prevalence of dissociative disorders among males and females were not statistically significant.

Credit: Johnson, J., Cohen, P., Kasen, S., & Brook, J. (2006). Dissociative disorders among adults in the community, impaired functioning, and Axis I and Axis II comorbidity. *Journal of Psychiatric Research, 40*, 131–140, p. 135, with permission from Elsevier.

Dissociative experiences can last for a few minutes or hours, but they reoccur. They can also last for longer periods of time. Some of these experiences are severe and represent significant disruptions in the organization of identity, memory, perception, or consciousness (Lynn et al., 2022; Maldonado & Spiegel, 2015; Spiegel et al., 2013). More pathological symptoms of dissociation are often connected with trauma and experiences beyond the individual's control. This was seen in one study of children of war and traumatized refugee youth (Gušić et al., 2018), who showed signs both of trauma-related disorders and dissociation.

In another study of individuals who had been subject to torture, all those who had been tortured showed signs of post-traumatic stress disorder (PTSD) but varied in terms of their level of dissociation (Ray et al., 2006). This suggests that dissociation is a separate process from PTSD. In addition, the number of these individuals' dissociative experiences directly and positively correlated with magnetoencephalography (MEG) activity in the left frontal cortex and negatively correlated with MEG activity in the right frontal cortex. This suggests that brain changes associated with becoming detached from the overwhelming experience of torture permanently disrupt the networks involved in integrating emotional experience with the language features and executive control associated with the left hemisphere.

Verbatim histories and family reports were once the basic methodologies used to study dissociation. At the beginning of the 1900s, a number of dissociation studies were published in the United States in the *Journal of Abnormal Psychology*. These case histories led to the view that dissociation was the narrowing of the field of one's consciousness. Trauma was seen as critical and the cause of dissociation, since one's mind could not integrate traumatic experiences and memories of trauma in a coherent manner.

Dissociation and hypnosis have been connected in a variety of theoretical discussions of the underlying processes since at least the 1880s. However, in a nonclinical population of more than 800 individuals, hypnosis and dissociation have been shown not to be correlated with one another (Faith & Ray, 1994). That is to say, there are those who score high or low on both or low on one and high on the other, as well as others who show no relationship. Although dissociation and the hypnotic experience both represent an incomplete integration of sensory and other experiences, they are brought forth in different ways. Dissociation happens to a person without voluntary awareness, whereas one allows oneself to enter a hypnotic trance.

DISSOCIATIVE DISORDERS

Now let's examine the specific dissociative disorders that are included in *DSM-5-TR*.

Depersonalization/Derealization Disorder

Depersonalization is the perception of not experiencing the reality of one's self. This experience can include feeling detached or observing the self as if one were an outside observer. One model suggests that depersonalization is the result of a difficulty in integrating external stimuli with internal experiences (Saini et al., 2022). **Derealization**, on the other hand, is the experience that the external world is not solid. One's world is experienced with a sense of detachment, as if in a fog or a dream, or in other ways distorted or unreal. Immediately following an automobile accident, for example, many individuals report feeling as if the world and what is occurring are not real.

Unlike in psychotic experiences, reality testing, or the ability to distinguish between external and internal events, is available to individuals experiencing depersonalization and derealization. It is estimated that at least 50% of all adults in the United States have experienced depersonalization/derealization symptoms at some time in their life (APA, 2022).

Depersonalization and derealization are seen as normal responses to many types of acute stress. However, when they cause distress or impairment in important areas of one's life, they qualify as a *DSM* disorder. The prevalence rate is estimated to be 0 to 1.9% in the general population but higher in those with other psychopathological disorders (Yang et al., 2023), and there are no gender differences.

To better understand depersonalization, Simeon and colleagues (1997) interviewed 30 individuals with the disorder who ranged in age from 18 to 56 years. The average age at onset of the disorder was during adolescence, with no one having an onset after age 25. The mean duration of the illness was 15.7 years. Half of the individuals reported a sudden onset of the experience of depersonalization, whereas the other half reported a gradual onset over weeks to months. In comparison with a control group without depersonalization symptoms, individuals with the disorder reported more traumatization. Also, comorbid mood, anxiety, and personality disorders were common among those with depersonalization disorder. The case studies that follow are based on this research.

Immediately following an automobile accident, many individuals report feeling as if the world and what is occurring is not real.

iStock.com/RuslanDashinsky. Stock photo. Posed by model.

> **TWO CASE STUDIES**
>
> DEPERSONALIZATION
>
> This first case study describes a 43-year-old woman who was living with her mother and worked at a clerical job. She reports a trauma history of her mother fondling her and frequently giving her enemas until the time she was 10 years old. From the earliest times, this person reports having depersonalization experiences. She explains them this way: "It is as if the real me is taken out and put on a shelf or stored somewhere inside of me. Whatever makes me me is not there. It is like an opaque curtain . . . like going through the motions and having to exert discipline to keep the unit together." Each year, she experiences several such depersonalization episodes.
>
> The second case study is that of a 37-year-old married professional man who had suffered from depersonalization disorder. He describes his life as a child as one with little human contact. His parents gave him food and clothing but rarely touched or kissed him. His parents also rarely showed emotions. At the age of 10, he was playing football when he was tackled by another boy. As he was tackled, he felt his body disappear. Initially, similar experiences of depersonalization would happen from time to time. By age 14, he recounts a more continuous experience. He describes it as "not being in this world . . . I am disconnected from my body. It is as if my body is not there."
>
> *Source:* Based on Simeon, D., Gross, S., Guralnik, O., Stein, D. J., Schmeidler, J., & Hollander, E. (1997). Feeling unreal: 30 cases of *DSM*-III-R depersonalization disorder. *American Journal of Psychiatry, 154,* 1107–1113.

Some researchers have even suggested that experiences of depersonalization are a hardwired, inhibitory response to acute stress that increases survival by reducing arousal and anxiety (Sierra, 2008). One study examined skin conductance response, which is a direct measure of the autonomic nervous system's reaction to unpleasant, pleasant, and neutral stimuli (Sierra et al., 2002). These researchers compared individuals with depersonalization disorder, those with anxiety disorders, and those without these disorders. As seen in Figure 9.1, individuals with depersonalization disorder showed reduced autonomic responses to unpleasant stimuli in comparison with the other groups. This suggests that individuals with depersonalization disorder show inhibitory responses to negative emotional information. The factors that allow these stress responses to move to a pathological state are still being determined.

Brain imaging studies of depersonalization disorder have been limited. One of the first studies used positron emission testing (PET) measures to compare individuals with depersonalization disorder and a matched set of controls (Simeon et al., 2000; see Figure 9.2). Overall, individuals with depersonalization disorder had lower metabolic activity in sensory areas as well as brain areas responsible for an integrated body schema. Other studies showed less cortical thickness in those with depersonalization disorder (Sierra et al., 2014).

Dissociative Amnesia

The main diagnostic element of **dissociative amnesia** is an inability to recall important autobiographical information. **Dissociative fugue**, which was listed as a separate disorder in *DSM-IV*, falls under the diagnosis of dissociative amnesia in *DSM-5-TR*. Dissociative fugue is sudden, unexpected travel away from one's home or place of work with an inability to recall one's past. Memory loss in terms of dissociative amnesia appears to be of a particular first-person nature rather than a global memory disorder. In fact, interacting with these individuals would seem like nothing out of the ordinary until they are asked about their personal history. At that point, they are unable to remember any of their historical experiences. However, our memory of events is different from our memory of how to do things, such as riding a bike. This type of memory, referred to as procedural memory, is not lost, nor is the ability to create new long-term memories. Dissociative amnesia may last for a few days to years. Unlike the other dissociative disorders, dissociative amnesia is generally diagnosed between the ages of 20 and 40, although it has been seen in both children and older adults (Staniloiu & Markowitsch, 2014). There are few large-scale epidemiological studies about dissociative amnesia. Twelve-month prevalence is estimated to be about 1.8% with a 2.6-to-1 female-to-male ratio (APA, 2013, 2022).

FIGURE 9.1 ■ How Do Individuals With Depersonalization Disorder Respond to Emotional Stimuli?

Individuals with depersonalization disorder showed reduced autonomic responses to unpleasant stimuli. This suggests that individuals with depersonalization disorder show inhibitory responses to negative emotional information. The control group and those with anxiety show larger responses to these stimuli. Responses are standardized as range-corrected scores (for each participant, skin conductance response magnitudes were computed as a proportion of that participant's largest response).

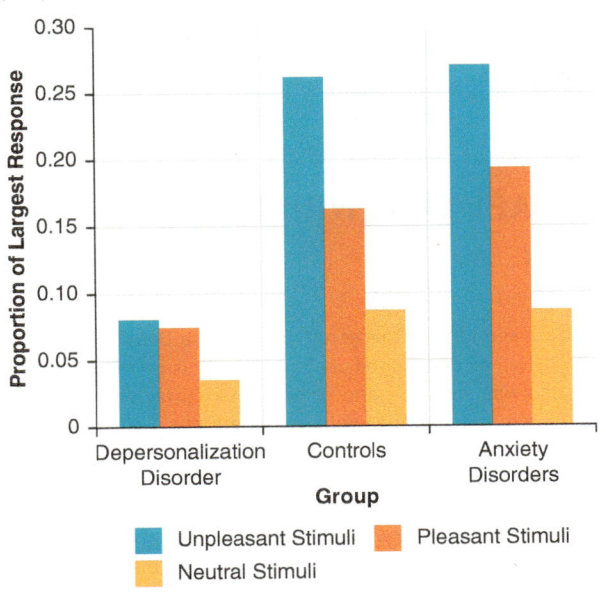

Source: Sierra, M., Senior, C., Dalton, J., McDonough, M., Bond, A., Phillips, M., O'Dwyer, A., & David, A. (2002). Autonomic response in depersonalization disorder. *American Journal of General Psychiatry, 59*, 833–838, p. 835).

FIGURE 9.2 ■ Do Those With Depersonalization Disorder Show Less Response in Brain Areas Related to Self-Image?

This figure shows PET images of the brains of a healthy comparison subject and a patient with depersonalization disorder at two consecutive levels in the parietal lobe.

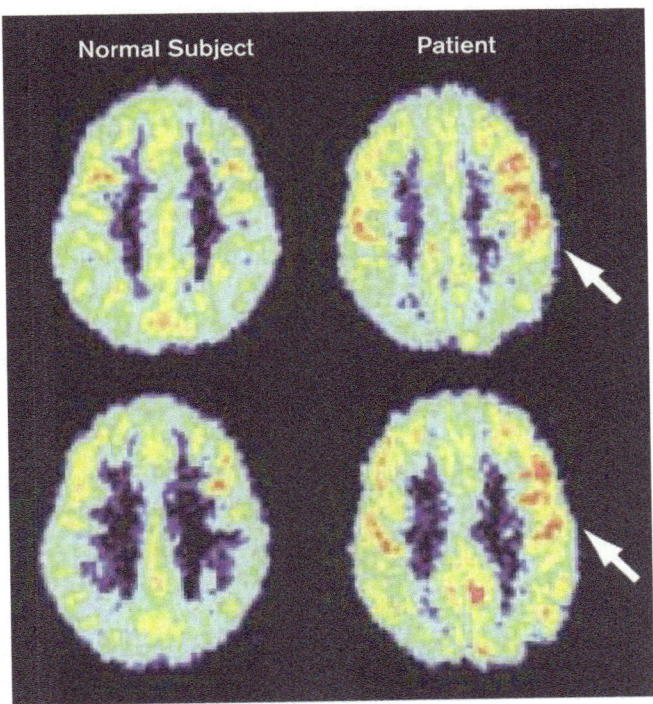

Credit: Reprinted with permission from the *American Journal of Psychiatry*, Volume 157, Issue 11, "Feeling Unreal: A PET Study of Depersonalization Disorder" Simeon et al, (Copyright 2000), Figure 1, PET Images of the Brains of a Healthy Comparison Subject and a Patient with Depersonalization Disorder at Two Consecutive Levels in the Parietal Lobe.

In the psychological literature, fugue has been discussed for at least the past 100 years. William James described the case of Reverend Ansel Bourne, who reported leaving his home and adopting a new identity after he had become amnesic about his previous life. However, most individuals with dissociative amnesia do not show the adoption of a new identity but just the forgetting of their past. During World War II and other periods of armed conflict, fugue states were frequently documented. Cases of dissociative amnesia continue to be seen today, in fact, and are often reported in the newspapers as medical staff seek to obtain information about the person. The following case study reports an incident that took place in 2013.

CASE OF MICHAEL BOATWRIGHT

DISSOCIATIVE AMNESIA

Michael Boatwright was taken to the emergency room of the Desert Regional Medical Center in Palm Springs, California. He had been found unconscious in his motel room. When he awoke in the hospital, he said his name was Johan Ek and he only spoke Swedish. He had with him five tennis rackets, two cell phones, a duffel bag filled with casual athletic clothes, some money, photos, and identification cards. Each of the cards—including a passport, a VA card, and a social security card—said he was Michael Boatwright. When asked by a translator about the identification cards, the man reported that he was Johan and did not know Michael. The hospital determined it would be unsafe to release this person without any memory who only spoke Swedish. He remained in a nursing facility for a few weeks so his condition could be evaluated. He had nightmares almost every night. During this time, hospital personnel sought to determine his past through his ID cards. They discovered that he recently flew in from China where he had taught English and was a graphic designer for the previous 4 years. Before that, he had worked in Japan for 10 years. The hospital staff also found that he did live in Sweden when he was younger. Through contacts in these countries, they were able to obtain some pictures of him with others. He reported that although he did not recognize the pictures, they gave him a sense of comfort and security. The hospital staff also sought to determine if he showed any signs of faking, which he did not. He was diagnosed with dissociative amnesia.

Michael Boatwright then returned to Sweden and worked as a private tennis coach. Some 14 months after he left California, he was found dead in his apartment in Uddevalla, Sweden. The Swedish police described his death as a suicide.

Source: Pelham, V. (2013, July 7). Michael Boatwright awakes in Palm Springs with apparent amnesia. *The Desert Sun.* The death was reported in *The Desert Sun,* April 23, 2014. Retrieved from http://www.desertsun.com/story/news/2014/04/23/michael-boatwright-dead-amnesia-sweden-palm-springs/8055511/

Unless a mental health or medical professional suspects that dissociation is involved, documentation that would lead to a diagnosis of dissociative amnesia is often lacking. For example, dissociation information is rarely asked for even in those who would be at risk for dissociative processes, such as adolescents who have run away from abusive homes or people experiencing homelessness.

Dissociative Identity Disorder

Dissociative identity disorder (DID) has received considerable attention from the media and popular press. Previously referred to as *multiple personality disorder*, there is a large amount of misinformation concerning its existence. Most television and film depictions of DID are not true to life. Some of this information is described in the LENS: Multiple Personality and the Media. Current views suggest that DID is less a disorder of multiple personalities than it is a developmental disorder where one consistent sense of self does not occur; that is, the person does not experience their thoughts, feelings, or actions in terms of a well-developed "I" or sense of self. Rather, the person experiences different "personalities" at different times. DID is seen as a complex disorder related to an experience of trauma before the age of 5 or 6 (Loewenstein, 2018; Reinders & Veltman, 2021). This is the time at which a sense of self is in development.

During World War II and other periods of armed conflict, fugue states were frequently documented.

Dave Bagnall Collection/Alamy Stock Photo

LENS

MULTIPLE PERSONALITY AND THE MEDIA

Dissociative identity disorder (DID), commonly called *multiple personality disorder* in the media, became popular through films, television shows, and books. One movie was *The Three Faces of Eve*, released in 1957. The book *Sybil* was published in 1973 and sold in the millions. It was followed by the made-for-television movie *Sybil* in 1976, which was watched by millions of people. These brought further attention to the concept of DID.

The film *The Three Faces of Eve* (1957) portrayed a real woman, Chris Sizemore, who showed signs of at least three separate personalities, the primary two of which are referred to as Eve White and Eve Black. In the film, Eve White is portrayed as a timid wife and mother with headaches. During treatment, a fun-loving personality, Eve Black, appears. Eve Black knows about Eve White, but Eve White does not know about Eve Black. Her therapy sessions explored the traumatic events from Eve's childhood, which were believed to be the source of her developing different identities, or "alters." Although the film was fairly melodramatic, there has been little controversy concerning the fact that Sizemore experienced DID. However, that was not the case with *Sybil*.

The book *Sybil* (Schreiber, 1973) was published as the purportedly true story of a woman with multiple personalities. Her story is that of a person who had difficulty functioning in day-to-day activities. The basic idea was that to cope with trauma, including abuse by her mother, Sybil developed multiple personalities—as many as 16. Sybil experienced "blank spells," which could last from a few minutes to a couple of days, in which she had no idea what had happened to the time. It was during these periods that other personalities appeared who were unknown to Sybil. By the end of the book, Sybil was able to integrate her personalities and become a functioning individual, thanks to a caring therapist. It was both a book and a movie that fascinated the public, especially since it was sold as a "true" story.

Sybil was a pseudonym for a real woman named Shirley Mason. Mason grew up in the Midwest in a strict Seventh-day Adventist family. Feeling emotionally unstable, she sought help from mental health professionals. Mason's psychiatrist, Dr. Connie Wilbur, was interested in multiple personality disorder. One suggestion is that to gain more attention, Mason said, "I'm not Shirley—I'm Peggy," in a childish voice and started acting like there were other people inside her. Soon other personalities followed and were seen during therapy.

The 1957 film *The Three Faces of Eve* brought the existence of dissociative identity disorder to the public consciousness.
John Springer Collection/Corbis Historical/via Getty Images

According to a 2011 exposé, *Sybil Exposed*, by the journalist Debbie Nathan, Mason wrote a letter to Dr. Wilbur to say that she did not have multiple personalities. She admitted, "I do not really have any multiple personalities. . . . I do not even have a 'double.' . . . I am all of them. I have been lying in my pretense of them. . . . as trying to show you I felt I needed help. . . . Quite thrilling. Got me a lot of attention." Wilbur believed that Mason had other motives for recanting her claims of multiple identities, and she dismissed the letter. Based on the papers and letters available at the John Jay College of Criminal Justice concerning those involved, however, the story of Mason having 16 personalities is now considered to be a fake.

Dr. Herbert Spiegel, a New York psychiatrist who treated Mason when her psychiatrist was on vacation, suggested that she did not have DID. Rather, she was a highly suggestible person. Another psychiatrist, Dr. Paul McHugh, who has worked with DID individuals at Johns Hopkins in Baltimore, said, "I don't believe she had identity disorder, multiple personality or anything. I think she did have an intensely suggestible personality, and she was in a situation where she was open to the suggestions—looking, as she was, for help for the conditions that she suffered from."

At this point, the general consensus is that *Sybil* does not represent a true portrayal of DID. Rather, through a complicated situation in which a suggestible person with close connections to her psychiatrist became involved in a plan to write a book by her psychiatrist and a writer, storytelling became more important than truth. The original broadcast of *Sybil*, like the book itself, led to a huge increase in the reported incidents of DID. According to a National Public Radio report, the number of cases reported went from fewer than 100 to thousands.

Thought Question

If you were a mental health professional, how might you determine if a person was experiencing DID or following the suggestions of others?

Source: Flatow, I. (Host). (2011, October 21). Exploring Multiple Personalities in "Sybil Exposed" [Audio podcast episode]. In *Talk of the Nation*. NPR. http://www.npr.org/2011/10/21/141591185/exploring-multiple-personalities-in-sybil-exposed

Epidemiological studies suggest the prevalence of DID to be between 1% and 3% with slightly more men than women showing the disorder (Vermetten et al., 2006). Although the prevalence is similar across genders, the manner of presentation is different (APA, 2013, 2022). Women with DID are more likely to be seen in adult clinical settings. Men, on the other hand, tend to deny their symptoms and trauma history. However, the symptoms can be seen following combat conditions or acts of physical or sexual assault. Cultural differences are also seen. In developing countries and rural communities, the fragmented identities may become part of religious or other experiences. For example, possessions by gods or spirits are seen in a number of cultures.

In *DSM-5-TR*, as seen in Table 9.3, an important feature of DID is the presence of two or more distinct personality states or an experience of possession. These can be influenced by a number of psychological factors, including the person's current experience of stress, ability to cope, internal conflicts, and cultural factors.

Disruptions in memory are also an important part of DID. These memory problems can appear in three different ways. First, the person may not remember significant parts of their life, such as what occurred between 12 and 14 years of age or an event that would be considered important to most people. Second, the person may not remember how to perform an act or well-learned skills such as driving or using a computer. Third, the person may discover evidence of actions that they do not remember doing. For example, the person may find notes written in their handwriting with no memory of having written them, or clothes in the closet that they do not remember buying. These disruptions may occur without any significant psychologically stressful event taking place.

Marlene Steinberg (1994) developed a screening device for dissociative disorders, the *Structured Clinical Interview for DSM-IV Dissociative Disorders* (SCID-D). She described DID as a situation in which a person shifts between distinct personality states that take control of their behavior and thoughts (Steinberg & Schnall, 2000). These alternate personalities, or *alters*, are clearly defined, and each may have its own name, memories, traits, and behavioral patterns. However, it is possible for one alter not to know of the existence or experiences of another. At times, an alter may take control of the host without the host's awareness of the situation. This amnesia may lead to the person being told by others of events, conversations, or agreements that took place out of their awareness. At other times, the "host" personality may experience the alters as arguing with one another. One of Steinberg's patients described one such situation:

> I was about to walk into a meeting that I needed to attend, and the only chair that was available was between two men. I didn't turn around and walk out, but my body turned around and walked out. And I couldn't talk to save my soul because there was this battle going on about whether or not I should go into the meeting, and someone wanting some memory to come up and someone else suppressing it. I tried to walk into that meeting, but I couldn't do it. (Steinberg & Schnall, 2000, p. 109)

TABLE 9.3 ■ *DSM-5-TR* Diagnostic Criteria for Dissociative Identity Disorder

A. Disruption of identity characterized by two or more distinct personality states, which may be described in some cultures as an experience of possession. This disruption in identity involves marked discontinuity in sense of self and sense of agency, accompanied by related alterations in affect, behavior, consciousness, memory, perception, cognition, and/or sensory-motor functioning. These signs and symptoms may be observed by others or reported by the individual.

B. Recurrent gaps in the recall of everyday events, important personal information, and/or traumatic events that are inconsistent with ordinary forgetting.

C. The symptoms cause clinically significant distress or impairment in social, occupational, or other important areas of functioning.

D. The disturbance is not a normal part of a broadly accepted cultural or religious practice. Note: In children, the symptoms are not better explained by imaginary playmates or other fantasy play.

E. The symptoms are not attributable to the physiological effects of a substance (e.g., blackouts or chaotic behavior during alcohol intoxication) or another medical condition (e.g., complex partial seizures).

Credit: Reprinted with permission from the *Diagnostic and Statistical Manual of Mental Disorders*, fifth edition, text revision, DSM-V-TR, p. 330 (Copyright © 2022). American Psychiatric Association. All rights reserved.

Historically, DID was commonly understood in terms of possession by an outside force or possession in which an individual loses their identity to become another person. Descriptions seen as early as 1787 referred to an "umgetauschte Personlichkeit," German for exchanged personality. Likewise, Benjamin Rush described such patients in the early 1800s, followed by Charcot, Janet, and Morton Prince in the early 1900s. Prince wrote the classic book *The Dissociation of a Personality* in 1905. Swiss psychiatrist Eugen Bleuler included DID under the rubric of schizophrenia, resulting in disuse of the DID diagnosis for a time during the mid-20th century.

Gleaves, May, and Cardeña (2001) reviewed a variety of studies that examined DID populations and their core features. As seen in Table 9.4, amnesia was reported in almost 100% of the individuals studied. Further, previous child abuse was present on average in over 90% of the individuals with DID.

Neuroscience research related to DID has been relatively limited. In one study, the volume of the hippocampus and amygdala was studied using MRI (Vermetten et al., 2006; see Figure 9.3). Those

FIGURE 9.3 ■ The Size of the Hippocampus and Amygdala in Those With DID

This figure shows the volume of the hippocampus and amygdala using magnetic resonance imaging (MRI) for those with DID and healthy controls. Those with DID show smaller structures. Each comparison shows a significant difference between groups.

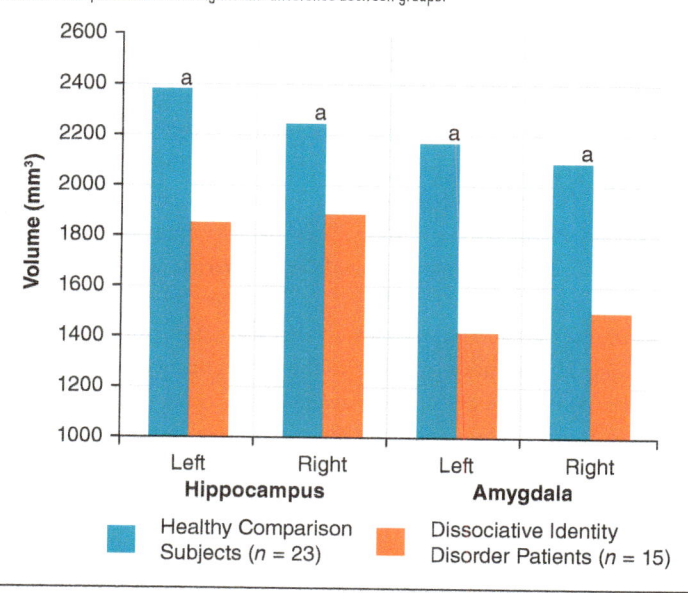

Source: Vermetten, E., Schmahl, C., Lindner, S., Loewenstein, R., & Bremner, J. (2006). Hippocampal and amygdalar volumes in dissociative identity disorder. *American Journal of Psychiatry, 163*, 630–636, p. 633.

TABLE 9.4 ■ Frequency of Core Features of Dissociative Identity Disorder From Large-Scale Investigations

Core Feature	Putnam et al., 1986 (n = 100)	Coons et al., 1988 (n = 50)	Ross et al., 1989 (n = 236)	Ross et al., 1990a, b (n = 102)	Boon & Draijer, 1993a, b (n = 71)
Amnesia	98.0	100.0	94.9	100.0	99.0
Identity alteration	–	–	–	81.4	100.1
Depersonalization	55.0	38.0	–	–	100.0
Derealization	–	–	–	56.9	73.1
Auditory hallucinations	29.0	72.0	71.7	82.4	94.0
Childhood abuse	97.0	96.0	88.5	95.1	94.4

Note: All values are percentages of persons reportedly experiencing the symptom.

Credit: Gleaves, D., May, M., & Cardeña, E. (2001). An examination of the diagnostic validity of dissociative identity disorder. *Clinical Psychology Review, 21*, 577–608, p. 579, with permission from Elsevier.

with DID had hippocampal volume that was 19.2% smaller and amygdala volume that was 31.6% smaller compared with a control group of people without DID. Reduced volume of the hippocampus and amygdala has also been reported in stress-related disorders, including PTSD. In a script-driven imagery study, the act of writing descriptions of previous trauma events was associated with similar patterns of PET brain activation in those with DID as had been previously seen in individuals with PTSD (Reinders et al., 2014). The authors of this study suggest that DID uses similar networks to PTSD and may be a severe childhood onset form of PTSD.

One large-scale review of the literature proposes that neurofunctional biomarkers of pathological dissociation are the dorsomedial and dorsolateral prefrontal cortex, bilateral superior frontal regions, (anterior) cingulate, posterior association areas, and basal ganglia (Roydeva & Reinders, 2021). This review found hyperactivity of the frontal regions, the cingulate, parietal regions, and the basal ganglia to be neurobiomarkers of pathological dissociation, underpinning previously proposed neurobiological models for severe pathological dissociation. Brain volume measures of pathological dissociation are decreased hippocampal volume, basal ganglia volume, and thalamus volume.

Treatment for Dissociative Disorders

Although some dissociative disorders such as dissociative amnesia may resolve on their own, others such as DID require long-term treatment. Often, clients with DID seek treatment for a different type of psychological distress. The basic procedure for treating DID is typically long-term psychotherapy. In therapy, a focus on the relationship between the client and the therapist is important. The emphasis is on developing a safe place where individuals can experience and integrate the various parts of themselves. At present, no empirically supported principles have been tested beyond the exploratory stages in terms of dissociation (Maxwell et al., 2018). However, techniques from cognitive behavioral therapy (CBT), humanistic-existential therapy, and dynamic approaches have been used in various combinations (Ross, 1997). There are also no established medications directed solely to DID. However, medication may be used for comorbid conditions.

In summary, the common theme seen in all dissociative disorders is a loss of the normal integration of cognitive functioning. This includes the person's sense of self, autobiographical memory, a sense of control and agency, and an integrated awareness of functioning. Historically, dissociative disorders have been a way to avoid the distress of trauma and other psychologically changing events. In the next section of this chapter, those disorders that focus on a person's reaction to bodily symptoms, referred to as somatic symptom disorders, will be discussed.

The television series *Mr. Robot* follows Elliot, a cybersecurity expert recruited to join a hacking operation, as he develops dissociative identity disorder.

UNIVERSAL CABLE PRODUCTIONS/Album/Alamy Stock Photo

> ## UNDERSTANDING CHANGES IN *DSM-5* AND *DSM-5-TR*
> ### DISSOCIATIVE DISORDERS
>
> In *DSM-5*, dissociative disorders were placed immediately after trauma and stress-related disorders to indicate the close relationship between them (Spiegel et al., 2013). Both acute stress disorder and PTSD can contain dissociative symptoms such as amnesia, flashbacks, and emotional numbing.
>
> In terms of dissociative identity disorder, one important change was to distinguish psychopathological states of dissociation from those that are part of one's cultural experience. For example, religious rituals and experiences from around the world may result in dissociative experiences. In some cases, the person may speak in the voice of another person or spirit. These cultural experiences are considered normal from the standpoint of *DSM-5*.
>
> In *DSM-IV*, a person who suddenly left home and found themselves in another city without any sense of their own identity or where they came from was seen to have a separate disorder referred to as dissociative fugue. In *DSM-5*, this condition is seen as a subtype of dissociative amnesia. The basic idea is that one component of dissociative fugue is amnesia.
>
> A third change in *DSM-5* dissociation categories is the renaming of depersonalization disorder to depersonalization/derealization disorder. This is based on the fact that those who experience derealization do not significantly differ from those who experience depersonalization and derealization together.
>
> In developing *DSM-5*, there was also a suggestion that conversion disorder, which you will read about in the next section, be classified as a dissociative disorder. A person with a conversion disorder will report that they cannot see, hear, move their limbs, or feel pain, yet there is no physiological process that would explain any of these inabilities. Although symptoms of conversion disorders can overlap with those of dissociative disorders, they also overlap with other diagnostic categories. Thus, it was decided to leave conversion disorder as part of the Somatic Symptom and Related Disorders grouping. Overall, the changes made to both dissociative and somatic symptom disorders were less controversial than the changes made in the criteria for other disorders.

> ## CONCEPT CHECK
>
> - In what ways are dissociative disorders similar to the types of dissociative experiences common to most people? In what ways are they different?
> - What can we say about when and how the following dissociative disorders occur and their prevalence in the general population?
>   - Depersonalization/derealization
>   - Dissociative amnesia
>   - DID
> - What methods are currently available for the assessment and treatment of individuals with dissociative disorders?

SOMATIC SYMPTOM AND RELATED DISORDERS

Most of us experience some sort of somatic, or bodily, symptom regularly. We may feel tired, feel a pain in our leg, or have a stomachache. In fact, it is estimated that 60% to 80% of the general population experiences some sort of somatic symptom in a given week (Kellner, 1985). Further, how you understand your symptoms can be related to your culture, as described in *Cultural LENS: Culture and Somatic Symptoms*.

CULTURAL LENS
CULTURE AND SOMATIC SYMPTOMS

Anthropologists who have researched cultures around the world have found that individuals' descriptions of distress are influenced by cultural beliefs and the manner in which their particular culture treats health concerns. In some cultures, individuals report bodily symptoms, whereas individuals in other cultures describe emotional or social distress. This pattern of describing distress in bodily terms has been referred to as *idioms of distress*. Another strand of research shows that conversion symptoms are more common in some cultures than others.

Many cultures show some of these bodily presentations (Kirmayer & Young, 1998). There is a Korean condition called *hwa-byung*, which includes stomach distress, headaches, and other pains. This condition is understood by those who experience it as the result of not expressing anger or resentment that results in a mass in the chest. In Nigeria, students experience a condition known as *brain fag*. Brain fag is experienced as a heaviness or heat in the head associated with the effort of studying. This condition is often reported by those who are the first in their families to become educated and is related to their experience of no longer being part of their larger community. In South Asia, there is a belief that vital essence can be lost through semen. It is assumed that the semen can be lost in urine. This is called *dhat* and is experienced as fatigue and weakness as well as anxiety and depression.

Since the 1970s, a series of research studies conducted in China have found that people in that country emphasize somatic symptoms more than do people in Western cultures, especially when experiencing depression (Zhou et al., 2016). This pattern is referred to as *Chinese somatization*. The research suggests that emphasizing somatic symptoms rather than psychological ones may be more culturally acceptable and less likely to bring shame on one's family. Somatic symptoms may also lead to faster treatment in the health care system. In a factor-analytic study, Xiaolu Zhou and her colleagues suggested that Chinese somatization can be understood in terms of two factors. The first involves the experience of distress, and the second involves the conceptualization and communication of distress. These researchers also demonstrated that these two factors are culturally shaped.

As more people in China have moved from rural communities to large cities, there has also been a change in how they view mental health problems (Kolstad & Gjesvik, 2014). Traditionally, mental health problems were seen in rural communities as challenges in daily life and relationship strain. With movement to the cities and Western influences, mental health problems are now being seen more from a disorder perspective.

Similar changes have been seen in the United States. Traditionally, people living in rural communities looked to their religious leaders for help with mental health concerns. Today, there is a greater willingness to use mental health professionals as an alternative source of help. However, there is also a tendency to describe mental health issues as bodily problems or a case of *nerves*.

Thought Question

Given the issue of somatization, what health and mental health policies and principles could countries like China consider to help their population successfully transition from rural communities to large cities?

The most common symptoms include chest pain, headache, fatigue, and dizziness. Most of us consider these experiences as part of life and assume they will go away. If they don't, or if the symptoms concern us, we may go see our physician, who may do an examination, run some tests, or perform other procedures. The physician may diagnose a possible cause or say that they can find nothing wrong. If our physician says that nothing is wrong, most of us will feel relieved.

Some people, however, do not feel relieved. They may continue to search for organic problems by going to other physicians or request more tests. They are certain something is wrong with them. Others may feel excessive anxiety and worry that the simple symptoms they have are really something serious, perhaps cancer or the beginning of a heart attack. These are two aspects of what are referred to as **somatic symptom and related disorders** (Table 9.5). Another related phenomenon is the situation in

TABLE 9.5 ■ Somatic Symptom and Related Disorders in *DSM-5-TR*
Somatic Symptom Disorder
Illness Anxiety Disorder
Conversion Disorder (Functional Neurological Symptom Disorder)
Psychological Factors Affecting Medical Condition
Factitious Disorder
Other Specified Somatic Symptom and Related Disorder

which a person shows signs of a physical disability but does not present with what we know to be the underlying physiology of that disability. These disorders were previously referred to as *hysteria* and are now called conversion disorders.

Before *DSM-5*, somatic symptom and related disorders were referred to as *somatoform disorders*. *Somatoform*, easily confused with *psychosomatic illness* or *somatization*, was an ambiguous term to many clinicians and researchers. A *psychosomatic disorder* is an actual physical illness in which psychological factors play an important role. *Somatoform* was also a difficult term to translate into different languages, and this made cross-cultural studies difficult. Because of these and other reasons, the specific diagnosis of somatoform disorder was changed to *somatic symptom and related disorders* in *DSM-5*. The manual also removed the diagnosis of *pain disorder*. It was removed because, in *DSM-IV*, it was assumed that some pain was associated with psychological factors, and other types of pain were not psychological. However, research has shown that psychological factors influence all types of pain, and thus the prior diagnosis of pain disorder lacked reliability and validity.

Somatic symptom disorders represent an interface between psychological processes and medical ones. Individuals with these disorders do not seek mental health professionals. Thus, it is one set of disorders in which the professional doing the diagnosis, typically a physician, is a person who does not specialize in the treatment of mental disorders. This will influence the estimates of the prevalence of these disorders, since few physicians will use this diagnosis. For example, if an individual went to an emergency room, the physician would perform an examination and then release the person if they found no physical problems. The physician would not make a diagnosis since no physical disorder was evident. It is only when the person's behavior is seen in a larger context—such as going to a series of different physicians—that the possibility of a somatic symptom disorder becomes apparent.

Physicians in emergency rooms will also describe cases in which individuals fake medical disorders for other types of gain. In some cases, they may be trying to avoid going to work or doing other activities they do not want to do. This is referred to as *malingering*. Some individuals may actually take substances to create a disorder. This is referred to as a *factitious disorder*.

Somatic Symptom Disorder

Somatic symptom disorder is the condition in which a person's somatic or bodily symptoms cause distress or disruption in physical health that is not consistent with a medical disorder. For a diagnosis of the disorder, the person must do one of the following: have persistent thoughts about the seriousness of their symptoms, have a high level of anxiety about their health or symptoms, or spend excessive time and energy on their health. Further, these characteristics must have lasted for longer than 6 months.

These individuals may go from physician to physician or from emergency room to emergency room seeking to be told that they have a medical disorder. They are not satisfied when the professional cannot find the cause of their symptoms. This leads to inconsistent statistics concerning the disorder and a lack of research compared with other disorders. One estimate suggests the prevalence of somatic symptom disorder is around 5% to 7% (APA, 2013, 2022). Since women seek medical advice more often than men and are more willing to report symptoms, a gender difference would be expected.

Illness Anxiety Disorder

Illness anxiety disorder is the diagnosis when a person is preoccupied with the possibility of having a serious illness (Scarella et al., 2019). However, unlike somatic symptom disorders, the person experiences few, if any, symptoms. This disorder was previously referred to as *hypochondriasis* but was

Even if diagnosed, some people with somatic symptoms may not feel relieved and may continue to search for organic problems.

iStock.com/Creativeye99

Chuck on *Better Call Saul* has what's known as self-perceived electromagnetic hypersensitivity, a condition with no accepted medical diagnosis, which shares many characteristics with somatic symptom disorder.

PictureLux/The Hollywood Archive/Alamy Stock Photo

renamed in *DSM-5*. In illness anxiety disorder, the anxiety is focused on health issues; the person may become alarmed at any suggestion or thought that they may have a health problem. For example, the person might read an article about symptoms of cancer or have a sensation in their body and decide that they have cancer. In addition to anxiety, behavioral components such as checking one's body for changes may be present. Although it would be reasonable to be concerned if a particular disorder was part of one's family history, illness anxiety disorder takes this to the extreme. Generally, reassurance from a health care worker will not reduce the anxiety. Paradoxically, some individuals with this disorder actually avoid seeing a health professional since this would increase their anxiety, fearing that the doctor might confirm a serious condition.

In many ways, it is not the symptom itself but the person's reaction to the symptom that is the critical feature of illness anxiety disorder. *DSM-5-TR* makes a distinction between those whose major concern is the symptoms versus those whose concern is the possibility of having a disorder. Those whose concern is with the symptoms themselves would be diagnosed with somatic symptom disorder. Those whose concern is with the possibility of developing a particular illness would be diagnosed with illness anxiety disorder.

As you think about illness anxiety disorder, you might wonder if it is just an anxiety disorder with a different focus: the body. A number of studies have suggested that individuals with illness anxiety disorder are different from those with other disorders in the manner in which they conceptualize bodily processes. For example, in one study, those with illness anxiety disorder reported that they believed bodily complaints are always a sign of disease, which was not the case for those with other disorders such as depression (Rief et al., 1998). In comparison with individuals with other anxiety disorders and a control group without mental disorders, individuals with illness anxiety disorder were shown to have a different concept of what "good health" means (Weck et al., 2012). Those with illness anxiety disorder were shown to have a more restrictive concept in that they saw bodily symptoms as incompatible with good health. This was not true of those with other anxiety disorders. Further, if asked to compare their symptoms to those of other people, those with illness anxiety disorder saw symptoms in themselves as more severe than those in others. Other studies have shown that those with illness anxiety disorder also can be distinguished from those with panic disorder (Hiller et al., 2005).

Conversion Disorder

Conversion disorder refers to what has historically been called *hysteria*. In this situation, a person reports sensory or motor symptoms such as not being able to hear, see, feel pain, or move a part of the body. However, the symptoms do not follow known physiological or neurological patterns. **Glove anesthesia**, for example, refers to the phenomenon when a person says, "I cannot feel anything in my hand." The pattern of insensitivity is that of a glove. However, the touch receptors in our hand do not follow this pattern. The ulnar nerve is involved in sensitivity beginning in the ring finger and little finger and continuing up the wrist. The area of sensitivity is shown in Figure 9.4. The medial nerve is involved

FIGURE 9.4 ■ How Would Nerve Damage Influence Our Sense of Touch?

Depending on which nerve in the hand was damaged, one would lose sensation in either the left or right part of the hand. This figure shows the region of skin innervation of the ulnar nerve in blue. The sensitivity of the other part of the hand would be controlled by the radial nerve.

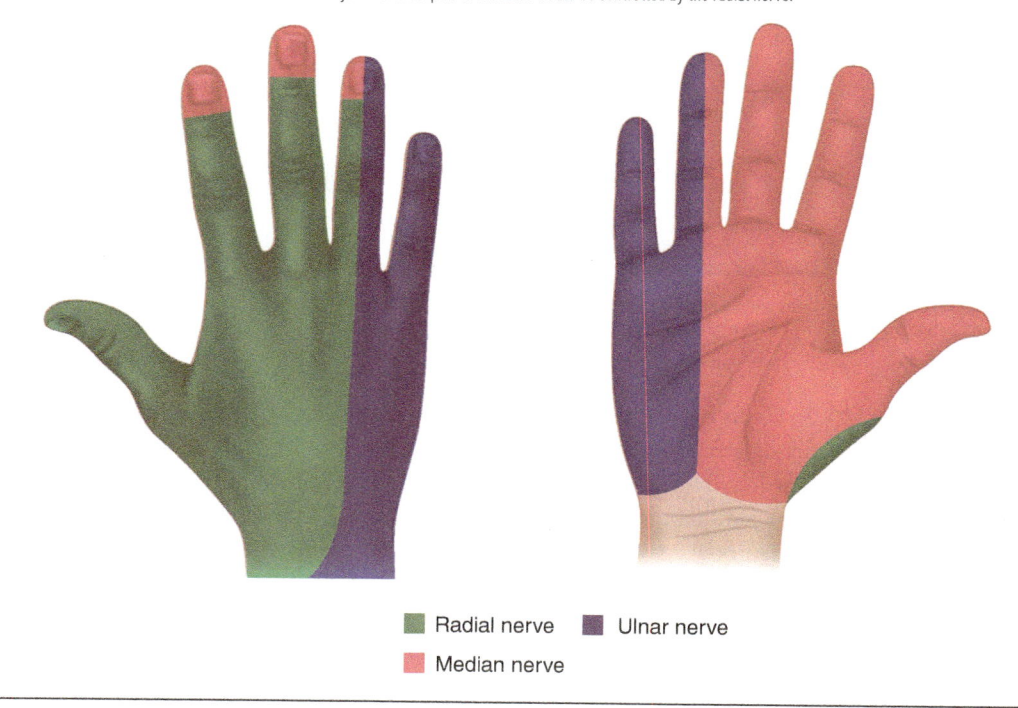

■ Radial nerve ■ Ulnar nerve
■ Median nerve

Credit: Dailey, T. M., & Vallabhaneni, M. (2022). Ulnar, median, radial, and antebrachial cutaneous nerve blocks. In D. Souza & L. Kohan (Eds.), *Bedside pain management interventions* (pp. 571–586). Springer. https://doi.org/10.1007/978-3-031-11188-4_57

with sensitivity on the other part of the hand (thumb, second and third fingers). The radial nerve is involved in the area of the finger below the medial nerve. There is less involvement of the radial nerve on the palm compared with the back of the hand. Thus, if there was damage to one of these nerves, we would see a very different pattern of insensitivity.

In comparison to malingering and factitious disorder, in which a person voluntarily creates their symptoms, conversion disorder is considered to take place in an involuntary manner outside of the person's consciousness. Common symptoms include paralysis, seizures, tremor, blindness, anesthesia, and problems with movement. In the clinical literature, conversion disorders show a high comorbidity with anxiety, depression, and personality disorders. In some cases, the conversion symptoms develop after an emotional stress or trauma. Some individuals show what is referred to as *la belle indifférence* (the beautiful indifference) and seem unconcerned about their symptoms.

A form of conversion disorder seen as particular to women has been recorded for at least 2,000 years. The unfounded view was that the disorder resulted from movement of the uterus, actually referred to as "wandering uterus." The medical literature of the 5th century CE took the Greek word for uterus (*hystera*) and described the disorder as *hysteria*. In 1859 in France, Paul Briquet wrote a landmark monograph, *Traité Clinique et Thérapeutique de L'hystérie*, which has influenced the conceptualization of conversion disorder to the present day. He used the term *hysteria* in describing a series of patients who showed medical symptoms without a known cause. They described their symptoms in a dramatic and excessive manner.

These were the types of patients with whom Freud did his early work. In fact, the term **conversion reaction** refers to Freud's idea that psychic energy was converted into physical symptoms. The basic concept, in Freud's thinking, is that painful memories or trauma are not consciously experienced in an emotional manner but rather converted into physical processes. Freud learned from Charcot that individuals with a conversion disorder (e.g., glove anesthesia) would, under hypnosis, be able to recall painful memories and have normal feeling in their hands.

After Freud left his study with Charcot in Paris, he went to Vienna and worked with Dr. Josef Breuer. One of Breuer's patients was referred to as Anna O, whom we now know was Bertha Pappenheim (Ellenberger, 1970; Sulloway, 1979). At the age of 21, Pappenheim developed a variety of medical symptoms. During this time, her father became ill and eventually died. Prior to this time, she had led the life of a young woman raised in a wealthy family. Breuer described her as attractive, intelligent, and with much imagination. Freud described her in terms of her treatment with Breuer as a woman "whose numerous hysterical symptoms disappeared one by one, as Breuer was able to make her evoke the specific circumstances that had led to their appearance" (Ellenberger, 1970, p. 480). Many historians see this case as one that led Freud to have the patient talk about trauma in treatments for conversion disorder.

Today, the term *conversion disorder* is used in *DSM-5* and *DSM-5-TR* without reference to psychoanalytic theory. *DSM-5-TR* also refers to conversion disorder as *functional neurological symptom disorder*, a common term in neurology. In the medical literature, conversion reactions are also called *psychogenic disorders* or *functional disorders*. There has been a resurgence of interest in conversion disorders with recent conferences, articles, and books (Fobian & Elliott, 2019 Hallett et al., 2011). One focus has been psychogenic movement disorders and psychogenic seizures.

The specific neuroscience mechanisms that underlie conversion disorder are not yet fully understood. Pavlov (1941) suggested that an overexcitation of the subcortical centers due to strong emotions could, in turn, produce cortical inhibition. This inhibition of the frontal lobes could affect sensory and motor areas and functionally turn them off. These basic ideas continue in current hypotheses, which suggest that activation of motor pathways might be suppressed by inhibitory processes related to emotional experiences. Others have suggested that conversion symptoms are related not to inhibitory cognitive processes but to midline brain regions associated with representations of the self and emotional regulation (Cojan et al., 2009; Nowak & Fink, 2009). Beginning in the late 1990s, brain imaging studies began to examine individuals with various types of conversion reaction. Let's look at three of these studies.

Bertha Pappenheim (Anna O.)
Chronicle/Alamy Stock Photo

Ghaffar, Staines, and Feinstein (2006) examined three individuals with conversion disorder using fMRI. The first person was a 34-year-old woman with an 8-month history of numbness and tingling on her left side, mainly her left hand. The second person was a 44-year-old woman with left-sided numbness, most prominently in her foot, that had persisted for 9 years. The third person was a 35-year-old woman who had a left-sided numbness on her foot. When the limb without numbness was stimulated, as expected, the researchers saw brain activity on the contralateral side of the brain in the sensory area related to that limb. When the limb experienced as numb was stimulated, there was no brain activity. However, if both sides were stimulated, then activity was seen on both sides of the brain for all three patients (Figure 9.5). The exact mechanism that made this happen is not fully understood.

Mirror neurons in our brain are active when we observe movement in others; that is, if we watch someone move their left hand, then we display activity in our brain as if had we made the same movement. Markus Burgmer and his colleagues (2006) wondered if they would see mirror neuron activity in functional motor paralysis. To answer this question, they performed brain imaging on four individuals with functional paralysis and seven individuals without it. These results are shown in Figure 9.6. The top two rows show brain activation for the control group while they moved or watched movement. As expected, moving the left hand showed greater activation in the right motor strip.

FIGURE 9.5 ■ Do People With Conversion Reaction Show Brain Responses to Sensory Stimulation?

The answer is no if the stimulation was only presented to the limb involved in the conversion reaction. This figure shows three conditions: *Left panel:* As expected, stimulation of the limb in which stimulation is felt is shown on the contralateral side. *Middle panel:* No stimulation influences the brain response on the side of the conversion reaction. *Right panel:* When both sides are stimulated, the brain shows activity as if both were normal.

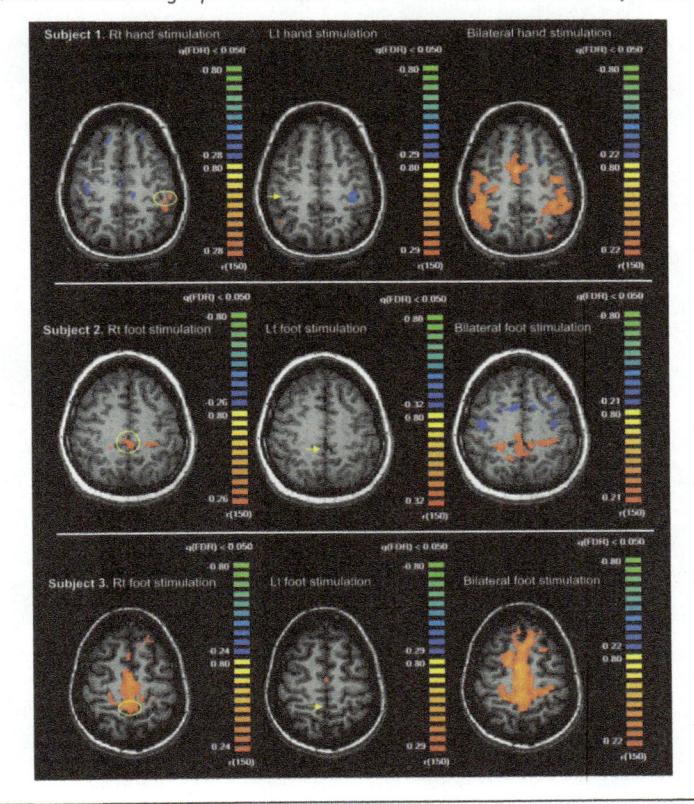

Credit: Ghaffar, O., Staines, W., & Feinstein, A. (2006). Unexplained neurologic symptoms: An fMRI study of sensory conversion disorder. *Neurology, 67,* 2036–2038. © 2012 American Academy of Neurology.

Right-hand movement showed greater activation in the left motor area. Also, making a movement resulted in greater activation than just watching the movement. The bottom four rows show the observation of movement for each of the four individuals with functional paralysis. The arrows in the figure represent where activation was expected. Patient 2 showed paralysis on the right side, whereas the other three patients showed it on the left. As you can see, in individuals with functional paralysis, there was no brain activity when they observed movement on the side of their paralysis. However, brain activity was seen in the control group while they observed movement. This suggests that individuals with a conversion disorder do not create an internal representation or motor map while watching movement, as is the case with healthy controls.

Yann Cojan and his colleagues (2009) used a "go–no go" task to study a person with a single-sided conversion paralysis in comparison with a control group without paralysis. In the brain scanner, the woman with paralysis was given a cue to prepare to make a movement. This was followed by a gray image of a hand that conveyed to her which of her hands she was to move. The hand either became a green hand, which meant she was to make a movement (go), or a red hand, which meant she was not to make a movement (no go). The ratio of green to red hands was 3 to 1 (Figure 9.7).

The fMRI data showed that the patient's right motor cortex was suppressed when she was instructed to make a movement. However, it did show activation when she saw the green hand and prepared to make a movement. This suggests that the functional paralysis did not influence motor preparation in the brain but only the actual movement. When examining the difference between preparation of left-hand movement and right-hand movement in this patient, these researchers

FIGURE 9.6 ■ What Influences the Activity of Mirror Neurons?

(A) The brain activity in healthy controls while they observed movement reflects activity in the motor areas of the brain. (B) For those with functional paralysis, there is no brain activity when they observe movement on the side of their paralysis.

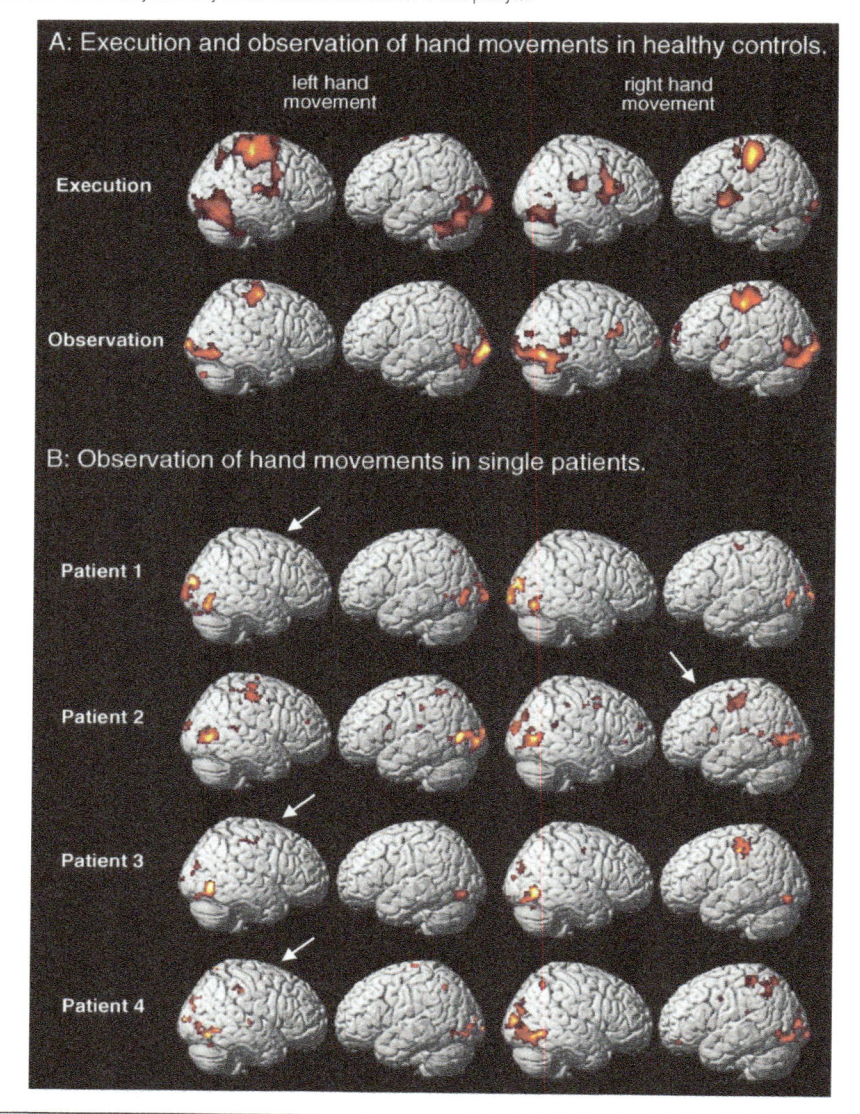

Credit: Burgmer, M., Konrad, C., Jansen, A., Kugel, H., Sommer, J., Heindel, W., Ringelstein, E., Heuft, G., & Knecht, S. (2006). Abnormal brain activation during movement observation in patients with conversion paralysis. *NeuroImage, 29,* 1336–1343, with permission from Elsevier.

discovered different areas of the brain being activated as compared with the control group. In the preparatory movement stage, the patient showed increases in the left orbitofrontal cortex (OFC), the ventromedial prefrontal cortex (vmPFC), and the posterior cingulate cortex. These are areas involved in the default network and suggest that conversion disorder may include an inability to turn off the default network and remain in a more internally focused state. This fMRI activity was not seen in the control group.

Overall, the brain imaging data suggest that individuals with conversion disorder show differences in their cortical networks. As you can see from the three fMRI studies, there is a clear difference when the person is asked to respond or make a movement. However, the mechanisms that *create* these differences are still to be discovered. In *LENS: Awareness of the Body and the Brain*, the manner in which our brains give us our sense of our bodies is explored.

FIGURE 9.7 ■ Does Functional Paralysis Influence Both Preparation to Move as Well as the Actual Movement?

The figure shows the outline of the study in which the participant must make a movement (green) or not make a movement (red). Functional paralysis did not influence motor preparation in the brain, only the actual movement.

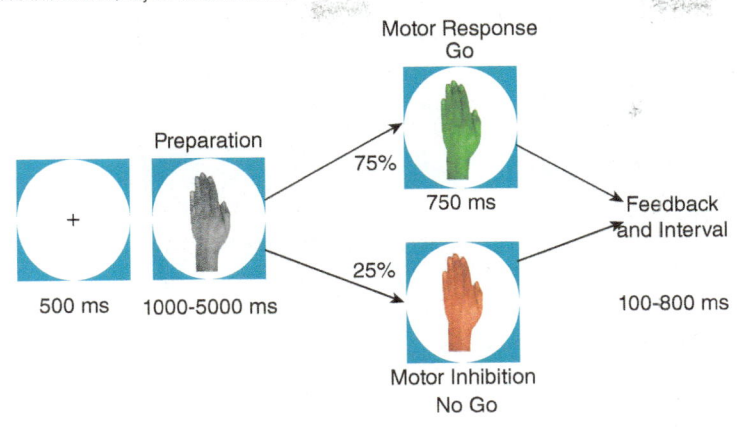

Note: 1000 ms = 1 second.

Credit: Cojan, Y., Waber, L., Carruzzo, A., & Vuilleumier, P. (2009). Motor inhibition in hysterical conversion paralysis. *NeuroImage, 47*(3), 1026–1037. https://doi.org/10.1016/j.neuroimage.2009.05.023, p. 1028, with permission from Elsevier.

LENS
AWARENESS OF THE BODY AND THE BRAIN

Tom was driving home from soccer practice when a car crossed over into his lane. He put on his brake, but his car went out of control and he was thrown out of it. As a result of the accident, Tom lost his left arm just above the elbow. Strangely, he could still feel it as if it were there. He had the sense of moving each finger of his hand and being able to grab an object. Tom is not alone in his sensation of a lost limb. This phenomenon has been reported since antiquity, and following the U.S. Civil War, it came to be known as *phantom limb*. Not only do individuals with a lost limb experience its presence, but over 70% of them also experience pain in the missing limb, which can last for years after the amputation surgery or accident.

An intriguing way to treat the pain, which may involve the mirror neuron system, is referred to as a *mirror box*. It is literally a box with a mirror that divides it in half. On each side of the mirror is a hole in the box such that a person could put a hand in each side. A person who had lost his left arm could put his right arm through the hole. Looking at the right hand and arm, the person would see both the limb and its reflection, creating the illusion of having two hands. What is amazing is that the person has the sensation of moving not only the right hand but the left one as well. The person has the experience of moving the phantom limb, and for some individuals, the pain can also be modified.

As scientists have examined phantom limb with neuroscience techniques, it turns out that our sense of our body is all in our heads—just not in the way that most people think. It is not "made up"; it is real. Wilder Penfield in the 1940s and 1950s was able to map how the body is represented in the brain (Figure 9.8). What became clear is that the body is represented on a thin strip in the brain. Some areas such as the hands and lips have more brain areas devoted to them than do other body parts. However, the body's representation is not how it appears in real life. The hands—not the neck—are next to the face in the brain.

Experiences such as learning a new skill can change the connections in the brain. Losing a body part can do the same. If a person lost their middle finger, for example, then the area represented by it in the brain could be taken over by the fingers on each side of it. If the individual lost their arm, then the brain area that represents the arm could be taken over by the face. Now when the person touches their face, they not only experience their face, but they also experience the sensation of their arm being touched. What if someone lost their leg? As Penfield's map suggests, both men and women have reported sensations in their lost leg when they are having sex. The brain areas

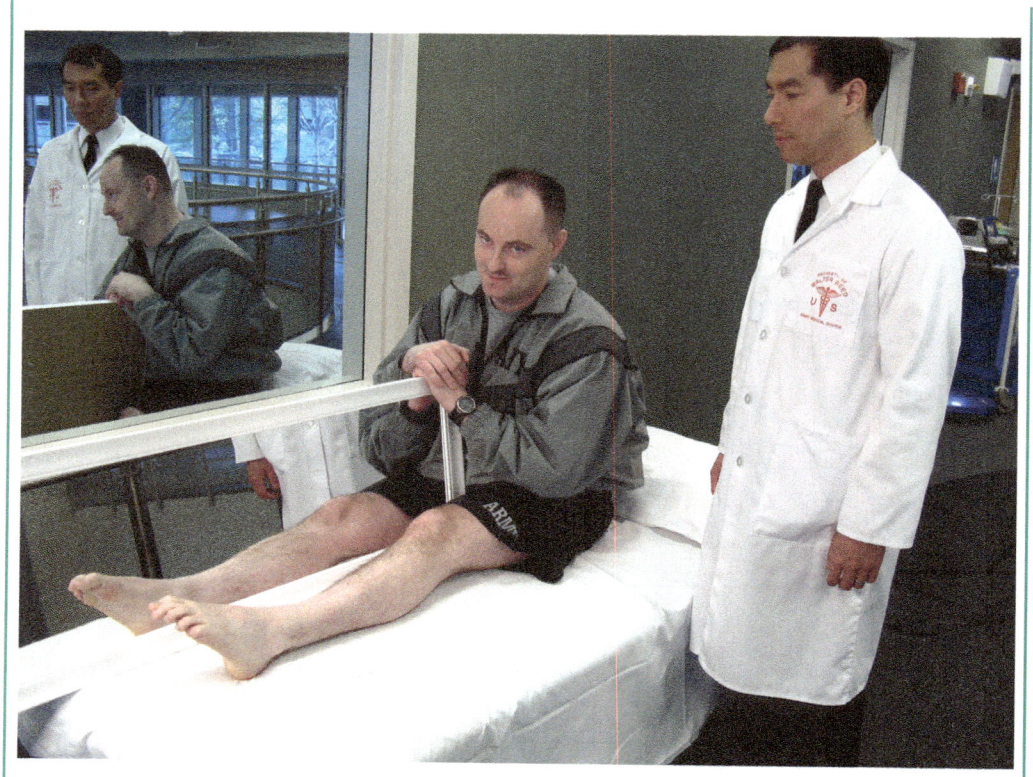

The mirror box technique has been expanded beyond just the arm to also treat phantom limb of a person's leg. In the photo, Navy Cmdr. (Dr.) Jack Tsao shows Army Sgt. Nicholas Paupore how to perform mirror therapy to treat phantom pain in his right leg.

U.S. Defense Department photo/Donna Miles

FIGURE 9.8 ■ How Is Your Body Represented in Your Brain?

This figure presents Penfield's homunculus showing the representation of the body in the brain. Note that some body areas have more representation in the brain than others.

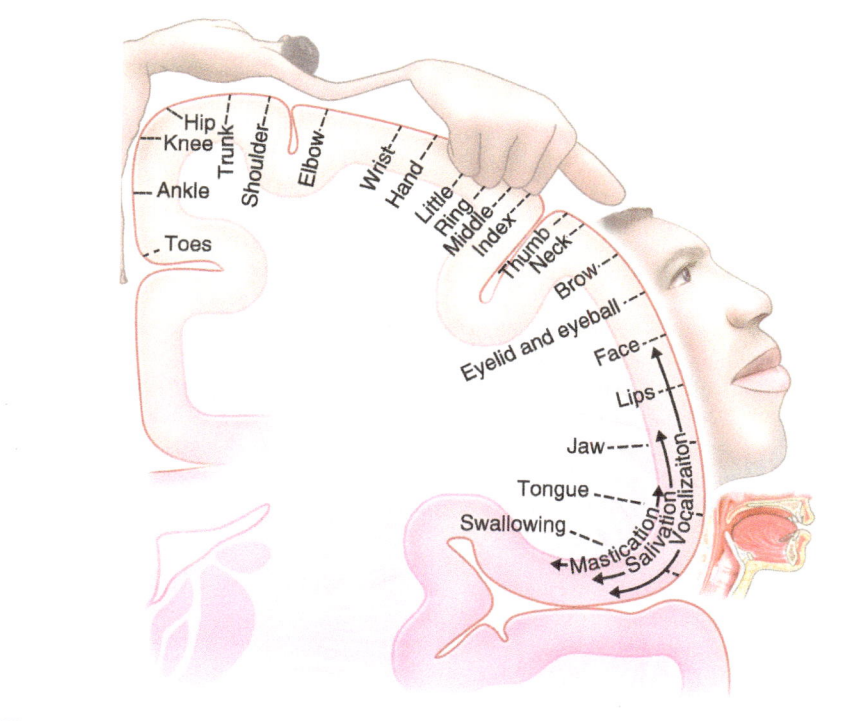

Source: Adapted from *The Cerebral Cortex of Man* by W. Penfield and T. Rasmussen, 1950, New York: Macmillan. © 1950 Gale, a part of Cengage Learning, Inc.

representing both male and female genitalia are located next to that of the toes and leg and farther from the hands. This may also help to explain why it is more common to have a foot fetish than a hand fetish.

Thought Question

If it's true that "our sense of our body is all in our heads," how might it be possible to use video games or virtual reality to lessen or eliminate the negative effects of phantom limb?

Source: Based on Ramachandran, V. S., & Blakeslee, S. (1998). *Phantoms in the brain.* William Morrow.

Factitious Disorder

Medical records describe a man who went to the emergency room with a history of fever and bilateral pain (Turner & Reid, 2002). He had a tender abdomen, so blood tests and images were taken. While waiting for the test results, a nurse realized she had seen the man at another hospital. In fact, he had gone to the other hospital 3 times over 6 months with the same symptoms. At no time was any pathology found. When confronted after a number of these trips to the hospital, the man admitted that he had falsified his condition.

A factitious disorder is a situation in which a person creates the symptoms seen by the health care professional. Such an individual may take laxatives or even inject insulin to mimic an actual physical disorder such as a stomach flu or low blood sugar. Although it seems strange that someone would actually hurt themselves for only the gain of receiving medical attention, this is indeed the case. The person with a factitious disorder will attempt to manipulate the health care system by seeking extra medical tests or even medical procedures such as surgery. The disorder can be initially difficult to determine if the person has medical training, since they can accurately describe and produce known symptoms. When the person does not receive the attention sought, they may become angry and claim mistreatment. There is some indication that factitious disorder is seen more often in women than men, although epidemiological studies are lacking.

DSM-5-TR makes a distinction between factitious disorder imposed on self and factitious disorder imposed on another. In a factitious disorder imposed on another, typically, a caregiver such as a parent would produce symptoms in their child. The parent would then seek medical attention and procedures for the child. They may even be seen as a devoted parent who cares for their child, whereas they are actually the one causing the symptoms.

Current streaming video shows have used factitious disorders in their plots. One of these is the Gypsy Rose Blanchard case, in which her mother claimed she had a number of different disorders. This is now the subject of a popular show on Hulu (*The Act*) as well as an HBO documentary (*Mommy Dead and Dearest*). Gypsy Rose's mother even managed to get her treated for leukemia at one point.

Historically, those with a factitious disorder imposed on self have also been referred to as having *Munchausen syndrome.* The disorder is named after a German baron who liked to embellish his stories of military adventures and came to be known as the "Baron of Lying." Those who produce the symptoms in another have been referred to as having *Munchausen syndrome by proxy.* Munchausen by proxy is seen almost exclusively in women (Sheridan, 2003).

One classic case study describes more than 400 pages of medical records in which a child beginning at age 2 was brought to the hospital for treatment of conditions brought on by the mother (Bryk & Siegel, 1997). As a 2-year-old girl, the patient was initially brought to the hospital for a trivial injury to the right ankle that had not healed. It was reported that the infant had fallen down the stairs. What was not known by the medical professional at the time was that the mother had inflicted repeated blows to her daughter's foot with a hammer. Over the next 8 years, the patient experienced 28 hospitalizations, 24 surgeries, and a number of other medical procedures related to swelling and bone problems as well as high temperature. Not only did the mother cause the damage, but she also added soil or coffee grounds to infected wounds to prevent healing. What complicated the situation even more was that the mother was a nurse. Thus, hospital personnel assumed she was giving correct care to her own daughter.

In the period of more than half a century since this case occurred, medical personnel have been better trained to determine potential child abuse and look for alternative explanations for continuing unexplained medical conditions. However, short-term cases of factitious disorder imposed on another person continue to be seen. Some examples include altering a child's diet to produce medical conditions, use of fecal or other material to induce infections, and describing a child's symptoms seen only by the mother.

Factitious disorder should be differentiated from malingering in that malingering involves deceiving to obtain external rewards such as not going to work, obtaining financial compensation through an insurance claim, receiving paid sick leave, or avoiding undesired activities. Also, some individuals fake symptoms as a means of obtaining drugs that they can use or sell. These individuals would not be diagnosed with a factitious disorder.

Treatment for Somatic Symptom Disorders

Since individuals with somatic symptom disorders are generally seen in a medical setting, the most common approach for treatment is an educational one. With conversion disorder, the health care professional will discuss aspects of the patient's stress and suggest that their symptoms will improve. This is consistent with reports that about 50% of these individuals will not have symptoms by the time of discharge from a general hospital (Folks et al., 1984). It is common for individuals with somatic symptom disorder not to seek therapy.

One review of treatments for somatic symptom disorders noted that three approaches exist (Sumathipala, 2007): antidepressant medication, CBT, and other treatments such as family therapy or a problem-solving approach. Although there is little empirical research related to the treatment of somatic symptom disorders, CBT shows the most success at reducing physical symptoms, psychological distress, and disability (Woolfolk et al., 2007). CBT treatments for illness anxiety disorder are typically modeled after those for panic disorder and have been shown to be effective (Hollon & Beck, 2013). However, treatment research in the area of somatic symptom disorders overall is somewhat limited.

Overall, somatic symptom disorders represent an interface between psychological and medical processes. Individuals with these disorders do not seek treatment from mental health professionals. Thus, it is one set of disorders in which the professional doing the diagnosis, typically a physician, is a person

In the case of Gypsy Rose Blanchard, the subject of the documentary *Mommy Dead and Dearest*, Blanchard's mother claimed she had a number of different disorders and even managed to get her treated for leukemia at one point.

Steve Mack/Alamy Stock Photo

who does not specialize in the treatment of mental disorders. This will influence the estimates of the prevalence of these disorders, since few physicians will use this diagnosis.

> **CONCEPT CHECK**
>
> - What is the difference between a somatic symptom disorder and a psychosomatic disorder? How are they the same?
> - What are the primary diagnostic criteria for each of the following somatic symptom and related disorders?
>   - Somatic symptom disorder
>   - Illness anxiety disorder
>   - Conversion disorder
>   - Factitious disorder
> - What are important implications for the diagnosis and treatment of somatic symptom disorders due to the fact that many individuals seek help from medical professionals instead of mental health professionals?

SUMMARY

Many researchers see dissociation as a normal experience. Dissociative experiences can last for a few minutes or hours but reoccur, or they can also last for a longer period of time. In times of stress, dissociation is a mechanism that protects the individual and allows that person to survive. Pathological dissociative symptoms are generally experienced as involuntary disruption of the normal integration of consciousness, memory, identity, or perception. *DSM-5-TR* describes four dissociative disorders: (1) depersonalization/derealization disorder, (2) dissociative amnesia, (3) dissociative identity disorder (DID), and (4) other specified dissociative disorder. Depersonalization is the experience of not sensing the reality of one's self; derealization, on the other hand, is the experience that the external world is not solid. The main diagnostic element of dissociative amnesia is an inability to recall important autobiographical information. Dissociative fugue—a sudden, unexpected travel away from one's home or place of work with an inability to recall one's past—also falls under the diagnosis of dissociative amnesia. DID is less a case of multiple personalities than it is a developmental disorder where one consistent sense of self does not occur. Although some dissociative disorders, such as dissociative amnesia, may resolve on their own, others, such as DID, require long-term psychotherapy.

Most of us experience some sort of somatic, or bodily, symptom regularly. We consider these experiences to be part of life and assume they will go away. Some people, however, do not feel this way. They may continue to search for organic problems—certain that something is wrong with them—or may feel anxiety that the simple symptoms they have are really something serious. These are two aspects of somatic symptom and related disorders. Another aspect is the situation in which a person shows the signs of a physical illness, but it does not follow the underlying physiology. Some individuals may actually take substances to create a disorder. Somatic symptom disorders represent an interface between psychological processes and medical ones in that it is one set of disorders in which the professional doing the diagnosis, typically a physician, does not specialize in the treatment of mental disorders.

Major somatic symptom and related disorders described in *DSM-5-TR* include (1) somatic symptom disorder, (2) illness anxiety disorder, (3) conversion disorder, and (4) factitious disorder. Somatic symptom disorder is the condition in which a person's somatic or bodily symptoms cause distress or disruption in physical health that are not consistent with a medical disorder. Illness anxiety disorder is when a person is preoccupied with the possibility of having a serious illness. However, unlike somatic symptom disorders, the person experiences few, if any, symptoms. Conversion disorder, or functional neurological symptom disorder, refers to the situation in which the person reports sensory or motor symptoms such as not being able to hear or see or feel pain or move a part of the body; however, the symptoms do not follow known physiological or neurological patterns. A factitious disorder is the situation in which a person creates the symptoms in order to be seen by a health care professional. *DSM-5-TR* makes a distinction between factitious disorder imposed on self and factitious disorder imposed on another, where a caregiver such as a parent would produce symptoms in her child. Since individuals with somatic symptom disorders are generally seen in a medical setting, the most common approach for treatment is an educational one.

STUDY RESOURCES

Review Questions

1. "In times of stress, dissociation is a mechanism that protects the individual and allows her to survive." Considering all of the dissociative disorders, how do they protect the individual? What are they protecting her from? What are some of the costs of that protection?

2. Most of us have had experiences of dissociation including "spacing out." Does that mean that dissociative disorders are just at the extreme end of normal processes? In what ways are psychopathologies an extension of normal human functioning? In what ways are they categorically different?

3. Somatic symptom disorders represent a set of disorders in which the professional doing the diagnosis, typically a physician, does not specialize in the treatment of mental disorders. As an expert on somatic symptom disorders, you are called on to create a program to educate physicians about the characteristics, diagnosis, and treatment of these disorders. What are the critical areas of information you include in your program?

4. "Somatic symptom disorders represent an interface between psychological processes and medical ones." What evidence can you cite from neuropsychological research that shows disordered brain functioning in individuals with somatic symptom disorder? How might medical professionals use this information in diagnosis and treatment in the future?

For Further Reading

Ananthaswamy, A. (2015). *The man who wasn't there*. Dutton.

Dell, P., & O'Neil, J. (Eds.). (2009). *Dissociation and the dissociative disorders: DSM-V and beyond*. Taylor & Francis.

Hyman, J. (2007). *I am more than one*. McGraw-Hill.

Steinberg, M., & Schnall, M. (2000). *The stranger in the mirror*. Cliff Street Books.

Walker, M., & Antony-Black, J. (Eds.). (1999). *Hidden selves: An exploration of multiple personality*. Open University Press.

KEY TERMS

conversion disorder
conversion reaction
depersonalization
derealization
dissociation
dissociative amnesia
dissociative fugue
dissociative identity disorder (DID)

factitious disorder
factitious disorder imposed on another
factitious disorder imposed on self
glove anesthesia
illness anxiety disorder
SCID-D
somatic symptom and related disorders
somatic symptom disorder

10 EATING DISORDERS

LEARNING OBJECTIVES

10.1 Describe the characteristics and prevalence of the major feeding disorders.

10.2 Discuss the factors that influence obesity and its impact worldwide.

10.3 Identify the three major eating disorders and discuss their prevalence.

10.4 Describe anorexia nervosa and its treatment.

10.5 Define bulimia nervosa and binge eating disorder and discuss their treatment.

Eating seems simple. We eat to give ourselves energy and live life. However, as you will see in this chapter, eating is in fact extremely complicated. Consider this account from Marya Hornbacher-Beard:

> One minute I was your average nine-year-old, shorts and a T-shirt and long brown braids, sitting in the yellow kitchen, watching Brady Bunch reruns, munching on a bag of Fritos, scratching the dog with my foot. The next minute I was walking, in a surreal haze I would later compare to the hum induced by speed, out of the kitchen, down the stairs, into the bathroom, shutting the door, putting the toilet seat up, pulling my braids back with one hand, sticking my first two fingers down my throat, and throwing up until I spat blood. (Hornbacher-Beard, 1998, p. 9)

And this description from an edited volume by Kate M. Taylor:

> I started losing weight in the spring of my freshman year in college, but in some miracle of denial, I didn't initially see it as a problem. Nor did I see it as intentional; it was merely a side effect of discovering how much I loved being hungry. . . . I didn't even notice I'd lost weight until it was pointed out to me by my roommate's boyfriend. . . . In any case, I continued my new eating habits, which involved fasting until I was light-headed and then rewarding myself with a big meal. In my view, I didn't really eat less than other people, just differently. But I continued to lose weight. . . . By the end of my sophomore year, though, I could no longer convince myself I was okay. The telltale symptom was back: namely, that even when I knew I should eat more, I often couldn't make myself do it. (Taylor, 2008)

What we eat and how we eat represent a complex relationship across all levels of human functioning including culture, evolutionary history, genetics, our physiology, preferences, and psychological attitudes toward our appearance and that of others. Some people eat substances that have no obvious nutritional value, such as dirt. Some people continue to eat food long after they have consumed sufficient calories for their daily needs. Others, like the protagonist of Taylor's narrative, starve themselves because they believe they are fat when they are actually extremely underweight.

Although we often suggest that our views of ideal appearance are related to the media and movies, humans have had ideas of ideal appearance for thousands of years. In fact, one of the earliest known human figures is that of a woman with excess weight estimated to be carved from limestone around 25,000 BCE. Besides this figure found in southern Austria, other similar figures of women with large breasts have been found throughout Europe. With recorded history came the possibility of knowing attitudes toward appearance and what we now call **obesity**. Both Hippocrates and Galen in ancient Greece saw a connection between excess weight and physical disorders and wrote that those who were overweight died early. They also understood how food intake and exercise were related to weight and used exercise and diet as a treatment for being overweight (Christopoulou-Aletra & Papavramidou, 2004; Shepard, 2019). Many of the concerns they had surrounding weight continue to this day.

Some upper-class women in ancient Rome starved themselves to look thin, but it was not until the Middle Ages that medical texts began to describe what we now call *anorexia*. Records from that period also reference women who starved themselves for religious and other purposes. By the late 1800s,

One of the earliest figures of a human, referred to as the Venus of Willendorf, was created around 25,000 BCE.
iStock.com/WHPics

disorders related to eating were considered to merit a place in medical diagnosis and treatment. This history will be continued later in the chapter.

In this chapter, you will learn about three separate areas related to eating. The first is **feeding disorders**, which includes the eating of substances that do not have nutritional value. The second topic covered will be *obesity*. While obesity is not an identified psychological disorder in *DSM-5* and *DSM-5-TR*, there is an increasing understanding among psychologists that obesity is frequently evidence of and often contributes to mental illness. The third topic to be discussed is **eating disorders**.

FEEDING DISORDERS

Unlike *DSM-IV*, *DSM-5* combines feeding and eating disorders into one category. Previously, feeding disorders were considered a distinct category of disorders usually first diagnosed in infancy, childhood, or adolescence (Bryant-Waugh, 2019; Bryant-Waugh et al., 2010). Even normally developing children show changes in eating patterns and preferences for particular foods. It has been estimated that 25% to 45% of normally developing children and up to 80% of those who are developmentally delayed show such changes.

According to Bryant-Waugh et al. (2010), some of the types of eating problems seen in clinics and other mental health settings include the following:

- Delayed or absent development of feeding or eating skills
- Difficulty managing or tolerating fluids or foodstuffs
- Reluctance or refusal to eat based on taste, texture, and other sensory factors
- Lack of appetite or interest in food
- Utilizing feeding behaviors to comfort, self-soothe, or self-stimulate

However, since feeding disorders can be seen in individuals of all ages, they were made part of a larger feeding and eating disorders category in *DSM-5-TR*. The three major feeding disorders are *pica*, *rumination disorder*, and *avoidant/restrictive food intake disorder* (Table 10.1).

Pica

Pica is a feeding disorder in which the person eats something that would not be considered food. Some common substances include clay, cornstarch, charcoal, paste, newspaper, coffee grounds, paint chips, and blackboard chalk. This is different than a child swallowing a plaything. The process of eating nonnutritive substances has been described historically for more than 2,500 years using various terms (Young, 2010, 2011). The onset of eating nonnutritive substances can begin in childhood, adolescence, or adulthood. Prevalence rates for pica are unknown.

Historically, pica has generally been described as part of another disorder such as obsessive-compulsive disorder (OCD) or developmental disorder or as part of the normal condition of being pregnant. In the 1970s, the medical journal *Lancet* suggested that pica is a worldwide practice found more commonly in underdeveloped countries (Lacey, 1990). In addition, it was seen more often in individuals who were poor compared with those who were well off, Black people more than white people, pregnant women more than those who were not pregnant, and children more than adults. Some researchers have tried to determine if there is any positive value to eating nonnutritive substances

TABLE 10.1 ■ Feeding Disorders in *DSM-5-TR*

Pica—Persistent eating of nonnutritive substances
Rumination disorder—Repeated regurgitation of food
Avoidant/restrictive food intake disorder—Lack of interest in certain food, which can lead to weight loss and/or nutritional deficiency

(Stokes, 2006). Indeed, there is some suggestion that clay, for example, may bind to trace elements in the stomach and thus help to clean the gastrointestinal tract.

The nutritional problem with pica is that it leads to health problems, including vitamin deficiency, possible poisoning, and visits to the emergency room for stomach pain and other distress. *DSM-5-TR* restricts the conditions for a clinical diagnosis of pica; it states that pica should not be considered part of a cultural practice but that pica can be considered part of another condition (pregnancy) or disorder (e.g., intellectual developmental disorder, autism spectrum, schizophrenia). It also requires that the eating behavior have lasted for longer than 1 month.

Rumination Disorder

A rumination disorder is a condition in which a person regurgitates their food. This regurgitated food is then re-chewed, re-swallowed, or spit out. The choice of what to do with the food is often determined by whether the person is in a social situation or not. To be diagnosed as a rumination disorder, the condition must occur for more than 1 month and not be part of any other medical or eating disorder. In fact, it should be noted that pica and rumination disorder are rarely seen in individuals with bulimia or other eating disorders (Delaney et al., 2015). However, rumination disorder can result in a number of problems, including halitosis, malnutrition, electrolyte imbalance, and dental problems.

Avoidant/Restrictive Food Intake Disorder

Avoidant/restrictive food intake disorder is, as the name implies, the condition in which an individual does not eat certain foods, which leads to such conditions as weight loss or nutritional deficiency. A person may avoid certain foods because of the foods' sensory characteristics, such as taste, hardness, color, or any other characteristic.

How common is picky eating itself? One study examined 4,018 young children's eating habits (Cano et al., 2015). The researchers found the prevalence of picky eating was 26.9% at 1.5 years of age and 27.6% at 3 years of age. However, picky eating declines to 13.2% at 6 years of age. In this sample, 55% of the children were never picky eaters, whereas almost 46% were. This suggests that in children, picky eating is common but decreases with age.

Picky eating has not been shown to be a predictor of later eating disorders. Even though most people have foods they like and dislike, their avoidance of certain foods does not lead to significant weight loss or nutritional deficiency as would be the case with avoidant/restrictive food intake disorder. Further, many individuals have had the experience of eating a food and becoming sick. It could be any food—fish, soup, dessert, or vegetable. If a person has eaten a food that made them sick, they will normally avoid it for at least 2 or 3 years. This is referred to as the *Garcia effect* or *one-trial learning*. However, these individuals will eat other foods to obtain the energy and nutrition necessary for a healthy life.

CONCEPT CHECK

- "With recorded history came the possibility of knowing attitudes toward appearance and obesity." What are some historical examples of such attitudes described in this section? How are historical attitudes different from, and similar to, current views?
- What do we know about the prevalence of feeding disorders? What are some common examples?
- What is the defining characteristic of each of the following feeding disorders, and what is a negative consequence of each?
  - Pica
  - Rumination disorder
  - Avoidant/restrictive food intake disorder

OBESITY

DSM-5 notes that obesity is not a mental disorder. However, it notes that there are strong associations between obesity and other disorders such as binge eating disorder. Childhood obesity has also been shown to be an important negative health condition (J. D. Smith et al., 2020). It should be noted that the term *obesity* has a number of imprecise meanings. In fact, in the Middle Ages in Europe, it was a sign of wealth. It is more appropriate to speak of "excessive body fat." Current scientific research sees excessive body fat as related to a complex set of conditions including genes, gut bacteria, physiological factors (including metabolism), and environmental and cultural factors. It is more complicated than just the number of calories that one consumes. Although controversial, many research studies define obesity in terms of body mass index (BMI). BMI will be discussed later in the chapter.

Everyone has certain foods that they love and foods that they hate. Some of us have comfort foods that give us a good feeling. Some of our food choices are cultural and related to the foods we grew up with. Other choices are genetic, such as the ability to drink and digest milk into adulthood, which was described in Chapter 1. Also, our genetic makeup influences if the herb cilantro tastes like soap or something we like. Further, some people find themselves addicted to foods that are high in fat, salt, or sugar. Eating processed foods that are high in these substances can be related to weight gain. Further, the time of day you eat a desired food, such as chocolate, can influence a number of physiological processes (Hernández-González et al., 2021).

Throughout humans' evolutionary history, not having enough food was a more frequent event than having too much. An examination of current hunter-gatherer groups around the world showed lower weight and more energy expenditure in these societies than in other societies (Shepard, 2019). One theory, referred to as the *thrifty gene hypothesis*, suggests that times of scarce food sources helped to shape humans' genetic makeup (Neel, 1962).

Current conditions of food abundance and low levels of exercise do not match our evolutionary history and can lead people to develop body fat. Everywhere you look in a city, there are restaurants, cafes, and food stores. In the United States, bookstores have cafes, as do many other shops. Fast-food snacks with high calorie content are everywhere. Most of these fast foods are designed to engage physiological

Our body seeks sweets even when we want less.
iStock.com/PeopleImages

and psychological mechanisms that compel us to seek food and experience it as rewarding. Just looking at a piece of chocolate cake can lead to our seeking it even when we are not hungry.

Our evolutionary history may have us seeking calorie-rich substances. For example, in our early history thousands of years ago, sugar was not easy to come by. It was only found in foods that were not constantly available, such as fruits. Since sugar gives us a pleasant feeling, we came to seek it. In fact, we consume sugars even when full. One study showed that rodents are more likely to work for sweet rewards, even when not hungry, than to work for cocaine (Lenoir et al., 2007). The constant availability of sugars and other such substances today plays a critical role in obesity and some eating disorders, although other factors also play a role (Drewnowski, 1997).

Overall, obesity can be defined as the condition of being extremely overweight. It is seen to result from a mismatch between the amount of calories a person eats and the amount of energy they expend (Shepard, 2019). The factors that influence these two variables are complicated. Other factors related to obesity include the environment in which a person lives, psychological factors, and biological factors (Bouchard, 2010; Wadden & Bray, 2018). These factors can influence both the intake of calories and their expenditure through exercise. Environmental factors can include our family and culture, which influence the foods we cook as well as how much we eat. The environment of our towns and cities can also permit us to safely walk or ride bikes or may require us to drive a car. Psychological factors such as self-esteem or need for comfort can also determine how and when we eat. Some people love eating with others and associating food with friends. Others worry about being or becoming fat. Denying certain types of foods, as some diets advise, will actually increase our desire for that food. Biological factors such as genetic makeup have also been shown to be an important factor in terms of the risk of becoming obese.

Twin studies have shown that children's weight tends to be more like that of their biological parents, even when they are adopted (Moustafa & Froguel, 2013). It is also the case that genetics can influence the amount and distribution of body fat. This is greatly influenced by environmental factors. In Finnish twins who have low physical activity, the heritability of body fat has been estimated to be 90%. However, if the twins engage in high levels of physical activity, the heritability is reduced to 20%. Another study showed that intake of sugar-sweetened beverages increased weight gain in a low-income population in South Africa over a 4- to 5-year period (Okop et al., 2019).

These studies suggest that environmental factors such as exercise and sugar consumption can influence the manner in which genetic influences are related to body fat. Further, someone who overeats for a period of time will develop additional fat cells in their body. If this person then loses weight, their fat cells can become smaller, but the number of them will not decrease. This is thought to make losing weight more difficult for someone who was heavier as a child. In summary, the more common form of obesity results from the combined effects of multiple genes acting in relation to environmental factors. However, it should be noted that there is a rare form of obesity that results from the action of a single gene.

Neuroscience Aspects of Obesity

In terms of the brain, a homeostatic system regulates body weight. Its basic task is to produce energy for the body. This system involves the hypothalamus, which has been seen as important for appetite and weight regulation. Fat is deposited in adipose tissue so that we can store energy to be available during times of famine. When nutrients are easily accessible, humans and other animals tend to overload with nutrients and gain weight. Research points to brain processes involving the limbic system that encode the rewarding aspect of food intake along with emotional and cognitive aspects. These brain processes lead to an overconsumption of food even when the person feels full.

Since humans and other animals will continue to eat even when they feel full and do not need additional energy, researchers have asked if similar mechanisms are involved in excess weight gain and drug addiction (Volkow et al., 2013). Both involve disruptions in the dopamine pathways of the brain. These pathways modulate behavioral responses to environmental cues. With both food and drugs, psychological processes interact in a complex manner. For example, when we see a food or drug we like, there are memory (hippocampus), emotional reactivity (amygdala), arousal (thalamus), and cognitive control (prefrontal cortex [PFC] and cingulate) as well as autonomic nervous system reactions related

FIGURE 10.1 ■ How Is the Intake of Food and Drugs Similar and Different?

The intake of food and drugs can be described in terms of three systems: a cognitive system, a dopamine reward system, and an energy system. With food, our bodies make a computation in terms of energy needs and the feelings of hunger and satiety. Drugs, on the other hand, mainly influence the reward pathways of the brain.

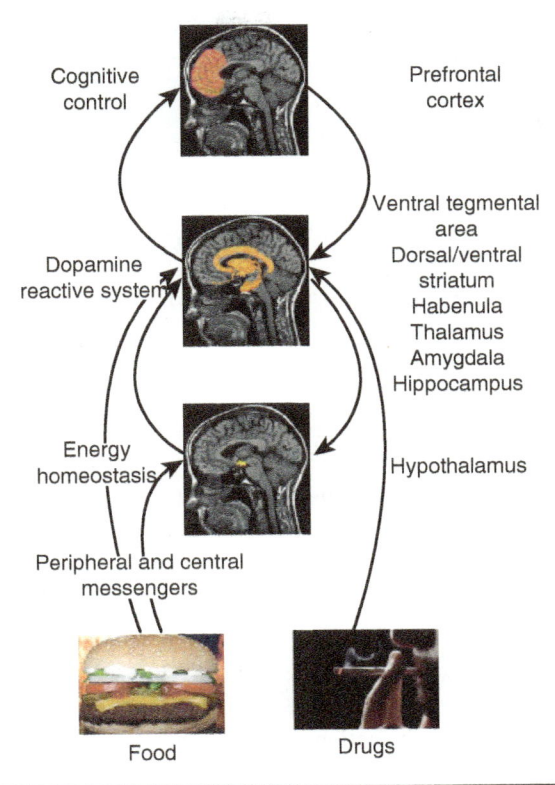

Credit: Volkow, N., Wang, G., Tomasi, D., & Baler, R. (2013). Obesity and addiction: Neurobiological overlaps. *Obesity Reviews, 14*, 2–18, p. 6.

to consuming the substance. In the case of food, a number of peripheral mechanisms involving such organs as the stomach, pancreas, and intestine, as well as brain structures such as the hypothalamus, signal when food is needed. With food, our bodies also make a computation in terms of energy needs and the feelings of hunger and satiety. Drugs, on the other hand, mainly influence the reward pathways of the brain (Figure 10.1). These pathways are described in greater detail in Chapter 12.

Although our bodies tell us when we are hungry, environmental factors can lead to cravings and to ingesting more calories than we need. These environmental factors may include how attractive the food is, how expensive it is, what kind of deal we get with supersizing, and so forth. We also have memories of eating the food previously and may have other personal associations connected with the food. In addition, psychological stress increases our consumption of food and thus can lead to weight gain. One important new finding is that brain mechanisms related to these systems are changeable even in adulthood (Dietrich & Horvath, 2013). If you start a new diet or find yourself in situations in which food intake is reduced or even increased, your brain circuits will change in relation to how your body uses energy. That is, as environmental conditions change, metabolic brain circuits change in relation to eating.

Based on brain imaging studies, obese adolescent girls process the anticipation and consumption of food differently from lean adolescent girls (Stice et al., 2008). Individuals who are obese show less activation of reward circuits in the brain when they consume food than lean individuals. However, they show greater activation of somatosensory brain areas when they anticipate consumption. Further, the amount of activation was found to be related to body mass index in terms of anticipation but inversely related in terms of consumption. Less activation of the dopamine reward circuits in obese individuals may be one mechanism that leads to greater consumption of food.

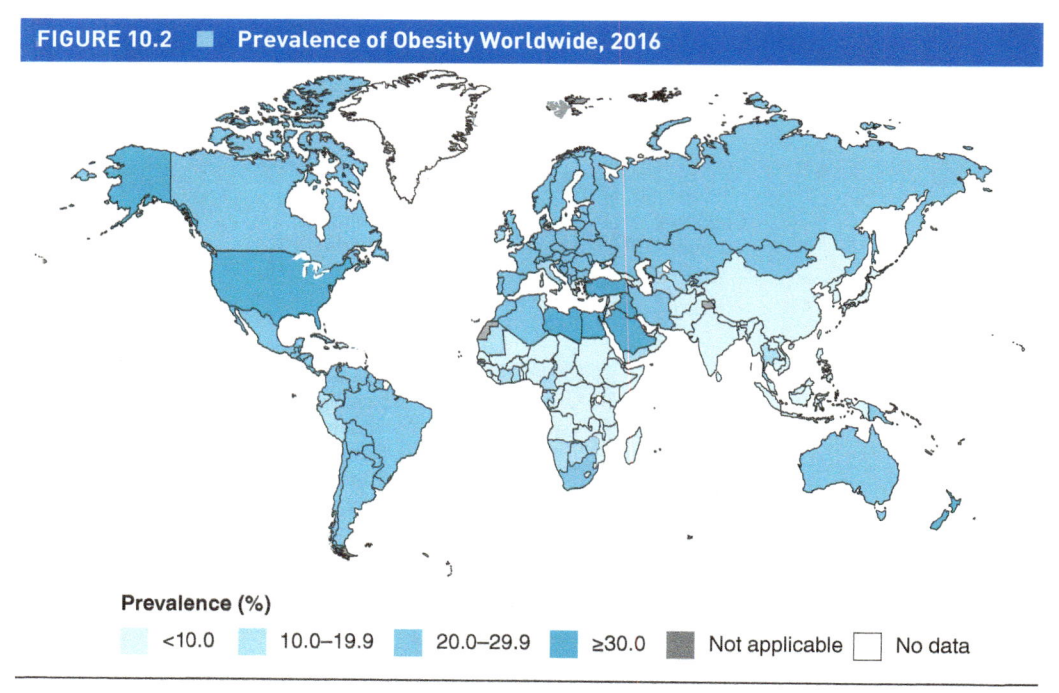

FIGURE 10.2 ■ Prevalence of Obesity Worldwide, 2016

Prevalence (%): <10.0 | 10.0–19.9 | 20.0–29.9 | ≥30.0 | Not applicable | No data

Credit: Adapted from World Health Organization. (2023). *Prevalence of obesity among adults, BMI ≥ 30 (age-standardized estimate) (%)*. https://www.who.int/data/gho/data/indicators/indicator-details/GHO/prevalence-of-obesity-among-adults-bmi-=-30-(age-standardized-estimate)-(-)

Prevalence of Obesity

According to the World Health Organization, obesity worldwide has doubled since 1980. In 2016, more than 1.9 billon adults (age 18 and over) were overweight, and 650 million adults were obese (Figure 10.2; see also For Further Reading). That works out to 39% of the world population being overweight and 13% obese. By 2020, the overweight percentage increased to 41.9%. In 2013, an estimated 42 million children under the age of 5 were overweight. These overweight children are found not only in high-income countries but also in low- and medium-income countries. As described in *Cultural LENS: Reducing Obesity Worldwide*, many countries around the world are beginning to focus on obesity in the same way they previously focused on tobacco smoking.

CULTURAL LENS
REDUCING OBESITY WORLDWIDE

Nations around the world are now examining obesity as a public health problem. The current approach is similar to how tobacco use was previously approached—that is, to consider it as an epidemic with the goal of reducing its occurrence. Developed countries have the most accurate statistics concerning obesity. Besides the United States, Mexico and South America are also making efforts to reduce obesity (Elder & Arredondo, 2013; Holub et al., 2013). Mexico is second only to the United States in the developed countries in terms of an obesity epidemic. In the United States, obesity is present in all ethnic groups, but it is higher in adult Latino Americans (38.7%) compared with white Americans (25.6%). This relationship is also seen in adolescents.

A number of intervention programs intended to lower rates of obesity have been implemented and evaluated in terms of outcomes (Holub et al., 2013). School-based programs to increase physical activity have been established in Mexico, Brazil, and Chile. Other studies in Latin America were directed at teaching individuals how to eat in a healthy manner. Currently, the best outcomes have been with programs that help high-weight individuals rather than prevention programs.

A street vendor in Thailand serves food to customers.
iStock.com/Brostock

Thought Question

Why do you think programs aimed at high-weight individuals work better than prevention programs? Does that mean we shouldn't have any prevention program? Why or why not?

The Centers for Disease Control and Prevention (CDC) has a number of resources to help individuals eat well; likewise, the U.S. Department of Health and Human Services has a series of dietary guidelines (see For Further Reading). However, Americans consume more calories than do people in many other places in the world. Daily calorie intake for various countries in the world is shown in Figure 10.3. As can be seen in this figure, people living in Africa and China consume fewer calories than those in the United States, Canada, and Western Europe. Comparing this figure with Figure 10.2 showing obesity worldwide, it is clear there is a connection between calorie intake and obesity.

A common measure of weight in relation to obesity is body mass index (BMI). BMI is defined as weight in kilograms divided by height in meters squared (kg/m2). This is an indirect measure of body fat based on a person's height and weight, which can also be calculated in inches and pounds. It should be noted that body weight includes fat, muscle, and bone. Thus, athletes may show a higher BMI that reflects muscles and not fat. For any given individual, BMI may not be the best measure. In fact, the American Medical Association (2023) adopted a policy in 2023 that recommended that BMI not be used as the sole measure of body fat in a given individual. However, BMI is useful for worldwide comparisons in large populations, as is done by the World Health Organization (WHO). In general, a BMI score below 18.5 is considered underweight, 18.5 to 24.9 is considered normal, 25 to 29.9 is considered overweight, and 30 and above is obese. CDC data suggest that 39.8% of Americans over the age of 20 are obese and another 31.8% are overweight (see For Further Reading). There are differences in these statistics by U.S. states; however, all states have shown an increase in obesity over the past 30 years (Figure 10.4).

There is currently a debate in terms of whether this increase in obesity results from lack of activity, supersizing foods, or a combination of factors. In terms of adolescents, the latest data also show an increase in obesity for both boys and girls over the past 30 years. Data also show that from 1971 to 2006, BMI ratios in the United States increased no matter when the person was born (Figure 10.5). This suggests it is not a cohort or age effect.

FIGURE 10.3 ■ Daily Supply of Calories per Person, 2018

Kcal per person per day

| No data | 1,250 kcal | 1,500 kcal | 1,750 kcal | 2,000 kcal | 2,250 kcal | 2,500 kcal | 3,000 kcal | 3,250 kcal | 3,500 kcal |

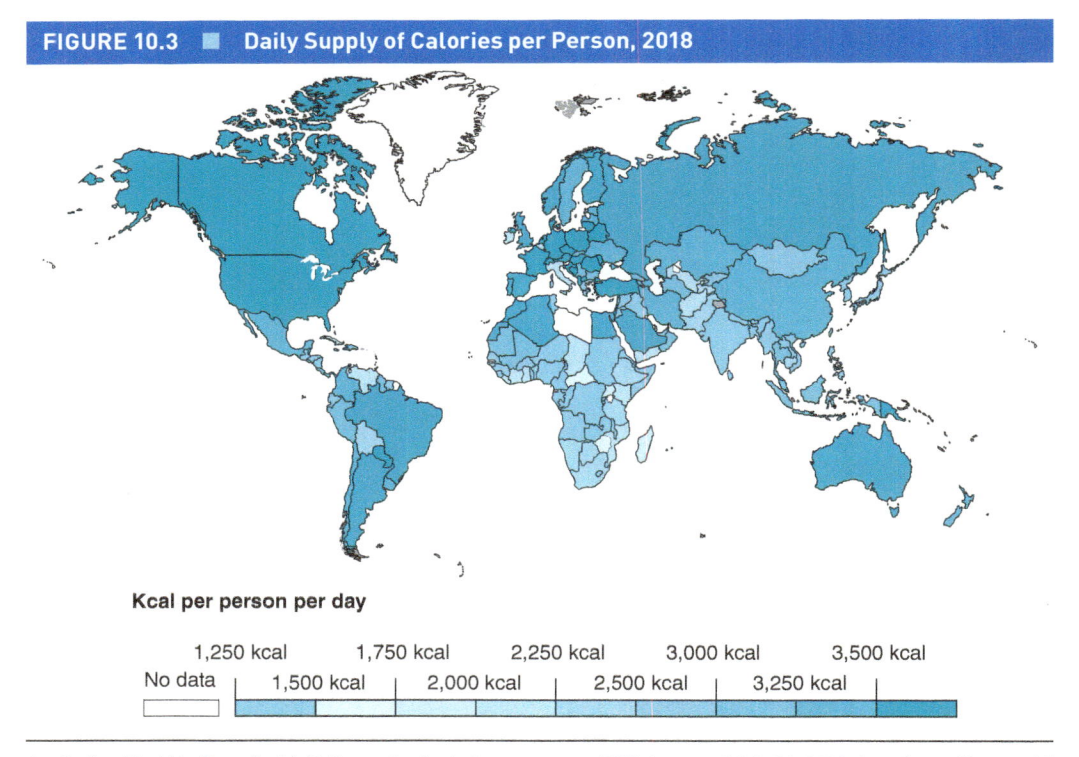

Credit: Our World in Data. (n.d.). *Daily supply of calories per person, 2018.* Accessed July 26, 2023, from https://ourworldindata.org/grapher/daily-per-capita-caloric-supply, licensed under CC BY 4.0 https://creativecommons.org/licenses/by/4.0/deed.en_US.

FIGURE 10.4 ■ Obesity Rates in the United States 1990, 2000, 2010, 2021

The first row shows the changes in obesity trends by state in the United States. The bottom map shows the adult obesity rate by state in 2021.

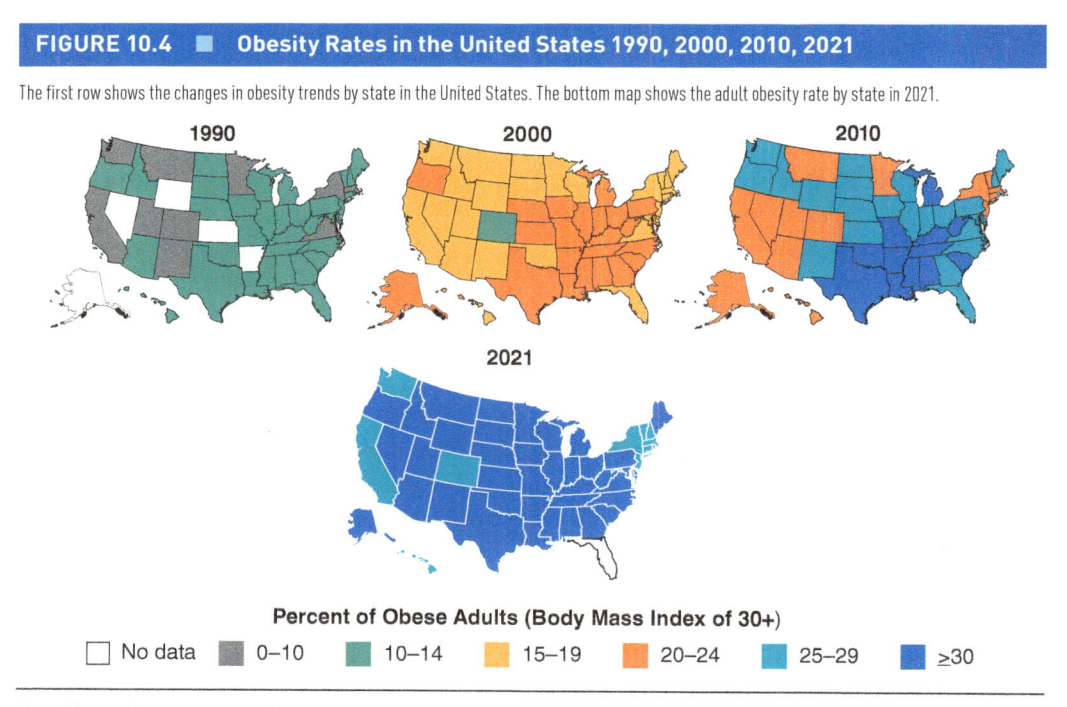

Percent of Obese Adults (Body Mass Index of 30+)

| No data | 0–10 | 10–14 | 15–19 | 20–24 | 25–29 | ≥30 |

Note: The methodology for collecting these data changed in 2011, so figures from before and after 2011 cannot be directly compared.

Source: Centers for Disease Control and Prevention. (2023, March 17). *Adult obesity prevalence maps.* U.S. Department of Health and Human Services. https://www.cdc.gov/obesity/data/prevalence-maps.html

FIGURE 10.5 ■ Does When You Were Born Influence Your BMI?

BMI ratios in the United States have increased no matter when the person was born. This figure shows changes in BMI by when a person was born (data from 1971 to 2006).

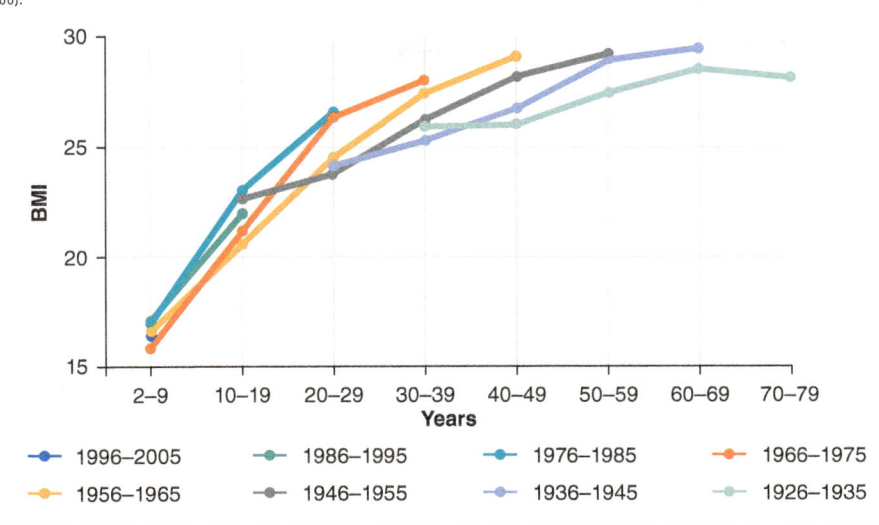

Credit: Lee, J., Pilli, S., Gebremariam, A., Keirns, C., Davis, M., Vijan, S., Freed, G., Hermar, W., & Gurney, J. (2010). Getting heavier, younger: Trajectories of obesity over the life course. *International Journal of Obesity, 34*, 614–623, p. 619.

According to the CDC, overweight and obese individuals are at higher risk for the following health problems:

- Hypertension
- Dyslipidemia (e.g., high LDL cholesterol, low HDL cholesterol, or high levels of triglycerides)
- Type 2 diabetes
- Coronary heart disease
- Stroke
- Gallbladder disease
- Osteoarthritis
- Sleep apnea and respiratory problems
- Some cancers (endometrial, breast, and colon)

In addition to physical disorders, depression has also been linked to obesity (Roberts et al., 2003). More than 2,000 individuals age 50 or older were followed for 5 years. At the beginning of the study, both BMI and depression were measured. Obesity, as measured by a BMI over 30, was associated with increased risk for depression 5 years later. Depression at baseline, however, was not related to obesity some 5 years later.

Body Image and Attitudes Toward Weight

In addition to an individual's actual weight, there is also the person's attitude toward their weight. Attitudes toward body size are culturally determined: In some cultures, being larger is seen as positive, whereas in others, thinness is sought. In the United States, for instance, dieting is an obsession for millions of people. Popular magazine articles, television advertisements, Internet sites, and dozens of new books every year cover the latest dietary fads.

Many Pacific Island people, on the other hand, find a fuller-figured body more attractive, as seen in the art of Paul Gauguin (1848–1903). One study examined 433 Maori individuals in New Zealand, 657 Pacific Islanders, and 4,464 Europeans in terms of their perceptions of body size (Metcalf et al., 2000). Although both the Maori and Pacific people had a larger BMI than the Europeans, they perceived themselves as having a smaller body size compared with Europeans. Thus, culture influences what individuals see as overweight.

Gender factors also play a role in a person's attitude toward body size. Men and women think about their weight differently. Studies have shown that women tend to overestimate their weight, whereas men tend to underestimate their weight (Fallon & Rozin, 1985). In one study, women were asked to rate illustrations of female figures in terms of their ideal weight, what would be considered attractive to men their own current weight, and the attractive weight of men. Men were asked to do the same task. Figure 10.6 shows the results of this study. As can be seen in the figures, men rated a higher weight for women seen as attractive than women did. Women chose a weight lower than their own as attractive or ideal. Men, on the other hand, rated all three categories (attractive, current, and ideal) as very similar. Overall, this suggests that women are more dissatisfied with their current weight than men.

Similar findings were also seen in 22 countries around the world (Wardle et al., 2006). In this study, BMI was calculated from 18,512 university students. No matter their BMI, more women than men felt overweight. The perception of being overweight was similar in all regions of the world. One interesting difference between regions was that in Asian countries, where body weight tends to be lower overall, most individuals were attempting to lose weight. Overall, this study showed that young adult women around the world tend to overestimate their weight, whereas men tend to underestimate their own weight.

A number of studies have also shown a relationship between body image concerns and sexual orientation. In one study in Australia comparing 52 gay men with 51 straight men and 55 straight women, gay men scored higher than straight men on scales of disordered eating (Yelland & Tiggemann, 2003). Although similar to straight women on scales of desire for thinness or engaging in bulimia, the gay men did not differ from straight men on measures of body esteem. A study in the United States collected data from 130 straight men, 116 gay or bisexual men, 361 straight women, and 86 gay or bisexual women

FIGURE 10.6 ■ Do Men and Women Differ in Terms of Ideal and Attractive Ratings?

Men are more likely to see their current body as more attractive and ideal than women are. This figure shows the mean rating by women (*top*) and men (*bottom*) of their current figure, ideal figure, and the figure most attractive to the opposite sex. Participants were shown four figures varying in size and asked to make a mark along the arbitrary scale in terms of ideal, attractive, current, and most attractive to the opposite sex.

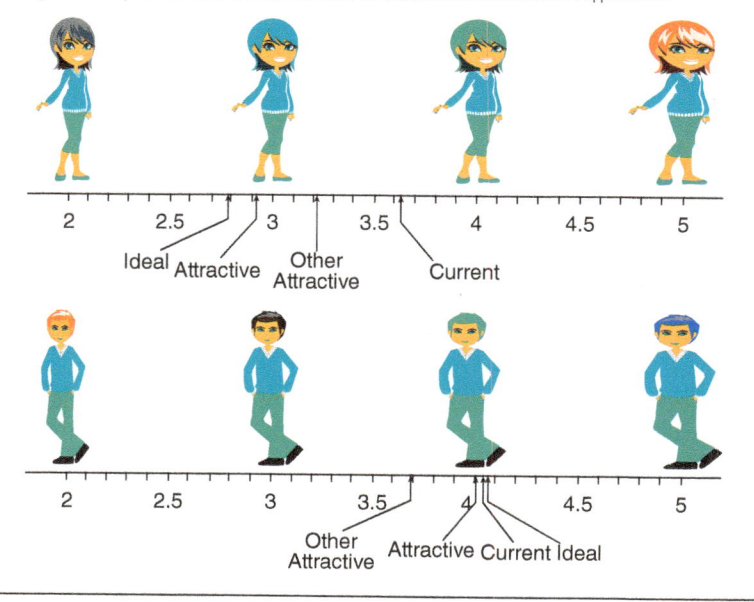

Credit: Adapted from Fallon, A., & Rozin, P. (1985). Sex differences in perceptions of desirable body shape. *Journal of Abnormal Psychology, 94*, 102–105, p. 103. https://doi.org/10.1037/0021-843X.94.1.102

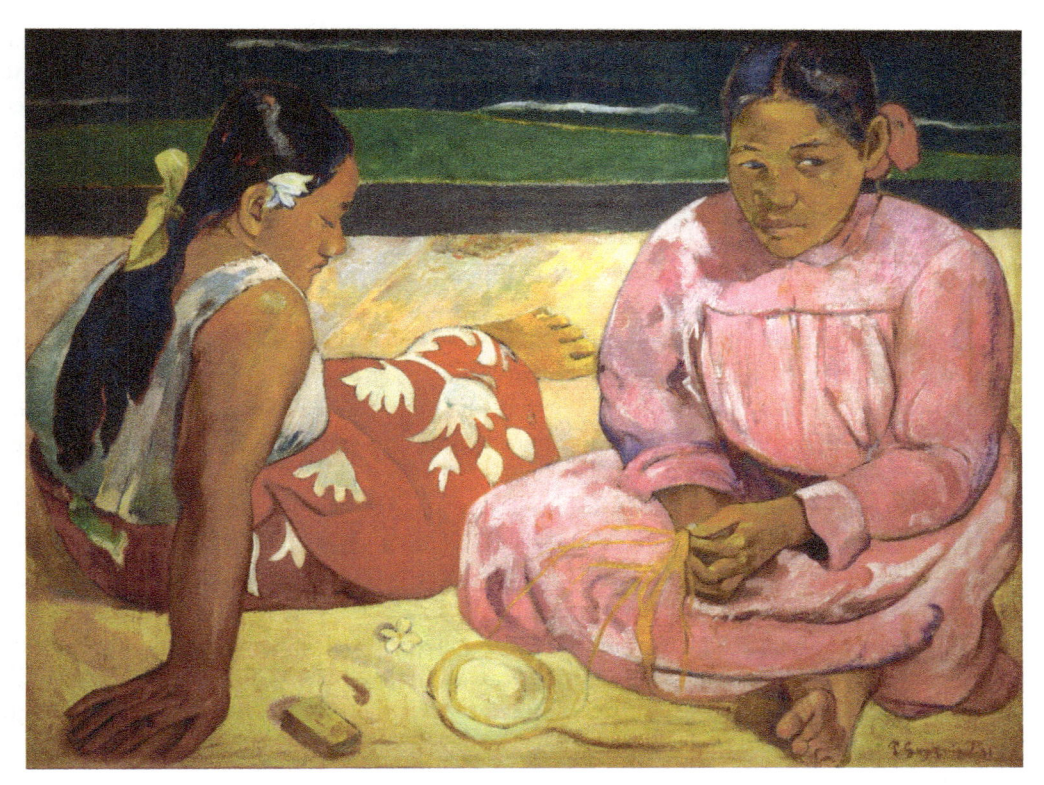

Some cultures see heavier women as more attractive than less heavy women. This 1891 painting of Tahitian women is by the French artist Paul Gauguin.

Nigel Reed QEDimages/Alamy Stock Photo

(Yean et al., 2013). There were no differences between straight and gay women in terms of body dissatisfaction, drive for thinness, or disordered eating. Gay women, however, reported lower self-esteem and an increased drive for muscularity. In this study, gay men reported more disordered eating patterns and body dissatisfaction compared to straight men. Further, body fat dissatisfaction rather than muscular dissatisfaction predicted disordered eating in gay men (A. R. Smith et al., 2011). In a large study of transgender and nonbinary young adults, weight over perception and thin-ideal overvaluation were associated with less positive mental health and, in turn, elevated eating disorder pathology (Romano & Lipson, 2022).

> **CONCEPT CHECK**
>
> - How do our evolutionary history and current conditions of food abundance interact to promote obesity?
> - What are some of the environmental, psychological, and biological factors involved in obesity?
> - How is the brain involved in obesity?
> - What are some of the physical and psychological disorders for which obese individuals are at higher risk?
> - What are some of the factors at different weights that influence views of ideal weight?

OVERVIEW OF EATING DISORDERS

The three major eating disorders in *DSM-5-TR* are *anorexia nervosa, bulimia nervosa*, and *binge eating disorder* (Bhattacharya et al., 2015; Keel et al., 2012; Treasure et al., 2020). Anorexia nervosa and bulimia nervosa are the most commonly discussed eating disorders. They tend to have an onset before puberty and mainly influence women. Various studies suggest that anorexia nervosa affects 0.5% of the population at any one time. Its lifetime prevalence is 0.9% in women and 0.3% in men. Bulimia is seen to have lifetime prevalence of around 1% to 2% in women in the United States. Binge eating tends to affect both genders with a somewhat varied onset. Its lifetime prevalence is seen to be 3.5% in women and 2% in men (Hudson et al., 2007; see Table 10.2). Similar data in terms of prevalence have been found in Australian populations for these same disorders (Hay et al., 2015). One consideration with the three major eating disorders is that they have a high rate of relapse, as high as 50% for anorexia nervosa (Sala et al., 2023).

There is a developmental pattern seen in eating disorders. Both anorexia nervosa and bulimia show onset during adolescence, with increased risk occurring from middle adolescence into young adulthood (Bhattacharya et al., 2020). Symptoms such as weight preoccupation, body dissatisfaction, and disordered eating also show an increasing trajectory with a peak at middle to late adolescence. This increase was shown in a sample of 745 female twins who were followed from age 11 to age 25 (Slane et al., 2014). Although symptoms of bulimia tended to increase among those in this sample up to age 18, they then stabilized.

There is good evidence that eating disorders have a partial genetic component (Bulik et al., 2022; Rankinen & Bouchard, 2006). As you will see, this genetic component may influence temperament, which sets the stage for an eating disorder. Adverse childhood experiences are also associated with eating disorders (Rienecke et al., 2022). Although at one time it was suggested that family factors could be a primary cause of eating disorders, data does not support this position (Le Grange et al., 2010). That is, parents or caregivers should not be blamed for their child's anorexia or bulimia. However, parents and caregivers can play an important role in treatment. Further, one group who may show eating disorders are athletes, as described in *LENS: Eating Disorders and Sports*.

TABLE 10.2 ■ Prevalence and Its Standard Error for Eating Disorder by Gender

	Men		Women		Total	
	%	(SE)	%	(SE)	%	(SE)
I. Lifetime prevalence						
Anorexia nervosa	.3*	(.1)	.9*	(.3)	.6	(.2)
Bulimia nervosa	.5*	(.3)	1.5*	(.3)	1.0	(.2)
Binge eating disorder	2.0*	(.5)	3.5*	(.5)	2.8	(.4)
Subthreshold binge eating disorder	1.9*	(.5)	.6*	(.1)	1.2	(.2)
Any binge eating	4.0	(.7)	4.9	(.6)	4.5	(.4)
II. Twelve-month prevalence†						
Bulimia nervosa	.1*	(.1)	.5*	(.2)	.3	(.1)
Binge eating disorder	.8*	(.3)	1.6*	(.2)	1.2	(.2)
Subthreshold binge eating disorder	.8	(.3)	.4	(.1)	.6	(.2)
Any binge eating	1.7	(.4)	2.5	(.3)	2.1	(.2)
(n)	(1,220)		(1,760)		(2,980)	

Note: SE = standard error.

*Significant sex difference based on a .05 level, 2-sided test.

†None of the respondents met criteria for 12-month anorexia nervosa.

Source: Hudson, J., Hiripi, E., Pope, H., Jr., & Kessler, R. (2007). The prevalence and correlates of eating disorders in the National Comorbidity Survey Replication. *Biological Psychiatry, 61*, 348–358, p. 350, with permission from Elsevier.

LENS
EATING DISORDERS AND SPORTS

Most of us think of athletes being in great shape, ready to perform well in their sport. Elite athletes undergo rigorous training, follow prescribed diets, and are careful about factors that would influence their performance. Thus, it may be surprising that eating disorders have been found to be more common among elite athletes than the general population (Sundgot-Borgen & Torstviet, 2004). In fact, eating disorders were seen in both male and female athletes, although more commonly in women than men. For men, the most common disorder was bulimia, found especially in weight category sports such as wrestling (9%). For women, the highest rates for eating disorders were in aesthetic sports such as figure skating or gymnastics, with a rate of 12% for anorexia and a rate of 15% for bulimia.

iStock.com/wundervisuals

In some sports such as wrestling, an athlete must "make weight." That is, to compete in a certain weight category, the person must show their weight to be at a certain level. Some athletes feel pressure as they consider ways to make their required weight, which has implications for their health (Lakicevic et al., 2022). One way to make weight follows the purging pattern seen in bulimia.

Besides making weight, a number of sports are most effectively performed with a lean body. These include distance running, gymnastics, swimming, and diving. These so-called lean sports, along with weight-class sports such as wrestling, show more eating disorders than other sports (Thompson & Sherman, 2010). It is also the case that judged sports such as figure skating or gymnastics are associated with more cases of eating disorders. A judged sport is one in which the person is given a score by a judge rather than being rewarded simply for being the fastest to run or swim a distance.

Student athletes are influenced by a number of individuals, including their coaches. In one case study of a 12-year-old runner, his coach suggested he might do better competing in a different track and field event such as shot put (Dosil, 2008). Since this student had wanted to be a lean runner as he had seen on TV, he became upset at this advice. Rather than discuss it, he went home and said to himself that he should stop eating so he could become lean. This upset his parents, as he refused to eat and began to lose weight. Fortunately in this case, a psychologist was able to work with the adolescent, his parents, and his coach to reduce the problematic eating behaviors.

Another case involved a 22-year-old taekwondo national champion competing to go to the Olympics (Dosil, 2008). He was at a higher weight level than he would have liked and argued with his coach about his weight. The coach thought the athlete was "letting himself go" and putting on weight. With the competition coming soon, he considered a number of ways to lose weight in order to compete in a lower weight-class category. These included taking laxatives and diuretics, going

> to a sauna, and training in plastic clothing. Feeling the athlete was not working at his potential, the coach involved a sports psychologist who was able to work with the athlete and his coach in terms of the advantages and disadvantages of remaining in the current weight class. This turned into a more long-term collaboration, which resulted in adequate food intake with the athlete performing well.
>
> These two case studies show the beginning of disordered eating patterns and behaviors concerning weight spurred on by involvement in athletic competition. What is less well known is how many of these disordered patterns develop into clinical eating disorders. At this point, longitudinal studies that would help us scientifically understand this relationship are lacking. Eating disorder prevention programs are just beginning to be implemented to educate all those involved in athletics and to identify athletes at risk (De Oliveira Coelho et al., 2014).
>
> ### Thought Question
>
> What factors can lead athletes to disordered eating patterns?

There is also a cultural component to eating disorders. When eating disorders are examined in terms of ethnic diversity within the United States, ethnic differences are seen. One common finding is that there is a higher prevalence of disordered eating in Hispanic and Native American adolescent girls and a lower prevalence in white, Black, and Asian American adolescent girls (Lynch et al., 2011). Although at one time it was suggested that family factors could be a primary cause of eating disorders, data do not support this position (Le Grange et al., 2010). That is, parents should not be blamed for their child's anorexia or bulimia. However, parents can play an important role in treatment.

There are also secondary problems related to eating disorders. Those with eating disorders experience a number of serious medical conditions related to reducing body weight or purging. They also show a higher death rate, including suicide rates of between 4% and 5% (Crow et al., 2009). Often, those with eating disorders conceal their symptoms and do not seek treatment. Even when they seek help for medical disorders related to purging, such as problems with their teeth and gastrointestinal system, they continue to hide the underlying eating disorder. Although limited in number, prevention programs for children and adolescents experiencing body image and eating problems show positive results when parents are involved (Hart et al., 2015).

ANOREXIA NERVOSA

Anorexia nervosa has been described in the medical literature since the 1600s. In 1689, Richard Morton, an English physician, described an adolescent boy and girl who suffered from "want of appetite" and "nervous consumption" (Gordon, 1990). These adolescents lost weight but did not appear to have any medical disorder. Sir William Gull is credited with first using the term *anorexia nervosa* in his description in 1870. In Latin, *anorexia* refers to a loss of appetite and *nervosa* to nervous. Gull (1874) described a condition affecting young adolescent women who starved themselves. In France, Charles Lasègue described young women with significant weight loss as *anorexie hystérique*. The major clinical features described over 100 years ago are similar to those seen today.

Characteristics of Anorexia Nervosa

From the 1600s to the present, the disorder has commonly been described in terms of three characteristics:

1. Food refusal
2. Onset in adolescence
3. Lack of concern about the consequences of not eating

The onset of anorexia nervosa takes place in a narrow range in adolescence. There is a consistency in symptoms. These include a preoccupation with food while at the same time showing a resistance to eating. Body image is also distorted. Even when significantly underweight, individuals with anorexia nervosa see themselves as fat. They also show a lack of concern for being underweight. This lack of concern also results in these individuals not seeking treatment for their condition. Those with anorexia nervosa always have a lower-than-normal BMI. The following description describes the experience of a daughter with anorexia nervosa as seen from the perspective of her mother:

> It was 6 months ago when I realized my daughter, Jen, had an eating disorder. Jen has always been a picky eater. But I started to see that she moved food around her plate. And she never ate very much. She exercised all the time—even when she was sick. And she was sick a lot. She became very skinny and pale. Her hair thinned. Jen became moody and seemed sad—I thought that's what teens act like. But once I put the signs together, I talked to Jen about anorexia. She denied she had a problem. But I knew she needed help. I took her to our doctor, and she asked me to put Jen in the hospital. Jen's treatment helped her return to a normal weight. It's been a tough road since then for all of us, but Jen is back home now. She is still seeing her doctors, and may need help for some time. But she's doing much better. (Office on Women's Health, 2009)

DSM-5-TR criteria for a diagnosis of anorexia nervosa (Table 10.3) include a restriction of food, which results in a weight that is below normal, a fear of gaining weight, and a lack of recognition of

TABLE 10.3 ■ *DSM-5-TR* Diagnostic Criteria for Anorexia Nervosa

A. Restriction of energy intake relative to requirements, leading to a significantly low body weight in the context of age, sex, developmental trajectory, and physical health. *Significantly low weight* is defined as a weight that is less than minimally normal or, for children and adolescents, less than that minimally expected.

B. Intense fear of gaining weight or of becoming fat, or persistent behavior that interferes with weight gain, even though at a significantly low weight.

C. Disturbance in the way in which one's body weight or shape is experienced, undue influence of body weight or shape on self-evaluation, or persistent lack of recognition of the seriousness of the current low body weight.

Coding note: The ICD-10-CM code depends on the subtype (see below).

Specify whether:

F50.01 Restricting type: During the last 3 months, the individual has not engaged in recurrent episodes of binge-eating or purging behavior (i.e., self-induced vomiting or the misuse of laxatives, diuretics, or enemas). This subtype describes presentations in which weight loss is accomplished primarily through dieting, fasting, and/or excessive exercise.

F50.02 Binge-eating/purging type: During the last 3 months, the individual has engaged in recurrent episodes of binge-eating or purging behavior (i.e., self-induced vomiting or the misuse of laxatives, diuretics, or enemas).

Specify if:

In partial remission: After full criteria for anorexia nervosa were previously met, Criterion A (low body weight) has not been met for a sustained period, but either Criterion B (intense fear of gaining weight or becoming fat or behavior that interferes with weight gain) or Criterion C (disturbances in self-perception of weight and shape) is still met.

In full remission: After full criteria for anorexia nervosa were previously met, none of the criteria have been met for a sustained period of time.

Specify current severity:

The minimum level of severity is based, for adults, on current body mass index (BMI) (see below) or, for children and adolescents, on BMI percentile. The ranges below are derived from World Health Organization categories for thinness in adults; for children and adolescents, corresponding BMI percentiles should be used. The level of severity may be increased to reflect clinical symptoms, the degree of functional disability, and the need for supervision.

Mild: BMI $\geq$ 17 kg/m^2.

Moderate: BMI 16–16.99 kg/m^2.

Severe: BMI 15–15.99 kg/m^2.

Extreme: BMI <15 kg/m^2.

Credit: Reprinted with permission from the *Diagnostic and Statistical Manual of Mental Disorders, fifth edition, text revision*, DSM-V-TR, p. 381 (Copyright © 2022). American Psychiatric Association. All rights reserved.

the seriousness of current body weight and a distortion of how body weight is experienced. Unlike other mental disorders such as depression, in which different types of symptoms can lead to the overall diagnosis, individuals with anorexia nervosa show a similar pattern in their behavior and attitudes. This consistency has led some researchers to suggest that anorexia nervosa has the most homogeneous presentation of any psychiatric disorder (Kaye et al., 2009).

Within this consistency, *DSM-5-TR* describes two subtypes. The first subtype is referred to as the *restricting type*. As the name implies, individuals of this subtype accomplish weight loss through dieting, fasting, and/or excessive exercise. The second subtype is referred to as the *binge eating/purging type*. Low-weight individuals with this subtype display episodes of binge eating or purging through self-induced vomiting or the use of laxatives, diuretics, or enemas. Although this second type may sound similar to bulimia nervosa (described later in this chapter), individuals with bulimia nervosa generally maintain normal or higher body weight, whereas those with anorexia nervosa have a lower than normal body weight.

Although adolescents are often concerned about their body image, only about 1% of adolescent women go on to develop anorexia nervosa. What can we say about these individuals? One thing is that they tend to have certain personality characteristics that can be thought of as an endophenotype (Kaye et al., 2013). They tend to be anxious, and this anxiety exists before the onset of anorexia nervosa and will continue even after treatment and weight gain. They also tend to be perfectionistic, with an overemphasis on self-imposed standards. Perfectionism is also seen prior to the onset and continues after treatment. The higher the level of perfectionism, the poorer the recovery from treatment and the shorter the duration before relapse. These individuals also have difficulty with flexibility and changing rule structures. This is also seen in terms of an obsessiveness around order, exactness, and symmetry. Figure 10.7 shows a pathway by which these characteristics become part of the development of anorexia nervosa.

In addition to the outward signs of anorexia nervosa, there are also distortions in body image (Gaudio & Quattrocchi, 2012). One common characteristic is for the person to see both specific body parts and their overall weight as being heavier than they are. The body image distortion has been described as having perceptual, emotional, and cognitive components. The perceptual component has to do with whether one's self or others are underweight, normal, or overweight. The affective

FIGURE 10.7 ■ Developmental Contributions to Anorexia Nervosa

Anorexia nervosa begins in adolescence and reflects an endophenotype associated with anxiety and perfectionism.

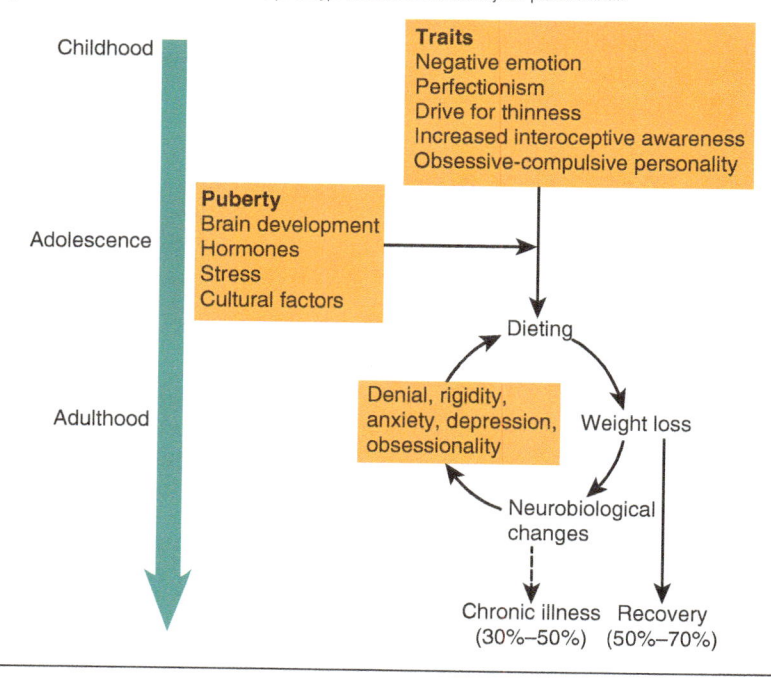

Credit: Kaye, W., Fudge, J., & Paulus, M. (2009). New insights into symptoms and neurocircuit function of anorexia nervosa. *Nature Reviews Neuroscience, 10,* 573–584, p. 575.

In the film *To the Bone*, Lily Collins plays a woman with anorexia nervosa who is in treatment working to change the discrepancy between her actual weight and how she views herself.

AMBI GROUP/SPARKHOUSE MEDIA/MOCKINGBIRD PIC/FOXTAIL ENT/BOND/Album/Alamy Stock Photo

(emotional) component involves whether the person is satisfied or dissatisfied with their own body. The cognitive component consists of beliefs concerning one's body image as well as the mental representation of one's body. These beliefs exist separately without actually viewing body types.

One problem in assessing individuals with anorexia nervosa is that they commonly deny that they have a problem. They may also not give you straightforward descriptions of their view of their weight or how they approach eating. They will tell you various reasons for why they eat or exercise as they do, which may not fit their actual behaviors. However, it is helpful to have the person describe how and what they eat during the day. In doing so, the person's sense of control can be assessed. Also, questions related to binge eating can help to assess the subtype. Mental health professionals often seek to include family members or other significant people to obtain information. If possible, getting the history of a person's weight, including the highest and lowest weights, is important. For females, knowing the person's weight at which menstruation last occurred may also give the professional a sense of that individual's more normal body weight.

Neuroscience and Anorexia

In a review of brain imaging studies concerning differences between those with anorexia nervosa and those without anorexia, it was found that each of the condition's three components involves different areas of the brain (Gaudio & Quattrocchi, 2012). As can be seen in Figure 10.8, the perception component shows differences in the precuneus and the inferior parietal lobe. The affective component involves the PFC, the insula, and the amygdala. One task of the insula is to process internal information that gives rise to a sense of self. Those individuals with anorexia nervosa may experience different internal information that leads to a distorted body image, lack of response to hunger, and lack of motivation to change.

In previous studies, the cognitive component was often combined with a negative affective component. This made it impossible to study beliefs concerning body image alone. However, when the cognitive network is considered to modulate selective attention, planning, and effortful regulation of affective states, it is possible to see changes in the hippocampus, anterior cingulate cortex (ACC), dorsolateral prefrontal cortex (DLPFC), and parietal areas (Kaye et al., 2009). Brain imaging in a resting state found that regions of two main networks were associated with body dissatisfaction and drive for thinness, which are key features of anorexia (Gupta et al., 2022). Specifically, anorexia is associated with greater network communication from the basal ganglia and lower information propagation in the sensorimotor cortices.

FIGURE 10.8 ■ What Areas of the Brain Are Involved in Anorexia Nervosa?

fMRI findings related to affective and cognitive involvement in anorexia nervosa. These include the precuneus and the inferior parietal lobe (perceptive component). The affective component involves the PFC, the insula, and the amygdala.

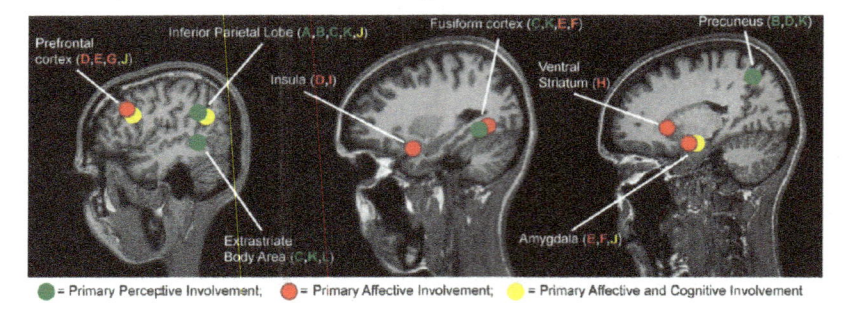

● = Primary Perceptive Involvement; ● = Primary Affective Involvement; ● = Primary Affective and Cognitive Involvement

Credit: Gaudio, S., & Quattrocchi, C. (2012). Neural basis of a multidimensional model of body image distortion in anorexia nervosa. *Neuroscience and Biobehavioral Reviews, 36*, 1839–1847, p. 1844, with permission from Elsevier.

On a neurotransmitter level, both serotonin and dopamine systems have been shown to be different in those with eating disorders (Kaye et al., 2009). The serotonin system is thought to play a role in eating disorders by influencing the feeling of being full, impulse control, and mood. That is, those with anorexia nervosa may feel full quicker and experience more anxiety and behavioral inhibition. The binding potential of the serotonin (5-HT) receptor is increased in individuals with eating disorders, whereas it is decreased in those with depression, social phobia, and panic disorder.

Research also suggests that the dopamine system and its relationship to reward is different in those with eating disorders (Kaye et al., 2013). That is, individuals with anorexia nervosa do not show signs of reward in the dopamine system in relation to eating. Thus, individuals with anorexia nervosa do think about food but do not find satisfaction or reward from this or even other activities. One recent discovery is that gut bacteria differ in those with eating disorders and that there is a pathway between the gut and the brain. This relationship is described in *LENS: Eating Disorders and Your Gut.*

LENS
EATING DISORDERS AND YOUR GUT

An important new discovery concerning a possible contributing factor to eating disorders involves bacteria in the gut (Roubalová et al., 2020). As you will see, gut bacteria are involved in the emotionality and eating patterns of those with eating disorders.

Gut bacteria develop during an individual's first year of life.
iStock.com/Dr_Microbe

For all of us, there are more bacteria in our gut than there are cells in our body (Herd et al., 2018). It is estimated that there are approximately 150 to 200 species of common bacteria in the gut as well as 1,000 less common species (Dinan et al., 2015). Although there are similarities among people, each individual has a unique set of gut bacteria (Kleiman et al., 2015). We now know that these gut bacteria (called the *microbiome* when referring to their genes) are associated with both health and illness. They also play a role in stress and a number of types of psychological disorders (De Palma et al., 2015; Foster et al., 2017). Gut bacteria can influence how medications affect you, and they may reduce the effects of some psychotropic medications. That is, the medication interacts with the bacteria in your gut, and the bacteria in turn may influence how these substances are taken up by your body. In turn, the types of food you eat can influence the types of bacteria in your gut.

Gut bacteria develop during an individual's first year of life and are influenced by such factors as breast feeding (Bäckhed et al., 2015). We supply these gut bacteria with a constant source of nutrition, and they in turn are involved in brain development and functioning. Without gut bacteria, the brain, such as those processes involved in emotionality, does not develop appropriately. Gut bacteria are also associated with temperament during early childhood, although it is not known

FIGURE 10.9 ■ How Do Your Brain and Gut Communicate With Each Other?

There are multiple pathways, which go in both directions, between the brain and the gut. These pathways include the vagus nerve, the hypothalamic–pituitary–axis (HPA), the immune system (cytokines), and short-chain fatty acids (SCFAs).

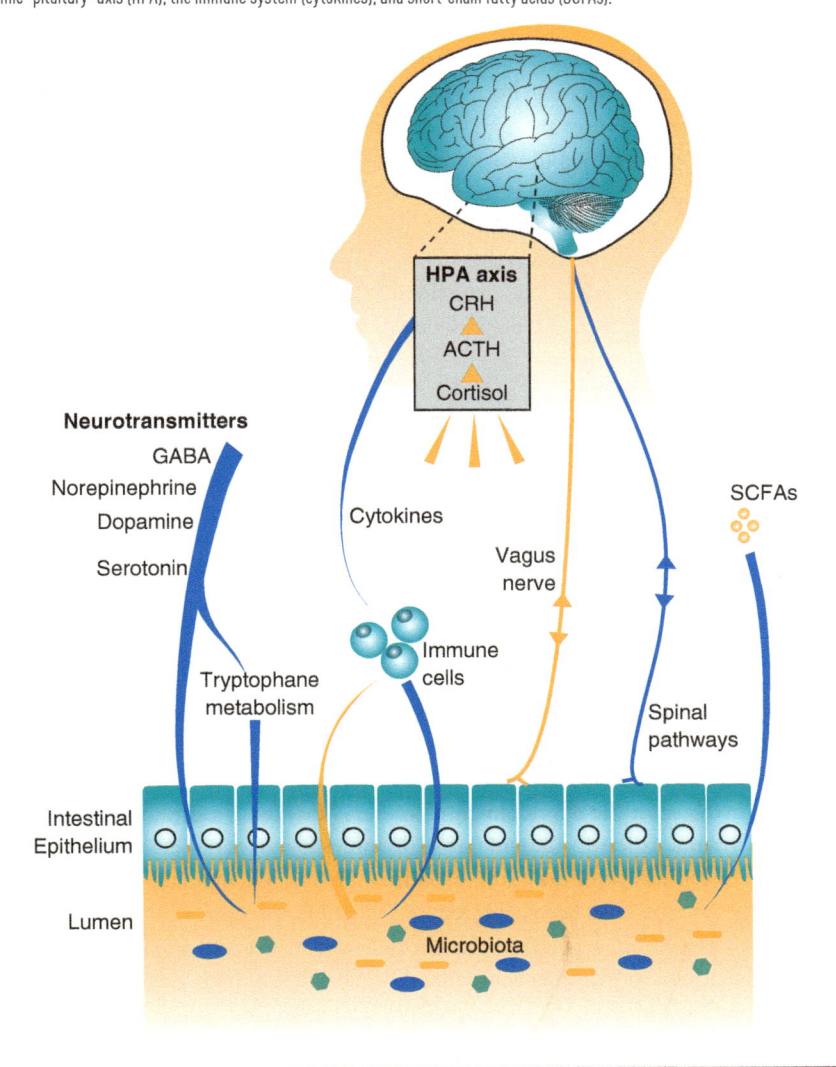

Credit: Dinan, T. G., Stilling, R. M., Stanton, C., & Cryan, J. F. (2015). Collective unconscious: How gut microbes shape human behavior. *Journal of Psychiatric Research, 63*, 1–9. http://doi.org/10.1016/j.jpsychires.2015.02.021, with permission from Elsevier.

> whether temperament influences gut bacteria or gut bacteria influence temperament (Christian et al., 2015). Recent investigations indicate that these microbes have a major impact on cognitive function and fundamental behavior patterns, such as social interaction and stress management. One mechanism is through changes in underlying biochemistry. That is, different forms of gut bacteria can generate specific neurotransmitters such as GABA, which is involved in anxiety. There are multiple pathways that go in both directions between the brain and the gut, as shown in Figure 10.9.
>
> What is exciting to scientists is how these gut bacteria are involved in the emotionality and eating patterns of those with eating disorders. Initial research is beginning to offer a better understanding of the specific pathways in which gut bacteria influence disordered eating (Tennoune et al., 2014). There is also compelling evidence that intestinal microbiota influence key features of anorexia nervosa, including weight regulation, energy metabolism, anxiety, and depression (Kleiman et al., 2015). One case study showed fewer types of bacteria in a person with anorexia nervosa (Gouba et al., 2014). Other research is currently underway to see if modifying gut bacteria can influence disordered eating (e.g., Chen et al., 2014). Further research into gut bacteria may provide new insights into how we can alleviate certain factors that contribute to eating disorders.
>
> ### Thought Question
>
> What are the different ways bacteria in your gut can influence mental health disorders?

Individuals with anorexia nervosa develop a variety of additional medical problems that may be related to lack of nutrition and changes in hormones such as lower levels of estrogen and higher levels of cortisol. The most serious outcome of anorexia is death, although a number of other conditions are also seen. One of these is a decreased level of bone density, which increases the chances of fracture. Other problems related to cardiovascular functioning and reduced motility of the gastrointestinal tract are also seen in individuals with anorexia nervosa. It is possible to reverse these disorders when the individual returns to a normal weight. This was shown is a study of women who were diagnosed and treated for anorexia nervosa when they were adolescents (Flamarique et al., 2022). Twenty years later, normal cardiovascular parameters were seen in those individuals who had maintained normal weight.

Causes of Anorexia Nervosa

The specific causes of anorexia nervosa are still being researched. However, a variety of factors appear to be involved (see Kaye et al., 2009, for an overview). Table 10.4 lists some of these factors, although not every person will have all of these.

One factor is genetics. Twin studies suggest that 50% to 80% of the variance in both anorexia nervosa and bulimia can be accounted for by genetics (Kaye et al., 2009). With the development of genome-wide association studies (GWAS) that compare individual genes in thousands of individuals with and without eating disorders, results are beginning to show more specific genes that are involved in eating disorders (Bulik et al., 2022). As noted previously, studies also look for endophenotypes that include psychological personality factors and food intake. Overall, these genetic influences appear to show heritability of global attitudes toward food and dieting, including the restriction of eating, binge eating, and self-induced vomiting.

Another factor involved in the development of anorexia nervosa is restricting the intake of food. For example, brain volume is less in individuals with anorexia nervosa. There is also a reduction in brain metabolism in specific areas of the brain, including the frontal, cingulate, temporal, and parietal areas. Also, even when puberty has been achieved, individuals with anorexia nervosa show characteristics of prepubertal functioning. As a way of conserving energy, these and other physiological changes may actually lead the person to increase their desire to reduce food intake. As such, it becomes a dangerously self-perpetuating situation. As with other physical conditions, these characteristics tend to return to normal after the individual gains weight in treatment.

Cultural factors also play an important role. For example, individuals with anorexia nervosa in Hong Kong, Japan, Singapore, and Malaysia do not show the same phobic response to fat that is seen in Western

TABLE 10.4	Suggestive Risk Factors in Anorexia Nervosa

A. Familial
1. A family member or relative with anorexia nervosa, bulimia nervosa
2. A family member or relative with depression or alcohol/drug abuse/dependence

B. Individual Biological Factors
1. Early menarche
2. Mildly overweight

C. Individual Psychological Factors
1. Perfectionistic—obsessional personality
2. Sense of ineffectiveness, lack of confidence, low self-esteem
3. Affective disorders (depression)

D. Individual Behaviors
1. Dieting
2. Involvement in activities or professions that emphasize weight control: gymnastics, ballet, wrestling, jockeys, actors, and models

E. Cultural
1. Living in an industrialized country
2. Emphasis on thinness as beauty
3. General significant weight increase in the general population in the U.S. over the past 40 years

F. Stressful life events
1. Death of a close relative or friend
2. Sexual abuse

Credit: Halmi, K. (2005). Psychopathology of anorexia nervosa. *International Journal of Eating Disorders, 37,* S20–S21, p. S21.

cultures (Becker, 2011). This has led some professionals to question the diagnostic criteria in the *DSM*, since one requirement of anorexia nervosa is a fear of becoming fat. Likewise, screenings in countries with high rates of poverty will identify individuals who are preoccupied with food as the result of hunger rather than an eating disorder. In general, anorexia is seen more in developed economies. Paradoxically, the rate of anorexia nervosa is higher in cultures where food is abundant. As a country develops, there is an increase in the occurrence of anorexia. It has been suggested that with economic development come changing roles for women, a shift in eating patterns, and an emphasis on thinness (Nasser et al., 2001).

It is interesting to note that starvation in itself may lead to similar psychological characteristics in individuals who do not have anorexia. In a classic study performed during World War II, 36 men who were conscientious objectors volunteered to be part of a study of starvation (Franklin et al., 1948). During the first 3 months of the study, these men ate a diet of some 3,492 calories a day. (This is actually higher than the recommendation today that males should consume roughly 2,500 calories a day based on physical size for a healthy lifestyle.) For the next 6 months, these men began a semi-starvation diet of 1,570 calories a day. This was followed by 3 months of rehabilitation when calorie intake was increased.

By the end of the semi-starvation period, the men had lost about 24% of their previous weight. Physically, their faces and bodies showed emaciation. Also, they lost muscle and adipose tissue such that sitting on hard surfaces was uncomfortable. They experienced some of their hair falling out. They reported feeling cold, even in the summer. They played with the food they ate. Food also became part of their conversations, reading, and daydreams. They showed periods of emotional instability and depression. Overall, they became indecisive, unable to make personal plans, and unwilling to participate in group activities. These men showed a narrowing of focus and mainly stayed alone. During the rehabilitation phase, recovery to normal as seen before the start of the experiment was very slow. Although these men did not begin with an eating disorder, their experiences parallel the cognitive and emotional changes seen in anorexia nervosa.

Treating Anorexia Nervosa

Anorexia nervosa is seen as one of the most difficult disorders to treat (Candea et al., 2018; Halmi, 2005). To begin with, here is a troubling truth: Many individuals with anorexia do not want to be

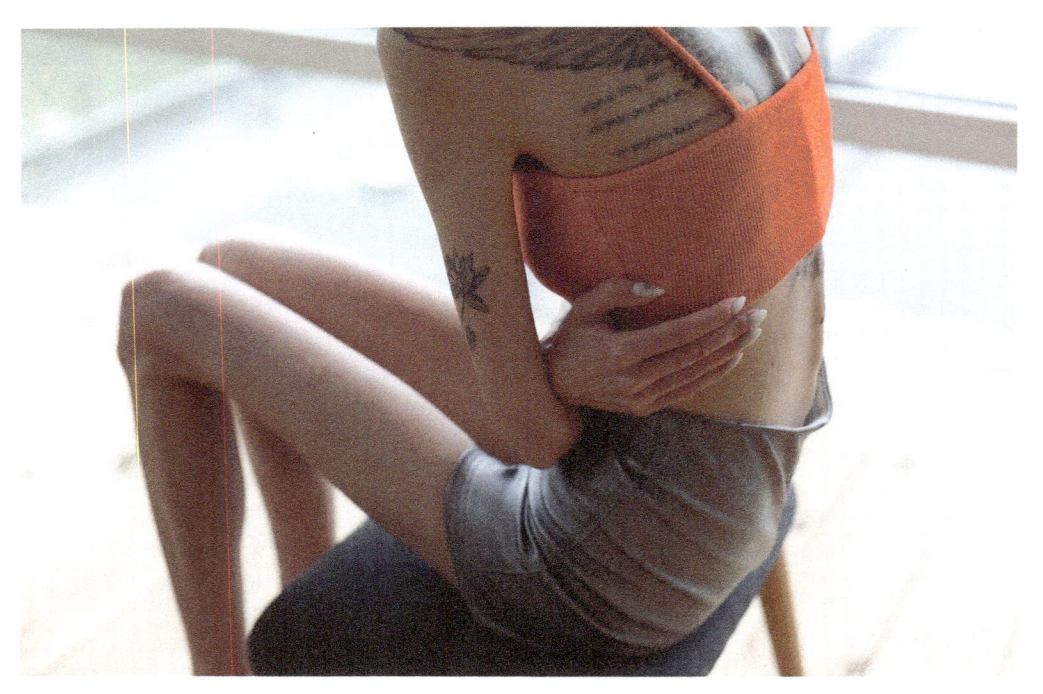

A patient with anorexia nervosa.
iStock.com/Zinkevych. Stock photo. Posed by model.

treated. In fact, there are some websites on which individuals with anorexia nervosa share with one another techniques for remaining underweight and avoiding recognition that they have the disorder. The disorder itself has resulted in psychological and physiological changes, and many individuals deny that they actually have a disorder even when they have agreed to treatment. With adolescents, it is often the family that pushes for treatment.

One of the first tasks for someone to heal from anorexia nervosa is to gain weight. This often requires a hospital stay in which the individual's consumption of food is gradually increased. This also includes analysis of the person's nutritional needs. Following this, psychological or family therapy is typically the next step. Family therapy has proven quite successful in treating adolescents with anorexia. A critical component is the person's willingness to be involved in treatment and experience change, such as bodily and psychological feelings.

One family-based treatment approach for adolescents with anorexia nervosa is referred to as the **Maudsley approach** (Doyle & Le Grange, 2015; Lock et al., 2001; see also their website in For Further Reading). The Maudsley approach is based on treatment research on anorexia nervosa at the Maudsley Hospital in the United Kingdom and is used by a number of university-based medical centers in the United States. The approach is designed to take place within the family rather than at a hospital.

There are three basic phases to the Maudsley approach. The first phase is weight restoration. In this phase, the mental health professional works with the parents or caregivers to encourage their child to eat during family meals without blaming the adolescent for having the eating disorder. The second phase focuses on having the adolescent take more control over their eating problems. This phase takes place after the adolescent has begun to gain weight associated with increased food intake. Once the individual approaches a normal body weight, the third phase begins. This phase emphasizes developing a healthy adolescent identity as well as developing personal autonomy. The current limited research suggests that the Maudsley approach is effective, especially for those adolescents who have experienced anorexia nervosa for less than 3 years (Le Grange & Eisler, 2009).

With adults, cognitive behavioral therapy (CBT) has been shown to be an effective approach. The basic CBT approach is to help the person develop productive thoughts and feelings around their eating and view of self. As with the treatment of other disorders, CBT focuses on the irrational thoughts and conclusions of an individual with anorexia nervosa. Some of these irrational thoughts can include the need to follow strict rules and the belief that self-control can only be achieved through dieting.

There are currently two versions of CBT for use with any eating disorder, including anorexia and bulimia (Fairburn, 2008; Fairburn, Cooper, & Doll, 2009; Fairburn, Cooper, & Shafran, 2003, 2008). The first version focuses on pathology related to eating disorders exclusively. The second form is more complex and also addresses mood intolerance, clinical perfectionism, low self-esteem, and interpersonal difficulties. Both of these approaches have been shown to be effective in reducing symptoms in about 50% of those with eating disorders (Fairburn et al., 2009; Waller et al., 2018).

A number of medications have been tried with anorexia nervosa (Walsh, 2008). Generally, these have been neuroleptics, the main focus of which is in treating psychosis. The basic idea is that these medications are associated with weight gain and the reduction of disordered thinking and might help those with anorexia nervosa. Tricyclic antidepressants have also been tried without any apparent benefits. Currently, there is no good evidence to suggest a critical role for medication in the treatment of anorexia nervosa (Walsh, 2008).

There are a limited number of studies evaluating treatment approaches for anorexia nervosa. The dropout rates for adults in treatment are high. In one treatment outcome study comparing CBT with medication treatment and a combination of the two, the dropout rate was 46% (Halmi, 2005). Only 27% of those in the medication group completed treatment, whereas 38% in the combination group and 43% in the CBT group completed treatment. In another study that compared nutritional counseling with CBT, all of the individuals in the nutritional counseling group dropped out, whereas 8% of the CBT condition dropped out. In another similar study, the numbers were 73% dropout rate for nutritional counseling and 22% for CBT. Although this suggests that individuals are more willing to be part of CBT treatments than other types of treatments, the dropout rates made it difficult to know the effectiveness of therapy.

In addition, individuals—especially adults with anorexia nervosa—may refuse treatment. At the beginning of another study for the treatment of anorexia nervosa with a particular drug, there were 139 individuals who met criteria for the study (Bissada et al., 2008). Of these, 63 individuals refused day hospital treatment. Out of the remaining 76 individuals, 42 declined to be part of the study, leaving only 14 individuals in the drug treatment group and 14 in the placebo group. Among adolescents, parental pressure increases the involvement in treatment and treatment studies.

Individuals with anorexia nervosa show a great variety in the outcomes of the disorder (Zerwas et al., 2013). Previous research showed that about one third of individuals recover about 4 years after the onset of anorexia nervosa. By year 10 after onset, about 50% recover. Beyond this time, it increases to 73%. The other individuals either experience medical complications from the disorder or die of suicide. Given these data, researchers have sought to determine the factors associated with successful outcomes (Zerwas et al., 2013). These researchers looked at eating disorder features, personality traits, and comorbid psychological disorders. Presence of vomiting and higher levels of trait anxiety were associated with lower positive levels of recovery. Impulsivity, on the other hand, was associated with recovery.

BULIMIA NERVOSA AND BINGE EATING DISORDER

Although overeating followed by purging has been described since Roman times more than 2,000 years ago, the eating disorder bulimia nervosa was not introduced into the medical literature until 1979 (Russell, 1979). Since that time, there have been no major changes to its conceptualization.

Characteristics and Prevalence of Bulimia Nervosa

The main characteristics of bulimia are periods of overeating in which the person feels out of control followed by an inappropriate attempt to compensate. In general, individuals with bulimia nervosa report that once they begin eating, they are unable to stop until a large amount of food has been consumed. To prevent weight gain associated with excessive eating, the person self-induces vomiting or takes laxatives or other medications to eliminate the food. The person may also overexercise or fast to prevent weight gain. However, as noted previously, those with bulimia nervosa typically show normal body weights compared to those with anorexia nervosa.

To avoid weight gain, individuals with bulimia nervosa induce vomiting.
iStock.com/LukaTDB. Stock photo. Posed by model.

This disorder is generally reported in women and is associated with an overconcern related to weight and appearance. Twelve-month prevalence in women is around 1% to 1.5% (APA, 2013). Although it is seen to have a 10-to-1 female-to-male ratio, it may be missed in men such as those involved in sports where they are required to "make weight." The prevalence of bulimia nervosa is low in developing countries. The prevalence is higher in developed countries such as the United States, Canada, Japan, Australia, and countries of Europe.

The typical onset is described as one in which a young woman who sees herself as overweight begins to diet (Walsh, 2008). After some initial success, she experiences a lack of control and begins to overeat. Fearing that she will become fat and not having a sense of control in her eating, the person then looks for ways to overeat and not be fat at the same time. She then learns techniques from friends, the media, or the Internet. Initially, these techniques may work and give her a sense of control. However, afterward she will find herself using these techniques more often and feeling guilty and not wanting to be discovered. If fact, those with bulimia nervosa will generally stop bingeing if interrupted by another person such as a roommate. The binge eating tends to occur in the late afternoon or evening when the person is alone. The eating often involves sweet foods such as ice cream or cake. Some individuals describe themselves as "numb" when they are engaging in binge eating episodes. Purging usually follows shortly after the eating.

Bulimia nervosa can also lead to secondary medical problems related to vomiting and the overuse of medications such as laxatives. These can include menstrual disturbances, dental erosion (especially of the upper front teeth), and electrolyte imbalances. More serious complications can involve the heart and esophagus.

Causes of Bulimia Nervosa

The causes of bulimia nervosa are uncertain at this time (Glasofer et al., 2015; Keel et al., 2012). Since bulimia nervosa is seen more often in relatives, including twins, it is assumed to have some genetic basis (Trace et al., 2013). However, a study of 745 individuals with anorexia nervosa, 245 individuals with bulimia nervosa, and 321 controls found no differences in the genetic components of 20 markers related to appetite and weight (Yilmaz et al., 2014). In terms of brain volume, reductions are seen in those with anorexia nervosa but not in those with bulimia nervosa (Amianto et al., 2013). Although psychological studies have shown differences in anxiety, self-esteem, and reported sexual abuse in those with bulimia nervosa, at this point these appear to be more of an associative rather than causal nature. Likewise, cultural factors clearly influence the disorder but cannot alone account for its presence.

Overall, there are three major aspects of bulimia nervosa in terms of *DSM-5-TR* (Table 10.5). The first is binge eating, in which the person consumes large amounts of food. Typically, the individual consumes 2,000 calories in one sitting, which is equal to the amount of calories recommended for a woman's daily intake for a healthy lifestyle. The person also experiences a lack of control over their eating. The second aspect is the purging. **Purging** is where a person eliminates food from the body by such means as vomiting or taking laxatives, diuretics, or enemas. The third aspect is a psychological one in which one's self-worth is seen in relation to one's weight or body shape.

The assessment for bulimia nervosa is similar to that for anorexia nervosa. It is important to have the person describe their eating behaviors in terms of amount and types of foods eaten. The mental health professional needs to be direct in assessing compensating behaviors such as the use of self-induced vomiting, laxatives, and other medications. In *DSM-5-TR*, the bingeing and inappropriate compensatory behaviors need to occur at least once a week for 3 months. The person's view of their body and weight history should also be assessed. The following case study of Anne Hart (not her real name) shows such an assessment.

TABLE 10.5 ■ *DSM-5-TR* Diagnostic Criteria for Bulimia Nervosa

A. Recurrent episodes of binge eating. An episode of binge eating is characterized by both of the following:
  1. Eating, in a discrete period of time (e.g., within any 2-hour period), an amount of food that is definitely larger than what most individuals would eat in a similar period of time under similar circumstances.
  2. A sense of lack of control over eating during the episode (e.g., a feeling that one cannot stop eating or control what or how much one is eating).

B. Recurrent inappropriate compensatory behaviors in order to prevent weight gain, such as self-induced vomiting; misuse of laxatives, diuretics, or other medications; fasting; or excessive exercise.

C. The binge eating and inappropriate compensatory behaviors both occur, on average, at least once a week for 3 months.

D. Self-evaluation is unduly influenced by body shape and weight.

E. The disturbance does not occur exclusively during episodes of anorexia nervosa.

Specify if:

In partial remission: After full criteria for bulimia nervosa were previously met, some, but not all, of the criteria have been met for a sustained period of time.

In full remission: After full criteria for bulimia nervosa were previously met, none of the criteria have been met for a sustained period of time.

Specify current severity:
The minimum level of severity is based on the frequency of inappropriate compensatory behaviors (see below). The level of severity may be increased to reflect other symptoms and the degree of functional disability.

Mild: An average of 1–3 episodes of inappropriate compensatory behaviors per week.

Moderate: An average of 4–7 episodes of inappropriate compensatory behaviors per week.

Severe: An average of 8–13 episodes of inappropriate compensatory behaviors per week.

Extreme: An average of 14 or more episodes of inappropriate compensatory behaviors per week.

Credit: Reprinted with permission from the *Diagnostic and Statistical Manual of Mental Disorders, fifth edition, text revision*, DSM-V-TR, pp. 387–388 (Copyright © 2022). American Psychiatric Association. All rights reserved.

> ## CASE OF ANNE HART
> ### BULIMIA NERVOSA
>
> Anne Hart is an 18-year-old single white woman who is in her junior year at a local university. She is majoring in theater. She lives in an off-campus apartment with two female roommates and works part-time as a waitress in a local restaurant. She is very involved in athletics and is on the collegiate gymnastics team, through which she received a scholarship that has enabled her to pursue her goal of attending college. Ms. Hart initially reported that she had a largely "uneventful childhood" where she grew up in an intact family along with three older siblings, although she did acknowledge that her parents "didn't like each other." She also reported that her parents frequently engaged in loud verbal arguments for "as long as she can remember." As a result, she noted that her home environment was stressful and chaotic, where minor disagreements tended to result in "shouting matches" between family members. As a result, Ms. Hart reported that she tended to spend most of her time alone in her room or outside the home with friends. She also reported that although she was never without basic necessities while growing up, she was also aware that her parents often struggled to make ends meet, which she believes also intensified their arguments and tensions within the home.
>
> Although Ms. Hart described herself as high functioning throughout her primary and secondary school years, she also noted that she has always been somewhat shy and reserved, with a tendency to be perfectionistic about her academics and unassertive in social relationships. Ms. Hart was initially referred for therapy by her collegiate coach when she was observed to appear increasingly more dysphoric, at which time she also started to voice greater ambivalence about her future in college athletics. When presenting for therapy, Ms. Hart acknowledged that she has been feeling increasingly distressed by her problems. This has been compounded by her strong reluctance to openly share her concerns with her coach or any of her friends, especially in relation to worsening problems with her body image and concerns about maintaining the "right weight" in order to successfully compete alongside her teammates, as well as feeling trapped in remaining on the team given her financial reliance on her collegiate athletic scholarship.
>
> She indicated that her preoccupation with weight began when she was initially encouraged to lose 8 pounds in order to optimize her physical performance in athletics approximately 2 years ago. Although Ms. Hart was successful with that goal, she noted that since then she has become increasingly more preoccupied with her body weight and eating habits, which she believes were further intensified given her major in theater, where she believes there is also an emphasis on physical appearance. Although Ms. Hart reported that purging, in particular, was initially limited to times when she was actively focused on losing weight, she reported that the frequency of binge/purge cycles has progressively increased within the past year, where she now reports that she has purged several times per week in the last few months. Perhaps most distressing to Ms. Hart, she has noticed that the binge/purge cycles have been increasingly triggered at times when she is experiencing general feelings of pressure or distress, such as when dealing with academic pressures, relationship difficulties, and uncertainties related to prioritizing responsibilities and goals.
>
> Ms. Hart was diagnosed with bulimia nervosa and accepted recommendations to participate in therapy focused on eating-related issues.
>
> *Credit:* Clinical vignette provided by Sandra Testa Michelson, PhD.

Treating Bulimia Nervosa

CBT is the best-evaluated treatment for bulimia (Anderson & Maloney, 2001; Candea et al., 2018). Outcome research suggests that about 40% to 50% of those treated with CBT recover from bulimia in terms of bingeing and purging. In one randomized control treatment study, CBT was compared with psychoanalytic psychotherapy (Poulsen et al., 2014). Both therapies resulted in improvement, but CBT showed the best results. In CBT, therapy is most effective for those individuals who are willing to keep a food diary and self-monitor their feelings and thoughts concerning eating and binge–purge episodes. In two studies, those who were able to reduce purging by Session 6 showed the best outcomes (Agras et al., 2000; Fairburn et al., 2004).

CBT typically begins with a psychoeducational and monitoring phase, including discussions of regular eating. This is followed by a more cognitive phase that emphasizes techniques to eliminate binge eating and challenge obstacles to normal eating behavior. The final sessions discuss ways to cope with relapse, which is experienced by a number of individuals with bulimia. Antidepressant medications such as fluoxetine (Prozac) have been used to treat the depressive aspects of bulimia and have been shown to be more effective than a placebo. However, CBT is more effective than medication in the treatment of bulimia nervosa.

Binge Eating Disorder

Jane Brody, who writes health books and columns for the *New York Times*, has described her own experience with binge eating. She begins by telling of her first newspaper job in which she felt bored and had a difficult boss. Her answer to this was to eat, since food was associated with love and happiness for her. This started a pattern of gaining weight and going on a diet. Feeling desperate when she could not stop eating, she would fast during the day and binge eat at night. She would spend the night eating and could go through 3,000 calories in one sitting. Something sweet and then something salty—she could eat a half-gallon of ice cream and go on from there. Brody continued to gain weight until she was one-third more than her normal weight. She became suicidal. Calling a psychologist she knew at 2:00 a.m. got her into treatment. She said, "Just talking about my behavior and learning from the psychologist that I was not the only person with this problem helped relieve my despair. Still, he was not able to help me stop bingeing. That was something I would have to do on my own" (Brody, 2007).

Binge eating was a term used by Stunkard in 1959 to describe obese individuals in terms of recurrent episodes of eating excessive amounts without purging. It was not categorized as a separate disorder until *DSM-5* (Striegel-Moore & Franko, 2008). **Binge eating disorder** is characterized in *DSM-5-TR* by the consumption of large amounts of food and the sense that one cannot control their eating behavior. Although the amount of food ingested in a binge eating episode varies from person to person, it can go as high as 10,000 calories. Binge eating rates are higher in those who are overweight than those who are a normal weight. The prevalence is 2.9% in overweight individuals and 1.5% in normal weight individuals. Also, obese individuals take in a larger number of calories during binge eating and non–binge eating episodes.

There is evidence to suggest that binge eating runs in families and is not related to obesity per se. Thus, it should be considered to be different from familial obesity. It is estimated to have a lifetime prevalence rate of 3.5% in women and 2% in men (Hudson et al., 2007). Similar frequency of the disorder is seen in developed countries around the world (APA, 2022). In the United States, there are few ethnic differences found between Latino, Asian, Black, and white Americans.

In addition to binge eating and a lack of control, *DSM-5-TR* requires three of the following five criteria: (1) eating much more rapidly than normal; (2) eating until feeling uncomfortably full; (3) eating large amounts of food when not feeling physically hungry; (4) eating alone because of feeling embarrassed by how much one is eating; and (5) feeling disgusted with oneself, depressed, or very guilty after overeating.

Treating Binge Eating

Overall, the goals of treatment are to cease binge eating, to reduce negative emotions and cognitions, and to lose weight. Psychosocial treatments, especially CBT, have been shown to be effective for treating binge eating disorder. At times, other approaches such as exercise have been added to CBT treatments. Drug treatments such as the use of antidepressant medication show limited evidence of success.

UNDERSTANDING CHANGES IN *DSM-5* AND *DSM-5-TR*
EATING DISORDERS

Based on research, a number of changes were made in *DSM-5* in terms of eating disorders. One of these changes in anorexia nervosa was the removal of the requirement for not having three menstrual cycles. This was removed since not having a menstrual cycle is related more to the state of one's nutrition. Thus, it is a secondary factor to not eating. This also allowed for the disorder to be diagnosed in males. For bulimia nervosa, the frequency of binge eating and inappropriate compensatory behavior was reduced from twice a week for 3 months to at least once a week for 3 months.

One goal of *DSM-5* was to reduce the use of the diagnosis of *eating disorder not otherwise specified (EDNOS)* (Keel et al., 2012). For example, previously, in *DSM-IV*, binge eating disorder was not listed. A large proportion of individuals who would now be diagnosed with binge eating disorder were diagnosed in *DSM-IV* with an EDNOS. It was the goal of *DSM-5* to minimize the use of this category by adding binge eating disorder.

In order to determine the effects of anticipated changes to the eating disorder criteria in *DSM-5*, Eric Stice and his colleagues (2012) reclassified the female participants in an 8-year prospective community sample. This study annually assessed 496 adolescents for 8 years beginning at age 13. Overall, they found that the changes in *DSM-5* eating disorders resulted in higher prevalence rates as compared with *DSM-IV*. These findings suggest 1 in 8 young women experience some type of eating disorder before they reach the age of 21.

DSM-5 also includes a category of *other specified feeding or eating disorder*. This category includes examples of the other eating disorders but with fewer symptoms. One example is atypical anorexia nervosa in which all criteria except weight loss are met. Another example is bulimia nervosa of low frequency or limited duration. Other examples are binge eating disorder of low frequency or limited curation, purging disorder without binge eating, and night eating disorder in which excessive food is consumed after the evening meal.

From a research standpoint, Kate Fairweather-Schmidt and Tracey Wade (2014) interviewed 699 female twins three times between 12 and 20 years of age. In particular, they were interested in differences between the eating disorder categories in *DSM-IV* and *DSM-5*. Just over 10% of this sample had an eating disorder. These results were similar whether using *DSM-IV* or *DSM-5*. Further, genetic influences that were associated with traditional eating disorders such as anorexia nervosa and bulimia were also associated with similar symptoms when diagnosed as *other specified feeding or eating disorder*. The authors concluded that there is less clinical utility to the diagnosis of *other specified feeding or eating disorder*.

The changes in the eating disorders section of *DSM-5* have also brought forth more large-scale controversies. One perspective asks if mental health professionals are trying to turn some common behaviors such as overeating into mental disorders (Frances, 2013; Frances & Widiger, 2012). That is, should we view binge eating as a clinical disorder? Further, should binge eating of low frequency be included as an *other specified feeding or eating disorder*? While it is true that binge eating is seen as a part of other disorders such as bulimia nervosa and anorexia nervosa, should it be considered a disorder on its own, especially at low frequencies? Moreover, is it logical to consider binge eating a mental disorder but not label obesity as one also?

CONCEPT CHECK

- What are some of the negative consequences of eating disorders?
- How are the following factors implicated in "causing" anorexia nervosa?
  - Genetics
  - Physiological changes
  - Cultural factors
- Considering the three eating disorders described in this section—anorexia nervosa, bulimia nervosa, and binge eating disorder—answer the following questions:
  - What are the primary diagnostic criteria for each?
  - What are the prevalence rates of each in terms of lifetime and gender differences?
  - Is there a genetic component to the disorder?
  - What is the treatment of choice for each, and what do we know about the effectiveness of treatment?

SUMMARY

Eating seems simple; however, it is extremely complicated. What we eat and how we eat represent a complex relationship between all levels of human functioning, including culture, evolutionary history, genetics, our physiology, preferences, and psychological attitudes toward our appearance and that of others. Humans have had notions of ideal appearance for thousands of years, and many of the concerns they had about obesity continue to this day.

Previously, feeding disorders were considered part of a category of disorders usually first diagnosed in infancy, childhood, and adolescence. However, since feeding disorders can be seen in individuals of all ages, they were made part of a larger feeding and eating disorders category in *DSM-5*. The three major feeding disorders are (1) pica, in which the person eats something that would not be considered food; (2) rumination disorder, in which a person regurgitates food; and (3) avoidant/restrictive food intake disorder, in which an individual does not eat certain foods, which leads to such conditions as weight loss or nutritional deficiency.

Current conditions of food abundance and lack of exercise do not match our evolutionary history and can lead to obesity. Our evolutionary history may have us seeking substances that do not lead to a healthy lifestyle. However, obesity itself is not a *DSM-5* disorder. Overall, obesity is seen to result from a mismatch between the amount of calories that we eat and the amount of energy that we expend, complicated by (1) environmental factors such as family and culture, (2) psychological factors such as self-esteem or need for comfort, and (3) biological factors such as genetic makeup. In terms of the brain, a homeostatic system regulates body weight. Its basic task is to produce energy for the body. When nutrients are easily accessible, humans and other animals tend to overload with nutrients and become obese. Research points to brain processes involving the limbic system encoding the rewarding aspect of food intake along with emotional and cognitive aspects. These brain processes lead to an overconsumption of food even when the person feels full. Obesity, like drug addiction, involves disruptions in the dopamine pathways of the brain, which modulate behavioral responses to environmental cues.

According to the WHO, obesity worldwide has doubled since 1980. Data also show that from 1971 to 2006, BMI ratios in the United States increased no matter when the person was born. This suggests that the reason for the rise in the rate of obesity is not a cohort or age effect. According to the CDC, overweight and obese individuals are at higher risk for a number of physical disorders. Depression has also been linked to obesity. In addition to an individual's actual weight, there is the person's attitude toward their weight. In some cultures, being heavier in weight is seen as positive, whereas in others, it is thinness that is sought. Men and women think about their weight differently. Studies around the world have shown that women tend to overestimate their weight, whereas men tend to underestimate their weight.

The three major eating disorders in *DSM-5-TR* are anorexia nervosa, bulimia, and binge eating disorder. There is good evidence that eating disorders have a partial genetic component. Those with eating disorders experience a number of serious medical conditions related to reducing body weight or purging.

DSM-5-TR criteria for a diagnosis of anorexia nervosa include a restriction of food that results in a weight that is below normal, a fear of gaining weight, and a lack of recognition of the seriousness of current body weight along with a distortion of how body weight is experienced. The body image distortion has been described as having a perceptual, an emotional, and a cognitive component, and research shows that each component involves different areas of the brain. *DSM-5-TR* describes two subtypes of anorexia: (1) the restricting type and (2) the binge eating or purging type.

Individuals with anorexia tend to have certain personality characteristics that can be thought of as an endophenotype: (1) anxious with anxiety that exists before the onset of anorexia nervosa and continues even after treatment; (2) perfectionistic with an overemphasis on self-imposed standards; (3) having difficulty in flexibility and changing rule structures; and (4) obsessive around order, exactness, and symmetry. Individuals with anorexia nervosa develop a variety of medical problems that may be related to lack of nutrition and changes in hormones. The specific causes of anorexia nervosa are still being researched. However, there appear to be a variety of factors involved, including genetics, physiological factors resulting from restricting the intake of food, and cultural factors.

Anorexia nervosa is seen as one of the most difficult disorders to treat. Many individuals with anorexia do not want to be treated. The disorder itself results in psychological and physiological changes, and many individuals deny that they actually have a disorder. One of the first tasks for someone to heal from anorexia nervosa is to gain weight. This often requires a hospital stay. Psychological or family therapy is typically the next step. Family therapy has good success with adolescents. With adults, CBT has been shown to be an effective approach. Currently, there is no good evidence to suggest a critical role for medication in the treatment of anorexia nervosa.

There are three major characteristics of bulimia nervosa: (1) binge eating in which the person consumes large amounts of food; (2) purging where a person eliminates food from the body by such means as vomiting, taking laxatives, diuretics, or enemas; and (3) a psychological aspect in which one's self-worth is seen in relation to one's weight or body shape. Bulimia nervosa can also lead to secondary medical problems related to vomiting and the overuse of medications such as laxatives. CBT is more effective than medication in the treatment of bulimia nervosa.

Binge eating disorder is characterized by the consumption of large amounts of food and the sense that one cannot control their eating behavior. It is more prevalent in those who are overweight than in those who are of normal weight. There is evidence to suggest that binge eating runs in families and is not related to obesity per se. Overall, the goals of treatment are to cease binge eating, to reduce negative emotions and cognitions, and to lose weight. Psychosocial treatments, especially CBT, have been shown to be effective. At times, other approaches such as exercise have been added to CBT treatments. Drug treatments such as the use of antidepressant medication show limited evidence of success.

STUDY RESOURCES

Review Questions

1. What we eat and how we eat represent a complex relationship between all levels of human functioning, including culture, evolutionary history, genetics, our physiology, preferences, and psychological attitudes toward our appearance and that of others. What is an example of each of these levels?

2. Historically, feeding disorders were categorized with other childhood disorders; now they are part of a more general feeding and eating disorders grouping. What are some of the advantages of this change? Are there any disadvantages, and if so, what are they?

3. "Researchers have asked if similar mechanisms are involved in both obesity and drug addiction." What evidence can you cite to support the position that obesity is like drug addiction? Does the evidence convince you? Why or why not?

4. What is it about eating disorders that makes them so difficult to treat? If you were asked to put together an awareness program about eating disorders targeting a college-age audience, what information would you include, and what approach would you take?

For Further Reading

Centers for Disease Control and Prevention. (2023, February 15). *Food assistance and food systems resources*. U.S. Department of Health and Human Services. https://www.cdc.gov/nutrition/

Centers for Disease Control and Prevention. (2023, January 5). *Obesity and overweight*. U.S. Department of Health and Human Services. https://www.cdc.gov/nchs/fastats/obesity-overweight.htm

Eating Disorder Hope. (2023). *Maudsley method family therapy*. https://www.eatingdisorderhope.com/treatment-for-eating-disorders/therapies/maudsley-method

Hornbacher, M. (2014). *Wasted: A memoir of anorexia and bulimia* (Updated ed.). Harper Perennial.

Le Grange, D., & Lock, J. (Eds.). (2011). *Eating disorders in children and adolescents: A clinical handbook*. Guilford Press.

National Heart, Lung, and Blood Institute. (n.d.). *Calculate your body mass index*. U.S. Department of Health and Human Services. https://www.nhlbi.nih.gov/health/educational/lose_wt/BMI/bmicalc.htm

Office of Disease Prevention and Health Promotion. (2023, July 26). *Eat healthy*. U.S. Department of Health and Human Services. https://health.gov/myhealthfinder/health-conditions/diabetes/eat-healthy

Taylor, K. (Ed.). (2008). *Going hungry*. Anchor Books.

World Health Organization. (2021, June 9). *Obesity and overweight* [Fact sheet]. www.who.int/mediacentre/factsheets/fs311/en/

KEY TERMS

- anorexia nervosa
- avoidant/restrictive food intake disorder
- binge eating disorder
- bulimia nervosa
- eating disorders
- feeding disorders
- Maudsley approach
- obesity
- pica
- purging
- rumination disorder

11 SEXUAL DISORDERS, PARAPHILIC DISORDERS, AND GENDER DYSPHORIA

LEARNING OBJECTIVES

- 11.1 Discuss the scientific approach to human sexuality from a historical perspective.
- 11.2 Summarize the major scientific findings about human sexual desire, arousal, and response.
- 11.3 Distinguish among the sexual dysfunction disorders and treatments.
- 11.4 Distinguish among the paraphilic dysfunction disorders and treatments.
- 11.5 Discuss the development, characteristics, and prevalence of gender dysphoria.

> I am not talking about my many—indeed many thousands—instances of lusting after girls' and women's bodies while giving little thought to relating to them as persons. As I noted before, frotteurism was a ubiquitous part of my life from my fifteenth year to my nineteenth year—during which time I bestrode the New York subways (and many of my female fellow passengers) with vim, vigor, and vitality. Lusting after women's fore and aft parts is only moderately reprehensible. Debatably, it can be viewed as minimally harassing as long as one keeps one's big mouth shut—which I invariably did.
>
> From Albert Ellis (with Debbie Joffe-Ellis), *All Out! An Autobiography* (2010), p. 302.

> Many people may not understand how, being born female, I can state with total clarity and certainty that as a child I felt like a boy. That's mainly because most people don't know the difference between gender and gender identity. Gender is the sex that one is born as, and for most of us that sex is either female or male. Your gender identity, however, is based on feelings and not biology. I like to say that your gender identity is between your ears, not between your legs. I am here to attest to the fact that you can be born one sex and yet feel with every fiber of your being that you really are the opposite. And as a kid, it was no more complicated to me than this: I felt like a little boy.
>
> From Chaz Bono, *Transition: The Story of How I Became a Man* (2011).

The World Health Organization (WHO) estimates that more than 100 million acts of sexual intercourse between humans take place each day around the world. Thus, sexuality is a driving force in humans, as it is in other species. However, unlike most other species, humans engage in sexual intercourse while looking at one another. This suggests that sexual activity has an important pair-bonding and social component for humans beyond that of procreation. In fact, studies of sexuality across the life span show that both sexual and nonsexual responses to one's partner influence the relationship in a positive manner, which is seen in both men and women (Dewitte et al., 2015). In particular, positive feelings about the relationship predicted more sexual activity and intimacy in both men and women.

Humans also spend more time in the sex act itself than other species do. For example, unlike male chimpanzees who go from penile penetration to ejaculation in only 90 seconds, humans take around 7 minutes preceded by 12 minutes of foreplay (Miller & Byers, 2004). Seven out of 10 American adults questioned reported spending 15 minutes to 1 hour overall making love. Other species, such as some primates, engage in sexual activity only when there is a high probability of producing offspring. Humans, on the other hand, can and do engage in sexual activity at any time. Overall, humans use the internal experience of sexual arousal and the external experience of sexual activity for a variety of purposes (LeVay & Baldwin, 2012). Some of these experiences enhance people and their relationships with themselves and others. Other sexual experiences, on the other hand, can lead to distress.

In this chapter, these various aspects of sexuality will be discussed. The chapter then concludes with a section on gender dysphoria, with considerations about one's biological gender, the gender that one is attracted to, and the gender that one feels oneself to be.

SEXUALITY IN CONTEXT

Sexuality is more than the sexual experience itself. WHO describes sexuality as

> a central aspect of being human throughout life [that] encompasses sex, gender identities and roles, sexual orientation, eroticism, pleasure, intimacy and reproduction. Sexuality is experienced and expressed in thoughts, fantasies, desires, beliefs, attitudes, values, behaviors, practices, roles and relationships. While sexuality can include all of these dimensions, not all of them are always experienced or expressed. Sexuality is influenced by the interaction of biological, psychological, social, economic, political, cultural, legal, historical, religious and spiritual factors. (World Health Organization, 2023)

In this section, you will learn about sexuality as seen and practiced by humans. Let us begin with a historical perspective and then move to data concerning the sexual activity of Americans. Later in the chapter, *Cultural LENS: Sexuality and the Clashing of Cultures* examines sexual practices from a cultural perspective.

Historical Perspectives

Humans have depicted sexual activities in paintings and carvings for thousands of years. Some of the more famous are the Etruscan ceramic plates showing a variety of sexual positions dating from some 2,500 years ago in Italy. With the excavation of Pompeii and Herculaneum near Naples, Italy, a variety of scenes were discovered on the walls in the cities that graphically depicted sexual activities. These towns were covered by volcanic ash when Mount Vesuvius erupted in 79 CE. Similar sexual illustrations have been found throughout the world.

However, at certain times, some cultures have seen sexual activity as a negative force in human life. In the 18th and 19th centuries in Europe and the United States, there were

Erotic collection fresco from Pompeii
funkyfood London—Paul Williams/Alamy Stock Photo

those in the medical profession who suggested that sexual stimulation, especially masturbation, could lead to mental illness. In the 1800s, both graham crackers and unsweetened corn flakes were introduced as aids for reducing sexual desire. John Kellogg was a physician who ran the Battle Creek Sanitarium in Michigan and crusaded against masturbation and supported sexual abstinence. The approach at the sanitarium included a holistic approach to medicine. However, when John's brother Will suggested adding sugar to the corn flakes, a decade-long feud commenced. Will created a separate company and sold corn flakes with sugar.

In the 1800s, a number of scientists began to approach sexuality from a scientific perspective. Charles Darwin presented the manner in which sexual selection and self-preservation were important instincts seen across many species. Sigmund Freud emphasized the way in which sexuality was an important driving force in humans. Havelock Ellis in England was one of the first to study human sexuality itself. From 1897 to 1910, Ellis published a series of books titled *Studies in the Psychology of Sex*. In these books, he suggested that variations in sexuality should be viewed statistically in terms of frequency. He also suggested that variations in sexual practices had their roots in normal sexual practices. Ellis also went against a common notion at that time and suggested that women—like men—have sexual desires and seek and enjoy sex. Further, he suggested that a gay or lesbian orientation was a normal variation of human sexuality and should not be viewed as a disorder. He also suggested that tendencies toward same-sex attraction were present at birth.

In the 1930s, Alfred Kinsey, a zoologist, was asked to teach a course on marriage. In preparing for the course, Kinsey realized that little was known about the sexual behavior of Americans. Further, students found it difficult to obtain factual information free of moral or social perspectives. This led Kinsey to conduct a large-scale survey of some 12,000 individuals across the United States. The results of these surveys were published in two books: *Sexual Behavior in the Human Male* (Kinsey, 1948) and *Sexual Behavior in the Human Female* (Kinsey, 1953). In 1947, the Institute for Sex Research was established at Indiana University with Alfred Kinsey as director. This was later renamed the Kinsey Institute, and it continues performing research related to sexuality today (see For Further Reading).

The original Kinsey survey focused on six different outlets to sexual orgasm, which were described at the time as masturbation, petting, nocturnal dreams, heterosexual coitus, homosexual behaviors, and bestiality. These six outlets were related in terms of frequency to various socioeconomic variables such as age, education, marital status, occupation, and religious identification. The prevailing cultural myth in this era was that women engaged in sex merely for procreative purposes or to please their partners, who were generally men. Many Americans in the 1950s were shocked to learn that women are as capable as men of sexual response. Further, 50% of the women interviewed had engaged in premarital coitus, and 25% had engaged in extramarital sex. In addition, 84% of the men and 69% of the women reported being aroused by sexual fantasies. Also, 89% of the men and 64% of the women used fantasy as part of masturbation. Even more shocking to some was the number of men and women who reported they had masturbated (92% for men and 62% for women). Some newspapers and magazines refused to publish stories about this survey and its data. Some lawmakers even suggested it undermined the moral fiber of the nation. In the 1960s, William Masters and Virginia Johnson began actual studies of the human sexual response itself in both men and women. Since that time, a number of journals have focused on sexual behaviors as well as psychological and physiological responses involved in sexual activity. These will be discussed later in this chapter.

Recent Studies on the Sexual Activities of Americans

To understand sexual disorders, it is important to gain a perspective on sexual activities in the general population. From 2011 to 2013, the Centers for Disease Control and Prevention (CDC) performed a survey that included face-to-face interviews with a national sample of 10,416 men and women in the United States. In order to obtain more accurate information, the information in this survey related to sexuality was collected using a laptop computer without the participant communicating directly with the interviewer.

As can be seen in Figure 11.1, among a sample of 9,175 men and women 18 to 44 years of age, 92% of men and 94% of women have had vaginal intercourse with a member of the opposite sex. Further, 87% of men and 86% of women have had oral sex with a member of the opposite sex. The percentage of people who had had anal sex with the opposite sex was lower: 42% for men and 36% for women. In this survey, the percentage of those who had had same-sex contact was 7% for men and 17% for women (Copen et al., 2016).

According to the National Survey of Sexual Health and Behavior (NSSHB) conducted in 2009, 2012, 2014, 2015, 2016, and 2018 by Indiana University's Center for Sexual Health Promotion, about 8% of men and 7% of women identify as gay, lesbian, or bisexual (see For Further Reading). Further, more women than men see themselves as bisexual (about 3.6% vs. 2.5%).

In 2017, the Center for Sexual Health Promotion published the results of the 2015 NSSHB, which included descriptions of more than 40 combinations of sexual acts that people perform during sexual events, the use of condoms, and the percentage of Americans participating in same-sex encounters. The survey, which gathered information from 2,021 adults ages 18 to 70+, shows that sexual activity continues across the life span and that humans engage in a variety of types of sexual acts (see Table 11.1;

FIGURE 11.1 ■ Sexual Activities Ever Engaged in by Americans, 2011–2013

This figure shows the percentage of American men and women 18 to 44 years of age who have ever engaged in various types of sexual contact.

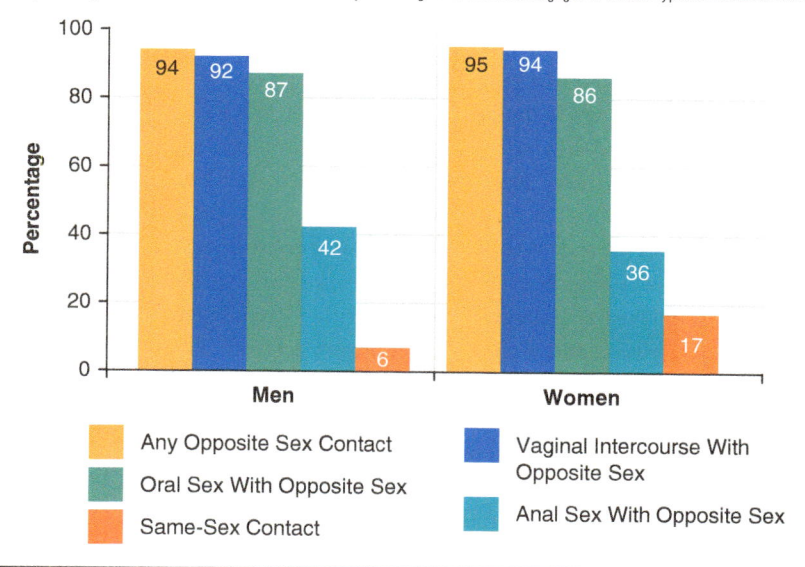

Category	Men	Women
Any Opposite Sex Contact	94	95
Vaginal Intercourse With Opposite Sex	92	94
Oral Sex With Opposite Sex	87	86
Anal Sex With Opposite Sex	42	36
Same-Sex Contact	6	17

Source: Copen, C. E., Chandra, A., & Febo-Vazquez, I. (2016, January 7). *Sexual behavior, sexual attraction, and sexual orientation among adults aged 18–44 in the United States: Data from the 2011–2013 National Survey of Family Growth* (National Health Statistics Reports No. 88). U.S. Department of Health and Human Services. https://www.cdc.gov/nchs//data/nhsr/nhsr088.pdf

TABLE 11.1 Percentage of Americans Performing Certain Sexual Behaviors in the Past Year and Across Their Lifetime

	Total (%)	Total Men	Men (%) 18–24	25–29	30–39	40–49	50–59	60–69	70+	Total Women	Women (%) 18–24	25–29	30–39	40–49	50–59	60–69	70+
Vaginal intercourse																	
Past month	52.4	52.1	39.3	68.9	63.2	62.3	49.1	44.1	37.2	52.6	52.1	72.6	77.3	62.0	52.8	32.6	14.6
Past year	64.1	65.8	53.3	74.4	74.9	79.3	65.6	57.5	50.6	62.4	62.1	83.6	85.3	74.2	64.5	39.3	23.8
Lifetime	88.5	85.6	59.4	87.4	85.0	90.2	90.6	93.2	87.4	91.1	65.8	90.9	92.7	92.5	95.0	94.1	96.1
Gave partner oral sex																	
Past month	34.9	34.0	32.9	50.7	41.5	34.0	36.8	21.7	21.4	35.7	44.7	53.5	53.0	41.6	31.9	19.7	8.0
Past year	54.6	56.7	49.5	69.4	71.3	67.9	57.7	42.3	33.7	52.6	57.3	76.4	73.8	63.0	54.3	27.4	15.2
Lifetime	82.7	83.0	61.3	84.8	88.2	88.4	87.9	86.8	76.1	82.5	62.3	85.5	89.0	89.0	86.4	85.1	66.9
Received oral sex																	
Past month	35.0	38.4	36.4	66.0	44.9	42.4	36.7	27.9	19.2	31.8	35.8	48.1	51.3	34.7	28.3	17.0	8.5
Past year	54.8	60.9	61.7	76.1	71.0	75.1	59.6	46.2	33.4	49.2	59.7	69.5	68.7	54.9	49.4	27.7	16.2
Lifetime	84.8	85.0	67.1	89.2	88.3	92.2	89.1	88.4	74.1	84.6	64.2	87.4	87.9	89.9	87.3	88.0	76.9
Insertive anal sex																	
Past month	–	5.7	2.7	8.1	10.1	8.7	6.3	1.4	0.8	–	–	–	–	–	–	–	–
Past year	–	15.2	12.4	21.1	26.1	21.9	12.7	7.5	3.4	–	–	–	–	–	–	–	–
Lifetime	–	42.6	20.2	44.3	55.1	57.9	45.3	35.5	29.7	–	–	–	–	–	–	–	–
Received anal sex																	
Past month	3.5	2.5	7.2	3.3	3.9	0.4	2.2	0.7	1.4	4.4	6.7	9.9	5.0	5.0	5.0	0.6	0.0
Past year	8.7	5.3	8.9	5.6	10.5	7.0	2.6	1.2	1.4	11.8	17.0	25.5	18.3	14.7	9.8	1.2	0.0
Lifetime	23.8	9.3	9.8	5.6	15.4	11.3	7.7	7.2	6.4	37.3	27.7	41.2	46.2	44.2	39.9	33.6	20.1

(Continued)

TABLE 11.1 ■ Percentage of Americans Performing Certain Sexual Behaviors in the Past Year and Across Their Lifetime *(Continued)*

	Total (%)	Total Men	Men (%)							Total Women	Women (%)						
			18–24	25–29	30–39	40–49	50–59	60–69	70+		18–24	25–29	30–39	40–49	50–59	60–69	70+
Worn sexy underwear or lingerie for a partner*																	
Past month	10.3	3.0	3.9	8.4	2.3	1.4	3.8	1.8	0.8	16.9	23.9	29.5	27.0	15.1	16.3	7.2	2.6
Past year	22.7	8.9	8.2	17.7	10.1	10.4	8.6	6.4	1.9	35.5	45.9	63.3	55.0	36.1	31.7	15.1	7.1
Lifetime	51.8	26.2	13.5	23.5	30.8	33.3	33.9	28.1	10.1	75.4	61.9	81.0	85.2	75.0	00.8	72.8	61.4
Had sex with someone in public place																	
Past month	1.2	1.5	1.2	3.7	0.0	3.0	1.4	0.7	0.7	0.9	0.0	4.9	0.7	0.5	0.6	0.0	0.0
Past year	5.3	6.0	11.0	12.5	2.9	7.5	4.7	3.7	1.9	4.7	7.4	12.7	6.3	4.7	4.2	0.0	0.0
Lifetime	44.1	45.4	21.2	49.6	42.2	59.9	53.9	47.1	32.8	42.9	27.0	49.2	50.9	52.8	51.3	38.1	16.1
Tied up your partner or been tied up as part of sex																	
Past month	1.3	1.4	3.1	4.1	1.6	0.4	1.1	0.6	0.0	1.3	2.4	4.2	3.8	0.0	0.0	0.0	0.0
Past year	4.5	4.3	7.9	15.1	3.8	3.2	2.5	1.4	0.3	4.8	7.6	15.0	8.4	1.9	3.8	0.0	0.0
Lifetime	21.1	21.7	11.7	40.7	25.9	31.4	19.5	15.0	8.2	20.6	14.7	30.8	34.2	20.3	26.4	7.9	5.2
Sucked/licked partner's feet/toes*																	
Past month	1.6	2.3	1.3	5.3	3.7	1.5	3.6	0.0	0.8	0.9	2.0	2.1	1.5	0.5	0.4	0.5	0.0
Past year	5.3	8.3	6.2	14.3	8.3	10.3	11.9	1.8	3.9	2.6	2.0	8.1	4.0	1.6	1.8	1.5	0.0
Lifetime	18.0	25.6	14.6	28.6	25.5	28.7	33.1	27.1	15.6	10.9	5.1	12.3	14.4	11.7	13.1	8.8	6.8
Masturbated with someone else (spouse, boy/girlfriend, friend, someone else)																	
Past month	18.8	18.4	21.9	19.6	18.8	24.0	19.0	13.7	9.6	19.1	21.6	30.9	30.8	24.3	16.5	9.3	0.7
Past year	33.2	35.5	35.8	43.0	49.4	48.3	28.9	25.1	16.8	31.1	27.6	50.7	51.7	38.1	29.9	13.8	3.2
Lifetime	55.2	57.5	46.2	62.2	69.6	71.4	55.8	48.0	44.0	53.1	42.0	62.8	70.0	67.7	56.7	42.6	18.0

	Total (%)	Total Men	Men (%)							Total Women	Women (%)						
			18–24	25–29	30–39	40–49	50–59	60–69	70+		18–24	25–29	30–39	40–49	50–59	60–69	70+
Masturbated in front of partner																	
Past month	10.2	10.7	10.0	16.6	11.2	13.2	10.3	8.4	5.5	9.8	7.2	25.0	19.2	9.2	7.8	1.0	0.7
Past year	20.6	21.3	17.0	28.8	25.9	31.0	19.9	12.8	11.7	19.8	18.3	40.0	32.4	27.1	16.2	5.7	0.7
Lifetime	41.5	43.7	24.8	49.7	56.3	56.2	44.2	42.9	24.1	39.4	25.1	53.4	55.3	55.4	42.5	25.3	7.6
Role played with partner																	
Past month	2.2	2.6	3.7	7.1	2.3	3.5	2.4	0.6	0.0	1.7	3.9	4.2	2.5	1.2	1.1	0.7	0.0
Past year	7.6	8.1	12.9	17.1	6.1	10.2	8.5	2.3	1.1	7.2	7.6	13.3	13.8	5.3	5.7	4.3	0.9
Lifetime	23.7	25.8	19.2	38.7	27.6	35.0	26.6	18.3	12.9	21.8	14.7	31.0	33.8	22.3	24.8	13.9	7.1
Playfully whipped or been whipped by partner as part of sex																	
Past month	2.5	2.2	4.6	3.8	2.3	3.1	2.1	0.0	0.0	2.7	2.3	9.3	5.4	3.3	0.4	0.0	0.0
Past year	6.0	5.6	6.9	12.9	5.6	6.3	5.9	3.1	0.0	6.4	6.7	15.6	14.1	6.9	3.1	0.6	0.0
Lifetime	15.0	16.2	9.2	22.7	17.9	23.8	18.3	13.3	4.1	13.8	8.4	30.3	20.4	18.3	10.4	7.2	2.6
Spanked or been spanked as part of sex																	
Past month	8.1	6.1	9.2	15.2	12.4	5.7	2.8	0.5	0.3	10.0	23.2	25.4	17.9	7.5	4.3	0.7	0.0
Past year	17.2	14.2	13.4	39.2	27.5	13.6	8.7	3.8	0.3	20.0	40.3	50.8	37.0	16.4	10.2	0.7	0.0
Lifetime	31.9	29.5	16.8	49.4	46.0	41.2	25.9	18.3	7.4	34.1	46.0	58.8	56.6	39.5	27.3	11.9	5.2

Credit: Herbenick, D., Bowling, J., Fu, T. J., Dodge, B., Guerra-Reyes, L., & Sanders, S. (2017, July 20). Sexual diversity in the United States: Results from a nationally representative probability sample of adult women and men. *PLOS ONE.* https://doi.org/10.1371/journal.pone.0181198, licensed under CC BY 4.0 https://creativecommons.org/licenses/by/4.0/.

Herbenick et al., 2017). It should be noted that the CDC study asked if a person had ever performed a specific sexual act, whereas the Center for Sexual Health Promotion study asked if the sexual act had been performed in the past 12 months as well as in one's lifetime.

> **CONCEPT CHECK**
>
> - What were the contributions of the following scientists in advancing our understanding of sexuality from a scientific perspective?
>   - Charles Darwin
>   - Sigmund Freud
>   - Havelock Ellis
>   - Alfred Kinsey
> - What have we learned about the sexual attitudes and behaviors of Americans from comprehensive surveys? Are you surprised by these results? What would you have expected?

SEXUAL DESIRE, AROUSAL, AND RESPONSE

The scientific literature has described the desire for sex in various ways, using words such as *drive, arousal, need, desire, obsession*, and *motivation*. Heiman and Pfaff (2011) have attempted to clarify these descriptions in terms of sexual activity. *Arousal* has traditionally been seen as a general term in relation to central nervous system activity. An organism can be aroused or triggered without being sexually motivated. However, sexual motivation and arousal go together. *Motivation* has been described in terms of an organism performing an act that has a positive reward. A related concept is that of *drive*, which traditionally reflects a state of need. In this sense, hunger or thirst is seen as a drive when the organism lacks food or water, and this is reflected in internal physiological processes. Freud and Havelock Ellis described sex as a drive, although current theories suggest this concept may not be appropriate in explaining human sexuality. Human sexuality also carries with it a social or pair-bonding relationship that moves it beyond a simple drive.

Since the term *sexual arousal* was introduced to the scientific literature in the 1930s, it has referred to a number of distinct processes (Janssen, 2011; Sachs, 2007). It has been used in a psychological sense to refer to the internal experience of both cognitive and emotional processes. It has also been used in a physiological sense to refer to hormonal changes, brain changes, and changes in sexual organs related to blood flow. It is also the case that the subjective experience of arousal and genital physiological responses and arousal may not go together. In terms of gender differences, men show a higher correlation between genital responses and subjective sexual arousal than women; in other words, if a man achieves orgasm, he is satisfied (Chivers et al., 2011). Women, on the other hand, do not always show a direct relationship between arousal and satisfaction. Female sexual arousal is a multifaceted process that includes emotional, behavioral, and physiological components (Velten et al., 2016). This has led some researchers to suggest that women are more sensitive to the situational context in which sexual activity takes place than are men.

Like many human processes, sexual arousal and desire take place on a number of levels in a complex manner. Through certain cognitive-level considerations, an individual may increase desire or choose to inhibit sexual activity. Thoughts, images, and other human cognitive processes, for instance, can either increase or decrease desire. This level of functioning is only beginning to be understood in terms of sexual disorders. There are also emotional-level experiences, which may include joy and love, contained within the sexual experience. There is also the physical level of functioning, which includes the activities involved in sexual encounters. More recent research is beginning to examine arousal and desire in the LGBTQ community. Although this research is limited, it reports similar responses (Nimbi et al., 2020; Nimbi et al., 2023). Our experience of sexual arousal and desire also involves our culture, as shown in *Cultural LENS: Sexuality and the Clashing of Cultures*.

CULTURAL LENS
SEXUALITY AND THE CLASHING OF CULTURES

From an evolutionary perspective, all humans seek sexual experiences. Let us begin with the culture of the U.S. college student (McAnulty, 2012). Over the past 100 years, relationships between college students in the United States have gone from "dating" to "hooking up." In between were periods of openness and free love in the 1960s. By the 1970s, few colleges tried to "protect" women with required curfews, as most had done for decades. Co-ed dorms were set up in many colleges, and the enactment of similar rules for both men and women and other changes within the culture led to a greater sense of empowerment. Rates of premarital sex among 20-year-olds increased from 48% in the 1950s to 65% in the 1960s to over 70% for the rest of the century (Finer, 2007).

Eleventh-century carving on the Rajarani temple, known as the love temple, in Bhubaneshwar, India.

ephotocorp/Alamy Stock Photo

According to recent studies on college students, 61% of young women and 70% of young men report having initiated sex within 6 months of beginning a relationship (McAnulty, 2012). For a variety of reasons, there is less research on the sexual activity of LGBTQ individuals and their dating practices. Although the popular press emphasizes "hooking up" (i.e., meeting up purely for sex) among college students, surveys indicate it is less frequent than suggested, and what begins as a hooking-up experience does not always lead to sexual intercourse. In addition, it is estimated that 24% of college students are virgins.

> Both implicit and explicit rules related to sexuality vary greatly from culture to culture. Some nonindustrialized cultures encourage adolescents to experiment with and engage in sex play, whereas others discourage any display of public affection. Among the industrial countries, Europe, Australia, and the United States report the greatest satisfaction with sexual experiences, and East Asian countries report the least (Laumann et al., 2006). There is also a strong association between relationship satisfaction and sexual satisfaction. This is reflected in a WHO report that a quarter of married couples in Japan had not had sex in the past year, whereas the Kinsey Institute reported a 5% to 10% rate for American couples (although the rate goes up after age 50 in the United States). Likewise, in one survey, the average number of times a 16- to 45-year-old in Hong Kong had sex in a year was 57 compared with 138 times for an American and 141 for a French person ("Durex Global Sex Surveys," 1996, 1998).
>
> Although people in all cultures find mates and engage in sexual behaviors, the ease of migration throughout the world brings together a plethora of attitudes toward sexual relationships. This has occasionally resulted in conflict. For example, Germany has banned forced marriage, a custom of some of its immigrants. In 2006, the Netherlands introduced changes in its immigration laws. One change requires that those seeking to immigrate to the Netherlands watch a 108-minute film that depicts nudity at a beach and same-sex couples kissing. The basic idea is that people who seek to move to the Netherlands should understand the types of acceptable sexual attitudes and activities in the country. Although all humans share a search for sexuality, culture shapes this process.
>
> ### Thought Question
>
> What are some of the methods different cultures use to shape sexuality among their people? Give some specific examples.

One important research question across the cognitive, emotional, and physical levels has to do with the manner in which measurements can be made. With the advent of psychophysiological techniques to measure blood flow in sexual organs, a different type of precision is possible. However, as with a number of psychophysiological measures, the relationship between changes in physiology and the experienced cognitions and feelings may not be exact. More recently, measures of brain activity using such brain imaging techniques as electroencephalography (EEG) and functional magnetic resonance imaging (fMRI) have allowed for an understanding of cortical involvement. Sexual response in a variety of species is related to specific external signals tied to the possibility of conception. Humans, on the other hand, can also respond to internal thoughts and continued sexual arousal even without external stimuli.

In the popular media, men are often portrayed as thinking about sex much more often than women. However, clear research evidence for this has not been available. In order to study the differences between men and women in terms of cognition, college students were asked to click a small counter every time they thought about sex, food, and sleep (Fisher et al., 2012). These data showed that men did indeed think more about sex than women. However, they also thought more about food and about sleep than women did. Thus, the gender differences may relate to appetites in general rather than a specific domain.

In studies of sexual orientation, including both straight and LGBTQ individuals, it has been shown that different groups are aroused by different types of stimuli. One study examined self-reported arousal in men as well as changes in penis size in relation to videos of explicit sexual interactions (Cerny & Janssen, 2011). Men who identified themselves as straight, gay, or bisexual were asked to watch videos of men and women engaging in sex, men engaging in sex, and scenes including both men and women in bisexual encounters. As in previous research, straight males showed the most changes in erections and self-report arousal in response to the videos of men and women engaging in sex. They also showed the least changes in response to the videos of men engaging in sex. Both bisexual and gay men showed similar changes in response to the videos of men engaging in sex. However, the bisexual men showed the greatest changes in response to the bisexual videos. In another study, lesbians showed more sexual arousal in response to same-sex stimuli than to other-sex stimuli (Rieger et al., 2016). Another study using fMRI found that lesbians showed more subjective and neural responses to stimuli involving women than did bisexual or heterosexual women (Safron et al., 2018). Overall, this research suggests that men and women show both subjective and physiological arousal in a manner that is consistent with their sexual orientation.

Your Brain and Sexual Activity

Brain imaging studies allow for cortical measures of arousal in addition to self-report and blood flow changes in sexual organs. Overall, when both men and women achieve orgasm, there are changes in the brain. In males, areas involved in vigilance shut down. Positron emission tomography (PET) studies show that when males experience ejaculation, the same areas of the midbrain (e.g., the ventral tegmental area [VTA]) show activity as when a person takes heroin. In females, orgasm results in areas involved in controlling thoughts and emotions becoming silent (Portner, 2008).

Antonio Ferretti and his colleagues (2005) showed males erotic videos in an fMRI scanner. By using longer videos, these researchers were able to measure changes in penile tumescence, or erection, along with self-reports of arousal and fMRI data. In comparison with a sports film, the erotic video was associated with brain changes in the inferior parietal lobule and precuneus, cuneus, extrastriatal visual cortices, frontal cortices, hippocampus, and amygdala (Figure 11.2). Further, specific areas of the brain were correlated with the transition from no erection to the beginning of erection to a full erection. These areas include the anterior cingulate, insula, amygdala, hypothalamus, and secondary somatosensory cortices. Overall, the processing of sexual arousal engages complex brain networks involving cognitive, emotional, and self processes.

Do men and women look at different aspects of a picture depicting sexual activity? One way to answer this question is to use eye tracking, which measures where a person looks when viewing stimuli in real time. One study suggests that both males and females look at the bodies rather than the faces of opposite-sex nudes (Lykins et al., 2006). In another study, while viewing sexually explicit photographs of heterosexual couples engaged in intercourse or oral sex, males spent more time looking at the face of the female, whereas females spent more time looking at genitals (Rupp & Wallen, 2007). Females who were taking birth control pills spent less time looking at the sexual characteristics of the picture. These females also spent less time looking at sexually related characteristics in nonsexual pictures (Nielsen & Pernice, 2008). From an evolutionary perspective, this suggests that there is a close relationship between what attracts one's attention and the ability to conceive.

FIGURE 11.2 ■ Differences Evident in the Brain When Watching Erotic Videos Versus Sports Videos

This figure shows cortical areas that are significantly more active (larger fMRI BOLD signal) during erotic as compared with sport visual stimulation in video clips. Light and dark gray indicate folds (gyri) and grooves (sulci), respectively.

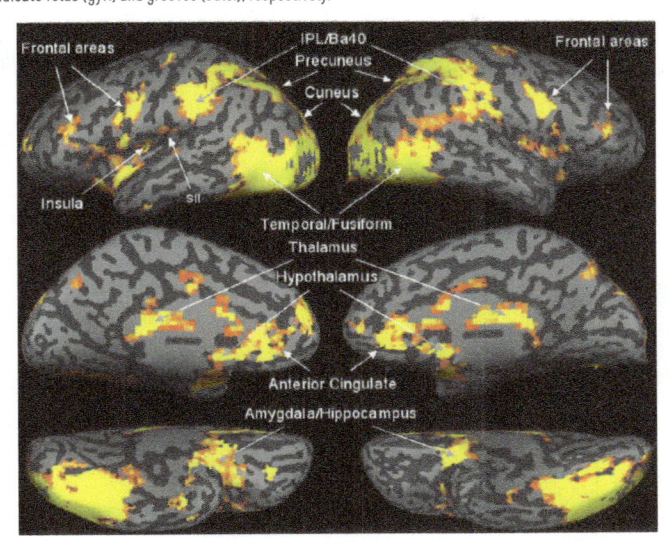

Credit: Ferretti, A., Caulo, M., Del Gratta, C., Di Matteo, R., Merla, A., Montorsi, F., . . . Romani, G. (2005). Dynamics of male sexual arousal: Distinct components of brain activation revealed by fMRI. *NeuroImage, 26,* 1086–1096. p. 1090, with permission from Elsevier.

Normal Sexual Functioning

Although sexual activity has been studied in animals for at least 200 years, human laboratory studies were first undertaken in the 1960s by William Masters and Virginia Johnson. Before this time, little was known concerning what happens to human bodies as we become aroused and engage in sexual activity. In order to understand these processes, Masters and Johnson created instruments that were able to film and measure changes in male and female sexual responsiveness during arousal and sex. Masters and Johnson also studied clinical populations to help treat sexual and reproductive problems. Their major books include *Human Sexual Response* (1966), *Human Sexual Inadequacy* (1970), and *Homosexuality in Perspective* (1979). Figures 11.3 through 11.5 show male and female anatomy in relation to sexual functioning.

In studying the sexual responses of males and females, Masters and Johnson (1966) realized that there was a similarity in how men and women experienced sexual activity. They identified four phases of human sexual response: (1) excitement, (2) plateau, (3) orgasm, and (4) resolution (Figures 11.6 and 11.7). The four phases of sexual response can be described on a variety of levels. The two main ones are blood flow, which is referred to

FIGURE 11.3 ■ Male Reproductive System

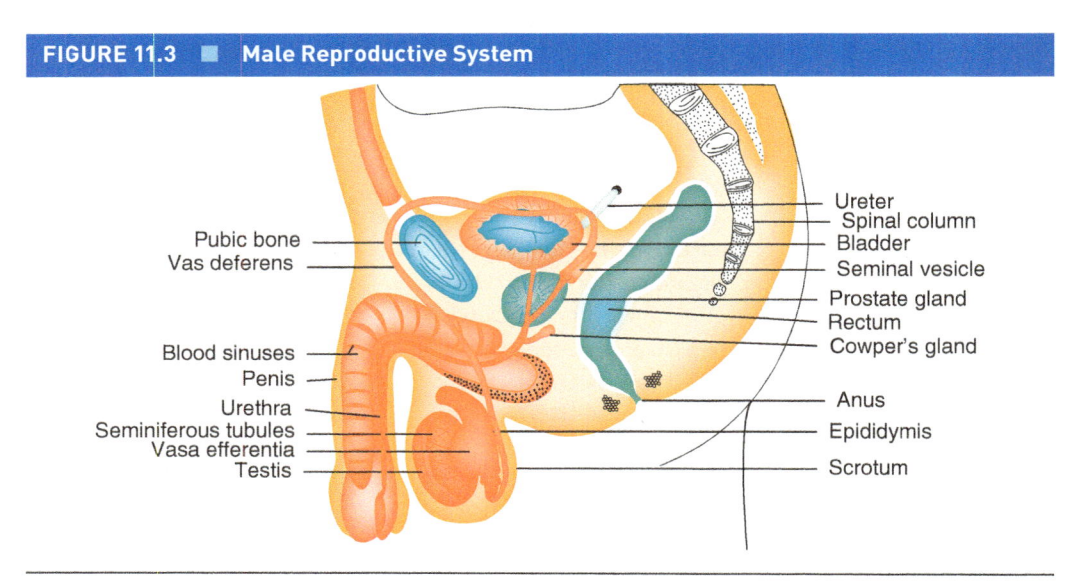

Credit: Kimball's Biology Pages © John W. Kimball. https://www.biology-pages.info

FIGURE 11.4 ■ Female Reproductive System

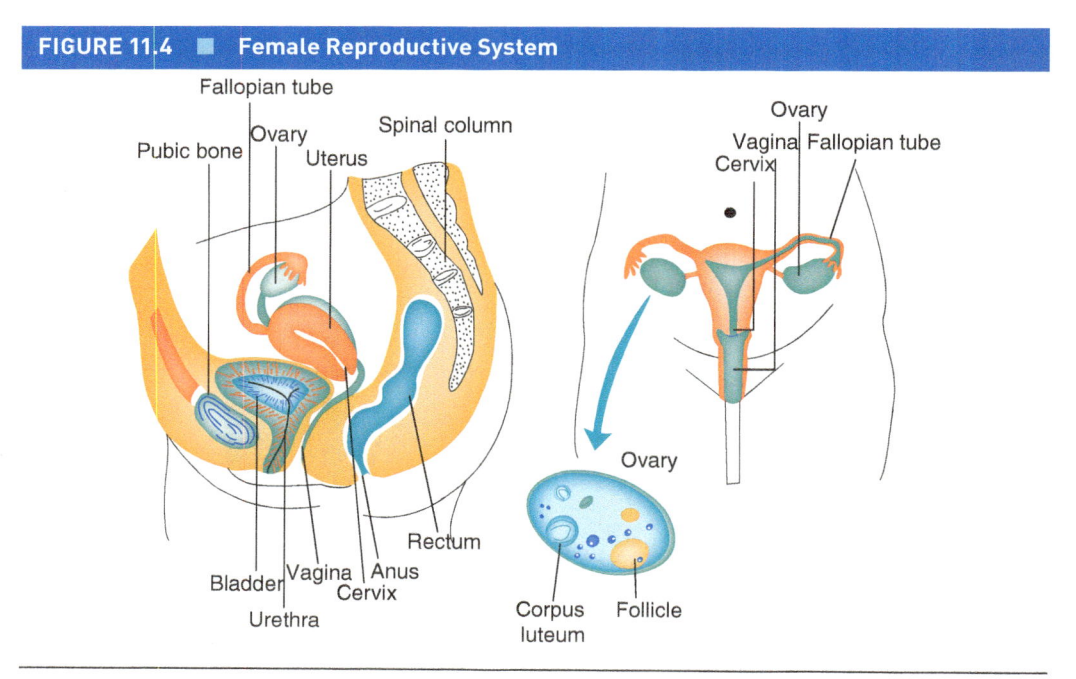

Credit: Kimball's Biology Pages © John W. Kimball. https://www.biology-pages.info

FIGURE 11.5 ■ Female External Sexual Anatomy

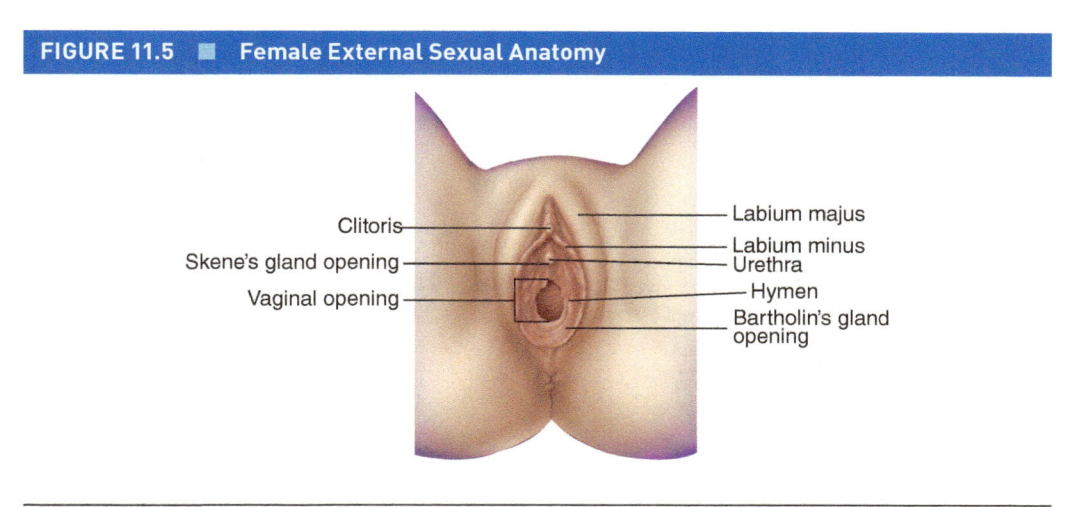

Clitoris
Skene's gland opening
Vaginal opening
Labium majus
Labium minus
Urethra
Hymen
Bartholin's gland opening

Credit: © Brian Evans/Science Source.

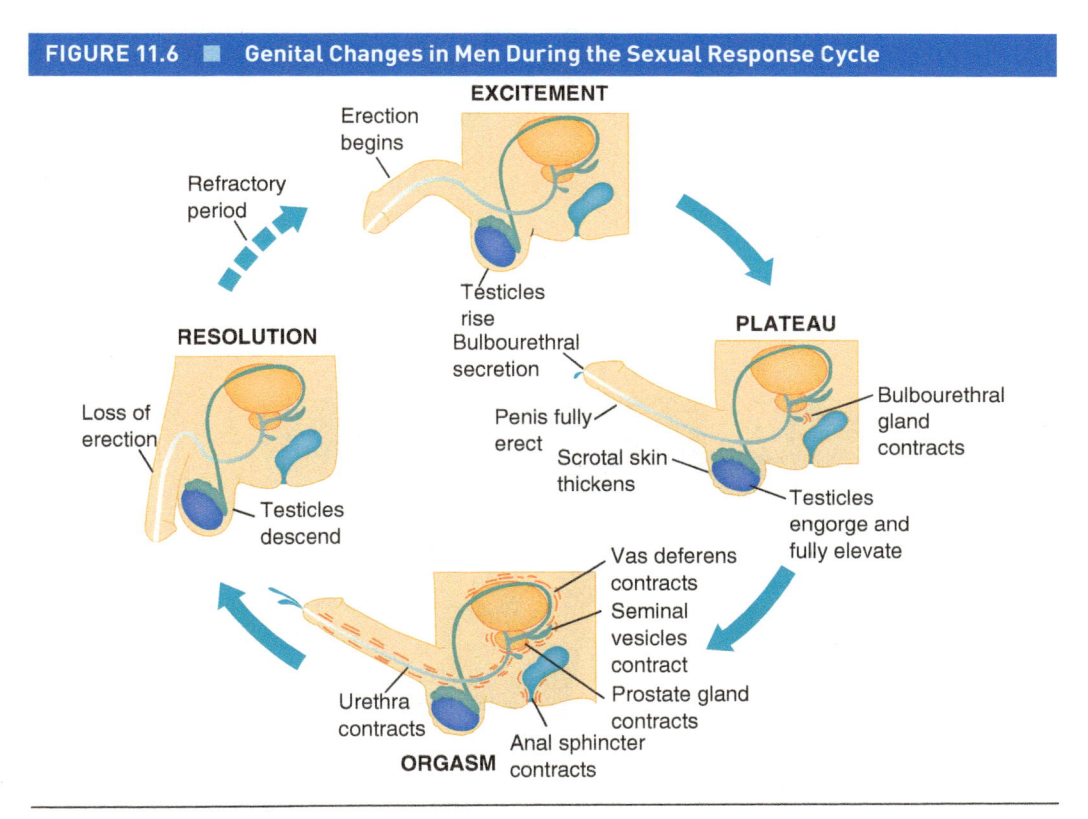

FIGURE 11.6 ■ Genital Changes in Men During the Sexual Response Cycle

EXCITEMENT
Erection begins
Testicles rise
Bulbourethral secretion
Refractory period

PLATEAU
Penis fully erect
Scrotal skin thickens
Bulbourethral gland contracts
Testicles engorge and fully elevate

ORGASM
Vas deferens contracts
Seminal vesicles contract
Prostate gland contracts
Anal sphincter contracts
Urethra contracts

RESOLUTION
Loss of erection
Testicles descend

Credit: From Simon LeVay and Janice Baldwin. *Human Sexuality, Fourth Edition.* Reprinted with permission from Sinauer Associates.

as *vasocongestion*, and muscular tension, which is referred to as *myotonia*. It should be noted that Masters and Johnson saw dividing the sexual experience into four parts as arbitrary, and other researchers have used slightly different categories. Also, outside the laboratory, sexual activity begins with desire, and this should be considered as an initial step preceding Masters and Johnson's four phases (Wincze & Carey, 2001).

In the excitement phase, blood flow is increased in the genital region in both males and females. This is both a physiological and a psychological state. In males, this results in an erection of the penis and the testes becoming elevated. In females, blood flow swells the clitoris and enlarges the labia. Also, the vagina begins to moisten. Excitement is felt throughout the body with increased muscle tension. Both the penis and the clitoris are richly endowed with nerve endings, which make them highly sensitive to touch, pressure, and temperature, and this leads to the sensation of pleasure.

FIGURE 11.7 ■ Genital Changes in Women During the Sexual Response Cycle

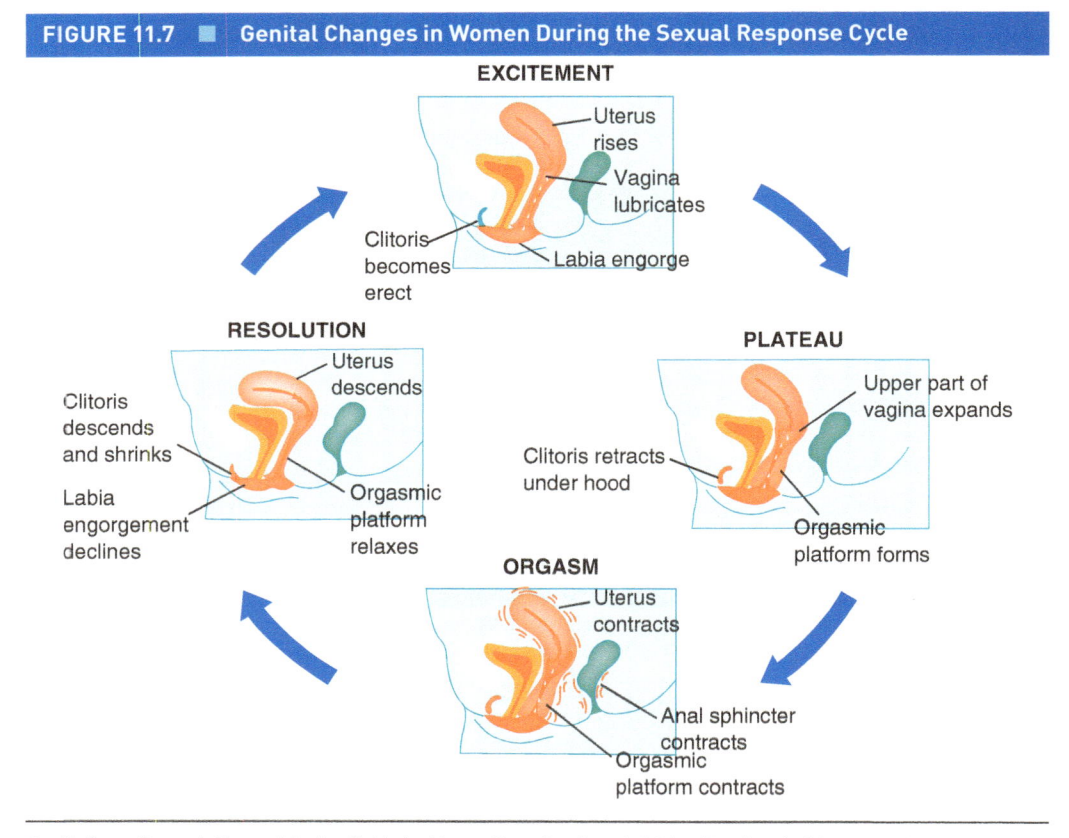

EXCITEMENT
- Uterus rises
- Vagina lubricates
- Clitoris becomes erect
- Labia engorge

PLATEAU
- Upper part of vagina expands
- Clitoris retracts under hood
- Orgasmic platform forms

ORGASM
- Uterus contracts
- Anal sphincter contracts
- Orgasmic platform contracts

RESOLUTION
- Uterus descends
- Clitoris descends and shrinks
- Labia engorgement declines
- Orgasmic platform relaxes

Credit: From Simon LeVay and Janice Baldwin. *Human Sexuality, Fourth Edition.* Reprinted with permission from Sinauer Associates.

Masters and Johnson conducted some of the first laboratory studies of human sexual response.
Ben Martin/Contributor/Archive Photos/via Getty Images

The experiences begun in the excitement phase continue during the second of Masters and Johnson's phases: the plateau. During this phase, most individuals pay little attention to external stimuli as the pleasurable internal experiences continue. In the male, the Cowper's glands, which are two pea-sized glands, release a substance that changes the pH of the urethra from the acidity of urine to make it more alkaline, so as to protect the sperm that will be released during orgasm. Since this slippery substance appears between erection and ejaculation, it is colloquially referred to as pre-ejaculate or "pre-cum." During the plateau phase, there is also an increase in heart rate and breathing. In addition, some individuals show a flush throughout their body.

The tension of the plateau stage climaxes in the third phase—orgasm. Muscular contractions in the male cause sperm from the testes to be released, become part of the seminal fluid from the prostate, and be expelled. This experience lasts only a few seconds. In the process of ejaculation, the internal sphincter of the bladder closes in a manner that both prevents semen under pressure from entering the bladder and urine from the bladder from becoming part of the seminal fluid. In females, pelvic muscles also contract in a somewhat rhythmical manner, which may lead to the experience of a climax. Both men and women experience muscular spasms throughout their bodies.

The fourth phase is the resolution following orgasm. Both males and females return to pre-arousal levels during the resolution phase (Figure 11.8). This includes a decrease in blood flow and muscle tension. During resolution, males—unlike females—experience a time period in which they cannot achieve another orgasm. This time period generally increases with age.

Before completing this section, it should be noted that approximately 1 in 4,500 individuals are born with atypical patterns of chromosomes, gonads, or genitals that do not fit binary notions of male and female bodies (Cools et al., 2018; Profeta et al., 2022; Witchel, 2018). In these individuals, sexual development can follow a variety of paths that require different medical and psychological treatments over their life span. These individuals are commonly referred to as intersex individuals. Research into the unique sexual development patterns of these individuals is emerging.

We turn now from our discussion of the physiology of sexual experience and behavior to a consideration of disorders related to sexual functioning listed in the fifth edition text revision of the *Diagnostic and Statistical Manual of Mental Disorders* (*DSM-5-TR*) (American Psychiatric Association [APA], 2022).

FIGURE 11.8 ■ The Human Sexual Response in Terms of Masters and Johnson's Four Stages

The colors show different patterns of sexual responses seen in the study. Yellow in males and red in females show an orgasm. Blue shows multiple orgasms. Yellow in females shows a pattern that does not lead to orgasm.

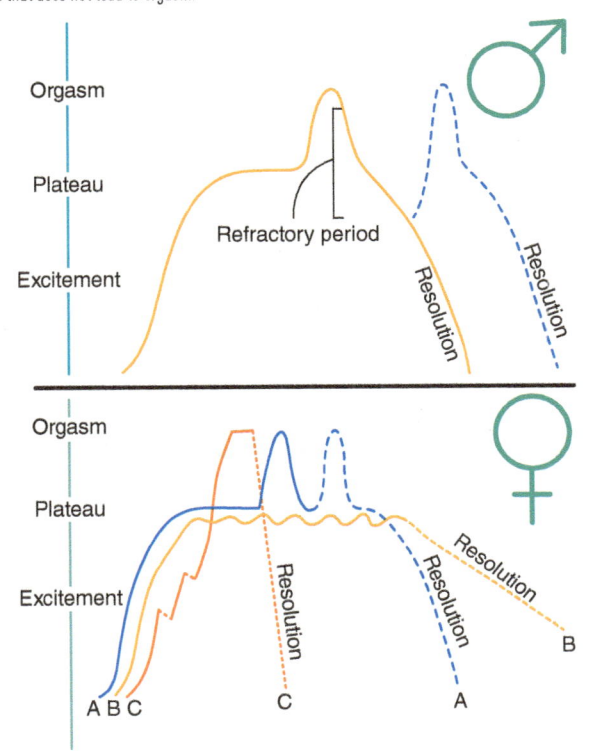

Source: Masters, W. H., & Johnson. V. E. (1966). *Human sexual response.* Little, Brown, p. 5.

> **CONCEPT CHECK**
>
> - Do men think more about sex than women? What evidence do we have from scientific research that adds context to your answer?
> - How is the brain involved with sexual activity?
> - What are some of the issues concerning the term *sexual arousal* from the perspectives of psychology, physiology, subjective experience, and gender differences?
> - What are the four phases of the human sexual response defined by Masters and Johnson? What are some of the different levels on which they can be described?

SEXUAL DYSFUNCTION DISORDERS

We all think about sexual activities. As humans, sexual functioning is important to us. We have ideas and fantasies concerning sexual relationships. We also share our ideas with our partners, which may lead to emotional intimacy. Some couples find emotional connectedness to be critical to a meaningful sex life. Emotional connections may also include touch and physical contact, which leads to the physical sexual response.

As with any activity, there are times when our sexual functioning is not optimal. There may be a physical problem, such as diabetes, that interferes. Mental disorders such as depression and anxiety as well as medications used to treat these disorders have also been shown to interfere with sexuality. At other times, our attitude or desire at the moment may interfere; for example, we may have been trying to impress the other person, we may be concerned about our performance, or we may not be in the mood. This, in turn, interferes with the relationship. In other situations, one partner may move faster or slower than the other partner in their sexual experience of the moment. In addition, sexual patterns change as we age. Most couples can adjust to the changes they experience, but sometimes there are difficulties. Of course, all of this takes place within a historical and cultural context that dictates expectations in terms of sexuality and what is considered normal (Kleinplatz, 2018).

All of these aspects make sexual activity both complex and complicated. Thus, it is not surprising that sexual relations do not always end up the way we wish them to. However, it is important to distinguish between temporary sexual problems, including relationship issues, and more long-term **sexual dysfunction disorders**. *DSM-5-TR* requires that the dysfunction exist for at least 6 months and cause significant distress or impairment in order to be considered a sexual disorder. Table 11.2 lists the sexual dysfunction disorders described in *DSM-5-TR*.

As with other disorders, it is important to consider three perspectives in order to understand sexual dysfunction. The first includes medical and biological factors. A number of medical disorders, such as diabetes and vascular disease, can interfere with normal sexual functioning. Also, medications used to treat specific medical disorders may influence sexual desire and functioning. Further, health conditions such as lack of exercise, an unhealthy weight, and smoking or drinking alcohol can influence sexual response. Shakespeare, referring to alcohol, noted in *Macbeth*, "It provoketh desire and taketh away the capacity."

TABLE 11.2 ■ Sexual Dysfunction Disorders in *DSM-5-TR*

Erectile Disorder
Female Orgasmic Disorder
Delayed Ejaculation
Early Ejaculation
Female Sexual Interest/Arousal Disorder
Male Hypoactive Sexual Desire Disorder
Genito-Pelvic Pain/Penetration Disorder
Substance/Medication-Induced Sexual Dysfunction
Sexual Dysfunction Not Elsewhere Classified

The second perspective is the psychological one. This can include previous experiences, such as childhood abuse. It can also include such factors as performance anxiety. For example, if a person did not perform in the way they wished in a previous sexual encounter, they may try too hard at the next one. Psychological conditions such as anxiety and depression have also been shown to influence sexual functioning. Some individuals also carry with them religious or cultural prohibitions that interfere with their sexual activity.

The third perspective involves the relationship itself. If there is an argument or previous situation in which someone had their feelings hurt, then this may inhibit sexual responding. Of course, good communication with a partner, including expressing desires and expectations, can reduce some problems of sexual functioning.

Epidemiological data collected in the 1990s suggests that sexual dysfunctions are common. However, they are less common in one's 20s and become more common as a person ages (Levin, 2012). In a national sample of 1,749 women and 1,410 men ranging in age from 18 to 59, it was found that 43% of the women and 31% of the men reported sexual dysfunctions (Laumann et al., 1999). Specific dysfunctions reported by women were lack of interest in sex (31%), inability to achieve orgasm (approximately 26%), the experience of pain during sex (16%), not finding sex pleasurable (23%), anxiety about performance (12%), and difficulty lubricating (21%). Sexual dysfunctions reported by men were lack of interest (15%), inability to achieve orgasm (8%), climaxing too early (30%), not finding sex pleasurable (8%), anxiety about performance (18%), and trouble maintaining or achieving an erection (10%). As part of a larger health study, it was found that age, health, and stress were associated with sexual dysfunctions.

A later study sought to update these data with results from an older population. Table 11.3 shows the sexual problems reported by those 57 to 85 years of age. With aging, testosterone levels decline in men and influence a decrease in sexual desire. Many men also show erectile dysfunction as they age. Women following menopause show a reduction in estrogen, which increases vaginal dryness. This, in turn, reduces their desire to engage in sexual acts. Other medical conditions associated with aging can also influence sexual desire and responsiveness. Interestingly, while sexual dysfunction increases with age, personal *distress* associated with sexual dysfunction appears to *decrease* with age. Couples are also able to adjust their expectations and experiences.

In reviews, it has been shown that sexual dysfunction is common in the United States and worldwide in both men and women (DeRogatis & Burnett, 2008; IsHak, 2018; Lewis et al., 2010). At this point, it is difficult to compare rates of sexual dysfunction across countries since the manner in which epidemiological data related to sexual functioning are collected differs by country. There are also cultural factors involved in how candidly individuals respond to questions about their sexual functioning.

Sexual dysfunction disorders can be thought of in terms of four categories. These are related to desire, arousal, orgasm, and pain. In *DSM-5-TR*, sexual dysfunction disorders are characterized by changes in sexual desire as well as problems in the experience of the sexual act. These include problems of low interest or desire in both males and females, male erectile dysfunction, delayed or early ejaculation, and problems with women feeling pain during intercourse or not experiencing orgasm. There is also a classification having to do with changes in sexual functioning related to taking a drug or medication.

Erectile Disorder

Erectile disorder requires that a male has a problem in one of three areas. The first is that he cannot obtain an erection during sexual activity. The second is that he cannot maintain an erection until the completion of sexual activity. The third is a decrease in the rigidity of the penis in a way that interferes with sexual activity. Further, the experience of the erectile problem produces significant distress. As noted previously, 10% of the men in one general population survey reported difficulties maintaining or achieving an erection. The ability to establish and maintain an erection changes with aging. For example, various studies suggest that around 2.3% of 30- to 39-year-olds experience erectile dysfunction; this increases to 11% to 55% in one's 50s, 47% to 53% in the 70s, and 64% to 76% in those men

TABLE 11.3	Prevalence of Sexual Problems in Older Americans by Age and Gender							
	Women				Men			
	Percentage				Percentage			
	Age 57–64	Age 65–74	Age 75–85	Trend Test	Age 57–64	Age 65–74	Age 75–85	Trend Test
Lack of sexual interest	44.2 (3.7)	38.4 (4.4)	49.3 (6.2)	0.403	28.2 (3.5)	28.6 (2.9)	24.2 (3.9)	0.920
Erectile problems					30.7 (2.7)	44.6 (2.9)	43.5 (4.5)	<0.001
Vaginal lubrication problems	35.9 (3.2)	43.2 (4.2)	43.6 (7.8)	0.125				
Premature climax	9.2 (1.5)	6.9 (2.1)	8.5 (3.7)	0.874	29.6 (3.0)	28.1 (2.4)	2.13 (4.0)	0.406
Inability to climax	34.0 (3.0)	32.8 (3.9)	38.2 (7.2)	0.129	16.2 (2.1)	22.7 (2.6)	33.2 (4.1)	<0.001
Pain during intercourse	17.8 (2.2)	18.6 (3.9)	11.8 (3.7)	0.450	3.0 (0.9)	3.2 (1.0)	1.0 (0.7)	0.125
Lack of pleasure in sex	24.0 (3.0)	22.0 (3.5)	24.9 (5.0)	0.909	3.8 (0.7)	7.0 (1.7)	5.1 (1.9)	0.075
Performance anxiety	10.4 (2.1)	12.5 (3.2)	9.9 (4.1)	0.850	25.1 (2.0)	28.9 (3.0)	29.3 (4.7)	0.094
Avoided sex due to problems	34.3 (4.7)	30.5 (4.5)	22.7 (6.6)	0.114	22.1 (2.4)	30.1 (3.4)	25.7 (5.4)	0.256

Credit: Waite, L. J., Laumann, E. O., Das, A., & Schumm, L. P. (2009). Sexuality: Measures of partnerships, practices, attitudes, and problems in the national social life, health, and aging study. *Journal of Gerontology: Social Sciences, 64B*(S1), i56–i66. doi:10.1093/geronb/gbp038, p. 62, by permission of Oxford University Press.

Notes: These questions were asked only of participants reporting sex in the preceding year.

older than 80 years of age (see Beutel et al., 2006; Tobia et al., 2017, for a review of these studies). By middle age, most men require some manual stimulation to achieve an erection.

A number of lifestyle factors can influence erectile dysfunction. For example, smoking can double the risk. Likewise, not exercising, being obese, and abusing alcohol can increase the probability of erectile dysfunction. Medical conditions such as diabetes, hypertension, and atherosclerosis as well as some psychotropic medications have an influence. Many psychological factors, including stress and relationship problems, also influence erectile dysfunction.

Female Orgasmic Disorder

Female orgasmic disorder is the condition in which a woman either does not experience an orgasm or has a reduced intensity of the sensation of the orgasm. Moreover, this condition causes significant distress. The female orgasm has been a topic of much confusion (Graham, 2009). Unlike males, in whom orgasm is closely tied to puberty, the initial experience of orgasm in females may follow puberty by a number of years. Also, data suggest that females are more likely to have an orgasm during masturbation than with a partner. Another difference is that females are less likely to complain of having an orgasm too early in the sex act. Studies performed in both the United States and Europe suggest that orgasmic disorder is seen in between 20% and 30% of females (Palacios et al., 2009).

Delayed Ejaculation

Delayed ejaculation is the situation (over at least a 6-month period) in which a male shows an unwanted delay in ejaculation or shows a lack of ejaculation, and this causes significant distress (Segraves, 2010). Using a definition of ejaculatory problems as occurring in 75% of a person's sexual experiences, the worldwide prevalence is somewhere around 2%. However, there is no clear agreement as to what would be considered "delayed."

Early Ejaculation

Early ejaculation is diagnosed when a man experiences an ejaculation within approximately the first minute of sexual activity, over at least a 6-month period, and this causes significant distress (see Segraves, 2010, for a *DSM* overview). *Premature ejaculation* (as the disorder has traditionally been called) was first noted in the medical literature in 1887 (Waldinger, 2008). Initially, early ejaculation was seen mainly as a psychological disorder and treated with psychoanalytic techniques. In the mid-20th century, there was a realization that both psychological and biological factors were involved. In the 1990s, it was discovered that selective serotonin reuptake inhibitors (SSRIs) would delay ejaculation.

As noted earlier in this chapter, some 30% of the men in one study reported problems with early ejaculation, although other studies show slightly lower numbers. There are few data in terms of the number of males affected using *DSM-5* and *DSM-5-TR* criteria. In one study of men who had reported experiencing premature ejaculation, their female partners were asked to use a stopwatch at home to time ejaculation over a 4-week period. What was found was that 90% of the men reporting problems ejaculated within 1 minute, with 40% of these men ejaculating within 15 seconds after penetration (Waldinger, 2008).

Female Sexual Interest/Arousal Disorder

In studies from around the world, approximately 30% of women report a significantly decreased desire to engage in sexual activities (see Palacios et al., 2009, for an overview). In particular, sexual desire decreases with age. According to *DSM-5-TR* criteria, female sexual interest/arousal disorder requires significant distress or impairment along with at least three specific symptoms. The symptoms include a reduction or absence of interest in sexual activity, reduced occurrence of sexual fantasies, less excitement or pleasure during sex, and fewer internal or external sexual cues or sexual sensations.

Male Hypoactive Sexual Desire Disorder

Male hypoactive sexual desire disorder refers to a situation in which a male has little desire for sexual activity or even erotic thoughts for at least 6 months. Further, this condition causes significant distress. Overall, lack of sexual desire is reported more frequently by females than by males. As noted previously, some 15% of men in the general population report a lack of interest in sexual activities. Other studies have found similar numbers throughout the world. However, when asked if this is a significant problem lasting for 6 months, the numbers drop to only a few percent.

Genito-Pelvic Pain/Penetration Disorder

In females, pain during sexual activity has traditionally been divided into two types. The first is *dyspareunia*. This type of pain is experienced during intercourse. The pain may be experienced initially as the penis is inserted into the vagina. It may also be present once the penis is inserted and associated with thrusting. The causes of dyspareunia can be varied. Dryness of the vagina can result from aging or certain medications. Infections and previous injury such as from childbirth or operations can also cause painful experiences. The second type is *vaginismus*. When penetration of the vagina is attempted, the muscles of the vaginal wall or the pelvic floor begin to spasm. This is accompanied by either pain or fear of pain, and penetration is impossible. This condition is not limited to sexual experiences and includes the penetration of any object, such as a speculum used by a gynecologist, a tampon, or even a finger. In the *DSM-5-TR*, genito-pelvic pain/penetration disorder refers to conditions associated with dyspareunia or vaginismus or the fear or anxiety associated with these conditions. As noted previously, some 16% of women report painful sexual experiences. Unlike with other sexual disorders, younger women report more painful sexual experiences than older women.

Treatment Approaches for Sexual Dysfunction Disorders

Given the complexity of factors that can be involved in sexual dysfunction disorders, a thorough assessment is critical. It is important to understand the person's attitudes toward sexual behavior and their understanding of the presenting problems. Often, during the initial assessment it becomes apparent that the person is missing some critical information regarding sexual activity. Thus, part of successful future treatment may include teaching the individual the basics of sexual activity or filling in gaps in their knowledge. This may also include behavioral techniques such as directed masturbation. The second important assessment procedure is to determine if there is a medical problem that contributes to the sexual dysfunction. In addition to specific medical conditions, some medications have side effects that influence sexual desire and responsiveness. The third important assessment procedure is understanding the psychological factors involved. These can include relationship problems or family or cultural prohibitions toward sexual practices. Some individuals may also have expectations concerning how a sexual encounter should progress that are incompatible with the expectations of their partner. Based on a psychological assessment, couples therapy can be directed at helping the two people to communicate about their needs and desires in terms of sexual activity.

Sex Therapy

Sex therapy begins with a thorough assessment as described and then uses straightforward techniques to help a couple achieve a more fulfilling sexual life. Many of the techniques were initiated by Masters and Johnson in their clinic and described in their 1970 book *Human Sexual Inadequacy*. Masters and Johnson believed that performance anxiety was a factor in a number of sexual dysfunction disorders. That is, the person was worried about being aroused, or having a climax, or not getting an erection. These worries could indeed interfere with satisfying sexual relationships. Also, some individuals had

Good communication can reduce some problems of sexual functioning.
iStock.com/vgajic

never had the experience of slowly moving through a sexual experience. Thus, part of their treatment was designed to reduce worries and help individuals understand how their body functions sexually.

Masters and Johnson's treatment procedure lasted for 2 weeks. In their clinic, they initially requested that the couple not engage in sexual activity. The couple would begin by each talking individually with a therapist of their same gender, and a thorough social and sexual assessment was made. The overall approach was to see problems in sexual functioning as an issue for the couple rather than the individual to work on. Beginning on the third day, the couple was to use what Masters and Johnson (1970) referred to as "sensate focus," which meant that they were to pleasure each other through kissing, touching, and massaging and engage in these behaviors without attempting sexual intercourse or involving genital areas. Part of this was the opportunity to communicate to the other person what was pleasurable. The next step in the sequence was to include genital stimulation without the goal of having an orgasm. Part of this technique was to have a time in which the woman directed the activity of the couple and determined the timing of the interaction. In their sessions, both the man and the woman learned to listen to the other as well as ask for what they wanted in the sexual encounter. Many couples reported more satisfying intercourse as a result of the treatment.

Masters and Johnson collected data on their 2-week treatment program followed by a 5-year follow-up. They reported complete success with 29 of 29 women with vaginismus and 182 out of 186 men with premature ejaculation. These high rates of success may have resulted in part from the high motivation of the clients involved. That is, these couples had to agree to take 2 weeks off, fly to St. Louis, and spend this time working on their sexual relationship. More recent work with similar procedures has shown positive but lower rates of success.

Since the work of Masters and Johnson, a variety of specific techniques have been used by sex therapists. Some have required changes in the sex act. With premature ejaculation, for example, the couple would be instructed to practice foreplay and penile stimulation to the point prior to ejaculation. Stimulation is then paused until the arousal level is decreased. Stimulation is then applied again. This technique is performed at least three times before ejaculation. A variant on this is referred to as the squeeze technique. In this case, as the man approaches ejaculation, his partner squeezes the penis near the top, which reduces arousal. This is then repeated. For a female with vaginismus, it is important for her to learn to tense and relax the muscles of her vagina. In a comfortable setting, she is instructed to insert her finger into her vagina and practice relaxation. Later, she can insert two fingers or a vaginal dilator. Slowly she learns to insert larger dilators while practicing relaxation. After she is comfortable and feels in control, a partner can be involved with the woman remaining in control.

Medications and Other Treatments

Pharmacological approaches are also used to treat a number of sexual dysfunction disorders. With painful sexual activity in women, creams that contain antifungals, corticosteroids, or estrogen can be applied to the vaginal area. Medications such as Addyi (flibanserin) have been designed to increase sexual desire in females. It should also be noted that some antidepressants may reduce sexual desire. With male erectile disorder, drugs such as Viagra, Levitra, or Cialis increase blood flow to the penis and nearby areas. This allows for an erection. However, these drugs do not influence sexual desire. It is generally reported that these drugs work in over half of men who take them, although the satisfaction of the sexual experience varies. Traditional psychological treatments such as mindfulness have also been used to treat sexual dysfunctions (Brotto & Goldmeier, 2015). The best results have been found when pharmacological techniques for a sexual dysfunction are combined with behavioral techniques, psychosocial approaches such as cognitive behavioral therapy, and therapy focused on the interpersonal relationship.

In this section, you have seen problems associated with experiencing the sex act itself. These disorders include lack of desire and inability to initiate or complete sexual intercourse successfully. You also learned about treatment approaches for these disorders. In the next section, you will learn about disorders in which the person experiences distress in relation to their object of desire.

> ## CONCEPT CHECK
>
> - What factors distinguish temporary sexual problems from sexual dysfunction disorders?
> - Sexual dysfunction disorders can be thought of in terms of four categories related to desire, arousal, orgasm, and pain. Into which category would you place each of the sexual dysfunction disorders covered in this section?
> - What are key diagnostic criteria for each of the sexual dysfunction disorders covered in this section?
> - What are examples from each of the following categories of factors that influence erectile dysfunction: age, lifestyle, medical, and psychological factors?
> - What are the similarities and differences between female sexual interest/arousal disorder and male hypoactive sexual desire disorder?
> - What are the two types of genito-pelvic pain/penetration disorder? What are the causes of each?
> - Therapy for sexual dysfunction disorders begins with a thorough assessment focusing on three factors. What are these factors, and how are they important in successful treatment?

PARAPHILIC DISORDERS

As demonstrated by the popularity of sexual themes in novels and online, humans are attracted to and enjoy reading about and imagining different types of sexual encounters. In fact, there is a long history of sexual images in art and literature. Sexual surveys also demonstrate that humans engage in a variety of sexual activities. In addition to traditional sexual activities, humans may play erotic games with each other and act out various sexual roles. Some individuals experience sexual arousal in seeing themselves or their partner dress in a particular manner. For example, some people like to wear leather or dress in the traditional clothes of the opposite sex. Imagining oneself in nontraditional sexual activities or actually engaging in them with a consenting partner does not constitute a mental disorder.

Professionals involved with *DSM-5* wanted to distinguish between nontraditional sexual activities and sexual disorders. That is, they wanted to distinguish between **paraphilia** and **paraphilic disorders**

The film *Secretary* portrays the relationship between two people exploring a consensual dominant/submissive relationship.
Photo 12/Alamy Stock Photo

(Moser, 2019). The term *philia* is derived from Greek and refers to love or affection. The term *para*, as in paranormal, refers to something that exists alongside of the traditional or normal. Thus, the term *paraphilia* refers to practices that exist alongside traditional expressions of sexuality and offer a sense of pleasure for many individuals.

Research suggests that for many individuals there is no difference in sexual distress when engaged in traditional versus nontraditional sexual activities (Pascoal et al., 2015). This was also true for psychological distress. A large-scale Australian study involving over 19,000 individuals reported that those who engage in sexual dominance and submission actually showed lower scores on measures of psychological distress (Richters et al., 2008). The popularity of novels and movies such as *Fifty Shades of Grey*, with its theme of sexual dominance and submission, shows that paraphilias are increasingly accepted in Western popular culture as within a broad range of sexual expression. In the same way that short-term experiences of anxiety or depression do not qualify as a mental disorder, nontraditional sexual practices in themselves do not qualify as a disorder.

The term *paraphilias* was coined by Wilhelm Stekel, a Viennese physician and psychologist, in his 1925 work *Sexual Aberrations* (Stekel, 1925/1996). The term was used in *DSM-III* to describe nontraditional sexual arousal in response to objects, situations, or nonconsenting individuals (Beech et al., 2016; Krueger & Kaplan, 2015). When sexual desires or behaviors become problematic, they can be classified under the heading of paraphilic disorders. This is analogous to situations with eating disorders or addictions in which individuals no longer have control or can make decisions in terms of their cognitions and behaviors.

For a sexual desire or sexual behavior to qualify as a disorder, it must cause distress to the person or interfere with important areas of the person's life. Thus, just engaging in nontraditional sexual activity without distress or interference in one's life would not be considered a disorder. However, the acts associated with any sexual activity may also be illegal when they involve other nonconsenting individuals.

Illegal activity such as acting on urges related to pedophilia, exhibitionism, and voyeurism has received the most attention in the clinical literature. Because those who have been convicted of an illegal sexual act are easier to track and study scientifically, much of the current research has focused on these individuals. At present, a scientific understanding of the development of paraphilic disorders and their treatment in both legal and illegal forms is very incomplete (Marshall & Kingston, 2018).

In general, the paraphilic disorders included in *DSM-5-TR* are long-term in nature, cause distress to the person involved, and may cause distress or harm to others. Significantly more men than women display paraphilic disorders, though they appear across ethnic and socioeconomic groups. These disorders may encompass behaviors such as exposing oneself to others, being sexually aroused by inanimate objects, being aroused by touching or rubbing against others without their consent, becoming aroused by children, gaining sexual arousal by seeking humiliation or suffering perpetrated by others, gaining sexual arousal by making another person suffer, gaining sexual arousal from cross-dressing, and gaining sexual arousal by watching unknowing individuals disrobe or engage in sexual activities. *DSM-5-TR* describes these types of behaviors in terms of the eight paraphilic disorders covered next, as well as *otherwise specified* and *unspecified paraphilic disorders*. Table 11.4 lists the paraphilic disorders described in *DSM-5-TR*.

TABLE 11.4 ■ Paraphilic Disorders in *DSM-5-TR*

Exhibitionistic Disorder
Fetishistic Disorder
Frotteuristic Disorder
Pedophilic Disorder
Sexual Masochism Disorder
Sexual Sadism Disorder
Transvestic Disorder
Voyeuristic Disorder
Otherwise Specified Paraphilic Disorder
Unspecified Paraphilic Disorder

Exhibitionistic Disorder

A person with an exhibitionistic disorder becomes sexually aroused by exposing their genitals to an unsuspecting stranger (Morin & Levenson, 2008). Although *DSM-5-TR* describes the disorder as gender neutral, it is infrequently displayed by women. Prevalence is suggested to be 2% to 4% in the male population and less frequent in females. Often called a *flasher*, a male exhibitionist will find a place where women are expected to be, such as a park. A common scenario is that upon seeing a woman, he will move in front of her and open his coat so that his genitals are exposed, or he will wear baggy shorts without underwear and allow his genitals to fall out. He may use this experience later as part of his sexual fantasies.

Exhibitionism is also a crime in the United States, referred to as *indecent exposure*. Society has treated exhibitionism as a nuisance crime since it involves no physical contact. However, there are reasons to take it seriously (Firestone et al., 2006). First, one third to two thirds of all sexual offenses reported are related to exhibitionism, but this is probably an underreported crime. Putting together a variety of studies, research suggests that 32% to 39% of college female students and 40% to 48% of community samples of women have experienced someone exposing themselves (Murphy & Page, 2008). Second, those individuals who engage in exhibitionism tend to perform the act frequently and show high recidivism after treatment. Firestone and his colleagues studied 208 men diagnosed with exhibitionism. They found over a 19-year period that these men showed recidivism rates of 23.6% for sexual crimes, 31.3% for violent crimes, and 38.9% for criminal offenses. Third, there is a tendency for exhibitionists to move from exhibitionism to more serious sexual assaults. Fourth, an important result is that victims of exposure experience distress and trauma.

Snaith and Collins (1981) described five patients referred to a psychosexual clinic in the United Kingdom. One of these descriptions is as follows:

> Mr. D. was 30 years old when he referred himself to the clinic. He said that he felt that an arrest for his deviant sexual behaviour would be inevitable unless he could gain some degree of self-control. He spent many hours a week prowling around the neighbourhood in the evenings and exposed himself to adolescent girls, masturbating as he did so. In addition to exhibitionism he indulged in frotteurism in crowded public places. He had been exposing since the age of 17 and in view of the very blatant nature of the behaviour it was remarkable that he had never been arrested. (p. 128)

Mr. D. would qualify for an exhibitionistic disorder diagnosis since he engaged in exhibitionism for more than 6 months and this behavior caused him distress. Unlike with other paraphilic disorders, there is not a higher rate of prior physical or sexual abuse among those who display exhibitionism.

Few individuals with an exhibitionistic disorder seek treatment on their own. Thus, most of the treatment literature has been related to those who were prescribed treatment as part of a legal punishment. One approach to treatment is group therapy in which the individual has an opportunity to discuss their exhibitionistic tendencies and receive feedback from others. Whether presented in groups or individually, the majority of treatment programs have a cognitive behavioral orientation. This is often combined with an approach directed at relapse prevention in which the individuals discuss how they will handle future situations in which desires to expose themselves are present. Some approaches also seek to develop empathy in those with the disorder so that they can better understand their impact on their victims. Some health care professionals have also used SSRIs as a psychopharmacological approach. This is based on the finding that serotonin has an inhibitory effect on male ejaculatory functioning. SSRIs have been shown to reduce sexual fantasies and impulsivity.

Frotteuristic Disorder

Frotteuristic disorder refers to the condition in which an individual gains sexual arousal from touching or rubbing against another nonconsenting person (Lussier & Piché, 2008). The word *frottage* means rubbing or friction in French. *DSM-5-TR* reports the prevalence of frotteuristic disorder to be 10% to 14% as seen in outpatient settings for paraphilic disorders.

This disorder has been seen only in men. Men with this condition will report that they seek crowded situations, such as a subway, in which they can make contact with others as if by accident. Generally, the contact is from the side or behind with little eye or face-to-face contact. In extremely crowded situations, the actual contact may go unnoticed. Women undercover police officers, seeking to stop theft and other crimes on subways, have discovered frotteurism to be more common than these other crimes. Some subway systems, such as the one in Tokyo, have established women-only cars during rush hours.

A frotteuristic disorder diagnosis requires two conditions. The first is that the experiences of sexual arousal that result from touching or rubbing against a nonconsenting person have lasted for at least 6 months. The second is that these urges occur with a nonconsenting person or the urges result in clinically significant distress or impairment in the individual's functioning. As with other paraphilic disorders, few individuals seek treatment on their own as opposed to being court ordered. Treatment approaches for paraphilic disorders in general will be described later in this chapter.

Fetishistic Disorder

A *fetish* is an erotic fixation on a nonsexual object or body part (Darcangelo, 2008). The word *fetish* comes from the French *fétiche*, which may have come from the Portuguese *feitiço*, which means spell or magic charm. In this sense, an object casts a spell over the person. A person with a particular fetish experiences sexual arousal from focusing on the object. High-heeled shoes and feet are common fetish objects. Although sound epidemiological data are lacking, fetishes appear to be more common in men than women. It is an open question why certain objects or parts of the body take on a sexual connotation for these individuals.

Masters, Johnson, and Kolodny (1986) described a man who had a fetish for women's high-heeled shoes. He had collected more than 1,000 of these shoes, which he had catalogued and concealed from his wife in his attic. Other fetish objects may involve a particular type of material, such as latex, leather, or silk. A person with a fetish may feel or stroke the object or even masturbate while doing this. Sometimes a picture or drawing of the object may be enough for sexual arousal. Although many couples use clothing such as lingerie or other objects to enhance their sexual experience, a **fetishistic disorder** involves a fixation that lasts for more than 6 months and results in clinically significant distress or impairment in important areas of functioning. Treatment approaches for paraphilic disorders in general will be described later in this chapter.

Dressing in latex or rubber, or seeing someone else in these outfits, is a common fetish.
iStock.com/nullplus

Pedophilic Disorder

I believe that I was born a pedophile, because I have had feelings of sexual attraction toward children and love for them as long as I can remember. . . . I remember being fascinated by children even during my own childhood. . . . By now, it was clear to me that I loved children, especially boys, and was happiest when I was in their company. What I took pleasure in most was seeing them happy and developing healthily in mind and body. So, I encouraged their interests if I felt these interests were healthy, or I exposed them to experiences that I thought would contribute to their educational or cultural edification. . . . Even in sex, producing pleasure in the children was the most gratifying aspect to me.

From Donald Silva. (1990). Pedophilia: An Autobiography *(1990, p. 464). In Jay Feierman (Ed.),* Pedophilia: Biosocial Dimensions. *New York: Springer, reprinted with kind permission from Springer Science+Business Media.*

Donald Silva, who wrote the quote you just read, is in prison in Europe. Not only is *pedophilia* a mental disorder, but acting on these urges is also a crime in most countries. **Pedophilic disorder** involves a persistent sexual interest in prepubescent or early pubescent children. In the popular media, the word *pedophilia* carries with it the connotation of sexual acts with children. The clinical definition of pedophilic disorder does not require an actual sexual act, although this can be the case. Some individuals with pedophilic disorder do not act on their urges. However, others may pick out a particular child and "groom" them by giving attention or gifts to make the child feel special. Over a period of time, the child is led into more behaviors that the person with pedophilic disorder finds sexually arousing. As seen in the quote from Donald Silva, many of these individuals claim they are only trying to make the child happy.

In the *DSM-5-TR* criteria for pedophilic disorder, a number of conditions are required. The first is that the person gains more sexual arousal from children than from adults. The second is that the person has acted on these urges or that these urges cause problems in the person's functioning and distress. Third, the condition has lasted for more than 6 months.

The term *pedophile* was coined in 1886 by the German psychiatrist Richard Freiherr von Krafft-Ebing. The term comes from the Greek meaning love of children. In his work, Krafft-Ebing differentiated the attraction to children from the act of sexual abuse. Some people with pedophilia may use child pornography and have limited contact with children, while others seek out child contact.

Separating the desire for children from child abuse helps to define who has pedophilia. Thus, not everyone who performs a sexual act with a child has pedophilia. Some adults who abuse children may not gain arousal from thinking of the child as a sexual object. They just abuse the child as a matter of convenience. For example, it would be considered child abuse for a teacher to have sexual relations with a student, as it would for a parent to have sexual relations with one of their children. This, of course, is against the law but may not qualify as a pedophilic disorder. Although both men and women can sexually abuse children, pedophilic disorder appears mainly in men. Only a small percentage of those with the disorder are women.

Any type of abuse of children brings out a strong emotional reaction in people hearing about specific situations as portrayed in the media. Part of the emotional reaction to pedophilia is that many of these children have yet to experience their own sexuality. Pedophilic disorder is the most common paraphilia discussed in both the scientific and legal literature.

Pedophilic disorder is seen to develop during adolescence (Seto, 2008). Studies suggest that 40% to 50% of offenders against unrelated boys and 35% to 40% of offenders against unrelated girls reported this attraction before the age of 20. Although solid longitudinal research has yet to be conducted, the general consensus is that a sexual interest in children lasts across the life span for individuals with this disorder.

In terms of the brain, there is evidence to suggest both structural and functional brain differences in those with pedophilia (Mohnke et al., 2014). Brain imaging research has shown volume reduction in the right amygdala in individuals with pedophilic disorder as compared to those without pedophilia

(Poeppl et al., 2013). In addition, within the pedophilic group, sexual interest in children and sexual recidivism were correlated with gray matter decrease in the left dorsolateral prefrontal cortex ($r = -.64$) and insular cortex ($r = -.45$). In addition, pedophilic individuals were shown to display reduced levels of the neurotransmitter GABA (Ristow et al., 2018).

Another study compared fMRI brain networks in individuals with pedophilia who engaged in child abuse with a control group (Kärgel et al., 2015). The former showed reduced network activity and functional connections between the left amygdala and frontal regions of the brain in comparison to the control group. These areas are involved in the social and emotional awareness of others. Differences are seen in those with pedophilia not only in relation to sexual stimuli but also in relation to nonsexual material involving cognitive and executive functions (Poeppl et al., 2015). Further, when presented with moral and legal decisions involving sexual offenses against children, people with pedophilia and controls show opposite brain activation patterns (Massau et al., 2017). Overall, these studies suggest individuals with pedophilia show differences in brain structure, which in turn affect both network connections and the ability to process information.

At this point, there is no evidence that an individual with pedophilic disorder can change their sexual attraction to children (Seto, 2008). Treatment approaches tend to focus on teaching the individual how to control their sexual arousal as well as other self-regulation skills in order to reduce risk factors (Beier et al., 2015). Currently, there is no effective treatment for pedophilic disorder. A number of school-based programs are designed to teach children how to protect themselves from individuals with this disorder.

Sexual Masochism Disorder

> The blows fell rapidly and powerfully on my back and arms. Each one cut into my flesh and burned there, but the pains enraptured me. They came from her whom I adored, *and for whom I was ready at any hour to lay down my life.*
>
> *From Leopold von Sacher-Masoch. (2013).* Venus in Furs. *New York: Dover Publications.*
> *(Original work published 1888)*

The term *masochism* comes from the Austrian author Sacher-Masoch, who in the 1800s described men who derived sexual satisfaction from being whipped or beaten. Masochism involves deriving sexual pleasure from being subjected to pain or humiliation. This may include being restrained by ropes or other devices, blindfolded, humiliated, or dominated as well as being whipped or beaten. Judging from masochism themes in popular press books and the number of websites devoted to themes or objects involved in masochistic activity, it cannot be a rare fantasy in humans. Fewer individuals act on these fantasies, however. Some surveys suggest that 5% to 10% of men and women find these activities to be sexually pleasurable on an occasional basis (Masters et al., 1986).

However, masochistic fantasies or activities can also become a compulsion that limits human functioning. **Sexual masochism disorder** is present when the person experiences sexual arousal from the act of being humiliated, beaten, bound, or otherwise made to suffer, as manifested by fantasies, urges, or behaviors for more than 6 months. Further, these urges or behaviors cause distress or impairment in the person's life. This is one of the paraphilic disorders that can be seen in both men and women, although the number of women is much smaller.

Although there is limited neuroscience research related to masochism, both sexual stimuli and pain stimuli can heighten central nervous system states of arousal and motivation (Bodnar et al., 2002). Further, there is an overlap between the neuroanatomical pathways and mechanisms of pain and sex. Thus, it is possible that in some individuals, those stimuli that would normally produce an avoidance or withdrawing process would activate approach-like sexual processes.

The criteria for sexual masochism disorder also ask if asphyxiation is present. This is the process by which a person puts a plastic bag over their head or a rope around their neck to cut off oxygen temporarily and enhance the sexual experience, especially during masturbation. A tragic number of individuals lose consciousness and die before they can remove the bag or noose.

Sexual Sadism Disorder

She stopped. "I am beginning to enjoy it," she said, "but enough for today. I am beginning to feel a demonic curiosity to see how far your strength goes. I take a cruel joy in seeing you tremble and writhe beneath my whip, and hearing your groans and wails; I want to go on whipping without pity until you beg for mercy, until you lose your senses. You have awakened dangerous elements in my being. But now get up."

From Leopold von Sacher-Masoch. (1888). Venus in Furs. *New York: Dover Publications. (Original work published 1888)*

The term *sadism* is derived from the French author Marquis de Sade, who in the 1700s described sadistic features in his novels. Sadism is characterized by the experience of sexual arousal from violent sexual fantasies or by subjecting another to pain or humiliation. This may include restraining, blindfolding, humiliating, or dominating another. This may also include producing physical pain such as by whipping another. Although prevalence rates have not been fully determined, it is believed to be more common in men than women.

Sexual sadism disorder involves deriving sexual pleasure from inflicting pain or humiliation on others. To be referred to as a disorder, the occurrence of sexual arousal from the suffering of another must have been present for at least 6 months. The person also must have acted out these impulses with a nonconsenting individual or experienced distress or impairment from these impulses. Some individuals with the disorder require a nonconsenting person to experience the sexual arousal. Sexual sadism does not appear in isolation but is often comorbid with other disorders. These include impulse control disorders, antisocial personality disorder, and borderline personality disorder.

Transvestic Disorder

Transvestism refers to dressing in clothing that is culturally associated with the opposite sex. This in itself may not produce sexual arousal and would not be considered a fetish. However, it can become a fetish when this cross-dressing produces sexual arousal. In general, it is men who experience arousal from dressing in items of clothing associated with women. Most researchers differentiate individuals whose gender identity aligns with their assigned sex at birth and who engage in drag performance from those whose gender identity and sex assigned at birth do not align and would be commonly referred to as transgender (Newring et al., 2008). Typically, transgender individuals do not experience sexual arousal from dressing in clothes of the opposite sex.

Early research mainly examined straight men who dressed in traditional women's clothes and accessories culturally associated with women. Similar patterns were found in both Australia and the United States (Buhrich & Beaumont, 1981). Half of the individuals studied began this behavior before puberty, and a majority had established it by late puberty. Långström and Zucker (2005) examined a random sample of 2,450 individuals in the general population of Sweden. The overall survey was related to health with questions related to sexuality embedded within the larger survey. They found that 2.8% of men and 0.4% of women reported being sexually aroused from dressing in the clothes culturally associated with the other gender. Fifty percent of these individuals reported that they did not find this behavior acceptable to themselves. It is these individuals who would be diagnosed with transvestic disorder. The other 50% would not seek treatment unless there were relationship problems or other difficulties related to the behavior.

Transvestic disorder is characterized by recurrent and intense sexual arousal from cross-dressing, as manifested by fantasies, urges, or behaviors. It also needs to last for a period of at least 6 months and cause distress or impairment.

Voyeuristic Disorder

Voyeurism is the act of watching unsuspecting others engage in nonpublic activities such as undressing, having sexual relations, or engaging in other such behaviors. In some countries such as England, Wales, and the United States, it is an illegal activity. It is seen mainly in men and usually begins before the age of 15. *DSM-5-TR* reports a lifetime prevalence for voyeuristic disorder as 12% for males and 4% for females. Voyeurs are also called *peeping Toms* after the Lady Godiva story. Lady Godiva rode through the town on her horse nude to protest a tax. She asked the townspeople not to look at her. Tom the tailor was the only person who looked at her and thus became known as "peeping Tom." A number of recent cases have gone to court where a person was recorded through a peephole as they changed clothes in their hotel room or vacation rental.

It can also be a fetish when the individual gains sexual arousal from watching others. Voyeurs generally are not interested in meeting or having a relationship with the person they are watching. Rather, they use voyeurism as a means for sexual excitement, which may include masturbation. Generally, voyeurs seek a place outside a house or apartment where they can observe the other person without being seen, although some use the risk of being caught as an additional source of excitement. In a city, voyeurs may use a telescope or other device to watch others in their apartments. They may also hide webcams in locker rooms or other places where people undress. Hacking into another person's computer can allow someone to turn on the camera without this being noticed. Paradoxically, most voyeurs do not go to places such as nude beaches or nude stage shows where nudity is acceptable.

Voyeuristic disorder involves obtaining sexual arousal from watching unsuspecting people when they are undressing, naked, performing sexual acts, or going to the bathroom. To be categorized as a disorder, this activity needs to have existed for at least 6 months. It also needs to involve a nonconsenting individual or cause marked distress or impairment for the voyeur.

Other Paraphilic Disorders

There are two additional categories of paraphilic disorders. The first is referred to as *other specified paraphilic disorder*. This category includes symptoms that cause significant distress or impairment in important areas of one's life but do not satisfy the criteria in any of the disorders previously described in this chapter. This can include intense sexual arousal from making obscene phone calls, corpses, animals, feces, urine, enemas, or other such sexually arousing events for the individual. The second disorder is referred to as *unspecified paraphilic disorder*. The requirements for this disorder are the same as the first except that there may be insufficient information to make a more specific diagnosis.

At times, individuals are mandated by courts to receive treatment for a sexually related crime. Some of these crimes, such as rape, are not seen to have resulted from the person having a mental disorder, although there could be a relationship in terms of sexual sadism or a personality disorder. Other crimes, such as child pornography, can be directly related to a paraphilic disorder. The following case study of George Nadel (not his real name) describes someone who was mandated for treatment for the crime of possessing child pornography. Although a mental health professional would initially consider a diagnosis of pedophilic disorder, George Nadel, as you will see, reported being more sexually attracted to adults than children and came to have an interest in child pornography later in his life. Thus, the mental health professional might choose *other specified paraphilic disorder* as the *DSM-5-TR* diagnosis.

CASE OF GEORGE NADEL
COURT-MANDATED TREATMENT FOR CHILD PORNOGRAPHY POSSESSION

George Nadel is a 47-year-old unemployed, twice-divorced male who presented to the Rising Sun Center for Treatment of Sexual Offenders with complaints of depressed mood, anxiety, and impulsive behavior. He reports that he is heterosexually oriented. The client reports a history of depression since childhood, which he has managed through what he describes as self-destructive behaviors. In addition to substance abuse and impulsive spending, the client has a recent history of possessing child pornography (depicting boys and girls ages 9–16), which resulted in pending legal charges for possession (and possible distribution) of child pornography. His pending charges cause him a significant amount of anxiety and shame.

> George reports behavior that is consistent with a preoccupation with sexual behaviors. He has engaged in anonymous fellatio in the back rooms of bookstores. He also spends significant portions of his income on legal pornography and preparations used to reverse erectile dysfunction. George says that while he feels he can stop downloading child pornography, he claims an addiction to pornography depicting adults. The client said that he became interested in child pornography more than 7 years ago when he heard a television news report that caused him to become curious regarding images of child pornography. Since that time, George has downloaded nearly 20,000 images of child pornography. At his intake, George expressed his concern over his pending legal charges, which have lasted over the past 2 years.
>
> Clinical vignette provided by Clifford Evans, MEd, RN.

Causes and Treatment Approaches for Paraphilic Disorders

At this point, we do not have a clear picture of factors that produce paraphilia or paraphilic disorders. Certainly, a person's internal hormonal environment, which is experienced as a sexual drive, is important (Bradford & Ahmed, 2014). Bradford and Ahmed suggest that a relationship exists between the hormone androgen, which is experienced only by males in the 6th week in the womb, and future sexual behavior. They further suggest this may help to explain why paraphilia and paraphilic disorders are seen more commonly in males than females. In addition, *DSM-5-TR* describes paraphilic disorders as first becoming apparent during adolescence. Although in humans the experience of basic needs such as food, sexuality, and social relationships occurs in complex ways, including seeking pleasure, bonding with others, and procreation, current research does not suggest that predilections for certain sexual behaviors can be totally the result of some type of learning. Likewise, there is little documented evidence to suggest that paraphilia can be extinguished in a traditional learning paradigm. However, cultural factors and the availability of pornographic websites can play a role.

Since individuals who experience one paraphilia tend to experience another, this suggests that there may be an endophenotype or other common factors that influence their expression. Further, a number of psychological disorders are comorbid with paraphilic disorders (Marshall, 2007). The highest comorbidity is with personality disorders, but substance abuse–related comorbidity is also strong. This suggests that no single paraphilic disorder should be viewed as if it exists in isolation or as if it has a separate causal pathway.

Because many individuals with paraphilic disorders do not seek treatment, sound studies of treatment efficacy are lacking. Those that do exist suggest that positive treatment effects are not strong (Beech & Harkins, 2012). Case studies and research studies are available in which the paraphilic disorder was treated in terms of other comorbid problems. In some paraphilic disorders, the individuals themselves may have experienced physical, emotional, or sexual trauma in childhood, which would influence the nature of the treatment.

When treatment is sought, it generally has one of three sources. The first is through the courts. These are individuals who were arrested for paraphilia involving nonconsenting others. The second source is when a partner or spouse encourages the person to seek treatment to improve their relationship. The third source is when the person finds their own fantasies or behaviors distressing or is afraid of being caught doing the behavior.

Psychopharmacological treatments have been used to reduce sexual drive in general (Briken & Kafka, 2007; Holoyda & Kellaher, 2016). SSRIs have been shown to reduce sexual drive and have been used with a number of paraphilic disorders. These have been shown to have the best effects with disorders that have a strong affective component. Likewise, leuprolide acetate (Lupron) has been used alone or in combination with cognitive behavioral therapy to reduce recidivism (Gallo et al., 2019). Other drugs that influence sexual hormones directly have also been tried. Inconsistent results and the occurrence of side effects do not make these the treatment of choice for paraphilic disorders.

At one time, aversion therapy was used to treat paraphilic disorders (Beech & Harkins, 2012). This treatment involved pairing an aversive experience such as a mild electric shock with the person imagining the paraphilic fantasy. Covert sensitization has also been used in which the person imagined an unpleasant experience that was then paired with the focus of the paraphilia. However, the effectiveness of these treatments has not been strong, and their use has decreased over the past 20 years.

Cognitive behavioral orientations make up the majority of treatment approaches to paraphilic disorders. This approach focuses on how the person interprets their thoughts and emotions in relation to others. This is often combined with an approach directed at relapse prevention. This is similar to the approach used with those addicted to drugs in which discussions focus on how to avoid future high-risk situations.

In 2016, the World Federation of Societies of Biological Psychiatry published a set of guidelines for the treatment of paraphilic disorders in adolescents (Thibaut et al., 2016). Overall, they note that both psychopharmacological treatments and psychological approaches (particularly cognitive behavioral therapy) have been shown to be effective. They also note that most of the studies involve only males. These adolescents were often referred through the courts and may include a variety of sexual offenses, making an exact diagnosis of paraphilic disorder difficult.

CONCEPT CHECK

- What factors distinguish paraphilia from paraphilic disorders?
- What are the diagnostic criteria for each of the paraphilic disorders covered in this chapter?
- Exhibitionism is a crime in the United States as well as a *DSM-5-TR* paraphilic disorder. What are some of the reasons to treat it seriously as a crime?
- Does the clinical definition of *pedophilic disorder* require an actual sexual act with a child? Does anyone who performs a sexual act with a child have pedophilia? Why, or why not?
- In terms of treatment approaches for paraphilic disorders overall, please answer the following questions:
  - What are the three primary sources through which treatment is initiated?
  - What pharmacological approaches are used, and what aspects of the disorder do they target?
  - What psychotherapy approaches are used to treat paraphilic disorders, and what aspects of these disorders do they target?

GENDER DYSPHORIA

The truth that was slowly emerging had a hazy beginning. Since I was a child, I'd been aware of a part of me that did not fit. At first, I thought this sense of not fitting in was about me being gay. But as time went on, and I tried different ways of "being a lesbian"—from lipstick to stone butch—I had to admit to myself that the "something" nagging at me was a lot more complicated than just my sexual orientation. Even when I was active in the gay community, I never felt completely at ease. There was something else about me that didn't make sense, something that was much more profound and a lot more threatening. . . .

It would take me almost ten more years before I truly understood the significance of my gender dysphoria, a clinical description that gets to the disconnection between how the body presents its sex and how the brain experiences its sex. In essence, when these two are different (the brain feels itself to be a man but the body is a woman's, and vice versa), the confusion and discomfort is so deep, so disturbing, that most of us try anything to either deny our true feelings or otherwise avoid dealing with ourselves.

From Chaz Bono, Transition: The Story of How I Became a Man *(2011).*

The hours I spent as Renée were a very small part of my active life, but they cast a continuing shadow over all the relationships I formed. There was no time as a child or teenager when I could say that anyone really knew me. They knew Dick, but I kept the female component of my personality deeply buried. The idea that it might get out haunted me. Had I been able to talk to someone, it would have decreased my isolation, but I never met anyone to whom I gave even passing consideration to telling my secret. No matter how kind or understanding people seemed, even my good friends, I couldn't imagine that they would forgive me.

From Renée Richards, Second Serve *(1983, p. 41).*

Gender Roles, Gender Identity, and Gender Dysphoria

There is great variety in the traditional **gender roles** that children experience. These gender roles are typically defined by one's culture in terms of the kinds of activities boys and girls are expected to engage in. Some girls enjoy activities that are seen as stereotypically male, such as playing sports or playing with toy cars and trucks. Some boys may enjoy stereotypically female activities, such as dressing up or playing with dolls. Some individuals stay with their childhood interests and continue in occupations that follow. Women who become construction workers or men who design clothes are two examples. However, even though their culture has negative attitudes toward their interests, these individuals' experience of their gender aligns with their assigned sex at birth. This is referred to as **gender identity**.

Gender identity is the internal experience of knowing that you are a man or a woman. Even if individuals find themselves sexually attracted to members of their same sex, they would describe themselves as a man attracted to another man or as a woman attracted to another woman. Being gay, lesbian, or bisexual does not change one's gender identity. However, some individuals experience a discrepancy between their assigned sex at birth and their understanding of their own gender. The common term used for these individuals is *transgender*. If the transgender individual has sought medical intervention such as hormone treatment or gender confirmation surgery, the term **transsexual** is sometimes used in the scientific literature. Both Chaz Bono and former professional tennis player Renée Richards, whose experiences are described earlier, underwent medical treatment to change their biological sexual characteristics.

The home page of Laverne Cox's website declares: "MY LIFE changed when I realized I deserve to be seen, to dream, to be fully included, always striving to bring my full humanity." Cox is the first transgender woman of color to have a leading role on a mainstream TV series, *Orange Is the New Black*. She has also advocated for a better understanding of gender identity.

Chaz Bono has been another advocate for better understanding of gender identity. As noted in the previous account, Bono, who was born as Chastity Bono to the singing duo Sonny and Cher, experienced life as being in the wrong body. In 2015, Caitlyn Jenner described her journey from living as Olympic star Bruce Jenner, who won a gold medal in the decathlon in 1976, to living as a transgender

Actress and gender identity activist Laverne Cox
Moviestore Collection Ltd/Alamy Stock Photo

woman (see For Further Reading). Jenner felt as if "nature had made a mistake." *LENS: Transgender: Bruce Jenner's Journey to Caitlyn Jenner* describes this transformation. These individuals may have been born as one gender in terms of their body, but their internal experience is that of the other gender. In *DSM-5-TR*, this is referred to as **gender dysphoria**. *Dysphoria* is defined as a sense of unease or suffering.

LENS

TRANSGENDER: BRUCE JENNER'S JOURNEY TO CAITLYN JENNER

The transition of Olympic gold-medal winner Bruce Jenner to transgender woman Caitlyn Jenner became public in 2015. In remarkable self-revealing television and magazine interviews that year, Jenner described her long-term struggle to come to terms with gender dysphoria. For millions of Americans, this was an amazing story about someone they admired and whose personal struggle with gender identity had never been evident.

Caitlyn Jenner on the cover of *Vanity Fair*, June 2015
Richard Levine/Alamy Stock Photo

As a child, Jenner was popular and excelled at athletics. She continued sports in college and was part of the U.S. Olympic Teams in the 1972 and 1976 Summer Olympics, becoming widely known after winning the gold medal in the grueling decathlon competition during the 1976 events. These tremendous achievements gave her instant fame, including a prominent placement on the front of Wheaties cereal boxes. To many, Jenner seemed to be living a perfect life, the American dream. Jenner was quickly offered a job as a television broadcaster, gave speeches across the country in the following years, and was the face of a number of advertising campaigns.

However, in private life, Jenner was keeping a secret. Going back to around 10 years of age, she would sneak into her mother's or sister's closet, put on a dress or other feminine items of clothing, and walk around dressed this way. She was both fascinated and scared that someone would find out. Internally, Jenner had always wanted to be a woman and had fantasies of what this would mean. Over time, Jenner had three wives and four children, but these relationships ended as Jenner revealed more to her partners about her internal feelings.

In 2015, when Jenner was in her mid-60s and her children were all grown up and in careers of their own, she decided it was time to embrace her gender identity as a woman. With the help of psychological therapy and hormones, she transitioned into Caitlyn. Jenner had taken hormones previously but had discontinued their use. This time, as Caitlyn, Jenner continued with the hormones and underwent plastic surgery to feminize her face. By late 2015, with increasing confidence, Jenner publicly embraced her new identity. As with about 75% of all transgender women, Jenner did not undergo gender confirmation surgery. In fact, health professionals suggest that if genital surgery is conducted, it should be delayed until at least a year after transitioning.

On July 15, 2015, Jenner was awarded the Arthur Ashe Courage Award at the ESPY Awards in Los Angeles.

Thought Question

What factors influence how a society understands gender dysphoria?

The Vanity Fair article on Caitlyn Jenner from 2015 can be found at http://www.vanityfair.com/hollywood/2015/06/caitlyn-jenner-bruce-cover-annie-leibovitz

Development, Characteristics, and Prevalence of Gender Dysphoria

Gender dysphoria can be seen in children, adolescents, and adults (Zucker et al., 2016). In children, the gender dysphoria diagnosis requires that the condition last for at least 6 months and cause the child significant distress or impairment in school, social relationships, or other areas. In order to make the diagnosis, six of eight criteria must be present. These include (1) a strong desire to be the other gender; (2) a strong preference for wearing clothes culturally associated with the opposite gender; (3) a strong preference for acting out the other gender in make-believe play; (4) a strong preference for toys, games, or activities culturally associated with the opposite gender; (5) a strong preference for playmates of the opposite gender; (6) a strong rejection of toys or games culturally associated with one's assigned sex at birth; (7) a strong dislike of one's sexual anatomy; and (8) a strong desire to have the physical sexual anatomy of the opposite gender. There is greater variety in the patterns of behaviors seen in children than those seen in adolescents and adults with gender dysphoria. Not all children who show gender dysphoria will continue to show it into adolescence or adulthood. Its continuance has been estimated to range from 2% to 39% in those assigned male at birth as opposed to 12% to 50% in those assigned female at birth (APA, 2022).

In adolescents and adults, the experience of the situation is seen as more stable. For a diagnosis, it also requires 6 months' duration and significant distress or impairment in social, occupational, or other areas of functioning. Also, two of the following six criteria must be present. These are (1) a marked incongruence between one's experienced gender and one's assigned sex at birth; (2) a strong desire to be rid of one's primary sex characteristics because of a marked incongruence with one's experience; (3) a strong desire for the sex characteristics of the other gender; (4) a strong desire to be of the other gender; (5) a strong desire to be treated as the other gender; and (6) a strong conviction that one has the typical feelings and reactions of the other gender.

Estimates of prevalence indicate around 1 in 10,000 for those who are assigned male at birth and experience a gender identity of woman and slightly lower for those who are assigned female at birth and experience a gender identity of man (APA, 2022). This is seen as an underestimate, since many adults do not seek treatment programs for a variety of reasons, including cultural factors. Also, this information is not generally sought in studies of epidemiology. However, individuals who experience gender dysphoria are found throughout the world.

The Brain and Gender Dysphoria

For adolescents and adults, the relatively infrequent occurrence of gender dysphoria has limited the research directed at the topic. However, a number of medical centers have begun to collect data related to gender dysphoria, such as the Amsterdam Cohort of Gender Dysphoria Study (1972–2015) (Wiepjes et al., 2018). One of the findings from this study was that brain activity and structure in transgender adolescents more closely resembles the typical activation patterns of their experienced gender.

As noted, gender dysphoria is a complicated and politically charged topic that brings forth many issues around the meaning of sexuality and gender. When examined in non-dysphoria conditions, neuroscience research suggests that brain differences exist in relation to gender and that these differences begin when an individual is in the womb (Bao & Swaab, 2011; Savic et al., 2010; Swaab & Garcia-Falgueras, 2009). Using this knowledge, some researchers have sought to determine similarities between non-dysphoric males and females and those who experience gender dysphoria. One study found that white matter fiber pathways in female-to-male transgender individuals were more similar to those found in non-dysphoric males (Rametti et al., 2011). The brain imaging took place before any hormonal treatment was applied and was not influenced by medical intervention. Thus, fiber pathways in those who experienced themselves as male did indeed look similar to those non-dysphoric individuals who were assigned male at birth.

Another study examined cortical thickness in male-to-female transgender individuals (Luders et al., 2012). This study compared non-dysphoric males and individuals who experienced male-to-female gender dysphoria before any hormonal treatment had taken place. As seen in Figure 11.9, cortical thickness was greater in several regions. There was no area in which the control group showed greater thickness. Previous research had shown greater cortical thickness in non-dysphoric women as compared with non-dysphoric men. Other research has also shown that a cluster of cells in the hypothalamus (bed nucleus of stria terminalis) that is involved in sexual activity is not only smaller in women as compared with men but also smaller in men with gender dysphoria (Zhou et al., 1995). Thus, individuals with gender dysphoria who experience their gender as women have brain structures that are more similar to those of non-dysphoric females. Overall, these neuroscience studies suggest that the experience of gender is reflected in brain structures.

Providing Assistance for Individuals With Gender Dysphoria

Gender dysphoria is a topic of great debate. One position is that although there exist individuals who exemplify the characteristics of the condition, it should not be considered a mental health disorder. This would be parallel to cultural shifts related to same-sex attraction. Until 1973, "homosexuality" was listed in the *DSM* as a sexual disorder. However, mental health professionals believed that this

FIGURE 11.9 ■ The Brain and Gender

Individuals assigned male at birth who have gender dysphoria and experience themselves as women have brain structures that are more similar to those of non-dysphoric women. The right side of the figure shows cortical thickness for the control and transgender groups separately in terms of millimeter thickness. The left side of the figure shows brain areas in which cortical thickness significantly differed between the two groups. Note that differences are mainly shown for the transgender group (yellow and red show greater thickness for this group).

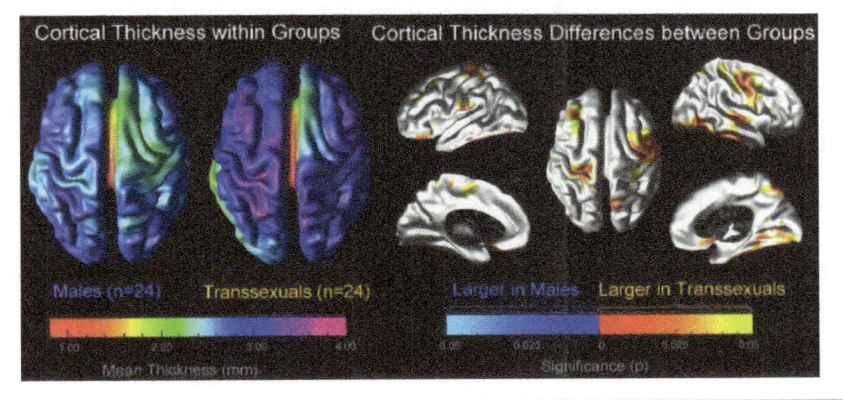

Credit: Luders, E., Sánchez, F., Tosun, D., Shattuck, D., Gaser, C., Vilain, E., & Toga, W. (2012). Increased cortical thickness in male-to-female transsexualism. *Journal of Behavioral and Brain Science*, 2, 357–362, licensed under CC BY 4.0 https://creativecommons.org/licenses/by/4.0/.

resulted in making a common condition a pathology. Similarly, the question arises as to whether the clinical and scientific evidence exists for seeing gender dysphoria as a mental disorder.

The task force that created *DSM* criteria reviewed the evidence for including gender dysphoria in *DSM-5* (Byne et al., 2012). One aspect related to childhood diagnosis. It was noted that it was not uncommon for children to show cross-gender behaviors. However, the majority of these children do not show these behaviors as they move through puberty and into adolescence. Further, few studies have been able to identify which of these children will continue these behaviors in adolescence. There are also few treatment studies with this population.

The overall question involves what a mental health professional would seek to treat. No treatment to date has shown any effect on gender identity or sexual orientation in young adulthood (Byne et al., 2012). Clearly, if a child is not gaining the support they need for psychological development from those around them, then psychological interventions designed to create positive ways of coping and techniques for dealing with negative emotions and self-esteem would be important. These treatments could involve family therapy and child-based therapy.

Often, both adolescents and adults experiencing gender dysphoria initially come to treatment for another psychological disorder. Also, suicidal ideation and attempts may be present. In one study with adolescents, those seeking a female-to-male change reported more suicide attempts than those seeking a male-to-female change (Peterson et al., 2017). Similar findings were found in other studies (Toomey et al., 2018). In the Toomey et al. study, female-to-male adolescents reported the highest rate of attempted suicide (50.8%), followed by adolescents who identified as not exclusively male or female (41.8%), male-to-female adolescents (29.9%), questioning adolescents (27.9%), female adolescents (17.6%), and male adolescents (9.8%). Identifying with a sexual orientation other than heterosexual exacerbated the risk for all adolescents except for those who did not exclusively identify as male or female. For transgender adolescents, no other sociodemographic characteristic was associated with suicide attempts.

Some adults with gender dysphoria seek gender transition surgery. This is a complicated procedure that carries with it a variety of mental health concerns along with political and medical concerns. Some individuals want to talk with a mental health professional to help them clarify their concerns about engaging in medical transition procedures. Certain providers may make counseling mandatory, especially in cases involving adolescents. Medical transition procedures may include hormonal supplements that will produce secondary sex characteristics such as facial hair growth voice deepening, in the case of transgender men, or skin softening and fat distribution alterations, in the case of transgender women. These may be followed by surgical procedures to modify sexual organs and other sexual characteristics.

As with any major life change, a variety of positive and negative experiences have been reported by those who engage in medical transition. One review of the research involving more than 1,000 people who medically transitioned from male to female and more than 400 who medically transitioned from female to male reported a general reduction of psychological distress (Pfäfflin & Junge, 1998). Overall, there was a general satisfaction and lack of regret for engaging in the procedure. Another review reported that 80% of those who had a medical transition procedure experienced improved quality of life and decreased gender dysphoria (Murad et al., 2010). Strong regrets or ambivalence were estimated to have occurred in less than 2% of individuals. This is a change from earlier reviews in which a higher proportion of individuals reported regrets. The positive change may have resulted from the number of clinics around the world that have created teams of mental health, medical, and surgical professionals to thoroughly evaluate and offer comprehensive services to individuals with gender dysphoria. In general, it is not recommended that medical transition procedures take place before young adulthood.

At this time, gender dysphoria is not well understood. Most cultures do not offer much support for individuals who experience gender dysphoria, and many U.S. states offer no antidiscrimination laws to protect them. Many individuals who experience gender dysphoria often find support within the larger LGBTQ community. Stigmatization is a common experience for these individuals. Research in relation to gender dysphoria is in its early stages, although a literature search in PubMed (pubmed.gov) shows research on the topic from around the world.

UNDERSTANDING CHANGES IN *DSM-5* AND *DSM-5-TR*
SEXUAL AND GENDER-RELATED EXPERIENCES

Our understanding of sexual feelings and experiences has been an important topic for society and for scientific study. Although such experiences as being attracted to members of one's own sex have been reported throughout human history, many cultures currently see this as abnormal. Until the 1970s, the *DSM* considered "homosexuality" to be a mental disorder. However, scientific evidence and cultural changes within American society have led to changes in our view of sexual orientation. As society has become more aware of and accepting of varieties of sexual orientation, both legal and psychological perspectives have changed. Likewise, organizations such as the Association for Lesbian, Gay, Bisexual & Transgender Issues in Counseling have developed guidelines related to counseling (see For Further Reading).

With *DSM-5-TR*, two other previously considered disorders have been updated to avoid stigma and encourage health care for those who seek it. These conditions are paraphilia and gender dysphoria. In terms of paraphilia, the *DSM-5-TR* fact sheet clearly states that most people with atypical sexual interests do *not* have a mental disorder. In fact, studies have shown similar levels of sexual satisfaction for those who engage in culturally atypical practices and more traditional practices (Pascoal et al., 2015). Likewise, many so-called atypical sexual fantasies such as submission and domination are common among both men and women (Joyal et al., 2015). For a paraphilia to be considered a disorder, people with such interests must either

- feel personal distress about their interest, not merely distress resulting from society's disapproval; or
- have a sexual desire or behavior that involves another person's psychological distress, injury, or death, or a desire for sexual behaviors involving unwilling persons or persons unable to give legal consent.

The other sexual condition that has been updated is gender dysphoria. In *DSM-5*, people whose gender at birth is contrary to the one they experience are diagnosed with gender dysphoria. In the previous edition of the *DSM*, the term was *gender identity disorder*. In *DSM-5*, the word *disorder* was dropped in order to avoid stigma while still allowing the person to seek health care. That is, the condition needs to be specified such that the person can access insurance coverage for their treatment. According to the *DSM-5* fact sheet, this allows these individuals to undergo hormone therapy, related surgery, and psychological treatment to support their gender transition.

The text of *DSM-5-TR* was also updated to reflect culturally sensitive language. For example, "desired gender" was changed to "experienced gender," "cross-sex medical procedure" was updated to "gender affirming medical procedure," "cross-sex hormone treatment" to "gender affirming hormone treatment," "natal male" to "individual assigned male at birth" and "natal female" to "individual assigned female at birth." *ICD-11*, which took effect in 2022, replaced "transsexualism" and "gender identity disorder of children" with "gender incongruence of adolescence and adulthood" and "gender incongruence of childhood," respectively. Likewise, a number of Northern European countries have moved gender identity clinics away from psychiatric departments to those of medicine and endocrinology. Further, in *DSM-5*, gender dysphoria was placed in a section of its own and separated from other sexual disorders.

CONCEPT CHECK

- What are the definitions for the following terms, and what relationships exist among them?
  - Gender roles
  - Gender identity
  - Gender dysphoria
  - Transgender
  - Transvestism
- What changes have occurred in the *DSM* in regard to paraphilia and gender dysphoria? Why were these changes made?

SUMMARY

Sexuality is a driving force in many species, including humans. Humans use the internal experience of sexual arousal and the external experience of sexual activity for a variety of purposes. Humans have depicted sexual activities in paintings and carvings for thousands of years. At certain times, some cultures have seen sexual activity as a negative force in human life. In the 1800s, a number of scientists—including Charles Darwin, Sigmund Freud, and Havelock Ellis—began to approach sexuality from a scientific perspective. In the 1930s, Alfred Kinsey, a zoologist, conducted a large-scale survey on the sexual activities of some 12,000 individuals across the United States. It is important to gain a perspective on sexual activities in the general population to understand sexual disorders scientifically. It is also important to understand normal sexual functioning.

In studying the sexual responses of males and females, Masters and Johnson realized that there was a similarity in how men and women experienced sex. They identified four phases of the human sexual response: (1) excitement, (2) plateau, (3) orgasm, and (4) resolution. Outside the laboratory, sexual activity begins with desire, and this should be considered as an initial step preceding Masters and Johnson's four phases. The four phases of sexual response can be described on a variety of levels—the two main ones are blood flow (*vasocongestion*) and muscular tension (*myotonia*).

Like many human processes, sexual arousal and desire take place on a number of levels in a complex manner. These levels include (1) cognitive considerations, (2) emotional experiences, and (3) the physical level of functioning. Within these three levels, one important research question has been the manner in which measurements can be made. With the advent of psychophysiological techniques to measure blood flow in the sexual organs of males and females, a different type of precision is possible. However, as with a number of psychophysiological measures, the relationship between changes in physiology and the experienced cognitions and feelings may not be exact. More recently, measures of brain activity using such brain imaging techniques as EEG or fMRI allow for an understanding of cortical involvement.

Research suggests that gender differences between men and women in the amount of time spent thinking about sex may relate to appetites in general rather than a specific domain. Research also suggests that males show both subjective and physiological arousal in a manner that is consistent with their sexual orientation. Brain imaging studies allow for cortical measures of arousal in addition to self-report and blood flow changes in sexual organs. Overall, when both males and females achieve orgasm, there are changes in the brain. The processing of sexual arousal involves complex brain networks involving cognitive, emotional, and self processes.

Sexual functioning is important to humans. Sexual relations encompass all aspects of human behavior—thinking, feeling, and doing all interact to contribute to a satisfying sex life. However, there are times when our sexual functioning is not optimal. It is important to distinguish between temporary sexual problems, including relationship issues, and more long-term sexual dysfunction disorders. As with other disorders, it is important to consider three perspectives in order to understand sexual dysfunction: (1) medical and biological factors, (2) psychological factors, and (3) relationship factors. Epidemiological data suggest that sexual dysfunctions are common. Sexual dysfunction disorders can be thought of in terms of four categories. These are desire, arousal, orgasm, and pain.

Erectile disorder requires that a male has a problem in at least one of three areas—obtaining an erection, maintaining an erection, or having a decrease in rigidity of erection—and that the experience of the erectile problem produces significant distress. Female orgasmic disorder is the condition in which a woman either does not experience an orgasm or has a reduced intensity of the sensation of the orgasm. Delayed ejaculation is the situation in which a male shows either a delay in or a lack of ejaculation. Early ejaculation is diagnosed when a man experiences an ejaculation within approximately the first minute of sexual activity. Female sexual interest/arousal disorder requires significant distress or impairment along with at least three specific symptoms, including a reduction or absence of interest in sexual activity, sexual fantasies, or sexual activity; lack of excitement or pleasure during sex; and reduced internal or external sexual cues or sexual sensations. Male hypoactive sexual desire disorder refers to the situation in which a male has little desire for sexual activity or even erotic thoughts. Genito-pelvic pain/penetration disorder refers to conditions (in females) associated with dyspareunia or vaginismus or the fear or anxiety associated with these conditions.

Sex therapy begins with a thorough assessment and then uses straightforward techniques to help a couple achieve a more fulfilling sexual life. Assessment includes evaluation of (1) the individual's attitudes and understanding, (2) any medical problems, and (3) psychological factors. Many of the techniques were initiated by Masters and Johnson in the 1960s in their clinic and described in their book *Human Sexual Inadequacy*. Since the work of Masters and Johnson, a variety of specific techniques have been used by sex therapists. Best results have been found when pharmacological techniques for a sexual dysfunction are combined with behavioral techniques, psychosocial approaches such as cognitive behavioral therapy, and therapy focused on the interpersonal relationship.

Humans are attracted to and enjoy reading about and imagining different types of sexual encounters, and they engage in a variety of sexual activities. *DSM-5-TR* distinguishes between nontraditional sexual activities and sexual disorders—that is, between paraphilia and paraphilic disorders. In general, paraphilic disorders in *DSM-5-TR* are long-term in nature, cause distress to the person involved, and may cause distress or harm to others. The acts associated with the disorder may also be illegal when they involve other nonconsenting individuals. Overall, there is a large gender difference with considerably more men than women displaying paraphilic disorders.

An exhibitionistic disorder is the case in which a person becomes sexually aroused by exposing his genitals to an unsuspecting stranger. Exhibitionism is also a crime in the United States referred to as *indecent exposure*. Frotteuristic disorder refers to the condition in which an individual gains sexual arousal from touching or rubbing against a nonconsenting person. A fetishistic disorder involves an erotic fixation with a nonsexual body part or object that lasts for more than 6 months and results in clinically significant distress or impairment. Pedophilic disorder involves a persistent sexual interest in prepubescent or early pubescent children. Not only is *pedophilia* a mental disorder, but acting on these urges is also a crime in most countries. Sexual masochism disorder is present when the person experiences sexual arousal from the act of being humiliated, beaten, bound, or otherwise made to suffer, as manifested by fantasies, urges, or behaviors. Sexual sadism disorder involves deriving sexual pleasure from inflicting pain or humiliation on others. Transvestic disorder is characterized by recurrent and intense sexual arousal from wearing clothing culturally associated with the opposite gender, as manifested by fantasies, urges, or behaviors. Voyeuristic disorder involves obtaining sexual arousal from watching unsuspecting people when they are undressing, naked, performing sexual acts, or going to the bathroom.

Many individuals with paraphilic disorders do not seek treatment. When treatment is sought, it generally has one of three sources: (1) the courts, (2) a partner or spouse, or (3) the person themselves. Psychopharmacological treatments have been used to reduce sexual drive in general. Cognitive behavioral orientations make up the majority of treatment approaches to paraphilic disorders.

There is great variety in the traditional gender roles that children experience. These gender roles are typically defined by one's culture. Gender identity is the internal experience of knowing one's gender. Being gay, lesbian, or bisexual does not change one's gender identity. However, some individuals experience a discrepancy between their assigned sex at birth and their sense of their own gender. In *DSM-5-TR*, this is referred to as gender dysphoria. *Dysphoria* is defined as a sense of unease or suffering.

Gender dysphoria can be seen in children, adolescents, and adults. Not all children who show gender dysphoria will continue to show it into adolescence or adulthood. In adolescents and adults, the experience of the situation is seen as more stable. Individuals who experience gender dysphoria are found throughout the world. The common term used for individuals who have the anatomy of one sex and the gender identity of the other is *transgender*. Gender dysphoria is a topic of great debate. One position is that although there exist individuals who exemplify the characteristics of the condition, it should not be considered as a mental health disorder. This would be parallel to cultural shifts related to same-sex attraction, in which mental health professionals believed that treating it as a mental disorder resulted in making a common condition a pathology. The overall question involves what a mental health professional would seek to treat.

No treatment to date has shown any effect on gender identity or sexual orientation in young adulthood. For adolescents and adults, the relatively infrequent occurrence of gender dysphoria has limited the research directed at the topic. However, overall, neuroscience studies suggest that the experience of gender is reflected in brain structures. Some adults with gender dysphoria seek gender confirmation surgery. As with any major life change, a variety of positive and negative experiences have been reported by those who engage medical transition. In general, it is not recommended that such procedures take place before young adulthood. At this time, gender dysphoria is not well understood.

STUDY RESOURCES

Review Questions

1. How are sexual arousal and drive described scientifically?
    a. What are the relationships in the scientific literature among the terms *drive, arousal, need, desire, obsession*, and *motivation*?
    b. Sexual arousal and desire take place on a number of levels in a complex manner. What are these levels?
    c. What advances have been made in psychophysiological measures to support research?

2. What are the treatment approaches for sexual dysfunction disorders?
    a. How would you describe the complexity of factors that can be involved in sexual dysfunction disorders, thus making thorough assessment critical?
    b. What was the procedure Masters and Johnson introduced? What issues were they targeting with their treatment protocol?
    c. What are some of the techniques that have been developed since the period of Masters and Johnson?
    d. What pharmacological techniques are available for treating sexual dysfunction disorders?

3. Please answer the following questions for each of the paraphilic disorders:
    a. What neuroscience research informs our understanding of the disorder?
    b. What are the treatment issues?
    c. What are the legal issues related to this disorder, if any?
    d. What do we know about gender and life span prevalence rates?

4. There is a debate in the mental health community as to whether gender dysphoria should be considered a disorder in the *DSM*. Choose one side of the debate, and provide evidence in support of your position. What questions would you ask of proponents of the other side of the debate?

For Further Reading

Bissinger, B. (2015, June 25). *Caitlyn Jenner: The full story. Vanity Fair.* https://www.vanityfair.com/hollywood/2015/06/caitlyn-jenner-bruce-cover-annie-leibovitz

Bono, C. (2011). *Transition: The story of how I became a man.* Dutton.

Indiana University. (2023). *About the National Survey of Sexual Health and Behavior.* https://nationalsexstudy.indiana.edu/

Kinsey Institute. (2023). *Explore Kinsey.* https://kinseyinstitute.org/about/

Laws, D., & O'Donohue, W. (Eds.). (2008). *Sexual deviance: Theory, assessment, and treatment* (2nd ed.). Guilford Press.

Masters, W., & Johnson, V. (1966). *Human sexual response.* Little, Brown.

Masters, W., & Johnson, V. (1970). *Human sexual inadequacy.* Little, Brown.

McAnulty, R. (Ed.). (2012). *Sex in college: The things they don't write home about.* Praeger.

Meana, M. (2012). *Sexual dysfunction in women.* Hogrefe.

Rowland, D. (2012). *Sexual dysfunction in men.* Hogrefe.

Society for Sexual, Affectional, Intersex, and Gender Expansive Identities. (2020). *SAIGE [formerly ALGBTIC] competencies for counseling LGBTQQIA individuals and transgender clients.* https://saigecounseling.org/competencies-2/

World Health Organization. (2023). *Sexual and reproductive health and research (SRH)*. https://www.who.int/teams/sexual-and-reproductive-health-and-research/key-areas-of-work/sexual-health/defining-sexual-health

KEY TERMS

- delayed ejaculation
- early ejaculation
- erectile disorder
- exhibitionistic disorder
- female orgasmic disorder
- female sexual interest/arousal disorder
- fetishistic disorder
- frotteuristic disorder
- gender dysphoria
- gender identity
- gender roles
- genito-pelvic pain/penetration disorder
- male hypoactive sexual desire disorder
- paraphilia
- paraphilic disorders
- pedophilic disorder
- sexual dysfunction disorders
- sexual masochism disorder
- sexual sadism disorder
- transgender
- transsexual
- transvestic disorder
- voyeuristic disorder

12 SUBSTANCE-RELATED AND ADDICTIVE DISORDERS

LEARNING OBJECTIVES

12.1 Discuss the history and prevalence of drug use in the United States.

12.2 Describe the characteristics of disordered substance use, dependence, and addiction.

12.3 Discuss alcohol-related disorders and alcohol's effects on the human body and brain.

12.4 Identify common hallucinogens and their effects on the human body and brain.

12.5 Identify common stimulants and their effects on the human body and brain.

12.6 Discuss gambling as an addictive disorder.

12.7 Identify the treatments available to individuals with substance-related disorders.

As she walks toward the subway station, Janice thinks about the life she used to have. Before drugs, Janice had her own apartment, worked several jobs (as a nurse's aide, a chambermaid, and an office assistant), and was a good mother to her two kids. In fact, in Janice's twenties and early thirties, friends of the plump, friendly Baptist often poked fun at her for being too good for her own good. They wanted her to take more risks, to live a little. Eventually, that meant trying what it seemed like everyone in Harlem was trying in the 1980s: crack cocaine. . . .

Janice finally did try it, and before long she was shipping her kids off to her sister's or a baby-sitter so she could smoke crack in peace. When a neighbor finally called Child Protective Services to complain that Janice could no longer care for her children, Janice sent them to her sister's permanently. She visited several times a week, until one day her family wouldn't let her inside the house. "Not until you get some help," her eldest daughter, then twenty, told her.

From America Anonymous: Eight Addicts in Search of a Life *(2009), by Benoit Denizet-Lewis.*

Throughout human evolutionary history, we have discovered that some plants change the way we feel. The betel nut has been chewed for its nicotine-like effects for at least 13,000 years in Timor (Saah, 2005). Cocaine is naturally available in coca leaves, and morphine is available from poppy plants. Archaeological evidence suggests that Peruvian foraging societies were chewing coca leaves some 8,000 years ago. Poppy seeds were recovered from a 4,500-year-old settlement in Switzerland. Other evidence shows that opium was available in Europe in the Neolithic, Copper, and Bronze Ages. There is evidence that cannabis smoking existed in western China at least 2,500 years ago (Ren et al., 2019). We as humans thus discovered naturally occurring psychoactive substances, and we have used them throughout history.

When we began to move away from being hunter-gatherers about 10,000 years ago, we also discovered how to make alcoholic beverages such as beer and wine, although it may have happened earlier. In fact, there is some suggestion that we made beer as early as 13,000 years ago (Liy et al., 2018). Beer may have been made before we humans made bread (Hayden et al., 2013).

Throughout the world, many natural ingredients are used to make alcohol (McGovern, 2009). One of these is honey. Other ingredients are region-specific. In the Middle East, barley, wheat, and grapes are used; in China, rice, millet, and hawthorn fruit. In present-day Lebanon, Syria, Jordan, and Israel, figs and dates are used; in Africa, grasses and palm sap; in the Americas, corn, cacao, cactus fruit, and yucca. Pottery artifacts have been found in China dating from 7000 BCE with residue of fermented beverages. Other pottery has been found in Iran from around 3500 BCE that was used to store wine. Thus, whether it was cocaine, opium, alcohol, or some other form, the use of psychoactive substances has been an enduring part of our human experience. *Cultural LENS: Cultural and Historical Factors Related to Using Drugs* explores this history further.

CULTURAL LENS
CULTURAL AND HISTORICAL FACTORS RELATED TO USING DRUGS

Humans have used various forms of drugs throughout our history, including alcohol, poppy derivatives, cactus derivatives, and coffee and tea. Their uses have ranged from medical (e.g., pain management) to religious and cultural rituals to recreational uses. Historically, the particular type of drug used was largely related to where one lived. Tobacco (nicotine) and coca (cocaine) grew only in the Americas (Crocq, 2007). Poppy (opium) and hemp (cannabis) originated in Eurasia, whereas tea originated in China. Although alcohol has been derived for centuries from yeast, it did not appear in North America until the Europeans arrived. It was with the worldwide trading patterns first seen in the 15th and 16th centuries that most drugs became available around the world.

In some cultures, the use of drugs was restricted to priests or shamans. Mushrooms that produce trance states have been used in religious ceremonies in Central Asia for at least 4,000 years. In Central America, psilocybin has been used to influence consciousness. Likewise, peyote has been used in Mexico and among the Navajo in the southwest United States as part of religious ceremonies.

A poppy plant. Opium has been cultivated in many cultures worldwide since prehistoric times.
iStock.com/Goja1

Cultural and religious practices have largely directed which drugs are seen as acceptable and which are seen as illicit. In Christian and Jewish religious texts, Noah was seen to plant a vineyard and drink wine after leaving the ark (Genesis 9, 20–21). In Islamic cultures, coffee has been consumed, and hashish, a drug made from cannabis, has been smoked, although cannabis probably came to the Islamic world from ancient Chinese cultures. Alcohol has been restricted for at least 1,400 years in the Islamic world (Baasher, 1981). The banishment of strong drink was seen as part of being faithful to Islam and involved not only those who would drink alcohol but also those who produce it.

In the United States and Europe, alcohol, nicotine, and caffeine have historically been popular drugs. Throughout North America and Europe, there are coffee houses and bars in almost every city. Although cigars and cigarettes as a source of nicotine have seen a decrease in use for health reasons, electronic cigarettes, especially flavored ones, have seen an increase in use among high school students. Cannabis is also beginning to see an increase in use in both the United States and Europe, as it did in the 1800s.

Thought Question

As you learn about the various psychoactive substances in this chapter, notice the maps of their use worldwide. Ask yourself: What cultural or religious factors could be influencing differences in their use?

To begin the chapter, an overview of drug use in the United States will be provided. Following this section, the use of specific drugs, including alcohol, cannabis, opioids, amphetamines, and tobacco, will be discussed, as will disorders associated with their use. Gambling is now considered an addictive disorder in *DSM-5* and *DSM-5-TR* and will be examined after coverage of substances linked with misuse or dependence. The final section of the chapter will look at various approaches used in the treatment of addiction.

DRUG USE IN THE UNITED STATES

In the United States, our attitude toward drug use has changed drastically over the past 200 years (Musto, 1991). Benjamin Franklin often took a substance made of opium and alcohol for medical reasons. During the 1800s, drugs such as cocaine and opiates were seen as everyday compounds to be used by all. In fact, the original formula for Coca-Cola, which was introduced in 1886, included cocaine.

In 1898, the Bayer Company was able to synthesize a substance from morphine, which they named heroin. This was the year before they introduced the Bayer aspirin. Opium imports rose until the drug was made illegal in the United States in 1909. During the 1800s, it was discovered that drugs could be made in the laboratory, and this helped to propel the pharmaceutical industry (Jones, 2011). Although synthetic drugs have been useful in medical treatment, those made and sold on the black market have resulted in impure substances even to this day. Some of these impure substances have even led to severe illness and death.

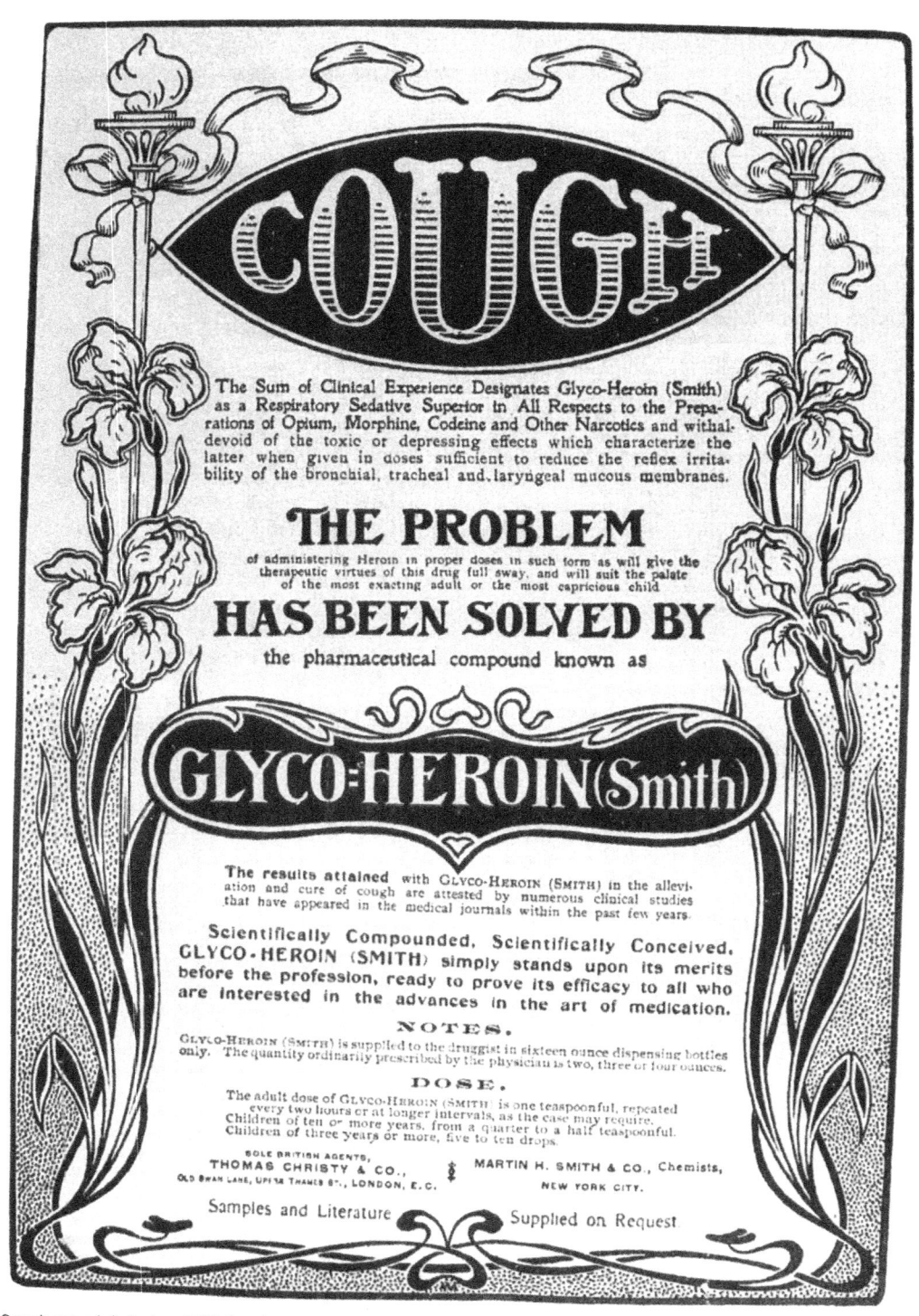

Cough syrup label, circa 1900. Cough syrup containing heroin was legally sold in the United States more than a century ago.
H.S. Photos/Alamy Stock Photo

From the early 1900s through the 1940s, the U.S. government's view of drugs changed in a dramatic fashion. Drugs were increasingly seen as dangerous and in need of strict control. During the 1920s, even alcohol was made illegal by constitutional amendment. Known as *Prohibition*, this era lasted until another constitutional amendment repealed the ban on alcohol in 1933. The decades of tougher laws against drugs were followed by the 1960s, during which drugs were viewed by many as a form of recreation and a method for changing consciousness, and drug use skyrocketed. Cannabis, which was originally used for its fiber (hemp) properties in clothes and rope, became more of a recreational drug during the period of alcohol prohibition. It was widely used in the 1960s, especially by teenagers and young adults, as were opiates and cocaine. Synthesized substances such as LSD were also freely available for a number of years. Society's view of drugs began to change in the 1970s and 1980s, with the popular media running stories on a "crisis of addiction." The U.S. government under President Richard Nixon began its "war on drugs." In 2011, the head of the Center for Disease Control (CDC), Tom Frieden, spoke of an epidemic of opioid addiction. In 2017, the U.S. government declared opioid misuse and addiction related to pain relief a national emergency.

Since 1971, the U.S. government through the Department of Health and Human Services has collected data on drug use through the U.S. Substance Abuse and Mental Health Services Administration (SAMHSA; see For Further Reading). According to recent data collected by this agency, a significant percentage of Americans over 12 years of age use a variety of both illegal and legal drugs (Figure 12.1). In 2021, over 45.1% of Americans age 12 or older said they had used alcohol in the past month, while 22% said they had used tobacco or vaped nicotine. Those 18 and older with any mental illness showed higher rates of tobacco use or vaping (32.6%). Among those under the age of 18, 7% reported drinking alcohol, and 6.7% reported tobacco use or nicotine vaping (see For Further Reading).

In 2021, SAMHSA estimated that approximately 61.2 million Americans age 12 or older had used an illicit drug in the past year. This is roughly 1 in 5 Americans overall but increases to 2 in 5 (38%) for the 18- to 25-year age range. Illicit drugs according to the U.S. government include marijuana, cocaine (including crack), heroin, hallucinogens, inhalants, and prescription-type psychotherapeutics (pain relievers, tranquilizers, stimulants, and sedatives) used nonmedically. Some illicit drugs are not illegal in themselves—prescription drugs, for example—but are used in ways a health professional would not support. Figure 12.2 shows the illicit drug use in 2021 by drug in the last year. This figure shows that marijuana is the most commonly used illicit drug—used by some 52.5 million people or 18.7% of the

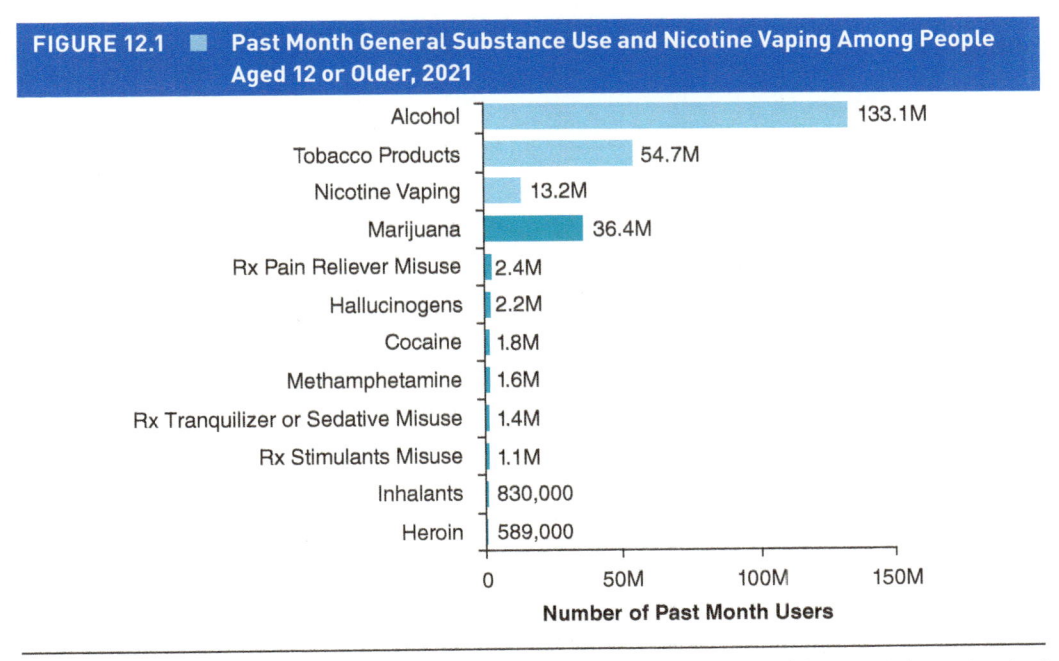

FIGURE 12.1 ■ Past Month General Substance Use and Nicotine Vaping Among People Aged 12 or Older, 2021

Substance	Number of Past Month Users
Alcohol	133.1M
Tobacco Products	54.7M
Nicotine Vaping	13.2M
Marijuana	36.4M
Rx Pain Reliever Misuse	2.4M
Hallucinogens	2.2M
Cocaine	1.8M
Methamphetamine	1.6M
Rx Tranquilizer or Sedative Misuse	1.4M
Rx Stimulants Misuse	1.1M
Inhalants	830,000
Heroin	589,000

Source: Substance Abuse and Mental Health Services Administration. (2023, January 4). *2021 NSDUH annual national report* (Publication No. PEP22-07-01-005). U.S. Department of Health and Human Services. https://www.samhsa.gov/data/report/2021-nsduh-annual-national-report

FIGURE 12.2 ■ Percentage of People in the United States Who Used Illicit Drugs in the Past Year

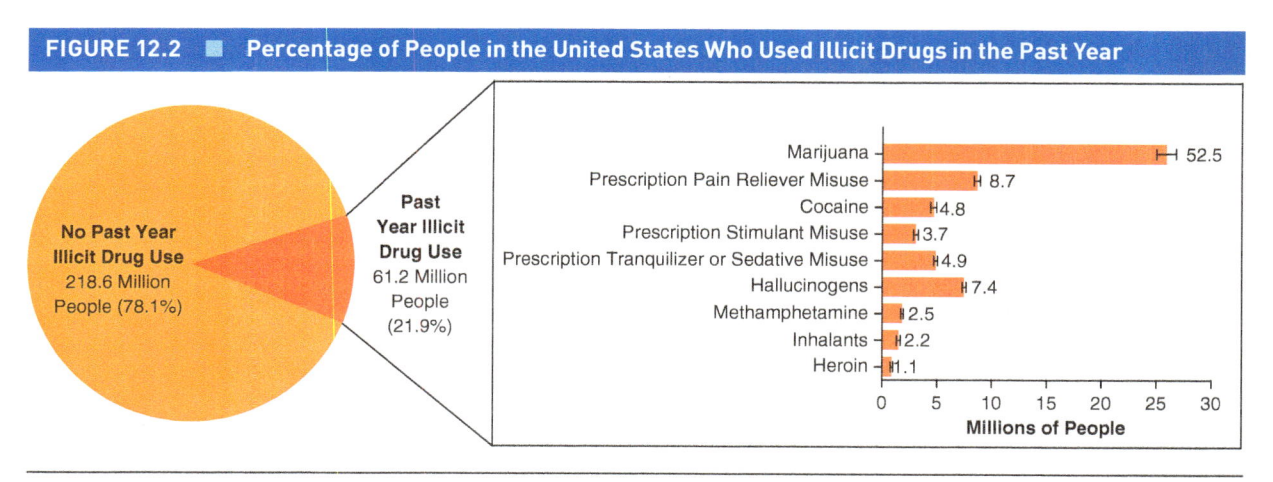

- No Past Year Illicit Drug Use: 218.6 Million People (78.1%)
- Past Year Illicit Drug Use: 61.2 Million People (21.9%)

Millions of People (Past Year Illicit Drug Use):
- Marijuana: 52.5
- Prescription Pain Reliever Misuse: 8.7
- Cocaine: 4.8
- Prescription Stimulant Misuse: 3.7
- Prescription Tranquilizer or Sedative Misuse: 4.9
- Hallucinogens: 7.4
- Methamphetamine: 2.5
- Inhalants: 2.2
- Heroin: 1.1

Source: Substance Abuse and Mental Health Services Administration. (2023, January 4). *2021 NSDUH annual national report* (Publication No. PEP22-07-01-005). U.S. Department of Health and Human Services. https://www.samhsa.gov/data/report/2021-nsduh-annual-national-report

U.S. population age 12 or older. Although not shown in the figure, the use of cocaine and amphetamines has decreased significantly since the 1980s. Marijuana has shown a recent increase in use as many states have changed its legal status. In terms of age group, individuals 18 to 25 years old currently show the highest percentage of illicit drug use.

The United Nations also collects data on drug use. Figure 12.3 shows trends in the use of illicit drugs throughout the world. As can be seen in this figure, the use of cocaine, amphetamines, and "ecstasy" has decreased worldwide, whereas opioid (e.g., heroin, pain medication, morphine, codeine) and cannabis use has increased. Overall, drugs are used more by men than women throughout the world. Illicit drugs can have economic consequences for countries in terms of health care costs and the loss of work productivity. They also have personal consequences in terms of social and family relationships.

FIGURE 12.3 ■ Recent Patterns in the Use of Illicit Drugs

The use of cocaine, amphetamines, and ecstasy (MDMA) has decreased worldwide, whereas opioid (e.g., heroin, pain medication, morphine, codeine) and cannabis use has increased. This figure shows global trends in the prevalence of the use of various drugs, 2009–2013. The figures are based on changes from 2009 for each drug. This particular graph distinguishes between naturally occurring opium drugs (opiates) and synthetic opium drugs (opioids). This distinction is not commonly used.

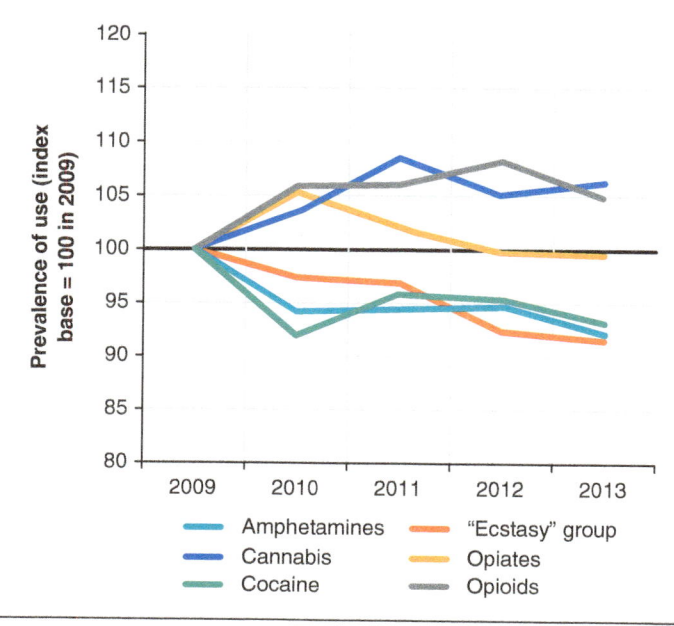

Credit: United Nations Office on Drugs and Crime, World Drug Report 2015 (United Nations publication, Sales No. E.15.XI.6). Reprinted with the permission of the United Nations.

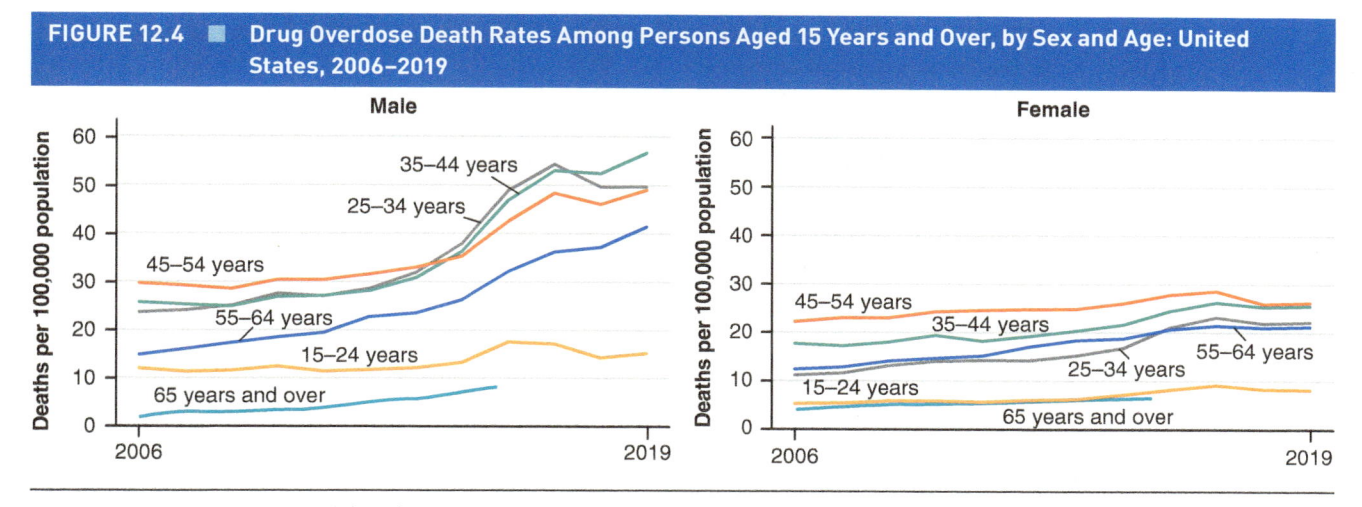

FIGURE 12.4 ■ Drug Overdose Death Rates Among Persons Aged 15 Years and Over, by Sex and Age: United States, 2006–2019

Source: Centers for Disease Control. (2023). *Health, United States, 2020-2021.* www.cdc.gov/nchs/hus/contents2017.htm#Figure_026; https://www.cdc.gov/nchs/data/hus/2020-2021/ODMort.pdf

Note: Data for persons age 65 and older are not available from 2017 to 2019.

Drug use in the United States is higher than it is worldwide. The United States is one of the larger users of illicit drugs such as marijuana, amphetamines, opioids such as heroin and opium, and cocaine. Fentanyl, which is a synthetic opioid drug, is some 100 times more potent than morphine. Its use is at crisis proportions in some parts of the United States. In fact, U.S. deaths due to opioid overdose increased from 17,500 in 2006 to 42,200 in 2016. Further the number of deaths is estimated to increase to 81,700 by 2025 (Chen et al., 2019). Figure 12.4 shows drug overdose death rates from 2006 to 2019. Although this figure includes all drug overdoses, over two thirds of these involve an opioid including fentanyl. Other countries with developed economies, such as Australia and European countries, show greater drug use than countries with developing economies. In the next section, you will be introduced to the nature of addiction and how drugs can influence and change your brain.

DISORDERED SUBSTANCE USE, DEPENDENCE, AND ADDICTION

Using psychoactive substances is part of human culture, social life, and our evolutionary history. In fact, it is probably our evolutionary history that makes us vulnerable to the desire for psychoactive substances. More broadly, there are many motivations behind our desire to use drugs and alcohol. Some of these can be based on liking the experience associated with their use. In these cases, we make a choice of when and where to have the experience. In other instances, individuals experience a stronger motivation, which results in a wanting and seeking of the drug. In comparison with liking a substance, the wanting and seeking behavior uses a different pathway in the brain, which is related to **addiction**. Many researchers make a distinction between drug use, drug misuse (e.g., binge drinking), and addiction. This section of the chapter will focus on the addictive properties of drugs and the manner in which drugs are processed by our bodies as well as experienced in emotional and cognitive terms.

Addiction is also described in terms of substance **dependence**. There are three major components to dependence: (1) the desire to seek and take a certain substance, (2) the inability to avoid or limit the intake of the substance, and (3) the experience of negative emotional states when the substance is not available. SAMHSA estimates that, in 2021, some 46.3 million individuals could be considered has having had a substance use disorder in the past year.

As you will see in this chapter's discussion of the mechanisms of different drugs, there are often complex relationships between addiction and dependence. Coffee is a common substance on which many individuals show physical dependence. That is, they show signs of withdrawal such as a headache if they stop drinking coffee. They may even drink coffee to avoid these negative experiences. However, just avoiding withdrawal symptoms is not a sign of addiction in itself. Other drugs such as cocaine can produce addiction without withdrawal symptoms. Thus, psychoactive substances can show different patterns of addiction and dependence.

Disordered substance use and addiction are a burden not only to the individual but also to the family and society at large. It is estimated that approximately half a trillion dollars is lost to the U.S. economy from disordered substance use and addiction each year. This includes medical problems, loss of productivity, accidents, and crime. Family relationships are also disturbed, including the person's relationship with their children.

Substance Disorders in *DSM-5-TR* and *ICD-11*

Both *DSM-5-TR* and *ICD-11* examine a disordered level of involvement with a psychoactive substance (Witkiewitz et al., 2022). Both systems include symptoms related to one's loss of control over substance use, and substance use taking over other activities, and use resulting in life-health problems, tolerance, and physiological withdrawal. To be considered a disorder, an individual's use of a psychoactive substance must cause distress or impairment that interferes with normal functioning. **Disordered use** refers to the condition in which this distress or impairment is significant, related to such factors as the person taking more of the substance than was intended, not being able to reduce the use of the substance, spending time trying to obtain the substance, not being able to work or keep up with other obligations, having the substance interfere with social relationships, reducing one's activities because of the substance, having the substance create medical problems, and engaging in hazardous activities such as driving while on the substance.

Intoxication refers to the effects of the psychoactive substance, typically including psychological changes and effects on behavioral abilities. Alcohol intoxication, for example, may produce such symptoms as slurred speech, problems with attention and memory, inability to make coordinated motor movements (including walking), and passing out. Cannabis intoxication, on the other hand, may lead to increased appetite, a different experience of time, a withdrawal into inner experience, a cognitive and emotional overvaluation of ideas, and, at times, anxiety.

Withdrawal refers to the symptoms experienced when a psychoactive substance is no longer used. Withdrawal symptoms may also be seen when the amount of a drug is reduced, especially when this follows a long period of use. These symptoms are typically specific to the drug. Alcohol withdrawal can produce tremors, problems with sleep, nausea or vomiting, anxiety, and autonomic nervous system

A lethal combination of drugs may have contributed to the death in 2022 of Foo Fighters drummer Taylor Hawkins.
Daniel DeSlover/ZUMA Press, Inc./Alamy Stock Photo

(ANS) overactivity such as sweating or a fast heart rate. An extreme form of alcohol withdrawal is referred to as *delirium tremens (DTs)*. After a long period of heavy drinking, withdrawal of alcohol can produce not only the normal symptoms of withdrawal but also hallucinations, confusion, and seizures. Individuals with delirium tremens may believe they are picking bugs off their body or think they see various insects crawling on the walls when there is nothing there. The cultural idea that alcohol causes one to see pink elephants comes from DTs.

DSM-5-TR and *ICD-11* describe use of, intoxication with, and withdrawal from a number of psychoactive substances, including alcohol, caffeine, cannabis, hallucinogens, opioids, sedatives, stimulants, and tobacco. They also include a general category of inhalant-related disorders. Gambling as a disorder is now part of substance use and addictive disorders. The criteria for substance use and addictive disorder for each drug are very similar.

Who Becomes Addicted?

There is no one answer as to who becomes addicted and why (Volkow & Li, 2005). One factor is related to timing of first use. With alcohol, those who begin using alcohol before the age of 15 in the United States are 4 times more likely to become addicted in their lifetime in comparison with those who begin at age 20 or older. Current research suggests that drugs affect adolescents in a different manner than they do adults. Further, it has been shown that societal attitudes at the time a person grew up will later influence their drug use (Keyes et al., 2012). It has been suggested that since European youth are introduced to alcohol use, such as wine with meals, earlier than American youth, they have fewer problems with alcohol. However, data from the U.S. Department of Justice suggest this is not the case (Friese & Grube, n.d.). While 15- and 16-year-olds in Europe do report drinking more than American adolescents (as shown in Figure 12.5), European youth in general do not report less intoxication in the past month than American adolescents.

As discussed in Chapter 5, adolescence is clearly a time when the brain is reestablishing connections and networks and is sensitive to environmental and internal changes. Related to these brain changes is the development of better impulse control, social understanding, self-awareness, and other executive

FIGURE 12.5 ■ Countries in Which Adolescents Report the Most Intoxication

This figure shows the percentage of 15- to 16-year-olds reporting intoxication in the past 30 days, based on 2007 data.

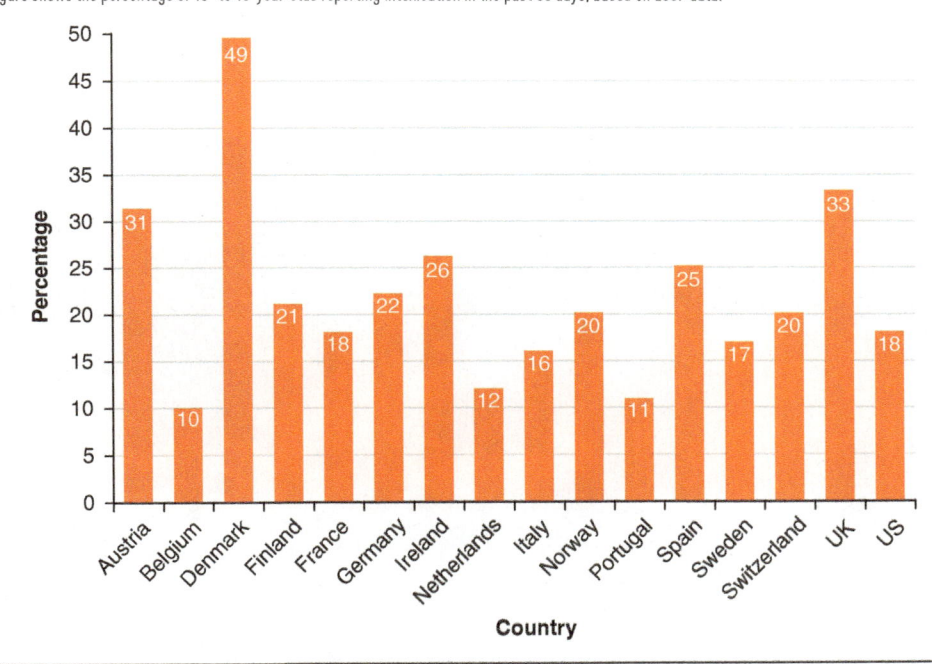

Country	Percentage
Austria	31
Belgium	10
Denmark	49
Finland	21
France	18
Germany	22
Ireland	26
Netherlands	12
Italy	16
Norway	20
Portugal	11
Spain	25
Sweden	17
Switzerland	20
UK	33
US	18

Source: Friese, B., & Grube, J. (n.d.). *Youth drinking rates and problems: A comparison of European countries and the United States.* U.S. Department of Justice. https://www.ojp.gov/ncjrs/virtual-library/abstracts/youth-drinking-rates-and-problems-comparison-european-countries-and

functioning in the frontal lobes. As you will see, drugs have a direct influence on the frontal lobes in individuals of all ages. Adolescents are particularly at risk for changes in both short-term and long-term brain development associated with drug use (Blakemore, 2013; Westbrook et al., 2020).

Genetic, Environmental, and Evolutionary Influences

An important factor for understanding addiction is genetics (Bogdan et al., 2023). Research has shown that 40% to 60% of vulnerability to addiction can be attributed to genetic factors. Genome-wide association study (GWAS) approaches can explain only about a quarter of this heritability (Bogdan et al., 2023). Genetic factors and their relationship with the environment can be seen in the manner in which different drugs show different levels of reinforcing factors and influence an individual's metabolism. That is, some drugs are more addictive than others. Also, individuals show different sensitivities to particular drugs, and thus some people can become addicted to certain drugs more quickly than to other drugs as well as more quickly than other individuals become addicted to a particular drug (Volkow et al., 2019; Volkow et al., 2012). Studies to identify specific genes such as those associated with cannabis dependence are just beginning (Sherva et al., 2016).

The environments in which both adults and adolescents live play a crucial role. Environmental factors such as stress and low socioeconomic level are associated with greater drug use, which can lead to addiction (Koob & Schulkin, 2018). Among adolescents, peer pressure can play an important role in deciding whether to try new types of drugs. Adolescence is also a time when individuals take risks and try new things. This is compounded, research shows, by the fact that drugs may disrupt networks of the brain involved in making decisions. Drugs influence not only what people seek for reinforcement but also their ability to inhibit these desires.

Another way in which the environment plays a role is in terms of epigenetics (Robison & Nestler, 2011). Although numerous studies suggest that the genetic contribution to the risk for addiction is about 50%, it is not known which genes are involved. An alternative suggestion is that epigenetic mechanisms relate to addiction by determining how genes are turned on and off. Specifically, teenage alcohol consumption is associated with the development of alcohol use disorder and anxiety in adulthood (Bohnsack et al., 2022; Teague & Nestler, 2022). This is related to the epigenetic expression of a particular gene expression, activity-regulated cytoskeleton-associated protein (Arc) in the amygdala (Bohnsack et al., 2022).

With the advent of brain imaging and other neuroscience techniques, research has suggested that a common process underlies a variety of disorders, including drug addiction, bulimia nervosa, pathological gambling, and sexual addiction (Goodman, 2007). These disorders are also associated with affective disorders, anxiety disorders, attention deficit disorder, and personality disorders at frequencies that are higher than in the general population.

During adolescence, peer pressure and a tendency to take risks can lead to drug use.
iStock.com/gorodenkoff

Addiction to psychoactive substances is not unique to humans. Neuroscience research has shown that other mammals exhibit compulsive behaviors to take in the same addictive substances as humans (Wise, 1998). This supports an evolutionary perspective but also raises some interesting questions as to why a number of species seek these substances. Clearly, addiction can cause harm, but is there another side to understanding addiction? From an evolutionary perspective, we can ask if taking psychoactive substances helps us to protect ourselves, or to mate, or to engage in social activities.

It can also be noted that psychoactive substances use the same networks in the brain that are associated with a feeling of social well-being. In particular, the opioid system in the brain, which is involved in addiction to morphine and heroin, is also involved in the satisfaction derived from social relationships, sexual stimulation, and tasty food. Opioids also modify learning and memory through the hippocampus (Kibaly et al., 2019). One of the ways these processes may be influenced is through our emotions (Panksepp et al., 2002). We perform activities such as eating, sleeping, and being with others that not only make us feel good but also increase our ability to take care of ourselves and have sexual and social relationships. As infants, feeling taken care of in terms of food, closeness, and attachment is critical for successful development. Research with other mammals such as rats and monkeys shows that isolation in early life leads to a greater sensitivity to psychoactive substances, including alcohol. This suggests that early environmental factors can play a role in later drug use.

Pattern of Addiction

There is a pattern that is seen in addiction (Figure 12.6). Initially, the positive experience of taking the drug—a rush or a sense of well-being—leads to a compulsion to seek and take it again. This period of intoxication is also associated with impaired cognitive abilities. This is followed by a *craving* in which the individual loses control of their ability to limit intake of the drug. For example, even when the blood alcohol level of a person with an alcohol addiction is high, they still drink more. The next condition is the emergence of a negative emotional state when the substance is unavailable or access to it is limited. What once gave a positive feeling now does little. In fact, the person needs the drug to feel normal. There is a paradox in that by this last stage, people who are addicted want their psychoactive substance more than they enjoy it. It should also be noted that with drugs there is an increased tolerance. That is, people at this stage need more of the drug to experience the effect they are seeking.

A more detailed pattern of addiction is described by Goodman (2007) in Table 12.1.

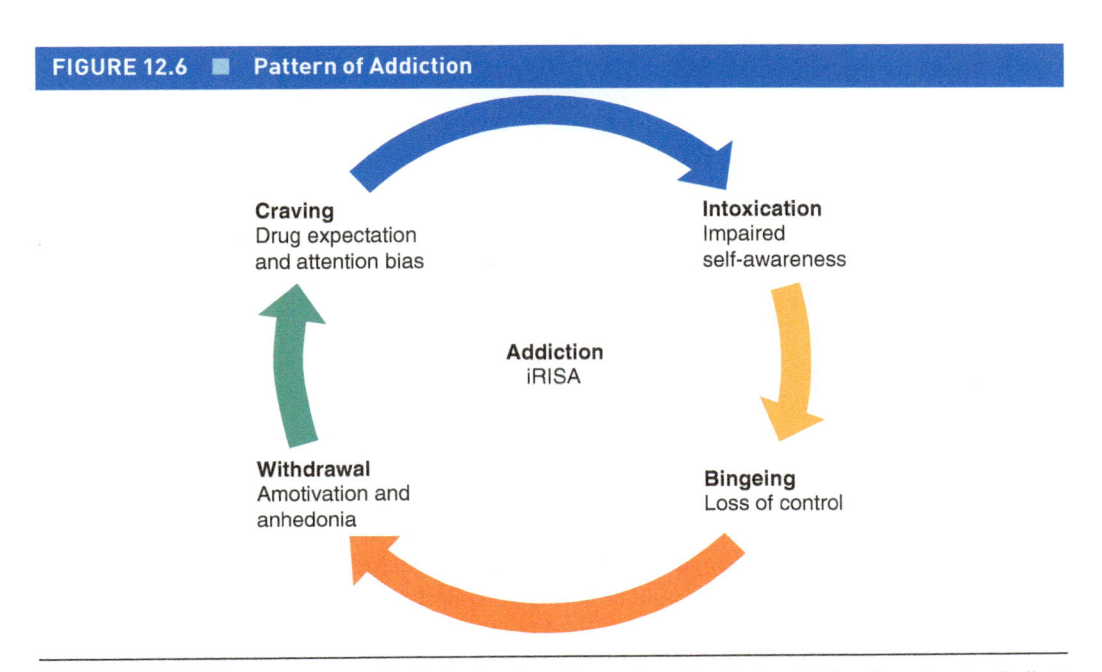

FIGURE 12.6 ■ Pattern of Addiction

Craving — Drug expectation and attention bias

Intoxication — Impaired self-awareness

Bingeing — Loss of control

Withdrawal — Amotivation and anhedonia

Addiction — iRISA

Credit: Goldstein, R. Z., & Volkow, N. D. (2011). Dysfunction of the prefrontal cortex in addiction: Neuroimaging findings and clinical implications. *Nature Reviews Neuroscience, 12*(11), 652–669. http://doi.org/10.1038/nrn3119, p. 653.

Note: iRISA refers to impaired response inhibition and salience attribution.

TABLE 12.1 ■ Detailed Pattern of Addiction

Topic	Details
Course of Illness	The disorder typically begins in adolescence or early adulthood and follows a chronic course with remissions and exacerbations.
Behavioral Features	Behavioral repertoire narrows, and the behavior is continued despite harmful consequences.
Individuals' Subjective Experience of the Condition	Individuals feel a sense of craving, preoccupation, excitement during preparatory activity, mood-altering effects, and a sense of loss of control.
Progressive Development of the Condition	Craving, loss of control, narrowing of behavioral repertoire, and harmfulness of consequences all tend to increase as the duration of the condition increases.
Experience of Tolerance	As the behavior is repeated, its potency to produce reinforcing effects tends to diminish.
Experience of Withdrawal Phenomena	Psychological or physical discomfort is felt when the behavior is discontinued.
Tendency to Relapse	Individual tends to return to harmful patterns of behavior after a period of abstinence or control has been achieved.
Propensity for Behavioral Substitution	When the behavioral symptoms of the disorder have come under control, addictive engagement in other behaviors tend to emerge or intensify.
Relationship Between the Condition and Other Aspects of Affected Individuals' Lives	Other areas of life are neglected as the behavior assumes priority.
Recurrent Themes in the Ways Individuals With These Conditions Relate to Others and to Themselves	Condition can result in low self-esteem, self-centeredness, denial, rationalization, and conflicts over dependency and control.

Credit: Goodman, A. (2007). Neurobiology of addiction: An integrative review. *Biochemical Pharmacology*, 75, 266–322, with permission from Elsevier.

Can Drugs Change Your Brain?

The quick answer is yes—drugs change your brain. In fact, for someone addicted to a particular drug, whether heroin, whiskey, or another addictive substance, just seeing the paraphernalia associated with it can produce physiological changes before the drug is actually ingested. This works in a manner similar to how all learning changes your brain, although drug addiction seems to last longer than simple learning (Nestler & Malenka, 2004). It can last for weeks, months, or even years after the last ingestion of the drug. This sets up the possibility of relapse, since a person has a difficult time forgetting the drug's effects.

On one level, drugs are rewarding to our body and give us experiences we seek (Lüscher & Janak, 2021; Ray & Grodin, 2021). They use the same neural networks as those found in the reward values of food and sex. This can result in some surprising situations. For example, if an animal is given the choice of drugs or food, it will choose drugs. Catnip is one example seen outside of the laboratory. In the lab, the typical procedure is to use a Skinner box in which the animal can press a lever for food or a different lever for the drug. If the animal has previous experience with the drug, it will ignore the food lever and press the drug lever. If the ratio is set so that the animal will need to press the lever a number of times before the drug is administered, the animal will actually spend much of its waking hours working for the drug. This is not unlike the human addicted to a drug who spends considerable energy to obtain it, including engaging in illegal activities to acquire the money to purchase it.

Drugs take over the brain mechanisms that are involved in reward (Hyman et al., 2006). Neuroscience studies show that their rewarding effect is based on their ability to increase *dopamine* (Bogdan et al., 2023; Hyman et al., 2006; Lüscher & Janak, 2021; Volkow et al., 2012). One important pathway related to addiction is the mesolimbic dopamine system (Lüscher & Janak, 2021; Ostroumov & Dani, 2018). This system begins in the ventral tegmental area (VTA), which is located near the base of the brain (Figure 12.7).

These pathways connect with the nucleus accumbens, prefrontal cortex (PFC), dorsal striatum, and amygdala, all structures that release dopamine. Dopamine was initially thought to be the neurobiological correlate of reward or pleasure. However, more recent research has clarified dopamine's function, which includes signaling what the person can expect. That is, dopamine is not so much associated with pleasure as with the *expectation* of pleasure. In this sense, it is involved in driving motivated behavior. Thus, it is involved in predicting reward or non-reward as well as in facilitating consolidation of memory for salient events. The important point is that many drugs of addiction increase activity in the VTA and the nucleus accumbens.

Molecular mechanisms of many drugs leave excessive dopamine available in the brain (Figure 12.8). This works by different mechanisms. Cocaine either blocks dopamine uptake in the synapse or increases dopamine released by the terminals of VTA cells, which increases dopamine signaling in the nucleus accumbens. Alcohol and opiates such as opium and heroin enhance dopamine release by quieting neurons that would otherwise inhibit dopamine-secreting neurons. Nicotine induces VTA cells to release dopamine into the nucleus accumbens.

The rewarding mechanisms are seen as the main reason humans and laboratory animals choose to self-administer drugs. The main mechanism for these rewarding effects is the ability of drugs to increase dopamine in the nucleus accumbens (Volkow et al., 2019; Volkow et al., 2012). Dopamine appears to encode the prediction of reward, whereas endogenous opioids and cannabinoids mediate the experience of pleasure. Nicotine, alcohol, stimulants, and marijuana all increase dopamine in the dorsal striatum and ventral striatum (VS). Interestingly, research suggests that individuals with a low dopamine level—as seen in Parkinson's disease, for example—when given dopamine as a treatment may show pathological gambling, hypersexuality, compulsive shopping, compulsive eating, and compulsive medication use (Voon & Fox, 2007). Through classical conditioning, a neutral stimulus that is linked to a drug (such as a syringe used to inject a drug or a small mirror used to snort a line of cocaine) can by itself produce increased dopamine.

FIGURE 12.7 ■ Addiction and the Brain: The Mesolimbic Dopamine Pathway

This figure shows the mesolimbic dopamine pathway, beginning with the VTA and ending in the prefrontal cortex. Dopamine is a critical component of the brain reward circuitry.

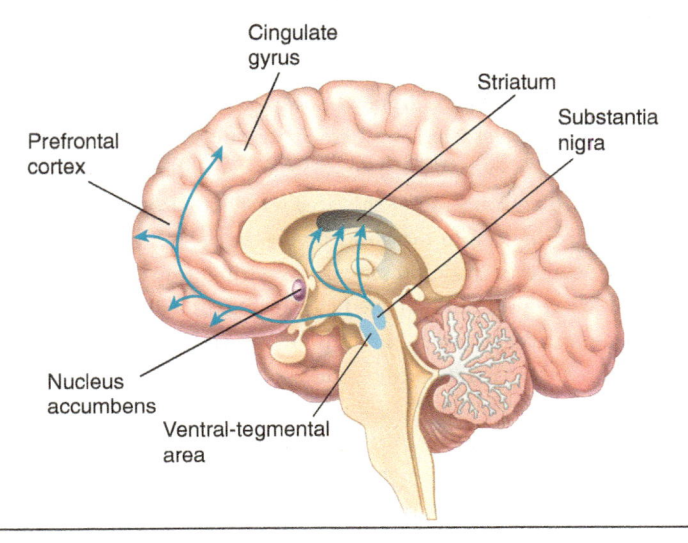

Credit: Hyman, S., Malenka, R., & Nestler, E. (2006). Neural mechanisms of addiction: The role of reward-related learning and memory. *Annual Review of Neuroscience, 29,* 565–598. Reprinted with permission from Annual Reviews.

FIGURE 12.8 ■ Drug Effects on Dopamine in the Brain

This figure shows the manner in which drugs can affect the operation of dopamine in the brain.

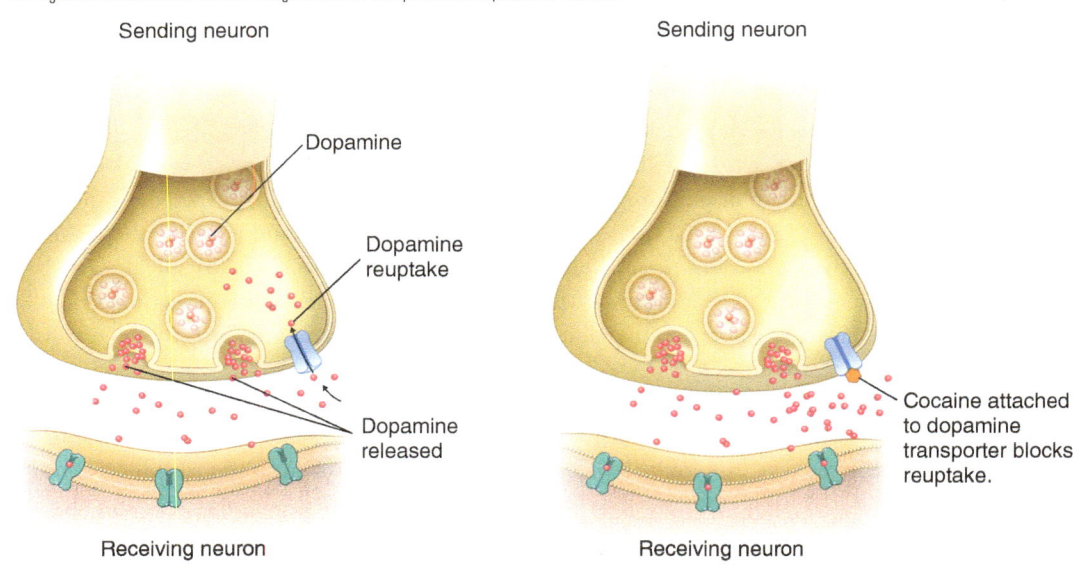

Thus, dopamine plays an important role in motivation, which includes activation, effort, and persistence. Drug addiction can be seen as one form of enhanced motivation. At this point, five dopamine receptors have been identified, which are labeled by the letter D and a number. Short-term exposure to drugs triggers the dopamine system. The release of dopamine in relation to addictive drugs changes drug use into drug-seeking behavior (Kalivas, 2009). Over time, other neurotransmitters such as glutamate and GABA become involved (Uys & Reissner, 2011).

Not only can drugs change your brain, but they can also take over the cognitive, emotional, and physiological mechanisms that we use for everyday life. In an addicted state, compulsive drug use largely reduces our level of human functioning to seeking means for obtaining the drug. This results in decreased social functioning, personal creativity, and productivity. In addition, brain changes in areas such as the frontal lobe lead us to deny we even have a problem and reduce our desire to make changes.

The speed at which specific drugs enter the brain is related to the experience of reward and the nature of the felt "high." This can happen with the same drug administered in different ways. For example, cocaine that is snorted through the nose produces a slower and less intense high than if it is given intravenously. Further, the peak experience of different drugs happens at different times. Nicotine has a peak level at around 2 to 3 minutes. Cocaine has a peak level at around 4 to 6 minutes. Methamphetamines have a peak level at around 10 to 15 minutes.

Given the role of the PFC in executive functions such as inhibitory control and decision making, it is not surprising to see a disruption of this area with addiction (Goldstein & Volkow, 2011). It appears that the PFC is connected to networks involving the striatum, which are modulated by dopamine. In studies that compare those who use drugs with non-users, the worst task performance was found on tasks that are connected with the PFC. It is assumed that dysfunction of these areas contributes to the development of craving, compulsive use, and the denial that a problem exists or there is need for treatment. Table 12.2 describes processes associated with the PFC that are disrupted in addiction.

With our current understanding of brain mechanisms in addiction, it is possible to redraw Figure 12.6 and add the brain mechanisms involved (Figure 12.9). Once a person has taken a drug and experiences its pleasant or euphoric effects, this person has been reinforced to want more. This reward circuit, which involves the neurotransmitter dopamine and is related to reward and expectation and memory of the drug experience, includes the VTA, nucleus accumbens, amygdala, and hippocampus. Following the reinforcing effects of a drug comes the expectation of or craving for using the drug again. This is a conscious experience involving the PFC, the orbitofrontal cortex (OFC), and the anterior cingulate cortex (ACC). Next comes a loss of control or bingeing in which the VTA and nucleus accumbens reward circuit is increased and the normal inhibition of the frontal cortex is decreased. These areas are also thought to be involved in the experience of withdrawal when an addicted individual does not receive the drug.

TABLE 12.2 ■ Processes Associated With the Prefrontal Cortex (PFC) That Are Disrupted in Addiction

Process	Possible Disruption in Addiction	Probable PFC Region
Self-control and behavioral monitoring: response inhibition, behavioral coordination, conflict and error prediction, detection, and resolution	Impulsivity, compulsivity, risk taking and impaired self-monitoring (habitual, automatic, stimulus-driven, and inflexible behavioral patterns)	DLPFC, dACC, IFG, and vlPFC
Emotion regulation: cognitive and affective suppression of emotion	Enhanced stress reactivity and inability to suppress emotional intensity (e.g., anxiety and negative affect)	mOFC, vmPFC, and subgenual ACC
Motivation: drive, initiative, persistence, and effort toward the pursuit of goals	Enhanced motivation to procure drugs but decreased motivation for other goals, and compromised purposefulness and effort	OFC, ACC, vmPFC, and DLPFC
Awareness and interoception: feeling one's own bodily and subjective state, insight	Reduced satiety, denial of illness or need for treatment, and externally oriented thinking	rACC and dACC, mPFC, OFC, and vlPFC
Attention and flexibility: set formation and maintenance versus set-shifting, and task switching	Attention bias toward drug-related stimuli and away from other stimuli and reinforcers, and inflexibility in goals to procure the drug	DLPFC, ACC, IFC, and vlPFC
Working memory: short-term memory enabling the construction of representations and guidance of action	Formation of memory that is biased toward drug-related stimuli and away from alternatives	DLPFC
Learning and memory: stimulus–response associative learning, reversal learning, extinction, reward devaluation, latent inhibition (suppression of information), and long-term memory	Drug conditioning and disrupted ability to update the reward value of non-drug reinforcers	DLPFC, OFC, and ACC
Decision making: valuation (coding reinforcers) versus choice, expected outcome, probability estimation, planning and goal formation	Drug-related anticipation, choice of immediate reward over delayed gratification, discounting of future consequences, and inaccurate predictions or action planning	lOFC, mOFC, vmPFC, and DLPFC
Salience attribution: affective value appraisal, incentive salience, and subjective utility (alternative outcomes)	Drugs and drug cues have a sensitized value, non-drug reinforcers are devalued and gradients are not perceived, and negative prediction error (actual experience worse than expected)	mOFC and vmPFC

Credit: Goldstein, R. Z., & Volkow, N. D. (2011). Dysfunction of the prefrontal cortex in addiction: Neuroimaging findings and clinical implications. *Nature Reviews Neuroscience, 12*(11), 652–669. http://doi.org/10.1038/nrn3119, p. 654.

Note: Brain areas are prefrontal cortex (PFC), anterior cingulate cortex (ACC), orbitofrontal cortex (OFC), and interior orbitofrontal cortex (lOFC). These various processes and regions participate to a different degree in craving, intoxication, bingeing, and withdrawal.

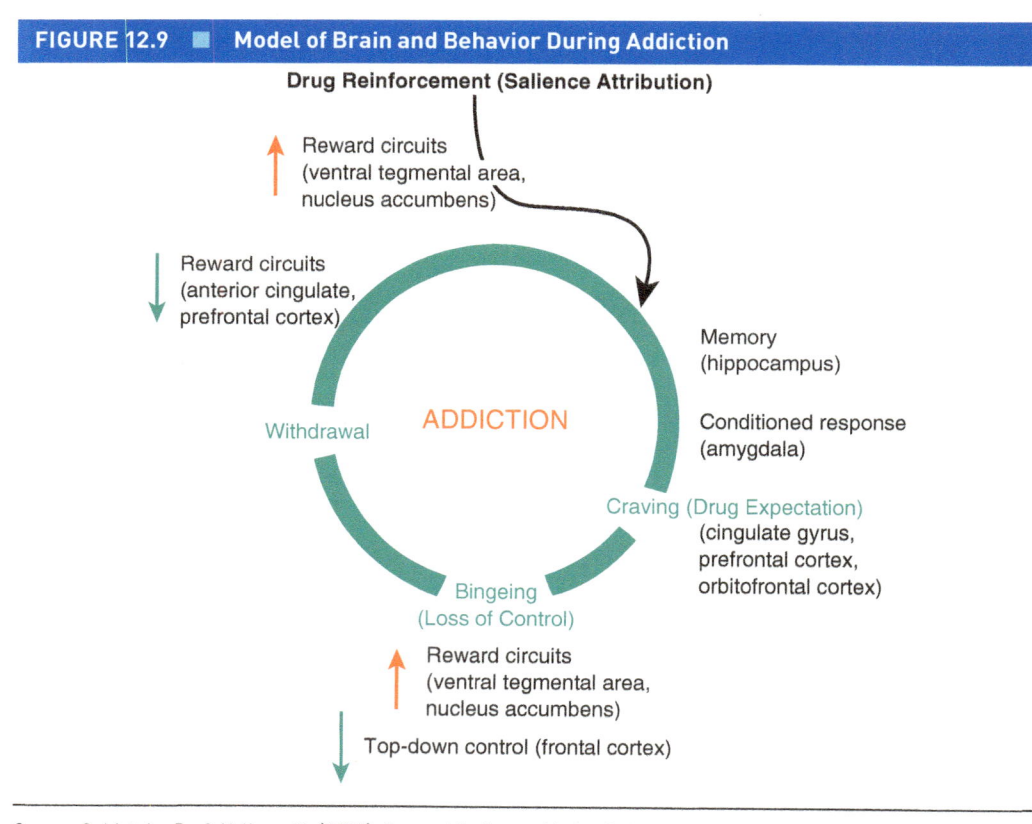

FIGURE 12.9 ■ Model of Brain and Behavior During Addiction

Drug Reinforcement (Salience Attribution)

↑ Reward circuits (ventral tegmental area, nucleus accumbens)

↓ Reward circuits (anterior cingulate, prefrontal cortex)

ADDICTION

- Withdrawal
- Memory (hippocampus)
- Conditioned response (amygdala)
- Craving (Drug Expectation) (cingulate gyrus, prefrontal cortex, orbitofrontal cortex)
- Bingeing (Loss of Control)

↑ Reward circuits (ventral tegmental area, nucleus accumbens)

↓ Top-down control (frontal cortex)

Source: Goldstein, R., & Volkow, N. (2002). Drug addiction and its underlying neurobiological basis: Neuroimaging evidence for the involvement of the frontal cortex. *American Journal of Psychiatry, 159*, 1642–1652.

CONCEPT CHECK

- What can we say about the use of both legal and illegal substances in the United States? What are the worldwide patterns of drug use?
- What is the distinction between drug use, drug misuse such as binge drinking, and addiction? What are the three major components to dependence?
- *DSM-5* and *ICD-11* identify the level of involvement with a psychoactive substance in terms of use, intoxication, and withdrawal. What are the characteristics of each of these levels? Do they apply across the board, or are they substance related, or both?
- What factors play a role in who becomes addicted and who doesn't?
- What are the steps in the pattern of addiction? What mechanisms move the process from one step to the next?
- How do drugs change your brain? In what ways can they be said to control it?

ALCOHOL

Until recently, I hadn't gone to bed sober in twenty-five years. I was a drunk when I first met my wife of twenty-three years, and I have been one ever since. I have been a pretty good drunk, as drunks go, without the usual DWIs, abusive behavior, or too dear a price paid for being too honest after my seventh or tenth drink. I am a flirt when drunk but have never been unfaithful.

I worked hard while I drank, and once wrote three novels and hundreds of nonfiction articles in four years. I believe my work was more lyrical with the help of alcohol. The problem was that my love affair with the bottle finally began to threaten my continued existence on this shaky earth.

iStock.com/Baranova Valentina

In the past year, I started drinking in the shower each morning. I was drunk by nine, drunk at noon, drunk at three, drunk at seven, and drunk at ten o'clock. I had pretty much stopped eating, although I still made dinner for my wife, our dogs, and myself, and pretended to enjoy a fine meal in a fine little house on a pretty street in a nice little town. Eventually, my body started eating itself to stay alive. Ketosis is the medical term.

Why my drinking got so out of control after so many years of my being a functioning and productive alcoholic remains a mystery to me. I just know that I had become (and still am) one sick son of a bitch just a step away from the grave because I suffer from the disease of alcoholism. I drank too much. It is as simple, and as difficult, as that.

I love drinking, and am having a hard time accepting that being sober is somehow a superior state of being. It's also hard to accept that I have to expend even more energy to stay clean than I did when the first thing I thought about in the morning was whether I had enough Scotch for the following night. Never having had hangovers, I don't feel any better when I wake up now than I did when I drank, and I literally have to remind myself that I didn't drink yesterday.

I do not, however, miss all those questions for which I seldom found answers: Did I black out last night? Are apologies due? Is my wife pissed? How did I get home, and where the hell is the car? Who did I call, and did I insult them? What happened to all the money I had in my wallet? How much did I put on the card? Think now, Davidson. These are questions most drunks have had to ask themselves at one time or another. After a while, I just stopped asking them.

From Neil Davidson, "Goodbye, Johnnie Walker." Originally published in *The Sun*, July 1998, Issue 271.

Alcohol has been available to humans for a large part of our history. For at least 10,000 years, humans have made wine, beer, and other drinks through a process of fermentation. During fermentation, yeast breaks down sugar found in grains, such as barley, and fruits, such as grapes, into ethanol (alcohol) and carbon dioxide. Once carbon dioxide is removed, the ethanol and water remain in the form of wine or beer. Alcohol levels above about 12% will greatly slow down fermentation and above 14% will kill the yeast. Higher alcohol drinks such as gin, vodka, rum, and whiskey

Part of the reason for alcohol's use in celebrations is its effect on our central nervous system.

iStock.com/jacoblund

are further heated after fermentation in a process of distilling to remove the water. The percentage of alcohol in a substance is measured in terms of *proof*, which is twice the percentage of alcohol (e.g., 20% alcohol equals 40 proof). Researchers consider 12 oz. of beer, 5 oz. of wine, and 1.5 oz. of liquor to contain .5 oz. of pure alcohol.

Alcohol is consumed throughout most of the world, and Figure 12.10 shows the amount of alcohol—in liters—consumed annually by people over 15 years of age. A bottle of wine is three fourths of a liter, and a gallon contains not quite 4 liters. In many cultures around the world, alcohol is used for celebrations such as weddings and parties. In some cultures, alcohol is even part of funerals, such as the traditional Irish wake. In other cultures—Islamic, for example—it is not used and is even banned in some places. Some individuals, such as those with East Asian heritage, have a genetic makeup that causes their faces or body to become flushed when drinking alcohol, which results in lower alcohol consumption. Thus, there are both cultural and genetic factors related to the use of or abstinence from alcohol in a given country or region.

Part of the reason for alcohol's use in celebrations is its effect on our central nervous system. In most humans, the experience of alcohol intake includes pleasant subjective experiences that may lead to increased social interactions. This is partly related to the effects of alcohol on such neurotransmitters as serotonin, endorphins, and dopamine. Alcohol will also decrease inhibition by reducing the effects of the GABA system, which is associated with anxiety. However, when alcohol intake is increased, it increases the effects of GABA, which can lead to sedation. This is why alcohol is generally listed as a depressant.

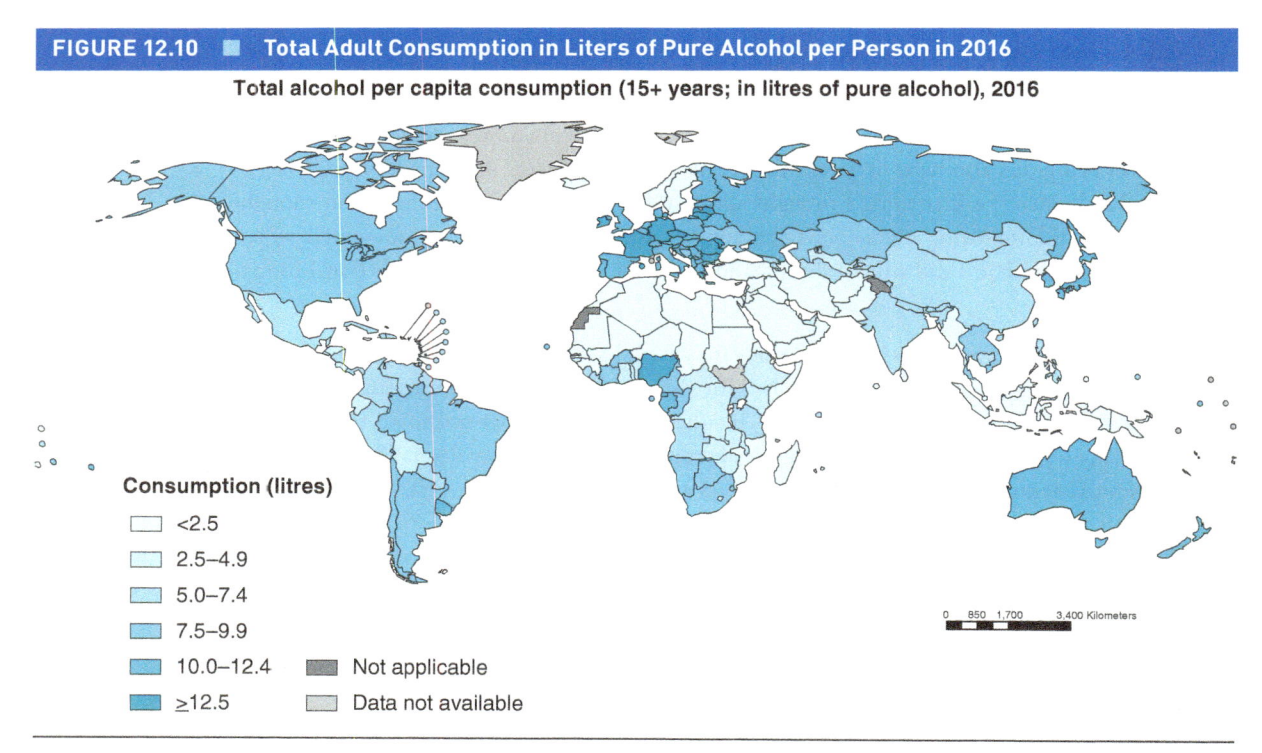

FIGURE 12.10 ■ Total Adult Consumption in Liters of Pure Alcohol per Person in 2016

Total alcohol per capita consumption (15+ years; in litres of pure alcohol), 2016

Consumption (litres)
- <2.5
- 2.5–4.9
- 5.0–7.4
- 7.5–9.9
- 10.0–12.4
- ≥12.5
- Not applicable
- Data not available

Credit: World Health Organization. (2018). *Total alcohol per capita consumption (15+ years; in litres of pure alcohol), 2016.* http://gamapserver.who.int/mapLibrary/Files/Maps/Global_adult_percapita_consumption_2016.png

Note: A bottle of wine is three quarters of a liter.

As an addictive substance, alcohol can also lead to social, legal, and medical problems (GBD 2016 Alcohol Collaborators, 2018). It often causes problems within the family, as shown in the following case study of Richard Thompson (not his real name).

> **CASE OF RICHARD THOMPSON**
> ALCOHOL USE DISORDER
>
> Richard Thompson, a 28-year-old white male, presented at the Serene Oaks Recovery Center with his wife and parents. Richard and his family had just participated in an intervention where family members shared their concerns and expressed their collective desire to see him get help for his drinking. Richard's drinking had escalated quite rapidly since losing his job last year. Richard had always had a "high tolerance." Prior to the job loss, he was drinking mostly on the weekends, consuming 8 to 12 beers on occasion, yet at times reportedly he consumed much more. He had a DUI when he was 21, but other than that, Richard denied having any problems with drinking prior to losing his job and described himself as a "social" drinker. Since the job loss, Richard has been drinking most days of the week and has begun consuming hard liquor in addition to beer, sometimes including a fifth of vodka per day. He has been having trouble remembering events while intoxicated and has been asked by his wife to leave the home on several occasions because of his belligerent behavior while drinking. At one point, the police were called to the home due to Richard's aggressive behavior. This incident prompted the recent family intervention and subsequent admission to Serene Oaks Recovery Center.
>
> Clinical vignette provided by Michael Cameron Wolff, PhD, CADC

Through loss of productivity, automobile accidents, and medical problems such as alcohol-related cancers, alcohol is estimated to cost the United States $185 billion annually (see For Further Reading). The World Health Organization (WHO) lists alcohol as the leading risk factor for death in men ages 15 to 59 (see For Further Reading). This is due to injuries, violence, and cardiovascular disease. Worldwide, they estimate that 6.2% of all deaths among men are related to alcohol compared with 1.1% for women. Overall, alcohol consumption is the world's third largest risk factor for disease and disability. It is also the third leading cause of preventable death in the United States.

Effects of Alcohol on the Human Body

Unlike most of the other foods you eat, alcohol is absorbed directly into the bloodstream without digestion. When you drink a beer or other alcoholic beverage, it goes to your stomach. In your stomach, only a small amount of alcohol is absorbed, and most is absorbed in the small intestine. However, if there is food in your stomach, your body absorbs the alcohol more slowly. If the alcoholic drink contains food substances, as beer does, it is also absorbed more slowly. On the other hand, drinks with carbon dioxide, such as champagne or a mixed drink with a carbonated beverage, are moved from the stomach to the small intestine more rapidly. Alcohol's effects are felt once it is carried through the bloodstream to the brain. So, champagne will give you the experience of alcohol faster than beer will, because it gets to your brain faster. Alcohol influences the brain through changes in gene expression as well as epigenetic processes and, in turn, the activity of neuronal circuits (Egervari et al., 2021).

Once in the bloodstream, alcohol also goes to the other organs of the body, such as the brain, heart, lungs, and liver. In the lungs, it is vaporized and exhaled. This is the basis for breathalyzers used by the police to measure alcohol levels. In the liver, it is broken down into carbon dioxide and water. Alcohol is absorbed into the bloodstream faster than it is metabolized by the liver. The speed at which your body breaks down or metabolizes alcohol is fairly constant, although women absorb and metabolize alcohol differently than men do (McHugh et al., 2018). This means that a woman may have a higher blood alcohol concentration (BAC) level than a man, even if they both drink the same amount of alcohol. Alcohol can have both positive and negative long-term effects on the body (Figure 12.11).

FIGURE 12.11 ■ Effects of Alcohol on Your Body

Alcohol can have both positive and negative long-term effects on the body.

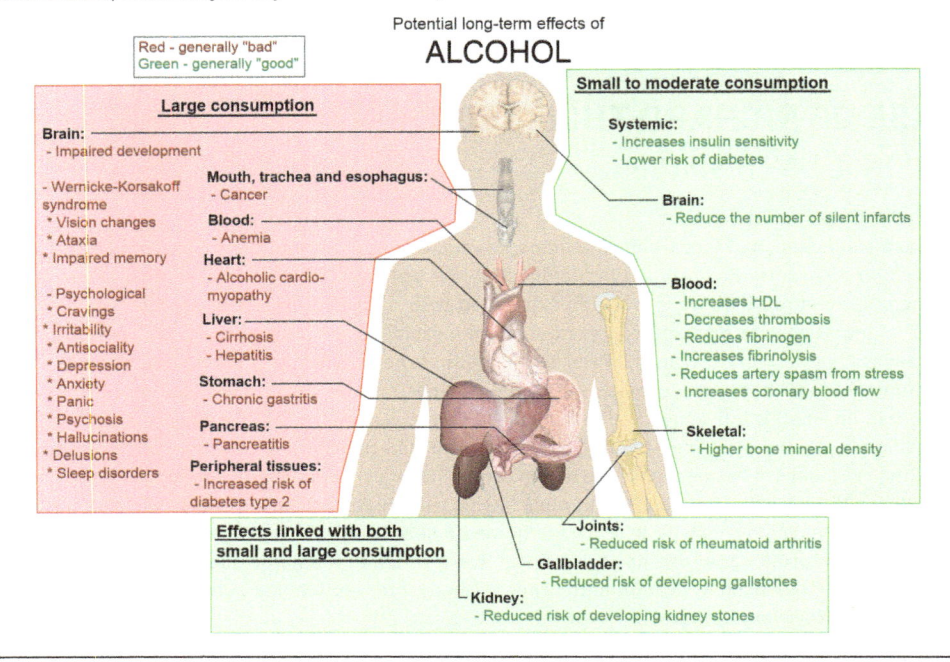

Potential long-term effects of ALCOHOL

Red - generally "bad"
Green - generally "good"

Large consumption

Brain:
- Impaired development
- Wernicke-Korsakoff syndrome
  * Vision changes
  * Ataxia
  * Impaired memory
- Psychological
  * Cravings
  * Irritability
  * Antisociality
  * Depression
  * Anxiety
  * Panic
  * Psychosis
  * Hallucinations
  * Delusions
  * Sleep disorders

Mouth, trachea and esophagus:
- Cancer

Blood:
- Anemia

Heart:
- Alcoholic cardiomyopathy

Liver:
- Cirrhosis
- Hepatitis

Stomach:
- Chronic gastritis

Pancreas:
- Pancreatitis

Peripheral tissues:
- Increased risk of diabetes type 2

Effects linked with both small and large consumption

Small to moderate consumption

Systemic:
- Increases insulin sensitivity
- Lower risk of diabetes

Brain:
- Reduce the number of silent infarcts

Blood:
- Increases HDL
- Decreases thrombosis
- Reduces fibrinogen
- Increases fibrinolysis
- Reduces artery spasm from stress
- Increases coronary blood flow

Skeletal:
- Higher bone mineral density

Joints:
- Reduced risk of rheumatoid arthritis

Gallbladder:
- Reduced risk of developing gallstones

Kidney:
- Reduced risk of developing kidney stones

Credit: Image by Mikael Häggström, MD (2009), https://en.wikipedia.org/wiki/File:Possible_long-term_effects_of_ethanol.svg, licensed under CC0 1.0 https://creativecommons.org/publicdomain/zero/1.0/deed.en

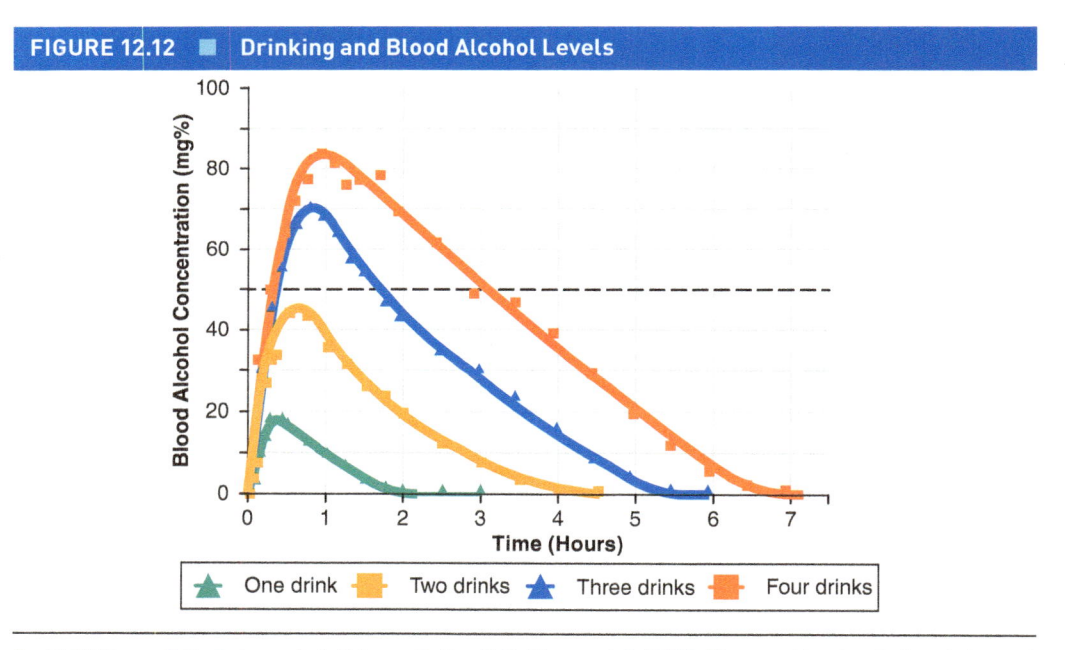

FIGURE 12.12 ■ Drinking and Blood Alcohol Levels

Credit: Wilkinson, P. K., Sedman, A. J., Sakmar, E., Kay, D. R., Wagner, J. G. (1977). Pharmacokinetics of ethanol after oral administration in the fasting state. *Journal of Pharmacokinetics and Biopharmaceutics, 5*(3), 207–224; with kind permission from Springer Science+Business Media B.V.

As seen in Figure 12.12, which charts the BAC level of men who have not recently eaten food, BAC peaks within 30 to 45 minutes of ingesting one standard drink, and it returns to zero after about 2 hours. Thus, having one drink every couple of hours would not lead to intoxication, because the alcohol would be metabolized and removed from the bloodstream. However, since alcohol is absorbed faster than it is metabolized, drinking more than one drink in an hour leads to increased BAC levels. Also as seen in Figure 12.12, drinking two, three, or four drinks in an hour both increases BAC and increases the amount of time it takes for alcohol to be removed from the bloodstream. As noted earlier, having food in the stomach will also delay the absorption of alcohol.

Alcohol and Genetics

Alcohol dependence runs in families (Treutlein et al., 2009). Twin studies suggest that 40% to 60% of the variance in dependence can be accounted for by genetics. One study showed that a gene influencing the activity of serotonin is related to impulsivity (Tikkanen et al., 2015). Individuals with this gene showed more impulsive and aggressive behavior both when drinking and not drinking, but particularly under the influence of alcohol, including physical fights when drinking and arrests for drunk driving. Further, GWASs suggest that a number of genes contribute to alcohol dependence, which are separate from those genes involved in nonpathological drinking behaviors (Walters et al., 2018). Further, neurotransmitters such as serotonin and dopamine can bind to histones and act as epigenetic marks to regulate gene expression, which could influence addiction (Egervari et al., 2021).

Overall, research suggests there is a common genetic component involved in alcohol, tobacco, and cannabis dependence across adolescence and young adulthood (Palmer et al., 2013). What is interesting is that this genetic influence increases from adolescence to young adulthood, and at the same time, the influence of the environment decreases. Since dopamine pathways have a large genetic component, this may be the critical dimension that influences alcohol dependence. The overall picture suggests that environmental influences such as friends, peer pressure, and one's culture influence the *use* of drugs. However, genetics have more influence on the person becoming drug *dependent*. These genetic effects appear to be slightly stronger for women than men.

Moderate, Heavy, and Binge Drinking

Light drinking of alcohol, such as a glass of wine, has been associated with better health outcomes—even better than the outcomes associated with not drinking at all. For example, individuals who drink a glass of wine daily show fewer cardiovascular problems. Additional health benefits are seen when one drinks slowly and eats while drinking. Moderate drinking is defined by the National Institute on Alcohol Abuse and Alcoholism (NIAAA) as no more than 4 drinks in a single day and no more than 14 drinks a week for a man. Women, who metabolize alcohol differently, have lower levels for moderate drinking—no more than three drinks on a single day and no more than seven drinks a week.

Those who drink more than these amounts are considered to be heavy or "at-risk" drinkers who are susceptible to a number of health and other problems. **Binge drinking** is defined by NIAAA as consuming enough alcohol in a 2-hour period to have a BAC of 0.08g/dL. Figures 12.13

FIGURE 12.13 ■ BAC Chart for Men

Men

Approximate Blood Alcohol Percentage

Drinks	Body Weight in Pounds								
	100	120	140	160	180	200	220	240	
0	.00	.00	.00	.00	.00	.00	.00	.00	Only Safe Driving Limit
1	.04	.03	.03	.02	.02	.02	.02	.02	Driving Skills Significantly Affected
2	.08	.06	.05	.05	.04	.04	.03	.03	
3	.11	.09	.08	.07	.06	.06	.05	.05	
4	.15	.12	.11	.09	.08	.08	.07	.06	Possible Criminal Penalties
5	.19	.16	.13	.12	.11	.09	.09	.08	
6	.23	.19	.16	.14	.13	.11	.10	.09	Legally Intoxicated
7	.26	.22	.19	.16	.15	.13	.12	.11	
8	.30	.25	.21	.19	.17	.15	.14	.13	Criminal Penalties
9	.34	.28	.24	.21	.19	.17	.15	.14	
10	.38	.31	.27	.23	.21	.19	.17	.16	Death Possible

Subtract 0.01% for each 40 minutes of drinking.

One drink is 1.25 oz. of 80-proof liquor, 12 oz. of beer, or 5 oz. of table wine.

Credit: Campus Alcohol Abuse Prevention Center, Virginia Tech.

and 12.14 show BAC levels for men and women. Currently, all 50 U.S. states consider 0.08 to be the legal definition of being intoxicated. Since BAC levels are often not available, for example in surveys of previous use, NIAAA uses four or more drinks for women and five or more for men as the definition of binge drinking. Table 12.3 shows changes in psychological and physical functions as BAC increases.

FIGURE 12.14 ■ BAC Chart for Women

Women
Approximate Blood Alcohol Percentage

Drinks	Body Weight in Pounds									
	90	100	120	140	160	180	200	220	240	
0	.00	.00	.00	.00	.00	.00	.00	.00		Only Safe Driving Limit
1	.05	.05	.04	.03	.03	.03	.02	.02	.02	Driving Skills Significantly Affected
2	.10	.09	.08	.07	.06	.05	.05	.04	.04	
3	.15	.14	.11	.10	.09	.08	.07	.06	.06	
4	.20	.18	.15	.13	.11	.10	.09	.08	.08	Possible Criminal Penalties
5	.25	.23	.19	.16	.14	.13	.11	.10	.09	
6	.30	.27	.23	.19	.17	.15	.14	.12	.11	Legally Intoxicated
7	.35	.32	.27	.23	.20	.18	.16	.14	.13	
8	.40	.36	.30	.26	.23	.20	.18	.17	.15	Criminal Penalties
9	.45	.41	.34	.29	.26	.23	.20	.19	.17	
10	.51	.45	.38	.32	.28	.25	.23	.21	.19	Death Possible

Subtract 0.01% for each 40 minutes of drinking.

One drink is 1.25 oz. of 80-proof liquor, 12 oz. of beer, or 5 oz. of table wine.

Credit: Campus Alcohol Abuse Prevention Center, Virginia Tech.

TABLE 12.3 ■ Psychological and Physical Effects at Various Blood Alcohol Levels

Progressive Effects of Alcohol		
Blood Alcohol Concentration	**Changes in Feelings and Personality**	**Physical and Mental Impairments**
0.01–0.06	Relaxation, sense of well-being, inhibition lowered, alertness, joyous	Thought, judgment. coordination, concentration
0.06–0.10	Blunted feelings, disinhibition, extraversion, impaired sexual pleasure	Reflexes, impaired reasoning, perception distance acuity, peripheral vision, glare recovery
0.11–0.20	Over-expression, emotional, swings angry or sad boisterous	Reaction time, gross motor control, staggering slurred speech
0.21–0.29	Stupor, lose understanding, impaired sensations	Severe motor impairment, loss of consciousness, memory blackout
0.30–0.39	Severe depression, unconsciousness, death possible	Bladder function, breathing, heart rate
=>0.40	Unconsciousness, death	Breathing, heart rate

Credit: Campus Alcohol Abuse Prevention Center, Virginia Tech.

About two thirds of all Americans over 18 have had at least one drink in the past year (Table 12.4). Around 40% of men and 20% of women have at least one drink a week. Results from the 2014 National Survey on Drug Use and Health: Summary of National Findings suggest that 21.5% of the population participated in binge drinking in the past 30 days. Binge drinking was highest in college-age populations (Figure 12.15).

TABLE 12.4 ■ Frequency of Drinking in the United States for Individuals Age 18 and Over

Percentage Who Drank	Women	Men
Daily	2.45%	5.78%
Nearly every day	2.39%	4.98%
3–4 times a week	5.55%	10.00%
2 times a week	5.82%	10.46%
Once a week	6.77%	10.33%
2–3 times a month	8.27%	9.55%
Once a month	7.19%	6.72%
7–11 times in the past year	4.44%	3.51%
3–6 times in the past year	9.26%	5.67%
1–2 times in the past year	8.73%	4.91%
Never in the past year (former drinker or lifetime abstainer)	39.13%	28.09%

Source: National Institute on Alcohol Abuse and Alcoholism.

FIGURE 12.15 ■ Binge Drinking and Alcohol Use by Age Group

This figure shows current binge drinking and alcohol use by age group. The largest amount of binge drinking is seen in the young adult years, especially 21–25.

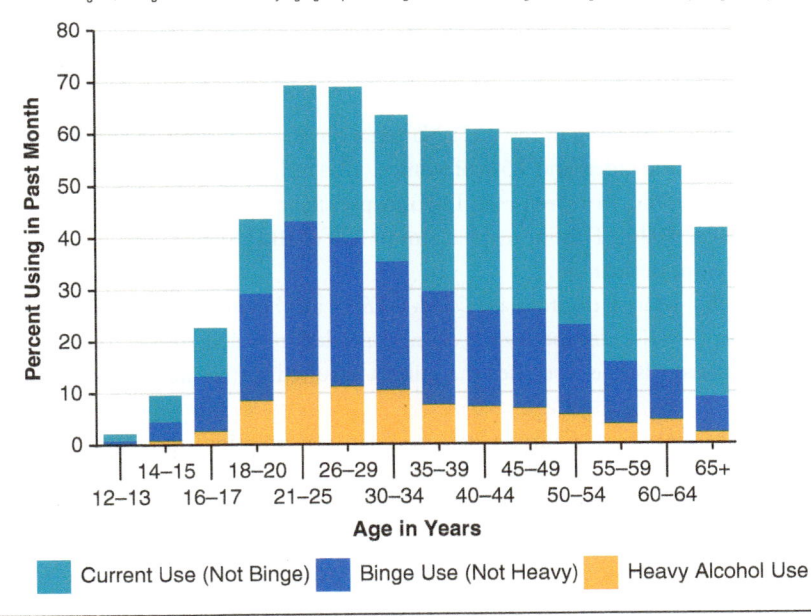

Source: SAMHSA. (2014). *Results from the 2013 National Survey on Drug Use and Health: Summary of national findings* (NSDUH Series H-48, HHS Publication No. [SMA] 14-4863).

College-age young adults who engage in binge drinking generally believe that they do not have a drinking problem. They also believe that they have no problem driving in these conditions. Similar to risk-taking behaviors seen in adolescence, these types of cognitive distortions and lack of inhibition can lead to problems ranging from passing out to traffic accidents to problematic sexual and physical encounters. In fact, WHO data worldwide show a larger proportion of deaths related to alcohol in this age group than in any other.

Do People Who Drink More Like It More?

Given that people who binge drink take in more alcohol than others, the question arises as to whether they experience more positive effects from drinking than do light drinkers. You might think that those who drink more would like it more. However, some individuals want or crave alcohol even though they might not like it that much (Pool et al., 2016; Tibboel et al., 2015). This is related to the expectation of pleasure associated with dopamine.

It turns out that the relationship between wanting and liking depends on how much you drink. The role of drinking and its experience was studied by following 104 weekly binge drinkers and 86 light drinkers over 2 years (King et al., 2011). In the initial part of the study, the researchers used a double-blind design in which the participants did not know if they were receiving a drink with alcohol or a similar-tasting placebo. Participants rated their experience of both alcohol and the placebo. Over the next 2 years, participants were asked to report on their drinking habits. Heavy drinkers, as compared with light drinkers, reported they wanted alcohol more and liked it more. Further, light drinkers found less stimulation from alcohol and were more sedated by its effects than were heavy drinkers. Light drinkers liked alcohol but did not want it more than heavy drinkers did.

DSM-5-TR Alcohol-Related Disorders

Alcohol use disorder is defined in *DSM-5-TR* as a pattern of alcohol use that leads to significant impairment or distress. As seen in Table 12.5, the criteria also require two or more other factors, such as the person taking more of the substance than was intended, not being able to reduce the use of the substance, spending time trying to obtain the substance, not being able to do one's work or other obligations, having the substance interfere with social relationships, reducing one's activities because of the substance, having the substance create medical problems, and engaging in hazardous activities such as driving while on the substance.

In the United States, according to the 2021 National Survey on Drug Use and Health, 13.2% of men (16.3 million age 18 and older) and 9.5% of women (12.4 million age 18 and older) would meet the criteria for alcohol use disorder in a given year. Lifetime prevalence is estimated to be 42% for men and 22.7% for women (APA, 2022). This means that almost half of all U.S. men will qualify for an alcohol use disorder at some point in their life.

The second alcohol-related disorder in *DSM-5-TR* is alcohol intoxication disorder (see Table 12.6). The criteria for this disorder specify the changes needed for a diagnosis of alcohol intoxication. The third alcohol-related disorder specifies the criteria required for an alcohol withdrawal disorder (see Table 12.7).

Overall, alcohol has been part of human history, and its consumption represents a complex interaction of psychological factors, cultural factors, and brain processes. Addiction and reduction of cognitive and motor functions are related to its overuse. However, these factors are not unique, as we will see in the next section on marijuana, hallucinogens, and opioids.

TABLE 12.5 ■ *DSM-5-TR* Diagnostic Criteria for Alcohol Use Disorder

A. A problematic pattern of alcohol use leading to clinically significant impairment or distress, as manifested by at least two of the following, occurring within a 12-month period:

1. Alcohol is often taken in larger amounts or over a longer period than was intended.
2. There is a persistent desire or unsuccessful effort to cut down or control alcohol use.
3. A great deal of time is spent in activities necessary to obtain alcohol, use alcohol, or recover from its effects.
4. Craving, or a strong desire or urge to use alcohol.
5. Recurrent alcohol use resulting in a failure to fulfill major role obligations at work, school, or home.
6. Continued alcohol use despite having persistent or recurrent social or interpersonal problems caused or exacerbated by the effects of alcohol.
7. Important social, occupational, or recreational activities are given up or reduced because of alcohol use.
8. Recurrent alcohol use in situations in which it is physically hazardous.
9. Alcohol use is continued despite knowledge of having a persistent or recurrent physical or psychological problem that is likely to have been caused or exacerbated by alcohol.
10. Tolerance, as defined by either of the following:
    a. A need for markedly increased amounts of alcohol to achieve intoxication or desired effect.
    b. A markedly diminished effect with continued use of the same amount of alcohol.
11. Withdrawal, as manifested by either of the following:
    a. The characteristic withdrawal syndrome for alcohol (refer to Criteria A and B of the criteria set for alcohol withdrawal).
    b. Alcohol (or a closely related substance, such as a benzodiazepine) is taken to relieve or avoid withdrawal symptoms.

Specify if:
In early remission: After full criteria for alcohol use disorder were previously met, none of the criteria for alcohol use disorder have been met for at least 3 months but for less than 12 months (with the exception that Criterion A4, "Craving, or a strong desire or urge to use alcohol," may be met).
In sustained remission: After full criteria for alcohol use disorder were previously met, none of the criteria for alcohol use disorder have been met at any time during a period of 12 months or longer (with the exception that Criterion A4, "Craving, or a strong desire or urge to use alcohol," may be met).
Specify if:
In a controlled environment: This additional specifier is used if the individual is in an environment where access to alcohol is restricted.
Code based on current severity/remission: If an alcohol intoxication, alcohol withdrawal, or another alcohol-induced mental disorder is also present, do not use the codes below for alcohol use disorder. Instead, the comorbid alcohol use disorder is indicated in the 4th character of the alcohol-induced disorder code (see the coding note for alcohol intoxication, alcohol withdrawal, or a specific alcohol-induced mental disorder). For example, if there is comorbid alcohol intoxication and alcohol use disorder, only the alcohol intoxication code is given, with the 4th character indicating whether the comorbid alcohol use disorder is mild, moderate, or severe: F10.129 for mild alcohol use disorder with alcohol intoxication or F10.229 for a moderate or severe alcohol use disorder with alcohol intoxication.
Specify current severity/remission:
F10.10 Mild: Presence of 2–3 symptoms.
F10.11 Mild, In early remission
F10.11 Mild, In sustained remission
F10.20 Moderate: Presence of 4–5 symptoms.
F10.21 Moderate, In early remission
F10.21 Moderate, In sustained remission
F10.20 Severe: Presence of 6 or more symptoms.
F10.21 Severe, In early remission
F10.21 Severe, In sustained remission

Credit: Reprinted with permission from the *Diagnostic and Statistical Manual of Mental Disorders, fifth edition, text revision* (DSM-V-TR), pp. 553–554 (Copyright © 2022). American Psychiatric Association. All rights reserved.

TABLE 12.6 ■ *DSM-5-TR* Diagnostic Criteria for Alcohol Intoxication

A. Recent ingestion of alcohol.

B. Clinically significant problematic behavioral or psychological changes (e.g., inappropriate sexual or aggressive behavior, mood lability, impaired judgment) that developed during, or shortly after, alcohol ingestion.

C. One (or more) of the following signs or symptoms developing during, or shortly after, alcohol use:
   1. Slurred speech.
   2. Incoordination.
   3. Unsteady gait.
   4. Nystagmus.
   5. Impairment in attention or memory.
   6. Stupor or coma.

D. The signs or symptoms are not attributable to another medical condition and are not better explained by another mental disorder, including intoxication with another substance.

Coding note: The ICD-10-CM code depends on whether there is a comorbid alcohol use disorder. If a mild alcohol use disorder is comorbid, the ICD-10-CM code is F10.120, and if a moderate or severe alcohol use disorder is comorbid, the ICD-10-CM code is F10.220. If there is no comorbid alcohol use disorder, then the ICD-10-CM code is F10.920.

Credit: Reprinted with permission from the *Diagnostic and Statistical Manual of Mental Disorders, fifth edition, text revision (DSM-V-TR)*, p. 561 (Copyright 2022). American Psychiatric Association. All rights reserved.

TABLE 12.7 ■ *DSM-5-TR* Diagnostic Criteria for Alcohol Withdrawal

A. Cessation of (or reduction in) alcohol use that has been heavy and prolonged.

B. Two (or more) of the following, developing within several hours to a few days after the cessation of (or reduction in) alcohol use described in Criterion A:
   1. Autonomic hyperactivity (e.g., sweating or pulse rate greater than 100 bpm).
   2. Increased hand tremor.
   3. Insomnia.
   4. Nausea or vomiting.
   5. Transient visual, tactile, or auditory hallucinations or illusions.
   6. Psychomotor agitation.
   7. Anxiety.
   8. Generalized tonic-clonic seizures.

C. The signs or symptoms in Criterion B cause clinically significant distress or impairment in social, occupational, or other important areas of functioning.

D. The signs or symptoms are not attributable to another medical condition and are not better explained by another mental disorder, including intoxication or withdrawal from another substance.

Specify if:
With perceptual disturbances: This specifier applies in the rare instance when hallucinations (usually visual or tactile) occur with intact reality testing, or auditory, visual, or tactile illusions occur in the absence of a delirium.
Coding note: The ICD-10-CM code depends on whether or not there is a comorbid alcohol use disorder and whether or not there are perceptual disturbances.
For alcohol withdrawal, without perceptual disturbances: If a mild alcohol use disorder is comorbid, the ICD-10-CM code is F10.130, and if a moderate or severe alcohol use disorder is comorbid, the ICD-10-CM code is F10.230. If there is no comorbid alcohol use disorder, then the ICD-10-CM code is F10.930.
For alcohol withdrawal, with perceptual disturbances: If a mild alcohol use disorder is comorbid, the ICD-10-CM code is F10.132, and if a moderate or severe alcohol use disorder is comorbid, the ICD-10-CM code is F10.232. If there is no comorbid alcohol use disorder, then the ICD-10-CM code is F10.932.

Credit: Reprinted with permission from the *Diagnostic and Statistical Manual of Mental Disorders, fifth edition, text revision (DSM-V-TR)*, pp. 564–565 (Copyright © 2022). American Psychiatric Association. All rights reserved.

> # UNDERSTANDING CHANGES IN *DSM-5* AND *DSM-5-TR*
> ## SUBSTANCE-RELATED AND ADDICTIVE DISORDERS
>
> There were a number of changes in *DSM-5* related to substance use and addiction. In *DSM-IV*, substance abuse and substance dependence were considered as two different and separate disorders. In *DSM-5*, substance abuse and substance dependence form a single disorder. This "use disorder" phrase is employed to describe each substance, for example, alcohol use disorder, cannabis use disorder, opioid use disorder, and so forth.
>
> Further, each substance use disorder is measured on a continuum ranging from mild to severe. The determination of severity level is related to how many symptoms are present. As can be seen in the presentation of alcohol use disorder (Table 12.5), there are 11 possible symptoms—mild would be noted if two or three symptoms were present, moderate if four or five symptoms were present, and severe if six or more symptoms were present. In addition, a criterion of substance craving was added. Another condition was removed that was present in *DSM-IV*, and that was problems with law enforcement. This was removed to make it easier to apply the criteria internationally. That is, cultural and legal restrictions vary around the world in terms of substance use.
>
> Not everyone agrees with the current *DSM-5* changes. With the current changes in criteria for addiction, Stanford professor Keith Humphreys estimated that as many as 20 million additional individuals will be diagnosed with a substance abuse problem (Urbina, 2012). This will have implications for health care services as well as legal ramifications.
>
> Also, based on research that shows similar physiological and psychological processes between substance use and some behavioral addictions, gambling was added to the Substance-Related and Addictive Disorders section of *DSM-5*. Other research has shown similar brain processes in addiction and obesity (Volkow et al., 2013). This has raised a question for some critics of the *DSM-5* addiction criteria (e.g., Frances, 2013)—namely, will we make what is our passion, whether using the Internet, playing video games, shopping, or other such activities, into mental disorders?

> # CONCEPT CHECK
>
> - What are the effects of alcohol on an individual's body and brain?
> - What can we say about the prevalence rates of alcohol use disorder in terms of genetics, gender, age, and culture?
> - What is considered moderate, heavy, and binge drinking?

CANNABIS, HALLUCINOGENS, AND OPIOIDS

Cannabis, hallucinogens, and opioids are naturally occurring substances. These three different types of drugs are seen in cultures throughout the world. However, they have different effects on the body and are generally used for different purposes.

Cannabis

Cannabis has been used worldwide for at least 4,000 years for its psychoactive effects. During this period, it has been seen as an important medical compound and as a religious and recreational substance. The physician Galen in 200 CE wrote that it was customary to give cannabis to guests to promote hilarity and enjoyment (Stuart, 2004). It has a history of use in China, India, Europe, and the Middle East. It came to the United States during the 1900s, where during the 1960s, it became a recreational drug of choice for many. Since that time, views have changed as to whether the drug should be decriminalized for all adults, made available strictly for medical purposes such as pain relief, or banned completely. Table 12.8 shows a timeline up to 2022 of cultural and scientific views of cannabis.

Individuals who use cannabis report a wide variety of experiences. Small doses produce enjoyable positive feelings associated with being "high." This can include states in which time stands still. The person often may see their own ideas as exceptionally creative and important. Cannabis can also influence

TABLE 12.8	A Brief History of Cannabis
2727 BC	The Pên-ts'ao Ching, the oldest known pharmacopoeia, describes medicinal properties of cannabis, as well as psychiatric side effects from excessive use.
~1200 BC	In the Indus Valley civilization, cannabis is regarded as one of five sacred plants: "a source of happiness and bringer of freedom."
1894	The seven-volume report of the Indian Hemp Drugs Commission concludes, "There is no evidence of any weight regarding mental and moral injuries from moderate use of these drugs."
1928	Recreational use of cannabis is banned in the United Kingdom.
1937	The Marijuana Tax Act effectively prohibits recreational cannabis use in the United States.
1942	Cannabis is removed from the American Pharmacopoeia.
1961	60 nations sign the Uniform Drug Convention, which pledges to end cannabis use within 25 years.
1965	Mechoulam and colleagues isolate and subsequently synthesize delta-9-tetrahydrocannabinol (THC).
1967	Groups such as NORML (National Organization for the Reform of Marijuana Laws), in the United States, and SOMA, in the United Kingdom, lobby for the legalization of cannabis. Over 3,000 people attend a smoke-in in Hyde Park, London.
1970	It becomes clear that the psychological effects of cannabis are attributable to THC.
1976	In the Netherlands, the Opium Act separates cannabis from hard drugs. Subsequently, the sale of cannabis is tolerated under strict conditions. In the United States, government funding for medical research on cannabis is banned.
1982	The National Institutes of Health–sponsored Relman study concludes that "there is no evidence that cannabis causes permanent health damage,.... affects brain structure, ... is addictive or leads to harder drug [use]."
1987	The link between cannabis use and the development of schizophrenia is shown for the first time.
1988	Cannabis receptors are discovered by Howlett and Devane.
1990	The cannabinoid 1 (CB1) receptor is cloned by Bonner and colleagues.
1992	The first endocannabinoid is discovered and termed anandamide.
1994	SR141716 (rimonabant), the first selective CB1 antagonist, is discovered. Germany decriminalizes possession of small quantities of cannabis for occasional use. In the United Kingdom, the maximum fine for possession increases from £500 to £2500.
1995	A second endocannabinoid, 2-arachidonylglycerol, is identified.
1996	California becomes the first state in the United States to legalize the use of medical cannabis.
1997	A leading British newspaper, the Independent on Sunday, launches a "decriminalize cannabis" campaign.
2001	Endocannabinoids are shown to inhibit the release of amino-acid neurotransmitters in the hippocampus and the cerebellum.
2002	Endocannabinoids are shown to be involved in long-term synaptic plasticity.
2003	The first evidence that endocannabinoids mediate spike-timing dependent plasticity is discovered.
2004	In the United Kingdom, cannabis is moved from a Class B to a Class C drug; possession drops to a maximum 2-year, rather than 5-year, prison sentence.
2005	In Canada, a cannabis-based medicine is licensed for the treatment of spasticity in multiple sclerosis.

2012	Washington and Colorado become the first states to legalize recreational cannabis use. By this year, Montana, New Mexico, Vermont, Michigan, New Jersey, Arizona, and Massachusetts have legalized medical cannabis use as well.
2016	29 U.S. states allow for medical cannabis use and 8 states allow recreational use.
2018	33 U.S. states and Washington, D.C., allow for medical cannabis and 10 states and Washington, D.C., allow recreational use. Thirteen states have decriminalized (but not legalized) marijuana. Canada legalizes cannabis for both medical and recreational uses.
2022	38 U.S. states and Washington, D.C., allow for medical cannabis, and 18 states and Washington, D.C., allow recreational use. U.S. president Joe Biden pardons those convicted of simple marijuana possession under federal law.

Source: Based on Murray, R., Morrison, P., Henquet, C., & Di Forti, M. (2007). Cannabis, the mind and society: The hash realities. *Nature Reviews Neuroscience, 8*, 885–895, with updates.

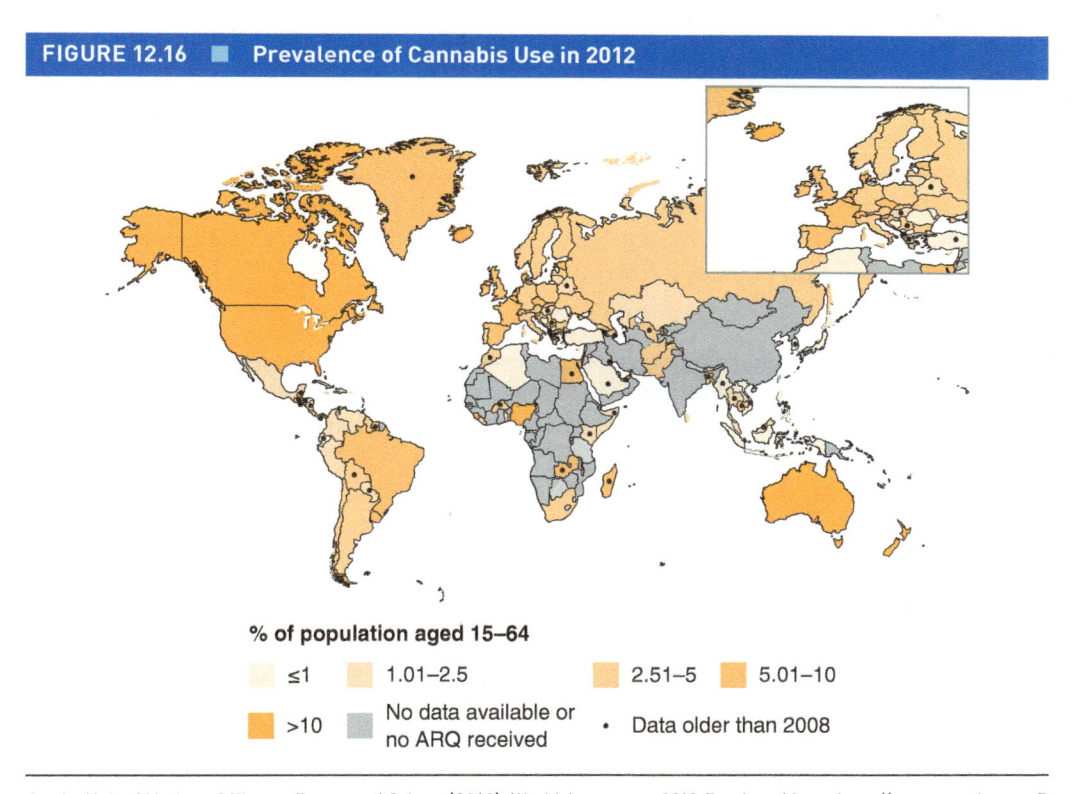

FIGURE 12.16 ■ Prevalence of Cannabis Use in 2012

% of population aged 15–64
- ≤1
- 1.01–2.5
- 2.51–5
- 5.01–10
- >10
- No data available or no ARQ received
- Data older than 2008

Credit: United Nations Office on Drugs and Crime. (2012). *World drug report 2012*. Retrieved from http://www.unodc.org. Reprinted with the permission of the United Nations.

appetite, with short-term users reporting increasing hunger or "the munchies." Larger doses can produce negative feelings such as anxiety and paranoia. Hallucinations and persecutory delusions have also been reported. Most of these experiences are short-lived but in some cases can last longer. More long-term use is also associated with cognitive impairment in executive functions (Crean et al., 2011).

One important area of research is the effects of cannabis on the developing brain. Pregnant women, young mothers who breastfeed their infants, and adolescents whose brains are changing can be affected by cannabis (Bara et al., 2021). The current research suggests that these individuals may be at risk for later developmental problems, although a number of factors such as genetics, amount of exposure to cannabis, gender, and so forth are still being researched. With increased legalization of cannabis, it should be possible to better describe the positive and negative effects of the drug (Hasin, 2017).

Cannabis is a plant species also referred to as *marijuana*. Cannabis resin is known as *hashish*. The cannabis plant can easily be cultivated both indoors and outdoors, and it is grown and used throughout the world. The United Nations estimates that 4% of the population of the world uses cannabis, and the United States is one of the larger users (Figure 12.16).

The main psychoactive ingredient in cannabis, THC (Δ9-tetrahydrocannabinol), was first described in the 1960s. THC particularly affects receptors in the hippocampus, the cerebellum, the basal ganglia, and the neocortex. THC affects receptors in the brain that also release GABA, an inhibitory neurotransmitter related to anxiety. As with other drugs, dopamine and the VTA play a role. THC also increases dopamine release in the striatum of healthy subjects (Figure 12.17). Cannabis also influences the salience networks in the brain, which results in impaired neurocognitive task performance (Ramaekers et al., 2021).

The brain also produces substances, referred to as cannabinoids, that are similar to those found in cannabis. Cannabinoids and their receptors are found throughout the body (Bridgeman & Abazia, 2017; Lutz, 2020). These appear to be related to reducing the negative memories associated with troubling past experiences, a function similar to the effects of cannabis. Overall, cannabinoids produced by our bodies are involved in eating, sleeping, relaxing, forgetting, and protecting.

A number of different cannabinoids are found in the cannabis plant, one of which is the basis of medical cannabis. Typically, the major component of medical cannabis is cannabidiol (CBD). CBD does not produce any psychoactive effects. Medical cannabis is available is different forms, including lotions, sprays, oils, creams, and food products, and its flowers and leaves are smoked. It should be noted that many of these components have not been tested in well controlled scientific studies. The components of medical cannabis (CBD and THC) are determined by the laws of each state. Each state also differs in terms of which health concerns, such as seizures, pain, nausea, glaucoma, and anxiety, can treated by medical cannabis. Society is currently debating how cannabis should be legalized for its medical benefits, a debate that is further discussed in *LENS: The Legalization of Cannabis*.

FIGURE 12.17 ■ Changes in the Brain Related to Cannabis Use Disorder

Dots indicate brain regions in which neurochemical marks reflective of CB1R, dopamine transporter (DAT) and dopamine (DA) synthesis have been detected in individuals with cannabis use disorder. ACC, anterior cingulate cortex; DS, dorsal striatum; PCC, posterior cingulate cortex; VS, ventral striatum.

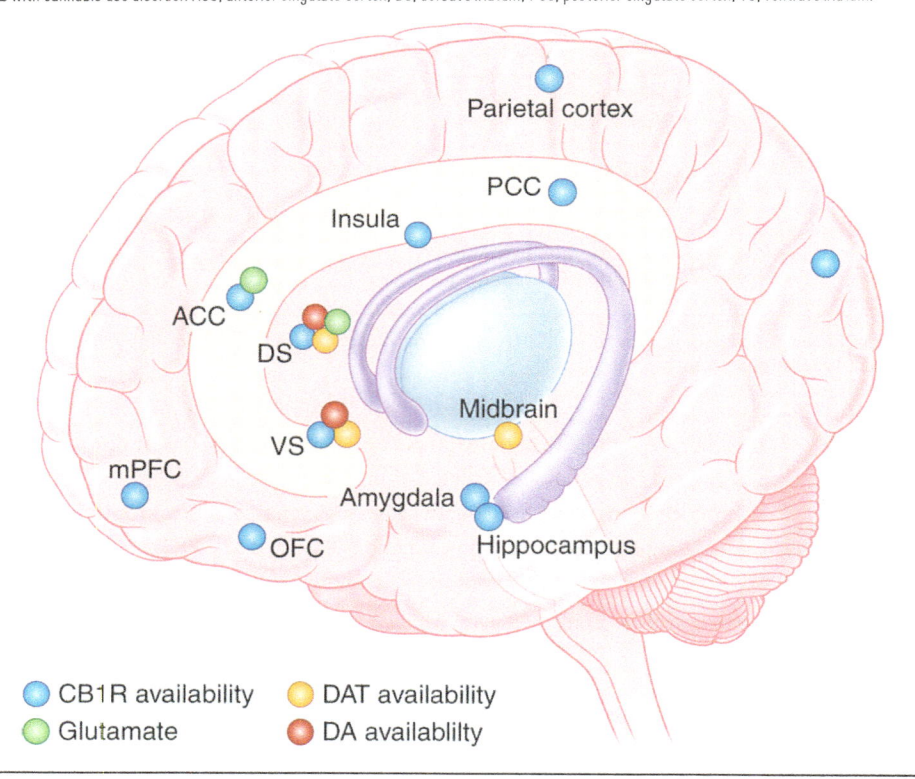

Credit: Ferland, J. N., & Hurd, Y. L. (2020). Deconstructing the neurobiology of cannabis use disorder. *Nature Neuroscience*, 23(5), 600–610. https://doi.org/10.1038/s41593-020-0611-0

LENS

THE LEGALIZATION OF CANNABIS

The United States and many other countries have gone through periods in which drugs were legal and times in which they were illegal. Alcohol is one classic example of a drug that was legal, then banned completely, and then re-legalized. Currently, there is a vigorous debate in the United States concerning the legalization of cannabis. Many polls, including a recent survey from Pew Research Center, suggest that only around 10% of Americans believe that cannabis should not be legal in any form. On the other side, the federal government has suggested that legalizing cannabis is "a bad idea" since it would increase the availability and use of other illicit drugs and pose significant health and safety risks (see For Further Reading).

Although cannabis is still illegal in many states, there is increasing support for its medical and recreational use in the United States.

Bill Clark/Associated Press

Those who want to legalize cannabis suggest a number of different reasons that regulating it like alcohol would benefit society. They begin with the fact that it is the most commonly used illegal drug on the planet. This means that a wide variety of government resources are being devoted to police illegal cannabis use. These range from public information campaigns to law enforcement procedures, to spending money on jail terms, and missing out on taxes available from legal drugs. The economic benefits can be seen if you consider all of the businesses related to production, distribution, and sale of such legal drugs as alcohol and coffee, including advertising. In any given town, the number of bars and coffeehouses is typically quite large. With cannabis being legal, it is also suggested that the price would decrease and illegal drug dealers would be unnecessary. On another level, cannabis has been shown to have medical benefits, including combating nausea produced by chemotherapy treatment for cancer.

Those who are opposed to the legalization of cannabis often begin with its health effects. The U.S. government information arguing against the legalization of cannabis lists the following problems:

- Cannabis use is associated with dependence, respiratory and mental illness, poor motor performance, and impaired cognitive and immune system functioning, among other negative effects.
- Cannabis intoxication can cause distorted perceptions, difficulty in thinking and problem solving, and problems with learning and memory.

- Studies have shown an association between chronic cannabis use and increased rates of anxiety, depression, suicidal thoughts, and schizophrenia.
- Other research cited by the U.S. government has shown cannabis smoke to contain carcinogens and to be an irritant to the lungs. Cannabis smoke, in fact, contains 50% to 70% more carcinogenic hydrocarbons than does tobacco smoke.

California was the first state to legalize medical cannabis in 1996. Although the federal government was antagonistic to this move, other states followed. As of 2022, 38 states and Washington, D.C., allow for medical cannabis, and 18 states and Washington, D.C., allow for recreational use. Also, more recent research has called into question the relationship between marijuana and schizophrenia (Gillespie & Kendler, 2021). In 2022, President Biden published a statement on marijuana reform in an effort to make its use not a criminal offense (White House, 2022).

Thought Question

Should cannabis be treated like alcohol by the federal government?

Cannabis and Psychosis

Although a number of reports from governments around the world suggest no negative medical effects from using cannabis, a persistent question relates to its relationship to psychosis (R. Murray et al., 2007; Volkow et al., 2016). As noted, larger doses of cannabis can produce hallucinations and delusions. However, it has also been reported that individuals with an established psychosis had worse outcomes with continued cannabis use. In particular, a continued use of cannabis by those with a recent onset of psychosis was associated with earlier relapse of the psychotic symptoms, more frequent hospitalization, and poorer social functioning over a 4-year period.

Research that followed about 2,000 individuals for 10 years suggests a more direct relationship between the use of cannabis and symptoms such as hallucinations and delusions (Kuepper et al., 2011). It should be noted that just having these symptoms might not in itself result in a diagnosis of psychosis or schizophrenia. In this study, cannabis use and psychotic symptoms were assessed at baseline, some 3.5 years later and 8.4 years later. These researchers first looked at individuals who had not used cannabis at baseline and reported no psychotic symptoms. They then examined those from this group who used cannabis between the baseline and the session 3.5 years later. They found that this group showed an increased risk for displaying psychotic symptoms prior to the 8.4 years later session.

In reviewing the evidence from a number of studies, R. Murray et al. (2007) noted strong evidence that heavy cannabis use increases the risk of both psychotic symptoms and schizophrenia. These studies were conducted around the world and are presented in Table 12.9. The odds ratio column reflects the odds that cannabis use is related to psychotic symptoms. If there was no relationship, then the odds would be 1. Thus, odds above 1 suggest that cannabis use is related to having psychotic symptoms. It can be noted that all of the studies reviewed show an odds ratio from 1.5 to 3.1, suggesting a relationship.

Other research looked at individuals with psychosis and their unaffected siblings (van Winkel et al., 2011). These studies suggest that genetic factors may play a role in those individuals who use cannabis and go on to develop psychosis. A later meta-analysis also showed that the use of cannabis was associated with an earlier age of onset of psychotic disorders (Large et al., 2011). This relationship was not found for alcohol. At this point a causal relationship between cannabis use and later psychosis has not been determined, but the association between the two is commonly reported. One related factor is that those individuals with a psychosis that used cannabis frequently before the illness have a greater genetic predisposition to schizophrenia than those who did not use cannabis before the onset of their illness (Aas et al., 2018). Thus, those who have a genetic predisposition to developing psychosis also have a genetic predisposition to greater use of cannabis before the onset of the psychosis.

TABLE 12.9 ■ Effects of Cannabis Use and Psychosis

Country in Which the Study Was Conducted	Number of Participants	Follow-up	Odds Ratio (95% Confidence Interval)	Study Design
United States	4,494	NA	2.4 (1.2, 7.1)	Population based
Sweden	50,053	25 years	2.1 (1.2, 3.7)	Conscript cohort
The Netherlands	4,045	3 years	2.8 (1.2, 6.5)	Population based
Israel	9,724	4–15 years	2.0 (1.3, 3.1)	Population based
New Zealand (Christchurch)	1,265	3 years	1.8 (1.2, 2.6)	Birth cohort
New Zealand (Dunedin)	1,253	15 years	3.1 (0.7, 13.3)	Birth cohort
The Netherlands	1,580	14 years	2.8 (1.79, 4.43)	Population based
Germany	2,436	4 years	1.7 (1.1, 1.5)	Population based
United Kingdom	8,580	18 months	1.5 (0.55, 3.94)	Population based

NA: not applicable.

Credit: Murray, R., Morrison, P., Henquet, C., & Di Forti, M. (2007). Cannabis, the mind and society: The hash realities. *Nature Reviews Neuroscience*, 8, 885–895.

The psilocybin mushroom
iStock.com/mindhive

Hallucinogens

Hallucinogens are drugs that alter perceptual experiences (Nichols, 2004). The word *hallucinate* comes from Latin, meaning "to wander in the mind." Some of these drugs occur in nature and have been used by various cultures for thousands of years. These include mescaline, which comes from the peyote cactus, and psilocybin, which comes from a variety of mushroom. Historians suggest that these drugs were often part of religious ceremonies to give people experiences beyond those of everyday life. Other hallucinogens, such as LSD (d-lysergic acid diethylamide), begin with a grain fungus called ergot. Although the fungus is naturally occurring, LSD was first made in the laboratory. Other laboratory-made hallucinogens include MDMA, commonly known as ecstasy; MDA, sometimes referred to as the love drug; and PCP, also known as angel dust.

Hallucinogens, also called *psychedelics*, can alter users' perception, mood, and cognitive processes in often unpredictable ways (Hollister, 1984; Kwan et al., 2022). These can be described as follows:

1. Somatic symptoms: dizziness, weakness, tremors, nausea, drowsiness, paresthesia (numbness or tingling), and blurred vision

2. Perceptual symptoms: altered shapes and colors, difficulty in focusing on objects, sharpened sense of hearing, and, at times, synesthesia

3. Psychic symptoms: alterations in mood (happy, sad, or irritable at varying times), tension, distorted sense of time, difficulty in expressing thoughts, depersonalization, dreamlike feelings, and visual hallucinations

Although these are possible experiences from hallucinogens, in reality these drugs are quite unpredictable, and experiences vary based on both the expectations of the user and the situation in which the drug is taken. This also makes research with the drugs more difficult to perform.

In order to conduct human research with hallucinogens, a self-administered rating scale, the Altered States of Consciousness (ASC) scale, was developed (Dittrich, 1998). Dittrich suggested that the subjective effects of taking hallucinogens can be divided into three major components. The first is oceanic boundlessness. This is similar to what has been described as mystical experiences such as depersonalization and derealization. The second component is anxious ego dissolution. This would include such experiences as anxiety, delusions, fear of losing control, and loss of a sense of self. The third component is visionary restructuralization. This component includes visual hallucinations and illusions, synesthesia, and changes in the meaning of perceptions.

Although illegal in the United States, hallucinogens do not produce dependence and are relatively safe (Nichols, 2004). They also do not show withdrawal symptoms. However, as with any process, misuse and dependence are possible, although the pattern is not the same. Addictive drugs typically affect the dopamine system and the experience of reward. It is also possible to train animals to self-administer addictive drugs, but this is not the case with hallucinogens. Hallucinogens do not directly affect dopamine neurotransmission as alcohol, cannabis, tobacco, and cocaine do. They also appear to lack the toxic effects on human organs seen in alcohol and tobacco, for example. However, not all experiences with hallucinogens are positive. A so-called "bad trip" can include extreme anxiety and fearful psychotic-like experiences.

Structurally, the chemical makeup of hallucinogens is similar to that of the neurotransmitter serotonin. In fact, early theories suggested that hallucinogens produced their effects by increasing serotonin in specific brain areas. It is now known that hallucinogens bind to the 5-HT serotonin receptor.

LSD was first experienced on April 16, 1943. Albert Hoffmann, who worked for Sandoz Pharmaceuticals in Basel, Switzerland, was studying naturally occurring products and their modification in the laboratory. He was working on the ergot fungus, which is found on grains. On his way home from work, he experienced strange perceptual experiences, including hallucinations. To determine if his experiences were due to LSD, Hoffmann purposely ingested LSD some 3 days later. Indeed, it was LSD that had given Hoffman the psychotic-like experiences. This was also confirmed by other scientists in the lab who had similar experiences. LSD has been shown to be the most potent of all hallucinogens with effects that can last up to 12 hours.

Whereas LSD is the most potent hallucinogen, mescaline is the least potent. Mescaline comes from the peyote cactus and has a long history in the Western Hemisphere. Mescaline was widely used in pre-Columbian Mexico, where it was considered magical and divine (Carson-DeWitt, 2001). From there, it spread to North America, and certain Native American tribes used it in religious ceremonies. In 1990, the U.S. Supreme Court ruled that mescaline could not be used legally for religious ceremonies. Mescaline produces vivid mental images and an altered sense of space and time with a loss of a sense of reality.

Psilocybin comes from a type of fungus often referred to as "magic mushrooms." These mushrooms are found throughout the world and have been used for centuries. Psilocybin affects the central nervous system through the functioning of serotonin, to which it is chemically similar (Kwan et al., 2022). The active ingredient was identified by Sandoz Pharmaceuticals and found to be similar to LSD in its altering of perception, mood, and thought (Studerus et al., 2011). Psilocybin produces heightened sensory experiences and perceptual distortions. It induces milder negative experiences compared to LSD, such as anxiety and panic reaction. It is considered to be relatively safe in terms of dependence.

Erich Studerus and his colleagues (2011) examined a number of psilocybin sessions conducted in their lab using the ASC questionnaire, a standardized measure of altered states of consciousness. These are shown in Figure 12.18. This figure shows that the larger the dose, the greater the effect across the three domains of oceanic boundlessness, anxious ego dissolution, and visionary restructuralization. Note also that the placebo had no effect.

Brain blood flow research from this lab showed increases in the frontal areas of the brain, the insula, and the anterior and posterior cingulate from hallucinogens (see Figure 12.19). These are areas involved in cognitive and affective processes, including one's sense of self. Decreased blood flow was found in areas related to integration of information, such as the thalamus.

Current research is being directed at using hallucinogens in clinical treatment (Fuentes et al., 2020). For example, experiments are underway to examine the use of psilocybin in the treatment of obsessive-compulsive disorder (OCD) and MDMA as an adjunct to psychotherapy. At this point, psilocybin has been shown to be effective in the treatment of major depressive disorder (Carhart-Harris et al., 2021; Davis et al., 2021; Marwaha et al., 2023; Pearson et al., 2022).

FIGURE 12.18 ■ Rating Altered States of Consciousness From Psilocybin Use

This figure shows how different amounts of psilocybin affected research participants, using the Altered States of Consciousness (ASC) rating scale.

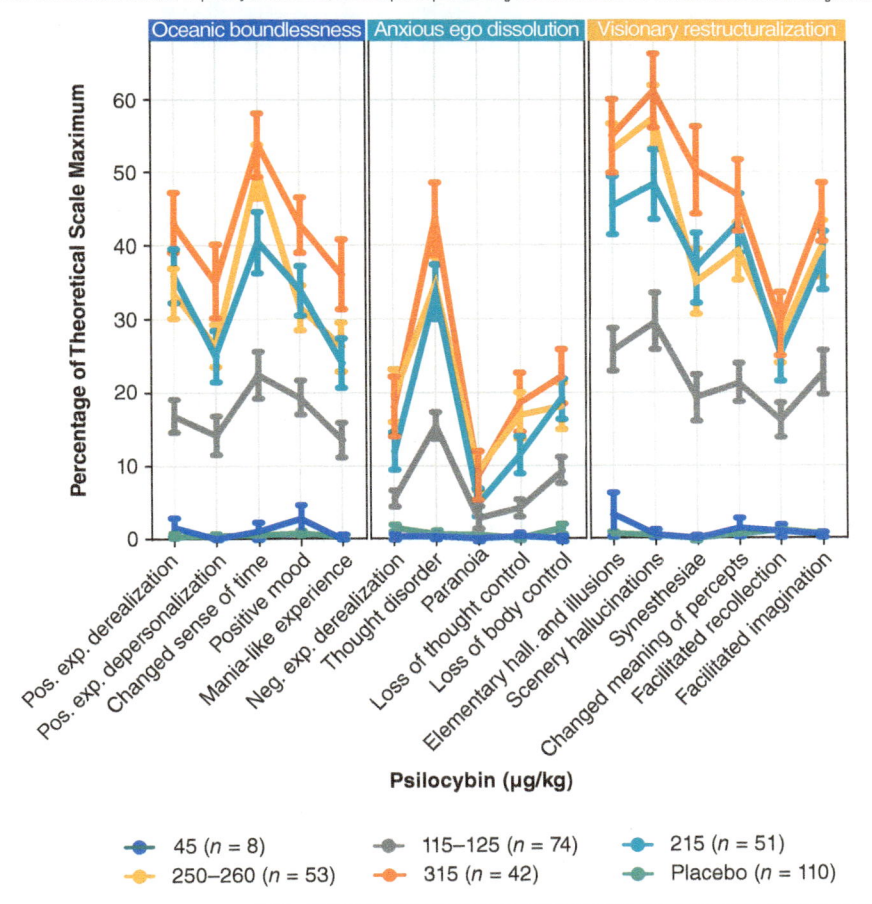

Credit: Studerus, E., Kometer, M., Hasler, F., & Vollenweider, F. (2011). Acute, subacute and long-term subjective effects of psilocybin in healthy humans: A pooled analysis of experimental studies. *Journal of Psychopharmacology, 25*, 1434–1452.

FIGURE 12.19 ■ The Effect of Hallucinogens on Your Brain

This figure shows the effects of psilocybin on brain activity in healthy human volunteers as indicated by changes in cerebral blood flow (CBF) using H2O-PET. Red shows relative increases, and yellow indicates relative decreases in regional brain activity. Marked increases in activity are seen in areas important for cognitive and affective processes, such as the frontomedial cortex extending into the anterior cingulate (1 and 2); the dorsolateral (3), insula (4), and temporal poles (5); and the left posterior cingulate (6). Decreased flow was observed in brain areas important for gating or integrating cortical information processing, such as the bilateral thalamus (7), right globus pallidus and bilateral pons (8), and in the cerebellum (9). Psilocybin also reduced neuronal activity in components responsible for higher-order visuospatial processing, such as the precuneus (11) and angular gyrus, as well as in supplementary eye fields of the pre-motor area (10) (unpublished data from F. X. Vollenweider).

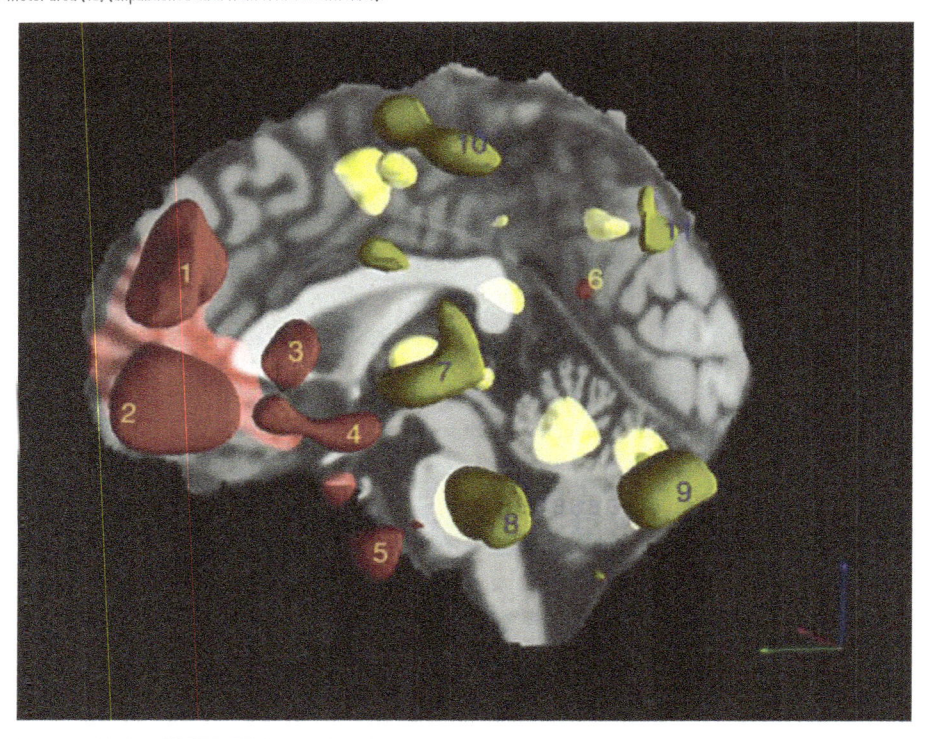

Credit: Nichols, D. (2004). Hallucinogens. *Pharmacology & Therapeutics, 101*, 131–181, with permission from Elsevier.

Opioids

Opioids are substances derived from the opium poppy plant that have been used for thousands of years to control pain and bring on euphoric feelings. In fact, poppy seeds have been found at Neanderthal burial sites from 30,000 years ago (Stuart, 2004). Around 3400 BCE, Sumerians referred to the opium poppy as the "joy plant." From there, it spread throughout the world. Opium was available in the street markets of ancient Rome. In 1860, Britain imported some 220,000 pounds of opium for medical and recreational use.

Opioids affect the brain and spinal cord by influencing neurotransmitters at the level of the synapse. The effects of these changes include blocking pain and general calming and slowing of the breath. Opioids can also influence your gut and may cause problems for those with stomach disorders. The effects of opioids can be blocked by the injection of an opiate antagonist such as naloxone. One of the problems with using opioids is that the person develops a tolerance to the drug. Thus, after a time period, a greater amount of the opioid is needed to product the same effects of pleasure and pain relief. Further, when the opioid is no longer available in the body, the person experiences symptoms of withdrawal.

The more common opioids are heroin, opium, morphine, methadone, and oxycodone (OxyContin, Percocet). Variations of these drugs are currently used in medical settings primarily for pain relief following operations or pain experienced with some types of cancer. Opioids became popular in the United States after the Civil War for their ability to control pain. However, some individuals given these drugs became addicted to them. Misuse took the form of the opium den, where people gathered to smoke the drug. With the availability of the hypodermic needle, individuals began to inject it

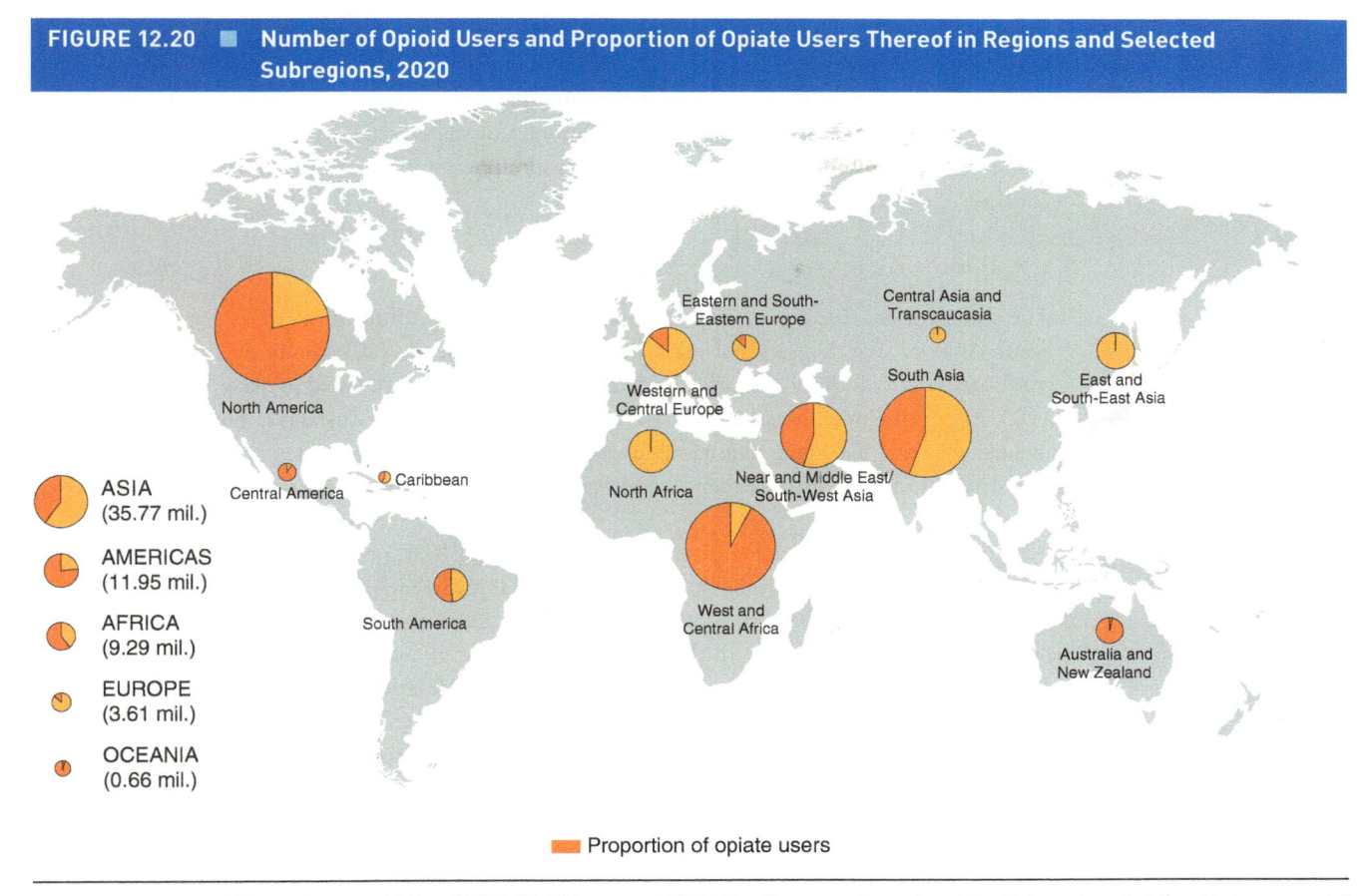

FIGURE 12.20 ■ **Number of Opioid Users and Proportion of Opiate Users Thereof in Regions and Selected Subregions, 2020**

ASIA (35.77 mil.)
AMERICAS (11.95 mil.)
AFRICA (9.29 mil.)
EUROPE (3.61 mil.)
OCEANIA (0.66 mil.)

Regions shown: North America, Central America, Caribbean, South America, Eastern and South-Eastern Europe, Western and Central Europe, North Africa, West and Central Africa, Central Asia and Transcaucasia, Near and Middle East/South-West Asia, South Asia, East and South-East Asia, Australia and New Zealand.

■ Proportion of opiate users

Credit: United Nations Office on Drugs and Crime. (2022). *World drug report 2022.* https://www.unodc.org/unodc/en/data-and-analysis/world-drug-report-2022.html. Reprinted with the permission of the United Nations.

directly into the bloodstream. As noted earlier, before the early 1900s, opioids were available legally in the United States. More recently, there has been an increase in the use of opioid prescriptions for the treatment of pain, especially the synthetic opioids fentanyl and carfentanil, which are more potent than morphine. This has led to an addiction epidemic, with a number of individuals turning to illegal heroin and other drugs, as these can be cheaper than traditional pain medications (Volkow & Blanco, 2021). Figure 12.20 shows the prevalence of opioid use worldwide.

Do You Have Opium Receptors in Your Brain?

Surprisingly, you do have receptors in your brain that are sensitive to opioid drugs (Darcq & Kieffer, 2018; Kibaly et al., 2019). The reason for this is that our bodies make a naturally occurring substance that also reduces the experience of pain and makes us feel good. Endorphins are produced at times of stress and allow individuals to continue in combat or a sports activity even when they are hurt. Endorphins also play a role in the placebo effect in relation to pain.

CONCEPT CHECK

- What is the primary psychoactive ingredient in cannabis? What are its impacts on an individual's body and brain?
- What is the relationship between cannabis and psychosis?
- Hallucinogens are not addictive, but in what other ways can they cause impairments to the individual using them?
- What are some common opioids? What is it about opioids that makes them sought after as medicines as well as for recreational use?

STIMULANTS: COCAINE, AMPHETAMINES, CAFFEINE, AND NICOTINE

In this section, you will learn about stimulants that are associated with positive feelings, bursts of energy, and alertness. One of the most common of these is coffee, which contains the stimulant caffeine. You will also learn about cocaine, amphetamines, and nicotine. Let us begin with cocaine.

Cocaine

The stimulant **cocaine** comes from the naturally occurring coca plant, which is grown primarily in South America. For thousands of years, individuals have chewed the leaves of the coca plant for their psychoactive effects. As noted earlier in the chapter, cocaine was even used to make Coca-Cola around 1900. About this time, Freud tried the drug and found it to be very pleasant. The effects of cocaine include a mental alertness often combined with feelings of euphoria, energy, and a desire to talk. The drug also heightens the experience of sensory processes, such as our responses to sound, touch, and sight.

Cocaine produces physiological effects such as increased heart rate and blood pressure. It also influences the default network in the brain, suggesting that it impedes flexibility and the ability to move between tasks (Zhang et al., 2018). Cocaine has been administered by smoking, snorting through the nose, or injecting directly into the bloodstream. The form of cocaine that is smoked is referred to as *crack*. Crack refers to the sounds made when the white cocaine crystals are heated to turn it into a form that can be smoked. Taking it through the nose results in a slower high than the high that results from taking it intravenously, which occurs in 4 to 6 minutes. Cocaine has a shorter effect in comparison with other drugs. That is, most of its effect is completed in 15 to 40 minutes. Like alcohol, some individuals may use cocaine in binges.

In 2014, there were 1.5 million current cocaine users (Substance Abuse and Mental Health Services Administration, 2015) in the United States. That is about one half of 1% of the population, a drop from previous years. The United Nations (UN) estimates of cocaine use are a little higher, as shown in the map in Figure 12.21. You might note that rates of cocaine use in North America and Australia are some of the highest in the world.

For thousands of years, individuals have chewed the leaves of the coca plant for its psychoactive effects.
iStock.com/Al Gonzalez

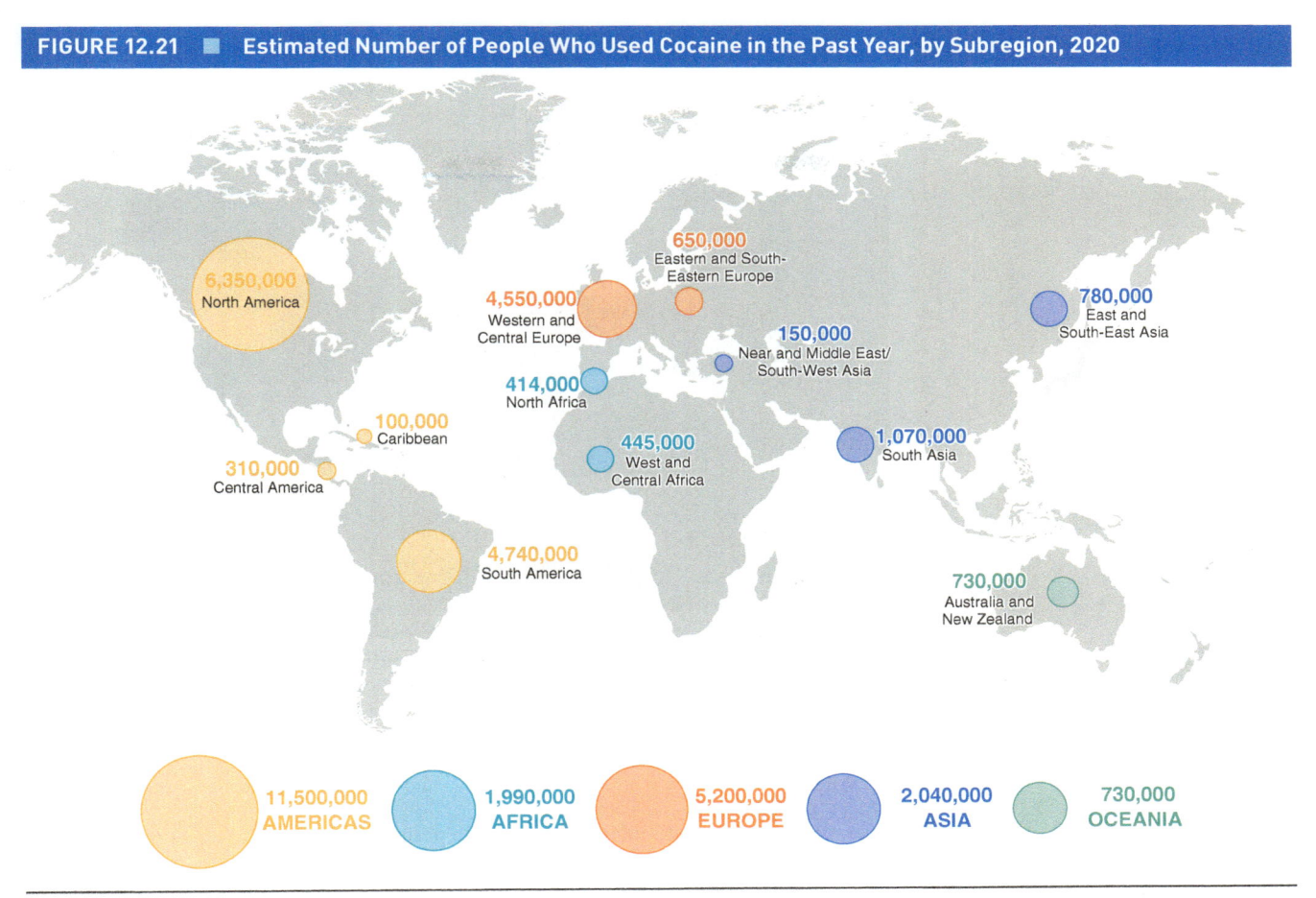

FIGURE 12.21 ■ Estimated Number of People Who Used Cocaine in the Past Year, by Subregion, 2020

- 6,350,000 North America
- 650,000 Eastern and South-Eastern Europe
- 4,550,000 Western and Central Europe
- 780,000 East and South-East Asia
- 150,000 Near and Middle East/South-West Asia
- 414,000 North Africa
- 100,000 Caribbean
- 310,000 Central America
- 445,000 West and Central Africa
- 1,070,000 South Asia
- 4,740,000 South America
- 730,000 Australia and New Zealand

- 11,500,000 AMERICAS
- 1,990,000 AFRICA
- 5,200,000 EUROPE
- 2,040,000 ASIA
- 730,000 OCEANIA

Credit: United Nations Office on Drugs and Crime. (2022). *World drug report 2022.* https://www.unodc.org/unodc/en/data-and-analysis/world-drug-report-2022.html. Reprinted with the permission of the United Nations.

Cocaine, Dopamine, and Your Brain

Normally, when there is an action potential, dopamine is released at the terminals. Dopamine is then removed from the receptors by a process called reuptake. However, the introduction of cocaine interferes with this natural process, resulting in an increase of dopamine (recall Figure 12.8). This increased dopamine signaling is involved in the effects experienced with cocaine.

The parts of your brain affected by cocaine depend on whether you are a new user or have taken cocaine for a long time. In short-term users, the brain regions involved are primarily the nucleus accumbens and parts of the PFC. However, with long-term use, more of the brain becomes involved, including the striatum, amygdala, hippocampus, and additional areas. New pathways in the amygdala also develop, which reduce the information available to the PFC (J. E. Murray et al., 2015). This change in the brain is seen to represent a shift from the voluntary seeking of the drug to habitual use—a state of craving without the voluntary component.

Cocaine's effects on the brain are different from those of other drugs, such as hallucinogens, in that they are long lasting, even when the person ceases to use cocaine. This is shown in the positron emission tomography (PET) images in Figure 12.22. The top row depicts a person who has never used cocaine, which shows normal brain functioning in the area of the basal ganglia in four different brain slices. The middle row depicts a person who has not used cocaine for a month. The bottom row depicts the same person after 4 months of not using cocaine. Note that there is still lower activity, which the researchers attribute to a continued blockage of dopamine receptors (Volkow et al., 1993).

FIGURE 12.22 ■ Cocaine Continues to Change a Human Brain, Even After Non-Use

Brain image of a non–cocaine user (top row) and a cocaine user for 1 month of non-use (middle row), and a cocaine user after 4 months of non-use (bottom row). Even after stopping use of cocaine, brain changes remain for a period of time.

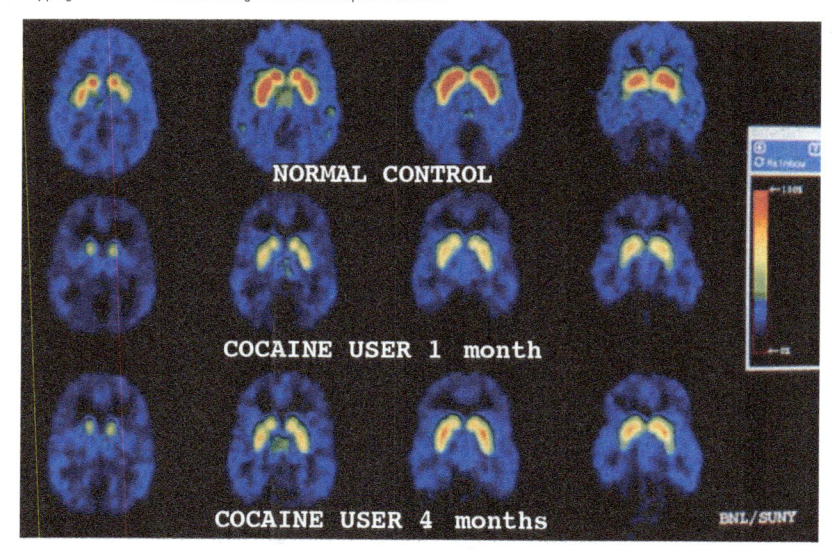

Credit. Volkow, N., Fowler, J., Wang, G., Hitzemann, R., Logan, J., Schlyer, D., . . . Wolf, A. (1993). Decreased dopamine D2 receptor availability is associated with reduced frontal metabolism in cocaine abusers. *Synapse, 14*, 169–177.

Amphetamines

Like cocaine, **amphetamines** are stimulants that result in positive feelings, a burst of energy, and alertness. However, unlike cocaine, amphetamine is a substance produced in the laboratory rather than found in nature. Amphetamine was first developed in the 1880s. It was not until the 1930s that it was introduced as a medicine in the form of an inhaler for the treatment of a stopped-up nose. Also during this time, it was introduced in the form of pills with the trade name Benzedrine, which were called "bennies" (Iversen, 2006; Koob et al., 2008).

During the 1930s and 1940s, amphetamines were prescribed by health professionals for the treatment of more than 30 disorders, including epilepsy, Parkinson's disease, schizophrenia, migraines, and even behavioral problems in children. They were also prescribed to reduce addictions to other substances such as alcohol, morphine, and tobacco. During World War II, amphetamines were given to soldiers as "pep pills" to give them an edge in combat. The common ones were Benzedrine, Dexedrine, and Methedrine, the last one being methamphetamine. Although there are chemical differences between amphetamine and methamphetamine (also known as "speed," "crystal meth," or "crank"), they both function as stimulants.

As people experienced the stimulant effects of amphetamines, they began to misuse them. In the 1950s, long-distance truck drivers would use the drugs to help them drive farther. After they were publicized for use as a recreational drug from Hollywood to New York, the U.S. government began to pay attention. Amphetamines were also making their way into teenage parties. In 1959, the U.S. Food and Drug Administration (FDA) required that amphetamines be available by prescription only.

Amphetamine-like drugs do not require the cultivation of plants. Instead, they can be manufactured almost anywhere without an advanced knowledge of chemistry. They are easy to take in the form of a pill, which can be conveniently purchased one pill at a time on the illegal market. Amphetamines are not considered to be harmful by many individuals, and indeed they have fewer negative effects than methamphetamines. However, amphetamines can have negative effects in some individuals, including psychotic-like experiences (Berman et al., 2009). Taking these drugs through intravenous injection or smoking increases the feeling of a rush.

In its 2011 global assessment, the UN noted that amphetamine-type drugs are the second most widely used drugs throughout the world, the first being cannabis (United Nations Office on Drugs and

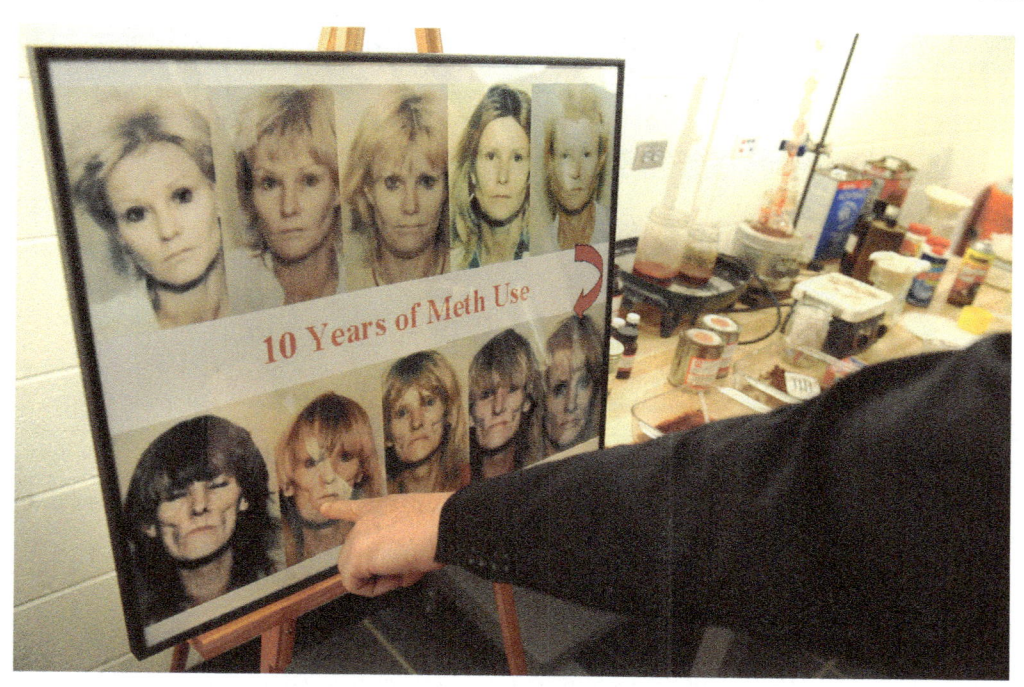

Chronic users of methamphetamine show dramatic changes in their physical appearance.
TIM SLOAN/Staff/AFP/via Getty Images

Crime, 2011). This makes amphetamine use greater than heroin or cocaine use worldwide. From 2015 to 2019, methamphetamine use increased greatly with additional overdose deaths (Han et al., 2021).

The main reasons people take amphetamines is that they believe they enhance performance and help them feel good. The common experience is euphoria, increased alertness, and hyperactivity. As with other stimulant drugs, amphetamines affect the dopamine system to produce the initial euphoric experience. In addition to the short-term experience, there are also less positive long-term effects (Marshall & O'Dell, 2012). These long-term effects, especially from methamphetamine, create brain changes in three areas. The first is the development of compulsive patterns of use. The second produces negative brain changes consistent with brain injury. Third, methamphetamine produces changes in the individual's cognitive functioning.

Cognitive deficits in people who use methamphetamine include problems with motor activities, such as skill movements or perceptual speed. These individuals also experience problems in their ability to shift their attention. Finally, research suggests memory, attention, and decision-making problems. These types of problems make it difficult for individuals to objectively see their addiction as well as be able to engage in therapy requiring cognitive responses. Methamphetamine also has a devastating effect on physical appearance.

One of the first studies to examine the effects of methamphetamine and methcathinone (also known as "cat") on the brain was performed by Una McCann and her colleagues (1998). Both of these drugs have been shown to be toxic to dopamine and serotonin neurons in animals. Parkinson's disease also shows a reduction in dopamine in the brain. Figure 12.23 shows PET images from four individuals. The first is from a healthy control person. This person shows dopamine activity in the striatum, as seen with the brighter colors. The next two PET images show a person who had not taken methamphetamine for 3 years and a person who had not taken methcathinone for 3 years, respectively. Notice that there is less dopamine activity. The last image is from a person who had just been diagnosed with Parkinson's disease and shows even less dopamine activity. This suggests that damage to dopamine mechanisms is long-lasting in methamphetamine users, although improvement over time has been shown.

Thus far, our focus in this chapter has been on illegal substances, except for alcohol. In the next sections, we will discuss two legal substances: caffeine, which is contained in coffee, and nicotine, which is found in tobacco.

FIGURE 12.23 ■ **Conditions That Can Influence Dopamine in the Human Brain**

Positron emission tomography (PET) image from a control person, a person who had not taken methamphetamine for 3 years, a person who had not taken methcathinone for 3 years, and a person who had just been diagnosed with Parkinson's disease.

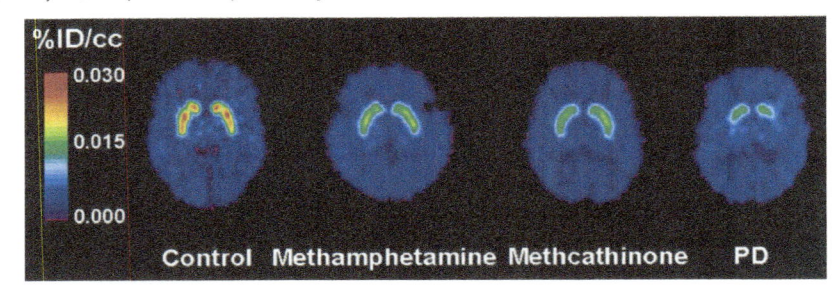

Credit: McCann, U. D., Wong, D. F., Yokoi, F., Villemagne, V., Dannals, R. F., & Ricaurte, G. A. (1998). Reduced striatal dopamine transporter density in abstinent methamphetamine and methcathinone users: Evidence from positron emission tomography studies with [11C]WIN-35,428. *The Journal of Neuroscience, 18*(20), 8417–8422. https://doi.org/10.1523/JNEUROSCI.18-20-08417.1998. Copyright 1998 Society for Neuroscience.

Caffeine

DSM-5-TR includes caffeine and tobacco in its substance-related and addictive disorders category. Caffeine is usually described as a stimulant, although it has beneficial effects beyond stimulation (Glade, 2010). Caffeine works through the central nervous system and increases resting energy expenditure within 30 minutes of ingestion. Its effects will last for about 4 hours. Caffeine also increases serotonin concentration in the region of the brain stem. This, in turn, postpones fatigue and increases endurance. Overall, caffeine consumption increases alertness, ability to concentrate, problem solving, wakefulness, and feelings of energy, and it elevates mood. These effects have also been shown in studies in which caffeine was compared with a placebo in a double-blind situation.

Caffeine comes from a number of sources. It is found naturally in different amounts in the leaves and seeds of various plants, including coffee beans, tea leaves, and cocoa beans, which are used to make chocolate. Caffeine amounts even vary in different types of coffee beans. The average 8 oz. cup of coffee has about 100 milligrams of caffeine, with black tea having about half this amount and chocolate even less. Caffeine is also added to energy drinks, weight loss drugs, some sodas, and drugs for colds. It is estimated that over 85% of children and adults in the United States consume caffeine daily, with adults consuming around 280 mg each day (APA, 2013). This equates to about 2 to 3 cups of coffee per day. Headaches are reported in about 10% of regular users who have not used caffeine for the past 24 hours.

In large-scale studies involving more than 100,000 individuals who were followed for up to 24 years, the consumption of coffee for those over 60 years of age was related to individuals having less risk for heart disease (Glade, 2010). Even drinking six cups of coffee a day did not increase the risk of developing heart disease. However, some individuals are more sensitive to caffeine than others. These individuals may experience stomach problems, trouble sleeping, anxiety, irritability, and nervousness from increased caffeine intake.

Individuals who experience such symptoms along with clinically significant distress or impairment in important areas of functioning after ingesting a large dose of caffeine can be diagnosed with caffeine intoxication per criteria *in DSM-5-TR*. There is also a caffeine withdrawal disorder in which the individual experiences clinically significant distress or impairment in important areas of functioning after an abrupt reduction in caffeine. In addition, the individual with this disorder also experiences at least three of the following: headache, fatigue, depressed mood, difficulty concentrating, and flu-like symptoms. Although individuals can experience symptoms related to increased caffeine intake or abrupt reduction, there is little evidence that a person can become addicted to caffeine as with other drugs. However, individuals can become addicted to tobacco, as you will see in the next section.

Tobacco and Nicotine

Tobacco originated in the Americas, with Indigenous populations smoking or chewing the leaves of the plant (Dani & Balfour, 2011). After Columbus's voyages to the Americas beginning in 1492, tobacco was carried back home by sailors and began to spread throughout Europe. In 1623, the English scientist Francis Bacon described the addictive nature of tobacco. Also in the 1600s, tobacco was grown in the Jamestown colony. During the next few hundred years, it became a cash crop. After 1880, when the cigarette rolling machine was invented, billons of cigarettes and cigars were smoked worldwide.

In the 1950s, tobacco use was associated with cancer. Today, tobacco use is seen by the CDC as the leading cause of preventable disease, disability, and death in the United States (see For Further Reading). In 2016, an estimated 17% of adults 25 years of age and older in the United States were cigarette smokers. Since 2006, smoking has decreased around 1% a year. Incidence of cigarette smoking is related to level of education (see Figure 12.24). It should be noted that e-cigarettes contain nicotine and carry the same risk factors as those found in regular cigarettes (see For Further Reading). The majority of tobacco use worldwide is in less developed countries.

The addictive substance in tobacco is nicotine (Dani & Balfour, 2011). **Nicotine** is a stimulant substance found in plants of the nightshade family. Nicotine may be produced by the plant to inhibit insects. In humans, research has shown that nicotine influences dopamine neurons in the midbrain. It increases dopamine and thus functions similarly to other drugs of addiction. Also similar to other drugs, the environmental cues associated with tobacco use play a critical role. For some, it is the smell of the smoke from another smoker. For others, it can be a cue such as finishing a meal or having sexual relations. Nicotine is able to alter the inhibitory effects of GABA and thus enhance the learning of external cues with tobacco use and experience. In terms of learning, nicotine acts throughout the brain and influences attention, memory, emotion, and motivation.

Nicotine can have varied effects on the body, which makes it function as both a stimulant and a depressant (see For Further Reading). Some of these include the following:

FIGURE 12.24 ■ Cigarette Smoking in the United States by Level of Education

There is an inverse relationship between cigarette smoking and education: Those with more education are the least likely to be smokers.

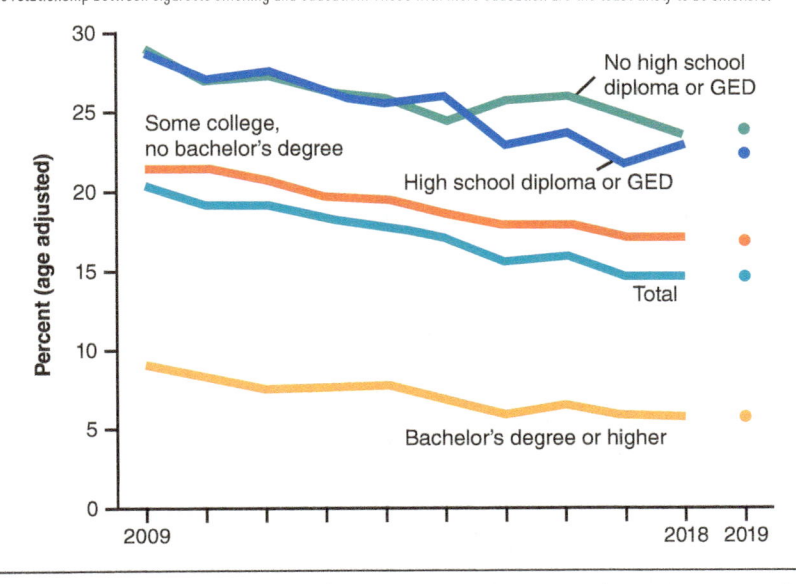

Source: National Center for Health Statistics. (2023). *Health, United States, 2020–2021: Annual perspective.* https://www.ncbi.nlm.nih.gov/books/NBK589555/figure/healthus20_21.fig8/

Note: Data are based on household interviews of a sample of the civilian noninstitutionalized population.

- Decreases the appetite (for this reason, the fear of weight gain reduces some people's willingness to stop smoking)
- Boosts mood and may even relieve minor depression; many people will feel a sense of well-being
- Raises the level of blood sugar (glucose) and increases insulin production
- Increases bowel activity, saliva, and phlegm
- Increases heart rate by around 10 to 20 beats per minute
- Increases blood pressure by 5 to 10 mmHg (because it tightens the blood vessels)
- May cause sweating, nausea, and diarrhea
- Stimulates memory and alertness; people who use tobacco often depend on it to help them accomplish certain tasks and perform well

As with other drugs of addiction, nicotine will effect changes in the brain that result in the symptoms of withdrawal if it is not available. These include the following:

- An intense craving for nicotine
- Anxiety, tension, restlessness, frustration, or impatience
- Difficulty concentrating
- Drowsiness or trouble sleeping, as well as bad dreams and nightmares
- Headaches
- Increased appetite and weight gain
- Irritability or depression

As with other addictive disorders, *DSM-5-TR* includes tobacco use disorder and tobacco withdrawal disorder, which involve clinically significant distress or impairment in important areas of functioning.

It wasn't until the 1950s that tobacco use was associated with cancer. Today, it is seen by the CDC as the leading cause of preventable disease in the United States.

Allan Cash Picture Library/Alamy Stock Photo

> **CONCEPT CHECK**
>
> - What factors impact the brain changes that occur from the use of cocaine?
> - What are some of the factors that promote the use and abuse of amphetamines?
> - How do amphetamines affect the body?
> - What are the primary effects of caffeine on the body? An individual can experience intoxication and withdrawal in regard to caffeine, but what about addiction?
> - What is the addictive ingredient in tobacco, and what are its impacts on an individual's body and brain?

GAMBLING

Gambling has long been part of human existence worldwide, at least since the beginning of written history. Currently, lottery tickets are available throughout the world. Many countries have some form of legal gambling, such as that seen in the United States in Las Vegas and many additional places. Poker tournaments are televised, online poker is popular, and sports betting has become more prevalent in recent years.

In one national community survey, four out of five respondents, or 78.4% of the more than 9,000 people in the sample, reported gambling at least once in their lifetime (Kessler et al., 2008). Some 54% gambled more than 10 times, 27% gambled more than 100 times, and 10.1% gambled more than 1,000 times. Table 12.10 shows these data by type of gambling. In some individuals, gambling becomes a problem that appears similar to drug addiction.

Whereas *DSM-IV* categorized pathological gambling as an *impulse control disorder* (Shaffer & Martin, 2011), *DSM-5* and *DSM-5-TR* consider pathological gambling an addictive disorder. Like drug addiction, pathological gambling continues despite negative consequences, such as consistent losses and an inability to control one's gambling behavior. The *DSM-5-TR* criteria for gambling disorder have similarities to criteria for other addictive disorders. This includes at least four of the following: a need to gamble with increasing amounts of money, restlessness or irritability when attempting to cut down on gambling, past attempts to cut down on gambling, thinking about gambling, gambling when feeling distressed,

A pachinko parlor in Japan, similar to Western slot machine parlors.
iStock.com/fotoVoyager

TABLE 12.10 ■ Lifetime Prevalence by Gambling Type

Gambling Type	Prevalence (%)
I. Sports betting	
Office sports pool	44.3
Sports with bookie or parlay cards	5.8
Betting on horse/dog races or cock/dog fights	25.0
Gambling at a casino	44.7
II. Other types of gambling that involve some aspect of mental or physical skill	
Games involving mental skill (e.g., cards)	35.8
Games involving physical skill (e.g., pool)	22.7
Speculating on high-risk investments	8.4
Internet gambling	1.0
III. Types of gambling that largely involve chance rather than skill	
Playing numbers/lotto	62.2
Gambling machines (e.g., video poker)	26.1
Slot machines, bingo, or pull tabs	48.9

Credit: Kessler, R. C., Hwang, I., LaBrie, R., Petukhova, M., Sampson, N., Winters, K., & Shaffer, H. (2008). The prevalence and correlates of DSM-IV pathological gambling in the National Comorbidity Survey Replication. *Psychological Medicine, 38*, 1351–1360.

trying to recoup losses, lying to conceal involvement in gambling, jeopardizing significant opportunities, and relying on others to supply money lost in gambling. The pattern of gambling disorder's development can be unpredictable and is not related to any age group. It is seen to develop in adolescence, young adulthood, middle age, and even old age. Men tend to develop gambling disorder when they are younger, whereas women develop it late in life. It has only recently been studied from a scientific standpoint.

In a study by Kessler and his colleagues (2008), those with pathological gambling symptoms showed a lifetime prevalence of 2.3% and a 12-month prevalence of less than 1% (0.3%). Those with pathological gambling symptoms also show comorbidity on a number of mental disorders. Table 12.11 presents these data. Notice that individuals with pathological gambling show the highest comorbidity for other substance use disorders.

Psychological studies suggest that pathological gambling is more than just an impulse control disorder but is another example of an addiction disorder (Wareham & Potenza, 2010). Individuals with both gambling and substance use disorder show **substance tolerance**. With drugs, individuals develop tolerance and must consume more of the drug to have the same effect. With gambling, the individual needs to bet more to keep the same level of excitement. Withdrawal is also a common factor in both gambling and substance use disorder. As the person cuts down on or quits either, they become anxious or irritable. Both gambling and substance use can lead to illegal activity to keep them available.

Researchers suggest that four cognitive–emotional processes play a role in pathological gambling (van Holst et al., 2010). The first is behavioral conditioning. People are sensitive to rewards in their life. Early wins when playing games of chance will keep an individual gambling longer. Also, those who win are more likely than those who lose to attribute the win to their behavior. Finally, as seen in various studies of conditioning, a variable intermittent pattern of reinforcement, which is impossible to predict, is one of the most difficult to extinguish.

The second cognitive–emotional process that plays a role in pathological gambling is the experience of cues that bring forth urges to gamble. As with other addictive disorders such as alcohol use disorder, just seeing an item such as a glass of beer will produce arousal and the desire to drink. The same is true of gambling, and the person will show attentional processes in which they are quick to notice gambling-related items.

The third process is impulsivity. Studies of pathological gambling show more impulsiveness on behavioral inhibition tasks as well as questionnaires for pathological gamblers.

The fourth process is impaired executive functioning in pathological gamblers. This leads to decision making that results in an inaccurate evaluation of the situation; that is, individuals continue to

TABLE 12.11 ■ Lifetime Comorbidity of Pathological Gambling With Other Mental Disorders

Mental Disorder	Prevalence (%)
I. Mood disorders	
Major depressive disorder or dysthymia	38.6
Bipolar disorder	17.0
Any mood disorder	55.6
II. Anxiety disorders	
Panic disorder	21.9
Generalized anxiety disorder	16.6
Phobia	52.2
PTSD	14.8
Any anxiety disorder	60.3
III. Impulse control disorders	
ADHD	13.4
Oppositional-defiant disorder	15.4
Conduct disorder	24.9
Intermittent explosive disorder	27.0
Any impulse control disorder	42.3
IV. Substance use disorders	
Alcohol or drug abuse	46.2
Alcohol or drug dependence	31.8
Nicotine dependence	63.0
Any substance use disorder	76.3
V. Number of disorders	
Any disorder	96.3
Exactly one disorder	22.0
Exactly two disorders	9.9
Three or more disorders	64.4

Credit: Kessler, R. C., Hwang, I., LaBrie, R., Petukhova, M., Sampson, N., Winters, K., & Shaffer, H. (2008). The prevalence and correlates of DSM-IV pathological gambling in the National Comorbidity Survey Replication. *Psychological Medicine, 38*, 1351–1360.

gamble even when external factors show negative consequences. Pathological gamblers often ignore the long-term consequences in favor of short-term experiences. One common research paradigm is to use the Iowa Gambling Task. In this task, individuals must choose between four decks of cards. Unknown to the person, two decks give low payouts but with fewer penalties. The other two give higher payouts but also greater penalties. Since the task is to accumulate money, the best strategy is to consistently choose the low payout/low penalty decks. The Iowa Gambling Task is able to differentiate healthy individuals who choose the low penalty decks from individuals with frontal lobe disorders who do not move to the better strategy decks. People with a pathological gambling disorder also show a tendency to choose short-term gain over the more successful long-term strategy.

CONCEPT CHECK

- What are the characteristics of pathological gambling that make it an addictive disorder?

TREATMENT OF SUBSTANCE-RELATED DISORDERS

Addictive drugs create brain changes that affect one's ability to accurately conceptualize their addiction. The person with an addiction will often deny that an addiction is present. Thus, those with addiction are slow to seek help until they experience the negative consequences of their situation. The changes that occur in the brain from taking psychoactive drugs on a prolonged basis also create an increased need for additional amounts of the drug to obtain the same effect. Physiological states of need, such as feeling hungry, can interfere with cognitive and emotional processes such that we tend to pay more attention to these need states. Drugs with their rewarding effects and withdrawal experiences make it difficult for an individual to reverse a drug addiction without help.

Treating addiction is a difficult process. Many individuals who engage in some type of substance misuse do not want to seek treatment. As noted, many have other comorbid mental disorders. This raises the question of what type of treatment is needed. Overall, there are two broad categories of treatment. The first is psychosocial approaches, including cognitive behavioral therapy (CBT), motivational interviewing, and family or couples approaches (MacKillop et al., 2018; Witkiewitz et al., 2022). Motivational interviewing is a technique that seeks to use the client's own motivations to produce change. Community support and relapse prevention groups such as Alcoholics Anonymous (AA) also play a role. The second treatment approach involves using psychopharmacological agents. These agents can be directed at problems of withdrawal, relapse prevention, or comorbid mental disorders. Given the large number of approaches used in the clinical setting, systematic evaluation of these treatments has been limited (Luquiens et al., 2019).

The first step in treating addiction is to help the individual remove the drug from their system. For some, this requires a stay in a hospital or rehabilitation center during the initial phases of withdrawal and subsequent cravings. This is usually followed by some type of psychosocial treatment to help the person understand other factors related to the addiction and develop a plan for future action. One important goal is to help individuals gain a feeling of control over their substance use. For some, this may mean no further use of the substance. For others, this may result in using alcohol, for example, in a limited manner. In this section, some of the more effective means of treatment will be presented, including both psychosocial and psychopharmacological approaches and the way in which they should be used.

Alcoholics Anonymous (AA) sobriety coins. Support and prevention groups such as AA play a role in treating addiction.
Christina Kennedy/Alamy Stock Photo

Principles of Effective Treatment

The National Institute on Drug Abuse (2018), of the U.S. Department of Health and Human Services, examined and updated the complex question of how to treat drug addiction. In their summary publication, *Principles of Drug Addiction Treatment: A Research-Based Guide (Third Edition)*, 13 principles are suggested. These principles are as follows:

1. *Addiction is a complex but treatable disease that affects brain function and behavior.* Drugs of abuse alter the brain's structure and function, resulting in changes that persist long after drug use has ceased. This may explain why drug abusers are at risk for relapse even after long periods of abstinence and despite the potentially devastating consequences.

2. *No single treatment is appropriate for everyone.* Treatment varies depending on the type of drug and the characteristics of the patients. Matching treatment settings, interventions, and services to an individual's particular problems and needs is critical to his or her ultimate success in returning to productive functioning in the family, workplace, and society.

3. *Treatment needs to be readily available.* Because drug-addicted individuals may be uncertain about entering treatment, taking advantage of available services the moment people are ready for treatment is critical. Potential patients can be lost if treatment is not immediately available or readily accessible. As with other chronic diseases, the earlier treatment is offered in the disease process, the greater the likelihood of positive outcomes.

4. *Effective treatment attends to multiple needs of the individual, not just his or her drug abuse.* To be effective, treatment must address the individual's drug abuse and any associated medical, psychological, social, vocational, and legal problems. It is also important that treatment be appropriate to the individual's age, gender, ethnicity, and culture.

5. *Remaining in treatment for an adequate period of time is critical.* The appropriate duration for an individual depends on the type and degree of the patient's problems and needs. Research indicates that most addicted individuals need at least 3 months in treatment and that the best outcomes occur with longer durations of treatment. Recovery from drug addiction is a long-term process and frequently requires multiple episodes of treatment. As with other chronic illnesses, relapses to drug abuse can occur and should signal a need for treatment to be reinstated or adjusted. Because individuals often leave treatment prematurely, programs should include strategies to engage and keep patients in treatment.

6. *Behavioral therapies—including individual, family, or group counseling—are the most commonly used forms of drug abuse treatment.* Behavioral therapies vary in their focus and may involve addressing a patient's motivation to change, providing incentives for abstinence, building skills to resist drug use, replacing drug-using activities with constructive and rewarding activities, improving problem-solving skills, and facilitating better interpersonal relationships. Also, participation in group therapy and other peer support programs during and following treatment can help maintain abstinence.

7. *Medications are an important element of treatment for many patients, especially when combined with counseling and other behavioral therapies.* For example, methadone, buprenorphine, and naltrexone (including a new long-acting formulation) are effective in helping individuals addicted to heroin or other opioids stabilize their lives and reduce their illicit drug use. Acamprosate, disulfiram, and naltrexone are medications approved for treating alcohol dependence. For persons addicted to nicotine, a nicotine replacement product (available as patches, gum, lozenges, or nasal spray) or an oral medication (such as bupropion or varenicline) can be an effective component of treatment when part of a comprehensive behavioral treatment program.

8. *An individual's treatment and services plan must be assessed continually and modified as necessary to ensure that it meets his or her changing needs.* A patient may require varying combinations of services and treatment components during the course of treatment and recovery. In addition

to counseling or psychotherapy, a patient may require medication, medical services, family therapy, parenting instruction, vocational rehabilitation, and/or social and legal services. For many patients, a continuing care approach provides the best results, with the treatment intensity varying according to a person's changing needs.

9. *Many drug-addicted individuals also have other mental disorders.* Because drug abuse and addiction—both of which are mental disorders—often co-occur with other mental illnesses, patients presenting with one condition should be assessed for the other(s). And when these problems co-occur, treatment should address both (or all), including the use of medications as appropriate.

10. *Medically assisted detoxification is only the first stage of addiction treatment and by itself does little to change long-term drug abuse.* Although medically assisted detoxification can safely manage the acute physical symptoms of withdrawal and can, for some, pave the way for effective long-term addiction treatment, detoxification alone is rarely sufficient to help addicted individuals achieve long-term abstinence. Thus, patients should be encouraged to continue drug treatment following detoxification. Motivational enhancement and incentive strategies, begun at initial patient intake, can improve treatment engagement.

11. *Treatment does not need to be voluntary to be effective.* Sanctions or enticements from family, employment settings, and/or the criminal justice system can significantly increase treatment entry, retention rates, and the ultimate success of drug treatment interventions.

12. *Drug use during treatment must be monitored continuously, as lapses during treatment do occur.* Knowing their drug use is being monitored can be a powerful incentive for patients and can help them withstand urges to use drugs. Monitoring also provides an early indication of a return to drug use, signaling a possible need to adjust an individual's treatment plan to better meet his or her needs.

13. *Treatment programs should test patients for the presence of HIV/AIDS, hepatitis B and C, tuberculosis, and other infectious diseases, as well as provide targeted risk-reduction counseling, linking patients to treatment if necessary.* Typically, drug abuse treatment addresses some of the drug-related behaviors that put people at risk of infectious diseases. Targeted counseling focused on reducing infectious disease risk can help patients further reduce or avoid substance-related and other high-risk behaviors. Counseling can also help those who are already infected to manage their illness. Moreover, engaging in substance abuse treatment can facilitate adherence to other medical treatments. Substance abuse treatment facilities should provide on-site, rapid HIV testing rather than referrals to off-site testing—research shows that doing so increases the likelihood that patients will be tested and receive their test results. Treatment providers should also inform patients that highly active antiretroviral therapy (HAART) has proven effective in combating HIV, including among drug-abusing populations, and help link them to HIV treatment if they test positive.

These 13 principles seek to describe the reality of drug addiction. They suggest that addiction is a treatable disorder but one that requires an individualized approach. These principles also acknowledge that the person may have other disorders or problems and that these should be considered in the treatment. In addition, these principles consider the complex nature of addiction. One of these realities is that those who use drugs may also engage in risky behavior, including committing crime, having unprotected sex, and using dirty needles, which can result in getting HIV, hepatitis C, and other diseases. Pregnant women may also negatively impact the health of their fetus through drug use. From a treatment standpoint, both behavioral approaches and medications should be considered for treating drug addiction. Additionally, as described in the *LENS: Drug Use—Rehabilitation, Not Jail*, some police departments are taking drug users who turn themselves in to rehabilitation rather than charging them with a crime.

LENS

DRUG USE—REHABILITATION, NOT JAIL

During the 1960s and early 1970s, there was a dramatic increase in drug use in the United States, especially among those under 30. This rise in drug use was celebrated by many but caused great concern for others. The era is sometimes looked back on as the period of "sex, drugs, and rock 'n' roll," where old social norms were challenged and a "do your own thing" spirit took hold. To many of the 1960s generation, the use of drugs was a way to free the mind from conventional limits, which was a striking contrast to the conformity-minded years of the 1950s. However, the widespread use of cannabis, pills (uppers and downers), LSD, heroin, and other psychoactive substances struck many other Americans as evidence of a dangerous social breakdown.

In Gloucester, Massachusetts, drug addicts who turn themselves in at a police station will not be charged but instead are helped toward recovery.

iStock.com/shiyali

In 1971, President Richard Nixon declared a "war on drugs." With this came an increase in the size of federal drug control agencies. Cannabis became a restricted drug, and mandatory jail sentences were added for drug use. This tougher policy was followed by an extension of the war on drugs during the presidency of Ronald Reagan. Between 1980 and 1997, the number of people placed in jail for nonviolent drug use increased from 50,000 to 400,000. Large sums of federal money were used in the various drug control programs. Many of these moved from police action to more military-type actions. More recently, the entire "war on drugs" approach has been called into question, as data have not supported the efforts to use the legal system as the way to regulate drug use and punish users. Many in government have concluded that the war on drugs has not worked.

More recently, there has been a shift in focus from drug supply and use to that of drug demand. For example, the police chief of Gloucester, MA, said that the old drug war was lost and over. Instead, he is treating addiction as a disease and not a crime. He said, "Any addict who walks into the police station with the remainder of their drug equipment (needles, etc.) or drugs and asks for help will NOT be charged. Instead we will walk them through the system toward detox and recovery" and send them for treatment "on the spot" (Seelye, 2016). Since he began this approach, 391 addicts have turned themselves in. It is reported that the program not only has human benefits but economic ones as well. Whereas it cost $220 to arrest, process, and hold a person with an addiction in custody for a single day, it costs only $55 for the police to send that person to treatment. Also, the Gloucester community has been supportive with in-kind donations to the program.

> This new approach in treating drug addiction is not limited to Gloucester. At least 56 police departments in 17 states—from Orlando, Florida, to Port Angeles, Washington—have started similar programs, with about twice that number preparing to do so. One important aspect is for treatment programs to work with the police departments, which is happening in Gloucester and elsewhere.
>
> ### Thought Question
>
> What are the promises and problems of focusing on demand rather than supply in relation to drug use?

Psychosocial Therapies and Addiction

Given the difficulty that most individuals face in reducing drug use, a number of procedures have been developed. Some of these, such as an educational approach, have been shown not to be effective (Miller et al., 2006). That is, just telling a person with an addiction about the problems related to addiction does not change their behavior. Other psychosocial approaches, such as those discussed previously in terms of other disorders, have also been utilized with disordered substance use. However, the evaluation of these psychosocial approaches is complex, as most of these methods are used in the context of other treatment types. Thus, it is difficult to determine which aspects of the treatment constitute the effective component.

One approach that has been found to have empirical support is CBT for individuals and for couples. CBT has mainly been used as a means to prevent relapse. As with CBT for other mental disorders, it is designed to help the person understand their thoughts toward substance abuse and create means to cope. One part of this is an exploration of positive and negative aspects of continued use. Another part is to anticipate problems associated with no longer using a substance and to consider alternative ways to act and reason in the situation. This would include teaching the person techniques of self-monitoring related to their emotions and internal sensations such that they are able to anticipate when a craving will develop. Likewise, the person can consider which future situations would put them at risk for misuse. With the opioid crisis in the United States, psychological organizations such as the American Psychological Association have summarized empirical supported treatments such as CBT (see For Further Reading).

Another approach is that of motivational interviewing (Miller & Rollnick, 2012). Motivational interviewing focuses on the client's own goals and motivations as a way to change addictive behaviors. It is similar to the client-centered approach of Carl Rogers in that the focus is on the client's internal thoughts and feelings. In the therapy, the client focuses on their own feelings about the situation and their current plan for making changes. Typically, changes that represent small steps are emphasized.

The 12-Step Program

The **12-step program** forms the basis of Alcoholics Anonymous (AA). Variations of this approach have also been used with other addictions (e.g., Narcotics Anonymous, Gamblers Anonymous). The 12-step program and AA were established in the 1930s by William Wilson and Robert Holbrook Smith. These individuals are better known as "Bill W." and "Dr. Bob." They created a community in which individuals with alcohol problems would meet and follow the principles described in the 12 steps. AA is not considered a treatment in the usual sense since no health care professional is involved, nor is there a desire to change their procedures based on empirical research.

AA groups are found throughout the world. According to AA (see For Further Reading) in a 2014 survey, there are more than 115,000 groups worldwide. In the United States and Canada, 62% of the members are men and 38% women with an average age of 50 years. The average length of time since

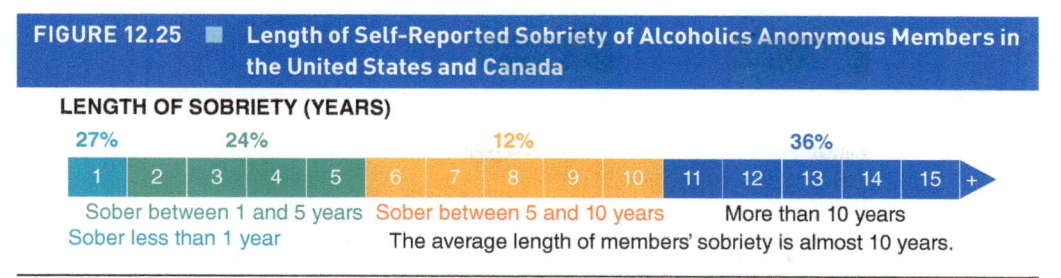

FIGURE 12.25 ■ **Length of Self-Reported Sobriety of Alcoholics Anonymous Members in the United States and Canada**

LENGTH OF SOBRIETY (YEARS)

27%	24%		12%		36%	
1	2 3 4 5	6 7 8 9 10	11 12 13 14 15 +

Sober less than 1 year
Sober between 1 and 5 years
Sober between 5 and 10 years
More than 10 years
The average length of members' sobriety is almost 10 years.

Source: Alcoholics Anonymous. (2011). *Alcoholics Anonymous 2011 membership survey.* http://www.aa.org/pdf/products/p-48_membershipsurvey.pdf

members' last drink is around 10 years (see Figure 12.25). In this sense, AA is a support group designed to help an individual not to drink or relapse.

The first step suggests that the individual is powerless over alcohol. Therefore, individuals must look to a higher power to help them. The Twelve Steps are presented here (see For Further Reading):

1. We admitted we were powerless over alcohol—that our lives had become unmanageable.
2. Came to believe that a Power greater than ourselves could restore us to sanity.
3. Made a decision to turn our will and our lives over to the care of God *as we understood Him*.
4. Made a searching and fearless moral inventory of ourselves.
5. Admitted to God, to ourselves, and to another human being the exact nature of our wrongs.
6. Were entirely ready to have God remove all these defects of character.
7. Humbly asked Him to remove our shortcomings.
8. Made a list of all persons we had harmed, and became willing to make amends to them all.
9. Made direct amends to such people wherever possible, except when to do so would injure them or others.
10. Continued to take personal inventory, and when we were wrong, promptly admitted it.
11. Sought through prayer and meditation to improve our conscious contact with God *as we understood Him*, praying only for knowledge of His will for us and the power to carry that out.
12. Having had a spiritual awakening as the result of these steps, we tried to carry this message to alcoholics, and to practice these principles in all our affairs.

Credit: The Twelve Steps are reprinted with permission of Alcoholics Anonymous World Services, Inc. ("AAWS"). Permission to reprint the Twelve Steps does not mean that AAWS has reviewed or approved the contents of this publication, or that AAWS necessarily agrees with the views expressed herein. A.A. is a program of recovery from alcoholism only—use of the Twelve Steps in connection with programs and activities which are patterned after A.A., but which address other problems, or in any other non-A.A. context, does not imply otherwise.

As an individual moves through these steps, they come to see their own emotional reactions to the world as well as the manner in which their behavior has affected other individuals. The majority of individuals in AA have a sponsor—a recovering addict who is further along in the program—who helps them consider their life. The typical participant goes to two or three meetings a week. Although no formal evaluation of the program has been conducted, it appears to be useful for those committed to changing their relationship to drugs of addiction.

In the TV show *Mom*, Allison Janney and Anna Faris star as a mother and daughter who are both recovering from addiction who attend Alcoholics Anonymous meetings to continue with their recovery.

CBS Photo Archive/Contributor/CBS/via Getty Images

Controlled Drinking Approaches

Controlled drinking is based on the idea that a person can learn to use alcohol in moderation (Saladin & Santa Ana, 2004). This is in contrast to the AA approach, which suggests that total abstinence is required. It was commonly assumed in both the United States and Europe that a person with alcoholism could not learn to drink alcohol in moderation. This view was challenged in the United Kingdom when D. L. Davies published a paper in 1962 reporting that 7 of 97 individuals with serious alcoholism were able to control their consumption of alcohol over a 7- to 11-year period. There was also a Rand Report based on data from 45 treatment centers in the United States that suggested that around 20% of those who had been treated were able to drink moderately after 4 years (Polich et al., 1981).

The controlled drinking approach gained additional scientific credibility when Mark Sobell and Linda Sobell (1978) conducted a study of men with an alcohol problem at a state hospital. Half of the men were assigned to a treatment group in which they were taught to drink in moderation, whereas the other group focused on abstinence. These individuals were followed and at the end of 2 years, it was reported that the controlled drinking group was doing well 85% of the time, whereas in the abstinence group, it was only 42% of the time. Clearly, in men picked because of their potential for a good prognosis, controlled drinking offered an alternative.

However, this conclusion was challenged in 1982 with a publication in the journal *Science* (Pendery et al., 1982). These researchers reported that when they followed up on the individuals in the controlled drinking group some 10 years later, the results were not impressive. Only 1 out of 20 men had maintained a pattern of controlled drinking. However, they did not follow up with the abstinence-focused group. This stirred great debate in the research and treatment community as to whether controlled drinking works. In 1995, the Sobells wrote an editorial for the journal *Addiction* with the title "Controlled Drinking After 25 Years: How Important Was the Great Debate?" which was followed by eight commentaries on the editorial by other researchers (Sobell & Sobell, 1995).

Although there was great debate during the end of the 1900s concerning whether an individual with alcohol problems could achieve controlled use of alcohol, more recent research suggests it is possible (Saladin & Santa Ana, 2004). Treatment alternatives to abstinence are known by a number of names besides controlled drinking, including moderated drinking, reduced-risk drinking, asymptomatic drinking, and behavioral self-control training. Various studies suggest these approaches are as effective as other approaches in treating those who experience problems with alcohol. Currently, these approaches are found worldwide, including in Europe and Asia (e.g., Higuchi et al., 2014; Luquiens et al., 2011).

Medications Used to Treat Addiction

Medications are used with at least three different approaches to treating addiction that utilize the manner in which the drug of addiction works in the brain. The first approach is to use agonists. An **agonist drug** is a substance that binds to the receptor and produces cellular activity. Methadone is an opioid agonist. When given, it functions like heroin at the receptor site. However, it does not give the same rush as heroin. If taken orally, it will also lessen the effects of using heroin or other opioids. Thus, if a person wants to lessen the withdrawal effects of heroin, methadone would offer that opportunity. By giving the body the molecular experience of taking a drug without the experience of a high, it aids in the reduction of opioid use. Most U.S. states offer methadone treatment programs. Methadone maintenance works better if it is combined with a psychosocial treatment program.

The second approach is to use an **antagonist drug**. Whereas an agonist drug acts similarly to the illicit drug, an antagonist drug blocks the receptor site so that the illicit drug does not produce an effect. By blocking or counteracting the effects of the illicit drug, it no longer is experienced as rewarding and addictive. One such antagonist is naloxone (brand name Narcan), which is used for opioid overdose reversal. Naloxone is available in many states without a prescription. Another such antagonist is naltrexone, which is used to treat alcohol and opioid addiction. It is also used in emergency rooms to counteract opioid overdose. In terms of tobacco use, varenicline (Chantix) blocks the ability of nicotine to activate dopamine. By reducing the rewarding effects of tobacco use, varenicline reduces craving. Naltrexone triggers a similar effect for alcohol.

The third approach is to use an **aversive drug** that becomes aversive when the drug of abuse is taken. One example is disulfiram (Antabuse). Antabuse interferes with the metabolism of alcohol and produces unpleasant reactions. If a person on Antabuse drinks alcohol, they will experience nausea and other physiological reactions such as increased heart rate. Other substances, such as those that leave a bad taste in one's mouth, have been used in reducing tobacco use.

CONCEPT CHECK

- What are the primary steps in a treatment for drug addiction? Why is treating addiction such a difficult process?
- What are the principles for effective treatment as proposed by the National Institute of Drug Abuse?
- What psychosocial therapy approaches have been used with addiction?
- What are the primary characteristics that describe a 12-step program? Is it a treatment for addiction? Why or why not?
- What is the main principle behind the controlled drinking approach? Is it an effective treatment for alcohol addiction? Why or why not?
- It seems paradoxical to treat drug addiction with drugs. What three different approaches do pharmacological treatments use?

SUMMARY

The use of psychoactive substances has been part of our evolutionary history. Psychoactive substances use the same networks in the brain that are associated with a feeling of social well-being. In particular, the opioid system in the brain that is involved in the addiction to morphine and heroin is also involved in the satisfaction derived from social relationships, sexual stimulation, and eating tasty food.

Researchers make a distinction between drug use, drug misuse such as binge drinking, and addiction. In this chapter, the focus was on the addictive properties of drugs and the manner in which they are processed by our bodies, experienced in emotional and cognitive terms, and treated. Addiction was also described in terms of substance dependence. There are three major components to dependence: (1) the desire to seek and take a certain substance, (2) the inability to avoid or limit the intake of the substance, and (3) the experience of negative emotional states when the substance is not available. Substance abuse and addiction are burdens not only to the individual person but also to the family and society at large.

There is no one answer as to what causes addiction, but related factors include (1) timing of first use, (2) genetic factors and their relationship with the environment, and (3) environmental factors such as stress and/or low socioeconomic level and their role in terms of epigenetics. There is a pattern seen in addiction: (1) intoxication—the initial positive experience of taking the drug leads to a compulsion to seek and take it; (2) bingeing—the individual loses control in the ability to limit intake of the drug; (3) withdrawal—emergence of a negative emotional state when the substance is unavailable or access to it is limited; and (4) what once gave a positive feeling now does little, and the individual needs the drug to feel normal.

Drugs change the brain. This works in a manner similar to how all learning changes your brain, although drug addiction seems to last longer than simple learning. Neuroscience studies show the rewarding effect of drugs is their ability to increase dopamine. Drug addiction can be seen as one form of enhanced motivation. Not only can drugs change your brain, but they can also take over the cognitive, emotional, and physiological mechanisms that we use for everyday life. They take over the brain mechanisms that are involved in reward. In addiction, compulsive drug use limits our level of human functioning. It is largely reduced to seeking means for obtaining the drug.

DSM-5-TR describes three substance-related disorders for each of the substances covered in this chapter: (1) substance use disorder, which is a pattern of use that leads to significant impairment or distress; (2) substance intoxication disorder, which develops during or shortly after substance ingestion; and (3) substance withdrawal disorder, which occurs following the cessation of, or reduction in, prolonged substance use.

In most humans, the experience of alcohol intake includes pleasant subjective experiences that may lead to increased social interactions. This is partly related to the effects of alcohol on such neurotransmitters as serotonin, endorphins, and dopamine. Alcohol will also decrease inhibition by reducing the effects of the GABA system, which is associated with anxiety. However, if the amount of alcohol intake is increased, it will increase the effects of GABA, which can lead to sedation, which is why alcohol is generally listed as a depressant. As an addictive substance, it can also lead to social, legal, and medical problems. An individual's alcohol intake is assessed at three levels: (1) moderate drinking of alcohol, especially wine, has been associated with better health outcomes; (2) heavy drinking—drinking more than the limits for moderate drinking—places individuals "at risk" for a number of health and other problems; and (3) binge drinking. Binge drinking is highest in college-age populations.

Individuals who use cannabis report a wide variety of experiences: (1) Small doses produce enjoyable positive feelings; (2) larger doses can produce negative feelings, such as anxiety and paranoia; and (3) long-term use is associated with cognitive impairment, for example, to attention or memory. The main psychoactive ingredient in cannabis is THC. A persistent question about cannabis relates to its relationship to psychosis.

Hallucinogens are also called psychedelics and are able to alter perception, mood, and cognitive processes in often unpredictable ways. The subjective effects of taking hallucinogens can be divided into three major components: (1) oceanic boundlessness, (2) anxious ego dissolution, and (3) visionary restructuralization. Although illegal in the United States, hallucinogens do not produce dependence and ceasing use does not create withdrawal symptoms. However, misuse is possible, and not all experiences with hallucinogens are positive.

Opioids are substances derived from the opium poppy used to control pain and bring on euphoric feelings. Opioids are currently used in medical settings primarily for reduction of pain following operations or pain experienced with some types of cancer. There are receptors in the brain that are sensitive to opioid drugs; our bodies make a similar naturally occurring substance—endorphins—which also reduce the experience of pain and makes us feel good.

Cocaine is a stimulant that comes from the coca plant. Its effects include (1) a mental alertness including feelings of euphoria, energy, and desire to talk; (2) a heightened experience of sensory processes such as sound, touch, and sight; (3) physiological effects such as increased heart rate and blood pressure; and (4) increased dopamine signaling in the brain. Brain changes are long lasting, even when the person ceases to use cocaine.

Amphetamines are stimulants produced in the laboratory that result in positive feelings, a burst of energy, and alertness. They have been used as a medicine and even prescribed to reduce addictions to other substances. Amphetamines affect the dopamine system to produce the initial euphoric experience but also less positive long-term brain changes, especially from the use of methamphetamines: (1) development of compulsive patterns of use, (2) negative brain changes consistent with brain injury, and (3) changes in the individual's cognitive functioning.

Caffeine is a stimulant that enhances alertness, ability to concentrate, problem solving, wakefulness, energy, and overall mood. However, some individuals are more sensitive to caffeine than others and may experience stomach problems, trouble sleeping, anxiety, irritability, and nervousness from increased caffeine intake. In *DSM-5-TR*, individuals who experience such symptoms along with clinically significant distress or impairment in important areas of functioning after ingesting a large dose of caffeine can be diagnosed with caffeine intoxication. There is also a caffeine withdrawal disorder. However, there is little evidence that a person can become addicted to caffeine.

The addictive substance in tobacco is nicotine, which increases dopamine and thus functions similarly to other drugs of addiction. Similar to those for other drugs, the environmental cues associated with tobacco use play a critical role. Nicotine acts throughout the brain and influences attention, memory, emotion, and motivation. Nicotine can have varied effects on the body, which makes it function as both a stimulant and a depressant.

Like drug addiction, pathological gambling continues despite negative consequences and because of an inability to control one's gambling behavior. Individuals with pathological gambling show the highest comorbidity for other substance use disorders. Psychological studies led *DSM-5* to recategorize pathological gambling as an addiction disorder, rather than an impulse control disorder as it had been categorized previously. Researchers suggest that four cognitive–emotional processes play a role in pathological gambling: (1) behavioral conditioning, (2) the experience of cues that bring forth urges to gamble, (3) impulsivity, and (4) impaired executive functioning.

Treating addiction is a difficult process because many do not want to seek treatment, and many have other comorbid mental disorders. There are several broad categories of treatment: (1) psychosocial approaches, including CBT, motivational interviewing, and family or couple approaches; (2) community support and relapse prevention groups, such as AA with its 12-step program; (3) controlled drinking approaches for alcohol; and (4) using psychopharmacological agents. Given the large number of approaches used, systematic evaluation of treatments has been limited. Steps in treating addiction include helping the individual remove the drug from their system and some type of psychosocial treatment to help the person understand other factors related to the addiction and develop a plan for future action. Medications are used with at least three different approaches to treating addiction, which utilize the manner in which the drug of addiction works in the brain. The classes of drugs used for treatment include agonists, antagonists, and a drug that becomes aversive when the drug of abuse is taken.

STUDY RESOURCES

Review Questions

1. A number of the substances that have been covered in this chapter provide benefits as medicines—for example, opioids, cannabis, and amphetamines. On the other hand, it is clear that individuals can misuse or become addicted to these substances, which can lead to negative consequences. What principles would you use in developing a policy surrounding their use,

including who could use them, what types of illnesses they could be used for, and who would regulate that use?

2. What are the similarities across substance-related and addictive disorders in terms of onset, diagnostic criteria, brain processes, and treatment?

3. Pathological gambling is the only addictive disorder considered in this chapter that is not substance related. Are there other disorders that you think should be included as an addictive disorder?

4. What is it about substance-related and addictive disorders that make them so difficult to treat? If you were asked to put together an awareness program about these disorders targeting a college-age audience, what information would you include, and what approach would you take?

FOR FURTHER READING

Alcoholics Anonymous. (n.d.). https://www.aa.org/

Centers for Disease Control. (n.d.). *Alcohol*. U.S. Department of Health and Human Services. https://www.cdc.gov/alcoholportal/

Centers for Disease Control. (n.d.). *Quick facts on the risks of e-cigarettes for kids, teens, and young adults*. U.S. Department of Health and Human Services. https://www.cdc.gov/tobacco/basic_information/e-cigarettes/Quick-Facts-on-the-Risks-of-E-cigarettes-for-Kids-Teens-and-Young-Adults.html

Denizet-Lewis, B. (2009). *America anonymous: Eight addicts in search of a life*. Simon & Schuster.

Levy, M. (2007). *Take control of your drinking . . . and you may not need to quit*. Johns Hopkins University Press.

Lewis, M. (2015). *The biology of desire*. PublicAffairs.

McGreal, C. (2018). *American overdose: The opioid tragedy in three acts*. Public Affairs.

National Center for Health Statistics. (2018). *Health, United States, 2017: With special feature on mortality*. https://www.cdc.gov/nchs/data/hus/hus17.pdf

National Library of Medicine.U.S. Department of Health and Human Services. (2022). *Nicotine and tobacco*. https://medlineplus.gov/ency/article/000953.htm

Society of Clinical Psychology. (2022). *Treatment target: Substance and alcohol use disorders*. https://div12.org/diagnosis/substance-and-alcohol-use-disorders/

Substance Abuse and Mental Health Services Administration. (n.d.). www.samhsa.gov

World Health Organization. (n.d.). *Drugs (psychoactive)*. https://www.who.int/health-topics/drugs-psychoactive#tab=tab_1

KEY TERMS

addiction
agonist drug
alcohol
amphetamines
antagonist drug
aversive drug
dependence
binge drinking
caffeine
cannabis
cocaine

craving
disordered use
hallucinogens
intoxication
nicotine
opioids
pathological gambling
substance tolerance
tobacco
12-step program
withdrawal

13 SCHIZOPHRENIA

LEARNING OBJECTIVES

13.1 Describe the prevalence of schizophrenia, the time course of its development, and its positive and negative symptoms.

13.2 Discuss the historical and evolutionary contexts of schizophrenia.

13.3 Identify genetic and environmental factors in the development of schizophrenia.

13.4 Describe the brain changes seen in individuals with schizophrenia.

13.5 Identify the treatments available to individuals with schizophrenia.

Schizophrenia is one of the most debilitating of the mental disorders, as is made clear in the following personal accounts from those living with it. In this chapter, you will learn about the nature of schizophrenia, its prevalence around the world, its symptoms, and the time course of symptom development.

> The voices arrived without warning on an October night in 1962, when I was fourteen years old. Kill yourself. . . . Set yourself afire, they said. Only moments before, I'd been listening to a musical group called Frankie Valli and the Four Seasons singing "Walk like a man, fast as I can . . ." on the small radio that sat on the night table beside my bed. But the terrible words that I heard now were not the lyrics to that song. I stirred, thinking I was having a nightmare, but I wasn't asleep; and the voices—low and insistent, taunting and ridiculing—continued to speak to me from the radio. Hang yourself, they told me. The world will be better off. You're no good, no good at all.
>
> *From Ken Steele and Claire Berman. (2001).* The Day the Voices Stopped.

> After a time I began to hate work, and Bruce sometimes got on my nerves. I got depressed and crashed out of an evening, staying up all night listening to Pink Floyd's "The Wall." One day I was at work, Bruce was out and the phone rang. I picked it up. "We are following your every move," said a voice; then nothing. Instantly the PA system from the next factory, which was quite loud, said, "Telephone for did-you-get-that? Telephone call for we-know-you're-listening."
>
> *From Richard McLean. (2003).* Recovered, Not Cured: A Journey Through Schizophrenia.

> At the beginning of that summer, I felt well, a happy healthy girl—I thought—with a normal head and heart. By summer's end, I was sick, without any clear idea of what was happening to me or why. And as the Voices evolved into a full-scale illness, one that I only later learned was called schizophrenia, it snatched from me my tranquility, sometimes my self-possession, and very nearly my life.
>
> I spent my junior year abroad. While I was in Spain my first semester, the Voices were softer, but I was so revved up, my motor seemed to be working overtime. When the Voices did speak to me, sometimes they did so in Spanish: "Puta! Puta!" they yelled. "Vaya con el diablo." Go to hell, whore.
>
> Along the way I have lost many things: the career I might have pursued, the husband I might have married, the children I might have had. During the years when my friends were marrying, having their babies and moving into houses I once dreamed of living in, I have been behind locked doors, battling the Voices who took over my life without even asking my permission.
>
> Sometimes these Voices have been dormant. Sometimes they have been overwhelming. At times over the years they have nearly destroyed me. Many times over the years I was ready to give up, believing they had won.
>
> Today this illness, these Voices, are still part of my life. But it is I who have won, not they. A wonderful new drug, caring therapists, the support and love of my family and my own fierce battle—that I know now will never end—have all combined in a nearly miraculous way to enable me to master the illness that once mastered me.
>
> Today, nearly eighteen years after that terrifying summer, I have a job, a car, an apartment of my own. I am making friends and dating. I am teaching classes at the very hospital at which I was once a patient.
>
> *From Lori Schiller and Amanda Bennett. (1996).* The Quiet Room: A Journey Out of the Torment of Madness.

SCHIZOPHRENIA BASICS: PREVALENCE, COURSE, AND SYMPTOMS

Schizophrenia is part of a broad category of disorders referred to as schizophrenia spectrum and other psychotic disorders. According to *DSM-5-TR*, these disorders are defined by abnormalities in one or more of five domains. The five domains are delusions, hallucinations, disorganized thinking, disorganized or abnormal motor behavior, and negative symptoms.

Psychotic disorders involve a loss of touch with reality and are characterized by abnormal thinking and sensory processes. Individuals with a psychotic disorder may show problems in any of the five domains. Studies of intelligence in the first 20 years of life show a decline in both verbal and spatial abilities in those with a psychotic disorder (Mollon et al., 2018). People with psychotic disorders other than schizophrenia may show psychotic symptoms for a brief period of time or for a longer duration. They may also show delusions, affective problems outside the normal range, or simply seem odd to those around them. Psychotic symptoms not part of schizophrenia can be induced through drugs, lack of sleep, and other medical conditions. Also, it should be noted that although the term *schizophrenia* comes from the Greek meaning "to split the mind," it is very different from dissociative disorders, such as dissociative identity disorder. The *Diagnostic and Statistical Manual of Mental Disorders, Fifth Edition, Text Revision* (*DSM-5-TR;* American Psychiatric Association, 2022) describes these conditions separately from schizophrenia. This chapter will focus on schizophrenia since it is a long-term disorder with substantial research to describe its occurrence. All of the disorders on the schizophrenia spectrum and other psychotic disorders are described in Table 13.1.

Schizophrenia affects one's ability to express oneself clearly, to have close social relationships, to express positive emotions, and to plan for the future. Not everyone with schizophrenia displays the same symptoms. Individuals with schizophrenia may hear voices, see images not seen by others, believe that others wish to harm or control them, and have bizarre thoughts. The most common set of symptoms seen in individuals with schizophrenia over the past 100 years is a belief that others are out to get them and the hearing of voices that others do not hear (Insel, 2010).

TABLE 13.1 ■ *DSM-5-TR* **Schizophrenia Spectrum and Other Psychotic Disorders**

DSM-5-TR Diagnosis	Characteristics
Schizophrenia	Symptoms such as delusions, hallucinations, disorganized thinking and speech, abnormal motor behaviors, and negative symptoms, continuously present for at least 6 months
Brief Psychotic Disorder	Symptoms such as delusions, hallucinations, disorganized thinking and speech, abnormal motor behaviors, and negative symptoms lasting for less than a month
Schizophreniform Disorder	Symptoms such as delusions, hallucinations, disorganized thinking and speech, abnormal motor behaviors, and negative symptoms lasting for at least 1 month but less than 6 months
Schizoaffective Disorder	Symptoms such as delusions, hallucinations, disorganized thinking and speech, abnormal motor behaviors, and negative symptoms along with those of a major mood disorder (major depressive or manic)
Substance/Medication-Induced Psychotic Disorder	Delusions or hallucinations related to drugs or medications
Psychotic Disorder Due to Another Medical Condition	Delusions or hallucinations related to a medical condition
Catatonic Disorder Due to Another Medical Condition	Non-normal activity of the motor system such as stupor, holding of a posture, mutism, mannerisms, or grimacing
Unspecified Catatonia	Non-normal activity of the motor system such as stupor, holding of a posture, mutism, mannerisms, or grimacing
Other Specified Schizophrenia Spectrum and Other Psychotic Disorder	Symptoms such as delusions, hallucinations, disorganized thinking and speech, abnormal motor behaviors, and negative symptoms that do not meet the criteria for other categories
Unspecific Schizophrenia Spectrum and Other Psychotic Disorder	Symptoms such as delusions, hallucinations, disorganized thinking and speech, abnormal motor behaviors, and negative symptoms that do not meet the criteria for other categories
Delusional Disorder	Presence of delusions for 1 month or longer without criteria for another schizophrenia spectrum disorder

Individuals with psychotic disorder may experience delusions, hallucinations, disorganized thinking and speech, abnormal motor behaviors, and negative symptoms.

iStock.com/Marjan_Apostolovic. Stock photo. Posed by model.

Individuals with schizophrenia can display problems in terms of cognitive processes, emotional processes, and motor processes. Cognitive problems can be seen as a disorganization of thinking and behavior. In listening to a person with schizophrenia, you may note a speech style that, although detailed, does not seem to have a coherent focus and may seem to constantly change themes. Technically, these characteristics are referred to as *circumstantiality* and *tangentiality*, respectively. In more severe cases, the speech is actually incoherent and contains a stream of words that are unrelated to one another, which is referred to as *word salad*.

Mood symptoms include impairments in affective experience and expression. Depression and thoughts of suicide are common experiences with schizophrenia. A number of individuals with schizophrenia hear voices that tell them to kill themselves. Ken Steele's voices told him, "Hang yourself. The world will be better off. You're no good, no good at all" (Steele & Berman, 2001). Motor symptoms can range from repetitive behaviors such as rocking to total stiffness or lack of change in posture, referred to as *catatonia*.

Prevalence and Course of Schizophrenia

Schizophrenia affects about 1% of the population. It is seen throughout the world with similar symptoms regardless of culture or geographical location. However, the experience of schizophrenia differs by culture, as described in the *Cultural LENS: Schizophrenia Around the World*. Onset of schizophrenia occurs in the late teens or early 20s. Men show an earlier onset than women by about 5 years. Some individuals with schizophrenia display the symptoms throughout their life. However, there is a subgroup of individuals who, a few years after the initial display of symptoms, show a lack of symptoms even without treatment (Jobe & Harrow, 2010). Even with symptoms, some people with schizophrenia are able to be part of the social and economic world experienced by healthy individuals. In fact, two of the individuals whose self-reports are included in this chapter work at major universities in the United States.

The symptoms of schizophrenia are not constantly present. Some individuals with schizophrenia are able to finish college and maintain jobs, even high-level jobs. Thus, individuals with schizophrenia may show periods in which they are able to function in terms of external realities. Symptoms for some people tend to appear in times of change or stress. Different individuals with schizophrenia may show very different symptoms. For example, some individuals may hear voices but never see a visual hallucination. Others show a different presentation of symptoms. This has led some researchers to conclude that a variety of similar disorders exist that are currently described by the term *schizophrenia*—in other words, that schizophrenia is not a single disorder but a number of related disorders. Some have even suggested that the term *schizophrenia* be replaced with the concept of a psychosis spectrum disorder, since not every case of schizophrenia looks the same but may vary in terms of the five domains (Guloksuz & van Os, 2018).

CULTURAL LENS
SCHIZOPHRENIA AROUND THE WORLD

Although schizophrenia is seen in similar rates globally, it is expressed and understood differently in different cultures (Fabrega, 1989; López & Guarnaccia, 2000; Wüsten et al., 2018). That is, cultural factors not only influence how the disorder is experienced by the person with the disorder but also how it is understood by others. This can result in individuals with schizophrenia describing symptoms differently based on where they live (McLean et al., 2014). For example, those who live in developing, low-income countries show less distress to psychotic experiences than those who live in high-income developed countries (Wüsten et al., 2018).

The Māori, who are Indigenous Polynesian people of New Zealand, view health within the context of spiritual, mental/emotional, family, and physical aspects of life. If someone reports hearing voices or seeing individuals others do not see, they are seen as a different type of person who may actually possess spiritual gifts that reflect alternative realities. However, the person could also be seen as someone who is in a state of darkness and not able to fully function. In interviews with the Māori, it was clear that they could hold multiple explanatory models of psychosis and schizophrenia that Western individuals would see as competing (Taitimu et al., 2018). This study highlights the importance of asking users of mental health services about the meaning they place on their experiences to ensure valid assessment and treatment.

The Māori of New Zealand view symptoms of schizophrenia in ways mediated by their culture.
iStock.com/MollyNZ

Cultural and gender roles within a society can also influence how schizophrenia is experienced. For example, in India, men with schizophrenia hide their illness in job applications and from others (Loganathan & Murthy, 2011), since this is associated with shame, ridicule, and difficulty in getting married. For women whose gender role is that of homemaker and child-bearer, especially in lower socioeconomic levels, their experience of schizophrenia may be withheld during the initial marriage proposal. According to the researchers, an understanding of schizophrenia may be lacking, and marriage may even be seen as a remedy for the illness in young women of certain social groups.

Another way in which cultural factors influence the experience of schizophrenia involves help-seeking behaviors. For example, in a society with a collectivist and familial orientation such as China, elders in the family hold the belief that they are responsible for other family members (Wong, 2007). This may lead to younger members of the family not seeking help for schizophrenia. This can be especially true if a person's understanding of schizophrenia involves supernatural or societal explanations. Likewise, in cultures in which schizophrenia is stigmatized, interaction with health care professionals may be delayed.

Even in countries like the United States, Asian Americans and Latino Americans with schizophrenia are more likely to live with family members than are white or Black individuals with schizophrenia (Snowden, 2007). Specifically, Asian Americans with schizophrenia were 4 times more likely and Latinos 3 times more likely to live with their families than were whites or Blacks with schizophrenia. Although this is generally positive, families with more volatile negative emotions are associated with greater relapse.

Overall, it is important to understand that psychological disorders are experienced within a social and cultural context that has implications for care, especially for people of marginalized populations (Jason, 2015). As such, organizations such as the American Psychological Association (APA) have developed guidelines that emphasize cultural and diversity perspectives for working with individuals who seek psychological services (APA, 2017). Likewise, the Association for Psychological Science devoted an issue of the journal *Perspectives on Psychological Science* to the importance of understanding psychological research from a multicultural perspective (Sternberg, 2017).

Thought Question

What are some specific ways the consideration of cultural, social, and gender contexts broadens our perspective on schizophrenia, for example, in manifestation, treatment, or research?

Schizophrenia generally first becomes evident in adolescence or young adulthood (Tandon et al., 2009). The course of the disorder is shown in Figure 13.1. The initial phase is referred to as the *premorbid phase*. During this phase, only subtle or nonspecific problems with cognition, motor, or social functioning can be detected. These are accompanied by poor academic achievement and social functioning. This is followed by a *prodromal phase* in which initial positive symptoms, along with declining functioning, can be seen. Based on prospective studies, this phase can last from a few months to years, with the mean duration being about 5 years. Next is the *psychotic phase*, in which positive psychotic

FIGURE 13.1 ■ Phases in the Development of Schizophrenia

Schizophrenia has been described in terms of four phases: premorbid, prodromal, psychotic, and stable. This figure shows the natural history and course of schizophrenia.

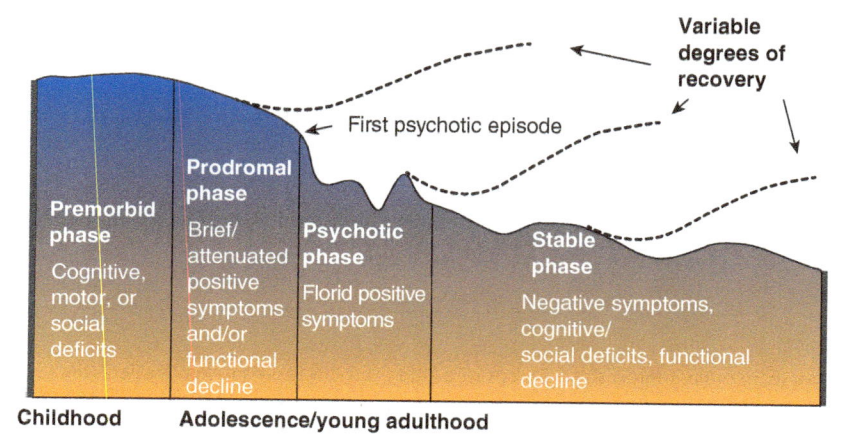

Credit: Tandor, R., Nasrallah, H. A., & Keshavan, M. S. (2009). Schizophrenia, "Just the facts": Clinical features and conceptualization. *Schizophrenia Research, 110*, 1–23, with permission from Elsevier.

symptoms are apparent. For most individuals, this phase occurs between 15 and 45 years of age, with the onset being about 5 years earlier in males than females. This phase is marked by repeated episodes of psychosis with remission in between. The greatest decline in functioning is generally seen during the first 5 years after the initial episode. This phase is followed by a *stable phase* characterized by fewer positive symptoms and an increase in negative ones (see definitions of positive and negative symptoms in the next subsection of this chapter). Stable cognitive and social deficits also characterize this phase. The actual course of the disorder varies greatly across individuals.

Individuals with schizophrenia tend to die earlier than those their age in the general population. These higher age-standardized mortality rates are approximately double those of the general population. The life span of individuals with schizophrenia is abbreviated by 15 to 20 years. Of those with this abbreviated life span, approximately 25% of deaths can be attributed to suicide and 10% to accidents. The remainder are related to medical conditions, particularly cardiovascular disease.

Positive and Negative Symptoms

Based on initial descriptions used by neurologist John Hughlings Jackson in the 1800s, schizophrenia symptoms are referred to as positive or negative. The more familiar **positive symptoms** are hallucinations, delusions, disorganized thinking, and disorganized behavior. The more familiar **negative symptoms** include lack of affect in situations that call for it, poor motivation, and social withdrawal. Hughlings Jackson saw positive symptoms as reflecting a lack of high cortical control over more primitive brain processes. Negative symptoms, on the other hand, were the result of loss of function—what today we would refer to as a dysfunctional network of the brain. It should be noted that "positive" and "negative" are not evaluative terms when applied to symptoms of schizophrenia. Instead, they indicate either what is present (positive) or what is not present (negative). Symptoms characterized by the presence of something unusual, such as hearing voices or seeing hallucinations, are described as positive symptoms. Symptoms characterized by the lack of a normal human process, such as poor motivation or social withdrawal, are referred to as negative symptoms.

Positive Symptoms

Hallucinations are sensory experiences that can involve any of the senses, although auditory hallucinations are the ones most commonly reported by individuals with schizophrenia. The two examples of hallucinations presented at the beginning of this chapter illustrate the unusual experiences that individuals with schizophrenia can have. Ken Steele, while listening to music on the radio, heard it tell him to kill himself. Richard McLean picked up a phone to hear voices telling him that they were following his every move. These auditory hallucinations were experienced as coming from outside the person. Other individuals experience the voices or thoughts as coming from within their head. Individuals with schizophrenia report that they may hear voices throughout the day and on more than one day. Elyn Saks describes her experiences in a TED Talk in which she explains her thoughts during a psychotic episode and aspects of her treatment that helped her to improve (see For Further Reading). Her experience of giving a lecture at law school is related in *LENS: Elyn Saks Describes Her Day-to-Day Experiences With Schizophrenia*.

LENS

ELYN SAKS DESCRIBES HER DAY-TO-DAY EXPERIENCES WITH SCHIZOPHRENIA

As you read about schizophrenia, you generally learn of the symptoms such as hearing voices or feeling that others are out to get you. What you don't hear about is the way those with the disorder are successful. You also don't often read about how an individual with schizophrenia lives their day-to-day life. In the following essay, Elyn Saks describes her experience of teaching a law school class.

Elyn Saks

John D. and Catherine T. MacArthur Foundation, used with permission; licensed under CC BY 4.0 https://creativecommons.org/licenses/by/4.0/

My students filled the room. They were interested and eager, unusually so, given that they were second- and third-year law students for whom the fear and trembling that came with the first year had long since faded. The course was "Advanced Mental Health Law." The day's topic: Billie Boggs. A street person who lived over a hot air vent in midtown Manhattan, she threw food at people who wanted to help her and chased them across the street. Her rantings and ravings seemed crazy to most of the students, and we were discussing whether she should be sent to a psychiatric hospital.

I heard myself speak, surprising myself by the steady sound of my voice as I tried to restore my attention to the group before me: "What if Billie Boggs were your sister—would you put her in a psychiatric hospital then?" Up shot the hands.

Concentrate. These are your students. You have an obligation to them. Canceling class would be admitting defeat. But there are explosions in my head. They're testing nuclear devices on my brain. They're very little and they can get inside. They are powerful.

I pulled myself together, enough to point to a young woman who spoke often in class. "I couldn't let my sister live like that," she said from across the classroom, which held the students in curved rows, like a giant palm before me. "I know my sister. That wouldn't be her. There's one and only one of her—and that's the one before she got sick."

Is she trying to kill me? No, she's a student. But what about the others? The voices inside my head, the explosions. What do they want? Are they trying to interdict me, to hit me with the Kramer device? I went to the store and they said "interdiction." Interdiction, introduction, exposition, explosion. Voicemail is the issue.

I knew not to say those thoughts out loud. Not because they were crazy thoughts—they were every bit as real as the students sitting right in front of me—but I kept silent because others would think them crazy. People would think me as deranged as Billie Boggs.

But I'm not crazy. I simply have greater access to the truth.

"Good," I replied. "But why isn't it the case that your sister has two selves, the sick one you see now and the healthy one you've known all your life? Why should you get to pick which is real? Shouldn't your sister make that choice?" Up shot more hands.

My brain is on fire! My head is going to explode right here, right in front of my class!

"But isn't health always preferred to illness?" a bright-eyed young man countered. "We should prefer the healthy self."

Mercifully, the class ended. A law-school dean spotted me as I walked back to my office. He said I looked as if I were in pain. "Just a lot on my mind," I heard myself reply as I continued quickly down the hall. Keys out, door open, door shut. I crumpled into my chair and buried my face in my hands.

That was in September of 1991, and it was one of my worst such incidents. Ten years before, in my mid-20s, during my third psychiatric hospitalization, I had been given the diagnosis "chronic paranoid schizophrenia with acute exacerbation." My prognosis? "Grave." I was, in other words, expected to be unable to live independently, let alone work. At best I would be in a board-and-care, holding a minimum-wage job—perhaps flipping burgers—when my symptoms had become less severe.

That has not turned out to be my life. I am the Orrin B. Evans professor of law, psychology, and psychiatry and the behavioral sciences at the University of Southern California's law school; adjunct professor of psychiatry at the University of California at San Diego's medical school; and an assistant faculty member at the New Center for Psychoanalysis, where I am also a research clinical associate.

My schizophrenia has not gone away. I still become psychotic, as happened in class that day in 1991. Today my symptoms, while not as severe, still recur and I struggle to stay in the world, so to speak, doing my work. I have written about my illness in a memoir and much of the narrative takes place after I had accepted a tenure-track appointment at USC.

Barring a medical breakthrough of Nobel-Prize-winning proportions, I will never fully recover from schizophrenia. I will remain on antipsychotic medication and in talk therapy for the rest of my life. Yet I have learned to manage my illness.

[There] are steps that everyone with mental illness should take. First, learn about the illness you have—the typical signs, symptoms, and course. Many excellent sources are available. You may want to start with the Diagnostic and Statistical Manual of Mental Disorders [DSM-5], [and] psychiatric textbooks, e.g., Kaplan and Sadock's, can be helpful. I have also discovered excellent lay accounts of mental illness.

Second, understand how your illness affects you. What are your triggers? What are your early warning signs? What can you do to minimize your symptoms when they worsen—e.g., call your therapist, increase your medication, listen to music, exercise? Try to devise some techniques for your own situation. Some colleagues and I are studying how a group of high-functioning people with schizophrenia manage their symptoms. You are in the best position to determine what works for you.

Put a good treatment team in place. You need a therapist you can trust and can turn to in times of difficulty. Does he or she respond if you call in crisis? The same is true of a psychopharmacologist. Make friends and family members part of your team.

Sometimes your team can see early warning signs before you can. For instance, my closest friend, Steve, and my husband, Will, often identify when I am slipping. Will says I become quieter in a particular way that signals all is not well. It's a blessing to have such people in your life. Seek them out.

We also need to put a face on mental illness. Being open about one's own illness will probably do more good than all the laws we can pass.

My own "outing" of myself was a bit of a risk, but has turned out well. I am glad and relieved I no longer have to hide. And my story seems to be meaningful to people—it has helped people understand mental illness more and perhaps has led to a decrease in the stigma. I was lucky in that my law school accommodated my teaching needs without my having to invoke the ADA. My colleagues are supportive, and I no longer feel ashamed about needing their help.

Perhaps most important: Seek help when you need it. Mental illness is a no-fault disease like any other, such as cancer or diabetes. Help is available, but you need to ask for it. Don't let the threat of stigma deter you. You shouldn't have to suffer.

And you shouldn't allow mental illness to stand in the way of the wonderful contributions you are poised to make to your students and to your field.

Thought Question

What are the important components of Elyn Saks's treatment plan? How do they apply to other psychological disorders?

From "Mental Illness in Academe," The Chronicle of Higher Education, November 25, 2009 (edited part of a longer article).

Elyn R. Saks is a professor of law, psychology, and psychiatry and the behavioral sciences at the University of Southern California's law school. She is the author of a memoir, *The Center Cannot Hold: My Journey Through Madness* (Hyperion, 2007).

Of course, all of us misinterpret our experiences once in a while. It is common for people to mistakenly believe that they heard someone call their name or that the phone rang while they were taking a shower. It is also common to mistake a stick on a path in the woods for a snake or to imagine an experience while falling asleep. These experiences are different from true hallucinations in that we check to see what the reality of the situation is or whether we are mistaken. Individuals with schizophrenia treat their hallucinations as real. In hallucinations in which individuals are instructed to perform an act, it is suggested that the instructions are obeyed by some 40% of people (Junginger, 1990). It should be noted that hallucinations can be produced by other disorders, such as Charles Bonnet syndrome, or the medications used to treat Parkinson's disease. In these situations, the person experiences the hallucination but generally knows that it is not real.

Delusions are beliefs that have no support for their occurrence and are at odds with the individual's current environment. One hospitalized patient believed that the CIA had cameras in the drawer pulls of her dresser. Elyn Saks, whose story was presented in the previous *LENS*, believed that powerful individuals could put thoughts in her head. John Hinckley, who tried to kill President Ronald Reagan, believed that Jodie Foster, the actress, would be impressed by this event. Another patient believed that God spoke to her when the dogs outside her house barked.

The most common delusions can be organized into categories. The first is *persecution*. This is the belief that other people or groups such as the CIA are plotting against the individual. Mathematician John Nash (introduced at the beginning of Chapter 1) wrote letters to the U.S. government describing attempts of others to take over the world. The second category is *grandeur*. This is the belief that one is really a very famous person. The individual with schizophrenia may tell everyone that they are Jesus or some other famous figure. The third delusion is *control*. As in the case of Elyn Saks, the delusion is that someone or some entity such as aliens can put thoughts into one's mind. A related delusion is that *others* can hear or understand one's thoughts without being told what they are. Finally, one common delusion is that one is *special* and that God or important individuals are speaking directly to the person.

Long-term delusional activity varies from person to person. One narrative study examined 373 individuals described in 24 studies to examine the nature of the delusions (Ritunnano et al., 2022). Three superordinate themes relating to experiential changes and meanings in delusion were identified: (1) a radical rearrangement of the lived world dominated by intense emotions; (2) doubting, losing, and finding oneself again within delusional realities; and (3) searching for meaning, belonging, and coherence beyond mere dysfunction. In another study, 43 individuals with schizophrenia were assessed six times over a 20-year period (Jobe & Harrow, 2010). Twenty-nine percent of those individuals had no delusional activity over that time, another 26% displayed delusions at each of the six assessments, and the remaining individuals had some delusions (see Figure 13.2).

Negative Symptoms

Negative symptoms seen in schizophrenia tend to be more constant and stable than positive symptoms. Several studies have linked negative symptoms with a poorer prognosis (see Foussias & Remington, 2010, for a review). Whereas it is usually the positive symptoms that result in a diagnosis of schizophrenia, it is the negative symptoms that tend to persist over time. Many individuals with schizophrenia have little interest in doing simple day-to-day activities such as taking a bath or shopping for food. This lack of will or volition is technically referred to as **avolition**. Individuals with schizophrenia also show a lack of interest in talking with others or answering questions with more than a one- or two-word answer. This is referred to as **alogia**. They also show a flattening of affect or difficulty expressing emotion. Another symptom is referred to as **anhedonia** or the inability to experience pleasure.

Multilevel Process for Diagnosing Schizophrenia

The text revision of the fourth edition of the *DSM* (*DSM-IV-TR*) and *DSM-5* set forth a multilevel process for diagnosing schizophrenia. The first level is *symptoms*, which includes delusions, hallucinations, or disorganized speech. At least one of these must be present. In addition, abnormal psychomotor behaviors, such as catatonia, and negative symptoms, such as a lack of volition or social processing, may also be present. The second level is *functioning*. A reduction in functioning in the areas of work,

FIGURE 13.2 ■ Variations in Delusional Activity

Not all individuals with schizophrenia show long-term delusional activity. In this study, 29% had no delusional activity over the 20 years, another 26% displayed delusions at each of the six assessments, and the remaining individuals had some delusions. The figure shows the presence of delusional activity over a 20-year period for individuals with schizophrenia, other psychotic disorders, and others.

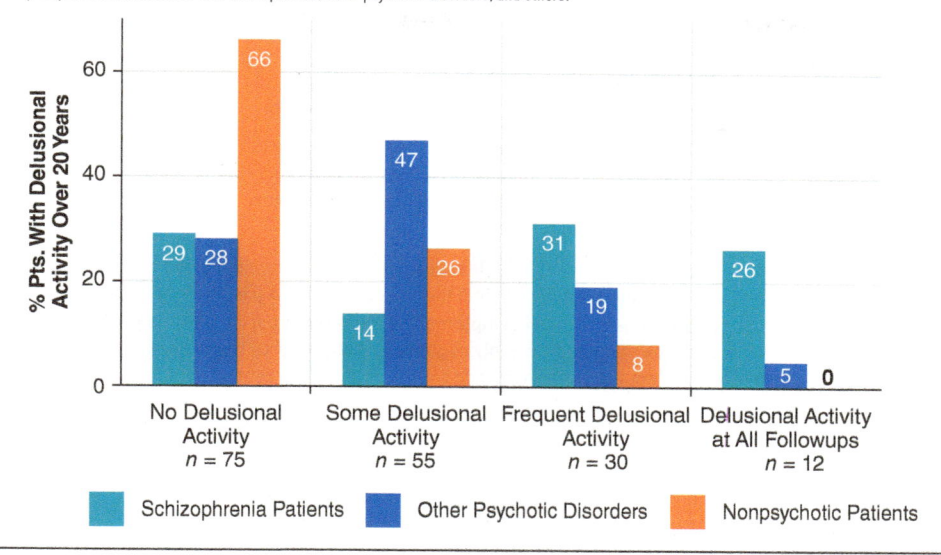

Credit: Martin Harrow and Thomas H. Jobe, "How Frequent Is Chronic Multiyear Delusional Activity and Recovery in Schizophrenia: A 20-Year Multi-Follow-up," *Schizophrenia Bulletin* (2010) 36(1): 192–204, by permission of Oxford University Press.

interpersonal relations, and/or self-care should be present. The third level is *duration*, in which the presence of the positive or negative symptoms should have existed for 6 months with at least 1 month of positive symptoms. The final levels are designed to rule out psychotic-like symptoms found in other disorders such as mania or depression or those related to specific medical conditions such as drug abuse. The *DSM-5-TR* criteria are shown in Table 13.2.

Are There Subtypes of Schizophrenia?

Individuals with schizophrenia have a variety of different symptoms and exhibit an inconsistent picture of the disorder. This has led some to suggest that there is not a single schizophrenia disorder but rather a variety of syndromes. Historically, one approach to this variety of presentations was to look for subtypes, a development we will discuss later in the chapter. The fourth edition of the *DSM* divided schizophrenia into five subtypes: paranoid, disorganized, catatonic, undifferentiated, and residual subtypes. *DSM-5* removed the classification of subtypes but left the diagnostic criteria for schizophrenia almost identical to *DSM-IV-TR*. *DSM-5* also uses the subtype descriptions in classifying other psychotic disorders. Although *ICD-10* used subtypes, *ICD-11* removed the subtypes to be more similar to *DSM-5*. The subtypes are included in this section since they are of historical importance and will aid you in reading previous research.

The **paranoid subtype** is characterized by delusions whose themes generally center on ideas of grandiosity or persecution. Individuals with this subtype might tell stories of how the FBI or CIA is out to get them and they must be constantly vigilant. Normal everyday occurrences such as seeing a person with a camera or encountering problems running a computer program would be interpreted as proof of the persecution. Others with the disorder might tell of how they have special powers, such as the ability to read someone's mind. The criteria for being diagnosed with this subtype exclude disorganized speech, disorganized or catatonic behavior, or flat or inappropriate affect. Overall, these individuals show the greatest possibility of improvement.

The **disorganized subtype**, which was previously referred to as *hebephrenic schizophrenia*, is characterized by disorganized speech patterns and behavior. Individuals with this subtype display odd speech patterns often referred to as *word salad* in which a variety of words are put together in incoherent ways.

TABLE 13.2 ■ *DSM-5-TR* Diagnostic Criteria for Schizophrenia

A. Two (or more) of the following, each present for a significant portion of time during a 1-month period (or less if successfully treated). At least one of these must be (1), (2), or (3).
   1. Delusions.
   2. Hallucinations.
   3. Disorganized speech (e.g., frequent derailment or incoherence).
   4. Grossly disorganized or catatonic behavior.
   5. Negative symptoms (i.e., diminished emotional expression or avolition).

B. For a significant portion of the time since the onset of the disturbance, level of functioning in one or more major areas, such as work, interpersonal relations, or self-care, is markedly below the level achieved prior to the onset (or when the onset is in childhood or adolescence, there is failure to achieve expected level of interpersonal, academic, or occupational functioning).

C. Continuous signs of the disturbance persist for at least 6 months. This 6-month period must include at least 1 month of symptoms (or less if successfully treated) that meet Criterion A (i.e., active-phase symptoms) and may include periods of prodromal or residual symptoms. During these prodromal or residual periods, the signs of the disturbance may be manifested by only negative symptoms or by two or more symptoms listed in Criterion A present in an attenuated form (e.g., odd beliefs, unusual perceptual experiences).

D. Schizoaffective disorder and depressive or bipolar disorder with psychotic features have been ruled out because either 1) no major depressive or manic episodes have occurred concurrently with the active phase symptoms, or 2) if mood episodes have occurred during active-phase symptoms, they have been present for a minority of the total duration of the active and residual periods of the illness.

E. The disturbance is not attributable to the physiological effects of a substance (e.g., a drug of abuse, a medication) or another medical condition.

F. If there is a history of autism spectrum disorder or a communication disorder of childhood onset, the additional diagnosis of schizophrenia is made only if prominent delusions or hallucinations, in addition to the other required symptoms of schizophrenia, are also present for at least 1 month (or less if successfully treated).

Specify if:
The following course specifiers are only to be used after a 1-year duration of the disorder and if they are not in contradiction to the diagnostic course criteria.
First episode, currently in acute episode: First manifestation of the disorder meeting the defining diagnostic symptom and time criteria. An acute episode is a time period in which the symptom criteria are fulfilled.
First episode, currently in partial remission: Partial remission is a period of time during which an improvement after a previous episode is maintained and in which the defining criteria of the disorder are only partially fulfilled.
First episode, currently in full remission: Full remission is a period of time after a previous episode during which no disorder-specific symptoms are present.
Multiple episodes, currently in acute episode: Multiple episodes may be determined after a minimum of two episodes (i.e., after a first episode, a remission and a minimum of one relapse).
Multiple episodes, currently in partial remission
Multiple episodes, currently in full remission
Continuous: Symptoms fulfilling the diagnostic symptom criteria of the disorder are remaining for the majority of the illness course, with subthreshold symptom periods being very brief relative to the overall course.
Unspecified
Specify if:
With catatonia (refer to the criteria for catatonia associated with another mental disorder, p. 135, for definition).
Coding note: Use additional code F06.1 catatonia associated with schizophrenia to indicate the presence of the comorbid catatonia.
Specify current severity:
Severity is rated by a quantitative assessment of the primary symptoms of psychosis, including delusions, hallucinations, disorganized speech, abnormal psychomotor behavior, and negative symptoms. Each of these symptoms may be rated for its current severity (most severe in the last 7 days) on a 5-point scale ranging from 0 (not present) to 4 (present and severe). (See Clinician-Rated Dimensions of Psychosis Symptom Severity in the chapter "Assessment Measures.")

Credit: *Diagnostic and Statistical Manual of Mental Disorders*, fifth edition, text revision, (*DSM-V-TR*), pp. 113–115 (Copyright © 2022). Reprinted with permission from the American Psychiatric Association. All rights reserved.

Note: Diagnosis of schizophrenia can be made without using this severity specifier.

A Beautiful Mind tells the true story of John Nash, a mathematician with schizophrenia who often experienced delusions of situations that did not exist, including government conspiracies.

Pictorial Press Ltd/Alamy Stock Photo

Affective responses also appear odd to others in that little affect is shown in response to what should be significant events. Instead, silly or childlike responses are shown almost randomly. Whereas individuals with the paranoid subtype tend to have a consistent theme to their delusions, individuals with the disorganized subtype do not.

The **catatonic subtype** is characterized by non-normal activity of the motor system. One classic symptom is referred to as *waxy flexibility* in that the individual will remain in a fixed position. If someone moves the individual's arms or legs, they will then remain in this new position. Motor movement can also be characterized by the opposite condition, in which the individual shows excessive, purposeless activity of their motor system. Other possible manifestations of this subtype include the repeating of someone else's speech, referred to as *echolalia*, and the repeating of someone else's movements, referred to as *echopraxia*. Although these individuals may copy the speech or movements of others, they may not follow instructions and they may even refuse to speak.

Some researchers have suggested that catatonia should be considered a separate disorder and not part of the schizophrenia group (Fink et al., 2010). Part of the support for this position is that these individuals do not respond as frequently to antipsychotic medication, and about 70% respond to the drug lorazepam alone. Lorazepam is a benzodiazepine associated with relaxation and is often given for treatment of anxiety disorders.

If an individual shows signs of schizophrenia but does not fit in any of the three major subtypes—paranoid, disorganized, or catatonic—then they would be diagnosed with an *undifferentiated subtype*.

A final subtype is referred to as the *residual subtype*. Individuals with this subtype have had schizophrenic episodes but no longer display the traditional positive symptoms of delusions and hallucinations. They may still display strange ideas or odd behaviors.

There has been considerable debate as to the value of using the five subtypes for diagnosis and treatment. Part of this debate involves a larger question of whether schizophrenia should be considered in terms of discrete categories or existing along a dimension. If schizophrenia exists along a dimension, then it would be meaningless to consider categories or subtypes (Linscott et al., 2010). An additional question is whether the subtype information is actually used in making diagnoses and designing treatment. As noted, *DSM-5* dropped the use of subtypes.

UNDERSTANDING CHANGES IN *DSM-5* AND *DSM-5-TR*
SCHIZOPHRENIA

Since the 1800s, there have been constant debates concerning the nature of schizophrenia. Most researchers do not consider schizophrenia to be a single disorder but rather a number of different disorders (Tandon, 2012). From this perspective, there are problems in determining exact criteria for schizophrenia.

With this in mind, a number of changes were made in *DSM-5*. First, two of five key symptoms are now required in *DSM-5* for a diagnosis of schizophrenia, whereas *DSM-IV* required only one. These symptoms include (1) delusions, (2) hallucinations, (3) disorganized speech, (4) disorganized or catatonic behavior, and (5) negative symptoms. Second, *DSM-5* requires that the individual have at least one of the most blatant symptoms: (1) delusions, (2) hallucinations, or (3) disorganized speech. Third, the subtypes such as paranoid, catatonic, undifferentiated, and so on, were removed. The basic reason for dropping the subtypes from *DSM-5* was that research has shown that these subtypes are not stable, and their differentiation is not supported by clinical evidence. Except for the paranoid and undifferentiated subtypes, the others are rarely used in diagnoses. Fourth, a dimensional approach was introduced to rate the severity of the core symptoms of schizophrenia. This was established since different individuals with schizophrenia show different types of symptoms such as auditory or visual hallucinations.

Overall, these changes to the schizophrenia category were less controversial than the changes made to the diagnostic criteria for many other disorders. Some have criticized the *DSM-5* for not relying more on neuroscience-based criteria. However, as shown in this chapter, an exact one-to-one relationship has yet to be established between brain measures of function, connections, chemistry, or structure and the presence of schizophrenia. Others see *DSM-5* as a transition point toward the goal of basing criteria on neuroscience perspectives (e.g., Nemeroff et al., 2013). Finally, *DSM-5* is also seen as a step toward bringing it and the newest version of *ICD* closer together on the criteria to be used in diagnosing schizophrenia (Tandon et al., 2013).

CONCEPT CHECK

- The symptoms of schizophrenia are characterized as positive symptoms and negative symptoms.
  - What is the definition of each symptom type?
  - What are primary examples of each type?
  - What role does each type play in the course of schizophrenia?
- How are the four stages of the course of schizophrenia defined, and when do they typically occur? Is the course the same for each individual? If not, how does it differ?
- What can we say about the prevalence of schizophrenia across the life span? Across genders?
- The *DSM* has set forth a multilevel process for diagnosing schizophrenia. What are the characteristics of each of the levels?
- What are the five subtypes of schizophrenia as defined by *DSM-IV*, and how are they characterized? How are they used in the current edition, *DSM-5*, and what led to the change?

HISTORICAL AND EVOLUTIONARY PERSPECTIVES ON SCHIZOPHRENIA

As you will see in this section, schizophrenia has been described for thousands of years. As professionals began to study the disorder through case studies in the 1800s, different aspects were emphasized. As techniques from evolution and genetics were applied in the 1900s, it became apparent that schizophrenia is a very old disorder. In fact, schizophrenia was probably present when humans moved out of Africa some 100,000 years ago. As will be evident, genetics points to schizophrenia as a complex disorder that cannot be explained by single genes. A current focus of research is to discover underlying features of the disorder.

Historical Perspective

Disorders with psychotic-like symptoms have been described for at least 4,000 years (Tandon, 2012; Tandon et al., 2009; Woo & Keatinge, 2008). In addition, medical texts have been found throughout the ancient world that suggest that psychosis was present in all cultures. By the 1800s, the present-day terms of schizophrenia were being introduced. The German physician Ewald Hecker in the 1870s referred to a silly, undisciplined mind as *Hebephrenia*, named after the Greek goddess of youth and frivolity, Hebe. Figure 13.3 shows the evolution of the concept of schizophrenia.

In 1874, the German physician Karl Ludwig Kahlbaum used the terms *paranoid* and *catatonic*. Paranoid referred to the idea that one felt oneself to be in danger. Catatonic referred to the mannequin-like muscle stiffness associated with unusual postures. In 1878, Emil Kraepelin combined these various disorders into a single disease entity, which he termed *dementia praecox* or *dementia of early onset*. The word *early* referred to the fact that schizophrenia developed early in life rather than as part of a decline in mental function associated with the dementias of old age. Overall, Kraepelin established what we now refer to as schizophrenia as a disorder with an onset in early adulthood that shows chronic and deteriorating progression and results in pervasive impairments in mental functions over the life span.

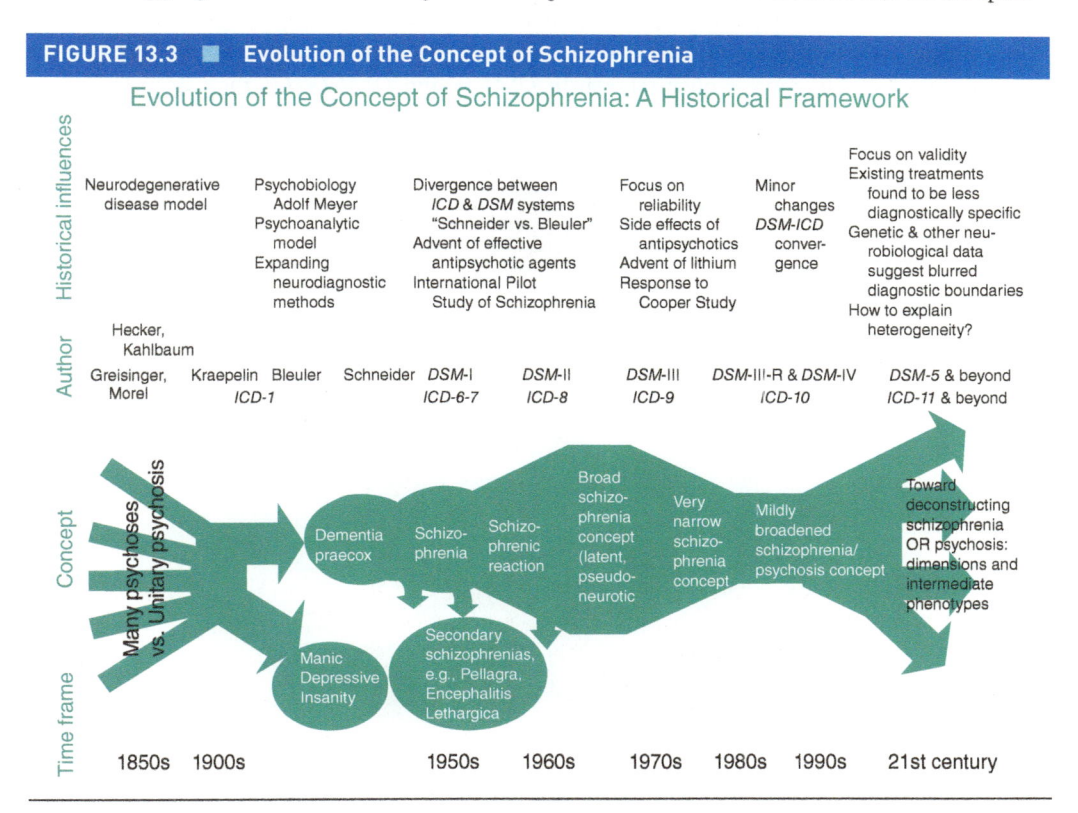

FIGURE 13.3 ■ **Evolution of the Concept of Schizophrenia**

Credit: Tandon, R., Nasrallah, H. A., & Keshavan, M. S. (2009). Schizophrenia, "Just the facts": Clinical features and conceptualization. *Schizophrenia Research, 110*, 1–23, with permission from Elsevier.

Kraepelin suggested there were four subtypes of dementia praecox. The first was the *simple* type, which was characterized by a slow decline along with social withdrawal and apathy. The second type was *paranoid*, characterized by fear of persecution. The third type was *hebephrenic*, characterized by a mania-like presentation. The fourth type was *catatonia*, characterized by a lack of movement. Kraepelin differentiated dementia praecox from what French psychiatrist Jean-Pierre Falret in 1854 referred to as *folie circulaire*. Kraepelin referred to *folie circulaire* as manic–depressive insanity. Thus, Kraepelin established manic depression, which we refer to today as bipolar disorder, as a separate category from schizophrenia.

In 1911, Eugen Bleuler introduced the term *schizophrenia*, from the Greek meaning "to split the mind." Bleuler was critical of the term *dementia praecox* and suggested that there was not a single schizophrenia but a number of different disorders or schizophrenias with different etiologies and prognoses. There were, however, a series of characteristics described by Bleuler often referred to as *the four As*.

1. *Affect*—Blunted or diminished emotional response
2. *Associations*—Loosening or inability to think in a logical manner
3. *Ambivalence*—Inability to make decisions
4. *Autism*—Social aloofness and an inability to remain in contact with the external world

Emil Kraepelin
GL Archive/Alamy Stock Photo

These four As were thought to be unique to schizophrenia and present in those with the condition.

In the 1950s, the *DSM* was introduced and described psychosis in broad terms as a disorder resulting in serious functional impairment. Schizophrenia was differentiated from organic disorders such as neurocognitive disorders (dementia) that may produce psychotic behaviors. By *DSM-III*, schizophrenia was defined by more explicit criteria. In *DSM-IV* and *DSM-IV-TR*, the criteria for schizophrenia were broadened. The *DSM* diagnostic criteria used in the United States became more similar

Eugen Bleuler
Retrieved from the National Library of Medicine, http://resource.nlm.nih.gov/101434737

to the *ICD* system used in Europe, thus reducing the differential diagnosis rates. In September 2020, the National Institutes of Health (NIH) announced the AMP-SCZ initiative (Accelerating Medicines Partnership–Schizophrenia), bringing together the NIH, the U.S. Food and Drug Administration, and multiple nonprofit and private organizations to seek biomarkers for the diverse array of clinical trajectories and adverse outcomes observed in individuals identified as at elevated risk of psychosis using the research domain criteria (RDoC) perspective (Cuthbert & Morris, 2021).

As noted earlier in this chapter, like *DSM-IV-TR* before it, *DSM-5* includes a multilevel process for making a diagnosis of schizophrenia: symptoms, functioning, and duration. The case of James Stern (not his real name) illustrates difficulties in all three areas of functioning.

CASE OF JAMES STERN
SCHIZOPHRENIA

James Stern is a 20-year-old, single, white male who is a full-time student at a nearby university where he also works part-time to offset living expenses. He resides off campus with three roommates and has been in an off-again, on-again relationship with his girlfriend since high school. He first sought treatment at a local student counseling center for anxiety, depression, and general distress at the urging of his family but was then referred for longer-term individual psychotherapy due to the increasing severity of symptoms that were described by his therapist as paranoid ideation, ideas of reference, increasing distress, and dysphoric affect.

Mr. Stern confirmed that he had experienced symptoms that "others described as sounding paranoid" since high school. He also reported that throughout his developmental years he felt a lack of connection with his family and had few, if any, close friends throughout his primary and secondary school years. While he noted that he was always somewhat suspicious and guarded, he also reported that these feelings became much more intense after he relocated to the current local university from a much smaller college near his hometown. James reported that during this same time period, he became increasingly reliant on the daily use of marijuana to ease/cope with associated symptoms of anxiety and distress. He was eventually "forced" to eliminate his usage because of his growing realization that the marijuana magnified feelings of paranoia that resulted in isolating himself in his room for days amid a growing suspicion that his roommates and classmates had been infiltrated by "dark forces" that posed an increasing threat to mankind.

Following his cessation of marijuana use, James continued to struggle with perceptions that his professors were dropping surreptitious clues for him to decipher regarding the "dark forces" he still feared were infiltrating society, and he began to believe that those forces may have already "taken over" at least two of his roommates. At this point, his paranoia and fears about "evil forces" escalated rapidly, and he began to intermittently see "demons" moving among people. His distress elevated to the point that he refused to leave his apartment bedroom, which forced his withdrawal from school and termination of employment. Mr. Stern has been diagnosed with schizophrenia. Since beginning psychotherapy and pharmacotherapy, he has reported moderate to marked reductions in paranoia and distress, although he continues to report intermittent suspiciousness and ongoing uncertainty about his future in multiple domains (e.g., relationship, academic, and career goals).

Clinical vignette provided by Sandra Testa Michelson, PhD.

Evolutionary Perspective

There is an evolutionary paradox with schizophrenia (Huxley et al., 1964)—individuals with schizophrenia have fewer children than others, and men with schizophrenia have even fewer children than women with schizophrenia. Given this situation, one would expect that the disorder would disappear over evolutionary time, and the genes of individuals with schizophrenia would not be passed on to the next generation. This, however, is not the case. How can the disorder exist without a reproductive advantage? A number of suggestions have been made. One is that the genes associated with schizophrenia are also associated with positive traits such as creativity, cognitive abilities, and language (Srinivasan et al., 2015). Natural selection is seen to play a less prominent role in genetic selection for schizophrenia (Keller, 2018).

A number of Nobel laureates had family members who were thought to have schizophrenia, including Albert Einstein.
Harris & Ewing, photographer. Retrieved from the Library of Congress, https://www.loc.gov/item/2016885961/.

It has been noted that many highly gifted and creative individuals manifest schizophrenic-like traits, referred to as **schizotypal traits**, without having the disorder. However, it is not uncommon for these individuals to have a first-degree relative with schizophrenia, suggesting a genetic component. Andreasen (2005) suggested there may be a connection with scientific creativity and schizophrenia within one's family. She noted that a number of Nobel laureates had family members who were thought to have schizophrenia, including physicist Albert Einstein, philosopher Bertrand Russell, and John Nash. (As mentioned in Chapter 1, John Nash's story was described in the book and film *A Beautiful Mind*.) But this still leaves open the question of how schizophrenia came about.

Two separate theories related to the evolutionary existence of schizophrenia were proposed by Tim Crow (2000) and Jonathan Burns (2004). Both of these theories note that schizophrenia is found throughout the world in approximately the same prevalence across cultures, and it is found in populations that have been separate from one another for at least 50,000 years. Since similar rates are seen in both industrialized and agrarian societies, this suggests that schizophrenia has existed as a part of the human experience since at least the time humans began migrations out of Africa some 100,000 years ago. If it were a newer disorder, then one would expect to find different rates in populations of humans in different parts of the world.

Tim Crow (2000) suggested that the development of language and the genetic changes required for producing and understanding speech were associated with the development of schizophrenia. Since the time of both Paul Broca and Hughlings Jackson in the 1800s, it has been known that the brain is lateralized, with linguistic functions associated with left hemispheric networks. In 1879, psychiatrist James Crichton-Browne suggested that since language processes evolved more recently than many other brain processes, these might be the first involved with mental disorders. Crow noted how one common positive symptom in schizophrenia around the world is the experience of hearing voices separate from one's normal thought processes. This suggests a disruption in normal language processes resulting from incomplete differentiation of the hemispheres, leading to a loss of the ability to differentiate thought and speech. Using electroencephalography (EEG), Crow and his colleagues (Angrilli et al., 2009) showed that individuals with schizophrenia compared with normal controls failed to show a left hemispheric dominance when processing language.

Jonathan Burns (2004) suggested that schizophrenia is better understood as a disorder of the social brain rather than a disorder of language ability. For Burns, schizophrenia results from disordered connections from the frontal to temporal areas and the frontal to parietal areas, which are critical brain connections related to social functioning. According to Burns, schizophrenia exists as the result of a trade-off at two separate stages of cognitive evolution in humans.

The first trade-off occurred between 2 and 16 million years ago. It was during this period that human brains evolved the specialized neural processing and complex interconnections required to respond to group living. To perform the tasks required for social living, a higher level of cognitive functioning was required. To permit the brain to develop the circuits required, brain maturation was lengthened. That is, given the physical constraints of the developing brain in the human fetus, brain development time needed to be lengthened. This trade-off meant that the developing brain experienced a long period of time in which complex gene interactions or accidents could happen.

The second trade-off for Burns (2004) happened more recently, about 100,000 to 150,000 years ago. This date is important. Since schizophrenia is seen in all cultures with similar symptoms, it is assumed that the genes involved in its manifestation would have evolved before human groups began migrations out of Africa. What happened at this point was that some individuals experienced non-normal connections in the frontal areas of the brain. These connections resulted in some individuals being especially creative and thinking in different ways. These individuals may have been able to make important contributions to culture, much as our present-day artists and creative thinkers do. However, some individuals demonstrated a more severe version of these connections, which resulted in psychopathological experiences. Burns further suggested that this different way of experiencing the world in either its mild or severe form did not have any reproductive advantage. However, since the genes that controlled these experiences evolved as a part of the larger cortical networks needed for the cognitive and intellectual demands of social life, these genes continued to be passed on through their connections with adaptive mechanisms. Thus, according to Burns, schizophrenia represents one of the prices paid for evolving complex cognitive and social abilities. Further, it should be noted that ancient burial sites have bones of older individuals with various deformities. Since these individuals could not have survived without care from others, this suggests to some that individuals with schizophrenia-like symptoms may also have been cared for and made part of the community.

CONCEPT CHECK

- What can we say about the prevalence of schizophrenia across history? Across the world?
- "Disorders with psychotic-like symptoms have been described for at least 4,000 years." Describe four important advancements in the development of the concept of schizophrenia since 1850.
- Describe the evolutionary paradox that schizophrenia presents. What different theories did Crow and Burns present to explain the paradox?

FACTORS IN THE DEVELOPMENT OF SCHIZOPHRENIA

Schizophrenia typically is first noted during the transition from late adolescence to adulthood. However, theories related to the development of the disorder generally see its onset as the culmination of a process that may have begun before the individual was born (Uhlhaas, 2011). In a review of birth cohort studies in which individuals are followed from birth, there is evidence to suggest that children who later develop schizophrenia show different profiles from those who do not (Welham et al., 2009). These data from seven different countries show subtle deficits in terms of behavioral disturbances, intellectual and language deficits, and early motor delays.

The current research literature suggests that schizophrenia begins early in life. This has led some researchers to call for a reconsideration of schizophrenia as a neurodevelopmental disorder (Insel,

2010). A variety of negative events can happen to a developing fetus, including infections and malnutrition. It has been shown, for example, that vitamin D deficiency during pregnancy can be a risk for developing schizophrenia (McGrath et al., 2010). Likewise, maternal infection is now regarded as a potential risk factor for schizophrenia (A. Brown & Patterson, 2011; Paquin et al., 2021). This type of thinking has led researchers to examine the role of the gut microbiome in relation to schizophrenia (Golofast & Vales, 2020).

Overall, the theory that development of schizophrenia involves events experienced during pregnancy is referred to as the *neurodevelopmental hypothesis*. The basic idea is that during the time the fetus is in utero, an insult happens that influences changes to the brain that take place later, during adolescence.

Weinberger (1987) was one of the originators of the neurodevelopmental view and suggested that problems during the second trimester lead to an incomplete development of frontal lobe networks in the brain during adolescence. Currently, the neurodevelopmental hypothesis itself is not completely developed. However, the second trimester has clearly been noted as an important period in brain development.

What can be described about the reorganization of brain processes during adolescence in relation to schizophrenia? We know that adolescence is a time of great reorganization of cortical networks. Gogtay and colleagues (2011) reviewed two longitudinal studies with this question in mind. The first data set was composed of individuals who developed schizophrenia before puberty and has been studied at the National Institute of Mental Health (NIMH). The second data set was from Melbourne, Australia, and included adolescents at ultra-high risk for schizophrenia. Imaging studies showed larger ventricles and greater gray matter loss in the parietal and frontal areas in children who developed schizophrenia before puberty as compared with those who developed schizophrenia in adulthood. The data set from Australia indicated that those adolescents who developed schizophrenia showed greater gray matter loss, especially in the prefrontal cortex (PFC), as compared with those who did not develop the disorder.

Environmental factors can also play a role in the development of schizophrenia (van Os et al., 2010). The basic idea is that environmental factors can influence the developing social brain and lead to the development of schizophrenia in those at risk. Such factors as early life adversity, growing up in an urban environment, and cannabis use have been associated with the development of the disorder. While being part of a particular ethnic group is not associated with schizophrenia per se, there is an association if one lives within a small minority enclave of a larger ethnic group. Also, if one moves from an urban environment to a rural one, then the chance of having schizophrenia decreases. Overall, greater amounts of stress are associated with greater chances of developing schizophrenia. Further, childhood trauma is associated with the severity of hallucinations and delusions (Bailey et al., 2018). Overall, environmental factors continue to reflect an interaction with genetic influences and are not a sole condition in themselves for developing schizophrenia (Sariaslan et al., 2016).

Genetic Factors in Schizophrenia

Since schizophrenia tends to run in families and is seen throughout the world, it is assumed to have a genetic component. That is to say, the risk of developing schizophrenia is much higher if someone else in your family also has the disorder. As can be seen in Figure 13.4, schizophrenia indeed has a strong genetic component. The more similar the genes between two individuals, one of whom has schizophrenia, the more likely the other person will also develop its characteristics. However, the genetic underpinnings of schizophrenia are not simple. It is clearly not the result of a single gene, as is the case with some other neurological disorders such as Huntington's disease.

Genome-wide association study (GWAS) research suggests that the number of genetic variants seen in individuals with schizophrenia is very large (Cheng et al., 2021; Keller, 2018). There may be 1,000 different genes contributing to the disorder, including rare genetic variants (Cannon, 2015; Coyle et al., 2020; Walker et al., 2010; Wray & Visscher, 2010). These genes may act in an additive or interactive manner to produce the disorder. It is assumed that these genes act by altering gene expression. In

FIGURE 13.4 ■ Endophenotype Anomalies and Schizophrenia

In terms of endophenotype anomalies, those with schizophrenia show the most, followed by their relatives, and the least are shown by healthy controls. This figure shows the average percentage abnormal for each endophenotype category for those with schizophrenia (SCZ), their relative (REL), and healthy controls (HC).

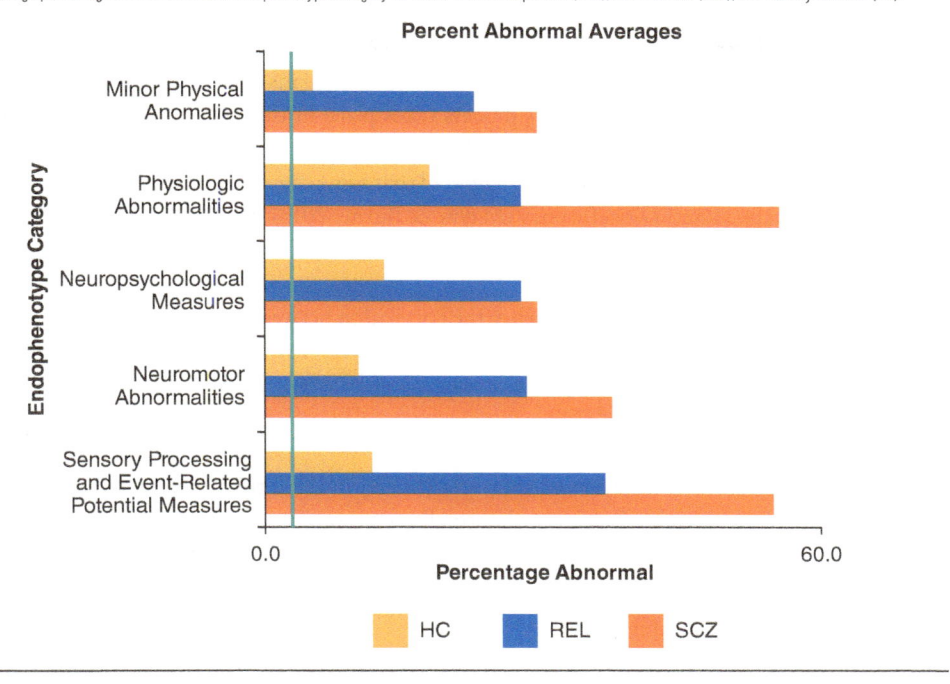

Percent Abnormal Averages

[Bar chart showing Percentage Abnormal (0.0 to 60.0) across five Endophenotype Categories: Minor Physical Anomalies, Physiologic Abnormalities, Neuropsychological Measures, Neuromotor Abnormalities, and Sensory Processing and Event-Related Potential Measures, with bars for HC, REL, and SCZ.]

Credit: Allen, A. J., Griss, M. E., Folley, B. S., Hawkins, K. A., & Pearlson, G. D. (2009). Endophenotypes in schizophrenia: A selective review. *Schizophrenia Research, 109*, 24–37, with permission from Elsevier.

Adopted children from families with schizophrenia show a similar rate of schizophrenia development to those raised with their birth families. This implies that the manner in which individuals are reared is not directly related to the development of schizophrenia.

iStock.com/fizkes

other words, there may be a variety of genetic combinations that are associated with schizophrenia. For example, heritable traits such as white matter connections and the thickness of gray matter in the brain are reduced in individuals with schizophrenia.

Those with schizophrenia show both fewer connections that link different parts of the brain and a reduction of dendrite connections at the level of the neuron. Adolescence and early adulthood bring extensive elimination of synapses in distributed association regions of the cerebral cortex, such as the prefrontal cortex. An impairment of this process takes place in those with schizophrenia. Research suggests that this is related to variations in the HMC locus, particularly the genetic allele called component 4 (C4) (Sekar et al., 2016). It is also suggested that some cognitive deficits seen in schizophrenia can be influenced by vitamin D deficiency (Mayne & Burne, 2019). Taken together, this suggests that schizophrenia should be viewed as a developmental disorder that takes place as the brain is reorganized in adolescence.

Further, the genetic factors that influence the correlation between schizophrenia and white matter measures were found to be different from the genetic factors that influence the correlation between schizophrenia and reduced gray matter thickness (Bohlken et al., 2015). That is, there are different genetic pathways for each type of deficit.

In addition, individuals with schizophrenia compared with individuals without the disorder show more abnormalities in their deoxyribonucleic acid (DNA) in the form of deletions or duplications of DNA sequences. Surprisingly, these gene abnormalities are even seen in the monozygotic (MZ) twin who does not develop schizophrenia as compared with the one who does. This suggests that these abnormalities are the result of both inherited and non-inherited factors.

If schizophrenia were a totally inherited disorder, then if one MZ twin developed the disorder, the other would also. However, this is not the case. There are three factors that may be playing a role in this situation. First, as genes are reproduced during fetal and later development, there may be slight changes in one twin as compared with the other. These are referred to as *copy number variations.* Maiti and colleagues (2011) studied copy number variations in MZ twins from families with schizophrenia and found genetic differences in the twins. Thus, even identical twins can show differences in their total genetic makeup. Second, differences in twins may not result from differences in the DNA itself but from the results of epigenetic factors in which genes of an affected individual may be turned on differently from those of a non-affected individual, suggesting that internal and external environmental factors play a role (King et al., 2010). And third, environmental factors may play a role that does not involve genetic changes.

A number of studies over the years have shown that there is a higher concordance rate for MZ twins than for DZ twins. However, because of differences in how these studies were conducted in terms of diagnostic characteristics of schizophrenia, the concordance rates differ. Yet, in every study, MZ twins show a higher rate than DZ twins, supporting the importance of genetics. The initial studies of the 1990s show a 48% concordance rate for MZ twins. This suggests that the environment plays an important role. Although environmental stress is known to exacerbate the disorder, there is little evidence that psychological stress can actually cause schizophrenia. Further, adopted children from families with schizophrenia show a similar rate to children raised with their birth families. This implies that the manner in which individuals are reared is not directly related to the development of schizophrenia.

As noted earlier, other work has suggested a role for poor maternal nutrition or infections during fetal periods, but this work is also inconclusive. Review of the genetics of schizophrenia indicates a higher concordance rate (80%–82%) for MZ twins and schizophrenia (Besteher et al., 2020; Rutter, 2006). Recent speculation suggests that epigenetics (see Chapter 2) may offer a more viable mechanism for the development of schizophrenia (Petronis, 2004).

Another way to examine the genetic factor is to look at adolescents whose parents had schizophrenia. When compared with a control group, adolescents who did not have schizophrenia but whose parents did were shown to have dysfunctional interactions within cortical networks involved in emotional processing (Diwadkar et al., 2012). This suggests an endophenotype could be connected with schizophrenia.

Endophenotypes Associated With Schizophrenia

At present, there is no one biomarker that can identify a person with schizophrenia. A number of researchers have sought to find endophenotypes related to schizophrenia (Miller & Rockstroh, 2013, 2016). As described in Chapter 2, an *endophenotype* is a pattern of processes that lies between the gene (the genotype) and the manifestations of the gene in the external environment (the phenotype). These processes can be biological, such as white and gray matter integrity or patterns of EEG activity. They can also involve higher-level psychological processes, such as difficulties with memory or difficulties in recognizing emotional changes or empathy. One set of studies suggests that the genetic pathway to the development of schizophrenia begins with cognitive deficits (Toulopoulou et al., 2019). The only requirement in this type of research is that there is a pathway from the gene to the endophenotype to the phenotype. In the case of psychopathology, the phenotype is typically the clinical expression of a disorder.

These stable internal physiological or psychological markers associated with schizophrenia have been found in a variety of areas. In one review of the literature, which compared individuals with schizophrenia, their relatives, and healthy control individuals, endophenotypes were found in five major areas (A. J. Allen et al., 2009).

- The first area is *minor physical anomalies*, which include differences in head or body size or motor movements.

- The second area, *physiologic abnormalities*, is based on the membrane theory of schizophrenia. This theory suggests that normal metabolism in the brain is disturbed in individuals with schizophrenia.

- The third area is *neuropsychological measures*. Studies reviewed in this area include such measures as the Wisconsin Card Sorting Test (WCST), in which the person must respond to changing demands, and the Continuous Performance Task, which measures attentional abilities.

- The fourth area involves *neuromotor abnormalities*. One task has to do with smooth pursuit eye movement. Individuals with schizophrenia show a different pattern of eye movement if asked to follow a person's finger moving from right to left in front of them. Rather than showing a smooth motion of eye movement, they show periods of quick pursuit in which they attempt to catch up with the finger movement.

- The fifth area is *sensory processing and event-related potentials*. Numerous studies have shown EEG differences between individuals with schizophrenia and others. In response to cognitive tasks, the evoked potential waveforms of P50, P300, and N400 were noted as important.

As can be seen in Figure 13.4, individuals with schizophrenia and their first-degree relatives without schizophrenia show similar responses to tasks in the five areas. This suggests an endophenotype related to schizophrenia but not a definitive biomarker of the disorder.

Recent reviews of the literature suggest that cognitive deficits are among the most important symptoms of schizophrenia, especially in terms of their impact on society and quality of life (Miller & Rockstroh, 2016). Factor analyses by Seidman et al. (2015) of data from 83 schizophrenia patients, 151 unaffected siblings, and 209 community comparison participants yielded five distinct cognitive factors: episodic memory, working memory, perceptual vigilance, inhibitory processing, and visual abstraction. Each of these factors was shown to be significantly heritable. Another review emphasizes the importance of social cognition in schizophrenia (Green et al., 2015). Deficits in the ability to perceive social cues, regulate social emotions, and share with others are seen as potential endophenotypes related to schizophrenia. At this point, research studies are focused on determining appropriate biological and psychological endophenotypes related to schizophrenia, although a final list has yet to be determined.

In a series of papers, Rajiv Tandon and his colleagues (Tandon, 2012; Tandon et al., 2009; Tandon et al., 2013) reviewed the literature to determine what aspects of schizophrenia have been shown to be stable through a number of replications. These are presented in Table 13.3. These researchers also suggested that a dimensional approach including the study of endophenotypes will be important in future conceptualizations of schizophrenia.

TABLE 13.3 ■ Clinical "Facts" of Schizophrenia

- Schizophrenia is generally diagnosed on the basis of the presence of positive symptoms in conjunction with impaired social function in the absence of significant mood symptoms, other recognizable neurological illness, or substance use that can account for the psychotic symptoms.
- The nosological boundaries between schizophrenia and other psychiatric disorders are indistinct.
- There is significant heterogeneity in neurobiology, clinical manifestations, course, and treatment response across patients.
- Schizophrenia is characterized by an admixture of positive, negative, disorganization, cognitive, psychomotor, and mood symptoms.
- The severity of different symptom clusters varies across patients and through the course of the illness.
- There is a generalized but highly variable cognitive impairment.
- There may be additional specific impairment in a range of cognitive functions (such as executive functions, memory, psychomotor speed, attention, and social cognition).
- Cognitive impairments are present prior to onset of psychosis and persist during the course of the illness.
- There is a higher occurrence of obesity and cardiovascular disease.
- There is increased prevalence of cigarette smoking and other substance use disorders.
- There is increased suicidality.
- There is some phase-specific increase in violent behavior.
- There are significant premorbid impairments in a substantial proportion of patients.
- Onset of psychotic symptoms is usually during adolescence or early adulthood.
- The age of onset is earlier in males.
- There is an approximate doubling of age-standardized mortality.
- Schizophrenia is frequently a chronic and relapsing disorder with generally incomplete remissions.
- Social outcomes include reduced rates of employment and financial independence, and increased likelihood of homelessness and incarceration.
- Poor outcome is predicted by male gender, early age of onset, prolonged period of untreated illness, and severity of cognitive and negative symptoms.

Credit: Adapted from Tandon, R., Nasrallah, H. A., & Keshavan, M. S. (2009). Schizophrenia, "Just the facts": Clinical features and conceptualization. *Schizophrenia Research, 110*, 1–23, with permission from Elsevier.

RESEARCH TERMS TO KNOW
FACTOR ANALYSIS

Factor analysis is a statistical technique that allows us to know which variables go together. Typically, a factor analysis study will collect a large number of variables on a group of individuals. The statistical technique creates factors that describe which of these variables are responded to in a similar way. For example, if a number of individuals were given a variety of cognitive tests, it is possible to see that those who do well on one type of problem also do well on another. One study found five factors related to intelligence. These were reasoning, spatial ability, memory, processing speed, and vocabulary (Deary et al., 2010). Another study examined psychopathology over 20 years in terms of personality functioning, life impairment, family histories and developmental histories of psychiatric disorders, and measures of brain integrity (Caspi et al., 2014). These researchers reported three factors. These were an internalizing liability related to depression and anxiety, an externalizing liability related to antisocial and substance-use disorders, and a thought disorder liability related to symptoms of psychosis.

CONCEPT CHECK

- Schizophrenia typically is first noted during the transition from late adolescence to adulthood, but current research suggests that the disorder begins early in life. What evidence from research into genetic and environmental factors points to this characterization?
- "Schizophrenia has a strong genetic component." But it's not simple and straightforward. What three factors that we've learned from research with MZ twins help to explain this genetic component?
- There is currently no one biomarker to identify an individual with schizophrenia. However, what five internal physiological or psychological markers associated with schizophrenia suggest a potential endophenotype related to schizophrenia?

CAUSES AND EFFECTS: NEUROSCIENCE FINDINGS ABOUT SCHIZOPHRENIA

This section will discuss structural and functional changes in the brain that are related to schizophrenia, including the manner in which chemical and electrical information moves throughout the brain. The section ends with a look at the cognitive changes found in individuals with schizophrenia.

Schizophrenia manifests on a variety of levels, including abnormal sensory experiences, such as hallucinations; problems in cognitive processes, such as delusions and disordered thought; changes in affect, such as lack of expression; and, in some cases, problems with language and future directed planning. Because these symptoms are so diverse, it is challenging to describe the manner in which brain processes relate to the disorder.

Schizophrenia and Brain Function

Current research examining individuals with schizophrenia has emphasized five different neuroscience measurements. The first is *anatomical changes*, such as the loss of brain volume in particular areas. The second is *functional processes*, such as the manner in which cortical areas and networks process information as seen in brain imaging. The third is *neural oscillations* that underlie the cortical networks. The fourth is *changes in neurotransmitters* such as dopamine, GABA, glycine, and glutamate. And the fifth is the *development of cortical processes beginning in utero*.

A variety of studies have shown that individuals with schizophrenia have emphasized differential activity in the dorsolateral prefrontal cortex (DLPFC), the ACC, and the thalamus (see Minzenberg et al., 2009, for a meta-analysis). Due to their involvement with executive function tasks such as planning and social tasks, the frontal lobes have been extensively studied. Other reviews, of studies examining the entire brain and schizophrenia, point to enlargement of the ventricles and abnormalities of the medial temporal lobe structures, including the amygdala, hippocampus, and neocortical temporal lobe functions (Shenton et al., 2001). Other reviews point to a connection between the DLPFC and disorganized symptoms (Goghari et al., 2010). In addition, the ventrolateral prefrontal cortex (VLPFC) was found to be associated with negative symptoms and the medial prefrontal activity with positive symptoms (Figure 13.5).

The EEG reflects the electrical activity of the brain at the level of the synapse (Nunez & Srinivasan, 2006). It is the product of the changing excitatory and inhibitory currents at the synapse. Neural oscillations seen in the EEG offer a window for understanding how brain processes

FIGURE 13.5 ■ Differential Activity in the Brain Related to Symptoms of Schizophrenia

The ventrolateral prefrontal cortex (VLPFC) is associated with negative symptoms (red) and medial prefrontal activity with positive symptoms (yellow). The figure shows differential brain activity exhibited in schizophrenia by positive symptoms, negative symptoms, and disorganization.

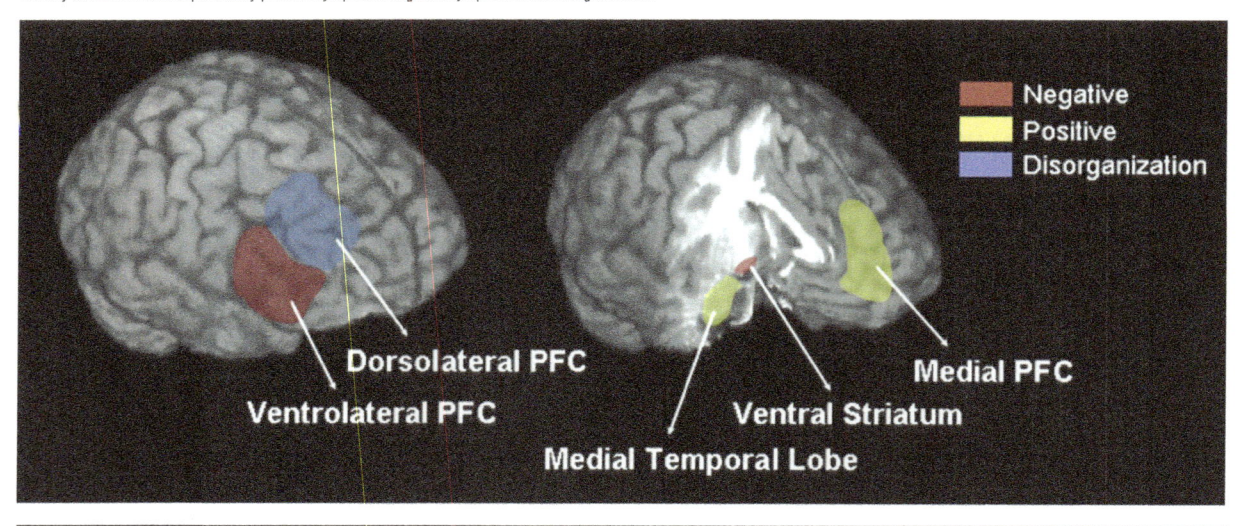

Credit: Goghari, V., Sponheim, S., & MacDonald, A. (2010). The functional neuroanatomy of symptom dimensions in schizophrenia: A qualitative and quantitative review of a persistent question. *Neuroscience and Biobehavioral Review, 34,* 468–486, with permission from Elsevier.

influence cortical networks, which can reflect normal cognitive, emotional, and motor processes. More low-frequency oscillations seen in the theta (4–7 Hz) and alpha (8–12 Hz) ranges reflect longer distant relationships in the brain, whereas higher frequency oscillations in the beta (13–30 Hz) and gamma (30–200 Hz) ranges reflect more local cortical networks (Uhlhaas & Singer, 2011, 2012). Activity in the four frequency bands has been associated with a variety of cognitive processes in normal functioning. Since individuals with schizophrenia may show deficits in these cognitive processes, the study of cortical oscillations offers important insights into how schizophrenic processes affect the brain.

Cortical networks in the brain begin in utero and the period following birth. However, the development of these networks is not perfectly continuous. There is also a fundamental reorganization of these networks in adolescence (Uhlhaas et al., 2009; Uhlhaas & Singer, 2011, 2012). The reorganization during adolescence is reflected in both cognitive performance and EEG synchrony (Uhlhaas et al., 2009). Prior to adolescence, there is a period of increase over the years in both cognitive performance and EEG synchrony. This synchrony is reflected in similar EEG activity displayed in a variety of sites throughout the brain. However, during adolescence there is a decrease in both. After this period, there is a reorganization of EEG activity such that the synchrony is more focused at specific EEG sites, especially parietal and occipital electrodes.

Figure 13.6 depicts three critical periods in which changes in the physiology and anatomy of cortical processes would show changes consistent with the neurodevelopmental hypothesis of schizophrenia. The first period is fetal development, in which genetic and epigenetic factors impair the electrical activity of the brain and with that the rhythmical activity associated with the formation of cortical circuits. Adverse experiences during fetal development are associated with the development of schizophrenia (Debnath et al., 2015). The second stage involves the reorganization of cortical networks seen in adolescence. Along with this come changes in white and gray matter as well as neurotransmitters. Although all adolescents show gray matter declines in the PFC during this period of synaptic pruning, declines are higher in individuals with schizophrenia (Karlsgodt et al., 2010). The third stage describes the situation in which individuals with schizophrenia fail to develop the coordinated networks necessary for normal cognitive processes.

FIGURE 13.6 ■ Critical Periods Related to the Brain and Schizophrenia

As schizophrenia develops, cortical networks cease to work as large-scale networks. This figure shows the three critical periods and key changes in the physiology and anatomy of these cortical processes.

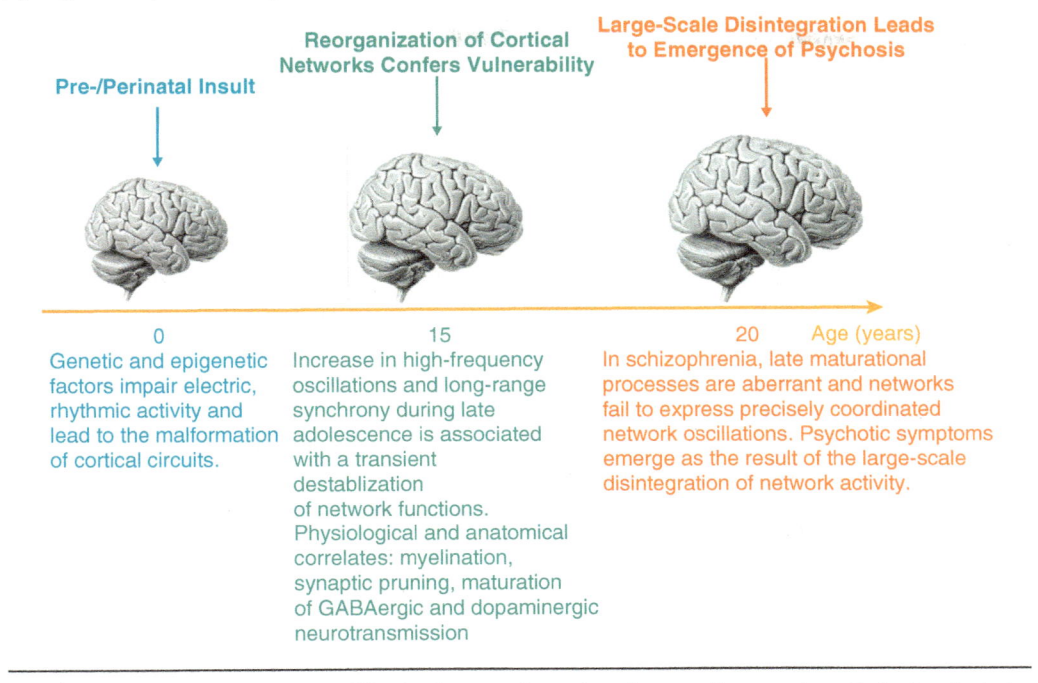

Pre-/Perinatal Insult — Age 0: Genetic and epigenetic factors impair electric, rhythmic activity and lead to the malformation of cortical circuits.

Reorganization of Cortical Networks Confers Vulnerability — Age 15: Increase in high-frequency oscillations and long-range synchrony during late adolescence is associated with a transient destablization of network functions. Physiological and anatomical correlates: myelination, synaptic pruning, maturation of GABAergic and dopaminergic neurotransmission.

Large-Scale Disintegration Leads to Emergence of Psychosis — Age 20: In schizophrenia, late maturational processes are aberrant and networks fail to express precisely coordinated network oscillations. Psychotic symptoms emerge as the result of the large-scale disintegration of network activity.

Credit: Peter J. Uhlhaas and Wolf Singer. "The development of neural synchrony and large-scale cortical networks during adolescence: Relevance for the pathophysiology of schizophrenia and neurodevelopmental hypothesis." *Schizophrenia Bulletin*, 2011 May; 37(3): 514–523, by permission of Oxford University Press.

CONCEPT CHECK

- According to current research, what are the five different neuroscience measurements related to individuals with schizophrenia?
- What are the three critical periods of neurological changes in the development of schizophrenia?

Schizophrenia and Brain Structure

Exactly when brain changes take place in those with schizophrenia is an important question. In order to better understand the role of timing in terms of brain structure, John Gilmore and his colleagues (2010) performed imaging studies before and after birth. These researchers used ultrasound scans prior to birth and magnetic resonance imaging (MRI) scans after birth while the babies slept. They compared children whose mothers had schizophrenia with a matched control group whose mothers did not have the disorder. Using ultrasound prior to birth, they found no differences between the two groups. After birth, males whose mothers had schizophrenia showed more gray matter in the brain, increased cerebrospinal fluid, and larger ventricles. Female infants did not show any differences. This suggests that at least the endophenotype for schizophrenia in males can be seen early in life.

Gray Matter and White Matter Changes in Individuals With Schizophrenia

Neuroimaging studies of those with schizophrenia have included both structural and functional approaches (Giraldo-Chica et al., 2018; Karlsgodt et al., 2010; Shenton & Turetsky, 2011). Structural approaches have focused on gray matter and white matter differences as well as the size of the ventricles (Cannon, 2015; Cheng et al., 2021; Thompson et al., 2001). In a variety of reviews, both general and specific reductions in gray matter have been reported for individuals with schizophrenia. Specifically, reductions have been noted in the temporal cortex, especially the hippocampus, the frontal lobe, and the parietal lobe. In addition, the striatum part of the basal ganglia has been shown to be reduced (Shenton et al., 2001). Gray matter reductions have also been seen in cases when one identical twin has schizophrenia and the other does not (see Figure 13.7).

Since brain changes in chronic schizophrenia can be influenced by both the disorder itself and the medications that the individual has taken over a number of years, researchers have sought to determine gray matter changes in individuals who display their first episode of schizophrenia. These studies also suggest a reduction in gray matter in schizophrenia (Whitford et al., 2011). Further, similar reduction in gray matter was seen in a group of individuals who had been diagnosed with schizophrenia for an average of 21 years but had never taken medications (Zhang et al., 2015). Overall, these studies rule out the possibility that brain volume reductions result from medication alone.

What might be at the heart of this gray matter reduction? One possibility is that the neurons actually die. However, a number of studies suggest this is not the case. What has been found is that the neurons in the brains of individuals with schizophrenia are more densely packed. This implies that the substance found between neurons—neuropil—is reduced, resulting in a greater density of neurons. Further, gray matter abnormalities have been shown to be partly hereditary and also related to trauma during pregnancy (Karlsgodt et al., 2010). Figure 13.8 shows the reduction of gray matter in the same set of individuals with schizophrenia over a 5-year period (Thompson et al., 2001). Figure 13.9 shows the differences in gray matter between individuals with schizophrenia and normal controls.

FIGURE 13.7 ■ Gray Matter Reductions in Individuals With Schizophrenia

Even if they are identical (monozygotic, or MZ) twins, if one has schizophrenia there are gray matter reductions. This figure shows average gray matter deficit between identical twins. One twin has schizophrenia, and the other does not.

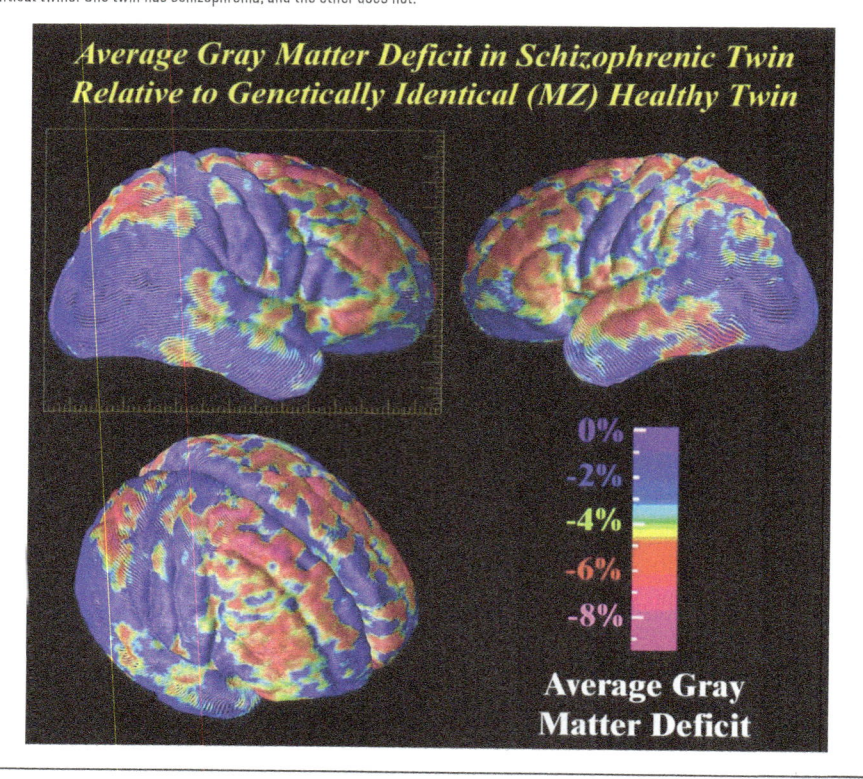

Credit: Cannon, T. D., Thompson, P. M., van Erp, T., Toga, A. W., Poutanen, V.-P., Huttunen, M., Lonnqvist, J., Standertskjold-Nordenstam, C.-G., Narr, K. L., Khaledy, M., Zoumalan, C. I., Dail, R., Kaprio, J. (2001, June). A probabilistic atlas of cortical gray matter changes in monozygotic twins discordant for schizophrenia [Paper presentation]. Organization for Human Brain Mapping 7th Annual Meeting, Brighton, England. http://www.loni.ucla.edu/~thompson/HBM2001/ty_HBM2001.html

Note: Color represents the difference in gray matter between the twins.

Chapter 13 • Schizophrenia   529

FIGURE 13.8 ■ Gray Matter Reductions After 5 Years

Gray matter continues to decrease as schizophrenia develops. This figure shows early and late gray matter deficits in schizophrenia.

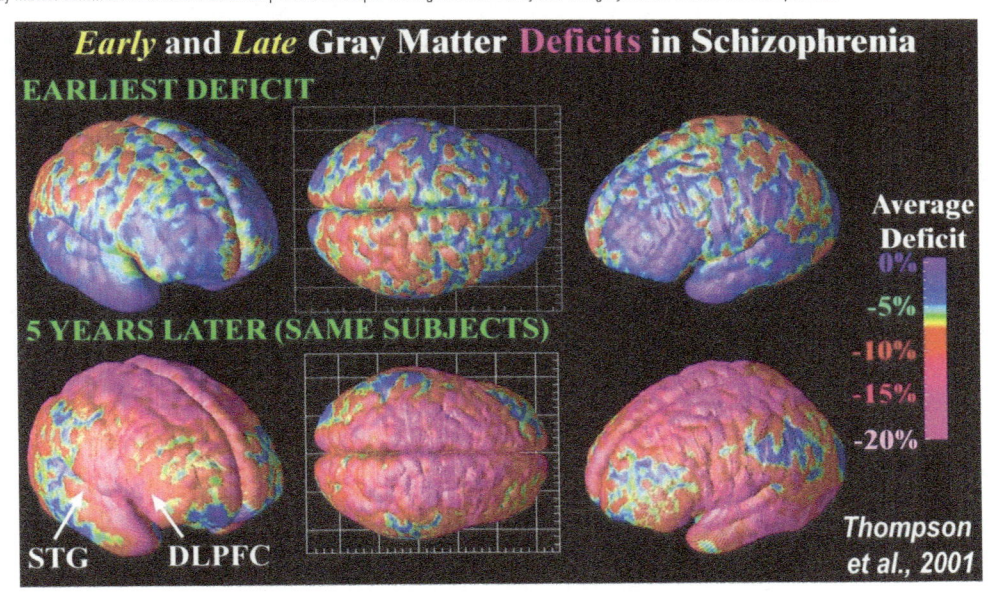

Credit: Paul M. Thompson, et al. "Mapping adolescent brain change reveals dynamic wave of accelerated gray matter loss in very early-onset schizophrenia." Proceedings of the National Academy of Sciences of the United States of America. 2001 September 25; 98(20). © 2001 National Academy of Sciences, U.S.A.

Note: Color represents the difference in gray matter between individuals with schizophrenia and matched controls.

FIGURE 13.9 ■ Annual Loss of Gray Matter in Those With Schizophrenia

As shown, gray matter loss is less in typical adolescents as compared to those with schizophrenia. Typical adolescents show around 1% or 2%, whereas those with schizophrenia show as much as 4% or 5% in some areas of the brain. The color represents percentage of gray loss.

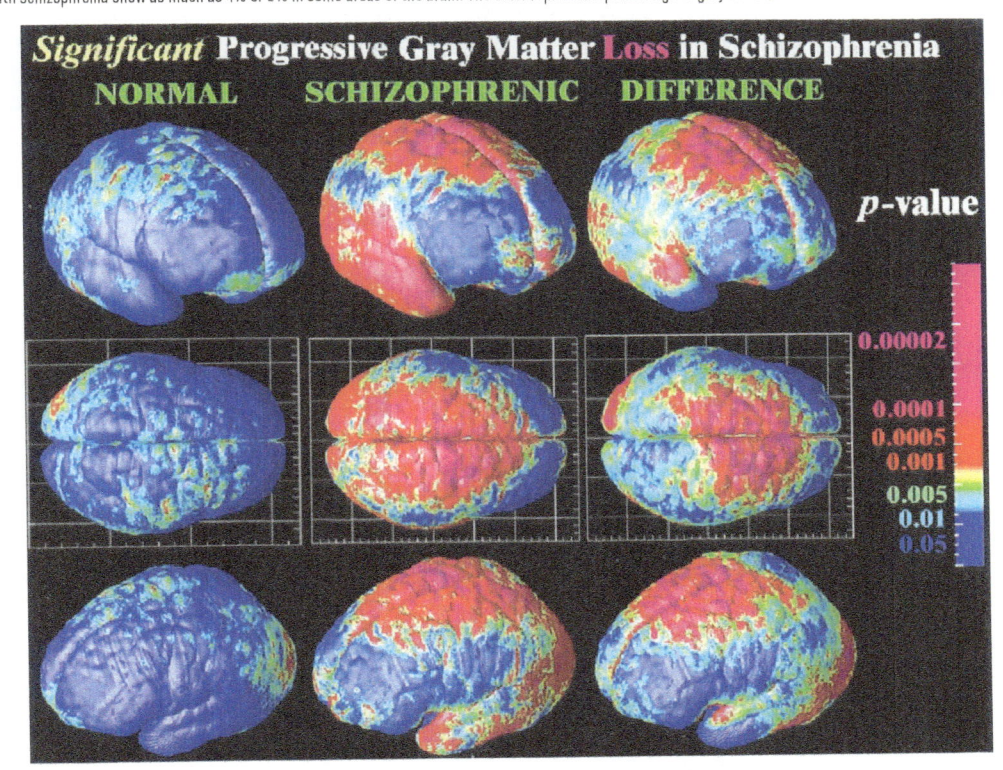

Credit: Paul M. Thompson, et al. "Mapping adolescent brain change reveals dynamic wave of accelerated gray matter loss in very early-onset schizophrenia." Proceedings of the National Academy of Sciences of the United States of America. 2001 September 25; 98(20). © 2001 National Academy of Sciences, U.S.A.

White matter changes have also been observed in individuals with schizophrenia. One study compared the white matter in 114 individuals with schizophrenia and 138 matched controls (White et al., 2011). Using a brain imaging technique—diffusion tensor imaging (DTI)—sensitive to white matter, individuals with chronic schizophrenia, individuals with first episode (FE) schizophrenia, and matched controls were compared. Figure 13.10 shows an example of tracking white matter through DTI. Measures of white matter were lower for individuals with chronic schizophrenia in the four lobes of the brain but not in the cerebellum or brain stem. Individuals experiencing their first episode of schizophrenia did not show significant differences from controls, which suggests that white matter reduction is part of the progression of the disorder over time.

One scientific report using worldwide data from a number of sites examined brain related MRI measures from over 3,000 individuals (ENIGMA Working Group, 2021). They compared the cortical thickness of specific brain areas in a group of individuals who were at high risk for developing psychosis and a control group. They further examined those individuals at risk who did develop a psychotic disorder and those who did not. In those who developed a psychotic disorder, they found a lower cortical thickness in paracentral, superior temporal, and fusiform regions of the brain.

In summary, gray matter and white matter changes in individuals with schizophrenia have been found in a large number of studies.

Ventricle Changes in Individuals With Schizophrenia

There are four ventricles in the brain (Figure 13.11). These ventricles contain cerebrospinal fluid. Findings from a number of studies have shown that individuals with schizophrenia have larger ventricles (see Vita et al., 2006, for a meta-analysis). Since the walls of the ventricles are not rigid, it is assumed that larger ventricles result from a decrease in volume in other areas of the brain. Some of the other areas that have been shown to be smaller in individuals with schizophrenia are the frontotemporal cortices, the anterior cingulate cortex (ACC), and the right insular cortex. One question is whether this reduction could be related to the medications that individuals with schizophrenia take. To answer this question, one study examined individuals with first episode schizophrenia and compared their brain structure with that of matched healthy controls (Rais et al., 2012). These researchers found brain volume loss in

FIGURE 13.10 ■ White Matter Reductions Throughout the Whole Brain in Those With Schizophrenia

Those with long-term schizophrenia show white matter reductions throughout the brain, whereas those who have just begun to experience symptoms appear more like their matched controls. This figure shows differences in z-transformed DTI measures of cortical white matter between first episode and chronic patients with schizophrenia and matched controls.

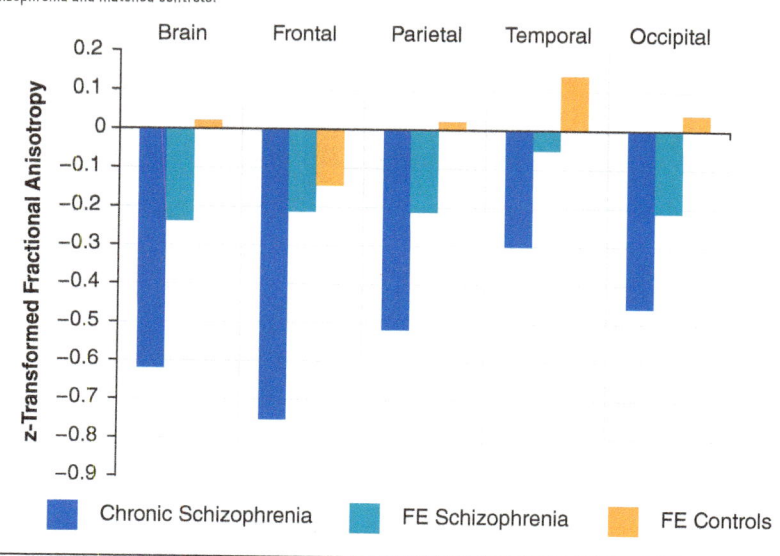

Credit: White, T. Magnotta, V., Bockholt, H., Williams, S., Wallace, S., Ehrlich, S., . . . Lim, K. (2011). Global white matter abnormalities in schizophrenia: A multisite diffusion tensor imaging study. *Schizophrenia Bulletin, 37,* 222–232, by permission of Oxford University Press.

Note: The z score for the chronic control group was set to zero; FE = first episode.

FIGURE 13.11 ■ Location of Ventricles in the Brain

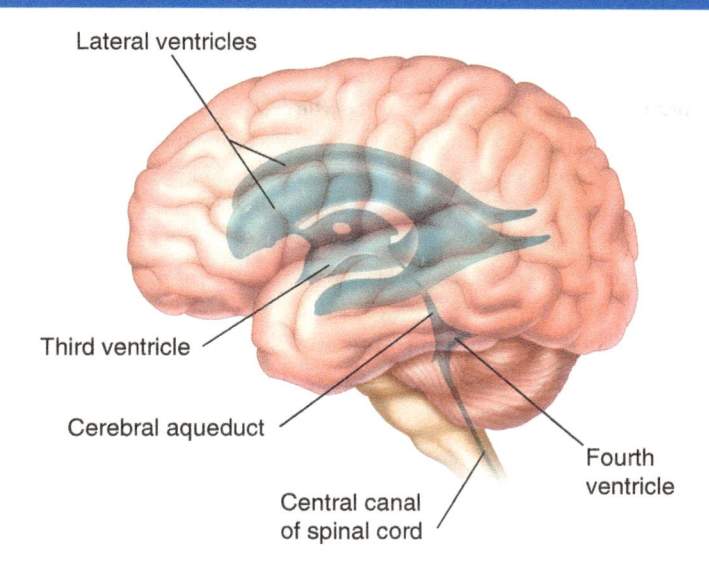

FIGURE 13.12 ■ Magnetic Resonance Imaging Showing Differences in Brain Ventricle Size in Twins—One With Schizophrenia, One Without Schizophrenia

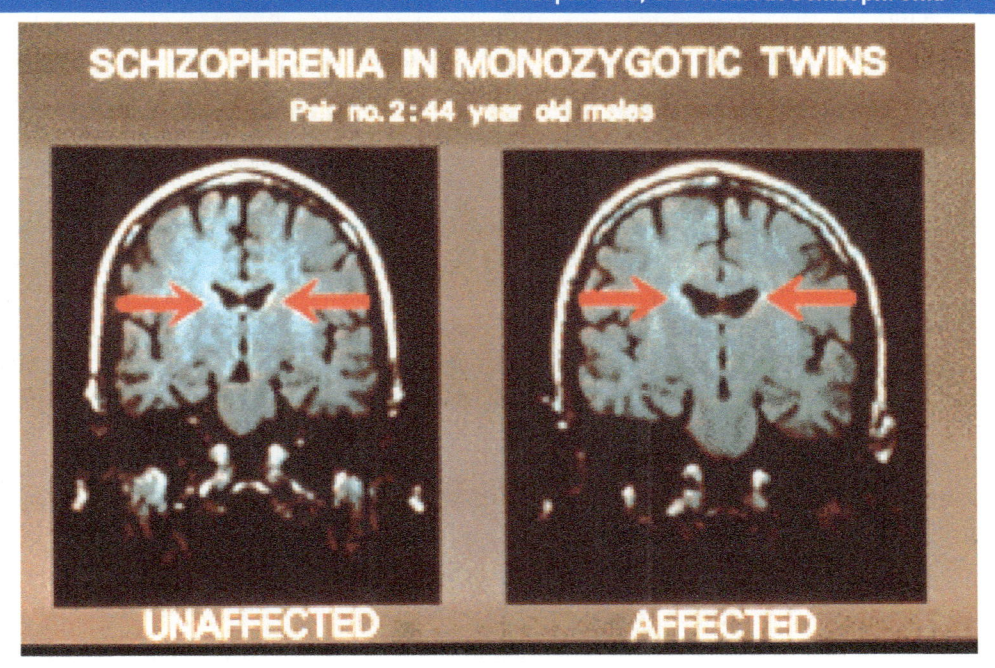

Source: Image courtesy of National Institute of Health, Dr. Daniel Weinberger, Clinical Brain Disorders Branch.

the individuals with schizophrenia, which suggests that the brain volume loss is present when symptoms begin. They found reduced volume in the temporal and insular cortex. Figure 13.12 shows a larger ventricle in an MZ twin who had schizophrenia and a smaller one in the twin who did not.

Schizophrenia and Brain Networks

One common network studied in functional magnetic resonance imaging (fMRI) research is the default mode network (Raichle et al., 2001). This network is activated when individuals are not performing a task and are letting their mind wander. The network involves both the frontal part of the brain (i.e., ventromedial prefrontal cortex [vmPFC]) and the posterior part of the brain (e.g., posterior cingulate and the angular gyrus/inferior parietal lobe). Once an individual engages in a task, this network is suppressed, and specific task-related networks become active.

In healthy individuals, greater suppression of the default network during a task is associated with better performance on that task (Kelly et al., 2008). Individuals with schizophrenia and their first-degree relatives do not show the normal suppression of the default network when performing cognitive tasks (Whitfield-Gabrieli et al., 2009). Further, individuals who experience auditory hallucinations also show non-typical brain connections in the default network (Alderson-Day et al., 2015). They also show a different organization of the auditory cortex when listening to simple tones (Doucet et al., 2019). Individuals with schizophrenia also show weaker connections between brain areas than individuals without schizophrenia, and the strength of connections is correlated with measures of memory, attention, and negative symptoms (Bassett et al., 2012; Gao et al., 2018).

A recent network model of schizophrenia examined the relationship between the default network, the salience network, and the frontal parietal network (Menon et al., 2022). According to this perspective, a central role for the salience network is when important external stimuli and self-referential mental events are not processed correctly by the brain. This leads to altered dynamic temporal interactions with the frontoparietal network (FPN) and the default mode network (DMN). Disrupted processing of salient and rewarding stimuli in schizophrenia is closely linked to dysregulated striatal dopamine signaling, which has been related to problems in predicting rewards common with schizophrenia.

Current brain imaging technology has allowed researchers to better identify cortical areas involved in hallucinations (P. Allen et al., 2008; Ford & Hoffman, 2013; Jardri & Sommer, 2013). It is suggested that in addition to dysfunctions in sensory cortices, dysfunctions in prefrontal premotor, cingulate, subcortical, and cerebellar regions also seem to contribute to hallucinatory experiences. One model suggests that a disruption in the information transfer from the left inferior frontal gyrus to Wernicke's area contributes to the failure to perceive that inner experiences are actually coming from one's self (Ford & Hoffman, 2013). That is, the person has the experience without knowing that it comes from their own brain.

Brain imaging research has suggested that individuals with schizophrenia show fewer connections between frontal and temporal areas of the brain while performing tasks. EEG measures offer one way of determining degree of connectivity. In a number of studies, Ford and her colleagues (e.g., Ford et al., 2007) have shown that individuals without schizophrenia show a cortical reduction of responsiveness to hearing their own voice talking, whereas those with schizophrenia do not. These researchers also reported that less connectivity between the frontal and temporal regions of the brain was seen when people with schizophrenia were talking compared with individuals without schizophrenia (Figure 13.13; Ford et al., 2002). Since there was even less connectivity in those individuals prone to hallucinating, this may be one mechanism involved in the mistaken experience that internal voices are produced externally (see also Fletcher & Frith, 2009).

Neurotransmitters Involved in Schizophrenia

Certain neurotransmitters are especially important in relation to schizophrenia. The first is dopamine. It has been suggested that dopamine neurons are overactive in schizophrenia in midbrain areas and underactive in higher cortical areas (Abi-Dargham & Grace, 2011; Gründer & Cumming, 2016). These activations can, in turn, influence other brain areas with dopamine projections (McCutcheon et al., 2019). This is referred to as the *dopamine imbalance hypothesis.* Supporting this hypothesis is the finding that there is a direct relationship between drugs that treat schizophrenia and their ability to bind to dopamine receptors in the brain. Further, stress not only increases symptoms in schizophrenia but also causes an activation of the hippocampus and an increase in dopamine activity (Gomes et al., 2019).

On a broader level, creative ability in humans has been associated with dopamine functioning, especially in the thalamus. Specifically, decreased dopamine D_2 receptor densities in the thalamus

FIGURE 13.13 ■ Brain Connections and Schizophrenia

Individuals with schizophrenia show fewer and weaker connections between frontal and temporal areas of the brain when performing tasks. This figure shows differences in connectivity between the frontal and temporal regions of the brain for normal controls and patients with schizophrenia.

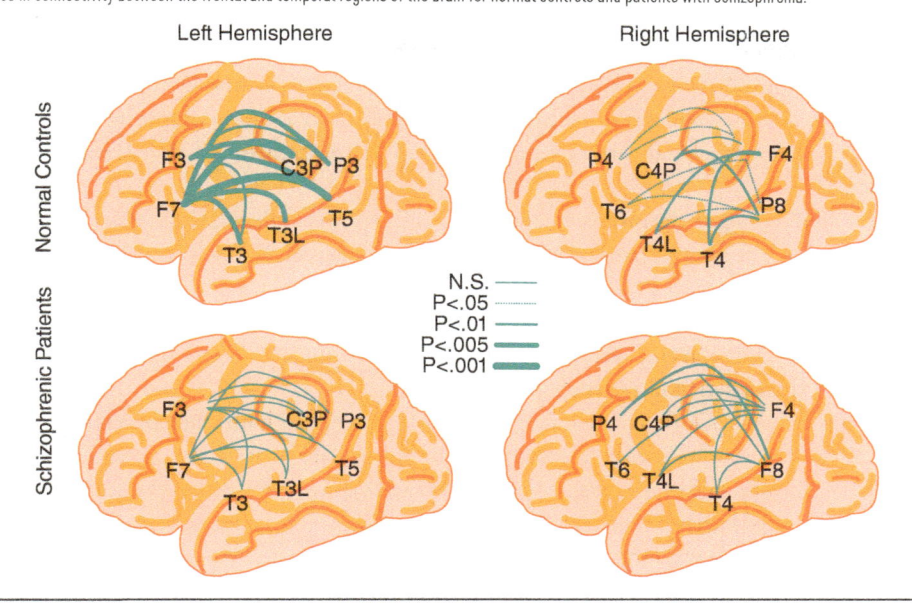

Credit: Ford, J. M., Mathalon, D. H., Whitfield, S., Faustman, W. O., & Roth, W. T. (2002). Reduced communication between frontal and temporal lobes during talking in schizophrenia. *Biological Psychiatry, 21*, 485–492, with permission from Elsevier.

Note: Thickness of the lines reflects the difference in strength of the connections between brain areas in those with schizophrenia and matched controls.

resulted in a lower gating threshold and thus increased information flow. This, in turn, could result in more creative thinking (Manzano et al., 2010).

Other researchers have suggested it is not the dopamine system per se that is involved in schizophrenia but that schizophrenia is the result of other transmitters that regulate the dopamine system (Grace, 2010). This is supported by the fact that dopamine levels are not strongly elevated in schizophrenia. What is greater in individuals with schizophrenia is the induced release of dopamine by amphetamines. Further, the increased release is proportional to the ability of amphetamines to exacerbate psychosis. In addition, GWASs suggest that only a few of the genes involved in schizophrenia are related to dopamine (Konopaske & Coyle, 2023).

The second neurotransmitter involved in schizophrenia is glutamate (Coyle et al., 2020; Konopaske & Coyle, 2023; Krystal & Moghaddam, 2011). Glutamate is an excitatory neurotransmitter in the brain. Further, another neurotransmitter, GABA (γ-aminobutyric acid), is involved in nearly all neuronal processes that engage the glutamate system. If the glutamate receptors in the brain are blocked in normal individuals, those individuals display psychotic-like symptoms.

At one time, the dopamine hypothesis and the *glutamate hypothesis* were seen as competing explanations involving the mechanisms of schizophrenia. Research has shown that giving substances that modify the activity of dopamine or glutamate could produce psychotic-like symptoms in healthy humans (Krystal et al., 2005). However, the type of psychotic presentation differed according to whether dopamine or glutamate receptors were affected.

Schizophrenia and Cognitive Processes

Since cognitive tasks utilize specific cognitive networks, one approach to understanding the brains of individuals with schizophrenia is to note deficits in solving cognitive problems (Barch & Ceaser, 2012; Pearlson, 2011). Individuals with schizophrenia show deficits in a variety of cognitive domains, including executive function, working memory, and episodic memory. Overall, these cognitive processes all involve the DLPFC and its connections to other brain areas.

One suggestion is to develop a *cognitive stress test* similar to physical stress tests that determine the integrity of the heart. Two types of cognitive tasks that distinguish individuals with schizophrenia from those without schizophrenia are those using working memory and those using attention. Working memory is the ability to keep information available for a short period of time, including its manipulation in planning and goal-directed behaviors. Disturbances in working memory are found in individuals with both acute and chronic schizophrenia as well as in their first-degree relatives without the disorder.

Imaging studies suggest the involvement of the DLPFC as well as the ACC, inferior parietal lobule, and hippocampus. The inferior parietal lobule is located just behind Wernicke's area and is connected with large fiber tracts to both Broca's and Wernicke's areas. Overall, this area is associated with processing and integrating auditory, visual, and sensorimotor information. As suggested by DTI brain imaging measures, the problems seen with schizophrenia are probably better thought of as network problems rather than a deficit in a particular brain area.

One classic example of differential brain processing in individuals with schizophrenia is the *Charlie Chaplin illusion*. If individuals without schizophrenia look at a mask of Charlie Chaplin as it rotates, they will see the reverse side of the mask not as hollow but as convex. A video of the mask rotating can be seen online (see For Further Reading). As you can see in the video, as the mask turns, an individual initially sees the hollow mask, but this changes into a normal face. Individuals with schizophrenia do not see the illusion and view the reverse side of the mask as hollow.

The Charlie Chaplin illusion has been studied with fMRI (Dima et al., 2009). What these researchers found was that individuals with schizophrenia and those without showed different types of connectivity in the brain. Specifically, individuals without schizophrenia showed more top-down processing when perceiving the illusion. This suggests that part of the illusion is the sensory expectation of how a face should appear. Thus, in individuals without schizophrenia, the brain creates the face as it should appear and not hollow as it actually is. Individuals with schizophrenia, on the other hand, show weakened top-down processes and stronger bottom-up ones. As a result, they see the sensory stimuli as they are without expectation. Overall, this is consistent with other research that suggests that individuals with schizophrenia lack the top-down expectations necessary to predict future events (e.g., P. Allen et al., 2008).

Individuals with schizophrenia may describe complex emotional processes when writing in a journal while at the same time showing limited emotional expression when interacting with others (Kring & Elis, 2013). Further, people with schizophrenia report similar emotional experiences as those without schizophrenia. However, individuals with schizophrenia do appear to have problems connecting the emotions of others in a social situation with the context in which they occur. For example, in one study, those with schizophrenia as compared to control individuals showed less brain activity in the amygdala and visual cortex when shown faces of fear or happiness (Maher et al., 2015). Moreover, they tend to experience positive and neutral situations as more negative than those who do not have schizophrenia.

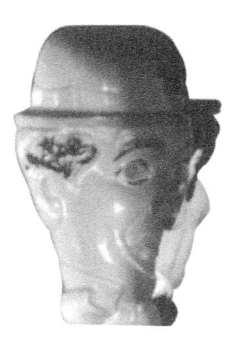

Charlie Chaplin Illusion

© Gregory RL. "Knowledge in perception and illusion." *Philosophical Transactions of the Royal Society of London B* 1997; 352:1 121–8, by permission of the Royal Society.

CONCEPT CHECK

- What structural brain changes in white matter and gray matter are characteristic of those with schizophrenia?
- Individuals with schizophrenia show larger ventricles in the brain. What do larger ventricles represent? When do they appear?
- What are the impacts of deficits in the brain's default network and connectivity within and across networks in individuals with schizophrenia?
- "At one time, the dopamine hypothesis and the glutamate hypothesis were seen as competing explanations involving the mechanisms of schizophrenia." What is the support for each hypothesis? What evidence suggests a more complex relationship?
- What is a cognitive stress test? What are three cognitive domains that show deficits in individuals with schizophrenia that would be the focus of the stress test?
- What are some of the problems in emotional processing experienced by individuals with schizophrenia?

TREATING INDIVIDUALS WITH SCHIZOPHRENIA

Until about the 1960s, individuals with schizophrenia were placed in mental hospitals, often with little real treatment other than controlling them. With the advent of medications in the mid-20th century, it became possible for individuals with schizophrenia to live in community or home settings. In fact, individuals with schizophrenia tend to show more positive mental health behaviors when living within a community. In some cultures, small towns saw it as their duty to take care of these individuals. In 2008 the National Institute of Mental Health (NIMH) began research studies aimed at how to best treat individuals with schizophrenia after their first episode was experienced (Dixon et al., 2018). This NIMH program was referred to as Recovery After an Initial Schizophrenia Episode (RAISE) (see For Further Reading).

Today, after initial hospitalizations to gain control over symptoms, many individuals with schizophrenia return to their family. Other individuals continue their education or work. Some individuals, such as the ones noted at the beginning of this chapter, are able to be productive and succeed in high-level jobs with appropriate support. However, some individuals with schizophrenia become homeless and are at the mercy of their community. *LENS: Mercy Bookings of Mental Patients* describes how police around the United States try to protect these individuals.

LENS
MERCY BOOKINGS OF MENTAL PATIENTS

During the 1800s, individuals with mental disorders were placed in jails and prisons in the United States. Dorothea Dix and others pushed for more humane treatment, and state mental hospitals began to be built. During the 1950s, another movement began to overcome the lack of adequate treatment found in many state hospitals. This community mental health movement sought to give individuals with mental disorders more freedom and dignity by moving their care and treatment out of institutions and into the community. However, the lack of funding for community facilities has left many of these individuals without treatment and literally on the streets of many cities. In these circumstances, police must often interact with those with mental illness.

Traditionally, law enforcement is there to protect the public, while the mental health system is there to treat the individual. However, these roles become more ambiguous in what is referred to as *mercy booking*. As mental hospitals were closed in the last half of the 20th century, many of the individuals who would previously have been hospitalized found themselves in the community or homeless. Mental hospitals or wards currently give priority to those who are a danger to themselves or others. Others with mental disorders find themselves released to the community, their family, or the streets. This leaves some of these individuals, especially women, open to becoming victims of robbery or even rape. Mercy booking is the situation in which police fabricate a charge to enable jailing the person in order to protect them.

Police from around the United States have described their involvement in mercy booking (see Reisig & Kane, 2014; Torrey, 1997). One police officer in Los Angeles, California, described mercy booking as crisis intervention in that the individuals arrested were malnourished, in need of medical care, and often hallucinating. By arresting the individuals, they were able to obtain shelter and food and the necessary medications.

Sometimes, the person with a mental disorder creates an arrest situation, committing a minor crime near a police station so they can be arrested and live in the protected context of a jail. In other cases, families are unable to care for an individual who refuses their medications and shows disruptive behaviors. The family will often use the police to protect the individual through having them arrested.

It is critical for society to determine who should be responsible for treating individuals with mental disorders and how that should be done. In the 1800s, jails were shown not to be the best solution. In the 1900s, mental hospitals offered an alternative that came to have a number of problems in terms of humane treatment. Today, those with mental disorders experience a patchwork of agencies, including law enforcement, that determine their treatment. A consistent approach is sorely lacking and seems long overdue.

Thought Question

What do you think are the pros and cons of mercy booking? What would you recommend as a consistent approach to community mental health treatment?

Over the past 100 years, there has been a shift in viewing schizophrenia as a disorder with inevitable deterioration to one in which recovery is possible (Frese et al., 2009). Recovery includes having a career. Living with schizophrenia depends on the resources of the individual in terms of intellectual abilities, coping techniques, and willingness to accept the advice of professionals.

Treatment for schizophrenia involves addressing the specific stage of the illness. Figure 13.14 shows the major stages of the development of schizophrenia and some suggested treatment approaches at each stage. One major focus of treatment and research is the manner in which early intervention at each stage can reduce the severity of that stage. There are studies currently underway that are seeking to identify reliable indicators as to who will develop schizophrenia later in life (e.g., Cornblatt & Carrión, 2016). However, at this point the research is not definitive. Thus, knowing who should

FIGURE 13.14 ■ Interventions Used at Each Stage of the Development of Schizophrenia

This figure shows the stages of schizophrenia and opportunities for intervention at each stage.

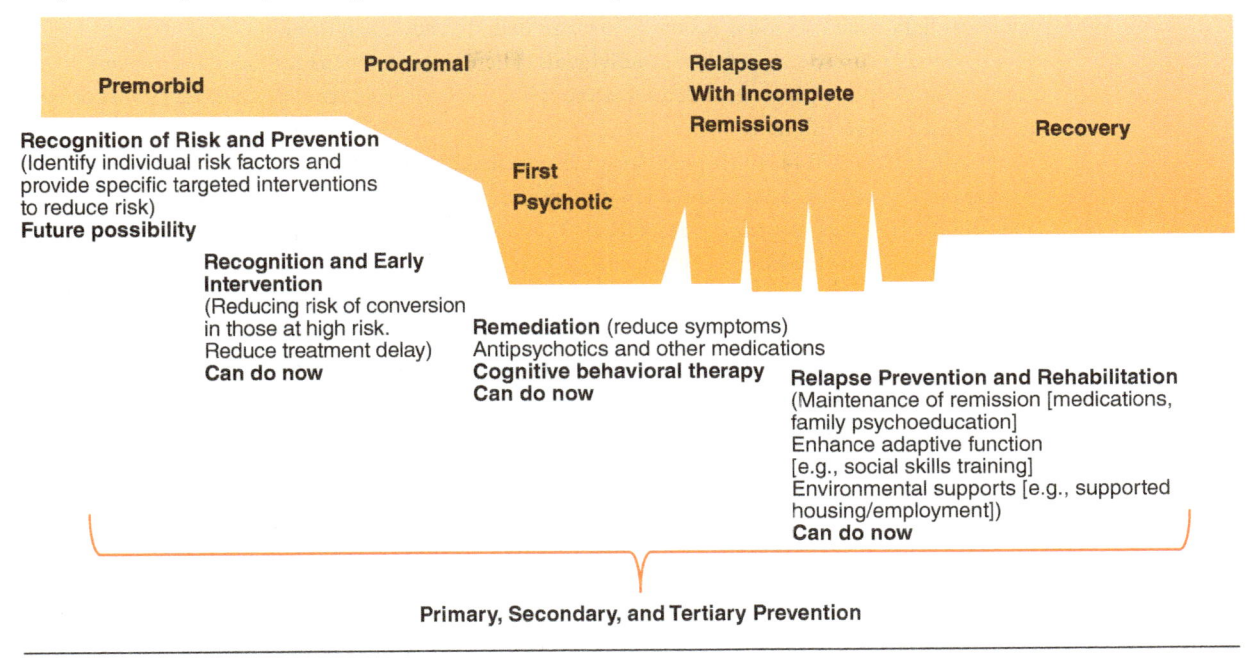

Premorbid • Prodromal • First Psychotic • Relapses With Incomplete Remissions • Recovery

Recognition of Risk and Prevention (Identify individual risk factors and provide specific targeted interventions to reduce risk)
Future possibility

Recognition and Early Intervention (Reducing risk of conversion in those at high risk. Reduce treatment delay)
Can do now

Remediation (reduce symptoms) Antipsychotics and other medications
Cognitive behavioral therapy
Can do now

Relapse Prevention and Rehabilitation (Maintenance of remission [medications, family psychoeducation] Enhance adaptive function [e.g., social skills training] Environmental supports [e.g., supported housing/employment])
Can do now

Primary, Secondary, and Tertiary Prevention

Credit: Tandon, R. (2012). The nosology of schizophrenia: Toward DSM-5 and ICD-11. Psychiatric Clinics of North America, 35(3), 557–569. http://doi.org/10.1016/j.psc.2012.06.001, with permission from Elsevier.

intervene and how remains a future possibility, although a number of programs are testing it out. Once signs of schizophrenia develop, early intervention becomes important. With signs of a psychotic episode, antipsychotic medication and psychological treatments are essential. Following this, supportive mechanisms such as family therapy and the creation of living and work conditions that help to reduce relapse are critical.

The Internet provides access to local and national groups that offer support for those with schizophrenia as well as their caregivers. For example, researchers in San Francisco are using mobile apps to help adolescents with schizophrenia improve their treatments (Schlosser et al., 2018). A number of other support procedures have been developed to help individuals with schizophrenia cope in the community. These include antipsychotic medications as well as educational procedures to help the individual with schizophrenia and their family understand the course of the illness and the types of support available. As with other mental health disorders, specific psychotherapies for individuals with schizophrenia have also been developed. Research suggests that the most effective treatment of schizophrenia should involve both medication and psychosocial approaches (Beck & Rector, 2005; Kane et al., 2016).

Antipsychotic Medications

A variety of medications have been used in the treatment of schizophrenia (Gopalakrishna et al., 2016; Hyman & Cohen, 2013; Kutscher, 2008; Marder & Cannon, 2019; Minzenberg et al., 2010; Taipale et al., 2018). The treatment of schizophrenia changed drastically in 1954 with the discovery of chlorpromazine (brand name Thorazine). When effective, this drug reduced agitation, hostility, and aggression. It also reduced positive symptoms such as hallucinations and delusions and increased the time between hospitalizations associated with schizophrenia. However, negative symptoms and cognitive deficits were not changed by the drug.

One problem with this and other initial drugs were side effects such as *tardive dyskinesia*, which is a movement disorder that results in involuntary movement of the lower face and at times the limbs. These purposeless movements include sucking, smacking the lips, and making tongue movements. These and other movement side effects were difficult to reverse if the medication was given over a period of time. Weight gain is also seen with antipsychotic medications. In subsequent years, new and different classes of *neuroleptic* medications have been developed with different or fewer side effects (Gopalakrishna et al., 2016). These newer drugs tend to reduce the positive symptoms of schizophrenia such as hallucinations and delusions. They also help the individual think more clearly and remain calmer. Not all medications work for all individuals. There is also some suggestion that different ethnic groups respond differently to neuroleptics, although it is less clear whether it is genetic factors or diet that influences these differences.

Overall, medications for schizophrenia have been referred to as first-generation or second-generation antipsychotics. Second-generation antipsychotics are also known as *atypical antipsychotics*. First-generation antipsychotics influence dopamine receptors (D_2), although the exact mechanism by which they work is still being studied. One example of a first-generation antipsychotic medication is haloperidol, which has a number of trade names worldwide, one being Haldol. Second-generation or atypical antipsychotic medications, such as Seroquel or Risperdal, influence the dopamine receptors differently. Both first- and second-generation antipsychotics are successful in treating the positive symptoms seen in schizophrenia. One advantage of the second-generation antipsychotics is that they are also able to treat the negative symptoms. Initially, it was thought that the second-generation antipsychotics had fewer motor side effects, but this has not always been shown to be the case (Peluso et al., 2012). In fact, large-scale studies suggest that second-generation drugs are no more effective than the older ones (Hyman & Cohen, 2013).

One large-scale study of effectiveness of antipsychotic medication was conducted at 57 clinical sites in the United States in the early 2000s and involved almost 1,500 individuals with schizophrenia (see Lieberman & Stroup, 2011, for an overview and update). This is referred to as the CATIE (Clinical Antipsychotic Trials of Intervention Effectiveness) study. Individuals with schizophrenia were randomly assigned to one of four second-generation antipsychotic medications (olanzapine [Zyprexa], quetiapine [Seroquel], risperidone [Risperdal], ziprasidone [Geodon]) or a first-generation antipsychotic medication (perphenazine [Trilafon]) and followed for 18 months. An important aspect of the study was to compare first- and second-generation antipsychotic medications. One surprising result was that the second-generation medications did not show greater effectiveness than the first-generation medication, perphenazine. This included no greater effectiveness in terms of negative symptoms and cognitive impairment. These results had implications not only for treatment effectiveness but also for economic considerations, since first-generation medications are less expensive. The CATIE study brought forth much controversy in the years following its publication (Lieberman & Stroup, 2011).

Psychosocial Interventions for Schizophrenia

Psychosocial factors play an important role in the overall treatment of individuals with schizophrenia. It has been estimated that over 60% of people with a first episode of a major mental illness return to live with relatives. Thus, families play an important role in supporting these individuals. In fact, *family interventions* for schizophrenia reduce relapse and hospitalizations. A number of meta-analyses have looked at evidence supporting family interventions (see Barrowclough & Lobban, 2008, for an overview). In general, family interventions involve the following key components:

1. Provide practical emotional support to family members.
2. Provide information about schizophrenia, what mental health services are available in the community, and nationwide support services (such as those found on the Internet).
3. Help the family develop a model of schizophrenia (including not blaming themselves).
4. Modify beliefs about schizophrenia that are unhelpful or inaccurate.
5. Increase coping for all family members.
6. Enhance problem-solving skills.
7. Enhance positive communications.
8. Involve everyone in a relapse prevention plan.

Families play an important role in supporting individuals with schizophrenia.
iStock.com/Imagesbybarbara. Stock photo. Posed by model.

A number of manuals involving *cognitive behavioral therapy (CBT) approaches* to schizophrenia are available (e.g., Kingdon & Turkington, 1994; Smith et al., 2003). The basic model suggests that what is important is the manner in which individuals interpret psychotic phenomena (Beck & Rector, 2005; Ellenberg et al., 2018; Morrison, 2008). The overall model suggests that neurocognitive impairment in the premorbid state makes the individual vulnerable to difficulties in school or work, which leads to nonfunctional beliefs such as "I am inferior," maladaptive cognitive appraisals, and in turn nonfunctional behavior such as social withdrawal (Beck & Rector, 2005). The cognitive approach is aimed at helping the client understand the psychotic experience as well as cope with the experience and reduce distress. One key feature of schizophrenia is the disruption of thought processes, and one part of the treatment is directed at these illogical associations. Another focus of the treatment is directed at interpersonal relationships and success at work. This approach may also involve skills training such as self-monitoring and activity scheduling. Since individuals with schizophrenia may also show mood and anxiety problems, CBT aimed at these processes can also be utilized. The key features of CBT for schizophrenia can be summarized as follows (Beck & Rector, 2005; Turkington et al., 2006):

1. Develop a therapeutic alliance based on the client's perspective.
2. Understand the client's interpretation of past and present events.
3. Develop alternative explanations of schizophrenia symptoms.
4. Normalize and reduce the impact of positive and negative symptoms.
5. Educate the client in terms of the role of stress.
6. Teach the client about the cognitive model, including the relationships between thoughts, feelings, and behaviors.
7. Offer alternatives to the medical model to address medication adherence.

Developing a therapeutic alliance, that is, a relationship between the therapist and client that helps the work of therapy, is an initial task of therapy. Part of this may include talking with the client about their delusional beliefs. For example, if a client claims to have invented a machine to solve the world's problems, then the therapist might ask when the person had this idea and what the person has done to create the machine. The therapist might also ask about others who had helped with these ideas. As with CBT for other disorders, the basic idea is to look for inconsistent thoughts and conclusions that do not follow logically. For example, if no one would help the person with their machine, it does not follow logically that everyone is out to get that person.

Another major task of therapy is helping the individual develop an alternative understanding of their symptoms. For example, some individuals with schizophrenia experience the voices that they hear as coming from outside of them. One goal of therapy would be to help the client reinterpret the source of the voices. Part of this may also include a cognitive assessment of alternatives to obeying the voices.

The role of stress in increasing symptoms of schizophrenia is an important concept for clients to understand. It is also important for them to understand the problems associated with not taking medication to control the symptoms of schizophrenia. Keeping individuals with schizophrenia on their medications is a difficult problem. In studies involving active medication alone versus a placebo alone, the relapse rates are about one half with medication compared with a placebo (32% vs. 72%) (Hogarty & Goldberg, 1973). Based on current studies, treating individuals with schizophrenia with both CBT and psychotropic medication appears to be the most effective approach (see Beck & Rector, 2005, for outcome studies).

In the 1950s, George Brown in London, England, sought to understand why some individuals with schizophrenia were readmitted soon after their hospital discharge with their symptoms reoccurring (G. Brown, 1985). He discovered that one important factor was the emotional environment in the home. This came to be referred to as *expressed emotion*, which refers to the emotions that the person with schizophrenia would experience from others. That is, homes in which the person experienced critical comments, hostility, and angry arguments were associated with relapse, whereas homes with warmth and positive remarks were not. Since that time, a number of intervention programs have been developed involving caregivers and others who live with people with schizophrenia (Amaresha & Venkatasubramanian, 2012).

As noted earlier, *early intervention* is being tried as a new approach in the treatment of schizophrenia (Fisher et al., 2013). This approach seeks out those who are at high risk for developing the disorder. The basic approach is to help these individuals develop cognitive skills as a way to increase attention, memory, executive control, and other cognitive processes. In addition, cognitive therapy is being used to reduce the reactivity to stress seen in the period prior to the development of psychosis and to better understand these individuals' thoughts and feelings. Although some success has been reported, this approach for the prevention of schizophrenia is still early in its development. Finally, corporations are establishing networks to help those with serious mental disorders, as described in the *LENS: Mental Health Networks of Those With Serious Mental Health Disorders*.

LENS

MENTAL HEALTH NETWORKS OF THOSE WITH SERIOUS MENTAL HEALTH DISORDERS

Something new is happening in major corporations and institutions in this country. Successful individuals who have experienced such disorders as schizophrenia, depression, and bipolar disorder are forming networks to support and educate others. One of these was The Stability Network (see Web Resources). This particular network consisted of over 30 individuals who would speak publicly about their mental health experiences. They were also successfully employed in all lines of work. One of these people is Robert Boorstin, a former director of public policy at Google. Another is Elyn Saks, whose experiences with schizophrenia are offered in the *LENS: Elyn Saks Describes Her Day-to-Day Experiences With Schizophrenia*. All of the people involved can describe their experiences and beliefs. One person thought she could walk on the Charles River in Boston when she was at the Harvard Business School. Another believed his hotel room was the *Starship Enterprise*. However, each has worked with professionals and developed routines for stabilizing his or her condition.

The Stability Network sought people who were successfully employed in business, government, the nonprofit sector, academia, or the arts who were successfully living with a mental health condition. These individuals gave presentations and sought to improve work place conditions and improve the lives of others. The Stability Network ceased operation in 2023, although other such groups exist.

Mental health disorders often carry with them a stigma. However, psychological research tells us that actually meeting and talking with someone about his or her condition can change that stigma.

Thought Question

You've now read a lot of psychological research concerning mental health disorders. What specific actions would you recommend that your university or community take to reduce the stigma of psychological disorders?

Another new approach, referred to as *NAVIGATE*, has been designed for the treatment of first-episode psychosis (Kane et al., 2016). NAVIGATE is a multidisciplinary, team-based approach that emphasizes low-dose antipsychotic medications, cognitive behavioral psychotherapy, family education and support, and vocational and educational support. The program also helps the person to engage in their community. One advantage of this approach is that the individual with first-episode psychosis receives all of these different treatment approaches. In a randomized control study involving 34 community mental health centers in 21 U.S. states, the NAVIGATE program was shown to be more effective than the standard care found in the community health center. Further, the earlier the person entered treatment after the first psychotic episode, the better their outcome measures were. Based on these types of results, the National Institute of Mental Health has announced the Early Psychosis Intervention Network (EPINET) (see For Further Reading) that seeks to link evidence-based treatment centers around the United States.

Many professionals involved in the treatment of schizophrenia have come to realize that people are more likely to accept treatment and follow directions if they are involved in their own treatment. A number of states have coordinated treatment approaches such as NAVIGATE that use a multidisciplinary team as well as input from the person with schizophrenia. Researchers worldwide are also testing mobile app–based interventions for adolescents with first-episode psychosis (Barbeito et al., 2019). These types of interventions are critical, since many youth in the early stages of schizophrenia drop out of conventional medication-alone treatment.

CONCEPT CHECK

- What are three critical shifts in the past 60 years that have transformed the treatment of schizophrenia from institution-based to community-based?
- "Treatment for schizophrenia involves addressing the specific stage of the illness." What specific treatments are suggested for different stages of the illness, and why?
- A variety of classes of medications have been used in the treatment of schizophrenia. What are they, and what are the advantages and disadvantages of each?
- What four psychosocial approaches are currently used in the treatment of individuals with schizophrenia, and what is the primary focus of each approach?

SUMMARY

Schizophrenia is one of the most debilitating of the mental disorders. It is part of a broad category of mental illness referred to as psychotic disorders, all of which involve a loss of touch with reality and problems with cognitive, emotional, and motor processes. Schizophrenia affects about 1% of the population. It is seen throughout the world with similar symptoms regardless of culture or geographical location. Onset of schizophrenia occurs in the late teens or early twenties. Men show an earlier onset than women by about 5 years. Symptoms are referred to as positive or negative. The more familiar positive symptoms are hallucinations, delusions, disorganized thinking, and disorganized behavior. The more familiar negative symptoms include lack of affect in situations that call for it, poor motivation, and social withdrawal. Not everyone with schizophrenia displays the same symptoms. This has led some researchers to suggest that a variety of similar disorders exist that are currently described by the term *schizophrenia*.

Disorders with psychotic-like symptoms have been described for at least 4,000 years, and ancient medical texts suggest that psychosis was present in all cultures. The present-day concept of schizophrenia began to evolve in the mid-1800s. Beginning in the 1950s, the *DSM* was introduced and described psychosis in broad terms. By *DSM-III*, schizophrenia was defined by more explicit criteria, and in *DSM-IV* and *DSM-IV-TR*, the criteria for schizophrenia were broadened to become similar to the diagnostic criteria used by *ICD*. Most recently, the text revision of the fourth edition of *DSM* (*DSM-IV-TR*) and *DSM-5* set forth a multilevel process for diagnosing schizophrenia: (1) symptoms, (2) functioning, and (3) duration; the final levels are designed to rule out psychotic-like symptoms found in other disorders. Because individuals with schizophrenia have a variety of different symptoms and show an inconsistent presentation of the disorder, some have suggested that there is not a single schizophrenia disorder but rather a variety of syndromes. *DSM-IV* divided schizophrenia into five subtypes: paranoid, disorganized, catatonic, undifferentiated, and residual. There has been considerable debate as to the value of using the five subtypes due to the larger question of whether schizophrenia should be considered in terms of discrete categories or existing along a dimension. Although *ICD-10* uses subtypes, *DSM-5* removed the classification of subtypes but left the diagnostic criteria.

There is an evolutionary paradox with schizophrenia: How can the disorder exist without a reproductive advantage? One possible answer is that the genes associated with schizophrenia are also associated with positive traits such as creativity, since it has been noted that highly gifted and creative individuals manifest schizophrenic-like characteristics, referred to as schizotypal traits, without having the disorder. Other scientists propose different evolutionary paths: Crow theorizes that the development of language and the genetic changes required for producing and understanding speech were associated with the development of schizophrenia, while Burns suggests that schizophrenia is better understood as a disorder of the social brain rather than language.

Schizophrenia typically is first manifested during the transition from late adolescence to adulthood at a time of great reorganization of cortical networks. However, current research literature suggests that we consider schizophrenia as a neurodevelopmental disorder that begins early in life. The basic idea is that during the time the fetus is in utero, an insult happens that influences the changes to the brain that take place during adolescence. Schizophrenia has a strong genetic component; however, the genetic underpinnings of schizophrenia are not simple. The number of genetic variants seen in individuals with schizophrenia is very large, and these genes may act in an additive or interactive manner, leading to a variety of genetic combinations associated with schizophrenia. Genetic differences may result not from differences in the DNA itself but from epigenetic factors, suggesting internal and external environmental factors play a role. Finally, environmental factors that do not involve genetic changes may also play a role.

Presently, there is no one biomarker that can identify a person with schizophrenia. However, in comparing individuals with schizophrenia, their relatives, and healthy control individuals, endophenotypes have been found in six major areas: (1) minor physical anomalies, (2) physiologic abnormalities due to normal metabolism in the brain being disturbed, (3) neuropsychological measures, (4) neuromotor abnormalities, and (5) sensory processing and event-related potentials. Another physiological marker that distinguishes individuals with schizophrenia is larger ventricles in the brain resulting from a decrease in volume in other areas of the brain.

Schizophrenia manifests on a variety of levels, including abnormal sensory experiences such as hallucinations, problems in cognitive processes such as delusions and disordered thought, changes in affect such as lack of expression, and in some cases problems with language and future directed planning. This presents a challenge to describe the manner in which brain processes relate to the disorder. Current research examining individuals with schizophrenia has emphasized five different levels of analysis from a neuroscience perspective. The first is anatomical changes, such as the loss of brain volume in particular areas. The second is functional processes, such as the manner in which cortical areas and networks process information as seen in brain imaging. The third is neural oscillations that underlie the cortical networks. The fourth is changes in neurotransmitters, such as dopamine and glutamate. And the fifth is the development of cortical processes beginning in utero.

Until about the 1960s, individuals with schizophrenia were placed in mental hospitals, often with little real treatment other than controlling them. With the advent of medications in the mid-20th century, it became possible for individuals with schizophrenia to live within community or home settings. In fact, they tend to show more positive mental health behaviors when living within a community. In addition, over the past 100 years, there has been a shift in viewing schizophrenia as a disorder with inevitable deterioration to one in which recovery is possible. In order to help individuals with schizophrenia cope in the community, a number of support procedures have been developed. These include antipsychotic medications; educational procedures to help the individual with schizophrenia and his or her family to understand the course of the illness and the types of support available; and specific psychotherapies, particularly CBT approaches. Research suggests that the most effective treatment of schizophrenia should involve both medication and psychosocial approaches.

STUDY RESOURCES

Review Questions

1. This chapter states that "individuals with schizophrenia have a variety of different symptoms and show an inconsistent picture of the disorder. This has led some to suggest that there is not a single schizophrenia disorder but rather a variety of syndromes." What do you think: Is schizophrenia one disorder? What evidence would you cite to support your position?

2. What are the environmental and genetic factors that play a role in the development of schizophrenia?

3. "Current research examining individuals with schizophrenia has emphasized five different levels of research from a neuroscience perspective." For each type, what has been the focus of the research, and what brain changes have been found in schizophrenia?
    a. Anatomical changes
    b. Functional processes
    c. Neural oscillations
    d. Neurotransmitters
    e. Development of cortical processes

4. "Psychosocial factors play an important role in the overall treatment of individuals with schizophrenia." What are the characteristics of each factor, and what role does each play in treatment?
    a. Family interventions
    b. CBT approach
    c. Early intervention

5. "Over the past 100 years, there has been a shift in viewing schizophrenia as a disorder with inevitable deterioration to one in which recovery is possible." What impact does this shift suggest for changes in research, education, and public policy?

For Further Reading

Charlie Chaplin mask illusion [Video]. (n.d.). https://www.youtube.com/watch?v=hoLg23xn3HM

McLean, R. (2003). *Recovered, not cured: A journey through schizophrenia.* Allen Unwin.

Mukherjee, S. (2016, March 28). *Runs in the family: New findings about schizophrenia rekindle old questions about genes and identity.*

Nasar, S. (1998). *A beautiful mind.* Simon & Schuster.

National Institute of Mental Health. (2015, February 6). *Early Psychosis Intervention Network (EPINET): A learning healthcare system for early serious mental illness.* U.S. Department of Health and Human Services. http://www.nimh.nih.gov/concept-clearance/EPINET

National Institute of Mental Health. (2022, October). *Recovery After an Initial Schizophrenia Episode (RAISE).* U.S. Department of Health and Human Services. https://www.nimh.nih.gov/research/research-funded-by-nimh/research-initiatives/recovery-after-an-initial-schizophrenia-episode-raise

Saks, E. (2007). *The center cannot hold: My journey through madness.* Hyperion.

Saks, E. (2012, June). *A tale of mental illness—from the inside.* [Video]. TED Conferences. https://www.ted.com/talks/elyn_saks_a_tale_of_mental_illness_from_the_inside

Schiller, L., & Bennett, A. (1994). *The quiet room.* Warner Books.

The Stability Network. (2023). https://www.thestabilitynetwork.org/

Steele, K., & Berman, C. (2001). *The day the voices stopped.* Basic Books.

Torrey, E. (1997). *Out of the shadows: Confronting America's mental illness crisis.* Wiley.

KEY TERMS

- alogia
- anhedonia
- avolition
- catatonic subtype
- delusions
- disorganized subtype
- hallucinations
- negative symptoms
- paranoid subtype
- positive symptoms
- psychotic disorders
- schizophrenia
- schizotypal traits

14 PERSONALITY DISORDERS

LEARNING OBJECTIVES

14.1 Identify personality disorders, personality traits, and the characteristics of a healthy self.

14.2 Distinguish among the paranoid, schizoid, and schizotypal personality disorders.

14.3 Distinguish among the antisocial, borderline, histrionic, and narcissistic personality disorders.

14.4 Distinguish among the anxious fearful personality disorders.

14.5 Identify the treatments available to individuals with personality disorders.

Stephen Westwood
Photo courtesy of Stephen Westwood

Am I completely selfish? Is that what all this is about? I must be because the one thing that scares me more than living, more than death, is surviving another suicide attempt. Then I would have to face up to my actions. Then I would have to try and mend the relationships that my selfishness has destroyed. So why do it? Why do I have such strong suicidal urges? Why have I had these urges all these years? Why does it seem to bear no relation to what is actually going on in my life? Why won't the God damn shrinks tell me that one? Have I got too much of the suicidal gene in my DNA? Are there too many suicidal chemicals in my brain? Can't they give me a pill that deals with that? They can't, can they? They send me to therapy with three different people and not one of them has been able to touch on just why. Why a kid from the country village of Wymondley grew up from catching newts and making camps to slashing his wrists and taking overdoses. Surely there is something in between those two events that has made me this way? . . . But no one can help me and I have always been meant to kill myself, so that's what will have to happen. It is my unwritten destiny. It gets to the point where I feel that I really have to do it. It is not even a choice anymore. I must obey.

You might ask how I can do it to my family. How I can do this to the girl I love. Well, the guilt I feel about my plans to die is just as strong as my urge to carry them out. It is as if someone else, the other me, made those plans for me. When Ashley comes home from work I usually put that other me aside and I am there for her, but sometimes he stays like a great dark cloud smothering my thoughts. Living for the sake of someone else is not easy. I wish that I wanted to live for myself, but I probably never will.

From Stephen Westwood (2007), Suicide Junkie *(p. 5).*

PERSONALITY DISORDERS AND PERSONALITY

As you read the self-report from Stephen Westwood above, you probably had a number of reactions. You might have thought of others you know who react in similar ways. You might have thought about how you would react and what upsets you. You might have wondered why some people seem to be so dramatic in everything they do. Some people will tell you that they cut themselves or burn themselves when they experience psychological pain. Westwood tells you that all he thinks about is suicide. However, he also tells you that he can have a relationship with a girlfriend. People who have these types of relationships with themselves and others are described in terms of personality disorders.

What Is a Personality Disorder?

The basic definition of a **personality disorder** is "an enduring pattern of inner experience and behavior that deviates markedly from the expectations of the individual's culture" (American Psychiatric Association, 2022, p. 733). Further, the pattern is inflexible, stable, and generally begins in adolescence, and it leads to distress or impairment. The characteristics of these disorders are especially apparent when these individuals find themselves in situations that are beyond their ability to cope. *DSM-5-TR* describes a general set of criteria seen in varying degrees in all personality disorders. These are shown in Table 14.1. It should be noted that mental health professionals do not use the category of *general personality disorder* as a diagnosis. Rather, they diagnose individuals with 1 of 10 specific personality disorders.

DSM-5-TR identifies 10 personality disorders that form separate categories. These disorders can be organized into three clusters, as presented in Table 14.2.

The first cluster is referred to as Cluster A and covers *odd or eccentric disorders.* These include *schizoid personality disorder, paranoid personality disorder,* and *schizotypal personality disorder.* Individuals

Personality disorders are most apparent when individuals find themselves in situations that are beyond their ability to cope.
iStock.com/Dima Berlin

TABLE 14.1 ■ *DSM-5-TR* Diagnostic Criteria for General Personality Disorder

A. A. An enduring pattern of inner experience and behavior that deviates markedly from the expectations of the individual's culture. This pattern is manifested in two (or more) of the following areas:
   1. Cognition (i.e., ways of perceiving and interpreting self, other people, and events).
   2. Affectivity (i.e., the range, intensity, lability, and appropriateness of emotional response).
   3. Interpersonal functioning.
   4. Impulse control.

B. The enduring pattern is inflexible and pervasive across a broad range of personal and social situations.

C. The enduring pattern leads to clinically significant distress or impairment in social, occupational, or other important areas of functioning.

D. The pattern is stable and of long duration, and its onset can be traced back at least to adolescence or early adulthood.

E. The enduring pattern is not better explained as a manifestation or consequence of another mental disorder.

F. The enduring pattern is not attributable to the physiological effects of a substance (e.g., a drug of abuse, a medication) or another medical condition (e.g., head trauma).

Credit: Reprinted with permission from the *Diagnostic and Statistical Manual of Mental Disorders, fifth edition, text revision (DSM-V-TR)*, pp. 734–735 (Copyright © 2022). American Psychiatric Association. All rights reserved.

with these disorders typically feel uncomfortable around or suspicious of others or restrict their relationships. Schizoid personality disorder is characterized by a pervasive pattern of detachment from social relationships and a restricted range of emotional expression. Paranoid personality disorder is characterized by a pervasive distrust and suspiciousness of others. Schizotypal personality disorder is characterized by odd beliefs and behaviors.

The second cluster is referred to as Cluster B and covers *dramatic, emotional, or erratic disorders.* These include *antisocial personality disorder, borderline personality disorder (BPD), histrionic personality disorder,* and *narcissistic personality disorder.* Individuals with these disorders show a wide diversity of patterns of social and emotional interactions with others. Antisocial personality disorder is characterized by a disregard for the other person. BPD is characterized by instability in relationships. Histrionic personality disorder is characterized by excessive emotional responding and the seeking of attention. Narcissistic personality disorder is characterized by grandiosity in terms of one's abilities and a lack of empathy.

TABLE 14.2 ■ Three Clusters of Personality Disorders

Disorder	Characteristics	Prevalence
Cluster A	**Odd or eccentric disorders**	**5.7%**
Paranoid	Pervasive distrust and suspiciousness of others; sees others as having malevolent intentions	2.3–4.4%
Schizoid	Detachment from social relationships and restriction of the expression of emotions in interpersonal settings	3.1–4.9%
Schizotypal	Discomfort with close relationships; cognitive and perceptual distortions and eccentricities of behavior	3.3–3.9%
Cluster B	**Dramatic, emotional, or erratic disorders**	**1.5%**
Antisocial	Disregard for and violation of the rights of others	0.2–3.3%
Borderline	Instability of interpersonal relationships and impulsivity	1.6–5.9%
Histrionic	Excessive emotionality and attention seeking	1.8%
Narcissistic	Grandiosity, need for admiration, and lack of empathy	6.2%
Cluster C	**Anxious or fearful disorders**	**6%**
Avoidant	Social inhibition, feelings of inadequacy and hypersensitivity to negative evaluation	2.4–5.2%
Dependent	Need to be taken care of, clinging behaviors, and fear of separation	0.49–0.6%
Obsessive-compulsive	Preoccupation with orderliness, perfectionism, and control at the expense of flexibility, openness, and efficiency	2.1–7.9%

Sources: Prevalence based on American Psychiatric Association. (2022). *Diagnostic and statistical manual of mental disorders* (5th ed., text rev.); Lenzenweger, M., Lane, M., Loranger, A., & Kessler, R. (2007). *DSM-IV* personality disorders in the National Comorbidity Survey Replication. *Biological Psychiatry, 62,* 553–564.

The third cluster is referred to as Cluster C and covers *anxious or fearful disorders.* These include *avoidant personality disorder, dependent personality disorder*, and *obsessive-compulsive personality disorder.* Avoidant personality disorder is characterized by a pattern of social inhibition, feelings of inadequacy, and hypersensitivity to negative evaluation. Dependent personality disorder is characterized by an excessive need to be taken care of, and it includes clinging behavior. Obsessive-compulsive personality disorder is characterized by a preoccupation with orderliness, perfectionism, and interpersonal control.

Prevalence of Personality Disorders

In a number of community samples, personality disorders have been found in 9% to 13% of the population (Lawton et al., 2011; Lenzenweger, 2008; Tyrer et al., 2015). This suggests that 1 in every 10 people suffers from a personality disorder. Overall, similar numbers of men and women are seen in each personality disorder. The only exception is antisocial personality disorder, which is seen more frequently in men. In terms of the three clusters, Cluster A shows a prevalence of 5.7%, Cluster B shows a prevalence of 1.5%, and Cluster C shows a prevalence of 6% in a community sample (Lenzenweger et al., 2007), although prevalence rates vary by a few percent in different studies. Estimates from World Health Organization (WHO) surveys of 13 countries suggest a worldwide prevalence of around 6.1% for having any one personality disorder and 3.6% for Cluster A, 1.5% for Cluster B, and 2.7% for Cluster C (Huang et al., 2009). The prevalence of personality disorders worldwide is discussed in the *Cultural LENS: Global Mental Health: Personality Disorders.*

It was long believed that personality disorders were highly resistant to change and difficult to treat effectively. One characteristic of personality disorders is the stable occurrence of the personality structure. This would lead one to expect only minor changes in the expression of these disorders over the life span. However, current research findings suggest that personality disorders may be more plastic than previously expected, which makes treatment important (Newton-Howes et al., 2015; Onken & Nielsen, 2019; Roberts et al., 2017). A number of recent studies have followed individuals with personality disorders over the life span. Initially, there is stability of personality pathology in adolescence (van den Akker et al., 2015). Further, aspects of personality pathologies remain stable until one's 20s or 30s and then decrease over the life span. One exception to this is the schizoid personality disorder, which increases with age. Figure 14.1 displays changes in diagnostic criteria for personality disorders for different age groups (Gutiérrez et al., 2012). As you can see, there is a decrease in the number of criteria met over time, except for schizoid personality disorder.

FIGURE 14.1 ■ Changes in Personality Disorder Symptoms Over the Life Span

As can be seen in the figure, individuals as they age meet fewer criteria for being diagnosed with a personality disorder. The only exception is that of schizoid personality.

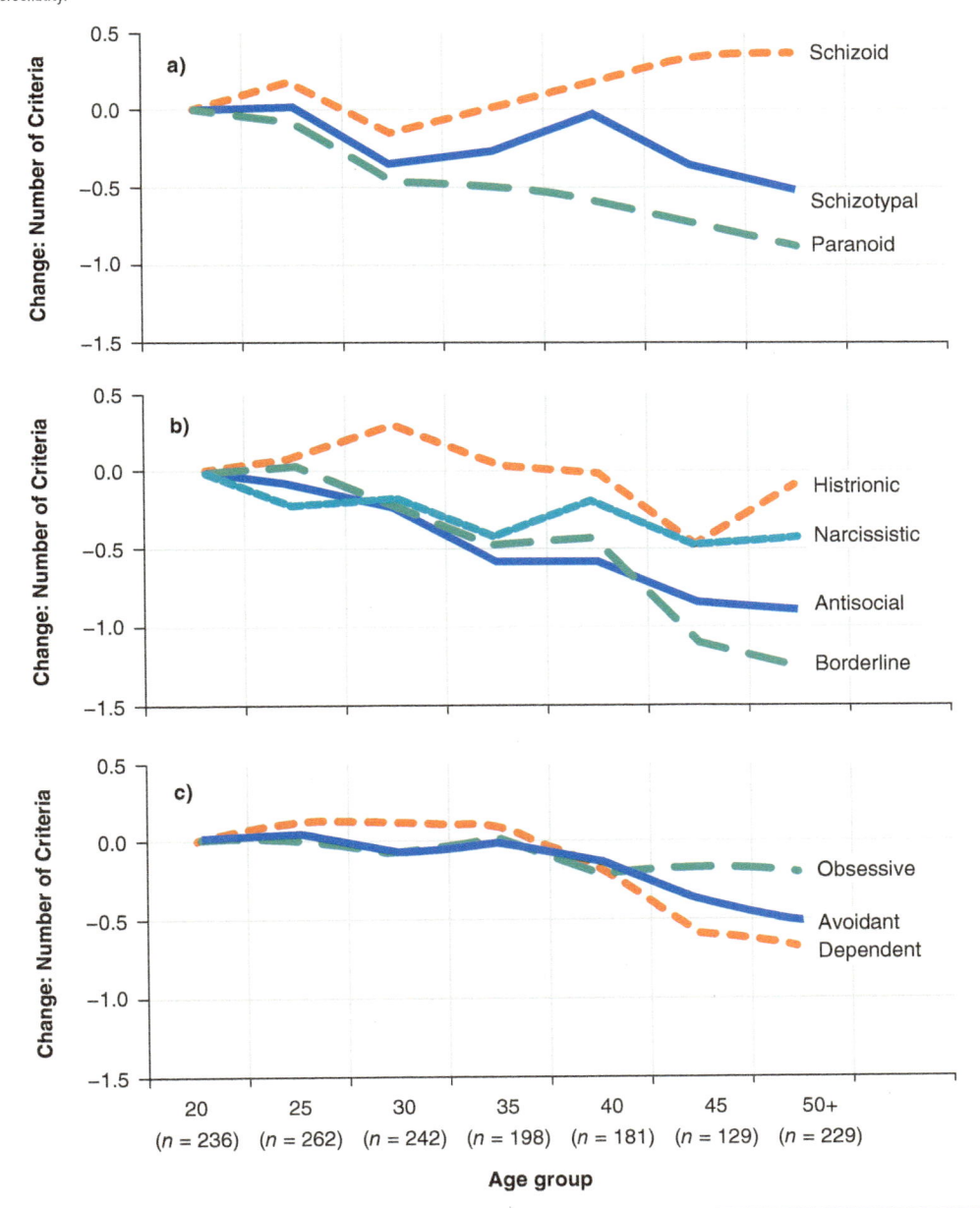

Source: Gutiérrez, F., Vall, G., Peri, J., Baillés, E., Ferraz, L., Gárriz, M., & Caseras, X. (2012). Personality disorder features through the life course. *Journal of Personality Disorders, 26*, 763–774.

CULTURAL LENS
GLOBAL MENTAL HEALTH: PERSONALITY DISORDERS

Until the beginning of this century, little was known about the prevalence of personality disorders worldwide. One complicating factor was that countries used different diagnostic approaches to determine the presence of personality disorders. In order to address this problem, the WHO surveyed individuals in 13 countries using the same screening questions based on *DSM-IV* (Huang et al., 2009; Kessler & Üstün, 2008). The screening included face-to-face interviews. In all, 21,162 individuals responded to the survey questions. Those who were screened were chosen to reflect the demographics of their particular country. The 13 countries were widely distributed and included both economically developed and developing countries, including one in Asia (China), two in Africa (Nigeria and South Africa), six in Europe (Belgium, France, Germany, Italy, the Netherlands, and Spain), one in the Middle East (Lebanon), and three in the Americas (Colombia, Mexico, and the United States).

Table 14.3 shows the prevalence of personality disorders by cluster. In addition to the data presented in the table, there were several other interesting findings related to the prevalence of personality disorders worldwide. First, more men than women were found in Cluster A and Cluster C. Second, all three clusters showed an inverse relationship with education. Third, over half of the individuals with a personality disorder also met criteria for an additional *DSM* disorder such as anxiety, mood, substance use, or externalizing disorders. Those areas with the highest socioeconomic status (SES) showed the greatest percentage of respondents in treatment, including United States at 37.3%, the countries of Western Europe collectively at 21.6%, and South Africa at 19.9%. The countries with the lowest percentage of respondents in treatment were Nigeria (6%), China (6.6%), and Lebanon (7.8%).

TABLE 14.3 ■ Prevalence of Personality Disorders Worldwide

	Cluster A % (SE)	Cluster B % (SE)	Cluster C % (SE)	Any Personality Disorder, % (SE)	n
Colombia	5.3 (0.6)	2.1 (0.4)	3.6 (0.5)	7.9 (1.1)	2381
Lebanon	4.2 (1.7)	1.7 (0.9)	2.9 (0.8)	6.2 (1.7)	10.31
Mexico	4.6 (0.7)	1.6 (0.4)	2.4 (0.5)	6.1 (0.8)	2362
Nigeria	1.6 (0.5)	0.3 (0.2)	0.9 (0.3)	2.7 (0.7)	2143
People's Republic of China	3.1 (0.7)	1.3 (0.7)	1.4 (0.6)	4.1 (1.1)	1628
South Africa	3.4 (0.5)	1.5 (0.3)	2.5 (0.5)	6.8 (0.7)	4315
United States	4.0 (0.4)	2.0 (0.3)	4.2 (0.4)	7.6[b] (0.5)	5692
Western Europe[a]	1.1 (0.6)	0.4 (0.3)	1.2 (0.5)	2.4 (0.9)	1610
Total	3.6 (0.3)	1.5 (0.1)	2.7 (0.2)	6.1 (0.3)	21162

[a] Includes Belgium, France, Germany, Italy, and Spain.

[b] This prevalence estimate differs from the estimate reported in a previous study based on U.S. data owing to the use of an improved imputation equation in the current analysis.

IPDE, International Personality Disorder Examination; WMH, World Mental Health.

Credit: Huang, Y., Kotov, R., de Girolamo, G., Preti, A., Angermeyer, M., Benjet, C., Demyttenaere, K., de Graaf, R., Gureje, O., Karam, A., Lee, S., Lépine, J. P., Matschinger, H., Posada-Villa, J., Suliman, S., Vilagut, G., & Kessler, R. (2009). DSM-IV personality disorders in the WHO World Mental Health Surveys. *British Journal of Psychiatry, 195,* 46–53.

Thought Question

What follow-up research questions would you want to study after reviewing the data in this table or in the related findings presented here?

Comorbidity of Personality Disorders

A number of studies have shown that those with a personality disorder also meet criteria for other disorders—especially anxiety, mood, and substance use disorders (Lenzenweger et al., 2007; Links & Eynan, 2013; Welander-Vatn et al., 2016). These comorbidities are seen in both clinic-based studies and large-scale studies of the general population. There is also a high comorbidity between bipolar disorder and borderline personality disorder (Frías et al., 2016; Henriques-Calado et al., 2021; Parker et al., 2022). This comorbidity is seen more often in community samples (Parker et al., 2022).

Lenzenweger and his colleagues (2007) used data from the National Comorbidity Survey Replication, which is a nationally representative, face-to-face household survey of 9,282 adults (ages 18 and older) in the continental United States. What these researchers did was compute the percentage of individuals with a personality disorder who also met criteria for an anxiety disorder, mood disorder, impulse control disorder, or substance use disorder. These percentages are shown in Table 14.4.

TABLE 14.4 ■ Percentage of Individuals With a Personality Disorder Who Also Meet Criteria for an Anxiety, Mood, Impulse Control, or Substance Use Disorder

	Personality Disorder					
	Cluster A	Antisocial	Borderline	Any Cluster B	Cluster C	Any PD
Anxiety						
General anxiety disorder	8.1%	20.2%	20.3%	22.0%	11.%	15.2%
Specific phobia	14.1%	12.5%	30.3%	26.7%	21.1%	23.4%
Social phobia	11.4%	19.5%	28.4%	26.4%	22.8%	26.3%
Panic disorder	5.5%	15.9%	16.8%	14.4%	7.3%	10.0%
Adult separation anxiety disorder	4.3%	13.0%	12.4%	15.9%	5.4%	8.9%
PTSD	7.9%	19.1%	17.0%	19.6%	10.0%	14.1%
Any anxiety	31.0%	47.5%	60.5%	61.4%	41.4%	52.4%
Mood						
Major depressive disorder	7.2%	9.1%	16.1%	13.1%	9.1%	13.4%
Dysthymia	5.3%	18.4%	19.0%	20.8%	8.1%	10.8%
Bipolar I or II	3.4%	15.1%	15.5%	14.5	5.3%	8.1%
Any mood disorder	12.4%	27.7%	34.3%	33.0%	16.8%	24.1%
Impulse control						
Intermittent explosive disorder	10.1%	34.2%	38.0%	35.0%	9.4%	15.9%
Attention deficit disorder	5.2%	22.4%	21.5%	21.5%	7.0%	11.0%

(Continued)

TABLE 14.4	Percentage of Individuals With a Personality Disorder Who Also Meet Criteria for an Anxiety, Mood, Impulse Control, or Substance Use Disorder (*Continued*)					
	Personality Disorder					
	Cluster A	**Antisocial**	**Borderline**	**Any Cluster B**	**Cluster C**	**Any PD**
Any impulse control disorder	13.5%	41.4%	49.0%	45.1%	13.7%	23.2%
Substance						
Alcohol abuse or dependence	5.8%	23.9%	27.0%	26.7%	5.4%	10.9%
Drug abuse or dependence	2.3%	13.6%	11.1%	12.9%	2.7%	5.6%
Tobacco dependence	6.2%	21.0%	13.7%	15.5%	6.8%	11.8%
Any substance use disorder	11.9%	40.5%	38.2%	39.9%	12.4%	22.6%

Credit: Lenzenweger, M., Lane, M., Loranger, A., & Kessler, R. (2007). *DSM-IV* personality disorders in the National Comorbidity Survey Replication. *Biological Psychiatry, 62*, 553–564, with permission from Elsevier.

They also looked at the opposite relationship. That is, they looked at individuals who met criteria for an anxiety disorder, mood disorder, impulse control disorder, or substance use disorder to see if they also met criteria for a personality disorder. Although these data are not shown in the table, there tends to be a greater number of individuals with a personality disorder who qualify for another disorder than the other way around. For example, individuals with a personality disorder are more likely to also have an anxiety disorder than individuals with an anxiety disorder are to also have a personality disorder.

Not only do individuals with a personality disorder often meet criteria for non-personality disorders, but they also often meet criteria for other personality disorders (Lenzenweger et al., 2007). Overall, the highest co-occurrence of personality disorders is seen within each of the clusters. That is, someone with one Cluster A disorder is more likely to have another Cluster A disorder than a Cluster C disorder. The relationships between different personality disorders are shown in Table 14.5. Throughout the chapter, we will discuss some of the implications of this comorbidity.

Environmental and Genetic Studies of Personality Disorders

A number of studies have shown that emotional abuse, sexual abuse, and neglect are related to the later development of personality disorders (Battle et al., 2004; Pereda et al., 2011). In the study by Cynthia Battle and her colleagues, the prior histories of 600 adults with a personality disorder were examined. In this sample, 73% of these individuals reported prior abuse and 82% reported childhood neglect. Childhood maltreatment was particularly common among individuals with borderline personality disorder (BPD). Thus, abuse and neglect reflect important contributions to the development of personality disorders.

Behavioral genetic research offers an opportunity to help clarify the role of genetics and the environment in personality and personality disorders (Livesley & Jang, 2008; Polderman et al., 2015). In general, heritability estimates for personality disorders are in the 40% to 60% range, suggesting that both genetic and environmental factors are involved. Except for BPD, the other personality disorders show more environmental than genetic factors in their development. However, there are inconsistent findings related to the heritability of personality disorders. For example, impulsivity shows a higher genetic component than does BPD itself. At this point, future research is needed to clarify the role of genetic contributions to the development of a personality disorder.

TABLE 14.5 ■ Correlations Between the Personality Disorders

	Cluster A			Cluster B		Cluster C		
	Paranoid	**Schizoid**	**Schizotypal**	**Antisocial**	**Borderline**	**Avoidant**	**Dependent**	**OCD**
Cluster A								
Paranoid								
Schizoid	.77[a]							
Schizotypal	.48	.96[a]						
Cluster B								
Antisocial	.73[a]	−.84[a]	.13	—				
Borderline	.76[a]	.56[a]	.34	.64[a]				
Cluster C								
Avoidant	.70[a]	.55[a]	.53[a]	.05	.54[a]			
Dependent	.20[a]	−.84[a]	−.86[a]	−.83[a]	.82[a]	.70[a]		
OCD	.59[a]	.40	.49	.45	.67[a]	.63[a]	.80[a]	

[a]Significant at the .05 level, two-sided test.

Credit: Lenzenweger, M., Lane, M., Loranger, A., & Kessler, R. (2007). DSM-IV personality disorders in the National Comorbidity Survey Replication. *Biological Psychiatry, 62*, 553–564, with permission from Elsevier.

Personality Disorders and Typical Personality Traits

Not only do the 10 separate personality disorders show considerable overlap with other mental disorders, but they also show considerable overlap with traits found in typical personality patterns (Costa & Widiger, 2002; Krueger & Markon, 2014; Samuel & Widiger, 2008; South et al., 2011). In one study, measures of typical and pathological personality functioning showed a shared dimensional structure (Samuel et al., 2010). That is, personality characteristics reflected in personality disorders can be seen as an extreme version of typical personality characteristics. These findings suggest the value of viewing personality characteristics from a variety of perspectives, including the *DSM-5-TR*, the five-factor model described next, the HiTOP model, and the NIMH RDoC model of psychopathology (Gore & Widiger, 2018). Initially, the studies concerning typical personality factors and personality disorders were conducted separately. Based on *DSM-5*, scales were constructed and analyzed in terms of the symptoms of personality disorder. Separate studies have found a five-factor structure of personality disorder characteristics (DeYoung et al., 2016). These five factors emphasize the opposite poles of typical personality dimensions, which will be discussed in the next section. These factors have been labeled *detachment, negative affectivity, antagonism, disinhibition,* and *psychoticism.* Detachment, for example, can be seen as the extreme and opposite version of extraversion.

It should also be noted that *DSM-5* and *DSM-5-TR* include an alternative model for personality disorders. The alternative model involves two determinations. First, personality disorders are characterized by impairments in personality functioning. That is, does an individual show problems in self-identity and self-direction as well as relationships with others in terms of empathy and intimacy? Second, does an individual show pathological personality traits? These traits include the five domains of *detachment, negative affectivity, antagonism, disinhibition,* and *psychoticism.* The *DSM-5* alternative model allows for an individual's functioning to be rated along a continuum with specific pathologic traits. This more dimensional model is currently being discussed in the literature and has generated much research (Krueger & Hobbs, 2020; Zimmermann et al., 2019).

Thus, there are both healthy and maladaptive personality styles. An individual can be extraverted in a healthy manner, seeking engagement with others and developing warm and meaningful relationships. They may also enjoy large parties and feel fulfilled by meeting new people. These same traits could manifest in a maladaptive manner, in which the individual has a need to always be with others and ties their self-worth to being in a relationship. An individual can also be introverted in a healthy way by valuing inner experiences such as writing poetry or enjoying walks alone or with another friend. One could also be introverted in a maladaptive manner by avoiding or distrusting others and living a life without meaningful contact with others. Figure 14.2 shows some of the maladaptive factors of introversion and extraversion.

The Characteristics of a Healthy Self

In order to understand personality disorders, one needs to consider what a healthy personality looks like. That is, what is a healthy self? One conceptualization suggested in *DSM-5* and *DSM-5-TR* is to consider the healthy self in terms of a self and an interpersonal functioning continuum. The first aspect of this continuum is identity. In terms of identity, the healthy individual sees oneself as a unique person with stable boundaries between oneself and others. The self would have a history that the person understands. The person would also have an accurate sense of who they are and what they can accomplish. This person also appreciates their own abilities.

Another aspect of the self is self-direction. Healthy self-direction reflects the ability to have both meaningful short-term and long-term goals consistent with one's identity. Self-direction also includes a sense of what would be productive for society and how to interact with others. Internally, healthy self-direction also includes the ability to reflect on one's life in a productive manner.

The healthy personality also suggests the ability to have positive interpersonal relationships. One aspect of this is *empathy*. This includes understanding how another person experiences their own life and what that person might want to accomplish. It also includes the ability to experience and accept

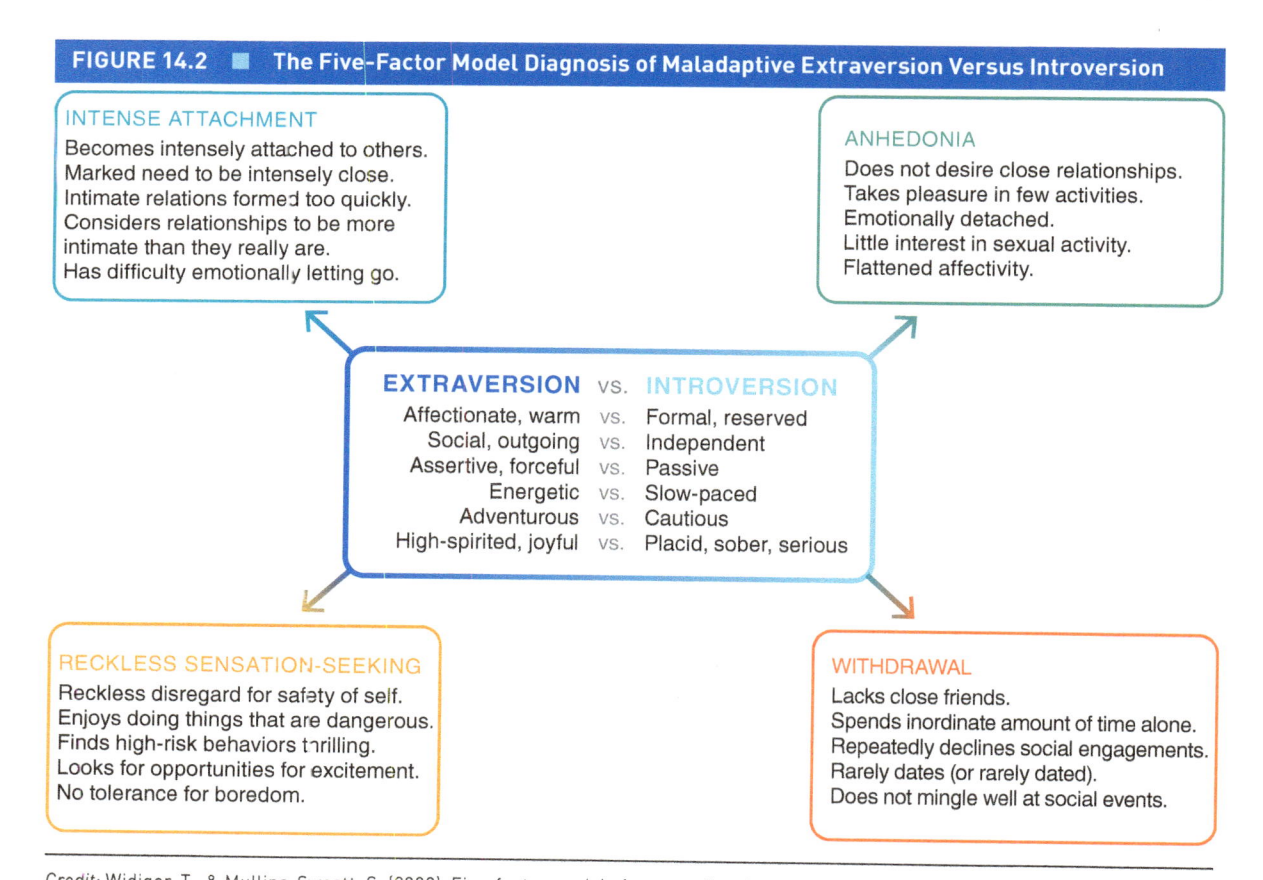

FIGURE 14.2 ■ The Five-Factor Model Diagnosis of Maladaptive Extraversion Versus Introversion

INTENSE ATTACHMENT
Becomes intensely attached to others.
Marked need to be intensely close.
Intimate relations formed too quickly.
Considers relationships to be more intimate than they really are.
Has difficulty emotionally letting go.

ANHEDONIA
Does not desire close relationships.
Takes pleasure in few activities.
Emotionally detached.
Little interest in sexual activity.
Flattened affectivity.

EXTRAVERSION vs. **INTROVERSION**
Affectionate, warm vs. Formal, reserved
Social, outgoing vs. Independent
Assertive, forceful vs. Passive
Energetic vs. Slow-paced
Adventurous vs. Cautious
High-spirited, joyful vs. Placid, sober, serious

RECKLESS SENSATION-SEEKING
Reckless disregard for safety of self.
Enjoys doing things that are dangerous.
Finds high-risk behaviors thrilling.
Looks for opportunities for excitement.
No tolerance for boredom.

WITHDRAWAL
Lacks close friends.
Spends inordinate amount of time alone.
Repeatedly declines social engagements.
Rarely dates (or rarely dated).
Does not mingle well at social events.

Credit: Widiger, T., & Mullins-Sweatt, S. (2009). Five-factor model of personality disorder: A proposal for *DSM-V. Annual Review of Clinical Psychology, 5*, 197–220. Reprinted with permission from *Annual Reviews.*

The healthy personality values closeness and seeks it when appropriate.
iStock.com/whitebalance.oatt

different perspectives toward life and goals and the ability to understand how one's own behavior may influence others. In healthy relationships, **intimacy** is also critical. Intimacy involves having a relationship with another person that includes mutual connectedness and a valuing of the other person. The healthy personality values closeness and seeks it when appropriate.

Thus, a person can develop a stable self that has an identity and has the ability for self-direction and the fulfillment of goals. This person can also have positive interpersonal relationships in which they relate to others in an intimate and empathetic manner. This person we would describe as healthy.

Not having a stable self or the ability to have intimate and empathetic relationships with others is a significant part of a personality disorder (Kernberg, 1984). One consideration for future versions of *DSM* is whether it may make sense to place personality disorders on a continuum in terms of the person's disturbance of self and others as just described (Bender et al., 2011). That is, the person's level of identity, self-direction, empathy, and intimacy, could be rated on 5-point scales. This would more clearly reflect those areas in which there are fundamental personality disturbances.

Another way to consider relationships between the individual and others is from an evolutionary perspective: Personality disorders can be viewed as a failure to solve adaptive life tasks relating to identity or self, intimacy and attachment, and prosocial behavior (Livesley, 2007; Millon & Strack, 2015). From this perspective, it has been the evolutionary task of a human to perform on three levels. The first is the individual level and the development of a self. The second is the interpersonal level, which reflects attachment processes. The third is the group level and involves prosocial behavior, altruism, and the cooperation needed for the functioning of society.

Typical Personality Traits

In the early 20th century, most psychologists who discussed personality used a theoretical perspective that emphasized the descriptive nature of specific traits. Outgoing individuals were described in terms of extraversion, for example. Those who frequently took risks in activities such as skydiving were referred to as sensation seekers. The problem was that there were far too many personality terms to describe a person's behavior and experiences. This made it difficult to create a coherent theory of personality. Mathematical techniques that compared the similarity of responses between the different measures offered an alternative to this descriptive approach.

Such a psychometric approach was directed by Robert McCrae and Paul Costa (1987; see also McCrae, Gaines, & Wellington, 2013). Their factor analytic approach to personality, referred to as the **five-factor model (FFM)**, suggested five major personality dimensions: *extraversion, neuroticism, openness, agreeableness,* and *conscientiousness*.

Extraversion is associated with sociability, cheerfulness, energy, and a sense of fun. This dimension ranges from being passive, quiet, and inner-directed to being active, talkative, and outer-directed. **Neuroticism** is associated with a tendency to express distressing emotions and difficulty experiencing stressful situations. This dimension ranges from being calm, even-tempered, and comfortable to being worried, temperamental, and self-conscious. **Openness** as a personality trait is associated with curiosity, flexibility, and an artistic sensitivity, including imaginativeness and the ability to create a fantasy world. This dimension ranges from inventive and curious to cautious and conservative. **Agreeableness** is associated with being sympathetic, trusting, cooperative, modest, and straightforward. This dimension ranges from being friendly and compassionate to being competitive and outspoken. **Conscientiousness** as a personality trait is associated with being diligent, disciplined, well-organized, punctual, and dependable. This dimension ranges from being efficient and organized to being easygoing and careless. These five dimensions are shown in Table 14.6.

Solid research on the FFM has also demonstrated that there is a consistency of results across a variety of cultures (McCrae, 2009). However, there are changes across the life span (Costa, McCrae, & Löckenhoff, 2019). In one study, McCrae and colleagues (1999) gave personality measures to individuals in five countries. In all of the cultures studied, they found some changes in the levels of the five factors over the life span. Overall, life span data suggest that from age 18 to 30, individuals show declines in neuroticism, extraversion, and openness to experience and increases in agreeableness and conscientiousness. McCrae and Costa (1996, 1999) suggested that the five factors of personality should be considered as biologically based tendencies as opposed to culturally conditioned characteristic adaptations. Genetic research has supported this perspective.

Evolution and Different Personality Characteristics

Nettle (2006) examined the FFM in relation to an evolutionary perspective. He suggested that each of the dimensions has a particular advantage given certain environmental conditions. Extraversion, for example, is associated with success in mating, having social allies, and exploring the environment. Neuroticism, on the other hand, is associated with greater vigilance and labeling situations as dangerous. In times of little stress, extraversion would be a successful strategy. However, in dangerous times, it may not afford the necessary caution that would be found with neuroticism. Nettle's summary of the costs and benefits of each of the five-factor dimensions is presented in Table 14.7.

TABLE 14.6   Five-Factor Model

Factor	Low Scorers	High Scorers
Extraversion (positive emotionality)	Passive Quiet Inwardly directed	Active Talkative Outwardly directed
Neuroticism (negative emotionality)	Calm Even-tempered Comfortable	Worried Temperamental Self-conscious
Openness	Not curious Less flexibility Down-to-earth	Curious Flexible Imaginative
Agreeableness	Suspicious Aggressive Antagonistic	Trusting Sympathetic Cooperative
Conscientiousness	Less dependable Undisciplined Disorganized	Dependable Disciplined Well-organized

Credit: Widiger, T., & Mullins-Sweatt, S. (2009). Five-factor model of personality disorder: A proposal for *DSM-V*. *Annual Review of Clinical Psychology, 5*, 197–220. Reprinted with permission from *Annual Reviews*.

Extraversion is associated with sociability, cheerfulness, energy, and a sense of fun.
iStock.com/wundervisuals

TABLE 14.7 ■ **Summary of Hypothesized Fitness Benefits and Costs of Increasing Levels of Each of the Five-Factor Personality Dimensions**

Domain	Benefits	Costs
Extraversion	Mating success; social allies; exploration of environment	Physical risks; family stability
Neuroticism	Vigilance to dangers; striving and competitiveness	Stress and depression, with interpersonal and health consequences
Openness	Creativity, with effect on attractiveness	Unusual beliefs; psychosis
Conscientiousness	Attention to long-term fitness benefits; life expectancy and desirable social qualities	Missing of immediate fitness gains; obsessionality; rigidity
Agreeableness	Attention to mental states of others; harmonious interpersonal relationships; valued coalitional partner	Subject to social cheating; failure to maximize selfish advantage

Credit: Nettle, D. (2006). The evolution of personality variation in humans and other animals. *American Psychologist, 61,* 622–631.

Maladaptive Personality Traits and Personality Disorders

As *DSM-5* was being developed, many studies were addressing the question of how the personality dimensions of the FFM could be related to the personality disorder categories of the *DSM* (Bagby & Widiger, 2018; Widiger & Mullins-Sweatt, 2009). The simple answer is that the three clusters representing 10 types of personality disorders can be understood as maladaptive variants of the FFM. Using data from clinicians and researchers, Table 14.8 shows the relationship between different facets of each of the five factors and the 10 personality disorders described in the *DSM*. An H in the table means that this personality trait would be high for that particular personality disorder. An L means low occurrence. For example, individuals with antisocial personality disorder show high scores in the facets of extraversion and low scores in the facets of agreeableness and conscientiousness.

TABLE 14.8	*DSM* Personality Disorders From the Perspective of the Five-Factor Model									
	PRN	SZD	SZT	ATS	BDL	HST	NCS	AVD	DPD	OCP
Neuroticism (vs. emotional stability)										
Anxiousness (vs. unconcerned)			H	L	H			H	H	H
Angry hostility (vs. dispassionate)	H			H	H		H			
Depressiveness (vs. optimistic)					H					
Self-consciousness (vs. shameless)			H	L	H	L	L	H	H	
Impulsivity (vs. restrained)				H	H	H				L
Vulnerability (vs. fearless)				L	H			H	H	
Extraversion (vs. introversion)										
Warmth (vs. coldness)	L	L	L					L		H
Gregariousness (vs. withdrawal)	L	L	L	H		H		L		
Assertiveness (vs. submissiveness)				H			H	L	L	
Activity (vs. passivity)		L		H		H				
Excitement seeking (vs. dullness)		L		H		H	H	L		L
Positive emotionality (vs. anhedonia)		L	L			H				
Openness (vs. closedness)										
Fantasy (vs. concrete)						H				
Aesthetics (vs. disinterest)										
Feelings (vs. alexithymia)		L			H	H	L			L
Actions (vs. routine)	L	L		H	H	H	H	L		L
Ideas (vs. closed-minded)			H							L
Values (vs. dogmatic)	L									L
Agreeableness (vs. antagonism)										
Trust (vs. mistrust)	L		L	L	L	H	L		H	
Straightforwardness (vs. deception)	L			L			L			
Altruism (vs. exploitation)				L			L			

	PRN	SZD	SZT	ATS	BDL	HST	NCS	AVD	DPD	OCP
Compliance (vs. opposition, aggression)	L			L	L		L		H	
Modesty (vs. arrogance)				L			L	H	H	
Tender-mindedness (vs. tough-mindedness)	L			L			L			
Conscientiousness (vs. disinhibition)										
Competence (vs. ineptitude)									L	H
Order (vs. disordered)			L							H
Dutifulness (vs. irresponsibility)				L						H
Achievement striving (vs. lackadaisical)										H
Self-discipline (vs. negligence)				L	L					H
Deliberation (vs. rashness)				L	L	L				H

Credit: Costa, P. T., & Widiger, T. (Eds.). (2002). *Personality disorders and the five-factor model of personality* (2nd ed.). American Psychological Association.

Note: PRN, paranoid; SZD, schizoid; SZT, schizotypal; ATS, antisocial; BDL, borderline; HST, histrionic; NCS, narcissistic; AVD, avoidant; DPD, dependent; OCP, obsessive-compulsive; H, high; L, low.

Categories and Dimensions

One complex aspect of understanding personality disorders is that they are described in terms of 10 categories, and the FFM is related to five dimensions. That is to say, a person can score along a continuum in terms of a personality trait such as extraversion. However, a person is either diagnosed with one of the personality disorders or not. Currently, for the 10 personality disorders, there are 79 descriptive criteria. A continuum approach would simplify this.

Some have suggested that there would be advantages to considering personality disorders along a spectrum as is the case with autism spectrum disorder. This would allow for a mapping of personality disorders and personality traits in the FFM. Since each dimension of the FFM has been shown to have a genetic component and these five dimensions are found worldwide, a spectrum approach would help clarify this aspect of personality disorders.

CONCEPT CHECK

- What is a personality disorder?
- Individuals with a personality disorder are more prone to meet the diagnostic criteria of what other types of psychological disorders?
- What are the characteristics of a healthy self? Why is it important to understand the concept of the healthy self when considering personality disorders?
- What are the five dimensions that describe typical personality traits in the FFM proposed by McCrae and Costa? What kinds of evidence support this model?
- What is the evolutionary advantage of different personality characteristics?

ODD, ECCENTRIC PERSONALITY DISORDERS

The three personality disorders included in the odd, eccentric personality disorders (Cluster A) grouping are paranoid personality disorder, schizoid personality disorder, and schizotypal personality disorder. The behavior of individuals with these disorders may seem similar to the behavior of individuals with schizophrenia, except that individuals with Cluster A disorders show a greater grasp of reality. These disorders are sometimes seen in first-degree relatives of those with schizophrenia. Each of the three odd, eccentric personality disorders shows a prevalence rate of about 1%. However, these rates may be 10 times higher in relatives of those with schizophrenia.

Paranoid Personality Disorder

Paranoid personality disorder is characterized by a pervasive distrust and suspiciousness of others (Bernstein & Useda, 2007). Individuals with this disorder might tell you how others are trying to exploit or deceive them. This may make them unwilling to confide in others. They may also focus much of their internal thoughts on the possible breaks in loyalty of their friends or significant others. Even if they were able to tell you about their concerns of loyalty or harm, you might find it difficult to understand how they reached the conclusions they did. These individuals could be correct in all the details that they recount concerning an interaction, and in fact they may be better observers than many people would be. However, they may draw unusual conclusions from normal interactions. You would have difficulty understanding, for instance, how a person with paranoid personality disorder goes from seeing a real event such as a smile or frown to the conclusion that their boss is about to fire them.

The interpersonal style of these individuals is often quarrelsome, stubborn, and rigid in their own beliefs. This can create a self-fulfilling prophecy in that if an individual acts coldly to another, the other person will misinterpret the individual's intentions. This leads to the other person breaking off the interaction. Although the individual with paranoid personality may interpret noise coming from a neighbor's apartment as an attempt to get back at them for something, the individual would not go so far as to suggest that the neighbor was working for the CIA and gathering information, as a person with schizophrenia might. Prevalence rates vary from 4.4% in the National Epidemiologic Survey on Alcohol and Related Conditions (Grant et al., 2004) to 2.3% in the National Comorbidity Survey Replication (Lenzenweger et al., 2007).

The diagnostic criteria in *DSM-5-TR* for paranoid personality disorder describe a person who is distrustful and suspicious of others such that the motives of others are seen as malevolent. To meet the diagnosis, this personality style should begin in early adulthood. At least four of the following specific characteristics should also be present: (1) believing that others are exploiting or deceiving the person, (2) having a preoccupation with unjustified doubts about the trustworthiness of a friend or colleague, (3) being reluctant to confide in others, (4) seeing simple statements as having hidden meanings, (5) bearing grudges, (6) seeing others as attacking the person's reputation, and (7) not trusting one's sexual partner as being faithful.

Schizoid Personality Disorder

Schizoid personality disorder is characterized by a pervasive pattern of detachment from social relationships and a restricted range of emotional expression (Mittal et al., 2007; Triebwasser et al., 2012). These individuals are traditional loners. Others see them as unavailable, aloof, or detached. The *DSM* has traditionally described these individuals as not desiring close relationships, lacking friends, and seeking solitary activities. Schizoid personality is one of the least studied disorders with very little empirical research. Prevalence rates vary from 3.1% in the National Epidemiologic Survey on Alcohol and Related Conditions (Grant et al., 2004) to 4.9% in the National Comorbidity Survey Replication (Lenzenweger et al., 2007).

The diagnostic criteria in *DSM-5-TR* for schizoid personality disorder describe a person who shows a pattern of detachment and a limited expression of emotions in social relationships. This personality style should begin in early adulthood. At least four of the following specific characteristics should also be present: (1) not desiring or enjoying social relationships, (2) mainly engaging in solitary activities, (3) showing little interest in sexual activities with others, (4) finding little pleasure in any activity, (5) having no close friends, (6) showing indifference to both praise and criticism, and (7) showing emotional coldness or detachment.

Schizotypal Personality Disorder

Schizotypal personality disorder is characterized by odd beliefs and behaviors (Bollini & Walker, 2007). An individual with schizotypal personality disorder may show excessive social anxiety as well as unusual ideas. This can include *magical thinking*, such as the person believing that thinking about an event can actually make it happen. Historically, it was noted that first-degree relatives of those with schizophrenia had odd behavioral propensities. Early behavioral genetic studies also noted that oddities in social behavior, perception, and ideation were found in relatives of those with schizophrenia (Gottesman, 1991).

Schizotypal personality disorder was first included in *DSM-III* in 1980. Currently, it is defined by odd behavior, cognitive distortions, and inappropriate affect. Although these behaviors, thoughts, and affects are similar to those seen in individuals with schizophrenia, the person with this disorder is not out of touch with reality. Unlike those with schizophrenia, although the person's speech may be odd or vague, you would still be able to understand it. Prevalence rates were found to be 3.3% in the National Comorbidity Survey Replication (Lenzenweger et al., 2007). The case study of Nathan James (not his real name) illustrates the manner in which others experience the person as odd. Initially, it was thought by mental health professionals that this person might have schizophrenia, but this was determined not to be the case.

CASE OF NATHAN JAMES
SCHIZOTYPAL PERSONALITY DISORDER

Nathan James is a 35-year-old single white male who has been in outpatient treatment since early childhood. He is currently in an outpatient clinic at a university medical center. He is now in his eighth year of treatment. Prior to the current treatment, he had been diagnosed with a range of disorders, including schizophrenia. However, he denied having hallucinations and delusions. He did, however, report that when he was younger, he claimed to be having hallucinations to avoid going to school. At present, he is living at home with his mother and is unemployed despite a high intelligence. Although he desires intimate relationships with women, he has never had this experience. He also has no long-term friends.

Mr. James has also never held a job for more than a few days before being fired. This includes volunteer work for which he was fired after a few days because he came across as odd. He would often say competitive and derogatory things toward others. He volunteered for a political campaign where he had many ideas that were different than those of the campaign. He told others that this low-level volunteer position was one of great responsibility. He has a hard time reading the emotions of others and thought at times others were jealous of him. He has little insight into how his behavior influences others. He is currently receiving disability for his mental illness.

Several years ago, he was reevaluated since there were questions concerning his diagnosis of schizophrenia. After the evaluation, it was determined he met criteria for schizotypal personality disorder and not schizophrenia. During treatment, he reported that he wanted to be working at a high-level job that was consistent with his intelligence. He interviewed for a number of high-level jobs. Many of these were beyond his level of training and degrees achieved. He became upset when he received feedback from employment interviewers that he was not qualified for a high-level position such as CEO of a major television company. He was an avid TV watcher and president of a fan club for a girl act, which he thought qualified him for understanding television production. He would dress for these interviews in unconventional clothing such as a cowboy hat although he lived in a major East Coast city. He would blame not getting the job on being late to the meeting and in turn blaming that on public transportation. He would then write letters to public officials complaining about the delay of public transit. He sees himself as a victim who is not involved in the events that happen to him.

> Following 3 years of therapy, he showed much progress. He moved from his mother's house to an apartment of his own. He was also able to obtain a job more consistent with his abilities. He became a good salesperson and was nominated for a management training program. He also met a woman, and they formed a positive relationship.
>
> *Clinical vignette provided by Kenneth Levy, PhD*

The diagnostic criteria in *DSM-5-TR* for schizotypal personality disorder describe a person who shows a pattern of discomfort in social relationships and a limited expression of emotions in social relationships. This personality style should begin in early adulthood. Five specific characteristics should also be present. These characteristics include that the person (1) makes connections between ideas that are not related to one another, (2) holds odd beliefs or engages in magical thinking such as a belief in telepathy, (3) experiences unusual perceptual experiences, (4) engages in odd thinking and speech, (5) is suspicious, (6) shows inappropriate affect, (7) appears odd to others, (8) does not have close friends, and (9) shows excessive social anxiety that does not lessen as the situation becomes more familiar.

Brain imaging studies show a similarity between those with schizotypal personality disorder and schizophrenia (Asami et al., 2013). Both show a reduction of gray matter in the brain. However, those with schizotypal personality disorder do not show more loss of gray matter volume with age as individuals with schizophrenia do. It can be noted that gray matter loss is seen in those areas that involve the default network, which is associated with internal tasks.

CONCEPT CHECK

- What are the primary defining characteristics of paranoid personality disorder? How do they create a self-fulfilling prophecy in maintaining the disorder?
- Schizoid personality is one of the least studied disorders with very little empirical research. What is it about the characteristics of this disorder that contributes to this?
- How are the behaviors, thoughts, and affect in an individual with schizotypal personality disorder similar to an individual with schizophrenia? How are they different?

DRAMATIC EMOTIONAL PERSONALITY DISORDERS

There are four personality disorders included in the dramatic emotional personality disorders (Cluster B) grouping: antisocial, borderline, histrionic, and narcissistic. The behavior of individuals with these disorders can be dramatic and impulsive. However, as you will see, there are also real differences between these four disorders.

Antisocial Personality Disorder and Psychopathy

Although the media interchange the terms *antisocial personality disorder* and *psychopathy*, there are differences in manner in which these terms have been used in research and *DSM-5-TR*. Although *DSM-5-TR* notes that antisocial personality disorder has also been referred to as psychopathy, sociopathy, and dyssocial personality disorder, the *DSM-5-TR* criteria for antisocial personality disorder emphasize the breaking of society's rules, including laws. A majority of individuals in prisons would qualify for this disorder. The *DSM-5-TR* criteria tend to focus on observable behaviors, whereas historical research studies have also noted internal processes of the person, such as their lack of feeling for others and lack of empathy.

It has been estimated that only about 10% to 25% of individuals with an antisocial personality disorder would be classified as having psychopathy. Further, not all individuals who would be described as having psychopathy would show conduct disorders early in their life or have found themselves in trouble with the law. Psychopathy is not a formal definition of *DSM-5-TR* but has been studied in both clinical and research settings for a number of years.

Antisocial Personality Disorder

The *DSM-5-TR* criteria for **antisocial personality disorder** begin with the individual being at least 18 years of age. The person would also meet the requirements for a *child conduct disorder* before the age of 15. As described in the chapter on developmental disorders, child conduct disorder includes aggression toward animals or people, destruction of property, deception or stealing, and serious rule violations. The diagnostic criteria in *DSM-5-TR* for antisocial personality disorder describe a person who shows a pattern of disregard for the rights of others, including such behaviors as repeated participation in illegal acts, deceitfulness, impulsiveness, hostility and aggression, engagement in dangerous acts, irresponsible behavior, and absence of remorse. Three of the following specific characteristics should also currently be present: (1) a failure to observe social norms, which can result in legal arrest; (2) a deceitfulness, including lying to and using others; (3) a failure to plan ahead; (4) an irritability and aggressiveness that lead to physical fights; (5) a reckless disregard for the safety of others; (6) an irresponsibility, such as a failure to pay debts or perform duties at work; and (7) a lack of remorse when another person is hurt.

Using *DSM* criteria, the prevalence rate for antisocial personality disorder is around 3%, with more men than women having the disorder. There is a high comorbidity of around 80% with substance use disorders (Patrick, 2007). However, the opposite is not the case. The prevalence of antisocial personality disorder also tends to be higher in correctional and forensic settings, where base rates have been recorded between 50% and 80% (Hare, 2003). Often, those who are mandated by the courts for treatment of sexual offenses would qualify for an antisocial personality disorder. The following case study describes Jim Nelson (not his real name), who was court mandated for treatment due to his involvement in child sexual abuse. This is a complex case, but Jim Nelson displays many of the characteristics seen in those with antisocial personality disorder.

CASE OF JIM NELSON
MANDATED TREATMENT FOR CHILD SEXUAL ABUSE

Jim is a 71-year-old employed white male who presented at the Rising Sun Center for Treatment of Sexual Offenders. He was court mandated into sexual offender treatment as a consequence of his conviction for incest and endangering the welfare of a child. This was related to charges of molesting his stepson when the victim was 12 years old. The client denies the current charges but says that prosecutors used a previous conviction of incest to coerce him into a plea bargain. Jim states that he did not have sexual contact with his stepson but admits to having engaged in sexual intercourse twice with his stepdaughter (Lisa) when she was 17 years old. The stepdaughter became pregnant and now has a daughter. The client states that the sexual activity was consensual and calls it "an affair." Jim remains married to and actively involved with his victims' mother, although because of a court order he cannot cohabitate with his wife.

The client's parole records state that he was charged with forcing his stepson to engage in oral and anal penetration as a discipline measure to make the boy comply with household rules. Jim denied any contact with his stepson and claims that the charges were brought by the victim's biological father as retaliation for Jim's sexual contact with his stepdaughter. The client reports that he had sexual intercourse with his stepdaughter on two occasions, including once when she was a minor and once when she was aged 18 years. Jim claims that the first sexual contact occurred because his stepdaughter took advantage of him when he was intoxicated and asleep in his bed. The client states that his stepdaughter initiated sexual intercourse, which resulted in a pregnancy.

Jim has a history of behavior that might be deemed as predatory. His current wife, the mother of his stepchildren, was best friends with Jim's daughter from an earlier marriage and is the same age as his daughter. The client said he would "help" the girl escape her chaotic family life and take her for outings with his family. Jim said that later, he helped the young woman "escape" an abusive marriage by relocating her to another state.

Jim claims to have never initiated sexual contact with anyone and that all of his partners have come to him for sex.

Clinical vignette provided by Clifford Evans, MEd, RN

Psychopathy

Individuals who display signs of **psychopathy** show emotional detachment with a lack of empathy for the experiences of others (Patrick, 2010, 2022). They also show impulsive behavior and a callousness concerning their actions. These patterns are stable and difficult to change. Although individuals with this condition take a real toll on society, many people are fascinated by these individuals. They are portrayed in such movies as *No Country for Old Men, The Shining*, and *The Silence of the Lambs*, although you don't need to be violent to be diagnosed as a psychopath. These are the classic "con men," who are able to manipulate others and get what they want. Often, the victims find the con man charming and may not even know they are being taken.

Historically, in the early 1800s, both Philippe Pinel in France and Benjamin Rush in America described individuals who experienced no shame or guilt in relation to their actions. In 1835, the British physician J. C. Pritchard used the term *moral insanity*. The basic idea was that these individuals had a deficit in moral reasoning, which led them to disregard normal senses of decency, fairness, and responsibility. In 1891, the German psychiatrist J. L. Koch introduced the term *psychopathic*, which was followed by Emil Kraepelin in 1904 using the term *psychopathic personality* in his textbook on psychiatry. In 1909, the German psychiatrist Karl Birnbaum offered the term *sociopathic* to suggest that the condition resulted from environmental factors. However, the terms *psychopathic* and *sociopathic* have been used interchangeably over the years.

In the 1940s, the American psychiatrist Hervey Cleckley published a major work on people with psychopathy, *The Mask of Sanity* (1941/1988). This was based on his work with a large number of patients at the VA hospital in Augusta, Georgia. One of his insights, as implied by the title of his book, was that beneath the appearance of being well adjusted and socially appealing, there exists severe pathology. Cleckley described these individuals in terms of 16 diagnostic criteria, which can be categorized in terms of three conceptual categories (Lilienfeld et al., 2018). The categories are positive adjustment, chronic behavioral deviance, and emotional-interpersonal deficits (Table 14.9).

Based on the descriptive characteristics of Cleckley, Robert Hare and his colleagues developed a checklist that serves as an assessment tool (Hare, 2003; Hare & Neumann, 2008). The checklist includes such items as glibness and superficial charm, grandiose sense of self-worth, pathological lying, lack of remorse, shallow affect, lack of empathy, need for stimulation, lack of long-term goals, poor behavioral control, and impulsivity. These can be divided into four facets, as shown in Table 14.10.

In a 2014 analysis published in the *Journal of Forensic Sciences*, researchers submitted 126 film characters to a panel of senior forensic psychologists and found Anton Chigurh from the Coen Brothers' film *No Country for Old Men* to be among the most "realistic idiopathic psychopathic characters" in film.

RGR Collection/Alamy Stock Photo

TABLE 14.9 ■ Cleckley's 16 Diagnostic Criteria for Psychopathy

Item Category	No.	Description
Positive adjustment	1.	Superficial charm and good "intelligence"
	2.	Absence of delusions and other signs of irrational thinking
	3.	Absence of "nervousness" or psychoneurotic manifestations
	14.	Suicide rarely carried out
Behavioral deviance	7.	Inadequately motivated antisocial behavior
	8.	Poor judgment and failure to learn by experience
	4.	Unreliability
	13.	Fantastic and uninviting behavior with drink and sometimes without
	15.	Sex life impersonal, trivial, and poorly integrated
	16.	Failure to follow any life plan
Emotional-interpersonal deficits	5.	Untruthfulness and insincerity
	6.	Lack of remorse or shame
	10.	General poverty in major affective reactions
	9.	Pathologic egocentricity and incapacity for love
	11.	Specific loss of insight
	12.	Unresponsiveness in general interpersonal relations

Credit: Patrick, C. J. (2006). Back to the future: Cleckley as a guide to the next generation of psychopathy research. In C. J. Patrick (Ed.), *Handbook of psychopathy* (pp. 605–617). Guilford Press.

TABLE 14.10 ■ Psychopathy Checklist—Revised

Factor 1: Interpersonal-Affective Scale		Factor 2: Antisocial Scale	
Facet 1 Interpersonal	**Facet 2 Affective**	**Facet 3 Lifestyle**	**Facet 4 Antisocial**
Glibness/superficial charm Grandiose sense of self-worth Pathological lying Conning/manipulative	Lack of remorse or guilt Shallow affect Callousness/lack of empathy Failure to accept responsibility for own actions	Need for stimulation/proneness to boredom Parasitic lifestyle Lack of realistic long-term goals Impulsivity Irresponsibility	Poor behavioral controls Early behavioral problems Juvenile delinquency Revocation of conditional release Criminal versatility

Credit: Hare Psychopathy Checklist-Revised: 2nd Edition™. Copyright © 2003, Multi-Health Systems Inc. All rights reserved.

Note: Two PCL-R items are not included in this factor structure: namely, promiscuous sexual behavior, many short-term marital relationships.

Psychopathy has often been described in terms of a deficit in emotional processing. Christopher Patrick and Edward Bernat (2009) have suggested that two factors, determined from factor analytic studies, better explain psychopathy. The first factor is *fearlessness*. This reflects an underreactivity of the brain's defensive motivational system. The second factor is *externalizing vulnerability*. This factor reflects impairments in the frontocortical system of the brain, the system involved in anticipation,

Ted Bundy was a famous psychopath.
Bettmann/Contributor/Bettmann/via Getty Images

planfulness, and affective/behavioral control. This model suggests there are two separate processes in the same individual. The first involves the lack of fear, and the second involves a weakness in impulse control. Further, it should be noted that the *DSM* descriptions of antisocial personality disorder do not include such characteristics as superficial charm, which were included in a previous description of psychopathy. Thus, research may show inconsistencies depending on the measures used.

Evolutionary perspectives suggest that there is an advantage in certain environmental conditions for an individual who is cunning, manipulative, and not considerate of the well-being of others. Such individuals would create resources for themselves and in certain situations would do well in business and politics. They would also be able to function well under conditions that would be extremely stressful for others. Such characteristics may be protective in terms of stress and anxiety disorders.

Brain Involvement in Psychopathy

Unlike many other psychological disorders in which the volume of specific brain structures is shown to be smaller, the research has shown the amygdala to be larger in people with psychopathy (Boccardi et al., 2011). Research also found larger white matter volumes in the parietal, occipital, and left cerebellar lobes. However, gray matter reductions have been observed in the frontopolar, orbitofrontal, and anterior temporal cortices, as well as the superior temporal sulcus region and insula (Oliveira-Souza et al., 2008). Other studies have also found reduced gray matter volume in relation to psychopathy, which may contribute to problems in decision making, emotional regulation, and moral judgments.

Reviews of current studies suggest two major brain areas are involved in both structural and functional approaches to the study of psychopathy (N. Anderson & Kiehl, 2011; Raine, 2018). The first area involves the frontal lobes, and the second involves temporal regions, including the hippocampus and the amygdala. It may not be that the structures are not functioning but rather that they are being used for processing tasks for different purposes. One study showed pictures of people in pain (e.g., slamming a door on one's finger) to those with psychopathy and control individuals (Decety et al., 2013). Participants in the psychopathy group exhibited significantly less activation in the ventromedial prefrontal cortex (vmPFC), lateral orbitofrontal cortex (OFC), and periaqueductal gray relative to controls. It is these areas that are seen to form the essential neural circuit of empathy (Decety & Svetlova, 2012).

There is some suggestion that psychopathy can be considered a result of neurodevelopmental abnormalities with a significant genetic component (Gao et al., 2009; Miskovich et al., 2018; Raine, 2018). Specifically, psychopathic behaviors can be associated with the lack of frontal lobe development at a critical time. This might allow for the development of intellectual abilities but limit the development of social and moral behavior. Also, structural differences between individuals with psychopathic behaviors and controls show differences in gyri or folds in the brain, which suggests that psychopathy results from a different pattern of brain development (Miskovich et al., 2018).

One intriguing study examined two adults who had prefrontal lesions before the age of a year and a half (S. Anderson et al., 1999). The first person was run over by a vehicle at 15 months of age. She recovered fully within days with no apparent abnormalities. However, at the age of 3, she was unresponsive to verbal or physical punishment. She became more disruptive and by the age of 14 was placed in a treatment facility. She was seen by her teachers to be intelligent, but she showed little moral development. She stole from others, lied to others, and was abusive. The second individual had a frontal lobe tumor at age 3 months. His recovery appeared to be normal, and he met typical developmental landmarks. By age 9, however, he showed a general lack of motivation. Although he graduated from high school, he would threaten others, lie often, and steal. He showed no guilt or remorse for his behavior. These case studies suggest that early dysfunction in the prefrontal cortex (PFC) is related to abnormal development of social and moral behavior.

CONCEPT CHECK

- What are the differences between antisocial personality and psychopathy? How are they related?
- What is the organizing model Cleckley introduced to help us understand the diagnostic criteria for psychopathy? How did Hare and colleagues change the model in developing an assessment tool?
- Psychopathy has often been described in terms of a deficit in emotional processing. What are the factors in the competing model that Patrick and colleagues developed?
- What evidence exists to support the idea that psychopathy is the result of neurodevelopmental abnormalities?

Borderline Personality Disorder

Borderline personality disorder (BPD) is characterized by an instability in mood, interpersonal relationships, and sense of self (Bohus et al., 2021; Bradley et al., 2007). These three factors interact with each other in such a manner that the person with BPD experiences a changing world without a solid sense of self. At one point, the person may feel rejected and abandoned due to a misinterpretation of an event and lash out in anger. At other times, they may see another person as perfect and form an intense relationship, only to have that go to its opposite without warning. The movie *Fatal Attraction* shows this type of intense relationship seen in people with BPD. The television show *Crazy Ex-Girlfriend* also features a character who shows signs of BPD.

In her book *Borderline Traits*, Arlene Roberson (2010) quotes a person describing life with BPD: "I go from feeling panicked and angry to feeling depressed and hurt to feeling anxious." It continues: "I have to react to this pain by lashing out at everything and everyone around me." This lashing out includes not only angry outbursts at others but also self-mutilating behaviors and suicide attempts. It is estimated that 75% of those with BPD engage in self-injurious behavior. Two common behaviors are to cut or burn themselves. Some say that the external pain from burning or cutting gives them an experience that they are alive compared with feeling that they do not exist. For those with BPD, feelings of emptiness and boredom are common, as are feelings of being special or having exceptional talents. An analysis of self-reported experiences found those high in BPD characteristics could be grouped in terms of loneliness, recklessness, and mood instability as compared to those who reported fewer BPD characteristics (Southward & Cheavens, 2018). Table 14.11 shows some of the common functions of self-injurious behavior as reported by inpatient women.

TABLE 14.11	Functions of Self-Injurious Behavior	
Feel pain		60%
Punish self		50%
Control feelings		40%
Exert control		22%
Express anger		22%
Feel		20%

Source: Shearer, S., Peters, C., Quaytman, S., & Wadman, B. (1988). Intent and lethality of suicide attempts among female borderline inpatients. *American Journal of Psychiatry, 145*, 1424–1427.

Self-harm is closely related to attempts to regulate one's emotions. That is, self-harm may interrupt the intense feeling of distress reported by those with BPD. One review of the literature suggests three aspects of this relationship (Klonsky, 2007). The first aspect is that acute negative affect precedes self-injury. The second aspect is that after self-injury, individuals report relief. The third aspect is that individuals engage in self-injury as a means to reduce their experience of negative affect. Although many studies involve self-report, similar findings were seen in research studies performed in the lab.

Self-harm is different from suicide, but a suicide attempt resulting in death is estimated to be about 9% in clinical samples of those with BPD. Also, suicide threats or gestures are estimated to occur in 90% of clinical samples (Gunderson & Ridolfi, 2001).

For those with BPD, their view of self and others is sometimes described in terms of *splitting* or having things be all good or all bad without the nuance most individuals experience in their relationships. Thus, people with BPD have a sense of self that is fluid and can change quickly.

The conceptualization of BPD has been greatly influenced by the work of Kernberg (1984, 1995), who viewed these individuals as using immature ways of dealing with impulses and emotions. Historically, the term *borderline*, as the name implies, denoted individuals who were neither neurotic nor psychotic. Although not out of touch with reality, when under stress, these individuals can become disorganized in their view of self and others. On the other hand, their experiences go beyond those seen in anxiety or depression where the tendency is to withdraw when experiencing psychological distress.

One term that has been used to describe individuals with BPD is *fearful preoccupation* (Levy, 2005). This reflects an intense need for attention and closeness on the one hand and a deep fear of rejection and abandonment on the other. Thus, these individuals want to be close but become fearful and then angry when they experience closeness. Anger is also seen whenever individuals perceive they are being rejected. These characteristics can be seen in the case of Amy James (not her real name).

CASE OF AMY JAMES
BORDERLINE PERSONALITY DISORDER

Amy James is in her mid-20s. Amy has a history of multiple violent suicide attempts dating back to early adolescence. She reported that over time her suicide attempts have become more serious and aggressive. She describes her suicide attempts as more of a tantrum than a desire to die. She first entered therapy as a child for what she describes as an "unhappy childhood" and for being a "weird kid." However, it was not until she was 22 years old that she was first diagnosed with BPD.

She is the only child in a family that was chaotic and had unclear relationships with each other. This was partly because of a major traumatic accident that occurred before her birth. She had a brother who was killed due to injuries sustained when a car hit him. Amy's mother developed a chronic illness and depended on her for emotional and physical caretaking. Her father, a research scientist, was an alcoholic who was alternatively cruel, seductive, and pathetic. The parents frequently separated and reunited during Amy's childhood, and both eroticized their relationship with her by engaging in a number of overt and covert sexualized interactions. In addition, she recollects various bizarre and traumatic incidents from her childhood, including witnessing her father drowning her pets.

Amy James is currently married and has no children. Amy describes being very unsatisfied in her relationship with her husband, whom she perceives as inept, unhelpful, or overly intrusive and irrelevant but whom she had frequent fantasies of being saved by. She has numerous affairs and would frequently torture her husband by telling him the details of the relationships. She states that she "did my best to ruin my marriage." One night, she even made a pass at her husband's brother, whom she dated before her husband.

Amy is very intelligent and college educated but not working in her chosen field. At the time she entered therapy, she was underemployed working as a clerk. She did not enjoy her work, feeling that it was uninteresting. She calls in sick frequently and sometimes fails to show up for work due to overdoses. She describes the overdoses as a way of getting out of working while attempting to garner sympathy from her coworkers. However, because of these difficulties she is frequently fired from these jobs, despite the fact that they are relatively low-stress and low-level jobs.

Her prior psychotherapies all have a similar pattern. First, she would find the therapist helpful and begin to depend more on him or her. Then, her dependency would put pressure on the therapist to be increasingly available. Nevertheless, there would always come a moment when she felt let down by the therapist and engaged in non-suicidal, self-injurious behaviors, some of which were very serious. During her current therapy, she also showed suicidal attempts—some resulting in hospitalization. After a year of treatment, she became more committed to her marriage and obtained a job consistent with her college degree. At the 3-year follow-up, she reported career success and giving birth to a child.

Clinical vignette provided by Kenneth Levy, PhD

Source: Adapted from Levy, K. N., Yeomans, F. E., & Diamond, D. (2007). Psychodynamic treatments of self-injury. *Journal of Clinical Psychology, 63*(11), 1105–1120.

Although genetic factors may play a role in terms of the trait of impulsivity, environmental factors also play an important role. Around 70% of individuals with BPD report some type of physical, emotional, or sexual abuse. Overall, there is evidence to suggest that the development of BPD is related to heightened risk from chaotic family life, increased stress experienced by the parents, and disruptive communications between the caregiver and the child.

The disorder is also related to attachment (Levy, 2005). In general, individuals with BPD present with an insecure pattern of attachment. Only some 6% to 8% show secure attachment patterns. Studies that used dimensional measures of BPD indicate an inverse relationship between secure attachment and BPD. Further, studies that have looked at early loss or separation in children found that it occurred in 37% to 64% of individuals with BPD. Additional research has examined the role of early maltreatment and how this affects attachment relationships and symptoms of borderline personality disorder differently in males and females (Godbout et al., 2019). In females, both maternal and paternal maltreatment were associated with borderline symptoms, whereas with males, only paternal maltreatment was associated with borderline symptoms.

The diagnostic criteria in *DSM-5-TR* for BPD describe a person who shows a pattern of impulsivity in social relationships and an unstable self-image. This personality disorder begins in early adulthood. For a diagnosis of BPD, five of the following specific characteristics should also be present: (1) a frantic effort to avoid abandonment, whether real or imagined; (2) a pattern of unstable and intense interpersonal relationships characterized by alternating idealization and devaluation; (3) an unstable self-image and sense of self; (4) impulsivity in areas that can be damaging such as sexual relations, substance abuse, reckless driving, and binge eating; (5) recurrent suicidal or self-mutilating behaviors; (6) emotional instability lasting only a few hours; (7) chronic feelings of emptiness; (8) inappropriate anger and inability to control anger; and (9) short-term, stress-related dissociative experiences or paranoid ideation. Given the nine current *DSM-5-TR* criteria for BPD, there are at least 150 different ways that a person can receive the diagnosis based on various combinations of the criteria. This suggests that the instability of the self and its functioning can be manifested in a number of ways.

Actor and comedian Pete Davidson has been open about his diagnosis of borderline personality disorder.
Album/Alamy Stock Photo

One way the instability manifests for society is that individuals with BPD are high consumers of emergency room services, crisis lines, and referrals from health professionals to mental health services (Bradley et al., 2007). It is estimated that individuals with BPD represent 20% of inpatients and 10% of outpatients in mental health clinics. Prevalence rates in community samples are around 1.6% as found in the National Comorbidity Survey Replication (Lenzenweger et al., 2007).

Comparing individuals with major depressive disorder (MDD) and BPD over a 10-year period, it was found that 85% of the individuals with BPD showed a reduction in their symptoms (Gunderson et al., 2011). However, they also found persistent impairment in social relationships. This study and Grilo et al. (2004) found that those with MDD showed a reduction in symptoms earlier than those with personality disorders.

Brain Studies of Those With Borderline Personality Disorder

Studies looking at both structural and functional aspects of the brain have shown differences in those with BPD. Structurally, individuals with BPD have less volume in a number of brain areas (Soloff et al., 2012). The regions with reductions include the insula, the middle and superior temporal cortex (Mid-Sup T), the fusiform gyrus (FG), the anterior cingulate cortex (ACC), the hippocampus and the parahippocampus, and the amygdala (Amyg) (Figure 14.3). Overall, the precise neurobiological processes of BPD are unknown, though disturbances in a corticolimbic circuitry involving the amygdala, hippocampus, insula, anterior cingulate, orbitofrontal cortex, and medial prefrontal cortex seem to contribute to problems in emotion regulation, interpersonal disturbances, and inconsistent identity (Bohus et al., 2021; Karas et al., 2021).

Empathy has been a focus of research in those with BPD. In terms of brain processes, Isabel Dziobek and her colleagues (2011) examined empathy using brain imaging tasks. These researchers divided empathy into two categories: cognitive empathy and emotional empathy. Cognitive empathy required participants to assess the mental states of individuals shown in pictures. Emotional empathy required participants to rate their concern for the person shown in the picture. Thus, a picture of a little girl standing in front of a destroyed house could be rated in terms of both how the little girl would feel as well as how much one would be concerned about her.

FIGURE 14.3 ■ BPD and Brain Volume

Individuals with BPD have less volume in a number of brain areas. These areas include the insula, the middle and superior temporal cortex (Mid-Sup T), the fusiform gyrus (FG), the anterior cingulate cortex (ACC), the hippocampus and the parahippocampus, and the amygdala (Amyg).

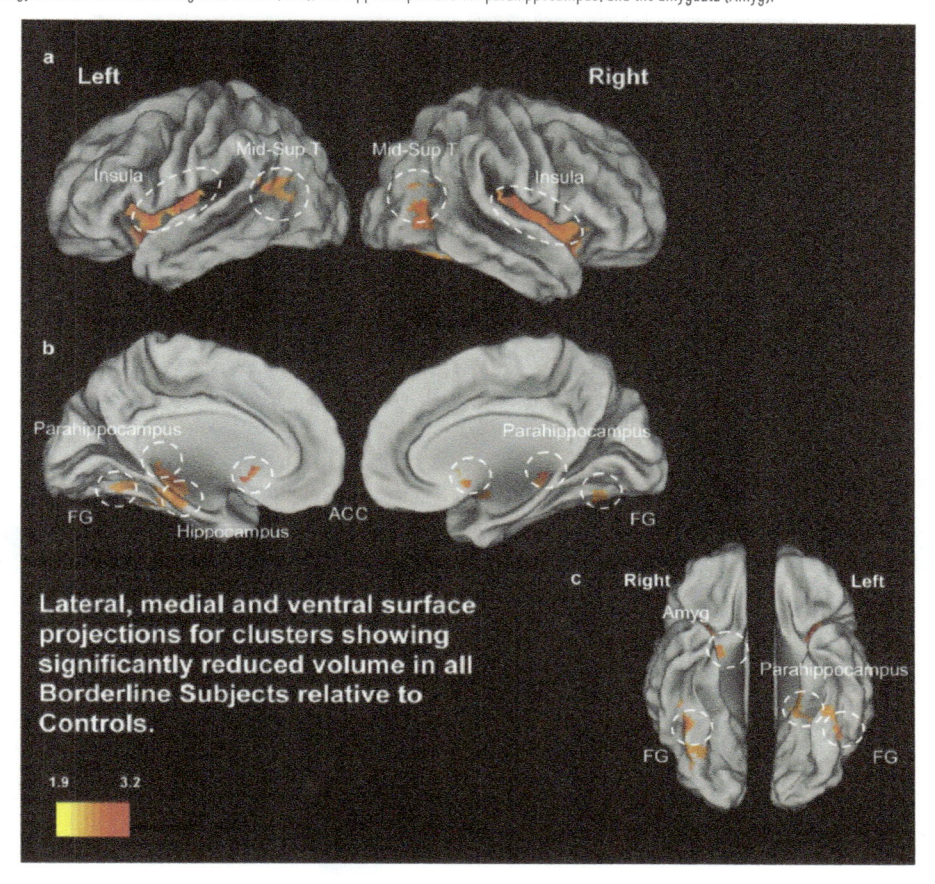

Credit: Soloff, P., Pruitt, P., Sharma, M., Radwan, J., White, R., & Diwadkar, V. (2012). Structural brain abnormalities and suicidal behavior in borderline personality disorder. *Journal of Psychiatric Research, 46,* 16–25, with permission from Elsevier.

In terms of emotional empathy, individuals with BPD showed different responses from controls in the right insula (Figure 14.4). The functional magnetic resonance imaging (fMRI) bold signal was larger in those with BPD, suggesting greater arousal when performing empathy tasks (Figure 14.5).

Trust and Borderline Personality Disorder

An important method of research in this area is to have individuals with borderline personality play computer games. One of these is the *trust game.* In this game, money is exchanged between an investor, who decides how much money to commit, and a trustee, who decides how much of the investment to repay the investor. During the game, the investment is tripled. If both cooperate, then both the investor and the trustee benefit. However, this involves a degree of trust between the two. This trust builds up from playing the game a number of times. Individuals with BPD do not trust the situation and invest less money than do non-BPD controls.

During the game, activity in the anterior insula is measured. This area is traditionally related to a sense of self and the physiological state of the body. It has also been shown to react to unfairness and the emotional states of others. With the healthy control, activation of the anterior insula was related to the size of the investment. Small investments related to large activation and large investments corresponded

FIGURE 14.4 ■ The Experience of Empathy Evident in the Brains of Those With BPD

In terms of emotional empathy, individuals with BPD showed different responses from controls, as evident in the right insula. This figure shows differences between control participants and those with borderline personality disorder.

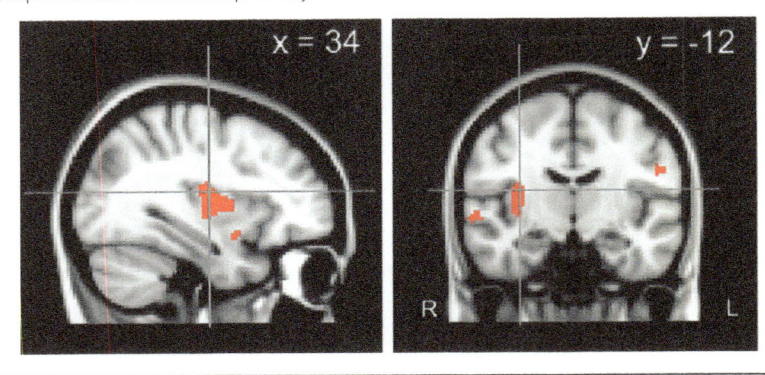

Credit: Dziobek, I., Preissler, S., Grozdanovic, Z., Heuser, I., Heekeren, H. R., & Roepke, S. (2011). Neuronal correlates of altered empathy and social cognition in borderline personality disorder. *NeuroImage, 57*, 539–548, with permission from Elsevier.

Note: Figure uses radiological format in terms of right and left side.

FIGURE 14.5 ■ BPD and Greater Brain Activation When Performing Empathy Tasks

Bold (fMRI) differences show more brain activation when performing both cognitive and emotional empathy tasks as compared with control participants.

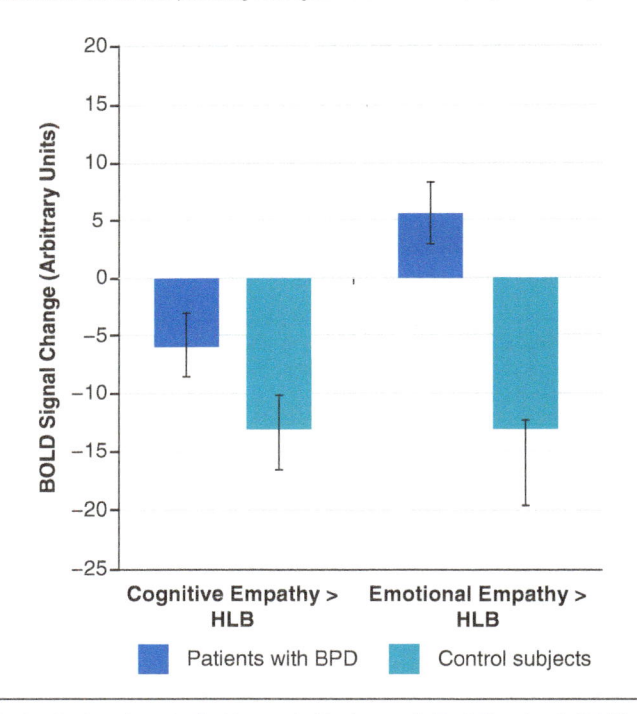

Credit: Dziobek, I., Preissler, S., Grozdanovic, Z., Heuser, I., Heekeren, H. R., & Roepke, S. (2011). Neuronal correlates of altered empathy and social cognition in borderline personality disorder. *NeuroImage, 57*, 539–548, with permission from Elsevier.

to small activations. Thus, it is activated when the person does not cooperate. On the other hand, the insula of the person with BPD did not differentiate between the size of the offer. According to these researchers (King-Casas et al., 2008), those with BPD did not have the gut feeling that cooperation, and thus the relationship, was in jeopardy (Figure 14.6).

Another game that is used to examine physiological responses of those with borderline personality is a simple ball toss game called *cyberball*. Imagine that you are sitting at a computer terminal and see Figure 14.7 on the screen. You are told that there are two other people playing with you, represented by the two cartoon characters on the screen.

At the beginning of the game, you see the other two people throwing to each other and then to you, and you, in turn, throw to them (Figure 14.8). However, near the end of the game, the other two people throw only to each other. Individuals in a control group without personality disorders will experience distress and feel rejected.

FIGURE 14.6 ■ BPD and Difficulty With Trust

In playing the trust game, those with BPD found it more difficult to develop trust. They also showed less activation of the anterior insula, which was not related to the degree of investment as it was with individuals without BPD.

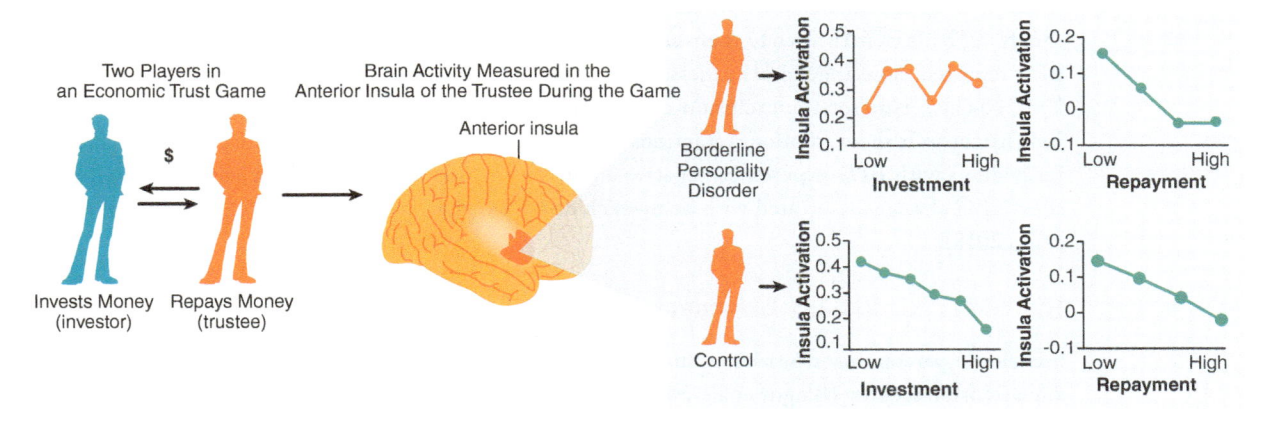

Credit: From Andreas Meyer-Lindenberg, "Trust Me on This." *Science* Volume: 321, Issue: 5890. 2008, August 15. Reprinted with permission from AAAS. Illustration adapted by N. Kevitiyagala/Science.

FIGURE 14.7 ■ Image of Computer Screen Representing Two Other People Throwing a Ball. Your Hand Is Represented at the Bottom of the Screen

Credit: Williams, K. D., Cheung, C. K. T., & Choi, W. (2000). Cyberostracism: Effects of being ignored over the Internet. *Journal of Personality and Social Psychology, 79*, 748–762.

FIGURE 14.8 ■ Cyberball Game in Which All Three Individuals Throw the Ball to Each Other

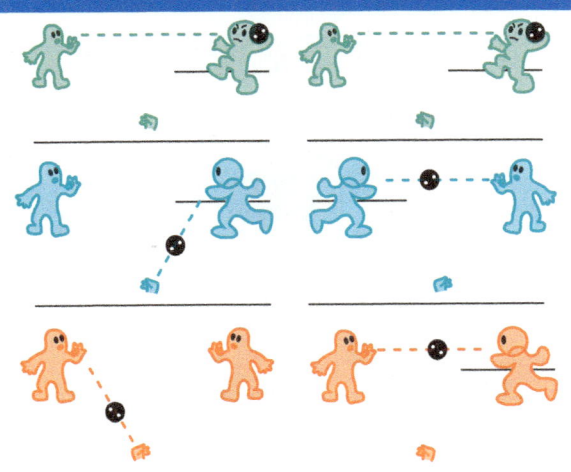

Source: Williams, K. D., Cheung, C. K. T., & Choi, W. (2000). Cyberostracism: Effects of being ignored over the Internet. *Journal of Personality and Social Psychology, 79*, 748–762.

In one study, these individuals showed greater activation of the ACC and right ventral prefrontal cortex (RVPFC) during exclusion (Eisenberger et al., 2003). Further, greater activity in the ACC was associated with more self-reported social distress, and the opposite was true for the RVPFC (Figures 14.9 and 14.10). Interestingly, the experience of social distress paralleled that of physical pain. That is, activity in the ACC, which has been previously linked with pain, was also associated with social rejection. Likewise, increased activity in the RVPFC, previously linked with the regulation of pain, was associated with diminished distress after rejection.

When individuals with BPD played the cyberball game, they felt more excluded than controls, whether it was the inclusion or exclusion condition (Renneberg et al., 2012). They also believed that fewer balls were thrown to them than did controls. In the inclusion condition, individuals with BPD reported more anger and sadness both before and after the inclusion condition (Figure 14.11). This was also true for the exclusion condition (Figure 14.12). These figures show that, whereas healthy controls show emotional reactions only to the situation in which they are actually excluded, individuals with BPD experience negative emotions in both situations. Those with BPD will also show EEG changes associated with being excluded even when they were not excluded (Weinbrecht et al., 2018).

Histrionic Personality Disorder

Histrionic personality disorder is characterized by a pervasive pattern of excessive emotionality and attention seeking (Blagov et al., 2007). Being the center of attention is one key element, and the person may use a number of means for gaining attention. They may be highly dramatic, dress provocatively, be seductive, and even make up stories or describe physical complaints to draw attention to themselves. If they are not the center of attention, they become uncomfortable. Prevalence rates are 1.8% based on the National Epidemiologic Survey on Alcohol and Related Conditions (Grant et al., 2004).

DSM-5-TR describes histrionic personality disorder in terms of eight possible facets. These include (1) discomfort in situations in which the person is not the center of attention; (2) interaction with others characterized by inappropriate sexually seductive or provocative behavior; (3) displaying of rapidly shifting and shallow expression of emotions; (4) consistent use of physical appearance to draw attention to self; (5) a style of speech that is excessively impressionistic and lacking in detail; (6) self-dramatization, theatricality, and exaggerated expression of emotion; (7) suggestibility, that is, easily influenced by others or circumstances; and (8) considering relationships to be more intimate than they actually are. The case of Amy Porter (not her real name) illustrates many of these characteristics.

FIGURE 14.9 ■ The Experience of Social Distress as Shown in the Brain

During exclusion, there is increased activity in the anterior cingulate cortex (A). During inclusion, there is increased activity in the right ventral prefrontal cortex (B). Greater activity in the ACC was associated with more self-reported social distress, and the opposite was true for the RVPFC.

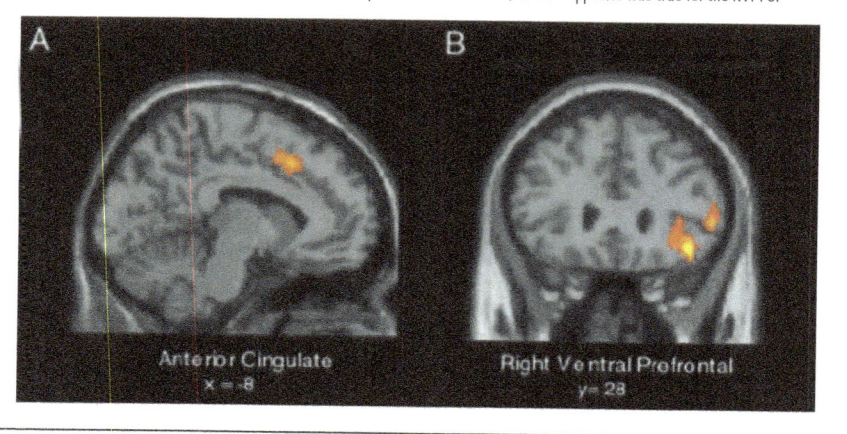

Credit: Eisenberger, N., Lieberman, M., & Kipling, K. (2003). Does rejection hurt? An fMRI study of social exclusion. *Science, 302*, 290–292. Reprinted with permission from AAAS.

FIGURE 14.10 Relationship Between Social Distress and Brain Activity

Scatterplots showing a positive correlation between anterior cingulate cortex activity and self-reported distress (Graph A) and a negative correlation between the right ventral prefrontal cortex and self-reported distress (Graph B). Each dot represents a participant in the study.

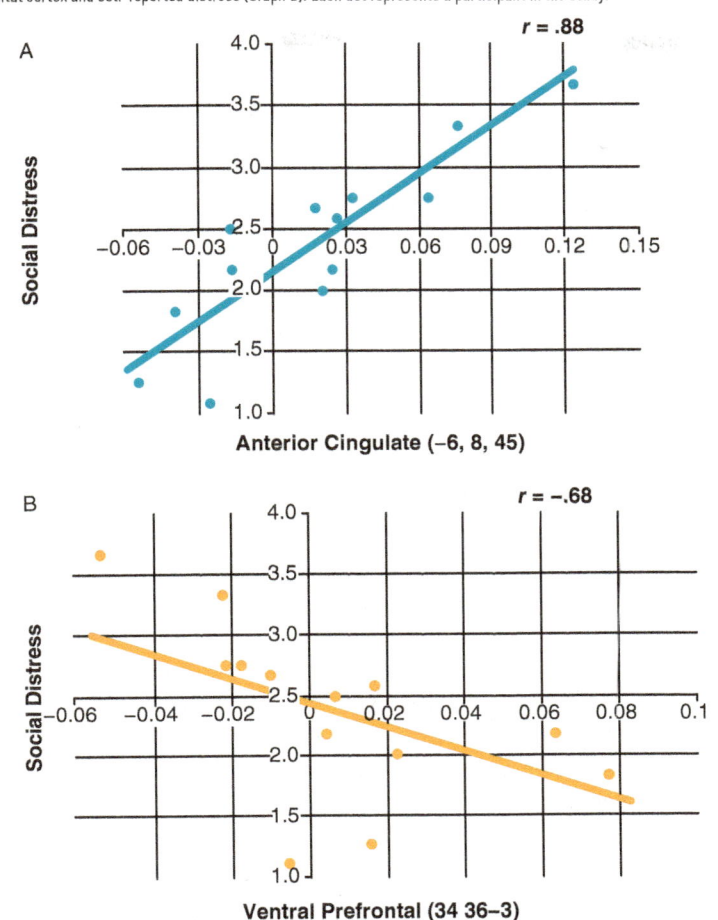

A — Social Distress vs. Anterior Cingulate (−6, 8, 45), $r = .88$

B — Social Distress vs. Ventral Prefrontal (34 36−3), $r = −.68$

Credit: Eisenberger, N., Lieberman, M., & Kipling, K. (2003). Does rejection hurt? An fMRI study of social exclusion. *Science, 302,* 290–292. Reprinted with permission from AAAS.

CASE OF AMY PORTER
HISTRIONIC PERSONALITY DISORDER

Amy Porter is a 50-year-old divorced woman with two young children. She had been in treatment off and on over the past 20 years. She would typically enter treatment when distressed by difficult situations. She would end treatment when she began a new romantic relationship. At that point, she would feel excited about the person she was dating and would idealize the person and the future. Prior to her marriage, Ms. Porter would date one man after another. She was very attractive and dressed in a provocative manner. She even described herself as a "Barbie doll." She enjoyed all the men looking at her at a party. She had a romance novel view of relationships. Her idea was that she would meet someone and that they would live happily ever after in a big house. She was often surprised that the men she met only wanted a short-term relationship. This pattern had repeated itself a large number of times. As she became older, she wanted to have a child with someone but tended to be dissatisfied with relationships with men her own age. As she moved into her 40s, she viewed men her age as inferior, referred to them in derogatory terms, and was intolerant of their physical imperfections. However, she did meet a man her age that she felt attracted to and quickly they married and had children. After that, he left her.

At some point, she found herself in the dating world again. Although she was still attractive as a 50-year-old, she was negative toward her appearance. She continued to be uninterested in men her age but felt desperate to find a suitable partner. In therapy, she wanted more from the therapist and showed a dependency. She had difficulty reflecting on her own internal experiences. She imagined the therapist to have a very different life than was the case and would become angry at what she imagined. After around 2 years of therapy, she was able to obtain a job more consistent with her education. She also was able to have a long-term relationship with a man her age.

Clinical vignette provided by Kenneth Levy, PhD

Narcissistic Personality Disorder

Narcissistic personality disorder is characterized by a pervasive pattern of grandiosity, a need for admiration, a sense of privilege or entitlement, and a lack of empathy for others (Levy, Reynoso, et al., 2007). Individuals with narcissistic personality disorder often think about how special they are and all the ways in which they will succeed, including in business, love, and so forth. They may also make unreasonable demands on others in relation to their view of themselves. In doing so, they ignore others' experiences or needs. Prevalence rates have been estimated as high as 6% in community samples (American Psychiatric Association, 2013).

The diagnostic criteria in *DSM-5-TR* for narcissistic personality disorder describe a person who shows a pattern of grandiosity, a need for admiration, and a lack of empathy for others. This personality style should begin by early adulthood. Five of the following specific characteristics should also be present: (1) having a grandiose sense of self-importance; (2) being preoccupied with ideas of unlimited success or attractiveness; (3) seeing one's self as special and being understood only by other exceptional individuals; (4) needing excessive admiration; (5) having a sense of entitlement, which can include unreasonable expectations; (6) taking advantage of others for one's own needs; (7) lacking empathy; (8) being envious of others or believing that others envy the person; and (9) being arrogant.

The word *narcissism* comes from the Greek myth of Narcissus, who saw his image in a pool of water and fell in love with it. Unable to remove himself from his own image, he died at the pool. In a similar manner, people with narcissistic personality disorder think only of their own image and lose close

FIGURE 14.11 ■ BPD and Feelings of Inclusion

Being included in social situations elicits different feelings for those with BPD and those without. Note the anger and sadness before and after the inclusion condition for those with borderline personality disorder (BPD) and controls (C).

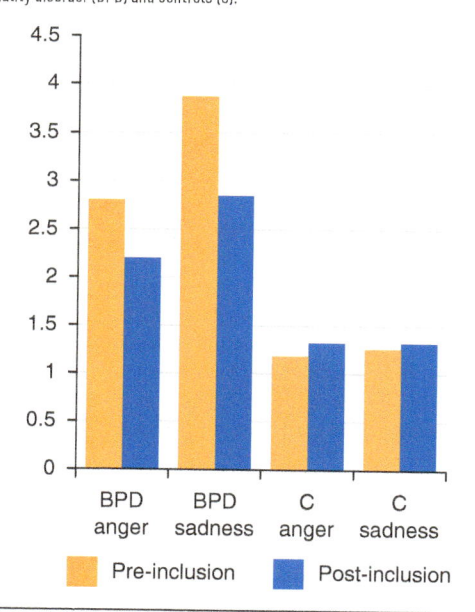

Credit: Renneberg, B., Herm, K., Hahn, A., Staebler, K., Lammers, C., & Roepke, S. (2012). Perception of social participation in borderline personality disorder. *Clinical Psychology and Psychotherapy, 19,* 473–480.

FIGURE 14.12 ■ BPD and Experiencing Exclusion

Control participants showed less anger and sadness before the exclusion task. Those with BPD showed different responses.

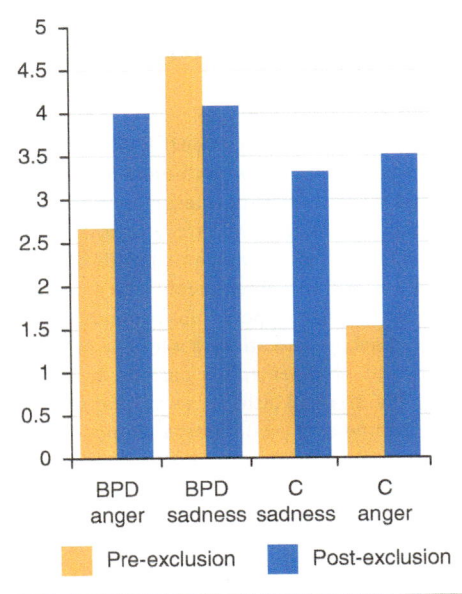

Credit: Renneberg, B., Herm, K., Hahn, A., Staebler, K., Lammers, C., & Roepke, S. (2012). Perception of social participation in borderline personality disorder. *Clinical Psychology and Psychotherapy, 19*, 473–480.

In Ovid's *Metamorphoses*, Narcissus fell in love with his own reflection.
GL Archive/Alamy Stock Photo

contact with others and the world. They may believe that they are so unique that they can be understood only by others who are similarly special. They need others only insofar as they provide validation of their own views. In fact, all of the individual's resources, including regulating their emotions and interpersonal processes, are directed at maintaining a positive self-image. This may be accomplished by seeking validation and self-enhancement experiences from others. When others cease to admire the person, an individual with narcissistic personality disorder will move on and seek someone who will. Although everyone likes to receive positive responses from others, those with narcissistic personality disorder take this to the extreme. The case study of Dawn Nichols (not her real name) shows the characteristics of a person with narcissistic personality disorder.

CASE OF DAWN NICHOLS
NARCISSISTIC PERSONALITY DISORDER

Dawn Nichols was a tall, attractive married woman in her mid-30s with three children. A friend of hers helped her to find a therapist. Her chief complaints were feelings of long-term depression and a general feeling of anxiety. Others in her life reported that she could become angry quickly and that these outbursts could occur in businesses and when traveling with others. She grew up in a home in which her father was an extremely successful businessman. Her father was "all business" and too busy for his children. He was also hostile and derogatory toward her. Although her mother provided for Dawn's basic needs as a child, her mother was emotionally distant and physically absent. Both in childhood and after Dawn grew up, her mother sought to coerce her into doing what she wanted.

Dawn Nichols believed that she had superior intelligence and abilities. However, she also reported difficulty doing well in school and sticking with any of her activities such as horseback riding, acting, and singing. Overall, she blamed her parents for not helping her develop her abilities. Although she was in her 30s, she had little sense of what she wanted to do with her life. She would change her mind and become angry with others. She once sold a horse since she had not gone horseback riding for years, only to buy another horse a few days later because she admired it.

In addition to feeling depressed and anxious, Dawn reported angry outbursts, significant alcohol and marijuana use, concerns about rapidly shifting interests, and unhappiness with the lack of success in her life. She also reported that her husband was concerned that she was disconnected from her three children and that she would often become angry with them for typical behaviors of children. She experienced this anger in spite of the fact that she had a housekeeper, a gardener, an au pair, and a number of babysitters to help her. She also blamed her husband for not helping her succeed. She was part of local acting workshops and sang with some local bands. She often fantasized about leaving her family and touring Europe with a younger man who would produce her music and help her achieve fame and fortune.

Clinical vignette provided by Kenneth Levy, PhD

Source: Adapted from Levy, K. N. (2012). Subtypes, dimensions, levels, and mental states in narcissism and narcissistic personality disorder. *Journal of Clinical Psychology: In Session, 8,* 886–897.

CONCEPT CHECK

- What three factors characterize BPD?
- What role do self-mutilating behaviors and suicide attempts play in individuals with BPD? What do we know about the prevalence of these behaviors?
- What evidence do we have that the brains of individuals with BPD differ from the brains of other people?
- Two computer games—the trust game and a ball toss game—are used in research with individuals with BPD. What is the purpose of each of these games, and what have they revealed about personality disorder?
- What environmental factors play a role in the development of BPD?
- What is the defining characteristic of histrionic personality disorder? What eight facets does *DSM-5-TR* use to describe the disorder?
- How would you explain the paradox that individuals with narcissistic personality disorder need other people at the same time that they have no empathy for others themselves?

ANXIOUS FEARFUL PERSONALITY DISORDERS

There are three personality disorders included in the **anxious fearful personality disorders (Cluster C)** grouping; these are avoidant, dependent, and obsessive-compulsive personality disorders. The behavior of individuals with these disorders is one of fearfulness and avoidance.

Avoidant Personality Disorder

Avoidant personality disorder is characterized by a pervasive pattern of social inhibition, feelings of inadequacy, and hypersensitivity to negative evaluation (Herbert, 2007; Marian et al., 2022). Individuals with avoidant personality disorder avoid many social interactions, especially those involving close relationships with other people. One key feature is the fear of being criticized or evaluated by others. This, in turn, results in the person interacting only with their family or a few trusted others. Prevalence rates range between 2.3% based on the National Epidemiologic Survey on Alcohol and Related Conditions (Grant et al., 2004) and 5.1% in the National Comorbidity Survey Replication (Lenzenweger et al., 2007).

The diagnostic criteria in *DSM-5-TR* for avoidant personality disorder describe a person who shows a pattern of social inhibition, feelings of inadequacy, and an increased sensitivity to negative evaluation. This personality style should begin by early adulthood. Four of the following specific characteristics should also be present: (1) an avoidance of occupational activities that involve interpersonal contact that could lead to criticism; (2) an unwillingness to be involved with others, unless it is certain that the person will be liked; (3) restraint within an intimate relationship for fear of being ridiculed; (4) a preoccupation with being criticized or rejected in social situations; (5) an inhibition in new interpersonal situations because of feelings of inadequacy; (6) a view of one's self as socially inept, unappealing, or inferior; and (7) a reluctance to take personal risks or engage in new activities for fear of being embarrassed.

Dependent Personality Disorder

Dependent personality disorder is characterized by a pervasive pattern of clinging and being submissive (Bornstein, 2007). The person with dependent personality disorder has difficulties making everyday decisions without reassurance from others. This results in a desire for others to assume responsibility for most areas of one's life. Their lack of experiencing a self who can plan and direct their behavior leaves them in a position that requires that they always be with another person. Otherwise, they tend to feel anxious and helpless when alone. They tend not to be thoughtful in choosing a partner, which may result in choosing partners who are not reliable or empathic. Prevalence rates range from 0.4% based on the National Epidemiologic Survey on Alcohol and Related Conditions (Grant et al., 2004) to 0.6% in the National Comorbidity Survey Replication (Lenzenweger et al., 2007).

The diagnostic criteria in *DSM-5-TR* for dependent personality disorder describe a person who shows a pattern of excessive need to be taken care of that leads to submissive and clinging behavior and fears of separation. This personality style should begin by early adulthood. Five of the following specific characteristics should also be present: (1) an inability to make everyday decisions without an excessive amount of advice and reassurance from others; (2) a need for others to assume responsibility for one's life; (3) difficulty disagreeing with another person; (4) difficulty beginning projects; (5) a need to work hard to receive support from others; (6) an uncomfortable feeling when alone, resulting from the idea that the person cannot take care of one's self; (7) beginning a new relationship when an old one is over as a source of care; and (8) feeling fearful that one cannot take care of one's self.

Obsessive-Compulsive Personality Disorder

Obsessive-compulsive personality disorder is characterized by a pervasive pattern of preoccupation with orderliness, perfectionism, and control of one's environment (Bartz et al., 2007). Individuals with obsessive-compulsive personality would be described as workaholics. They themselves would see little need for taking time off or just spending time with other people. In dealing with others, they may appear to be rigid and using standards not called for in the current situation.

Obsessive-compulsive personality disorder is not the same as obsessive-compulsive disorder (OCD). How are they different, since they appear to have similar characteristics? The traditional distinction between the two is the relation of the object of control to the person's self. In OCD, individuals typically attempt to control something that takes place outside of themselves. For example, some individuals with OCD fear germs and constantly wash their hands or clean their houses. However, in obsessive-compulsive personality disorder, the need for control is part of the individual's self in every domain that the person experiences. Thus, it is a way of life rather than a reaction to external processes. Prevalence rates range from 2.4% in the National Comorbidity Survey Replication (Lenzenweger et al., 2007) to 7.8% based on the National Epidemiologic Survey on Alcohol and Related Conditions (Grant et al., 2004). A meta-analysis that examined research on obsessive-compulsive personality disorder across 28 years estimated worldwide prevalence to be 6.5%; it further suggested that rates of the disorder have remained stable and do not vary significantly around the world (Clemente et al., 2022). This disorder has one of the highest prevalence rates of any of the personality disorders.

The diagnostic criteria in *DSM-5-TR* for obsessive-compulsive personality disorder describe a person who shows a pattern of being concerned with orderliness, perfectionism, and control. This control reduces flexibility and openness. This personality style should begin by early adulthood. Four of the following specific characteristics should also be present: (1) a preoccupation with details, rules, lists, order, or schedules; (2) a perfectionism that interferes with task completion; (3) an excessive preoccupation with work to the exclusion of fun and friendships; (4) an inflexibility concerning morals and values; (5) an inability to discard worthless objects even when there is no emotional connection to the object; (6) a reluctance to delegate tasks to others unless they are performed in a particular way; (7) a hoarding of money; and (8) rigidity and stubbornness.

CONCEPT CHECK

- What are the similar characteristics that run through the personality disorders in Cluster C? What are the distinct characteristics of each disorder?
- How is obsessive-compulsive personality disorder similar to OCD? How is it different?

TREATMENT OF PERSONALITY DISORDERS

Personality disorders are difficult to treat. This is in part related to the fact that one individual with a personality disorder may show different signs and symptoms from another. In addition, individuals with personality disorders find it difficult to maintain a close, intimate relationship with their therapist. Because of this, psychotherapy for personality disorders is more individually focused than it tends to be for other disorders. The focus of treatment is also based on conceptualizations of the disorder (Gunderson et al., 2018). At this point, research studies have shown that treatments based on both cognitive behavioral and dynamic perspectives have been effective (Cristea et al., 2017). Medications have not been used as a direct treatment, but only as an adjunct (Bateman et al., 2015).

Although psychosocial treatment approaches come from different traditions, the effective approaches show many common factors (Bateman et al., 2015). BPD has been the focus of the most empirical treatment studies. The common factors seen in the treatment of BPD are as follows:

1. A structured, manualized approach is used, which focuses on the commonly seen problems.
2. Clients are encouraged to assume control of themselves.
3. The therapist helps the client to understand the connections of his or her feelings to events and actions. The therapist helps the client to consider the situation rather than just experiencing anxiety.
4. Therapists are active, responsive, and validating.
5. Therapists are willing to discuss their own reactions in the therapy session. For example, the therapist might say, "I misunderstood."

We will now discuss specific treatment approaches.

Dialectical Behavior Therapy

One of the first researched treatment approaches for BPD is **dialectical behavior therapy (DBT)**. Dialectical refers to the balancing of opposites in spite of the desire of individuals with BPT to see things in a black or white manner. Some of the key features are acceptance of the moment, being able to tolerate negative emotions, regulating these emotions, and the ability to engage in effective communication with others.

DBT was developed by Marsha Linehan, based on her work with clients with suicidal ideation, and then expanded to those with BPD (Linehan, 1993; Linehan & Dexter-Mazza, 2008). Numerous studies have shown DBT to be effective in reducing suicide and increasing positive changes. This is especially true when a group skills training component is included (Linehan et al., 2015).

DBT therapy begins with the acceptance of the fact that individuals with BPD experience extreme emotional reactions and are particularly sensitive to changes in the environment. Anger toward the therapist is not uncommon. Individuals with BPD take longer to return to baseline conditions after their emotional reactivity. They may be impulsive. Suicidal considerations are common. This makes these clients difficult to work with, and therapy sessions are often very challenging.

DBT is described by Marsha Linehan and her colleagues (Crowell et al., 2009; Linehan, 1993) as a blend of behavioral science, dialectical philosophy, and Zen practice. The cornerstone of DBT is based on problem solving and acceptance of the experience of the moment. This acceptance is sought even when the individual with BPD seeks to escape from their experience of negative emotions. That is, the therapist acknowledges and accepts that a person felt rejected at the moment but not that the appropriate response to the rejection would be self-harm. The therapy itself is conceptualized in terms of a number of stages.

The *pretreatment stage* is a time when the client and the therapist arrive at a mutually informed decision to work together. Traditionally, this includes a 6-month contract between the individual and the therapist. The pretreatment stage includes an understanding of the client's history and decisions concerning which processes should receive high priority. This pretreatment stage also includes a discussion concerning what can reasonably be expected from therapy and the roles of the therapist and the client. One emphasis is on the therapist and the client as a team, whose goal is to help the client create a life worth living. In the service of creating a productive life, the individual will develop problem-solving skills for their own life.

The *first stage of therapy* is directed at helping the client develop a stable life. This includes reducing suicide-related behaviors and other behaviors that interfere with therapy and life. This stage typically lasts for 1 year. During this stage, dialectical thinking encourages clients to see reality as complex and not something that can be reduced to a single idea. This includes developing the ability to experience thoughts and feelings that are thought to be contradictory. This is a difficult task for those with BPD. Four specific goals of Stage 1 include reducing suicidal ideation, reducing behavior that interferes with therapy, achieving a stable lifestyle, and developing skills in emotional regulation, such as mindfulness. Stage 1 has been most researched in terms of empirically supported procedures.

The *second stage of therapy* moves to processing previously experienced traumatic events. One approach is to have the person reexperience prior trauma inside the therapy session. This stage can only occur once the person's life is stable and their emotional responding is under their control. The four specific goals of this stage include remembering and accepting the facts of earlier trauma, reducing any self-blame involving the earlier trauma, reducing the intrusive material associated with the earlier trauma as well as any denial associated with it, and resolving dialectical tensions associated with blame for the trauma.

The *third stage of therapy* is directed at helping the person develop a sense of self that allows them to live independently. The goal is to help the person experience both happiness and unhappiness with the ability to trust in their experiences. The *fourth and final stage of therapy* focuses on the ability to sustain joy and be part of an ever-changing world. The following *LENS* describes Marsha Linehan's own experiences, which led to the creation of DBT.

LENS

MARSHA LINEHAN, CREATING DIALECTICAL BEHAVIOR THERAPY FROM HER OWN EXPERIENCES

Growing up in Tulsa, Oklahoma, in the 1960s, Marsha Linehan was an excellent student and played the piano well. However, she felt deeply inadequate compared with others. She also found herself at odds with her parents and spent much of her senior year of high school in bed with headaches. That year, she was taken to local mental health professionals, who recommended she be institutionalized. Thus, at age 17, Linehan found herself in a locked ward at the Institute of Living in Hartford, Connecticut. Previously, she displayed the characteristics often seen in those with BPD. She burned herself and slashed her arms, legs, and other parts of her body. In the hospital without sharp objects, she hit her head on the wall or floor.

Marsha Linehan
Courtesy of the University of Washington

This is how she currently describes that time: "My whole experience of these episodes was that someone else was doing it; it was like 'I know this is coming, I'm out of control, somebody help me; where are you, God?'" She further stated, "I felt totally empty, like the Tin Man; I had no way to communicate what was going on, no way to understand it." After more than 2 years, she was released from the ward and returned home. While at home, she attempted suicide.

She later moved to Chicago in an attempt to start over. She lived at the YMCA and took a job as a clerk in an insurance company. She reports that her Catholic faith was vital to her and that she prayed often. A religious experience took her to a place where she accepted herself as she was. In Chicago, Linehan also took classes and was able to complete a PhD in psychology. As she continued her career, she became a therapist who worked with people with suicidal ideation who often had a personality disorder. She helped them to focus on life as it is rather than how the person thought it should be. She also emphasized acceptance. She built on these principles to develop DBT and to test its empirical efficacy.

Linehan, along with Elyn Saks (whom you met in Chapter 13) and Kay Jamison (whom you met in Chapter 6), has become a productive scholar and advocate of reforming our current mental health system with its frequently inadequate care. This also means sharing an understanding of the experiences of those with mental disorders, including the way in which society stigmatizes these individuals. A growing number of voices, some of whom are profiled in the *New York Times* series "Lives Restored," have demonstrated the reality of those with mental illness moving from distress to productivity (see For Further Reading).

Thought Question

What kinds of unique contributions can an individual who has experienced mental illness make to our understanding of the experience and treatment of mental illness that would otherwise be missing?

This LENS is based on a talk given by Dr. Linehan at the Institute of Living as reported in the New York Times (see For Further Reading; Carey, B. (2011, June 23). Expert on mental illness reveals her own fight. The New York Times. https://www.nytimes.com/2011/06/23/health/23lives.html).

Other Proven Therapies for Treating Borderline Personality Disorder

In addition to DBT, there are a number of dynamic-oriented therapies that are empirically supported. One of these is **dynamic deconstructive psychotherapy (DDP)**. DDP was developed for clients who find therapy difficult as well as for those who may also have substance abuse problems (Gregory & Remen, 2008). This approach is partly based on neuroscience research, which shows that individuals with BPD show difficulties with memory, emotional regulation, and decision making. This is seen as preventing these individuals from building a coherent self-system independent of other people. DDP is designed to help individuals with BPD develop a coherent sense of self.

DDP is divided into four distinct stages. The *first stage* is for the client and the therapist together to identify the client's difficulties and establish a series of goals and tasks for working on them. They also create an agreement as to how the client will keep themself safe. By the end of this stage, the relationship between the therapist and client should be stable and give the client comfort. This stage is similar in both dynamic and cognitive behavioral approaches.

The first stage of DDP is for the client and the therapist together to identify the client's difficulties and establish a series of goals and tasks for working on these difficulties.

iStock.com/Antonio_Diaz

The *second stage* involves the development of the client's ability to understand complex ideas related to their relationships with others. For example, when a relationship with another ended, they would be able to say, "I felt both horrified and relieved." As this stage ends, the client begins to give up an idealized image of themselves and their abilities. As this idealized image is given up, there can be a better understanding of self-limitations, which is the focus of the *third stage*. During this stage, the client can learn to verbalize their disappointments and experience the loss associated with them. This can lead to fears of personal incompetence, but it can also help the person understand these fears. The *fourth and final stage* moves to the relationship between the client and therapist and how the person will experience the termination of therapy.

Another empirically supported therapy is **transference-focused psychotherapy (TFP)**. This is a twice-weekly therapy based on Otto Kernberg's object relations model (Clarkin et al., 2006; see also Levy & Scala, 2012). As with other approaches, TFP seeks to reduce symptoms of BPD, especially self-destructive behaviors. The technique involves an exploration of how the person views themself and may combine their identity with that of another. That is, the person does not have a stable view of self. During the first year of treatment, behaviors involved with self-harm are limited, and a therapy contract is developed. In the sessions, the therapist follows the affect that the client brings to the session. The emphasis is on the relationship between the client and therapist. Questions of whether this relationship can also be seen in the client's other relationships can be addressed. Many of these techniques are similar to those of Hans Strupp, as described in Chapter 1.

Treatments for Other Personality Disorders

Most of our knowledge of the treatment of personality disorders other than BPD is based on the experience of health care professionals, case studies, or simple descriptions of treatments. These include approaches to treating BPD. The individuals with other personality disorders about whom we have information present problems with their self and in their behavior toward, or relationships with, others in a number of different ways. This requires the mental health professional to pay attention to the specific way in which an individual is interacting with their world. Thus, manualized, empirically validated treatments for disorders other than BPD are less available. However, a general approach is often taken in therapy.

The fundamental aspect of this general approach for all personality disorders is to focus on the relationship between the mental health professional and the individual. This approach includes six general components—four related to the relationship and two related to assisting the individual in developing certain skills (Livesley et al., 2016):

1. *Structure:* Specify the model of treatment, describe the framework of therapy, define the therapy, and establish a treatment contract.

2. *Treatment alliance:* Establish and maintain a relationship between the therapist and the client.

3. *Consistency:* Maintain a consistent treatment process.

4. *Validation:* Acknowledge the reality of the experiences of the client. This does not require that the therapist agree with the client's explanation but only acknowledge that the experiences have taken place.

5. *Motivation:* Help the client develop motivation and commitment to change.

6. *Metacognition:* Promote the client's ability to observe and reflect on their behaviors and experiences.

As part of this overall treatment perspective, it is important to help the client feel safe and contain their experiences. From this perspective, there is more focus on aspects that can be changed, such as maladaptive thinking styles, attitudes about the self, and interpersonal patterns (McMurran & Crawford, 2016). These more integrated treatment approaches have been used with a number of personality disorders.

The type of personality disorder experienced determines the nature of the problems focused on in treatment (Tufekcioglu & Muran, 2016). Cluster A disorders of the schizotypal, schizoid, and paranoid types show particular problems in relation to the therapeutic relationship. The client may question the therapist's intentions, show aloofness, or be very sensitive to what the therapist says. Clients with Cluster B (borderline, narcissistic, and histrionic) personality disorders push the limits of the therapeutic relationship by being demanding or seeking constant approval. Those being treated for Cluster C (dependent, avoidant, and obsessive-compulsive) disorders tend to be emotionally inhibited and avoid interpersonal conflict.

As you can imagine, individuals with certain personality disorders such as schizoid or avoidant personality disorder rarely seek treatment, which makes systematic treatment studies more difficult. Those with antisocial personality disorder initially may come in contact with the legal system and may receive treatment while in prison. The focus of this treatment is often the prevention of future criminal or violent acts (Wong, 2016). In addition to psychotherapy, medications have been used for specific aspects of different personality disorders, such as depression or impulsivity. However, unlike psychotherapy, there are no medications that target all aspects of a personality disorder. Currently, alternative therapies are in the process of being tested empirically as to their effectiveness.

UNDERSTANDING CHANGES IN *DSM-5* AND *DSM-5-TR*
PERSONALITY DISORDERS

In the development of the personality disorders section of *DSM-5*, there was much discussion concerning whether personality disorders should continue to be presented in a categorical manner or reconfigured to place along a dimension (Gøtzsche-Astrup & Moskowitz, 2016; Krueger & Markon, 2014). With a categorical approach, a person either has the disorder or does not, based on certain criteria. A dimensional approach, on the other hand, allows for the health care professional to place the person on a continuum ranging from adaptive personality functioning to disordered personality functioning. For example, a dimensional approach was adopted for autism spectrum disorders.

There was considerable debate in the *DSM-5* workgroup as to which approach to adopt for personality disorders. Much of this was based on scientific considerations. Initially, there was agreement that the categorical approach seen in *DSM-IV* had problems. However, as the debates continued, certain conflicting forces began to influence the debate as reflected in the American Psychiatric Association Board of Trustees. A few of the workgroup members suggested that personality disorders and the five-factor model of personality were unrelated. Other members even resigned from the workgroup. The results of these debates ended in a manner that was not seen with any other *DSM-5* disorder: Both approaches were adopted. In the main part of *DSM-5* that is used for diagnosis, the same criteria as in *DSM-IV* are used for personality disorders. In a separate section of *DSM-5* referred to as Emerging Measures and Models, a combination of the dimensional approach and categorical approach was presented.

The alternative model reflects the understanding that personality disorders involve problems with the person's sense of self. In many of the disorders, there is not a coherent sense of self as an independent identity. Further, the experience of being directed by one's goals and plans is missing. Instead, the experience of the moment may dictate the emotional reactions of the individual. In addition to a lack of a sense of self, there are also problems with interpersonal relationships. Specifically, there are problems with understanding others as well as being intimate with another person.

This has led researchers to ask whether personality disorders could initially be conceptualized along a continuum based on ratings of each of these four dimensions: self-identity, self-direction, interpersonal empathy, and interpersonal intimacy. If this dimensional model were adopted for diagnosis, the health care professional would rate the person's level of personal functioning in these four areas. After the level of functioning was determined, the health care professional would rate pathological personality traits in five broad categories. These are (1) negative affectivity, (2) detachment, (3) antagonism, (4) disinhibition, and (5) psychoticism. A further consideration is how pervasive and stable these factors are. At this point, many researchers suggest that future versions of the *DSM* will be more like the alternative model of personality. The alternative approach is used in much of the research on personality disorders today. It should be noted that the *ICD-11* released in 2018 has adapted a dimensional approach that involves assigning the severity of the disorder followed by trait characteristics (Bach et al., 2022; Tyrer et al., 2019).

CONCEPT CHECK

- What is it about personality disorders that makes them difficult to treat? What factors do effective treatments have in common to address those difficulties?
- BPD has been the focus of most empirical treatment studies of personality disorders. What is the state of knowledge about treatments for other personality disorders? What do you think should be the top priority in future treatment research?
- Personality disorders are said to involve problems with the person's sense of self. What are these problems? What conceptual models have been proposed for helping us understand how the sense of self is disrupted in personality disorders?

SUMMARY

The basic definition of a personality disorder is one that (1) represents an enduring pattern of inner experience and behavior that deviates markedly from the expectations of the individual's culture; (2) exhibits a pattern that is inflexible, stable, and generally begins in adolescence; and (3) has characteristics that are especially apparent when these individuals find themselves in situations that are beyond their ability to cope. Research has shown that those with a personality disorder also meet criteria for other disorders—especially anxiety, mood, and substance use disorders. Not only do individuals with a personality disorder meet criteria for another non-personality disorder, but they also meet criteria for other personality disorders where the highest co-occurrence is seen within each of the clusters. Some researchers have suggested that personality characteristics reflected in personality disorders can be seen as an extreme version of typical personality characteristics. Thus, there can be both healthy and maladaptive personality styles. A healthy self is considered to have the following characteristics: (1) identity, (2) self-direction, and (3) positive interpersonal relationships characterized by empathy and intimacy. Some researchers, from an evolutionary perspective, view personality disorders as a failure to solve adaptive life tasks relating to identity or self, intimacy and attachment, and prosocial behavior.

Typical personality traits can be described by the dimensions of the five-factor model (FFM). The five personality dimensions are (1) extraversion, which ranges from active and outer-directed on one end to passive and inner-directed on the other; (2) neuroticism, which ranges from being worried and temperamental on one side of the continuum to being even-tempered and confident on the other; (3) openness, which is associated with curiosity, flexibility, and an artistic sensitivity, including imaginativeness and the ability to create a fantasy world; (4) agreeableness, which is associated with being sympathetic, trusting, cooperative, modest, and straightforward; and (5) conscientiousness, which is associated with being diligent, disciplined, well-organized, punctual, and dependable. From an evolutionary perspective, each of the personality dimensions may have particular advantages, as well as disadvantages, in specific environmental conditions. Research has shown that personality disorders can be understood as maladaptive variants of the FFM. Some have suggested that there would be advantages to considering personality disorders along a spectrum, which would allow for a mapping of personality disorders and personality traits in the FFM. Since each dimension of the FFM has been shown to have a genetic component and these five dimensions are found worldwide, a spectrum approach would help clarify another aspect of personality disorders.

DSM-5-TR identifies 10 personality disorders that can be organized into three clusters. Cluster A includes odd or eccentric disorders. Individuals with these disorders typically feel uncomfortable around or suspicious of others or restrict their relationships. Cluster A includes (1) schizoid personality disorder, which is characterized by a pervasive pattern of detachment from social relationships and a restricted range of emotional expression; (2) paranoid personality disorder, which is characterized by a pervasive distrust and suspiciousness of others; and (3) schizotypal personality disorder, which is characterized by odd beliefs and behaviors. The behavior of individuals with odd, eccentric personality disorders may seem similar to individuals with schizophrenia except that these individuals show a greater grasp of reality. These disorders are sometimes seen in first-degree relatives of those with schizophrenia.

The second cluster of personality disorders is referred to as Cluster B and includes dramatic, emotional, or erratic disorders. Individuals with these disorders show a wide diversity of patterns of social and emotional interactions with others: (1) antisocial personality disorder, which is characterized by a disregard for the other person; (2) borderline personality disorder (BPD), which is characterized by the three factors of instability in mood, interpersonal relationships, and a sense of self, which interact with each other in such a manner that the person experiences a changing world without a solid sense of self; (3) histrionic personality disorder, which is characterized by a pervasive pattern of excessive emotionality and attention seeking; and (4) narcissistic personality disorder, which is characterized by a pervasive pattern of grandiosity, a need for admiration, a sense of privilege or entitlement, and a lack of empathy for others.

Although the media interchange the words *antisocial personality disorder* and *psychopathy*, there are differences in the formal definitions of the two terms. Psychopathy is not a formal definition of *DSM-5-TR* but has been studied in both clinical and research settings. Individuals who display signs of psychopathy show (1) emotional detachment with a lack of empathy for the experiences of others and (2) impulsive behavior and a callousness concerning their actions. These patterns are stable and difficult to change. Recent research suggests there are two separate processes in the same individual with psychopathy: (1) the lack of fear and (2) a weakness in impulse control that has the effect of externalizing vulnerability. Only about 10% to 25% of individuals with an antisocial personality disorder would be classified as having psychopathy, and not all individuals who would be described as having psychopathy would show a conduct or antisocial personality disorder.

Cluster C includes anxious or fearful disorders: (1) avoidant personality disorder, which is characterized by a pattern of social inhibition, feelings of inadequacy, and hypersensitivity to negative evaluation; (2) dependent personality disorder, which is characterized by an excessive need to be taken care of, including clinging behavior; and (3) obsessive-compulsive personality disorder, which is characterized by a preoccupation with orderliness, perfectionism, and interpersonal control. In OCD, the individual typically attempts to control something that takes place outside of herself, whereas in obsessive-compulsive personality disorder, the need for control is part of the individual's self in every domain that the person experiences.

Personality disorders are difficult to treat for the following reasons: (1) One individual with a personality disorder may show different signs and symptoms from another, and (2) individuals with personality disorders find it difficult to maintain a close, intimate relationship with their therapist. Most of our knowledge of the treatment of personality disorders other than BPD is based on the experience of health care professionals, case studies, or simple descriptions of treatments. Medications have been used for specific aspects of different personality disorders; however, there are no medications that target all aspects of a personality disorder. BPD has been the focus of the most empirical treatment studies. Research has shown that treatments based on both cognitive behavioral and dynamic perspectives have been effective, including (1) DBT, whose cornerstone is based on problem solving and acceptance of the experience of the moment; (2) DDP, which was developed for clients who find therapy difficult as well as for those who may also have substance abuse problems; and (3) TFP, which seeks to reduce symptoms of BPD, especially self-destructive behaviors.

STUDY RESOURCES

Review Questions

1. A number of models have been presented in this chapter relating personality disorders to typical personality patterns. What are those models? What evidence is presented to support them?

2. What are the advantages and disadvantages of describing personality disorders in terms of categories versus dimensions?

3. The *DSM* places personality disorders in multiple groups. For each of the three groups, or clusters, of personality disorders, describe the cluster in terms of the following:
   a. The name and defining characteristics of the cluster
   b. The specific personality disorders included in the cluster, as well as the defining characteristics of each disorder

4. Historically, the term *borderline*, as the name implies, denoted individuals who were neither neurotic nor psychotic. From what you have read in this chapter, what additional meanings do you think the term *borderline* implies about that personality disorder?

5. What are three examples of effective treatment approaches for BPD? What is the overall approach of each therapy, and what are the goals for each stage of these therapies? How are the therapies similar, and how are they different?

For Further Reading

Beck, A., Freeman, A., & Davis, D. (2004). *Cognitive therapy of personality disorders* (2nd ed.). Guilford Press.

Gunderson, J., & Hoffman, P (Eds.). (2005). *Understanding and treating borderline personality disorder.* American Psychiatric Publishing.

Carey, E. (2011, June 23). *Expert on mental illness reveals her own fight. The New York Times.* https://www.nytimes.com/2011/06/23/health/23lives.html

Carey, B., Donaldson, N., Kang, S.-J., Louttit, M., & Winter, D. (2015). *Lives restored [Series]. The New York Times.* https://archive.nytimes.com/www.nytimes.com/interactive/science/lives-restored-series.html

Huprich, S (Ed.). (2015). *Personality disorders: Toward theoretical and empirical integration in diagnosis and assessment.* American Psychological Association.

Oldham, J., Skodol, A., & Bender, D (Eds.). (2009). *Essentials of personality disorders.* American Psychiatric Publishing.

Paris, J. (2007). *Half in love with death.* Routledge.

KEY TERMS

agreeableness
antisocial personality disorder
anxious fearful personality disorders (Cluster C)
avoidant personality disorder
borderline personality disorder (BPD)
conscientiousness
dependent personality disorder
dialectical behavior therapy (DBT)
dramatic emotional personality disorders (Cluster B)
dynamic deconstructive psychotherapy (DDP)
empathy
extraversion
five-factor model (FFM)
healthy self
histrionic personality disorder

identity
intimacy
narcissistic personality disorder
neuroticism
obsessive-compulsive personality disorder
odd, eccentric personality disorders (Cluster A)
openness
paranoid personality disorder
personality disorder
positive interpersonal relationships
psychopathy
schizoid personality disorder
schizotypal personality disorder
self-direction
transference-focused psychotherapy (TFP)

iStock.com/Carlos Pintau. Stock photo. Posed by models.

15 NEUROCOGNITIVE DISORDERS

LEARNING OBJECTIVES

15.1 Summarize the major cognitive and brain changes in older adulthood.

15.2 Distinguish between delirium and mild and major neurocognitive disorder.

15.3 Describe the characteristics, prevalence, and diagnosis of Alzheimer's disease.

15.4 Describe the characteristics, prevalence, and diagnosis of other mild and major neurocognitive disorders.

15.5 Identify methods of prevention, treatment, and support for individuals with neurocognitive disorders.

November 5, 1994

My fellow Americans, I have recently been told that I am one of the millions of Americans who will be afflicted with Alzheimer's disease.

Upon learning this news, Nancy and I had to decide whether as private citizens we would keep this a private matter or whether we would make this news known in a public way. In the past, Nancy suffered from breast cancer and I had my cancer surgeries. We found through our open disclosures we were able to raise public awareness. We were happy that as a result, many more people underwent testing. They were treated in early stages and able to return to normal, healthy lives.

So now we feel it is important to share it with you. In opening our hearts, we hope this might promote greater awareness of this condition. Perhaps it will encourage a clearer understanding of the individuals and families who are affected by it.

At the moment I feel just fine. I intend to live the remainder of the years God gives me on this Earth doing the things I have always done. I will continue to share life's journey with my beloved Nancy and my family. I plan to enjoy the great outdoors and stay in touch with my friends and supporters.

Unfortunately, as Alzheimer's disease progresses, the family often bears a heavy burden. I only wish there was some way I could spare Nancy from this painful experience. When the time comes, I am confident that with your help she will face it with faith and courage.

In closing, let me thank you, the American people, for giving me the great honor of allowing me to serve as your president. When the Lord calls me home, whenever that day may be, I will leave with the greatest love for this country of ours and eternal optimism for its future.

I now begin the journey that will lead me into the sunset of my life. I know that for America there will always be a bright dawn ahead.

Thank you, my friends. May God always bless you.

Sincerely, Ronald Reagan

From Ronald Reagan's Letter to the American People Concerning His Alzheimer's Disease. http://www.reagan.utexas.edu/archives/reference/alzheimerletter.html

President Ronald Reagan announced to the public in November 1994 that he had Alzheimer's disease.
Carol M. Highsmith, photographer. Retrieved from the Library of Congress, https://www.loc.gov/pictures/item/2011633940/

The loss of past memory was not as extreme as it is in amnesia. When I came out of the coma I had been in for 6 weeks, I knew who I was, and I knew that I was a husband, a father, and a psychologist. I knew my family, but I had difficulty recognizing some of my friends. In the beginning I thought I had two children, but I have but one. I thought my daughter was 13, but she was 15 at that point. I also thought I was 33, but I was 44.

During the drive home from the hospital (after 11 weeks), I saw that I did not recognize the route home, even though it was a route quite familiar to me. At that point, I realized that some of the geography of the city was lost to me. But I did recognize my home and the neighborhood when we arrived there. My house was familiar to me, but I didn't remember where some things were kept and how some things were used. I had to relearn how to play the stereo, set the alarm clock, use the calculator, change a razor blade, etc. All of these things were relearned, but because of the short-term memory problem, it often took several trials to relearn and keep these things in mind.

So, many things I had learned and that had made me feel like a competent person seemed to have been lost, and I wondered if I could be an adequate husband, father, or worker again. Combined with this, I felt to some extent that I had lost my identity. This was not total or extreme, but there were some questions in my mind about beliefs, values, and purposes in life. In addition, I felt that I had lost some of my cultural background when I had difficulty remembering some of the customs, traditions, and beliefs of the groups to which I belonged. This produces a feeling of being somewhat alone.

From Malcolm Meltzer. (1983). Poor Memory: A Case Report. Journal of Clinical Psychology, *39, 3–10.*

We all age. As we age, our mental and physical abilities change. Some of these changes happen gradually and appear to be related to genetic differences. Huntington's disease and Alzheimer's disease are examples of such genetic disorders. The letter from Ronald Reagan shows that he understood that he was experiencing gradual memory changes. Other changes happen more quickly. Events such as a stroke or heart attack may lead to not only physical changes but also changes in mental processing. The description of Malcolm Meltzer, who was both the author and the subject of the case report, resulted from a heart attack that influenced brain function and was a sudden event. This chapter focuses on **neurocognitive disorders** typically seen in older individuals. These disorders represent a loss of cognitive abilities not related to normal aging. Previously, these disorders were referred to as **dementias**.

The aging of each of us is related to a number of factors. These include the genes we received from our parents. These also include the experiences that happen to us, including the stresses of everyday life as well as the positive events in our lives. Aging also involves choices we make in terms of what we eat, how we exercise, and the type of work we do. Scientists are also asking what one can do to increase brain health (Brem & Sensi, 2018). To place neurocognitive changes in perspective, it is important to have an understanding of normal aging. This chapter begins by noting the worldwide changes in aging. This is followed by research considerations of factors that may prevent or delay neurocognitive disorders. After a section on delirium, the major neurocognitive disorders are described, with special attention given to Alzheimer's disease.

NORMAL COGNITIVE CHANGES RELATED TO AGING

We all know individuals or relatives who, as they age, show problems with memory or physical activities. Most of us also know individuals who continue to be productive well into their 80s and 90s. This has come to be called **successful aging** (Rowe & Kahn, 1987). The characteristics of successful aging include the following:

1. Freedom from disability and disease
2. High cognitive and physical functioning
3. Social activity, including both having friends and being productive

The idea of successful aging emphasizes that life is more than just living a long time. It also includes a sense of connectedness and a close interaction with one's environment and self. For example, many of the aging performers associated with 1960s and 1970s music, such as Bob Dylan, Keith Richards, Carole King, Rod Stewart, and Cher, still perform today.

Throughout the world, better public health conditions, such as clean water and sanitation as well as medical and disease-prevention procedures, have led to an increasing life expectancy. In the United States, individuals age 65 and older went from less than 2% of the population in 1900 to over 16% of the population in 2020 (Figure 15.1). It is estimated that by 2060, over 20% of the U.S. population will be over 65 (Figure 15.2). Aging worldwide is discussed in *Cultural LENS: Aging Around the World*.

Singer-songwriter Willie Nelson has continued to perform into his 90s.

James Jeffrey Taylor/Alamy Stock Photo

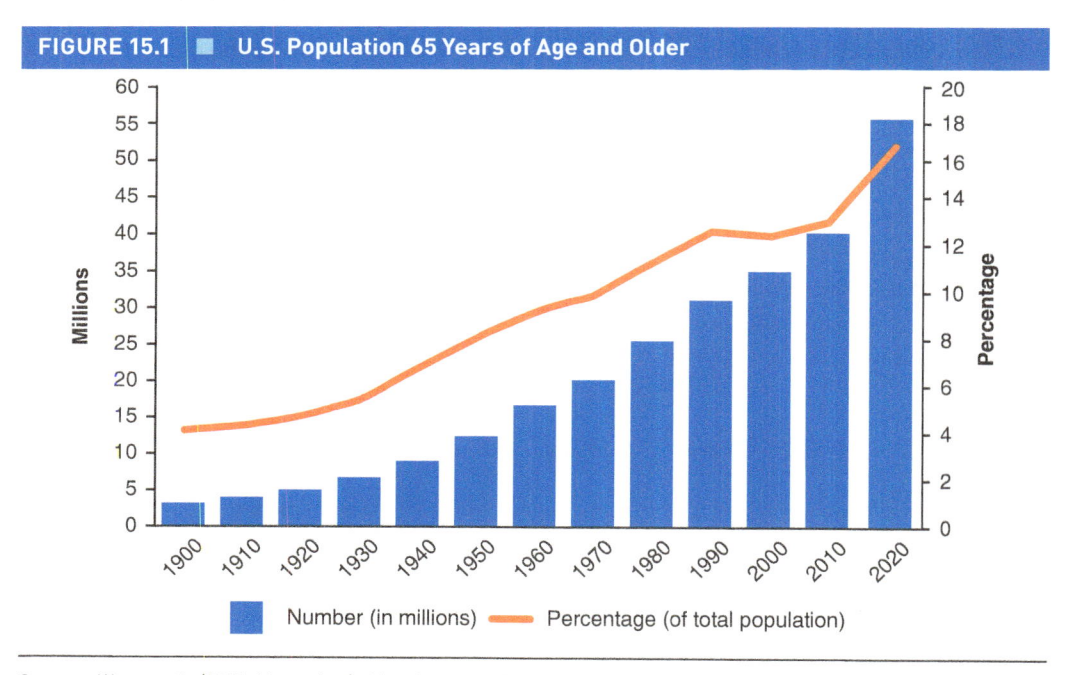

FIGURE 15.1 ■ U.S. Population 65 Years of Age and Older

Sources: Werner, C. (2011, November). The older population: 2010. 2010 census briefs (Figure 2). U.S. Government Printing Office. http://www.census.gov/prod/cen2010/briefs/c2010br-09.pdf; Caplan, Z. (2023, May 25). *U.S. older population grew from 2010 to 2020 at fastest rate since 1880 to 1890.* U.S. Census Bureau. https://www.census.gov/library/stories/2023/05/2020-census-united-states-older-population-grew.html

FIGURE 15.2 ■ Population Projections Into 2060

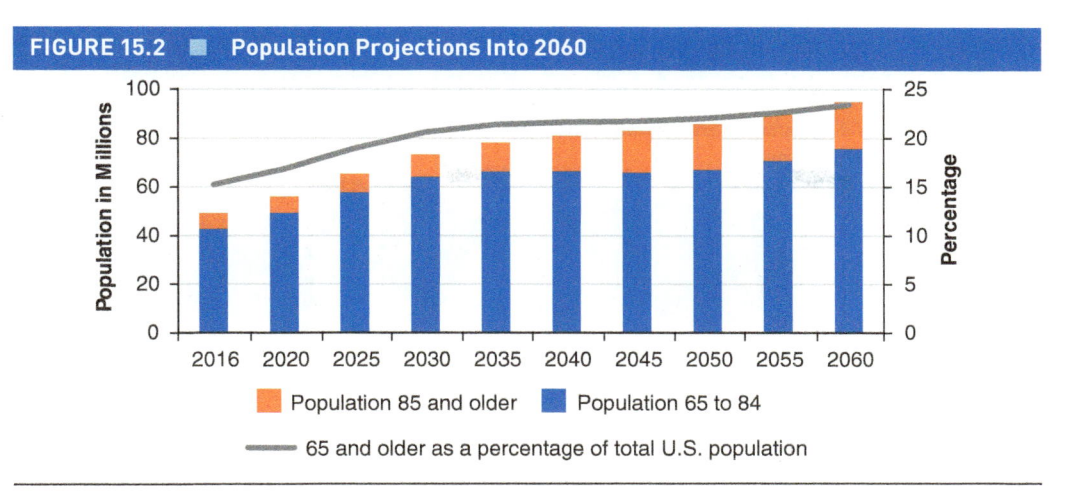

- Population 85 and older
- Population 65 to 84
- 65 and older as a percentage of total U.S. population

Source: U.S. Census Bureau, Population Division. (2012). Table 12. Projections of the Population by Age and Sex for the United States: 2015 to 2060 (NP2012-T12).

CULTURAL LENS
AGING AROUND THE WORLD

How old will you be in 2050 or 2060? You may be in your 50s or 60s or even older. With better access to clean water, fresh food, sanitation, and improved health care, individuals worldwide are living longer. In fact, in 2020 there were more people over age 65 than children under 5 worldwide (Figure 15.3). Data show that in North America, Europe, and Russia, over 11% of the population is 65 and older (Figure 15.4). In fact, in Japan, Italy, and Germany, over 20% of their populations are 65 years and older. These data are influenced by a number of factors, including birth rate and immigration as well as improved health practices.

FIGURE 15.3 ■ World Population of Individuals Over 65 Years and Those Under 5 Years of Age

By 2020 there were more people in the world aged 65 and older than there were children younger than 5. This figure shows young children and older people as a percentage of the global population.

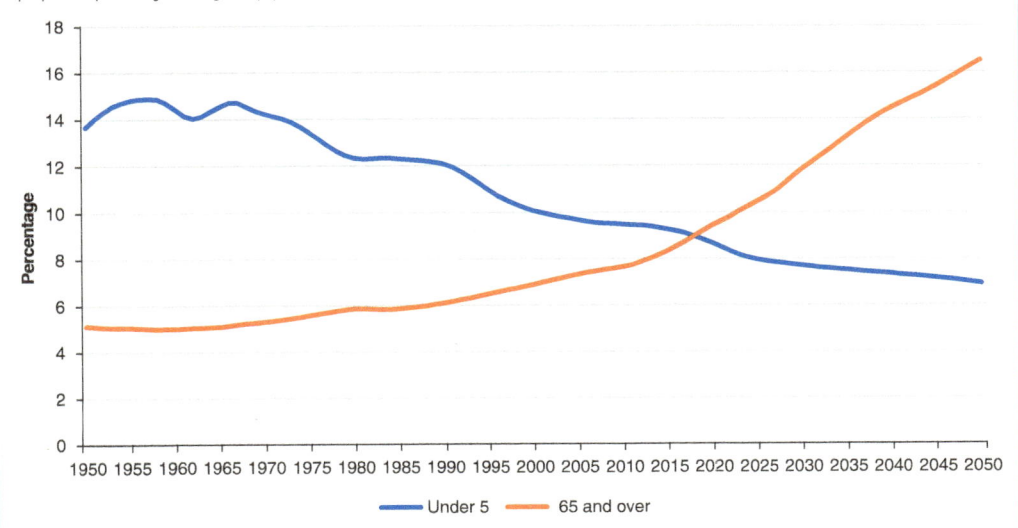

- Under 5
- 65 and over

Source: United Nations, Department of Economic and Social Affairs, Population Division. (2022). *World Population Prospects 2022*, Online Edition. https://population.un.org/wpp/Download/Standard/Population/

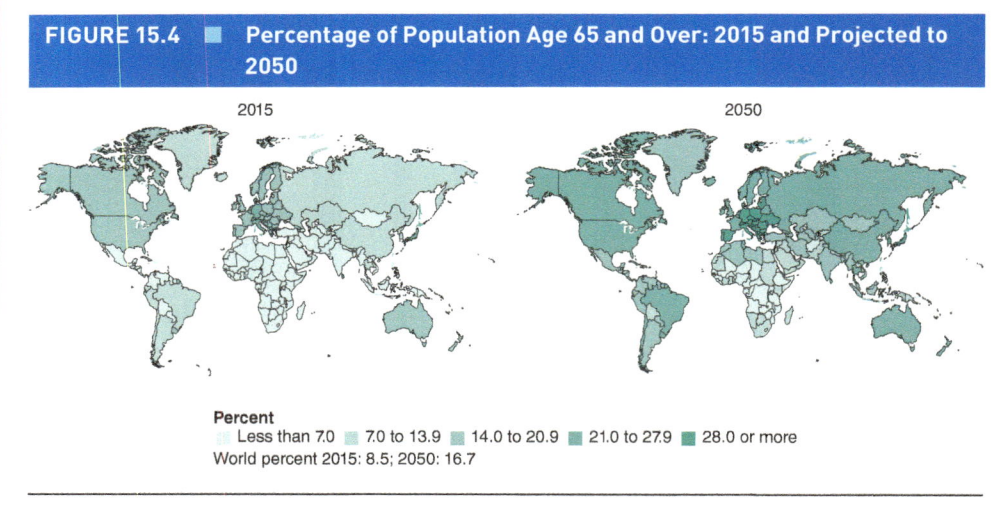

FIGURE 15.4 ■ Percentage of Population Age 65 and Over: 2015 and Projected to 2050

2015 | 2050

Percent
Less than 7.0 ■ 7.0 to 13.9 ■ 14.0 to 20.9 ■ 21.0 to 27.9 ■ 28.0 or more
World percent 2015: 8.5; 2050: 16.7

Source: He, W., Goodkind, D., & Kowal, P. (2016). An aging world: 2015. *International Population Reports*, P95-16-1. www.census.gov/content/dam/Census/library/publications/2016/demo/p95-16-1.pdf

With the expectation of an increasing percentage of the population being older, many countries are asking what facilities and resources will be needed for this older population. A large number of cities in more than 37 countries are participating in the World Health Organization (WHO) Global Network of Age-Friendly Cities and Communities. In addition, the American Association for Retired People (AARP) has developed reports on how different countries are planning and developing programs for older individuals (see http://arc.aarpinternational.org/home).

Since we know that an active life with social contacts can help to prevent cognitive decline (Ballesteros et al., 2015; Evans, Llewellyn, et al., 2018; Evans, Martyr, et al., 2018), communities in many countries have focused on healthy aging. One important component is accessibility in terms of transportation, access to and within buildings, and affordable housing. Another important component is social engagement. This includes creating community centers as well as providing opportunities for older adults to volunteer with community organizations, especially those that cut across generations. A third component is assistance in helping older individuals maintain their well-being. Such programs as Meals on Wheels, help with daily chores around the home, and regular check-ins can help to maintain quality of life for older individuals.

One innovative program in Japan uses the post offices and postal workers around the country to check on individuals and report back to their families if problems are apparent. Parts of Canada use a help line as a way to identify "at-risk" older adults. China, which has almost 25% of the world's population of those 60 and older, is developing an integrated care system for older adults. The United States offers health care to those over 65 through its Medicare and Medicaid programs.

Although many people think of technology and social media as mainly involving young adults, they are playing an important role in the lives of older adults, as well. For example, ride hailing services such as Uber or Lyft offer those who no longer drive an easy way to travel throughout their community. With limited effort, social media also offer a way for older adults to stay connected with family and friends and be involved with their children and grandchildren. Also, devices in a smart home can be used to increase safer living conditions. Online courses let older adults learn new information at their own rate. Likewise, telemedicine allows those in remote communities to check in with health care professionals. Some countries, such as Germany, train senior volunteers to help other older adults use technology to improve their lives. In countries such as the United States, South Korea, and Canada, programs have been developed to help fund early- to late-stage innovation-focused companies whose mission is to improve the lives of older adults.

In summary, the rate of aging in almost all countries is increasing as the result of both an increase in life span and a decrease in birth rate. This has required all countries to rethink how to utilize older individuals to increase productivity as well as give these individuals an optimal and meaningful lifestyle. There is also a critical role for young adults to consider how to plan for a long and productive life.

Thought Question

You're a young adult—from what you read in this chapter and in this LENS feature, what factors are important for you to consider in planning for your own long and productive life?

With better public health conditions, it is noncommunicable diseases such as cardiovascular problems and cancer that are the major causes of death among older individuals in both developed and developing countries. With individuals living longer, there is also a greater chance of developing neurocognitive disorders such as Alzheimer's and Parkinson's. Within the same age group, mortality is higher for people with neurocognitive disorders than for those without. Figure 15.5 shows the incidence of mild and moderate neurocognitive disorders for Europe, East Asia, and the United States. From this figure, one can note that the increase in neurocognitive disorders over the life span is similar throughout the world.

Do Cognitive Abilities Change With Age?

Cognitive abilities do change as one ages (Khammash et al., 2023). In order to understand the changes seen in neurocognitive disorders, it is important to examine normal changes in cognitive abilities across the life span. Timothy Salthouse (2004, 2011) combined data from 33 separate studies with 6,832 individuals to follow cognitive changes in terms of five major categories. Although memory is often seen as a problem of aging, other abilities are also affected. As can be seen in the graphs (Figures 15.6 through 15.10), there is a consistent picture of change over the life span for each category, with the sole exception of vocabulary ability, which does not decrease over the life span.

The first category examined by Salthouse is vocabulary, based on measures in which the individual provided definitions of words, named an object in a picture, or selected antonyms or synonyms. As seen in Figure 15.6, vocabulary ability remains fairly constant across the life span, with even a slight increase as individuals approach their 60s.

The second ability is perceptual speed. This reflects the ability to quickly compare patterns of letters or match symbols. As can be seen in Figure 15.7, this ability declines steadily from age 20 on.

The third factor is episodic memory. Episodic memory in these studies refers to the ability to recall information from stories or other stimulus items. As can be seen from Figure 15.8, these types of memory abilities remain fairly stable until around 60 years of age, and then they begin to drop off.

The fourth category is spatial visualization. Tests of spatial visualization require someone to move between a two-dimensional and a three-dimensional figure or determine shapes to fill a larger shape or imagine how a pattern would appear in a folded piece of paper. As can be seen from Figure 15.9, this

FIGURE 15.5 ■ Does Where You Live Influence the Development of Neurocognitive Disorders?

The development of neurocognitive disorders increases with age at similar rates in Europe, the United States, and Asia. This figure shows the incidence of mild and moderate neurocognitive disorders for Europe, East Asia, and the United States.

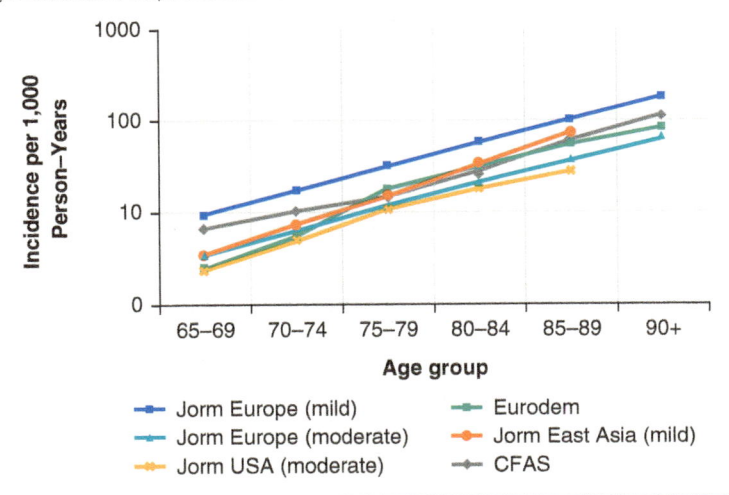

Credit: Brayne, C. (2007). The elephant in the room—Healthy brains in later life, epidemiology and public health. *Nature Reviews Neuroscience, 8*, 233–239.

Note: CFAS is a study from England and Wales. Eurodem is results from Europe. Jorm is based on research in Europe, the United States, and Asia.

FIGURE 15.6 ■ Does Your Vocabulary Increase or Decrease as You Age?

It tends to increase until your 60s. This figure shows vocabulary abilities across the life span based on the Wechsler Adult Intelligence Scale (WAIS) vocabulary, picture vocabulary, and synonym and antonym measures.

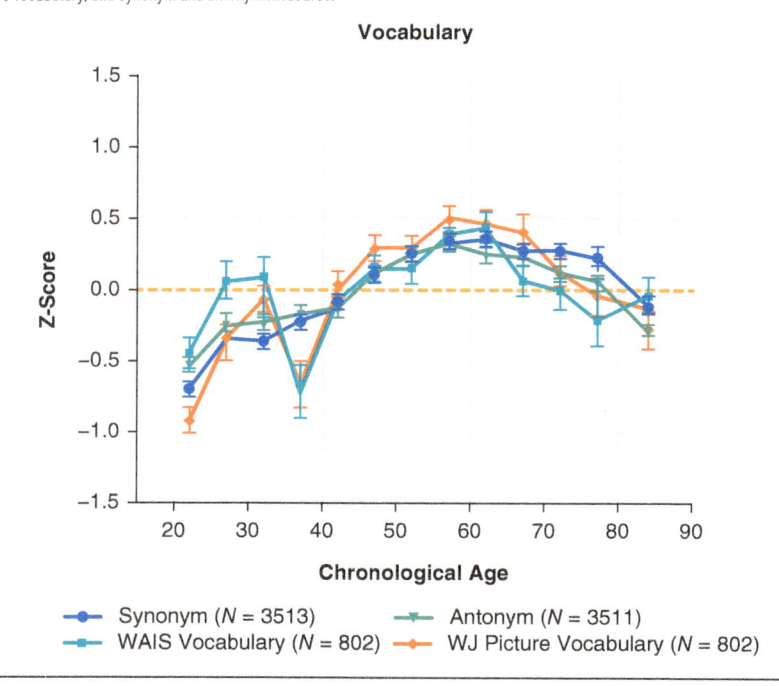

- Synonym (N = 3513)
- Antonym (N = 3511)
- WAIS Vocabulary (N = 802)
- WJ Picture Vocabulary (N = 802)

Credit: Salthouse, T. (2004). Localizing age-related individual differences in a hierarchical structure. *Intelligence, 32,* 541–561, with permission from Elsevier.

FIGURE 15.7 ■ How Does Aging Affect Your Processing Speed?

After 20 years of age, the perceptual speed across the life span decreases. This figure is based on three different measures.

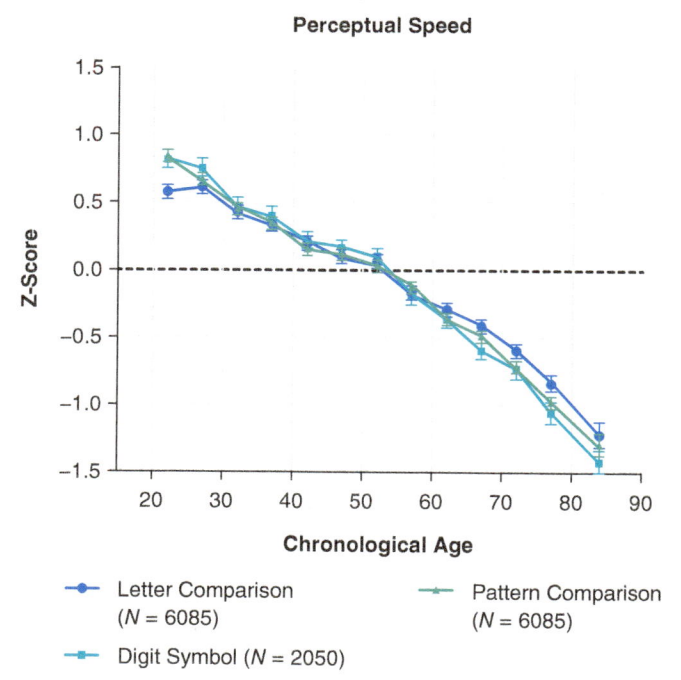

- Letter Comparison (N = 6085)
- Pattern Comparison (N = 6085)
- Digit Symbol (N = 2050)

Credit: Salthouse, T. (2004). Localizing age-related individual differences in a hierarchical structure. *Intelligence, 32,* 541–561, with permission from Elsevier.

FIGURE 15.8 ■ Does Your Episodic Memory Increase or Decrease as You Age?

It stays about the same until age 60 and then decreases. This figure shows episodic memory across the life span based on measures of free recall, logical memory, and paired associates.

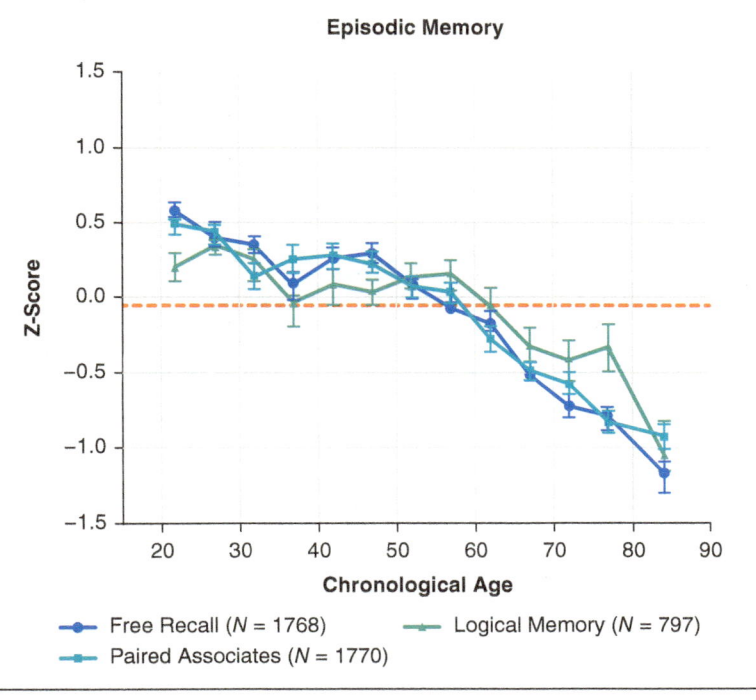

Episodic Memory

- Free Recall ($N = 1768$)
- Paired Associates ($N = 1770$)
- Logical Memory ($N = 797$)

Credit: Salthouse, T. (2004). Localizing age-related individual differences in a hierarchical structure. *Intelligence, 32,* 541–561, with permission from Elsevier.

FIGURE 15.9 ■ Do Your Spatial Visualization Abilities Increase or Decrease as You Age?

After our 30s, there is a decrease in spatial visualization across the life span. This figure is based on measures of spatial relations, paper folding, and form board skills.

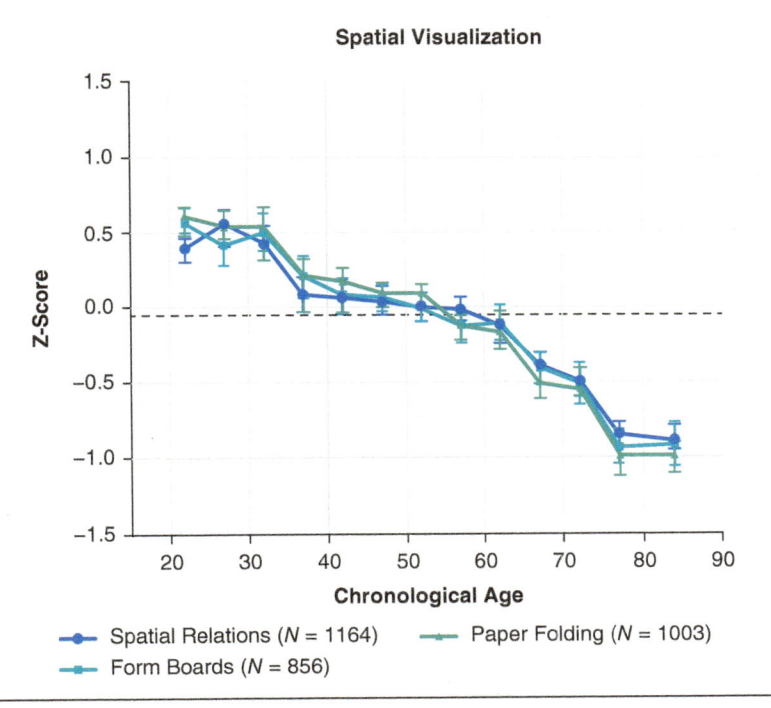

Spatial Visualization

- Spatial Relations ($N = 1164$)
- Form Boards ($N = 856$)
- Paper Folding ($N = 1003$)

Credit: Salthouse, T. (2004). Localizing age-related individual differences in a hierarchical structure. *Intelligence, 32,* 541–561, with permission from Elsevier.

FIGURE 15.10 ■ Does Your Reasoning Ability Increase or Decrease as You Age?

There is an initial drop in our 20s, and then it is stable until our 60s. This graph shows reasoning across the life span based on Raven's, Shipley abstraction, and letter sets tests.

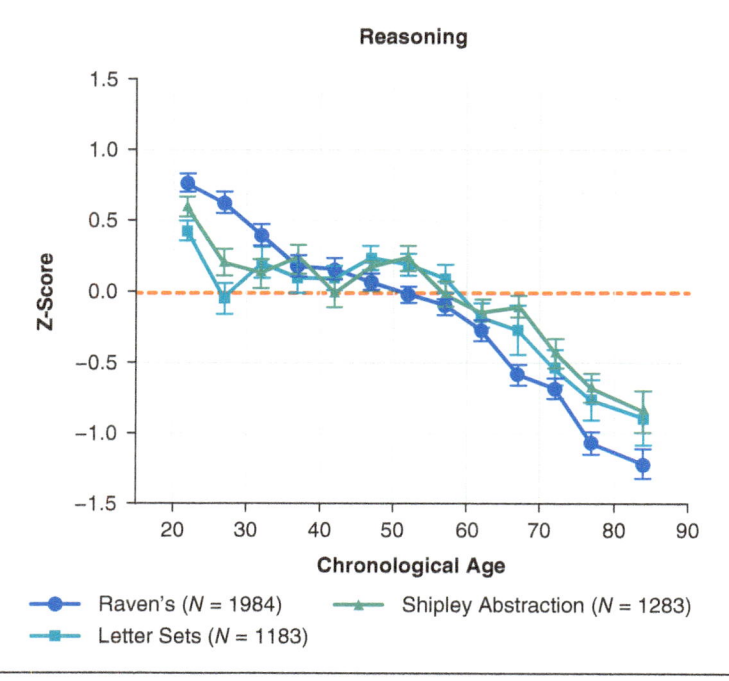

Credit: Saltnouse, T. (2004). Localizing age-related individual differences in a hierarchical structure. *Intelligence, 32*, 541–561, with permission from Elsevier.

ability is best in a person's 20s and 30s. It decreases but remains stable through a person's 40s to 60s. It then decreases rapidly.

The fifth category is reasoning. This includes determining geometric patterns needed to complete a sequence or completing word or letter patterns. As can be seen from Figure 15.10, the ability to determine the next symbol in a set of geometric patterns is best in individuals in their 20s and then decreases gradually into their 80s.

RESEARCH TERMS TO KNOW

Z-SCORE

When a researcher has more than one measure of a particular concept, they need a way to show the different measures on the same scale. In the case of cognitive abilities across the life span (see Figures 15.6 through 15.10), each graph is based on three or four different measures of the same cognitive ability. Since each measure has a different mean and standard deviation, plotting each measure could give a confusing picture. However, if you converted these to standard scores such that each had the same mean, then you could plot them. This is what a z-score does. Every measure when converted to a z-score has a mean of zero. What you plot in these graphs is the standard deviation or differences from the mean. The actual formula for a z-score is the difference between a particular score and the mean of the scores divided by the standard deviation. Simply put, z-scores allow for the comparison of different measures on the same scale.

How the Brain Changes With Age

Two consistent findings are (1) that older adults, generally defined as 65 years of age or older, show changes in brain structure and (2) that they use their brains in different ways from younger adults (Khammash et al., 2023; Mather, 2015 Park & Reuter-Lorenz, 2009; Reuter-Lorenz & Park, 2010).

In terms of brain volume, volume reduction is seen in the hippocampus, cerebellum, dorsolateral prefrontal cortex (dlPFC), and caudate nucleus, which are areas related to executive control and memory. Along with hippocampus changes, reductions of dopamine with age also play a role in the inability to remember events (Leal & Yassa, 2015). Specific genes can also change during aging for a variety of reasons. As with cancer, some researchers have examined mutations in a subset of genes in the brain that could produce neurocognitive disorders such as Alzheimer's disease (Miller et al., 2021).

Areas involved in emotional processes such as the amygdala and ventromedial prefrontal cortex show little structural and functional decline compared with other areas. Likewise, the visual cortex and the *entorhinal cortex* show little reduction in volume with age. The entorhinal cortex is located in the temporal lobe and serves as a hub that connects the hippocampus and the neocortex. It is involved in memory and spatial navigation. It is one of the first areas affected in Alzheimer's disease.

In order to solve problems, older individuals use their brains differently. Even when both younger and older adults perform a memory task successfully, the older adults recruit more brain regions than do younger adults. One interpretation is that older adults need additional executive resources to perform the same task. This is referred to as *compensation*. That is, in order to optimize their performance, older adults perform the same task using additional neural circuitry (Figure 15.11). When older adults use just the brain areas that are activated in younger individuals, they do not perform the tasks as well as younger adults.

As you are sitting and doing nothing, the default network in your brain turns on. When you start performing a task, more task-related networks are activated, and the default network is inhibited. In younger individuals, the same pattern of activity in the frontal lobes, the parietal lobes, the temporal lobes, and the cingulate is seen across a variety of tasks in numerous studies (Beason-Held, 2011). In older individuals, the number of brain areas involved in the default network is larger, especially in the frontal lobes. Older adults also have a more difficult time turning off the default network. It is assumed that this is related to the problems some older adults have in shifting cortical resources to new tasks.

One interesting study followed a group of individuals in Scotland who were given an IQ test at age 11 and then again at age 79 (see For Further Reading). Beginning at age 79, a subset of the original participants were also followed until they were 87. Overall, a number of behavioral factors, such as not smoking and being more physically active and fit, were associated with better mental aging. Also, eating fresh fruits and vegetables was associated with better health (Corley et al., 2015). The effect of alcohol consumption on cognitive abilities in aging was related to one's ability to metabolize alcohol (Ritchie et al., 2014). Individuals with higher genetic ability to process alcohol showed relative improvements

FIGURE 15.11 ■ Do Older Individuals Use Their Brain Differently When Solving Problems Compared With Younger Individuals?

Older adults recruit more of their brain to solve the same task as younger adults.

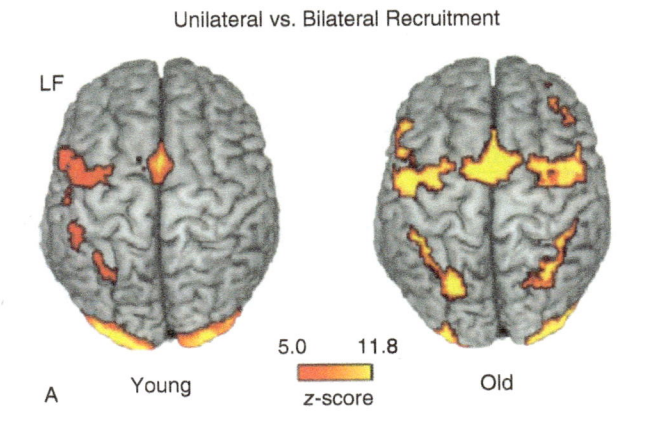

Unilateral vs. Bilateral Recruitment

Credit: Schneider-Garces, N. J., Gordon, B. A., Brumback-Peltz, C. R., Shin, E., Lee, Y., Sutton, B. P., & Fabiani, M. (2010). Span, CRUNCH and beyond: Working memory capacity and the aging brain. *Journal of Cognitive Neuroscience, 15,* 655–669. Reprinted by permission of MIT Press Journals.

FIGURE 15.12 ■ Can Genes Influence Cognitive Decline?

Yes, the presence of the APOE4 allele is associated with cognitive decline, even in individuals without a neurocognitive disorder.

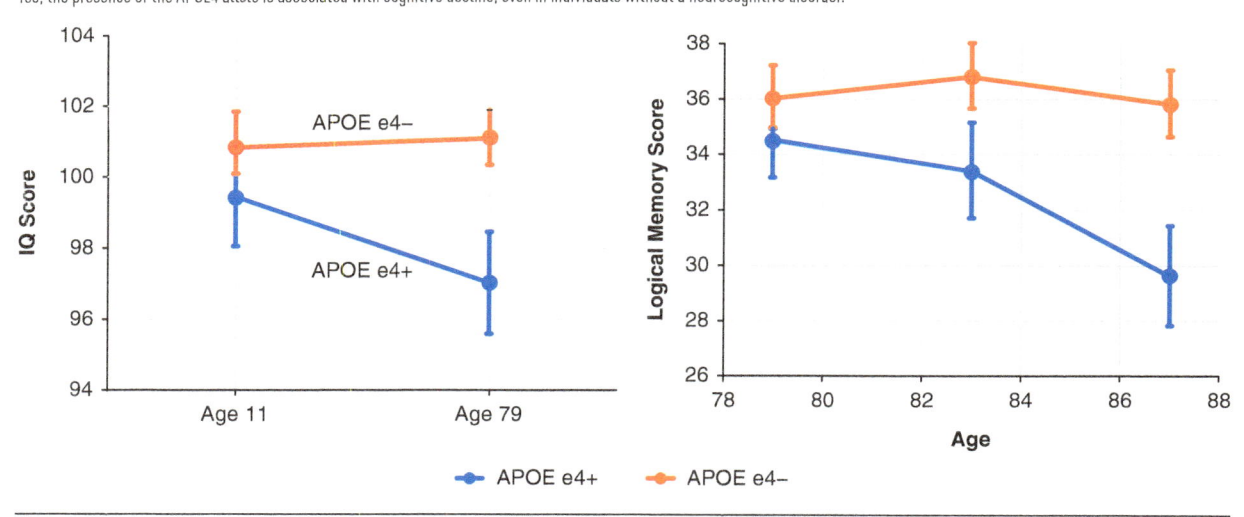

Credit: Harris, S., & Deary, I. (2011). The genetics of cognitive ability and cognitive ageing in healthy older people. *Trends in Cognitive Sciences, 15,* 388–394, with permission from Elsevier.

in cognitive ability with more consumption, whereas those with low processing capacity showed a negative relationship between cognitive change and alcohol consumption. In terms of personality and cognitive abilities, low levels of neuroticism were associated with better cognitive aging (Zammit et al., 2014). It was also found that those individuals who had stimulating lifestyles, including complex work environments, showed better cognitive abilities in later life (Smart et al., 2014). Although reduced, this association continued even when the age 11 IQ was considered.

A person's genetics was also related to their cognitive functioning (Cacciaglia et al., 2019). What the researchers discovered was that those individuals with a variant of the APOE gene, known as the APOE4 allele, showed more cognitive decline even in the absence of a neurocognitive disorder. Figure 15.12 shows that at age 11, there was little difference in the IQ scores of those with and without the APOE4 allele. However, by age 79, those with the APOE4 allele showed a lower IQ score, whereas those without this allele showed a similar IQ score to that seen when they were age 11. On the logical memory task, those with the APOE4 allele showed a decline over the next 8 years.

CONCEPT CHECK

- What are the primary characteristics of successful aging? What can individuals and communities do to promote successful aging, and why is that important?
- What is the relationship between cognitive changes in older adults and mental illness?

CATEGORIES OF NEUROCOGNITIVE DISORDERS

Neurocognitive disorders represent a condition in which a person shows cognitive deficits that are greater than those experienced with normal aging. In its section on these disorders, the fifth edition text revision of the *Diagnostic and Statistical Manual of Mental Disorders* (*DSM-5-TR*) (American Psychiatric Association, 2022) discusses delirium, mild neurocognitive disorder, and major neurocognitive disorder. This section of the chapter will cover the typical characteristics, prevalence, and *DSM-5-TR* criteria for these three broad categories.

Delirium: Characteristics, Prevalence, and Causes

Delirium is a short-term state of confusion. This short-term condition is characterized by a change in cognitive processing such as an inability to focus attention or problems with language, memory, or orientation. The idea of delirium dates back to at least the time of Hippocrates (Caraceni & Grassi, 2011; Lindesay et al., 2002). In the 19th century, the term *confusion* was often used in relation to delirium. Physical illness, toxins (including alcohol), and infections were historically seen as causes of delirium. The modern concept of delirium is based largely on the work of Lipowski (1980), who brought together a spectrum of acute cognitive problems that influence consciousness and are associated with medical illness. The fact that signs and symptoms associated with delirium fluctuate and are seen to be reversible has been used to differentiate it from more stable neurocognitive disorders.

The *DSM-5-TR* (American Psychiatric Association, 2022) describes delirium as a disturbance in attention and awareness. That is, the person is less aware of their environment and has a reduced ability to direct and change the focus of attention. Additional cognitive disturbances such as memory, language, or perceptual disorders are seen. Further, delirium develops over a short period of time and shows fluctuations in severity during the day. In general, delirium develops in relation to another medical condition, including medication side effects or toxins.

Delirium occurs in up to 56% of older adults in general hospital populations (Jones et al., 2010). It is seen in 15% to 53% of older individuals after a medical operation and in 70% to 87% of those in intensive care (American Psychiatric Association, 2013). In a community sample, the prevalence of delirium is low (1%–2%) but increases with age to where the prevalence is 14% among those over 85. Overall, delirium is seen as a disturbance of consciousness that cannot be accounted for by neurocognitive disorders. Its onset is typically abrupt and lasts for only a few hours or days. It can be caused by a number of underlying physiological disturbances. Those who show weakened connection between brain areas may be more at risk for delirium (Montfort et al., 2019). As seen in the prevalence data, it is a frequent complication of hospitalization for older populations.

Delirium can manifest in a number of ways and be related to a number of causes. Problems with memory of recent events is one common manifestation of delirium. However, memory of older experiences also occurs. Language problems are such that the person sounds incoherent, disorganized, and rambling. Writing problems may also be present. The person may also appear disoriented. Although delirium more often occurs in older individuals, it can also be seen in young children. The following is the case study of Bobby Baldwin (not his real name).

CASE OF BOBBY BALDWIN
DELIRIUM

Bobby Baldwin is a 7-year-old white male. He was taken to the hospital because he appeared to have ingested insecticide. While at the hospital, he was interviewed by a health care professional. When asked his address, he answered correctly but then spelled the name of the city as the word *house*. When asked about his birthday, he gave the wrong year for when he was born. He then said, "Jerry, get up and stand on this. Who said you could wear a blue jacket?" When asked about his hospital experience, he said, "Whose funeral—all the cars around mean a funeral—I was in the hospital 2 or 3 days." When asked about what he last ate, he said, "Today is Thursday—it's April—A B C. That is the alphabet. Jerry doesn't know the alphabet." He misperceived the 6'4," 200-pound male health care worker as his mother. When identifying common objects, he answered all incorrectly—that is, a pen clip was a cross, a pen point was a cross and then a tent, and to the remaining objects he said, "How many hamburgers did you get?" He was unable to draw the geometric objects. Bobby also lost track in the middle of some of the tasks, such as counting backward.

When reexamined some 3 days later, Bobby was alert. He gave his correct birthday and address and knew what day it was. He could remember what he had last eaten. He could also draw geometric

> objects. He did complain of fatigue during the examination. The health care professional who examined Bobby concluded that there were no longer signs of delirium. Bobby did, however, show signs of mild central nervous system problems related to having ingested the insecticide.
>
> Source: Based on Prugh, D. G., Wagonfeld, S., Metcalf, D., & Jordan, K. (1980). A Clinical Study of Delirium in Children and Adolescents [Suppl.]. *Psychosomatic Medicine*, *42*, 177–195.

Neurocognitive Disorders: Characteristics, Prevalence, and Diagnosis

Neurocognitive declines are typically shown in memory-related processes. Some older individuals call mild memory problems "senior moments," in which they cannot remember someone's name or a particular word. Some individuals show a progression in which it becomes more difficult to encode recent information or retrieve it from long-term memory. It is not uncommon for people with memory problems in old age to be able to remember events in great detail from their distant past while showing real problems remembering recent events.

In addition to memory problems, there can also be problems in a number of other cognitive processes. Complex attentional tasks in which the individual must divide their attention or pay attention to more than one process at a time may be difficult. Problems in executive functions that require planning, mental flexibility, and learning from mistakes can also be compromised. Declines in other tasks involving language and spatial abilities also occur in neurocognitive disorders. In addition to cognitive tasks, the person may show declines in social processes such as recognizing the intentions or emotions of others and being able to regulate one's own behavior.

As noted previously, a number of cognitive abilities are shown to decline with age. However, in many older individuals, these do not interfere with living a normal life. They may rely more on lists or friends to help them live independently. When cognitive or social deficits are greater than those seen with normal aging, this decline is diagnosed as a **mild neurocognitive disorder** (Table 15.1). If the declines are severe and interfere with one's ability to function independently, then this is diagnosed as a **major neurocognitive disorder** (Table 15.2). In *DSM-5-TR*, the diagnosis of major neurocognitive disorder replaced the term *dementia*.

The diagnosis of a neurocognitive disorder is a two-step process. The first step is to determine if the person is showing normal changes related to aging, a mild neurocognitive disorder, or a major neurocognitive disorder. This initially can be accomplished by using the Mental Status Exam as described in Chapter 4. With mild neurocognitive disorder, the person is still able to function independently and perform activities such as paying bills and taking medications on their own. When the person is no longer able to function independently, the diagnosis is major neurocognitive disorder. The second step is to determine what caused the neurocognitive disorder. Potential causes include Alzheimer's disease, frontotemporal lobar degeneration, Lewy body disease, vascular disease, substance/medication use, human immunodeficiency virus (HIV) infection, prion disease, Parkinson's disease, Huntington's disease, or another medical condition. These major causes of neurocognitive disorders will be described in the next sections.

It has been estimated that some type of neurocognitive disorder will impact around 15% of all individuals over age 65 and up to 45% of those over age 80. Since more extreme cases will require extensive care in a facility such as a nursing home, neurocognitive disorders require a large expenditure of resources on the part of the individual, their family, and society as a whole. Family members and caregivers in turn are at risk for a number of psychological problems, including depression, anxiety, and stress. It has been estimated that about 10% of all health care costs are used for neurocognitive disorders. Costs are expected to increase in the future. However, the actual prevalence of neurocognitive disorders has decreased 44% from the 1980s to the 2010s, according to one large-scale U.S. study (Satizabal et al., 2016). In the United Kingdom, a 20% drop in these disorders was seen in the two decades between 1989 and 2011 (Matthews et al., 2016). This suggests that neurocognitive disorders may be reduced over time. Although both studies only looked at prevalence, the U.S. study also showed a reduction in cardiovascular disorders, suggesting that exercise, diet, or health habits could help to explain these results.

TABLE 15.1 ■ *DSM-5-TR* Diagnostic Criteria for Mild Neurocognitive Disorder

A. Evidence of modest cognitive decline from a previous level of performance in one or more cognitive domains (complex attention, executive function, learning and memory, language, perceptual-motor, or social cognition) based on:

    Concern of the individual, a knowledgeable informant, or the clinician that there has been a mild decline in cognitive function; and

    A modest impairment in cognitive performance, preferably documented by standardized neuropsychological testing or, in its absence, another quantified clinical assessment.

B. The cognitive deficits do not interfere with capacity for independence in everyday activities (i.e., complex instrumental activities of daily living such as paying bills or managing medications are preserved, but greater effort, compensatory strategies, or accommodation may be required).

C. The cognitive deficits do not occur exclusively in the context of a delirium.

D. The cognitive deficits are not better explained by another mental disorder (e.g., major depressive disorder, schizophrenia).

Specify whether due to:

Note: Each subtype listed has specific diagnostic criteria and corresponding text, which follow the general discussion of major and mild neurocognitive disorders (NCDs).

- **Alzheimer's disease**
- **Frontotemporal degeneration**
- **Lewy body disease**
- **Vascular disease**
- **Traumatic brain injury**
- **Substance/medication use**
- **HIV infectionPrion disease**
- **Parkinson's disease**
- **Huntington's disease**
- **Another medical condition**
- **Multiple etiologies**
- **Unknown etiology**

Coding note: Code based on medical or substance etiology. An additional code indicating the etiological medical condition must immediately precede the diagnostic code **F06.7z** for mild NCD due to a medical etiology. An additional code is not used for medical etiologies that are judged to be "possible" (i.e., mild NCD due to possible Alzheimer's disease, due to possible frontotemporal degeneration, due to possible Lewy body disease, possibly due to vascular disease, possibly due to Parkinson's disease). See coding table on pp. 682–683. For substance/medication-induced mild NCD, code based on type of substance; see "Substance/Medication-Induced Major or Mild Neurocognitive Disorder."

Note: **G31.84** is used for mild NCD due to unknown etiology and for mild NCD due to a possible medical etiology (e.g., possible Alzheimer's disease); no additional code for medical or substance etiology is used.

Specify (see coding table for details):

Without behavioral disturbance: If the cognitive disturbance is not accompanied by any clinically significant behavioral disturbance.

With behavioral disturbance *(specify disturbance):* If the cognitive disturbance is accompanied by a clinically significant behavioral disturbance (e.g., apathy, agitation, anxiety, mood symptoms, psychotic disturbance, or other behavioral symptoms).

Coding note: Use additional disorder code(s) to indicate clinically significant psychiatric symptoms due to the same medical condition causing the mild NCD (e.g., **F06.2** psychotic disorder due to traumatic brain injury, with delusions; **F06.32** depressive disorder due to HIV disease, with major depressive–like episode). Note: Mental disorders due to another medical condition are included with disorders with which they share phenomenology (e.g., for depressive disorders due to another medical condition, see the chapter "Depressive Disorders").

Coding and Recording Procedures

The following are examples of coding and recording different types of mild NCDs. *(For more information, see coding table on pp. 682–683 and coding notes in the specific diagnostic criteria for each major and mild NCD subtype):*

Mild neurocognitive disorder due to probable Alzheimer's disease, without behavioral disturbance: G30.9 Alzheimer's disease, **F06.70** mild neurocognitive disorder due to probable Alzheimer's disease, without behavioral disturbance.

Mild neurocognitive disorder due to possible Alzheimer's disease, without behavioral disturbance: G31.84 mild neurocognitive disorder due to possible Alzheimer's disease, without behavioral disturbance.

Credit: Reprinted with permission from the *Diagnostic and Statistical Manual of Mental Disorders, fifth edition, text revision (DSM-V-TR)*, pp. 680–683 (Copyright © 2022). American Psychiatric Association. All rights reserved.

TABLE 15.2 ■ *DSM-5-TR* Diagnostic Criteria for Major Neurocognitive Disorder

A. Evidence of significant cognitive decline from a previous level of performance in one or more of the cognitive domains (complex attention, executive function, learning and memory, language, perceptual-motor, or social cognition) based on: Concerns of the individual, a knowledgeable informant, or the clinician that there has been a substantial decline in cognitive function; and a substantial impairment in cognitive performance, preferably documented by standardized neuropsychological testing or, in its absence, another quantified clinical assessment.

B. The cognitive deficits interfere with independence in everyday activities (i.e., at a minimum, requiring assistance with complex instrumental activities of daily living such as paying bills or managing medications).

C. The cognitive deficits do not occur exclusively in the context of a delirium.

D. The cognitive deficits are not better explained by another mental disorder (e.g., major depressive disorder, schizophrenia).

Specify whether due to:
Note: Each subtype listed has specific diagnostic criteria and corresponding text, which follow the general discussion of major and mild neurocognitive disorders (NCDs).

    Alzheimer's disease

    Frontotemporal degeneration

    Lewy body disease

    Vascular disease

    Traumatic brain injury

    Substance/medication use

    HIV infection

    Prion disease

    Parkinson's disease

    Huntington's disease

    Another medical condition

    Multiple etiologies

    Unknown etiology

Coding note: Code based on medical or substance etiology. An additional code indicating the etiological medical condition, if known, must immediately precede the diagnostic code for major NCD in most cases, as noted in the coding table on pp. 682–683. An additional code is not used for medical etiologies that are judged to be "possible" (i.e., major NCD due to possible Alzheimer's disease, due to possible frontotemporal degeneration, due to possible Lewy body disease, possibly due to vascular disease, possibly due to Parkinson's disease).
Specify current severity *(see coding table for details)*:
Mild: Difficulties with instrumental activities of daily living (e.g., housework, managing money).
Moderate: Difficulties with basic activities of daily living (e.g., feeding, dressing).
Severe: Fully dependent.
Specify (see coding table for details):
With agitation: If the cognitive disturbance is accompanied by clinically significant agitation.
With anxiety: If the cognitive disturbance is accompanied by clinically significant anxiety.
With mood symptoms: If the cognitive disturbance is accompanied by clinically significant mood symptoms (e.g., dysphoria, irritability, euphoria).
With psychotic disturbance: If the cognitive disturbance is accompanied by delusions or hallucinations.
With other behavioral or psychological disturbance: If the cognitive disturbance is accompanied by other clinically significant behavioral or psychological disturbance (e.g., apathy, aggression, disinhibition, disruptive behaviors or vocalizations, sleep or appetite/eating disturbance).
Without accompanying behavioral or psychological disturbance: If the cognitive disturbance is not accompanied by any clinically significant behavioral or psychological disturbance.
Coding and Recording Procedures
The following are examples of coding and recording different types of major NCDs. In cases where there is more than one type of associated behavioral or psychological disturbance, each is coded separately. *(For more information, see coding table on pp. 682–683 and coding notes in the specific diagnostic criteria for each major and mild NCD subtype):*
Major neurocognitive disorder due to probable Alzheimer's disease, mild, with anxiety: G30.9 Alzheimer's disease, **F02.A4** major neurocognitive disorder due to probable Alzheimer's disease, mild, with anxiety.

Major neurocognitive disorder due to traumatic brain injury, moderate, with psychotic disturbance and agitation: S06.2XAS diffuse traumatic brain injury with loss of consciousness of unspecified duration, sequela; **F02.B2** major neurocognitive disorder due to traumatic brain injury, moderate, with psychotic disturbance; **F02.B11** major neurocognitive disorder due to traumatic brain injury, moderate, with agitation.
Major neurocognitive disorder due to unknown etiology, severe, with mood symptoms: F03.C3 major neurocognitive disorder due to unknown etiology, severe, with mood symptoms.

Credit: Reprinted with permission from the *Diagnostic and Statistical Manual of Mental Disorders, fifth edition, text revision (DSM-5-TR)*, pp. 679–680 (Copyright © 2022). American Psychiatric Association. All rights reserved.

There is also a complex relationship between cognitive changes in older adults and mental illness (O'Hara, 2012). One clear example is depression in older adults. With depression in this age group, memory and executive function are generally impaired. Similar findings are seen in anxiety in older populations. They show problems in cognitive performance, the ability to divide their attention, and memory recall. In one study looking at women 85 years of age and older, the researchers measured depressive symptoms and performed a battery of neurocognitive tests. The participants then retook the tests 5 years later. The researchers found that depressive symptoms were associated with cognitive impairment over that time (Spira et al., 2012). In fact, these individuals had 3 times the risk of developing mild neurocognitive impairment. Other studies have shown an increased prevalence of symptoms of mental illness in those with a mild neurocognitive disorder compared with similar-age adults with normal cognitive processes (Teng et al., 2012). These symptoms of mental illness actually decreased the person's quality of life more than decreases in their cognitive abilities did.

UNDERSTANDING CHANGES IN *DSM-5* AND *DSM-5-TR*
NEUROCOGNITIVE DISORDERS

The changes made in *DSM-5* for this category are related to how neurocognitive disorders are described. In *DSM-IV*, these disorders were described in terms of delirium, dementia, amnestic, and other disorders. In *DSM-5*, the overall category is referred to as *neurocognitive disorders*. The category still includes specific conditions such as Alzheimer's disease, Lewy body, traumatic brain injury, Parkinson's disease, and so forth.

A further change, which was common already among health care professionals before *DSM-5*, is to classify the disorder as either major or mild. This is an initial step toward seeing severity on a continuum. Neurocognitive disorders that do not reach the threshold for diagnosis of a major disorder are referred to as a mild neurocognitive disorder. Generally, the distinction between mild and major is based on the results obtained from neuropsychological testing.

CONCEPT CHECK

- What are the characteristics of each of the following in terms of triggering event, symptoms, treatment, and prevalence?
  - Delirium
  - Mild neurocognitive disorder
  - Major neurocognitive disorder

NEUROCOGNITIVE DISORDER DUE TO ALZHEIMER'S DISEASE

Neurocognitive disorder due to Alzheimer's disease is a progressive disorder characterized by problems with memory (Breijyeh & Karaman, 2020; Selkoe et al., 2012; Ulrich & Holtzman, 2021). It is associated with a disruption of cortical networks followed by a loss of neurons, which results in cognitive problems. This dysfunction is initially shown in the entorhinal cortex, which represents an interface between the hippocampus and the neocortex (Igarashi, 2023).

Characteristics, Prevalence, and Diagnosis of Alzheimer's Disease

Initial memory problems may include forgetting names, misplacing household items, and forgetting the task one was about to undertake. As the disorder progresses, the person has more problems with finding words and may not be able to follow a familiar path from one location to another. The individual may

William Utermohlen, an American artist in London, drew self-portraits over a period of years to document the progressive effect on his brain of Alzheimer's disease.

AP Photo/JOSEPH KACZMAREK

also not undertake new tasks and may withdraw socially. The health care professional may also see the person looking to their family for answers to personal questions that should be part of their own personal knowledge. In the later stages of the disorder, motor problems become apparent. This includes urinary incontinence. The person may also spend time in bed without acknowledging other people, including family, or speaking to those around them. Delusions and hallucinations are seen in a subset of individuals. On average, the full course of the disorder encompasses 10 to 20 years. Currently, research is focusing on procedures that postpone or reduce the symptoms of Alzheimer's disease (Reiman et al., 2016). The artist William Utermohlen drew self-portraits as his Alzheimer's disease developed. Look over the series, which provides a vivid illustration of the artist's gradual decline due to the disease.

As noted in President Reagan's letter to the American public, reprinted at the beginning of this chapter, it is the family who experiences the greatest toll from the disorder, as the person with Alzheimer's disease loses their memories and sense of self. At one point, Reagan's wife Nancy said, "Ronnie's long journey has finally taken him to a distant place where I can no longer reach him." It is also hard for the children who had a relationship with their parent to lose this connection as well as watch it slowly disappear.

Alzheimer's disease is the most common neurodegenerative disorder in the world, and its prevalence is fairly similar worldwide (Hebert, Weuve, Scherr, & Evans, 2013; Prince et al., 2013). In 2020, it was estimated that the prevalence of Alzheimer's in the United States was 5.3% in those 65 to 74 years of age and 13.8% in those 75 to 84 years of age. After 85, the prevalence goes to 34.6% (Rajan et al., 2021). It affects women more often than men. Also in 2020, the Centers for Disease Control and Prevention (CDC) estimated that more than 5.8 million people in the United States had Alzheimer's disease and ranked the disease seventh overall as the cause of death. (It had been previously ranked sixth, but COVID-19 became a leading cause of death in 2020; see For Further Reading.) At present, it is the only disorder in the top 10 causes of death that cannot be prevented, cured, or even slowed in its progression. Presently, Alzheimer's disease can only be diagnosed with certainty from brain studies after death, although a number of imaging studies are suggesting alternatives to diagnosis for those who are living. Table 15.3 shows the *DSM-5-TR* diagnostic criteria for Alzheimer's disease.

Brain Changes With Alzheimer's Disease

The disorder was first described by Alois Alzheimer in his report of a 51-year-old woman who displayed progressive memory loss and disorientation (Alzheimer, 1907; see Alzheimer et al., 1995, for English translation). Alzheimer had followed this woman for a number of years. At one point, she could no longer orient herself, even in her own home. She also believed that people intended to murder her. After she died, Alzheimer examined her brain and identified two major factors that came to be seen as hallmarks of Alzheimer's disease. These are *neurofibrillary tangles* and *neuritic plaques* (Figure 15.13).

Neurofibrillary Tangles and Neuritic Plaques

The neurofibrillary tangles are found within the cell body of neurons, whereas the neuritic plaques are extracellular deposits. Today, we know that β-amyloid (beta amyloid) is the core protein involved in extracellular amyloid plaques and that tau is the core protein of intracellular neurofibrillary tangles (Edwards, 2019; Iaccarino et al., 2018; Iqbal et al., 2015 Y. Wang & Mandelkow, 2016). Using brain imaging techniques such as PET, β-amyloid and tau buildup can be seen in individuals with Alzheimer's disease (Figure 15.14).

TABLE 15.3 ■ *DSM-5-TR* Diagnostic Criteria for Neurocognitive Disorder Due to Alzheimer's Disease

The criteria are met for major or mild neurocognitive disorder.

A. There is insidious onset and gradual progression of impairment in one or more cognitive domains (for major neurocognitive disorder, at least two domains must be impaired).

B. Criteria are met for either probable or possible Alzheimer's disease as follows:

   For major neurocognitive disorder:

   Probable Alzheimer's disease is diagnosed if either of the following is present; otherwise, **possible Alzheimer's disease** should be diagnosed.
   1. Evidence of a causative Alzheimer's disease genetic mutation from family history or genetic testing.
   2. All three of the following are present:
      a. Clear evidence of decline in memory and learning and at least one other cognitive domain (based on detailed history or serial neuropsychological testing).
      b. Steadily progressive, gradual decline in cognition, without extended plateaus.
      c. No evidence of mixed etiology (i.e., absence of other neurodegenerative or cerebrovascular disease, or another neurological, mental, or systemic disease or condition likely contributing to cognitive decline).

   For mild neurocognitive disorder:

   Probable Alzheimer's disease is diagnosed if there is evidence of a causative Alzheimer's disease genetic mutation from either genetic testing or family history.

   Possible Alzheimer's disease is diagnosed if there is no evidence of a causative Alzheimer's disease genetic mutation from either genetic testing or family history, and all three of the following are present:
   1. Clear evidence of decline in memory and learning.
   2. Steadily progressive, gradual decline in cognition, without extended plateaus.
   3. No evidence of mixed etiology (i.e., absence of other neurodegenerative or cerebrovascular disease, or another neurological, mental, or systemic disease or condition likely contributing to cognitive decline).
      a. The disturbance is not better explained by cerebrovascular disease, another neurodegenerative disease, the effects of a substance, or another mental, neurological, or systemic disorder.

Coding note (see coding table on pp. 682–683):
For major neurocognitive disorder (NCD) due to probable Alzheimer's disease: 1) code first **G30.9** Alzheimer's disease, 2) followed by **F02**. 3) Next, code the current severity of the cognitive disturbance (mild, moderate, severe) and 4) whether or not there is an accompanying behavioral or psychological disturbance. For example, for major NCD due to probable Alzheimer's disease, moderate, with psychotic disturbance, the ICD-10-CM code is **F02.B2**.
For major NCD due to possible Alzheimer's disease: 1) code first **F03** (there is no additional medical code). 2) Next, code the current severity of the cognitive disturbance (mild, moderate, severe) and 3) whether or not there is an accompanying behavioral or psychological disturbance. For example, for major NCD due to possible Alzheimer's disease, mild, with mood symptoms, the ICD-10-CM code is **F03.A3**.
For mild NCD due to probable Alzheimer's disease: 1) code first **G30.9** Alzheimer's disease, 2) followed by either **F06.70** for mild NCD due to Alzheimer's disease without behavioral disturbance or **F06.71** for mild NCD due to Alzheimer's disease with behavioral disturbance. Use additional code(s) to indicate clinically significant psychiatric symptoms also due to Alzheimer's disease (e.g., **F06.2** psychotic disorder due to Alzheimer's disease, with delusions; **F06.32** depressive disorder due to Alzheimer's disease, with major depressive–like episode).
For mild NCD due to possible Alzheimer's disease, code **G31.84**. (Note: There is no additional medical code. "With behavioral disturbance" and "Without behavioral disturbance" cannot be coded but should still be recorded.)

Credit: Reprinted with permission from the *Diagnostic and Statistical Manual of Mental Disorders, fifth edition, text revision (DSM-5-TR)*, pp. 690–691 (Copyright © 2022). American Psychiatric Association. All rights reserved.

Research to understand the pathological forms of amyloid and tau has led to the conclusion that we should consider Alzheimer's in two stages (Ulrich & Holtzman, 2021). The first is a presymptomatic phase of 15 to 25 years during which amyloid builds up in the cerebral cortex in the absence of cognitive symptoms. In the second phase, tau tangles develop in the cortex, and neurodegeneration begins, with cognitive dysfunction appearing as brain cells die.

Alzheimer's disease is also associated with widespread synaptic and neuronal loss (Nath et al., 2012). During the progression of the disorder, the development of tangles follows a fixed pattern. It begins in an area in the temporal lobe and serves as a hub that connects the hippocampus and the neocortex, the entorhinal cortex. This then progresses to the hippocampus, which is associated with memory, and then to other cortical areas along anatomical connections. The development of neuritic plaques does not follow a fixed pattern. The development of tangles is better correlated with cognitive decline than is the development of plaques.

FIGURE 15.13 ■ Brain Changes With Alzheimer's Disease

The size of the brain shrinks as a result of Alzheimer's disease.

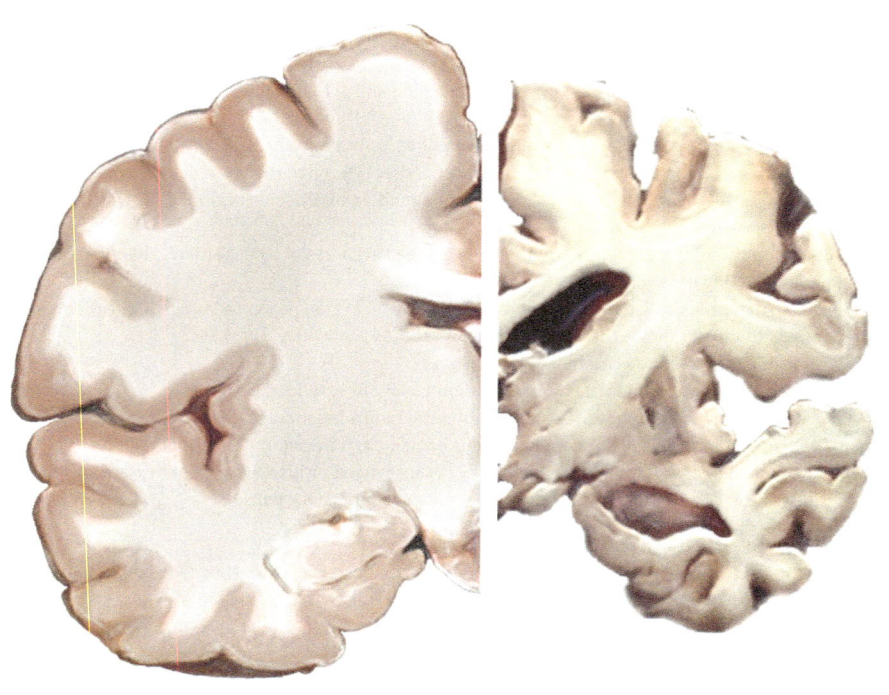

Credit: Science History Images/Alamy Stock Photo

FIGURE 15.14 ■ What Happens as a Person Develops Alzheimer's Disease?

As Alzheimer's disease develops, β-amyloid and tau build up in the brain and become visible in PET scans (red and yellow). Healthy controls do not show these changes.

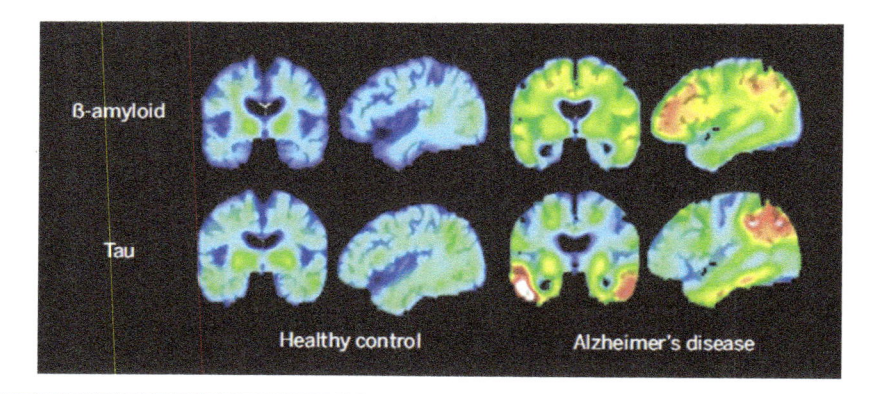

Credit: Underwood, E. (2015). Alzheimer's amyloid theory gets modest boost. *Science, 349*(6247), 464. https://doi.org/10.1126/science.349.6247.464. Reprinted with permission from AAAS.

Microglia

During Alzheimer's examination of his initial patient's brain, he also noted changes in the structural makeup of glia cells (Ulrich & Holtzman, 2021). One type of glia, the microglia, are now seen to play an important role in both the early and late stages of the development of Alzheimer's disease. Microglia are the main form of immune cells in the brain and can influence the relationship between amyloid and tau. In the developing brain, microglia are related to protecting the brain against infection and pruning excess synapses. Recent research has suggested that microglia processes could be a target for drugs to influence Alzheimer's disease (Kulkama et al., 2022).

Genes and Alzheimer's Disease

Family studies of those with Alzheimer's disease suggest that first-degree relatives (parents, siblings, and children) are at a greater risk for developing Alzheimer's. In fact, they have about 3 times the risk of developing the disorder. The photo of the DeMoe family from North Dakota shows a family in which all but one of the individuals pictured have a genetic makeup associated with early onset Alzheimer's.

Genetic studies also distinguish between those who show signs of the disorder before age 65 (early onset) and those who show signs of the disorder after age 65 (Rademakers & Rovelet-Lecrux, 2009; Savonenko et al., 2023). Individuals with early onset Alzheimer's show a stronger familial risk than the others. Early onset is associated with mutations in genes involved in encoding amyloid, called APP and β-amyloid (beta amyloid) processing, especially the genes PSEN1 and PSEN2. That is, the presence of the β-amyloid protein is the primary component in the development of plaques (van Norden et al., 2012).

Late onset Alzheimer's has been consistently associated with an allele of the APOE gene (Raichlen & Alexander, 2014; Sanes & Holtzman, 2021; Savonenko et al., 2023). In humans, there are three alleles of the APOE gene—APOE2, APOE3, and APOE4. Individuals with one APOE4 allele have an increased risk that is about 2 to 3 times more than individuals without it. If an individual has two APOE4 alleles, the risk increases to between 7 and 15 times. By contrast, the APOE2 gene is associated with a longer life and not having Alzheimer's disease. The gene APOE is involved with removing β-amyloid. GWAS approaches are also identifying risk locations of additional genes (Bellenguez et al., 2022; Lill & Bertram, 2022; Wightman et al., 2021).

One current theory of Alzheimer's disease is that the substances involved in the development and removal of plaques are not functioning correctly, allowing for their buildup. Current drug treatments for Alzheimer's disease seek to lower the production of β-amyloid. It has also been shown that those who engage in cognitively stimulating activities in their early and middle life show fewer problems associated with β-amyloid (Landau et al., 2012).

With a better understanding of the microglia processes related to Alzheimer's disease, new genes such as *TREM2*, which is related to the protein also referred to as TREM2, have come to light. The TREM2 receptor is exclusively expressed in microglia (Damisah et al., 2020). Variants of this protein

The DeMoe family from North Dakota; all of the family (except Karla) have a genetic makeup associated with early onset Alzheimer's.

AP Photo/Manuel Balce Ceneta

have been shown to be associated with an increase in Alzheimer's disease (Olufunmilayo & Holsinger, 2022). Overall, the fewer microglia that surrounded a plaque, the more damaged the nearby axons were. The basic idea is that microglia protect against amyloid's toxic effects.

One surprising finding is that healthy older adults who do not show cognitive problems may also have abundant plaques. In addition, plaques and tangles are found in individuals who do not show the loss of neurons seen in Alzheimer's disease. Thus, the presence of plaques and tangles is not related to dementia in all cases. Cognitive reserve and the brain's ability to reorganize networks to compensate may play a role in these individuals. At this point, the role of plaques and tangles in Alzheimer's disease is still being worked out, although all individuals with Alzheimer's disease show tangles and plaques and a loss of neurons (van Norden et al., 2012).

Neuroimaging of Alzheimer's Disease

There would be an advantage to knowing who will develop Alzheimer's disease in the future (Koch et al., 2012; Mevel et al., 2011). One promising approach is to study brain metabolism. In one study, it was found that those areas that correspond to the default network in young adults corresponded to those areas with amyloid deposits in older individuals with Alzheimer's (Figure 15.15). In addition, the connection between the posterior cingulate and the hippocampus appears to be impaired in Alzheimer's disease. Individuals with Alzheimer's show less activation of the default network than older individuals without Alzheimer's. It is assumed that the deposit of amyloid plaques in these areas is related to lower glucose metabolism as well as atrophy. Thus, changes in the default network could be an important biomarker of those at risk for Alzheimer's disease.

FIGURE 15.15 ■ Brain Activity Is Related to the Severity of Neurocognitive Disorders

The magnitude of impairment in brain metabolism for patients with Alzheimer's disease is greater than for those with mild impairment and normal controls.

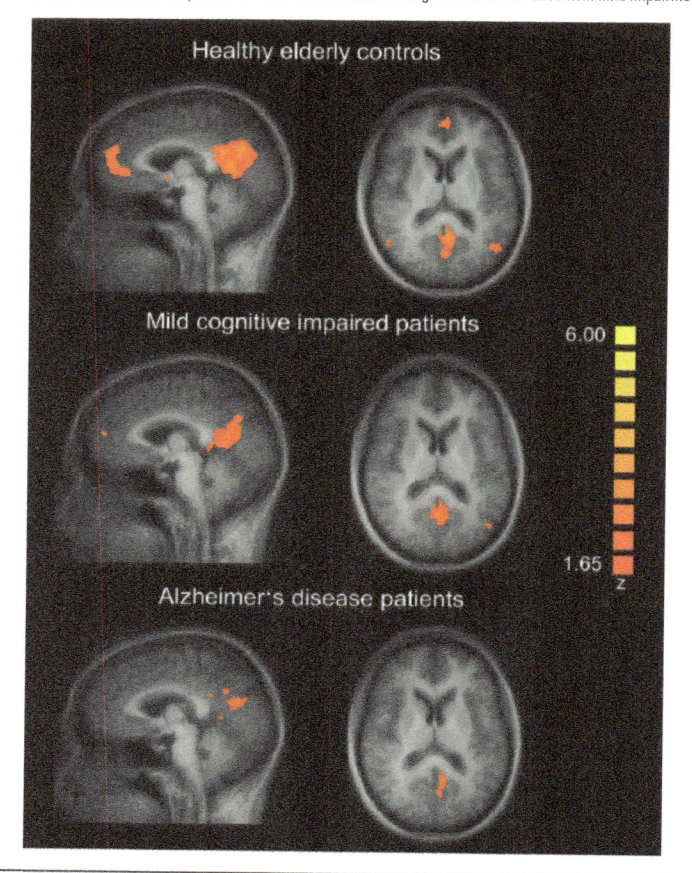

Credit: Koch, W., Teipel, S., Mueller, S., Benninghoff, J., Wagner, M., Bokde, A., . . . Meindl, T. (2012). Diagnostic power of default mode network resting state fMRI in the detection of Alzheimer's disease. *Neurobiology of Aging, 33*, 466–478, with permission from Elsevier.

> **CONCEPT CHECK**
>
> - What are the primary changes in the brain related to Alzheimer's disease?
> - What is the characteristic progression of symptoms in Alzheimer's disease?
> - What is the genetic risk for Alzheimer's disease?

OTHER CAUSES OF NEUROCOGNITIVE DISORDER

In addition to Alzheimer's disease, there are other types of neurocognitive disorders. This section will briefly note these other disorders and describe their characteristics.

Vascular Neurocognitive Disorder

Vascular problems such as strokes can lead to a neurocognitive disorder. It can be one large stroke or a series of smaller ones. Approximately 8% of individuals who have a stroke go on to develop a neurocognitive disorder. **Vascular neurocognitive disorder** is the second most frequent cause of neurocognitive problems after Alzheimer's disease. Problems in cognitive performance are usually seen as abrupt changes following the stroke. These abrupt changes are one characteristic that differentiates vascular neurocognitive disorder from Alzheimer's disease, although the symptoms may appear similar.

In the late 1800s, the disorder was referred to as *arteriosclerotic dementia* (Erkinjuntti, 2005). With increased research related to blood flow in the brain, it became apparent that a number of factors influence how blood is delivered to the brain and converted for cognitive and motor processes. Without blood flow, there is a lack of oxygen, which can lead to brain damage. The term *vascular neurocognitive disorder* reflects the role of blood flow in cognitive performance.

Frontotemporal Neurocognitive Disorder

Frontotemporal neurocognitive disorder was originally known as *Pick's disease*, since Arthur Pick, a professor of psychiatry in Prague, first described brain changes in those with this disorder in 1892. The disorder is characterized by a reduction of the anterior lobes of the frontal and temporal areas. The parietal and occipital lobes do not show this reduction. Prevalence rates are about 2 to 3 per 100,000 people (Neary, 2005). This disorder may be seen as early as the third decade of life.

Frontotemporal neurocognitive disorder is seen in different variants depending on the brain areas involved. Anne Adams, who will be introduced in the next section, had a variant that shows a loss of language abilities. Another variant gives a pattern of impairment not unlike that seen in Phineas Gage, the railroad worker who received a rod through his brain (see Chapter 3). It is not so much cognitive impairment that is seen but rather behavioral and personality changes that come to the forefront. These include a lack of social awareness, a lack of insight, indifference, inappropriate behaviors, stereotyped behaviors, aggression, and a loss of inhibition. Some of these characteristics may be manifested in terms of eating. That is, the person will eat indiscriminately and may even take food from others' plates. The person may also show repetitive motor behaviors such as hand rubbing or foot tapping. They may repeat the same phrase or do the same activity at the same time each day. Visuospatial skills tend not to be impaired, as you will see in the extended case study of Anne Adams (her real name).

The Development of Frontotemporal Neurocognitive Disorder in a Scientist and Artist

Let's look at an extended case study in which an individual with frontotemporal neurocognitive disorder shows deficits in cognitive abilities, especially language. However, as she experienced these deficits, other areas of the brain became more active and increased her creativity.

Dr. Anne Adams graduated from college with honors degrees in physics and chemistry. She taught college chemistry before taking time off to raise her children. After returning to work, she received a PhD in cell biology and taught for the next 4 years. At that point, her son was involved in a life-threatening motor vehicle accident. While taking care of her son, she went back to an old interest in art and began to paint. Surprisingly, her son recovered in 7 weeks, but rather than return to teaching, she continued to paint and would spend all day in her studio.

Unknown to her, she was developing a neurocognitive disorder, which changed the relationship of networks in her brain. Around age 60, she began to have language difficulties and was evaluated at the University of California, San Francisco. William Seeley and his colleagues (2008) followed these changes in her brain processes and in her art and published their findings in the journal *Brain*. Using structural and functional imaging, these researchers were able to show that as Anne Adams lost brain processing in the frontal and temporal areas, she was able to create enhanced connections in the right posterior areas including the right parietal, which is involved in spatial relationships as would be necessary for creativity in art. One intriguing scientific question relates to the manner in which loss in one area may increase abilities in another. In this case, the loss of spoken language was associated with an increase in creativity and artistic abilities. Fortunately, before her difficulty with spoken language, Anne Adams kept extensive notes on the nature of her paintings, which detailed the manner in which she related her paintings to music and mathematics.

In a strange coincidence, Anne Adams became interested in the French composer Maurice Ravel (1875–1937), best known for his work *Boléro*, a piece of music that is highly structured. The strange coincidence is that Ravel at the time in his life that he was writing *Boléro* may have begun to develop the same neurocognitive disorder that was to be manifested in Anne Adams a century later. At this point, at age 53, she turned the music of *Boléro* into art in the form of a visual analysis of the piece (Figure 15.16). Each of the vertical panels represents a specific bar in the music. This was some 7 years before any of her symptoms appeared. At age 58, she moved from painting music to more abstract patterns such as those found in mathematics. One of Anne Adams's paintings with this theme is called *Pi* (Figure 15.17). This was 2 years before her symptoms appeared. There is a podcast describing her case and Ravel (see For Further Reading).

Anne Adams's symptoms began to appear around age 60 with difficulties in speech. However, her comprehension remained intact. By age 64, she was nearly mute, able to speak only 3- or 4-word phrases at best. As she was losing her speech, she emphasized a spatial language in her paintings (Figure 15.18). With the development of her symptoms, she also shifted her painting style to one of realism with high surface fidelity. Her paintings at this time were very symmetrical.

FIGURE 15.16 ■ *Unraveling Boléro.* Painting by Anne Adams.

Credit: Courtesy of Robert A. Adams.

FIGURE 15.17 ■ *Pi.* Painting by Anne Adams.

Credit: Courtesy of Robert A. Adams.

FIGURE 15.18 ■ Examples From Anne Adams's *ABC Book of Invertebrates*

Credit: Courtesy of Robert A. Adams.

FIGURE 15.19 ■ *Arbutus Leaves.* Painting by Anne Adams

Credit: Courtesy of Robert A. Adams.

FIGURE 15.20 ■ *Amsterdam.* Painting by Anne Adams

Credit: Courtesy of Robert A. Adams.

During the next 4 years, her paintings emphasized a certain type of realism (Figure 15.19), including surfaces of buildings (Figure 15.20). Figure 15.21 shows the loss of brain areas in Anne Adams relative to the painting she was producing at the time.

The case of Dr. Anne Adams portrays a person with frontotemporal neurocognitive disorder who shows deterioration in language abilities over time. However, as she was losing language abilities, she began to display greater creativity according to those who worked with her. Thus, she showed compensation and increased reliance on other areas of the brain related to creativity. Unlike the artist William Utermohlen, for whom you could see the deterioration of his artistic abilities in his painting due to Alzheimer's disease, Anne Adams showed shifts in the types of images that she focused on and the levels of detail that she emphasized (Seeley et al., 2008).

FIGURE 15.21 ■ Magnetic Resonance Imaging With Paintings

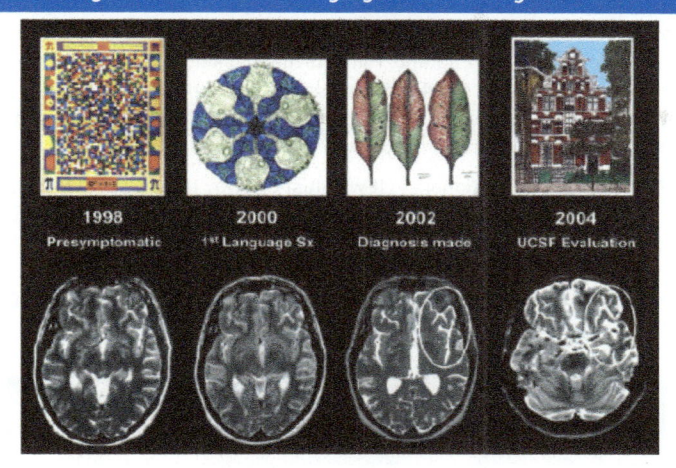

Credit: Seeley, W., Matthews, B., Crawford, R., Gorno-Tempini, M., Foti, D., Mackenzie, I., & Miller, B. (2008). Unravelling Boléro: Progressive aphasia, transmodal creativity and the right posterior neocortex. *Brain, 131,* 39–49, by permission of Oxford University Press.

Neurocognitive Disorder Due to Traumatic Brain Injury

Traumatic brain injuries (TBIs) are seen across the life span (Silver et al., 2011). Acceleration and deceleration forces on the brain as it impacts with the skull commonly lead to injuries, which often produce diffuse microstructural injury. The severity of these injuries can range from mild to severe. Mild TBIs are often referred to as *concussions*. Common sources of TBIs are sports, transportation accidents, and falls by older adults. Some are one-time-only events and others are repeated, such as concussions in contact sports. Aging boxers may show what's called "punch drunk" syndrome, which is characterized by slowed thought as well as changes in emotional processing.

The National Football League (NFL) and college football associations in the United States have recently begun a number of studies to determine the long-term effects of concussions on players. The U.S. military has also noted an increase in TBIs, at times along with post-traumatic stress disorder (PTSD), in soldiers involved in the conflicts in the Middle East. Worldwide, TBIs are a critical public health problem that can lead to a variety of neurocognitive and psychological problems. For example, one meta-analysis involving over 700,000 individuals suggested that concussion and mild TBIs are associated with a higher risk of suicide, suicide attempts, and suicidal ideation (Brenner & Bahraini, 2018; Fralick et al., 2018).

Problems associated with TBIs can include loss of consciousness, cognitive deficits, depression, and—at a later period—the onset of neurocognitive disorder. For example, chronic traumatic encephalopathy (CTE), which is a degenerative brain disease, has been found in athletes, soldiers, and others with a history of brain trauma. The types of deficits seen in individuals with TBI vary in terms of the areas of the brain affected by the injury. It is estimated by the Centers for Disease Control and Prevention (CDC) that in the United States, some 1.7 million occurrences of TBI happen each year, with about 2% of the population having TBI-related disabilities (Faul et al., 2010; see For Further Reading). *LENS: The Silent Epidemic of Concussion in Sports* describes what has been called a silent epidemic: the presence of concussion in sports.

LENS
THE SILENT EPIDEMIC OF CONCUSSION IN SPORTS

For years, few people paid attention to the potential dangers of hard-hitting encounters that occur frequently in contact sports. One of the most common injuries—concussion—has been referred to as a "silent epidemic." It was once assumed that there were no long-term consequences of concussion. However, this has recently changed, as more individuals have come forward to discuss the effects of having played such sports as football years ago. Research has suggested that older, retired professional football players experience neurocognitive disorders at 5 times the national rate. Ted Johnson, a former New England Patriots linebacker, had multiple concussions that resulted in significant memory and emotional problems throughout his 30s. Previously, athletes just "played through the pain." The former Denver Broncos and Washington Redskins running back Clinton Portis described his experiences as follows:

> The truth is I had a lot of concussions. . . . It was just the way things were at the time. I'd get hit hard and be woozy. I'd be dizzy. I'd take a play off and then go back in. Sometimes when I went back into the game, I still couldn't see straight. This happened all the time. Sometimes once or twice a game. (Davenport, 2013)

It is now known that a person is most susceptible to another concussion for about 10 days after the first.

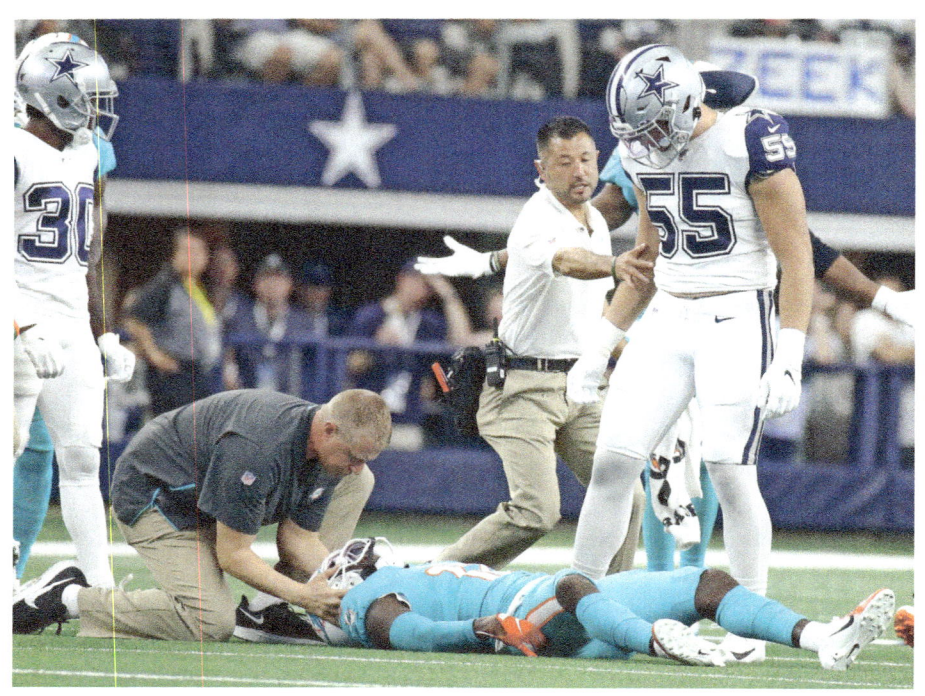

Charles Trainor Jr./Miami Herald/Tribune News Service via Getty Images

It is becoming more apparent that repetitive blows to the head affect the brain in negative ways, which can lead to neurocognitive disorders. Often, it is not contact with another person but a person's head hitting the ground that produces the concussion. This is not limited to men; women who play such sports as field hockey and soccer are also at risk. The symptoms of concussion in men and women are very similar. Even a fall from a bicycle can result in a concussion.

In response to a new recognition of the effects of concussion, a number of groups have changed their approach. The NFL now supports studies of the long-term effects of concussion in professional athletes. A number of older athletes such as the Hall of Fame professional quarterback Ken Stabler, who played for the Oakland Raiders, developed chronic traumatic encephalopathy (CTE), a degenerative brain disease believed to be caused by repeated blows to the head (Montenigro, Corp, Stein, Cantu, & Stern, 2015).

Many universities have established centers for the study of concussion, and all but three U.S. states have established laws related to concussion assessment and management in high school athletics as well as return-to-play guidelines. High school athletes are particularly at risk, since surveys suggest that this group believes there is not a problem playing sports with a concussion. Returning to play before the concussion has been fully resolved can increase long-term injuries.

Since adolescence is a time in which an individual's brain goes through a series of cortical reorganizations, brain insults at this time put the adolescent at greater risk for serious injury. Further, as risk takers, adolescent athletes may even deny there is a problem so they can continue to play. For college and professional athletes, different pressures may cause them to ignore information concerning the effects of concussion. Overall, this can lead to a lack of candor when athletes at all levels describe their symptoms.

> The CDC now offers a number of programs directed at athletics at all levels for the care and prevention of concussion, and the organization also works with the National Collegiate Athletic Association (NCAA; see For Further Reading). Professional football now has individuals in the press box who look for potential concussions on the field and immediately report this to team physicians. Many college programs engage in intensive baseline neuropsychological and neuroscience testing, which can be compared with a person's performance after a concussion to help determine when the person should return to play. There is also a best practices guideline for athletic trainers (Broglio et al., 2014). It is no longer the case that a concussion should be seen as unimportant.
>
> ### Thought Question
>
> Since young people are at particular risk for serious injury from concussions while playing sports, what recommendations would you offer to make it safer?
>
> *Source:* Based on Slobounov, S., & Sebastianelli, W. (2021). *Concussions in Athletics: From Brain to Behavior* (2nd ed.). Springer.

Neurocognitive Disorder Due to Lewy Body Dementia

Lewy bodies are substances found in the neuron (Figure 15.22). When these Lewy bodies build up, symptoms of a neurocognitive disorder, called **Lewy body dementia**, become apparent. The symptoms include changes in alertness and attention, which can result in drowsiness or staring into space. Other symptoms include visual hallucinations and Parkinson's-like symptoms, which start a year after the cognitive impairment begins. The prevalence of this disorder is estimated to be less than 5% of the older adult population (American Psychiatric Association, 2013). When autopsies have been conducted, Lewy bodies are seen in 20% to 35% of those with a neurocognitive disorder. The comedian Robin Williams was diagnosed with Lewy body dementia at the end of his life. His condition was described by his wife in an editorial in the journal *Neurology* (Williams, 2016).

Neurocognitive Disorder Due to Parkinson's Disease

Parkinson's disease is a neurological condition that affects the motor system. The symptoms generally include tremors, which may involve the hands, arms, legs, jaw, and face. In addition, the person shows a slowness of movement and stiffness in their limbs. Other motor problems such as poor balance and coordination may be present. In addition, there may be problems with sleep patterns. As the disorder progresses, the ability to walk may be lost and a wheelchair is required. Parkinson's disease typically begins after the age of 60 and affects about 1% of people over age 60 and 3% over age 85. It affects men more often than women.

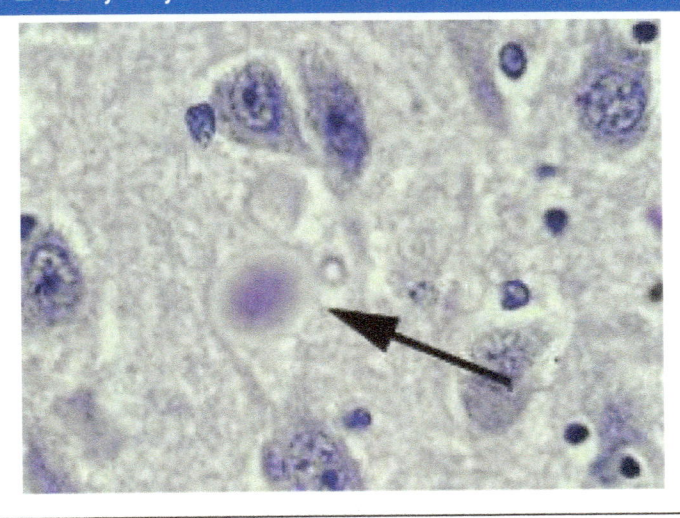

FIGURE 15.22 ■ Lewy Body

Source: U.S. National Library of Medicine, National Institutes of Health.

Actor Bruce Willis retired from his profession after a diagnosis of aphasia caused by frontotemporal dementia.
Sydney Alford/Alamy Stock Photo

In Parkinson's disease, damaged nerve cells are found in the part of the brain stem called the substantia nigra. There are two types of problems seen in this area. The first is a loss of neurons that create dopamine. Parkinson's disease does not become apparent until 60% of the dopamine neurons in the substantia nigra are lost or dopamine levels in the basal ganglia fall by 80%. Treatment of Parkinson's disease typically involves drugs that replace the lost dopamine. The second type of problem is the presence of Lewy bodies in the substantia nigra and locus coeruleus in the brain stem.

About a third of individuals with Parkinson's disease continue to develop a neurocognitive disorder. Neurocognitive symptoms are generally not seen in the early stage of Parkinson's but are found in about 40% of 70-year-olds. The cognitive characteristics are similar to those found in neurocognitive disorder due to Lewy body dementia. These include inflexibility and problems with executive functions. It is suggested that the progression of the neurocognitive disorder is related to the migration of the Lewy bodies from the motor areas to the cortex. Hallucinations may also be seen, but this may be related to the increase of dopamine in the brain from medications. These hallucinations tend to be of a visual rather than auditory nature.

Neurocognitive Disorder Due to HIV Infection

The **human immunodeficiency virus (HIV)** can be passed on by coming in contact with the bodily fluids of an infected person. Common means of contact include unprotected sex, sharing a needle for drug use, or tainted blood such as from a transfusion. It can also be seen in infants born to infected women. The virus affects the person's immune system in a negative manner. In the later stages, this is referred to as **acquired immune deficiency syndrome (AIDS)**. About a third of individuals with AIDS will also show neurocognitive problems such as slowing in both cognitive and motor functions. These include memory problems, confusion, depression, and difficulty with fine motor tasks. Prior to the development of effective AIDS drugs, many individuals died of disorders related to a compromised immune system from HIV. Today, drug treatments have successfully increased the life span and reduced neurocognitive problems of those with HIV/AIDS.

Substance-Induced Neurocognitive Disorder

The abuse of drugs over a period of time can lead to neurocognitive deficits, known as **substance-induced neurocognitive disorder**. These drugs can include illegal substances as well as medications.

Toxins such as lead, mercury, and carbon monoxide are also included as potential causes of neurocognitive problems. One common substance that can lead to cognitive changes is alcohol. This is especially the case when combined with poor nutrition. There is also some suggestion that the toxic effects of alcohol make the person more susceptible to the negative effects of a head injury. Alcohol is seen as the third leading cause of neurocognitive disorder and affects more women than men.

Neurocognitive Disorder Due to Huntington's Disease

Huntington's disease is a genetic disorder that causes a degeneration of neurons in the brain (Ahveninen et al., 2018; Gusella & MacDonald, 2006; Parsons & Raymond, 2023). It is one of the few disorders that has a single cause—a gene on chromosome 4—in all people who are diagnosed with it. The gene that is associated with this disorder is dominant. Thus, a child of an individual with Huntington's disease has a 50–50 chance of inheriting the gene that produces the disorder. Typically, this disorder does not become apparent until around age 40, which is after the primary childbearing years. The loss of brain cells results in cognitive, emotional, and motor disturbances. The cognitive deficits include problems with executive function, memory, arithmetic, and spatial ability. There are fewer problems with language functions. Emotional disturbances include mood swings and depression. Motor problems include both voluntary movements, in which the person may appear clumsy, and involuntary movements, such as jerking of the body.

Neurocognitive Disorder Due to Prion Disease

Prions are infectious pathogens that are different in structure—and the diseases they cause are different—from other pathogens such as bacteria, fungi, parasites, and viruses (Walker & Jucker, 2015). They produce tiny holes in the brain, which give it a spongy appearance and result in **neurocognitive disorder due to prion disease**. Prion proteins occur in their natural form in all brains and are harmless. The general public became aware of prions with the advent of "mad cow disease," also called *bovine spongiform encephalopathy*, which spread through the food chain to humans in the United Kingdom in the 1990s. Prion disease is not infectious in the usual sense of the word but is spread through eating the brain tissue of a diseased organism. A similar disorder was found in an isolated tribe in Papua New Guinea whose members ate brains as a part of funeral rites.

A related disease that also causes brain degeneration is *Creutzfeldt-Jakob disease*, a disorder described by German neuroscientists Creutzfeldt and Jakob in the 1920s. This disorder can also have a genetic component that is estimated to be related to 10% of the occurrences of the disorder. Overall, these disorders affect about 1 in a million people. Creutzfeldt-Jakob disease typically occurs in individuals over 60, with about 90% dying within a year. During this time, there are cognitive impairments including memory loss, motor problems, personality changes, and impaired judgment. Although the cognitive problems may be similar to those seen in other neurocognitive disorders, it has a more rapid course of development and can be distinguished on autopsy by the sponge-like changes in the brain.

> **CONCEPT CHECK**
>
> - What are the defining characteristics of each of these neurocognitive disorders, including triggering event, time of onset, symptoms, and treatment?
>   - Vascular neurocognitive disorder
>   - Frontotemporal neurocognitive disorder
>   - Neurocognitive disorder due to TBI
>   - Neurocognitive disorder due to Lewy body dementia
>   - Neurocognitive disorder due to Parkinson's disease
>   - Neurocognitive disorder due to HIV infection
>   - Substance-induced neurocognitive disorder
>   - Neurocognitive disorder due to Huntington's disease
>   - Neurocognitive disorder due to prion disease

PREVENTION, TREATMENT, AND SUPPORT

As our life span has increased, with many of us living into our 80s, 90s, and even beyond, it is becoming clear that not all older individuals develop neurocognitive disorders. This has led scientists to search for the characteristics of those who do and do not develop neurocognitive disorders. This research has helped us to better understand the environmental factors and genetic predispositions that are involved. This section will describe both prevention and treatment approaches to neurocognitive disorders. There will also be examples of support networks that have been developed to help those with the disorder live successfully in their communities.

Prevention of Neurocognitive Disorders

Although many people assume that these disorders are a normal part of old age, it is suggested that perhaps 50% of neurocognitive disorders could be prevented (Brayne, 2007). Some of the prevention factors are related to lifestyle. Such life changes as exercising, eating better, and not using tobacco have been shown to be related to a reduction in both physical and mental health problems.

Cognitive challenges and social relations have also been shown to help reduce cognitive decline (Ballesteros et al., 2015). One large-scale cognitive training program (the Advanced Cognitive Training for Independent and Vital Elderly [ACTIVE]) was directed at 2,832 individuals age 65 and older who lived independently (Rebok et al., 2014). These individuals received 10 training sessions for memory, reasoning, or speed of processing. Cognitive measures and self-reported daily abilities showed beneficial effects of the training, especially during the period 3 to 5 years after training. In comparison to control individuals, those who received training showed benefits after 10 years in reasoning and processing speed but not memory. These results suggest that cognitive training can delay the onset of cognitive decline.

Other prevention factors can be found through medical checkups. For example, studies that have examined blood pressure readings in childhood, midlife, and later life have shown that those with a higher blood pressure when young will have higher pressure throughout their life. High blood pressure at an earlier age, in turn, puts one at greater risk for neurocognitive disorders through strokes.

Can an Individual's Activities Be Protective in Brain Changes?

The answer to this question is *yes*. It was first noticed that not all individuals showed the same changes from similar neurocognitive disorders or brain injury. From this observation, the concept of **reserve** was developed. That is, high-functioning individuals tend to show less loss of cognitive abilities in relation to neurocognitive disorders. The concept of reserve suggests that the brain can compensate for problems in neural functioning. This is illustrated by the case in which the brains of older individuals expand their networks to solve problems, as shown earlier in Figure 15.10. High functioning or intelligence is often associated with greater reserve.

Additional research has shown a role for exercise and social support. Exercise is thought to play an important role in aging by promoting healthy cardiovascular function. That is, exercise increases blood flow to the entire brain. Exercise has also been shown to slow the expression of Alzheimer's-like disorders in a mouse model. In a review of literature from different areas, Kramer and Erickson (2007) suggested that exercise provides multiple routes to enhancing cognitive vitality across the life span. These include the reduction of disease risk as well as improvement in molecular and cellular structures of the brain. This, in turn, increases brain function. Further, aerobic exercise has been demonstrated to affect executive function more than other cognitive processes. Exercise has also been associated with lowering the risk for future Parkinson's disease (Xu et al., 2010).

Following more than 700 older individuals without neurocognitive disorders for several years, Aron Buchman and his colleagues (2012) found that daily physical activity slowed cognitive decline. Exercise was also associated with a lower risk for developing Alzheimer's disease. Although performing various types of cognitive tasks such as crossword puzzles or speaking a second language are also associated with successful aging, these brain effects appear to be more localized in those areas of the brain related to the specific task.

In order to better articulate the causal role of exercise, Lindsay Nagamatsu and her colleagues (2013) randomly assigned older individuals who were beginning to show mild cognitive impairment to one of three groups. The first group received resistance training and lifted weights. The second group received aerobic training and walked outdoors at levels that increased their heart rate. The third group received balance and stretching exercises. The third group served as the control group. After 6 months of twice-weekly exercise, the first two groups showed improvement in memory functions. This was seen more strongly on a difficult spatial memory test. The aerobic group also improved performance on the verbal memory test. The important point of this study is that 6 months of exercise can improve memory in 70-year-olds.

Social support has also been associated with a reduced risk for neurocognitive disorders and better physiological functioning (Yang et al., 2016). Two of these factors are the size of one's network of friends and whether one is married or not. As suggested in studies of the social brain, understanding and maintaining networks of friends require a variety of cognitive resources, which in turn offer a reserve for dealing with brain pathologies. One study followed 16,638 individuals over the age of 50 for 6 years. Those individuals who were more socially integrated and active showed less memory loss during the 6-year period (Ertel et al., 2008).

One comprehensive study of aging is The 90+ Study (see For Further Reading). Initial members of this study started as part of another study of aging, which began in 1981 in Orange County, California. The 90+ Study was begun in 2003 to study the oldest old. By studying 14,000 individuals of the original study, the researchers were able to ask, what allows people to live to age 90 and beyond? Participants in The 90+ Study are visited by researchers every 6 months. A comprehensive battery of information including diet, activities, medical history, and medications is collected. In addition, neurological, cognitive, and neuropsychological tests are administered.

Researchers from The 90+ Study have published many scientific papers (e.g., Bilousova et al., 2016; Kawas, 2008; Kawas et al., 2015; Robinson et al., 2018). Some of the major findings are as follows: People who drank moderate amounts of alcohol or coffee lived longer than those who abstained. People who were overweight in their 70s lived longer than normal or underweight people did. Over 40% of people aged 90 and older suffer from dementia, while almost 80% are disabled. Both are more common in women than men. About half of people with dementia over age 90 do not have sufficient neuropathology in their brain to explain their cognitive loss. People aged 90 and older with an APOE2 gene are less likely to have clinical Alzheimer's dementia but are much more likely to have Alzheimer's neuropathology in their brains.

Treatment of and Support for Those With Neurocognitive Disorders

In the same way that cognitive training has been used to delay the negative effects of aging, it has been used to help individuals with neurocognitive disorders recover cognitive functions that can be restored. Most of these training programs seek to help individuals maximize their strengths while bypassing their weaknesses. An example of such a training program is CogSMART (Cognitive Symptom Management and Rehabilitation Therapy), developed by Elizabeth Twamley at the University of California, San Diego (Twamley et al., 2014). This is a manualized, empirically supported approach that helps the individual with a neurocognitive disorder recover cognitive functioning and compensate for cognitive difficulties. For example, in one's daily life, cell phones, calendars, and lists can be used to remember meetings, grocery products, and tasks to do. Likewise, when talking with others, eye contact, reducing distractions, and paraphrasing what was said can improve the accuracy of conversations. The approach also includes formal steps in solving problems and learning new information. An additional advantage of these types of approaches is that they have been shown to reduce the burden on caregivers of those with dementia (Germain et al., 2018).

In addition to psychological approaches, medications are used for the treatment of neurocognitive disorders (Gatchel et al., 2016). The neurocognitive disorders described in this chapter, except for delirium, cannot be cured. However, sometimes the symptoms can be reduced. There are also secondary symptoms such as anxiety and depression that can be treated separately. Further, at times, it is difficult to distinguish depression from dementia. Also, it should be noted that with aging, medications can influence the body differently from how they influence younger or middle-aged individuals. That is, medications can be absorbed and distributed in the body differently. Also, there can be more adverse side effects with older individuals.

Many communities across the world are taking strides to become more accessible to and navigable for people with dementia.

PA Images/Alamy Stock Photo

Different medications are used for different neurocognitive disorders. In Alzheimer's disease, drugs such as cholinesterase inhibitors are used to increase memory and other cognitive functions by increasing concentrations of ACh in the hippocampus. Although useful, the memory effects are modest. Because Parkinson's disease is the result of dopamine neurons not functioning correctly, treatment of Parkinson's disease typically involves drugs that replace the lost dopamine such as L-dopa. However, it should be noted that dopamine replacement drugs are not always effective. There are currently no medications directed at the other neurocognitive disorders such as frontotemporal neurocognitive disorder and Lewy body disease.

A different approach for Parkinson's disease is deep brain stimulation (DBS), which was approved by the FDA in 2002. Deep brain stimulation for depression was described in Chapter 6. DBS involves placing an electrode in the areas of the brain related to movement, usually the basal ganglia. This in turn is connected to a pulse generator that is placed under the person's skin, usually near the collarbone. The pulse generator can be programmed to stimulate the brain in a number of ways related to the individual. Although not a treatment that is recommended for all who have Parkinson's disease, it has proven useful for improving movement in a number of individuals.

While the search continues to discover more effective treatments for those with neurocognitive disorders, describes a movement has formed to make cities and towns more livable for those with dementia (see *LENS: Dementia-Friendly Communities*).

LENS

DEMENTIA-FRIENDLY COMMUNITIES

As people around the world live longer, there are more opportunities for individuals to develop neurocognitive disorders. Alzheimer's is the most common of these disorders. In 2015, it was estimated that the prevalence of Alzheimer's was 4% in those 65 years or younger, 15% in those 65 to 74 years of age, and 43% of those 75 to 84 years of age. After 85 years of age, the prevalence drops to 38%. Often, a person with Alzheimer's disease will require living in a nursing home or assisted living facility. However, a number of individuals with milder forms of dementia are still able to interact with those in their town or community. In fact, being able to shop for food, attend church, and be with others is important for the health of many of these individuals.

Many retirement communities have trained staff on how to interact with those who have cognitive difficulties. This type of training is now moving to the larger community. There is currently a movement in a number of states such as Minnesota to help communities become more dementia friendly. The Minnesota plan began as part of a 2009 legislative mandate aimed at preparing the state for the social, economic, and personal impacts of Alzheimer's disease. More than 50 communities in Minnesota have undertaken dementia-friendly planning and action. In Paynesville, Minnesota, a small town of 2,400 people, there are twice-monthly "Fridays and Friends" events for those with dementia and other townspeople designed for socializing. Volunteers also help those with cognitive difficulties with various basic tasks such as buying groceries at the local market (Figure 15.23).

Other U.S. states and nations such as Canada and the United Kingdom are also seeking to make communities more dementia friendly. In Watertown, Wisconsin, there are programs to train businesses in the community to institute minor changes in their daily operations to make life easier for those with cognitive difficulties. For example, servers who work in coffee shops or restaurants are taught to ask yes-or-no questions rather than naming all of the specials or menu items for the day. Cashiers are taught to slow down the transactions if the person finds it difficult to count their money. Even more complicated transitions such as estate planning or money management can be presented in shorter, more understandable segments of a larger presentation. In some other towns, local shops have created special areas of their store where those with dementia can feel calm, comfortable, and in control. Building designers are also considering how features such as lighting, sound, and pathways can make an environment more user friendly.

Thought Question

Think about your hometown or school environment: What specific changes would you recommend to make it more dementia-friendly? How would those changes also help other segments of your local population?

Reproduced from ACT on Alzheimer's® developed tools and resources.

FIGURE 15.23 ■ Aspects of a Dementia-Friendly Community

Additional descriptions can be found online (see For Further Reading).

- Health care that promotes early diagnosis and uses dementia care best practices along the care continuum
- Residential settings that offer memory loss services and supports
- Dementia-aware and responsive legal and financial planning
- Welcoming and supportive faith communities
- Businesses with dementia-informed services and environments for customers and employee caregivers
- Dementia-friendly public environments and accessible transportation
- Dementia-aware local government services, planning and emergency responses
- Supportive options for independent living and meaningful community engagement

Source: Reproduced from ACT on Alzheimer's® developed tools and resources.

CONCEPT CHECK

- It is suggested that perhaps 50% of neurocognitive disorders could be prevented. What are some specific examples of each of the following areas of prevention?
  - Cognitive challenges
  - Social relations
  - Exercise
  - Lifestyle
- Describe the concept of reserve. What role does it play in protecting individuals from neurocognitive disorders?
- What are some strategies used to help an individual with a neurocognitive disorder recover cognitive functionality or compensate for cognitive losses?
- Medications can't cure neurocognitive disorders, but what are some of the ways they can be useful in treating some of them?

SUMMARY

As we age, our mental and physical abilities change. Some of these changes happen gradually and appear to be related to genetic differences. Other changes happen more quickly. They may involve not only physical changes but also changes in mental processing, including neurocognitive disorders. This contrasts with what has come to be called normal successful aging. Perhaps 50% of neurocognitive disorders could be prevented through lifestyle changes and preventive medical care. In order to understand the changes seen in neurocognitive disorders, it is important to examine the normal changes in cognitive abilities across the life span, including (1) vocabulary, (2) perceptual speed, (3) episodic memory, (4) spatial visualization, and (5) reasoning. Two consistent findings are that older adults show changes in brain structure and that they use their brains in different ways from younger adults, using compensation to improve their performance. High functioning or intelligence, exercise, and social support are all associated with a greater reserve and overall brain health to provide for compensation.

There is a complex relationship between cognitive changes in older adults and mental illness. Studies have shown that symptoms of mental illness actually decreased the person's quality of life more than did decreases in their cognitive abilities. Delirium is a short-term condition characterized by a change in cognitive processing and can be caused by a number of underlying physiological disturbances. When cognitive or social deficits are greater than those seen with normal aging, this decline can be described in terms of a mild neurocognitive disorder. If the declines are severe and interfere with one's ability to function independently, then these can be described in terms of major neurocognitive disorders. *DSM-5-TR* defines a variety of neurocognitive disorders.

Neurocognitive disorder due to Alzheimer's disease is a progressive disorder characterized by problems with memory. It is associated with a loss of neurons and disruption of cortical networks, which result in cognitive problems. Alzheimer's disease is the most common neurodegenerative disorder in the world, and its prevalence is fairly similar worldwide. Neurofibrillary tangles and neuritic plaques as well as widespread synaptic and neuronal loss in the brain are the hallmarks of Alzheimer's disease. There is a genetic risk for developing Alzheimer's disease. Changes in the default network, as shown in neuroimaging studies, could prove to be an important biomarker or predictor of those at risk for Alzheimer's disease.

Vascular neurocognitive disorder can result from vascular problems such as strokes—either one large stroke or a series of smaller ones. Frontotemporal neurocognitive disorder has different variants depending on the brain areas involved. It can present as cognitive impairment or behavioral and personality changes. Neurocognitive disorder due to traumatic brain injury (TBI) occurs across the life span as a result of a one-time-only traumatic event or a series of smaller injuries. It results in slowed thought as well as changes in emotional processing.

Neurocognitive disorder due to Lewy body dementia results in a buildup of Lewy bodies in the neuron. Symptoms include changes in alertness and attention. Parkinson's disease is a condition that affects the motor system. About a third of the individuals with Parkinson's disease continue to develop a neurocognitive disorder. The cognitive characteristics are similar to those found in the neurocognitive disorder due to Lewy body dementia. About a third of individuals with AIDS will also show neurocognitive problems, referred to as neurocognitive disorder due to HIV infection, such as slowing in both cognitive and motor functions. The abuse of drugs or alcohol over a period of time can lead to neurocognitive deficits, referred to as substance-induced neurocognitive disorder.

Huntington's disease is a genetic disorder that causes a degeneration of neurons in the brain, referred to as neurocognitive disorder due to Huntington's disease, resulting in cognitive, emotional, and motor disturbances. It is one of the few disorders that has a single cause—a gene—in all people who have it. Prions are infectious pathogens that produce tiny holes in the brain, which give it a spongy appearance and result in neurocognitive disorder due to prion disease. A related disease that also causes brain degeneration is Creutzfeldt-Jakob disease, which can have a genetic component. These two diseases have a rapid course of development, and cognitive impairments include memory loss, motor problems, personality changes, and impaired judgment.

The treatment approaches for neurocognitive disorders are basically designed to slow the progression of the disorder and to offer the person support to live with the disorder. The neurocognitive disorders described in this chapter, except for delirium, cannot be cured. At times, the symptoms can be reduced using medication such as drugs that attempt to increase dopamine in those with Parkinson's disease or memory abilities in other dementias. Deep brain stimulation has also been used to reduce the tremors in Parkinson's disease. Psychological disorders such as anxiety and depression have been seen with dementia, and these have been treated using traditional approaches. There is also a worldwide movement to make communities more dementia friendly.

STUDY RESOURCES

Review Questions

1. This chapter on neurocognitive disorders devotes a considerable amount of space to describing the process of aging and the diseases experienced (typically) by older adults. Does that mean it has no personal meaning for you or your friends—at least for a few more years? Present an argument that this information is vitally important for young people to know. What evidence would you cite to support your position and convince them that they should care?

2. Alzheimer's disease is the most common neurodegenerative disorder in the world, and currently, it is the only disorder in the top 10 causes of death that cannot be prevented, cured, or even slowed in its progression. What would be your focus of research in each of these three important areas: prevention, cure, and slowing progression? Which one would you start with and why?

3. "One intriguing question relates to the manner in which loss in one area may increase abilities in another." This question arises in relation to the case of Anne Adams, whose creativity and artistic abilities increased at the same time she was developing frontotemporal neurocognitive disorder. Using this example, as well as the concepts of brain reserve and compensation presented at the beginning of the chapter, what can we say about the plasticity of the brain, that is, the brain's ability to reorganize and repurpose itself to be able to function?

For Further Reading

Abumrad, J., & (Hosts), Krulwich, R. (2018, May 22). Unraveling Bolero [Audio podcast episode]. *Radiolab*. WNYC Studios. https://radiolab.org/podcast/unraveling-bolero

Arnett, P (Ed.). (2013). *Secondary influences on neuropsychological test performance*. Oxford University Press.

Bayley, J. (1999). *Elegy for Iris*. Picador.

Campo-Flores, A. (2015, October 22). *More cities aim to be "dementia-friendly."*. The Wall Street Journal. https://www.wsj.com/articles/more-cities-aim-to-be-dementia-friendly-1445539091

Centers for Disease Control and Prevention. (2010). *Traumatic brain injury in the United States*. U.S. Department of Health and Human Services. https://www.cdc.gov/traumaticbraininjury/pdf/blue_book.pdf

Centers for Disease Control and Prevention. (2020). *Alzheimer's disease and related dementias*. U.S. Department of Health and Human Services. https://www.cdc.gov/aging/aginginfo/alzheimers.htm

Centers for Disease Control and Prevention. (2023). *Traumatic brain injury & concussion*. U.S. Department of Health and Human Services. https://www.cdc.gov/traumaticbraininjury/

Favdin, L., & Katzen, H (Eds.). (2013). *Handbook on the neuropsychology of aging and dementia*. Springer.

Kawas, C., Corrada, M., Paganini-Hill, A., & Greenia, D. (n.d.). *The 90+ Study*. UC Irvine Institute for Memory Impairments and Neurological Disorders. http://www.mind.uci.edu/research/90plus-study/

Lipton, A., & Marshall, C. (2013). *The common sense guide to dementia for clinicians and caregivers*. Springer.

University of Edinburgh. (2023). *Lothian birth cohorts*. https://www.ed.ac.uk/lothian-birth-cohorts

Wisconsin Healthy Brain Initiative. (n.d.). *A toolkit for building dementia-friendly communities*. https://www.dhs.wisconsin.gov/publications/p01000.pdf

KEY TERMS

- acquired immune deficiency syndrome (AIDS)
- delirium
- dementias
- frontotemporal neurocognitive disorder
- human immunodeficiency virus (HIV)
- Huntington's disease
- Lewy body dementia
- major neurocognitive disorder
- mild neurocognitive disorder
- microglia
- neuritic plaques
- neurocognitive disorder due to Alzheimer's disease
- neurocognitive disorder due to prion disease
- neurocognitive disorders
- neurofibrillary tangles
- Parkinson's disease
- reserve
- substance-induced neurocognitive disorder
- successful aging
- traumatic brain injuries (TBIs)
- vascular neurocognitive disorder

16 THE LAW AND MENTAL HEALTH

LEARNING OBJECTIVES

16.1 Discuss the meaning and history of the insanity defense.

16.2 Identify the criteria used to determine competency to stand trial.

16.3 Discuss the ethical and legal considerations for mental health professionals and individuals seeking psychological treatment.

16.4 Explain how sexual predator laws work.

16.5 Discuss neuroscience and evolutionary perspectives on the legal aspects of psychopathology.

3/30/81

12:45 P.M.

Dear Jodie,

There is a definite possibility that I will be killed in my attempt to get Reagan. It is for this very reason that I am writing you this letter now.

As you well know by now I love you very much. Over the past seven months I've left you dozens of poems, letters and love messages in the faint hope that you could develop an interest in me. Although we talked on the phone a couple of times I never had the nerve to simply approach you and introduce myself. Besides my shyness, I honestly did not wish to bother you with my constant presence. I know the many messages left at your door and in your mailbox were a nuisance, but I felt that it was the most painless way for me to express my love for you.

I feel very good about the fact that you at least know my name and know how I feel about you. And by hanging around your dormitory, I've come to realize that I'm the topic of more than a little conversation, however full of ridicule it may be. At least you know that I'll always love you.

Jodie, I would abandon this idea of getting Reagan in a second if I could only win your heart and live out the rest of my life with you, whether it be in total obscurity or whatever.

I will admit to you that the reason I'm going ahead with this attempt now is because I just cannot wait any longer to impress you. I've got to do something now to make you understand, in no uncertain terms, that I am doing all of this for your sake! By sacrificing my freedom and possibly my life, I hope to change your mind about me. This letter is being written only an hour before I leave for the Hilton Hotel.

Jodie, I'm asking you to please look into your heart and at least give me the chance, with this historical deed, to gain your respect and love.

I love you forever,

John Hinckley

From *Text of letter in suspect's room.* (1981, April 2). The New York Times, A25.

A courtroom drawing of John Hinckley

Freda Leibowitz Reiter; archived in Library of Congress Web Archives at https://www.loc.gov/pictures/item/2017646661/

The story goes that John Hinckley became obsessed with the film *Taxi Driver* in which a character played by Robert De Niro plans to kill a presidential candidate. After watching the film a number of times, John Hinckley became infatuated with the actress Jodie Foster, who was in the film. He followed her when she went to college at Yale. He left her notes, but she did not respond. After a period of time, he decided that he would need to do something serious to get her attention. He considered a number of extreme situations to get her attention. As his letter to Jodie Foster states, "*Jodie, I would abandon this idea of getting Reagan in a second if I could only win your heart and live out the rest of my life with you, whether it be in total obscurity or whatever. I will admit to you that the reason I'm going ahead with this attempt now is because I just cannot wait any longer to impress you.*"

The next day, John Hinckley tried to kill President Reagan. At his trial, John Hinckley was found not guilty by reason of insanity.

As we watch and listen to the media, we are at times told about horrific events. In 2015, there were 273 mass shootings in the United States including the San Bernardino, California, case in which terrorists killed 14 people. In 2016, an American who had pledged allegiance to ISIS killed 49 people at a gay nightclub in Orlando, Florida. This was seen as a hate crime. At the beginning of 2023, 12 people were killed at a dance hall in Monterey Park, California. Just a few days later, 7 people were killed in Half Moon Bay, California. From 2015 to 2018, the number of mass killings in the United States was in the upper 300s. This number increased in 2020 to 2022 to numbers in the 600s. In all of these crimes, a critical question is whether mental illness played a factor. Not all of these killings involved individuals that would be considered mentally ill, but many of them were. Understanding whether mental illness was involved in an individual's commission of a crime has been a critical question in many countries.

In 2011 and 2012, three mass killings occurred in which the media suggested mental illness was involved. A U.S. House of Representatives member, Gabby Giffords, was shot and injured outside a grocery store in Tucson, Arizona, and six other people were killed. In Aurora, Colorado, a young man in tactical clothes appeared inside a movie theater during a midnight showing. The audience initially thought it was part of the movie event. But then James Holmes began to shoot people randomly. A young adult, Adam Lanza, went into a school in Newtown, Connecticut, and shot and killed children and teachers. Before going to the school, Lanza shot and killed his mother at their home. Each of these individuals clearly was involved in a crime. As with any other crime, the person would have the opportunity for a trial and be found guilty or innocent. However, the media often

Scene outside a Washington, D.C., hotel as John Hinckley was trying to kill the president of the United States.

Archived in National Archives at https://catalog.archives.gov/id/75852773

labels these individuals as "mentally ill," whereas research does not support this conclusion for every individual (Sullivan, 2021; Varshney et al., 2016). In fact, it is suggested that even if mental illness could be eliminated as a violence risk factor, the population prevalence of violent acts toward others would go down by less than 4% (Swanson et al., 2015). However, if someone who commits a crime does have a mental disorder, how does this influence the manner in which the justice system views the actions of these people? This chapter will discuss the manner in which the U.S. legal system understands mental illness.

THE AMERICAN LEGAL SYSTEM AND THE INSANITY DEFENSE

Insanity is a legal term, not a psychological one. As such, the definition of insanity varies both by state and by country. In contrast to neuroscience perspectives, which view mental illness as a complex process that is influenced by a number of factors, legal perspectives are more narrowly focused on questions of responsibility, guilt, and innocence. Law courts are designed to determine who is responsible for an event, so legal considerations focus on determining if an individual is responsible or not. In turn, juries are asked to determine whether someone is guilty. The underlying assumption is that a person has free will and should be held accountable for their actions. If the person breaks the law, then they are found guilty. What if the person does not have free will? Are they still responsible for their actions? Societies have long debated this question.

All cultures throughout time have sought to determine the role of individual responsibility in committing criminal acts. The American system of justice in relation to insanity was initially influenced by an event that happened in England more than 170 years ago. An individual named Daniel M'Naghten (pronounced *McNaughton*) believed that he was being persecuted by the Tory party, one of the political parties of England. In response to this belief, M'Naghten planned to kill the British prime minister, Sir Robert Peel. However, he ended up attacking and killing the prime minister's secretary rather than the prime minister himself. When M'Naghten was tried for the crime, medical experts said he was psychotic. Today, he would be described as someone with paranoid schizophrenia. He was acting under the delusion that the pope and the prime minister were conspiring against him. The court found M'Naghten not guilty by reason of insanity. There was some concern about the verdict on the part of the public, which resulted in a more formal definition of mental insanity. However, many decades later, in 1843, it was determined that mental insanity could be used as a defense only if the following was found:

> At the time of the committing of the act, the party accused was labouring under such a defect of reason, from a disease of the mind, as not to know the nature and quality of the act he was doing; or, if he did know it, that he did not know what he was doing was wrong. (*Queen v. M'Naghten*, 1843)

This came to be known as the **M'Naghten rule**. The two basic conditions for the M'Naghten rule to apply are (1) that there is the presence of a mental disorder and (2) that there is a lack of comprehension of the nature or wrongfulness of the act. As you can imagine, it is difficult to determine someone's state of mind at a previous time, such as when the crime was committed. Further, it is difficult to determine if a disease of the mind is present and what even constitutes a disease of the mind. Generally, the "disease of the mind" in these cases is thought to be psychosis. However, many of the disorders you have considered in this book, such as post-traumatic stress disorder (PTSD), substance abuse, and bipolar disorder, could all impair judgment and action. The M'Naghten rule continues to be used in many states but is also challenged as not being the best criteria for determining the responsibility of those convicted (Geary, 2015).

In the United States, a number of variations based on mental capacity and knowledge have been applied in determining sanity. In the 1880s, the state of Alabama found an individual not guilty by reason of insanity because mental illness made the person unable to control himself even though he knew the difference between right and wrong. This came to be known as the **volitional test**, often described as the "elbow test." That is, if a policeman was standing next to the person, would they still commit

The M'Naghten rule was created as a reaction to the 1843 acquittal of Daniel M'Naghten, who was found not guilty by reason of insanity.

Historic Images/Alamy Stock Photo

the crime? Again, it is difficult to determine an individual's state of mind after the fact. In reality, this volitional test is a legal principle used rarely in modern times.

In the 1950s, a decision based on an 1871 New Hampshire ruling became known as the **Durham rule,** or "product test." The basic idea is that an individual is not "criminally responsible if their unlawful act is the product of a mental disease or defect." One problem with this approach is that a person could understand that they were committing a crime and still be found not guilty by reason of insanity. As with other approaches, it was hard to define and limit the definition of a mental disease. Most U.S. states dropped this approach by the 1970s, and federal judges rejected the approach in 1972.

With all of the problems experienced with the insanity plea, the American Law Institute (ALI) in 1962 developed a broader approach to "not guilty by reason of insanity." Its formulation, known as the **ALI rule,** is defined as follows:

> A person is not responsible for criminal conduct if at the time of such conduct as the result of mental disease or defect he lacks substantial capacity either to appreciate the criminality (wrongfulness) of his conduct or to conform his conduct to the requirements of the law.

This approach broadens the M'Naghten rule. Instead of requiring a defendant to have no understanding whatsoever of the nature of their acts or the difference between right and wrong, the ALI rule requires merely that they lack a "substantial capacity" to understand right from wrong and expands the M'Naghten rule to include an "irresistible impulse" component.

The insanity defense was changed drastically by an event on March 30, 1981. On that day in Washington, D.C., John Hinckley tried to kill the president of the United States, Ronald Reagan. Rushed to the hospital with a serious chest wound, President Reagan survived the shooting. John Hinckley was a person who, after 2 years of college where he played his guitar, listened to music, and watched television, dropped out and moved to Hollywood. He planned to make it as a songwriter, although he had no musical training. While in Hollywood, Hinckley saw the movie *Taxi Driver*, the story of a psychotic taxi driver who contemplates political assassination and rescues a young prostitute who was played by the actress Jodie Foster. This movie influenced Hinckley, who saw the movie 15 times over the next few years. He even began to dress like the main character. He also became obsessed with Foster, as you saw in his letter to her at the beginning of this chapter. He moved to the East Coast and began to stalk the president, Jimmy Carter. Hinckley traveled around the country and to his parents' home in Colorado. By this time, there was a new president: Ronald Reagan.

At Hinckley's trial, the mental health professional for the prosecution testified that Hinckley was sane and knew at the time of the shooting that his acts were wrong. The mental health professional for the defense diagnosed Hinckley as having a psychosis and thus being insane. The testimony during the trial and Hinckley's behavior in terms of his defense were complex. Hinckley was found not guilty by reason of insanity. This verdict upset the American public. Following the Hinckley trial, a number of states changed their laws related to the insanity plea. These changes included the following:

1. Twenty states changed the insanity plea to "guilty but mentally ill."
2. Some states abolished the insanity defense.
3. Expert witness testimony was limited in terms of ability to express an opinion.
4. Burden of proof was increased to require clear and convincing evidence.

On the federal level, the Comprehensive Crime Control Act of 1984 was passed. The act provides that for persons prosecuted in federal courts, the insanity defense may be asserted only when "the defendant, as a result of severe mental disease or defect, was unable to appreciate the nature and quality or the wrongfulness of his acts." The act also states the following: "Mental disease or defect does not otherwise constitute a defense." In addition, this act removed any use of the defense that the person was not able to control themselves. Table 16.1 summarizes the various legal standards used for determining insanity.

In practice, the insanity defense is used less than 1% of the time. A person found not guilty by reason of insanity faces indeterminate confinement in an institution. They may be released if it is determined that they are not a risk to self or others. However, studies suggest that these individuals serve as much or even more time in an institution than those who are found guilty of the crime.

"Guilty but mentally ill," which is legally the same as finding a person guilty, is a verdict possible in a number of states, including Nevada and Alaska. The person who is guilty but mentally ill is sentenced exactly as a defendant without identified mental illness, but their sentence must include mental health treatment. If they are deemed to have recovered from their disorder, they would continue to serve the sentence as would any other person convicted of a crime.

TABLE 16.1 ■ Historical Criteria for Determining Insanity

Test	Date	Legal Criteria
M'Naghten rule	1843	1. There is the presence of a mental disorder. 2. There is a lack of comprehension of the nature or wrongfulness of the act.
Volitional test	1880s	Mental illness made the person unable to control themself even though they knew the difference between right and wrong.
Durham rule	1954	An individual is not criminally responsible if their unlawful act is the product of a mental disease or defect.
American Law Institute (ALI) rule	1962	A person is not responsible for criminal conduct if at the time of such conduct as the result of mental disease or defect they lacked substantial capacity either to appreciate the criminality (wrongfulness) of their conduct or to conform their conduct to the requirements of the law.
Comprehensive Crime Control Act	1984	The defendant, as a result of severe mental disease or defect, was unable to appreciate the nature and quality or the wrongfulness of their acts.

As you think about who is guilty of a crime and who should be treated as mentally ill, you may realize that at times the demands of different aspects of society come into conflict with each other. In *LENS: Mental Health and the Law in the Real World—Failure of a System?* you will read about an actual situation in New York City in which the legal and medical systems were working at cross purposes.

LENS

MENTAL HEALTH AND THE LAW IN THE REAL WORLD—FAILURE OF A SYSTEM?

On January 3, 1999, Andrew Goldstein, who was 29 years of age, pushed 32-year-old Kendra Webdale in front of a New York subway train. She died from the impact of the train. Who was Goldstein, and what did he know about his actions?

Andrew Goldstein in 1999

AP Photo/MARTY LEDERHANDLER

Some 10 years earlier, Goldstein had been diagnosed with schizophrenia after pushing his mother into a wall. In 1992, he had committed himself to a state psychiatric hospital in New York. Some 8 months later, he was transferred to a group home. Four years after that, he was living on his own in New York City. However, he continued to seek help by going to emergency rooms when showing delusional behavior. In 1998, he committed himself to another New York hospital complaining that he had severe schizophrenia. This hospital released him after less than a month with a referral for outpatient therapy. Some have suggested he was released because the state only funds hospital stays for 21 days. Hospital records showed disordered thought and delusional and psychotic behavior. Three weeks after the last release, he pushed Webdale in front of the subway train.

The legal system treated Webdale's death as a crime. It would take three trials before the case could be resolved. In the first trial, Goldstein claimed that he pushed Webdale during a psychotic episode. The jury could not reach a unanimous decision. A second trial was held, and Goldstein was found guilty. However, this verdict was thrown out since the prosecution psychiatrist had quoted conversations from individuals who were not available for the defense to question. Thus, he did not have a fair trial. The third trial took a different turn. In this trial, Goldstein said he knew what he was doing when he pushed Webdale. Here is some of his testimony, as reported in the *New York Times* (Hartocollis, 2006).

> "On Jan. 3, 1999, did you push a woman you came to know as Kendra Webdale to her death?" Justice Berkman asked him yesterday.
>
> Mr. Goldstein answered, "As much as I can understand, I did that."
>
> Justice Berkman said she was not sure what he meant, and Mr. Goldstein's lawyers whispered to him at the defense table. He then changed his answer to a simple "yes."
>
> The judge asked whether he had intended to cause serious injury.
>
> "Yes," he said. "But not necessarily death." After another conference with his lawyers, he added, "Yes, yes."

The story of Goldstein shows the different purposes of the mental health and legal systems. It also shows the problems in getting each to work for the individual and society. Following these trials, the New York legislature passed a law referred to as "Kendra's Law," which authorizes courts to force individuals living in the community to take medication for their disorder. Webdale's mother, Patricia Webdale, has become an advocate for better mental health treatment. Follow-up studies have shown this approach has had positive results (Robertson, Swanson, Van Dorn, & Swartz, 2014). The results show that individuals who were compelled to take their medication were less likely to be readmitted to psychiatric hospitals and less likely to be arrested. Although the use of outpatient treatment increased, the costs to the mental health system dropped by over half. Currently, 45 states have some version of Kendra's Law.

Thought Question

In this case of Andrew Goldstein, the mental health system failed to protect both him and his victim. What recommendations would you make so that the legal and mental health systems could work together to better serve both individuals with mental illness and society as a whole?

CONCEPT CHECK

- What are the critical milestones in the evolution of the concept "not guilty by reason of insanity"?

LEGAL COMPETENCE: STANDING TRIAL AND MAKING DECISIONS

The first step before a trial is to determine if a person is competent to stand trial. One important tenet of our legal system is that an individual must understand the charges against them. Individuals should also be rational enough to be able to participate in their own defense. To see how this played out in one tragic, high-profile case involving mental illness, consider Andrea Yates.

It was June 2001 in Clear Lake, Texas. Andrea Yates, who was 36 years old and the mother of five, drew a bath. Her husband had left for work at NASA. She then drowned each of her five children, one at a time—her 3-year-old son, her 2-year-old son, her 5-year-old son, her 6-month-old daughter, and her 7-year-old son. After each had died, she laid them out on the bed. She then called 9–1–1 and then her husband.

Andrea Yates was a high school valedictorian, swimming champion, college graduate, and professional nurse. Her family was described as loving and happy. What happened? She did have postpartum depression. She had taken her antidepressant medication that morning. She had tried to kill herself when taking care of her father with Alzheimer's disease. In fact, she tried to kill herself a number of times. She had seen a psychiatrist and was diagnosed as severely depressed with psychotic features.

During the 2-year period after she experienced postpartum depression, she attempted suicide and was hospitalized on more than one occasion. Also during this period, her father died and she gave birth to another child. At times, she would no longer take her medication and displayed psychotic behaviors. This led up to the day that police arrived at her house and found the five dead children. Andrea Yates was arrested. While under arrest, she was evaluated by a clinical psychologist. He found her to be psychotic. She was experiencing hallucinations and saw Satan on the walls of her jail cell. She would also take up to 2 minutes to respond to questions from the psychologist. A psychologist appointed by the prosecution also evaluated her. He reported that she had some difficulties with attention and concentration, took a long time to respond to questions, and did not show any evidence of faking.

After 3 months in the county jail, where she was also treated for psychosis, a competency hearing was held. The purpose of this hearing was to determine if she could understand the court proceedings and assist in her defense. In Texas, a pretrial competency hearing can be held in front of a jury, which it was. Eleven women and one man were to determine if Yates was competent to stand trial. The judge instructed the jury to determine only the issue of whether Andrea Yates was able at the present time to understand the court proceedings and to assist in her defense. They also heard the testimony from the two clinical psychologists who had evaluated Yates. One suggested that she was not competent because of her religious delusions. The psychologist appointed by the prosecution suggested that she was competent to stand trial despite her mental illness. Although the jury found her not to be competent in an initial vote, they changed their minds after further deliberation and found her competent to stand trial.

Now that she was found competent to stand trial, the question became whether she was insane at the time she drowned her five children. In determining insanity, many states require that the individual (1) know the nature of consequences of her act or (2) know that the act was right or wrong. Texas, where the trial was being held, based its insanity test on the second proposition, that is, knowing the act was wrong. Yates herself believed that if she were convicted and received the death penalty, then she would be able to kill Satan. Some of the experts testified that she believed that by killing her children, she was saving them from the devil. Although both the prosecution and the defense believed that Yates was mentally ill, the trial focused on whether Yates met the Texas legal definition of insanity: Did she know that drowning her children was wrong?

To add to the difficulty, one of the expert witnesses who consulted for the television show *Law and Order* reported that an episode that portrayed a woman with postpartum depression who had killed her children had been aired prior to the death of Andrea Yates's children. Thus, it was suggested that Yates obtained the idea to kill her children from television. However, it was later discovered that such an episode had never been written, produced, or televised. The defense asked the judge for a mistrial since the jurors were led to believe that Yates had planned the murders based on the television show. The judge denied the motion. She was not found insane. She was found guilty and sentenced to life in prison.

Some 3 years later, a Texas Court of Appeals reversed the conviction and required a new trial. In the second trial, Andrea Yates was found not guilty by reason of insanity. She was placed in a state mental hospital.

Source: Based on Ewing, C., & McCann, J. (2006). Minds on Trial: Great Cases in Law and Psychology. *Oxford University Press.*

As seen in the Yates story, although the decision of competency rests with the court, mental health professionals as experts are often asked to evaluate whether someone is competent to stand trial. The type of information that psychologists consider is determined from tests similar to those used for evaluating neurocognitive disorders. The mental health history of the person is considered. One looks for medical disorders that may influence the person. Interviews may also be conducted with family and

Yates family photos. Yates admitted to killing her four sons and her infant daughter in 2001.
Pam Francis/Contributor/Getty Images Entertainment/via Getty Images

friends of the person. As we saw with Yates, different states have different legal requirements and procedures for determining competency.

Decision-Making Competence

On January 8, 2011, Jared Lee Loughner shot and injured U.S. Rep. Gabby Giffords and killed six other people in Tucson, Arizona. He was initially evaluated and found incompetent to stand trial and showing signs of schizophrenia. He refused to take medication. A crucial question for the courts was whether Loughner could be forced to take antipsychotic medications to make him competent to stand trial. The prison medical doctors, on one hand, began giving him antipsychotic medications not to make him competent but because he had become violent and was a danger to himself and others, including other inmates and the prison staff. The medical staff saw medications as part of his treatment. On the other hand, there were a number of court challenges to the forced use of antipsychotic medications. The question being asked was whether a person before being convicted of a crime had the ability to make a choice in his treatment. This question of using medication to restore competency continues to be raised in court trials throughout the nation (Hicks & West, 2020; Wasser & Trueblood, 2015). Although the question was not formally settled in the Loughner case, the court allowed the medication to continue. After about a year and a half, Jared Loughner was reevaluated and found competent to stand trial. He pleaded guilty in November 2012 and was sentenced to life in prison without parole.

Historically, it was assumed that those with mental illness could not make rational decisions and were placed in hospitals without their consent. It was not until the 1880s that the idea of voluntary hospitalization was made part of the legal system in Massachusetts, the first state to do this. By the 1970s, it was realized that those with a mental illness could have different types of cognitive, emotional, or motor deficits. Thus, it became critical to determine if a person could consent to their own treatment.

In terms of legal standards, four factors have been used for determining decision-making competence (Appelbaum & Grisso, 1995). The first is ability to communicate a choice. This is the simplest of the requirements in that simple communication does not necessarily require understanding. However, if a client makes a choice but then constantly changes their mind, it would be concluded that they cannot make a choice. The second is the ability to understand relevant information. This requirement is that the client understands what they are being told. It was initially developed in contract law to

Well wishes for U.S. Representative Gabby Giffords, survivor of a 2011 shooting by Jared Lee Loughner. Six others were killed in the shooting.

John Moore/Staff/Getty Images News/Getty Images

determine if the person knew the consequences of signing a contract. The third factor is the ability to appreciate the nature of the situation and its consequences. In terms of legal proceedings, this requirement emphasizes that the client understands what a trial is and what could be its potential outcomes. The client must understand not only the concept of trials but what their specific trial could mean for them personally. The fourth is what is referred to as the ability to rationally manipulate information. That is, the person must be able to understand and consider alternatives to the information available to them. This requirement seeks to determine whether the client can logically and rationally reason based on the information they have. Neuropsychological testing offers one way to determine areas of strengths and weaknesses in terms of cognitive abilities related to decision-making competence.

Competence and Mental Health Courts

In addition to high-profile individuals such as John Hinckley and Andrea Yates, the court system in the United States encounters many individuals with mental disorders who are involved in minor or other types of offenses. Some of these individuals were convicted and sent to jail, then released, and then reappeared in court again for a repeat offense. This revolving door was not seen to serve society or these individuals well, and special courts were established to consider their cases that sought to add treatment as part of the consequences of a guilty conviction (Steadman et al., 2001; see also For Further Reading). In 1989, the first of the drug treatment courts was established, and such courts are now found all around the country. Following the model of drug courts, mental health courts were established. In 1996, the first mental health treatment court was established in Indianapolis, Indiana. Currently, the U.S. Department of Justice funds projects involving mental health courts that improve the treatment for adults with mental illness who are convicted of crimes (see For Further Reading).

Both drug and mental health courts share two common goals (Callahan et al., 2012). The first is to reduce recidivism and the revolving door phenomenon. The second is to increase community-based treatment for the participants. This is accomplished by holding both the individual and the community responsible for treatment success. To be part of such a program, the individual must agree to follow the conditions of the court, which specify their treatment. Most treatment courts require the person to enter a guilty plea in lieu of the criminal sentence. Currently, the treatment goal of mental health courts is one of recovery, whereas drug courts focus on abstinence from drug use. Both courts use sanctions and incentives to ensure that the person remains involved in their treatment. It is an incentive for the individual to be receiving treatment in the community as opposed to being in jail. Such programs also use reduced supervision and rewards such as gift cards for those who take responsibility for their treatment. Sanctions can include the requirement of more frequent meetings with court officials and, if the person does not become involved in the treatment procedure, jail time. Research studies suggest this approach offers an effective alternative to traditional treatment if developed correctly (Fox et al., 2021; Hiday et al., 2013; Loong et al., 2019; Redlich & Han, 2013).

> **CONCEPT CHECK**
>
> - What four criteria do mental health professionals use to determine an individual's competency to stand trial?

ETHICAL AND LEGAL ISSUES IN MENTAL HEALTH TREATMENT

In the 1970s, Prosenjit Poddar, a graduate student from India studying at the University of California, Berkeley, met another student, Tatiana Tarasoff, at a social event. They saw each other for a time and on New Year's Eve, they kissed. Poddar felt they had a special relationship, although he knew little of dating or American social patterns. He felt betrayed when she had relationships with other men. Feeling depressed, he went to the student health center. During the course of his therapy, he told the therapist that he intended to get a gun and shoot Tarasoff. The mental health professional sent a letter to the campus police, who then interviewed Poddar. He convinced them that he was not a risk to anyone, and he promised that he would stay away from and not harm Tarasoff. In a strange move, he moved in with Tarasoff's brother while she was visiting relatives in Brazil. When she returned, Poddar stalked her and stabbed her to death. What was to follow changed the nature of the therapeutic relationship with respect to the legal system.

After her death, Tarasoff's parents sued the campus police, health service employees, and regents of the University of California for failing to warn them that their daughter was in danger, but the trial court initially dismissed the suit. At the time, most courts had ruled that a doctor had a duty to a patient but not to a third party. The appeals court supported the dismissal. An appeal was then taken to the California Supreme Court.

In 1974, the California Supreme Court reversed the appeals court ruling. The court held that a therapist bears a duty to use reasonable care to give threatened persons such warnings as are essential to avert foreseeable danger arising from a patient's condition. This is known as the *Tarasoff I* decision, and it meant that the trial court was instructed to hear the lawsuit against the police and various employees of the University of California. Due to great uproar among psychiatrists and police, the California Supreme Court took the very unusual step of rehearing the same case in 1976. The decision from this case came to be known as *Tarasoff II*.

The legal statement that the court issued was as follows:

> When a therapist determines, or pursuant to the standards of his profession should determine, that his patient presents a serious danger of violence to another, he incurs an obligation to use reasonable care to protect the intended victim against such danger. The discharge of this duty may require the therapist to take one or more of various steps. Thus, it may call for him to warn the intended victim, to notify the police, or to take whatever steps are reasonably necessary under the circumstances.

Following the California decision, a number of U.S. states adopted the *Tarasoff* decision of **duty to protect**, which in the original decision included a *duty to warn* provision. That is, the professional must

The *Tarasoff* decision stemmed from the murder of Tatiana Tarasoff (*left*) by fellow UC Berkeley student Prosenjit Poddar (*right*).
AP Photo

not only protect intended victims but must also warn the intended victims or others at risk. However, it should be noted that there are differences in how various states interpret the duty to protect provision (Johnson et al., 2014). Further, California as of January 1, 2013, removed the "duty to warn" phrase (Weinstock et al., 2014). What is required is that the therapist has a duty to protect, which can be accomplished without actually warning the potential victim.

Ethical and Legal Aspects of the Initial Contract for Treatment

Ethical and legal considerations are part of every professional interaction. This is particularly true in relation to the mental health system. Let's use psychotherapy as an example. After the client describes the initial reason for seeking treatment, the therapist begins a dialogue to help the client understand what will take place in the therapy session and the nature of the therapist–client relationship. One major aspect of this dialogue involves **informed consent**. That is to say, the client has the right to know what will happen during the therapy sessions, what is expected of them, and the potential outcomes. The client also has the right to know the experience and expertise of the therapist with a given psychological problem and if there are alternative choices for treatment. After being informed of the nature of therapy, the client can consent to be treated or not.

In addition to being informed about the nature of therapy, the client also needs to understand the ethical and legal aspects of therapy. The first point is that the information discussed in the psychotherapy session is confidential. **Confidentiality (in health care)** means that the therapist is not to discuss information learned in a therapy session in any other context. Confidentiality as part of treatment has a long history in many cultures. Today, confidentiality is legally required for those who are licensed to practice psychotherapy. All 50 U.S. states and the District of Columbia have confidentiality laws that protect the information revealed in therapy.

The legal term for confidentiality is **privileged communication**. In most states, privileged communication may take place in a number of situations, including between an attorney and client, married partners, a priest and penitent, and a health care professional and client. Information obtained in these situations cannot be released in court. Thus, a court could not compel a therapist to reveal information learned in the therapy session. However, the privilege is controlled by the client. Thus, if a client wants the therapist to reveal what was discussed in therapy in court, then the therapist must comply. The situation becomes more complicated if a couple was seen by the same therapist in family therapy, for instance, or if there is a child involved in the court or custody proceedings.

In addition, health care records are protected by the **Health Insurance Portability and Accountability Act of 1996 (HIPAA).** This law regulates the manner in which medical and psychological records are maintained and shared with insurance companies and other health care professionals. If you wanted your current therapist to have access to work you did with a previous therapist, you would need to consent to having these records transferred. In addition to legal laws, which determine what information must be protected, there are also ethical guidelines from such organizations as the American Psychological Association (Table 16.2).

Based on the findings of *Tarasoff* and other court rulings, the therapist needs to discuss with the client exceptions to confidentiality. One of these is *duty to protect*. This may vary slightly from state to state, but the general guideline is that the therapist must take action if they believe the client will harm themself or another person. This may require that the therapist warn the other person, talk with the authorities or the police, or suggest hospitalization. These requirements are a direct consequence of the *Tarasoff* court ruling.

Another exception to confidentiality is related to the legal requirement for **mandated reporting**. Mandated reporting is the requirement that when health care professionals learn firsthand of child abuse or neglect as well as elder abuse, they report this information to the appropriate state agency. More specific information by state is available from the U.S. Department of Health and Human Services website (see For Further Reading).

TABLE 16.2 ■ Ethical Principles From the American Psychological Association—Some Highlights

Privacy and Confidentiality

Maintaining Confidentiality

Psychologists have a primary obligation and take reasonable precautions to protect confidential information obtained through or stored in any medium, recognizing that the extent and limits of confidentiality may be regulated by law or established by institutional rules or professional or scientific relationship. (See also Standard 2.05, Delegation of Work to Others.)

Discussing the Limits of Confidentiality

a. Psychologists discuss with persons (including, to the extent feasible, persons who are legally incapable of giving informed consent and their legal representatives) and organizations with whom they establish a scientific or professional relationship (1) the relevant limits of confidentiality and (2) the foreseeable uses of the information generated through their psychological activities. (See also Standard 3.10, Informed Consent.)

b. Unless it is not feasible or is contraindicated, the discussion of confidentiality occurs at the outset of the relationship and thereafter as new circumstances may warrant.

c. Psychologists who offer services, products, or information via electronic transmission inform clients/patients of the risks to privacy and limits of confidentiality.

Therapy

Informed Consent to Therapy

a. When obtaining informed consent to therapy as required in Standard 3.10, Informed Consent, psychologists inform clients/patients as early as is feasible in the therapeutic relationship about the nature and anticipated course of therapy, fees, involvement of third parties and limits of confidentiality and provide sufficient opportunity for the client/patient to ask questions and receive answers. (See also Standards 4.02, Discussing the Limits of Confidentiality, and 6.04, Fees and Financial Arrangements.)

Credit: American Psychological Association. (2017). *Ethical Principles of Psychologists and Code of Conduct.* http://www.apa.org/ethics/code/

Emergency Commitment

Most mental health professionals rarely are required to make emergency commitments. In therapy, they work closely with clients who are at risk to themselves to prevent suicide attempts. When there is concern for imminent danger, the first approach is to help the client decide to seek treatment at a mental health facility on a voluntary basis. When this is not possible, an emergency commitment may be required. If the person refuses the treatment, mental health professionals will involve the courts. The courts may require a civil commitment to an inpatient facility. Many states allow for an initial 72-hour involuntary commitment in an inpatient facility if the person is dangerous to themself or others. If, after 72 hours, health care professionals believe the person is still in need of inpatient treatment, they request that the person be committed for a longer period of time through the court system.

A *civil commitment* is the legal process by which a court orders the involuntary commitment of an individual (Zander, 2005). In general, the court needs to determine that the person has a mental illness, is dangerous to themself or others, or is unable to care for themself. The inability to take care of one's self is legally referred to as *grave disability*. The goal of a civil commitment is to protect the public or to protect, or treat, the person.

The legal precedent for civil commitment is based on two principles. The first is based on the government's need to invoke police powers to ensure public health, safety, welfare, and morality. Thus, it is the task of the government to protect the public. The second legal principle is referred to as *parens patriae* ("parent of the nation") authority, which is derived from English common law. Since the 1500s, the king or queen held the authority to take care of those who could not take care of themselves. In the United States, courts have held this authority to take care of children in certain situations or those with certain types of mental disorders.

A tragic use of these child treatment laws are cases in which parents transfer legal and physical custody of a child to the state so that the child can receive treatment for a serious psychological disorder that they would not be able to access otherwise. In 2019, National Public Radio (NPR) profiled parents who could access treatment for their child only if they relinquished custody (see For Further Reading). Currently, a number of legal proceedings in state and federal courts are examining the manner in which children with serious psychological disorders can receive treatment for their conditions.

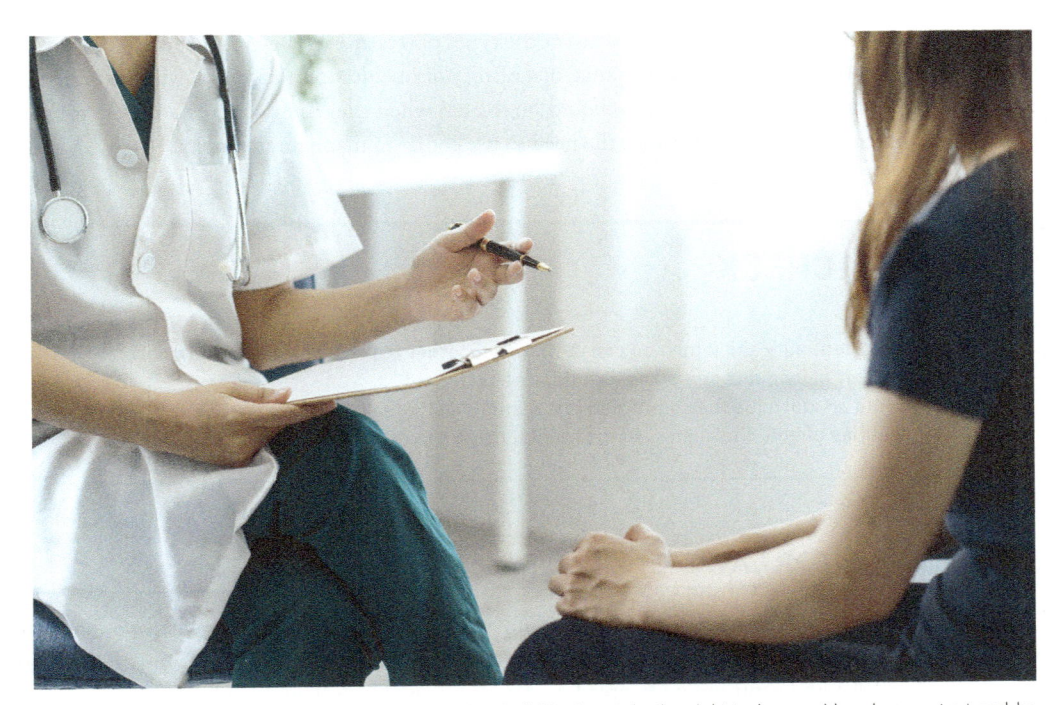

Even if involuntarily committed to an inpatient facility, individuals retain the right to be considered competent and be involved in their own treatment. This includes the right in many states to refuse medication.

iStock.com/AmnajKhetsamtip

Until the 1970s, involuntary commitment of adults with mental illness required only that there was a need for treatment. This was changed in a landmark federal court decision in 1972 referred to as *Lessard v. Schmidt*. This was the first of many court decisions based on the due process requirements of the Fourteenth Amendment to the U.S. Constitution, which concluded that civil commitment could not be solely justified based on the *parens patriae* authority. That is, a court needed to meet additional requirements other than just the person's need for treatment.

The additional requirement was to show that individuals about to be involuntarily committed were dangerous to themselves or others. By showing that there was danger, the court could draw upon another responsibility of the government. Legally, this is referred to as the *police power authority*. It is the job of government to ensure the safety of the people, which is traditionally performed by the police. For involuntary commitment, the person must also be shown to be dangerous to themself or others. Thus, needing treatment is not enough for a civil commitment. This was formally decided by the U.S. Supreme Court in 1975 in *O'Connor v. Donaldson*. The court ruled that there is no constitutional basis for confining people involuntarily if they are dangerous to no one and can live safely in freedom. In the 1980s, the Supreme Court ruled that being dangerous to the self and others also applied to sexual offenders.

From the 1970s until today, those with mental illness have gained more rights within the law. Even if involuntarily committed to an inpatient facility, the person still retains the right to be considered competent and be involved in their own treatment. This includes the right in many states to refuse medication. If the health care professionals deem that medication is critical, they, in turn, can involve the courts or their representatives.

Psychiatric Advance Directives

In health care, the **Patient Self-Determination Act (PSDA) of 1991** was introduced. This is a set of federal requirements intended to implement advance directive policies at all health care facilities that receive federal funding through Medicaid and Medicare programs. Today, many individuals have "living wills" or advance directives that direct how they will be treated if they become seriously ill or are near death. What became apparent was that this approach could also be applied to mental health.

This approach is referred to as **psychiatric advance directives (PADs).** PADs have been written into law in a number of states. These laws allow a person to submit directives or designate individuals to consent on their behalf. This enables someone who has a history of periods in which they would not be competent to make a rational decision to direct the types of treatments they would accept or refuse. Thus, an individual with schizophrenia, mania, or a history of suicide attempts could, when experiencing periods of incapacity, direct how they would be treated when they are not able to make rational decisions on their own. This would reduce the need to use courts to mandate treatment.

CONCEPT CHECK

- How do confidentiality and informed consent work together to provide legal and ethical protections for individuals seeking psychological treatment?
- When should an individual be committed to a mental health facility? What are the rights and responsibilities of both the client and the mental health professionals in that situation?

SEXUAL PREDATOR LAWS

Issues of mental health, involuntary commitment, and recidivism collide powerfully when we consider people convicted of sexual offenses. One of the most gruesome strings of sexual crimes in U.S. history came to light in 1991 and captured widespread media attention. The following public case details the chilling story of Jeffrey Dahmer.

In 1988, Jeffrey Dahmer, age 28, offered a group of teenage boys $50 to take nude photographs of them. Most of them said no, but one 13-year-old said yes. He took him to a nearby apartment and had him pose on a bed. Dahmer took Polaroid photos, fondled the boy's penis, and kissed his stomach. He then offered him an alcoholic drink, which was laced with a strong sleep medication. The boy was able to find his way out of the apartment and go to his home where his parents took him for medical care. The 13-year-old boy explained what happened.

The next morning, Dahmer was arrested and charged with sexual assault. He was released on bail. Although Dahmer later pleaded guilty to sexual assault, he denied any involvement and said only that he wanted to take pictures. What no one knew at the time was that over the preceding 11 years, Jeffrey Dahmer had sexually assaulted and killed five males aged 14 to 48. When it was time for the sentencing, the judge did not send Jeffrey Dahmer to prison. Rather, Dahmer received probation and was told to stay away from minors. He worked during the day but was required to sleep in a jail dormitory at night. This ended after 10 months.

In a little more than a year following this, Dahmer sexually assaulted and killed at least 12 additional boys and men ranging in age from 14 to 33. His way of approaching the men and killing them was very similar. He would go to gay bars, bath houses, and other similar gathering places. He would invite the men to his apartment and offer them money for sex or photographs. Dahmer would drug their drinks, and they would be sexually molested and killed. After death, they might be further molested. They were then cut into pieces and, in some cases, even cooked and eaten by Dahmer.

In a strange twist of fate, Dahmer's next victim was actually the younger brother of one of his earlier victims whom he had killed. Thinking his victim would be passed out for a while from the drugs he had given him, Dahmer went out to get some beer. However, the boy escaped during this time. Those in the neighborhood saw the boy naked and called the police. When the police arrived, Dahmer had returned. He told the police that the boy was actually 19, had been staying with him, and had too much to drink. He further told them that they were boyfriends. At the apartment, they found the boy's clothes neatly folded and concluded that he did indeed live there. Thinking it was a domestic situation, the police left. Dahmer then strangled the boy.

The killing continued. With the next victim, Dahmer changed his routine. Rather than drug the 32-year-old man he had picked out, he handcuffed him and pulled a knife on him. At that point, Dahmer showed the man a human skull and told him that he too would be staying with him. After some hours, the man was able to punch and kick Dahmer and escape. He found a police car and told the officers the story. They returned to Dahmer's apartment with the man. After asking Dahmer if they could look around, they began to discover the horrors of Dahmer's activities. They found body parts throughout the apartment but mostly in refrigerators and freezers. There were photos of mutilated bodies and the victims posed in sex acts.

Dahmer cooperated with the police and admitted to killing 17 men. The prosecution and defense in the case appointed a number of psychologists and psychiatrists to evaluate Dahmer. Most believed he was competent to stand trial but differed on whether he should be considered legally sane at the time of the crimes. The jury also could not reach a unanimous verdict in terms of insanity. Jeffrey Dahmer was found guilty of murder and sentenced to 957 years in prison. After less than 2 years in prison, he was killed by a mentally ill inmate.

Source: Based on Ewing, C., & McCann, J. (2006). Minds on Trial: Great Cases in Law and Psychology. *Oxford University Press.*

Most people believed Jeffrey Dahmer was competent to stand trial but differed on whether he should be considered legally sane at the time of the crimes.

TCD/Prod.DB/Alamy Stock Photo

Sexual crimes such as those committed by Jeffrey Dahmer bring forth repulsion in the public. Since the 1990s, a total of 20 U.S. states and the federal government have passed laws that allow for civil commitment of individuals who are considered to be sexually dangerous (Felthous & Ko, 2018; Sreenivasan et al., 2010). These laws are referred to as **sexually violent predator (SVP) or sexually dangerous person (SDP) statutes.** In general, these laws allow for a person who committed a sexual crime to be held after their criminal sentence has been completed. The idea is that these individuals represent a threat to public safety if they are released.

A number of groups, including the American Psychiatric Association, have opposed these laws. One argument is that such laws do not allow the person to have due process. They may also invalidate an earlier plea bargain by which the person was sentenced. These laws represent a form of preventive detention whereby individuals are being held for an activity they have yet to commit, based on past convictions. Psychological and psychiatric organizations are also concerned that in the name of public safety, other individuals with mental illness might be included. They also object because detention is not an effective form of treatment.

Child sexual abuse and other sexual offenses greatly concern a community that seeks various ways to prevent such behaviors. This has resulted in laws being passed by both the federal government and the states to address these issues (Agan, 2011; Felthous & Ko, 2018; Prescott & Rockoff, 2011). The laws are typically named for victims. In 1994, the Jacob Wetterling Act directed states to create registries of sex offenders to be used by law enforcement. This was updated in 2006 by the Adam Walsh Act to include more categories of sex offenders. In 1996, Megan's Law required that states provide public notification of the identities of sexual offenders. The basic motivation suggested that this information would help communities protect themselves and prevent future crimes. Although research suggests that these laws may reduce sexual incidents for those who know the sexual predator personally, they do not increase overall public safety.

It is currently a critical question to determine the role of mental illness in commitment of sexual crimes. Sexual predator laws have been upheld by the Supreme Court in *Kansas v. Hendricks* and *Kansas v. Crane* (Zander, 2005). The claim is that these laws do not define a crime but rather relate to mental illness. However, individuals who qualify for involuntary commitment are not sent for treatment but remain in prison. This continues to raise questions related to the treatment of people with mental illness who have committed crimes versus imprisonment for the protection of society. *Cultural LENS: Global Mental Health: Incarcerationand Mental Health* describes the relationship between mental health and being a prisoner throughout the world.

CULTURAL LENS
GLOBAL MENTAL HEALTH: INCARCERATION AND MENTAL HEALTH

It is estimated that 9 million people are imprisoned worldwide (Fazel & Danesh, 2002). Seena Fazel and John Danesh examined 62 surveys from 12 Western countries that examined mental disorders in 22,790 people in prison. They found that, in comparison with the general population, people in prison were several times more likely to have a psychotic disorder and major depression and 10 times more likely to have an antisocial personality disorder. Specifically, they found that 3.7% of the men had a psychotic illness, 10% had major depression, and 65% had a personality disorder. Among women in prison, they found that 4% had a psychotic illness, 10% had major depression, and 42% had a personality disorder. Overall, this suggests that 1 in 7 people in prison in Western countries have psychotic illness or major depression. About 1 in 2 men in prison and 1 in 5 women in prison have antisocial personality disorder. Unfortunately, mental health data in prisons in many countries such as those of Latin America are underestimated for lack of scientific studies (Almanzar et al., 2015).

An inmate with mental health conditions in the Twin Towers Correctional Facility in Los Angeles, California.
Robert Gauthier/Contributor/Los Angeles Times/via Getty Images

In the United States, there are now more than 3 times more seriously mentally ill individuals in jails and prisons than in hospitals (Torrey et al., 2010). This varies by state, with Arizona and Nevada having almost 10 times more mentally ill individuals in jails and prisons than hospitals, whereas North Dakota has a nearly equal number.

Placing individuals who commit crimes in jail does serve a societal function. Particular mental disorders, such as psychopathy, are strongly associated with a high risk for criminal and violent behavior. However, there are individuals with a mental disorder who are jailed merely because a particular community does not want them on their streets, or as a means of protecting those individuals with a mental disorder from becoming victims of crime themselves. Many believe that society is not being served well by using jails and prisons as a place to put individuals with mental disorders who have not committed a crime.

Thought Question

What are possible alternatives that a society might consider rather than using prisons as a place to put those with a mental illness?

As described in the *Cultural LENS*, there is concern about how prisons around the world are being used to house those with mental disorders, even if they have not committed a crime. There is also concern about what prison life may do to those with a mental illness. In the past decade, society has become more aware of how some aspects of prison life such as solitary confinement affect both those with and without a mental disorder. The implications of solitary confinement are described in *LENS: The Implications of Solitary Confinement*.

LENS

THE IMPLICATIONS OF SOLITARY CONFINEMENT

Solitary confinement is when a person in prison is kept in their cell alone for 22 or 23 hours a day without access to the activities that other inmates engage in. These people eat in their cell, sleep in their cell, and perform normal bathroom functions in their cell. It is estimated that some 80,000 people in the United States are currently being held in solitary confinement. That is more than any other country in the world.

Demonstrators rally in Oakland, California, to reform the practice of solitary confinement.

San Francisco Chronicle/Hearst Newspapers via Getty Images

Solitary confinement is used in American prisons for a number of reasons. Sometimes, the person is violent and a danger to other inmates and prison workers. Other times, the person is seen to be a member of a prison gang. Sometimes, it is to protect the person from other inmates, as seen with LGBTQ individuals or those who committed certain types of crimes. Other times, it is part of an administrative procedure that precedes the introduction of a new person into a larger prison unit. Others who are often put in solitary are those who find it difficult to follow the rules of the prison and those who respond to guards in a confrontational manner. This may include those with mental illness. Most prisons do not have the resources to respond to mental illness, and therefore solitary confinement became one way to handle those with mental disorders. However, these individuals may not have the skills to endure the environment experienced in solitary confinement.

Although the person's basic physical needs are taken care of in solitary confinement, they have little or no social contact or interaction with others. What is the result of this lack of true human interaction? Psychologists have begun to ask this question. One psychologist who has studied solitary confinement over a number of years is Craig Haney (Haney, 2018; Heng et al., 2023). In 1993, Haney interviewed a group of inmates in solitary confinement at Pelican Bay State Prison in

California. During this period, new super-maximum security prisons were being built. It was also a time when the nation viewed prisons as punishment and not rehabilitation for those incarcerated.

Haney returned to Pelican Bay some 20 years later and talked to some of the same individuals he had seen previously. He was shocked by what he experienced. He reported that not only did solitary confinement make those with mental illness worse, but even individuals without any disorders showed negative consequences. He found a similar pattern: Some individuals respond with panic to the isolation. Once this has passed, they may become depressed and feel hopeless. Without human contact and other important activities, some lose contact with reality. Others do outrageous things just to know that they still exist or to get a reaction from the guards. After a time, they no longer want to see others, even their family.

Recently, a number of media outlets have begun to pay attention to the consequences of solitary confinement. What little research there is suggests that solitary confinement does not make a prison safer and is a negative experience for the individuals involved. In 2012, the Center for Constitutional Rights filed suit in federal court against state officials on behalf of Pelican Bay inmates who had spent more than 10 years in solitary confinement, claiming that their prolonged isolation violated their Eighth Amendment protection against cruel and unusual punishment. In 2015, a settlement by the state of California reformed the way in which solitary confinement is used (see https://ccrjustice.org/key-reforms-california-s-use-solitary-confinement). Further, in June 2015, Supreme Court Justice Anthony Kennedy wrote that in relation to solitary confinement, "near-total isolation exacts a terrible price." In 2015, President Barack Obama became the first president to visit a federal prison and asked whether "we really think it makes sense to lock so many people alone in tiny cells for 23 hours a day, sometimes for months or even years at a time." In 2016, President Obama banned solitary confinement for juvenile offenders in federal prisons.

Source: Based on information presented on PBS's *Frontline* (Childress, S. [2014, April 22]. *Craig Haney: Solitary confinement is a "tried-and-true" torture device.* PBS. http://www.pbs.org/wgbh/frontline/article/craig-haney-solitary-confinement-is-a-tried-and-true-torture-device/) and the *New York Times* (Goode, E. [2015, August 3]. *Solitary confinement: Punished for life. New York Times.* https://www.nytimes.com/2015/08/04/health/solitary-confinement-mental-illness.html).

Thought Question

How would you research the effects of solitary confinement? What would be your control group?

CONCEPT CHECK

- What is the purpose of SVP or SDP laws?
- What have communities put in place to try to prevent pedophilia and other sexual offenses?

NEUROSCIENCE AND EVOLUTIONARY PERSPECTIVES ON THE LEGAL ASPECTS OF PSYCHOPATHOLOGY

The legal profession and the courts have been greatly influenced by neuroscience discoveries and methods (Jones & Wagner, 2020; Roskies et al., 2013). Today, deoxyribonucleic acid (DNA) is commonly used to help to convict or demonstrate innocence in court trials. Hundreds of individuals who were previously serving prison sentences have been exonerated through DNA and other types of biological testing. The legal system is also seeking information from neuroscience researchers. In 2012, the Connecticut Medical Examiner asked geneticists at the University of Connecticut to examine the DNA of Adam Lanza, the 20-year-old who killed 27 people at Sandy Hook Elementary School in Newtown, Connecticut. Although Lanza died by suicide, the medical examiner sought to determine if there were clues in the DNA to help explain the killings (see For Further Reading). Using neuroscience to arrive at answers to legal questions is a field referred to as *forensic neuroscience*.

Neuroscience information also requires that the legal system ask questions it is not used to asking. For example, how should we understand the fact that in 1966, Charles Whitman, who was an Eagle

Scout and marine, killed 15 people from the University of Texas tower with a rifle? Had he lived and gone to court, juries would have likely said he was responsible for the killings. Yet, should we consider the fact that he had a brain tumor that pressed on his amygdala? The relationship between neuroscience research and the law is not easy, especially when the task is to determine responsibility or predict violent behavior (Alces, 2018; Poldrack et al., 2018; Slobogin, 2018).

Neuroscience research is currently being included in legal decisions. It has been used to help establish responsibility. The U.S. Supreme Court has used neuroscience data to help determine if an individual is responsible for their actions (Steinberg, 2013). In one important case, the Court considered the question of whether an adolescent who killed another person should be tried as an adult. Sixteen- and 17-year-olds could receive the death penalty in some states before 2005, and those even younger could be sentenced to life in prison without parole for killing another person. In 2005, the U.S. Supreme Court in the *Roper v. Simmons* case abolished the death penalty for crimes committed while under the age of 18. In 2012, in the *Miller v. Alabama* and *Jackson v. Hobbs* cases, the Supreme Court banned the use of the life without parole sentence for adolescents on constitutional grounds. In 2016, the Supreme Court expanded this ruling in *Montgomery v. Louisiana* with the decision that their 2012 ruling should be applied retroactively to more than 2,000 cases nationwide. In these cases, it was noted that neuroscience research shows the adolescent brain to be different from an adult's, as you read in Chapter 5. Thus, an adolescent should be held responsible for their actions to a different degree than should an adult. This, in turn, should be reflected in the sentencing of the convicted individual.

Another situation in which neuroscience research has changed legal procedures is in terms of memory and the ability to influence another individual's recollection of an event (Loftus, 2003; Schacter & Loftus, 2013; Wade et al., 2018; Wixted et al., 2018). Schacter and Loftus described a crime that happened in Camden, New Jersey, on New Year's Day, 2003. Larry Henderson was accused of holding a gun on James Womble while another man shot Rodney Harper to death. Almost 2 weeks after the murder, Womble identified Henderson from a photograph. Womble again identified Henderson at trial, and Henderson was easily convicted of reckless manslaughter and aggravated assault, among other charges. The case was appealed to the New Jersey Supreme Court, which resulted in the court issuing a new set of guidelines that reflected the reconstructive nature of memory and the various factors that can influence it. Specifically, jurors are now to be told that memory is not like a video recording, and it is not foolproof but can be influenced. Research has also shown that those in positions of authority, such as police officers, military personnel, and emergency responders, are susceptible to memory errors during challenging incidents (Hope et al., 2015).

The relationship between neuroscience research and the law is not easy. In 1966 Charles Whitman killed 15 people, including himself, at the University of Texas clock tower; should we consider the fact that he had a brain tumor that pressed on his amygdala?

iStock.com/dszc

Juries in some states are told how eyewitness memory may be problematic. This also includes a statement that those of a different race may be harder to identify than a person of one's own race. These are common findings from neuroscience research. By the way, in the original trial of Larry Henderson, the jury was never told that the witness, James Womble, who identified Larry Henderson, had used crack cocaine and had drunk wine and champagne on that New Year's Day when the crime happened.

Although neuroscience approaches have potential for clarifying legal questions in relation to mental illness, as noted previously, current neuroscience techniques are not able to diagnose a given individual. Even in areas in which neuroscience research has been directed at criminal behavior, such as convicted criminals with antisocial personality disorder, it is still impossible to predict which individual will commit another crime from brain imaging studies (Eastman & Campbell, 2006). At this time, neither neuroscience nor brain imaging research can determine whether or not a specific individual person is telling a lie (Langleben & Moriarty, 2013). Research can, of course, suggest which groups of individuals, such as those with antisocial personality disorder, are more likely to seek to deceive others.

As you have seen in this book, neuroscience research is largely characterized by studies that reflect the differences between one group of individuals with specific psychopathologies and another group of individuals without the disorder. These data represent the average of measures from all individuals in a given group and the probability of these results being found if the study was performed again. These results are described in terms of statistical probabilities. On the other hand, courts do not say a person has a 95% probability of being guilty. The legal system seeks a different type of answer than does neuroscience research. Of course, as with the U.S. Supreme Court, neuroscience has extremely important information to help the legal system make informed judgments.

Evolutionary perspectives in relation to the legal system have been less well studied. However, we know that our long history of social relationships has resulted in a rich calculus of how we make moral judgments and exact punishments on others. For example, if you are asked who you would save from a burning building, a 2-year-old or a 70-year-old, most people quickly answer a 2-year-old. It is a gut reaction with little thinking required. What if you see someone hurt a helpless animal? How do you respond? It is also a quick response, unless you have an antisocial personality or a conduct disorder. Our evolutionary history leads us to approach social and moral situations in a particular manner. It does not matter if we are out in the world or part of a jury.

Someone who thinks that rape or killing is wrong does not think that this only applies to their hometown but to the entire world. In this sense, moral judgments are experienced differently from cultural ones. It is also the case that humans believe that committing immoral acts should be followed by punishment. People often say it is wrong to let someone "get away with it." That is, humans not only make moral judgments but also believe that what they consider to be immoral behavior should be punished. These are two critical elements that juries consider, although often outside of conscious awareness, as they determine guilt and innocence. Thus, neuroscience and evolutionary perspectives have the potential to help inform the legal system in relation to the types of questions it considers.

UNDERSTANDING CHANGES IN *DSM-5* AND *DSM-5-TR*
LEGAL ISSUES

Although we usually think about *DSM-5-TR* in terms of the diagnosis of mental illness, it is also used in a variety of legal and other situations (Appelbaum, 2014). For example, *DSM-5 and DSM-5-TR* are used in courts to determine disability, criminal responsibility, and the capacity to perform tasks and understand actions. Forensic evaluations can be required to determine if a person is capable of writing a will, running a business, or consenting to medical treatment (Simpson, 2014).

Courts typically determine who is responsible for a specific act. As such, they want to say this situation or this person is responsible. Thus, conditions that result in injury, stress, or trauma are treated differently in courts than they are treated by health care professionals. For example, there are a number of lawsuits related to the National Football League as well as the Veterans Administration in terms of responsibility for care. This is part of a larger situation in which brain injury from sports or military service related to over a decade of combat and the aging of the population are playing a critical role in our society. How neurocognitive disorders are defined in *DSM-5* and *DSM-5-TR* play an important role in these decisions.

Another disorder that was changed in *DSM-5* and is often found in court proceedings is PTSD (Levin et al., 2014). With the original introduction of the diagnosis of PTSD in the 1980s, a variety of victims have come before the courts as either defendants or plaintiffs. Likewise, studies have shown higher rates of PTSD in prison populations. As noted in Chapter 7 on stress and trauma, changes in the *DSM-5* criteria for PTSD resulted in different individuals being diagnosed with the disorder. This, in turn, could influence the outcomes of court proceedings. That is, *DSM-5* includes work situations such as those experienced by firefighters, police, and emergency medical personnel as well as the military in exposure to stress-related disorders. This could change the nature of the legal rulings.

The larger conceptual shift in *DSM-5* from categorical to more dimensional descriptions of mental disorders should have important implications for its use in the legal system. In particular, the legal system seeks to determine who is guilty or responsible for a particular act. This underlying legal goal may be at odds with a psychological understanding of human behavior. It will be some time before we know how *DSM-5* will influence the legal system.

CONCEPT CHECK

- What are five ways in which the legal profession and the courts have been greatly influenced by neuroscience discoveries and methods?
- What are some specific ways that evolutionary perspectives help inform the legal profession and the courts?

SUMMARY

Individuals seeking treatment for a psychological disorder have both legal and ethical protections, including (1) informed consent; (2) confidentiality, or in legal terms, privileged communication; and (3) protection of health care records through HIPAA. Exceptions to confidentiality include duty to protect and mandated reporting. Commitment to a mental health facility may be necessary if it is determined that the person has a mental illness, is dangerous to self or others, or is unable to care for self. Even if involuntarily committed to an inpatient facility, the person still retains the right to be considered competent and be involved in their own treatment. A new approach, referred to as psychiatric advance directives (PADs), allows a person with a psychological disorder to submit directives or designate individuals to consent on his behalf and direct how he would be treated when or if he is not able to make rational decisions on his own.

Insanity is a legal term, not a psychological one. All cultures throughout time have sought to determine the role of responsibility in committing criminal acts. In the United States, a number of variations based on capacity and knowledge have been applied in determining sanity, including the M'Naghten rule, the volitional test, the Durham rule, the ALI rule, and the Comprehensive Crime Control Act of 1984. In reality, the insanity defense is used less than 1% of the time. The first step before a trial is to determine if a person is competent to stand trial. Four factors have been used for determining decision-making competence: (1) ability to communicate a choice, (2) ability to understand relevant information, (3) ability to appreciate the nature of the situation and its consequences, and (4) ability to rationally manipulate information.

SVP or SDP statutes generally allow for individuals who committed a sexual crime to be held after their sentence has been completed. The idea is that these individuals represent a threat to public safety if they are released. A number of groups, including the American Psychiatric Association, have opposed these laws. Pedophilia and other sexual offenses greatly concern a community that seeks various ways to prevent such behaviors. Although research suggests that these laws may reduce sexual incidents in those who know the sexual predator personally, they do not increase overall public safety. It is currently a critical question to determine the role of mental illness in committing sexual crimes.

STUDY RESOURCES

Review Questions

1. Ethical and legal considerations are part of every professional interaction. How do the following concepts relate to the ethical and legal aspects of the therapy session and the nature of the therapist–client relationship:
   a. Duty to protect
   b. Informed consent
   c. Confidentiality
   d. Privileged communication
   e. Health Insurance Portability and Accountability Act of 1996 (HIPAA)
   f. Mandated reporting

2. The impact of mental illness on an individual's ability to think rationally and make rational decisions is an important consideration in their interactions within both the legal system and the mental health system. What are some situations where this is most problematic, and what are some ideas for improving those situations?

3. Why is it critical to both individuals and communities to determine the role of mental illness in the commitment of sexual crimes?

4. We know that neuroscience research shows the adolescent brain to be different from an adult's, and thus, an adolescent should be held responsible for his or her actions to a different degree than should an adult. This, in turn, should be reflected in the sentencing of the convicted individual. What do you think: Are adult sentences appropriate for an adolescent who has been convicted of a sexual crime?

5. Considering neuroscience and evolutionary perspectives on mental health is a thread that has run throughout this book. What are some specific ways in which your thinking has changed about how those with mental illness are treated within our legal system? What alternatives to the legal system would you want to consider?

For Further Reading

Alces, P. (2018). *The moral conflict of law and neuroscience*. University of Chicago Press.

Bureau of Justice Assistance. (2012). *Mental health courts program*. U.S. Department of Justice. https://bja.ojp.gov/program/mental-health-courts-program/overview?Program_ID=68

Child Welfare Information Gateway. (n.d.). www.childwelfare.gov/systemwide/sgm/index.cfm

Childress, S. (2014, April 22). *Craig Haney: Solitary confinement is a "tried-and-true" torture device*. PBS. http://www.pbs.org/wgbh/frontline/article/craig-haney-solitary-confinement-is-a-tried-and-true-torture-device/

Council of State Governments Justice Center. (2008). *Mental health courts: A primer for policymakers and practitioners*. https://bja.ojp.gov/sites/g/files/xyckuh186/files/Publications/MHC_Primer.pdf

Davis, K. (2017). *The Brain Defense*. Penguin Press.

Eagleman, D. (2011). *Incognito: The secret lives of the brain*. Pantheon Books.

Goode, E. (2015, August 3). *Solitary confinement: Punished for life*. New York Times. https://www.nytimes.com/2015/08/04/health/solitary-confinement-mental-illness.html

Herman, C. (2019, January 2). *To get mental health help for a child, desperate parents relinquish custody*. NPR. https://www.npr.org/sections/health-shots/2019/01/02/673765794/to-get-mental-health-help-for-a-child-desperate-parents-relinquish-custody

Lewis, R. (2013, January 3). *Comparing Adam Lanza's DNA to forensic DNA databases: A modest proposal. : DNA Science*. https://dnascience.plos.org/2013/01/03/comparing-adam-lanzas-dna-to-forensic-dna-databases-a-modest-proposal/

Morse, S., & Roskies, A. (Eds.). (2013). *A primer on criminal law and neuroscience*. Oxford University Press.

Tottey, E. (2008). *The insanity offense*. Norton.

KEY TERMS AND CONCEPTS

- ALI rule
- confidentiality (in health care)
- Durham rule
- duty to protect
- informed consent (in mental health treatment)
- insanity
- Health Insurance Portability and Accountability Act of 1996 (HIPAA)
- mandated reporting
- M'Naghten rule
- Patient Self-Determination Act (PSDA) of 1991
- privileged communication
- psychiatric advance directives (PADs)
- sexually violent predator (SVP) or sexually dangerous person (SDP) statutes
- volitional test

GLOSSARY

12-step program: a community in which individuals with addiction problems meet and follow the principles described in the 12 steps; forms the basis for Alcoholics Anonymous (AA), and variations of the approach have been used with other addictions

abnormal psychology: the study of psychological dysfunctions that the person experiences in terms of distress or impairment in functioning; a complete definition of abnormal behavior includes behaviors and experiences accepted in the person's culture

acquired immune deficiency syndrome (AIDS): a disorder caused by the human immunodeficiency virus (HIV), which affects the person's immune system in a negative manner; characterized by neurocognitive problems such as slowing in both cognitive and motor functions, including memory problems, confusion, depression, and difficulty with fine motor tasks

acute stress disorder: a short-term reaction to traumatic events that lasts from 3 days to 1 month

addiction: dependence on a substance (or process) in which an individual experiences a strong motivation that results in an active wanting and seeking of the substance, which may be experienced as compulsive

adjustment disorders: disorders in which reactions to events are out of proportion to the severity of the event

adoption study: research into the phenomenon where dizygotic (DZ) and monozygotic (MZ) twins have been raised apart, providing insights into the environmental and genetic influences on human development and behavior

agonist drug: as a treatment for addiction, it is a substance that binds to the receptor in the brain and produces cellular activity that mimics the function of the illicit drug without producing the high; methadone is an opioid agonist

agoraphobia: the condition in which a person experiences fear or anxiety when in public

agreeableness: associated with being sympathetic, trusting, cooperative, modest, and straightforward; as a dimension in the five-factor model (FFM), this dimension ranges from being friendly and compassionate to being competitive and outspoken

alcohol: a liquid created through a process of fermentation; in most humans, the experience of alcohol intake includes pleasant subjective experiences, which are partly related to the effects of alcohol on such neurotransmitters as serotonin, endorphins, and dopamine; alcohol will also decrease inhibition by reducing the effects of the GABA system, which is associated with anxiety

ALI rule: a broader approach to not guilty by reason of insanity developed by the American Law Institute (ALI) in 1962 that states the following: "A person is not responsible for criminal conduct if at the time of such conduct as the result of mental disease or defect he lacks substantial capacity either to appreciate the criminality (wrongfulness) of his conduct or to conform his conduct to the requirements of the law"

allele: the alternative molecular form of the same gene

allostasis: refers to the body's ability to achieve stability through an active process of change, often involving the brain. This is in contrast to the older term *stress* in which responses to change were seen as passive and fixed

allostatic load: cumulative wear and tear on the body from responding to stressful conditions

alogia: lack of interest in talking with others or answering questions with more than a one- or two-word answer

amphetamines: stimulants produced in the laboratory that result in positive feelings, a burst of energy, and alertness

anhedonia: the inability to experience pleasure

anonymity: a principle that requires that the personal identity of a given participant in a research study be kept separate from their data

anorexia nervosa: a serious eating disorder involving the restriction of food, a weight that is below normal, a fear of gaining weight, a lack of recognition of the seriousness of current body weight, and a distorted perception of one's body

antagonist drug: as a treatment for addiction, it is a substance that blocks the receptor site in the brain so that the illicit drug does not produce an effect; by blocking or counteracting the effects of the illicit drug, it no longer is experienced as rewarding and addictive; naltrexone is an antagonist used to treat opioid addiction

antisocial personality disorder: one of the dramatic emotional personality disorders (Cluster B); typically involving repeated participation in illegal acts, deceitfulness, impulsiveness, hostility and aggression, engagement in dangerous acts, irresponsible behavior, and absence of remorse

anxious/ambivalent attachment pattern: an attachment style in which the infant appears preoccupied with having access to the mother and shows protest on her separation; when she returns, the infant may show anger or ambivalence toward her

anxious fearful personality disorders (Cluster C): a grouping of personality disorders within *DSM-5-TR* characterized by fearfulness and avoidance

attachment: the quality of the relationship between an infant and parent or primary caregiver

attention deficit/hyperactivity disorder (ADHD): a disorder of childhood that includes two major dimensions: (1) inattention and (2) hyperactivity and impulsivity

autism spectrum disorder (ASD): the new *DSM-5* diagnosis for a neurodevelopmental disorder in which individuals have difficulty in three separate areas: (1) social interactions, (2) communication, and (3) behavioral processes

autonomic nervous system (ANS): a division of the nervous system that innervates a variety of organs, including the adrenal medulla, that results in the release of catecholamines (norepinephrine and epinephrine) from the terminal of sympathetic nerves

aversive drug: as a treatment for addiction, it becomes aversive when the drug of abuse is taken; Antabuse is an aversive drug that interferes with the metabolism of alcohol and produces unpleasant reactions

avoidant/restrictive food intake disorder: a feeding disorder in which an individual does not eat certain foods, which leads to such conditions as weight loss or nutritional deficiency

avoidant attachment pattern: an attachment style in which the infant shows more interest in the toys than the mother and shows less distress when the mother leaves and less positive emotion when she returns

avoidant personality disorder: one of the anxious fearful personality disorders (Cluster C); characterized by a pervasive pattern of social inhibition, feelings of inadequacy, and hypersensitivity to negative evaluation

avolition: lack of will or volition

Beck Depression Inventory (BDI): a questionnaire useful for determining the level of depressive symptoms that a person is reporting

behavioral and experiential perspective: examines the behavior and experience observed in psychopathology, especially the manner in which the signs and symptoms of a particular disorder are seen in a similar manner throughout the world

behavioral genetics: the study of genetic and environmental contributions to organisms' behavior

behavioral perspective: a psychological approach focused only on actions and behaviors, not internal processes or aspects of consciousness

binge drinking: imbibing numerous alcoholic drinks over a short period of time or, officially, consuming enough alcohol in a 2-hour period to have a blood alcohol concentration (BAC) of 0.08g/dL

binge eating disorder: characterized by the consumption of large amounts of food and the sense that one cannot control their eating behavior

bipolar disorder: previously known as manic depression; a mood disorder characterized by the experience of both depression and mania

blind controls: research participants who do not know whether they are in the experimental group or the control (placebo) group

body dysmorphic disorder: an obsessive-compulsive–related disorder characterized by a preoccupation with a perceived flaw in one's physical appearance

borderline personality disorder (BPD): one of the dramatic emotional personality disorders (Cluster B); characterized by an instability in mood, interpersonal relationships, and sense of self

bulimia nervosa: an eating disorder involving periods of overeating in which the person feels out of control, followed by purging

caffeine: a stimulant found naturally in different amounts in the leaves and seeds of various plants, including coffee beans, tea leaves, and cocoa beans

cannabis: a plant species also referred to as marijuana; the resin is referred to as hashish; the main psychoactive ingredient in cannabis is THC

case study: a research method that typically focuses on recording the experiences and behaviors of one individual

catatonic subtype: a type of schizophrenia characterized by non-normal activity of the motor system

categorical: in psychopathology, describes the approach to determining whether a person has or does not have a disorder based on the presence or absence of a certain set of symptoms

central executive network: the neural network involved in performing such tasks as planning, goal setting, directing attention, performing, inhibiting the management of actions, and coding representations in working memory

chromosomes: threadlike structures located inside the nucleus of animal and plant cells. Each chromosome is made of protein and a single molecule of deoxyribonucleic acid (DNA). Passed from parents to offspring, DNA contains the specific instructions that make each type of living creature unique

classical conditioning: the pairing of the unconditioned stimulus with a neutral stimulus eventually causing the neutral stimulus to produce the same response

classification: in psychopathology, a way to name, organize, and categorize the collections of symptoms seen in mental disorders

client-centered therapy: a treatment approach in psychology characterized by the therapist's empathic understanding, unconditional positive regard, and genuineness

clinically significant: the characterization of the results of a study when, beyond being statistically significant, the findings indicate clinically important outcomes

cocaine: a stimulant that comes from the naturally occurring coca plant largely grown in South America; its psychoactive effects include a mental alertness, heightening sensory experiences, and increased heart rate

cognitive avoidance model: a theoretical model that proposes that worry is the manner in which an individual with GAD attempts to reduce the negative emotional experiences associated with GAD

cognitive behavioral perspective: a treatment perspective that suggests that dysfunctional thinking is common to all psychological disturbances; by learning in therapy how to understand one's thinking, it is possible to change the way one thinks as well as one's emotional state and behaviors

cognitive behavioral therapy (CBT): a therapy based on the cognitive behavioral perspective, directed at changing the individual's faulty logic and maladaptive behaviors

cognitive bias: the tendency to pay attention to certain aspects of the situation differently from the norm. Those with anxiety disorders show more sensitivity than others to the possibility of potential threat

cognitive model of depression: a model that proposes that individuals with depression display a bias in the way they search for and process information

comorbid: descriptive term used when an individual has more than one disorder at the same time

compulsions: repetitive behaviors that one uses to respond to obsessive thoughts with the goal of decreasing anxiety

conduct disorder (CD): a disorder diagnosed in children and adolescents who engage in aggressive and violent behaviors that actively violate the rights and safety of others

confidentiality (for research participants): a principle that requires that the scientist not release data of a personal nature to other scientists or groups without the participant's consent

confidentiality (in health care): the principle that the health care professional is not to discuss information learned in a therapy session in any other context

confound: a factor that systematically biases the results of experimental research

confound hypothesis: a conceptual question that asks if results of an experiment could have been influenced by a factor other than the independent variable (IV)

confounding variables: unintended factors not chosen by the experimenter, but which influence the independent variable (IV)

connectivity: the concept that different areas of the brain work together in specific conditions

conscientiousness: as a personality trait, it is associated with being diligent, disciplined, well-organized, punctual, and dependable; as a dimension in the five-factor model (FFM), this dimension ranges from being efficient and organized to being easygoing and careless

Continuous Performance Test (CPT): a test that measures attentional characteristics

control group: in a research experiment, the group that is treated exactly like the experimental group except for not experiencing the independent variable (IV) being studied

conversion disorder: a somatic disorder in which a person shows the signs of a physical disability (such as blindness or a paralyzed limb), but the disorder does not follow what we know to be the underlying physiology; previously referred to as hysteria

conversion reaction: Freud's idea that psychic energy was converted into physical symptoms; the basic concept is that painful memories or trauma are not consciously experienced in an emotional manner but rather converted into physical processes

correlational approach: a research method designed to measure how specific factors are associated with one another

correlation coefficient: a statistic ranging from −1 to +1 that indicates the degree of association between two variables

cortisol: a hormone that is released in response to stress

covary: the degree to which variables are related to one another

craving: a step in the addiction pattern in which the individual loses control of the ability to limit intake of the drug

Cultural Formulation Interview (CFI): a set of questions developed to help mental health professionals obtain information concerning the person's culture and its influence on behavior and experience

cultural perspective: examines the social world in which a person lives and from which a person learns skills, values, beliefs, attitudes, and other information

cyclothymic disorder: a disorder characterized by mood changes that lack severity, number, and duration as would be required for a depressive or manic disorder

deep brain stimulation (DBS): a treatment for depression in which electrodes are placed in the brain and connected to a pulse generator in the chest, which influences electrical activity in certain parts of the brain

default or intrinsic network: neural network that is active during internal processing

delayed ejaculation: sexual dysfunction (lasting at least 6 months) in which a male shows a delay in ejaculation or shows a lack of ejaculation, and this causes significant distress

delirium: a short-term state of confusion characterized by a change in cognitive processing, such as an inability to focus attention, or problems with language, memory, or orientation

delusional thinking: an unrealistic pattern of thoughts forming a theme

delusions: beliefs without support for their occurrence and which are at odds with the individual's current environment

demand characteristics: bias that occurs when a participant's response is influenced more by the research setting than by the independent variable (IV)

dementias: term previously used to refer to a loss of cognitive abilities not related to normal aging; currently called neurocognitive disorders

deoxyribonucleic acid (DNA): a molecule that provides information necessary to produce proteins, which are involved in growth and functioning

dependence: a way to describe addiction to a substance; three major components are (1) the desire to seek and take a certain substance, (2) the inability to avoid or limit the intake of the substance, and (3) the experience of negative emotional states when the substance is not available

dependent personality disorder: one of the anxious fearful personality disorders (Cluster C), characterized by a pervasive pattern of clinging and being submissive; the lack of experiencing a self leaves the individual in a position that requires that he or she always be with another; otherwise, the person tends to feel anxious and helpless when alone

dependent variable (DV): in an experimental study, the variable that is said to depend on the action of another variable (the independent variable [IV])

depersonalization: the perception of not experiencing the reality of one's self; this experience can include feeling detached or observing one's self as an outside observer

depression in terms of attachment: the theory that offers an evolutionary explanation that depression is a protective mechanism that prevents further critical losses, as depressed mood reduces the desire of the individual to immediately enter a social relationship in which there could be an adverse outcome and behaviors send signals to others of submission and helplessness

depression in terms of resource conservation: the theory that depressive mood has an evolutionary benefit in that it protects the organism by conserving energy

depression in terms of social competition: the theory that offers an evolutionary explanation that depression is seen in the context of hierarchies as an involuntary de-escalating strategy, which signals to the other individual that he has won

derealization: the experience that the external world is not solid; one's world is experienced with a sense of detachment or as if in a fog or a dream, or in other ways distorted or unreal

Diagnostic and Statistical Manual of Mental Disorders (DSM): a publication of criteria for diagnosis by the American Psychiatric Association (APA), used in North America

dialectical behavior therapy (DBT): treatment approach for borderline personality disorders developed by Marsha Linehan; the cornerstone of DBT therapy is based on problem solving and acceptance of the experience of the moment

diffusion tensor imaging (DTI): procedure that uses the magnetic resonance imaging (MRI) magnet to measure fiber tracts (white matter) in the brain

dimensional: in psychopathology, describes the assessment of severity of a disorder on a continuum, in terms of differing degrees

disinhibited social engagement disorder: a disorder stemming from not being well cared for in which a child is overly willing to accept comfort and support from strangers who are not attachment figures

disordered use: the condition in which a person experiences significant impairment or distress from use of a psychoactive substance

disorganized/controlling attachment pattern: an attachment style in which the infant shows disruptions in processing during a strange situation

disorganized subtype: a type of schizophrenia characterized by disorganized speech patterns and behavior

disruptive, impulse control, and conduct disorders: a category of childhood disorders referred to as externalizing disorders

dissociation: experiencing a disruption in our normal ability to integrate information from our sensory and psychological processes such as memory and awareness

dissociative amnesia: a disorder characterized mainly by the inability to recall important autobiographical information.

dissociative fugue: sudden, unexpected travel away from one's home or place of work with an inability to recall one's past

dissociative identity disorder (DID): a developmental disorder where one consistent sense of self does not occur—that is, the person does not experience her thoughts, feelings, or actions in terms of a well-developed "I" or sense of self and instead experiences different "personalities" at different times; previously referred to as multiple personality disorder

dizygotic (DZ) twins: twins who arise from the situation in which two different eggs are fertilized by two different spermatozoa; these are called fraternal twins since their shared genes are approximately 50%—the same as that between any two siblings

double-blind experiment: research procedure in which participants do not know whether they are in the experimental group or the control (placebo) group, and the researchers involved in the study also do not know which participants are in which group

doubt: to question ideas and research and ask whether factors other than the ones that were originally considered might have influenced the results

Down syndrome: a disorder resulting in both physical and intellectual problems found in individuals with an extra copy of chromosome 21

dramatic emotional personality disorders (Cluster B): a grouping of personality disorders in which individuals show a wide diversity of problematic patterns of social and emotional interactions with others

Durham rule: also called the "product test," a rule based on an 1871 New Hampshire decision that an individual is not "criminally responsible if his unlawful act is the product of a mental disease or defect"

duty to protect: an exception to the principle of confidentiality; the general guideline is that the therapist must take action if she believes that the client will harm another person or himself—a direct consequence of the *Tarasoff* court ruling

dynamic deconstructive psychotherapy (DDP): psychological treatment developed for clients who find therapy difficult as well as for those who may also have substance abuse problems; designed to help individuals with borderline personality disorder develop a coherent sense of self

early ejaculation: sexual dysfunction diagnosed when a man experiences an ejaculation within approximately the first minute of sexual activity, over a period of 6 months or more, and this causes significant distress

eating disorders: inappropriate and unhealthy behaviors related to the intake of food. The three major eating disorders in *DSM-5-TR* are anorexia nervosa, bulimia, and binge eating disorder

effect size: the measured magnitude indicating the influence that a treatment has on the dependent variable (DV)

electroconvulsive therapy (ECT): a treatment for depression in which electrical current is passed through the brain for a brief period

electroencephalography (EEG): a technique for recording electrical activity from the scalp, which measures the electrical activity of the brain at the level of the synapse

emotion-focused therapy: therapeutic approach in which emotion is viewed as centrally important in the experience of self

empathizing-systemizing theory of autism: argument that among those with ASD, the inability to empathize with other people is coupled with a superior ability to systemize objects or events

empathy: understanding how another person experiences their life and what that person might feel about situations, relationships, events, etc.

empiricism: the process of understanding the world through observation and experimentation

encode: to lay out the process by which a particular protein is made; this is the job of a gene

endophenotypes: patterns of processes that lie between the gene (the genotype) and the manifestations of the gene in the external environment (the phenotype)

epidemiology: the study of the distribution and determinants of the frequency of a disorder in humans

epigenetic inheritance: a form of inheritance by which factors largely influenced by the environment of the organism that turn the genes on and off can be passed on to the next generation without influencing DNA itself

epigenetic marks or tags: factors that influence whether a gene segment is relaxed and able to be activated, or condensed, and thereby inhibited

epigenetics: study of the mostly environmental factors that turn genes on and off and are passed on to the next generation

erectile disorder: sexual dysfunction diagnosed when a male has a problem in at least one of three areas: (1) obtaining an erection, (2) maintaining an erection until the completion of sexual activity, or (3) decreased rigidity of the penis that interferes with sexual activity; in addition, the experience of the erectile problem produces significant distress

ethics: the study of proper action

event-related potentials (ERPs): also known as evoked potentials (EPs), they show electroencephalography (EEG) activity in relation to a particular event

evoked potentials (EPs): also known as event-related potentials (ERPs), they show electroencephalography (EEG) activity in relation to a particular event

evolutionary perspective: examines psychological disorders in terms of how certain aspects might be adaptive, asking if there is any advantage to behaving and feeling in certain ways that others consider abnormal or if the disordered behavior is secondary to another process that is beneficial

executive functions: cognitive functions involved in planning, understanding new situations, and cognitive flexibility

exhibitionistic disorder: a paraphilic disorder in which a person becomes sexually aroused by exposing his genitals to an unsuspecting stranger

existential-humanistic perspective: psychological therapy that focuses on the experience of the person in the moment and the manner in which the person interprets the experience

experimental group: a group that receives the independent variable (IV) in a study using the experimental method

experimental method: scientific research technique in which the influence of an independent variable (IV) on a dependent variable (DV) is determined, using carefully structured conditions

experimenter effects: bias that occurs due to the experimenter's expectations

exposure therapy for PTSD: a therapy designed to have the individual with post-traumatic stress disorder (PTSD) reexperience the original trauma; the person confronts their fears and expectations such that they are reduced

externalizing disorders: disorders that are manifested in the external world by the person's behavior, such as conduct disorder, antisocial personality disorder, and other behavior-based disorders

external validity: also known as generalizability, the ability to apply the results from an internally valid experiment to other situations and other research participants

extinction: the process by which, after a period of time, the conditioned stimulus, when presented alone, will no longer produce the response

extraversion: as a personality trait, it is associated with sociability, cheerfulness, energy, and a sense of fun; as a dimension in the five-factor model (FFM), this dimension ranges from being passive, quiet, and inner-directed to being active, talkative, and outer-directed

factitious disorder: a somatic disorder in which a person creates certain symptoms in order to be seen by a health care professional, with the goal of receiving attention or sympathy

factitious disorder imposed on another: a type of factitious disorder in which typically a caregiver such as a parent would produce symptoms in her child; historically referred to as Munchausen syndrome by proxy

factitious disorder imposed on self: a type of factitious disorder in which the person produces symptoms in himself or herself; historically referred to as Munchausen syndrome

facts: general conclusions drawn from observations

falsification: the scientific approach by which a claim or hypothesis is shown to be wrong

feeding disorders: inappropriate and unhealthy behaviors related to the types of substances eaten and attitude toward food. The three major feeding disorders in the *DSM-5-TR* are pica, rumination disorder, and avoidant/restrictive food intake disorder

female orgasmic disorder: sexual dysfunction in which a woman either does not experience an orgasm or has a reduced intensity of the sensation of the orgasm, causing significant distress

female sexual interest/arousal disorder: sexual dysfunction that requires significant distress or impairment along with at least three specific symptoms, including a reduction or absence of interest in sexual activity, fewer sexual fantasies, less excitement or pleasure during sex, and fewer internal or external sexual cues or sexual sensations

fetishistic disorder: a paraphilic disorder that involves an erotic fixation on a non-sexual object or body part, that lasts for at least 6 months, and that results in clinically significant distress or impairment in important areas of functioning

fight-or-flight response: the overall stress reaction in which the body prepares you either to fight or to leave the scene

five-factor model (FFM): a model of personality based on a factor analytic approach to personality developed by Robert McCrae and Paul Costa, which suggested five major personality dimensions: extraversion, neuroticism, openness, agreeableness, and conscientiousness

flight of ideas: spoken expression in which comments are not related to a question asked or jump abruptly from one topic to another unrelated topic

fragile X syndrome: a chromosome disorder that results in intellectual developmental disorder due to the FMR1 gene producing too little of a protein needed for brain development

frontotemporal neurocognitive disorder: a disorder characterized by a reduction of the anterior lobes of the frontal and temporal areas; it is seen in different variants depending on the brain areas involved

frotteuristic disorder: the condition in which an individual gains sexual arousal from touching or rubbing against a nonconsenting person

functional magnetic resonance imaging (fMRI): a brain imaging technique that measures increased blood flow in active areas of the cortex by determining the ratio of hemoglobin with and without oxygen

gamma-aminobutyric acid (GABA): the major inhibitory neurotransmitter in the brain and one of the major neurotransmitters involved in anxiety

gender dysphoria: a marked incongruence between one's gender at birth and the person's experienced and expressed gender that is associated with significant distress

gender identity: the internal experience of knowing that one is male or female

gender roles: typically defined by one's culture in terms of the kinds of activities boys and girls are expected to engage in and behaviors considered to be more typical of either males or females

gene by environment correlations: how certain genotypes and certain environments occur together

gene by environment interaction: the possibility that individuals with different genotypes may respond to the same environment in different ways

general adaptation syndrome (GAS): Selye's model of how the body reacts similarly to a variety of different stressors in three stages: the alarm stage, the resistance stage, and the exhaustion stage

generalizability: also known as external validity, the ability to apply the results from an internally valid experiment to other situations and other research participants

generalized anxiety disorder (GAD): a disorder characterized by excessive anxiety and worry that has been present for more than 3 months

genes: the basic physical and functional unit of heredity, made up of DNA; act as instructions to make proteins

genito-pelvic pain/penetration disorder: a sexual dysfunction disorder associated with dyspareunia or vaginismus or the fear or anxiety associated with pain from these conditions

genotype: the set of observable characteristics of an individual resulting from the interaction of its genotype with the environment

glove anesthesia: a specific type of conversion disorder in which the person reports not being able to feel anything in the hand, but the symptoms do not follow known physiological or neurological patterns

hallucinations: sensory experiences that can involve any of the senses and that are at odds with the individual's current environment

hallucinogens: drugs such as mescaline, LSD, and ecstasy that are able to alter perception, mood, and cognitive processes in often unpredictable ways; also called psychedelics

Health Insurance Portability and Accountability Act of 1996 (HIPAA): U.S. law that protects the privacy of health care records; regulates the manner in which medical and psychological records are maintained and shared with insurance companies and other health care professionals

healthy self: in *DSM-5*, the healthy self is described in terms of a self and interpersonal functioning continuum, which includes the aspects of identity, self-direction, empathy, and intimacy

heterozygotes or heterozygous: when a person has two different alleles at the same location

hierarchical integration: through inhibitory control, the various levels of the brain, such as the brain stem, the limbic system, and the neocortex, are able to interact with each other, and higher levels restrict or inhibit the lower levels

histrionic personality disorder: one of the dramatic emotional personality disorders (Cluster B); characterized by a pervasive pattern of excessive emotionality and attention seeking

hoarding disorder: an obsessive-compulsive–related disorder characterized by an excessive acquisition of objects and an inability to discard these objects

homozygotes or homozygous: when a person has two copies of the same allele

human immunodeficiency virus (HIV): a virus that can be passed on by coming in contact with the bodily fluids of an infected person; the virus affects the person's immune system in a negative manner; in the later stages, this is referred to as acquired immune deficiency syndrome (AIDS)

Huntington's disease: a genetic disorder that causes a degeneration of neurons in the brain; one of the few disorders that has a single genetic cause; characterized by the loss of brain cells resulting in cognitive, emotional, and motor disturbances

hypothalamic–pituitary–adrenal (HPA) axis: the hypothalamus, pituitary, and adrenal pathway, which is activated in times of stress

hypothesis: a formally stated expectation

identity: one aspect of a healthy self; this includes (1) seeing oneself as a unique person with stable boundaries between self and others, (2) having a history that the person understands, (3) having an accurate sense of who the person is and what she can accomplish, and (4) appreciating her abilities

illness anxiety disorder: type of somatic disorder in which an individual is preoccupied with the possibility of having a serious illness, despite having few if any symptoms; previously referred to as hypochondriasis

imitation learning: a brain system response to observing an action that leads to a motor representation of the observed action, essentially turning a visual image into a motor plan

immune system: the body's system for recognizing foreign agents in the body and then destroying them

incidence: the number of new cases of a disorder that develop during a certain period of time

independent variable (IV): the manipulated variable in an experimental study

Individuals with Disabilities Education Act (IDEA): the act by which the U.S. Department of Education defined the services required to be provided to students with learning disabilities

inference: the process by which we look at the evidence available and then use logic to reach a conclusion

inferential statistics: a method of analysis that concerns the relationship between the statistical characteristics of the population and those of the experimental sample

informed consent: a prospective participant in psychological research must be given complete information on which to base a decision, including information about what will be required of him or her during the study, and about any potential harm that may come from participation

informed consent (in mental health treatment): the principle that the client has the right to know what will take place in the therapy session and the nature of the therapist–client relationship; after being informed of the nature of therapy, the client can consent to be treated or not

insanity: a term used in the legal system instead of "mental illness," based on legal definitions of who is responsible for an event and the person's mental state at the time of the crime

institutional review board (IRB): a committee to determine whether the participants in a proposed research study are adequately protected in terms of both welfare and rights, and to determine when a risk is unreasonable

intellectual developmental disorder (IDD): a disorder characterized by intellectual disabilities in which the person does not meet normal developmental milestones

intergenerational transmission of depression: the concept that depression in an individual is influenced by having one or more parents who are depressed

internalizing disorders: disorders that are experienced internally, such as anxiety and depression

internal validity: the ability to make valid inferences between the independent variables (IVs) and dependent variables (DVs)

International Classification of Diseases (ICD): a publication of criteria for diagnosis by the World Health Organization (WHO), used in Europe

intimacy: the ability to have a relationship with another person that includes mutual connectedness and a valuing of the other person; the individual values closeness and seeks it when appropriate

intoxication: the effects of the psychoactive substance on the individual; effects are substance-related but typically involve impairment to psychological processes and behavioral abilities

learning disabilities: diagnosed when a child's achievement is lower than that expected from their scores on achievement or intelligence tests

levels of analysis: examination of psychopathology ranging from culture and society at a higher level to the individual at a middle level and physiology and genetics at the lower levels

Lewy body dementia: a neurocognitive disorder caused by the buildup of a substance called Lewy bodies in the neurons; the symptoms include changes in alertness and attention, which can result in drowsiness or staring into space as well as visual hallucinations and Parkinson's-like symptoms

lifetime prevalence: the percentage of a specific population that had the disorder at some point in their life, even if they no longer show symptoms of the disorder currently

longitudinal design: a research technique that allows the researcher to follow a

**specific group of individuals across a period of time to document any changes that take place

macrophage theory of depression:** the model that proposes that the malfunctioning of cytokines may be involved in depression

magnetoencephalography (MEG): brain imaging technique that measures the small magnetic field gradients exiting and entering the surface of the head that are produced when neurons are active

major depressive disorder (MDD): a mood disorder characterized by depressed mood for at least 2 weeks in which one feels sad or empty without any sense of pleasure in one's activities

major neurocognitive disorder: diagnosis made when an individual's cognitive or social deficits are severe and interfere with one's ability to function independently

male hypoactive sexual desire disorder: sexual dysfunction in which a male has little desire for sexual activity or even erotic thoughts for at least 6 months, and this condition causes significant distress

mandated reporting: an exception to the principle of confidentiality; requirement that when health care professionals learn firsthand of child abuse or neglect, they report this information to the appropriate state agency

manic depression: now known as bipolar disorder; a mood disorder characterized by the experience of both depression and mania

match subjects design: a design type in psychopathology research in which the closer a scientist can match individuals in the experimental and control groups, the stronger the logic of the design

Maudsley approach: a family-based approach to the treatment of anorexia nervosa developed at Maudsley Hospital in the UK; a three-phased approach involving weight restoration, taking control, and developing personal autonomy

melancholia: now known as depression; described by ancient Greek writers in terms of despondency, dissatisfaction with life, problems sleeping, restlessness, irritability, difficulties in decision making, and a desire to die

Mendel's first law or the law of segregation: for the dominant trait to appear, only one dominant element is needed; for the recessive trait to appear, both nondominant elements must be present

Mendel's second law or the law of independent assortment: the inheritance of the gene of one trait is not affected by the inheritance of the gene for another trait

mental status exam: clinical interview organized into major categories designed to determine a person's cognitive processes

meta-analysis: statistical examination of the results of studies taken together and treated as one study

microglia: the main form of immune cells in the brain and can influence the relationship between amyloid and tau

mild neurocognitive disorder: a diagnosis made when the cognitive or social deficits in an individual are greater than those declines seen with normal aging

mindfulness: a therapeutic technique involving an increased, focused, non-judgmental, purposeful awareness of the present moment

Minnesota Multiphasic Personality Inventory (MMPI): an assessment measurement of personality traits, used in psychopathology to identify response patterns suggesting a psychological disorder based on empirical comparison to the general population

mirror neurons: neurons in your brain that fire as if you had performed the same actions as you observe

mitochondrial DNA (mtDNA): deoxyribonucleic acid (DNA) of mitochondria structures within a cell; because mtDNA does not recombine sections of DNA from the mother and father, it is very stable and mutates slowly

mitochondrial inheritance: generally mitochondrial DNA (mtDNA) is inherited only from the mother; mtDNA is contained within each cell and is related to energy production

M'Naghten rule: a rule adopted in the British legal system in 1843 stating that mental illness could be used as a defense only if (1) there is the presence of a mental disorder and (2) there is a lack of comprehension of the nature or wrongfulness of the act

modularity: the concept that specific areas of the brain are dedicated to certain types of processing

monozygotic (MZ) twins: identical twins resulting from the zygote (fertilized egg) dividing during the first 2 weeks of gestation

narcissistic personality disorder: one of the dramatic emotional personality disorders (Cluster B), characterized by a pervasive pattern of grandiosity, a need for admiration, a sense of privilege or entitlement, and a lack of empathy for others

National Institute of Mental Health (NIMH): agency of the U.S. government that advances the understanding and treatment of mental disorders

naturalistic observation: research method based on observing and describing the phenomenon occurring naturally, without manipulating any variables

natural selection: Darwin's idea that if an organism has even slight variations that help it to compete successfully for survival, then over time the species will have more members with these characteristics and fewer individuals lacking these features

negative cognitive triad: the concept that an individual with depression has a negative pattern of thinking regarding the self, the world, and the prospects for the future

negative correlation: an association between two variables where a decrease in one variable correlates to a decrease in the other

negative symptoms: in schizophrenia, lack of affect in situations that call for it, poor motivation, and social withdrawal

neuritic plaques: also called senile plaques; a buildup of proteins outside of the neuron seen more frequently in dementias than in normal aging

neurocognitive disorder due to Alzheimer's disease: a progressive disorder characterized by problems with memory; associated with a loss of neurons and disruption of cortical networks that result in cognitive problems

neurocognitive disorder due to prion disease: neurocognitive disorder caused by prions, which are infectious pathogens that produce tiny holes in the brain, giving it a spongy appearance; it has a rapid course of development and is characterized by cognitive impairments, including memory loss, motor problems, personality changes, and impaired judgment

neurocognitive disorders: decline in brain function typically seen in older individuals but that represents a loss of cognitive abilities not related to normal aging

neurodevelopmental disorders: a category of childhood disorders, including autism spectrum disorder; attention deficit/hyperactivity disorder (ADHD); disorders of learning, intelligence, and communication; and motor disorders such as tics and Tourette's disorder

neuroethics: a field of ethical inquiry related to the ethical, legal, and social policy implications of neuroscience, which explores questions about who should have access to data and scans of an individual's internal processes

neurofibrillary tangles: buildup of tau protein within the neurons seen in a number of dementias including Alzheimer's disease to a greater degree than normal aging

neuroscience perspective: examines what we know about particular psychopathological experience from the standpoint of neuroscience, including the structure and function of the brain, the autonomic nervous system, and a genetic and epigenetic consideration as it relates to psychopathology

neuroticism: as a personality trait, it is associated with a tendency to express distressing emotions and difficulty experiencing stressful situations; as a dimension in the five-factor model (FFM), this dimension ranges from being calm, even-tempered, and comfortable to being worried, temperamental, and self-conscious

neurotransmitters: chemicals released into the synaptic space that are involved in increasing or decreasing the likelihood for action potentials to be produced; they also maintain the communication across the synapse. Their presence or lack is related to particular psychopathological disorders

nicotine: the addictive substance in tobacco; it is a stimulant substance found in plants of the nightshade family; it can have varied effects on the body, which makes it function as both a stimulant and a depressant

null hypothesis: a statistical hypothesis that is tested to determine if there are differences between the experimental and control groups; the null hypothesis states that there is no difference

obesity: the condition of being more than just overweight, seen to result from a mismatch between the amount of calories that we eat and the amount of energy that we expend; influenced by the environment in which we live, psychological factors, and biological factors

observational learning: also known as modeling; when humans imitate the behaviors of others, even without reinforcement

obsessional thinking: a pattern of repeated thoughts beyond the control of the person

obsessions: persistent, generally unwelcome thoughts or images that come into one's head, which the person experiences as disturbing

obsessive-compulsive disorder (OCD): a disorder characterized by repetitive, intrusive thoughts and feelings (obsessions) usually followed by behaviors in response to them (compulsions)

obsessive-compulsive personality disorder: one of the anxious fearful personality disorders (Cluster C), characterized by a pervasive pattern of preoccupation with orderliness, perfectionism, and control of one's environment

odd, eccentric personality disorders (Cluster A): a grouping of personality disorders in which individuals typically feel uncomfortable around or suspicious of others or restrict their relationships

openness: as a personality trait, it is associated with curiosity, flexibility, and an artistic sensitivity, including imaginativeness and the ability to create a fantasy world; as a dimension in the five-factor model (FFM), this dimension ranges from inventive and curious to cautious and conservative

operant conditioning: the concept that behavior can be elicited or shaped if reinforcement follows its occurrence

operational definition: a definition that presents a construct in terms of observable operation that can be measured and utilized in research

opioids: psychoactive substances derived from the opium poppy used to control pain and bring on euphoric feelings; more common opioids are heroin, opium, morphine, methadone, and oxycodone

oppositional defiant disorder (ODD): a disorder in which children and adolescents show excessive and persistent anger, irritability, and defiance to authority

panic attack: a sudden, intense feeling of apprehension, anxiety, or fear; happens without an actual situation that would suggest danger

panic disorder: an anxiety disorder defined by recurrent and unpredictable panic-like symptoms followed by at least 1 month of concern or change in lifestyle

paranoid personality disorder: one of the odd, eccentric personality disorders (Cluster A), characterized by a pervasive distrust and suspiciousness of others; the interpersonal style of these individuals is often quarrelsome, stubborn, and rigid in their own beliefs, which can create a self-fulfilling prophecy

paranoid subtype: a type of schizophrenia characterized by delusions whose themes generally center on ideas of grandiosity or persecution

paraphilia: nontraditional sexual practices that exist alongside the traditional sexual expressions

paraphilic disorders: to qualify as a disorder, a paraphilia must cause distress to the person involved or interfere with important areas of life, and/or cause distress or harm to others

parasympathetic division: the branch of the autonomic nervous system involved in the restoration of bodily reserves and the elimination of bodily waste

Parkinson's disease: a neurological condition that affects the motor system; symptoms generally include tremors that may involve the hands, arms, legs, jaw, and face; in addition, the person shows a slowness of movement and stiffness in the limbs

pathological gambling: a disorder in which gambling continues even despite negative consequences such as consistent losses and an inability to control one's gambling behavior

Patient Self-Determination Act (PSDA) of 1991: a set of federal requirements intended to implement advance directive policies at all health care facilities that receive federal funding through Medicaid and Medicare programs

pedophilic disorder: a paraphilic disorder that involves a persistent sexual interest in prepubescent or early pubescent children

personality disorder: an enduring pattern of inner experience and behavior that deviates markedly from the expectations of the individual's culture; the pattern is inflexible, stable, and generally begins in adolescence, and it leads to distress or impairment; characteristics of these disorders are especially apparent when these individuals find themselves in situations that are beyond their ability to cope

phenotype: an organism's observable characteristics

pica: a feeding disorder in which the person eats something that would not be considered food

placebo effect: the phenomenon that some people show psychological and physiological changes just from the suggestion that a change will take place

population: in a research study, the larger group of individuals to which the results can be generalized

positive correlation: an association between two variables where an increase in one variable correlates to an increase in the other

positive interpersonal relationships: one aspect of a healthy self; characterized by interpersonal relationships in which the person relates to others in an intimate and empathetic manner

positive symptoms: in schizophrenia, the presence of such characteristics as hallucinations, delusions, disorganized thinking, and disorganized behavior

positron emission tomography (PET): a brain imaging technique that measures the blood flow in the brain that is correlated with brain activity

post-traumatic stress disorder (PTSD): a long-term reaction to traumatic events that lasts longer than 1 month

prevalence: the proportion of individuals who have a particular disorder at a particular time period

private personality: the private thoughts of a person

privileged communication: the legal term for confidentiality; the privilege is controlled by the client

probability: the likelihood that a set of results in an experiment differed from what would be expected by chance

projective instruments: assessment tests that use ambiguous stimuli to elicit the internal cognitive and emotional organization of a person's primary thought processes

prolonged grief disorder: a disorder characterized by intense and persistent grief that causes problems and interferes with daily life

proteins: made up of amino chains from DNA, proteins do the work of the body and are involved in a variety of processes; functionally, proteins in the form of enzymes are able to make metabolic events speed up, whereas structural proteins are involved in building body parts

psychiatric advance directives (PADs): authorizations that allow a person with mental health problems to submit specific instructions for possible treatment or designate individuals to consent on that person's behalf; they enable a person who has a history of periods in which he would not be competent to make a rational decision to direct the types of treatments he would accept or refuse

psychoanalysis: treatment developed by Freud based on the search for ideas and emotions that are in conflict on an unconscious level

psychodynamic perspective: approach to psychological therapy that emphasizes how behaviors and experience may be influenced by internal processes that are outside of awareness, often due to internal conflicts

psychological assessment: the process of gathering information about a person so that you can make a clinical decision about that person's symptoms

psychological stress: the uncomfortable reaction when something we do not expect and cannot control happens to us

psychoneuroimmunology: the study of how psychological factors can influence the immune system

psychopathology: the scientific study of mental illness and its causes

psychopathy: an internal personality problem characterized by showing emotional detachment with a lack of empathy for the experiences of others, impulsive behavior, and a callousness concerning one's actions

psychotic disorders: disorders that involve a loss of being in touch with reality and are characterized by abnormal thinking and sensory processes

purging: an aspect of bulimia where a person eliminates food from the body by such means as vomiting, taking laxatives, taking diuretics, or using enemas

randomization: in an experiment, selection of participants solely by chance to either the experimental group or the control group

randomized controlled trial (RCT): an experimental procedure in which participants in the study are randomly assigned to the treatment group or the control group for the independent variable being studied

reactive attachment disorder (RAD): a diagnosis offered when a child does not seek comfort or support from an attachment figure when distressed, which is the result of inadequate caregiving

reinforcement: in operant conditioning, rewards that follow behaviors and increase their occurrence

reliability: consistency of the measurement by an assessment instrument

replication: the process whereby a study is performed in different laboratories with different participants and obtains the same results

Research Domain Criteria (RDoC): an alternative classification system for mental disorders that emphasizes evaluating five domains established by the National Institute of Mental Health (NIMH) to better clarify our understanding of psychopathology

research hypothesis: the formal statement of the manner in which the dependent variable (DV) is related to the independent variable (IV)

reserve: concept that suggests that the brain can compensate for problems in neural functioning; high functioning or intelligence is often associated with greater reserve

reward system: particular brain structures, especially the nucleus accumbens part of the ventral striatum, influenced by an increase in dopamine during a reward

ribonucleic acid (RNA): DNA information is carried as RNA, which determines the sequence of amino acids, the building blocks of proteins; it is made up of single strands rather than the dual strands in DNA

right to privacy: in an experiment, this means that information given by a participant to a scientist should be considered a private event, not a public one

risk: related to incidence, the likelihood that someone in a specific population will develop a particular disorder in a given time period

Rorschach inkblots: a projective test using inkblots; an individual's interpretation of the ambiguous ink patterns is evaluated to identify patterns in underlying thoughts and feelings

rumination disorder: a feeding disorder in which a person regurgitates food; this swallowed food is then re-chewed, re-swallowed, or spit out

salience network: the neural network involved in monitoring and noting important changes in biological and cognitive systems

sample: participants in a study

schizoid personality disorder: one of the odd, eccentric personality disorders (Cluster A); characterized by a pervasive pattern of detachment from social relationships and a restricted range of emotional expression; these individuals are traditional loners; others see them as unavailable, aloof, or detached

schizophrenia: a debilitating psychotic disorder in which individuals may hear voices, see images not seen by others, believe that others wish to harm or control them, and have bizarre thoughts

schizotypal personality disorder: one of the odd, eccentric personality disorders (Cluster A); characterized by odd beliefs and behaviors; an individual may show excessive social anxiety as well as unusual ideas

schizotypal traits: schizophrenic-like traits

SCID-D: a screening device for dissociative disorders developed by Marlene Steinberg

science: a process of understanding the world through observation and research, which includes developing theories

scientific knowledge: the known facts about a particular subject derived from the scientific method

secure attachment pattern: an attachment style characterized by the following pattern in the strange situation: The infant (1) engages in active exploration, (2) is upset when the mother leaves, and (3) shows positive emotions when the mother returns

self-direction: the ability to have both meaningful short-term and long-term goals consistent with one's identity as well as a sense of what would be productive for society and how to interact with others; internally, healthy self-direction also includes the ability to reflect on one's life in a productive manner

separation anxiety disorder: a disorder in which children as they develop do not show a normal sense of independence and continue to feel distress when not with their caregivers

sexual dysfunction disorders: a category in *DSM-5-TR* in which there are problems in sexual functioning, the condition exists for at least 6 months, and it causes significant distress or impairment

sexually violent predator (SVP) or sexually dangerous person (SDP) statutes: laws that allow for a person convicted of a sexual crime to be held after his or her sentence has been completed; based on the belief that these individuals represent a threat to public safety if they are released

sexual masochism disorder: a paraphilic disorder diagnosed when the person experiences sexual arousal from the act of being humiliated, beaten, bound, or otherwise made to suffer, as manifested by fantasies, urges, or behaviors, lasting for at least 6 months, and these urges or behaviors cause distress or impairment in the person's life

sexual sadism disorder: a paraphilic disorder in which an individual derives sexual pleasure from inflicting pain or humiliation on others; the person must have acted out these impulses with a nonconsenting individual or experienced distress or impairment from these impulses, and it must have been present for at least 6 months

sexual selection: the manner in which males and females choose a mate

signs: features observed by the clinician

single-subject design: also referred to as small-N design, an experiment that uses the data from one individual participant without averaging it as part of a group of participants

small world framework: a model of brain connectivity based on the idea that the ability to socially contact any two random individuals in the world can be accomplished in a limited number of connections

social anxiety disorder (SAD): a disorder characterized by marked fear or anxiety about one or more social situations in which the individual is exposed to possible scrutiny by others

somatic symptom and related disorders: category of disorders in *DSM-5* in which individuals are certain something is wrong with their bodies or health and display unwarranted anxiety and/or seek unnecessary medical attention

somatic symptom disorder: the condition in which a person's somatic or bodily symptoms cause distress or disruption in physical health that is not consistent with a medical disorder

specific learning disorder: a disorder in which a child shows problems in one of the major school tasks

specific phobia: an anxiety disorder in which an individual experiences fear of or anxiety about a particular situation or object

statistically significant: the probability that the independent variable (IV) influences the dependent variable (DV) by chance alone

stigma: negative attitudes and beliefs that cause the general public to avoid certain people, including those with a mental illness

Stroop test: a psychological test used to study cognitive bias; the traditional Stroop test has color names in ink of a different color. A variant of this procedure uses threat words rather than color names

Structured Clinical Interview for DSM Disorders (SCID): an interview that directly probes for the existence of the criteria for disorders within the current classification manual, the *DSM-5*

structured interview: an evaluation technique that is tightly systematized in terms of the questions asked, allowing for better consistency across interviewers and clients

substance-induced neurocognitive disorder: neurocognitive deficits caused by the abuse of drugs over a period of time

substance tolerance: the situation in which the individual must consume more of the drug to have the same effect, or with gambling, the individual needs to bet more to keep the same level of excitement

successful aging: individuals who continue to be productive well into their 80s and 90s; characterized by (1) freedom from disability and disease, (2) high cognitive and physical functioning, and (3) social activity, including both having friends and being productive

suicidal ideation: thinking often about suicide

suicide: to kill oneself

sympathetic division: the branch of the autonomic nervous system that connects with its target organs through the middle part of the spinal cord, responsible for the fight-or-flight response

symptoms: features observed by the patient

syndrome: determination of which signs and symptoms go together

tend-and-befriend response: a response to stress associated with the tendency of females to take care of others and form social connections in times of stress, as opposed to the fight-or-flight response by most males

Thematic Apperception Test (TAT): a projective testing instrument composed of black-and-white drawings of various scenes and people; by evaluating the individual's interpretive responses to the ambiguous drawings, it is possible to gain insight into their thoughts, emotions, and motivations, including areas of conflict

theory of mind: the ability to understand one's own or another person's mental state

tobacco: a plant that originated in the Americas with native populations smoking or chewing its leaves

transcranial magnetic stimulation (TMS): a treatment for depression in which an electromagnetic coil is placed on the scalp; from the coil, a magnetic field induces a small electrical current in the first few centimeters of the brain, which depolarizes the neurons

transference-focused psychotherapy (TFP): a twice-weekly psychological therapy based on Otto Kernberg's object relations model; as with other approaches, TFP seeks to reduce symptoms of borderline personality disorder, especially self-destructive behaviors

transgender: describes individuals who have the anatomy of one sex and the gender identity of the other

transsexual: describes a transgender individual who has sought medical intervention such as hormone treatment and sexual reassignment surgery to change their body into that of the opposite sex

transvestic disorder: a paraphilic disorder characterized by recurrent and intense sexual arousal from cross-dressing, as manifested by fantasies, urges, or behaviors that last for a period of at least 6 months and cause distress or impairment

trauma- and stressor-related disorders: a category of childhood disorders, including disorders of attachment

traumatic brain injuries (TBIs): significant injuries caused by hits to the head, with acceleration and deceleration forces on the brain as it impacts with the skull; the severity of the resulting injuries can range from mild to severe

twin studies: a major paradigm of behavioral genetics; the study of twins to examine and understand critical factors related to genetic influences

unipolar depression: the mood disorder characterized by the experience of depression without mania

vagal nerve stimulation (VNS): a treatment for depression in which an electrical stimulator is surgically implanted next to the vagus and then connected to a pulse generator in the person's chest; like a pacemaker in the heart, the pulse generator can be programmed to deliver electrical pulses at desirable frequencies and currents

validity: truth of the results and capability of being supported

variation: the assumption that heritable variations can and do occur in nature

vascular neurocognitive disorder: neurocognitive disorder caused by vascular problems such as strokes; problems in cognitive performance are usually seen as abrupt changes

volitional test: a test adopted in Alabama in the 1880s for not guilty by reason of insanity in which mental illness made the person unable to control himself even though he knew the difference between right and wrong

voluntary participation: a principle stating that a person should participate in an experiment only by free choice and should be free to leave an experiment at any time, whether or not the experiment has been completed

voyeuristic disorder: a paraphilic disorder that involves obtaining sexual arousal from watching unsuspecting people when they are undressing, performing sexual acts, or going to the bathroom; it lasts for a period of at least 6 months and causes distress or impairment

Wechsler Adult Intelligence Scale (WAIS): a common intelligence test with a number of subscales designed to measure verbal and performance tasks

Wisconsin Card Sorting Test (WCST): an assessment instrument that requires an individual to sort cards into four piles; each card has a specific shape on it and a specific number of these shapes, and each card is printed in a specific color; thus, the cards could be sorted by shape, number, or color. The sort criteria are changed throughout the test. The purpose of the test is to measure the person's ability to adjust to changes in sorting criteria.

withdrawal: the symptoms experienced when a psychoactive substance is used less or no longer used

REFERENCES

FM

Patalay, P., & MacDonald, A. W., III. (2022). New titles can give new perspectives: Reflections on language and equity in clinical science [Editorial]. *Journal of Psychopathology and Clinical Science*, *131*(1), 1–3. https://doi.org/10.1037/abn0000739

CHAPTER 1

Ambady, N., & Bharucha, J. (2009). Culture and the brain. *Current Directions in Psychological Science*, *18*, 342–345.

Barber, J. P., Muran, J. C., McCarthy, K. S., Keefe, J. R., & Zilcha-Mano, S. (2021). Research on dynamic therapies. In M. Barkham, W. Lutz, & L. G. Castonguay (Eds.), *Bergin and Garfield's handbook of psychotherapy and behavior change: 50th anniversary edition* (pp. 387–419). John Wiley & Sons.

Barlow, D. H., Allen, L. B., & Choate, M. L. (2016). Toward a unified treatment for emotional disorders–republished article. *Behavior Therapy*, *47*(6), 838–853.

Beck, A. T. (1967). *Depression: Clinical, experimental, and theoretical aspects.* Harper & Row.

Beck, A. T. (2019). A 60-year evolution of cognitive theory and therapy. *Perspectives on Psychological Science*, *14*, 16–20. https://doi.org/10.1177/1745691618804187

Benton, M. L., Abraham, A., LaBella, A. L., Abbot, P., Rokas, A., & Capra, J. A. (2021). The influence of evolutionary history on human health and disease. *Nature Reviews Genetics*, *22*(5), 269–283. https://doi.org/10.1038/s41576-020-00305-9

Boring, E. (1950). *A history of experimental psychology* (2nd ed.). Appleton-Century-Crofts.

Camprodon, J., Kaur, N., Rauch, S., & Dougherty, D. (2016). Neurotherapeutics. In T. A. Stern, M. Fava, T. E. Wilens, & J. F. Rosenbaum (Eds.), *Massachusetts General Hospital comprehensive clinical psychiatry* (2nd ed., pp. 518–524). Elsevier.

Carlucci, L., Saggino, A., & Balsamo, M. (2021). On the efficacy of the unified protocol for transdiagnostic treatment of emotional disorders: A systematic review and meta-analysis. *Clinical Psychology Review*, *87*, Article 101999. https://doi.org/10.1016/j.cpr.2021.101999

Centers for Disease Control and Prevention. (2012). *Attitudes toward mental illness: Results from the Behavioral Risk Factor Surveillance System.*

Cheney, T. (2008). *Manic*. William Morrow.

Chiao, J. (2011). Cultural neuroscience: Visualizing culture-gene influences on brain function. In J. Decety & J. Cacioppo (Eds.), *The Oxford handbook of social neuroscience* (pp. 742–761). Oxford University Press.

Clark, D. M. (2018). Realizing the mass public benefit of evidence-based psychological therapies : The IAPT program. *Annual Review of Clinical Psychology*, *14*, 159–183.

Creswell, J. D. (2017). Mindfulness interventions. *Annual Review of Psychology*, *68*, 491–516. https://doi.org/10.1146/annurev-psych-042716-051139

Darwin, C. (1859). *On the origin of species by means of natural selection*. John Murray.

David, D., Lynn, S., & Montgomery, G (Eds.). (2018). *Evidence-based psychotherapy: The state of science and practice.* Wiley Blackwell.

Ellenberger, H. F. (1970). *The discovery of the unconscious: The history and evolution of dynamic psychiatry.* Basic Books.

Elliott, R., Bohart, A. C., Watson, J. C., & Murphy, D. (2018). Therapist empathy and client outcome: An updated meta-analysis. *Psychotherapy*, *55*, 399–410.

Elliott, R., Greenberg, L., Watson, J., Timulak, L., & Freire, E. (2013). Humanistic-experiential psychotherapies. In M. Lambert (Ed.), *Handbook of psychotherapy and behavior change* (6th ed.). Wiley.

Elliott, R., Watson, J., Timulak, L., & Sharbanee, J. (2021). Research on humanistic-experiential psychotherapies: Updated review. In M. Barkham, W. Lutz, & L. G. Castonguay (Eds.), *Bergin and Garfield's handbook of psychotherapy and behavior change: 50th anniversary edition* (pp. 421–467). John Wiley & Sons.

Farber, B. A., Suzuki, J. Y., & Lynch, D. A. (2018). Positive regard and psychotherapy outcome: A meta-analytic review. *Psychotherapy*, *55*, 411–423.

Fava, M., & Papakostas, G. (2016). Antidepressants. In T. A. Stern, M. Fava, T. E. Wilens, & J. F. Rosenbaum (Eds.), *Massachusetts General Hospital comprehensive clinical psychiatry* (2nd ed., pp. 489–505). Elsevier.

Finger, S. (2000). *Minds behind the brain: A history of the pioneers and their discoveries.* Oxford University Press.

Fisher, W., Geller, J., & Pandiani, J. (2009). The changing role of state psychiatric hospital. *Health Affairs*, *28*, 676–684.

Fonagy, P. (2015). The effectiveness of psychodynamic psychotherapies: An update. *World Psychiatry*, *14*(2), 137–150.

Freudenreich, O., Goff, D., & Henderson, D. (2016). Antipsychotic drugs. In T. A. Stern, M. Fava, T. E. Wilens, & J. F. Rosenbaum (Eds.), *Massachusetts General Hospital comprehensive clinical psychiatry* (2nd ed., pp. 475–488). Elsevier.

Galen. (1944). *On medical experience* (R. Walzer, Trans.). Oxford University Press. (Original work published ca. 165–175 C.E.)

Garrett, B. (2010). *Brain & behavior: An introduction to biological psychology.* Sage.

Gerard, D. (1997). Chiarugi and Pinel considered: Soul's brain/person's mind. *Journal of the History of the Behavioral Sciences*, *33*, 381–403.

Greenberg, L. S. (2002). *Emotion-focused therapy: Coaching clients to work through their feelings.* American Psychological Association.

Greenberg, L. S., & Watson, J. C. (2006). *Emotion-focused therapy for depression.* American Psychological Association.

Grossman, P., Niemann, L., Schmidt, S., & Walach, H. (2004). Mindfulness-based stress reduction and health benefits: A meta-analysis. *Journal of Psychosomatic Research*, *57*, 35–43.

Gruber, H. (1974). *Darwin on Man: A psychological study of scientific creativity*. Dutton.

Hayes, S. C., & Hofmann, S. G. (2017). The third wave of cognitive behavioral therapy and the rise of process-based care. *World Psychiatry*, *16*(3), 245.

Hippocrates. (n.d.). *On the sacred disease*. (F. Adams, Trans.). The Internet Classics Archive. (Original work published 400 B.C.E.) http://classics.mit.edu/Hippocrates/sacred.html

Hofmann, S., Grossman, P., & Hinton, D. (2011). Loving-kindness and compassion meditation: Potential for psychological interventions. *Clinical Psychology Review, 31*, 1126–1132.

Hofmann, S. G., Sawyer, A., & Fang, A. (2010). The empirical status of the "New Wave" of CBT. *Psychiatric Clinics of North America, 33*, 701–710.

Hofmann, S., Sawyer, A., Witt, A., & Oh, D. (2010). The effect of mindfulness-based therapy on anxiety and depression: A meta-analytic review. *Journal of Consulting and Clinical Psychology, 78*, 169–183.

Hollon, S., & Beck, A. (2013). Cognitive and cognitive-behavioral therapies. In M. Lambert (Ed.), *Handbook of psychotherapy and behavior change* (6th ed.). Wiley.

Holton, G. (1952). *Introduction to concepts and theories in physical science*. Addison-Wesley.

Hong, J. (2018). Cognitive behavioral models, measures, and treatments for anxiety disorders in Asian Americans. In E. Chang, C. Downey, J. Hirsch, & E. Yu (Eds.), *Treating depression, anxiety, and stress in ethnic and racial groups*. American Psychological Association.

Huey, S. J. Jr., Tilley, J. L., Jones, E. O., & Smith, C. A. (2014). The contribution of cultural competence to evidence-based care for ethnically diverse populations. *Annual Review of Clinical Psychology, 10*, 305–338. https://doi.org/10.1146/annurev-clinpsy-032813-153729

Insel, T. (2015). RAISE-ing our expectations for first-episode psychosis. *American Journal of Psychiatry, 173*(4), 311–312.

Jackson, J. H. (1894). The factors of insanities. *The Medical Press and Circular, 108*, 615–619.

Kabat-Zinn, J. (1990). *Full catastrophe living*. Delta.

Kane, J., Robinson, D., Schooler, N., Mueser, K., Penn, D. L., Rosenheck, R. A., Addington, J., Brunette, M. F., Correll, C. U., Estroff, S. E., Marcy, P., Robinson, J., Meyer-Kalos, P. S., Gottlieb, J. D., Glynn, S. M., Lynde, D. W., Pipes, R., Kurian, B. T., Miller, A. L., . . . Heinssen, R. (2016). Comprehensive versus usual community care for first-episode psychosis: 2-year outcomes from the NIMH RAISE Early Treatment Program. *American Journal of Psychiatry, 173*, 362–372.

Knyazev, G. G., Savostyanov, A. N., Bocharov, A. V., Levin, E. A., & Rudych, P. D. (2021). The default mode network in self- and other-referential processing: effect of cultural values. *Culture and Brain, 9*, 144–160.

Krendl, A. C., & Pescosolido, B. A. (2020). Countries and cultural differences in the stigma of mental illness: The east-west divide. *Journal of Cross-Cultural Psychology, 51*(2), 149–167.

López, S., & Guarnaccia, P. (2000). Cultural psychopathology: Uncovering the social world of mental illness. *Annual Review of Psychology, 51*, 571–598.

Marsella, A. J., & Yamada, A. (2000). Culture and mental health: An introduction and overview of foundations, concepts, and issues. In I. Cuellar & F. Paniagua (Eds.), *Handbook of multicultural mental health* (pp. 3–24). Academic Press.

Mora, G. (1959). Vincenzo Chiarugi (1759–1820) and his psychiatric reform in Florence in the late 18th century. *Journal of the History of Medicine and Allied Sciences, 14*, 424–433.

Murphy, J. (1976). Psychiatric labeling in cross-cultural perspective. *Science, 191*, 1019–1028.

Nasar, S. (1998). *A beautiful mind*. Simon & Schuster.

Newman, M. G., Agras, W. S., Haaga, D. A. F., & Jarrett, R. B. (2021). Cognitive, behavioral, and cognitive behavioral therapy. In M. Barkham, W. Lutz, & L. G. Castonguay (Eds.), *Bergin and Garfield's handbook of psychotherapy and behavior change: 50th anniversary edition* (pp. 469–505). John Wiley & Sons.

Newton, I. (1969). *Mathematical principles* (F. Cajori, Trans.). Greenwood. (Original work published 1687)

Norcross, J. C., & Lambert, M. J. (2018). Psychotherapy relationships that work III. *Psychotherapy, 55*, 303–315.

Norton, P. J., & Roberge, P. (2017). Transdiagnostic therapy. *Psychiatric Clinics of North America, 40*(4), 675–687. https://doi.org/10.1016/j.psc.2017.08.003

Öhman, A. (1986). Face the beast and fear the face: Animal and social fears as prototypes for evolutionary analyses of emotion. *Psychophysiology, 23*, 123–145.

Ong, C. W., Smith, B. M., Levin, M. E., & Twohig, M. P. (2020). Mindfulness and acceptance. In J. S. Abramowitz & S. M. Blakey (Eds.), *Clinical handbook of fear and anxiety: Maintenance processes and treatment mechanisms* (pp. 323–344). American Psychological Association. https://doi.org/10.1037/0000150-018

Patalay, P., & MacDonald, A. W. (2022). New titles can give new perspectives: Reflections on language and equity in clinical science. *Journal of Psychopathology and Clinical Science, 131*(1), 1–3. https://doi.org/10.1037/abn0000739

Perkins, A. M., Meiser-Stedman, R., Spaul, S. W., Bowers, G., Perkins, A. G., & Pass, L. (2023). The effectiveness of third wave cognitive behavioural therapies for children and adolescents: A systematic review and meta-analysis. *British Journal of Clinical Psychology, 62*(1), 209–227.

Perlis, R., & Ostacher, M. (2016). Lithium and its role in psychiatry. In T. A. Stern, M. Fava, T. E. Wilens, & J. F. Rosenbaum (Eds.), *Massachusetts General Hospital comprehensive clinical psychiatry* (2nd ed., pp. 525–532). Elsevier.

Pinel, P. (1806). *A treatise on insanity* (D. D. Davis, Trans.). Cadell & Davies.

Ravitz, P., Watson, P., Lawson, A., Constantino, M. J., Bernecker, S., Park, J., & Swartz, H. A. (2019). Interpersonal psychotherapy: A scoping review and historical perspective (1974–2017). *Harvard Review of Psychiatry, 27*(3), 165–180. https://doi.org/10.1097/HRP.0000000000000219

Ray, W. J. (2013). *Evolutionary psychology: Neuroscience determinants of human behavior and experience*. Sage.

Richerson, P., & Boyd, R. (2005). *Not by genes alone: How culture transformed human evolution*. University of Chicago Press.

Sakiris, N., & Berle, D. (2019). A systematic review and meta-analysis of the Unified Protocol as a transdiagnostic emotion regulation based intervention. *Clinical Psychology Review, 72*, Article 101751. https://doi.org/10.1016/j.cpr.2019.101751

Sartorius, N., Jablensky, A., Korten, A., Ernberg, G., Anker, M., Cooper, J. E., & Day, R. (1986). Early manifestations and first-contact incidence of schizophrenia in different cultures. A preliminary report on the initial evaluation phase of the WHO Collaborative Study on determinants of outcome of severe mental disorders. *Psychological Medicine, 16*, 909–928.

Strupp, H., & Binder, J. (1984). *Psychotherapy in a new key: A guide to time-limited dynamic psychotherapy*. Basic Books.

Sulloway, F. (1979). *Freud, biologist of the mind*. Basic Books.

Torrey, E. (1997). *Out of the shadows: Confronting America's mental illness crisis*. Wiley.

Tuke, S. (1813). *Description of the Retreat, an institution near York, for insane persons of the Society of Friends*. Isaac Peirce.

Watson, J. (1924). *Behaviorism*. People's Institute.

Watson, J., & Rayner, R. (1920). Conditioned emotional reactions. *Journal of Experimental Psychology, 3*, 1–14.

Welch, C. (2016). Electroconvulsive therapy. In T. A. Stern, M. Fava, T. E. Wilens, & J. F. Rosenbaum (Eds.), *Massachusetts General Hospital comprehensive clinical psychiatry* (2nd ed., pp. 510–517). Elsevier.

Wielgosz, J., Goldberg, S. B., Kral, T. R. A., Dunne, J. D., & Davidson, R. J. (2019). Mindfulness meditation and psychopathology. *Annual Review of Clinical Psychology, 15*, 285–316.

Williamson, P. C., & Allman, J. M. (2011). *The human illnesses: Neuropsychiatric disorders and the nature of the human brain*. Oxford University Press

CHAPTER 2

Andreasen, N. (2001). *Brave new brain*. Oxford University Press.

Bana, B., & Cabreiro, F. (2019). The microbiome and aging. *Annual Review of Genetics, 53*, 239–261. https://doi.org/10.1146/annurev-genet-112618-043650

Bell, J. T., & Spector, T. D. (2011). A twin approach to unraveling epigenetics. *Trends in Genetics, 27*, 116–125.

Berger, H. (1969). Über das Elektrekephalogramm des Menschen. *Electro encephalography and Clinical Neurophysiology* (Supp. 28). (Reprinted from *Archive für Psychiatrie und Nervenkrankheiten, 87*, 527–570, 1929)

Bigdeli, T. B., & Harvey, P. D. (2021). Cognitive endophenotypes: Powerful tools for modern neuropsychiatric genomics research. *Biological Psychiatry, 90*(6), 354–355. https://doi.org/10.1016/j.biopsych.2021.06.019

Brainstorm Consortium, Anttila, V., Bulik-Sullivan, B., Finucane, H. K., Walters, R. K., Bras, J., Duncan, L., Escott-Price, V., Falcone, G. J., Gormley, P., Malik, R., Patsopoulos, N. A., Ripke, S., Wei, Z., Yu, D., Lee, P. H., Turley, P., Grenier-Boley, B., Chouraki, V., . . . Murray, R. (2018). Analysis of shared heritability in common disorders of the brain. *Science (New York, N.Y.), 360*(6395), eaap8757. https://doi.org/10.1126/science.aap8757

Breen, G., Li, Q., Roth, B. L., Donnell, P. O., Didriksen, M., Dolmetsch, R., O'Reilly, P., Gaspar, H., Manji, H., Huebel, C., Kelsoe, J., Malhotra, D., Bertolino, A., Posthuma, D., Sklar, P., Kapur, S., Sullivan, P., Collier, D., & Edenberg, H. (2016). Translating genome-wide association findings into new therapeutics for psychiatry. *Nature Neuroscience, 19*, 1392–1396.

Bressler, S., & Menon, V. (2010). Large-scale brain networks in cognition: Emerging methods and principles. *Trends in Cognitive Sciences, 14*, 277–290.

Brodin, P. (2022). Immune-microbe interactions early in life: A determinant of health and disease long term. *Science (New York, N.Y.), 376*(6596), 945–950. https://doi.org/10.1126/science.abk2189

Brown, E. G., Goldman, S. M. (2020). Modulation of the microbiome in Parkinson's disease: Diet, drug, stool transplant, and beyond. *Neurotherapeutics, 17*, 1406–1417. https://doi.org/10.1007/s13311-020-00942-2

Bruce, S., Buchholz, K., Brown, W., Yan, L., Durbin, A., & Sheline, Y. (2013). Altered emotional interference processing in the amygdala and insula in women with post-traumatic stress disorder. *NeuroImage: Clinical, 2*, 43–49.

Buchsbaum, M., & Haier, R. (1987). Functional and anatomical brain imaging: Impact on schizophrenia research. *Schizophrenia Bulletin, 13*, 115–132.

Buckner, R. L., Andrews-Hanna, J. R., & Schacter, D. L. (2008). The brain's default network: Anatomy, function, and relevance to disease. *Annals of the New York Academy of Science, 1124*, 1–38.

Buckner, R. L., & DiNicola, L. M. (2019). The brain's default network: Updated anatomy, physiology and evolving insights. *Nature Reviews Neuroscience, 20*(10), 593–608. https://doi.org/10.1038/s41583-019-0212-7

Carone, B. R., Fauquier, L., Habib, N., Shea, J. M., Hart, C. E., Li, R., Bock, C., Li, C., Gu, H., Zamore, P. D., Meissner, A., Weng, Z., Hofmann, H. A., Friedman, N., & Rando, O. J. (2010). Paternally induced transgenerational environmental reprogramming of metabolic gene expression in mammals. *Cell, 143*, 1084–1096.

Caspi, A., McClay, J., Moffitt, T., Mill, J., Martin, J., Craig, I., Taylor, A., & Poulton, R. (2002). Role of genotype in the cycle of violence in maltreated children. *Science, 297*, 851–854.

Cavalli, G., & Heard, E. (2019). Advances in epigenetics link genetics to the environment and disease. *Nature, 571*(7766), 489–499. https://doi.org/10.1038/s41586-019-1411-0

Chavlis, S., & Poirazi, P. (2021). Drawing inspiration from biological dendrites to empower artificial neural networks. *Current Opinion in Neurobiology, 70*, 1–10. https://doi.org/10.1016/j.conb.2021.04.007

Chiao, J. (2009). Cultural neuroscience: A once and future discipline. *Progress in Brain Research, 178*, 287–304.

Chiao, J. (2011). Cultural neuroscience: Visualizing culture-gene influences on brain function. In J. Decety & J. Cacioppo (Eds.), *The Oxford handbook of social neuroscience* (pp. 742–761). Oxford University Press.

Clemmensen, C., Müller, T. D., Woods, S. C., Berthoud, H. R., Seeley, R. J., & Tschöp, M. H. (2017). Gut-brain cross-talk in metabolic control. *Cell, 168*(5), 758–774. https://doi.org/10.1016/j.cell.2017.01.025

Coley, E. J. L., & Hsiao, E. Y. (2021). Malnutrition and the microbiome as modifiers of early neurodevelopment. *Trends in Neurosciences, 44*(9), 753–764. https://doi.org/10.1016/j.tins.2021.06.004

Correa-Ghisays, P., Vicent Sánchez-Ortí, J., Balanzá-Martínez, V., Fuentes-Durá, I., Martinez-Aran, A., Ruiz-Bolo, L., Correa-Estrada, P., Ruiz-Ruiz, J. C., Selva-Vera, G., Vila-Francés, J., Macias Saint-Gerons, D., San-Martín, C., Ayesa-Arriola, R., & Tabarés-Seisdedos, R. (2022). MICEmi: A method to identify cognitive endophenotypes of mental illnesses. *European Psychiatry, 65*(1), e85. https://doi.org/10.1192/j.eurpsy.2022.2348

Cropley, J., Suter, C., Beckman, K., & Martin, D. (2006). Germ-line epigenetic modification of the murine *Avy* allele by nutritional supplementation. *Proceedings of the National Academy of Science, 103*, 17308–17312.

Cross-Disorder Group of the Psychiatric Genomics Consortium. (2013). Identification of risk loci with shared effects on five major psychiatric disorders: A genome-wide analysis. *The Lancet, 381*, 1371–1379.

Cryan, J. F., & Mazmanian, S. K. (2022). Microbiota-brain axis: Context and causality. *Science (New York N.Y.), 376*(6596), 938–939. https://doi.org/10.1126/science.ab04442

Cubells, J., & Zabetian, C. (2004). Human genetics of plasma dopamine beta-hydroxylase activity: Applications to research in psychiatry and neurology. Psychopharmacology, 174, 463–476.

Eisenberg, D., & Berman, K. (2010). Executive function, neural circuitry, and genetic mechanisms in schizophrenia. Neuropsychopharmacology, 35, 258–277.

Fanibunda, S. E., & Vaidya, V. A. (2021). Serotonin minting new mitochondria in cortical neurons: implications for psychopathology. Neuropsychopharmacology, 46(1), 259–260. https://doi.org/10.1038/s41386-020-00824-3

Foster, J. A. (2022). Modulating brain function with microbiota. Science (New York N.Y.), 376(6596), 936–937. https://doi.org/10.1126/science.abo4220

Frick, A., Åhs, F., Engman, J., Jonasson, M., Alaie, I., Björkstrand, J., Frans, Ö., Faria, V., Linnman, C., Appel, L., Wahlstedt, K., Lubberink, M., Fredrikson, M., & Furmark, T. (2015). Serotonin synthesis and reuptake in social anxiety disorder. JAMA Psychiatry, 1–9. http://doi.org/10.1001/jamapsychiatry.2015.0125

Friedman, N. P., Banich, M. T., & Keller, M. C. (2021). Twin studies to GWAS: There and back again. Trends in Cognitive Sciences, 25(10), 855–869. https://doi.org/10.1016/j.tics.2021.06.007

Gamboa, H. (2005). [Image of EEG sample]. Hgamboa, licensed under CC BY-SA 3.0 https://commons.wikimedia.org/wiki/User : https://creativecommons.org/licenses/by-sa/3.0/

Giangrande, E. J., Weber, R. S., & Turkheimer, E. (2022). What do we know about the genetic architecture of psychopathology? Annual review of clinical psychology, 18, 19–42. https://doi.org/10.1146/annurev-clinpsy-081219-091234

Gibson, G. (2012). Rare and common variants: Twenty arguments. Nature Reviews Genetics, 13(2), 135–145. https://doi.org/10.1038/nrg3118

Gilbert, J. A., Blaser, M. J., Caporaso, J. G., Jansson, J. K., Lynch, S. V., & Knight, R. (2018). Current understanding of the human microbiome. Nature Medicine, 24(4), 392–400. https://doi.org/10.1038/nm.4517

Goldstone, R. L., Pestilli, F., & Börner, K. (2015). Self-portraits of the brain: Cognitive science, data visualization and communicating brain structure and function. Trends in Cognitive Sciences, 19(8). http://doi.org/10.1016/j.tics.2015.05.012

Gottesman, I., & Hanson, D. (2005). Human development: Biological and genetic processes. Annual Review of Psychology, 56, 263–286.

Gottesman, I., & Shields, J. (1972). Schizophrenia and genetics: A twin study vantage point. Academic Press.

Hallgrímsson, B., & Hall, B (Eds.). (2011). Epigenetics: Linking genotype and phenotype in development and evolution. University of California Press.

Harpending, H., & Sobus, J. (1987). Sociopathy as an adaptation. Ethology and Sociobiology, 8, 63–72.

Hartl, C. L., Ramaswami, G., Pembroke, W. G., Muller, S., Pintacuda, G., Saha, A., Parsana, P., Battle, A., Lage, K., & Geschwind, D. H. (2021). Coexpression network architecture reveals the brain-wide and multiregional basis of disease susceptibility. Nature Neuroscience, 24(9), 1313–1323. https://doi.org/10.1038/s41593-021-00887-5

Hauri, P. (1982). Current concepts: The sleep disorders. Upjohn.

Henderson, D., Vincenzi, B., Yeung, A., & Fricchione, G. (2016). Culture and psychiatry. In T. A. Stern, M. Fava, T. E. Wilens, & J. F. Rosenbaum (Eds.), Massachusetts General Hospital comprehensive clinical psychiatry (2nd ed., pp. 718–725). Elsevier.

Herbet, G., & Duffau, H. (2020). Revisiting the functional anatomy of the human brain: Toward a meta-networking theory of cerebral functions. Physiological Reviews, 100(3), 1181–1228. https://doi.org/10.1152/physrev.00033.2019

Hofman, M. (2001). Brain evolution in hominids: Are we at the end of the road? In D. Falk, & K. Gibson (Eds.), Evolutionary anatomy of the primate cerebral cortex, (pp. 113–127). Cambridge University Press.

Illes, J., & Bird, S. (2006). Neuroethics: A modern context for ethics in neuroscience. TRENDS in Neurosciences, 29, 511–517.

Insel, T., & Cuthbert, B. (2009). Endophenotypes: Bridging genomic complexity and disorder heterogeneity. Biological Psychiatry, 66, 988–989.

Iyegbe, C. O., & O'Reilly, P. F. (2022). Genetic origins of schizophrenia find common ground. Nature, 604(7906), 433–435. https://doi.org/10.1038/d41586-022-00773-5

Jeremian, R., Malinowski, A., Chaudhary, Z., Srivastava, A., Qian, J., Zai, C., Adanty, C., Fischer, C. E., Burhan, A. M., Kennedy, J. L., Borlido, C., Gerretsen, P., Graff, A., Remington, G., Vincent, J. B., Strauss, J. S., & De Luca, V. (2022). Epigenetic age dysregulation in individuals with bipolar disorder and schizophrenia. Psychiatry Research, 315, Article 114689. https://doi.org/10.1016/j.psychres.2022.114689

Johnson, K. V. (2020). Gut microbiome composition and diversity are related to human personality traits. Human Microbiome Journal, 15. https://doi.org/10.1016/j.humic.2019.100069

Katsnelson, A. (2010). Epigenome effort makes its mark. Nature, 467, 646.

Kelly, C., Biswal, B., Craddock, R., Castellanos, F., & Milham, M. (2012). Characterizing variation in the functional connectome: Promise and pitfalls. Trends in Cognitive Sciences, 16, 181–188.

Kelly, P., Alderton, G., Scanlon, S. T., & Ash, C. (2022). A multiplicity of microbiomes. Science (New York N.Y.), 376(6596), 932–933. https://doi.org/10.1126/science.adc9690

Keverne, E. B. (2015). Genomic imprinting, action, and interaction of maternal and fetal genomes. Proceedings of the National Academy of Sciences of the United States of America, 112(22), 6834–6840. https://doi.org/10.1073/pnas.1411253111

Khona, M., & Fiete, I. R. (2022). Attractor and integrator networks in the brain. Nature Reviews Neuroscience, 23(12), 744–766. https://doi.org/10.1038/s41583-022-00642-0

Kitayama, S., & Cohen, D. (2007). The handbook of cultural psychology. Guilford Press.

Knyazev, G. (2007). Motivation, emotion, and their inhibitory control mirrored in brain oscillations. Neuroscience and Biobehavioral Reviews, 31, 377–395.

Laton, J., Van Schependom, J., Gielen, J., Decoster, J., Moons, T., De Keyser, J., De Hert, M., & Nagels, G. (2014). Single-subject classification of schizophrenia patients based on a combination of oddball and mismatch evoked potential paradigms. Journal of the Neurological Sciences, 347(1-2), 262–267. http://doi.org/10.1016/j.jns.2014.10.015

Laughlin, S., & Sejnowski, T. (2003). Communication in neuronal networks. Science, 301, 1870–1974.

Li, B. J., Friston, K., Mody, M., Wang, H. N., Lu, H. B., & Hu, D. W. (2018). A brain network model for depression: From symptom understanding to disease intervention. CNS Neuroscience and Therapeutics, 24, 1004–1019. https://doi.org/10.1111/cns.12998

Liebe, S., Hoerzer, G., Logothetis, N. K., & Rainer, G. (2012). Theta coupling between V4 and prefrontal cortex predicts visual short-term memory performance. *Nature Neuroscience, 15*, 456–464.

Lu, Q., & Stappenbeck, T. S. (2022). Local barriers configure systemic communications between the host and microbiota. *Science (New York N.Y.), 376*(6596), 950–955. https://doi.org/10.1126/science.abo2366

Luck, S. J., Woodman, G. F., & Vogel, E. K. (2000). Event-related potential studies of attention. *Trends in Cognitive Sciences, 11*, 432–440.

Mack, K., & Mack, P. (1992). Induction of transcription factors in somatosensory cortex after tactile stimulation. *Brain Research: Molecular Brain Research, 12*, 141–147.

Mayneris-Perxachs, J., Arnoriaga-Rodríguez, M., Garre-Olmo, J., Puig, J., Ramos, R., Trelis, M., Burokas, A., Coll, C., Zapata-Tona, C., Pedraza, S., Pérez-Brocal, V., Ramió, L., Ricart, W., Moya, A., Jové, M., Sol, J., Portero-Otin, M., Pamplona, R., Maldonado., R., & Fernández-Real, J. M. (2022). Presence of blastocystis in gut microbiota is associated with cognitive traits and decreased executive function. *The ISME Journal, 16*(9), 2181–2197. https://doi.org/10.1038/s41396-022-01262-3

Mello, C., Vicario, D., & Clayton, D. (1992). Song presentation induces gene expression in the songbird forebrain. *Proceedings of the National Academy of Sciences, 89*, 6818–6822.

Menon, V. (2011). Large scale brain networks and psychopathology: A unifying triple network model. *Trends in Cognitive Sciences, 15*, 483–506.

Menon, V., Palaniyappan, L., & Supekar, K. (2023). Integrative brain network and salience models of psychopathology and cognitive dysfunction in schizophrenia. *Biological Psychiatry, 94*(2), 108–120. https://www.biologicalpsychiatryjournal.com/article/S0006-3223(22)01637-7/fulltext

Meyer-Lindenberg, A. (2010). From maps to mechanisms through neuroimaging of schizophrenia. *Nature, 468*, 194–202. https://doi.org/10.1038/nature09569

Mezzich, J., & Ruiperez, M. (2015). Culture and psychiatric diagnostic systems. In A. Tasman, J. Kay, J. Lieberman, M. First, & M. Riba (Eds.), *Psychiatry* (4th ed., pp. 639–653). Wiley.

Miller, G., & Rockstroh, B. (2013). Endophenotypes in psychopathology research: Where do we stand? *Annual Review of Clinical Psychology, 9*, 1–15.

Montenegro, J. D. (2022). Gene co-expression network analysis. *Methods in molecular biology (Clifton, N.J.), 2443*, 387–404. https://doi.org/10.1007/978-1-0716-2067-0_19

Moseley, R. L., Ypma, R. J. F., Holt, R. J., Floris, D., Chura, L. R., Spencer, M. D., Baron-Cohen, S., Suckling, J., Bullmore, E., & Rubinov, M. (2015). Whole-brain functional hypoconnectivity as an endophenotype of autism in adolescents. *NeuroImage: Clinical, 9*, 140–152. http://doi.org/10.1016/j.nic1.2015.07.015

Nadeau, S. (2004). *Medical neuroscience*. Saunders.

Nath, S., Agholme, L., Kurudenkandy, F. R., Granseth, B., Marcusson, J., & Hallbeck, M. (2012). Spreading of neurodegenerative pathology via neuron-to-neuron transmission of β-amyloid. *Journal of Neuroscience, 32*, 8767–8777.

Needham, B. D., Kaddurah-Daouk, R., & Mazmanian, S. K. (2020). Gut microbial molecules in behavioural and neurodegenerative conditions. *Nature Review Neuroscience, 21*(12), 717–731. https://doi.org/10.1038/s41583-020-00381-0

Nesse, R., & Williams, G. (1994). *Why we get sick: The new science of Darwinian medicine*. Vintage.

Nestler, E. (2011). Hidden switches in the mind. *Scientific American, 305*, 76–83.

Ng, S., Lin, R., Laybutt, D., Barres, R., Owens, J., & Morris, M. (2010). Chronic high-fat diet in fathers programs β-cell dysfunction in female rat offspring. *Nature, 467*, 963–966.

Nishida, K., Sawada, D., Kuwano, Y., Tanaka, H., Sugawara, T., Aoki, Y., Fujiwara, S., & Rokutan, K. (2017). Daily administration of paraprobiotic *Lactobacillus gasseri* CP2305 ameliorates chronic stress-associated symptoms in Japanese medical students. *Journal of Functional Foods, 36*, 112–121.

Northcutt, R. G., & Kaas, J. H. (1995). The emergence and evolution of mammalian neocortex. *Trends in Neuroscience, 18*, 373–379.

Nunez, P., & Srinivasan, R. (2006). *Electrical fields of the brain: The neurophysics of EEG*. Oxford University Press.

O'Donnell, K. J., & Meaney, M. J. (2020). Epigenetics, development, and psychopathology. *Annual Review of Clinical Psychology, 16*, 327–350. https://doi.org/10.1146/annurev-clinpsy-050718-095530

Ospelt, C. (2022). A brief history of epigenetics. *Immunology Letters, 249*, 1–4. https://doi.org/10.1016/j.imlet.2022.08.001

Palmer, D. S., Howrigan, D. P., Chapman, S. B., Adolfsson, R., Bass, N., Blackwood, D., Boks, M. P. M., Chen, C. Y., Churchhouse, C., Corvin, A. P., Craddock, N., Curtis, D., Di Florio, A., Dickerson, F., Freimer, N. B., Goes, F. S., Jia, X., Jones, I., Jones, L., . . . Neale, B. M. (2022). Exome sequencing in bipolar disorder identifies AKAP11 as a risk gene shared with schizophrenia. *Nature Genetics, 54*(5), 541–547. https://doi.org/10.1038/s41588-022-01034-x

Pembrey, M., Bygren, L., Kaati, G., Edvinsson, S., Northstone, K., Sjöström, M., Golding, J., & ALSPAC, Study Team. (2006). Sex-specific, male-line transgenerational responses in humans. *European Journal of Human Genetics, 14*, 159–166.

Phillips, O., Nuechterlein, K., Asarnow, R., Clark, K., Cabeen, R., Yang, Y., Woods, R., Toga, A., & Narr, K. (2011). Mapping corticocortical structural integrity in schizophrenia and effects of genetic liability. *Biological Psychiatry, 70*, 680–689.

Plomin, R. (2018). *Blueprint: How DNA makes us who we are*. MIT Press.

Preuss, T., & Kaas, J. (1999). Human brain evolution. In F. Bloom, S. Landis, J. Roberts, L. Squire, & M. Zigmond (Eds.), *Fundamental neuroscience* (pp. 1283–1311). Academic Press.

Purves, D., Cabeza, R., Huettel, S., LaBar, K., Platt, M., & Woldorff, M. (2013). *Principles of cognitive neuroscience* (2nd ed.). Sinauer Associates.

Raichle, M. E. (2011). The restless brain. *Brain Connectivity, 1*, 3–12.

Raichle, M. E. (2015a, April). The brain's default mode network. *Annual Review of Neuroscience*, 413–427. http://doi.org/10.1146/annurev-neuro-071013-014030

Raichle, M. E. (2015b). The restless brain: How intrinsic activity organizes brain function. *Philosophical Transactions of the Royal Society B, 370*, Article 20140172. https://doi.org/10.1098/rstb.2014.0172

Raichle, M., & Snyder, A. (2007). A default mode of brain function: A brief history of an evolving idea. *NeuroImage, 37*, 1083–1090.

Ramachandran, V. S. (1998). Consciousness and body image: Lessons from phantom limbs, Capgras syndrome and pain asymbolia. *Transitions of the Royal Society of London, B, 353*, 1851–1859.

Ramos, K. M., Grady, C., Greely, H. T., Chiong, W., Eberwine, J., Farahany, N. A., Johnson, L. S. M., Hyman, B. T., Hyman, S. E., Rommelfanger, K. S., Serrano, E. E., Churchill, J. D., Gordon, J. A., & Koroshetz, W. J. (2019). The NIH BRAIN Initiative: Integrating neuroethics and neuroscience. *Neuron, 101*(3), 394–398. https://doi.org/10.1016/j.neuron.2019.01.024

Rampon, C., Jiang, C., Dong, H., Tang, Y., Lockhart, D., Schultz, P., Tsien, J. Z., & Hu, Y. (2000). Effects of environmental enrichment on gene expression in the brain. *Proceedings of the National Academy of Sciences, 97*, 12880–12884.

Ray, W. J., & Cole, H. W. (1985). EEG alpha activity reflects attentional demands, and beta activity reflects emotional and cognitive processes. *Science, 228*, 750–752.

Regenold, W., Phatak, P., Marano, C., Sassan, A., Conley, R., & Kling, M. (2009). Elevated cerebrospinal fluid lactate concentrations in patients with bipolar disorder and schizophrenia: Implications for the mitochondrial dysfunction hypothesis. *Biological Psychiatry, 65*, 489–494.

Ribeiro, S., & Mello, C. (2000). Gene expression and synaptic plasticity in the auditory forebrain of songbirds. *Learning and Memory, 7*, 235–243.

Rich, B. A., Carver, F. W., Holroyd, T., Rosen, H. R., Mendoza, J. K., Cornwell, B. R., Fox, N. A., Pine, D. S., Coppola, R., & Leibenluft, E. (2011). Different neural pathways to negative affect in youth with pediatric bipolar disorder and severe mood dysregulation. *Journal of Psychiatry Research, 45*, 1283–1294.

Rieke, F., Warland, D., van Steveninck, R., & Bialek, W. (1999). *Spikes: Exploring the neural code*. MIT Press.

Rossignol, D., & Frye, R. (2012). Mitochondrial dysfunction in autism spectrum disorders: A systematic review and meta-analysis. *Molecular Psychiatry, 17*, 290–314.

Sartorius, N., Jablensky, A., Korten, A., Ernberg, G., Anker, M., Cooper, J. E., & Day, R. (1986). Early manifestations and first-contact incidence of schizophrenia in different cultures. A preliminary report on the initial evaluation phase of the WHO Collaborative Study on determinants of outcome of severe mental disorders. *Psychological Medicine, 16*, 909–928.

Schultz, T. (2006). [Image of DTI measurement of a human brain]. *Wikimedia Commons*. DTI-sagittal-fibers.jpg, licensed under CC BY-SA 3.0 https://commons.wikimedia.org/wiki/File: https://creativecommons.org/licenses/by-sa/3.0/

Serretti, A., Calati, R., Mandelli, L., & De Ronchi, D. (2006). Serotonin transporter gene variants and behavior: A comprehensive review. *Current Drug Targets, 7*, 1659–1669.

Singer, W. (2009). Distributed processing and temporal codes in neuronal networks. *Cognitive Neurodynamics, 3*, 189–196.

Singer, W., & Gray, C. (1995). Visual feature integration and the temporal correlation hypothesis. *Annual Review of Neuroscience, 18*, 555–586.

Singh, T., Poterba, T., Curtis, D., Akil, H., Al Eissa, M., Barchas, J. D., Bass, N., Bigdeli, T. B., Breen, G., Bromet, E. J., Buckley, P. F., Bunney, W. E., Bybjerg-Grauholm, J., Byerley, W. F., Chapman, S. B., Chen, W. J., Churchhouse, C., Craddock, N., Cusick, C. M., . . . Daly, M. J. (2022). Rare coding variants in ten genes confer substantial risk for schizophrenia. *Nature, 604*(7906), 509–516. https://doi.org/10.1038/s41586-022-04556-w

Skinner, M. (2010). Fathers' nutritional legacy. *Nature, 467*, 922–923.

Smith, L. K., & Wissel, E. F. (2019). Microbes and the mind: How bacteria shape affect, neurological processes, cognition, social relationships, development, and pathology. *Perspectives on Psychological Science: A Journal of the Association for Psychological Science, 14*(3), 397–418. https://doi.org/10.1177/1745691618809379

Spencer, W. (2011). The physiology of supraspinal neurons in mammals. In E. R. Kandel (Ed.), *Supplement 1: Handbook of physiology, the nervous system, cellular biology of neurons* (pp. 969–1021). American Physiological Society.

Sporns, O. (2011). *Networks of the brain*. MIT Press.

Sporns, O. (2022). The complex brain: connectivity, dynamics, information. *Trends in Cognitive Sciences, 26*(12), 1066–1067. https://doi.org/10.1016/j.tics.2022.08.002

Stebbins, G., & Murphy, C. (2009). Diffusion tensor imaging in Alzheimer's disease and mild cognitive impairment. *Behavioral Neurology, 21*, 39–49.

Sullivan, P. F., Agrawal, A., Bulik, C. M., Andreassen, O. A., Børglum, A. D., Breen, G., Cichon, S., Edenberg, H. J., Faraone, S. V., Gelernter, J., Mathews, C. A., Nievergelt, C. M., Smoller, J. W., & O'Donovan, M. C. (2018). Psychiatric genomics: An update and an agenda. *American Journal of Psychiatry, 175*, 15–27. https://doi.org/10.1176/appi.ajp.2017.17030283

Tabarés-Seisdedos, R., & Rubenstein, J. (2013). Inverse cancer comorbidity: A serendipitous opportunity to gain insight into CNS disorders. *Nature Reviews Neuroscience, 14*, 293–304.

Tallon-Baudry, C., & Bertrand, O. (1999). Oscillatory gamma activity in humans and its role in object representation. *Trends in Cognitive Sciences, 3*, 151–162.

Tan, Q. (2019). The epigenome of twins as a perfect laboratory for studying behavioural traits. *Neuroscience and Biobehavioral Reviews, 107*, 192–195. https://doi.org/10.1016/j.neubiorev.2019.09.022

Taylor-Colls, S., & Pasco Fearon, R. M. (2015). The effects of parental behavior on infants' neural processing of emotion expressions. *Child Development, 86*(3), 877–888. http://doi.org/10.1111/cdev.12348

Thomason, M., & Thompson, P. (2011). Diffusion imaging, white matter, and psychopathology. *Annual Review of Clinical Psychology, 7*, 63–85.

Travers, J., & Milgram, S. (1969). An experimental study of small world problem. *Sociometry, 32*, 425–443.

Tuganbaev, T., Yoshida, K., & Honda, K. (2022). The effects of oral microbiota on health. *Science (New York N.Y.), 376*(6596), 934–936. https://doi.org/10.1126/science.abn1890

Tye, C., Asherson, P., Ashwood, K., Azadi, B., Bolton, P., & McCloughlin, G. (2014). Attention and inhibition in children with ASD, ADHD, and co-morbid ASD+ADHD: An event-related potential study. *Psychological Medicine, 44*, 1101–1116.

Van Os, J. (2010). Are psychiatric diagnoses of psychosis scientific and useful? The case of schizophrenia. *Journal of Mental Health, 19*, 305–317.

Varela, R. B., Cararo, J. H., Tye, S. J., Carvalho, A. F., Valvassori, S. S., Fries, G. R., & Quevedo, J. (2022). Contributions of epigenetic inheritance to the predisposition of major psychiatric disorders: Theoretical framework, evidence, and implications. *Neuroscience and Biobehavioral Reviews, 135*, Article 104579. https://doi.org/10.1016/j.neubiorev.2022.104579

Walters, W. A., Xu, Z., & Knight, R. (2014). Meta-analyses of human gut microbes associated with obesity and IBD. *FEBS letters, 588*(22), 4223–4233. https://doi.org/10.1016/j.febslet.2014.09.039

Wang, H., Braun, C., Murphy, E. F., & Enck, P. (2019). Bifidobacterium longum 1714™ strain modulates brain activity of healthy volunteers during social stress. *American Journal of Gastroenterology, 114*(7), 1152–1162. https://doi.org/10.14309/ajg.0000000000000203

Wang, O., Su, T., Zhou, Y., Chou, K., Chen, I., Jiang, T., & Lin, C. (2012). Anatomical insights into disrupted small-world networks in schizophrenia. *NeuroImage, 59*, 1085–1093.

Waszczuk, K., Rek-Owodziń, K., Tyburski, E., Mak, M., Misiak, B., & Samochowiec, J. (2021). Disturbances in white matter integrity in the ultra-high-risk psychosis state—A systematic review. *Journal of Clinical Medicine, 10*(11), 2515. https://doi.org/10.3390/jcm10112515

Weaver, I., Cervoni, N., Champagne, F., D'Alessio, A., Sharma, S., Seckl, J., Dymov, S., Szyf, M., & Meaney, M. (2004). Epigenetic programming by maternal behavior. *Nature Neuroscience, 7*, 847–854.

Wedeen, V. J., Rosene, D. L., Wang, R., Dai, G., Mortazavi, F., Hagmann, P., Kaas, J. H., & Tseng, W. Y. (2012). The geometric structure of the brain fiber pathways. *Science, 335*, 1628–1634.

Whittingstall, K., & Logothetis, N. (2009). Frequency band coupling in surface EEG reflects spiffing activity in monkey visual cortex. *Neuron, 64*, 281–289.

Yates, D. (2021). Gene networking. *Nature Review Neuroscience, 22*, 589.

Young, M. J., Bodien, Y. G., Giacino, J. T., Fins, J. J., Truog, R. D., Hochberg, L. R., & Edlow, B. L. (2021). The neuroethics of disorders of consciousness: a brief history of evolving ideas. *Brain: A Journal of Neurology, 144*(11), 3291–3310. https://doi.org/10.1093/brain/awab290

Zhang, K., Johnson, B., Pennell, D., Ray, W., Sebastianelli, W., & Slobounov, S. (2010). Are functional deficits in concussed individuals consistent with white matter structural alterations: combined FMRI & DTI study. *Experimental Brain Research, 204*, 57–70.

Zhao, B., Li, T., Smith, S. M., Xiong, D., Wang, X., Yang, Y., Luo, T., Zhu, Z., Shan, Y., Matoba, N., Sun, Q., Yang, Y., Hauberg, M. E., Bendl, J., Fullard, J. F., Roussos, P., Lin, W., Li, Y., Stein, J. L., & Zhu, H. (2022). Common variants contribute to intrinsic human brain functional networks. *Nature Genetics, 54*(4), 508–517. https://doi.org/10.1038/s41588-022-01039-6

Zimmer, C. (2001). *Evolution: The triumph of an idea*. HarperCollins

CHAPTER 3

Anderson, M. L., Chiswell, K., Peterson, E. D., Tasneem, A., Topping, J., & Califf, R. M. (2015). Compliance with results reporting at ClinicalTrials.gov. *New England Journal of Medicine, 372*, 1031–1039. http://doi.org/10.1056/NEJMsa1409364

Barch, D., & Ceaser, A. (2012). Cognition in schizophrenia: Core psychological and neural mechanisms. *Trends in Cognitive Science, 16*, 27–34.

Borkovec, T. D., & Ruscio, A. (2001). Psychotherapy for generalized anxiety disorder. *Journal of Clinical Psychiatry, 62*, 37–42.

Bouchard, T., Lykken, D., McGue, M., Segal, N., & Tellegen, A. (1990). Sources of human psychological differences: The Minnesota Study of Twins Reared Apart. *Science, 250*, 223–228.

Bromley, D. (1986). *The case-study design in psychology and related disciplines*. Wiley.

Butler, A., Chapman, J., Forman, E., & Beck, A. (2006). The empirical status of cognitive-behavioral therapy: A review of meta-analyses. *Clinical Psychology Review, 26*, 17–31.

Campbell, D. T., & Stanley, J. C. (1963). *Experimental and quasi-experimental designs for research*. Rand McNally.

Carey, G. (2003). *Human genetics for the social sciences*. Sage.

Caspi, A., McClay, J., Moffitt, T., Mill, J., Martin, J., Craig, I., Taylor, A., & Poulton, R. (2002). Role of genotype in the cycle of violence in maltreated children. *Science, 297*, 851–854.

Castrén, E., & Hen, R. (2013). Neuronal plasticity and antidepressant actions. *Trends in Neurosciences, 36*, 259–267.

Chauhan, P., & Widom, C. (2012). Childhood maltreatment and illicit drug use in middle adulthood: The role of neighborhood characteristics. *Development and Psychopathology, 24*, 723–738.

Damasio, H., Grabowski, T., Frank, R., Galaburda, A. M., & Damasio, A. (1994). The return of Phineas Gage: Clues about the brain from the skull of a famous patient. *Science, 264*, 51–62.

Dias, A., Azariah, F., Anderson, S. J., Sequeira, M., Cohen, A., Morse, J. Q., Cuijpers, P., Patel, V., & Reynolds, C. F. (2019). Effect of a lay counselor intervention on prevention of major depression in older adults living in low- and middle-income countries: A randomized clinical trial. *JAMA Psychiatry, 76*(1), 13–20. https://doi.org/10.1001/jamapsychiatry.2018.3048

DiLalla, L (Ed.). (2004). *Behavior genetics principles: Perspectives in development, personality, and psychopathology*. American Psychological Association.

Donati, F. L., D'Agostino, A., & Ferrarelli, F. (2020). Neurocognitive and neurophysiological endophenotypes in schizophrenia: An overview. *Biomarkers in Neuropsychiatry, 3*, Article 100017. https://doi.org/10.1016/j.bionps.2020.100017

Dyer, K., Dunlap, G., & Winterling, V. (1990). Effects of choice making on the serious problem behaviors of students with severe handicaps. *Journal of Applied Behavior Analysis, 23*(4), 515–524. https://doi.org/10.1901/jaba.1990.23-515

Eckshtain, D., Kuppens, S., Ugueto, A., Ng, M. Y., Vaughn-Coaxum, R., Corteselli, K., & Weisz, J. R. (2020). Meta-analysis: 13-year follow-up of psychotherapy effects on youth depression. *Journal of the American Academy of Child and Adolescent Psychiatry, 59*(1), 45–63. https://doi.org/10.1016/j.jaac.2019.04.002

The Economist. (2015, July 25). Spilling the beans: Failure to publish the results of all clinical trials is skewing medical science. https://www.economist.com/science-and-technology/2015/07/25/spilling-the-beans

Elbert, T., Pantev, C., Wienbruch, C., Rockstroh, B., & Taub, E. (1995). Increased cortical representation of the fingers of the left hand in string players. *Science, 270*, 305–307.

Faludi, G., & Mirnics, K. (2011). Synaptic changes in the brain of subjects with schizophrenia. *International Journal of Developmental Neuroscience, 29*, 305–309.

Field, M., & Behrman, R (Eds.). (2004). *Ethical conduct of clinical research involving children*. National Academies Press.

Fisher, R. (1935). *The design of experiments*. Oliver & Boyd.

Galińska-Skok, B., & Waszkiewicz, N. (2022). Markers of schizophrenia—A critical narrative update. *Journal of Clinical Medicine, 11*(14), 3964. https://doi.org/10.3390/jcm11143964

Garrett-Bakelman et al. (2019). The NASA Twins Study: A multidimensional analysis of a year-long human spaceflight. *Science, 364*, 127. https://doi.org/10.1126/science.aau8650

Glasser, R. J. (1976). *The body is the hero*. Random House.

Gottesman, I. (1991). *Schizophrenia genesis: The origin of madness*. Freeman.

Hersen, M., & Bellack, A. S. (1976). A multiple-baseline analysis of social-skills training in chronic schizophrenia. *Journal of Applied Behavior Analysis, 9*(3), 239–245.

James, D. J., & Glaze, L. E. (2006, September). *Mental health problems of prison and jail inmates*. Bureau of Justice Statistics, U.S. Department of Justice. https://bjs.ojp.gov/content/pub/pdf/mhppji.pdf

Kendler, K., Jaffee, S., & Romer, D. (Eds.). (2011). *The dynamic genome and mental health: The role of genes and environments in youth development*, Oxford University Press.

Knopik, V., Neiderhiser, J., DeFries, J., & Plomin, R. (2017). *Behavioral genetics*, (7th ed.).

Lahey, B., & Willcutt, E. (2010). Predictive validity of a continuous alternative to nominal subtypes of attention-deficit hyperactivity disorder for *DSM-V*. *Journal of Clinical Child Adolescence Psychology, 39*, 761–775.

Landis, R. S. (2007). Measures of association/correlation coefficient. In S. G. Rogelberg (Ed.), *Encyclopedia of industrial and organizational psychology* (pp. 471–474), Sage.

Lin, T., Heckman, T. G., & Anderson, T. (2022). The efficacy of synchronous teletherapy versus in-person therapy: A meta-analysis of randomized clinical trials. *Clinical Psychology: Science and Practice, 29*(2), 167–178.

Luria, A. R. (1972). *The man with a shattered world*. Basic Books.

National Institute of Mental Health. (2005). *Generalized anxiety disorder*. U.S. Department of Health and Human Services. http://www.nimh.nih.gov/health/statistics/prevalence/generalized-anxiety-disorder-among-adults.shtml

Olshan, A. F., Diez Roux, A. V., Hatch, M., & Klebanoff, M. A. (2019). Epidemiology: Back to the future. *American Journal of Epidemiology, 188*(5), 814–817. https://doi.org/10.1093/aje/kwz045

Patel, V., Araya, R., Chatterjee, S., Chisholm, D., Cohen, A., De Silva, M., Hosman, C., McGuire, H., Rojas, G., & van Ommeren, M. (2007). Treatment and prevention of mental disorders in low-income and middle-income countries. *The Lancet, 370*(9591), 991–1005. https://www.thelancet.com/article/S0140-6736(07)61240-9/fulltext

Plomin, R. (2018). *Blueprint: How DNA makes us who we are*. MIT Press.

Plomin, R., DeFries, J., & Loehlin, J. (1977). Genotype–environment interaction and correlation in the analysis of human behavior. *Psychological Bulletin, 84*, 309–322.

Polusny, M., Erbes, C., Thuras, P., Moran, A., Lamberty, G. J., Collins, R. C., Rodman, J. L., & Lim, K. O. (2015). Mindfulness-based stress reduction for posttraumatic stress disorder among veterans. *JAMA, 314*(5), 456–465. http://doi.org/10.1001/jama.2015.8361

Prince, M. (1913). *The dissociation of a personality: A biographical study in abnormal psychology*. Longmans, Green.

Raebhausen, O. M., & Brim, O. G. (1967). Privacy and behavioral research. *American Psychologist, 22*, 423–437.

Ratiu, P., Talos, O., Haker, S., Lieberman, D., & Evert, P. (2004). The tale of Phineas Gage, digitally remastered. *Journal of Neurotrauma, 21*, 637–643.

Ray, W. J. (2012). *Methods toward a science of behavior and experience* (10th ed.). Wadsworth.

Ray, W. J. (2022). *Research methods for psychological science*. Sage.

Ray, W. J., Odenwald, M., Neuner, F., Schauer, M., Ruf, M., Wienbruch, C., Rockstroh, B., & Elbert, T. (2006). Decoupling neural networks from reality: Dissociative experiences in torture victims are reflected in abnormal brain waves in left frontal cortex. *Psychological Science, 17*, 825–829. https://journals.sagepub.com/doi/abs/10.1111/j.1467-9280.2006.01788.x

Rockstroh, B., Wienbruch, C., Ray, W. J., & Elbert, T. (2007). Abnormal oscillatory brain dynamics in schizophrenia: A sign of deviant communication in neural network? *BMC Psychiatry, 7*, Article 44

Savage, J. E., Jansen, P. R., Stringer, S., Watanabe, K., Bryois, J., de Leeuw, C. A., Nagel, M., Awasthi, S., Barr, P. B., Coleman, J. R. I., Grasby, K. L., Hammerschlag, A. R., Kaminski, J. A., Karlsson, R., Krapohl, E., Lam, M., Nygaard, M., Reynolds, A. C., Trampush, J. W., . . . Posthuma, D. (2018). Genome-wide association meta-analysis in 269,867 individuals identifies new genetic and functional links to intelligence. *Nature Genetics, 50*, 912–919.

Singh, T., Poterba, T., Curtis, D., Akil, H., Al Eissa, M., Barchas, J. D., Bass, N., Bigdeli, T. B., Breen, G., Bromet, E. J., Buckley, P. F., Bunney, W. E., Bybjerg-Grauholm, J., Byerley, W. F., Chapman, S. B., Chen, W. J., Churchhouse, C., Craddock, N., Cusick, C. M., . . . Daly, M. J. (2022). Rare coding variants in ten genes confer substantial risk for schizophrenia. *Nature, 604*(7906), 509–516. https://doi.org/10.1038/s41586-022-04556-w

Tackett, J. L., Brandes, C. M., King, K. M., & Markon, K. E. (2019). Psychology's replication crisis and clinical psychological science. *Annual Review of Clinical Psychology, 15*, 579–604.

Tomko, R., Brown, W., Tragesser, S., Wood, P., Mehl, M., & Trull, T. (2012). Social context of anger in borderline personality disorder and depressive disorders: Findings from a naturalistic observation study. *Journal of Personality Disorders, 28*(3), 434–438.

Torrey, E. (1994). *Schizophrenia and manic depressive disorder*. Basic Books.

Torrey, E., Kennard, A., Eslinger, D., Lamb, R., & Pavle, J. (2010). *More mentally ill persons are in jails and prisons than hospitals: A survey of the states*. Report for National Sheriffs Association & Treatment Advocacy Center.

Trubetskoy, V., Pardiñas, A. F., Qi, T., Panagiotaropoulou, G., Awasthi, S., Bigdeli, T. B., Bryois, J., Chen, C. Y., Dennison, C. A., Hall, L. S., Lam, M., Watanabe, K., Frei, O., Ge, T., Harwood, J. C., Koopmans, F., Magnusson, S., Richards, A. L., Sidorenko, J., Wu, Y., . . . Schizophrenia Working Group of the Psychiatric Genomics Consortium (2022). Mapping genomic loci implicates genes and synaptic biology in schizophrenia. *Nature, 604*(7906), 502–508. https://doi.org/10.1038/s41586-022-04434-5

Tsuang, M., Cohen, M., & Jones, P. (2011). *Textbook of psychiatric epidemiology* (3rd ed.). Wiley.

Van Horn, J. D., Irimia, A., Torgerson, C. M., Chambers, M. C., Kikinis, R., & Toga, A. (2012). Mapping connectivity damage in the case of Phineas Gage. *PLOS ONE, 7*(5), Article e37454. https://doi.org/10.1371/journal.pone.0037454

Yin, R. (2017). *Case study research and applications: Design and methods*. Sage

CHAPTER 4

American Psychiatric Association. (2022). *Diagnostic and statistical manual of mental disorders*. (5th ed., text rev.)

Andreasen, N. (2001). *Brave new brain*. Oxford University Press.

Beck, A. T., & Beck, R. W. (1972). Screening depressed patients in family practice: A rapid technic. *Postgraduate Medicine, 52*, 81–85.

Ben-Porath, Y. S. (2012). *Interpreting the MMPI-2-RF*. University of Minnesota Press.

Blashfield, R. K., Flanagan, E. H., & Raley, K. (2010). Themes in the evolution of the 20th century *DSMs*. In T. Millon, R. Krueger, & E. Simonsen (Eds.), *Contemporary directions in psychopathology* (2nd ed., pp. 53–71). Guilford Press.

Blashfield, R., & Draguns, J. (1976). Toward a taxonomy of psychopathology: The purpose of psychiatric classification. *British Journal of Psychiatry, 129*, 574–583.

Carhart-Harris, R., & Friston, K. (2010). The default-mode, ego-functions and free- energy: A neurobiological account of Freudian ideas. *Brain, 133*, 1265–1283.

Clark, L. A., Cuthbert, B., Lewis-Fernández, R., Narrow, W. E., & Reed, G. M. (2017). Three approaches to understanding and classifying mental disorder: *ICD-11, DSM-5*, and the National Institute of Mental Health's Research Domain Criteria (RDoC). *Psychological Science in the Public Interest, 18*, 72–145. https://doi.org/10.1177/1529100617727266

Conway, C. C., Forbes, M. K., & South, S. C. (2022). A Hierarchical Taxonomy of Psychopathology (HiTOP) primer for mental health researchers. *Clinical Psychological Science, 10*(2), 236–258.

Cronbach, L. J., & Meehl, P. (1955). Construct validity in psychological tests. *Psychological Bulletin, 52*, 281–302.

Cuthbert, B. N. (2022). Research Domain Criteria (RDoC): Progress and potential. *Current Directions in Psychological Science, 31*(2), 107–114. https://doi.org/10.1177/09637214211051363

Cuthbert, B., & Insel, T. (2010). Classification issues in women's mental health: Clinical utility and etiological mechanisms. *Archives of Women's Mental Health, 12*, 57–59.

Cuthbert, B., & Insel, T. (2013). Towards the future of psychiatric diagnosis: The seven pillars of RDoC. *BMC Medicine, 11*, Article 126.

DeRubeis, R., Siegle, G., & Hollon, S. (2008). Cognitive therapy versus medication for depression: Treatment outcomes and neural mechanisms. *Nature Reviews Neuroscience, 9*, 788–796.

DeYoung, C. G., Kotov, R., Krueger, R. F., Cicero, D. C., Conway, C. C., Eaton, N. R.,
Forbes, M. K., Hallquist, M. N., Jonas, K., Latzman, R. D., Rodriguez-Seijas, C., Ruggero, C. J., Simms, L. J., Waldman, I. D., Waszczuk, M. A., Widiger, T., & Wright, A. G. (2022). Answering questions about the Hierarchical Taxonomy of Psychopathology (HiTOP): Analogies to whales and sharks miss the boat. *Clinical Psychological Science, 10*(2), 279–284.

Draguns, J. (1973). Comparisons for psychopathology across cultures: Issues, findings, directions. *Journal of Cross-Cultural Psychology, 4*, 9–47.

Draguns, J., & Tanaka-Matsumi, J. (2003). Assessment of psychopathology across and within cultures: Issues and findings. *Behavior Research and Therapy, 41*, 755–776.

Ecker, C., Rocha-Rego, V., Johnston, P., Mourao-Miranda, J., Marquand, A., Daly, E. M., Brammer, M. J., Murphy, C., Murphy, D. G., & MRC AIMS Consortium. (2010). Investigating the predictive value of whole-brain structural MR scans in autism: A pattern classification approach. *NeuroImage, 49*, 44–56.

Ellenberger, H. F. (1970). *The discovery of the unconscious: The history and evolution of dynamic psychiatry*. Basic Books.

Erdberg, P. (2019). The Rorschach. In G. Goldstein, D. Allen, & J. DeLuca (Eds.), *Handbook of psychological assessment* (4th ed., pp. 419–432). Academic Press.

Erdelyi, M. (1985). *Psychoanalysis: Freud's cognitive psychology*. Freeman.

Evans, A., & Jackson, V. H. (2009). *Addressing diversity and health disparities in promoting health and wellness*. American College of Mental Health Administration & College for Behavioral Health Leadership. https://www.leaders4health.org/summits/2009-summit/

Exner, J. E. (1986). *The Rorschach: A comprehensive system: Vol. I. Basic foundations* (2nd ed.). Wiley.

Exner, J. E. (2003). *The Rorschach: A comprehensive system* (4th ed.). Wiley.

Forbes, M. K., Greene, A. L., Levin-Aspenson, H. F., Watts, A. L., Hallquist, M., Lahey, B. B., Markon, K. E., Patrick, C. J., Tackett, J. L., Waldman, I. D., Wright, A. G. C., Caspi, A., Ivanova, M., Kotov, R., Samuel, D. B., Eaton, N. R., & Krueger, R. F. (2021). Three recommendations based on a comparison of the reliability and validity of the predominant models used in research on the empirical structure of psychopathology. *Journal of Abnormal Psychology, 130*(3), 297–317. https://doi.org/10.1037/abn0000533

Frances, A. J., & Widiger, T. (2012). Psychiatric diagnosis: Lessons from the *DSM-IV* past and cautions for the *DSM-5* future. *Annual Review of Clinical Psychology, 8*(1), 109–130. http://doi.org/10.1146/annurev-clinpsy-032511-143102

Frick, P. J., Barry, C. T., & Kamphaus, R. W. (2010). *Clinical assessment of child and adolescent personality and behavior*. Springer.

Garb, H. N., Wood, J. M., Lilienfeld, S. O., & Nezworski, M. T. (2005). Roots of the Rorschach controversy. *Clinical Psychology Review, 25*, 97–118.

Giromini, L., Porcelli, P., Viglione, D., Parolin, L., & Pineda, J. (2010). The feeling of movement: EEG evidence for mirroring activity during the observations of static, ambiguous stimuli in the Rorschach cards. *Biological Psychology, 85*, 233–241.

Glannon, W. (2015). Research domain criteria: A final paradigm for psychiatry? *Frontiers in Human Neuroscience, 9*, 8–11. http://doi.org/10.3389/fnhum.2015.00488

Good, M.-J. D., & Hannah, S. D. (2015). "Shattering culture": Perspectives on cultural competence and evidence-based practice in mental health services. *Transcultural Psychiatry, 52*(2), 198–221. http://doi.org/10.1177/1363461514557348

Grob, G. (1991). Origins of *DSM-I*: A study in appearance and reality. *American Journal of Psychiatry, 148*, 421–431.

Hall, J. T., Menton, W. H., & Ben-Porath, Y. S. (2022). Examining the psychometric equivalency of MMPI-3 scale scores derived from the MMPI-3 and the MMPI-2-RF-EX. *Assessment, 29*(4), 842–853.

Halligan, P., & David, A. (2001). Cognitive neuropsychiatry: Towards a scientific psychopathology. *Nature Reviews Neuroscience, 2*, 209–215.

Helms, J. E. (2015). An examination of the evidence in culturally adapted evidence-based or empirically supported interventions. *Transcultural Psychiatry, 52*(2), 174–197. http://doi.org/10.1177/1363461514563642

Henderson, D., Vincenzi, B., Yeung, A., & Fricchione, G. (2016). Culture and psychiatry. In T. A. Stern, M. Fava, T. E. Wilens, & J. F. Rosenbaum (Eds.), *Massachusetts General Hospital comprehensive clinical psychiatry* (2nd ed., pp. 718–725). Elsevier.

Hong, J., Hwang, J., & Lee, J. H. (2023). General psychopathology factor (p-factor) prediction using resting-state functional connectivity and a scanner-generalization neural network. *Journal of Psychiatric Research, 158*, 114–125. https://doi.org/10.1016/j.jpsychires.2022.12.037

Hunsley, J., & Mash, E. (2007). Evidence-based assessment. *Annual Review of Clinical Psychology, 3*, 29–51.

Hyman, S. (2007). Can neuroscience be integrated into the *DSM–V*? *Nature Reviews Neuroscience, 8*, 725–732.

Hyman, S. (2010). The diagnosis of mental disorders: The problem of reification. *Annual Review of Clinical Psychology, 6*, 155–179.

Insel, T. (2009). Translating scientific opportunity into public health impact: A strategic plan for research on mental illness. *Archives of General Psychiatry, 66*, 128–133

Jackson, V. H. (2015). Practitioner characteristics and organizational contexts as essential elements in the evidence-based practice versus cultural competence debate. *Transcultural Psychiatry, 52*(2), 150–173. http://doi.org/10.1177/1363461515571625

James, P. A., Oparil, S., Carter, B. L., Cushman, W. C., Dennison-Himmelfarb, C., Handler, J., Lackland, D. T., LeFevre, M. L., MacKenzie, T. D., Ogedegbe, O., Smith, S. C., Svetky, L. P., Taler, S. J., Townsend, R. R., Wright, J. T., Narva, A. S., & Ortiz, E. (2014). 2014 evidence-based guideline for the management of high blood pressure in adults. *JAMA, 1097*(5), 1–14. http://doi.org/10.1001/jama.2013.284427

Jimura, K., Asari, T., & Nakamura, N. (2021). Can neuroscience provide a new foundation for the Rorschach variables? *Rorschachiana, 42*(2), 143–165.

Kendler, K. S., Jaffee, S., & Romer, D (Eds.). (2011). *The dynamic genome and mental health: The role of genes and environments in youth development.* Oxford University Press.

Kendler, K. S., Neale, M. C., Kessler, R. C., Heath, A. C., & Eaves, L. J. (1992). Major depression and generalized anxiety disorder: Same genes, (partly) different environments? *Archives of General Psychiatry, 49*, 716–722.

Kessler, R. C., McGonagle, K., Zhao, S., Nelson, C. B., Hughes, M., Eshleman, S., Whittchen, H. U., & Kendler, K. S. (1994). Lifetime and 12-month prevalence of *DSM-III-R* psychiatric disorders in the United States. Results from the National Comorbidity Survey. *Archives of General Psychiatry, 51*, 8–19.

Kotov, R., Krueger, R. F., Watson, D., Cicero, D. C., Conway, C. C., DeYoung, C. G., Eaton, N. R., Forbes, M. F., Hallquist, M. N., Latzman, R. D., Mullins-Sweatt, S. N., Ruggero, C. J., Simms, L. J., Waldman, I. D., Waszczuk, M. A., & Wright, A. G. (2021). The Hierarchical Taxonomy of Psychopathology (HiTOP): A quantitative nosology based on consensus of evidence. *Annual Review of Clinical Psychology, 17*, 83–108.

Lahey, B. B., Krueger, R. F., Rathouz, P. J., Waldman, I. D., & Zald, D. H. (2017). A hierarchical causal taxonomy of psychopathology across the life span. *Psychological Bulletin, 143*(2), 142–186. https://doi.org/10.1037/bul0000069

Marsella, A. J., & Yamada, A. M. (2007). Culture and psychopathology: Foundations, issues, and directions. In S. Kitayama & D. Cohen (Eds.), *Handbook of cultural psychology* (pp. 797–818). Guilford Press.

Marshall, M. (2020). Roots of mental illness. *Nature, 581*, 19–21.

Meyer, G. (2001). Introduction to the final special section in the special series on the utility of the Rorschach for clinical assessment. *Psychological Assessment, 13*, 419–422.

Meyer, G., & Archer, R. (2001). The hard science of Rorschach research: What do we know and where do we go? *Psychological Assessment, 13*, 486–502.

Meyer, G., Erdberg, P., & Shaffer, T. (2007). Toward international normative reference data for the comprehensive system. *Journal of Personality Assessment, 89*, S201–S216.

Michelini, G., Palumbo, I. M., DeYoung, C. G., Latzman, R. D., & Kotov, R. (2021). Linking RDoC and HiTOP: A new interface for advancing psychiatric nosology and neuroscience. *Clinical Psychology Review, 86*, Article 102025.

Mihura, J. L., Bombel, G., Dumitrascu, N., Roy, M., & Meadows, E. A. (2019). Why we need a formal systematic approach to validating psychological tests: The case of the Rorschach Comprehensive System. *Journal of Personality Assessment, 101*(4), 374–392.

Mihura, J. L., Meyer, G. J., Dumitrascu, N., & Bombel, G. (2013). The validity of individual Rorschach variables: Systematic reviews and meta-analyses of the comprehensive system. *Psychological Bulletin, 139*(3), 548–605. doi:10.1037/a0029406

Miller, G. (2010). The seductive allure of behavioral epigenetics. *Science, 329*, 24–27.

Mirsky, A., Bieliauskas, L., French, L., Van Kammen, D., Jönsson, E., & Sedvall, G. (2000). A 39-year followup of the Genain quadruplets. *Schizophrenia Bulletin, 26*, 699–708.

National Institute of Mental Health. (n.d.). *About RDoC.* U.S. Department of Health and Human Services. https://www.nimh.nih.gov/research/research-funded-by-nimh/rdoc/about-rdoc

Pittenger, C., & Etkin, A. (2008). Are there biological commonalities among different psychiatric disorders? In A. Tasman, J. Kay, J. A. Lieberman, M. B. First, & M. Maj (Eds.), *Psychiatry* (3rd ed., pp. 245–256). Wiley.

Raj, A., Kuceyeski, A., & Weiner, M. (2012). A network diffusion model of disease progression in dementia. *Neuron, 73*, 1204–1215.

Rocha-Rego, V., Jogia, J., Marquand, A., Mourao-Miranda, J., Simmons, A., & Frangou, S. (2013). Examination of the predictive value of structural magnetic resonance scans in bipolar disorder: A pattern classification approach. *Psychological Medicine, 5*, 1–14.

Russo, S., & Nestler, E. (2013). The brain reward circuitry in mood disorders. *Nature Reviews Neuroscience, 14*, 609–625.

Saks, E. (2007). *The center cannot hold: My journey through madness.* Hyperion.

Sanislow, C., Pine, D., Quinn, K., Kozak, M., Garvey, M., Heinssen, R., Wang, P. S., & Cuthbert, B. N. (2010). Developing constructs for psychopathology research: Research domain criteria. *Journal of Abnormal Psychology, 199*, 631–639.

Scott, L. N., Victor, S. E., Kaufman, E. A., Beeney, J. E., Byrd, A. L., Vine, V., Pilkonis, P. A., & Stepp, S. D. (2020). Affective dynamics across internalizing and externalizing dimensions of psychopathology. *Clinical Psychological Science, 8*(3), 412–427. https://doi.org/10.1177/2167702619898802

Smith, G. T., Atkinson, E. A., Davis, H. A., Riley, E. N., & Oltmanns, J. R. (2020). The general factor of psychopathology. *Annual Review of Clinical Psychology, 16*, 75–98. https://doi.org/10.1146/annurev-clinpsy-071119-115848

Sprooten, E., Franke, B., & Greven, C. U. (2022). The P-factor and its genomic and neural equivalents: An integrated perspective. *Molecular Psychiatry*, *27*(1), 38-48. https://doi.org/10.1038/s41380-021-01031-2

Sumner, J. A., Powers, A., Jovanovic, T., & Koenen, K. C. (2015). Genetic influences on the neural and physiological bases of acute threat: A research domain criteria (RDoC) perspective. *Neuropsychiatric Genetics*, *171*(1), 44-64. http://doi.org/10.1002/ajmg.b.32384

van Graan, L. A. (2021). A commentary on "Can neuroscience provide a new foundation for the Rorschach variables?" (Jimura et al., 2021). *Rorschachiana*, *42*(2), 166-174.

Vargas, S. M., Cabassa, L. J., Nicasio, A., De La Cruz, A. A., Jackson, E., Rosario, M., Guarnaccia, P. J., & Lewis-Fernández, R. (2015). Toward a cultural adaptation of pharmacotherapy: Latino views of depression and antidepressant therapy. *Transcultural Psychiatry*, *52*(2), 244-273. http://doi.org/10.1177/1363461515574159

Weisner, T. S., & Hay, M. C. (2015). Practice to research: Integrating evidence-based practices with culture and context. *Transcultural Psychiatry*, *52*(2), 222-243. http://doi.org/10.1177/1363461514557066

Westen, D., Gabbard, G. O., & Ortigo, K. (2008). Psychoanalytic approaches to personality. In O. John, R. Robins, & L. Pervin (Eds.), *Handbook of personality: Theory and research* (4th ed., pp. 61-113). Guilford Press.

Widiger, T. A. (2021). Alternative models of psychopathology: The *Diagnostic and Statistical Manual of Mental Disorders*, the hierarchical taxonomy of psychopathology, research domain criteria, network analysis, the Cambridge model, and the five-factor model. *Clinical Psychological Science*, *9*(3), 340-342.

Zald, D. H., & Lahey, B. B. (2017). Implications of the hierarchical structure of psychopathology for psychiatric neuroimaging. *Biological Psychiatry: Cognitive Neuroscience and Neuroimaging*, *2*(4), 310-317

CHAPTER 5

Adler, L., Spencer, T., & Wilens, T. (2015). *Attention-deficit hyperactivity disorder in adults and children*. Cambridge University Press.

Adolphs, R. (2003). Cognitive neuroscience of human social behaviour. *Nature Reviews Neuroscience*, *4*, 165-178.

Aguiar, A., Eubig, P., & Schantz, S. (2010). Attention deficit/hyperactivity disorder: A focused overview for children's environmental health researchers. *Environmental Health Perspective*, *118*, 1646-1653.

Ainsworth, M., Blehar, M., Waters, E., & Wall, S. (1978). *Patterns of attachment: A psychological study of the strange situation*. Erlbaum.

Amaral, D., Schumann, C., & Nordahl, C. (2008). Neuroanatomy of autism. *Trends in Neurosciences*, *31*, 137-145.

American, Psychiatric Association. (2022). *Diagnostic and statistical manual of mental disorders* (5th ed., text rev.).

Anastopoulos, A., & Farley, S. (2003). A cognitive-behavioral training program for parents of children with attention-deficit/hyperactivity disorder. In A. Kazdin & J. Weisz (Eds.), *Evidence-based psychotherapies for children and adolescents* (pp. 187-203). Guilford Press.

Arns, M., de Ridder, S., Strehl, U., Breteler, M., & Coenen, A. (2009). Efficacy of neurofeedback treatment in ADHD: The effects on inattention, impulsivity and hyperactivity: A meta-analysis. *Clinical EEG and Neuroscience*, *40*(3), 180-189. http://doi.org/10.1177/155005940904000311

Bardin, J. (2012). Neurodevelopment: Unlocking the brain. *Nature*, *487*, 24-26. https://doi.org/10.1038/487024a

Barker, K., & Galardi, T. R. (2015). Diagnostic domain defense: Autism spectrum disorder and the *DSM-5*. *Social Problems*, *62*(1), 120-140. http://doi.org/10.1093/socpro/spu001

Baron-Cohen, S. (2009). Autism: The empathizing-systemizing (E-S) theory. *Annals of the New York Academy of Science*, *1156*, 68-80.

Baron-Cohen, S., Ashwin, E., Ashwin, C., Tavassoli, T., & Chakrabarti, B. (2008). Talent in autism: Hyper-systemizing, hyper-attention to detail and sensory hypersensitivity. *Philosophical Transactions of the Royal Society B*, *364*, 1377-1383.

Baron-Cohen, S., & Belmonte, M. (2005). Autism: A window onto the development of the social and the analytic brain. *Annual Review of Neuroscience*, *28*, 109-126.

Ben-Ari, Y. (2015). Is birth a critical period in the pathogenesis of autism spectrum disorders? *Nature Reviews Neuroscience*, *16*(8), 498-505. http://doi.org/10.1038/nrn3956

Bick, J., Zhu, T., Stamoulis, C., Fox, N. A., Zeanah, C., & Nelson, C. A. (2015). Effect of early institutionalization and foster care on long-term white matter development. *JAMA Pediatrics*, 1-10. http://doi.org/10.1001/jamapediatrics.2014.3212

Bidwell, L., McClernon, F., & Kolins, S. (2011). Cognitive enhancers for the treatment of ADHD. *Pharmacology, Biochemistry and Behavior*, *99*, 262-274.

Blakemore, S. (2019). The art of medicine: Adolescence and mental health. *The Lancet*, *393*, 2030-2031. https://doi.org/10.1016/S0140-6736(19)31013-X

Blum, D. (2002). *Love at Goon Park: Harry Harlow and the science of affection*. Perseus.

Bonini, L., Rotunno, C., Arcuri, E., & Gallese, V. (2022). Mirror neurons 30 years later: implications and applications. *Trends in Cognitive Sciences*, *26*(9), 767-781. https://doi.org/10.1016/j.tics.2022.06.003

Bouziane, C., Caan, M. W. A., Tamminga, H. G. H., & Schrantee, A. (2018). ADHD and maturation of brain white matter: A DTI study in medication naive children and adults. *NeuroImage: Clinical*, *17*, 53-59. https://doi.org/10.1016/j.nicl.2017.09.026

Bowlby, J. (1951). *Maternal care and mental health*. World Health Organization.

Bowlby, J. (1961). Childhood mourning and its implications for psychiatry. The Adolf Meyer lecture. *American Journal of Psychiatry*, *118*, 481-497.

Bowlby, J. (1969). *Attachment and loss*: Vol. 1. *Attachment*. Hogarth.

Bowlby, J. (1982). Attachment and loss: Retrospect and prospect. *American Journal of Orthopsychiatry*, *52*, 664-678.

Bowlby, J. (1988). *A secure base: Clinical applications of attachment theory*. Routledge.

Boxer, P., & Frick, P. (2008). Treating conduct problems, aggression, and antisocial behavior in children and adolescents: An integrated view. In R. Steele, T. Elkin, & M. Roberts (Eds.), *Handbook of evidence-based therapies for children and adolescents* (pp. 241-260). Springer.

Brinkmeyer, M., & Eyberg, S. M. (2003). Parent-child interaction therapy for oppositional children. In A. E. Kazdin & J. R. Weisz (Eds.), *Evidence-based psychotherapies for children and adolescents* (pp. 204-223). Guilford Press.

Brothers, L. (1990). The social brain: A project for integrating primate behaviour and neurophysiology in a new domain. *Concepts in Neuroscience*, *1*, 27-51.

Burnette, M., & Cicchetti, D. (2012). Multilevel approaches toward understanding antisocial behavior: Current research and future directions. *Development and Psychopathology, 24*, 703–704.

Byrd, A. L., & Manuck, S. B. (2014). MAOA, childhood maltreatment, and antisocial behavior: Meta-analysis of a gene–environment interaction. *Biological Psychiatry, 75*(1), 9–17 doi:10.1016/j.biopsych.2013.05.004

Caspi, A., Hairi, A., Holmes, A., Uher, R., & Mofitt, T. (2010). Genetic sensitivity to the environment: The case of the serotonin transporter gene and its implications for studying complex diseases and traits. *American Journal of Psychiatry, 167*, 509–527.

Caspi, A., McClay, J., Moffitt, T., Mill, J., Martin, J., Craig, I., Taylor, A., & Poulton, R. (2002). Role of genotype in the cycle of violence in maltreated children. *Science, 297*, 851–854.

Castellanos, F., & Proal, E. (2012). Large-scale brain systems in ADHD: Beyond the prefrontal–striatal model. *Trends in Cognitive Science, 16*, 17–26.

Cerliani, L., Mennes, M., Thomas, R. M., Di Martino, A., Thioux, M., & Keysers, C. (2015). Increased functional connectivity between subcortical and cortical resting-state networks in autism spectrum disorder. *JAMA Psychiatry, 72*(8), 767–777. http://doi.org/10.1001/jamapsychiatry.2015.0101

Chang, J., Gilman, S. R., Chiang, A. H., Sanders, S. J., & Vitkup, D. (2015). Genotype to phenotype relationships in autism spectrum disorders. *Nature Neuroscience, 18*(2), 191–198. https://doi.org/10.1038/nn.3907

Chartrand, T. L., & Bargh, J. A. (1999). The chameleon effect: The perception–behavior link and social interaction. *Journal of Personality and Social Psychology, 76*, 893–910.

Chein, J., Albert, D., O'Brien, L., Uckert, K., & Steinberg, L. (2011). Peers increase adolescent risk taking by enhancing activity in the brain's reward circuitry. *Developmental Science, 14*, F1–F10.

Chen, H., Wang, J., Uddin, L. Q., Wang, X., Guo, X., Lu, F., Duan, X., Wu, L., & Chen, H. (2018). Aberrant functional connectivity of neural circuits associated with social and sensorimotor deficits in young children with autism spectrum disorder. *Autism Research, 11*(12), 1643–1652. https://doi.org/10.1002

Chisholm, K., Lin, A., Abu-Akel, A., & Wood, S. J. (2015). The association between autism and schizophrenia spectrum disorders: A review of eight alternate models of co-occurrence. *Neuroscience & Biobehavioral Reviews, 55*, 173–183. http://doi.org/10.1016/j.neubiorev.2015.04.012

Christakis, D. (2016). Rethinking attention-deficit/hyperactivity disorder. *JAMA Pediatrics, 170*, 109–110.

Coleman, M., & Gillberg, C. (2012). *The autisms* (4th ed.). Oxford University Press.

Costanzo, V., Chericoni, N., Amendola, F. A., Casula, L., Muratori, F., Scattoni, M. L., & Apicella, F. (2015). Early detection of autism spectrum disorders: From retrospective home video studies to prospective "high risk" sibling studies. *Neuroscience & Biobehavioral Reviews, 55*, 627–635. http://doi.org/10.1016/j.neubiorev.2015.06.006

Dapretto, M., Davies, M., Pfeifer, J., Scott, A., Sigman, M., Bookheimer, S., & Iacoboni, M. (2006). Understanding emotions in other: Mirror neuron dysfunction in children with autism spectrum disorder. *Nature Neuroscience, 8*, 781–789.

Dawson, G., Sterling, L., & Faja, S. (2009). Autism. In M. De Haan & M. Gunnar (Eds.), *Handbook of developmental social neuroscience* (pp. 435–458). Guilford Press.

Dawson, M., Soulières, I., Gernsbacher, M., & Mottron, L. (2007). The level and nature of autistic intelligence. *Psychological Science, 18*, 657–662.

DeKlyen, M., & Greenberg, M. (2008). Attachment and psychopathology in childhood. In J. Cassidy & P. Shaver (Eds.), *Handbook of attachment: Theory, research, and clinical applications* (2nd ed., pp. 637–665). Guilford Press.

Dozier, M., Stovall-McClough, K., & Albus, K. (2008). Attachment and psychopathology in adulthood. In J. Cassidy & P. Shaver (Eds.), *Handbook of attachment: Theory, research, and clinical applications* (2nd ed., pp. 461–489). Guilford Press.

Duan, K., Chen, J., Calhoun, V. D., Lin, D., Jiang, W., Franke, B., Buitelaar, J., Hoogman, M., Arias-Vasquez, A., Turner, J., & Liu, J. (2018). Neural correlates of cognitive function and symptoms in attention-deficit/hyperactivity disorder in adults. *NeuroImage: Clinical, 19*, 374–383. https://doi.org/10.1016/j.nicl.2018.04.035

Dykens, E., & Hodapp, R. (2001). Research in mental retardation: Toward an etiologic approach. *Journal of Child Psychology and Psychiatry, 42*, 49–71.

Edwards, F., Wakefield, S., Healy, K., & Wildeman, C. (2021). Contact with Child Protective Services is pervasive but unequally distributed by race and ethnicity in large US counties. *Proceedings of the National Academy of Sciences of the United States of America, 118*(30), Article e2106272118. https://doi.org/10.1073/pnas.2106272118

Elsabbagh, M., Mercure, E., Hudry, K., Chandler, S., Pasco, G., Charman, T., Pickles, A., Baron-Cohen, S., Bolton, P., Johnson, M., & BASIS, Team. (2012). Infant neural sensitivity to dynamic eye gaze is associated with later emerging autism. *Current Biology, 22*, 338–342.

Ernst, M., Torrisi, S., Balderston, N., Grillon, C., & Hale, E. A. (2014). fMRI functional connectivity applied to adolescent neurodevelopment. *Annual Review of Clinical Psychology, 11*(1), 361–377. http://doi.org/10.1146/annurev-clinpsy-032814-112753

Fairchild, G., Hawes, D. J., Frick, P. J., Copeland, W. E., Odgers, C. L., Franke, B., Freitag, C. M., & De Brito, S. A. (2019). Conduct disorder. *Nature Reviews Disease Primers, 5*(1). https://doi.org/10.1038/s41572-019-0095-y

Fairchild, G., Passamonti, L., Hurford, G., Hagan, C., von dem, Hagen., E., van Goozen, S, Goodyer, I., & Calder, A. (2011). Brain structure abnormalities in early-onset and adolescent-onset conduct disorder. *American Journal of Psychiatry, 168*, 624–633.

Fredriksen, M., Halmøy, A., Faraone, S., & Haavik, J. (2013). Long-term efficacy and safety of treatment with stimulants and atomoxetine in adult ADHD: A review of controlled and naturalistic studies. *European Neuropsychopharmacology, 23*, 508–527.

Frick, P., & Nigg, J. (2012). Current issues in the diagnosis of attention deficit hyperactivity disorder, oppositional defiant disorder, and conduct disorder. *Annual Review of Clinical Psychology, 8*, 77–107.

Friedman, N., Politte, L., Nowinski, L., & McDougle, C. (2015). Autism spectrum disorder. In A. Tasman, J. Kay, J. Lieberman, M. First, & M. Riba (Eds.), *Psychiatry* (4th ed., pp. 722–747). Wiley.

Frith, U., Happé, F., Amarakm, D., & Warren, S. (2013). Autism and other neurodevelopmental disorders affecting cognition. In E. Kandel, J. Schwartz, T. Jessell, S. Siegelbaum, & A. Hudspeth (Eds.), *Principles of neural science* (5th ed., pp. 1425–1440). McGraw-Hill.

Galván, A. (2013). The teenage brain: Sensitivity to rewards. *Current Directions in Psychological Science, 22*, 88–93.

Geschwind, D. (2009). Advances in autism. *Annual Review of Medicine, 60*, 367–380.

Gonzalez-Liencres, C., Shamay-Tsoory, S., & Brüne, M. (2013). Towards a neuroscience of empathy: Ontogeny, phylogeny, brain mechanisms, context and psychopathology. *Neuroscience and Biobehavioral Research, 37*, 1537–1548.

Grandin, T. (2009). How does visual thinking work in the mind of a person with autism? A personal account. *Philosophical Transactions of the Royal Society B, 364*, 1437–1442.

Grandin, T. (2010). *Thinking in pictures: My life with autism* (Expanded ed.). Vintage Books.

Hart, H., Radua, J., Nakao, T., Mataix-Cols, D., & Rubia, K. (2013). Meta-analysis of functional magnetic resonance imaging studies of inhibition and attention in attention-deficit/hyperactivity disorder. *JAMA Psychiatry, 70*, 185–198.

Heyes, C., & Catmur, C. (2022). What happened to mirror neurons? *Perspectives on Psychological Science, 17*(1), 153–168. https://doi.org/10.1177/1745691621990638

Hickman, R. A., O'Shea, S. A., Mehler, M. F., & Chung, W. K. (2022). Neurogenetic disorders across the lifespan: From aberrant development to degeneration. *Nature Reviews Neurology, 18*(2), 117–124. https://doi.org/10.1038/s41582-021-00595-5

Hinshaw, S. P. (2018). Attention deficit hyperactivity disorder (ADHD): Controversy, developmental mechanisms, and multiple levels of analysis. *Annual Review of Clinical Psychology, 14*, 291–316.

Hodges, H., Fealko, C., & Soares, N. (2020). Autism spectrum disorder: Definition, epidemiology, causes, and clinical evaluation. *Translational Pediatrics, 9*(Suppl. 1), S55–S65. https://doi.org/10.21037/tp.2019.09.09

Hodgson, H. (2004). A statement by The Royal Free and University College Medical School and The Royal Free Hampstead NHS Trust. *The Lancet, 363*, 824. http://doi.org/10.1016/S0140-6736(04)15711-5

Holtmann, M., Sonuga-Barke, E., Cortese, S., & Brandeis, D. (2014). Neurofeedback for ADHD: A review of current evidence. *Child and Adolescent Psychiatric Clinics of North America, 23*(4), 789–806. http://doi.org/10.1016/j.chc.2014.05.006

Hoza, B., Kaiser, N., & Hurt, E. (2008). Evidence-based treatments for attention-deficit/hyperactivity disorder (ADHD). In R. Steele, T. Elkin, & M. Roberts (Eds.), *Handbook of evidence-based therapies for children and adolescents: Bridging science and practice* (pp. 197–219). Springer.

Humphreys, K. L., Guyon-Harris, K. L., Tibu, F., Wade, M., Nelson, C. A., Fox, N. A., & Zeanah, C. H. (2020). Psychiatric outcomes following severe deprivation in early childhood: Follow-up of a randomized controlled trial at age 16. *Journal of Consulting and Clinical Psychology, 88*(12), 1079–1090. https://doi.org/10.1037/ccp0000613

Hyman, S., & Cohen, J. (2013). Disorders of thought and volition: Schizophrenia. In E. Kandel, J. Schwartz, T. Jessell, S. Siegelbaum, & A. Hudspeth (Eds.), *Principles of neural science* (5th ed., chap. 62). McGraw-Hill. https://neurology.mhmedical.com/content.aspx?bookid=1049&sectionid=59138698

Iacoboni, M. (2009). Imitation, empathy, and mirror neurons. *Annual Review of Psychology, 60*, 653–670.

Jabr, F. (2012, January 30). *By the numbers: Autism is not a math problem. Scientific American.* www.scientificamerican.com/article/autism-math-problem/

Jolles, D. D., van Buchem, M. A., Crone, E. A., & Rombouts, S. A. (2011). A comprehensive study of whole-brain functional connectivity in children and young adults. *Cerebral Cortex, 21*, 385–391.

Jones, E. J. H., Gliga, T., Bedford, R., Charman, T., & Johnson, M. H. (2014). Developmental pathways to autism: A review of prospective studies of infants at risk. *Neuroscience and Biobehavioral Reviews, 39*, 1–33. https://doi.org/10.1016/j.neubiorev.2013.12.001

Kaczkurkin, A. N., Raznahan, A., & Satterthwaite, T. D. (2019). Sex differences in the developing brain: insights from multimodal neuroimaging. *Neuropsychopharmacology, 44*(1), 71–85. https://doi.org/10.1038/s41386-018-0111-z

Kamio, Y., Tobimatsu, S., & Fukui, H. (2011). Developmental disorders. In J. Decety & J. Cacioppo (Eds.), *The handbook of social neuroscience* (pp. 848–858). Oxford University Press.

Kanner, L. (1943). Autistic disturbances of affective contact. *Nervous Child, 2*, 217–250.

Kazdin, A. E. (2005). *Parent management training: Treatment for oppositional, aggressive, and antisocial behavior in children and adolescents*. Oxford University Press.

Kazdin, A. E. (2018). Developing treatments for antisocial behavior among children: Controlled trials and uncontrolled tribulations. *Perspectives on Psychological Science, 13*, 634–650. https://doi.org/10.1177/1745691618767880

Kessler, R. C., Green, J. G., Gruber, M. J., Sampson, N. A., Bromet, E., Cuitan, M., Furukawa, T. A., Gureje, O., Hinkov, H., Hu, C.-Y., Lara, C., Lee, S., Mneimneh, A., Myer, L., Oakley-Browne, M., Posada-Villa, J., Sagar, R., Viana, M. C., & Zaslavsky, A. M. (2010). Screening for serious mental illness in the general population with the K6 screening scale: Results from the WHO World Mental Health (WMH) survey initiative. *International Journal of Methods in Psychiatric Research, 19*(S1), 4–22.

Klin, A., Shultz, S., & Jones, W. (2014). Social visual engagement in infants and toddlers with autism: Early developmental transitions and a model of pathogenesis. *Neuroscience & Biobehavioral Reviews, 50*, 189–203. http://doi.org/10.1016/j.neubiorev.2014.10.006

Konrad, K., & Eickhoff, S. B. (2010). Is the ADHD brain wired differently? A review on structural and functional connectivity in attention deficit hyperactivity disorder. *Human Brain Mapping, 31*(6), 904–916. http://doi.org/10.1002/hbm.21058

Kushak, R. I., & Winter, H. S. (2018). Intestinal microbiota, metabolome and gender dimorphism in autism spectrum disorders. *Research in Autism Spectrum Disorders, 49*, 65–74. https://doi.org/10.1016/j.rasd.2018.01.009

Lagercrantz, H., & Slotkin, T. (1986). The "stress" of being born can be important to the neonate's survival outside the womb. *Scientific American, 254*, 100–107.

Lahey, B., Rathouz, P., Applegate, B., Hulle, C., Garriock, H., Urbano, R., & Waldman, I. (2008). Testing structural models of DSM-IV symptoms of common forms of child and adolescent psychopathology. *Journal of Abnormal Child Psychology, 36*, 187–206.

Lahey, B., Van Hulle, C., Singh, A., Waldman, I., & Rathouz, P. (2011). Higher-order genetic and environmental structure of prevalent forms of child and adolescent psychopathology. *Archives of General Psychiatry, 68*, 181–189.

Lahey, B., & Waldman, I. (2012). Phenotypic and causal structure of conduct disorder in the broader context of prevalent forms of psychopathology. *Journal of Child Psychology and Psychiatry, 53*, 536–557.

Lamblin, M., Murawski, C., Whittle, S., & Fornito, A. (2017). Social connectedness, mental health and the adolescent brain. *Neuroscience and Biobehavioral Reviews, 80*, 57–68. https://doi.org/10.1016/j.neubiorev.2017.05.010

Layton, T. J., Barnett, M. L., Hicks, T. R., & Jena, A. B. (2018). Attention deficit–hyperactivity disorder and month of school enrollment. *New England Journal of Medicine, 379*, 2122–2130. https://doi.org/10.1056/NEJMoa1806828

Leung, A., & Lemay, J. (2004). Infantile colic: A review. *Journal of the Royal Society for the Promotion of Health, 124*, 162–166.

Lewis, M., & Rudolph, K (Eds.). (2014). *Handbook of developmental psychopathology*. Springer.

Lichtenstein, P., Carlstrom, E., Råstam, M., Gillberg, C., & Anckarsäter, H. (2010). The genetics of autism spectrum disorders and related neuropsychiatric disorders in childhood. *Archives of General Psychiatry, 167*, 1357–1363.

Logue, S., Chein, J., Gould, T., Holliday, E., & Steinberg, L. (2014). Adolescent mice, unlike adults, consume more alcohol in the presence of peers than alone. *Developmental Science, 17*(1), 79–85. http://doi.org/10.1111/desc.12101

Lombardo, M., Chakrabarti, B., Bullmore, E., Sadk, S., Pasco, G., Wheelwright, S., Suckling, J., MRC AIMS, Consortium., & Baron-Cohen, S. (2010). Atypical neural self-representation in autism. *Brain, 133*, 611–624.

Lord, C., & Bishop, S. L. (2015). Recent advances in autism research as reflected in *DSM*-5 criteria for autism spectrum disorder. *Annual Review of Clinical Psychology, 11*(1), 150112144717005. http://doi.org/10.1146/annurev-clinpsy-032814-112745

Lovaas, O., & Smith, T. (2003). Early and intensive behavioral intervention in autism. In A. Kazdin & J. Weisz (Eds.), *Evidence-based psychotherapies for children and adolescents* (pp. 325–340). Guilford Press.

Main, M., & Solomon, J. (1990). Procedures for identifying infants as disorganized/disoriented during the Ainsworth strange situation. In M. Greenberg, D. Cicchetti, & E. M. Cummings (Eds.), *Attachment in the preschool years: Theory, research and intervention* (pp. 121–160). University of Chicago Press.

Markon, K. E., & Krueger, R. F. (2005). Categorical and continuous models of liability to externalizing disorders: A direct comparison in NESARC. *Archives of General Psychiatry, 62*, 1352–1359.

Martinez, R., & Nellis, L. (2020). Learning disorders of childhood and adolescence. In J. E. Maddux & B. A. Winstead (Eds.), *Psychopathology* (5th ed., pp. 482–493). Routledge.

Maxwell, R., Merckelbach, H., Lilienfeld, S., & Lynn, S. (2018). The treatment of dissociation. In D. David, S. Lynn, & G. Montgomery (Eds.), *Evidence-based psychotherapy: The state of science and practice* (pp. 329–361). Wiley Blackwell.

Mayes, S. D., Calhoun, S. L., Murray, M. J., Pearl, A., Black, A., & Tierney, C. D. (2014). Final *DSM*-5 under-identifies mild autism spectrum disorder: Agreement between the *DSM*-5, CARS, CASD, and clinical diagnoses. *Research in Autism Spectrum Disorders, 8*(2), 68–73. http://doi.org/10.1016/j.rasd.2013.11.002

McLaughlin, K. A., Greif-Green, J., Gruber, M. J., Sampson, N. A., Zaslavsky, A. M., & Kessler, R. C. (2012). Childhood adversities and first onset of psychiatric disorders in a national sample of U.S. adolescents. *Archives of General Psychiatry, 69*, 1151–1160.

McLaughlin, K. A., Sheridan, M. A., Tibu, F., Fox, N. A., Zeanah, C. H., & Nelson, C. A. (2015). Causal effects of the early caregiving environment on development of stress response systems in children. *Proceedings of the National Academy of Sciences, 112*(18), 5637–5642. http://doi.org/10.1073/pnas.1423363112

McMahon, R. J., & Kotler, J. S. (2008). Evidence-based therapies for oppositional behavior in young children. In R. G. Steele, T. D. Elkin, & M. C. Roberts (Eds.), *Handbook of evidence-based therapies for children and adolescents* (pp. 221–240). Springer.

Mefford, H., Batshaw, M., & Hoffman, E. (2012). Genomics, intellectual disability, and autism. *New England Journal of Medicine, 366*, 733–743.

Miguel, P. M., Pereira, L. O., Silveira, P. P., & Meaney, M. J. (2019). Early environmental influences on the development of children's brain structure and function. *Developmental Medicine and Child Neurology, 61*(10), 1127–1133. https://doi.org/10.1111/dmcn.14182

Mikulincer, M., & Shaver, P. R. (2012). An attachment perspective on psychopathology. *World Psychiatry, 11*(1), 11–5.

Minichino, A., & Cadenhead, K. (2017). Mirror neurons in psychiatric disorders: From neuroception to bio-behavioral system dysregulation. *Neuropsychopharmacology Reviews, 42*, 366. https://doi.org/10.1038/npp.2016.220

Minshew, N., & Williams, D. (2007). The new neurobiology of autism. *Archives of Neurology, 64*, 945–950.

Moffitt, T. E. (1993). Adolescence-limited and life-course–persistent antisocial behavior: A developmental taxonomy. *Psychological Review, 100*, 674–701.

Moffitt, T. E., Houts, R., Asherson, P., Belsky, D. W., Corcoran, D. L., Hammerle, M., Harrington, H., Hogan, S., Meier, M., Polanczyk, G., Poulton, R., Ramrakha, S., Sugden, K., Williams, B., Rohde, L. A., & Caspi, A. (2015). Is adult ADHD a childhood-onset neurodevelopmental disorder? Evidence from a four-decade longitudinal cohort study. *American Journal of Psychiatry, 172*(10), 967–977. http://doi.org/10.1176/appi.ajp.2015.14101266

Moffitt, T. E., & Scott, S. (2008). Conduct disorders of childhood and adolescence. In M. Rutter, D. V. M. Bishop, D. S. Pine, S. Scott, J. Stevenson, E. Taylor, & A. Thapar (Eds.), *Rutter's child and adolescent psychiatry* (5th ed., pp. 543–564). Blackwell.

Monastra, V. J., Lynn, S., Linden, M., Lubar, J. F., Gruzelier, J., & LaVaque, T. J. (2005). Electroencephalographic biofeedback in the treatment of attention-deficit/hyperactivity disorder. *Applied Psychophysiology and Biofeedback, 30*(2), 95–114. https://doi.org/10.1300/J184v09n04_02

Moseley, R. L., Ypma, R. J. F., Holt, R. J., Floris, D., Chura, L. R., Spencer, M. D., Baron-Cohen, S., Suckling, J., Bullmore, E., & Rubinov, M. (2015). Whole-brain functional hypoconnectivity as an endophenotype of autism in adolescents. *NeuroImage: Clinical, 9*, 140–152. http://doi.org/10.1016/j.nicl.2015.07.015

Müller, R., & Fishman, I. (2018). Brain connectivity and neuroimaging of social networks in autism. *Trends in Cognitive Sciences, 22*(12), 1103–1116. doi.org/10.1016/j.tics.2018.09.008

National Center for Education Statistics. (2022). *Students with disabilities*. U.S. Department of Education, Institute of Education Sciences. https://nces.ed.gov/programs/coe/indicator/cgg

Nelson, C. A., Fox, N. A., & Zeanah, C. H. (2014). *Romania's abandoned children: Deprivation, brain development, and the struggle for recovery*. Harvard University Press.

Nelson, E., Leibenluft, E., McClure, E., & Pine, D. (2005). The social re-orientation of adolescence: A neuroscience perspective on the process and its relation to psychopathology. *Psychological Medicine, 35*, 163–174.

Newcorn, J. H., Ivanov, I., & Chacko, A. (2015). Recent progress in psychosocial and psychopharmacologic treatments for ADHD. *Current Treatment Options in Psychiatry, 2*, 14-27. http://doi.org/10.1007/s40501-015-0030-0

Newschaffer, C., Croen, L., Daniels, J., Giarelli, E., Grether, J., Levy, S., Mandell, D., Miller, L., Pinto-Martin, J., Reaven, J., Reynolds, A., Rice, C., Schendel, D., & Windham, G. (2007). The epidemiology of autism spectrum disorders. *Annual Review of Public Health, 28*, 235-258.

Nilsson, K. W., Åslund, C., Comasco, E., & Oreland, L. (2018). Gene-environment interaction of monoamine oxidase A in relation to antisocial behaviour: Current and future directions. *Journal of Neural Transmission, 125*, 1601-1626. https://doi.org/10.1007/s00702-018-1892-2

O'Connor, E., Bureau, J.-F., McCartney, K., & Lyons-Ruth, K. (2011). Risks and outcomes associated with disorganized/controlling patterns of attachment at age three in the NICHD Study of Early Child Care and Youth Development. *Infant Mental Health Journal, 32*, 450-472.

Passamonti, L., Fairchild, G., Goodyer, I. M., Hurford, G., Hagan, C. C., Rowe, J. B., & Calder, A. J. (2010). Neural abnormalities in early-onset and adolescence-onset conduct disorder. *Archives of General Psychiatry, 67*, 729-738.

Paus, T., Keshavan, M., & Giedd, J. (2008). Why do many psychiatric disorders emerge during adolescence? *Nature Reviews Neuroscience, 9*, 947-957.

Pechtel, P., & Pizzagalli, D. (2011). Effects of early life stress on cognitive and affective function: An integrated review of human literature. *Psychopharmacology, 214*, 55-70.

Pelphrey, K. A., & Carter, E. J. (2008). Brain mechanisms for social perception. *Annals of the New York Academy of Sciences, 1145*, 283-299.

Pelphrey, K. A., & McPartland, J. C. (2012). Brain development: Neural signature predicts autism's emergence. *Current Biology, 22*(4), R127-R128.

Pelphrey, K. A., Sasson, J. J., Reznick, J. S., Paul, G., Goldman, B., & Piven, J. (2002). Visual scanning of faces in autism. *Journal of Autism and Developmental Disorders, 32*(4), 249-261.

Pollok, T. M., Kaiser, A., Kraaijenvanger, E. J., Monninger, M., Brandeis, D., Banaschewski, T., Eickhoff, S. B., & Holz, N. E. (2022, April). Neurostructural traces of early life adversities: A meta-analysis exploring age-and adversity-specific effects. *Neuroscience & Biobehavioral Reviews, 135*, Article 104589.

Rizzolatti, G., & Craighero, L. (2004). The mirror-neuron system. *Annual Review of Neuroscience, 27*, 169-192.

Rizzolatti, G., & Fabbri-Destro, M. (2010). Mirror neurons: From discovery to autism. *Experimental Brain Research, 200*(3-4), 223-237. http://doi.org/10.1007/s00221-009-2002-3

Robison, J. (2007). *Look me in the eye: My life with Asperger's*. Crown.

Rogers, S., & Vismara, L. (2008). Evidence-based comprehensive treatments for early autism. *Journal of Clinical Child & Adolescent Psychology, 37*, 8-38.

Rozenkrantz, L., Zachor, D., Heller, I., Plotkin, A., Weissbrod, A., Snitz, K., Secundo, L., & Sobel, N. (2015). A mechanistic link between olfaction and autism spectrum disorder. *Current Biology, 25*(14), 1904-1910. http://doi.org/10.1016/j.cub.2015.05.048

Sacco, R., Gabriele, S., & Persico, A. M. (2015). Head circumference and brain size in autism spectrum disorder: A systematic review and meta-analysis. *Psychiatry Research: Neuroimaging, 234*(2), 239-251. http://doi.org/10.1016/j.pscychresns.2015.08.016

Selfe, L. (2011). *Nadia revisited*. Psychology Press.

Serra, D., Almeida, L. M., & Dinis, T. C. P. (2019). Polyphenols as food bioactive compounds in the context of autism spectrum disorders: A critical mini-review. *Neuroscience and Biobehavioral Reviews, 102*, 290-298. https://doi.org/10.1016/j.neubiorev.2019.05.010

Shapiro, B. K., & Batshaw, M. L. (2011). Intellectual disability. In R. M. Kliegman, R. E. Behrman, H. B. Jenson, & B. F. Stanton (Eds.), *Nelson textbook of pediatrics* (19th ed., chap. 33). Saunders Elsevier.

Sharon, G., Cruz, N. J., Kang, D., Gandal, M. J., Wang, B., Kim, Y.-M., Zink, E. M., Casey, C. P., Taylor, B. C., Lane, C. J., Bramer, L. M., Isern, N. G., Hoyt, D. W., Noecker, C., Sweredoski, M. J., Moradian, A., Borenstein, E., Jansson, J. K., Knight, R., & Mazmanian, S. K. (2019). Human gut microbiota from autism spectrum disorder promote behavioral symptoms in mice. *Cell, 177*, 1600-1618. https://doi.org/10.1016/j.cell.2019.05.004

Sharp, S. I., McQuillin, A., & Gurling, H. M. D. (2009). Genetics of attention-deficit hyperactivity disorder (ADHD). *Neuropharmacology, 57*(7-8), 590-600. http://doi.org/10.1016/j.neuropharm.2009.08.011

Sheridan, M. A., Fox, N. A., Zeanah, C. H., McLaughlin, K. A., & Nelson, C. A. (2012). Variation in neural development as a result of exposure to institutionalization early in childhood. *Proceedings of the National Academy of Sciences, 109*(32), 12927-12932. http://doi.org/10.1073/pnas.1200041109

Sigman, M., Spence, S., & Wang, A. (2006). Autism from developmental and neuropsychological perspectives. *Annual Review of Clinical Psychology, 2*, 327-355.

Sinigaglia, C., & Rizzolatti, G. (2011). Through the looking glass: Self and others. *Consciousness and Cognition, 20*, 64-74.

Slopen, N., McLaughlin, K., Fox, N., Zeanah, C., & Nelson, C. (2012). Alterations in neural processing and psychopathology in children raised in institutions. *Archives of General Psychiatry, 69*, 1022-1030. http://doi.org/10.1001/archgenpsychiatry.2012.444

South, M., Ozonoff, S., & Schultz, R. (2008). Neurocognitive development in autism. In C. Nelson & M. Luciana (Eds.), *Handbook of developmental cognitive neuroscience* (2nd ed., pp. 701-715). MIT Press.

Spalletta, G., Janiri, D., Piras, F., & Sani, G (Eds.). (2020). *Childhood trauma in mental disorders: a comprehensive approach*. Springer.

Sporns, O. (2011). *Networks of the brain*. MIT Press.

Sturman, D. A., & Moghaddam, B. (2011). The neurobiology of adolescents: Changes in brain architecture, functional dynamics, and behavioral tendencies. *Neuroscience and Behavioral Reviews, 35*, 1704-1712.

Takeda, T., Ambrosini, P., deBerardinis, R., & Elia, J. (2012). What can ADHD without comorbidity teach us about comorbity? *Research in Developmental Disabilities, 33*, 419-425.

Tasman, A., Kay, J., Lieberman, J. A., First, M. B., & Maj, M (Eds.). (2008). *Psychiatry* (3rd ed.). Wiley.

Tau, G., & Peterson, B. (2010). Normal development of brain circuits. *Neuropsychopharmacology Reviews, 35*, 147-168.

Tincani, M., & Bondy, A. (2014). *Autism spectrum disorders in adolescents and adults*. Guilford Press.

Treffert, D. (2009). The savant syndrome: An extraordinary condition. A synopsis: Past, present, future. *Philosophical

Transactions of the Royal Society of London, B, 364, 1351–1357.

Van Ewijk, H., Heslenfeld, D., Zwiers, M., Buitelaar, J., & Oosterlaan, J. (2011). Diffusion tensor imaging in attention deficit/hyperactivity disorder: A systematic review and meta-analysis. Neuroscience and Biobehavioral Reviews, 36, 1093–1106.

Vuong, H. E., & Hsiao, E. Y. (2017). Review emerging roles for the gut microbiome in autism spectrum disorder. Biological Psychiatry, 81(5), 411–423. https://doi.org/10.1016/j.biopsych.2016.08.024

Wakefield, A., Murch, S., Anthony, A., Linnell, J., Casson, D., Malik, M., Berelowitz, M., Dhillon, A., Thomson, M., Harvey, P., Valentine, A., Davies, S., & Walker-Smith, J. (1998). Retracted: Ileal-lymphoid-nodular hyperplasia, non-specific colitis, and pervasive developmental disorder in children. The Lancet, 351(9103), 637–641. http://doi.org/10.1016/S0140-6736(97)11096-0

Walsh, P., Elsabbagh, M., Bolton, P., & Singh, I. (2011). In search of biomarkers for autism: Scientific, social and ethical challenges. Nature Reviews Neuroscience, 20, 603–612.

Wang, L., Zhu, C., He, Y., Zang, Y., Cao, Q., Zhang, H., Zhong, Q., & Wang, Y. (2009). Altered small-world brain functional networks in children with attention-deficit/hyperactivity disorder. Human Brain Mapping, 30, 638–649.

Warrier, V., Zhang, X., Reed, P., Havdahl, A., Moore, T. M., Cliquet, F., Leblond, C. S., Rollanc, T., Rosengren, A., EU-AIMS LEAP, iPSYCH-Autism Working Group, Spectrum 10K and APEX Consortia, Rowitch, D. H., Hurles, M. E., Geschwind, D. H., Børglum, A. D., Robinson, E. B., Grove, J., Martin, H. C., Bourgeron, T., . . . Baron-Cohen, S. (2022). EU-AIMS LEAP, iPSYCH-Autism Working Group, Spectrum 10K. Nature Genetics, 54(9), 1293–1304. https://doi.org/10.1038/s41588-022-01072-5

Waterhouse, L. (2012). Rethinking autism. Academic Press.

Watson, S. M. R., Richels, C., Michalek, A. P., & Raymer, A. (2015). Psychosocial treatments for ADHD: A systematic appraisal of the evidence. Journal of Attention Disorders, 19(1), 3–10. http://doi.org/10.1177/1087054712447857

Whelan, R., Conrod, P. J., Polines, J.-B., Lourdusamy, A., Banaschewski, T., Barker, G. J., Bellgrove, M. A., Büchel, C., Byrne, M., Cummins, T. D. R., Fauth-Bühler, M., Flor, H., Gallinat, J., Heinz, A., Ittermann, B., Mann, K., Martinot, J.-L., Lalor, E. C., Lathrop, M., . . . The IMAGEN Consortium. (2012). Adolescent impulsivity phenotypes characterized by distinct brain networks. Nature Neuroscience, 15, 920–927.

Whitaker, K. J., Vértes, P. E., Romero-Garcia, R., Moutoussis, M., & Prabhu, G. (2016). Adolescence is associated with genomically patterned consolidation of the hubs of the human brain connectome. PNAS, 113(32), 9105–9110. https://doi.org/10.1073/pnas.1601745113

Wicker, B., & Gomot, M. (2011). The Asperger syndrome. In J. Decety & J. Cacioppo (Eds.), The Oxford handbook of social neuroscience. Oxford University Press.

Wilens, T., Biederman, J., & Spencer, T. (2002). Attention deficit/hyperactivity disorder across the lifespan. Annual Review of Medicine, 53, 113–131.

Williams, J. H. G., Whiten, A., Suddendorf, T., & Perrett, D. I. (2001). Imitation, mirror neurons and autism. Neuroscience and Biobehavioral Reviews, 25, 287–295.

Wolosin, S., Richardson, M., Hennessey, J., Denckla, M., & Mostofsky, S. (2009). Abnormal cerebral cortex structure in children with ADHD. Human Brain Mapping, 30, 175–184.

Yang, Y., Tian, J., & Yang, B. (2018). Targeting gut microbiome: A novel and potential therapy for autism. Life Sciences, 194, 111–119. https://doi.org/10.1016/j.lfs.2017.12.027

Zeanah, C. H., & Gleason, M. M. (2010). Reactive attachment disorder: A review for DSM–V. Report presented to the American Psychiatric Association, Washington, DC.

Zeanah, C. H., & Gleason, M. M. (2015). Annual research review: Attachment disorders in early childhood—Clinical presentation, causes, correlates, and treatment. Journal of Child Psychology and Psychiatry, 56(3), 207–222. doi:10.1111/jcpp.12347

Zeanah, C. H., Smyke, A. T., Koga, S. F., Carlson, E., & The Bucharest Early Intervention Project Core Group. (2005). Attachment in institutionalized and community children in Romania. Child Development, 76(5), 1015–1028, Table 2.

Zimmerman, F. J., & Christakis, D. A. (2007). Associations between content types of early media exposure and subsequent attentional problems. Pediatrics, 120(5), 986–992 http://doi.org/10.1542/peds.2006-3322

CHAPTER 6

Alasaari, J. S., Lagus, M., Ollila, H. M., Toivola, A., Kivimäki, M., Vahtera, J., Kronholm, E., Härmä, M., Puttonen, S., & Paunio, T. (2012). Environmental stress affects DNA methylation of a CpG rich promoter region of serotonin transporter gene in a nurse cohort. PLOS ONE, 7(9), 3–10. http://doi.org/10.1371/journal.pone.0045813

Alen, N. V. (2022). The cholinergic anti-inflammatory pathway in humans: State-of-the-art review and future directions. Neuroscience and Biobehavioral Reviews, 136, Article 104622. https://doi.org/10.1016/j.neubiorev.2022.104622

Allen, N., & Badcock, P. (2003). The social risk hypothesis of depressed mood: Evolutionary, psychosocial, and neurobiological perspectives. Psychological Bulletin, 129, 887–913.

American Psychiatric Association. (2022). Diagnostic and statistical manual of mental disorders. (5th ed., text rev.).

Andrade, C. (2017). Ketamine for depression, 1: Clinical summary of issues related to efficacy, adverse effects, and mechanism of action. Journal of Clinical Psychiatry, 78, e415–e419. doi.org/10.4088/JCP.17f11567

Andrews, P. (2007). Reconstructing the evolution of the mind is depressingly difficult. In S. Gangestad & J. Simpson (Eds.), The evolution of mind (pp. 45–52). Guilford Press.

Arnaldo, I., Corcoran, A. W., Friston, K. J., & Ramstead, M. J. D. (2022). Stress and its sequelae: An active inference account of the etiological pathway from allostatic overload to depression. Neuroscience and Biobehavioral Reviews, 135, Article 104590. https://doi.org/10.1016/j.neubiorev.2022.104590

Baddeley, J. L., Pennebaker, J. W., & Beevers, C. G. (2012). Everyday social behavior during a major depressive episode. Social Psychological and Personality Science, 4(4), 445–452. http://doi.org/10.1177/1948550612461654

Ballmaier, M., Toga, A., Blanton, R., Sowell, E., Havretsky, H., Peterson, J., Pham, D., & Kumar, A. (2004). Anterior cingulate, gyrus rectus, and orbitofrontal abnormalities in elderly depressed patients. American Journal of Psychiatry, 161, 99–108.

Barba, T., Buehler, S., Kettner, H., Radu, C., Cunha, B. G., Nutt, D. J., Erritzoe, D., Roseman, L., & Carhart-Harris, R. (2022). Effects of psilocybin versus escitalopram on rumination and thought suppression in depression. *BJPsych Open*, *8*(5), e163. https://doi.org/10.1192/bj0.2022.565

Barnhofer, T., Huntenburg, J. M., Lifshitz, M., Wild, J., Antonova, E., & Margulies, D. S. (2016). How mindfulness training may help to reduce vulnerability for recurrent depression: A neuroscientific perspective. *Clinical Psychological Science*, *4*(2), 328–343. http://doi.org/10.1177/2167702615595036

Basco, M. R., & Rush, A. J. (2005). *Cognitive-behavioral therapy for bipolar disorder* (2nd ed.). Guilford Press.

Beck, A. T. (1967). *Depression: Clinical, experimental, and theoretical aspects*. Harper & Row.

Beck, A. T. (2019). A 60-year evolution of cognitive theory and therapy. *Perspectives on Psychological Science*, *14*, 16–20. https://doi.org/10.1177/1745691618804187

Beck, A. T., & Alford, B. A. (2009). *Depression: Causes and treatments* (2nd ed.). University of Pennsylvania Press.

Beck, A. T., & Bredemeier, K. (2016). A unified model of depression: Integrating clinical, cognitive, biological, and evolutionary perspectives. *Clinical Psychological Science*, *4*(4), 596–619. http://doi.org/10.1177/2167702616628523

Beck, J. (2011). *Cognitive behavioral therapy* (2nd ed.). Guilford Press.

Bell, J. A., Kivimäki, M., Bullmore, E. T., Steptoe, A., MRC ImmunoPsychiatry Consortium, & Carvalho, L. A. (2017). Repeated exposure to systemic inflammation and risk of new depressive symptoms among older adults. *Translational Psychiatry*, *7*, e1208. https://doi.org/10.1038/tp.2017.155

Bellivier, F., Golmard, J., Rietschel, M., Schulze, T., Malafosse, A., Preisig, M., McKeon, P., Mynett-Johnson, L., Henry, C., & Leboyer, M. (2003). Age at onset in bipolar I affective disorder: Further evidence for three subgroups. *American Journal of Psychiatry*, *160*, 999–1001. https://ajp.psychiatryonline.org/doi/10.1176/appi.ajp.160.5.999

Bergfeld, I. O., Mantione, M., Hoogendoorn, M. L. C., Ruhé, H. G., Notten, P., van Laarhoven, J., Visser, I., Figee, M., de Kwaasteniet, B. P., Horst, F., Schene, A. H., van den Munckhof, P., Beute, G., Schuurman, G., & Denys, D. (2016). Deep brain stimulation of the ventral anterior limb of the internal capsule for treatment-resistant depression: A randomized clinical trial. *JAMA Psychiatry*, *73*(5), 456–464. http://doi.org/10.1001/jamapsychiatry.2016.0152

Blumberger, D., Mulsant, B., & Daskalakis, Z. (2013). What is the role of brain stimulation therapies in the treatment of depression? *Current Psychiatry Reports*, *15*, 368.

Boland, R. J., & Keller, M. B. (2009). Course and outcome of depression. In I. H. Gotlib & C. L. Hammen (Eds.), *Handbook of depression* (2nd ed., pp. 23–43). Guilford Press.

Boldrini, M., & Mann, J. J. (2023). Depression and suicide. In M. J. Zigmond, C. A. Wiley, & M.-F. Chesselet (Eds.), *Neurobiology of brain disorders* (2nd ed., pp. 861–883). Academic Press.

Brickman, H. M., & Fristad, M. A. (2022). Psychosocial treatments for bipolar disorder in children and adolescents. *Annual Review of Clinical Psychology*, *18*, 291–327. https://doi.org/10.1146/annurev-clinpsy-072220-021237

Bridge, J. A., Iyengar, S., Salary, C. B., Barbe, R. P., Birmaher, B., Pincus, H. A., Ren, L., & Brent, D. A. (2007). Clinical response and risk for reported suicidal ideation and suicide attempts in pediatric antidepressant treatment: A meta-analysis of randomized controlled trials. *JAMA*, *297*(15), 1683–1696.

Bryan, C. J., Sinclair, S., & Heron, E. A. (2016). Do military personnel "acquire" the capability for suicide from combat? A test of the interpersonal-psychological theory of suicide. *Clinical Psychological Science*, *4*(3), 376–385. http://doi.org/10.1177/2167702615595000

Bullmore, E. (2019). *The inflamed mind: A radical new approach to depression*. Picador.

Buss, D. (Ed.). (2005). *The handbook of evolutionary psychology*. Wiley.

Carpenter, L., Janicak, P., Aaronson, S., Boyadjis, T., Brock, D., Cook, I., Dunner, D. L., Lanocha, K., Solvason, H. B., & Demitrack, M. (2012). Transcranial magnetic stimulation (TMS) for major depression: A multisite, naturalistic, observational study of acute treatment outcomes in clinical practice. *Depression and Anxiety*, *29*, 587–596.

Center for Collegiate Mental Health. (2022, January). *2021 Annual report* (Publication No. STA 22-132). Pennsylvania State University. https://files.eric.ed.gov/fulltext/ED617358.pdf

Centers for Disease Control and Prevention. (2023, April). *Suicide mortality in the United States, 2001-2021* (NCHS Data Brief No. 464). https://www.cdc.gov/nchs/products/databriefs/db464.htm

Chang, E., Downey, C., Hirsch, J., & Yu, E. (Eds.). (2018). *Treating depression, anxiety, and stress in ethnic and racial groups*. American Psychological Association.

Chang, J. J., Ji, Y., Li, Y. H., Pan, H. F., & Su, P. Y. (2021). Prevalence of anxiety symptom and depressive symptom among college students during COVID-19 pandemic: A meta-analysis. *Journal of Affective Disorders*, *292*, 242–254. https://doi.org/10.1016/j.jad.2021.05.109

Chau, D. T., Fogelman, P., Nordanskog, P., Drevets, W. C., & Hamilton, J. P. (2018). Distinct neural-functional effects of treatments with selective serotonin reuptake inhibitors, electroconvulsive therapy, and transcranial magnetic stimulation and their relations to regional brain function in major depression. *Biological Psychiatry: Cognitive Neuroscience and Neuroimaging*, *2*(4), 318–326. https://doi.org/10.1016/j.bpsc.2017.01.003

Cheney, T. (2008). *Manic*. William Morrow.

Cohen, Z. D., & DeRubeis, R. J. (2018). Treatment selection in depression. *Annual Review of Clinical Psychology*, *14*, 209–236.

Coryell, W., Endicott, J., Winokur, G., Akiskal, H., Solomon, D., Leon, A., Mueller, T., & Shea, T. (1995). Characteristics and significance of untreated major depressive disorder. *American Journal of Psychiatry*, *152*, 1124–1129.

Courtet, P., Gottesman, I. I., Jollant, F., & Gould, T. D. (2011). The neuroscience of suicidal behaviors: What can we expect from endophenotype strategies? *Translational Psychiatry*, *1*. http://doi.org/10.1038/tp.2011.6

Craddock, N., & Owen, M. J. (2010). The Kraepelinian dichotomy: Going, going... but still not gone. *British Journal of Psychiatry*, *196*(2), 92–95. http://doi.org/10.1192/bjp.bp.109.073429

Craddock, N., & Sklar, P. (2009). Genetics of bipolar disorder: Successful start to a long journey. *Trends in Genetics*, *25*, 95–105.

Craddock, N., & Sklar, P. (2013). Bipolar disorder 1—Genetics of bipolar disorder. *The Lancet*, *381*(9878), 1654–1662. https://doi.org/10.1016/S0140-6736(13)60855-7

Cristea, I., Montgomery, G., Szamoskozi, S., & David, D. (2013). Key constructs in "classical" and "new wave" cognitive behavioral psychotherapies: Relationships among each other and with emotional distress. *Journal of Clinical Psychology*, *69*, 584–599.

Curry, J. F. (2015). Good news in the battle against military suicide. *American Journal* of Psychiatry, 172(5), 406–407. http://doi.org/10.1176/appi.ajp.2015.15020172

Dantzer, R. (2012). Depression and inflammation: An intricate relationship. Biological Psychiatry, 71, 4–5.

Dantzer, R., O'Connor, J., Freund, G., Johnson, R., & Kelley, K. (2008). From inflammation to sickness and depression: When the immune system subjugates the brain. Nature Reviews Neuroscience, 9, 46–57.

Daws, R. E., & Carhart-Harris, R. (2022). Psilocybin increases brain network integration in patients with depression. Nature Medicine, 28(4), 647–648. https://doi.org/10.1038/s41591-022-01769-4

Daws, R. E., Timmermann, C., Giribaldi, B., Sexton, J. D., Wall, M. B., Erritzoe, D., Roseman, L., Nutt, D., & Carhart-Harris, R. (2022). Increased global integration in the brain after psilocybin therapy for depression. Nature Medicine, 28(4), 844–851. https://doi.org/10.1038/s41591-022-01744-z

DeRubeis, R., Siegle, G., & Hollon, S. (2008). Cognitive therapy versus medication for depression: Treatment outcomes and neural mechanisms. Nature Reviews Neuroscience, 9, 788–796.

Dillon, D. G., & Pizzagalli, D. A. (2018). Mechanisms of memory disruption in depression. Trends in Neurosciences, 41, 137–149. https://doi.org/10.1016/j.tins.2017.12.006

Disner, S., Beevers, C. G., Haigh, E. P., & Beck, A. T. (2011). Neural mechanisms of the cognitive model of depression. Nature Reviews Neuroscience, 12, 467–477.

Dooley, L. N., Kuhlman, K. R., Robles, T. F., Eisenberger, N. I., Craske, M. G., & Bower, J. E. (2018). The role of inflammation in core features of depression: Insights from paradigms using exogenously-induced inflammation. Neuroscience and Biobehavioral Reviews, 94, 219–237. https://doi.org/10.1016/j.neubiorev.2018.09.006

Dowlati, Y., Herrmann, N., Swardfager, W., Liu, H., Sham, L., Reim, E. K., & Lanctôt, K. L. (2010). A meta-analysis of cytokines in major depression. Biological Psychiatry, 67(5), 446–457. https://doi.org/10.1016/j.biopsych.2009.09.033

Duman, R., & Aghajanian, G. (2012). Synaptic dysfunction in depression: Potential therapeutic targets. Science, 338, 68–72.

Ellicott, A., Hammen, C., Gitlin, M., Brown, G., & Jamison, K. (1990). Life events and the course of bipolar disorder. American Journal of Psychiatry, 147, 1194–1198.

Fava, G. (2003). Can long-term treatment with antidepressant drugs worsen the course of depression? Journal of Clinical Psychiatry, 64, 123–133.

Garraza, L., Walrath, C., Goldston, D., Reid, H., & McKeon, R. (2015). Effect of the Garrett Lee Smith Memorial Suicide Prevention Program on suicide attempts among youths. JAMA Psychiatry, 72, 1143–1149.

Geddes, J., Burgess, S., Hawton, K., Jamison, K., & Goodwin, G. (2004). Long-term lithium therapy for bipolar disorder: Systematic review and meta-analysis of randomized controlled trials. American Journal of Psychiatry, 161, 217–222.

Gilbert, P. (2005). Evolution and depression: Issues and implications. Psychological Medicine, 36, 287–297.

Gitlin, M. (2009). Pharmacotherapy and other somatic treatments for depression. In I. Gotlib & C. Hammen (Eds.), Handbook of depression (2nd ed., pp. 554–585). Guilford Press.

Goldfried, M., Castonguay, L., Hayes, A., Drozd, J., & Shapiro, D. (1997). A comparative analysis of the therapeutic focus in cognitive-behavioral and psychodynamic-interpersonal sessions. Journal of Consulting and Clinical Psychology, 65, 740–748.

Goldsmith, S. (2001). Rick factors for suicide. National Academy Press.

Goodwin, F., & Jamison, K. (2007). Manic depressive illness (2nd ed.). Oxford University Press.

Goodyer, I. (2001). Depressed child and adolescent (2nd ed.). Cambridge University Press.

Gordon, B., McDonwell, C., Hallgren, M., Meyer, J., Lyons, M., & Herring, M. (2018). Association of efficacy of resistance exercise training with depressive symptoms: Meta-analysis and meta-regression analysis of randomized clinical trials. JAMA Psychiatry, 75, 566–575. https://doi.org/10.1001/jamapsychiatry.2018.0572

Gordovez, F. J. A., & McMahon, F. J. (2020). The genetics of bipolar disorder. Molecular Psychiatry, 25(3), 544–559. https://doi.org/10.1038/s41380-019-0634-7

Gotlib, I. H., Goodman, S. H., & Humphreys, K. L. (2020). Studying the intergenerational transmission of risk for depression: Current status and future directions. Current Directions in Psychological Science, 29(2), 174–179.

Greenberg, L. S., & Watson, J. C. (2006). Emotion-focused therapy for depression. American Psychological Association.

Hammen, C. (2009). Children of depressed parents. In I. Gotlib & C. Hammen (Eds.), Handbook of depression (2nd ed., pp. 275–297). Guilford Press.

Haq, A., Sitzmann, A., Goldman, M., Maixner, D., & Mickey, B. (2015). Response of depression to electroconvulsive therapy. Journal of Clinical Psychiatry, 76, 1374–1384.

Harrison, P. J., Geddes, J. R., & Tunbridge, E. M. (2018). The emerging neurobiology of bipolar disorder. Trends in Neurosciences, 41(1), 18–30. https://doi.org/10.1016/j.tins.2017.10.006

Hasin, D. S., Sarvet, A. L., Meyers, J. L., Saha, T. D., Ruan, W. J., Stohl, M., & Grant, B. F. (2019). Epidemiology of adult DSM-5 major depressive disorder and its specifiers in the United States. JAMA Psychiatry, 75(4), 336–346. https://doi.org/10.1001/jamapsychiatry.2017.4602

Haukvik, U. K., Gurholt, T. P., Nerland, S., Elvsåshagen, T., Akudjedu, T. N., Alda, M., Alnaes, D., Alonso-Lana, S., Bauer, J., Baune, B. T., Benedetti, F., Berk, M., Bettella, F., Bøen, E., Bonnín, C. M., Brambilla, P., Canales-Rodríguez, E. J., Cannon, D. M., Caseras, X., . . . ENIGMA Bipolar Disorder Working Group. (2022). In vivo hippocampal subfield volumes in bipolar disorder—A mega-analysis from The Enhancing Neuro Imaging Genetics through Meta-Analysis Bipolar Disorder Working Group. Human Brain Mapping, 43(1), 385–398. https://doi.org/10.1002/hbm.25249

Hayes, S. C. (2004). Acceptance and commitment therapy, relational frame theory, and the third wave of behavioral and cognitive therapies. Behavior Therapy, 35, 639–665.

Hirota, K., & Lambert, D. G. (2018). Ketamine and depression. British Journal of Anaesthesia, 121(6), 1198–1202. https://doi.org/10.1016/j.bja.2018.08.020

Hodes, G. E., Kana, V., Menard, C., Merad, M., & Russo, S. J. (2015). Neuroimmune mechanisms of depression. Nature Neuroscience, 18(10). http://doi.org/10.1038/nn.4113

Hollon, S. D., & Beck, A. T. (2013). Cognitive and cognitive-behavioral therapies. In M. Lambert (Ed.), Handbook of psychotherapy and behavior change (6th ed., pp. 393–442). Wiley.

Hollon, S. D., Jarrett, R. B., Nierenberg, A. A., Thase, M. E., Trivedi, M., & Rush, A. J. (2005). Treatment of adult and geriatric depression. Journal of Clinical Psychology, 66, 455–468.

Holtzheimer, P., Kosel, M., & Schlaepfer, T. (2012). Brain stimulation therapies for neuropsychiatric disease. In M. Aminoff, F. Boller, & D. Swaab (Eds.), *Handbook of clinical neurology* (pp. 681–695). Elsevier.

Horwitz, A. G., Berona, J., Busby, D. R., Eisenberg, D., Zheng, K., Pistorello, J., Albucher, R., Coryell, W., Favorite, T., Walloch, J. C., & King, C. A. (2020). Variation in suicide risk among subgroups of sexual and gender minority college students. *Suicide and Life-Threatening Behavior, 50*(5), 1041–1053.

Howard, D. M., Adams, M. J., Clarke, T., Hafferty, J. D., Gibson, J., Shirali, M., Coleman, J. R. I., Hagenaars, S. P., Ward, J., Wigmore, E. M., Alloza, C., Shen, X., Barbu, M. C., Xu, E. Y., Whalley, H. C., Marioni, R. E., Porteous, D. J., Davies, G., Deary, I. J., ... McIntosh, A. M. (2019). Genome-wide meta-analysis of depression identifies 102 independent variants and highlights the importance of the prefrontal brain regions. *Nature Neuroscience, 22*, 343–352. https://doi.org/10.1038/s41593-018-0326-7

Hwang, W.-C., Ho, L. C., Chan, C. P., & Hong, K. K. (2018). Cognitive behavioral models, measures, and treatments for depressive disorders in Asian Americans. In E. Chang, C. Downey, J. Hirsch, & E. Yu (Eds.), *Treating depression, anxiety, and stress in ethnic and racial groups* (pp. 23–47). American Psychological Association.

Hyde, J. S., & Mezulis, A. H. (2020). Gender differences in depression: Biological, affective, cognitive, and sociocultural factors. *Harvard Review of Psychiatry, 28*(1), 4–13.

Jamison, K. (1996). *An unquiet mind*. Random House.

Johnson, S. (2005). Mania and dysregulation in goal pursuit: A review. *Clinical Psychology Review, 25*, 241–262.

Johnson, S., Cuellar, A., & Miller, C. (2009). Bipolar and unipolar depression: A comparison of clinical phenomenology, biological vulnerability and psychosocial predictors. In I. Gotlib & C. Hammen (Eds.), *Handbook of depression* (2nd ed., pp. 142–160). Guilford Press.

Johnson, S., Murray, G., Fredrickson, B., Youngstrom, E., Hinshaw, S., Bass, J., Deckersbach, T., Schooler, J., & Salloum, I. (2012). Creativity and bipolar disorder: Touched by fire or burning with questions? *Clinical Psychology Review, 32*, 1–12.

Joiner, T. (2005). *Why people die by suicide*. Harvard University Press.

Just, M. A., Pan, L., Cherkassky, V. L., McMakin, D. L., Cha, C., Nock, M. K., & Brent, D. (2017). Machine learning of neural representations of suicide and emotion concepts identifies suicidal youth. *Nature Human Behaviour, 1*, 911–919. https://doi.org/10.1038/s41562-017-0234-y

Kappelmann, N., Arloth, J., Georgakis, M. K., Czamara, D., Rost, N., Ligthart, S., Khandaker, G. M., & Binder, E. B. (2021). Dissecting the association between inflammation, metabolic dysregulation, and specific depressive symptoms: A genetic correlation and 2-sample mendelian randomization study. *JAMA Psychiatry, 78*(2), 161–170. https://doi.org/10.1001/jamapsychiatry.2020.3436

Kaufman, J., Yang, B., Douglas-Palumberi, H., Grasso, D., Lipschitz, D., Houshyar, S., Krystal, J., & Gelernter, J. (2006). Brain-derived neurotrophic factor-5-HTTLPR gene interactions and environmental modifiers of depression in children. *Biological Psychiatry, 59*, 673–680.

Kendler, K., Thornton, L., & Gardner, C. (2000). Stressful life events and previous episodes in the etiology of major depression in women: An evaluation of the "kindling" hypothesis. *American Journal of Psychiatry, 157*, 1243–1251.

Kerestes, R., Davey, C. G., Stephanou, K., Whittle, S., & Harrison, B. J. (2014). Functional brain imaging studies of youth depression: A systematic review. *NeuroImage: Clinical, 4*, 209–231. http://doi.org/10.1016/j.nicl.2013.11.009

Kessler, R. C., & Bromet, E. J. (2013). The epidemiology of depression across cultures. *Annual Review of Public Health, 34*(1), 119–138. http://doi.org/10.1146/annurev-publhealth-031912-114409

Kessler, R. C., Merikangas, K., & Wang, P. (2007). Prevalence, comorbidity, and service utilization for mood disorders in the United States at the beginning of the twenty-first century. *Annual Review of Clinical Psychology, 137*, 137–158.

Khandaker, G. M., Pearson, R. M., Zammit, S., Lewis, G., & Jones, P. B. (2014). Association of serum interleukin 6 and C-reactive protein in childhood with depression and psychosis in young adult life: A population-based longitudinal study. *JAMA Psychiatry, 71*(10), 1121–1128. http://doi.org/10.1001/jamapsychiatry.2014.1332

Kupka, R. W., Luckenbaugh, D. A., Post, R. M., Suppes, T., Altshuler, L. L., Keck, P. E., Jr., Frye, M. A., Denicoff, K. D., Grunze, H., Leverich, G. S., McElroy, S. L., Walden, J., & Nolen, W. A. (2005). Comparison of rapid-cycling and non-rapid-cycling bipolar disorder based on prospective mood ratings in 539 outpatients. *American Journal of Psychiatry, 162*, 1273–1280.

Kuyken, W., Warren, F., Taylor, R., Whalley, B., Crane, C., Bondolfi, G., Hayes, R., Huijbers, M., Ma, H., Schweizer, S., Segal, Z., Speckens, A., Teasdale, J. D., Van Heeringen, K., Williams, M., Byford, S., Byng, R., & Dalgleish, T. (2016). Efficacy of mindfulness-based cognitive therapy in prevention of depressive relapse: An individual patient data meta-analysis from randomized trials. *JAMA Psychiatry, 73*, 565–574. http://doi.org/10.1001/jamapsychiatry.2016.0076

Lazary, J., Viczena, V., Dome, P., Chase, D., Juhasz, G., & Bagdy, G. (2012). Hopelessness, a potential endophenotpye for suicidal behavior, is influenced by TPH2 gene variants. *Progress in Neuropsychopharmacology and Biological Psychiatry, 36*, 155–160.

Lemos, J. C., Wanat, M. J., Smith, J. S., Reyes, B. A. S., Hollon, N. G., Van Bockstaele, E. J., Chavkin, C., & Phillips, P. (2012). Severe stress switches CRF action in the nucleus accumbens from appetitive to aversive. *Nature, 490*, 402–406.

Li, B.-J., Friston, K., Mody, M., Wang, H. N., Lu, H. B., & Hu, D. W. (2018). A brain network model for depression: From symptom understanding to disease intervention. *CNS Neuroscience and Therapeutics, 24*, 1004–1019. https://doi.org/10.1111/cns.12998

Li, H.-J., Zhang, C., Hui, L., Zhou, D. S., Li, Y., Zhang, C. Y., Wang, C., Wang, L., Li, W., Yang, Y., Qu, N., Tang, J., He, Y., Zhou, J., Yang, Z., Li, X., Cai, J., Yang, L., Chen, J., ... GeseDNA Research Team. (2021). Novel risk loci associated with genetic risk for bipolar disorder among Han Chinese individuals: A genome-wide association study and meta-analysis. *JAMA Psychiatry, 78*(3), 320–330. https://doi.org/10.1001/jamapsychiatry.2020.3738

Linehan, M. M. (2008). Suicide intervention research: A field in desperate need of development. *Suicide & Life-Threatening Behavior, 38*(5), 483–485. http://doi.org/10.1521/suli.2008.38.5.483

Linehan, M. M., Korslund, K. E., Harned, M. S., Gallop, R. J., Lungu, A., Neacsiu, A. D., McDavid, J., Comtois, K. A., & Murray-Gregory, A. M. (2015). Dialectical behavior therapy for high suicide risk in individuals with borderline personality disorder. *JAMA Psychiatry, 72*(5), 475–482. http://doi.org/10.1001/jamapsychiatry.2014.3039

Liu, Q., He, H., Yang, J., Feng, X., Zhao, F., & Lyu, J. (2020). Changes in the global burden of depression from 1990 to 2017:

Findings from the Global Burden of Disease study. *Journal of Psychiatric Research, 126*, 134–140. https://doi.org/10.1016/j.jpsychires.2019.08.002

Liu, Z., Zhu, F., Wang, G., Xiao, Z., Wang, H., Tang, J., Wang, X., Qiu, D., Liu, W., Cao, Z., & Li, W. (2006). Association of corticotropin-releasing hormone receptor1 gene SNP and haplotype with major depression. *Neuroscience Letters, 404*, 358–362.

Loo, C., & Mitchell, P. (2005). A review of the efficacy of transcranial magnetic stimulation (TMS) treatment for depression, and current and future strategies to optimize efficacy. *Journal of Affective Disorders, 88*, 255–267.

Malhi, G. (2009). The impact of lithium on bipolar disorder. *Bipolar Disorders, Supplement, 2*, 1–3.

Marchand, W., & Yurgelun-Todd, D. (2011). Functional imaging of bipolar illness. In M. Shenton & B. Turetsky (Eds.), *Understanding neuropsychiatric disorders: Insights from neuroimaging* (pp. 109–124). Cambridge University Press.

Martins-Monteverde, C. M. S., Baes, C. V. W., Reisdorfer, E., Padovan, T., Tofoli, S. M. C., & Juruena, M. F. (2019). Relationship between depression and subtypes of early life stress in adult psychiatric patients. *Frontiers in Psychiatry, 10*, 19. https://doi.org/10.3389/fpsyt.2019.00019

Marwaha, S., Palmer, E., Suppes, T., Cons, E., Young, A. H., & Upthegrove, R. (2023). Novel and emerging treatments for major depression. *Lancet (London, England), 401*(10371), 141–153. https://doi.org/10.1016/S0140-6736(22)02080-3

McDonald, J., Ross, R., Kilwein, T., & Sargent, E. (2018). Cognitive behavioral models, measures, and treatments for depressive disorders in American Indians. In E. Chang, C. Downey, J. Hirsch, & E. Yu (Eds.), *Treating depression, anxiety, and stress in ethnic and racial groups* (pp. 91–121). American Psychological Association.

Miklowitz, D. J., Goldstein, M. J., Nuechterlein, K. H., Snyder, K. S., & Mintz, J. (1988). Family factors and the course of bipolar affective disorder. *Archives of General Psychiatry, 45*, 225–231.

Miklowitz, D., & Johnson, S. (2006). The psychopathology and treatment of bipolar disorder. *Annual Review of Clinical Psychology, 2*, 199–235.

Miller, M., Azrael, D., & Barber, C. (2012). Suicide mortality in the United States: The importance of attending to method in understanding population-level disparities in the burden of suicide. *Annual Review of Public Health, 33*, 393–408.

Monroe, S. M., & Harkness, K. L. (2022). Major depression and its recurrences: Life course matters. *Annual Review of Clinical Psychology, 18*, 329–357.

Morley, T., & Moran, G. (2011). The origins of cognitive vulnerability in early childhood: Mechanisms linking early attachment to later depression. *Clinical Psychology Review, 31*, 1071–1082.

Morrison, B. (2008). Depression: Disease, loneliness, social isolation, suicide, negative thoughts. *Social Alternative, 27*, 312–328.

Muñoz, R. F., Le, H. N., Clarke, G. N., Barrera, A. Z., & Torres, L. D. (2008). Preventing first onset and recurrence of major depressive episodes. In I. H. Gotlib & C. L. Hammen (Eds.), *Handbook of depression* (2nd ed., pp. 533–553). Guilford Press.

Neblett, E., Sosoo, E., Willis, H., Bernard, D., & Bae, J. (2018). Cognitive behavioral models, measures, and treatments for depressive disorders in African Americans. In E. Chang, C. Downey, J. Hirsch, & E. Yu (Eds.), *Treating depression, anxiety, and stress in ethnic and racial groups* (pp. 73–97). American Psychological Association.

Nemeroff, C. (2018). Ketamine: Quo vadis. *American Journal of Psychiatry, 175*, 297–299.

Nesse, R. M. (1990). Evolutionary explanations of emotions. *Human Nature, 1*, 261–289.

Newport, D. J., Carpenter, L. L., McDonald, W. M., Potash, J. B., Tohen, M., Nemeroff, C. B., & APA Council of Research Task Force on Novel Biomarkers and Treatments. (2015). Ketamine and other NMDA antagonists: Early clinical trials and possible mechanisms in depression. *American Journal of Psychiatry, 172*(10), 950–966. http://doi.org/10.1176/appi.ajp.2015.15040465

Ngo, V., & Miranda, J. (2018). Cognitive behavioral models, measures, and treatments for depressive disorders in Latin Americans. In E. Chang, C. Downey, J. Hirsch, & E. Yu (Eds.), *Treating depression, anxiety, and stress in ethnic and racial groups* (pp. 49–72). American Psychological Association.

Nock, M. K., Green, J. G., Hwang, I., McLaughlin, K. A., Sampson, N. A., Zaslavsky, A. M., & Kessler, R. C. (2013). Prevalence, correlates, and treatment of lifetime suicidal behavior among adolescents: Results from the National Comorbidity Survey Replication Adolescent Supplement. *JAMA Psychiatry, 70*(3), 300–310. http://doi.org/10.1001/2013.jamapsychiatry.55

Oathes, D. J., & Ray, W. J. (2006). Depressed mood, index finger force, and motor cortex stimulation: A transcranial magnetic stimulation (TMS) study. *Biological Psychology, 72*, 278–290.

Office of the U.S. Surgeon General & National Action Alliance for Suicide Prevention. (2012). *2012 national strategy for suicide prevention: Goals and objectives for action. A report of the U.S. Surgeon General and of the National Action Alliance for Suicide Prevention*. U.S. Department of Health and Human Services. https://www.ncbi.nlm.nih.gov/books/NBK109917/

Ophir, Y., Tikochinski, R., Brunstein Klomek, A., & Reichart, R. (2022). The hitchhiker's guide to computational linguistics in suicide prevention. *Clinical Psychological Science, 10*(2), 212–235.

Otte, C., Gold, S. M., Penninx, B. W., Pariante, C. M., Etkin, A., Fava, M., Mohr, D. C., & Schatzberg, A. F. (2016). Major depressive disorder. *Nature Reviews Disease Primers, 2*(September), 1–21. https://doi.org/10.1038/nrdp.2016.65

Palmer, D. S., Howrigan, D. P., Chapman, S. B., Adolfsson, R., Bass, N., Blackwood, D., Boks, M. P. M., Chen, C. Y., Churchhouse, C., Corvin, A. P., Craddock, N., Curtis, D., Di Florio, A., Dickerson, F., Freimer, N. B., Goes, F. S., Jia, X., Jones, I., Jones, L., . . . Neale, B. M. (2022). Exome sequencing in bipolar disorder identifies AKAP11 as a risk gene shared with schizophrenia. *Nature Genetics, 54*(5), 541–547. https://doi.org/10.1038/s41588-022-01034-x

Parker, G., Spoelma, M. J., Tavella, G., Alda, M., Hajek, T., Dunner, D. L., O'Donovan, C., Rybakowski, J. K., Goldberg, J. F., Bayes, A., Sharma, V., Boyce, P., & Manicavasagar, V. (2021). Categorical differentiation of the unipolar and bipolar disorders. *Psychiatry Research, 297*, Article 113719. https://doi.org/10.1016/j.psychres.2021.113719

Pearson, C., Siegel, J., & Gold, J. A. (2022). Psilocybin-assisted psychotherapy for depression: Emerging research on a psychedelic compound with a rich history. *Journal of the Neurological Sciences, 434*, Article 120096. https://doi.org/10.1016/j.jns.2021.120096

Peciña, M., Bohnert, A. S. B., Sikora, M., Avery, E. T., Langenecker, S. A., Mickey, B. J., & Zubieta, J.-K. (2015). Association between placebo-activated neural systems and antidepressant responses. *JAMA Psychiatry, 72*(11), 1087–1094. http://doi.org/10.1001/jamapsychiatry.2015.1335

Perrin, J., Merz, S., Bennett, D., Currie, J., Steele, D., Reid, I., & Schwarzbauer, C. (2012). Electroconvulsive therapy reduces frontal cortical connectivity in severe depressive disorder. *Proceedings of the National Academy of Science, 109*, 5464–5468.

Peterson, B. S., & Weissman, M. M. (2011). A brain-based endophenotype for major depressive disorder. *Annual Review of Medicine, 62*, 461–474. https://doi.org/10.1146/annurev-med-010510-095632

Petrican, R., Levine, B., Söderlund, H., Kumar, N., Daskalakis, J., & Flint, A. (2019). Electroconvulsive therapy "corrects" the neural architecture of visuospatial memory: Implications for typical cognitive-affective functioning. *NeuroImage: Clinical, 23*, Article 101816. https://doi.org/10.1016/j.nicl.2019.101816

Pine, D. (2009). A social neuroscience approach to adolescent depression. In M. De Haan & M. Gunnar (Eds.), *Handbook of developmental social neuroscience* (pp. 399–418). Guilford Press.

Price, P. (1996). *Biological evolution.* Brooks/Cole.

Prigerson, H. G., Kakarala, S., Gang, J., & Maciejewski, P. K. (2021). History and status of prolonged grief disorder as a psychiatric diagnosis. *Annual Review of Clinical Psychology, 17*, 109–126.

Regenold, W., Phatak, P., Marano, C., Sassan, A., Conley, R., & Kling, M. (2009). Elevated cerebrospinal fluid lactate concentrations in patients with bipolar disorder and schizophrenia: Implications for the mitochondrial dysfunction hypothesis. *Biological Psychiatry, 65*, 489–494.

Reger, M. A., Smolenski, D. J., Skopp, N. A., Metzger-Abamukang, M. J., Kang, H. K., Bullman, T. A., Perdue, S., & Gahm, G. A. (2015). Risk of suicide among U.S. military service members following Operation Enduring Freedom or Operation Iraqi Freedom deployment and separation from the U.S. military. *JAMA Psychiatry, 72*(6). http://doi.org/10.1001/jamapsychiatry.2014.3195

Reger, M. A., Tucker, R. P., Carter, S. P., & Ammerman, B. A. (2018). Military deployments and suicide: A critical examination. *Perspective on Psychological Science, 13*, 688–699. https://doi.org/10.1177/1745691618785366

Riggs, L. M., & Gould, T. D. (2021). Ketamine and the future of rapid-acting antidepressants. *Annual Review of Clinical Psychology, 17*, 207–231. https://doi.org/10.1146/annurev-clinpsy-072120-014126

Rosner, R., Comtesse, H., Vogel, A., & Doering, B. K. (2021). Prevalence of prolonged grief disorder. *Journal of Affective Disorders, 287*, 301–307.

Ross, E. L., Zivin, K., & Maixner, D. F. (2018). Cost-effectiveness of electroconvulsive therapy vs. pharmacotherapy/psychotherapy for treatment-resistant depression in the United States. *JAMA Psychiatry, 75*, 713–722. https://doi.org/10.1001/jamapsychiatry.2018.0768

Roy, A., Hodgkinson, C. A., Deluca, V., Goldman, D., & Enoch, M. A. (2012). Two HPA axis genes, CRHBP and FKBP5, interact with childhood trauma to increase the risk for suicidal behavior. *Journal of Psychiatric Research, 46*, 72–79.

Rudd, M. D., Bryan, C. J., Wertenberger, E. G., Peterson, A. L., Young-McCaughan, S., Mintz, J., Williams, S. R., Arne, K. A., Breitbach, J., Delano, K., Wilkinson, E., & Bruce, T. O. (2015). Brief cognitive-behavioral therapy effects on post-treatment suicide attempts in a military sample: Results of a randomized clinical trial with 2-year follow-up. *American Journal of Psychiatry, 172*(5), 441–449. http://doi.org/10.1176/appi.ajp.2014.14070843

Rudolf, K. (2009). Adolescent depression. In I. Gotlib & C. Hammen (Eds.), *Handbook of depression* (2nd ed., pp. 444–466). Guilford Press.

Rutter, M. (2006). *Genes and behavior: Nature–nurture interplay explained.* Blackwell.

Ryba, M. M., & Hopko, D. R. (2012). Gender differences in depression: Assessing mediational effects of overt behaviors and environmental reward through daily diary monitoring. *Depression Research and Treatment, 2012*, Article 865679. http://doi.org/10.1155/2012/865679

Savitz, J., & Drevets, W. (2009). Bipolar and major depressive disorder: Neuroimaging the developmental–degenerative divide. *Neuroscience and Biobehavioral Reviews, 333*, 699–771.

Sax, K., & Strakowski, S. (2001). Behavioral sensitization in humans. *Journal of Addiction Disorders, 20*, 55–65.

Schmaal, L., Veltman, D. J., van Erp, T. G. M., Sämann, P. G., Frodl, T., Jahanshad, N., Loehrer, E., Tiemeier, H., Hofman, A., Niessen, W. J., Vernooij, M. W., Ikram, M. A., Wittfeld, K., Grabe, H. J., Block, A., Hegenscheid, K., Völzke, H., Hoehn, D., Czisch, M., . . . Hibar, D. P. (2015). Subcortical brain alterations in major depressive disorder: Findings from the ENIGMA Major Depressive Disorder working group. *Molecular Psychiatry*, 1–7. http://doi.org/10.1038/mp.2015.69

Shapiro, D. A., Barkham, M., Rees, A., Hardy, G. E., Reynolds, S., & Startup, M. (1994). Effects of treatment duration and severity of depression on the effectiveness of cognitive-behavioral and psychodynamic-interpersonal psychotherapy. *Journal of Consulting and Clinical Psychology, 62*(3), 522–534. http://doi.org/10.1037/0022-006X.63.3.378

Slavich, G. M., & Irwin, M. R. (2014). From stress to inflammation and major depressive disorder: A social signal transduction theory of depression. *Psychological Bulletin, 140*(3), 774–815. https://doi.org/10.1037/a0035302

Slavich, G. M., O'Donovan, A., Epel, E. S., & Kemeny, M. E. (2010). Black sheep get the blues: A psychobiological model of social rejection and depression. *Neuroscience and Biobehavioral Reviews, 35*, 39–45.

Smeland, O. B., Bahrami, S., Frei, O., Shadrin, A., O'Connell, K., Savage, J., Watanabe, K., Krull, F., Bettella, F., Steen, N. E., Ueland, T., Posthuma, D., Djurovic, S., Dale, A. M., & Andreassen, O. A. (2020). Genome-wide analysis reveals extensive genetic overlap between schizophrenia, bipolar disorder, and intelligence. *Molecular Psychiatry, 25*(4), 844–853. https://doi.org/10.1038/s41380-018-0332-x

Smith, R. (1991). The macrophage theory of depression. *Medical Hypotheses, 35*, 298–306.

Stahl, E. A., Breen, G., Forstner, A. J., McQuillin, A., Ripke, S., Trubetskoy, V., Mattheisen, M., Wang, Y., Coleman, J. R. I., Gaspar, H. A., de Leeuw, C. A., Steinberg, S., Pavlides, J. M. W., Trzaskowski, M., Byrne, E. M., Pers, T. H., Holmans, P. A., Richards, A. L., Abbott, L., . . . Bipolar Disorder Working Group of the Psychiatric Genomics Consortium. (2019). Genome-wide association study identifies 30 loci associated with bipolar disorder. *Nature Genetics, 51*(5), 793–803. https://doi.org/10.1038/s41588-019-0397-8

Strakowski, S. M. (2011). Structural imaging of bipolar illness. In M. Shenton & B. Turetsky (Eds.), *Understanding neuropsychiatric disorders: Insights from* neuroimaging (pp. 93–108). Cambridge University Press.

Strakowski, S. M., Adler, C. M., Holland, S. K., Mills, N., & DelBello, M. P. (2004). A preliminary fMRI study of sustained attention in euthymic, unmedicated bipolar disorder. *Neuropsychopharmacology, 29*, 1734–1740.

Strupp, H., & Binder, J. (1984). *Psychotherapy in a new key: A guide to time-limited dynamic psychotherapy.* Basic Books.

Substance Abuse and Mental Health Services Administration. (2011). *Utilization of mental health services by adults with suicidal thoughts and behavior. National Survey on Drug Use and Health. The NSDUH Report.*

Suomi, S. J. Attachment in rhesus monkeys. (2016). In P. Shaver & J. Cassidy (Eds.), *Handbook of attachment: Theory, research, and clinical applications* (3rd ed., pp. 181–197). Guilford Press.

Szentágotai-Tătar, A., & David, D. (2018). Evidence-based psychological interventions for bipolar disorder. In D. David, S. Lynn, & G. Montgomery (Eds.), *Evidence-based psychotherapy: The state of science and practice* (pp. 37–62). Wiley Blackwell.

Taylor, C. L. (2017). Creativity and mood disorder: A systematic review and meta-analysis. *Perspectives on Psychological Science, 12*, 1040–1076. https://doi.org/10.1177/1745691617699653

Tekin, S. (2015). Against hyponarrating grief: Incompatible research and treatment interests in the *DSM-5.* In S. Demazeux & P. Singy (Eds.), *The DSM-5 in perspective* (pp. 179–197). Springer.

Thase, M., & Denko, T. (2008). Pharmacotherapy of mood disorders. *Annual Review of Clinical Psychology, 4*, 53–91.

Tolstoy, L. (1882). *My confession: My life had some to a sudden stop.* Crowell.

Turecki, G., Ernst, C., Jollant, F., Labonté, B., & Mechawar, N. (2012). The neurodevelopmental origins of suicidal behavior. *Trends in Neurosciences, 35*, 14–23.

Twenge, J. M., Cooper, A. B., Joiner, T. E., Duffy, M. E., & Binau, S. G. (2019). Age, period, and cohort trends in mood disorder indicators and suicide-related outcomes in a nationally representative dataset, 2005–2017. *Journal of Abnormal Psychology, 128*, 185–199.

Uher, R., Payne, J. L., Pavlova, B., & Perlis, R. H. (2014). Major depressive disorder in *DSM-5*: Implications for clinical practice and research of changes from *DSM-IV*. *Depression and Anxiety, 31*(6), 459–471. http://doi.org/10.1002/da.22217

Ursano, R. J., Kessler, R. C., Naifeh, J. A., Mash, H. H., Fullerton, C. S., Bliese, P. D., Zaslovsky, A. M., Ng, T. H., Aliaga, P. A., Wynn, G. H., Dinh, H. M., McCarroll, J. E., Sampson, N. A., Kao, T.-C., Schoenbaum, M., Heeringa, S. G., & Stein, M. B. (2017). Risk of suicide attempt among soldiers in army units with a history of suicide attempts. *JAMA Psychiatry, 74*, 924–931. https://doi.org/10.1001/jamapsychiatry.2017.1925

Ursano, R. J., Kessler, R. C., Stein, M. B., Naifeh, J. A., Aliaga, P. A., Fullerton, C. S., Sampson, N. A., Kao, T.-C., Colpe, L. J., Schoenbaum, M., Cox, K. L., & Heeringa, S. G. (2015). Suicide attempts in the U.S. Army during the wars in Afghanistan and Iraq, 2004 to 2009. *JAMA Psychiatry, 72*(9), 917–926. http://doi.org/10.1001/jamapsychiatry.2015.0987

Wakefield, J. C. (2016). Diagnostic issues and controversies in *DSM-5*: Return of the false positives problem. *Annual Review of Clinical Psychology, 12*, 105–132. http://doi.org/10.1146/annurev-clinpsy-032814-112800

Wolford-Clevenger, C., Stuart, G. L., Elledge, L. C., McNulty, J. K., & Spirito, A. (2020). Proximal correlates of suicidal ideation and behaviors: A test of the interpersonal-psychological theory of suicide. *Suicide and Life-Threatening Behavior, 50*(1), 249–262.

World Health Organization. (2014). *Preventing suicide: A global imperative.* https://www.who.int/publications/i/item/9789241564779

Wu, A., Wang, J.-Y., & Jia, C.-X. (2015). Religion and completed suicide: A meta-analysis. *PLOS ONE, 10*(6), Article e0131715 http://doi.org/10.1371/journal.pone.0131715

CHAPTER 7

Ader, R. (Ed.). (2007). *Psychoneuroimmunology* (4th ed., 2 vols.). Elsevier.

Albert, P. (2010). Epigenetics in mental illness: Hope or hype? *Journal of Psychiatry and Neuroscience, 35*, 366–368.

American Psychiatric Association. (2013). *Diagnostic and statistical manual of mental disorders.* (5th ed.).

American Psychiatric Association. (2022). *Diagnostic and statistical manual of mental disorders* (5th ed., text rev.).

Bale, T. L., & Epperson, C. N. (2015). Sex differences and stress across the lifespan. *Nature Neuroscience, 18*, 35–42. http://doi.org/10.1038/nn.4112

Belsky, J. (2005). Differential susceptibility to rearing influence: An evolutionary hypothesis and some evidence. In B. Ellis & D. Bjorklund (Eds.), *Origins of the social mind: Evolutionary psychology and child development* (pp. 139–163). Guilford Press.

Berntson, G. G., Cacioppo, J. T., & Quigley, K. S. (1991). Autonomic determinism: The modes of autonomic control, the doctrine of autonomic space, and the laws of autonomic constraint. *Psychological Review, 98*, 459–487.

Berntson, G. G., Cacioppo, J. T., & Quigley, K. S. (1993). Cardiac psychophysiology and autonomic space in humans: Empirical perspectives and conceptual implications. *Psychological Bulletin, 114*, 296–322.

Betancourt, T. S., Borisova, I. I., Williams, T. P., Brennan, R. T., Whitfield, T. H., de la Soudiere, M., Williamson, J., & Gilman, S. E. (2010). Sierra Leone's former child soldiers: A follow-up study of psychosocial adjustment and community reintegration. *Child Development, 81*(4), 1077–1095. https://doi.org/10.1111/j.1467-8624.2010.01455.x

Bisson, J., & Andrew, M. (2007, July 18). Psychological treatment of post-traumatic stress disorder (PTSD). *Cochrane Database of Systematic Reviews*, (3), Article CD003388. https://doi.org/10.1002/14651858.CD003388.pub3

Bradley, R., Greene, M., Russ, E., Dutra, L., & Westen, D. (2005). A multidimensional meta-analysis of psychotherapy of PTSD. *American Journal of Psychiatry, 162*, 214–227.

Bryant, R., Friedman, M., Spiegel, D., Ursano, R., & Strain, J. (2011). A review of acute stress disorder in *DSM-5*. *Depression and Anxiety, 28*, 802–817.

Bryant, R., Nickerson, A., Creamer, M., O'Donnell, M., Forbes, D., Galatzer-Levy, I., McFarlane, A. C., & Silove, D. (2015). Trajectory of post-traumatic stress following traumatic injury: 6-year follow-up. *British Journal of Psychiatry, 206*(5), 417–423. https://doi.org/10.1192/bjp.bp.114.145516

Calancie, O. G., Khalid-Khan, S., Booij, L., & Munoz, D. P. (2018). Eye movement desensitization and reprocessing as a treatment for PTSD: Current neurobiological theories and a new hypothesis. *Annals* of the New York Academy of Science, 1426(1), 127–145.

Cannon, W. (1932). *The wisdom of the body.* Norton.

Caspi, A., McClay, J., Moffitt, T., Mill, J., Martin, J., Craig, I., Taylor, A., & Poulton, R. (2002). Role of genotype in the cycle of violence in maltreated children. *Science, 297,* 851–854.

Chattarji, A. S., Tomar, A., Suvrathan, A., Ghosh, S., & Rahman, M. M. (2015). Neighborhood matters: Divergent patterns of stress-induced plasticity across the brain affiliations. *Nature Neuroscience, 18,* 1364–1375. http://doi.org/10.1038/nn.4115

Cohen, S., & Herbert, T. (1996). Health psychology: Psychological factors and physical disease from the perspective of human psychoneuroimmunology. *Annual Review of Psychology, 47,* 113–142.

Crombach, A., & Elbert, T. (2015). Controlling offensive behavior using narrative exposure therapy: A randomized controlled trial of former street children. *Clinical Psychological Science, 3*(2), 270–282. http://doi.org/10.1177/2167702614534239

Cruz-Pereira, J. S., Rea, K., Nolan, Y. M., O'Leary, O. F., Dinan, T. G., & Cryan, J. F. (2020). Depression's unholy trinity: dysregulated stress, immunity, and the microbiome. *Annual Review of Psychology, 71,* 49–78.

Curley, J., Davidson, S., Bateson, P., & Champagne, F. (2009). Social enrichment during postnatal development induces transgenerational effects on emotional and reproductive behavior in mice. *Frontiers in Behavioral Neuroscience, 3.* https://doi.org/10.3389/neuro.08.025.2009

Dantzer, R. (2012). Depression and inflammation: An intricate relationship. *Biological Psychiatry, 71,* 4–5.

Dantzer, R., O'Connor, J., Freund, G., Johnson, R., & Kelley, K. (2008). From inflammation to sickness and depression: When the immune system subjugates the brain. *Nature Reviews Neuroscience, 9,* 46–57.

Difede, J., & Eskra, D. (2002). Cognitive processing therapy for PTSD in a survivor of the World Trade Center bombing: A case study. *Journal of Trauma Practice, 1,* 155–165.

Dohrenwend, B., Turner, J., Turse, N., Adams, B., Koenen, K., & Marshall, R. (2006). The psychological risks of Vietnam for U.S. veterans: A revisit with new data and methods. *Science, 313,* 979–982.

Ehlers, A., & Clark, D. (2003). Early psychological interventions for adult survivors of trauma: A review. *Biological Psychiatry, 53,* 817–826.

Eisenberger, N., & Lieberman, M. (2004). Why rejection hurts: A common neural alarm system for physical and social pain. *Trends in Cognitive Sciences, 8,* 294–300.

Elbert, T., Schauer, M., & Moran, J. K. (2018). Two pedals drive the bi-cycle of violence: Reactive and appetitive aggression. *Current Opinion in Psychology, 19,* 135–138. https://doi.org/10.1016/j.copsyc.2017.03.016

Elbert, T., Weierstall, R., & Schauer, M. (2010). Fascination violence: On mind and brain of man hunters. *European Archives of Psychiatry and Clinical Neuroscience, 260,* 100–105.

Ertl, V., Pfeiffer, A., Schauer-Kaiser, E., Elbert, T., & Neuner, F. (2014). The challenge of living on: Psychopathology and its mediating influence on the readjustment of former child soldiers. *PLOS ONE, 9*(7). https://doi.org/10.1371/journal.pone.0102786

Felmingham, K. L., Falconer, E. M., Williams, L., Kemp, A. H., Allen, A., Peduto, A., & Bryant, R. A. (2014). Reduced amygdala and ventral striatal activity to happy faces in PTSD is associated with emotional numbing. *PLOS ONE, 9*(9), Article e03653. https://doi.org/10.1371/journal.pone.0103653

Finlay, S., Roth, C., Zimsen, T., Bridson, T. L., Sarnyai, Z., & McDermott, B. (2022). Adverse childhood experiences and allostatic load: A systematic review. *Neuroscience and Biobehavioral Reviews, 136,* Article 104605. https://doi.org/10.1016/j.neubiorev.2022.104605

Flinn, M. V. (2008). Why words can hurt us: Social relationships, stress, and health. In W. Trevathan, E. Smith, & J. McKenna (Eds.), *Evolutionary medicine and health* (pp. 242–258). Oxford University Press.

Flux, M. C., & Lowry, C. A. (2023). Inflammation as a mediator of stress-related psychiatric disorders. In M. J. Zigmond, C. A. Wiley, & M.-F. Chesselet (Eds.), *Neurobiology of brain disorders* (2nd ed., pp. 885–911). Academic Press.

Foa, E., Gillihan, S., & Bryant, R. (2013). Challenges and successes in dissemination of evidence-based treatments for posttraumatic stress: Lessons learned from prolonged exposure therapy for PTSD. *Psychological Science in the Public Interest, 14,* 65–111.

Friedman, M. J., & Davidson, J. (2014). Pharmacotherapy for PTSD. In M. J. Friedman, T. M. Keane, & P. A. Resick (Eds.), *Handbook of PTSD* (2nd ed., pp. 482–501). Guilford Press.

Friedman, M. J., Keane, T. M., & Resick, P. A. (Eds.). (2014). *Handbook of PTSD: Science and practice* (2nd ed.). Guilford Press.

Frueh, B., Grubaugh, A., Madan, A., Neer, S., Elhai, J., & Beidel, D. (2018). Evidence-based practice of posttraumatic stress disorder. In D. David, S. Lynn, & G. Montgomery (Eds.), *Evidence-based psychotherapy: The state of science and practice* (pp. 157–188). Wiley Blackwell.

Galea, S., Vlahov, D., Resnick, H., Ahern, J., Susser, E., Gold, J., Bucuvalas, M., & Kilpatrick, D. (2003). Trends of probable post-traumatic stress disorder in New York City after the September 11 terrorist attacks. *American Journal of Epidemiology, 158,* 514–524.

Gelernter, J., Sun, N., Polimanti, R., Pietrzak, R., Levey, D. F., Bryois, J., Lu, Q., Hu, Y., Li, B., Radhakrishnan, K., Aslan, M., Cheung, K. H., Li, Y., Rajeevan, N., Sayward, F., Harrington, K., Chen, Q., Cho, K., Pyarajan, S., . . . Department of Veterans Affairs Cooperative Studies Program (#575B) and Million Veteran Program. (2019). Genome-wide association study of post-traumatic stress disorder reexperiencing symptoms in >165,000 US veterans. *Nature Neuroscience, 22*(9), 1394–1401. https://doi.org/10.1038/s41593-019-0447-7

Gilbertson, M. (2011). Structural imaging of post-traumatic stress disorder. In M. Shenton & B. Turetsky (Eds.), *Understanding neuropsychiatric disorders: Insights from neuroimaging* (pp. 205–213). Cambridge University Press.

Hariri, A. R., & Holmes, A. (2015). Finding translation in stress research. *Nature Neuroscience, 18,* 1347–1352. http://doi.org/10.1038/nn.4111

Hecker, T., Hermenau, K., Maedl, A., Hinkel, H., Schauer, M., & Elbert, T. (2013). Does perpetrating violence damage mental health? Differences between forcibly recruited and voluntary combatants in DR Congo. *Journal of Traumatic Stress, 26,* 142–148. https://doi.org/10.1002/jts.21770

Himmerich, H., Patsalos, O., Lichtblau, N., Ibrahim, M. A. A., & Dalton, B. (2019). Cytokine research in depression: Principles, challenges, and open questions. *Frontiers in Psychiatry, 10,* 30. https://doi.org/10.3389/fpsyt.2019.00030

Hoge, C., Riviere, L., Wilk, J., Herrell, R., & Weathers, F. (2014). The prevalence of post-traumatic stress disorder (PTSD) in U.S. combat soldiers: A head-to-head comparison of *DSM-5* versus *DSM-IV-TR* symptom criteria with the PTSD checklist. *The Lancet Psychiatry*, 1, 269-277.

Hori, H., & Kim, Y. (2019). Inflammation and post-traumatic stress disorder. *Psychiatry and Clinical Neurosciences*, 73(4), 143-153. https://doi.org/10.1111/pcn.12820

Horn, S. R., & Feder, A. (2018). Understanding resilience and preventing and treating PTSD. *Harvard Review of Psychiatry*, 26(3), 158-174. https://doi.org/10.1097/HRP.0000000000000194

Huizink, A., Mulder, E., & Buitelaar, J. (2004). Prenatal stress and risk for psychopathology: Specific effects or induction of general susceptibility? *Psychological Bulletin*, 130, 115-142.

Hyman, S. (2009). How adversity gets under the skin. *Nature Neuroscience*, 12(3), 241-243. http://doi.org/10.1038/nn0309-241

Iwamoto, K., & Kato, T. (2009). Epigenetic profiling in schizophrenia and major mental disorders. *Neuropsychobiology*, 60, 5-11.

Jones, R., Yates, W., & Zhou, M. (2002). Readmission rates for adjustment disorders: comparison with other mood disorders. *Journal of Affective Disorders*, 71, 199-203.

Kemeny, M., & Schedlowski, M. (2007). Understanding the interaction between psychosocial stress and immune-related diseases: A stepwise progression. *Brain, Behavior, and Immunity*, 21, 1009-1018.

Khandaker, G. M., Cousins, L., Deakin, J., Lennox, B. R., Yolken, R., & Jones, P. B. (2015). Inflammation and immunity in schizophrenia: Implications for pathophysiology and treatment. *The Lancet Psychiatry*, 2(3), 258-270. http://doi.org/10.1016/S2215-0366(14)00122-9

Kiecolt-Glaser, J., Garner, W., Speicher, C., Penn, G., Holliday, J., & Glaser, R. (1984). Psychosocial modifiers of immunocompetence in medical students. *Psychosomatic Medicine*, 46, 7-14.

Kiecolt-Glaser, J., Gouin, J., & Hantsoo, L. (2010). Close relationships, inflammation, and health. *Neuroscience and Biobehavioral Review*, 35, 33-38.

Kiecolt-Glaser, J., McGuire, L., Robles, T., & Glaser, R. (2002). Psychoneuroimmunology: Psychological influences on immune function and health. *Journal of Consulting and Clinical Psychology*, 70, 537-547.

Kok, B. C., Herrell, R. K., Thomas, J. L., & Hoge, C. W. (2012). Posttraumatic stress disorder associated with combat service in Iraq or Afghanistan: Reconciling prevalence differences between studies. *Journal of Nervous and Mental Disease*, 200(5), 444-450. https://doi.org/10.1097/NMD.0b013e3182532312

Kulka, R. A., Schlenger, W. E., Fairbank, J. A., Hough, R. L., Jordan, B. K., Marmar, C. R., & Weiss, D. S. (1990). *Trauma and the Vietnam generation: Report of findings from the National Vietnam Veterans Readjustment Study*. Brunner/Mazel.

Lambert, H. K., & McLaughlin, K. A. (2019). Impaired hippocampus-dependent associative learning as a mechanism underlying PTSD: A meta-analysis. *Neuroscience and biobehavioral reviews*, 107, 729-749. https://doi.org/10.1016/j.neubiorev.2019.09.024

Lamers, F., Vogelzanga, N., Merikangas, K., de Jonge, P., Beekman, A., & Penninx, B. (2013). Evidence for a differential role of HPA-axis function, inflammation and metabolic syndrome in melancholic versus atypical depression. *Molecular Psychiatry*, 18, 692-699.

Lauzon, N., Bechard, M., Ahmad, T., & Laviolette, S. (2013). Supra-normal stimulation of dopamine D1 receptors in the prelimbic cortex blocks behavioral expression of both aversive and rewarding associative memories through a cyclic-AMP-dependent signaling pathway. *Neuropharmacology*, 67, 104-114.

Levy, B., & Sidel, V. (2009). Health effects of combat: A life-course perspective. *Annual Review of Public Health*, 30, 123-136.

Lucassen, P., Fitzsimons, C., Korosi, A., Hoels, M., Belzung, C., & Abrous, D. (2013). Stressing new neurons into depression? *Molecular Psychiatry*, 18, 396-397.

Marmar, C. R., Schlenger, W., Henn-Haase, C., Qian, M., Purchia, E., Li, M., Corry, N., Williams, C. S., Ho, C.-L., Horesh, D., Karstoft, K.-I., Shalev, A., & Kulka, R. A. (2015). Course of posttraumatic stress disorder 40 years after the Vietnam War: Findings from the National Vietnam Veterans Longitudinal Study. *JAMA Psychiatry*, 1, 269-277.

McEwen, B. (2010). Stress, sex, and neural adaptation to a changing environment: Mechanisms of neuronal remodeling. *Annals of the New York Academy of Science*, 1204, E38-E59.

McEwen, B. S. (1998). Protective and damaging effects of stress mediators. *New England Journal of Medicine*, 338, 171-179.

McEwen, B. S. (2013). The brain on stress: Toward an integrative approach to brain, body, and behavior. *Perspectives on Psychological Science*, 8(6), 673-675. http://doi.org/10.1177/1745691613506907

McEwen, B. S., Bowles, N. P., Gray, J. D., Hill, M. N., Hunter, R. G., Karatsoreos, I. N., & Nasca, C. (2015). Mechanisms of stress in the brain. *Nature Neuroscience*, 18, 1353-1363. http://doi.org/10.1038/nn.4086

McFarlane, A. C. (2014). PTSD and *DSM-5*: Unintended consequences of change. *The Lancet Psychiatry*, 1(4), 246-247.

McGowan, P., Sasaki, A., D'Alessio, A., Dymov, S., Labonté, B., Szyf, M., Turecki, G., & Meaney, M. (2009). Epigenetic regulation of the glucocorticoid receptor in human brain associates with childhood abuse. *Nature Neuroscience*, 12, 342-348.

McLean, C. P., Levy, H. C., Miller, M. L., & Tolin, D. F. (2022). Exposure therapy for PTSD: A meta-analysis. *Clinical Psychology Review*, 91, Article 102115. https://doi.org/10.1016/j.cpr.2021.102115

McNally, R. J., Bryant, R. A., & Ehlers, A. (2003). Does early psychological intervention promote recovery from posttraumatic stress? *Psychological Science in the Public Interest*, 4(2), 45-79. https://doi.org/10.1111/1529-1006.01421

Miller, G. (2010). The seductive allure of behavioral epigenetics. *Science*, 329, 24-27.

Mitchell, J. (1983). When disaster strikes: The critical incident stress debriefing process. *Journal of Emergency Medical Services*, 8, 36-39.

Murphy, M. D., & Heller, E. A. (2022). Convergent actions of stress and stimulants via epigenetic regulation of neural circuitry. *Trends in Neurosciences*, 45(12), 955-967. https://doi.org/10.1016/j.tins.2022.10.001

Najavits, L. (2002). *Seeking safety*. Guilford Press.

Nandi, C., Crombach, A., Elbert, T., & Weierstall, R. (2015). Predictors of posttraumatic stress and appetitive aggression in active soldiers and former combatants. *European Journal of Psychotraumatology*, 1, 1-9. http://doi.org/10.3402/ejpt.v6.26553

Nikulina, V., Widom, C. S., & Brzustowicz, L. M. (2012). Child abuse and neglect, MAOA, and mental health outcomes: A prospective examination. *Biological Psychiatry*, 71, 350-357.

North, C., Nixon, S., Shariat, S., Mallonee, S., McMillen, J. C., Spitznagel, E. L., & Smith, E. M. (1999). Psychiatric disorders among survivors of the Oklahoma City bombing. *JAMA, 282,* 755–62.

O'Connor, D. B., Thayer, J. F., & Vedhara, K. (2021). Stress and health: A review of psychobiological processes. *Annual Review of Psychology, 72,* 663–688. https://doi.org/10.1146/annurev-psych-062520-122331

Panksepp, J. (1998). *Affective neuroscience: The foundations of human and animal emotions.* Oxford University Press.

Pardo, C., Vargas, D., & Zimmerman, A. (2005). Immunity, neuroglia and neuroinflammation in autism. *International Review of Psychiatry, 17,* 485–495.

Price, D. D. (2000). Psychological and neural mechanisms of the affective dimension of pain. *Science, 288,* 1769–1772.

Prigerson, H. G., Boelen, P. A., Xu, J., Smith, K. V., & Maciejewski, P. K. (2021). Validation of the new DSM-5-TR criteria for prolonged grief disorder and the PG-13-Revised (PG-13-R) scale. *World Psychiatry, 20*(1), 96–106. https://doi.org/10.1002/wps.20823

Prigerson, H. G., Kakarala, S., Gang, J., & Maciejewski, P. K. (2021). History and status of prolonged grief disorder as a psychiatric diagnosis. *Annual Review of Clinical Psychology, 17,* 109–126.

Radtke, K., Ruf, M., Gunter, H., Dohrmann, K., Schauer, M., Meyer, A., & Elbert, T. (2011). Transgenerational impact of intimate partner violence on methylation in the promoter of the glucocorticoid receptor. *Translational Psychiatry, 1.* https://doi.org/10.1038/tp.2011.21

Rauch, S., Shin, L., & Phelps, E. (2006). Neurocircuitry models of posttraumatic stress disorder and extinction: Human neuroimaging research—Past, present, and future. *Biological Psychiatry, 60,* 376–382.

Repetti, R. L. (1989). Effects of daily workload on subsequent behavior during marital interaction: The roles of social withdrawal and spouse support. *Journal of Personality and Social Psychology, 57,* 651–659.

Ressler, K. J., Berretta, S., Bolshakov, V. Y., Rosso, I. M., Meloni, E. G., Rauch, S. L., & Carlezon, W. A., Jr. (2022). Post-traumatic stress disorder: clinical and translational neuroscience from cells to circuits. *Nature Reviews Neurology, 18*(5), 273–288. https://doi.org/10.1038/s41582-022-00635-8

Rockstroh, B., & Elbert, T. (2010). Traces of fear in the neural web—Magnetoencephalographic responding to arousing pictorial stimuli. *International Journal of Psychophysiology, 78,* 14–19.

Rogers, J., Raveendran, M., Fawcett, G., Fox, A., Shelton, S., Oler, J., Cheverud, J., Muzny, D., Gibbs, R., Davidson, R., & Kalin, N. (2013). CRHR1 genotypes, neural circuits and the diathesis for anxiety and depression. *Molecular Psychiatry, 18,* 700–707.

Roggers, A., Morgan, C., Bronson, S., Revello, S., & Bale, T. (2013). Paternal stress exposure alters sperm microRNA content and reprograms offspring HPA stress axis regulation. *Journal of Neuroscience, 33,* 9003–9012.

Rose, S., Bisson, J., Churchill, R., & Wessely, S. (2002). Psychological debriefing for preventing post traumatic stress disorder (PTSD). *Cochrane Database of Systematic Reviews.* https://doi.org/10.1002/14651858.CD000560

Rosner, R., Comtesse, H., Vogel, A., & Doering, B. K. (2021). Prevalence of prolonged grief disorder. *Journal of Affective Disorders, 287,* 301–307.

Roth, T., & Sweatt, J. (2011). Annual research review: Epigenetic mechanisms and environmental shaping of the brain during sensitive periods of development. *Journal of Child Psychology and Psychiatry, 52,* 398–408.

Russell, M. (2008). Scientific resistance to research, training and utilization of eye movement desensitization and reprocessing (EMDR) therapy in treating post-war disorders. *Social Science and Medicine, 67,* 1737–1746.

Sapolsky, R. M. (2015). Commentary: Stress and the brain: Individual variability and the inverted-U. *Nature Neuroscience, 18,* 1344–1346. http://doi.org/10.1038/nn.4109

Schaal, S., Koebach, A., Hinkel, H., & Elbert, T. (2015). Posttraumatic stress disorder according to *DSM*-5 and *DSM*-IV diagnostic criteria: A comparison in a sample of Congolese ex-combatants. *European Journal of Psychotraumatology, 6,* Article 24981. http://dx.doi.org/10.3402/ejpt.v6.24981

Schauer, E., & Elbert, T. (2010). The psychological impact of child soldiering. In E. Martz (Ed.), *Trauma rehabilitation after war and conflict* (pp. 311–360). Springer.

Schauer, M., Neuner, F., & Elbert, T. (2011). *Narrative exposure therapy: A short-term treatment for traumatic stress disorders.* Hogrefe & Huber.

Schnyder, U., Muller, J., Morina, N., Schick, M., Bryant, R., & Nickerson, A. (2015). A comparison of *DSM*-5 and *DSM*-IV diagnostic criteria for posttraumatic stress disorder in traumatized refugees. *Journal of Traumatic Stress, 28,* 267–274.

Scott, H. R., Stevelink, S. A. M., Gafoor, R., Lamb, D., Carr, E., Bakolis, I., Bhundia, R., Docherty, M. J., Dorrington, S., Gnanapragasam, S., Hegarty, S., Hotopf, M., Madan, I., McManus, S., Moran, P., Souliou, E., Raine, R., Razavi, R., Weston, D., . . . Wessely, S. (2023). Prevalence of post-traumatic stress disorder and common mental disorders in health-care workers in England during the COVID-19 pandemic: A two-phase cross-sectional study. *Lancet Psychiatry, 10*(1), 40–49.

Seah, C., Breen, M. S., Rusielewicz, T., Bader, H. N., Xu, C., Hunter, C. J., McCarthy, B., Deans, P. J. M., Chattopadhyay, M., Goldberg, J., Desarnaud, F., Makotkine, I., Flory, J. D., Bierer, L. M., Staniskyte, M., NYSCF Global Stem Cell Array® Team, Noggle, S. A., Huckins, L. M., Paull, D., . . . Yehuda, R. (2022). Modeling gene × environment interactions in PTSD using human neurons reveals diagnosis-specific glucocorticoid-induced gene expression. *Nature Neuroscience, 25*(11), 1434–1445. https://doi.org/10.1038/s41593-022-01161-y

Segerstrom, S., & Miller, G. (2004). Psychological stress and the human immune system: A meta-analytic study of 30 years of inquiry. *Psychological Bulletin, 130,* 601–630.

Shalev, A., Liberzon, I., & Marmar, C. (2017). Post-traumatic stress disorder. *New England Journal of Medicine, 376,* 2459–2469. https://doi.org/10.1056/NEJMra1612499

Shapiro, F. (2001). *Eye movement desensitization and reprocessing: Basic principles, protocols, and procedures* (2nd ed.). Guilford Press.

Shapiro, F. (2013). The case: Treating Jared through eye movement desensitization and reprocessing therapy. *Journal of Clinical Psychology, 69,* 494–496.

Shin, L., Brohawn, K., Pfaff, D., & Pitman, R. (2011). Functional imaging of posttraumatic stress disorder. In M. Shenton & B. Turetsky (Eds.), *Understanding neuropsychiatric disorders: Insights from neuroimaging.* Cambridge University Press.

Slavich, G. M., O'Donovan, A., Epel, E. S., & Kemeny, M. E. (2010). Black sheep get the blues: A psychobiological model of social rejection and depression. *Neuroscience and Biobehavioral Reviews, 35,* 39–45.

Sloan, D. M., Lee, D. J., Litwack, S. D., Sawyer, A. T., & Marx, B. P. (2013). Written exposure therapy for veterans diagnosed with PTSD: A pilot study. *Journal of Traumatic Stress, 26*(6), 776–779. http://dx.doi.org/10.1002/jts.21858

Sloan, D. M., Marx, B. P., Lee, D. J., & Resick, P. A. (2018). A brief exposure-based treatment vs cognitive processing therapy for posttraumatic stress disorder: A randomized noninferiority clinical trial. *JAMA Psychiatry, 75*, 233–239. https://doi.org/10.1001/jamapsychiatry.2017.4249

Smith, M. (2005). Bilateral hippocampal volume reduction in adults with post-traumatic stress disorder: A meta-analysis of structural MRI studies. *Hippocampus, 15*, 798–807.

Suliman, S., Troeman, Z., Stein, D. J., & Seedat, S. (2013). Predictors of acute stress disorder severity. *Journal of Affective Disorders, 149*, 277–281.

Tanielian, T., & Jaycox, L. (2008). *Invisible wounds of war*. RAND Corporation.

Taylor, S. E. (2011). Pathways linking early life stress to adult health. In J. Decety & J. Cacioppo (Eds.), *The Oxford handbook of social neuroscience* (pp. 776–786). Oxford University Press.

Taylor, S. E., Dickerson, S. S., & Klein, L. C. (2002). Toward a biology of social support. In C. R. Snyder & S. J. Lopez (Eds.), *Handbook of positive psychology* (pp. 556–569). Oxford University Press.

Taylor, S. E., Klein, L. C., Lewis, B. P., Gruenewald, T. L., Gurung, R. A. R., & Updegraff, J. A. (2000). Biobehavioral responses to stress in females: Tend-and-befriend, not fight-or-flight. *Psychological Review, 107*, 411–429.

Tost, H., Champagne, F. A., & Meyer-Lindenberg, A. (2015). Environmental influence in the brain, human welfare and mental health. *Nature Neuroscience, 18*(10), 4121–4131. http://doi.org/10.1038/nn.4108

Ulrich-Lai, Y., & Herman, J. (2009). Neural regulation of endocrine and autonomic stress responses. *Nature Reviews Neuroscience, 10*, 397–409.

Ursano, R., Li, H., Zhang, L., Hough, C., Fullerton, C., Benedek, D., Grieger, T., & Holloway, H. (2008). Models of PTSD and traumatic stress: The importance of research "from bedside to bench to bedside". *Progress in Brain Research, 167*, 203–215.

Vermetten, E., & Lanius, R. A. (2012). Biological and clinical framework for posttraumatic stress disorder. *Handbook of Clinical Neurology, 106*, 291–342.

Villani, A. C., Sarkizova, S., & Hacohen, N. (2018). Systems immunology: Learning the rules of the immune system. *Annual Review of Immunology, 36*, 813–842. https://doi.org/10.1146/annurev-immunol-042617-053035

Waheed, K. (n.d.). *Honoring the person I am*. Retrieved from Anxiety and Depression Association of America website: www.adaa.org/living-with-anxiety/personal-stories/honoring-person-i-am

Walker, E., McMillan, A., & Mittal, V. (2005). Neurohormones, neurodevelopment and the prodrome of psychosis in adolescence. In D. Romer & E. Walker (Eds.), *Adolescent psychopathology and the developing brain: Integrating brain and prevention science* (pp. 264–283). Oxford University Press.

Watkins, L. R., & Maier, S. F. (2002). Beyond neurons: Evidence that immune and glial cells contribute to pathological pain states. *Physiological Review, 82*, 981–1011.

Watkins, L. E., Sprang, K. R., & Rothbaum, B. O. (2018). Treating PTSD: A review of evidence-based psychotherapy interventions. *Frontiers in Behavioral Neuroscience, 12*, 258. https://doi.org/10.3389/fnbeh.2018.00258

Weaver, I., Cervoni, N., Champagne, F., D'Alessio, A., Sharma, S., Seckl, J., Dymov, S., Szyf, M., & Meaney, M. (2004). Epigenetic programming by maternal behavior. *Nature Neuroscience, 7*, 847–854.

Wesarg, C., Van Den Akker, A. L., Oei, N. Y., Hoeve, M., & Wiers, R. W. (2020). Identifying pathways from early adversity to psychopathology: A review on dysregulated HPA axis functioning and impaired self-regulation in early childhood. *European Journal of Developmental Psychology, 17*(6), 808–827.

World Health Organization. (2005). *Mental health atlas*.

Yu, L. W., Agirman, G., & Hsiao, E. Y. (2022). The gut microbiome as a regulator of the neuroimmune landscape. *Annual Review of Immunology, 40*, 143–167. https://doi.org/10.1146/annurev-immunol-101320-014237

Yuan, H., Phillips, R., Wong, C., Zotev, V., Misaki, M. et al., Tracking resting state connectivity dynamics in veterans with PTSD. *NeuroImage: Clinical, 19*, 260–270.

Zefferino, R., Di Gioia, S., & Conese, M. (2021). Molecular links between endocrine, nervous and immune system during chronic stress. *Brain and Behavior, 11*(2), Article e01960 https://doi.org/10.1002/brb3.1960

CHAPTER 8

Abel, J. L., & Borkovec, T. D. (1995). Generalizability of *DSM*-III-R generalized anxiety disorders to proposed *DSM*-IV criteria and cross-validation of proposed changes. *Journal of Anxiety Disorders, 9*, 303–315.

Abramowitz, J. S., & Jacoby, R. J. (2015). Obsessive-compulsive and related disorders: A critical review of the new diagnostic class. *Annual Review of Clinical Psychology, 11*, 165–186.

Abramowitz, J., Deacon, B., & Whiteside, S. (2011). *Exposure therapy for anxiety*. Guilford Press.

American Psychiatric Association. (2013). *Diagnostic and statistical manual of mental disorders*. (5th ed.).

American Psychiatric Association. (2022). *Diagnostic and statistical manual of mental disorders*. (5th ed., text rev.).

Andreescu, C., Mennin, D., Tudorascu, D., Sheu, L. K., Walker, S., Banihashemi, L., & Aizenstein, H. (2015). The many faces of anxiety: Neurobiological correlates of anxiety phenotypes. *Psychiatry Research: Neuroimaging, 234*(1), 96–105. http://doi.org/10.1016/j.pscychresns.2015.08.013

Antony, M. M., & Barlow, D. H. (2002). Specific phobia. In D. H. Barlow (Ed.), *Anxiety and its disorders: The nature and treatment of anxiety and panic* (2nd ed., pp. 380–417). Guilford Press.

Arcaro, M. J., Schade, P. F., & Livingstone, M. S. (2019). Universal mechanisms and the development of the face network: What you see is what you get. *Annual Review of Vision Science, 5*, 341–372. https://doi.org/10.1146/annurev-vision-091718-014917

Asok, A., Kandel, E. R., & Rayman, J. B. (2019). The neurobiology of fear generalization. *Frontiers in Behavioral Neuroscience, 12*, Article 329. https://doi.org/10.3389/fnbeh.2018.00329

Barber, J., Muran, J., McCarthy, K., & Keefe, J. (2013). Research on dynamic therapies. In M. Lambert (Ed.), *Handbook of psychotherapy and behavior change* (6th ed., pp. 443–494). Wiley.

Barlow, D. (2000). Unraveling the mysteries of anxiety and its disorders from the perspective of emotion theory. *American Psychologist, 55*, 1247–1263.

Barlow, D. (2002). *Anxiety and its disorders: The nature and treatment of anxiety and panic* (2nd ed.). Guilford Press.

Bas-Hoogendam, J. M., van Steenbergen, H., Cohen Kadosh, K., Westenberg, P. M., & van der Wee, N. J. A. (2021). Intrinsic functional connectivity in families genetically enriched for social anxiety disorder—An endophenotype study. *EBioMedicine, 69*, 103445. https://doi.org/10.1016/j.ebiom.2021.103445

Bas-Hoogendam, J. M., van Steenbergen, H., van der Wee, N. J. A., & Westenberg, P. M. (2020). Amygdala hyperreactivity to faces conditioned with a social-evaluative meaning—A multiplex, multigenerational fMRI study on social anxiety endophenotypes. *NeuroImage: Clinical, 26*, Article 102247. https://doi.org/10.1016/j.nic1.2020.102247

Bienvenu, O., Samuels, J., Wuyek, L., Liang, K., Wang, Y., Grados, M., Cullen, B., Riddle, M., Greenberg, B., Rasmussen, S., Fryer, A., Pinto, A., Rauch, S., Pauls, D., McCraken, J., Piacentini, J., Murphy, D., Knowles, J., & Nestadt, G. (2012). Is obsessive-compulsive disorder an anxiety disorder, and what, if any, are spectrum conditions? A family study perspective. *Psychological Medicine, 42*, 1–13.

Bishop, S. J. (2007). Neurocognitive mechanisms of anxiety: An integrative account. *Trends in Cognitive Sciences, 11*, 307–316.

Bishop, S. J., & Gagne, C. (2018). Anxiety, depression, and decision making: A computational perspective. *Annual Reviews of Neuroscience, 41*, 371–388. https://doi.org/10.1146/annurev-neuro-080317-062007

Bloch, M. H., Landeros-Weisenberger, A., Rosario, M. C., Pittenger, C., & Leckman, J. F. (2008). Systematic review of the factor structure of obsessive-compulsive disorder. *American Journal of Psychiatry, 165*, 1532–1542.

Borkovec, T. D. (1994). The nature, functions, and origins of worry. In G. C. L. Davey & F. Tallis (Eds.), *Worrying: Perspectives on theory, assessment and treatment* (pp. 5–33). Wiley.

Borkovec, T. D., Alcaine, O., & Behar, E. S. (2004). Avoidance theory of worry and generalized anxiety disorder. In R. Heimberg, D. Mennin, & C. Turk (Eds.), *Generalized anxiety disorder: Advances in research and practice* (pp. 77–108). Guilford Press.

Borkovec, T. D., & Ruscio, A. (2001). Psychotherapy for generalized anxiety disorder. *Journal of Clinical Psychiatry, 62*, 37–42.

Brown, T. A., Campbell, L. A., Lehman, C. L., Grisham, J. R., & Mancill, R. B. (2001). Current and lifetime comorbidity of the DSM-IV anxiety and mood disorders in a large clinical sample. *Journal of Abnormal Psychology, 110*, 585–599.

Calkins, A., Bui, E., Taylor, C., Pollack, M., LeBeau, R., & Simon, N. (2016). Anxiety disorders. In T. A. Stern, M. Fava, T. E. Wilens, & J. F. Rosenbaum (Eds.), *Massachusetts General Hospital comprehensive clinical psychiatry* (2nd ed., pp. 353–366). Elsevier.

Carl, E., Witcraft, S. M., Kauffman, B. Y., Gillespie, E. M., Becker, E. S., Cuijpers, P., Van Ameringen, M., Smits, J. A. J., & Powers, M. B. (2020). Psychological and pharmacological treatments for generalized anxiety disorder (GAD): A meta-analysis of randomized controlled trials. *Cognitive Behaviour Therapy, 49*(1), 1–21. https://doi.org/10.1080/16506073.2018.1560358

Castonguay, L., Nelson, D., Boswell, J., Nordberg, S., McAleavey, A., Newman, M., & Borkovec, T. (2012). Corrective experiences in cognitive behavior and interpersonal-emotional processing therapies: A qualitative analysis of a single case. In L. Castonguay & C. Hill (Eds.), *Transformation in psychotherapy: Corrective experiences across cognitive behavioral, humanistic, and psychodynamic approaches* (pp. 245–279). American Psychological Association.

Chamberlain, S., Menzies, L., Hampshire, A., Suckling, J., Fineberg, N., del Campo, N., Aitken, M., Craig, K., Owen, A., Bullmore, E., Robbins, T., & Sahakian, B. (2008). Orbitofrontal dysfunction in patients with obsessive-compulsive disorder and their unaffected relatives. *Science, 321*, 421–422.

Chang, E., Downey, C., Hirsch, J., & Yu, E. (Eds.). (2018). *Treating depression, anxiety, and stress in ethnic and racial groups*. American Psychological Association.

Colas, E. (1998). *Just checking: Scenes from the life of an obsessive-compulsive*. Washington Square Press.

Collins, L., Bragdon, L., & Coles, M. (2018). The treatment of obsessive–compulsive disorder. In D. David, S. Lynn, & G. Montgomery (Eds.), *Evidence-based psychotherapy: The state of science and practice* (pp. 123–156). Wiley Blackwell.

Craske, M. G., Kircanski, K., Epstein, A., Wittchen, H. U., Pine, D. S., Lewis-Fernández, R., Hinton, D., DSM V Anxiety, OC Spectrum, & Posttraumatic and Dissociative Disorder Work Group. (2010). Panic disorder: A review of DSM-IV panic disorder and proposals for DSM-V. *Depression and Anxiety, 27*, 93–112.

Curtis, G. C., Magee, W. J., Eaton, W. W., Wittchen, H.-U., & Kessler, R. C. (1998). Specific fears and phobias: Epidemiology and classification. *British Journal of Psychiatry, 173*, 212–217. https://doi.org/10.1192/bjp.173.3.212

Davis, T. E., 3rd, Ollendick, T. H., & Öst, L. G. (2019). One-session treatment of specific phobias in children: Recent developments and a systematic review. *Annual Review of Clinical Psychology, 15*, 233–256. https://doi.org/10.1146/annurev-clinpsy-050718-095608

Dray, K. (n.d.). Adele emotionally explains why she may never tour again. *Stylist*. https://www.stylist.co.uk/people/adele-panic-attack-anxiety-why-never-tour-again-concert-tickets/33141

English, H. (1929). Three cases of the "conditioned fear response". *Journal of Abnormal Psychology, 24*, 221–225.

Etkin, A., & Wager, T. D. (2007). Functional neuroimaging of anxiety: A meta-analysis of emotional processing in PTSD, social anxiety disorder, and specific phobia. *American Journal of Psychiatry, 164*, 1476–1488.

Fang, A., & Wilhelm, S. (2015). Clinical features, cognitive biases, and treatment of body dysmorphic disorder. *Annual Review of Clinical Psychology, 11*(1). http://doi.org/10.1146/annurev-clinpsy-032814-112849

Fava, L., & Morton, J. (2009). Causal modeling of panic disorder theories. *Clinical Psychology Review, 29*, 623–637.

Feng, C., Eickhoff, S. B., Li, T., Wang, L., Becker, B., Camilleri, J. A., Hétu, S., & Luo, Y. (2021). Common brain networks underlying human social interactions: Evidence from large-scale neuroimaging meta-analysis. *Neuroscience and Biobehavioral Reviews, 126*, 289–303. https://doi.org/10.1016/j.neubiorev.2021.03.025

Fernández de la Cruz, L., Isomura, K., Lichtenstein, P., Rück, C., & Mataix-Cols, D. (2022). Morbidity and mortality in obsessive-compulsive disorder: A narrative review. *Neuroscience and Biobehavioral Reviews, 136*, Article 104602. https://doi.org/10.1016/j.neubiorev.2022.104602

Feygin, D., Swain, J., & Leckman, J. (2006). The normalcy of neurosis: Evolutionary origins of obsessive-compulsive disorder and related behaviors. *Progress in Neuro-psychopharmacology & Biological Psychiatry, 30*, 854–864.

Figee, M., Luigjes, J., Smolders, R., Valencia-Alfonso, C.-E., van Wingen, G., de Kwaasteniet, B., Mantione, M., Ooms, P., de Koning, P., Vulink, N., Levar, N., Droge, L., van den Munckhof, P., Schuurman, P., Nederveen, A., van den Brink, W., Mazaheri, A., Vink, M., & Denys, D. (2013). Deep brain stimulation restores frontostriatal network activity in obsessive-compulsive disorder. *Nature Neuroscience, 16*(4), 386–387. http://doi.org/10.1038/nn.3344

Filippi, C. A., Valadez, E. A., Fox, N. A., & Pine, D. S. (2022). Temperamental risk for anxiety: emerging work on the infant brain and later neurocognitive development. *Current Opinion in Behavioral Sciences, 44*, Article 101105. https://doi.org/10.1016/j.cobeha.2022.101105

Foa, E., & Kozak, M. (1986). Emotional processing of fear: Exposure to corrective information. *Psychological Bulletin, 99*, 20–35.

Franklin, M., & Foa, E. (2008). Obsessive-compulsive disorder. In D. Barlow (Ed.), *Clinical handbook of psychological disorders: A step-by-step treatment manual* (4th ed., pp. 164–215). Guilford Press.

Franklin, M., & Foa, E. (2011). Treatment of obsessive-compulsive disorder. *Annual Review of Clinical Psychology, 7*, 229–243.

Fries, E., Moragues, N., Caldji, C., Hellhammer, D. H., & Meaney, M. J. (2004). Preliminary evidence of altered sensitivity to benzodiazepines as a function of maternal care in the rat. *Annals of the New York Academy of Science, 1032*, 320–324.

Ghasemi, M., Navidhamidi, M., Rezaei, F., Azizikia, A., & Mehranfard, N. (2022). Anxiety and hippocampal neuronal activity: Relationship and potential mechanisms. *Cognitive, Affective & Behavioral Neuroscience, 22*(3), 431–449. https://doi.org/10.3758/s13415-021-00973-y

Gilbert, A., Gilbert, A., de Almeida, J., & Szeszko, P. (2011). In M. Shenton & B. Turetsky (Eds.), *Understanding neuropsychiatric disorders: Insights from neuroimaging*. Cambridge University Press.

Goodman, W. K., Storch, E. A., & Sheth, S. A. (2021). Harmonizing the neurobiology and treatment of obsessive-compulsive disorder. *American Journal of Psychiatry, 178*(1), 17–29. https://doi.org/10.1176/appi.ajp.2020.20111601

Graeff, F., & Del-Ben, C. (2008). Neurobiology of panic disorder: From animal models to brain neuroimaging. *Neuroscience and Biobehavioral Review, 32*, 1326–1335.

Gray, J. A., & McNaughton, N. (2000). *The neuropsychology of anxiety* (2nd ed.). Oxford University Press.

Grazia, D. (2010). *On the outside looking in: My life with social anxiety disorder*. BookLocker.

Grill-Spector, K., Weiner, K. S., Kay, K., & Gomez, J. (2017). The functional neuroanatomy of human face perception. *Annual Review of Vision Science, 3*, 167–196. https://doi.org/10.1146/annurev-vision-102016-061214

Gross, C., & Hen, R. (2004). The developmental origins of anxiety. *Nature Reviews Neuroscience, 5*, 545–552.

Gu, B., Kang, D., & Kwon, J. (2011). Functional imaging of obsessive-compulsive disorder. In M. Shenton & B. Turetsky (Eds.), *Understanding neuropsychiatric disorders: Insights from neuroimaging* (pp. 247–259). Cambridge University Press.

Haddad, J., Strauss, E. M., & Muir, D. (2009, November 23). Germs: "No deal" for host Howie Mandel. ABC News. https://abcnews.go.com/2020/howie-mandel-public-obsessive-compulisve-disorder-fear-germs/story?id=9153966

Hahn, A., Stein, P., Windischberger, C., Weissenbacher, A., Spindelegger, C., Moser, E., Kasper, S., & Lanzenberger, R. (2011). Reduced resting-state functional connectivity between amygdala and orbitofrontal cortex in social anxiety disorder. *NeuroImage, 56*, 881–889.

Hayes, S. C. (2004). Acceptance and commitment therapy, relational frame theory, and the third wave of behavioral and cognitive therapies. *Behavior Therapy, 35*, 639–665.

Hayes, S. C., Strosahl, K. D., & Wilson, K. G. (2011). *Acceptance and commitment therapy: The process and practice of mindful change* (2nd ed.). Guilford Press.

Hayes-Skelton, S. A., Roemer, L., & Orsillo, S. M. (2013). A randomized clinical trial comparing an acceptance-based behavior therapy to applied relaxation for generalized anxiety disorder. *Journal of Consulting and Clinical Psychology, 81*(5), 761–773. https://doi.org/10.1037/a0032871

Hettema, J., Neale, M., & Kendler, K. (2001). A review and meta-analysis of the genetic epidemiology of anxiety disorders. *American Journal of Psychiatry, 158*, 1568–1578.

Hofmann, S. G., & Barlow, D. H. (2002). Social phobia (social anxiety disorder). In D. H. Barlow (Ed.), *Anxiety and its disorders: The nature and treatment of anxiety and panic* (2nd ed., pp. 454–476). Guilford Press.

Hoge, E. A., Bui, E., Marques, L., Metcalf, C. A., Morris, L. K., Robinaugh, D. J., Worthington, J. J., Pollack, M. H., & Simon, N. M. (2013). Randomized controlled trial of mindfulness meditation for generalized anxiety disorder: Effects on anxiety and stress reactivity. *Journal of Clinical Psychiatry, 74*.

Hoge, E. A., Bui, E., Mete, M., Dutton, M. A., Baker, A. W., & Simon, N. M. (2023). Mindfulness-based stress reduction vs escitalopram for the treatment of adults with anxiety disorders: A randomized clinical trial. *JAMA Psychiatry, 80*(1), 13–21. doi:10.1001/jamapsychiatry.2022.3679

Hölzel, B. K., Hoge, E. A., Greve, D. N., Gard, T., Creswell, J. D., Brown, K. W., Barrett, L. F., Schwartz, C., Vaitl, D., & Lazar, S. W. (2013). Neural mechanisms of symptom improvements in generalized anxiety disorder following mindfulness training. *NeuroImage: Clinical, 2*, 448–458.

Huys, Q. J. M., Daw, N. D., & Dayan, P. (2015, January). Depression: A decision-theoretic analysis. *Annual Review of Neuroscience, 38*, 1–23. http://doi.org/10.1146/annurev-neuro-071714-033928

Kagan, J. (2003). Biology, context, and developmental inquiry. *Annual Review of Psychology, 54*, 1–23. http://doi.org/10.1146/annurev.psych.54.101601.145240

Karas, P. J., Lee, S., Jimenez-Shahed, J., Goodman, W. K., Viswanathan, A., & Sheth, S. A. (2019). Deep brain stimulation for obsessive compulsive disorder: Evolution of surgical stimulation target parallels changing model of dysfunctional brain circuits. *Frontiers in Neuroscience, 12*, Article 998. https://doi.org/10.3389/fnins.2018.00998

Kendler, K., & Baker, J. (2007). Genetic influences on measures of the environment: A systematic review. *Psychological Medicine, 37*, 615–626.

Kessler, R. C., Aguilar-Gaxiola, S., Alonso, J., Chatterji, S., Lee, S., Ormel, J., Üstün, T. B., & Wang, P. S. (2009). The global burden of mental disorders: An update from the WHO World Mental Health (WMH) surveys. *Epidemiologia e Psichiatria Sociale, 18*(1), 23–33.

Kessler, R. C., Avenevoli, S., Costello, E. J., Georgiades, K., Green, J. G., Gruber, M. J., He, J., Koretz, D., McLaughlin, K. A., Petukhova, M., Sampson, N. A., Zaslavsky, A. M., & Merikangas, K. (2012). Prevalence, persistence, and sociodemographic correlates of *DSM*-IV disorders in the National

Comorbidity Survey Replication Adolescent Supplement. *Archives of General Psychiatry, 69*, 372–380.

Kessler, R. C., Chiu, W. T., Demler, O., & Walters, E. E. (2005). Prevalence, severity, and comorbidity of 12-month DSM-IV disorders in the National Comorbidity Survey replication. *Archives of General Psychiatry, 62*(6), 617–627. https://doi.org/10.1001/archpsyc.62.6.617

Kessler, R. C., Chiu, W. T., Jin, R., Ruscio, A. M., Shear, K., & Walters, E. E. (2006). The epidemiology of panic attacks, panic disorder, and agoraphobia in the National Comorbidity Survey replication. *Archives of General Psychiatry, 63*, 415–424.

Kessler, R. C., Green, J. G., Gruber, M. J., Sampson, N. A., Bromet, E., Cuitan, M., Furukawa, T. A., Gureje, O., Hinkov, H., Hu, H.-Y., Lara, C., Lee, S., Mneimneh, Z., Myer, L., Oakley-Browne, M., Posada-Villa, J., Sagar, R., Viana, M. C., & Zaslavsky, A. M. (2010). Screening for serious mental illness in the general population with the K6 screening scale: Results from the WHO World Mental Health (WMH) survey initiative. *International Journal of Methods in Psychiatric Research, 19*(S1), 4–22.

Klumpp, H., & Fitzgerald, J. M. (2018). Neuroimaging predictors and mechanisms of treatment response in social anxiety disorder: An overview of the amygdala. *Current Psychiatry Reports, 20*(10), Article 89. https://doi.org/10.1007/s11920-018-0948-1

Kreps, D. (2018, November 2). Watch Ariana Grande talk anxiety, perform "Sweetener" songs on BBC special. *Rolling Stone.* https://www.rollingstone.com/music/music-news/ariana-grande-anxiety-bbc-751525/

Lai, C. (2011). Gray matter deficits in panic disorder. *Journal of Clinical Psychopharmacology, 31*, 287–293.

LeBeau, R., Glenn, D., Liao, B., Wittchen, H., Beesdo-Baum, K., Ollendick, T., & Craske, M. (2010). Specific phobia: A review of *DSM-IV* specific phobia and preliminary recommendations for DSM-V. *Depression and Anxiety, 27*, 148–167.

Leckman, J., Denys, D., Simpson, H., Mataix-Cols, D., Hollander, E., Saxena, S., Miguel, E., Rauch, S., Goodman, W., Phillips, K., & Stein, D. (2010). Obsessive-compulsive disorder: A review of the diagnostic criteria and possible subtypes and dimensional specifiers for *DSM-V*. *Depression and Anxiety, 27*, 507–527.

LeDoux, J. (1994, June). Emotion, memory, and the brain. *Scientific American,* pp. 62–71.

LeDoux, J. (2000). Emotion circuits in the brain. *Annual Review of Neuroscience, 23*, 155–184.

LeDoux, J. (2003). The self: Clues from the brain. *Annals of the New York Academy of Science, 1001*, 295–304.

Leichsenring, F., & Steinert, C. (2018). Towards an evidence-based unified psychodynamic protocol for emotional disorders. *Journal of Affective Disorders, 232*, 400–416.

Li, R., Shen, F., Sun, X., Zou, T., Li, L., Wang, X., Deng, C., Duan, X., He, Z., Yang, M., Li, Z., & Chen, H. (2023). Dissociable salience and default mode network modulation in generalized anxiety disorder: A connectome-wide association study. *Cerebral Cortex, 33*(10), 6354–6365. https://doi.org/10.1093/cercor/bhac509

MacLeod, C., Grafton, B., & Notebaert, L. (2019). Anxiety-linked attentional bias: Is it reliable? *Annual Review of Clinical Psychology, 15*, 529–554.

MacLeod, C., & Mathews, A. (2012). Cognitive bias modification approaches to anxiety. *Annual Review of Clinical Psychology, 8*, 189–217.

Mandel, H. (2010). *Here's the deal: Don't touch me.* Bantam Books.

Maust, D. T., Lin, L. A., & Blow, F. C. (2019). Benzodiazepine use and misuse among adults in the United States. *Psychiatric Services, 70*(2), 97–106. https://doi.org/10.1176/appi.ps.201800321

Mayo-Wilson, E., Dias, S., Mavranezouli, I., Kew, K., Clark, D. M., Ades, A. E., & Pilling, S. (2014, October). Psychological and pharmacological interventions for social anxiety disorder in adults: A systematic review and network meta-analysis. *The Lancet Psychiatry, 1*(5), 368–376. http://doi.org/10.1016/S2215-0366(14)70329-3

McCabe, R. E., Antony, M. M., Summerfeldt, L. J., Liss, A., & Swinson, R. P. (2003). Preliminary examination of the relationship between anxiety disorders in adults and self-reported history of teasing or bullying experiences. *Cognitive Behaviour Therapy, 32*, 187–193.

McCabe-Bennett, H., Fracalanza, K., & Antony, M. (2018). The psychological treatment of generalized anxiety disorder. In D. David, S. Lynn, & G. Montgomery (Eds.), *Evidence-based psychotherapy: The state of science and practice* (pp. 95–122). Wiley Blackwell.

McNaughton, N., & Corr, P. J. (2004). A two-dimensional neuropsychology of defense: Fear/anxiety and defensive distance. *Neuroscience and Biobehavioral Reviews, 28*, 285–305.

Menzies, L., Chamberlain, S., Laird, A., Thelen, S., Sahakian, B., & Bullmore, E. (2008). Integrating evidence from neuroimaging and neuropsychological studies of obsessive-compulsive disorder: The orbitofronto-striatal model revisited. *Neuroscience and Biobehavioral Review, 32*, 525–549.

Millan, M. (2003). The neurobiology and control of anxious states. *Progress in Neurobiology, 70*, 83–244.

Mineka, S., & Oehlberg, K. (2008). The relevance of recent developments in classical conditioning to understanding the etiology and maintenance of anxiety disorders. *Acta Psychologica, 127*(3), 567–580. http://doi.org/10.1016/j.actpsy.2007.11.007

Mineka, S., & Zinbarg, R. (2006). A contemporary learning theory perspective on the etiology of anxiety disorders: It's not what you thought it was. *American Psychologist, 61*(1), 10–26. http://doi.org/10.1037/0003-066X.61.1.10

Miskovic, V., & Schmidt, L. (2012). Social fearfulness in the human brain. *Neuroscience and Biobehavioral Reviews, 36*, 459–478.

Mitte, K. (2005). A meta-analysis of the efficacy of psycho- and pharmacotherapy in panic disorder with and without agoraphobia. *Journal of Affective Disorders, 88*, 27–45.

Mizzi, S., Pedersen, M., Lorenzetti, V., Heinrichs, M., & Labuschagne, I. (2022). Resting-state neuroimaging in social anxiety disorder: A systematic review. *Molecular Psychiatry, 27*(1), 164–179. https://doi.org/10.1038/s41380-021-01154-6

Nashold, B. S. Jr., Wilson, N. P., & Slaughter, G. S. (1974). The midbrain and pain. In J. J. Bonica (Ed.), *Advances in neurology, international symposium on pain* (Vol. 4, pp. 191–196). Raven Press.

Nasir, M., Trujillo, D., Levine, J., Dwyer, J. B., Rupp, Z. W., & Bloch, M. H. (2020). Glutamate systems in DSM-5 anxiety disorders: Their role and a review of glutamate and GABA psychopharmacology. *Frontiers in Psychiatry, 11*, Article 548505. https://doi.org/10.3389/fpsyt.2020.548505

Oathes, D. J., Ray, W. J., Yamasaki, A. S., Borkovec, T. D., Newman, M. G., & Castonguay, L. G. (2008). Worry, generalized anxiety disorder, and emotion: Evidence from the EEG gamma band. *Biological Psychology, 79*, 165–170.

Öhman, A. (1986). Face the beast and fear the face: Animal and social fears as prototypes for evolutionary analyses of emotion. *Psychophysiology*, 23, 123–145.

Öhman, A. (2009). Of snakes and faces: An evolutionary perspective on the psychology of fear. *Scandinavian Journal of Psychology*, 50, 543–552.

Öhman, A., & Mineka, S. (2001). Fears, phobias, and preparedness: Toward an evolved module of fear and fear learning. *Psychological Review*, 108, 483–522.

Olfson, M., King, M., & Schoenbaum, M. (2015). Benzodiazepine use in the United States. *JAMA Psychiatry*, 72(2), 136–142. http://doi.org/10.1001/jamapsychiatry.2014.1763

Ollendick, T., Yang, B., King, N., Dong, Q., & Akande, A. (1996). Fears in American, Australian, Chinese, and Nigerian children and adolescents: A cross-cultural study. *Journal of Child Psychology and Psychiatry*, 37, 213–220.

Öst, L. (1989). One-session treatment for specific phobias. *Behavior Research and Therapy*, 27, 1–7.

Öst, L. (1996). One-session group treatment of spider phobia. *Behavior Research and Therapy*, 34, 707–715.

Panksepp, J. (Ed.). (2004). *Textbook of biological psychiatry*. Wiley.

Pauls, D. L., Abramovitch, A., Rauch, S. L., & Geller, D. A. (2014). Obsessive-compulsive disorder: An integrative genetic and neurobiological perspective. *Nature Reviews Neuroscience*, 15(6), 410–424. http://doi.org/10.1038/nrn3746

Phan, K. L., Fitzgerald, D. A., Nathan, P. J., & Tancer, M. E. (2006). Association between amygdala hyperactivity to harsh faces and severity of social anxiety in generalized social phobia. *Biological Psychiatry*, 59, 424–429.

Phillips, K. A., Stein, D. J., Rauch, S. L., Hollander, E., Fallon, B. A., Barsky, A., Fineberg, N., Mataix-Cols, D., Ferrão, Y. A., Saxena, S., Wilhelm, S., Kelly, M. M., Clark, L. E., Pirto, A., Bienvenu, O. J., Farrow, J., & Leckman, J. (2010). Should an obsessive-compulsive spectrum grouping of disorders be included in DSM–V? *Depression and Anxiety*, 27(6), 528–555. https://doi.org/10.1002/da.20705

Porcelli, S., Van Der Wee, N., van der Werff, S., Aghajani, M., Glennon, J. C., van Heukelum, S., Mogavero, F., Lobo, A., Olivera, F. J., Lobo, E., Posadas, M., Dukart, J., Kozak, R., Arce, E., Ikram, A., Vorstman, J., Bilderbeck, A., Saris, I., Kaas, M. J., & Serretti, A. (2019). Social brain, social dysfunction and social withdrawal. *Neuroscience & Biobehavioral Reviews*, 97, 10–33.

Rapee, R., Schniering, C., & Hudson, J. (2009). Anxiety disorders during childhood and adolescence: Origins and treatment. *Annual Review of Clinical Psychology*, 5, 311–341.

Robinson, O. J., Krimsky, M., Lieberman, L., Allen, P., Vytal, K., & Grillon, C. (2014). Towards a mechanistic understanding of pathological anxiety: The dorsal medial prefrontal-amygdala "aversive amplification" circuit in unmedicated generalized and social anxiety disorders. *The Lancet Psychiatry*, 1(4), 294–302. http://doi.org/10.1016/S2215-0366(14)70305-0

Rodebaugh, T., Holaway, R., & Heimberg, R. (2004). The treatment of social anxiety disorder. *Clinical Psychology Review*, 24, 883–908.

Roemer, L., & Orsillo, S. M. (2002). Expanding our conceptualization of and treatment for generalized anxiety disorder: Integrating mindfulness/acceptance-based approaches with existing cognitive-behavioral models. *Clinical Psychology: Science and Practice*, 9(1), 54–68.

Roemer, L., Orsillo, S. M., & Barlow, D. H. B. (2002). Generalized anxiety disorder. In D. Barlow (Ed.), *Anxiety and its disorders: The nature and treatment of anxiety and panic* (2nd ed., pp. 477–515). Guilford Press.

Roemer, L., Orsillo, S. M., & Salters-Pednault, K. (2008). Efficacy of an acceptance-based behavior therapy for generalized anxiety disorder: Evaluation in a randomized controlled trial. *Journal of Consulting and Clinical Psychology*, 76(6), 1083–1089. http://doi.org/10.1037/a0012720

Rolling Stone. (2011, April 13). Choice excerpts from Adele's cover story. https://www.rollingstone.com/music/music-lists/choice-excerpts-from-adeles-cover-story-19278

Schmidt-Wilcke, T., Fuchs, E., Funke, K., Vlachos, A., Müller-Dahlhaus, F., Puts, N. A. J., Harris, R. E., & Edden, R. A. E. (2018). GABA-from inhibition to cognition: Emerging concepts. *The Neuroscientist*, 24(5), 501–515. https://doi.org/10.1177/1073858417734530

Schweckendiek, J., Klucken, T., Merz, C., Tabbert, K., Walter, B., Ambach, W., Vietl, D., & Stark, R. (2011). Weaving the (neuronal) web: Fear learning in spider phobia. *NeuroImage*, 54, 681–688.

Sehlmeyer, C., Schöning, S., Zwitserlood, P., Pfleiderer, B., Kircher, T., Arolt, V., & Konrad, C. (2009). Human fear conditioning and extinction in neuroimaging: A systematic review. *PLOS ONE*, 4, Article e5865.

Simonelli, L., Ray, W. J., & Pincus, A. (2004). Attachment models and their relationships with anxiety, worry, and depression. *Counseling and Clinical Psychology Journal*, 1, 107–118.

Slee, A., Nazareth, I., Bondaronek, P., Liu, Y., Cheng, Z., & Freemantle, N. (2019). Pharmacological treatments for generalised anxiety disorder: A systematic review and network meta-analysis. *The Lancet*, 393, 768–777. https://doi.org/10.1016/S0140-6736(18)31793-8

Stein, D. J., Fineberg, N. A., Bienvenu, O. J., Denys, D., Lochner, C., Nestadt, G., Leckman, J. F., Rauch, S. L., & Phillips, K. A. (2010). Should OCD be classified as an anxiety disorder in DSM–V? *Depression and Anxiety*, 27(6), 495–506. https://doi.org/10.1002/da.20699

Stewart, S. E., Lafleur, D., Dougherty, D. D., Wilhelm, S., Keuthen, N. J., & Jenike, M. A. (2016). Obsessive-compulsive disorder and obsessive-compulsive and related disorders. In T. A. Stern, M. Fava, T. E. Wilens, & J. F. Rosenbaum (Eds.), *Massachusetts General Hospital comprehensive clinical psychiatry* (Vol. 33, pp. 367–379). Elsevier.

Straube, T., Glauer, M., Dilger, S., Mentzel, H., & Miltner, W. (2006). Effects of cognitive-behavioral therapy on brain activation in specific phobia. *NeuroImage*, 29, 125–135.

Sylvester, C., Corbetta, M., Raichle, M., Rodebaugh, T., Schlaggar, B., Sheline, Y., Zorumski, C., & Lenze, E. (2012). Functional network dysfunction in anxiety and anxiety disorders. *Trends in Neuroscience*, 35(9), 527–535.

Takagi, Y., Sakai, Y., Abe, Y., Nishida, S., Harrison, B. J., Martínez-Zalacaín, I., Soriano-Mas, C., Narumoto, J., & Tanaka, S. C. (2018, May 15). A common brain network among state, trait, and pathological anxiety from whole-brain functional connectivity. *NeuroImage*, 172, 506–516. https://doi.org/10.1016/j.neuroimage.2018.01.080

Tillfors, M., Furmark, T., Marteinsdottir, I., Fischer, H., Pissiota, A., Langstrom, B., & Fredrikson, M. (2001). Cerebral blood flow in subjects with social phobia during stressful speaking tasks: A PET study. *American Journal of Psychiatry*, 158, 1220–1226.

Tolin, D., Stevens, M., Villavicencio, A., Norberg, M., Calhoun, V., Frost, R.,

Steketee, G., Rauch, S., & Pearlson, G. (2012). Neural mechanisms of decision making in hoarding disorder. *Archives of General Psychiatry*, 69, 832–841.

Tomiyama, H., Murayama, K., Nemoto, K., Hasuzawa, S., Mizobe, T., Kato, K., Matsuo, A., Ohno, A., Kang, M., Togao, O., Hiwatashi, A., Ishigami, K., & Nakao, T. (2022). Alterations of default mode and cingulo-opercular salience network and frontostriatal circuit: A candidate endophenotype of obsessive-compulsive disorder. *Progress in Neuro-Psychopharmacology & Biological Psychiatry*, 116, Article 110516. https://doi.org/10.1016/j.pnpbp.2022.110516

Troller-Renfree, S. V., Buzzell, G. A., Bowers, M. E., Salo, V. C., Forman-Alberti, A., Smith, E., Papp, L. J., McDermott, J. M., Pine, D. S., Henderson, H. A., & Fox, N. A. (2019). Development of inhibitory control during childhood and its relations to early temperament and later social anxiety: Unique insights provided by latent growth modeling and signal detection theory. *Journal of Child Psychology and Psychiatry*, 60(6), 622–629.

Vigerland, S., Ljótsson, B., Thulin, U., Öst, L.-G., Andersson, G., & Serlachius, E. (2016). Internet-delivered cognitive behavioural therapy for children with anxiety disorders: A randomised controlled trial. *Behaviour Research and Therapy*, 76, 47–56. http://doi.org/http://dx.doi.org/10.1016/j.brat.2015.11.006

Watanabe, N., Churchill, R., & Furukawa, T. (2009, January). Combined psychotherapy plus benzodiazepines for panic disorder. *Cochrane Database Systematic Reviews*. https://www.cochranelibrary.com/cdsr/doi/10.1002/14651858.CD005335.pub2/full

Watson, J., & Rayner, R. (1920). Conditioned emotional reactions. *Journal of Experimental Psychology*, 3, 1–14.

Weiss, B., Hope, D., & Cohn, L. (2010). Treatment of social anxiety disorder: A treatments-by-dimensions review. In S. Hofmann & P. DiBartolo (Eds.), *Social anxiety* (2nd ed., pp. 519–554). Elsevier.

Wergeland, G. J. H., Fjermestad, K. W., Marin, C. E., Bjelland, I., Haugland, B. S. M., Silverman, W. K., Öst, L.-G., Bjaastad, J. F., Oeding, K., Havik, O. E., & Heiervang, E. R. (2016). Predictors of treatment outcome in an effectiveness trial of cognitive behavioral therapy for children with anxiety disorders. *Behaviour Research and Therapy*, 76, 1–12. http://doi.org/10.1016/j.brat.2015.11.001

Wittchen, H., Gloster, A., Beesdo-Baum, K., Fava, G., & Craske, M. (2010). Agoraphobia: A review of the diagnostic classificatory position and criteria. *Depression and Anxiety*, 27, 113–133.

Zinbarg, R. E., Williams, A. L., & Mineka, S. (2022). A current learning theory approach to the etiology and course of anxiety and related disorders. *Annual Review of Clinical Psychology*, 18, 233–258 https://doi.org/10.1146/annurev-clinpsy-072220-021010

CHAPTER 9

American Psychiatric Association. (2013). *Diagnostic and statistical manual of mental disorders*. (5th ed.).

American Psychiatric Association. (2022). *Diagnostic and statistical manual of mental disorders*. (5th ed., text rev.).

Bryk, M., & Siegel, P. T. (1997). My mother caused my illness: The story of a survivor of Munchausen by proxy syndrome. *Pediatrics*, 100, 1–7.

Burgmer, M., Konrad, C., Jansen, A., Kugel, H., Sommer, J., Heindel, W., Ringelstein, E., Heuft, G., & Knecht, S. (2006). Abnormal brain activation during movement observation in patients with conversion paralysis. *NeuroImage*, 29, 1336–1343.

Cojan, Y., Waber, L., Carruzzo, A., & Vuilleumier, P. (2009). Motor inhibition in hysterical conversion paralysis. *NeuroImage*, 47(3), 1026–1037. https://doi.org/10.1016/j.neuroimage.2009.05.023

Dailey, T. M., & Vallabhaneni, M. (2022). Ulnar, median, radial, and antebrachial cutaneous nerve blocks. In D. Souza & L. Kohan (Eds.), *Bedside pain management interventions* (pp. 571–586). Springer. https://doi.org/10.1007/978-3-031-11188-4_57

Ellenberger, H. F. (1970). *The discovery of the unconscious: The history and evolution of dynamic psychiatry*. Basic Books.

Faith, M., & Ray, W. (1994). Hypnotizability and dissociation in a college age population: Orthogonal individual differences. *Personality and Individual Differences*, 17, 211–216.

Fobian, A. D., & Elliott, L. (2019). A review of functional neurological symptom disorder etiology and the integrated etiological summary model. *Journal of Psychiatry & Neuroscience*, 44(1), 8–18. https://doi.org/10.1503/jpn.170190

Folks, D., Ford, C., & Regan, W. (1984). Conversion symptoms in a general hospital. *Psychosomatics*, 25, 285–289.

Ghaffar, O., Staines, W., & Feinstein, A. (2006). Unexplained neurologic symptoms: An fMRI study of sensory conversion disorder. *Neurology*, 67, 2036–2038.

Gleaves, D., May, M., & Cardeña, E. (2001). An examination of the diagnostic validity of dissociative identity disorder. *Clinical Psychology Review*, 21, 577–608.

Gušić, S., Maleševi, A., Cardeña, E., Bengtsson, H., & Søndergaard, H. P. (2018). "I feel like i do not exist :" A study of dissociative experiences among war-traumatized refugee youth. *Psychological Trauma*, 10(5), 542–550. http://dx.doi.org/10.1037/tra0000348

Hallett, M., Lang, A., Jankovic, J., Fahn, S., Halligan, P., Voon, V., & Cloninger, C. (Eds.). (2011). *Psychogenic movement disorders and other conversion disorders*. Cambridge University Press.

Hiller, W., Leibbrand, R., Rief, W., & Fichter, M. (2005). Differentiating hypochondriasis from panic disorder. *Journal of Anxiety Disorders*, 19, 29–49.

Hollon, S., & Beck, A. (2013). Cognitive and cognitive-behavioral therapies. In M. Lambert (Ed.), *Handbook of psychotherapy and behavior change* (6th ed., pp. 393–442). Wiley.

Johnson, J., Cohen, P., Kasen, S., & Brook, J. (2006). Dissociative disorders among adults in the community, impaired functioning, and Axis I and Axis II comorbidity. *Journal of Psychiatric Research*, 40, 131–140.

Kellner, R. (1985). Functional somatic symptoms and hypochondriasis. A survey of empirical studies. *Archives of General Psychiatry*, 42, 821–833.

Kirmayer, L. J., & Young, A. (1998). Culture and somatization: Clinical, epidemiological, and ethnographic perspectives. *Psychosomatic Medicine*, 60(4), 420–430.

Kolstad, A., & Gjesvik, N. (2014). Collectivism, individualism, and pragmatism in China: Implications for perceptions of mental health. *Transcultural Psychiatry*, 51(2), 264–285. http://doi.org/10.1177/1363461514525220

Loewenstein, R. J. (2018). Dissociation debates: Everything you know is wrong. *Dialogues in Clinical Neuroscience*, 20(3), 229–242. https://doi.org/10.31887/DCNS.2018.20.3/rloewenstein

Lukens, S., & Ray, W. (1995). Dissociative experiences and their relation to psychopathology. Paper presented at the Society for Psychopathology Research annual meeting, Iowa City, IA.

Lynn, S. J., Polizzi, C., Merckelbach, H., Chiu, C. D., Maxwell, R., van Heugten, D., & Lilienfeld, S. O. (2022). Dissociation and disscciative disorders reconsidered: Beyond Sociocognitive and trauma models toward a transtheoretical framework. *Annual Review of Clinical Psychology*, *18*, 259–289. https://doi.org/10.1146/annurev-clinpsy-081219-102424

Maldonado, J. R., & Spiegel, D. (2015). Dissociative disorders. In A. Tasman, J. Kay, J. Lieberman, M. First, & M. Riba (Eds.), *Psychiatry* (4th ed., pp. 1178–1198). Wiley.

Maxwell, R., Merckelbach, H., Lilienfeld, S., & Lynn, S. (2018). The treatment of dissociation. In D. David, S. Lynn, & G. Montgomery (Eds.), *Evidence-based psychotherapy: The state of science and practice* (pp. 329–361). Wiley Blackwell.

Nowak, D., & Fink, G. (2009). Psychogenic movement disorders: Aetiology, phenomenology, neuroanatomical correlates and therapeutic approaches. *NeuroImage*, *47*, 1015–1025.

Pavlov, I. P. (1941). Conditioned reflexes and psychiatry. In W. H. Gantt (Trans.), *Lectures on conditioned reflexes* (Vol. 2). International Publishers.

Pelham, V. (2013, July 7). Michael Boatwright awakes in Palm Springs with apparent amnesia. *The Desert Sun*. Retrieved from www.mydesert.com/

Penfield, W., & Rasmussen, T. (1950). *The cerebral cortex of man*. Macmillan.

Ramachandran, V. S., & Blakeslee, S. (1998). *Phantoms in the brain*. William Morrow.

Ray, W. J., Odenwald, M., Neuner, F., Schauer, M., Ruf, M., Wienbruch, C., Rockstroh, B., & Elbert, T. (2006). Decoupling neural networks from reality: Dissociative experiences in torture victims are reflected in abnormal brain waves in left frontal cortex. *Psychological Science*, *17*, 825–829.

Reinders, A. A. T. S., & Veltman, D. J. (2021). Dissociative identity disorder: Out of the shadows at last? *British Journal of Psychiatry*, *219*(2), 413–414.

Reinders, A. A. T. S., Willemsen, A. T. M., den Boer, J. A., Vos, H. P. J., Veltman, D. J., & Loewenstein, R. J. (2014). Opposite brain emotion-regulation patterns in identity states of dissociative identity disorder: A PET study and neurobiological model. *Psychiatry Research: Neuroimaging*, *223*(3), 236–243. http://doi.org/10.1016/j.pscychresns.2014.05.005

Rief, W., Hiller, W., & Margraf, J. (1998). Cognitive aspects of hypochondriasis and the somatization syndrome. *Journal of Abnormal Psychology*, *107*, 587–595.

Ross, C. A. (1997). *Dissociative identity disorder: Diagnosis, clinical features, and treatment of multiple personality disorder*. Wiley.

Ross, C. A., Joshi, S., & Currie, R. (1990). Dissociative experiences in the general population. *American Journal of Psychiatry*, *147*, 1547–1552.

Roydeva, M. I., & Reinders, A. A. (2021). Biomarkers of pathological dissociation: A systematic review. *Neuroscience & Biobehavioral Reviews*, *123*, 120–202.

Saini, F., Ponzo, S., Silvestrin, F., Fotopoulou, A., & David, A. S. (2022). Depersonalization disorder as a systematic downregulation of interoceptive signals. *Scientific Reports*, *12*(1), Article 22123. https://doi.org/10.1038/s41598-022-22277-y

Scarella, T. M., Boland, R. J., & Barsky, A. J. (2019). Illness anxiety disorder: Psychopathology, epidemiology, clinical characteristics, and treatment. *Psychosomatic Medicine*, *81*, 398–407. https://doi.org/10.1097/PSY.0000000000000691

Schreiber, F. R. (1973). *Sybil*. Regnery.

Sheridan, M. (2003). The deceit continues: An updated literature review of Munchausen syndrome by proxy. *Child Abuse and Neglect*, *27*, 431–451.

Sierra, M. (2008). Depersonalization disorder: Pharmacological approaches. *Expert Review of Neurotherapeutics*, *8*, 19–26.

Sierra, M., Nestler, S., Jay, E.-L., Ecker, C., Feng, Y., & David, A. S. (2014). A structural MRI study of cortical thickness in depersonalisation disorder. *Psychiatry Research*, *224*(1), 1–7. http://doi.org/10.1016/j.pscychresns.2014.06.007

Sierra, M., Senior, C., Dalton, J., McDonough, M., Bond, A., Phillips, M., O'Dwyer, A., & David, A. (2002). Autonomic response in depersonalization disorder. *American Journal of General Psychiatry*, *59*, 833–838.

Simeon, D., Gross, S., Guralnik, O., Stein, D. J., Schmeidler, J., & Hollander, E. (1997). Feeling unreal: 30 cases of DSM-III-R depersonalization disorder. *American Journal of Psychiatry*, *154*, 1107–1113.

Simeon, D., Guralnik, O., Hazlett, E., Spiegel-Cohen, J., Hollander, E., & Buchsbaum, M. (2000). Feeling unreal: A PET study of depersonalization disorder. *American Journal of Psychiatry*, *157*, 1782–1788.

Spiegel, D., Lewis-Fernández, R., Lanius, R., Vermetten, E., Simeon, D., & Friedman, M. (2013). Dissociative disorders in DSM-5. *Annual Review of Clinical Psychology*, *9*, 299–326.

Staniloiu, A., & Markowitsch, H. J. (2014). Dissociative amnesia. *The Lancet Psychiatry*, *1*(3), 226–241. http://doi.org/10.1016/S2215-0366(14)70279-2

Steinberg, M. (1994). *Interviewer's guide to the structured clinical interview for DSM-IV dissociative disorders (SCID-D)*. American Psychiatric Publishing.

Steinberg, M., & Schnall, M. (2000). *The stranger in the mirror*. Cliff Street Books.

Sulloway, F. (1979). *Freud, biologist of the mind*. Basic Books.

Sumathipala, A. (2007). What is the evidence for the efficacy of treatments for somatoform disorders? A critical review of previous intervention studies. *Psychosomatic Medicine*, *69*, 889–990.

Turner, J., & Reid, S. (2002). Munchausen's syndrome. *The Lancet*, *359*, 346–349.

Vermetten, E., Schmahl, C., Lindner, S., Loewenstein, R., & Bremner, J. (2006). Hippocampal and amygdalar volumes in dissociative identity disorder. *American Journal of Psychiatry*, *163*, 630–636.

Weck, F., Neng, J., Richtberg, S., & Stangier, U. (2012). The restrictive concept of good health in patients with hypochondriasis. *Journal of Anxiety Disorders*, *26*, 792–798.

Woolfolk, R., Allen, L., & Tiu, J. (2007). New directions in the treatment of somatization. *Psychiatric Clinics of North America*, *30*, 621–644.

Yang, J., Millman, L. S. M., David, A. S., & Hunter, E. C. M. (2023). The prevalence of depersonalization-derealization disorder: A systematic review. *Journal of Trauma & Dissociation*, *24*(1), 8–41. https://doi.org/10.1080/15299732.2022.2079796

Zhou, X., Peng, Y., Zhu, X., Yao, S., Dere, J., Chentsova-Dutton, Y. E., & Ryder, A. G. (2016). From culture to symptom: Testing a structural model of "Chinese somatization". *Transcultural Psychiatry*, *53*(1), 3–23. http://doi.org/10.1177/1363461515589708

CHAPTER 10

Agras, W., Walsh, T., Fairburn, C., Wilson, G., & Kraemer, H. (2000). A multicenter comparison of cognitive-behavioral therapy and interpersonal psychotherapy for bulimia nervosa. *Archives of General Psychiatry, 57*, 459–466.

American Medical Association. (2023, June 14). *AMA adopts new policy clarifying role of BMI as a measure in medicine* [Press release]. https://www.ama-assn.org/press-center/press-releases/ama-adopts-new-policy-clarifying-role-bmi-measure-medicine

American Psychiatric Association. (2013). *Diagnostic and statistical manual of mental disorders.* (5th ed.).

American Psychiatric Association. (2022). *Diagnostic and statistical manual of mental disorders.* (5th ed., text rev.).

Amianto, F., Caroppo, P., D'Agata, F., Spalatro, A., Lavagnino, L., Caglio, M., Righi, D., Bergui, M., Abbate-Daga, G., Rigardetto, R., Mortara, P., & Fassino, S. (2013). Brain volumetric abnormalities in patients with anorexia and bulimia nervosa: A Voxel-based morphometry study. *Psychiatry Research: Neuroimaging, 213*(3), 210–216. http://doi.org/10.1016/j.pscychresns.2013.03.010

Anderson, D., & Maloney, K. (2001). The efficacy of cognitive-behavioral therapy on the core symptoms of bulimia nervosa. *Clinical Psychology Review, 21*, 971–988.

Bäckhed, F., Roswall, J., Peng, Y., Feng, Q., Jia, H., Kovatcheva-Datchary, P., Li, Y., Xia, Y., Xie, H., Zhong, H., Khan, M. T., Zhang, J., Li, J., Xiao, L., Al-Aama, J., Zhang, D., Lee, Y. S., Kotowska, D., Colding, C., . . . Jun, W. (2015). Dynamics and stabilization of the human gut microbiome in the first year of life. *Cell Host & Microbe, 17*(5), 690–703. http://doi.org/10.1016/j.chom.2015.04.004

Becker, A. (2011). Culture and eating disorders classification. In R. Striegel-Moore, S. Wonderlich, B. Walsh, & J. Mitchell (Eds.), *Developing an evidence-based classification of eating disorders* (pp. 257–266). American Psychiatric Association.

Bhattacharya, A., DeFilipp, L., & Timko, C. A. (2020). Feeding and eating disorders. *Handbook of clinical neurology, 175*, 387–403. https://doi.org/10.1016/B978-0-444-64123-6.00026-6

Bissada, H., Tasca, G., Barber, A., & Bradwejn, J. (2008). Olanzapine in the treatment of low body weight and obsessive thinking in women with anorexia nervosa: A randomized, double-blind, placebo-controlled trial. *American Journal of Psychiatry, 165*, 1281–1288.

Bouchard, C. (2010). Genetics and genomics of obesity: Current status. *Progress in Molecular Biology and Translational Science, 94*, 1–8.

Brody, J. (2007, February 20). Out of control: A true story of binge eating. *New York Times.* https://www.nytimes.com/2007/02/20/health/20brod.html

Bryant-Waugh, R. (2019). Feeding and eating disorders in children. *Psychiatric Clinics of North America, 42*(1), 157–167. https://doi.org/10.1016/j.psc.2018.10.005

Bryant-Waugh, R., Markham, L., Kreipe, R., & Walsh, B. (2010). Feeding and eating disorders in childhood. *International Journal of Eating Disorders, 43*, 98–111.

Bulik, C. M., Coleman, J. R. I., Hardaway, J. A., Breithaupt, L., Watson, H. J., Bryant, C. D., & Breen, G. (2022). Genetics and neurobiology of eating disorders. *Nature Neuroscience, 25*(5), 543–554. https://doi.org/10.1038/s41593-022-01071-z

Candea, D., David, D., & Szentágotai-Tătar, A. (2018). Evidence-based psychological interventions for eating disorders. In D. David, S. Lynn, & G. Montgomery (Eds.), *Evidence-based psychotherapy: The state of science and practice* (pp. 189–208). Wiley Blackwell.

Cano, S., Tiemeier, H., Van Hoeken, D., Tharner, A., Jaddoe, V. W. V., Hofman, A., Verhulst, F. C., & Hoek, H. W. (2015). Trajectories of picky eating during childhood: A general population study. *International Journal of Eating Disorders, 48*(6). http://doi.org/10.1002/eat.22384

Centers for Disease Control and Prevention. (2023, March 17). *Adult obesity prevalence maps.* U.S. Department of Health and Human Services. https://www.cdc.gov/obesity/data/prevalence-maps.html

Chen, Z., Guo, L., Zhang, Y., Walzem, R. L., Pendergast, J. S., Printz, R. L., Morris, L. C., Matafonova, E., Stien, X., Kang, L., Coulon, D., McGuinness, O. P., Niswender, K. D., & Davies, S. S. (2014). Incorporation of therapeutically modified bacteria into gut microbiota inhibits obesity. *Journal of Clinical Investigation, 124*(8), 3391–3406.

Christian, L. M., Galley, J. D., Hade, E. M., Schoppe-Sullivan, S., Kamp Dush, C., & Bailey, M. T. (2015). Gut microbiome composition is associated with temperament during early childhood. *Brain, Behavior, and Immunity, 45*, 118–127. http://doi.org/10.1016/j.bbi.2014.10.018

Christopoulou-Aletra, H., & Papavramidou, N. (2004). Methods used by the Hippocratic physicians for weight reduction. *World Journal of Surgery, 28*, 513–517.

Crow, S., Peterson, C., Swanson, S., Raymond, N., Specker, S., Eckert, E., & Mitchell, J. (2009). Increased mortality in bulimia nervosa and other eating disorders. *American Journal of Psychiatry, 166*, 1342–1346.

De Oliveira Coelho, G. M., da Silva Gomes, A. I., Ribeiro, B. G., & de Abreu Soares, E. (2014). Prevention of eating disorders in female athletes. *Open Access Journal of Sports Medicine, 5*, 105–13. http://doi.org/10.2147/OAJSM.S36528

De Palma, G., Blennerhassett, P., Lu, J., Deng, Y., Park, A. J., Green, W., Denou, E., Silva, M. A., Santacruz, A., Sanz, Y., Surette, M. G., Verdu, E. F., Collins, S. M., & Bercik, P. (2015). Microbiota and host determinants of behavioural phenotype in maternally separated mice. *Nature Communications, 6*, 7735. http://doi.org/10.1038/ncomms8735

Delaney, C. B., Eddy, K. T., Hartmann, A. S., Becker, A. E., Murray, H. B., & Thomas, J. J. (2015). Pica and rumination behavior among individuals seeking treatment for eating disorders or obesity. *International Journal of Eating Disorders, 48*, 238–248. http://doi.org/10.1002/eat.22279

Dietrich, M., & Horvath, T. (2013). Hypothalamic control of energy balance: Insights into the role of synaptic plasticity. *Trends in Neuroscience, 36*, 65–73.

Dinan, T. G., Stilling, R. M., Stanton, C., & Cryan, J. F. (2015). Collective unconscious: How gut microbes shape human behavior. *Journal of Psychiatric Research, 63*, 1–9. http://doi.org/10.1016/j.jpsychires.2015.02.021

Dosil, J. (2008). *Eating disorders in athletes.* Wiley.

Doyle, A., & Le Grange, D. (2015). Family-based treatment for anorexia nervosa in adolescents. In H. Thompson-Brenner (Ed.), *Casebook of evidence-based therapy for eating disorders* (pp. 43–70). Guilford Press.

Drewnowski, A. (1997). Taste preferences and food intake. *Annual Review of Nutrition, 17*, 237–253.

Elder, J. P., & Arredondo, E. M. (2013). Strategies to reduce obesity in the U.S. and Latin America: Lessons that cross international borders. *American Journal of Preventive Medicine, 44*(5), 526–528.

Fairburn, C. G. (2008). *Cognitive behavior therapy and eating disorders*. Guilford Press.

Fairburn, C. G., Agras, W., Walsh, B., Wilson, G., & Stice, E. (2004). Prediction of outcome in bulimia nervosa by early change in treatment. *American Journal of Psychiatry, 161*, 2322-2324.

Fairburn, C. G., Cooper, Z., & Doll, H. A. (2009). Transdiagnostic cognitive behavioral therapy for patients with eating disorders: A two-site trial with 60-week follow-up. *American Journal of Psychiatry, 166*, 311-319.

Fairburn, C. G., Cooper, Z., & Shafran, R. (2003). Cognitive behaviour therapy for eating disorders: A "transdiagnostic" theory and treatment. *Behaviour Research and Therapy, 41*, 509-528.

Fairburn, C. G., Cooper, Z., & Shafran, R. (2008). Enhanced cognitive behavior therapy for eating disorders ("CBT-E"): An overview. In C. Fairburn (Ed.), *Cognitive behavior therapy and eating disorders* (pp. 23-34). Guilford Press.

Fairweather-Schmidt, A. K., & Wade, T. D. (2014). DSM-5 eating disorders and other specified eating and feeding disorders: Is there a meaningful differentiation? *International Journal of Eating Disorders, 47*(5), 524-533. http://doi.org/10.1002/eat.22257

Fallon, A., & Rozin, P. (1985). Sex differences in perceptions of desirable body shape. *Journal of Abnormal Psychology, 94*, 102-105. https://doi.org/10.1037/0021-843X.94.1.102

Flamarique, I., Vidal, B., Plana, M. T., Andrés-Perpiñá, S., Gárriz, M., Sánchez, P., Pajuelo, C., Mont, L., & Castro-Fornieles, J. (2022). Long-term cardiac assessment in a sample of adolescent-onset anorexia nervosa. *Journal of Eating Disorders, 10*(1), Article 12. https://doi.org/10.1186/s40337-022-00533-w

Foster, J. A., Rinaman, L., & Cryan, J. F. (2017). Stress & the gut-brain axis: Regulation by the microbiome. *Neurobiology of Stress, 7*, 124-136. https://doi.org/10.1016/j.ynstr.2017.03.001

Frances, A. (2013). *Saving normal*. William Morrow.

Frances, A., & Widiger, T. (2012). Psychiatric diagnosis: Lessons from the DSM-IV past and cautions for the DSM-5 future. *Annual Review of Clinical Psychology, 8*(1), 109-130. http://doi.org/10.1146/annurev-clinpsy-032511-143102

Franklin, J., Schiele, B., Brozek, J., & Keys, A. (1948). Observations on human behavior in experimental semistarvation and rehabilitation. *Journal of Clinical Psychology, 4*, 28-45.

Gaudio, S., & Quattrocchi, C. (2012). Neural basis of a multidimensional model of body image distortion in anorexia nervosa. *Neuroscience and Biobehavioral Reviews, 36*, 1839-1847.

Glasofer, D., Attia, E., & Walsh, B. (2015). Feeding and eating disorders. In A. Tasman, J. Kay, J. Lieberman, M. First, & M. Riba (Eds.), *Psychiatry* (4th ed., pp. 1231-1249). Wiley.

Gordon, R. (1990). *Anorexia and bulimia: Anatomy of a social epidemic*. Basil Blackwell.

Gouba, N., Raoult, D., & Drancourt, M. (2014). Gut microeukaryotes during anorexia nervosa: A case report. *BMC Research Notes, 7*, 33. http://doi.org/10.1186/1756-0500-7-33

Gull, W. (1874). Anorexia nervosa. *Transactions of the Clinical Society of London, 7*, 22-28.

Gupta, A., Bhatt, R. R., Rivera-Cancel, A., Makkar, R., Kragel, P. A., Rodriguez, T., Graner, J. L., Alaverdyan, A., Hamadani, K., Vora, P., Naliboff, B., Labus, J. S., LaBar, K. S., Mayer, E. A., & Zucker, N. (2022). Complex functional brain network properties in anorexia nervosa. *Journal of Eating Disorders, 10*(1), Article 13. https://doi.org/10.1186/s40337-022-00534-9

Halmi, K. (2005). Psychopathology of anorexia nervosa. *International Journal of Eating Disorders, 37*, S20-S21.

Hart, L. M., Cornell, C., Damiano, S. R., & Paxton, S. J. (2015). Parents and prevention: A systematic review of interventions involving parents that aim to prevent body dissatisfaction or eating disorders. *International Journal of Eating Disorders, 48*(2), 157-169. http://doi.org/10.1002/eat.22284

Herd, P., Palloni, A., Rey, F., & Dowd, J. B. (2018). Social and population health science approaches to understand the human microbiome. *Nature Human Behaviour, 2*, 808-815. https://doi.org/10.1038/s41562-018-0452-y

Hernández-González, T., González-Barrio, R., Escobar, C., Madrid, J. A., Periago, M. J., Collado, M. C., Scheer, F. A. J. L., & Garaulet, M. (2021). Timing of chocolate intake affects hunger, substrate oxidation, and microbiota: A randomized controlled trial. *FASEB Journal, 35*(7), Article e21649. https://doi.org/10.1096/fj.202002770RR

Holub, C., Elder, J., Arredondo, E., Barquera, S., Eisenberg, C., Sánchez Romero, L., Rivera, J., Lobelo, F., & Simoes, E. (2013). Obesity control in Latin American and U.S. Latinos: A systematic review. *American Journal of Preventive Medicine, 44*, 529-537.

Hornbacher, M. (1998). *Wasted: A memoir of anorexia and bulimia*. HarperFlamingo.

Hudson, J., Hiripi, E., Pope, H., Jr., & Kessler, R. (2007). The prevalence and correlates of eating disorders in the National Comorbidity Survey Replication. *Biological Psychiatry, 61*, 348-358.

Kaye, W., Fudge, J., & Paulus, M. (2009). New insights into symptoms and neurocircuit function of anorexia nervosa. *Nature Reviews Neuroscience, 10*, 573-584.

Kaye, W., Wierenga, C., Bailer, U., Simmons, A., & Bischoff-Grethe, A. (2013). Nothing tastes as good as skinny feels: The neurobiology of anorexia nervosa. *Trends in Neurosciences, 36*, 110-120.

Keel, P., Brown, T., Holland, L., & Bodell, L. (2012). Empirical classification of eating disorders. *Annual Review of Clinical Psychology, 8*, 381-404.

Kleiman, S. C., Carroll, I. M., Tarantino, L. M., & Bulik, C. M. (2015). Gut feelings: A role for the intestinal microbiota in anorexia nervosa? *International Journal of Eating Disorders, 48*(5), 449-451. http://doi.org/10.1002/eat.22394

Lacey, E. (1990). Broadening the perspective of pica: Literature review. *Public Health Reports, 105*, 29-35.

Lakicevic, N., Matthews, J. J., Artioli, G. G., Paoli, A., Roklicer, R., Trivic, T., Bianco, A., & Drid, P. (2022). Patterns of weight cycling in youth Olympic combat sports: A systematic review. *Journal of eating disorders, 10*(1), Article 75. https://doi.org/10.1186/s40337-022-00595-w

Le Grange, D., & Eisler, I. (2009). Family interventions in adolescent anorexia nervosa. *Child and Adolescent Psychiatric Clinics of North America, 18*, 159-173.

Le Grange, D., Lock, J., Loeb, K., & Nicholls, D. (2010). Academy for Eating Disorders position paper: The role of the family in eating disorders. *International Journal of Eating Disorders, 43*(1), 1-5. https://doi.org/10.1002/eat.20751

Lee, J., Pilli, S., Gebremariam, A., Keirns, C., Davis, M., Vijan, S., Freed, G., Herman, W., & Gurney, J. (2010). Getting heavier, younger: Trajectories of obesity over the life course. *International Journal of Obesity, 34,* 614–623, p. 619.

Lenoir, M., Serre, F., Cantin, L., & Ahmed, S. H. (2007). Intense sweetness surpasses cocaine reward. *PLOS ONE, 2,* Article e698.

Lock, J., Le Grange, D., Agras, W., & Dare, C. (2001). *Treatment manual for anorexia nervosa: A family-based approach.* Guilford Press.

Lynch, W. C., Crosby, R. D., Wonderlich, S. A., & Striegel-Moore, R. H. (2011). Eating disorder symptoms of Native American and white adolescents. In R. H. Striegel-Moore, S. A. Wonderlich, B. T. Walsh, & J. E. Mitchell (Eds.), *Developing an evidence-based classification of eating disorders: Scientific findings for DSM-5* (pp. 285–297). American Psychiatric Association.

Metcalf, P., Scragg, R., Willoughby, P., Finau, S., & Tipene-Leach, D. (2000). Ethnic differences in perceptions of body size in middle-aged European, Maori and Pacific people living in New Zealand. *International Journal of Obesity, 24,* 593–599.

Moustafa, J., & Froguel, P. (2013). From obesity genetics to the future of personalized obesity therapy. *Nature Reviews Endocrinology, 9,* 402–413.

Nasser, M., Katzman, M. A., & Gordon, R. A. (Eds.). (2001). *Eating disorders and cultures in transition.* Taylor & Francis.

Neel, J. V. (1962). Diabetes mellitus: A "thrifty" genotype rendered detrimental by "progress"? *American Journal of Human Genetics, 14,* 353–363.

Office on Women's Health. (2009, June 15). *Jen's story.* U.S. Department of Health and Human Services. Retrieved from www.womenshealth.gov/publications/our-publications/fact-sheet/anorexia-nervosa.html

Okop, K. J., Lambert, E. V., Alaba, O., Levitt, N. S., Luke, A., Dugas, L., Dover, R. V. H., Kroff, J., Micklesfield, L. K., Kolbe-Alexander, L., Warren, S., Dugmore, H., Bobrow, K., Odunitan-Wayas, F. A., & Puoane, T. (2019). Sugar-sweetened beverage intake and relative weight gain among South African adults living in resource-poor communities: Longitudinal data from the STOP-SA study. *International Journal of Obesity, 43,* 603–614. https://doi.org/10.1038/s41366-018-0216-9

Our World in Data. (n.d.). *Daily supply of calories per person, 2018.* https://ourworldindata.org/grapher/daily-per-capita-caloric-supply

Poulsen, S., Lunn, S., Daniel, S. I. F., Folke, S., Mathiesen, B. B., Katznelson, H., & Fairburn, C. G. (2014). A randomized controlled trial of psychoanalytic psychotherapy or cognitive-behavioral therapy for bulimia nervosa. *American Journal of Psychiatry, 171*(1), 109–16. http://doi.org/10.1176/appi.ajp.2013.12121511

Rankinen, T., & Bouchard, C. (2006). Genetics of food intake and eating behavior phenotypes in humans. *Annual Review of Nutrition, 26,* 413–434.

Rienecke, R. D., Johnson, C., Le Grange, D., Manwaring, J., Mehler, P. S., Duffy, A., McClanahan, S., & Blalock, D. V. (2022). Adverse childhood experiences among adults with eating disorders: comparison to a nationally representative sample and identification of trauma. *Journal of Eating Disorders, 10*(1), 1–10.

Roberts, R., Deleger, S., Strawbridge, W., & Kaplan, G. (2003). Prospective association between obesity and depression: Evidence from the Alameda County Study. *International Journal of Obesity, 27,* 514–521.

Romano, K. A., & Lipson, S. K. (2022). Weight misperception and thin-ideal overvaluation relative to the positive functioning and eating disorder pathology of transgender and nonbinary young adults. *Psychology of Sexual Orientation and Gender Diversity, 9*(4), 446–453. https://doi.org/10.1037/sgd0000524

Roubalová, R., Procháčková, P., Papežová, H., Smitka, K., Bilej, M., & Tlaskavová, H. (2020). Anorexia nervosa : Gut microbiota-immune-brain interactions. *Clinical Nutrition, 39*(3), 676–684. https://doi.org/10.1016/j.clnu.2019.03.023

Russell, G. (1979). Bulimia nervosa: An ominous variant of anorexia nervosa. *Psychological Medicine, 9,* 429–448.

Shepard, R. (2019). *Obesity: A kinesiologist's perspective.* Routledge.

Slane, J. D., Klump, K. L., McGue, M., & Iacono, W. G. (2014). Developmental trajectories of disordered eating from early adolescence to young adulthood: A longitudinal study. *International Journal of Eating Disorders, 47*(7), 793–801. http://doi.org/10.1002/eat.22329

Smith, A. R., Hawkeswood, S. E., Bodell, L. P., & Joiner, T. E. (2011). Muscularity versus leanness: An examination of body ideals and predictors of disordered eating in heterosexual and gay college students. *Body Image, 8*(3), 232–236. http://doi.org/10.1016/j.bodyim.2011.03.005

Smith, J. D., Fu, E., & Kobayashi, M. A. (2020). Prevention and management of childhood obesity and its psychological and health comorbidities. *Annual Review of Clinical Psychology, 16,* 351–378. https://doi.org/10.1146/annurev-clinpsy-100219-060201

Stice, E., Marti, C., & Rohde, P. (2012). Prevalence, incidence, impairment, and course of the proposed *DSM-5* eating disorder diagnoses in an 8-year prospective community study of young women. *Journal of Abnormal Psychology, 122,* 445–457.

Stice, E., Spoor, S., Bohon, C., Veldhuizen, M. G., & Small, D. M. (2008). Relation of reward from food intake and anticipated food intake to obesity: A functional magnetic resonance imaging study. *Journal of Abnormal Psychology, 117,* 924–935.

Stokes, T. (2006). The earth-eaters. *Nature, 444,* 543–544.

Striegel-Moore, R., & Franko, D. (2008). Should binge eating disorder be included in the *DSM-V*? A critical review of the state of the evidence. *Annual Review of Clinical Psychology, 4,* 305–324.

Sundgot-Borgen, J., & Torstveit, M. K. (2004). Prevalence of eating disorders in elite athletes is higher than in the general population. *Clinical Journal of Sport Medicine: Official Journal of the Canadian Academy of Sport Medicine, 14*(1), 25–32. http://doi.org/10.1097/00042752-200401000-00005

Taylor, K. (Ed.). (2008). *Going hungry.* Anchor Books.

Tennoune, N., Chan, P., Breton, J., Legrand, R., Chabane, Y. N., Akkermann, K., Järv, A., Ouelaa, K., Ghouzali, I., Francois, M., Lucas, N., Bole-Feysot, C., Pestel-Caron, M., do Rego, J-C., Vaudry, D., Harro, J., Dé, E., Déchelotte, P., & Fetissov, S. O. (2014). Bacterial ClpB heat-shock protein, an antigen-mimetic of the anorexigenic peptide α-MSH, at the origin of eating disorders. *Translational Psychiatry, 4*(10), e458. http://doi.org/10.1038/tp.2014.98

Thompson, R. A., & Sherman, R. T. (2010). *Eating disorders in sport.* Routledge.

Trace, S. E., Baker, J. H., Peñas-Lledó, E., & Bulik, C. M. (2013). The genetics of eating disorders. *Annual Review of Clinical Psychology, 9*(1), 589–620. http://doi.org/10.1146/annurev-clinpsy-050212-185546

Treasure, J., Duarte, T. A., & Schmidt, U. (2020). Eating disorders. *Lancet (London, England), 395*(10227), 899–911. https://doi.org/10.1016/S0140-6736(20)30059-3

Volkow, N., Wang, G., Tomasi, D., & Baler, R. (2013). Obesity and addiction: Neurobiological overlaps. *Obesity Reviews, 14,* 2–18.

Wadden, T., & Bray, G. (Eds.). (2018). *Handbook of obesity treatment* (2nd ed.). Guilford Press.

Waller, G., Tatham, M., Turner, H., Mountford, V., Bennetts, A., Bramwell, K., Dodd, J., & Ingram, L. (2018). A 10-session cognitive-behavioral therapy (CBT-T) for eating disorders: Outcomes from a case series of nonunderweight adult patients. *International Journal of Eating Disorders, 51,* 262–269.

Walsh, B. (2008). Eating disorders. In A. Tasman, J. Kay, J. Lieberman, M. First, & M. Maj (Eds.), *Psychiatry* (3rd ed., pp. 1609–1625). Wiley.

Wardle, J., Haase, A., & Steptoe, A. (2006). Body image and weight control in young adults: International comparisons in university students from 22 countries. *International Journal of Obesity, 30,* 644–651.

World Health Organization. (2023). *Prevalence of obesity among adults, BMI > 30 (age-standardized estimate) (%).* https://www.who.int/data/gho/data/indicators/indicator-details/GHO/prevalence-of-obesity-among-adults-bmi-=-30-(age-standardized-estimate)-(-)

Yean, C., Benau, E. M., Dakanalis, A., Hormes, J. M., Perone, J., & Timko, C. A. (2013, November). The relationship of sex and sexual orientation to self-esteem, body shape satisfaction, and eating disorder symptomatology. *Frontiers in Psychology, 4,* 1–11. http://doi.org/10.3389/fpsyg.2013.00887

Yelland, C., & Tiggemann, M. (2003). Muscularity and the gay ideal: Body dissatisfaction and disordered eating in homosexual men. *Eating Behaviors, 4*(2), 107–116. http://doi.org/10.1016/S1471-0153(03)00014-X

Yilmaz, Z., Kaplan, A. S., Tiwari, A. K., Levitan, R. D., Piran, S., & Bergen, A. (2014). The role of leptin, melanocortin, and neurotrophin system genes on body weight in anorexia nervosa and bulimia nervosa. *Journal of Psychiatric Research, 55,* 77–86.

Young, S. (2010). Pica in pregnancy: New ideas about an old condition. *Annual Review of Nutrition, 30,* 403–422.

Young, S. (2011). *Craving earth: Understanding pica.* Columbia University Press.

Zerwas, S., Lund, B., Von Holle, A., Thornton, L., Berrettini, W., Brandt, H., Crawford, S., Fichter, M., Halmi, K., Johnson, C., Kaplan, A., La Via, M., Mitchell, J., Rotondo, A., Strober, M., Woodside, D., Kaye, W., & Bulik, C. (2013). Factors associated with recovery from anorexia nervosa. *Journal of Psychiatric Research, 47,* 972–979

CHAPTER 11

American Psychiatric Association. (2022). *Diagnostic and statistical manual of mental disorders,* (5th ed., text rev.)

Bach, B., Kramer, U., Doering, S., di Giacomo, E., Hutsebaut, J., Kaera, A., De Panfilis, C., Schmahl, C., Swales, M., Taubner, S., & Renneberg, B. (2022). The ICD-11 classification of personality disorders: A European perspective on challenges and opportunities. *Borderline Personality Disorder and Emotion Dysregulation, 9*(1), 12. https://bpded.biomedcentral.com/articles/10.1186/s40479-022-00182-0

Bao, A. M., & Swaab, D. F. (2011). Sexual differentiation of the human brain: Relation to gender identity, sexual orientation and neuropsychiatric disorders. *Frontiers in Neuroendocrinology, 32*(2), 214–226. https://doi.org/10.1016/j.yfrne.2011.02.007

Beech, A. R., & Harkins, L. (2012). DSM-IV paraphilia: Descriptions, demographics and treatment interventions. *Aggression and Violent Behavior, 17*(6), 527–539. http://doi.org/10.1016/j.avb.2012.07.008

Beech, A. R., Miner, M. H., & Thornton, D. (2016). Paraphilias in the *DSM-5. Annual Review of Clinical Psychology, 12*(1), 383–406. http://doi.org/10.1146/annurev-clinpsy-021815-093330

Beier, K. M., Grundmann, D., Kuhle, L. F., Scherner, G., Konrad, A., & Amelung, T. (2015). The German Dunkelfeld Project: A pilot study to prevent child sexual abuse and the use of child abusive images. *Journal of Sexual Medicine, 12*(2), 529–542. http://doi.org/10.1111/jsm.12785

Beutel, M., Weidner, W., & Brähler, E. (2006). Epidemiology of sexual dysfunction in the male population. *Andrologia, 38,* 115–121.

Bodnar, R., Commons, K., & Pfaff, D. (2002). *Central neural states relating sex and pain.* Johns Hopkins Press.

Bono, C. (2011). *Transition: The story of how I became a man.* Dutton.

Bradford, J. M. W., & Ahmed, A. G. (2014). The natural history of the paraphilias. *Psychiatric Clinics of North America, 37*(2), xi–xv. http://doi.org/10.1016/j.psc.2014.03.010

Briken, P., & Kafka, M. P. (2007). Pharmacological treatments for paraphilic patients and sexual offenders. *Current Opinion in Psychiatry, 20*(6), 609–613. http://doi.org/10.1097/YCO.0b013e3282f0eb0b

Brotto, L. A., & Goldmeier, D. (2015). Mindfulness interventions for treating sexual dysfunctions: The gentle science of finding focus in a multitask world. *Journal of Sexual Medicine, 12*(8), 1687–1689. http://doi.org/10.1111/jsm.12941

Buhrich, N., & Beaumont, T. (1981). Comparison of transvestism in Australia and America. *Archives of Sexual Behavior, 26,* 589–605.

Byne, W., Bradley, S., Coleman, E., Eyler, A., Green, R., Menvielle, E., & Tompkins, D. (2012). Report of the American Psychiatric Association Task Force on Treatment of Gender Identity Disorder. *Archives of Sexual Behavior, 41,* 759–796.

Cerny, J., & Janssen, E. (2011). Patterns of sexual arousal in homosexual, bisexual, and heterosexual men. *Archives of Sexual Behavior, 40,* 687–697.

Chivers, M., Pittini, R., Grigoriadis, S., Villegas, L., & Ross, L. (2011). The relationship between sexual functioning and depressive symptomatology in postpartum women: A pilot study. *Journal of Sexual Medicine, 8,* 792–799.

Cools, M., Nordenström, A., Robeva, R., Hall, J., Westerveld, P., Flück, C., Köhler, B., Berra, M., Springer, A., Schweizer, K., Pasterski, V., & COST Action BM1303 Working Group 1, (2018). Caring for individuals with a difference of sex development (DSD): A consensus statement. *Nature Reviews Endocrinology, 14*(7), 415–429. https://doi.org/10.1038/s41574-018-0010-8

Copen, C. E., Chandra, A., & Febo-Vazquez, I. (2016, January 7). *Sexual behavior, sexual attraction, and sexual orientation among adults aged 18–44 in the United States: Data from the 2011–2013 National Survey of Family Growth.* (National Health Statistics Report No. 88). U.S. Department of Health and Human Services https://www.cdc.gov/nchs/data/nhsr/nhsr088.pdf

Darcangelo, S. (2008). Fetishism: Psychopathology and theory. In D. R. Laws & W. O'Donohue (Eds.), *Sexual deviance: Theory, assessment and treatment* (2nd ed., pp. 22–39). Guilford Press.

DeRogatis, L. R., & Burnett, A. L. (2008). The epidemiology of sexual dysfunctions. *Journal of Sexual Medicine, 5*(2), 289–300. http://doi.org/10.1111/j.1743-6109.2007.00668.x

Dewitte, M., Van Lankveld, J., Vandenberghe, S., & Loeys, T. (2015). Sex in its daily relational context. *Journal of Sexual Medicine*, *12*(12), 2436–2450. http://doi.org/10.1111/jsm.13050

Durex global sex surveys (1996). London International Group.

Durex global sex surveys (1998). London International Group.

Ellis, A. (2010). *All out*. Prometheus Books.

Ferretti, A., Caulo, M., Del Gratta, C., Di Matteo, R., Merla, A., Montorsi, F., . . . Romani, G. (2005). Dynamics of male sexual arousal: Distinct components of brain activation revealed by fMRI. *NeuroImage*, *26*, 1086–1096.

Finer, L. (2007). Trends in premarital sex in the United States, 1954–2003. *Public Health Reports*, *122*, 73–78.

Firestone, P., Kingston, D., Wexler, A., & Bradford, J. (2006). Long-term follow-up of exhibitionists: Psychological, phallometric, and offense characteristics. *Journal of the American Academy of Psychiatry and Law*, *34*, 349–359.

Fisher, T., Moore, Z., & Pittenger, M. (2012). Sex on the brain? An examination of frequency of sexual cognitions as a function of gender, erotophilia, and social desirability. *Journal of Sex Research*, *49*, 69–77.

Gallo, A., Abracen, J., Looman, J., Jeglic, E., & Dickey, R. (2019). The Use of Leuprolide Acetate in the Management of High-Risk Sex Offenders. *Sexual Abuse: A Journal of Research and Treatment*, *31*(8), 930–951. https://doi.org/10.1177/1079063218791176

Graham, C. (2009). The *DSM* diagnostic criteria for female orgasmic disorder. *Archives of Sexual Behavior*, *39*, 256–270.

Heiman, J., & Pfaff, D. (2011). Sexual arousal and related concepts: An introduction. *Hormones and Behavior*, *59*, 613–615.

Herbenick, D., Bowling, J., Fu, T. J., Dodge, B., Guerra-Reyes, L., & Sanders, S. (2017, July 20). *Sexual diversity in the United States: Results from a nationally representative probability sample of adult women and men*. PLOS ONE. https://journals.plos.org/plosone/article?id=10.1371/journal.pone.0181198

Holoyda, B. J., & Kellaher, D. C. (2016). The biological treatment of paraphilic disorders: An updated review. *Current Psychiatry Reports*, *18*(2), 1–7. https://doi.org/10.1007/s11920-015-0649-y

IsHak, W. (2017). *The textbook of clinical sexual medicine*. Springer.

Janssen, E. (2011). Sexual arousal in men: A review and conceptual analysis. *Hormones and Behavior*, *59*, 708–716.

Joyal, C. C., Cossette, A., & Lapierre, V. (2015). What exactly is an unusual sexual fantasy? *Journal of Sexual Medicine*, *12*(2), 328–340. http://doi.org/10.1111/jsm.12734

Kärgel, C., Massau, C., Weiss, S., Walter, M., Kruger, T. H. C., & Schiffer, B. (2015). Diminished functional connectivity on the road to child sexual abuse in pedophilia. *Journal of Sexual Medicine*, *12*(3), 783–795. http://doi.org/10.1111/jsm.12819

Kinsey, A. (1948). *Sexual behavior in the human male*. Indiana University Press.

Kinsey, A. (1953). *Sexual behavior in the human female*. Indiana University Press.

Kleinplatz, P. J. (2018). History of the treatment of female sexual dysfunction(s). *Annual Review of Clinical Psychology*, *14*(1), 1–26. https://doi.org/10.1146/annurev-clinpsy-050817-084802

Krueger, R., & Kaplan, M. (2015). Paraphilic disorders. In A. Tasman, J. Kay, J. Lieberman, M. First, & M. Riba (Eds.), *Psychiatry* (4th ed., pp. 1749–1758). Wiley.

Långström, N., & Zucker, K. (2005). Transvestic fetishism in the general population: Prevalence and correlates. *Journal of Sex and Marital Therapy*, *31*, 87–95.

Laumann, E., Paik, A., & Rosen, R. (1999). Sexual dysfunction in the United States: Prevalence and predictors. *Journal of the American Medical Association*, *281*, 537–544.

Laumann, E., Paik, A., Glasser, D., Kang, J., Wang, T., Levinson, B., Moreira, E. D., Jr, Nicolosi., A, & Gingell, C. (2006). A cross-national study of subjective sexual well-being among older women and men: Findings from the Global Study of Sexual Attitudes and Behaviors. *Archives of Sexual Behavior*, *35*, 145–161.

LeVay, S., & Baldwin, J. (2012). *Human sexuality* (4th ed.). Sinauer Associates.

Lewis, R. W., Fugl-Meyer, K. S., Corona, G., Hayes, R. D., Laumann, E. O., Moreira, E. D., Rellini, A. H., & Segraves, T. (2010). Definitions/epidemiology/risk factors for sexual dysfunction. *Journal of Sexual Medicine*, *7*(4, Part 2), 1598–1607. http://doi.org/10.1111/j.1743-6109.2010.01778.x

Luders, E., Sánchez, F., Tosun, D., Shattuck, D., Gaser, C., Vilain, E., & Toga, W. (2012). Increased cortical thickness in male-to-female transsexualism. *Journal of Behavioral and Brain Science*, *2*, 357–362.

Lussier, P., & Piché, L. (2008). Frotteurism: Psychopathology and theory. In D. R. Laws & W. O'Donohue (Eds.), *Sexual deviance: Theory, assessment and treatment* (2nd ed., pp. 111–130). Guilford Press.

Lykins, A., Meana, M., & Kambe, G. (2006). Detection of differential viewing patterns to erotic and non-erotic stimuli using eye-tracking methodology. *Archives of Sexual Behavior*, *35*, 569–575.

Marshall, W. L. (2007). Diagnostic issues, multiple paraphilias, and comorbid disorders in sexual offenders: Their incidence and treatment. *Aggression and Violent Behavior*, *12*(1), 16–35. http://doi.org/10.1016/j.avb.2006.03.001

Marshall, W. L., & Kingston, D. A. (2018). Diagnostic issues in the paraphilias. *Current Psychiatry Reports*, *20*, 1–8.

Massau, C., Kärgel, C., Weiß, S., Walter, M., Ponseti, J., HC, Krueger., T, Walter., H, & Schiffer, B. (2017). Neural correlates of moral judgment in pedophilia. *Social Cognitive and Affective Neuroscience*, *12*, 1490–1499. https://doi.org/10.1093/scan/nsx077

Masters, W., & Johnson, V. (1966). *Human sexual response*. Little, Brown.

Masters, W., & Johnson, V. (1970). *Human sexual inadequacy*. Little, Brown.

Masters, W., & Johnson, V. (1979). *Homosexuality in perspective*. Little, Brown.

Masters, W., Johnson, V., & Kolodny, R. (1986). *Masters and Johnson on sex and human loving*. Little, Brown.

McAnulty, R. (2012). *Sex in college*. Praeger.

Miller, S., & Byers, E. (2004). Actual and desired duration of foreplay and intercourse: Discordance and misperceptions within heterosexual couples. *Journal of Sex Behavior*, *41*, 301–309.

Mohnke, S., Müller, S., Amelung, T., Krüger, T. H. C., Ponseti, J., Schiffer, B., Walter, M., Beier, K. M., & Walter, H. (2014, August). Brain alterations in paedophilia: A critical review. *Progress in Neurobiology*, *122*, 1–23. http://doi.org/10.1016/j.pneurobio.2014.07.005

Morin, J., & Levenson, J. (2008). Exhibitionism: Assessment and treatment. In D. R. Laws & W. O'Donohue (Eds.), *Sexual deviance: Theory, assessment and treatment* (2nd ed., pp. 76–107). Guilford Press.

Moser, C. (2019). *DSM*-5, paraphilias, and the paraphilic disorders: Confusion reigns. *Archives of Sexual Behavior*, *48*, 681–689. https://doi.org/10.1007/s10508-018-1356-7

Murad, M., Elamin, M., Garcia, M., Mullan, R., Murad, A., Erwin, P., & Montori, V. (2010). Hormonal therapy and sex reassignment: A systematic review and meta-analysis of quality of life and psychosocial outcomes. *Clinical Endocrinology, 72*, 214–231.

Murphy, W., & Page, I. (2008). Exhibitionism: Psychopathology and theory. In D. R. Laws & W. O'Donohue (Eds.), *Sexual deviance: Theory, assessment and treatment* (2nd ed., pp. 40–74). Guilford Press.

Newring, K., Wheeler, J., & Draper, C. (2008). Transvestic fetishism: Assessment and treatment. In D. R. Laws & W. O'Donohue (Eds.), *Sexual deviance: Theory, assessment and treatment* (2nd ed., pp. 285–304). Guilford Press.

Nielsen, J., & Pernice, K. (2008). *Eyetracking web usability*. New Riders Press.

Nimbi, F. M., Ciocca, G., Limoncin, E., Fontanesi, L., Uysal, B., Flinchum, M., Tambelli, R., Jannini, E. A., & Simonelli, C. (2020). Sexual desire and fantasies in the LGBT+ community: Focus on lesbian women and gay men. *Current Sexual Health Reports, 12*, 153–161. https://doi.org/10.1007/s11930-020-00263-7

Nimbi, F. M., Galizia, R., Limoncin, E., Levy, T., Jannini, E. A., Simonelli, C., & Tambelli, R. (2023). Sexual Desire and Erotic Fantasies Questionnaire: The development and validation of the Erotic Fantasy Use Scale (SDEF2) on experience, attitudes, and sharing issues. *Healthcare (Basel, Switzerland), 11*(8). 1159. https://doi.org/10.3390/healthcare11081159

Palacios, S., Castaño, R., & Grazziotin, A. (2009). Epidemiology of female sexual dysfunction. *Maturitas, 63*, 119–123.

Pascoal, P., Cardoso, D., & Henriques, R. (2015). Sexual satisfaction and distress in sexual functioning in a sample of the BDSM community: A comparison study between BDSM and non-BDSM contexts. *Journal of Sexual Medicine, 12*(4), 1052–1061. http://doi.org/10.1111/jsm.12835

Peterson, C., Matthews, A., Copps-Smith, E., & Conard, L. (2017). Suicidality, self-harm, and body dissatisfaction in transgender adolescents and emerging adults with gender dysphoria. *Suicide and Life-Threatening Behavior, 47*, 475–482. https://doi.org/10.1111/sltb.12289

Pfäfflin, F., & Junge, A. (1998). *Sex reassignment. Thirty years of international follow-up studies after sex reassignment surgery: A comprehensive review, 1961–1991*. Retrieved from http://classic-web.archive.org/web/20070503090247/http://www.symposion.com/ijt/pfaefflin/1000.htm

Poeppl, T. B., Eickhoff, S. B., Fox, P. T., Laird, A. R., Rupprecht, R., Langguth, B., & Bzdok, D. (2015). Connectivity and functional profiling of abnormal brain structures in pedophilia. *Human Brain Mapping, 36*(6), 2374–2386. http://doi.org/10.1002/hbm.22777

Poeppl, T. B., Nitschke, J., Santtila, P., Schecklmann, M., Langguth, B., Greenlee, M., Osterheider, M., & Mokros, A. (2013). Association between brain structure and phenotypic characteristics in pedophilia. *Journal of Psychiatric Research, 47*, 678–685.

Portner, M. (2008, April/May). The orgasmic mind: The neurological roots of sexual pleasure. *Scientific American*, 67–71.

Profeta, G., Micangeli, G., Tarani, F., Paparella, R., Ferraguti, G., Spaziani, M., Isidori, A. M., Menghi, M., Ceccanti, M., Fiore, M., & Tarani, L. (2022). Sexual developmental disorders in pediatrics. *La Clinica terapeutica, 173*(5), 475–488. https://doi.org/10.7417/CT.2022.2466

Rametti, G., Carrillo, B., Gómez-Gil, E., Junque, C., Segovia, S., Gomez, A., & Guillamon, A. (2011). White matter microstructure in female to male transsexuals before cross-sex hormonal treatment: A diffusion tensor imaging study. *Journal of Psychiatric Research, 45*, 199–204.

Richards, R. (1983). *Second serve*. Stein and Day.

Richters, J., De Visser, R. O., Rissel, C. E., Grulich, A. E., & Smith, A. M. A. (2008). Demographic and psychosocial features of participants in bondage and discipline, "sadomasochism" or dominance and submission (BDSM): Data from a national survey. *Journal of Sexual Medicine, 5*, 1660–1668.

Rieger, G., Savin-Williams, R., Chivers, M. L., & Bailey, J. M. (2016). Sexual arousal and masculinity-femininity of women. *Journal of Personality and Social Psychology, 111*, 265–283.

Ristow, I., Li, M., Colic, L., Marr, V., Födisch, C., von Düring, F., Schlitz, K., Drumkova, K., Witzel, J., Walter, H., Beier, K., Kruger, T. H. C., Ponseti, J., Schiffer, B., & Walter, M. (2018). Pedophilic sex offenders are characterised by reduced GABA concentration in dorsal anterior cingulate cortex. *NeuroImage: Clinical, 18*, 335–341. https://doi.org/10.1016/j.nicl.2018.01.018

Rupp, H., & Wallen, M. (2007). Sex differences in viewing sexual stimuli: An eye-tracking study in men and women. *Hormones and Behavior, 51*, 524–533.

Sacher-Masoch, L. (2013). *Venus in furs*. Dover. (Original work published 1888)

Sachs, B. D. (2007). A contextual definition of male sexual arousal. *Hormones and Behavior, 51*, 569–578.

Safron, A., Klimaj, V., Sylva, D., Rosenthal, A. M., Li, M., Walter, M., & Bailey, J. M. (2018). Neural correlates of sexual orientation in heterosexual, bisexual, and homosexual women. *Scientific Reports*, 1–14. https://doi.org/10.1038/s41598-017-18372-0

Savic, I., Garcia-Falgueras, A., & Swaab, D. F. (2010). Sexual differentiation of the human brain in relation to gender identity and sexual orientation. *Progress in Brain Research, 186*, 41–62. https://doi.org/10.1016/B978-0-444-53630-3.00004-X

Segraves, R. (2010). Considerations for an evidence-based definition of premature ejaculation in the *DSM-V*. *Journal of Sexual Medicine, 7*, 672–679.

Seto, M. (2008). Pedophilia: Psychopathology and theory. In D. R. Laws & W. O'Donohue (Eds.), *Sexual deviance: Theory, assessment and treatment* (2nd ed., pp. 164–182). Guilford Press.

Snaith, R., & Collins, S. (1981). Five exhibitionists and a method of treatment. *British Journal of Psychiatry, 138*, 126–130.

Stekel, W. (1996). *Sexual aberrations*. Liveright. (Original work published 1925)

Swaab, D. F., & Garcia-Falgueras, A. (2009). Sexual differentiation of the human. *Functional Neurology, 24*(16), 17–28.

Thibaut, F., Bradford, J. M. W., Briken, P., De La Barra, F., Häßler, F., & Cosyns, P. (2016). The World Federation of Societies of Biological Psychiatry (WFSBP) guidelines for the treatment of adolescent sexual offenders with paraphilic disorders. *World Journal of Biological Psychiatry, 17*(1), 2–38. https://doi.org/10.3109/15622975.2015.1085598

Tobia, G., Chahal, K., & IsHak, W. (2017). Surveys of sexual behavior and sexual disorders. In W. IsHak (Ed.), *The textbook of clinical sexual medicine*. Springer.

Toomey, R., Syvertsen, A., & Shramko, M. (2018). Transgender adolescent suicide behavior. *Pediatrics, 142*(4). Article e20174218

Velten, J., Scholten, S., Graham, C. A., Adolph, D., & Margraf, J. (2016).

Investigating female sexual concordance: Do sexual excitation and sexual inhibition moderate the agreement of genital and subjective sexual arousal in women? *Archives of Sexual Behavior*, 45, 1957–1971. http://doi.org/10.1007/s10508-016-0774-7

Waite, L. J., Laumann, E. O., Das, A., & Schumm, L. P. (2009). Sexuality: Measures of partnerships, practices, attitudes, and problems in the National Social Life, Health, and Aging study. *Journal of Gerontology: Social Sciences*, 64B(S1), i56–i66. https://doi.org/10.1093/geronb/gbp038

Waldinger, M. (2008). Recent advances in the classification, neurobiology and treatment of premature ejaculation. In R. Balon (Ed.), *Sexual dysfunction: The brain–body connection* (pp. 50–69). Karger.

Wiepjes, C. M., Nota, N. M., de Blok, C. J. M., Klaver, M., de Vries, A. L. C., Wensing-Kruger, S. A., de Jongh, R. T., Bouman, M.-B., Steensma, T. D., Cohen-Kettenis, P., Gooren, L. J. G., Kreukels, B. P. C., & den Heijer, M. (2018). The Amsterdam Cohort of Gender Dysphoria Study (1972–2015): Trends in prevalence, treatment, and regrets. *Journal of Sexual Medicine*, 15, 582–590.

Wincze, J., & Carey, M. (2001). *Sexual dysfunction: A guide for assessment and treatment* (2nd ed.). Guilford Press.

Witchel, S. F. (2018). Disorders of sex development. Best practice & research. *Clinical Obstetrics & Gynaecology*, 48, 90–102. https://doi.org/10.1016/j.bpobgyn.2017.11.005

World Health Organization. (2023). *Sexual and reproductive health and research (SRH)*. https://www.who.int/teams/sexual-and-reproductive-health-and-research/key-areas-of-work/sexual-health/defining-sexual-health

Zhou, J., Hofman, M., Gooren, L., & Swaab, D. (1995). A sex difference in the human brain and its relation to transsexuality. *Nature*, 378, 68–70.

Zucker, K. J., Lawrence, A. A., & Kreukels, B. P. C. (2016). Gender dysphoria in adults. *Annual Review of Clinical Psychology*, 12(1), 217–247 https://doi.org/10.1146/annurev-clinpsy-021815-093034

CHAPTER 12

Aas, M., Melle, I., Bettella, F., Djurovic, S., Le Hellard, S., Bjella, T., & Ringen, P. A. (2018). Psychotic patients who used cannabis frequently before illness onset have higher genetic predisposition to schizophrenia than those who did not. *Psychological Medicine*, 48, 43–49. https://doi.org/10.1017/S0033291717001209

American Psychiatric Association. (2013). *Diagnostic and statistical manual of mental disorders* (5th ed.).

American Psychiatric Association. (2022). *Diagnostic and statistical manual of mental disorders* (5th ed., text rev.)

Baasher, T. (1981). The use of drugs in the Islamic world. *British Journal of Addiction*, 76, 233–243.

Bara, A., Ferland, J. N., Rompala, G., Szutorisz, H., & Hurd, Y. L. (2021). Cannabis and synaptic reprogramming of the developing brain. *Nature Reviews Neuroscience*, 22(7), 423–438. https://doi.org/10.1038/s41583-021-00465-5

Berman, S. M., Kuczenski, R., McCracken, J. T., & London, E. D. (2009). NIH public access. *Psychiatry: Interpersonal and Biological Processes*, 14(2), 123–142.

Blakemore, S. (2013). Teenage kicks: Cannabis and the adolescent brain. *The Lancet*, 381, 888–889.

Bogdan, R., Hatoum, A. S., Johnson, E. C., & Agrawal, A. (2023). The genetically informed neurobiology of addiction (GINA) model. *Nature reviews. Neuroscience*, 24(1), 40–57. https://doi.org/10.1038/s41583-022-00656-8

Bohnsack, J. P., Zhang, H., Wandling, G. M., He, D., Kyzar, E. J., Lasek, A. W., & Pandey, S. C. (2022). Targeted epigenomic editing ameliorates adult anxiety and excessive drinking after adolescent alcohol exposure. *Science Advances*, 8(18). Article eabn2748

Bridgeman, M. B., & Abazia, D. T. (2017). Medicinal cannabis: History, pharmacology, and implications for the acute care setting. *Pharmacy and Therapeutics*, 42(3), 180–188.

Carhart-Harris, R., Giribaldi, B., Watts, R., Baker-Jones, M., Murphy-Beiner, A., Murphy, R., Martell, J., Blemings, A., Erritzoe, D., & Nutt, D. J. (2021). Trial of psilocybin versus escitalopram for depression. *New England Journal of Medicine*, 384(15), 1402–1411. https://doi.org/10.1056/NEJMoa2032994

Carson-DeWitt, R. (2001). Mescaline. In R. Carson-DeWitt (Ed.), *Encyclopedia of drugs, alcohol, & addictive behavior* (2nd ed., pp. 714–715). Macmillan Reference.

Chen, Q., Larochelle, M. R., Weaver, D. T., Lietz, A. P., Mueller, P. P., Mercaldo, S., & Wakeman, S. E. (2019). Prevention of prescription opioid misuse and projected overdose deaths in the United States. *JAMA Network Open*, 2(2). https://doi.org/10.1001/jamanetworkopen.2018.7621

Crean, R., Crane, N., & Mason, B. (2011). An evidence-based review of acute and long-term effects of cannabis use on executive cognitive functions. *Journal of Addiction Medicine*, 5, 1–8.

Crocq, M. (2007). Historical and cultural aspects of man's relationship with addictive drugs. *Dialogues in Clinical Neuroscience*, 9, 355–360.

Dani, J., & Balfour, D. (2011). Historical and current perspective on tobacco use and nicotine addiction. *Trends in Neuroscience*, 34, 383–392.

Darcq, E., & Kieffer, B. L. (2018). Opioid receptors: Drivers to addiction? *Nature Reviews Neuroscience*, 19, 499–514, 018-0028-x. https://doi.org/10.1038/s41583-

Davis, A. K., Barrett, F. S., May, D. G., Cosimano, M. P., Sepeda, N. D., Johnson, M. W., Finan, P. H., & Griffiths, R. R. (2021). Effects of psilocybin-assisted therapy on major depressive disorder: A randomized clinical trial. *JAMA Psychiatry*, 78(5), 481–489. https://doi.org/10.1001/jamapsychiatry.2020.3285

Denizet-Lewis, B. (2009). *America anonymous: Eight addicts in search of a life*. Simon & Schuster.

Dittrich, A. (1998). The standardized psychometric assessment of altered states of consciousness (ASCs) in humans. *Pharmacopsychiatry*, 31, 80–84.

Egervari, G., Siciliano, C. A., Whiteley, E. L., & Ron, D. (2021). Alcohol and the brain: Rrom genes to circuits. *Trends in Neurosciences*, 44(12), 1004–1015. https://doi.org/10.1016/j.tins.2021.09.006

Ferland, J. N., & Hurd, Y. L. (2020). Deconstructing the neurobiology of cannabis use disorder. *Nature Neuroscience*, 23(5), 600–610. https://doi.org/10.1038/s41593-020-0611-0

Frances, A. (2013). *Saving normal*. William Morrow.

Fuentes, J. J., Fonseca, F., Elices, M., Farré, M., & Torrens, M. (2020). Therapeutic use of LSD in psychiatry: A systematic review of randomized-controlled clinical trials. *Frontiers in Psychiatry*, 10, 943. https://doi.org/10.3389/fpsyt.2019.00943

GBD 2016 Alcohol Collaborators. (2018). Alcohol use and burden for 195 countries and territories, 1990–2016: A systematic analysis for the Global Burden of Disease

Study 2016. *The Lancet, 392*, 1015–1035. https://doi.org/10.1016/S0140-6736(18)31310-2

Gillespie, N. A., & Kendler, K. S. (2021). Use of genetically informed methods to clarify the nature of the association between cannabis use and risk for schizophrenia. *JAMA Psychiatry, 78*(5), 467–468. https://doi.org/10.1001/jamapsychiatry.2020.3564

Glade, M. (2010). Caffeine—Not just a stimulant. *Nutrition, 26*, 932–938.

Goldstein, R., & Volkow, N. (2002). Drug addiction and its underlying neurobiological basis: Neuroimaging evidence for the involvement of the frontal cortex. *American Journal of Psychiatry, 159*, 1642–1652.

Goldstein, R. Z., & Volkow, N. D. (2011). Dysfunction of the prefrontal cortex in addiction: Neuroimaging findings and clinical implications. *Nature Reviews Neuroscience, 12*(11), 652–669. http://doi.org/10.1038/nrn3119

Goodman, A. (2007). Neurobiology of addiction: An integrative review. *Biochemical Pharmacology, 75*, 266–322.

Häggström, M. (2009). Possible long-term effects of ethanol. *Wikipedia*. http://en.wikipedia.org/wiki/File: Possible_long-term_effects_of_ethanol.svg

Han, B., Compton, W. M., Jones, C. M., Einstein, E. B., & Volkow, N. D. (2021). Methamphetamine use, methamphetamine use disorder, and associated overdose deaths among US adults. *JAMA Psychiatry, 78*(12), 1329–1342. https://doi.org/10.1001/jamapsychiatry.2021.2588

Hasin, D. S. (2017). U.S. epidemiology of cannabis use and associated problems. *Neuropsychopharmacology Reviews, 43*, 195–212. https://doi.org/10.1038/npp.2017.198

Hayden, B., Canuel, N., & Shanse, J. (2013). What was brewing in the Natufian? An archaeological assessment of brewing technology in the Epipaleolithic. *Journal of Archaeological Method and Theory, 20*, 102–150.

Higuchi, S., Maesato, H., Yoshimura, A., & Matsushita, S. (2014). Acceptance of controlled drinking among treatment specialists of alcohol dependence in Japan. *Alcohol and Alcoholism, 49*(4), 447–452. http://doi.org/10.1093/alcalc/agu036

Hollister, L. E. (1984). Effects of hallucinogens in humans. In B. L. Jacobs (Ed.), *Hallucinogens: Neurochemical, behavioral, and clinical perspectives* (pp. 19–33). Raven Press.

Hyman, S., Malenka, R., & Nestler, E. (2006). Neural mechanisms of addiction: The role of reward-related learning and memory. *Annual Review of Neuroscience, 29*, 565–598.

Iversen, L. (2006). Neurotransmitter transporters and their impact on the development of psychopharmacology. *British Journal of Pharmacology, 147*, S82–S88.

Jones, A. (2011). Early drug discovery and the rise of pharmaceutical chemistry. *Drug Testing and Analysis, 3*(6), 337–344. https://doi.org/10.1002/dta.301

Kalivas, P. (2009). The glutamate homeostasis hypothesis of addiction. *Nature Reviews Neuroscience, 10*, 561–572.

Kessler, R. C., Hwang, I., LaBrie, R., Petukhova, M., Sampson, N., Winters, K., & Shaffer, H. (2008). The prevalence and correlates of DSM-IV pathological gambling in the National Comorbidity Survey Replication. *Psychological Medicine, 38*, 1351–1360.

Keyes, K., Schulenberg, J., O'Malley, P., Johnston, L., Bachman, J., Li, G., & Hasin, D. (2012). Birth cohort effects on adolescent alcohol use: The influence of social norms from 1976 to 2007. *Archives of General Psychiatry, 69*, 1304–1313.

Kibaly, C., Xu, C., Cahill, C. M., Evans, C. J., & Law, P. (2019). Non-nociceptive roles of opioids in the CNS: Opioids' effects on neurogenesis, learning, memory and affect. *Nature Reviews Neuroscience, 20*, 5–18. https://doi.org/10.1038/s41583-018-0092-2

King, A., de Wit, H., McNamara, P., & Cao, D. (2011). Rewarding, stimulant, and sedative alcohol responses and relationship to future binge drinking. *Archives of General Psychiatry, 68*, 389–399.

Koob, G. F., Kandel, D., & Volkow, N. D. (2008). Pathophysiology of addiction. In A. Tasman, J. Kay, J. A. Lieberman, M. B. First, & M. Maj (Eds.), *Psychiatry* (3rd ed., Vol. 1, pp. 354–378). Wiley.

Koob, G. F., & Schulkin, J. (2018). Addiction and stress: An allostatic view. *Neuroscience and Biobehavioral Reviews*. https://doi.org/10.1016/j.neubiorev.2018.09.008

Kuepper, R., van Os, J., Lieb, R., Wittchen, H., Höfler, M., & Henquet, C. (2011). Continued cannabis use and risk of incidence and persistence of psychotic symptoms: 10-year follow-up cohort study. *BMJ*. doi:10.1136/bmj.d738 *342*

Kwan, A. C., Olson, D. E., Preller, K. H., & Roth, B. L. (2022). The neural basis of psychedelic action. *Nature Neuroscience, 25*(11), 1407–1419. https://doi.org/10.1038/s41593-022-01177-4

Large, M., Sharma, S., Compton, M., Slade, T., & Nielssen, O. (2011). Cannabis use and earlier onset of psychosis: A systematic meta-analysis. *Archives of General Psychiatry, 68*, 555–561.

Liu, L., Wang, J., Rosenberg, D., Zhao, H., Lengyel, G., & Nadel, D. (2018). Fermented beverage and food storage in 13,000 y-old stone mortars at Raqefet Cave, Israel: Investigating Natufian ritual feasting. *Journal of Archaeological Science: Reports, 21*, 783–793.

Luquiens, A., Miranda, R., Benyamina, A., Carré, A., & Aubin, H. (2019). Cognitive training: A new avenue in gambling disorder management? *Neuroscience and Biobehavioral Reviews, 106*, 227–233. https://doi.org/10.1016/j.neubiorev.2018.10.011

Luquiens, A., Reynaud, M., & Aubin, H. J. (2011). Is controlled drinking an acceptable goal in the treatment of alcohol dependence? A survey of French alcohol specialists. *Alcohol and Alcoholism, 46*(5), 586–591. http://doi.org/10.1093/alcalc/agr083

Lüscher, C., & Janak, P. H. (2021). Consolidating the circuit model for addiction. *Annual Review of Neuroscience, 44*, 173–195. https://doi.org/10.1146/annurev-neuro-092920-123905

Lutz, B. (2020). Neurobiology of cannabinoid receptor signaling. *Dialogues in Clinical Neuroscience, 22*(3), 207–222. https://doi.org/10.31887/DCNS.2020.22.3/blutz

MacKillop, J., Stojek, M., VanderBroekStice, L., & Owens, M. (2018). Evidence-based treatment for alcohol use disorders. In D. David, S. Lynn, & G. Montgomery (Eds.), *Evidence based psychotherapy: The state of science and practice* (pp. 219–252). Wiley Blackwell.

Marshall, J., & O'Dell, S. (2012). Methamphetamine influences on brain and behavior: Unsafe at any speed? *Trends in Neurosciences, 35*, 536–545.

Marwaha, S., Palmer, E., Suppes, T., Cons, E., Young, A. H., & Upthegrove, R. (2023). Novel and emerging treatments for major depression. *Lancet (London, England), 401*(10371), 141–153. https://doi.org/10.1016/S0140-6736(22)02080-3

McCann, U., Szabo, Z., Scheffel, U., Dannals, R., & Ricaurte, G. (1998). Positron emission tomographic evidence of toxic effect of MDMA ("Ecstasy") on brain serotonin neurons in human beings. *The Lancet, 352*, 1433–1437.

McCann, U. D., Wong, D. F., Yokoi, F., Villemagne, V., Dannals, R. F., & Ricaurte, G. A. (1998). Reduced striatal dopamine transporter density in abstinent methamphetamine and methcathinone users: Evidence from positron emission tomography studies with [11C]WIN-35,428. *The Journal of Neuroscience*, 18(20), 8417–8422. https://doi.org/10.1523/JNEUROSCI.18-20-08417.1998

McGovern, P. (2009). *Uncorking the past: The quest for wine, beer, and other alcoholic beverages*. University of California Press.

McHugh, R. K., Votaw, V. R., Sugarman, D. E., & Green, S. F. (2018). Sex and gender differences in substance use disorders. *Clinical Psychology Review*, 66, 12–23. https://doi.org/10.1016/j.cpr.2017.10.012

Miller, W., Sorensen, J., Selzer, J., & Brigham, G. (2006). Disseminating evidence-based practices in substance abuse treatment: A review with suggestions. *Journal of Substance Abuse and Treatment*, 31, 25–39.

Miller, W. R., & Rollnick, S. (2012). *Motivational interviewing* (3rd ed.). Guilford Press.

Murray, J. E., Belin-Rauscent, A., Simon, M., Giuliano, C., Benoit-Marand, M., Everitt, B. J., & Belin, D. (2015). Dependent cocaine-seeking habits. *Nature Communications*, 6, 1–9. http://doi.org/10.1038/ncomms10088

Murray, R., Morrison, P., Henquet, C., & Di Forti, M. (2007). Cannabis, the mind and society: The hash realities. *Nature Reviews Neuroscience*, 8, 885–895.

Musto, D. (1991). Opium, cocaine and marijuana in American history. *Scientific American*, 265, 40–47.

National Institute on Drug Abuse. (2018, January). *Principles of drug addiction treatment: A research-based guide*, 3rd https://d14rmgtrwzf5a.cloudfront.net/sites/default/files/675-principles-of-drug-addiction-treatment-a-research-based-guide-third-edition.pdf

Nestler, E., & Malenka, R. (2004). The addictive brain. *Scientific American*, 290, 78–85.

Nichols, D. (2004). Hallucinogens. *Pharmacology & Therapeutics*, 101, 131–181.

Ostroumov, A., & Dani, J. A. (2018). Inhibitory plasticity of mesocorticolimbic circuits in addiction and mental illness. *Trends in Neurosciences*, 41(12), 898–910. https://doi.org/10.1016/j.tins.2018.07.014

Palmer, R., Young, S., Corley, R., Hopfer, C., Stallings, M., & Hewitt, J. (2013). Stability and change of genetic and environmental effects on the common liability to alcohol, tobacco, and cannabis DSM-IV dependence symptoms. *Behavioral Genetics*, 43(5), 374–385.

Panksepp, J., Knutson, B., & Burgdorf, J. (2002). The role of brain emotional systems in addictions: A neuro-evolutionary perspective and new "self-report" animal model. *Addiction*, 97, 459–469.

Pearson, C., Siegel, J., & Gold, J. A. (2022). Psilocybin-assisted psychotherapy for depression: Emerging research on a psychedelic compound with a rich history. *Journal of the Neurological Sciences*, 434, Article 120096. https://doi.org/10.1016/j.jns.2021.120096

Pendery, M., Maltzman, & West, L. (1982). Controlled drinking by alcoholics? New findings and a reevaluation of a major affirmative study. *Science*, 217, 169–175.

Polich, J., Armor, D., & Braiker, H. (1981). *The course of alcoholism: Four years after treatment*. Wiley.

Pool, E., Sennwald, V., Delplanque, S., Brosch, T., & Sander, D. (2016). Measuring wanting and liking from animals to humans: A systematic review. *Neuroscience & Biobehavioral Reviews*, 63, 124–142. http://doi.org/10.1016/j.neubiorev.2016.01.006

Ramaekers, J. G., Mason, N. L., Kloft, L., & Theunissen, E. L. (2021). The why behind the high: Determinants of neurocognition during acute cannabis exposure. *Nature Reviews Neuroscience*, 22(7), 439–454. https://doi.org/10.1038/s41583-021-00466-4

Ray, L. A., & Grodin, E. N. (2021). Clinical neuroscience of addiction: What clinical psychologists need to know and why. *Annual Review of Clinical Psychology*, 17, 465–493. https://doi.org/10.1146/annurev-clinpsy-081219-114309

Ren, M., Tang, Z., Wu, X., Spengler, R., Jiang, H., Yang, Y., & Boivin, N. (2019). The origins of cannabis smoking: Chemical residue evidence from the first millennium BCE in the Pamirs. *Science Advances*, 5(6), Article eaaw1391. https://doi.org/10.1126/sciadv.aaw1391

Robison, A., & Nestler, E. (2011). Transcriptional and epigenetic mechanisms of addiction. *Nature Reviews Neuroscience*, 12, 623–637.

Saah, T. (2005). The evolutionary origins and significance of drug addiction. *Harm Reduction Journal*, 2, 2–8.

Saladin, M., & Santa Ana, E. (2004). Controlled drinking: More than just a controversy. *Current Opinion in Psychiatry*, 17, 175–187.

Seelye, K. Q. (2016, January 24). *Massachusetts chief's tack in drug war: Steer addicts to rehab, not jail*. The New York Times. https://www.nytimes.com/2016/01/25/us/massachusetts-chiefs-tack-in-drug-war-steer-addicts-to-rehab-not-jail.html

Shaffer, H., & Martin, R. (2011). Disordered gambling: Etiology, trajectory, and clinical considerations. *Annual Review of Clinical Psychology*, 7, 483–510.

Sherva, R., Wang, Q., Kranzler, H., Zhao, H., Koesterer, R., Herman, A., Farrer, L., & Gelernter, J. (2016). Genome-wide association study of cannabis dependence severity, novel risk variants, and shared genetic risks. *JAMA Psychiatry*, 73(5), 472–480. http://doi.org/10.1001/jamapsychiatry.2016.0036

Sobell, M., & Sobell, L. (1978). *Behavioral treatment of alcohol problems*. Plenum.

Sobell, M., & Sobell, L. (1995). Controlled drinking after 25 years: How important was the great debate? [Editorial]. *Addiction*, 90, 1149–1154.

Stuart, D. (2004). *Dangerous garden*. Harvard University Press.

Studerus, E., Kometer, M., Hasler, F., & Vollenweider, F. (2011). Acute, subacute and long-term subjective effects of psilocybin in healthy humans: A pooled analysis of experimental studies. *Journal of Psychopharmacology*, 25, 1434–1452.

Substance Abuse and Mental Health Services Administration. (2015). *Behavioral health barometer: United States, 2015* (Publication No. SMA16-BARO-2015)

Teague, C. D., & Nestler, E. J. (2022). Teenage drinking and adult neuropsychiatric disorders: An epigenetic connection. *Science Advances*, 8(18), Article eabq5934. https://doi.org/10.1126/sciadv.abq5934

Tibboel, H., De Houwer, J., & Van Bockstaele, B. (2015). Implicit measures of "wanting" and "liking" in humans. *Neuroscience and Biobehavioral Reviews*, 57, 350–364. http://doi.org/10.1016/j.neubiorev.2015.09.015

Tikkanen, R., Tiihonen, J., Rautiainen, M. R., Paunio, T., Bevilacqua, L., Panarsky, R., Goldman, D., & Virkkunen, M. (2015). Impulsive alcohol-related risk behavior and emotional dysregulation among individuals with a serotonin 2B receptor stop codon. *Translational Psychiatry*, 5(11), e681. http://doi.org/10.1038/tp.2015.170

Treutlein, J., Cichon, S., Ridinger, M., Wodarz, N., Soyka, M., Zill, P., Maier, W., Moessner, R., Gaebel, W., Dahmen, N., Fehr, C., Scherbaum, N., Steffens, M., Ludwig, K. U., Frank, J., Wichmann, H. E., Schreiber, S., Dragano, N., & Rietschel, M. (2009). Genome-wide association study of alcohol dependence. *Archives of General Psychiatry*, *47*, 2016–2022.

United Nations Office on Drugs and Crime. (2011). *Amphetamines and ecstasy. United Nations*. Retrieved from www.unodc.org/documents/ATS/ATS_Global_Assessment_2011.pdf

United Nations Office on Drugs and Crime. (2012). *World drug report 2012*. Retrieved from http://www.unodc.org

Urbina, I. (2012, May 11). *Addiction diagnoses may rise under guideline changes. The New York Times*. https://www.nytimes.com/2012/05/12/us/dsm-revisions-may-sharply-increase-addiction-diagnoses.html

Uys, J., & Reissner, K. (2011). Glutamatergic neuroplasticity in cocaine addiction. *Progress in Molecular Biology and Translational Science*, *98*, 367–400.

van Holst, R., van den Brink, W., Veltman, D., & Goudriaan, A. (2010). Brain imaging studies in pathological gambling. *Current Psychiatry Reports*, *12*, 418–425.

van Winkel, R., van Beveren, N., & Simons, C. (2011). & Genetic Risk and Outcome of Psychosis (GROUP). AKT1 moderation of cannabis-induced cognitive alterations in psychotic disorder. *Investigators. (, Neuropsychopharmacology*, *36*, 2529–2537.

Volkow, N., & Li, T. (2005). The neuroscience of addiction. *Nature Neuroscience*, *8*, 1429–1430.

Volkow, N. D., & Blanco, C. (2021). The changing opioid crisis: Development, challenges and opportunities. *Molecular Psychiatry*, *26*(1), 218–233. https://doi.org/10.1038/s41380-020-0661-4

Volkow, N. D., Fowler, J. S., Wang, G. J., Hitzemann, R., Logan, J., Schlyer, D. J., Dewey, S. L., & Wolf, A. (1993). Decreased dopamine D2 receptor availability is associated with reduced frontal metabolism in cocaine abusers. *Synapse*, *14*, 169–177.

Volkow, N. D., Michaelides, M., & Baler, R. (2019). The neuroscience of drug reward and addiction. *Physiological Reviews*, *99*(4), 2115–2140. https://doi.org/10.1152/physrev.00014.2018

Volkow, N. D., Swanson, J. M., Evins, A. E., DeLisi, L. E., Meier, M. H., Gonzalez, R., Bloomfield, M. A. P., Curran, H. V., & Baler, R. (2016). Effects of cannabis use on human behavior, including cognition, motivation, and psychosis: A review. *JAMA Psychiatry*, *73*(3), 292–297. http://doi.org/10.1001/jamapsychiatry.2015.3278

Volkow, N. D., Wang, G.-J., Fowler, J. S., & Tomasi, D. (2012). Addiction circuitry in the human brain. *Annual Review of Pharmacology and Toxicology*, *52*, 321–336.

Volkow, N. D., Wang, G.-J., Tomasi, D., & Baler, R. D. (2013). Obesity and addiction: Neurobiological overlaps. *Obesity Reviews*, *14*, 2–18.

Voon, V., & Fox, S. (2007). Medication-related impulse control and repetitive behaviors in Parkinson disease. *Archives of Neurology*, *64*, 1089–1096.

Walters, R., Polimanti, R., Johnson, E., McClintick, J., Adams, M., Adkins, A. E., Aliev, F., Bacanu, S.-A., Batzler, A., Bertelsen, S., Biernacka, J. M., Bigdeli, T. B., Chen, L.-S., Clarke, T.-K., Chou, Y.-L., Degenhardt, F., Docherty, A. R., Edwards, A. C., & Agrawal, A. (2018). Transancestral GWAS of alcohol dependence reveals common genetic underpinnings with psychiatric disorders. *Nature Neuroscience*, *21*, 1656–1669. https://doi.org/10.1038/s41593-018-0275-1

Wareham, J., & Potenza, M. (2010). Pathological gambling and substance use disorders. *American Journal of Drug and Alcohol Abuse*, *36*, 242–247.

Westbrook, S. R., Carrica, L. K., Banks, A., & Gulley, J. M. (2020). AMPed-up adolescents: The role of age in the abuse of amphetamines and its consequences on cognition and prefrontal cortex development. *Pharmacology, Biochemistry, and Behavior*, *198*, Article 173016. https://doi.org/10.1016/j.pbb.2020.173016

White House. (2022, October 6). *Statement from President Biden on marijuana reform*. https://www.whitehouse.gov/briefing-room/statements-releases/2022/10/06/statement-from-president-biden-on-marijuana-reform

Wilkinson, P. K., Sedman, A. J., Sakmar, E., Kay, D. R., & Wagner, J. G. (1977). Pharmacokinetics of ethanol after oral administration in the fasting state. *Journal of Pharmacokinetics and Biopharmaceutics*, *5*(3), 207–224.

Wise, R. A. (1998). Drug activation of brain reward pathways. *Drug and Alcohol Dependence*, *51*, 13–22.

Witkiewitz, K., Pfund, R. A., & Tucker, J. A. (2022). Mechanisms of behavior change in substance use disorder with and without formal treatment. *Annual Review of Clinical Psychology*, *18*, 497–525. https://doi.org/10.1146/annurev-clinpsy-072720-014802

Zhang, Y., Zhang, S., Ide, J. S., Hu, S., Zhornitsky, S., & Wang, W. (2018). Dynamic network dysfunction in cocaine dependence: Graph theoretical metrics and stop signal reaction time. *NeuroImage: Clinical*, *18*, 793–801 https://doi.org/10.1016/j.nicl.2018.03.016

CHAPTER 13

Abi-Dargham, A., & Grace, A. (2011). Dopamine and schizophrenia. In D. Weinberger & P. Harrison (Eds.), *Schizophrenia* (3rd ed., pp. 413–432). Wiley.

Alderson-Day, B., McCarthy-Jones, S., & Fernyhough, C. (2015). Hearing voices in the resting brain: A review of intrinsic functional connectivity research on auditory verbal hallucinations. *Neuroscience & Biobehavioral Reviews*, *55*, 78–87. http://doi.org/10.1016/j.neubiorev.2015.04.016

Allen, A. J., Griss, M. E., Folley, B. S., Hawkins, K. A., & Pearlson, G. D. (2009). Endophenotypes in schizophrenia: A selective review. *Schizophrenia Research*, *109*, 24–37.

Allen, P., Larøi, F., McGuire, P., & Aleman, A. (2008). The hallucinating brain: A review of structural and functional neuroimaging studies of hallucinations. *Neuroscience and Biobehavioral Reviews*, *32*, 175–191.

Amaresha, A. C., & Venkatasubramanian, G. (2012). Expressed emotion in schizophrenia: An overview. *Indian Journal of Psychological Medicine*, *34*(1), 12–20. doi:10.4103/0253-7176.96149

American, Psychiatric Association. (2022). *Diagnostic and statistical manual of mental disorders*, (5th ed., text rev.)

American Psychological Association. (2017). *Multicultural guidelines: An ecological approach to context, identity, and intersectionality*. Retrieved from http://www.apa.org/about/policy/multicultural-guidelines.pdf

Andreasen, N. (2005). *The creating brain: The neuroscience of genius*. Dana Press.

Angrilli, A., Spironelli, C., Elbert, T., Crow, T. J., Marano, G., & Stegagno, L. (2009). Schizophrenia as failure of left hemispheric dominance for the phonological component of language. *PLOS ONE*, *4*. http://doi.org/10.1371/journal.pone.0004507

Bailey, T., Alvarez-Jimenez, M., Garcia-Sanchez, A. M., Hulbert, C., Barlow, E., & Bendall, S. (2018). Childhood trauma is associated with severity of hallucinations and delusions in psychotic disorders: A systematic review and meta-analysis. *Schizophrenia Bulletin, 44*(5), 1111–1122. https://doi.org/10.1093/schbul/sbx161

Barbeito, S., Sánchez-Gutiérrez, T., Mayoral, M., Moreno, M., & Scott, A. J. (2019). Mobile app–based intervention for adolescents with first-episode psychosis: Study protocol for a pilot randomized controlled trial. *Frontiers in Psychiatry, 10*. https://doi.org/10.3389/fpsyt.2019.00027

Barch, D., & Ceaser, A. (2012). Cognition in schizophrenia: Core psychological and neural mechanisms. *Trends in Cognitive Science, 16*, 27–34.

Barrowclough, C., & Lobban, F. (2008). Family intervention. In K. Meser & D. Jeste (Eds.), *Clinical handbook of schizophrenia* (pp. 214–225). Guilford Press.

Bassett, D. S., Nelson, B. G., Mueller, B. A., Camchong, J., & Lim, K. O. (2012). Altered resting state complexity in schizophrenia. *NeuroImage, 59*, 196–207.

Beck, A. T., & Rector, N. A. (2005). Cognitive approaches to schizophrenia: Theory and therapy. *Annual Review of Clinical Psychology, 1*, 577–606.

Besteher, B., Brambilla, P., & Nenadić, I. (2020). Twin studies of brain structure and cognition in schizophrenia. *Neuroscience and Biobehavioral Reviews, 109*, 103–113. https://doi.org/10.1016/j.neubiorev.2019.12.021

Bohlken, M. M., Brouwer, R. M., Mandl, R. C. W., Van den Heuvel, M. P., Hedman, A. M., De Hert, M., Cahn, W., Kahn, R. S., & Hulshoff Pol, H. E. (2015). Structural brain connectivity as a genetic marker for schizophrenia. *JAMA Psychiatry, 73*(1), 11–19. http://doi.org/10.1001/jamapsychiatry.2015.1925

Brown, A., & Patterson, P. (2011). Maternal infection and schizophrenia: Implications for prevention. *Schizophrenia Bulletin, 37*, 284–290.

Brown, G. (1985). The discovery of expressed emotion: Induction or deduction? In J. Leff & C. Vaughn (Eds.), *Expressed emotion in families*. Guilford Press.

Burns, J. (2004). An evolutionary theory of schizophrenia: Cortical connectivity, metarepresentation, and the social brain. *Behavioral and Brain Sciences, 27*, 831–885.

Cannon, T. D. (2015). How schizophrenia develops: Cognitive and brain mechanisms underlying onset of psychosis. *Trends in Cognitive Sciences, 19*(12), 744–756. http://doi.org/10.1016/j.tics.2015.09.009

Caspi, A., Houts, R. M., Belsky, D. W., Goldman-Mellor, S. J., Harrington, H., Israel, S., Meier, M., Ramrakha, S., Shalev, I., Poulton, R., & Moffitt, T. (2014). The p factor: One general psychopathology factor in the structure of psychiatric disorders? *Clinical Psychological Science, 2*(2), 119–137. http://doi.org/10.1177/2167702613497473

Cheng, W., Frei, O., van der Meer, D., Wang, Y., O'Connell, K. S., Chu, Y., Bahrami, S., Shadrin, A. A., Alnæs, D., Hindley, G. F. L., Lin, A., Karadag, N., Fan, C. C., Westlye, L. T., Kaufmann, T., Molden, E., Dale, A. M., Djurovic, S., Smeland, O. B., & Andreassen, O. A. (2021). Genetic association between schizophrenia and cortical brain surface area and thickness. *JAMA Psychiatry, 78*(9), 1020–1030. https://doi.org/10.1001/jamapsychiatry.2021.1435

Cornblatt, B. A., & Carrión, R. E. (2016). Deconstructing the psychosis risk syndrome: Moving the field of prevention forward. *JAMA Psychiatry, 73*, 105–106. http://doi.org/10.1001/jamapsychiatry.2015.2324.3

Coyle, J. T., Ruzicka, W. B., & Balu, D. T. (2020). Fifty years of research on schizophrenia: The ascendance of the glutamatergic synapse. *American Journal of Psychiatry, 177*(12), 1119–1128. https://doi.org/10.1176/appi.ajp.2020.20101481

Crow, T. (2000). Schizophrenia as the price that *Homo sapiens* pays for language: A resolution of the central paradox in the origin of the species. *Brain Research Reviews, 31*, 118–129.

Cuthbert, B. N., & Morris, S. E. (2021). Evolving concepts of the schizophrenia spectrum: A research domain criteria perspective. *Frontiers in Psychiatry, 12*, Article 641319. https://doi.org/10.3389/fpsyt.2021.641319

Deary, I. J., Penke, L., & Johnson, W. (2010). The neuroscience of human intelligence differences. *Nature Reviews Neuroscience, 11*, 201–211. http://doi.org/10.1038/nrn2793

Debnath, M., Venkatasubramanian, G., & Berk, M. (2015). Fetal programming of schizophrenia: Select mechanisms. *Neuroscience & Biobehavioral Reviews, 49*, 90–104. http://doi.org/10.1016/j.neubiorev.2014.12.003

Dima, D., Roiser, J. P., Dietrich, D. E., Bonnemann, C., Lanfermann, H., Emrich, H. M., & Dillo, W. (2009). Understanding why patients with schizophrenia do not perceive the hollow-mask illusion using dynamic causal modelling. *NeuroImage, 15*, 1180–1186.

Diwadkar, V. A., Wadehra, S., Pruitt, P., Keshavan, M. S., Rajan, U., Zajac-Benitez, C., & Eickhoff, S. B. (2012). Disordered corticolimbic interactions during affective processing in children and adolescents at risk for schizophrenia revealed by functional magnetic resonance imaging and dynamic causal modeling. *Archives of General Psychiatry, 69*, 231–242.

Dixon, L. B., Goldman, H., Srihari, V. H., & Kane, J. (2018). Transforming the treatment of schizophrenia in the United States: The RAISE Initiative. *Annual Review of Clinical Psychology, 14*, 237–258.

Doucet, G. E., Luber, M. J., Balchandani, P., Sommer, I. E., & Frangou, S. (2019). Abnormal auditory tonotopy in patients with schizophrenia. *NPJ Schizophrenia, 5*(1), Article 16. https://doi.org/10.1038/s41537-019-0084-x

Ellenberg, S., Lynn, S., & Strauss, G. (2018). Psychotherapy for schizophrenia-spectrum disorder. In D. David, S. Lynn, & G. Montgomery (Eds.), *Evidence-based psychotherapy: The state of science and practice* (pp. 363–405). Wiley Blackwell.

ENIGMA Clinical High Risk for Psychosis Working Group, Jalbrzikowski, M., Hayes, R. A., Wood, S. J., Nordholm, D., Zhou, J. H., Fusar-Poli, P., Uhlhaas, P. J., Takahashi, T., Sugranyes, G., Kwak, Y. B., Mathalon, D. H., Katagiri, N., Hooker, C. I., Smigielski, L., Colibazzi, T., Via, E., Tang, J., Koike, S., Rasser, P. E., . . . Hernaus, D. (2021). Association of structural magnetic resonance imaging measures with psychosis onset in individuals at clinical high risk for developing psychosis: An ENIGMA Working Group mega-analysis. *JAMA Psychiatry, 78*(7), 753–766. https://doi.org/10.1001/jamapsychiatry.2021.0638

Fabrega, H. (1989). On the significance of an anthropological approach to schizophrenia. *Psychiatry, 52*, 45–65.

Fink, M., Shorter, E., & Taylor, M. (2010). Catatonia is not schizophrenia: Kraepelin's error and the need to recognize catatonia as an independent syndrome in medical nomenclature. *Schizophrenia Bulletin, 36*, 314–320.

Fisher, M., Loewy, R., Hardy, K., Schlosser, D., & Vinogradov, S. (2013). Cognitive interventions targeting brain plasticity in the prodromal and early phases of schizophrenia. *Annual Review of Clinical Psychology, 9*, 435–463.

Fletcher, P., & Frith, C. (2009). Perceiving is believing: A Bayesian approach to explaining the positive symptoms of schizophrenia. *Nature Reviews Neuroscience, 10*, 48–58.

Ford, J., & Hoffman, R. (2013). Functional brain imaging of auditory hallucinations: From self-monitoring deficits to co-opted neural resources. In R. Jardri, A. Cachia, P. Thomas, & D. Pins (Eds.), *The neuroscience of hallucinations* (pp. 359–373). Springer.

Ford, J. M., Mathalon, D. H., Whitfield, S., Faustman, W. O., & Roth, W. T. (2002). Reduced communication between frontal and temporal lobes during talking in schizophrenia. *Biological Psychiatry, 21*, 485–492.

Ford, J. M., Roach, B. J., Faustman, W. O., & Mathalon, D. H. (2007). Synch before you speak: Auditory hallucinations in schizophrenia. *American Journal of Psychiatry, 164*, 456–466.

Foussias, G., & Remington, G. (2010). Negative symptoms in schizophrenia: Avolition and Occam's razor. *Schizophrenia Bulletin, 36*, 359–369.

Frese, F., Knight, E., & Saks, E. (2009). Recovery from schizophrenia: With views of psychiatrists, psychologists, and others diagnosed with this disorder. *Schizophrenia Bulletin, 35*, 370–380.

Gao, X., Zhang, W., Yao, L., Xiao, Y., Liu, L., Liu, J., Li, S., Tao, B., Shah, C., Gong, Q., Sweeney, J. A., & Lui, S. (2018). Association between structural and functional brain alterations in drug-free patients with schizophrenia: A multimodal meta-analysis. *Journal of Psychiatry and Neuroscience, 43*, 131–142. https://doi.org/10.1503/jpn.160219

Gilmore, J. H., Kang, C., Evans, D. D., Wolfe, H. M., Smith, J. K., Lieberman, J. A., Lin, W., Hamer, R. M., Styner, M., & Gerig, G. (2010). Prenatal and neonatal brain structure and white matter maturation in children at high risk for schizophrenia. *American Journal of Psychiatry, 167*, 1083–1091.

Giraldo-Chica, M., Rogers, B. P., Damon, S. M., Landman, B. A., & Woodward, N. D. (2018). Prefrontal-thalamic anatomical connectivity and executive cognitive function in schizophrenia. *Biological Psychiatry, 83*(6), 509–517. https://doi.org/10.1016/j.biopsych.2017.09.022

Goghari, V., Sponheim, S., & MacDonald, A. (2010). The functional neuroanatomy of symptom dimensions in schizophrenia: A qualitative and quantitative review of a persistent question. *Neuroscience and Biobehavioral Review, 34*, 468–486.

Gogtay, N., Vyas, N., Testa, R., Wood, S., & Pantelis, C. (2011). Age of onset of schizophrenia: Perspectives from structural neuroimaging studies. *Schizophrenia Bulletin, 37*, 504–513.

Golofast, B., & Vales, K. (2020). The connection between microbiome and schizophrenia. *Neuroscience and Biobehavioral Reviews, 108*, 712–731. https://doi.org/10.1016/j.neubiorev.2019.12.011

Gomes, F. V., Zhu, X., & Grace, A. A. (2019, January 30). Stress during critical periods of development and risk for schizophrenia. *Schizophrenia Research*. Advance online publication. doi.org/10.1016/j.schres.2019.01.030

Gopalakrishna, G., Ithman, M. H., & Lauriello, J. (2016). Update on new and emerging treatments for schizophrenia. *Psychiatric Clinics of North America, 39*, 217–238. http://doi.org/10.1016/j.psc.2016.01.005

Grace, A. (2010). Ventral hippocampus, interneurons, and schizophrenia: A new understanding of the pathophysiology of schizophrenia and its implications for treatment and prevention. *Current Directions in Psychological Science, 19*, 232–237.

Green, M., Horan, W., & Lee, J. (2015). Social cognition in schizophrenia. *Nature Reviews Neuroscience, 16*, 620–631.

Gründer, G., & Cumming, P. (2016). The dopamine hypothesis of schizophrenia: Current status. In T. Abel & T. Nickl-Jockschat (Eds.), *Neurobiology of schizophrenia* (pp. 109–124). Academic Press.

Guloksuz, S., & van Os, J. (2018). The slow death of the concept of schizophrenia and the painful birth of the psychosis spectrum. *Psychological Medicine, 48*(2), 229–244. doi:10.1017/S0033291717001775

Harrow, M., & Jobe, T. (2010). How frequent is chronic multiyear delusional activity and recovery in schizophrenia: A 20-year multi-follow-up. *Schizophrenia Bulletin, 36*, 192–204.

Hogarty, G., & Goldberg, S. (1973). Drugs and sociotherapy in the after care of schizophrenic patients: One year relapse rates. *Archives of General Psychiatry, 28*, 54–64.

Huxley, J., Mayr, E., Osmond, H., & Hoffer, A. (1964). Schizophrenia as a genetic morphism. *Nature, 204*, 220–221.

Hyman, S., & Cohen, J. (2013). Disorders of thought and volition: Schizophrenia. In E. Kandel, J. Schwartz, T. Jessell, S. Siegelbaum, & A. Hudspeth (Eds.), *Principles of neural science* (5th ed., p. chap. 62). McGraw-Hill. https://neurology.mhmedical.com/content.aspx?bookid=1049&sectionid=59138698

Insel, T. (2010). Rethinking schizophrenia. *Nature, 468*, 187–193.

Jardri, R., & Sommer, I. (2013). Functional brain imaging of hallucinations: Symptom capture studies. In R. Jardri, A. Cachia, P. Thomas, & D. Pins (Eds.), *The neuroscience of hallucinations* (pp. 375–391). Springer.

Jason, L. (2015). Ethical and diversity challenges in ecologically sensitive systems-oriented interventions. *American Psychologist, 70*(8), 764–775.

Jobe, T., & Harrow, M. (2010). Schizophrenia course, long-term outcome, recovery, and prognosis. *Current Directions in Psychological Science, 19*, 220–225.

Junginger, J. (1990). Predicting compliance with command hallucinations. *American Journal of Psychiatry, 147*, 245–247.

Kane, J., Robinson, D., Schooler, N., Mueser, K., Penn, D. L., Rosenheck, R. A., Brunette, Addington, J., F, M., Correll, C. U., Estroff, S. E., Marcy, P., Robinson, J., Meyer-Kalos, P. S., Gottlieb, J. D., Glynn, S. M., Lynde, D. W., Pipes, R., Kurian, B. T., & Heinssen, R. (2016). Comprehensive versus usual community care for first-episode psychosis: 2-year outcomes from the NIMH RAISE Early Treatment Program. *American Journal of Psychiatry, 173*, 362–372.

Karlsgodt, K. H., Sun, D., & Cannon, T. D. (2010). Structural and functional brain abnormalities in schizophrenia. *Current Directions in Psychological Science, 19*, 226–231.

Keller, M. C. (2018). Evolutionary perspectives on genetic and environmental risk factors for psychiatric disorders. *Annual Review of Clinical Psychology, 14*(1), 1–23. https://doi.org/10.1146/annurev-clinpsy-050817-084854

Kelly, A., Uddin, L., Biswal, B., Castellanos, F., & Milham, M. (2008). Competition between functional brain networks mediates behavioral variability. *NeuroImage, 39*, 527–537.

King, S., St-Hilaire, A., & Heidkamp, D. (2010). Prenatal factors in schizophrenia. *Current Directions in Psychological Science, 19*, 209–213.

Kingdon, D., & Turkington, D. (1994). Cognitive behaviour therapy of schizophrenia. The amenability of delusions and hallucinations to reasoning. *British Journal of Psychiatry, 164*, 581–587.

Konopaske, G., & Coyle, J. (2023). The neurobiology of schizophrenia. In M. G.

Zigmond, C. A. Wiley, & M. F. Chesselet (Eds.), *Neurobiology of brain disorders* (2nd ed., pp. 843–860). Academic Press.

Kring, A., & Elis, O. (2013). Emotion deficits in people with schizophrenia. *Annual Review of Clinical Psychology, 9*, 409–433.

Krystal, J. H., & Moghaddam, B. (2011). Contributions of glutamate and GABA systems to the neurobiology and treatment of schizophrenia. In D. Weinberger & P. Harrison (Eds.), *Schizophrenia* (pp. 433–461). Wiley.

Krystal, J. H., Perry, E. B., Gueorguieva, R., Belger, A., Madonick, S. H., Abi-Dargham, A., Cooper, T. B., Macdougall, L., Abi-Saab, W., & D'Souza, D. C. (2005). Comparative and interactive human psychopharmacologic effects of ketamine and amphetamine: Implications for glutamatergic and dopaminergic model psychoses and cognitive function. *Archives of General Psychiatry, 62*, 985–995.

Kutscher, E. (2008). Antipsychotics. In K. Meser & D. Jeste (Eds.), *Clinical handbook of schizophrenia* (pp. 159–167). Guilford Press.

Lieberman, J., & Stroup, T. (2011). The NIMH-CATIE Schizophrenia study: What did we learn? *American Journal of Psychiatry, 168*, 770–775.

Linscott, R., Allardyce, J., & van Os, J. (2010). Seeking verisimilitude in a class: A systematic review of evidence that the criterial clinical symptoms of schizophrenia are taxonic. *Schizophrenia Bulletin, 36*, 811–829.

Loganathan, S., & Murthy, R. S. (2011). Living with schizophrenia in India: Gender perspectives. *Transcultural Psychiatry, 48*(5), 569–584. https://doi.org/10.1177/1363461511418872

López, S., & Guarnaccia, P. (2000). Cultural psychopathology: Uncovering the social world of mental illness. *Annual Review of Psychology, 51*, 571–598.

Maher, S., Ekstron, T., & Chen, Y. (2015). Impaired visual cortical processing of affective facial information in schizophrenia. *Clinical Psychological Science, 4*, 651–660.

Maiti, S., Kumar, K., Castellani, C., O'Reilly, R., & Singh, S. (2011). Ontogenetic de novo copy number variations (CNVs) as a source of genetic individuality: Studies on two families with MZD twins for schizophrenia. *PLOS ONE. 6*

Manzano, O., Cervenka, S., Karabanov, A., Farde, L., & Ullén, F. (2010). Thinking outside a less intact box: Thalamic dopamine D2 receptor densities are negatively related to psychometric creativity in healthy individuals. *PLOS ONE, 5*(5), Article e10670. https://doi.org/10.1371/journal.pone.0010670

Marder, S. R., & Cannon, T. D. (2019). Schizophrenia. *New England Journal of Medicine, 381*(18), 1753–1761. https://doi.org/10.1056/NEJMra1808803

Mayne, P. E., & Burne, T. H. J. (2019). Vitamin D in synaptic plasticity, cognitive function, and neuropsychiatric illness. *Trends in Neurosciences, 42*, 293–306. https://doi.org/10.1016/j.tins.2019.01.003

McCutcheon, R. A., Abi-Dargham, A., & Howes, O. D. (2019). Schizophrenia, dopamine and the striatum: From biology to symptoms. *Trends in Neurosciences, 42*, 205–220. https://doi.org/10.1016/j.tins.2018.12.004

McGrath, J., Burne, T., Féron, F., Mackay-Sim, A., & Eyles, D. (2010). Developmental vitamin D deficiency and risk of schizophrenia: A 10-year update. *Schizophrenia Bulletin, 36*, 1073–1078.

McLean, D., Thara, R., John, S., Barrett, R., Loa, P., McGrath, J., & Mowry, B. (2014). DSM-IV "criterion A" schizophrenia symptoms across ethnically different populations: Evidence for differing psychotic symptom content or structural organization? *Culture, Medicine and Psychiatry, 38*(3), 408–426. https://doi.org/10.1007/s11013-014-9385-8

Menon, V., Palaniyappan, L., & Supekar, K. (2022). Integrative brain network and salience models of psychopathology and cognitive dysfunction in schizophrenia. *Biological Psychiatry*. S0006-3223(22)01637-7. Advance online publication https://doi.org/10.1016/j.biopsych.2022.09.029

Miller, G., & Rockstroh, B. (2013). Endophenotypes in psychopathology research: Where do we stand? *Annual Review of Clinical Psychology, 9*, 1–15.

Miller, G., & Rockstroh, B. (2016). Progress and prospects for endophenotypes for schizophrenia in the time of genomics, epigenetics, oscillatory brain dynamics, and the research domain criteria. In T. Nickl-Jockschat & T. Abel (Eds.), *The neurobiology of schizophrenia* (pp. 17–38). Elsevier.

Minzenberg, M., Laird, A., Thelen, S., Carter, C., & Glahn, D. (2009). Meta-analysis of 41 functional neuroimaging studies of executive function in schizophrenia. *Archives of General Psychiatry, 66*, 811–822.

Minzenberg, M., Yoon, J., & Carter, C. (2010). Schizophrenia. In R. Hales, S. Yudofsky, & G. O. Gabbard (Eds.), *Essentials of psychiatry* (3rd ed., pp. 111–150). American Psychiatric Press.

Mollon, J., David, A. S., Zammit, S., Lewis, G., & Reichenberg, A. (2018). Course of cognitive development from infancy to early adulthood in the psychosis spectrum. *JAMA Psychiatry, 75*(3), 270–279. https://doi.org/10.1001/jamapsychiatry.2017.4327

Morrison, A. (2008). Cognitive-behavioral therapy. In K. Meser & D. Jeste (Eds.), *Clinical handbook of schizophrenia* (pp. 226–239). Guilford Press.

Nemeroff, C. B., Weinberger, D., Rutter, M., MacMillan, H. L., Bryant, R. A., Wessely, S., Stein, D. J., Pariante, C. M., Seemüller, C., Berk, M., Malhi, G. S., Preisig, M., Brüne, M., & Lysaker, P. (2013). DSM-5: A collection of psychiatrist views on the changes, controversies, and future directions. *BMC Medicine, 11*, Article 202. http://doi.org/10.1186/1741-7015-11-202

Nunez, P., & Srinivasan, R. (2006). *Electrical fields of the brain: The neurophysics of EEG*. Oxford University Press.

Paquin, V., Lapierre, M., Veru, F., & King, S. (2021). Early environmental upheaval and the risk for schizophrenia. *Annual Review of Clinical Psychology, 17*, 285–311. https://doi.org/10.1146/annurev-clinpsy-081219-103805

Pearlson, G. (2011). Functional imaging of schizophrenia. In M. Shenton & B. Turetsky (Eds.), *Understanding neuropsychiatric disorders: Insights from neuroimaging*. Cambridge University Press.

Peluso, M., Lewis, S., Barnes, T., & Jones, P. (2012). Extrapyramidal motor side-effects of first- and second-generation antipsychotic drugs. *British Journal of Psychiatry, 200*, 387–392.

Petronis, A. (2004). The origin of schizophrenia: Genetic thesis, epigenetic antithesis, and resolving synthesis. *Biological Psychiatry, 55*, 965–970.

Raichle, M., MacLeod, A., Snyder, A., Powers, W., Gusnard, D., & Shulman, G. (2001). A default mode of brain function. *Proceedings of the National Academy of Sciences of the United States of America, 98*, 676–682.

Rais, M., Cahn, W., Schnack, H. G., Hulshoff Pol, H. E., Kahn, R. S., & van Haren, N. E. (2012). Brain volume reductions in medication-naïve patients with schizophrenia in relation to intelligence quotient. *Psychosomatic Medicine, 42*, 1847–1856.

Reisig, M., & Kane, R (Eds.). (2014). *The Oxford handbook on police and policing*. Oxford University Press.

Ritunnano, R., Kleinman, J., Whyte Oshodi, D., Michail, M., Nelson, B., Humpston, C. S., & Broome, M. R. (2022). Subjective experience and meaning of delusions in psychosis: A systematic review and qualitative evidence synthesis. *The Lancet Psychiatry*, 9(6), 458–476. https://doi.org/10.1016/S2215-0366(22)00104-3

Rutter, M. (2006). *Genes and behavior: Nature–nurture interplay explained*. Blackwell.

Saks, E. (2007). *The center cannot hold: My journey through madness*. Hyperion.

Sariaslan, A., Fazel, S., D'Onofrio, B. M., Långström, N., Larsson, H., Bergen, S. E., Kuja-Halkola, R., & Lichtenstein, P. (2016). Schizophrenia and subsequent neighborhood deprivation: Revisiting the social drift hypothesis using population, twin and molecular genetic data. *Translational Psychiatry*, 6(5), e796. http://doi.org/10.1038/tp.2016.62

Schlosser, D., Campellone, T., Truong, B., Etter, K., Vergain, S., Komaiko, K., & Vinogradov, S. (2018). Efficacy of PRIME, a mobile app intervention designed to improve motivation in young people with schizophrenia. *Schizophrenia Bulletin*, 44, 1010–1020.

Seidman, L. J., Hellemann, G., Nuechterlein, K. H., Greenwood, T. A., Braff, D. L., Cadenhead, K. S., Calkins, M. E., Freedman, R., Gur, R. E., Gur, R. C., Lazzeroni, C, L., Light, G. A., Olincy, A., Radant, A. D., Siever, L. J., Silverman, J. M., Sprock, J., Stone, W. S., Sugar, C, & Green, M. F. (2015). Factor structure and heritability of endophenotypes in schizophrenia: Findings from the Consortium on the Genetics of Schizophrenia (COGS-1). *Schizophrenia Research*, 163(1), 73–79. http://doi.org/10.1016/j.schres.2015.01.027

Sekar, A., Bialas, A. R., de Rivera, H., Davis, A., Hammond, T. R., Kamitaki, N., Tooley, K., Presumey, J., Baum, M., Van Doren, V., Genovese, G., Rose, S., & Handsaker, R. (2016). Schizophrenia Working Group of the Psychiatric Genomics. Schizophrenia risk from complex variation of complement component 4. *Nature*, 530, 177–183. http://doi.org/10.1038/nature16549

Shenton, M., Dickey, C., Frumin, M., & McCarley, R. (2001). A review of MRI finding in schizophrenia. *Schizophrenia Bulletin*, 49, 1–52.

Shenton, M., & Turetsky, B (Eds.). (2011). *Understanding neuropsychiatric disorders: Insights from neuroimaging*. Cambridge University Press.

Smith, L., Nathan, P., Juniper, U., Kingsep, P., & Lim, L. (2003). *Cognitive behavioural therapy for psychotic symptoms: A therapist's manual*. Centre for Clinical Interventions.

Snowden, L. R. (2007). Explaining mental health treatment disparities: Ethnic and cultural differences in family involvement. *Culture, Medicine and Psychiatry*, 31(3), 389–402. https://doi.org/10.1007/s11013-007-9057-z

Srinivasan, S., Bettella, F., Mattingsdal, M., Wang, Y., Witoelar, A., Schork, A. J., Thompson, W. K., & Zuber, V. (2015). The Schizophrenia Working Group of the Psychiatric Genomics Consortium, The International Headache Genetics. Genetic markers of human evolution are enriched in schizophrenia. *Biological Psychiatry*, 1–9. http://doi.org/10.1016/j.biopsych.2015.10.009

Steele, K., & Berman, C. (2001). *The day the voices stopped*. Basic Books.

Sternberg, R. J. (2017). Some lessons from a symposium on cultural psychological science. *Perspectives on Psychological Science*, 12, 911–921. https://doi.org/10.1177/1745691617720477

Taipale, H., Mehtälä, J., Tanskanen, A., & Tiihonen, J. (2018). Comparative effectiveness of antipsychotic drugs for rehospitalization in schizophrenia—A nationwide study with 20-year follow-up. *Schizophrenia Bulletin*, 44(6), 1381–1387. https://doi.org/10.1093/schbul/sbx176

Taitimu, M., Read, J., & McIntosh, T. (2018). Ngā Whakāwhitinga (standing at the crossroads): How Māori understand what Western psychiatry calls "schizophrenia.". *Transcultural Psychiatry*, 55(2), 153–177. https://doi.org/10.1177/1363461518757800

Tandon, R. (2012). The nosology of schizophrenia: Toward *DSM-5* and *ICD-11*. *Psychiatric Clinics of North America*, 35(3), 557–569. http://doi.org/10.1016/j.psc.2012.06.001

Tandon, R., Gaebel, W., Barch, D. M., Bustillo, J., Gur, R. E., Heckers, S., Malaspina, D., Owen, M. J., Schultz, S., Tsuang, M., van Os, J., & Carpenter, W. (2013). Definition and description of schizophrenia in the *DSM–5*. *Schizophrenia Research*, 150, 3–10. http://doi.org/10.1016/j.schres.2013.05.028

Tandon, R., Nasrallah, H. A., & Keshavan, M. S. (2009). Schizophrenia, "Just the facts": Clinical features and conceptualization. *Schizophrenia Research*, 110, 1–23.

Thompson, P., Vidal, C., Giedd, J., Gochman, P., Blumenthal, J., Nicolson, R., Toga, A. W., & Rapoport, J. (2001). Mapping adolescent brain change reveals dynamic wave of accelerated gray matter loss in very early-onset schizophrenia. *Proceedings of the National Academy of Science*, 98, 11650–11655.

Torrey, E. (1997). *Out of the shadows: Confronting America's mental illness crisis*. Wiley.

Touloupoulou, T., Zhang, X., Cherny, S., Dickinson, D., Berman, K. F., Straub, R. E., Sham, P., & Weinberger, D. R. (2019). Polygenic risk score increases schizophrenia liability through cognition-relevant pathways. *Brain*, 142, 471–485. https://doi.org/10.1093/brain/awy279

Turkington, D., Kingdon, D., & Weiden, P. (2006). Cognitive behavior therapy for schizophrenia. *American Journal of Psychiatry*, 163, 365–373.

Uhlhaas, P. (2011). The adolescent brain: Implications for the understanding, pathophysiology, and treatment of schizophrenia. *Schizophrenia Bulletin*, 37, 480–483.

Uhlhaas, P., & Singer, W. (2011). The development of neural synchrony and large-scale cortical networks during adolescence: Relevance for the pathophysiology of schizophrenia and neurodevelopmental hypothesis. *Schizophrenia Bulletin*, 37, 514–523.

Uhlhaas, P., & Singer, W. (2012). Neuronal dynamics and neuropsychiatric disorders: Toward a translational paradigm for dysfunctional large-scale networks. *Neuron*, 75, 963–980.

Uhlhaas, P., Roux, F., Singer, W., Haenschel, C., Sireteanu, R., & Rodriguez, E. (2009). The development of neural synchrony reflects late maturation and restructuring of functional networks in humans. *Proceedings of the National Academy of Sciences*, 106, 9866–9871.

van Os, J., Kenis, G., & Rutten, B. P. (2010). The environment and schizophrenia. *Nature*, 468(7321). 203–212. https://doi.org/10.1038/nature09563

Vita, A., de Peri, L., Silenzi, C., & Dieci, M. (2006). Brain morphology in first-episode schizophrenia: A meta-analysis of quantitative magnetic resonance imaging studies. *Schizophrenia Research*, 82, 75–88.

Walker, E., Shapiro, D., Esterberg, M., & Trotman, H. (2010). Neurodevelopment and schizophrenia, broadening the focus. *Current Directions in Psychological Science, 19*, 204–208.

Weinberger, D. (1987). Implications of normal brain development for the pathogenesis of schizophrenia. *Archives of General Psychiatry, 44*, 660–669.

Welham, J., Isohanni, M., Jones, P., & McGrath, J. (2009). The antecedents of schizophrenia: A review of birth cohort studies. *Schizophrenia Bulletin, 35*, 603–623.

White, T., Magnotta, V., Bockholt, H., Williams, S., Wallace, S., Ehrlich, S., Mueller, B., Ho, B., Jung, R., Clark, V., Lauriello, J., Bustillo, J., Shultz, S., Gollub, R., Andreasen, N., Calhoun, V., & Lim, K. (2011). Global white matter abnormalities in schizophrenia: A multisite diffusion tensor imaging study. *Schizophrenia Bulletin, 37*, 222–232.

Whitfield-Gabrieli, S., Thermenos, H. W., Milanovic, S., Tsuang, M. T., Faraone, S. V., McCarley, R. W., Shenton, M. E., Green, A. I., Nieto-Castanon, A., LaViolette, P., Wojcik, J., Gabrieli, J. D. E., & Seidman, L. J. (2009). Hyperactivity and hyperconnectivity of the default network in schizophrenia and in first-degree relatives of persons with schizophrenia. *Proceedings of the National Academy of Sciences of the United States of America, 106*, 1279–1284.

Whitford, T., Kubicki, M., & Shenton, M. (2011). Structural imaging of schizophrenia. In M. Shenton & B. Turetsky (Eds.), *Understanding neuropsychiatric disorders: Insights from neuroimaging* (pp. 1–29). Cambridge University Press.

Wong, D. F. K. (2007). Uncovering sociocultural factors influencing the pathway to care of Chinese caregivers with relatives suffering from early psychosis in Hong Kong. *Culture, Medicine and Psychiatry, 31*(1), 51–71. https://doi.org/10.1007/s11013-006-9038-7

Woo, S., & Keatinge, C. (2008). *Diagnosis and treatment of mental disorders across the lifespan*. Wiley.

Wray, N., & Visscher, P. (2010). Narrowing the boundaries of the genetic architecture of schizophrenia. *Schizophrenia Bulletin, 36*, 14–23.

Wüsten, C., Schlier, B., Jaya, E. S., Genetic, Risk., Outcome of Psychosis (GROUP), Investigators., Fonseca-Pedrero, E., Peters, E., Verdoux, H., Woodward, T. S., Ziermans, T. B., & Lincoln, T. M. (2018). Psychotic experiences and related distress: A cross-national comparison and network analysis based on 7141 participants from 13 countries. *Schizophrenia Bulletin, 44*(6), 1185–1194. https://doi.org/10.1093/schbul/sby087

Zhang, W., Deng, W., Yao, L., Xiao, Y., Li, F., Liu, J., Sweeney, J. A., Lui, S., & Gong, Q. (2015). Brain structural abnormalities in a group of never-medicated patients with long-term schizophrenia. *American Journal of Psychiatry, 172*(10), 995–1003

CHAPTER 14

American, Psychiatric Association. (2013). *Diagnostic and statistical manual of mental disorders*, (5th ed.).

American, Psychiatric Association. (2022). *Diagnostic and statistical manual of mental disorders*, (5th ed., text rev.)

Anderson, N., & Kiehl, K. (2011). The psychopath magnetized: Insights from brain imaging. *Trends in Cognitive Sciences, 16*, 52–60.

Anderson, S., Bechara, A., Damasio, H., Tranel, D., & Damasio, A. (1999). Impairment of social and moral behavior related to early damage in human prefrontal cortex. *Nature Neuroscience, 2*, 1032–1037.

Asami, T., Whitford, T., Bouix, S., Dickey, C., Niznikiewicz, M., Shenton, M., Voglmeier, M., & McCarley, R. (2013). Globally and locally reduced MRI gray matter volumes in neuroleptic-naive men with schizotypal personality disorder. *JAMA Psychiatry, 70*, 361–372.

Bach, B., Kramer, U., Doering, S., di Giacomo, E., Hutsebaut, J., Kaera, A., De Panfilis, C., Schmahl, C., Swales, M., Taubner, S., & Renneberg, B. (2022). The *ICD-11* classification of personality disorders: A European perspective on challenges and opportunities. *Borderline Personality Disorder and Emotion Dysregulation, 9*(1), Article 12. https://bpded.biomedcentral.com/articles/10.1186/s40479-022-00182-0

Bagby, R. M., & Widiger, T. A. (2018). Five-factor model personality disorder scales: An introduction to a special section on assessment of maladaptive variants of the five-factor model. *Psychological Assessment, 30*(1), 1–9. http://dx.doi.org/10.1037/pas0000523

Bartz, J., Kaplan, A., & Hollander, E. (2007). Obsessive-compulsive personality disorder. In W. O'Donohue, K. A. Fowler, & S. O. Lilienfeld (Eds.), *Personality disorders: Toward the* DSM-V (pp. 325–352). Sage.

Bateman, A., Gunderson, J., & Mulder, R. (2015). Treatment of personality disorders. *The Lancet, 385*, 735–743.

Battle, C. L., Shea, M. T., Johnson, D. M., Yen, S., Zlotnick, C., Zanarini, M. C., Battle, C. L., Shea, M. T., Johnson, D. M., Yen, S., Zlotnick, C., Zanarini, M. C., Sanislow, C. A., Skodol, A. E., Gunderson, J. G., Grilo, C. M., McGlashan, T. H., & Morey, L. C. (2004). Childhood maltreatment associated with adult personality disorders: Findings from the Collaborative Longitudinal Personality Disorders Study. *Journal of Personality Disorders, 18*(2), 193–211.

Bender, D., Morey, L., & Skodol, A. (2011). Toward a model for assessing level of personality functioning in *DSM*-5, Part I: A review of theory and methods. *Journal of Personality Assessment, 93*, 332–346.

Bernstein, D., & Useda, J. (2007). Paranoid personality disorder. In W. O'Donohue, K. Fowler, & S. Lilienfeld (Eds.), *Personality disorders: Toward the* DSM-V (pp. 41–62). Sage.

Blagov, P. S., Fowler, K., & Lilienfeld, S. (2007). Histrionic personality disorder. In W. O'Dononue, S. O. Lilienfeld, & K. A. Fowler (Eds.), *Personality disorders: Toward the DSM-V* (pp. 203–232). Sage.

Boccardi, M., Frisoni, G., Hare, R., Cavedo, E., Najt, P., Pievani, M., Rasser, P., Laakso, M, Aronen, H., Repo-Tiihonen, E, Vaurio, O., Thompson, P, & Tiihonen, J (Eds.). (2011). Cortex and amygdala morphology in psychopathy. *Psychiatry Research, 193*, 85–92.

Bohus, M., Stoffers-Winterling, J., Sharp, C., Krause-Utz, A., Schmahl, C., & Lieb, K. (2021). Borderline personality disorder. *Lancet (London, England), 398*(10310), 1528–1540. https://doi.org/10.1016/S0140-6736(21)00476-1

Bollini, A., & Walker, E. (2007). Schizotypal personality disorder. In W. O'Donohue, K. Fowler, & S. Lilienfeld (Eds.), *Personality disorders: Toward the* DSM-5 (pp. 81–108). Sage.

Bornstein, R. (2007). Dependent personality disorder. In W. O'Donohue, K. A. Fowler, & S. O. Lilienfeld (Eds.), *Personality disorders: Toward the DSM-V* (pp. 307–324). Sage.

Bradley, R., Conklin, C. Z., & Westen, D. (2007). Borderline personality disorder. In W. O'Donohue, K. Fowler, & S. Lilienfeld (Eds.), *Sage handbook of personality disorders* (pp. 167–202). Sage.

Carey, B. (2011, June 23). *Expert on mental illness reveals her own fight*. The New York Times. Retrieved from http://nytimes.com

Clarkin, J. F., Yeomans, F. E., & Kernberg, O. F. (2006). *Psychotherapy for borderline personality: Focusing on object relations*. American Psychiatric Publishing.

Cleckley, H. (1988). *The mask of sanity: An attempt to clarify some issues about the so called psychopathic personality* (5th ed.). Mosby. (Original work published 1941)

Clemente, M. J., Martins Silva, A. S., Pozzolo Pedro, M. O., Paiva, H. S., de Azevedo Marques Périco, C., Torales, J., Ventriglio, A., & Castaldelli-Maia, J. M. (2022). A meta-analysis and meta-regression analysis of the global prevalence of obsessive-compulsive personality disorder. *Heliyon*, *8*(7), Article e09912. https://doi.org/10.1016/j.heliyon.2022.e09912

Costa, P. T., McCrae, R. R., & Löckenhoff, C. E. (2019). Personality across the life span. *Annual Review of Psychology*, *70*, 423–448. https://doi.org/10.1146/annurev-psych-010418-103244

Costa, P. T., & Widiger, T (Eds.). (2002). *Personality disorders and the five-factor model of personality* (2nd ed.). American Psychological Association.

Cristea, I., Gentili, C., Cotet, C., Palomba, D., Barbui, C., & Cuijpers, P. (2017). Efficacy of psychotherapies for borderline personality disorder: A systematic review and meta-analysis. *JAMA Psychiatry*, *74*, 319–328. https://doi.org/10.1001/jamapsychiatry.2016.4287

Crowell, S. E., Beauchaine, T. P., & Linehan, M. M. (2009). A biosocial developmental model of borderline personality: Elaborating and extending Linehan's theory. *Psychological Bulletin*, *135*(3), 495–510. http://doi.org/10.1037/a0015616

Decety, J., Skelly, L., & Kiehl, K. (2013). Brain response to empathy-eliciting scenarios involving pain in incarcerated individuals with psychopathy. *JAMA Psychiatry*, *70*, 638–645.

Decety, J., & Svetlova, M. (2012). Putting together phylogenetic and ontogenetic perspectives on empathy. *Developmental Cognitive Neuroscience*, *2*(1), 1–24. http://doi.org/10.1016/j.dcn.2011.05.003

DeYoung, C. G., Carey, B. E., Krueger, R. F., & Ross, S. R. (2016). Ten aspects of the Big Five in the personality inventory for *DSM-5*. *Personality Disorders: Theory, Research, and Treatment*, *2*, 113–123.

Dziobek, I., Preissler, S., Grozdanovic, Z., Heuser, I., Heekeren, H. R., & Roepke, S. (2011). Neuronal correlates of altered empathy and social cognition in borderline personality disorder. *NeuroImage*, *57*, 539–548.

Eisenberger, N., Lieberman, M., & Kipling, K. (2003). Does rejection hurt? An fMRI study of social exclusion. *Science*, *302*, 290–292.

Frías, Á., Baltasar, I., & Birmaher, B. (2016). Comorbidity between bipolar disorder and borderline personality disorder: Prevalence, explanatory theories, and clinical impact. *Journal of Affective Disorders*, *202*, 210–219.

Gao, Y., Glenn, A., Schug, R., Yang, Y., & Raine, A. (2009). The neurobiology of psychopathy: A neurodevelopmental perspective. *Canadian Journal of Psychiatry*, *54*, 813–823.

Godbout, N., Daspe, M-È., Runtz, M., Cyr, G., & Briere, J. (2019). Childhood maltreatment, attachment, and borderline personality-related symptoms: Gender-specific structural equation models. *Psychological Trauma*, *11*(1), 90–98. http://dx.doi.org/10.1037/tra0000403

Gore, W. L., & Widiger, T. A. (2018). Negative emotionality across diagnostic models: RDoC, *DSM-5* Section III, and FFM. *Personality Disorders: Theory, Research, and Treatment*, *9*(2), 155–164. http://dx.doi.org/10.1037/per0000273

Gottesman, I. (1991). *Schizophrenia genesis: The origin of madness*. Freeman.

Gøtzsche-Astrup, O., & Moskowitz, A. (2016). Personality disorders and the *DSM-5*: Scientific and extra-scientific factors in the maintenance of the status quo. *Australian and New Zealand Journal of Psychiatry*, *50*(2), 1–30. http://doi.org/10.1177/0004867415595872

Grant, B., Stinson, F., Dawson, D., Chou, S., Dufour, M., Compton, W., Pikering, R., & Kaplan, K. (2004). Prevalence and co-occurrence of substance use disorders and independent mood and anxiety disorders: Results from the National Epidemiologic Survey on Alcohol and Related Conditions. *Archives of General Psychiatry*, *61*, 807–816.

Gregory, R. J., & Remen, A. L. (2008). A manual-based psychodynamic therapy for treatment-resistant borderline personality disorder. *Psychotherapy Theory, Research, Practice, Training*, *45*, 15–27.

Grilo, C., Sanislow, C., Gunderson, J., Pagano, M., Yen, S., Zanarini, M., Shea, M., Skodol, A., Stout, R., Morey, L., & McGlashan, T. (2004). Two-year stability and change of schizotypal, borderline, avoidant, and obsessive-compulsive personality disorders. *Journal of Consulting and Clinical Psychology*, *72*, 767–775.

Gunderson, J. G., Fruzzetti, A., Unruh, B., & Choi-Kain, L. (2018). Competing theories of borderline personality disorder. *Personality Disorders*, *32*(2), 148–167. doi:10.1521/pedi.2018.32.2.148

Gunderson, J. G., & Ridolfi, M. E. (2001). Borderline personality disorder: Suicidality and self-mutilation. *Annals of the New York Academy of Science*, *932*, 61–77.

Gunderson, J. G., Stout, R., McGlashan, T., Shea, M., Morey, L., Grilo, C., Zanarini, M., Yen, S., Markowitz, J., Sanislow, C., Ansell, E., Pinto, A., & Skodol, A. (2011). Ten-year course of borderline personality disorder: Psychopathology and function from the Collaborative Longitudinal Personality Disorders Study. *Archives of General Psychiatry*, *68*, 827–837. https://doi.org/10.1001/archgenpsychiatry.2011.37

Gutiérrez, F., Vall, G., Peri, J., Baillés, E., Ferraz, L., Gárriz, M., & Caseras, X. (2012). Personality disorder features through the life course. *Journal of Personality Disorders*, *26*, 763–774.

Hare, R. (2003). *The Hare Psychopathy Checklist-Revised*. Multi-Health System.

Hare, R., & Neumann, C. (2008). Psychopathy as a clinical and empirical construct. *Annual Review of Clinical Psychology*, *4*, 17–46.

Henriques-Calado, J., Gonçalves, B., Marques, C., Paulino, M., Gama Marques, J., Grácio, J., & Pires, R. (2021). In light of the *DSM-5* dimensional model of personality: Borderline personality disorder at the crossroads with the bipolar spectrum. *Journal of Affective Disorders*, *294*, 897–907. https://doi.org/10.1016/j.jad.2021.07.047

Herbert, J. (2007). Avoidant personality disorder. In W. O'Donohue, K. A. Fowler, & S. O. Lilienfeld (Eds.), *Personality disorders: Toward the DSM-V* (pp. 279–306). Sage.

Huang, Y., Kotov, R., de Girolamo, G., Preti, A., Angermeyer, M., Benjet, C., Demyttenaere, K., de Graaf, R., Gureje, O., Karam, A., Lee, S., Lépine, J. P., Matschinger, H., Posada-Villa, J., Suliman, S., Vilagut, G., & Kessler, R. (2009). DSM-IV personality disorders in the WHO World Mental Health Surveys. *British Journal of Psychiatry*, *195*, 46–53.

Karas, K. H., Baharikhoob, P., & Kolla, N. J. (2021). Borderline personality disorder and its symptom clusters: A review of positron emission tomography and single photon emission computed tomography studies. *Psychiatry Research: Neuroimaging, 316*, Article 111357. https://doi.org/10.1016/j.pscychresns.2021.111357

Kernberg, O. (1984). *Severe personality disorders: Psychotherapeutic strategies*. Yale University Press.

Kernberg, O. (1995). *Love relations: Normality and pathology*. Yale University Press.

Kessler, R. C., & Üstün, T. B. (2008). The WHO mental health surveys. *Global perspectives on the epidemiology of mental disorders*. Cambridge University Press.

King-Casas, B., Sharp, C., Lomax-Bream, L., Lohrenz, T., Fonagy, P., & Montague, P. (2008). The rupture and repair of cooperation in borderline personality disorder. *Science, 321*, 806–810.

Klonsky, E. (2007). The functions of deliberate self-injury: A review of the evidence. *Clinical Psychology Review, 27*, 226–239.

Krueger, R. F., & Hobbs, K. A. (2020). An overview of the *DSM*-5 alternative model of personality disorders. *Psychopathology, 53*(3–4), 126–132. https://doi.org/10.1159/000508538

Krueger, R. F., & Markon, K. E. (2014). The role of the *DSM*-5 personality trait model in moving toward a quantitative and empirically based approach to classifying personality and psychopathology. *Annual Review of Clinical Psychology, 10*, 477–501. http://doi.org/10.1146/annurev-clinpsy-032813-153732

Lawton, E., Shields, A., & Oltmanns, T. (2011). Five-factor model personality disorder prototypes in a community sample: Self- and informant-reports predicting interview-based *DSM* diagnoses. *Personality Disorders, 2*, 279–292.

Lenzenweger, M. (2008). Epidemiology of personality disorders. *Psychiatric Clinics of North America, 31*, 395–403.

Lenzenweger, M., Lane, M., Loranger, A., & Kessler, R. (2007). *DSM*-IV personality disorders in the National Comorbidity Survey Replication. *Biological Psychiatry, 62*, 553–564.

Levy, K. N. (2005). The implications of attachment theory and research for understanding borderline personality disorder. *Development and Psychopathology, 17*, 959–986.

Levy, K. N. (2012). Subtypes, dimensions, levels, and mental states in narcissism and narcissistic personality disorder. *Journal of Clinical Psychology: In Session, 8*, 886–897.

Levy, K. N., Reynoso, J., Wasserman, R. H., & Clarkin, J. F. (2007). Narcissistic personality disorder. In W. O'Donohue, K. A. Fowler, & S. O. Lilienfeld (Eds.), *Personality disorders: Toward the* DSM-V (pp. 233–277). Sage.

Levy, K. N., & Scala, J. W. (2012). Transference, transference interpretations, and transference-focused psychotherapies. *Psychotherapy, 49*, 391–403.

Levy, K. N., Yeomans, F. E., & Diamond, D. (2007). Psychodynamic treatments of self-injury. *Journal of Clinical Psychology, 63*(11), 1105–1120.

Lilienfeld, S. O., Watts, A. L., Smith, S. F., Patrick, C. J., & Hare, R. D. (2018). Hervey Cleckley (1903–1984): Contributions to the study of psychopathy. *Personality Disorders, 9*(6), 510–520. http://dx.doi.org/10.1037/per0000306

Linehan, M. M. (1993). *Cognitive-behavioral treatment of borderline personality disorder*. Guilford Press.

Linehan, M. M., & Dexter-Mazza, E. T. (2008). Dialectical behavior therapy for borderline personality disorder. In D. H. Barlow (Ed.), *Clinical handbook of psychological disorders: A step-by-step treatment manual* (pp. 365–420). Guilford Press.

Linehan, M. M., Korslund, K. E., Harned, M. S., Gallop, R. J., Lungu, A., Neacsiu, A. D., McDavid, J., Comtois, K. A., & Murray-Gregory, A. M. (2015). Dialectical behavior therapy for high suicide risk in individuals with borderline personality disorder. *JAMA Psychiatry, 72*(5), 475–482. http://doi.org/10.1001/jamapsychiatry.2014.3039

Links, P. S., & Eynan, R. (2013). The relationship between personality disorders and Axis I psychopathology: Deconstructing comorbidity. *Annual Review of Clinical Psychology, 9*, 529–554, clinpsy-050212-185624. http://doi.org/10.1146/annurev-

Livesley, W. J. (2007). A framework for integrating dimensional and categorical classifications of personality disorders. *Journal of Personality Disorders, 21*, 199–224.

Livesley, W. J., Dimaggio, G., & Clarkin, J. F. (2016). *Integrated treatment for personality disorder: A modular approach*. Guilford Press.

Livesley, W. J., & Jang, K. L. (2008). The behavioral genetics of personality disorder. *Annual Review of Clinical Psychology, 4*, 247–274.

Marian, Ş., Sava, F. A., & Dindelegan, C. (2022). A network analysis of DSM-5 avoidant personality disorder diagnostic criteria. *Personality and Individual Differences, 188*, Article 111454.

McCrae, R. (2009). Personality profiles of cultures: Patterns of ethos. *European Journal of Personality, 23*, 205–227.

McCrae, R., & Costa, P. (1987). Validation of the five-factor model of personality across instruments and observers. *Journal of Personality and Social Psychology, 52*, 81–90.

McCrae, R., & Costa, P. (1996). Toward a new generation of personality theories: Theoretical contexts for the five-factor model. In J. S. Wiggins (Ed.), *The five-factor model of personality*. Guilford Press.

McCrae, R., & Costa, P. (1999). A five-factor theory of personality. In L. A. Pervin & O. P. John (Eds.), *Handbook of personality: Theory and research* (2nd ed., pp. 139–153). Guilford Press.

McCrae, R., Costa, P., de Lima, M., Simões, A., Ostendorf, F., Angleitner, A., Marušić, I., Bratko, D., Caprara, G., Barbaranelli, C., Chae, J., & Piedmont, R. (1999). Age differences in personality across the adult life span: Parallels in five cultures. *Developmental Psychology, 35*(2), 466–477. https://doi.org/10.1037/0012-1649.35.2.466

McCrae, R., Gaines, J., & Wellington, M. (2013). The five-factor model in fact and fiction. In I. Weiner, H. Tennen, & J. Suls (Eds.), *Handbook of Psychology: Personality and social psychology* (2nd ed., Vol. 5, pp. 65–91). Wiley.

McMurran, M., & Crawford, M. (2016). Personality disorders. In C. Nezu & A. Nezu (Eds.), *The Oxford handbook of cognitive and behavioral therapies* (pp. 438–462). Oxford University Press.

Meyer-Lindenberg, A. (2008, August 15). Trust me on this. *Science, 321*(5890).

Millon, T., & Strack, S. (2015). An integrating and comprehensive model of personality pathology based on evolutionary theory. In S. Huprich (Ed.), *Personality disorders: Toward theoretical and empirical integration in diagnosis and assessment* (pp. 367–393). American Psychological Association.

Miskovich, T. A., Anderson, N. E., Harenski, C. L., Harenski, K. A., Baskin-Sommers, A. R., Larson, C. L., Newman, J. P., Hanson, J. L., Stout, D. M., Koenigs, M., Shollenbarger, S. G., Lisdahl, K. M., Decety, J., Kosson, D. S., & Kiehl, K. A. (2018). Abnormal cortical gyrification in criminal psychopathy. *NeuroImage: Clinical, 19*,

876-882. https://doi.org/10.1016/j.nicl.2018.06.007

Mittal, V., Kalus, O., Bernstein, D., & Siever, L. (2007). Schizoid personality disorder. In W. O'Donohue, K. Fowler, & S. Lillenfeld (Eds.), *Personality disorders: Toward the DSM-V* (pp. 63–80). Sage.

Nettle, D. (2006). The evolution of personality variation in humans and other animals. *American Psychologist, 61*, 622–631.

Newton-Howes, G., Clark, L. A., & Chanen, A. (2015). Personality disorder across the life course. *The Lancet, 385*(9969), 727–734. http://doi.org/10.1016/S0140-6736(14)61283-6

Oliveira-Souza, R., Hare, R., Bramati, I., Garrido, G., Azevedo, F., Tovar-Moll, F., & Moll, J. (2008). Psychopathy as a disorder of the moral brain: Fronto-temporo-limbic grey matter reductions demonstrated by voxel-based morphometry. *NeuroImage, 40*, 1202–1213.

Onken, L. S., & Nielsen, L. (2019). Targeting psychological processes related to personality facets to promote healthy aging. *Personality Disorders, 10*(1), 1–3. http://dx.doi.org/10.1037/per0000311

Parker, G., Bayes, A., & Spoelma, M. J. (2022). Why might bipolar disorder and borderline personality disorder be bonded? *Journal of Psychiatric Research, 150*, 214–218. https://doi.org/10.1016/j.jpsychires.2022.03.051

Patrick, C. J. (2006). Back to the future: Cleckley as a guide to the next generation of psychopathy research. In C. J. Patrick (Ed.), *Handbook of psychopathy* (pp. 605–617). Guilford Press.

Patrick, C. J. (2007). Antisocial personality disorder and psychopathy. In W. O'Donohue, K. A. Fowler, & S. O. Lilienfeld (Eds.), *Personality disorders: Toward the DSM-V* (pp. 325–352). Sage.

Patrick, C. J. (2010). Conceptualizing psychopathic personality: Disinhibited, bold, or just plain mean? In R. J. Salekin & D. R. Lynam (Eds.), *Handbook of child and adolescent psychopathy* (pp. 15–48). Guilford Press.

Patrick, C. J. (2022). Psychopathy: Current knowledge and future directions. *Annual Review of Clinical Psychology, 18*, 387–415. https://doi.org/10.1146/annurev-clinpsy-072720-012851

Patrick, C. J., & Bernat, E. M. (2009). Neurobiology of psychopathy: A two-process theory. In G. G. Berntson & J. T. Cacioppo (Eds.), *Handbook of neuroscience for the behavioral sciences* (pp. 1110–1131). Wiley.

Pereda, N., Gallardo-Pujol, D., & Padilla, R. (2011). Personality disorders in child sexual abuse victims. *Actas Españolas de Psiquiatría, 39*, 131–139.

Polderman, T. J. C., Benyamin, B., de Leeuw, C. A., Sullivan, P. F., van Bochoven, A., Visscher, P. M., & Posthuma, D. (2015). Meta-analysis of the heritability of human traits based on fifty years of twin studies. *Nature Genetics, 47*(7), 702–709. https://doi.org/10.1038/ng.3285

Raine, A. (2018). Antisocial personality as a neurodevelopmental disorder. *Annual Review of Clinical Psychology, 14*, 259–289. https://doi.org/10.1146/annurev-clinpsy-050817-084819

Renneberg, B., Herm, K., Hahn, A., Staebler, K., Lammers, C., & Roepke, S. (2012). Perception of social participation in borderline personality disorder. *Clinical Psychology and Psychotherapy, 19*, 473–480.

Roberson, A. (2010). *Borderline traits: Her life with borderline personality disorder*. Xlibris.

Roberts, B. W., Luo, J., Briley, D. A., Chow, P. I., & Hill, P. L. (2017). A systematic review of personality trait change through intervention. *Psychological Bulletin, 143*(2), 117–141. http://dx.doi.org/10.1037/bul0000088

Samuel, D. B., Simms, L. J., Clark, L. A., Livesley, W. J., & Widiger, T. A. (2010). An item response theory integration of normal and abnormal personality scales. *Personality Disorders: Theory, Research, and Treatment, 1*, 5–21.

Samuel, D. B., & Widiger, T. A. (2008). A meta-analytic review of the relationships between the five-factor model and the *DSM*-IV-TR personality disorders: A facet level analysis. *Clinical Psychology Review, 28*, 1326–1342.

Shearer, S., Peters, C., Quaytman, S., & Wadman, B. (1988). Intent and lethality of suicide attempts among female borderline inpatients. *American Journal of Psychiatry, 145*, 1424–1427.

Soloff, P., Pruitt, P., Sharma, M., Radwan, J., White, R., & Diwadkar, V. (2012). Structural brain abnormalities and suicidal behavior in borderline personality disorder. *Journal of Psychiatric Research, 46*, 16–25.

South, S., Oltmanns, T., & Krueger, R. (2011). The spectrum of personality disorders. In D. Barlow (Ed.), *The Oxford handbook of clinical psychology* (pp. 530–550). Oxford University Press.

Southward, M. W., & Cheavens, J. S. (2018). Identifying core deficits in a dimensional model of borderline personality disorder features: A network analysis. *Clinical Psychological Science, 6*, 685–703. https://doi.org/10.1177/2167702618769560

Triebwasser, J., Chemerinski, E., Roussos, P., & Siever, L. (2012). Schizoid personality disorder. *Journal of Personality Disorders, 26*, 919–926.

Tufekcioglu, S., & Muran, J. (2016). A relational approach to personality disorder and alliance rupture. In W. Livesley, G. Dimaggio, & J. Clarkin (Eds.), *Integrated treatment for personality disorder* (pp. 123–147). Guilford Press.

Tyrer, P., Mulder, R., Kim, Y., & Crawford, M. J. (2019). The development of the *ICD-11* classification of personality disorders: An amalgam of science, pragmatism, and politics. *Annual Review of Clinical Psychology, 15*, 481–502.

Tyrer, P., Reed, G. M., & Crawford, M. J. (2015). Classification, assessment, prevalence, and effect of personality disorder. *The Lancet, 385*(9969), 717–726. http://doi.org/10.1016/S0140-6736(14)61995-4

van den Akker, A. L., Prinzie, P., & Overbeek, G. (2015). Dimensions of personality pathology in adolescence: Longitudinal associations with Big Five personality dimensions across childhood and adolescence. *Journal of Personality Disorders, 30*, 211–231. http://doi.org/10.1521/pedi_2015_29_190

Weinbrecht, A., Niedeggen, M., Roepke, S., & Renneberg, B. (2018). Feeling excluded no matter what? Bias in the processing of social participation in borderline personality disorder. *NeuroImage: Clinical, 19*, 343–350. https://doi.org/10.1016/j.nicl.2018.04.031

Welander-Vatn, A., Ystrom, E., Tambs, K., Neale, M. C., Kendler, K. S., Reichborn-Kjennerud, T., & Knudsen, G. P. (2016). The relationship between anxiety disorders and dimensional representations of *DSM*-IV personality disorders: A co-twin control study. *Journal of Affective Disorders, 190*, 349–356. http://doi.org/10.1016/j.jad.2015.09.038

Westwood, S. (2007). *Suicide junkie*. Chipmunka.

Widiger, T., & Mullins-Sweatt, S. (2009). Five-factor model of personality disorder: A proposal for *DSM*-V. *Annual Review of Clinical Psychology, 5*, 197–220.

Williams, K. D., Cheung, C. K. T., & Choi, W. (2000). Cyberostracism: Effects of being ignored over the Internet. *Journal of Personality and Social Psychology, 79*, 748–762.

Wong, S. C. P. (2016). Treatment of violence-prone individuals with psychopathic personality traits. In W. Livesley, G. Dimaggio, & J. Clarkin (Eds.), *Integrated treatment for personality disorder* (pp. 345–376). Guilford Press.

Zimmermann, J., Kerber, A., Rek, K., Hopwood, C. J., & Krueger, R. F. (2019). A brief but comprehensive review of research on the alternative DSM-5 model for personality disorders. *Current Psychiatry Reports, 21*(9), Article 92 https://doi.org/10.1007/s11920-019-1079-z

CHAPTER 15

Ahveninen, L. M., Stout, J. C., Georgiou-Karistianis, N., Lorenzetti, V., & Glikmann-Johnston, Y. (2018). Reduced amygdala volumes are related to motor and cognitive signs in Huntington's disease: The IMAGE-HD study. *NeuroImage: Clinical, 18*, 881–887. https://doi.org/10.1016/j.nicl.2018.03.027

Alzheimer, A. (1907). Über eine eigenartige Erkrankung der Hirnrinde. *Allgemeine Zeitschrift für Psychiatrie und Psychisch-gerichtliche Medizin, 64*, 146–148.

Alzheimer, A., Stelzmann, R. A., Schnitzlein, H. N., & Murtagh, F. R. (1995). An English translation of Alzheimer's 1907 paper, "Über eine eigenartige Erkrankung der Hirnrinde.". *Clinical Anatomy, 8*, 429–431.

American, Psychiatric Association. (2013). *Diagnostic and statistical manual of mental disorders*, 5th

American, Psychiatric Association. (2022). *Diagnostic and statistical manual of mental disorders*, (5th ed., text rev.)

Ballesteros, S., Kraft, E., Santana, S., & Tziraki, C. (2015). Maintaining older brain functionality: A targeted review. *Neuroscience & Biobehavioral Reviews, 55*, 453–477. http://doi.org/10.1016/j.neubiorev.2015.06.008

Beason-Held, L. (2011). Dementia and the default mode. *Current Alzheimer Research, 8*, 361–365.

Bellenguez, C., Küçükali, F., Jansen, I. E., Kleineidam, L., Moreno-Grau, S., Amin, N., Naj, A. C., Campos-Martin, R., Grenier-Boley, B., Andrade, V., Holmans, P. A., Boland, A., Damotte, V., van der Lee, S. J., Costa, M. R., Kuulasmaa, T., Yang, Q., de Rojas, I., Bis, J. C. ... Lambert, J. C. (2022). New insights into the genetic etiology of Alzheimer's disease and related dementias. *Nature Genetics, 54*(4). 412–436. https://doi.org/10.1038/s41588-022-01024-z

Bilousova, T., Miller, C. A., Poon, W. W., Vinters, H. V., Corrada, M., Kawas, C., Hayden, E. Y., Teplow, D. B., Glabe, C., Albay, R., III, Cole., M, G., Teng, E., & Gylys, K. H. (2016). Synaptic amyloid-β oligomers precede p-Tau and differentiate high pathology control cases. *American Journal of Pathology, 186*(1), 185–198. http://doi.org/10.1016/j.ajpath.2015.09.018

Brayne, C. (2007). The elephant in the room—Healthy brains in later life, epidemiology and public health. *Nature Reviews Neuroscience, 8*, 233–239.

Breijyeh, Z., & Karaman, R. (2020). Comprehensive review on Alzheimer's disease: Causes and treatment. *Molecules (Basel, Switzerland), 25*(24), Article 5789. https://doi.org/10.3390/molecules25245789

Brem, A. K., & Sensi, S. L. (2018). Towards combinatorial approaches for preserving cognitive fitness in aging. *Trends in Neuroscience, 41*(12), 885–897.

Brenner, L. A., & Bahraini, N. H. (2018). Concussion and risk of suicide: Who, when and under what circumstances? *Nature Reviews Neurology, 15*, 132–133. https://doi.org/10.1038/s41582-019-0136-x

Broglio, S. P., Robert, C., Gioia, G. A., Kevin, M., Kutcher, J., Palm, M., & McLeod, T. C. V. (2014). National Athletic Trainers' Association position statement: Management of sport concussion. *Journal of Athletic Training, 49*(2), 245–265. https://doi.org/10.4085/1062-6050-49.1.07

Buchman, A., Boyle, P., Yu, L., Shah, R., Wilson, R., & Bennett, D. (2012). Total daily physical activity and the risk of AD and cognitive decline in older adults. *Neurology, 24*, 1323–1329.

Cacciaglia, R., Luis, J., Falcón, C., Sánchez-Benavides, G., Gramunt, N., Brugulat-Serrat, A., Esteller, M., Morán, S., Fauria, K., & Gispert, J. D. (2019). APOE-ε4 risk variant for Alzheimer's disease modifies the association between cognitive performance and cerebral morphology in healthy middle-aged individuals. *NeuroImage: Clinical, 23*, Article 101818. https://doi.org/10.1016/j.nicl.2019.101818

Caraceni, A., & Grassi, L. (2011). *Delirium: Acute confusional states in palliative medicine* (2nd ed.). Oxford University Press.

Corley, J., Kyle, J. A. M., Starr, J. M., McNeill, G., & Deary, I. J. (2015). Dietary factors and biomarkers of systemic inflammation in older people: The Lothian Birth Cohort 1936. *British Journal of Nutrition, 114*(7), 1088–1098. http://doi.org/10.1017/S000711451500210X

Damisah, E. C., Rai, A., & Grutzendler, J. (2020). TREM2: Modulator of lipid metabolism in microglia. *Neuron, 105*(5), 759–761. https://doi.org/10.1016/j.neuron.2020.02.008

Davenport, G. (2013, July 1). *Why the NFL's concussion problem is bigger than you think*. Bleacher Report. http://bleacherreport.com/articles/1690768-why-the-nfls-concussion-problem-is-bigger-than-you-think

Edwards, F. A. (2019). A unifying hypothesis for Alzheimer's disease: From plaques to neurodegeneration. *Trends in Neurosciences, 42*(5), 310–322. https://doi.org/10.1016/j.tins.2019.03.003

Erkinjuntti, T. (2005). Vascular cognitive impairment. In A. Burns, J. O'Brien, & D. Ames (Eds.), *Dementia* (3rd ed., pp. 529–545). Hodder Arnold.

Ertel, K., Glymour, M., & Berkman, L. (2008). Effects of social integration on preserving memory function in a nationally representative U.S. elderly population. *American Journal of Public Health, 98*, 1215–1220.

Evans, I. E. M., Llewellyn, D. J., Matthews, F., Woods, B., Brayne, C., & Clare, L. (2018, August 17). Social isolation, cognitive reserve, and cognition in older people with mental health problems. *PLOS ONE*. https://doi.org/10.1371/journal.pone.0201008

Evans, I. E. M., Martyr, A., Collins, R., Brayne, C., & Clare, L. (2018). Social isolation and cognitive function in later life: A systematic review and meta-analysis. *Journal of Alzheimer's Disease, 70*, 1–26. https://doi.org/10.3233/jad-180501

Faul, M., Xu, L., Wald, M. M., & Coronad., V. G. (2010). *Traumatic brain injury in the United States: Emergency department visits, hospitalizations and deaths 2002–2006*. Centers for Disease Control and Prevention, National Center for Injury Prevention and Control http://www.cdc.gov/traumaticbraininjury/tbi_ed.html

Fralick, M., Sy, E., Hassan, A., Burke, M. J., Mostofsky, E., & Karsies, T. (2019). Association of concussion with the risk of suicide: A systematic review and meta-analysis. *JAMA Neurology, 76*(2). 144–151. https://doi.org/10.1001/jamaneurol.2018.3487

Gatchel, J., Wright, C., Falk, W., & Trinh, N. (2016). Dementia. In T. A. Stern, M. Fava, T. E. Wilens, & J. R. Rosenbaum (Eds.), *Massachusetts General Hospital Psychopharmacology and Neurotherapeutics*. Elsevier.

Germain, S., Wojtasik, V., Quittre, A., Olivier, C., Godichard, V., & Salmon, E. (2018). Efficacy of cognitive rehabilitation in Alzheimer disease: A 1-year follow-up study. *Journal of Geriatric Psychiatry and Neurology, 32*, 16–23. https://doi.org/10.1177/0891988718813724

Gusella, J., & MacDonald, M. (2006). Huntington's disease: Seeing the pathogenic process through a genetic lens. *Trends in Biochemical Sciences, 31*, 533–540.

Harris, S., & Deary, I. (2011). The genetics of cognitive ability and cognitive ageing in healthy older people. *Trends in Cognitive Sciences, 15*, 388–394.

He, W., Goodkind, D., & Kowal, P. (2016). *An aging world: 2015. International Population Reports*. www.census.gov/content/dam/Census/library/publications/2016/demo/p95-16-1.pdf

Hebert, L. E., Weuve, J., Scherr, P. A., & Evans, D. A. (2013). Alzheimer disease in the United States (2010–2050) estimated using the 2010 census. *Neurology, 80*(19), 1778–1783. https://doi.org/10.1212/WNL.0b013e31828726f5

Iaccarino, L., Tammewar, G., Ayakta, N., Baker, S. L., Bejanin, A., Boxer, A. L., Gorno-Tempini, M. L., Janabi, M., Kramer, J. H., Lazaris, A., Lockhart, S. N., Miller, B. L., Miller, Z. A., O'Neil, J. P., Ossenkoppele, R., Rosen, H. J., Schonhaut, D. R. Jagust., J, W., & Rabinovici, G. D. (2018). Local and distant relationships between amyloid, tau and neurodegeneration in Alzheimer's disease. *NeuroImage: Clinical, 17*, 452–464. https://doi.org/10.1016/j.nicl.2017.09.016

Igarashi, K. M. (2023). Entorhinal cortex dysfunction in Alzheimer's disease. *Trends in Neurosciences, 46*(2), 124–136. https://doi.org/10.1016/j.tins.2022.11.006

Iqbal, K., Liu, F., & Gong, C.-X. (2015). Tau and neurodegenerative disease: The story so far. *Nature Reviews Neurology, 12*(1), 1–14. http://doi.org/10.1038/nrneurol.2015.225

Jones, R., Kiely, D., & Marcantonio, E. (2010). Prevalence of delirium on admission to postacute care is associated with a higher number of nursing home deficiencies. *Journals of the American Medical Directors Association, 11*, 253–256.

Kawas, C. H. (2008). The oldest old and the 90+ Study. *Alzheimer's & Dementia, 4*(1. Suppl. 1), S56–S59. https://doi.org/10.1016/j.jalz.2007.11.007

Kawas, C. H., Kim, R. C., Sonnen, J. A., Bullain, S. S., Trieu, T., & Corrada, M. M. (2015). Multiple pathologies are common and related to dementia in the oldest-old: The 90+ Study. *Neurology, 85*(6), 535–542. http://doi.org/10.1212/WNL.0000000000001831

Khammash, D., Rajagopal, S. K., & Polk, T. A. (2023). The neurobiology of aging. In M. J. Zigmond, S. K. Rajagopal, & T. A. Polk (Eds.), *Neurobiology of brain disorders* (2nd ed., pp. 977–993). Academic Press.

Koch, W., Teipel, S., Mueller, S., Benninghoff, J., Wagner, M., Bokde, A., Hampel, H., Coates, U., Reiser, M., & Meindl, T. (2012). Diagnostic power of default mode network resting state fMRI in the detection of Alzheimer's disease. *Neurobiology of Aging, 33*, 466–478.

Kramer, A., & Erickson, K. (2007). Capitalizing on cortical plasticity: Influence of physical activity on cognition and brain function. *Trends in Cognitive Sciences, 11*, 342–348.

Kulkarni, B., Cruz-Martins, N., & Kumar, D. (2022). Microglia in Alzheimer's disease: An unprecedented opportunity as prospective drug target. *Molecular Neurobiology, 59*(5), 2678–2693. https://doi.org/10.1007/s12035-021-02661-x

Landau, S., Marks, S., Mormino, E., Rabinovici, G., Oh, H., O'Neil, J., Wilson, R., & Jagust, W. (2012). Association of lifetime cognitive engagement and low β-amyloid deposition. *Archives of Neurology, 69*, 623–629.

Leal, S. L., & Yassa, M. A. (2015). Neurocognitive aging and the hippocampus across species. *Trends in Neurosciences, 38*(12), 800–812. http://doi.org/10.1016/j.tins.2015.10.003

Lill, C. M., & Bertram, L. (2022). Genome-wide analysis furthers decoding of Alzheimer disease genetics. *Nature Reviews Neurology, 18*(7), 387–388. https://doi.org/10.1038/s41582-022-00678-x

Lindesay, J., Rockwood, K., & Macdonald, A. (2002). *Delirium in old age*. Oxford University Press.

Lipowski, Z. (1980). *Delirium*. Charles C Thomas.

Mather, M. (2015). The affective neuroscience of aging. *Annual Review of Psychology, 67*, 213–238. http://doi.org/10.1146/annurev-psych-122414-033540

Matthews, F. E., Stephan, B. C. M., Robinson, L., Jagger, C., Barnes, L. E., Arthur, A., Brayne, C., Comas-Herrera, A., Wittenberg, R., Dening, T., McCracken, C. F. M., Moody, C., Parry, E., Green, R., Barnes, R., Warwick, J., Gao, L., Mattison, A., Baldwin, S., & Forster, G. (2016). A two-decade dementia incidence comparison from the Cognitive Function and Ageing Studies I and II. *Nature Communications, 7*, Article 11398. http://doi.org/10.1038/ncomms11398

Meltzer, M. (1983). Poor memory: A case report. *Journal of Clinical Psychology, 39*, 3–10.

Mevel, K., Chételat, G., Eustache, F., & Desgranges, B. (2011). The default mode network in healthy aging and Alzheimer's disease. *International Journal of Alzheimer's Disease*. https://doi.org/10.4061/2011/535816

Miller, M. B., Reed, H. C., & Walsh, C. A. (2021). Brain somatic mutation in aging and Alzheimer's disease. *Annual Review of Genomics and Human Genetics, 22*, 239–256. https://doi.org/10.1146/annurev-genom-121520-081242

Montenigro, P. H., Corp, D. T., Stein, T. D., Cantu, R. C., & Stern, R. A. (2015). Chronic traumatic encephalopathy: Historical origins and current perspective. *Annual Review of Clinical Psychology, 11*, 309–330. https://doi.org/10.1146/annurev-clinpsy-032814-112814

Montfort, S. J. T. Van., Dellen, E. Van., Stam, C. J., Ahmad, A. H., Mentink, L. J., Kraan, C. W., Zalesky, A., & Slooter, A. J. C. (2019). Brain network disintegration as a final common pathway for delirium: A systematic review and qualitative meta-analysis. *NeuroImage: Clinical, 23*, Article 101809. https://doi.org/10.1016/j.nicl.2019.101809

Nagamatsu, L., Chan, A., Davis, J., Beattie, B., Graf, P., Voss, M., Sharma, C., & Liu-Ambrose, T. (2013). Physical activity improves verbal and spatial memory in older adults with probable mild cognitive impairment: A 6-month randomized controlled trial. *Journal of Aging Research*.

Nath, S., Agholme, L., Kurudenkandy, F. R., Granseth, B., Marcusson, J., & Hallbeck, M. (2012). Spreading of neurodegenerative pathology via neuron-to-neuron transmission of β-amyloid. *Journal of Neuroscience, 32*, 8767–8777.

Neary, D. (2005). Frontotemporal dementia. In A. Burns, J. O'Brien, & D. Ames (Eds.), *Dementia* (3rd ed.). Hodder Arnold.

O'Hara, R. (2012). The reciprocal relationship of neurocognitive and neuropsychiatric function in late life. *American Journal of Geriatric Psychiatry, 20*, 1001–1005.

Olufunmilayo, E. O., & Holsinger, R. M. D. (2022). Variant TREM2 signaling in Alzheimer's disease. *Journal of Molecular Biology, 434*(7). Article 167470. https://doi.org/10.1016/j.jmb.2022.167470

Park, D., & Reuter-Lorenz, P. A. (2009). The adaptive brain: Aging and neurocognitive scaffolding. *Annual Review of Psychology, 60*, 173–196.

Parsons, M. P., & Raymond, L. A. (2023). Huntington's disease. In M. G. Zigmond, C. A. Wiley, & M. F. Chesselet (Eds.), *Neurobiology of brain disorders* (2nd ed., pp. 275–292). Academic Press.

Prince, M., Bryce, R., Albanese, E., Wimo, A., Ribeiro, W., & Ferri, C. (2013). The global prevalence of dementia: A systematic review and metaanalysis. *Alzheimer's & Dementia, 9*, 63–75.

Prugh, D. G., Wagonfeld, S., Metcalf, D., & Jordan, K. (1980). A clinical study of delirium in children and adolescents [Suppl.]. *Psychosomatic Medicine, 42*, 177–195.

Rademakers, R., & Rovelet-Lecrux, A. (2009). Recent insights into the molecular genetics of dementia. *Trends in Neurosciences, 32*, 451–461.

Raichlen, D. A., & Alexander, G. E. (2014). Exercise, APOE genotype, and the evolution of the human lifespan. *Trends in Neurosciences, 37*(5). 247–255. https://doi.org/10.1016/j.tins.2014.03.001

Rajan, K. B., Weuve, J., Barnes, L. L., McAninch, E. A., Wilson, R. S., & Evans, D. A. (2021). Population estimate of people with clinical Alzheimer's disease and mild cognitive impairment in the United States (2020–2060). *Alzheimer's & Dementia, 17*(12), 1966–1975. https://doi.org/10.1002/alz.12362

Rebok, G. W., Ball, K., Guey, L. T., Jones, R. N., Kim, H. Y., King, J. W., Marsiske, M., Morris, J. N., Tennstedt, S. L., Unverzagt, F. W., & Willis, S. L. (2014). Ten-year effects of the advanced cognitive training for independent and vital elderly cognitive training trial on cognition and everyday functioning in older adults. *Journal of the American Geriatrics Society, 62*(1), 16–24. http://doi.org/10.1111/jgs.12607

Reiman, E. M., Langbaum, J. B., Tariot, P. N., Lopera, F., Bateman, R. J., Morris, J. C., Sperling, R. A., Aisen, P. S., Roses, A. D., Welsh-Bohmer, K. A., Carillo, M. C., & Weninger, S. (2016). CAP—advancing the evaluation of preclinical Alzheimer disease treatments. *Nature Reviews Neurology, 12*(1), 56–61. http://doi.org/10.1038/nrneurol.2015.177

Reuter-Lorenz, P. A., & Park, D. C. (2010). Human neuroscience and the aging mind: A new look at old problems. *Journal of Gerontology: Psychological Sciences, (65B)*, 405–415.

Ritchie, S. J., Bates, T. C., Corley, J., McNeill, G., Davies, G., Liewald, D. C., Starr, J. M., & Deary, I. J. (2014). Alcohol consumption and lifetime change in cognitive ability: A gene × environment interaction study. *Age (Dordrecht, Netherlands), 36*(3), 1493–1502. http://doi.org/10.1007/s11357-014-9638-z

Robinson, J. L., Corrada, M. M., Kovacs, G. G., Dominique, M., Caswell, C., Xie, S. X., Lee, V. M.-Y., Kawas, C. H., & Trojanowski, J. Q. (2018). Non-Alzheimer's contributions to dementia and cognitive resilience in the 90+ Study. *Acta Neuropathologica, 136*(3), 377–388. https://doi.org/10.1007/s00401-018-1872-5

Rowe, J., & Kahn, R. (1987). Human aging: Usual and successful. *Science, 237*, 143–149.

Salthouse, T. (2004). Localizing age-related individual differences in a hierarchical structure. *Intelligence, 32*, 541–561.

Salthouse, T. (2011). Neuroanatomical substrates of age-related cognitive decline. *Psychological Bulletin, 137*, 753–784.

Sanes, J., & Holtzman, D. (2021). The aging brain. In E. Kandel, J. Koester, S. Mack, & S. Siegelbaum (Eds.), *Principles of neural science* (6th ed., pp. 1561–1579). McGraw-Hill.

Satizabal, C. L., Beiser, A. S., Chouraki, V., Chêne, G., Dufouil, C., & Seshadri, S. (2016). Incidence of dementia over three decades in the Framingham Heart Study. *New England Journal of Medicine, 374*, 523–532. http://doi.org/10.1056/NEJMoa1504327

Savonenko, A. V., Wong, P. C., & Li, T. (2023). Alzheimer disease. In M. G. Zigmond, C. A. Wiley, & M. F. Chesselet (Eds.), *Neurobiology of brain disorders* (2nd ed., pp. 313–336). Academic Press.

Schneider-Garces, N., Gordon, B., Brumback-Peltz, C., Shin, E., Lee, Y., Sutton, B., Maclin, E., Gratton, G., & Fabiani, M. (2010). Span, CRUNCH, and beyond: Working memory capacity and the aging brain. *Journal of Cognitive Neuroscience, 22*, 655–669.

Seeley, W., Matthews, B., Crawford, R., Gorno-Tempini, M., Foti, D., Mackenzie, I., & Miller, B. (2008). Unravelling Boléro: Progressive aphasia, transmodal creativity and the right posterior neocortex. *Brain, 131*, 39–49.

Selkoe, D., Mandelkow, E., & Holtzman, D. (2012). *The biology of Alzheimer disease*. Cold Spring Harbor Laboratory Press.

Silver, J., McAllister, T., & Yudofsky, S. (2011). *Textbook of traumatic brain injury* (2nd ed.). American Psychiatric Publishing.

Slobounov, S., & Sebastianelli, W. (2021). *Concussions in athletics: From brain to behavior* (2nd ed.). Springer.

Smart, E. L., Gow, A. J., & Deary, I. J. (2014). Occupational complexity and lifetime cognitive abilities. *Neurology, 83*(24), 2285–2291. http://doi.org/10.1212/WNL.0000000000001075

Spira, A., Rebok, G., Stone, K., Kramer, J., & Yaffe, K. (2012). Depressive symptoms in oldest-old women: Risk of mild cognitive impairment and dementia. *American Journal of Geriatric Psychiatry, 20*, 1006–1015.

Teng, E., Tassniyom, K., & Lu, P. (2012). Reduced quality of life ratings in mild cognitive impairment: Analyses of subject and informant responses. *American Journal of Geriatric Psychiatry, 20*, 1016–1025.

Twamley, E. W., Jak, A. J., Delis, D. C., Bondi, M. W., & Lohr, J. B. (2014). Cognitive Symptom Management and Rehabilitation Therapy (CogSMART) for Veterans with traumatic brain injury: Pilot randomized controlled trial. *Journal of Rehabilitation Research and Development, 51*(1), 59–70. http://doi.org/10.1682/JRRD.2013.01.0020

Ulrich, J., & Holtzman, D. (2021). A new understanding of Alzheimer's disease. *Scientific American, 325*(2), 38–43.

Underwood, E. (2015). Alzheimer's amyloid theory gets modest boost. *Science, 349*(6247), 464. https://doi.org/10.1126/science.349.6247.464

Van Norden, A., van Dijk, E., de Laat, K., Scheltens, P., Olderikkert, M., & de Leeuw, F. (2012). Dementia: Alzheimer pathology and vascular factors: From mutually exclusive to interaction. *Biochimica et Biophysica Acta, 1822*, 340–349.

Walker, L. C., & Jucker, M. (2015). Neurodegenerative diseases: Expanding the prion concept. *Annual Review of Neuroscience, 38*(1), 87–103. http://doi.org/10.1146/annurev-neuro-071714-033828

Wang, Y., & Mandelkow, E. (2015). Tau in physiology and pathology. *Nature Reviews Neuroscience, 17*(1), 5–21. http://doi.org/10.1038/nrn.2015.1

Werner, C. (2011, November). *The older population: 2010. 2010 census briefs* (Figure 2). U.S. Government Printing Office. Retrieved from http://www.census.gov/prod/cen2010/briefs/c2010br-09.pdf

Wightman, D. P., Jansen, I. E., Savage, J. E., Shadrin, A. A., Bahrami, S., Holland, D., Rongve, A., Børte, S., Winsvold, B. S., Drange, O. K., Martinsen, A. E., Skogholt, A. H., Willer, C., Bråthen, G., Bosnes, I., Nielsen, J. B., Fritsche, L. G., Thomas, L. F., Pedersen, L. M. ... Posthuma, D. (2021). A genome-wide association study with 1,126,563 individuals identifies new risk loci for Alzheimer's disease. *Nature Genetics, 53*(9), 1276–1282. https://doi.org/10.1038/s41588-021-00921-z

Williams, S. (2016). The terrorist inside my husband's brain. *Neurology, 87*, 1308–1311.

Xu, Q., Park, Y., Huang, X., Hollenbeck, A., Blair, A., Schatzkin, A., & Chen, H. (2010). Physical activities and future risk of Parkinson disease. *Neurology, 75*(4). 341–348. https://doi.org/10.1212/WNL.0b013e3181ea1597

Yang, Y. C., Boen, C., Gerken, K., Li, T., Schorpp, K., & Harris, K. M. (2016). Social relationships and physiological determinants of longevity across the human life span. *Proceedings of the National Academy of Sciences, 113*(3), Article 201511085. http://doi.org/10.1073/pnas.1511085112

Zammit, A. R., Starr, J. M., Johnson, W., & Deary, I. J. (2014). Patterns and associates of cognitive function, psychosocial wellbeing and health in the Lothian Birth Cohort 1936. *BMC Geriatrics, 14*(1), Article 53 http://doi.org/10.1186/1471-2318-14-53

CHAPTER 16

Agan, A. (2011). Sex offender registries: Fear without function? *Journal of Law and Economics, 54*, 207–239.

Alces, P. (2018). *The moral conflict of law and neuroscience*. University of Chicago Press.

Almanzar, S., Katz, C. L., & Harry, B. (2015). Treatment of mentally ill offenders in nine developing Latin American countries. *Journal of the American Academy of Psychiatry and the Law, 43*, 340–49.

American Psychological Association. (2017). *Ethical principles of psychologists and code of conduct*. http://www.apa.org/ethics/code

Appelbaum, P. S. (2014). Commentary: DSM-5 and forensic psychiatry. *Journal of the American Academy of Psychiatry and the Law, 42*, 136–140.

Appelbaum, P. S., & Grisso, T. (1995). The MacArthur Treatment Competence Study: I. Mental illness and competence to consent to treatment. *Law and Human Behavior, 19*, 105–126.

Callahan, L., Steadman, H., Tillman, S., & Vesselinov, R. (2012). A multi-site study of the use of sanctions and incentives in mental health courts. *Law and Human Behavior, 37*, 1–9.

Eastman, N., & Campbell, C. (2006). Neuroscience and legal determination of criminal responsibility. *Nature Reviews Neuroscience, 7*, 311–318.

Ewing, C., & McCann, J. (2006). *Minds on trial: Great cases in law and psychology*. Oxford University Press.

Fazel, S., & Danesh, J. (2002). Serious mental disorder in 23,000 prisoners: A systematic review of 62 surveys. *The Lancet, 359*, 545–550.

Felthous, A. R., & Ko, J. (2018). Sexually Violent Predator Law in the United States. *East Asian Archives of Psychiatry/Dong Ya jing shen ke xue zhi, 28*(4), 159–173.

Fox, B., Miley, L. N., Kortright, K. E., & Wetsman, R. J. (2021). Assessing the effect of mental health courts on adult and juvenile recidivism: A meta-analysis. *American journal of criminal justice, 46*, 644–664.

Geary, R. C. (2015). Conflicting expert witness testimony in insanity defense. *Journal of the American Academy of Psychiatry and the Law, 43*, 511–512.

Haney, C. (2018). Restricting the use of solitary confinement. *Annual Review of Criminology, 1*, 285–310. https://www.annualreviews.org/doi/abs/10.1146/annurev-criminol-032317-092326

Hartocollis, A. (2006, October 11). *Nearly 8 years later, guilty plea in subway killing. New York Times*. www.nytimes.com/2006/10/11/nyregion/11kendra.html?_r=0

Heng, V., Haney, C., & Smeyne, R. J. (2023). The impact of isolation on brain health. In M. J. Zigmond, S. K. Rajagopal, & T. A. Polk (Eds.), *Neurobiology of brain disorders* (2nd ed., pp. 963–975). Academic Press.

Hicks, C., & West, S. (2020). Does your patient have the right to refuse medications? *Current Psychiatry, 19*(4), 23–30.

Hiday, V., Wales, H., & Ray, B. (2013). Effectiveness of a short-term mental health court: Criminal recidivism one year postexit. *Law and Human Behavior, 37*(6), 401–411.

Hope, L., Blocksidge, D., Gabbert, F., Sauer, J. D., Lewinski, W., Mirashi, A., & Atuk, E. (2015). Memory and the operational witness: Police officer recall of firearms encounters as a function of active response role. *Law and Human Behavior, 40*(1), 23–35. http://doi.org/10.1037/lhb0000159

Johnson, R., Persad, G., & Sisti, D. (2014). The *Tarasoff* rule: The implications of interstate variation and gaps in professional training. *Journal of the American Academy of Psychiatry and the Law, 42*(4), 469–477.

Jones, O. D., & Wagner, A. D. (2020). Law and neuroscience: Progress, promise, and pitfalls. In D. Poeppel, J. R. Mangun, & M. S. Gazzaniga (Eds.), *The cognitive neurosciences* (6th ed., pp. 1015–1026). MIT Press.

Langleben, D., & Moriarty, J. (2013). Using brain imaging for lie detection: Where science, law and research policy collide. *Psychology and Public Policy Law, 19*, 222–234.

Levin, A. P., Kleinman, S. B., & Adler, J. S. (2014). DSM-5 and posttraumatic stress disorder. *Journal of the American Academy of Psychiatry and the Law, 42*, 146–158.

Loftus, E. (2003). Our changeable memories: Legal and practical implications. *Nature Reviews Neuroscience, 4*, 231–234.

Loong, D., Bonato, S., Barnsley, J., & Dewa, C. S. (2019). The effectiveness of mental health courts in reducing recidivism and police contact: A systematic review. *Community Mental Health Journal, 55*(7), 1073–1098. https://doi.org/10.1007/s10597-019-00421-9

Miller v. Alabama, 567 U.S. 460 (2012).

Montgomery v. Louisiana, 577 U.S. ___ (2016).

O'Connor v. Donaldson, 422 U.S. 563 (1975).

Poldrack, R. A., Monahan, J., Imrey, P. B., Reyna, V., Raichle, M. E., Faigman, D., & Buckholtz, J. W. (2018). Predicting violent behavior: What can neuroscience add? *Trends in Cognitive Sciences, 22*(2), 111–123. https://doi.org/10.1016/j.tics.2017.11.003

Prescott, J., & Rockoff, J. (2011). Do sex offender registration and notification laws affect criminal behavior? *Journal of Law and Economics, 54*, 161–206.

Queen v. M'Naghten, 8 Eng. Rep. 718 (1843).

Redlich, A., & Han, W. (2013). Examining the links between therapeutic jurisprudence and mental health court completion. *Law and Human Behavior, 38*(2), 109-118.

Robertson, A. G., Swanson, J. W., Van Dorn, R. A., & Swartz, M. S. (2014). Treatment participation and medication adherence: effects on criminal justice costs of persons with mental illness. *Psychiatric Services (Washington, D.C.), 65*(10), 1189-1191. https://doi.org/10.1176/appi.ps.201400247

Roper v. Simmons, 543 U.S. 551 (2005).

Roskies, A. L., Schweitzer, N. J., & Saks, M. J. (2013). Neuroimages in court: Less biasing than feared. *Trends in Cognitive Sciences, 17*(3), 99-101. https://doi.org/10.1016/j.tics.2013.01.008

Schacter, D., & Loftus, E. (2013). Memory and law: What can cognitive neuroscience contribute? *Nature Neuroscience, 16*, 119-123.

Simpson, J. R. (2014). *DSM-5* and neurocognitive disorders. *Journal of the American Academy of Psychiatry and the Law Online, 42*(2), 159-164.

Slobogin, C. (2018). Principles of risk assessment: Sentencing and policing. *Ohio State Journal of Criminal Law, 15*, 583-596.

Sreenivasan, S., Frances, A., & Weinberger, L. (2010). Normative versus consequential ethics in sexually violent predator laws: An ethics conundrum for psychiatry. *Journal of the American Academy of Psychiatry and the Law, 38*, 386-391.

Steadman, H., Davidson, S., & Brown, C. (2001). Mental health courts: Their promise and unanswered questions. *Psychiatric Services, 52*, 457-458.

Steinberg, L. (2013). The influence of neuroscience on US Supreme Court decisions about adolescents' criminal culpability. *Nature Reviews Neuroscience, 14*(7), 513-518.

Sullivan, J. (2021). Mass shootings, mental "illness," and *Tarasoff*. *University of Pittsburgh Law Review, 82*, 685-845.

Swanson, J. W., McGinty, E. E., Fazel, S., & Mays, V. M. (2015). Mental illness and reduction of gun violence and suicide: bringing epidemiologic research to policy. *Annals of Epidemiology, 25*(5), 366-376. https://doi.org/10.1016/j.annepidem.2014.03.004

Torrey, E., Kennard, A., Eslinger, D., Lamb, R., & Pavle, J. (2010, May). *More mentally ill persons are in jails and prisons than hospitals: A survey of the states*. Report for National Sheriffs Association & Treatment Advocacy Center.

Varshney, M., Mahapatra, A., Krishnan, V., Gupta, R., & Deb, K. S. (2016). Violence and mental illness: What is the true story? *Journal of Epidemiology and Community Health, 70*(3), 3-5.

Wade, K. A., Nash, R. A., & Lindsay, D. S. (2018). Reasons to doubt the reliability of eyewitness memory: Commentary on Wixted, Mickes, and Fisher (2018). *Perspectives on Psychological Science, 13*(3), 339-342. https://doi.org/10.1177/1745691618758261

Wasser, T., & Trueblood, K. (2015, March). Forced medication to restore competency. *Journal of the American Academy of Psychiatry and the Law Online, 43*(1), 112-114.

Weinstock, R., Bonnici, D., Seroussi, A., & Leong, G. B. (2014). No duty to warn in California: Now unambiguously solely a duty to protect. *Journal of the American Academy of Psychiatry and the Law, 42*(1), 101-108.

Wixted, J. T., Mickes, L., & Fisher, R. P. (2018). Rethinking the reliability of eyewitness memory. *Perspectives on Psychological Science, 13*(3), 324-335. https://doi.org/10.1177/1745691617734878

Zander, T. (2005). Civil commitment without psychosis: The law's reliance on the weakest links in psychodiagnosis. *Journal of Sexual Offender Civil Commitment: Science and the Law, 1*, 17-82

AUTHOR INDEX

Aaronson, S., 230
Aas, M., 474
Abazia, D. T., 472
Abbate-Daga, G., 393
Abbot, P., 8
Abbott, L., 244, 245
Abe, Y., 302
Abel, J. L., 313
Abi-Dargham, A., 532, 533
Abi-Saab, W., 533
Abracen, J., 430
Abraham, A., 8
Abramovitch, A., 333, 334
Abramowitz, J., 320, 328, 329, 334
Abrous, D., 291
Abu-Akel, A., 191
Adams, B., 284
Adams, M., 220, 463
Adanty, C., 81
Addington, J., 32, 537, 541
Ader, R., 271
Ades, A. E., 320
Adkins, A. E., 463
Adler, C. M., 246
Adler, J. S., 650
Adler, L., 197, 201
Adolfsson, R., 84, 244
Adolph, D., 408
Adolphs, R., 180
Agan, A., 644
Aghajani, M., 319
Aghajanian, G., 220
Agholme, L., 53, 607
Agirman, G., 271
Agras, W., 39, 390, 394
Agrawal, A., 82, 452, 455, 463
Aguiar, A., 200
Aguilar-Gaxiola, S., 214, 309–311
Ahern, J., 280
Ahmad, A. H., 601
Ahmad, T., 292
Ahmed, A. G., 430
Ahmed, S. H., 372
Ahs, F., 63
Ahveninen, L. M., 619
Ainsworth, M., 171
Aisen, P. S., 606
Aitken, M., 333
Aizenstein, H., 301
Akande, A., 307
Akil, H., 83, 122
Akiskal, H., 243
Akkermann, K., 388
Akudjedu, T. N., 220
Al Eissa, M., 83, 122
Al-Aama, J., 387
Alaba, O., 372
Alaie, I., 63

Alasaari, J. S., 220
Alaverdyan, A., 385
Albanese, E., 606
Albay, R. III., 621
Albert, D., 178, 179
Albert, P., 273
Albucher, R., 251
Albus, K., 173
Alcaine, O., 313
Alces, P., 648
Alda, M., 220, 243
Alderson-Day, B., 532
Alderton, G., 54
Aleman, A., 532, 534
Alen, N. V., 222, 229
Alexander, G. E., 609
Alford, B. A., 231
Aliaga, P. A., 254
Aliev, F., 463
Allardyce, J., 514
Allen, A., 291, 523
Allen, L., 39, 364
Allen, N., 224, 226
Allen, P., 306, 532, 534
Allman, J. M., 23
Alloza, C., 220
Almanzar, S., 645
Almeida, L. M., 192
Alnaes, D., 220, 520, 528
Alonso, J., 214, 309–311
Alonso-Lana, S., 220
Altshuler, L. L., 244
Alvarez-Jimenez, M., 520
Alzheimer, A., 606
Amarakm, D., 191
Amaral, D., 193
Amaresha, A. C., 540
Ambach, W., 324
Ambady, N., 13
Ambrosini, P., 200
Amelung, T., 426, 427
Amendola, F. A., 191
Amianto, F., 393
Amin, N., 609
Ammerman, B. A., 254
Anastopoulos, A., 202
Anckarsater, H., 191
Anderson, D., 394
Anderson, M. L., 124
Anderson, N., 566, 567
Anderson, S., 114, 567
Anderson, T., 123
Andersson, G., 321
Andrade, C., 228
Andrade, V., 609
Andreasen, N., 48, 149, 518, 530
Andreassen, O. A., 82, 244, 520, 528
Andreescu, C., 301

Andres-Perpina, S., 388
Andrew, M., 292
Andrews, P., 224
Andrews-Hanna, J. R., 73
Angermeyer, M., 548, 550
Angleitner, A., 556
Angrilli, A., 518
Anker, M., 13, 86
Ansell, E., 570
Anthony, A., 191
Antonova, E., 232
Antony, M., 313, 318, 325
Anttila, V., 82
Aoki, Y., 56
Apicella, F., 191
Appel, L., 63
Appelbaum, P. S., 636, 649
Applegate, B., 183
Araya, R., 114
Arcaro, M. J., 319
Arce, E., 319
Archer, R., 145
Arcuri, E., 176
Arias-Vasquez, A., 201
Arloth, J., 222
Armor, D., 496
Arnaldo, I., 220
Arne, K. A., 255
Arnoriaga-Rodriguez, M., 55
Arns, M., 202
Arolt, V., 324
Aronen, H., 566
Arredondo, E., 374
Arthur, A., 602
Artioli, G. G., 381
Asami, T., 562
Asari, T., 146
Asarnow, R., 65
Ash, C., 54
Asherson, P., 61, 199, 200
Ashwin, C., 188
Ashwin, E., 188
Ashwood, K., 61
Aslan, M., 283
Aslund, C., 166
Asok, A., 302
Atkinson, E. A., 151
Attia, E., 392
Atuk, E., 648
Aubin, H., 490, 497
Avenevoli, S., 308
Avery, E. T., 234
Awasthi, S., 122
Ayakta, N., 606
Ayesa-Arriola, R., 81
Azadi, B., 61
Azariah, F., 114
Azevedo, F., 566

Azizikia, A., 327
Azrael, D., 251, 251, 494

Baasher, T., 445
Bacanu, S.-A., 463
Bach, B., 586
Bachman, J., 451
Backhed, F., 387
Badcock, P., 224, 226
Baddeley, J. L., 225
Bader, H. N., 283
Bae, J., 233
Baes, C. V. W., 220
Bagby, R. M., 557
Bagdy, G., 252
Baharikhoob, P., 570
Bahraini, N. H., 615
Bahrami, S., 244, 520, 528, 609
Bailer, U., 384, 386
Bailey, J. M., 410, 411
Bailey, M. T., 388
Bailey, T., 520
Bailles, E., 549
Baker, A. W., 314
Baker, J., 306, 392
Baker, S. L., 606
Baker-Jones, M., 477
Bakolis, I., 283
Balanza-Martinez, V., 81
Balchandani, P., 532
Balderston, N., 177, 178
Baldwin, J., 402
Baldwin, S., 602
Bale, T., 267, 277
Baler, R., 372, 452, 455, 469, 474
Balfour, D., 485
Ball, K., 620
Ballesteros, S., 594, 620
Ballmaier, M., 245
Balsamo, M., 40
Baltasar, I., 551
Balu, D. T., 520, 533
Bana, B., 56
Banaschewski, T., 166, 169, 177
Banich, M. T., 82–83
Banihashemi, L., 301
Banks, A., 452
Bao, A. M., 435
Bara, A., 471
Barba, T., 228
Barbaranelli, C., 556
Barbe, R. P., 228
Barbeito, S., 541
Barber, A., 391
Barber, C., 281, 281, 494
Barber, J., 34, 313
Barbu, M. C., 220
Barbui, C., 580
Barch, D., 121, 533
Barchas, J. D., 83, 122
Bardin, J., 167, 168
Bargh, J. A., 176
Barker, G. J., 177
Barker, K., 187

Barkham, M., 231
Barlow, D., 39, 309, 313–315, 320, 325
Barlow, E., 520
Barnes, L. E., 602
Barnes, L. L., 606
Barnes, R., 602
Barnes, T., 538
Barnett, M. L., 199
Barnhofer, T., 232
Barnsley, J., 638
Baron-Cohen, S., 81, 176, 186, 188, 190–192
Barquera, S., 374
Barr, P. B., 122
Barrera, A. Z., 235
Barres, R., 80
Barrett, F. S., 477
Barrett, L. F., 314
Barrett, R., 505
Barrowclough, C., 538
Barry, C. T., 147
Barsky, A., 330, 354
Bartz, J., 579
Basco, M. R., 248
Bas-Hoogendam, J. M., 319, 320
Baskin-Sommers, A. R., 567
Bass, J., 245
Bass, N., 83, 84, 122, 244
Bassett, D. S., 532
Bateman, A., 580
Bateman, R. J., 606
Bates, T. C., 599
Bateson, P., 274
Batshaw, M., 204
Battle, A., 83
Battle, C. L., 552
Batzler, A., 463
Bauer, J., 220
Baum, M., 522
Baune, B. T., 220
Bayes, A., 243, 551
Be chard, M., 292
Beason-Held, L., 599
Beattie, B., 621
Beauchaine, T. P., 581
Beaumont, T., 428
Bechara, A., 567
Beck, A., 39, 123, 142, 221–223, 225, 231, 364, 537, 539, 540
Beck, J., 221, 231
Beck, R. W., 142
Becker, A., 370, 389
Becker, B., 319
Becker, E. S., 314
Beckman, K., 80
Bedford, R., 190
Beech, A. R., 423, 430
Beekman, A., 268
Beeney, J. E., 151
Beesdo-Baum, K., 322, 323, 327
Beevers, C. G., 222, 223, 225
Behar, E., 313
Behrman, R., 127
Beidel, D., 292
Beier, K., 426, 427
Beiser, A. S., 602

Bejanin, A., 606
Belger, A., 533
Belin, D., 481
Belin-Rauscent, A., 481
Bell, J. A., 222
Bell, J. T., 81
Bellack, A. S., 117, 118
Bellenguez, C., 609
Bellgrove, M. A., 177
Bellivier, F., 244
Belmonte, M., 176, 186, 190, 192
Belsky, D. W., 199, 200, 525
Belsky, J., 265
Belzung, C., 291
Ben-Ari, Y., 167
Benau, E. M., 379
Bendall, S., 520
Bender, D., 555
Bendl, J., 83
Benedek, D., 292
Benedetti, F., 220
Bengtsson, H., 342
Benjet, C., 548, 550
Bennett, D., 229, 620
Bennetts, A., 391
Benninghoff, J., 610
Benoit-Marand, M., 481
Ben-Porath, Y. S., 143
Benton, M. L., 8
Benyamin, B., 552
Benyamina, A., 490
Bercik, P., 387
Berelowitz, M., 191
Bergen, A., 393
Bergen, S. E., 520
Berger, H., 57
Bergfeld, I. O., 230
Bergui, M., 393
Berk, M., 220, 514, 526
Berkman, L., 621
Berle, D., 40
Berman, C., 502, 504
Berman, K., 73, 523
Berman, S. M., 482
Bernard, D., 233
Bernat, E. M., 565
Bernecker, S., 32
Bernstein, D., 560
Berntson, G. G., 269
Berona, J., 251
Berra, M., 415
Berretta, S., 283
Berrettini, W., 391
Bertelsen, S., 463
Berthoud, H. R., 56
Bertolino, A., 82
Bertram, L., 609
Bertrand, O., 59
Besteher, B., 522
Betancourt, T. S., 285
Bettella, F., 220, 244, 474, 517
Beute, G., 230
Beutel, M., 418
Bevilacqua, L., 463
Bharucha, J., 13

Bhatt, R. R., 385
Bhattacharya, A., 380
Bhundia, R., 283
Bialas, A. R., 522
Bialek, W., 54
Bianco, A., 381
Bick, J., 175
Bidwell, L., 201
Biederman, J., 198
Bieliauskas, L., 149
Bienvenu, O., 330
Bierer, L. M., 283
Biernacka, J. M., 463
Bigdeli, T. B., 81, 83, 122, 463
Bilderbeck, A., 319
Bilej, M., 386
Bilousova, T., 621
Binau, S. G., 249
Binder, E. B., 222
Binder, J., 34, 234
Bird, S., 70
Birmaher, B., 228, 551
Bis, J. C., 609
Bischoff-Grethe, A., 384, 386
Bishop, S. J., 301, 304
Bishop, S. L., 187, 190, 191
Bissada, H., 391
Bisson, J., 281, 292
Biswal, B., 53, 273
Bjaastad, J. F., 321
Bjella, T., 474
Bjelland, I., 321
Bjorkstrand, J., 63
Black, A., 187
Blackwood, D., 84, 244
Blagov, P. S., 574
Blair, A., 620
Blakemore, S., 452
Blakeslee, S., 46, 363
Blalock, D. V., 380
Blanco, C., 479
Blanton, R., 245
Blaser, M. J., 54
Blashfield, R. K., 156, 158
Blehar, M., 171
Blemings, A., 477
Blennerhassett, P., 387
Bliese, P. D., 254
Bloch, M. H., 331
Block, A., 220
Blocksidge, D., 648
Bloomfield, M. A. P., 474
Blow, F. C., 316
Blum, D., 169
Blumberger, D., 230
Blumenthal, J., 528
Bobrow, K., 372
Boccardi, M., 566
Bocharov, A. V., 13
Bock, C., 81
Bockholt, H., 530
Bodell, L., 379, 392, 396
Bodien, Y. G., 70
Bodnar, R., 427
Boelen, P. A., 219, 281

Boen, C., 621
Boen, E., 220
Bogdan, R., 452, 455
Bohart, A. C., 32
Bohlken, M. M., 522
Bohnert, A. S. B., 234
Bohnsack, J. P., 452
Bohon, C., 373
Bohus, M., 567, 570
Boivin, N., 444
Bokde, A., 610
Boks, M. P. M., 84, 244
Boland, A., 609
Boland, R. J., 213, 354
Boldrini, M., 252
Bole-Feysot, C., 388
Boley, B., 609
Bollini, A., 561
Bolshakov, V. Y., 283
Bolton, P., 61, 192
Bombel, G., 145, 146
Bonato, S., 638
Bond, A., 344, 345
Bondaronek, P., 317
Bondi, M. W., 621
Bondolfi, G., 232
Bondy, A., 186
Bonini, L., 176
Bonnemann, C., 534
Bonnici, D., 639
Bonnin, C. M., 220
Bono, C., 402, 431
Booij, L., 295
Bookheimer, S., 176, 192
Borenstein, E., 192
Borglum, A. D., 82, 191
Boring, E., 15
Borisova, I. I., 285
Borkovec, T., 110, 313, 314, 315
Borlido, C., 81
Borner, K., 49, 71
Bornstein, R., 579
Borte, S., 609
Bosnes, I., 609
Boswell, J., 315
Bouchard, C., 372, 380
Bouchard, T., 122
Bouix, S., 562
Bouman, M.-B., 434
Bourgeron, T., 191
Bouziane, C., 201
Bower, J. E., 222
Bowers, G., 40
Bowers, M. E., 309
Bowlby, J., 166, 169, 171
Bowles, N. P., 268, 274, 275
Bowling, J., 408
Boxer, A. L., 606
Boxer, P., 183, 184
Boyadjis, T., 230
Boyce, P., 243
Boyd, R., 11
Boyle, P., 620
Bradford, J., 424, 430, 431
Bradley, R., 292, 567, 570

Bradley, S., 436
Bradwejn, J., 391
Braff, D. L., 523
Bragdon, L., 334
Brahler, E., 418
Braiker, H., 496
Bramati, I., 566
Brambilla, P., 220, 522
Bramer, L. M., 192
Brammer, M. J., 150
Bramwell, K., 391
Brandeis, D., 166, 169, 202
Brandes, C. M., 123
Brandt, H., 391
Bras, J., 82
Brathen, G., 609
Bratko, D., 556
Braun, C., 56
Bray, G., 372
Brayne, C., 594, 595, 602
Bredemeier, K., 222, 225
Breen, G., 82, 83, 122, 244, 245, 380, 388
Breen, M. S., 283
Breijyeh, Z., 605
Breitbach, J., 255
Breithaupt, L., 380, 388
Brem, A. K., 591
Bremner, J., 349, 350
Brennan, R. T., 285
Brenner, L. A., 615
Brent, D., 228, 252
Bressler, S., 72
Breteler, M., 202
Breton, J., 388
Brickman, H. M., 247
Bridge, J. A., 228
Bridgeman, M. B., 472
Bridson, T. L., 265, 277
Briere, J., 569
Brigham, G., 494
Briken, P., 430, 431
Briley, D. A., 549
Brim, O. G., 128
Brinkmeyer, M., 183
Brock, D., 230
Brodin, P., 55
Brody, J., 395
Broglio, S. P., 617
Brohawn, K., 290
Bromet, E., 83, 122, 198, 318
Bromley, D., 96
Bronson, S., 267
Brook, J., 243, 247, 341, 342
Broome, M. R., 510
Brosch, T., 466
Brothers, L., 180
Brotto, L. A., 421
Brouwer, R. M., 522
Brown, A., 520
Brown, C., 637
Brown, E. G., 55
Brown, G., 247, 540
Brown, K. W., 314
Brown, T., 312, 379, 392, 396
Brown, W., 64, 98

Brozek, J., 389
Bruce, S., 64
Bruce, T. O., 255
Brugulat-Serrat, A., 600
Brumback-Peltz, C., 599
Brune, M., 175, 514
Brunette, M. F., 32, 537, 541
Brunstein Klomek, A., 255
Bryan, C. J., 255
Bryant, C. D., 380, 388
Bryant, R., 278, 280, 291, 294, 514
Bryant-Waugh, R., 369
Bryce, R., 606
Bryk, M., 363
Bryois, J., 122, 283
Brzustowicz, L. M., 265
Buchel, C., 177
Buchholz, K., 64
Buchman, A., 620
Buchsbaum, M., 62, 344, 345
Buckholtz, J. W., 648
Buckley, P. F., 83, 122
Buckner, R. L., 73
Bucuvalas, M., 280
Buehler, S., 228
Buhrich, N., 428
Bui, E., 301, 314
Buitelaar, J., 200, 201, 272
Bulik, C. M., 82, 380, 387, 388, 391, 392
Bulik-Sullivan, B., 82
Bullain, S. S., 621
Bullman, T. A., 254
Bullmore, E., 81, 191, 192, 222, 333
Bunney, W. E., 83, 122
Bureau, J.-F., 172
Burgdorf, J., 453
Burgess, S., 248
Burgmer, M., 358, 360
Burhan, A. M., 81
Burke, M. J., 615
Burne, T., 520, 522
Burnett, A. L., 417
Burnette, M., 166
Burns, J., 518, 519
Burokas, A., 55
Busby, D. R., 251
Buss, D., 226
Bustillo, J., 530
Butler, A., 123
Buzzell, G. A., 309
Bybjerg-Grauholm, J., 83, 122
Byerley, W. F., 83, 122
Byers, E., 402
Byford, S., 232
Bygren, L., 81
Byne, W., 436
Byng, R., 232
Byrd, A. L., 151, 166
Byrne, E. M., 244, 245
Byrne, M., 177
Bzdok, D., 427

Caan, M. W. A., 201
Cabassa, L. J., 139

Cabeen, R., 65
Cabeza, R., 53
Cabreiro, F., 56
Cacciaglia, R., 600
Cacioppo, J. T., 269
Cadenhead, K., 175, 523
Caglio, M., 393
Cahill, C. M., 453, 479
Cahn, W., 522, 530
Calancie, O. G., 295
Calati, R., 82
Calder, A., 182
Caldji, C., 306
Calhoun, S. L., 187
Calhoun, V., 201, 334, 530
Califf, R., 124
Calkins, A., 301
Calkins, M. E., 523
Callahan, L., 637
Camchong, J., 532
Camilleri, J. A., 319
Campbell, C., 649
Campbell, D. T., 106
Campbell, L. A., 312
Campellone, T., 537
Campos-Martin, R., 609
Camprodon, J., 31
Canales-Rodriguez, E. J., 220
Candea, D., 220, 389, 394
Cannon, T. D., 520, 526–528, 537
Cannon, W., 266, 268
Cano, S., 370
Cantin, L., 372
Cantu, R. C., 616
Canuel, N., 444
Cao, D., 466
Cao, Q., 201
Cao, Z., 220
Caporaso, J., 54
Capra, J. A., 8
Caprara, G., 556
Caraceni, A., 601
Cararo, J. H., 81
Cardena, E., 342, 350
Cardoso, D., 423, 427
Carey, B., 413, 553, 583
Carey, G., 121
Carey, M., 413
Carhart-Harris, R., 153, 228, 477
Carillo, M. C., 606
Carl, E., 314
Carlezon, W. A., 283
Carlson, E., 174
Carlstrom, E., 191
Carlucci, L., 40
Carone, B. R., 81
Caroppo, P., 393
Carpenter, L., 228, 230
Carr, E., 283
Carre, A., 490
Carrica, L. K., 452
Carrillo, B., 435
Carrion, R. E., 536
Carroll, I. M., 387, 388
Carruzzo, A., 357, 359, 361

Carson-DeWitt, R., 476
Carter, B. L., 155
Carter, C., 525, 537
Carter, E. J., 192
Carter, S. P., 254
Carvalho, A. F., 81
Carvalho, L. A., 222
Carver, F. W., 61
Caseras, X., 220, 549
Casey, C. P., 192
Caspi, A., 84, 121, 151, 166, 199, 200, 265, 525
Casson, D., 191
Castaldelli-Maia, J. M., 580
Castano, R., 418, 419
Castellani, C., 522
Castellanos, F., 73, 201, 532
Castonguay, L., 231, 315
Castren, E., 105
Castro-Fornieles, J., 388
Casula, L., 191
Caswell, C., 621
Catmur, C., 175, 176
Caulo, M., 411
Cavalli, G., 79
Cavedo, E., 566
Ceaser, A., 121, 533
Ceccanti, M., 415
Cerliani, L., 192
Cerny, J., 410
Cervenka, S., 533
Cervoni, N., 80, 272
Cha, C., 252
Chabane, Y. N., 388
Chacko, A., 201
Chae, J., 556
Chahal, K., 418
Chakrabarti, B., 188, 191
Chamberlain, S., 333
Chambers, M. C., 98
Champagne, F., 80, 272, 274, 265
Chan, A., 621
Chan, C. P., 232
Chan, P., 388
Chandler, S., 192
Chandra, A., 404
Chanen, A., 549
Chang, E., 232, 320
Chang, J., 191, 217
Chapman, J., 123
Chapman, S. B., 83, 84, 122, 244
Charman, T., 190, 192
Chartrand, T. L., 176
Chase, D., 252
Chattarji, A. S., 267
Chatterjee, S., 114, 214, 309–311
Chattopadhyay, M., 283
Chau, D. T., 235
Chaudhary, Z., 81
Chauhan, P., 118
Chavkin, C., 220
Chavlis, S., 51
Cheavens, J. S., 567
Chein, J., 178–180
Chemerinski, E., 560

Chen, C. Y., 84, 122, 244
Chen, H., 167, 301, 620
Chen, I., 72
Chen, J., 201
Chen, L.-S., 463
Chen, Q., 283, 449
Chen, W. J., 83, 122
Chen, Y., 534
Chen, Z., 388
Chene, G., 602
Cheney, T., 237
Cheng, W., 520, 528
Cheng, Z., 317
Chentsova-Dutton, Y. E., 353
Chericoni, N., 191
Cherkassky, V. L., 252
Cherny, S., 523
Chetelat, G., 610
Cheung, C. K. T., 573
Cheung, K. H., 283
Cheverud, J., 268
Chiang, A. H., 191
Chiao, J., 13, 68
Chiong, W., 70
Chisholm, D., 114
Chisholm, K., 191
Chiswell, K., 124
Chiu, C. D., 340, 342
Chiu, W. T., 312, 326
Chivers, M., 408, 410
Cho, K., 283
Choate, M., 39
Choi, W., 573
Choi-Kain, L., 580
Chou, K., 72
Chou, S., 560, 574, 579, 580
Chou, Y.-L., 463
Chouraki, V., 82, 602
Chow, P. I., 549
Christakis, D., 201
Christian, L. M., 388
Christopoulou-Aletra, H., 368
Chu, Y., 520, 528
Chung, W. K., 204
Chura, L. R., 81, 192
Churchhouse, C., 83, 84, 122, 244
Churchill, J. D., 70
Churchill, R., 281, 327
Cicchetti, D., 166
Cicero, D. C., 151
Cichon, S., 82, 463
Ciocca, G., 408
Clare, L., 594
Clark, D., 32, 278, 320
Clark, K., 65
Clark, L. A., 149, 553, 549
Clark, L. E., 330
Clark, V., 530
Clarke, G. N., 235
Clarke, T., 220, 463
Clarkin, J. F., 576, 584
Clayton, D., 78
Cleckley, H., 564
Clemente, M. J., 580
Clemmensen, C., 56

Cliquet, F., 191
Cloninger, C., 357
Coates, U., 610
Coenen, A., 202
Cohen Kadosh, K., 320
Cohen, A., 114
Cohen, D., 68
Cohen, J., 178, 537, 538
Cohen, M., 119
Cohen, P., 243, 247, 341, 342
Cohen, S., 271
Cohen, Z. D., 227
Cohen-Kettenis, P., 434
Cohn, L., 320
Cojan, Y., 357, 359, 361
Colas, E., 328
Colding, C., 387
Cole, H. W., 73
Cole, M. G., 621
Coleman, E., 436
Coleman, J. R. I., 122, 220, 244, 245, 380, 388
Coleman, M., 186, 191
Coles, M., 334
Coley, E. J. L., 55
Colibazzi, T., 530
Colic, L., 427
Coll, C., 55
Collado, M. C., 371
Collier, D., 82
Collins, L., 334
Collins, R. C., 110, 594
Collins, S., 387, 424
Colpe, L. J., 254
Comasco, E., 166
Comas-Herrera, A., 602
Commons, K., 427
Compton, M., 474
Compton, W., 483, 560, 574, 579, 580
Comtesse, H., 219, 281
Comtois, K. A., 255, 581
Conard, L., 436
Conese, M., 265, 271
Conklin, C. Z., 567, 570
Conley, R., 81, 245
Conrod, P. J., 177
Cons, E., 227, 228, 477
Constantino, M. J., 32
Conway, C. C., 151
Cook, I., 230
Cools, M., 415
Cooper, A. B., 249
Cooper, J. E., 13, 86
Cooper, T. B., 533
Cooper, Z., 391
Copeland, W. E., 182
Copen, C. E., 404
Coppola, R., 61
Copps-Smith, E., 436
Corbetta, M., 306, 307
Corcoran, A. W., 220
Corcoran, D. L., 199, 200
Corley, J., 599
Corley, R., 463
Cornblatt, B. A., 536

Cornell, C., 382
Cornwell, B. R., 61
Corona, G., 417
Coronad, V. G., 615
Corp, D. T., 616
Corr, P. J., 327
Corrada, M., 621
Correa-Estrada, P., 81
Correa-Ghisays, P., 81
Correll, C. U., 32, 537, 541
Corry, N., 284
Cortese, S., 202
Corteselli, K., 123
Corvin, A. P., 84, 244
Coryell, W., 243, 251
Cosimano, M. P., 477
Cossette, A., 437
Costa, M. R., 609
Costa, P., 555, 556
Costanzo, V., 191
Costello, E., 308
Cosyns, P., 431
Cotet, C., 580
Coulon, D., 388
Courtet, P., 252
Cousins, L., 271
Cox, K. L., 254
Coyle, J., 520, 533
Craddock, N., 83, 84, 122, 244, 245
Craddock, R., 73
Craig, I., 84, 121, 166, 265
Craig, K., 333
Craighero, L., 175
Crane, C., 232
Crane, N., 471
Craske, M., 222, 322, 323, 326, 327
Crawford, M., 548, 584, 586
Crawford, R., 612, 614
Crawford, S., 391
Creamer, M., 280
Crean, R., 471
Creswell, J. D., 36, 314
Cristea, I., 232, 580
Crocq, M., 444
Croen, L., 186
Crombach, A., 284, 294
Cronbach, L. J., 141
Crone, E. A., 178
Cropley, J., 80
Crosby, R. D., 382
Crow, S., 382
Crow, T., 518
Crowell, S. E., 581
Cruz, N. J., 192
Cruz-Pereira, J. S., 265
Cryan, J. F., 56, 265, 387
Cubells, J., 82
Cuellar, A., 243
Cuijpers, P., 114, 314, 580
Cuitan, M., 198, 318
Cullen, B., 330
Cumming, P., 532
Cummins, T. D. R., 177
Cunha, B. G., 228
Curley, J., 272

Curran, H. V., 474
Currie, J., 229
Currie, R., 340
Curry, J. F., 254
Curtis, D., 83, 84, 122, 244
Curtis, G. C., 323
Cushman, W. C., 155
Cusick, C. M., 83, 122
Cuthbert, B., 81, 149, 152–155, 517
Cyr, G., 569
Czamara, D., 222
Czisch, M., 220

D'Agata, F., 393
D'Agostino, A., 121
D'Alessio, A., 80, 272
D'Onofrio, B. M., 520
D'Souza, D. C., 533
da Silva Gomes, A. I., 382
Dahmen, N., 463
Dai, G., 65
Dailey, T. M., 356
Dakanalis, A., 379
Dale, A. M., 244, 520, 528
Dalgleish, T., 232
Dalton, B., 271
Dalton, J., 344, 345
Daly, E., 150
Daly, M. J., 83, 122
Damasio, A., 97–99, 567
Damasio, H., 97–99, 567
Damiano, S. R., 382
Damisah, E. C., 609
Damon, S. M., 527
Damotte, V., 609
Danesh, J., 645
Dani, J., 455, 485
Daniel, S. I. F., 394
Daniels, J., 186
Dannals, R., 483, 484
Dantzer, R., 222, 271
Dapretto, M., 176, 192
Darcangelo, S., 425
Darcq, E., 479
Dare, C., 390
Darwin, C., 24
Das, A., 418
Daskalakis, J., 229
Daskalakis, Z., 230
Daspe, M.-E., 569
Davenport, G., 616
Davey, C. G., 221
David, A., 149, 152, 343–345, 503
David, D., 32, 232, 247, 389, 394
Davidson, J., 36, 283, 292
Davidson, R., 268
Davidson, S., 274, 637
Davies, G., 220, 599
Davies, M., 176, 192
Davies, S., 191, 388
Davis, A., 477, 522
Davis, H. A., 151
Davis, J., 621
Davis, M., 377

Davis, T. E., 325
Daw, N. D., 305
Daws, R. E., 228
Dawson, D., 560, 574, 579, 580
Dawson, G., 190, 191
Dawson, M., 188
Day, R., 13, 86
de Abreu Soares, E., 382, 388
de Almeida, J., 333
de Azevedo Marques Perico, C., 580
de Blok, C. J. M., 434
De Brito, S. A., 182
de Girolamo, G., 548, 550
de Graaf, R., 548, 550
De Hert, M., 61, 522
De Houwer, J., 466
de Jonge, P., 268
de Jongh, R. T., 434
De Keyser, J., 61
de Koning, P., 335
de Kwaasteniet, B., 320, 335
De La Barra, F., 431
De La Cruz, A. A., 139
de la Soudiere, M., 285
de Laat, K., 609, 610
de Leeuw, C. A., 122, 244, 245
de Leeuw, F., 609, 610
de Lima, M., 556
De Luca, V., 81
De Oliveira Coelho, G. M., 382
De Palma, G., 387
De Panfilis, C., 586
de Peri, L., 530
de Ridder, S., 202
de Rivera, H., 522
de Rojas, I., 609
De Silva, M., 114
De Visser, R. O., 423
de Vries, A. L. C., 434
de Wit, H., 466
Deacon, B., 320
Deakin, J., 271
Deans, P. J. M., 283
Deary, I., 220, 519, 524, 599, 600
Deb, K. S., 630
deBerardinis, R., 200
Debnath, M., 526
Decety, J., 566, 567
Dechelotte, P., 388
Deckersbach, T., 245
Decoster, J., 61
DeDayan, P., 305
DeFilipp, L., 380
DeFries, J., 121
Degenhardt, F., 463
DeKlyen, M., 173
Del Gratta, C., 411
Delaney, C. B., 370
Delano, K., 255
DelBello, M. P., 246
Del-Ben, C., 327
delCampo, N., 333
Deleger, S., 377
Delis, D. C., 621
DeLisi, L. E., 474

Dellen, E. Van., 601
Delplanque, S., 466
Deluca, V., 252
Demitrack, M., 230
Demler, O., 312
Demyttenaere, K., 548, 550
den Boer, J. A., 346, 351
den Heijer, M., 434
Denckla, M., 201
Deng, C., 301
Deng, W., 528
Deng, Y., 387
Denicoff, K. D., 244
Dening, T., 602
Denizet-Lewis, B., 444
Dennison, C. A., 122
Dennison-Himmelfarb, C., 155
Denou, E., 387
Denys, D., 230, 329–331, 335
Dere, J., 353
DeRogatis, L. R., 417
DeRonchi, D., 82
DeRubeis, R., 153, 227, 234, 235
Desarnaud, F., 283
Desgranges, B., 610
Dewa, C. S., 638
Dewey, S. L., 481
Dewitte, M., 402
Dexter-Mazza, E. T., 581
DeYoung, C. G., 151, 152, 227, 228, 477, 553
Dhillon, A., 191
Di Florio, A., 84, 244
Di Forti, M., 474
di Giacomo, E., 586
Di Gioia, S., 265, 271
Di Martino, A., 192
Di Matteo, R., 411
Diamond, D., 576
Dias, A., 114
Dias, S., 320
Dickerson, F., 84, 244
Dickerson, S. S., 276
Dickey, C., 525, 528, 562
Dickey, R., 430
Dickinson, D., 523
Didriksen, M., 82
Dieci, M., 530
Dietrich, D. E., 534
Dietrich, M., 373
Diez Roux, A. V., 119
Difede, J., 289
DiLalla, L., 121
Dilger, S., 325
Dillo, W., 534
Dillon, D. G., 221
Dima, D., 534
Dimaggio, G., 584
Dinan, T. G., 265, 387
Dindelegan, C., 579
Dinh, H. M., 254
DiNicola, L. M., 73
Dinis, T. C. P., 192
Disner, S., 222, 223
Dittrich, A., 476
Diwadkar, V., 522, 570

Dixon, L. B., 535
Djurovic, S., 244, 474, 520, 528
do Rego, J.-C., 388
Docherty, A. R., 463
Docherty, M. J., 283
Dodd, J., 391
Dodge, B., 408
Doering, B. K., 219, 281
Doering, S., 586
Dohrenwend, B., 284
Dohrmann, K., 272
Doll, H., 391
Dolmetsch, R., 82
Dome, P., 252
Dominique, M., 621
Donati, F. L., 121
Dong, H., 78
Dong, Q., 307
Donnell, P. O., 82
Dooley, L. N., 222
Dorrington, S., 283
Dosil, J., 381
Doucet, G. E., 532
Dougherty, D., 31, 329, 330, 333
Douglas-Palumberi, H., 221
Dover, R. V. H., 372
Dowd, J. B., 387
Dowlati, Y., 222
Downey, C., 232, 320
Doyle, A., 390
Dozier, M., 173
Dragano, N., 463
Draguns, J., 137, 156
Drancourt, M., 388
Drange, O. K., 609
Draper, C., 428
Dray, K., 300
Drevets, W., 235, 245
Drewnowski, A., 372
Drid, P., 381
Droge, L., 335
Drozd, J., 231
Drumkova, K., 427
Duan, K., 201
Duan, X., 167, 301
Duarte, T. A., 379
Duffau, H., 71
Duffy, A., 380
Duffy, M. E., 249
Dufouil, C., 602
Dufour, M., 560, 574, 579, 580
Dugas, L., 372
Dugmore, H., 372
Dukart, J., 319
Duman, R., 220
Dumitrascu, N., 145, 146
Duncan, L., 82
Dunlap, G., 117
Dunne, J. D., 36
Dunner, D. L., 230, 243
Durbin, A., 64
Dutra, L., 292
Dutton, M., 314
Dyer, K., 117
Dykens, E., 204

Dymov, S., 80, 272
Dziobek, I., 570

Eastman, N., 649
Eaton, N. R., 151
Eaton, W. W., 323
Eaves, L. J., 151
Eberwine, J., 70
Ecker, C., 150, 344
Eckert, E., 382
Eckshtain, D., 123
Edden, R. A. E., 306
Eddy, K. T., 370
Edenberg, H., 82
Edlow, B. L., 70
Edvinsson, S., 81
Edwards, A. C., 463
Edwards, F., 168, 606
Egervari, G., 461, 463
Ehlers, A., 278, 280
Ehrlich, S., 530
Eickhoff, S. B., 166, 167, 169, 201, 319, 427, 522
Einstein, E. B., 483
Eisenberg, C., 374
Eisenberg, D., 73, 251
Eisenberger, N., 222, 273, 574
Ekstron, T., 534
Elamin, M., 436
Elbert, T., 101, 104, 105, 272, 284, 285, 291, 292, 294, 342, 518
Elder, J., 374
Elhai, J., 292
Elia, J., 200
Elices, M., 477
Elis, O., 534
Elledge, L. C., 249
Ellenberg, S., 539
Ellenberger, H. F., 33, 144, 357
Ellicott, A., 247
Elliott, L., 357
Elliott, R., 32, 35
Ellis, A., 402
Elsabbagh, M., 192
Elvsashagen, T., 220
Emrich, H. M., 534
Enck, P., 56
Endicott, J., 243
English, H., 324
Engman, J., 63
Enoch, M. A., 252
Epel, E. S., 220, 265
Epperson, C. N., 277
Epstein, A., 326
Erbes, C., 110
Erdberg, P., 146
Erdelyi, M., 144
Erickson, K., 620
Erkinjuntti, T., 611
Ernberg, G., 13, 86
Ernst, C., 252
Ernst, M., 177, 178
Erritzoe, D., 228, 477
Ertel, K., 621

Ertl, V., 285
Erwin, P., 436
Escobar, C., 371
Escott-Price, V., 82
Eshleman, S., 151
Eskra, D., 289
Eslinger, D., 120, 645
Esteller, M., 600
Esterberg, M., 520
Estroff, S. E., 32, 537, 541
Etkin, A., 151, 152, 219, 220, 324
Etter, K., 537
Eubig, P., 200
Eustache, F., 610
Evans, A., 139
Evans, C. J., 453, 479
Evans, D. A., 606
Evans, D. D., 527
Evans, I. E. M., 594
Everitt, B. J., 481
Evert, P., 98
Evins, A. E., 474
Ewing, C., 635, 643
Exner, J. E., 145
Eyberg, S. M., 183
Eyler, A., 436
Eyles, D., 520
Eynan, R., 551

Fabbri-Destro, M., 176
Fabiani, M., 599
Fabrega, H., 505
Fahn, S., 357
Faigman, D., 648
Fairbank, J. A., 292
Fairburn, C., 391, 394
Fairchild, G., 182
Fairweather-Schmidt, A. K., 396
Faith, M., 342
Faja, S., 190, 191
Falcon, C., 600
Falcone, G. J., 82
Falconer, E. M., 291
Fallon, A., 378
Fallon, B. A., 330
Faludi, G., 123
Fan, C. C., 520, 528
Fang, A., 40, 332
Fanibunda, S. E., 81
Farahany, N. A., 70
Faraone, S., 82, 201, 532
Farber, B. A., 32
Farde, L., 533
Faria, V., 63
Farley, S., 202
Farre, M., 477
Farrer, L., 452
Farrow, J., 330
Fassino, S., 393
Faul, M., 615
Fauquier, L., 81
Fauria, K., 600
Faustman, W. O., 532
Fauth-Buhler, M., 177

Fava, G., 228, 327
Fava, L., 326
Fava, M., 31, 219, 220
Favorite, T., 251
Fawcett, G., 268
Fazel, S., 520, 630, 645
Fealko, C., 186, 187
Febo-Vazquez, I., 415
Feder, A., 265
Fehr, C., 463
Feinstein, A., 358, 359
Felmingham, K. L., 291
Felthous, A. R., 644
Feng, C., 319
Feng, Q., 387
Feng, X., 217
Feng, Y., 344
Ferland, J. N., 471, 472
Fernandez de la Cruz, L., 330
Fernandez-Real, J., 55
Fernyhough, C., 532
Feron, F., 520
Ferraguti, G., 415
Ferrao, Y. A., 330
Ferrarelli, F., 121
Ferraz, L., 549
Ferretti, A., 411
Ferri, C., 606
Fetissov, S. O., 388
Feygin, D., 330
Fichter, M., 356, 391
Field, M., 127
Fiete, I. R., 71
Figee, M., 230, 335
Filippi, C. A., 309
Finan, P. H., 477
Finau, S., 378
Fineberg, N., 330, 333
Finer, L., 409
Finger, S., 15, 23
Fink, G., 357
Fink, M., 513
Finlay, S., 265, 277
Fins, J. J., 70
Finucane, H. K., 82
Fiore, M., 415
Firestone, P., 424
First, M. B., 168, 177
Fischer, C. E., 81
Fischer, H., 319
Fisher, M., 540
Fisher, R., 113, 648
Fisher, T., 410
Fisher, W., 29
Fishman, I., 192
Fitzgerald, D. A., 320
Fitzgerald, J. M., 319
Fitzsimons, C., 291
Fjermestad, K. W., 321
Flamarique, I., 388
Flanagan, E. H., 156, 158
Fletcher, P., 532
Flinchum, M., 408
Flinn, M. V., 277
Flint, A., 229

Flor, H., 177
Floris, D., 81, 192
Flory, J. D., 283
Fluck, C., 415
Flux, M. C., 271
Foa, E., 294, 329, 335
Fobian, A. D., 357
Fodisch, C., 427
Fogelman, P., 235
Folke, S., 394
Folks, D., 364
Folley, B. S., 523
Fonagy, P., 34, 572
Fonseca, F., 477
Fonseca-Pedrero, E., 505
Fontanesi, L., 408
Forbes, D., 280
Forbes, M. F., 151
Forbes, M. K., 151
Ford, C., 364
Ford, J., 532
Forman, E., 123
Forman-Alberti, A., 309
Fornito, A., 178
Forster, G., 602
Forstner, A. J., 244, 245
Foster, J. A., 55
Foti, D., 612, 614
Fotopoulou, A., 343
Foussias, G., 510
Fowler, J. S., 452, 455, 481
Fowler, K., 574
Fox, A., 268
Fox, B., 638
Fox, N., 61, 174, 175, 309
Fox, P. T., 427
Fox, S., 455
Fracalanza, K., 313
Fralick, M., 615
Frances, A., 160, 396, 469, 644
Francois, M., 388
Frangou, S., 150, 532
Frank, J., 463
Frank, R., 97–99
Franke, B., 151, 182, 201
Franklin, J., 389
Franklin, M., 329, 335
Franko, D., 395
Frans, O., 63
Fredrickson, B., 245
Fredriksen, M., 201
Fredrikson, M., 63, 319
Freed, G., 377
Freedman, R., 523
Freemantle, N., 317
Frei, O., 122, 244, 520, 528
Freimer, N. B., 84, 244
Freire, E., 35
Freitag, C. M., 182
French, L., 149
Frese, F., 536
Freudenreich, O., 31
Freund, G., 222, 271
Frias, A., 551
Fricchione, G., 68, 137

Frick, A., 63
Frick, P., 147, 182, 183, 184, 197
Friedman, M., 278, 283, 292, 342, 352
Friedman, N., 81, 82–83, 196
Fries, E., 306
Fries, G. R., 81
Frisoni, G., 566
Fristad, M. A., 247
Friston, K., 72, 153, 220
Frith, C., 532
Frith, U., 191
Fritsche, L. G., 609
Frodl, T., 220
Froguel, P., 372
Frost, R., 334
Frueh, B., 292
Frumin, M., 525, 528
Fruzzetti, A., 580
Frye, M. A., 244
Frye, R., 81
Fryer, A., 330
Fu, E., 371
Fu, T. J., 408
Fuchs, E., 306
Fuentes, J. J., 477
Fuentes-Dura, I., 81
Fugl-Meyer, K. S., 417
Fujiwara, S., 56
Fukui, H., 186
Fullard, J. F., 83
Fullerton, C., 254, 292
Funke, K., 306
Furmark, T., 63, 319
Furukawa, T., 198, 318, 327
Fusar-Poli, P., 530

Gabbard, G. O., 144
Gabbert, F., 648
Gabriele, S., 190
Gabrieli, J. D. E., 532
Gaebel, W., 463
Gafoor, R., 283
Gagne, C., 301
Gahm, G., 254
Gaines, J., 555
Galaburda, A. M., 97–99
Galardi, T. R., 187
Galatzer-Levy, I., 280
Galea, S., 280
Galen, 15
Galińska-Skok, B., 121
Galizia, R., 408
Gallardo-Pujol, D., 552
Gallese, V., 176
Galley, J. D., 388
Gallinat, J., 177
Gallo, A., 430
Gallop, R. J., 255, 581
Galvan, A., 178
Gama Marques, J., 551
Gamboa, H., 59
Gandal, M. J., 192
Gang, J., 219, 281
Gao, L., 602

Gao, X., 532
Gao, Y., 567
Garaulet, M., 371
Garb, H. N., 144
Garcia, M., 436
Garcia-Falgueras, A., 435
Garcia-Sanchez, A. M., 520
Gard, T., 314
Gardner, C., 220
Garner, W., 270
Garraza, L., 256
Garre-Olmo, J., 55
Garrett-Bakelman, 122
Garrido, G., 566
Garriock, H., 183
Garriz, M., 388, 549
Garvey, M., 152
Gaser, C., 435
Gaspar, H., 82, 244, 245
Gaudio, S., 384–386
Ge, T., 122
Geary, R. C., 630
Gebremariam, A., 377
Geddes, J., 244, 248
Gelernter, J., 82, 221, 283, 452
Geller, D. A., 333, 334
Geller, J., 29
Genovese, G., 522
Gentili, C., 580
Georgakis, M. K., 222
Georgiades, K., 308
Georgiou-Karistianis, N., 619
Gerig, G., 527
Gerken, K., 621
Germain, S., 621
Gernsbacher, M., 188
Gerretsen, P., 81
Geschwind, D., 83, 186, 191
Ghaffar, O., 358, 359
Ghasemi, M., 327
Ghosh, S., 267
Ghouzali, I., 388
Giacino, J. T., 70
Giangrande, E. J., 82
Giarelli, E., 186
Gibbs, R., 268
Gibson, G., 83
Gibson, J., 220
Giedd, J., 177, 528
Gielen, J., 61
Gilbert, A., 333
Gilbert, J. A., 54
Gilbert, P., 224
Gilbertson, M., 290
Gillberg, C., 186, 191
Gillespie, E. M., 314
Gillespie, N. A., 474
Gillihan, S., 294
Gilman, S. E., 285
Gilman, S. R., 191
Gilmore, J. H., 527
Gingell, C., 410
Gioia, G. A., 617
Giraldo-Chica, M., 527
Giribaldi, B., 228, 477

Giromini, L., 146
Gispert, J. D., 600
Gitlin, M., 227, 247
Giuliano, C., 481
Gjesvik, N., 353
Glabe, C., 621
Glade, M., 484
Glahn, D., 525
Glannon, W., 149
Glaser, R., 270, 271
Glasofer, D., 392
Glasser, D., 410
Glasser, R. J., 94
Glauer, M., 325
Glaze, L., 121
Gleason, M. M., 181
Gleaves, D., 350
Glenn, A., 567
Glenn, D., 322, 323
Glennon, J. C., 319
Gliga, T., 190
Glikmann-Johnston, Y., 619
Gloster, A., 327
Glymour, M., 621
Glynn, S. M., 32, 537, 541
Gnanapragasam, S., 283
Gochman, P., 528
Godbout, N., 569
Godichard, V., 621
Goes, F. S., 84, 244
Goff, D., 31
Goghari, V., 525
Gogtay, N., 520
Gold, J., 228, 280, 477
Gold, S. M., 219, 220
Goldberg, J., 243, 283
Goldberg, S., 36, 540
Goldfried, M., 231
Golding, J., 81
Goldman, B., 193
Goldman, D., 252, 463
Goldman, H., 535
Goldman, M., 228
Goldman, S. M., 55
Goldman-Mellor, S., 525
Goldmeier, D., 421
Goldsmith, S., 249
Goldstein, M. J., 247
Goldstein, R., 453, 456–458
Goldston, D., 256
Goldstone, R. L., 49, 71
Gollub, R., 530
Golmard, J., 244
Golofast, B., 520
Gomes, F. V., 532
Gomez, A., 435
Gomez, J., 319
Gomez-Gil, E., 435
Gomot, M., 186, 188
Goncalves, B., 551
Gong, C.-X., 606
Gong, Q., 528, 532
Gonzalez, R., 474
Gonzalez-Barrio, R., 371
Gonzalez-Liencres, C., 175

Good, M.-J. D., 139
Goodkind, D., 594
Goodman, A., 452–454
Goodman, S. H., 217
Goodman, W., 329, 331, 333, 335
Goodwin, F., 238, 239, 244, 245, 248
Goodwin, G., 248
Goodyer, I., 182, 221
Gooren, L., 434, 435
Gopalakrishna, G., 537, 538
Gordon, B., 227, 599
Gordon, J. A., 70
Gordon, R., 382, 389
Gordovez, F. J. A., 244
Gore, W. L., 553
Gormley, P., 82
Gorno-Tempini, M., 606, 612, 614
Gotlib, I. H., 217
Gottesman, I., 81, 122, 252, 561
Gottlieb, J. D., 32, 537, 541
Gotzsche-Astrup, O., 585
Gouba, N., 388
Goudriaan, A., 488
Gould, T., 180, 228, 252
Gow, A. J., 600
Grabe, H. J., 220
Grabowski, T., 97–99
Grace, A., 532, 533
Gracio, J., 551
Grados, M., 330
Grady, C., 70
Graeff, F., 327
Graf, P., 621
Graff, A., 81
Grafton, B., 304
Graham, C., 408, 418
Gramunt, N., 600
Grandin, T., 164, 187, 188
Graner, J. L., 385
Granseth, B., 53, 607
Grant, B., 219, 560, 574, 579, 580
Grasby, K. L., 122
Grassi, L., 601
Grasso, D., 221
Gratton, G., 599
Gray, C., 59
Gray, J. A., 327
Gray, J. D., 268, 274, 275
Grazia, D., 300
Grazziotin, A., 418, 419
Greely, H. T., 70
Green, A. I., 532
Green, J. G., 198, 249, 308, 318
Green, M., 523
Green, R., 436, 602
Green, S. F., 461
Green, W., 387
Greenberg, B., 330
Greenberg, L., 35, 36, 231, 233
Greenberg, M., 173
Greene, A. L., 151
Greene, M., 292
Greenlee, M., 427
Greenwood, T. A., 523
Gregory, R. J., 583

Greif-Green, J., 167, 168
Grenier-Boley, B., 82, 609
Grether, J., 186
Greve, D. N., 314
Greven, C., 151
Grieger, T., 292
Griffiths, R. R., 477
Grigoriadis, S., 408
Grillon, C., 177, 178, 306
Grill-Spector, K., 319
Grilo, C., 552, 570
Grisham, J. R., 312
Griss, M. E., 523
Grisso, T., 636
Grob, G., 157
Grodin, E. N., 454
Gross, C., 306
Gross, S., 343, 344
Grossman, P., 36
Grove, J., 191
Grozdanovic, Z., 570
Grubaugh, A., 292
Gruber, H., 25, 308
Gruber, M. J., 167, 168, 198, 318
Gruenewald, T. L., 275
Grulich, A. E., 423
Grunder, G., 532
Grundmann, D., 427
Grunze, H., 244
Grutzendler, J., 609
Gruzelier, J., 202
Gu, B., 333
Gu, H., 81
Guarnaccia, P., 10, 139, 505
Gueorguieva, R., 533
Guerra-Reyes, L., 408
Guey, L. T., 620
Guillamon, A., 435
Gull, W., 382
Gulley, J. M., 452
Guloksuz, S., 505
Gunderson, J., 552, 568, 570, 580
Gunter, H., 272
Guo, L., 388
Guo, X., 167
Gupta, A., 385
Gupta, R., 630
Gur, R. C., 523
Gur, R. E., 523
Guralnik, O., 343–345
Gureje, O., 198, 318, 548, 550
Gurholt, T. P., 220
Gurling, H. M., 201
Gurney, J., 377
Gurung, R. A. R., 275
Gusella, J., 619
Gušić, S., 342
Gusnard, D., 531
Gutierrez, F., 549
Guyon-Harris, K. L., 175
Gylys, K. H., 621

Haaga, D. A., 39
Haase, A., 378

Haavik, J., 201
Habib, N., 81
Hacohen, N., 271
Hade, E. M., 388
Haenschel, C., 526
Hafferty, J. D., 220
Hagan, C., 182
Hagen, E., 182
Hagenaars, S. P., 220
Hagmann, P., 65, 462
Hahn, A., 319, 320, 574
Haier, R., 62
Haigh, E. P., 222, 223
Hairi, A., 166
Hajek, T., 243
Haker, S., 98
Hale, E. A., 177, 178
Hall, B., 79
Hall, J., 143, 415
Hall, L. S., 122
Hallbeck, M., 53, 607
Hallett, M., 357
Hallgren, M., 227
Hallgrimsson, B., 79
Halligan, P., 149, 152, 357
Hallquist, M., 151
Halmi, K., 389, 391
Halmoy, A., 201
Hamadani, K., 385
Hamer, R. M., 527
Hamilton, J. P., 235
Hammen, C., 221, 247
Hammerle, M., 199, 200
Hammerschlag, A. R., 122
Hammond, T. R., 522
Hampel, H., 610
Hampshire, A., 333
Han, B., 483
Han, W., 638
Handler, J., 155
Handsaker, R., 522
Haney, C., 646
Hannah, S. D., 139
Hanson, D., 81
Hanson, J. L., 567
Happe, F., 191
Haq, A., 228
Hardaway, J., 380, 388
Hardy, G. E., 231
Hardy, K., 540
Hare, R., 563, 564, 566
Harenski, C. L., 567
Hariri, A. R., 268
Harkins, L., 430
Harkness, K. L., 217
Harma, M., 220
Harned, M. S., 255, 581
Harpending, H., 88
Harrington, H., 199, 200, 525
Harrington, K., 283
Harris, K. M., 621
Harris, R. E., 306
Harris, S., 600
Harrison, B. J., 221, 302
Harrison, P. J., 244

Harro, J., 388
Harrow, M., 504, 510
Harry, B., 645
Hart, C. E., 81
Hart, H., 200
Hart, L. M., 382
Hartl, C. L., 83
Hartmann, A., 370
Hartocollis, A., 634
Harvey, P., 81, 191
Harwood, J. C., 122
Hasin, D., 219, 451, 471
Hasler, F., 477
Hassan, A., 615
Hasuzawa, S., 334
Hatch, M., 119
Hatoum, A. S., 45, 455
Hauberg, M. E., 83
Haugland, B., 321
Haukvik, U. K., 220
Hauri, P., 57
Havdahl, A., 191
Havik, O. E., 321
Havretsky, H., 245
Hawes, D. J., 182
Hawkeswood, S. E., 379
Hawkins, K. A., 523
Hawton, K., 248
Hay, M. C., 139
Hayden, B., 444
Hayden, E. Y., 621
Hayes, A., 231
Hayes, R., 232, 314, 417
Hayes, R. A., 530
Hayes, S. C., 40, 232, 314
Hayes-Skelton, S. A., 314
Hazlett, E., 344, 345
He, D., 452
He, H., 217
He, J., 308
He, W., 594
He, Y., 201
He, Z., 301
Healy, K., 168
Heard, E., 79
Heath, A. C., 151
Hebert, L. E., 606
Hecker, T., 284
Heckman, T. G., 123
Hedman, A. M., 522
Heekeren, H. R., 570
Heeringa, S. G., 254
Hegarty, S., 283
Hegenscheid, K., 220
Heidkamp, D., 522
Heiervang, E. R., 321
Heiman, J., 408
Heimberg, R., 320
Heindel, W., 358, 360
Heinrichs, M., 319
Heinssen, R., 32, 152, 537, 541
Heinz, A., 177
Hellemann, G., 523
Heller, E. A., 262, 271, 272, 273
Heller, I., 188

Hellhammer, D. H., 306
Helms, J. E., 139
Hen, R., 105, 306
Henderson, D., 31, 68, 137
Henderson, H. A., 309
Heng, V., 646
Hennessey, J., 201
Henn-Haase, C., 284
Henquet, C., 474
Henriques, R., 423, 427
Henriques-Calado, J., 551
Henry, C., 244
Herbenick, D., 408
Herbert, J., 579
Herbert, T., 271
Herbet, G., 71
Herd, P., 387
Herm, K., 574
Herman, A., 452
Herman, J., 267
Herman, W., 377
Hermenau, K., 284
Hernandez-Gonzalez, T., 371
Hernaus, D., 530
Heron, E. A., 255
Herrell, R., 283, 284, 291
Herring, M., 227
Herrmann, N., 222
Hersen, M., 117, 118
Heslenfeld, D., 200
Hettema, J., 306
Hetu, S., 319
Heuft, G., 358, 360
Heuser, I., 570
Hewitt, J., 463
Heyes, C., 175, 176
Hibar, D. P., 220
Hickman, R. A., 204
Hicks, C., 636
Hicks, T. R., 199
Hiday, V., 638
Higuchi, S., 497
Hill, M. N., 268, 274, 275
Hill, P. L., 549
Hiller, W., 356
Himmerich, H., 271
Hindley, G. F. L., 520, 528
Hinkel, H., 284, 291
Hinkov, H., 198, 318
Hinshaw, S., 196, 201, 245
Hinton, D., 36, 326
Hiripi, E., 380
Hirota, K., 228
Hirsch, J., 232, 320
Hitzemann, R., 481
Hiwatashi, A., 334
Ho, B., 530
Ho, C.-L., 284
Ho, L. C., 232
Hobbs, K. A., 553
Hochberg, L. R., 70
Hodapp, R., 204
Hodes, G. E., 222
Hodges, H., 186, 187
Hodgkinson, C. A., 252

Hodgson, H., 191
Hoehn, D., 220
Hoek, H. W., 370
Hoels, M., 291
Hoerzer, G., 59
Hoeve, M., 267
Hoffer, A., 517
Hoffman, E., 204
Hoffman, R., 532
Hofler, M., 474
Hofman, A., 220, 370
Hofman, M., 49, 435
Hofmann, H. A., 81
Hofmann, S., 36, 40, 320
Hogan, S., 199, 200
Hogarty, G., 540
Hoge, C., 283, 284, 291
Hoge, E. A., 314
Holaway, R., 320
Holland, D., 609
Holland, L., 379, 392, 396
Holland, S. K., 246
Hollander, E., 329–331, 343–345, 579
Hollenbeck, A., 620
Holliday, E., 180
Holliday, J., 270
Hollister, L. E., 476
Hollon, N. G., 220
Hollon, S., 39, 153, 231, 234, 235, 364
Holloway, H., 292
Holmans, P. A., 244, 245, 609
Holmes, A., 166, 268
Holoyda, B. J., 430
Holroyd, T., 61
Holsinger, R. M. D., 610
Holt, R. J., 81, 192
Holtmann, M., 202
Holton, G., 19
Holtzheimer, P., 228, 229
Holtzman, D., 605–609
Holub, C., 374
Holz, N. E., 166, 169
Holzel, B. K., 314
Honda, K., 55
Hong, J., 12, 151
Hong, K. K., 232
Hoogendoorn, M. L. C., 230
Hoogman, M., 201
Hooker, C. I., 530
Hope, D., 320
Hope, L., 648
Hopfer, C., 463
Hopko, D. R., 219
Hopwood, C. J., 553
Horan, W., 523
Horesh, D., 284
Hori, H., 265
Horn, S. R., 265
Hormes, J. M., 379
Hornbacher, M., 368
Horst, F., 230
Horvath, T., 373
Horwitz, A. G., 251
Hosman, C., 114
Hotopf, M., 283

Hough, C., 292
Hough, R. L., 292
Houshyar, S., 221
Houts, R., 199, 200, 525
Howard, D. M., 220
Howes, O. D., 532
Howrigan, D. P., 84, 244
Hoyt, D. W., 192
Hoza, B., 201
Hsiao, E. Y., 55, 192, 271
Hu, C.-Y., 198, 318
Hu, D. W., 72, 220
Hu, H.-Y., 198, 318
Hu, S., 480
Hu, Y., 78, 283
Huang, X., 620
Huang, Y., 548, 550
Huckins, L. M., 283
Hudry, K., 192
Hudson, J., 307, 380
Huebel, C., 82
Huettel, S., 53
Huey, S. J. Jr., 32
Hughes, M., 151
Huijbers, M., 232
Huizink, A., 272
Hulbert, C., 520
Hulle, C., 183
Hulshoff Pol, H. E., 522, 530
Humphreys, K. L., 175, 217
Humpston, C. S., 510
Hunsley, J., 145
Huntenburg, J. M., 232
Hunter, C. J., 283
Hunter, E. C. M., 343
Hunter, R. G., 268, 274, 275
Hurd, Y. L., 471, 472
Hurford, G., 182
Hurles, M. E., 191
Hurt, E., 201
Hutsebaut, J., 586
Huxley, J., 517
Huys, Q. J. M., 305
Hwang, I., 249, 457, 458, 550
Hwang, J., 151
Hwang, W.-C., 232
Hyde, J. S., 219
Hyman, B. T., 70
Hyman, S., 70, 149, 152, 178, 455, 537, 538

Iaccarino, L., 606
Iacoboni, M., 176, 192
Iacono, W. G., 380
Ibrahim, M. A. A., 271
Ide, J. S., 480
Igarashi, K. M., 605
Ikram, A., 319
Ikram, M. A., 220
Illes, J., 70
Imrey, P. B., 648
Ingram, L., 391
Insel, T., 32, 81, 149, 152, 153, 155
Iqbal, K., 606

Irimia, A., 98
Irwin, M. R., 222
Isern, N. G., 192
IsHak, W., 418
Ishigami, K., 334
Isidori, A. M., 415
Isohanni, M., 519
Isomura, K., 330
Israel, S., 525
Ithman, M. H., 537, 538
Ittermann, B., 177
Ivanov, I., 201
Ivanova, M., 151
Iversen, L., 482
Iwamoto, K., 273
Iyegbe, C. O., 84
Iyengar, S., 228

Jablensky, A., 13, 86
Jabr, F., 187
Jackson, E., 139
Jackson, J. H., 23
Jackson, V. H., 139
Jacoby, R. J., 328, 329, 334
Jaddoe, V. W. V., 370
Jaffee, S., 121, 151
Jagger, C., 602
Jagust, J. W., 606
Jagust, W., 609
Jahanshad, N., 220
Jak, A. J., 621
James, D. J., 121
James, P. A., 155
Jamison, K., 238, 239, 244, 245, 247, 248
Janabi, M., 606
Janak, P. H., 454, 455
Jang, K. L., 552
Janicak, P., 230
Janiri, D., 173
Jankovic, J., 357
Jannini, E. A., 408
Jansen, A., 358, 360
Jansen, I. E., 609
Jansen, P. R., 122
Janssen, E., 408, 410
Jansson, J. K., 54, 192
Jardri, R., 532
Jarrett, R. B., 39, 234
Jarv, A., 388
Jason, L., 506
Jay, E.-L., 344
Jaya, E. S., 505
Jaycox, L., 293
Jeglic, E., 430
Jena, A. B., 199
Jenike, M., 329–330, 333
Jeremian, R., 81
Ji, Y., 217
Jia, C.-X., 251
Jia, H., 387
Jia, X., 84, 244
Jiang, C., 78
Jiang, H., 444

Jiang, T., 72
Jiang, W., 201
Jimenez-Shahed, J., 335
Jimura, K., 146
Jin, R., 326
Jobe, T., 504, 510
Jogia, J., 150
John, S., 505
Johnson, B., 65
Johnson, C., 380, 391
Johnson, D. M., 552
Johnson, E., 452, 455, 463
Johnson, J., 243, 247, 341, 342
Johnson, K. V., 55
Johnson, L. S. M., 70
Johnson, M., 190, 192
Johnson, M. W., 477
Johnson, R., 222, 271, 639
Johnson, S., 243, 245, 247
Johnson, V., 412, 420, 421, 425, 427
Johnson, W., 524, 600
Johnston, L., 451
Johnston, P., 150
Joiner, T., 249, 379
Jollant, F., 252
Jolles, D. D., 178
Jonas, K., 151
Jonasson, M., 63
Jones, A., 446
Jones, C. M., 483
Jones, E. J. H., 190
Jones, E. O., 32
Jones, I., 84, 244
Jones, L., 84, 244
Jones, O. D., 647
Jones, P., 119, 271, 519, 538
Jones, R., 260, 278, 601, 620
Jones, W., 191
Jonsson, E., 149
Jordan, B. K., 292
Jordan, K., 602
Joshi, S., 340
Jovanovic, T., 149
Jove, M., 55
Joyal, C. C., 437
Jucker, M., 619
Juhasz, G., 252
Jun, W., 387
Jung, R., 530
Junge, A., 436
Junginger, J., 510
Juniper, U., 539
Junque, C., 435
Juruena, M. F., 220
Just, M. A., 252

Kaas, J., 49, 65
Kaas, M. J., 319
Kaati, G., 81
Kabat-Zinn, J., 36
Kaczkurkin, A. N., 178
Kaddurah-Daouk, R., 55
Kaera, A., 586
Kafka, M. P., 430

Kagan, J., 309
Kahn, R. S., 522, 530, 591
Kaiser, A., 166, 169
Kaiser, N., 201
Kakarala, S., 219, 281
Kalin, N., 268
Kalivas, P., 456
Kalus, O., 560
Kambe, G., 411
Kaminski, J. A., 122
Kamio, Y., 186
Kamitaki, N., 522
Kamp Dush, C., 388
Kamphaus, R., 147
Kana, V., 222
Kandel, D., 482
Kandel, E. R., 302
Kane, J., 32, 535, 537, 541
Kane, R., 536
Kang, C., 527
Kang, D., 192, 333
Kang, H. K., 254
Kang, J., 410
Kang, L., 388
Kang, M., 334
Kanner, L., 186
Kao, T.-C., 254
Kaplan, A., 391, 393, 579
Kaplan, G., 377
Kaplan, K., 560, 574, 579, 580
Kaplan, M., 423
Kappelmann, N., 222
Kapur, S., 82
Karabanov, A., 533
Karadag, N., 520, 528
Karam, A., 548, 550
Karaman, R., 605
Karas, K. H., 570
Karas, P. J., 335
Karatsoreos, I. N., 268, 274, 275
Kargel, C., 427
Karlsgodt, K. H., 526–528
Karlsson, R., 122
Karsies, T., 615
Karstoft, K.-I., 284
Kasen, S., 243, 247, 341, 342
Kasper, S., 319, 320
Katagiri, N., 530
Kato, K., 334
Kato, T., 273
Katsnelson, A., 81
Katz, C. L., 645
Katzman, M. A., 389
Katznelson, H., 394
Kauffman, B. Y., 314
Kaufman, E. A., 151
Kaufman, J., 221
Kaufmann, T., 520, 528
Kaur, N., 31
Kawas, C., 621
Kay, D. R., 462
Kay, J., 168, 177
Kay, K., 319
Kaye, W., 384, 385–386, 388, 391
Kazdin, A. E., 184

Keane, T. M., 283, 292
Keatinge, C., 515
Keck, P. E., 244
Keefe, J., 34, 313
Keel, P., 379, 392, 396
Keirns, C., 377
Kellaher, D. C., 430
Keller, M. B., 213
Keller, M. C., 82–83, 517, 520
Kelley, K., 222, 271
Kellner, R., 352
Kelly, A., 532
Kelly, C., 73
Kelly, M. M., 330
Kelly, P., 54
Kelsoe, J., 82
Kemeny, M., 220, 265, 271
Kemp, A. H., 291
Kendler, K. S., 121, 151, 220, 306, 474, 551
Kenis, G., 520
Kennard, A., 120, 645
Kennedy, J. L., 81
Kerber, A., 553
Kerestes, R., 221
Kernberg, O., 555, 568, 584
Keshavan, M., 177, 514, 522, 524
Kessler, R., 151, 167, 168, 198, 212, 214, 215, 249, 254, 308–312, 318, 323, 326, 380, 457, 458, 487, 548, 550–552, 560, 561, 570, 579, 580
Kettner, H., 228
Keuthen, N. J., 329, 330, 333
Keverne, E. B., 81
Kevin, M., 617
Kew, K., 320
Keyes, K., 451
Keys, A., 389
Keysers, C., 192
Khalid-Khan, S., 295
Khammash, D., 595, 598
Khan, M. T., 387
Khandaker, G. M., 222, 271
Khona, M., 71
Kibaly, C., 453, 479
Kiecolt-Glaser, J., 270, 271
Kieffer, B. L., 479
Kiehl, K., 566, 567
Kiely, D., 601
Kikinis, R., 98
Kilpatrick, D., 280
Kilwein, T., 233
Kim, H. Y., 620
Kim, R. C., 621
Kim, Y., 192, 265, 586
King, A., 251, 466
King, J. W., 620
King, M., 123, 316
King, N., 307
King, S., 520, 522
King-Casas, B., 572
Kingdon, D., 539
Kingsep, P., 539
Kingston, D., 423, 424
Kinsey, A., 403
Kipling, K., 574

Kircanski, K., 326
Kircher, T., 324
Kirmayer, L. J., 353
Kitayama, S., 68
Kivimaki, M., 220, 222
Klaver, M., 434
Klebanoff, M. A., 119
Kleiman, S. C., 387, 388
Klein, L. C., 275, 276
Kleineidam, L., 609
Kleinman, J., 510
Kleinman, S. B., 650
Kleinplatz, P. J., 416
Klimaj, V., 411
Klin, A., 191
Kling, M., 81, 245
Kloft, L., 472
Klonsky, E., 568
Klucken, T., 324
Klump, K. L., 380
Klumpp, H., 319
Knecht, S., 358, 360
Knight, E., 536
Knight, R., 54, 56, 192
Knopik, V., 121
Knowles, J., 330
Knudsen, G. P., 551
Knutson, B., 453
Knyazev, G., 13, 59
Ko, J., 644
Kobayashi, M. A., 371
Koch, W., 610
Koebach, A., 291
Koenen, K., 149, 284
Koenigs, M., 567
Koesterer, R., 452
Koga, S. F., 174
Kohler, B., 415
Koike, S., 530
Kok, B. C., 284
Kolbe-Alexander, L., 372
Kolins, S., 201
Kolla, N. J., 570
Kolodny, R., 425, 427
Kolstad, A., 353
Komaiko, K., 537
Kometer, M., 477
Konopaske, G., 533
Konrad, A., 427
Konrad, C., 324, 358, 360
Konrad, K., 167, 201
Koob, G. F., 482, 452
Koopmans, F., 122
Koretz, D., 308
Koroshetz, W. J., 70
Korosi, A., 291
Korslund, K. E., 255, 581
Korten, A., 13, 86
Kortright, K. E., 638
Kosel, M., 228, 229
Kosson, D. S., 567
Kotler, J. S., 183
Kotov, R., 151, 152, 548, 550
Kotowska, D., 387
Kovacs, G. G., 621

Kovatcheva-Datchary, P., 387
Kowal, P., 594
Kozak, M., 152, 335
Kozak, R., 319
Kraaijenvanger, E. J., 166, 169
Kraan, C. W., 601
Kraemer, H., 394
Kraft, E., 594, 620
Kragel, P. A., 385
Kral, T. R. A., 36
Kramer, A., 620
Kramer, J., 605, 606
Kramer, U., 586
Kranzler, H., 452
Krapohl, E., 122
Krause-Utz, A., 567, 570
Kreipe, R., 369
Krendl, A. C., 10
Kreps, D., 300
Kreukels, B. P. C., 434
Krimsky, M., 306
Kring, A., 534
Krishnan, V., 630
Kroff, J., 372
Kronholm, E., 220
Krueger, R., 151, 183, 423, 553
Krueger, T., 427
Kruger, T. H. C., 426, 427
Krull, F., 244
Krystal, J., 221, 533
Kubicki, M., 528
Kuceyeski, A., 150
Kucukali, F., 609
Kuczenski, R., 482
Kuepper, R., 474
Kugel, H., 358, 360
Kuhle, L. F., 427
Kuhlman, K. R., 222
Kuja-Halkola, R., 520
Kulka, R. A., 284, 292
Kumar, A., 245
Kumar, K., 522
Kumar, N., 229
Kupka, R. W., 244
Kuppens, S., 123
Kurian, B. T., 32, 537, 541
Kurudenkandy, F. R., 53, 607
Kushak, R. I., 192
Kutcher, J., 617
Kutscher, E., 537
Kuulasmaa, T., 609
Kuwano, Y., 56
Kuyken, W., 232
Kwak, Y. B., 530
Kwan, A. C., 476, 477
Kwon, J., 333
Kyle, J. A. M., 599
Kyzar, E. J., 452

La Via, M., 391
Laakso, M., 566
LaBar, K., 53, 385
LaBella, A. L., 8
Labonte, B., 252, 272

LaBrie, R., 457, 458, 550
Labus, J. S., 385
Labuschagne, I., 319
Lacey, E., 369
Lackland, D. T., 155
Lafleur, D., 329, 330, 333
Lage, K., 83
Lagercrantz, H., 167
Lagus, M., 220
Lahey, B., 151, 118, 183
Lai, C., 327
Laird, A., 427, 525
Lakicevic, N., 381
Lalor, E. C., 177
Lam, M., 122
Lamb, D., 283
Lamb, R., 120, 645
Lambert, D. G., 228
Lambert, E. V., 372
Lambert, H. K., 290
Lambert, J. C., 609
Lambert, M. J., 32
Lamberty, G. J., 110
Lamblin, M., 178
Lamers, F., 268
Lammers, C., 574
Lanctot, K. L., 222
Landau, S., 609
Landeros-Weisenberger, A., 331
Landis, R. S., 102
Landman, B. A., 527
Lane, C. J., 192
Lane, M., 548, 551, 552, 560, 561, 570, 579, 580
Lanfermann, H., 534
Lang, A., 357
Langbaum, J. B., 606
Langenecker, S. A., 234
Langguth, B., 427
Langleben, D., 649
Langstrom, B., 319
Langstrom, N., 428, 520
Lanius, R. A., 283, 342, 352
Lanocha, K., 230
Lanzenberger, R., 319, 320
Lapierre, M., 437, 520
Lara, C., 198, 318
Large, M., 474
Larochelle, M. R., 449
Laroi, F., 532, 534
Larson, C. L., 567
Larsson, H., 520
Lasek, A. W., 452
Lathrop, M., 177
Laton, J., 61
Latzman, R. D., 151, 152
Laughlin, S., 71
Laumann, E., 410, 413, 417, 418
Lauriello, J., 530, 537, 538
Lauzon, N., 292
Lavagnino, L., 393
LaVaque, T. J., 202
LaViolette, P., 532
Laviolette, S., 292
Law, P., 453, 479

Lawrence, A. A., 434
Lawson, A., 32
Lawton, E., 548
Laybutt, D., 80
Layton, T. J., 199
Lazar, S. W., 314
Lazaris, A., 606
Lazary, J., 251
Lazzeroni, C. L., 523
Le Grange, D., 380, 390
Le Hellard, S., 474
Le, H. N., 235
Leal, S. L., 599
LeBeau, R., 301, 322, 323
Leblond, C. S., 191
Leboyer, M., 244
Leckman, J., 329–331
LeDoux, J., 302, 303
Lee, D. J., 294
Lee, J., 151, 294, 377, 523
Lee, P. H., 82
Lee, S., 198, 214, 309–311, 318, 335, 548, 550
Lee, V. M.-Y., 621
Lee, Y., 387, 599
Leeuw, C. A., 552
LeFevre, M. L., 155
Legrand, R., 388
Lehman, C., 312
Leibbrand, R., 356
Leibenluft, E., 61, 178, 180
Leichsenring, F., 313
Lemay, J., 172
Lemos, J. C., 220
Lennox, B. R., 271
Lenoir, M., 372
Lenze, E., 306, 307
Lenzenweger, M., 548, 551, 552, 560, 561, 570, 579, 580
Leon, A., 243
Leong, G. B., 639
Lepine, J. P., 548, 550
Leung, A., 172
Levar, N., 335
LeVay, S., 402
Levenson, J., 424
Leverich, G. S., 244
Levey, D. F., 283
Levin, A. P., 650
Levin, E. A., 13
Levin, M. E., 36
Levin-Aspenson, H. F., 151
Levine, B., 229
Levinson, B., 410
Levitan, R. D., 393
Levitt, N. S., 372
Levy, B., 568, 569
Levy, H. C., 292, 294
Levy, K. N., 568, 569, 576, 578, 584
Levy, S., 186
Levy, T., 408
Lewinski, W., 648
Lewis, B. P., 275
Lewis, G., 503
Lewis, M., 164

Lewis, R. W., 417
Lewis, S., 538
Lewis-Fernandez, R., 139, 149, 326, 342, 352
Li, B., 72, 220, 283
Li, C., 81
Li, F., 528
Li, G., 451
Li, H., 292
Li, J., 387
Li, L., 301
Li, M., 284, 427, 411
Li, Q., 82
Li, R., 81
Li, S., 532
Li, T., 83, 319, 451, 609, 621
Li, W., 220
Li, Y., 83, 217, 283, 387
Liang, K., 330
Liao, B., 322, 323
Liberzon, I., 283
Lichtblau, N., 271
Lichtenstein, P., 191, 319, 320, 330, 343, 344, 520
Lieb, R., 474, 567, 570
Liebe, S., 59
Lieberman, D., 98
Lieberman, J., 168, 177, 527, 538
Lieberman, L., 306
Lieberman, M., 273, 574
Lietz, A. P., 449
Liewald, D. C., 599
Lifshitz, M., 232
Light, G. A., 523
Ligthart, S., 222
Lilienfeld, S., 144, 194, 340, 342, 351, 564, 574
Lill, C. M., 609
Lim, K., 110, 530, 532
Lim, L., 539
Limoncin, E., 408
Lin, A., 191, 520, 528
Lin, C., 72
Lin, D., 201
Lin, L. A., 316
Lin, R., 80, 301
Lin, T., 123
Lin, W., 83, 527
Lincoln, T. M., 505
Linden, M., 202
Lindesay, J., 601
Lindner, S., 349, 350
Lindsay, D. S., 648
Linehan, M. M., 255, 581
Links, P. S., 551
Linnell, J., 191
Linnman, C., 63
Linscott, R., 514
Lipowski, Z., 601
Lipschitz, D., 221
Lipson, S. K., 379
Lisdahl, K. M., 567
Liss, A., 318
Litwack, S. D., 294
Liu, F., 606

Liu, H., 222
Liu, J., 201, 528, 532
Liu, L., 532
Liu, Q., 217
Liu, W., 220
Liu, Z., 220
Liu-Ambrose, T., 621
Livesley, W. J., 552, 553, 555, 584
Livingstone, M. S., 319
Ljotsson, B., 321
Llewellyn, D. J., 594
Loa, P., 505
Lobban, F., 538
Lobelo, F., 374
Lobo, A., 319
Lobo, E., 319
Lochner, C., 330
Lock, J., 390
Lockhart, D., 78
Lockhart, S. N., 606
Loeb, K., 390
Loehlin, J., 121
Loehrer, E., 220
Loewenstein, R., 346, 349, 350, 351
Loewy, R., 540
Loeys, T., 402
Loftus, E., 648
Logan, J., 481
Loganathan, S., 505
Logothetis, N., 57, 59
Logue, S., 180
Lohr, J. B., 621
Lohrenz, T., 572
Lomax-Bream, L., 572
Lombardo, M., 191
London, E. D., 482
Loo, C., 230
Looman, J., 430
Loong, D., 638
Lopera, F., 606
Lopez, S., 10, 505
Loranger, A., 548, 551, 552, 560, 561, 570, 579, 580
Lord, C., 187, 190, 191
Lorenzetti, V., 319, 619
Lourdusamy, A., 177
Lovaas, O., 195
Lowry, C. A., 271
Lu, F., 167
Lu, H. B., 72, 220
Lu, J., 387
Lu, P., 605
Lu, Q., 55, 283
Lubar, J. F., 202
Lubberink, M., 63
Luber, M. J., 532
Lucas, N., 388
Lucassen, P., 291
Luck, S. J., 61
Luckenbaugh, D. A., 244
Luders, E., 435
Ludwig, K. U., 463
Lui, S., 528, 532
Luigjes, J., 335
Luis, J., 600

Luke, A., 372
Lukens, S., 341
Lund, B., 391
Lungu, A., 255, 581
Lunn, S., 394
Luo, J., 549
Luo, T., 83
Luo, Y., 319
Luquiens, A., 490, 497
Luria, A. R., 97
Luscher, C., 454, 455
Lussier, P., 424
Lutz, B., 472
Lykins, A., 411
Lykken, D., 122
Lynch, S. V., 54
Lynch, W. C., 382
Lynde, D. W., 32, 537, 541
Lynn, S., 32, 194, 202, 247, 340, 342, 351, 539
Lyons, M., 227
Lyons-Ruth, K., 172
Lysaker, P., 514
Lyu, J., 217

Ma, H., 232
MacDonald, A., xix, 3, 525, 601
MacDonald, M., 619
Macdougall, L., 533
Macias Saint-Gerons, D., 81
Maciejewski, P. K., 219, 281
Mack, K., 78
Mack, P., 78
Mackay-Sim, A., 520
Mackenzie, I., 612, 614
MacKenzie, T. D., 155
MacKillop, J., 490
MacLeod, A., 531
MacLeod, C., 304, 305
Maclin, E., 599
MacMillan, H. L., 514
Madan, A., 292
Madan, I., 283
Madonick, S. H., 533
Madrid, J. A., 371
Maedl, A., 284
Maesato, H., 497
Magee, W. J., 323
Magnotta, V., 530
Magnusson, S., 122
Mahapatra, A., 630
Maher, S., 534
Maier, S. F., 275
Maier, W., 463
Main, M., 171
Maiti, S., 522
Maixner, D. F., 228
Maj, M., 168, 177
Mak, M., 64
Makkar, R., 385
Makotkine, I., 283
Malafosse, A., 244
Maldonado, R., 55, 342
Malenka, R., 454, 455

Maleševi, A., 342
Malhi, G., 248, 514
Malhotra, D., 82
Malik, M., 191
Malik, R., 82
Malinowski, A., 81
Mallonee, S., 280
Maloney, K., 394
Maltzman, 496
Mancill, R. B., 312
Mandel, H., 329
Mandelkow, E., 605
Mandell, D., 186
Mandelli, L., 82
Mandl, R. C. W., 522
Manicavasagar, V., 243
Manji, H., 82
Mann, J. J., 252
Mann, K., 177
Mantione, M., 230, 335
Manuck, S. B., 166
Manwaring, J., 380
Manzano, O., 533
Marano, C., 81, 245
Marano, G., 518
Marcantonio, E., 601
Marchand, W., 245
Marcusson, J., 53, 607
Marcy, P., 32, 537, 541
Marder, S. R., 537
Margraf, J., 356, 408
Margulies, D., 232
Marian, Ş., 579
Marin, C. E., 321
Marioni, R. E., 220
Markham, L., 369
Markon, K. E., 123, 151, 183, 553
Markowitsch, H. J., 344
Markowitz, J., 570
Marks, S., 609
Marmar, C. R., 283, 284, 292
Marquand, A., 150
Marques, C., 551
Marques, L., 314
Marr, V., 427
Marsella, A. J., 12, 137
Marshall, J., 483
Marshall, M., 151
Marshall, R., 284
Marshall, W. L., 423, 430
Marsiske, M., 620
Marteinsdottir, I., 319
Martell, J., 477
Marti, C., 396
Martin, D., 80
Martin, H. C., 191
Martin, J., 84, 121, 166, 265
Martin, R., 487
Martinez, R., 202
Martinez-Aran, A., 81
Martinez-Zalacain, I., 302
Martinot, J.-L., 177
Martins Silva, A. S., 580
Martinsen, A. E., 609
Martins-Monteverde, C. M. S., 220

Martyr, A., 594
Marušić, I., 556
Marwaha, S., 227, 228, 477
Marx, B. P., 294
Mash, E., 145
Mash, H. H., 254
Mason, B., 471
Mason, N. L., 472
Massau, C., 427
Masters, W., 412, 420, 421, 425, 427
Matafonova, E., 388
Mataix-Cols, D., 200, 329–331
Mathalon, D. H., 530, 532
Mather, M., 598
Mathews, A., 82, 304, 305
Mathiesen, B. B., 394
Matoba, N., 83
Matschinger, H., 548, 550
Matsuo, A., 334
Matsushita, S., 497
Mattheisen, M., 244, 245
Matthews, A., 436
Matthews, B., 612, 614
Matthews, F., 594, 602
Matthews, J. J., 381
Mattingsdal, M., 517
Mattison, A., 602
Maust, D. T., 316
Mavranezouli, I., 320
Maxwell, R., 194, 198, 340, 342, 351
May, D. G., 477
May, M., 350
Mayer, E. A., 385
Mayes, S. D., 187
Mayne, P. E., 522
Mayneris-Perxachs, J., 55
Mayoral, M., 541
Mayo-Wilson, E., 320
Mayr, E., 517
Mays, V. M., 630
Mazaheri, A., 335
Mazmanian, S. K., 55, 56, 192
McAleavey, A., 315
McAllister, T., 615
McAninch, E. A., 606
McAnulty, R., 409
McCabe, R. E., 318
McCabe-Bennett, H., 313
McCann, J., 635, 643
McCann, U., 483, 484
McCarley, R., 525, 528, 532, 562
McCarroll, J. E., 254
McCarthy, B., 283
McCarthy, K. S., 34, 313
McCarthy-Jones, S., 532
McCartney, K., 172
McClanahan, S., 380
McClay, J., 84, 121, 166, 265
McClernon, F., 201
McClintick, J., 463
McCloughlin, G., 61
McClure, E., 178, 180
McCracken, J. T., 482, 602
McCrae, R., 555, 556
McCraken, J., 330

McCutcheon, R. A., 532
McDavid, J., 255, 581
McDermott, B., 265, 277
McDermott, J. M., 309
McDonald, J., 233
McDonald, W. M., 228
McDonough, M., 344, 345
McDonwell, C., 227
McDougle, C., 196
McElroy, S. L., 244
McEwen, B., 268, 274, 275
McFarlane, A. C., 280, 291
McGinty, E. E., 630
McGlashan, T., 552, 570
McGonagle, K., 151
McGovern, P., 444
McGowan, P., 272
McGrath, J., 505, 519, 520
McGue, M., 122, 380
McGuinness, O. P., 388
McGuire, H., 114
McGuire, L., 271
McGuire, P., 532, 534
McHugh, R. K., 461
McIntosh, A. M., 220
McIntosh, T., 505
McKeon, P., 244
McKeon, R., 256
McLaughlin, K. A., 167, 168, 175, 249, 290, 308
McLean, C. P., 292, 294
McLean, D., 505
McLeod, T. C. V., 617
McMahon, F. J., 244
McMahon, R. J., 183
McMakin, D. L., 252
McManus, S., 283
McMillan, A., 268
McMillen, J. C., 280
McMurran, M., 584
McNally, R. J., 280
McNamara, P., 466
McNaughton, N., 327
McNeill, G., 519, 599
McNulty, J. K., 249
McPartland, J. C., 192
McQuillin, A., 201, 244, 245
Meadows, E. A., 145
Meana, M., 411
Meaney, M., 80, 81, 166, 168, 272, 306
Mechawar, N., 252
Meehl, P., 141
Mefford, H., 204
Mehl, M., 98
Mehler, M. F., 204
Mehler, P. S., 380
Mehranfard, N., 327
Mehtala, J., 537
Meier, M., 199, 200, 474, 525
Meindl, T., 610
Meiser-Stedman, R., 40
Meissner, A., 81
Melle, I., 474
Mello, C., 78
Meloni, E. G., 283

Meltzer, M., 591
Menard, C., 222
Mendoza, J. K., 61
Menghi, M., 415
Mennes, M., 192
Mennin, D., 301
Menon, V., 72–74, 532
Mentink, L. J., 601
Menton, W. H., 143
Mentzel, H., 325
Menvielle, E., 436
Menzies, L., 333
Merad, M., 222
Mercaldo, S., 449
Merckelbach, H., 194, 340, 342, 351
Mercure, E., 192
Merikangas, K., 215, 268, 308
Merla, A., 411
Merz, C., 324
Merz, S., 229
Metcalf, C. A., 314
Metcalf, D., 602
Metcalf, P., 378
Mete, M., 314
Metzger-Abamukang, M. J., 254
Mevel, K., 610
Meyer, A., 272
Meyer, G., 145, 146
Meyer, J., 227
Meyer-Kalos, P. S., 32, 537, 541
Meyer-Linderberg, A., 68, 265, 573
Meyers, J. L., 219
Mezulis, A. H., 219
Mezzich, J., 69
Micangeli, G., 415
Michaelides, M., 452, 455
Michail, M., 510
Michalek, A. P., 201
Michelini, G., 151, 152
Mickes, L., 648
Mickey, B., 228, 234
Micklesfield, L. K., 372
Miguel, E., 329, 331
Miguel, P. M., 166, 168
Mihura, J. L., 145, 146
Miklowitz, D., 243, 247
Mikulincer, M., 173
Milanovic, S., 532
Miley, L. N., 638
Milgram, S., 71
Milham, M., 73, 532
Mill, J., 84, 121, 166, 265
Miller, A. L., 32, 537, 541
Miller, B., 606, 612, 614
Miller, C. A., 243, 621
Miller, G., 81, 149, 152, 271, 272, 523
Miller, L., 186
Miller, M., 251, 252, 292, 294, 494
Miller, M. B., 599
Miller, S., 271, 402
Miller, W., 251, 494
Miller, Z. A., 606
Millman, L. S. M., 343
Millon, T., 555
Mills, N., 246

Miltner, W., 325
Mineka, S., 302, 304, 309
Miner, M. H., 423
Minichino, A., 175
Minshew, N., 192
Mintz, J., 247, 255
Minzenberg, M., 525, 537
Miranda, J., 232
Miranda, R., 490
Mirashi, A., 648
Mirnics, K., 123
Mirsky, A., 149
Misaki, M., 290
Misiak, B., 64
Miskovich, T. A., 567
Mitchell, J., 281, 382, 391
Mitchell, P., 230
Mittal, V., 268, 560
Mitte, K., 327
Mizobe, T., 334
Mizzi, S., 319
Mneimneh, A., 198, 318
Mneimneh, Z., 198, 318
Mody, M., 72, 220
Moessner, R., 463
Moffitt, T., 84, 121, 166, 182, 199, 200, 265, 525
Mofitt, T., 84, 121, 166, 265
Mogavero, F., 319
Moghaddam, B., 177, 533
Mohnke, S., 426
Mohr, D. C., 219, 220
Mokros, A., 427
Molden, E., 520, 528
Moll, J., 566
Mollon, J., 503
Monahan, J., 648
Monastra, V. J., 202
Monninger, M., 166, 169
Monroe, S. M., 217
Mont, L., 388
Montague, P., 572
Montenegro, J. D., 83
Montenigro, P. H., 616
Montfort, S. J. T. Van., 601
Montgomery, G., 32, 232, 247
Montori, V., 436
Montorsi, F., 411
Moody, C., 602
Moons, T., 61
Moore, T. M., 191
Moore, Z., 410
Mora, G., 28
Moradian, A., 192
Moragues, N., 306
Moran, A., 110
Moran, G., 221
Moran, J., 284, 285
Moran, P., 283
Moran, S., 600
Moreira, E. D., 410, 417
Moreno, M., 541
Moreno-Grau, S., 609
Morey, L., 552, 555, 570
Morgan, C., 267

Moriarty, J., 649
Morin, J., 424
Morina, N., 291
Morley, T., 221
Mormino, E., 609
Morris, J. C., 606
Morris, J. N., 620
Morris, L., 314, 388
Morris, M., 80
Morris, S. E., 517
Morrison, A., 212, 539
Morrison, B., 212, 539
Morrison, P., 474
Morse, J. Q., 114
Mortara, P., 393
Mortazavi, F., 65
Morton, J., 326
Moseley, R. L., 81, 192
Moser, C., 423
Moser, E., 319, 320
Moskowitz, A., 585
Mostofsky, E., 615
Mostofsky, S., 201
Mountford, V., 391
Mourao-Miranda, J., 150
Moustafa, J., 372
Moutoussis, M., 177
Mowry, B., 505
Moya, A., 55
Mueller, B., 530, 532
Mueller, P. P., 449
Mueller, S., 610
Mueller, T., 243
Mueser, K., 32, 537, 541
Mulder, E., 272
Mulder, R., 580, 586
Mullan, R., 436
Muller, J., 291
Muller, R., 192
Muller, S., 83, 426
Muller, T. D., 56
Muller-Dahlhaus, F., 306
Mullins-Sweatt, S., 151, 557
Mulsant, B., 230
Munoz, D. P., 295
Munoz, R. F., 235
Murad, A., 436
Murad, M., 436
Muran, J., 34, 313, 585
Muratori, F., 191
Murawski, C., 178
Murayama, K., 334
Murch, S., 191
Murphy, C., 65, 150
Murphy, D., 32, 150, 330
Murphy, E. F., 56
Murphy, J., 14
Murphy, M. D., 262, 271, 272, 273
Murphy, R., 477
Murphy, W., 424
Murphy-Beiner, A., 477
Murray, G., 245
Murray, H. B., 370
Murray, J. E., 481
Murray, M. J., 187

Murray, R., 82, 474
Murray-Gregory, A. M., 255, 281
Murtagh, F. R., 606
Murthy, R. S., 505
Musto, D., 445
Muzny, D., 268
Myer, L., 198, 318
Mynett-Johnson, L., 244

Nadeau, S., 53
Nagamatsu, L., 621
Nagel, M., 122
Nagels, G., 61
Naifeh, J. A., 254
Naj, A. C., 609
Najavits, L., 295
Najt, P., 566
Nakamura, N., 146
Nakao, T., 200, 334
Naliboff, B., 385
Nandi, C., 284
Narr, K., 65
Narrow, W. E., 149
Narumoto, J., 302
Narva, A. S., 155
Nasar, S., 2
Nasca, C., 268, 274, 275
Nash, R. A., 648
Nasrallah, H. A., 514, 524
Nasser, M., 389
Nath, S., 53, 607
Nathan, P., 320, 539
Navidhamidi, M., 327
Nazareth, I., 317
Neacsiu, A. D., 255, 581
Neale, B. M., 84, 244
Neale, M., 151, 551, 306
Neary, D., 611
Neblett, E., 233
Nederveen, A., 335
Needham, B. D., 55
Neel, J. V., 371
Neer, S., 292
Neiderhiser, J., 121
Nellis, L., 202
Nelson, B., 510, 532
Nelson, C. A., 174, 175
Nelson, C. B., 151
Nelson, D., 315
Nelson, E., 178, 180
Nemeroff, C., 228, 514
Nemoto, K., 334
Nenadic, I., 522
Neng, J., 356
Nerland, S., 220
Nesse, R., 88, 225
Nestadt, G., 330
Nestler, E., 79, 81, 152, 452, 454, 455
Nestler, S., 344
Nettle, D., 556
Neumann, C., 564
Neuner, F., 101, 285, 294, 342
Newcorn, J. H., 201
Newman, J. P., 567

Newman, M., 39, 315
Newport, D. J., 228
Newring, K., 428
Newschaffer, C., 186
Newton, I., 19
Newton-Howes, G., 549
Nezworski, M. T., 144
Ng, M. Y., 123
Ng, S., 80
Ng, T. H., 254
Ngo, V., 232
Nicasio, A., 139
Nicholls, D., 390
Nichols, D., 475, 476, 478
Nickerson, A., 280, 291
Nicolosi, A., 410
Nicolson, R., 476, 477, 528
Niedeggen, M., 574
Nielsen, J., 411, 609
Nielsen, L., 549
Nielssen, O., 474
Niemann, L., 36
Nierenberg, A. A., 234
Niessen, W. J., 220
Nieto-Castanon, A., 532
Nievergelt, C. M., 82
Nigg, J., 197
Nikulina, V., 265
Nilsson, K. W., 166
Nimbi, F. M., 408
Nishida, K., 56
Nishida, S., 302
Niswender, K., 388
Nitschke, J., 427
Nixon, S., 280
Niznikiewicz, M., 562
Nock, M. K., 249, 252
Noecker, C., 192
Nolan, Y. M., 265
Nolen, W. A., 244
Norberg, M., 334
Norcross, J. C., 32
Nordahl, C., 193
Nordanskog, P., 235
Nordberg, S., 315
Nordenstrom, A., 415
Nordholm, D., 530
North, C., 280
Northcutt, R. G., 49
Northstone, K., 81
Norton, P. J., 39
Nota, N. M., 434
Notebaert, L., 304
Notten, P., 230
Nowak, D., 357
Nowinski, L., 196
Nuechterlein, K., 65, 247, 523
Nunez, P., 57, 525
Nutt, D., 228, 477
Nygaard, M., 122

O'Brien, L., 178, 179
O'Connell, K., 244, 520, 528
O'Connor, D. B., 265

O'Connor, E., 172
O'Connor, J., 222, 271
O'Dell, S., 483
O'Donnell, K. J., 81
O'Donnell, M., 280
O'Donovan, A., 220, 265
O'Donovan, C., 82, 243
O'Dwyer, A., 344, 345
O'Hara, R., 605
O'Leary, O. F., 265
O'Malley, P., 451
O'Neil, J., 606, 609
O'Reilly, P., 82, 84
O'Reilly, R., 522
O'Shea, S. A., 204
Oakley-Browne, M., 198, 318
Oathes, D. J., 230
Odenwald, M., 101, 342
Odgers, C. L., 182
Odunitan-Wayas, F. A., 372
Oeding, K., 321
Oei, N. Y., 267
Ogedegbe, O., 155
Oh, D., 36, 40
Oh, H., 609
Ohman, A., 39, 302, 304, 309, 319
Ohno, A., 334
Okop, K. J., 372
Olderikkert, M., 609, 610
Oler, J., 268
Olfson, M., 316
Olincy, A., 523
Oliveira-Souza, R., 566
Olivera, F. J., 319
Olivier, C., 621
Ollendick, T., 307, 322, 323, 325
Ollila, H. M., 220
Olshan, A. F., 119
Oltmanns, J. R., 151
Oltmanns, T., 553, 548
Olufunmilayo, E. O., 610
Ong, C. W., 36
Onken, L. S., 549
Ooms, P., 335
Oosterlaan, J., 200
Oparil, S., 155
Ophir, Y., 255
Oreland, L., 166
Ormel, J., 214, 309–311
Orsillo, S. M., 314, 315
Ortigo, K., 144
Ortiz, E., 155
Osmond, H., 517
Ospelt, C., 79
Ossenkoppele, R., 606
Ost, L., 321, 325
Ostacher, M., 31
Ostendorf, F., 556
Osterheider, M., 427
Ostroumov, A., 455
Otte, C., 219, 220
Ouelaa, K., 388
Overbeek, G., 549
Owen, A., 333
Owen, M. J., 245

Owens, J., 80
Owens, M., 490
Ozonoff, S., 186, 193

Padilla, R., 552
Padovan, T., 220
Pagano, M., 570
Page, I., 424
Paik, A., 410, 413
Paiva, H. S., 580
Pajuelo, C., 388
Palacios, S., 418, 419
Palaniyappan, L., 74, 532
Palloni, A., 387
Palm, M., 617
Palmer, D. S., 84, 244
Palmer, E., 227, 228, 477
Palmer, R., 463
Palomba, D., 580
Palumbo, I. M., 151, 152
Pamplona, R., 55
Pan, H. F., 217
Pan, L., 252
Panagiotaropoulou, G., 122
Panarsky, R., 463
Pandey, S. C., 452
Pandiani, J., 29
Panksepp, J., 273, 304, 453
Pantelis, C., 520
Pantev, C., 104, 105
Paoli, A., 381
Papakostas, G., 31
Paparella, R., 415
Papavramidou, N., 368
Papežova, H., 386
Papp, L. J., 309
Paquin, V., 520
Pardinas, A. F., 122
Pardo, C., 271
Pariante, C. M., 219, 220, 514
Park, A. J., 387
Park, D., 598
Park, J., 32
Park, Y., 620
Parker, G., 243, 551
Parolin, L., 146
Parry, E., 602
Parsana, P., 83
Parsons, M. P., 619
Pasco Fearon, R. M., 61
Pasco, G., 191, 192
Pascoal, P., 423, 427
Pass, L., 40
Passamonti, L., 182
Pasterski, V., 415
Patalay, P., xix, 3
Patel, V., 114
Patrick, C. J., 563–565, 151
Patsalos, O., 271
Patsopoulos, N. A., 82
Patterson, P., 520
Paul, G., 193
Paulino, M., 551
Paull, D., 283

Pauls, D., 330, 333, 334
Paunio, T., 220, 463
Paus, T., 177
Pavle, J., 120, 645
Pavlides, J. M. W., 244, 245
Pavlov, I. P., 357
Pavlova, B., 219
Paxton, S. J., 382
Payne, J. L., 219
Pearl, A., 187
Pearlson, G., 334, 523, 533
Pearson, C., 228, 477
Pechtel, P., 167
Pecina, M., 234
Pedersen, L. M., 609
Pedersen, M., 319
Pedraza, S., 55
Peduto, A., 291
Pelham, V., 346
Pelphrey, K. A., 192, 193
Peluso, M., 538
Pembrey, M., 81
Pembroke, W. G., 83
Penas-Lledo, E., 392
Pendergast, J. S., 388
Pendery, M., 496
Penfield, W., 361, 362
Peng, Y., 353, 387
Penke, L., 524
Penn, D. L., 32, 537, 541
Pennebaker, J. W., 225
Pennell, D., 65
Penninx, B. W., 219, 220
Penninz, B., 268
Perdue, S., 254
Pereda, N., 552
Pereira, L. O., 166, 168
Perez-Brocal, V., 55
Peri, J., 549
Periago, M. J., 371
Perkins, A. G., 40
Perkins, A. M., 40
Perlis, R. H., 31, 219
Pernice, K., 411
Perone, J., 379
Perrin, J., 229
Perry, E. B., 533
Pers, T. H., 244, 245
Persad, G., 639
Persico, A., 190
Pescosolido, B. A., 10
Pestel Caron, M., 388
Pestilli, F., 49, 71
Peters, C., 568
Peters, E., 505
Peterson, A. L., 255
Peterson, B., 178, 223, 224
Peterson, C., 382, 436
Peterson, E., 124
Peterson, J., 245
Petrican, R., 229
Petronis, A., 522
Petukhova, M., 308, 457, 458, 550
Pfaff, D., 290, 408, 427
Pfafflin, F., 436

Pfeifer, J., 176, 192
Pfeiffer, A., 285
Pfleiderer, B., 324
Pfund, R. A., 450, 490
Pham, D., 245
Phan, K. L., 320
Phatak, P., 81, 245
Phelps, E., 291
Phillips, K., 329–331
Phillips, M., 344, 345
Phillips, O., 65
Phillips, P., 220
Phillips, R., 290
Piacentini, J., 330
Piche, L., 424
Pickles, A., 192
Piedmont, R., 556
Pietrzak, R., 283
Pievani, M., 566
Pikering, R., 560, 574, 579, 580
Pilkonis, P. A., 151
Pilli, S., 377
Pilling, S., 320
Pincus, A., 309
Pincus, H. A., 228
Pine, D., 61, 152, 178, 180, 221, 309, 326
Pineda, J., 146
Pinel, P., 26
Pintacuda, G., 83
Pinto, A., 330, 570
Pinto-Martin, J., 186
Pipes, R., 32, 537, 541
Piran, S., 393
Piras, F., 173
Pires, R., 551
Pissiota, A., 319
Pistorello, J., 251
Pitman, R., 290
Pittenger, C., 151, 152, 331
Pittenger, M., 410
Pittini, R., 408
Piven, J., 193
Pizzagalli, D., 167, 221
Plana, M. T., 388
Platt, M., 53
Plomin, R., 75, 76, 82, 83, 121
Plotkin, A., 188
Poeppl, T. B., 427
Poirazi, P., 51
Polanczyk, G., 199, 200
Polderman, T. J. C., 552
Poldrack, R. A., 648
Polich, J., 496
Polimanti, R., 283, 463
Polines, J.-B., 177
Politte, L., 196
Polizzi, C., 340, 342
Polk, T. A., 595, 598
Pollack, M., 301, 314
Pollok, T. M., 166, 169
Polusny, M., 110
Ponseti, J., 426, 427
Ponzo, S., 343
Pool, E., 466
Poon, W. W., 621

Pope, H., 380
Porcelli, P., 146, 319
Porteous, D. J., 220
Portero-Otin, M., 55
Portner, M., 411
Posadas, M., 319
Posada-Villa, J., 198, 318, 548, 550
Post, R. 244
Posthuma, D., 82, 244, 552
Potash, J. B., 228
Potenza, M., 488
Poterba, T., 83, 122
Poulsen, S., 394
Poulton, R., 84, 121, 166, 199, 200, 265, 525
Powers, A., 149
Powers, M. B., 314
Powers, W., 531
Pozzolo Pedro, M. O., 580
Prabhu, G., 177
Preisig, M., 244, 514
Preissler, S., 570
Preller, K. H., 476, 477
Prescott, J., 644
Presumey, J., 522
Preti, A., 548, 550
Preuss, T., 49
Price, D. D., 273
Price, P., 226
Prigerson, H. G., 219, 281
Prince, M., 97, 606
Printz, R. L., 388
Prinzie, P., 549
Proal, E., 201
Prochackova, P., 386
Profeta, G., 415
Prugh, D. G., 602
Pruitt, P., 522, 570
Puig, J., 55
Puoane, T., 372
Purchia, E., 284
Purves, D., 53
Puts, N., 306
Puttonen, S., 220
Pyarajan, S., 283

Qi, T., 122
Qian, J., 81
Qian, M., 284
Qiu, D., 220
Quattrocchi, C., 384–386
Quaytman, S., 568
Quevedo, J., 81
Quigley, K. S., 269
Quinn, K., 152
Quittre, A., 621

Rabinovici, G., 606, 609
Radant, A. D., 523
Rademakers, R., 609
Radhakrishnan, K., 283
Radtke, K., 211, 272
Radu, C., 228
Radua, J., 200

Radwan, J., 570
Raebhausen, O. M., 128
Rahman, M. M., 267
Rai, A., 609
Raichle, M., 49, 72, 73, 306, 307, 531, 648
Raichlen, D. A., 609
Raine, A., 566, 567
Raine, R., 283
Rainer, G., 59
Rais, M., 530
Raj, A., 150
Rajagopal, S. K., 595, 598
Rajan, K. B., 606
Rajan, U., 522
Rajeevan, N., 283
Raley, K., 156, 158
Ramachandran, V. S., 46, 363
Ramaekers, J. G., 472
Ramaswami, G., 83
Rametti, G., 435
Ramio, L., 55
Ramos, K. M., 70
Ramos, R., 55
Rampon, C., 78
Ramrakha, S., 199, 200, 525
Ramstead, M. J. D., 220
Rando, O. J., 81
Rankinen, T., 380
Raoult, D., 388
Rapee, R., 307
Rapoport, J., 528
Rasmussen, S., 330
Rasmussen, T., 361, 362
Rasser, P., 530, 566
Rastam, M., 191
Rathouz, P., 151, 183
Ratiu, P., 98
Rauch, S., 31, 283, 291, 329, 330, 331, 333, 334
Rautiainen, M. R., 463
Raveendran, M., 268
Ravitz, P., 32
Ray, B., 638
Ray, L. A., 454
Ray, W., 10, 65, 73, 95, 101, 125, 230, 309, 341, 342
Rayman, J. B., 302
Raymond, L. A., 619
Raymond, N., 382
Rayner, R., 37, 324
Razavi, R., 283
Raznahan, A., 178
Rea, K., 265
Read, J., 505
Reaven, J., 186
Rebok, G., 605, 620
Rector, N. A., 537, 539, 540
Redlich, A., 638
Reed, G. M., 149, 548
Reed, H. C., 599
Reed, P., 191
Rees, A., 231
Regan, W., 364
Regenold, W., 81, 245
Reger, M. A., 254

Reichart, R., 255
Reichborn-Kjennerud, T., 551
Reichenberg, A., 503
Reid, H., 256
Reid, I., 229
Reid, S., 363
Reim, E. K., 222
Reiman, E. M., 606
Reinders, A. A., 346, 351
Reisdorfer, E., 220
Reiser, M., 610
Reisig, M., 536
Reissner, K., 456
Rek, K., 553
Rek-Owodziń, K., 64
Rellini, A. H., 417
Remen, A. L., 583
Remington, G., 81, 510
Ren, L., 228
Ren, M., 444
Renneberg, B., 574, 586
Repetti, R. L., 276
Repo-Tiihonen, E., 566
Resick, P. A., 283, 292, 294
Resnick, H., 280
Ressler, K. J., 283
Reuter-Lorenz, P. A., 598
Revello, S., 267
Rey, F., 387
Reyes, B. A. S., 220
Reyna, V., 648
Reynaud, M., 497
Reynolds, A., 122, 186
Reynolds, C. F., 114
Reynolds, S., 231
Reynoso, J., 576
Rezaei, F., 327
Reznick, J. S., 193
Ribeiro, B. G., 382
Ribeiro, S., 78
Ribeiro, W., 606
Ricart, W., 55
Ricaurte, G., 483, 484
Rice, C., 186
Rich, B. A., 61
Richards, A. L., 122, 244, 245
Richards, R., 432
Richardson, M., 201
Richels, C., 201
Richerson, P., 11
Richtberg, S., 356
Richters, J., 423
Riddle, M., 330
Ridinger, M., 463
Ridolfi, M. E., 568
Rief, W., 356
Rieger, G., 410
Rieke, F., 54
Rienecke, R. D., 380
Rietschel, M., 244, 463
Rigardetto, R., 393
Riggs, L. M., 228
Righi, D., 393
Riley, E. N., 151
Ringelstein, E., 358, 360

Ringen, P., 474
Ripke, S., 82, 244, 245
Rissel, C. E., 423
Ristow, I., 427
Ritchie, S. J., 599
Ritunnano, R., 510
Rivera, J., 374
Rivera-Cancel, A., 385
Riviere, L., 283, 291
Rizzolatti, G., 175, 176
Roach, B. J., 532
Robbins, T., 333
Roberge, P., 39
Roberson, A., 567
Robert, C., 617
Roberts, B. W., 549
Roberts, R., 377
Robertson, A. G., 634
Robeva, R., 415
Robinaugh, D. J., 314
Robinson, D., 32, 537, 541
Robinson, E. B., 191
Robinson, J., 32, 537, 541, 621
Robinson, L., 602
Robinson, O. J., 306
Robison, A., 452
Robison, J., 164
Robles, T., 222, 271
Rocha-Rego, V., 150
Rockoff, J., 644
Rockstroh, B., 81, 101, 104, 105, 291, 292, 342, 523
Rockwood, K., 601
Rodebaugh, T., 306, 307, 320
Rodman, J. L., 110
Rodriguez, E., 526
Rodriguez, T., 385
Rodriguez-Seijas, C., 151
Roemer, L., 314, 315
Roepke, S., 570, 574
Rogers, B. P., 527
Rogers, J., 268
Rogers, S., 195, 196
Roggers, A., 267
Rohde, L. A., 199, 200
Rohde, P., 396
Roiser, J. P., 534
Rojas, G., 114
Rokas, A., 8
Roklicer, R., 381
Rokutan, K., 56
Rolland, T., 191
Rollnick, S., 251
Romani, G., 411
Romano, K. A., 379
Rombouts, S. A., 178
Romer, D., 121, 151
Romero-Garcia, R., 177
Rommelfanger, K. S., 70
Rompala, G., 471
Ron, D., 461, 463
Rongve, A., 609
Rosario, M., 139, 331
Rose, S., 281, 522
Roseman, L., 228

Rosen, H. J., 606
Rosen, R., 61, 413
Rosene, D. L., 65
Rosengren, A., 191
Rosenheck, R. A., 32, 537, 541
Rosenthal, A. M., 411
Roses, A. D., 606
Roskies, A. L., 647
Rosner, R., 219, 281
Ross, C. A., 340, 351
Ross, E. L., 228
Ross, L., 408
Ross, R., 233
Ross, S. R., 553
Rossignol, D., 81
Rosso, I. M., 283
Rost, N., 222
Roswall, J., 387
Roth, B. L., 82, 476, 477
Roth, C., 265, 277
Roth, T., 272
Roth, W. T., 532
Rothbaum, B. O., 292
Rotondo, A., 391
Rotunno, C., 176
Roubalova, R., 386
Roussos, P., 83, 560
Roux, F., 526
Rovelet-Lecrux, A., 609
Rowe, J., 182, 591
Rowitch, D. H., 191
Roy, A., 252
Roy, M., 145
Roydeva, M. I., 351
Rozenkrantz, L., 188
Rozin, P., 378
Ruan, W. J., 219
Rubenstein, J., 82
Rubia, K., 200
Rubinov, M., 81, 192
Ruck, C., 330
Rudd, M. D., 255
Rudolf, K., 221
Rudolph, K., 164
Rudych, P. D., 13
Ruf, M., 101, 272, 342
Ruggero, C. J., 151
Ruhe, H. G., 230
Ruiperez, M., 69
Ruiz-Bolo, L., 81
Ruiz-Ruiz, J. C., 81
Runtz, M., 569
Rupp, H., 411
Rupprecht, R., 427
Ruscio, A., 110, 313, 314, 326
Rush, A. J., 234, 248
Rusielewicz, T., 283
Russ, E., 292
Russell, G., 391
Russell, M., 295
Russo, S., 152, 222
Rutten, B. P., 520
Rutter, M., 219, 514, 522
Ruzicka, W. B., 520, 533
Ryba, M. M., 219

Rybakowski, J. K., 243
Ryder, A., 353

Saah, T., 444
Sacco, R., 190
Sacher-Masoch, L., 427
Sachs, B. D., 408
Sadk, S., 191
Safron, A., 411
Sagar, R., 198, 318
Saggino, A., 40
Saha, A., 83
Saha, T. D., 219
Sahakian, B., 333
Saini, F., 343
Sakai, Y., 302
Sakiris, N., 40
Sakmar, E., 462
Saks, E., 134, 536
Saks, M. J., 647
Saladin, M., 496
Salary, C. B., 228
Salloum, I., 245
Salmon, E., 621
Salo, V. C., 309
Salters-Pedneault, K., 314, 315
Salthouse, T., 595–598
Samann, P. G., 220
Samochowiec, J., 64
Sampson, N., 167, 168, 198, 249, 254, 308, 318, 457, 458, 550
Samuel, D. B., 151, 553
Samuels, J., 330
Sanchez Romero, L., 374
Sanchez, F., 435
Sanchez, P., 388
Sanchez-Benavides, G., 600
Sanchez-Gutierrez, T., 541
Sander, D., 466
Sanders, S. J., 191, 408
Sanes, J., 609
Sani, G., 173
Sanislow, C., 152, 552, 570
San-Martin, C., 81
Santa Ana, E., 496
Santacruz, A., 387
Santana, S., 594, 620
Santtila, P., 427
Sanz, Y., 387
Sapolsky, R. M., 268
Sargent, E., 233
Sariaslan, A., 520
Saris, I., 319
Sarkizova, S., 271
Sarnyai, Z., 265, 277
Sartorius, N., 13, 86
Sarvet, A. L., 219
Sasaki, A., 272
Sassan, A., 81, 245
Sasson, J. J., 193
Satizabal, C. L., 602
Satterthwaite, T. D., 178
Sauer, J. D., 648
Sava, F. A., 579

Savage, J., 122, 244, 609
Savic, I., 435
Savin-Williams, R., 410
Savitz, J., 245
Savonenko, A. V., 609
Savostyanov, A. N., 13
Sawada, D., 56
Sawyer, A., 36, 40, 294
Sax, K., 247
Saxena, S., 329–331
Sayward, F., 283
Scala, J. W., 584
Scanlon, S. T., 54
Scarella, T. M., 354
Scattoni, M. L., 191
Schaal, S., 291
Schacter, D., 73, 648
Schade, P. F., 319
Schantz, S., 200
Schatzberg, A. F., 219, 220
Schatzkin, A., 620
Schauer, E., 285
Schauer, M., 101, 272, 284, 285, 291, 292, 294, 342
Schauer-Kaiser, E., 285
Schecklmann, M., 427
Schedlowski, M., 271
Scheer, F. A. J. L., 371
Scheffel, U., 483, 484
Scheltens, P., 609, 610
Schendel, D., 186
Schene, A. H., 230
Scherbaum, N., 463
Scherner, G., 427
Scherr, P. A., 606
Schick, M., 291
Schiele, B., 389
Schiffer, B., 426, 427
Schlaepfer, T., 228, 229
Schlaggar, B., 306, 307
Schlenger, W., 284, 292
Schlier, B., 505
Schlitz, K., 427
Schlosser, D., 537, 540
Schlyer, D. J., 481
Schmaal, L., 220
Schmahl, C., 349, 350, 567, 570, 586
Schmeidler, J., 343, 344
Schmidt, S., 36
Schmidt, U., 372
Schmidt-Wilcke, T., 306
Schnack, H. G., 530
Schnall, M., 340, 349
Schneider-Garces, N., 599
Schniering, C., 307
Schnitzlein, H. N., 606
Schnyder, U., 291
Schoenbaum, M., 254, 316
Scholten, S., 408
Schonhaut, D. R., 606
Schoning, S., 324
Schooler, J., 245
Schooler, N., 32, 537, 541
Schoppe-Sullivan, S., 388
Schork, A. J., 517

Schorpp, K., 621
Schrantee, A., 201
Schreiber, F. R., 347
Schreiber, S., 463
Schug, R., 567
Schulenberg, J., 451
Schulkin, J., 452
Schultz, P., 78
Schultz, R., 186, 193
Schultz, T., 67
Schulze, T., 244
Schumann, C., 193
Schumm, L. P., 418
Schuurman, G., 230
Schuurman, P., 335
Schwartz, C., 314
Schwarzbauer, C., 229
Schweckendiek, J., 324
Schweitzer, N. J., 647
Schweizer, K., 415
Schweizer, S., 232
Scott, A., 176, 192, 541
Scott, H. R., 151, 283
Scott, L. N., 151
Scott, S., 182
Scragg, R., 378
Seah, C., 283
Sebastianelli, W., 65, 617
Seckl, J., 80, 272
Secundo, L., 188
Sedman, A. J., 462
Sedvall, G., 149
Seedat, S., 280
Seeley, R. J., 56
Seeley, W., 612, 614
Seelye, K. Q., 493
Seemuller, C., 514
Segal, N., 122, 232
Segerstrom, S., 271
Segovia, S., 435
Segraves, R., 419
Segraves, T., 417
Sehlmeyer, C., 324
Seidman, L. J., 523, 532
Sejnowski, T., 71
Sekar, A., 522
Selfe, L., 195
Selkoe, D., 605
Selva-Vera, G., 81
Selzer, J., 494
Senior, C., 344, 345
Sennwald, V., 466
Sensi, S. L., 591
Sepeda, N. D., 477
Sequeira, M., 114
Serlachius, E., 321
Seroussi, A., 639
Serra, D., 192
Serrano, E. E., 70
Serre, F., 372
Serretti, A., 82, 319
Seshadri, S., 602
Seto, M., 426, 427
Sexton, J. D., 228
Shadrin, A., 244, 520, 528, 609

Shaffer, H., 457, 458, 487, 550
Shaffer, T., 146
Shafran, R., 391
Shah, C., 532
Shah, R., 620
Shalev, A., 283, 284
Shalev, I., 525
Sham, L., 222
Sham, P., 523
Shamay-Tsoory, S., 175
Shan, Y., 83
Shanse, J., 444
Shapiro, B. K., 204
Shapiro, D., 231, 520
Shapiro, F., 294
Sharbanee, J., 35
Shariat, S., 280
Sharma, C., 621
Sharma, M., 570
Sharma, S., 80, 272, 474
Sharma, V., 243
Sharon, G., 192
Sharp, C., 567, 570, 572
Sharp, S. I., 201
Shattuck, D., 435
Shaver, P. R., 173
Shea, J. M., 81
Shea, M., 552, 570
Shea, T., 243
Shear, K., 326
Shearer, S., 568
Sheline, Y., 64, 306, 307
Shelton, S., 268
Shen, F., 301
Shen, X., 220
Shenton, M., 525, 527, 528, 532, 562
Shepard, R., 368, 371, 372
Sheridan, M., 175, 363
Sherman, R. T., 381
Sherva, R., 452
Sheth, S. A., 333, 335
Sheu, L. K., 301
Shields, A., 548
Shields, J., 81
Shin, E., 599
Shin, L., 290, 291
Shirali, M., 220
Shollenbarger, S. G., 567
Shorter, E., 513
Shramko, M., 436
Shulman, G., 531
Shultz, S., 191, 530
Siciliano, C. A., 461, 463
Sidel, V., 568, 569
Sidorenko, J., 122
Siegel, J., 228, 477
Siegel, P. T., 363
Siegle, G., 153, 234, 235
Sierra, M., 344, 345
Siever, L., 523, 560
Sigman, M., 176, 186, 192
Sikora, M., 234
Silenzi, C., 530
Silove, D., 280
Silva, M. A., 387

Silveira, P. P., 166, 168
Silver, J., 615
Silverman, J. M., 523
Silverman, W. K., 321
Silvestrin, F., 343
Simeon, D., 342, 343–345, 352
Simmons, A., 150, 384, 386
Simms, L. J., 151, 553
Simoes, A., 556
Simoes, E., 374
Simon, M., 481
Simon, N., 301, 314
Simonelli, C., 408
Simonelli, L., 309
Simons, C., 474
Simpson, H., 329, 331
Simpson, J. R., 649
Sinclair, S., 255
Singer, W., 59, 526
Singh, A., 183
Singh, I., 192
Singh, S., 522
Singh, T., 83, 122
Sinigaglia, C., 175, 176
Sireteanu, R., 526
Sisti, D., 639
Sitzmann, A., 228
Sjostrom, M., 81
Skelly, L., 566
Skinner, M., 80
Sklar, P., 82, 244, 245
Skodol, A., 552, 555, 570
Skogholt, A. H., 609
Skopp, N., 254
Slade, T., 474
Slane, J. D., 380
Slavich, G. M., 220, 222, 265
Slee, A., 317
Sloan, D. M., 294
Slobogin, C., 648
Slobounov, S., 65, 617
Slooter, A. J. C., 601
Slopen, N., 175
Slotkin, T., 167
Small, D. M., 373
Smart, E. L., 600
Smeland, O. B., 244, 520, 528
Smeyne, R. J., 646
Smigielski, L., 530
Smith, A. M. A., 423
Smith, A. R., 379
Smith, B. M., 36
Smith, C. A., 32
Smith, E., 280, 309
Smith, G. T., 151
Smith, J. D., 371
Smith, J. K., 527
Smith, J. S., 220
Smith, K. V., 219, 281
Smith, L., 54, 539
Smith, M., 290
Smith, R., 222
Smith, S. C., 155
Smith, S. F., 564
Smith, S. M., 83

Smith, T., 195
Smitka, K., 386
Smits, J. A. J., 314
Smolders, R., 335
Smolenski, D. J., 254
Smoller, J. W., 82
Smyke, A. T., 174
Snaith, R., 424
Snitz, K., 188
Snowden, L. R., 506
Snyder, A., 73, 531
Snyder, K. S., 247
Soares, N., 186, 187
Sobel, N., 188
Sobell, L., 496
Sobell, M., 496
Sobus, J., 88
Soderlund, H., 229
Sol, J., 55
Soloff, P., 570
Solomon, D., 243
Solomon, J., 171
Solvason, H. B., 230
Sommer, I., 532
Sommer, J., 358, 360
Sondergaard, H., 342
Sonnen, J. A., 621
Sonuga-Barke, E., 202
Sorensen, J., 494
Soriano-Mas, C., 302
Sosoo, E., 233
Soulieres, I., 188
Souliou, E., 283
South, M., 186, 193
South, S., 151, 553
Southward, M. W., 567
Sowell, E., 245
Soyka, M., 463
Spalatro, A., 393
Spalletta, G., 173
Spaul, S. W., 40
Spaziani, M., 415
Speckens, A., 232
Specker, S., 382
Spector, T. D., 81
Speicher, C., 270
Spence, S., 186
Spencer, M. D., 81, 192
Spencer, T., 197, 198, 201
Spencer, W., 55
Spengler, R., 444
Sperling, R. A., 606
Spiegel, D., 278, 342, 352
Spiegel-Cohen, J., 344, 345
Spindelegger, C., 319, 320
Spira, A., 605
Spirito, A., 249
Spironelli, C., 518
Spitznagel, E. L., 280
Spoelma, M. J., 243, 551
Sponheim, S., 525
Spoor, S., 373
Sporns, O., 71, 72, 201
Sprang, K. R., 292
Springer, A., 415

Sprock, J., 523
Sprooten, E., 151
Sreenivasan, S., 644
Srihari, V. H., 535
Srinivasan, R., 57, 525
Srinivasan, S., 517
Srivastava, A., 81
Staebler, K., 574
Stahl, E. A., 244, 245
Staines, W., 358, 359
Stallings, M., 463
Stam, C. J., 601
Stamoulis, C., 175
Stangier, U., 356
Staniloiu, A., 344
Staniskyte, M., 283
Stanley, J. C., 106
Stanton, C., 387
Stappenbeck, T. S., 55
Stark, R., 324
Starr, J. M., 599, 600
Startup, M., 231
Steadman, H., 637
Stebbins, G., 65
Steele, D., 229
Steele, K., 502, 504
Steen, N. E., 244
Steensma, T. D., 434
Steffens, M., 463
Stegagno, L., 518
Stein, D., 280, 329–331, 514
Stein, J. L., 83
Stein, M. B., 254
Stein, T. D., 616
Steinberg, L., 178–180, 648
Steinberg, M., 340, 349
Steinberg, S., 244, 245
Steinert, C., 313
Stekel, W., 423
Steketee, G., 334
Stelzmann, R. A., 606
Stephan, B. C. M., 602
Stephanou, K., 221
Stepp, S. D., 151
Steptoe, A., 222, 378
Sterling, L., 190, 191
Stern, R. A., 616
Sternberg, R. J., 506
Stevelink, S. A. M., 283
Stevens, M., 334
Stewart, S. E., 329, 330, 333
St-Hilaire, A., 522
Stice, E., 373, 394, 396
Stien, X., 388
Stilling, R. M., 387
Stinson, F., 560, 574, 579, 580
Stoffers-Winterling, J., 567, 570
Stohl, M., 219
Stojek, M., 490
Stokes, T., 370
Stone, K., 605
Stone, W. S., 523
Storch, E. A., 333
Stout, D. M., 567
Stout, J. C., 619

Stout, R., 570
Stovall-McClough, K., 173
Strack, S., 555
Strain, J., 278
Strakowski, S., 245–247
Straub, R. E., 523
Straube, T., 325
Strauss, E. M., 539
Strauss, J. S., 81
Strawbridge, W., 377
Strehl, U., 202
Striegel-Moore, R., 382, 395
Stringer, S., 122
Strober, M., 391
Strosahl, K. D., 314
Stroup, T., 538
Strupp, H., 34, 234
Stuart, D., 469, 478
Stuart, G. L., 249
Studerus, E., 477
Sturman, D. A., 177
Styner, M., 527
Su, P. Y., 217
Su, T., 72
Suckling, J., 81, 191, 192, 333
Suddendorf, T., 176
Sugar, C., 523
Sugarman, D. E., 461
Sugawara, T., 56
Sugden, K., 199, 200
Sugranyes, G., 530
Suliman, S., 280, 548, 550
Sullivan, J., 630
Sullivan, P., 82, 83, 552
Sulloway, F., 33, 357
Sumathipala, A., 364
Summerfeldt, L. J., 318
Sumner, J. A., 149
Sun, D., 526–528
Sun, N., 283
Sun, Q., 83
Sun, X., 301
Sundgot-Borgen, J., 381
Suomi, S. J., 219
Supekar, K., 74, 532
Suppes, T., 244, 227, 228, 244, 477
Surette, M. G., 387
Susser, E., 280
Suter, C., 80
Sutton, B., 599
Suvrathan, A., 267
Svetky, L. P., 155
Svetlova, M., 566
Swaab, D., 435
Swain, J., 330
Swales, M., 586
Swanson, J. M., 474
Swanson, J. W., 630, 634
Swanson, S., 382
Swardfager, W., 222
Swartz, H. A., 32
Swartz, M. S., 634
Sweatt, J., 272
Sweeney, J. A., 528, 532
Swerdoski, M. J., 192

Swinson, R. P., 318
Sy, E., 615
Sylva, D., 411
Sylvester, C., 306, 307
Syvertsen, A., 436
Szabo, Z., 483, 484
Szamoskozi, S., 232
Szentagotai-Tătar, A., 247, 389, 394
Szeszko, P., 333
Szutorisz, H., 471
Szyf, M., 80, 272

Tabares-Seisdedos, R., 81, 82
Tabbert, K., 324
Tackett, J. L., 123, 151
Taipale, H., 537
Taitimu, M., 505
Takagi, Y., 302
Takahashi, T., 530
Takeda, T., 200
Taler, S. J., 155
Tallon-Baudry, C., 59
Talos, O., 98
Tambelli, R., 408
Tambs, K., 551
Tammewar, G., 606
Tamminga, H. G. H., 201
Tan, Q., 81
Tanaka, H., 56
Tanaka, S. C., 302
Tanaka-Matsumi, J., 137
Tancer, M. E., 320
Tandon, R., 514, 515, 524
Tang, J., 220, 530
Tang, Y., 78
Tang, Z., 444
Tanielian, T., 293
Tanskanen, A., 537
Tao, B., 532
Tarani, F., 415
Tarani, L., 415
Tarantino, L. M., 387, 388
Tariot, P. N., 606
Tasca, G., 391
Tasman, A., 168, 177
Tasneem, A., 124
Tassniyom, K., 605
Tatham, M., 391
Tau, G., 178
Taub, E., 104, 105
Taubner, S., 586
Tavassoli, T., 188
Tavella, G., 243
Taylor, A., 84, 121, 166, 265
Taylor, B. C., 192
Taylor, C., 245, 301
Taylor, K., 399
Taylor, M., 513
Taylor, R., 232
Taylor, S. E., 265, 275, 276
Taylor-Colls, S., 61
Teague, C. D., 452
Teasdale, J. D., 232

Teipel, S., 610
Tekin, S., 219
Tellegen, A., 122
Teng, E., 605, 621
Tennoune, N., 388
Tennstedt, S. L., 620
Teplow, D. B., 621
Testa, R., 520
Thara, R., 505
Tharner, A., 370
Thase, M., 234, 248
Thayer, J. F., 265
Thelen, S., 525
Thermenos, H. W., 532
Theunissen, E. L., 472
Thibaut, F., 431
Thioux, M., 192
Thomas, J. J., 370
Thomas, J. L., 284
Thomas, L. F., 609
Thomas, R. M., 192
Thomason, M., 64
Thompson, P., 64, 528
Thompson, R. A., 381
Thompson, W. K., 517
Thomson, M., 191
Thornton, L., 220, 391, 423
Thulin, U., 321
Thuras, P., 110
Tian, J., 192
Tibboel, H., 466
Tibu, F., 175
Tiemeier, H., 220, 370
Tierney, C. D., 187
Tiggemann, M., 378
Tiihonen, J., 463, 537
Tikkanen, R., 463
Tikochinski, R., 255
Tilley, J. L., 32
Tillfors, M., 319
Tillman, S., 637
Timko, C. A., 380
Timmermann, C., 228
Timulak, L., 35
Tincani, M., 186
Tipene-Leach, D., 378
Tiu, J., 364
Tiwari, A. K., 393
Tlaskavova, H., 386
Tobia, G., 418
Tobias, G., 418
Tobimatsu, S., 186
Tofoli, S. M. C., 220
Toga, A., 65, 98, 245, 528
Toga, W., 435
Togao, O., 334
Tohen, M., 228
Toivola, A., 220
Tolin, D., 292, 294, 334
Tolstoy, L., 212
Tomar, A., 267
Tomasi, D., 372, 452, 455, 469
Tomiyama, H., 334
Tomko, R., 98
Tompkins, D., 436

Tooley, K., 522
Toomey, R., 436
Topping, J., 124
Torales, J., 580
Torgerson, C. M., 98
Torrens, M., 477
Torres, L. D., 235
Torrey, E., 29–30, 110, 120, 536, 645
Torrisi, S., 177, 178
Torstveit, M. K., 381
Tost, H., 265
Tosun, D., 435
Touloupoulou, T., 523
Tovar-Moll, F., 566
Townsend, R. R., 155
Trace, S. E., 392
Tragesser, S., 98
Trampush, J. W., 122
Tranel, D., 567
Travers, J., 71
Treasure, J., 379
Treffert, D., 193
Trelis, M., 55
Treutlein, J., 463
Triebwasser, J., 560
Trieu, T., 621
Trivedi, M., 234
Trivic, T., 381
Troeman, Z., 280
Trojanowski, J. Q., 621
Troller-Renfree, S. V., 309
Trotman, H., 520
Trubetskosky, V., 122, 244, 245
Trueblood, K., 636
Trull, T., 98
Truog, R. D., 70
Truong, B., 537
Trzaskowski, M., 244, 245
Tschop, M. H., 56
Tseng, W. Y., 65
Tsien, J. Z., 78
Tsuang, M., 119, 532
Tucker, R. P., 254, 450, 490
Tudorascu, D., 301
Tufekcioglu, S., 585
Tuganbaev, T., 55
Tuke, S., 28
Tunbridge, E. M., 244
Turecki, G., 252, 272
Turetsky, B., 527
Turkheimer, E., 82
Turkington, D., 539
Turley, P., 82
Turner, H., 391
Turner, J., 201, 284, 363
Turse, N., 284
Twamley, E. W., 621
Twenge, J. M., 249
Twohig, M. P., 36
Tyburski, E., 64
Tye, C., 61
Tye, S. J., 81
Tyrer, P., 548, 586
Tziraki, C., 594, 620

Uckert, K., 178, 179
Uddin, L., 167, 532
Ueland, T., 244
Ugueto, A., 123
Uher, R., 166, 219
Uhlhaas, P., 519, 526, 530
Ullen, F., 533
Ulrich, J., 605, 607, 608
Ulrich-Lai, Y., 267
Underwood, E., 608
Unruh, B., 580
Unverzagt, F. W., 620
Updegraff, J. A., 275
Upthegrove, R., 227, 228, 477
Urbano, R., 183
Urbina, I., 469
Ursano, R., 254, 278, 292
Useda, J., 560
Ustun, T. B., 214, 309–311, 487
Uys, J., 456
Uysal, B., 408

Vahtera, J., 220
Vaidya, V. A., 81
Vaitl, D., 314
Valadez, E. A., 309
Valencia-Alfonso, C.-E., 335
Valentine, A., 191
Vales, K., 520
Vall, G., 549
Vallabhaneni, M., 356
Valvassori, S. S., 81
Van Ameringen, M., 314
van Beveren, N., 474
van Bochoven, A., 552
Van Bockstaele, B., 466
Van Bockstaele, E. J., 220
van Buchem, M. A., 178
Van Den Akker, A. L., 267, 549
van den Brink, W., 335, 488
Van den Heuvel, M. P., 522
van den Munckhof, P., 230, 335
van der Lee, S. J., 609
van der Meer, D., 520, 528
van der Wee, N. J. A., 319, 320
van der Werff, S., 319
van Dijk, E., 609, 610
Van Doren, V., 522
Van Dorn, R. A., 634
van Erp, T. G. M., 220
Van Ewijk, H., 200
van Goozen, S., 182
van Graan, L. A., 146
van Haren, N. E., 530
Van Heeringen, K., 232
van Heugten, D., 340, 342
van Heukelum, S., 319
Van Hoeken, D., 370
van Holst, R., 488
Van Horn, J. D., 98
Van Hulle, C., 183
Van Kammen, D., 149
van Laarhoven, J., 230

Van Lankveld, J., 402
Van Norden, A., 609, 610
Van Ommeren, M., 114
Van Os, J., 81, 474, 505, 514, 520
Van Schependom, J., 61
van Steenbergen, H., 319, 320
van Steveninck, R., 54
van Wingen, G., 335
van Winkel, R., 474
Vandenberghe, S., 402
VanderBroek-Stice, L., 490
Varela, R. B., 81
Vargas, D., 271
Vargas, S. M., 139
Varshney, M., 630
Vaudry, D., 388
Vaughn-Coaxum, R., 123
Vaurio, O., 566
Vedhara, K., 265
Veldhuizen, M. G., 373
Velten, J., 408
Veltman, D., 220, 346, 351, 488
Venkatasubramanian, G., 526, 540
Ventriglio, A., 580
Verdoux, H., 505
Verdu, E. F., 387
Vergain, S., 537
Verhulst, F. C., 370
Vermetten, E., 283, 342, 349–350, 352
Vernooij, M. W., 220
Vertes, P. E., 177
Veru, F., 520
Vesselinov, R., 637
Via, E., 530
Viana, M. C., 198, 318
Vicario, D., 78
Vicent Sanchez-Orti, J., 81
Victor, S. E., 151
Viczena, V., 252
Vidal, B., 388
Vidal, C., 528
Vietl, D., 324
Vigerland, S., 321
Viglione, D., 146
Vijan, S., 377
Vila-Frances, J., 81
Vilagut, G., 548, 550
Vilain, E., 435
Villani, A. C., 271
Villavicencio, A., 334
Villegas, L., 408
Villemagne, V., 483, 484
Vincent, J. B., 81
Vincenzi, B., 68, 137
Vine, V., 151
Vink, M., 335
Vinogradov, S., 537, 540
Vinters, H. V., 621
Virkkunen, M., 463
Vismara, L., 195, 196
Visscher, P., 520, 552
Visser, I., 230
Viswanathan, A., 335
Vita, A., 530

Vitkup, D., 191
Vlachos, A., 306
Vlahov, D., 280
Vogel, A., 219, 281
Vogel, E. K., 61
Vogelzanga, N., 268
Voglmeier, M., 562
Volkow, N., 372, 451, 452, 453, 455–458, 462, 469, 474, 479, 481, 482, 483
Vollenweider, F., 477
Volzke, H., 220
von dem, 182
von During, F., 427
Von Holle, A., 391
Voon, V., 357, 455
Vora, P., 385
Vorstman, J., 319
Vos, H. P. J., 346, 351
Voss, M., 621
Votaw, V. R., 461
Vuilleumier, P., 357, 359, 361
Vulink, N., 335
Vuong, H. E., 192
Vyas, N., 520
Vytal, K., 306

Waber, L., 357, 359, 361
Wadden, T., 372
Wade, K. A., 648
Wade, M., 175
Wade, T. D., 396
Wadehra, S., 522
Wadman, B., 568
Wager, T. D., 324
Wagner, A. D., 647
Wagner, J. G., 462
Wagner, M., 610
Wagonfeld, S., 602
Waheed, K., 282
Wahlstedt, K., 63
Waite, L. J., 418
Wakefield, A., 191
Wakefield, J. C., 219
Wakefield, S., 168
Wakeman, S. E., 449
Walach, H., 36
Wald, M. M., 615
Walden, J., 244
Waldinger, M., 419
Waldman, I., 151, 183
Wales, H., 638
Walker, E., 268, 520, 561
Walker, L. C., 619
Walker, S., 301
Walker-Smith, J., 191
Wall, M. B., 228
Wall, S., 171
Wallace, S., 530
Wallen, M., 411
Waller, G., 391
Walloch, J. C., 251
Walrath, C., 256
Walsh, B., 369, 391, 392, 394

Walsh, C. A., 599
Walsh, P., 192
Walsh, T., 394
Walter, B., 324
Walter, H., 426, 427
Walter, M., 426, 427, 411
Walters, E. E., 312, 326
Walters, R., 82, 463
Walters, W. A., 56
Walzem, R. L., 388
Wanat, M. J., 220
Wandling, G. M., 452
Wang, A., 186
Wang, B., 192
Wang, G., 220, 372, 452, 455, 469, 481
Wang, H., 56, 72, 220
Wang, J., 167, 251
Wang, L., 201, 319
Wang, O., 72
Wang, P., 152, 214, 215, 309–311
Wang, Q., 452
Wang, R., 65
Wang, T., 410
Wang, W., 480
Wang, X., 83, 167, 220, 301
Wang, Y., 201, 244, 245, 330, 517, 520, 528
Ward, J., 220
Wardle, J., 378
Wareham, J., 488
Warland, D., 54
Warren, F., 232
Warren, S., 191, 372
Warrier, V., 191
Warwick, J., 602
Wasser, T., 636
Wasserman, R. H., 576
Waszkiewicz, N., 121
Waszczuk, K., 64
Waszczuk, M. A., 151
Watanabe, K., 122, 244
Watanabe, N., 327
Waterhouse, L., 192
Waters, E., 171
Watkins, L. E., 292
Watkins, L. R., 275
Watson, D., 151
Watson, H. J., 380, 388
Watson, J., 32, 35–37, 231, 233, 324
Watson, P., 32
Watson, S. M. R., 201
Watts, A. L., 151, 564
Watts, R., 477
Weathers, F., 283, 291
Weaver, D. T., 449
Weaver, I., 80, 272
Weber, R. S., 82
Weck, F., 356
Wedeen, V. J., 65
Wei, Z., 82
Weiden, P., 539
Weidner, W., 418
Weierstall, R., 284, 285, 291, 292
Weinberger, D., 514, 520, 523
Weinberger, L., 644
Weinbrecht, A., 574

Weiner, K. S., 319
Weiner, M., 150
Weinstock, R., 639
Weisner, T. S., 139
Weiss, B., 320
Weiss, D. S., 292
Weiss, S., 427
Weissbrod, A., 188
Weissenbacher, A., 319, 320
Weissman, M. M., 223, 224
Weisz, J. R., 123
Welander-Vatn, A., 551
Welch, C., 31
Welham, J., 519
Wellington, M., 555
Welsh-Bohmer, K. A., 606
Weng, Z., 81
Weninger, S., 606
Wensing-Kruger, S. A., 434
Wergeland, G. J. H., 321
Werner, C., 592
Wertenberger, E. G., 255
Wesarg, C., 267
Wessely, S., 281, 514
West, L., 496
West, S., 636
Westbrook, S. R., 452
Westen, D., 144, 292, 567, 570
Westenberg, P. M., 319, 320
Westerveld, P., 415
Westlye, L. T., 520, 528
Weston, D., 283
Westwood, S., 546
Wetsman, R. J., 638
Weuve, J., 606
Wexler, A., 424
Whalley, B., 232
Whalley, H. C., 220
Wheeler, J., 428
Wheelwright, S., 191
Whelan, R., 177
Whitaker, K. J., 177
White House, 474
White, R., 570
White, T., 530
Whiteley, E., 461, 463
Whiten, A., 176
Whiteside, S., 320
Whitfield, S., 532
Whitfield, T. H., 285
Whitfield-Gabrieli, S., 532
Whitford, T., 528, 562
Whittchen, H. U., 151
Whittingstall, K., 57
Whittle, S., 178, 221
Whyte Oshodi, D., 510
Wichmann, H. E., 463
Wicker, B., 186, 188
Widiger, T., 151, 160, 396, 553, 556, 557
Widom, C., 118, 265
Wielgosz, J., 36
Wienbruch, C., 101, 104, 105, 342
Wiepjes, C. M., 434
Wierenga, C., 384, 386
Wiers, R. W., 267

Wightman, D. P., 609
Wigmore, E. M., 220
Wild, J., 232
Wildeman, C., 168
Wilens, T., 197, 198, 201
Wilhelm, S., 329, 330, 332, 333
Wilk, J., 283, 291
Wilkinson, E., 255
Wilkinson, P. K., 462
Willcutt, E., 118
Willemsen, A. T. M., 346, 351
Willer, C., 609
Williams, A. L., 309
Williams, B., 199, 200
Williams, C. S., 284
Williams, D., 192
Williams, G., 88
Williams, J. H. G., 176
Williams, K. D., 573
Williams, L., 291
Williams, M., 232
Williams, S., 255, 530, 670
Williams, T. P., 285
Williamson, J., 285
Williamson, P. C., 23
Willis, H., 233
Willis, S. L., 620
Willoughby, P., 378
Wilson, G., 394
Wilson, K. G., 314
Wilson, R., 606, 609, 620
Wimo, A., 606
Wincze, J., 413
Windham, G., 186
Windischberger, C., 319, 320
Winokur, G., 243
Winsvold, B. S., 609
Winter, H. S., 192
Winterling, V., 117
Winters, K., 457, 458, 550
Wise, R. A., 453
Wissel, E. F., 54
Witchel, S. F., 415
Witcraft, S. M., 314
Witkiewitz, K., 450, 490
Witoelar, A., 517
Witt, A., 36, 40
Wittchen, H., 322, 323, 326, 327, 474
Wittenberg, R., 602
Wittfeld, K., 220
Witzel, J., 427
Wixted, J. T., 648
Wodarz, N., 463
Wojcik, J., 532
Wojtasik, V., 621
Woldorff, M., 53
Wolf, A., 481
Wolfe, H. M., 527
Wolford-Clevenger, C., 249
Wolosin, S., 201
Wonderlich, S., 382
Wong, C., 290
Wong, D. F., 483, 484, 506
Wong, P. C., 609
Wong, S. C. P., 585

Woo, S., 515
Wood, J. M., 144
Wood, P., 98
Wood, S., 191, 520, 530
Woodman, G. F., 61
Woods, B., 594
Woods, R., 65
Woods, S. C., 56
Woodside, D., 391
Woodward, T. S., 505, 527
Woolfolk, R., 364
Worthington, J. J., 314
Wray, N., 520
Wright, A. G., 151
Wright, J. T., 155
Wu, A., 251
Wu, L., 167
Wu, X., 444
Wu, Y., 122
Wusten, C., 505
Wuyek, L., 330
Wynn, G. H., 254

Xia, Y., 387
Xiao, L., 387
Xiao, Y., 528, 532
Xiao, Z., 220
Xie, H., 387
Xie, S. X., 621
Xiong, D., 83
Xu, C., 283, 453, 479
Xu, E. Y., 220
Xu, J., 219, 281
Xu, L., 615
Xu, Q., 620
Xu, Z., 56

Yaffe, K., 605
Yamada, A., 12, 137
Yan, L., 64
Yang, B., 192, 221, 307
Yang, J., 217, 343
Yang, M., 301
Yang, Q., 609
Yang, Y., 65, 83, 192, 444, 567, 621
Yao, L., 528, 532
Yao, S., 353

Yassa, M. A., 599
Yates, D., 83
Yates, W., 278
Yean, C., 379
Yehuda, R., 283
Yelland, C., 378
Yen, S., 552, 570
Yeomans, F. E., 576, 584
Yeung, A., 68, 137
Yilmaz, Z., 393
Yin, R., 96
Yokoi, F., 483, 484
Yolken, R., 271
Yoon, J., 537
Yoshida, K., 55
Yoshimura, A., 497
Young, A., 227, 228, 353, 477
Young, M. J., 70
Young, S., 369, 463
Young-McCaughan, S., 255
Youngstrom, E., 245
Ypma, R. J. F., 81, 192
Ystrom, E., 551
Yu, D., 82
Yu, E., 232, 320
Yu, L., 271, 620
Yuan, H., 290
Yudofsky, S., 615
Yurgelun-Todd, D., 245

Zabetian, C., 82
Zachor, D., 188
Zai, C., 81
Zajac-Benitez, C., 522
Zald, D. H., 151
Zalesky, A., 601
Zammit, A. R., 600
Zammit, S., 503
Zamore, P. D., 81
Zanarini, M., 552, 570
Zander, T., 641, 644
Zang, Y., 201
Zapata-Tona, C., 55
Zaslavsky, A. M., 167, 168, 198, 249, 254, 308, 318
Zeanah, C. H., 174, 175, 181
Zefferino, R., 265, 271
Zerwas, S., 391

Zhang, D., 387
Zhang, H., 201, 452
Zhang, J., 387
Zhang, K., 65
Zhang, L., 292
Zhang, S., 480
Zhang, W., 528, 532
Zhang, X., 191, 523
Zhang, Y., 388, 480
Zhao, B., 83
Zhao, F., 217
Zhao, H., 452
Zhao, S., 151
Zheng, K., 251
Zhong, H., 387
Zhong, Q., 201
Zhornitsky, S., 480
Zhou, J., 435, 530
Zhou, M., 278
Zhou, X., 353
Zhou, Y., 72
Zhu, C., 201
Zhu, F., 220
Zhu, H., 83
Zhu, T., 175
Zhu, X., 353, 532
Zhu, Z., 83
Ziermans, T. B., 505
Zilcha-Mano, S., 34
Zill, P., 463
Zimmer, C., 76
Zimmerman, A., 271
Zimmerman, F. J., 201
Zimmermann, J., 553
Zimsen, T., 265, 277
Zinbarg, R. E., 309
Zink, E. M., 192
Zivin, K., 228
Zlotnick, C., 552
Zorumski, C., 306, 307
Zotev, V., 290
Zou, T., 301
Zuber, V., 517
Zubieta, J.-K., 234
Zucker, K., 434, 428
Zucker, N., 385
Zwiers, M., 200
Zwitserlood, P., 324

SUBJECT INDEX

AA. *See* Alcoholics Anonymous (AA)
ABAB single-subject reversal design, 117, 117 (figure)
ABBT. *See* Acceptance-based behavioral therapy (ABBT)
Abnormal psychology, 3
ACC. *See* Anterior cingulate cortex (ACC)
Acceptance and commitment therapy (ACT), 40
Acceptance-based behavioral therapy (ABBT), 40
Acquired immune deficiency syndrome (AIDS), 618
ACT. *See* Acceptance and commitment therapy (ACT)
ACTH. *See* Adrenocorticotropic hormone (ACTH)
ACTIVE. *See* Advanced Cognitive Training for Independent and Vital Elderly (ACTIVE)
Active dendrites, 51
Acute stress disorder, 277, 278–280, 279 (table)
Addiction, 449
  brain and behavior, 456, 458 (figure)
  pattern of, 453, 453 (figure), 454 (table)
Addictive disorders, 447
  gambling, 445
  pathological gambling, 487
  substance-related and, 469, 484
ADHD. *See* Attention deficit/hyperactivity disorder (ADHD)
Adjustment disorders, 277, 278
Adolescence
  genetic, environmental, and evolutionary influences, 452–453
  impulsivity, 177
  intoxication, 451, 451 (figure)
  psychopathology, 177 (figure)
  risk taking, 177, 178–180, 179 (figure)
  social brain, 178
Adoption study, 122
Adrenocorticotropic hormone (ACTH), 268, 269 (figure), 290
Advanced Cognitive Training for Independent and Vital Elderly (ACTIVE), 620
Aggression, 104
Aging, 593–594
  brain, 598–600, 599–600 (figure)
  cognitive abilities, 595, 596–598 (figure)
  neurocognitive disorders, 595, 595 (figure)
  population projections in 2060, 592, 593 (figure)
  successful aging, 591–592
  U.S. Population, 592, 592 (figure)

Agonist drug, 497
Agoraphobia, 327–328
Agreeableness, 556
AIDS. *See* Acquired immune deficiency syndrome (AIDS)
Alcohol, 458–459
  adult consumption, 460, 460 (figure)
  DSM-5-TR, 466, 468–469 (table)
  fermentation, 460
  GABA system, 460
  and genetics, 463
  human body, 461–462, 462 (figure)
  moderate, heavy, and binge drinking, 463–466, 464–465 (figure), 464–465 (table)
Alcoholics Anonymous (AA), 490, 494, 495
Alcoholics Anonymous World Services (AAWS), 495
Alcohol use disorder, 450, 461, 466, 467–468 (table)
ALI (American Law Institute) rule, 631
Allele, 76
Allostasis, 274
Allostatic load, 274
Allostatic systems, 274, 275
AllTrials campaign, 125
Alogia, 510
Alpha activity, 59
Altered States of Consciousness (ASC) scale, 476
Alternate-form reliability, 140
Alzheimer's disease
  brain, 606–609
  characteristics, prevalence, and diagnosis, 605–606
  genes and, 609–610
  neuroimaging, 610, 610 (figure)
American attitudes, mental illness, 6–7
American mental health movement, 28
American Psychiatric Association (APA), 150, 154, 644
American Psychological Association (APA), 126, 640, 640 (table)
Amniocentesis, 204
Amphetamines, 482–484, 484 (figure)
Amplitude, 59
Amsterdam Cohort of Gender Dysphoria Study, 434
Amygdala (Amyg), 47, 47 (figure), 65 (figure), 69 (figure), 570, 571 (figure)
Anhedonia, 510
Anonymity, 128
Anorexia nervosa, 382
  brain imaging, 385–386, 386 (figure)
  causes, 388–389
  CBT approach, 390–391

characteristics, 382–385
developmental contributions, 384, 384 (figure)
DSM-5-TR diagnostic criteria, 383–384, 383 (table)
Maudsley approach, 390
medical problems, 388
risk factors, 388–389, 389 (table)
treatment, 389–391
ANS. *See* Autonomic nervous system (ANS)
Antagonist drug, 497
Anterior cingulate cortex (ACC), 222, 273, 457, 570, 571 (figure), 574
Antidepressants, 31
Antipsychotic medications, 537–538
Antisocial behaviors, 84
Antisocial personality disorder, 5, 87, 547, 563, 564
Anxiety, 120 (figure)
Anxiety disorders, 158
  agoraphobia, 327–328
  cognitive bias, 305
  cognitive processes, 304–306
  developmental aspects, 306–307
  in *DSM-5-TR*, 301, 301 (table)
  environmental and genetic factors, 306
  evolutionary explanations, 301–304
  four functional networks, 306, 307 (figure)
  GABA, 306
  GAD, 301, 312–317
  lifetime prevalence rates, 307, 308 (table), 310, 310 (table)
  models, 309
  neurobiology, 306
  overview, 300–301
  panic disorder, 301, 326–327, 326 (table)
  phobias, 321–325
  SAD, 301, 317–320
  separation, 320–321
  specific phobias, 321–325
  Stroop effect, 305, 305 (figure)
  twelve-month prevalence, 310, 311 (table)
Anxious/ambivalent attachment pattern, 171
Anxious fearful personality disorders (Cluster C), 578
  avoidant personality disorder, 579
  dependent personality disorder, 579
  OCD, 579–580
APOE2 gene, 621
APOE4 allele, 600

749

Appetitive aggression, 284
Arteriosclerotic dementia, 611
ASC scale. *See* Altered States of Consciousness (ASC) scale
Asperger's syndrome, 186–187, 190
Assessment models
    neuropsychological testing, 147–149
    neuroscience techniques, mental illness, 149–150, 149 (figure)
    personality tests, 142–144
    projective tests, 144–147, 148 (table)
    symptom questionnaires, 142
Attachment disorders, 181
Attachment patterns, 172–175
Attachment theories
    adolescence, 177–180
    brain systems, social relations, 180
    definition, 169
    Harry Harlow's experiments, 169–170, 170 (figure)
    imitation learning, 175–176
    institution effects, 174 (table)
    John Bowlby's research, 170–171
    long-term consequences, early attachment patterns, 172–175
    Mary Ainsworth's work and styles, 171–172
    theory of mind, 176
Attention deficit/hyperactivity disorder (ADHD), 61, 117, 151, 165
    causes, 200–201
    childhood/adulthood, 199–200, 200 (figure)
    definition, 196–197
    dimensions, 197–198
    DSM-5-TR, 197–198 (table)
    prevalence and characteristics, 198–200
    treatment, 201–202
Atypical sexual fantasies, 437
Auditory system, 47
Autism
    definition, 186
    development, 190–191
    intelligence, 188
    neuroanatomy, 194 (figure)
    prevalence, 191
    social and behavioral patterns, 189
    spectrum, 186–188
Autism spectrum disorder (ASD), 159, 164, 165, 167. *See also* Autism
    brain contributions, 192–193, 193 (figure)
    causes, 191–193
    characteristics, 186–191
    definition, 186
    DSM-5, 187
    DSM-5-TR, 187, 189–190 (table)
    environmental contributions, 191
    genetic contributions, 191–192
    talents, 193–194
    treatment, 194–196
Autistic disorder, 186
Autogenous obsessions, 328

Autonomic nervous system (ANS), 47, 266, 267 (figure), 268–269, 270 (figure), 450–451
Autopsy, 94
Aversive drug, 497
Avoidant attachment pattern, 171
Avoidant personality disorder, 579
Avoidant/restrictive food intake disorder, 370
Avolition, 510
Awareness of body and brain, 361–363

BAC. *See* Blood alcohol concentration (BAC)
BDI. *See* Beck Depression Inventory (BDI)
A Beautiful Mind (Nash), 2
Beck Depression Inventory (BDI), 103, 142
Behavioral/externalizing dysfunction (BXD), 143
Behavioral genetics, 121–122
Behavioral perspective, 7, 36–40
Behaviorism, 38 (figure)
The Behavior of Organisms (Skinner), 37
Belmont Report, 126
Benzodiazepines, 31, 306, 315–317, 317 (figure), 327
Beta activity, 59
Binge drinking, 463
    and alcohol use, 465, 465 (figure)
    college-age populations, 465
    light drinkers, 466
Binge eating disorder, 380, 384, 395–396
Biofeedback, 201
Biopsychosocial approach, 9, 10 (figure)
Bipolar disorder, 81, 213
    bipolar I, 239–243
    bipolar II, 243
    brain imaging, 245–247, 246 (figure)
    causes, 244–247
    characteristics, 238–239
    and creativity, 245
    cyclothymic disorder, 243–244
    environmental factors, 247
    genetics of, 244–245
    medications, 248
    neurotransmitter dysregulation, 247
    overview, 236–238
    prevalence, 244
    psychological treatments, 247–248
Bipolar I disorder, 239–243
Bipolar II disorder, 243
Blind controls, 108
Blood alcohol concentration (BAC), 461–462
    chart for men, 463, 463 (figure)
    chart for women, 464, 464 (figure)
    psychological and physical effects, 464, 464 (table)
BMI. *See* Body mass index (BMI)
Body dysmorphic disorder, 332
Body mass index (BMI), 371, 375, 377, 377 (figure), 378, 383
Borderline personality disorder (BPD), 98, 547, 567

    brain studies, 570–571, 571–572 (figure)
    diagnostic criteria, 569
    genetic factors, 569
    prevalence rates, 570
    self-harm, 568
    self-injurious behavior, 567, 568 (table)
    treatment, 580–585
    trust and, 569–574, 573–577 (figure)
Borderline Traits (Roberson), 567
Bovine spongiform encephalopathy, 619
BPD. *See* Borderline personality disorder (BPD)
Brain
    during addiction, 456, 458 (figure)
    addiction and, 455, 455 (figure)
    aging, 598–600, 599–600 (figure)
    Alzheimer's disease, 606–609
    and behavior, addiction, 456, 458 (figure)
    BPD, 570–571, 571–572 (figure)
    development, 167–169, 168 (figure)
    drugs and, 454–458, 455–456 (figure), 457 (table)
    fag, 353
    gender dysphoria and, 434–435, 435 (figure)
    gray and white matter changes, schizophrenia, 527–530, 528–529 (figure)
    imaging techniques, 48, 48 (figure), 65, 66, 68–69, 98
    molecular mechanisms, 455
    neural networks, 454
    pathways, 455
    PFC, 456–457, 457 (table)
    plasticity, 166
    psychopathy, 566–567
    and schizophrenia, 525–526, 526–527 (figure)
    sexual activities and, 411, 411 (figure)
    Skinner box, 454
    systems, 180
    ventricle changes in individuals, 531–532, 531 (figure)
Brain (Seeley), 612
Brain anatomy
    anatomical structures, 50 (figure)
    function, 49–50
    location, 49 (figure)
    structural and functional anatomy, 50 (figure)
Brain function
    evolution, 24–25
    head, Gall's structure, 22 (figure)
    lobes, 20, 21 (figure)
    nervous system, 20, 21 (figure)
    organization, 25
    parts, 23 (figure)
    signs, 25
    symptoms, 25
    syndrome, 25
    1700s to 1900s, 20–24
Brain networks
    default/intrinsic network, 73
    neuronal connections, 71

neurons, 71–73, 72 (figure)
psychopathology, 71
structural image, 74 (figure)
synaptic connections, 71
tasks, 73–74
Broca's area, 23
Bucharest Early Intervention Project, 174
Bulimia nervosa, 391
   Anne Hart, case of, 394
   causes, 392–393
   CBT, 394–395
   characteristics, 391
   DSM-5-TR diagnostic criteria, 393, 393 (table)
   prevalence, 392
   purging, 393
BXD. *See* Behavioral/externalizing dysfunction (BXD)

Caffeine, 484
Cannabidiol (CBD), 472
Cannabis, 469
   brain, 472, 472 (figure)
   hallucinations, 471
   history of, 469, 470–471 (table)
   legalization of, 473–474
   marijuana, 471
   prevalence, 469, 471 (table)
   and psychosis, 474, 475 (table)
   THC (Δ9-tetrahydrocannabinol), 472
Capgras syndrome, 46
Case studies
   Amy James, borderline personality disorder, 568–569
   Amy Porter, histrionic personality disorder, 575–576
   Bobby Baldwin delirium, 601–602
   child sexual abuse, mandated treatment, 563
   Dawn Nichols, narcissistic personality disorder, 578
   George Nadel, child pornography possession, 429–430
   James Stern, schizophrenia, 517
   Nathan James, schizotypal personality disorder, 561
   psychological research, 96–98
CAT. *See* Computerized axial tomography (CAT)
Catatonic subtype, 513
Categorical *vs.* dimensional approaches, 150–151
Catnip, 454
CBD. *See* Cannabidiol (CBD)
CBT. *See* Cognitive behavioral therapy (CBT)
CD. *See* Conduct disorder (CD)
Centers for Disease Control and Prevention (CDC), 199, 447, 606
Central dogma, molecular biology, 79
Central executive network, 72
Central sulcus, 50

CFI. *See* Cultural formulation interview (CFI)
Chemical synapse, 52
Child-based therapy, 436
Childhood development
   attachment theories, 169–175
   brain development, 167–169, 168 (figure)
   brain's plasticity, 166
   disruptions, 166
   evolutionary perspective, 166
   social and emotional processes, 166
Childhood disorders, 165 (table)
Childhood psychopathology, 173
Child pornography possession case, 429–430
Child protective services (CPS), 168
Chinese somatization, 353
Chlorpromazine, 31
Chromosomes, 76, 79, 204–205
Chronic traumatic encephalopathy (CTE), 615
Cigarette smoking, 485
Circumstantiality, 504
Civil commitment, 641
Classical conditioning, 36
Classification systems, 156–160
Client-centered therapy, 35
Clinical interview, 135–136, 135 (figure)
Clinically significant, 122–123
Closing mental hospitals, 29–30, 29–30 (figure)
Cocaine, 455, 480
   dopamine and brain, 481, 482 (figure)
   human brain, 481, 482 (figure)
Cognitive avoidance model, 313
Cognitive behavioral perspective, 36–40
Cognitive behavioral therapy (CBT), 39, 231–233, 431, 490, 539
   anorexia nervosa, 390–391
   antidepressant medication, 234, 235 (figure)
   bulimia nervosa, 394–395
   EFT, 233
   GAD, 313–315
   OCD, 334–335
   panic disorder, 327
   PTSD, 292, 295
   SAD, 320, 321
   somatic symptom disorders, 364
   suicide, 255
Cognitive deficits, 482
Cognitive development, 175
Cognitive model of depression, 221–222, 223 (figure)
Cognitive processes, 22
Cognitive therapy, 231–233, 232 (table)
   vs. medication, 153
CogSMART (Cognitive Symptom Management and Rehabilitation Therapy), 621
Comorbid, 151–152
Component 4 (C4), 522

Comprehensive Crime Control Act of 1984, 632
Computerized axial tomography (CAT), 98
Concurrent validity, 141
Conditioned stimulus, 37
Conduct disorder (CD), 166, 181–184
Confidentiality
   in health care, 639
   research participants, 128
Confound hypothesis, 111, 113
Confounding variables, 104
Connectivity, 74
Conscientiousness, 556
Construct validity, 141
Content validity, 141
Continuous performance test (CPT), 148
Control group, 103
Controlled drinking, 496–497
Conversion disorder, 356
   conversion reaction, 357, 359 (figure)
   fMRI, 359–360
   functional paralysis, 359, 361 (figure)
   glove anesthesia, 356
   mirror neuron activity, 358–359, 360 (figure)
   nerve, sensitivity area, 356–357, 356 (figure)
   neuroscience mechanisms, 357
   symptoms, 357
Conversion reaction, 357, 359 (figure)
Correlational approach, 100–103
Correlation coefficient, 101
Corticotropin-releasing hormone (CRH), 268, 269 (figure), 290
Cortisol, 220, 268, 269 (figure), 272, 327
Covary, 104
COVID-19 pandemic, 123, 217, 283, 606
Cowper's glands, 414
CPS. *See* Child protective services (CPS)
CPT. *See* Continuous performance test (CPT)
Crack babies, 205
Craving, 453
Creutzfeldt-Jakob disease, 619
CRH. *See* Corticotropin-releasing hormone (CRH)
CTE. *See* Chronic traumatic encephalopathy (CTE)
Cultural assessment, 138
Cultural competence, 138–139, 138 (figure)
Cultural formulation interview (CFI), 137–138
Cultural identity, 137
Cultural perspective, 10
Cultures, 8 (figure), 11
Cyberball game, 572, 573 (figure)
Cyclothymic disorder, 243–244

DALYs. *See* Disability-adjusted life years (DALYs)
DBS. *See* Deep brain stimulation (DBS)

DBT. *See* Dialectical behavior therapy (DBT)
Decision-making competence, 636–637
Deep brain stimulation (DBS), 32, 230, 622
Default/intrinsic network, 72, 73
Default mode network (DMN), 532
Deinstitutionalization, 30
Delayed ejaculation, 419
Delirium, 601
Delirium tremens (DTs), 451
Delusional thinking, 136
Delusions, 510, 511 (figure)
Demand characteristics, 108
Dementia-friendly communities, 622–623, 623 (figure)
Dementias, 591
  of early onset, 515
  praecox, 515, 516
Deoxyribonucleic acid (DNA), 51, 77–78, 271–273, 647
Dependence, 449
Dependent personality disorder, 579
Dependent variable (DV), 104, 111–114
Depersonalization/derealization disorder, 343–344, 345 (figure)
Depression, 32, 39 (figure), 87. *See also Specific depression*
  bipolar disorder, 236–248
  MDD. *See* Major depressive disorder (MDD)
  suicide, 249–257
Depression in terms of attachment, 225
Depression in terms of resource conservation, 225
Depression in terms of social competition, 225, 226
The Descent of Man (Darwin), 24, 25
Developmental psychopathology perspective, 164
Diagnostic and Statistical Manual of Mental Disorders (DSM), 150, 154–155, 157
Dialectical behavior therapy (DBT), 32, 255, 581–583
DID. *See* Dissociative identity disorder (DID)
Diffusion tensor imaging (DTI), 57, 64–65, 67 (figure), 201
Disability-adjusted life years (DALYs), 4, 214, 216 (figure)
Disinhibited social engagement disorder, 181
Disordered use, 450
Disorganized/controlling attachment pattern, 171
Disorganized subtype, 511
Disruptive, 166
Dissociation, 340–342
The Dissociation of a Personality (Prince), 97, 350
Dissociative amnesia, 344–346
Dissociative disorders
  depersonalization, 343–344, 345 (figure)
  derealization, 343–344
  DID, 346–351
  dissociation, 340–342

dissociative amnesia, 344–346
DSM-5 and *DSM-5-TR*, 341 (table), 352
prevalence, 341, 342 (table)
treatment, 351
Dissociative fugue, 344
Dissociative identity disorder (DID), 97, 346
  disruptions, in memory, 349
  DSM-5-TR diagnostic criteria, 349, 349 (table)
  hippocampus and amygdala, 350–351, 350 (figure)
  multiple personality and media, 347–348
  neurobiomarkers, pathological dissociation, 351
  prevalence, 349
  PTSD, 351
  SCID-D, 349
Dissolutions, 24
Distress, cultural conceptualizations of, 137
Dizygotic (DZ) twins, 122
DLPFC. *See* Dorsolateral prefrontal cortex (DLPFC)
DMN. *See* Default mode network (DMN)
DNA. *See* Deoxyribonucleic acid (DNA)
Dopamine, 455, 456 (figure), 481, 482 (figure)
Dorsolateral prefrontal cortex (DLPFC), 525
Double-blind experiment, 108
Doubt, 95
Down syndrome, 204–205, 204 (figure), 206 (figure)
Dramatic emotional personality disorders (Cluster B), 562
  antisocial personality disorder, 563
  BPD, 567–574
  DSM-5-TR criteria, 562
  histrionic personality disorder, 574
  narcissistic personality disorder, 576–577
  psychopathy, 564–566, 565 (table)
Drugs
  brain and, 454–458, 455–456 (figure), 457 (table)
  cannabis. *See* Cannabis
  cultural and historical factors, 444–445
  hallucinogens, 475–477, 477–478 (figure)
  opioids, 478–480, 479 (figure)
  rehabilitation, 493–494
  in the United States, 445–449
DSM. *See* Diagnostic and Statistical Manual of Mental Disorders (DSM)
DSM-5, 158–160, 187
  childhood disorder, 207
  cultural formulation interview, 137
  grief and the grief exception, 219
  legal issues, 649–650
  personality disorders, 557, 558–559 (table)
  schizophrenia, 514
  sexual and gender-related experiences, 437
  substance-related and addictive disorders, 469

DSM-5-TR (Diagnostic and Statistical Manual of Mental Disorders, fifth edition text revision), 158–160, 159 (table), 165, 165 (table), 181, 187, 197–198 (table), 415
  addictive disorders, 469
  alcohol-related disorders, 466, 467–468 (table)
  delirium, 601
  dramatic emotional personality disorders (Cluster B), 562
  early ejaculation, 419
  female sexual interest/arousal disorder, 419
  gambling, 487–489, 488–489 (table)
  and *ICD-11*, 450–451
  legal issues, 649–650
  personality disorders, 546, 547 (table), 585–586
  psychotic disorders and schizophrenia spectrum, 503, 503 (table)
  schizophrenia, 511, 512 (table), 514
  sexual dysfunction disorders, 416, 416 (table)
  substance-related disorder, 469
DSM-5-TR diagnostic criteria, 219. *See also* Anxiety disorders; Dissociative disorders; Eating disorders; Somatic symptom disorder
  acute stress disorder, 277, 278–280, 279 (table)
  adjustment disorders, 277, 278
  bipolar I disorder, 239, 240–242 (table)
  bipolar II disorder, 243
  feeding disorders, 369–370, 369 (table)
  grief exception, 219
  MDD, 217–218 (table), 217–219
  OCD, 329 (table), 330–333
  prolonged grief disorder, 277, 281
  PTSD, 286, 286–289 (table), 291
DSM-III-R, 158
DSM-IV-TR, 158
DTI. *See* Diffusion tensor imaging (DTI)
Durham rule, 631
Duty to protect, 638
DV. *See* Dependent variable (DV)
Dynamic deconstructive psychotherapy (DDP), 583
Dyspareunia, 419, 420, 438

Early ejaculation, 419
Early Psychosis Intervention Network (EPI-NET), 541
Eating disorder not otherwise specified (EDNOS), 396
Eating disorders
  anorexia nervosa, 382–391
  binge eating, 380, 384, 395–396
  bulimia nervosa, 391–395
  DSM-5 and *DSM-5-TR*, 395–396
  feeding disorders, 369–370, 369 (table)
  and gut, 386–388

obesity, 368, 371–379
overview, 368–369, 379–382
prevalence and standard error, 380, 380 (table)
and sports, 381–382
Ecological validity, 141
ECT. See Electroconvulsive therapy (ECT)
EDA. See Electrodermal activity (EDA)
EEG. See Electroencephalography (EEG)
Effect size, 123
EFT. See Emotion-focused therapy (EFT)
EID. See Emotional/internalizing dysfunction (EID)
Electroconvulsive therapy (ECT), 31, 228–229
Electrodermal activity (EDA), 47, 49
Electroencephalography (EEG), 49, 410, 518, 523, 526
definition, 57
electrodes, 58, 58 (figure)
evoked potentials, 60–61, 61 (figure)
oscillations, 59
patterns, 59 (figure)
sleep stages, 57 (figure)
wavelet analysis, 60 (figure)
EMDR. See Eye movement desensitization and reprocessing (EMDR)
Emotional conflict, 46
Emotional/internalizing dysfunction (EID), 143
Emotion-focused therapy (EFT), 35, 36, 233–234
Empathizing-systemizing theory of autism, 192
Empathy, 547, 570
Empirically based principles, 32, 138, 139
Empirically based treatments, 32, 138
Empiricism, 15, 96
Encode, 77
Endophenotypes, 81–82, 121, 252
Epidemiology, 119–120
Epigenetic inheritance, 79
Epigenetic marks/tags, 79
Epigenetics, 8–9, 79–81, 79 (figure), 271–273
EPINET. See Early Psychosis Intervention Network (EPINET)
EPs. See Evoked potentials (EPs)
Erectile disorder, 417–418
Erotic collection, Pompeii, 403, 403 (figure)
Erotic videos, 411, 411 (figure)
Ethics
beneficence, 126
definition, 125
experiment problem, 126
institutional review board, 129, 129 (figure)
justice, 126
relationship, 129–130
research participant and the responsibilities, 128
respect for persons, 126
scientist-participant dialogue, 127–128

Eugenics, 70
Event-related potentials (ERPs). See Evoked potentials (EPs)
Evidence-based medicine, 32, 138
Evoked potentials (EPs), 60–61, 61 (figure), 192
Evolutionary perspective, 7–8, 47–49, 86–89
Excoriation (skin picking disorder), 331
Executive functions, 73
Exhibitionism, 424
Exhibitionistic disorder, 424
Existential-humanistic perspective, 34–36
Experiential perspective, 7
Experimental group, 103
Experimental method
definition, 103–104
dependent vs. independent variable, 111–114
designing and structuring, 110–111
groups participants, 109–110
logic and inference, 106–107
participants study, 109
playing music, brain affect, 104–105, 105 (figure)
research considerations, 116–125
steps, 109 (figure), 114 (figure)
Experimenter effects, 108
Exposure therapy for PTSD, 292, 294
Externalizing/disinhibition dimension, 183
Externalizing disorders, 151, 200
External validity, 107
Extinction, 37
Extraversion, 556
Eye movement desensitization and reprocessing (EMDR), 294–295

Factitious disorder, 354, 363–364
Factitious disorder imposed on another, 363
Factitious disorder imposed on self, 363
Facts, 95
Falsification, 96
Family therapy, 436
FAS. See Fetal alcohol syndrome (FAS)
Fatal Attraction (movie), 567
FDA. See Food and Drug Administration (FDA)
Feeding disorders, 369–370, 369 (table)
Female orgasmic disorder, 418
Female sexual interest/arousal disorder, 419
Fetal alcohol syndrome (FAS), 205
Fetishistic disorder, 425
FFM. See Five-factor model (FFM)
Fiber tracts, 21
Fifty Shades of Grey (movie), 423
Fight-or-flight response, 268, 275–277
File drawer problem, 124
Fissures, 20
Five-factor model (FFM), 553–556, 556 (table)
agreeableness, 555, 556
categories and dimensions, 559

conscientiousness, 555, 556
extraversion, 555, 556
hypothesized fitness benefits and costs, 556, 557 (table)
maladaptive extraversion vs. introversion, 554, 554 (figure)
neuroticism, 555, 556
openness, 555, 556
Flight of ideas, 136
fMRI. See Functional magnetic resonance imaging (fMRI)
Food and Drug Administration (FDA), 482
Forensic neuroscience, 647
FPN. See Frontoparietal network (FPN)
Fragile X syndrome, 205
Frontal lobe tasks, 73
Frontal lobotomy, 32
Frontoparietal network (FPN), 532
Frontotemporal neurocognitive disorder, 611
Adams's symptoms, 612, 613 (figure)
Amsterdam, 614, 614 (figure)
Arbutus Leaves painting, 614, 614 (figure)
cognitive abilities, 611
magnetic resonance imaging with paintings, 614, 615 (figure)
Pi painting, 612, 613 (figure)
Frotteuristic disorder, 424–425
F test, 113
Functional magnetic resonance imaging (fMRI), 178, 410, 411, 531, 571
blood flow measurements, 63, 63 (figure)
brain anatomy, 63, 64 (figure)
DTI, 64–65
hemoglobin, 63
Functional neurological symptom disorder, 357. See also Conversion disorder
Fusiform gyrus (FG), 570, 571 (figure)

GABA. See Gamma-aminobutyric acid (GABA)
GAD. See Generalized anxiety disorder (GAD)
Gambling, 445
cognitive–emotional process, 488
DSM-5 and DSM-5-TR, 487
DSM-IV, 487
lifetime comorbidity, 489
lifetime prevalence, 487, 488 (table)
national community survey, 487
substance tolerance, 488
Gamma-aminobutyric acid (GABA), 53
anxiety, 306, 315
Garcia effect, 370
GAS. See General adaptation syndrome (GAS)
Gender dysphoria, 431–433
assistance for individuals, 435–436
brain and, 434–435, 435 (figure)
development, characteristics, and prevalence, 434
gender roles and gender identity, 432–433

Gender identity, 432
Gender-related experiences, 437
Gender roles, 432
Gene by environment correlation, 121
Gene by environment interactions, 121
Gene co-expression analysis, 83
General adaptation syndrome (GAS), 274, 296
Generalizability, 107
Generalized anxiety disorder (GAD), 110, 119, 301
   Adam Caldwell, case of, 315
   behaviors, 312
   benzodiazepines, 315–317, 317 (figure)
   CBT approach, 313–315
   cognitive avoidance model, 313
   DSM-5-TR diagnostic criteria, 312, 312 (table)
   mindfulness, 314–315
   prevalence rates, 312–313
   psychological treatment, 313–315
Genes, 76–77
Genetics, 47–49, 463
   components, 76
   disorders, 82
   DNA, 77–78
   genes, 76–77
   genes influence behavior, 78–82
   historical study, 75–76
   psychological disorders, 75
   research, 120–122
   SERT gene, 82
Genito-pelvic pain/penetration disorder, 419–420
Genome, 78
Genome-wide association studies (GWAS), 82, 83 (figure), 122, 244, 388, 452, 520
Genotype, 77
Global mental health, 11–12
Glove anesthesia, 356
Glutamate, 53
Grave disability, 641
Gray matter, 20, 20 (figure)
Gut biome, 56, 56 (figure)
Gut microbiome, 55
GWAS. *See* Genome-wide association studies (GWAS)
Gyri, 20

HAART. *See* Highly active antiretroviral therapy (HAART)
Hallucinations, 507
Hallucinogens
   addictive drugs, 476
   in brain, effect of, 477, 478 (figure)
   human research, 476
   LSD, 475–477
   perception, mood, and cognitive processes, 476
   psilocybin, 476–477, 477 (figure)
   psychedelics, 476

Health Insurance Portability and Accountability Act (HIPAA), 156, 640
Healthy self, 554
   DSM-5 and *DSM-5-TR*, 554–555
   empathy, 554
   evolutionary perspective, 555
   interpersonal functioning, 554
   intimacy, 555
Hebephrenia, 515
Heterozygotes/heterozygous alleles, 77
Hierarchical integration, 23
Hierarchical Taxonomy of Psychopathology (HiTOP), 151, 152 (figure)
Highly active antiretroviral therapy (HAART), 492
HIPAA. *See* Health Insurance Portability and Accountability Act (HIPAA)
Hippocampus, 570, 571 (figure)
Histones, 79, 79 (figure) 271, 273
Histrionic personality disorder, 87, 88, 547, 574
HiTOP. *See* Hierarchical Taxonomy of Psychopathology (HiTOP)
HIV. *See* Human immunodeficiency virus (HIV)
Hoarding disorder, 331–332
Homosexuality, 160
Homosexuality in Perspective (Masters and Johnson), 412
Homozygotes/homozygous alleles, 77
Hooking-up experience, 409
Hormones, 53
HPA axis. *See* Hypothalamic–pituitary–adrenal (HPA) axis
Human Genome Project, 78
Human immunodeficiency virus (HIV), 618
Human infants, 85 (figure)
Humanistic-experiential therapies, 35
Human organs, 18 (figure)
Human Sexual Inadequacy (Masters and Johnson), 412, 420
Human Sexual Response (Masters and Johnson), 412
Huntington's disease, 619
Hwa-byung, 353
Hypochondriasis, 142, 354–355
Hypothalamic–pituitary–adrenal (HPA) axis, 266–268, 267 (figure), 269 (figure)
Hypothesis, 95, 96
Hysteria, 25, 26 (figure), 143, 356, 357

ICD. *See* International Classification of Diseases (ICD)
IDEA. *See* Individuals with Disabilities Education Act (IDEA)
Identity, 554
Idioms of distress, 353
Illicit drug use
   drug overdose death rates, 448, 449 (figure)
   recent patterns, 448, 448 (figure)
   in United States, 447, 448 (figure)

Illness anxiety disorder, 354–356
Imitation learning, 175–176
Immune system, 270–271
Impulse control, 166
Incidence, 120
Incidental findings, 70
Independent variable (IV), 104, 111–114
Individuals with Disabilities Education Act (IDEA), 202
Inference, 106–107
Inferential statistics, 112–113, 112 (figure)
Informal networks, 10 (figure)
Informed consent, 127–128, 639
Insanity, 630
   American legal system, 630–634
   historical criteria, 632, 632 (table)
   manic–depressive, 516
Insight therapy, 34
Institutional review board (IRB), 129, 129 (figure)
Insula, 65 (figure)
Intellectual developmental disorder (IDD)
   causes, 204–205
   characteristics, 203
   chromosomes, 204–205
   definition, 203
   gestation, 205
   levels of functioning, 203–204
   metabolism, 205
   treatment, 205–206
Intellectual disabilities, 203
Intellectual functioning, 136
Intergenerational transmission of depression, 221
Internalizing disorders, 151
Internalizing/emotional dimension, 183
Internal reliability, 140
Internal validity, 106–107
International Classification of Diseases (ICD), 150, 156
International List of Causes of Death, 156
Interpersonal-psychological theory of suicide (IPTS), 255
Inter-rater reliability, 140
Intimacy, 555
Intoxication, 450
Invisible Wounds of War (Tanielian & Jaycox), 293
Involuntary/reflexive movement, 19 (figure)
Iowa Gambling Task, 489
IRB. *See* Institutional review board (IRB)
IV. *See* Independent variable (IV)

Jackson v. Hobbs (2012), 648
Journal of Abnormal Psychology, 3
Journal of Psychopathology and Clinical Science, 3

Lactose tolerance, 13
Lateral fissure, 50
Law and mental health, 628–630, 633–634

American legal system, 630–634, 632 (table)
    emergency commitment, 641–642
    ethical and legal aspects, 639–640, 640 (table)
    global mental health, 645
    legal competence, 634–638
    neuroscience and evolutionary perspectives, 647–649
    psychiatric advance directives, 642
    sexual predator laws, 642–647
Learning disabilities, 202–203
Legal competence, 634–636
    decision-making competence, 636–637
    and mental health courts, 637–638
Lessard v. Schmidt (1972), 642
Levels of analysis, 8–9
Lewy body dementia, 617, 617 (figure)
Lifetime prevalence, 119
Limbic system, 47
Longitudinal design, 117–119, 119 (figure)
Low- and middle-income countries, RCT, 114–116, 115 (table)
LSD (d-lysergic acid diethylamide), 475–476

Macrophage theory of depression, 222
Magical thinking, 561
Magnetoencephalography (MEG), 61, 62 (figure), 101
Mainstreaming, 206
Major depressive disorder (MDD), 216, 570
    adolescence, 221
    biological and neuroscience treatments, 227–230
    brain imaging, 223, 224 (figure)
    causes, 220–223
    characteristics, 216–219
    chronic stress, 220
    cognitive model of depression, 221–222, 223 (figure)
    cognitive therapy, 231–233, 232 (table)
    cortisol, 220
    deep brain stimulation (DBS), 230
    DSM-5 and *DSM-5-TR* criteria, 217–218 (table), 217–219
    ECT, 228–229
    EFT, 233–234
    environmental stress, 220
    everyday social behavior, 225–226
    evolutionary perspectives, 224–227
    inflammation, 222
    intergenerational transmission of depression, 221
    medications, 227–228
    prevention, 235
    psychodynamic therapy, 234
    psychological treatments, 230–235
    resource conservation, 225
    social competition, 226
    social risk hypothesis, 226–227
    TMS, 229–230
    VNS, 229

Major neurocognitive disorder, 602, 604 (table)
Maladaptive personality traits, 557, 558–559 (table)
Male hypoactive sexual desire disorder, 419
Malingering, 354
Malleus Maleficarum (The Hammer of the Witches), 16
Mandated reporting, 640
Manic (Cheney), 2
Manic depression, 212. *See also* Bipolar disorder
MAOIs. *See* Monoamine oxidase inhibitors (MAOIs)
The Mask of Sanity (Cleckley), 564
Masturbation, 403
Match subjects design, 110
Maudsley approach, 390
MDD. *See* Major depressive disorder (MDD)
Medical science, treatment and clinical perspectives, 124–125
Medical transition, 436
MEG. *See* Magnetoencephalography (MEG)
Melancholia, 213
Mendel's first law (law of segregation), 75
Mendel's second law (law of independent assortment), 75
Menopause, 277, 417
Mental disorders, 3
    American attitudes, 6–7
    bedlam, 26, 27 (figure)
    biological approaches, 31–32
    classification systems, 156–160
    genetic and environmental factors, 84 (figure)
    historical approaches, 26–30
    impact of, 4
    neuropsychological tests, 149
    neuroscience techniques, 149–150, 149 (figure)
    prevalence, 5 (figure)
    psychologists, 11 (figure)
    risk development, 168 (figure)
    stigma, 5–6
    suicide, 249
Mental health problems, 121 (figure)
Mental health professionals, 135, 166
Mental health workers, high-income countries, 12 (figure)
Mental retardation, 203
Mental status exam, 136
Mercy booking, mental patients, 535–536
Meta-analysis, 123
Microbiome, 54–56
Microglia, 608–609
Middle and superior temporal cortex (Mid-Sup T), 570, 571 (figure)
Mild neurocognitive disorder, 602, 603 (table)
Miller v. Alabama (2012), 648
Mind-body problem, 18
Mindfulness, 36

Mindfulness-based cognitive therapy (MBCT), 232 (table)
Mind reading. *See* Theory of mind
Minnesota Multiphasic Personality Inventory (MMPI), 142–144
Mirror box technique, 361, 362
Mirror neurons, 175–176
Mitochondria, 81
Mitochondrial DNA (mtDNA), 81
Mitochondrial dysfunction hypothesis, 81
Mitochondrial inheritance, 81
MMPI. *See* Minnesota Multiphasic Personality Inventory (MMPI)
M'Naghten rule, 630
Modularity, 74
Monoamine oxidase A (MAOA) gene, 265
Monoamine oxidase inhibitors (MAOIs), 31, 227
Monozygotic (MZ) twins, 122, 522
Montgomery v. Louisiana (2012), 648
Mood disorders, 14
    bipolar disorder, 236–248
    DALY measures, 214, 216 (figure)
    lifetime prevalence, 214, 215 (table)
    MDD. *See* Major depressive disorder (MDD)
    overview, 212–214
    standard error, 216
    suicide, 249–257
MST. *See* Multisystemic therapy (MST)
Multiple personality disorder. *See* Dissociative identity disorder (DID)
Multisystemic therapy (MST), 184
Munchausen syndrome, 363
Muscular/effector system, 21
Myelin sheath, 52
Myotonia, 413
MZ twins. *See* Monozygotic (MZ) twins

Narcissistic personality disorder, 547, 576–577
Narrative exposure therapy (NET), 294
National Comorbidity Survey, 151, 177
National Football League (NFL), 615
National Institute of Mental Health (NIMH), 4, 119, 153, 154, 520, 535
National Institute on Alcohol Abuse and Alcoholism (NIAAA), 463–464
National Institute on Drug Abuse, 491
National Institutes of Health (NIH), 517
National Public Radio (NPR), 641
National Survey of Sexual Health and Behavior (NSSHB), 404
National Survey on Drug Use and Health, 466
Naturalistic observation, 98–100
Natural selection, 24
Negative cognitive triad, 222
Negative correlation, 101
Negative symptoms, 507, 510
Nerve impulse, 21
Nervous system, 20, 21 (figure)

NET. See Narrative exposure therapy (NET)
Neuritic plaques, 606
Neurocognitive disorder due to Alzheimer's disease, 605. See also Alzheimer's disease
Neurocognitive disorder due to prion disease, 619
Neurocognitive disorders, 157, 591
　aging, 591–600
　categories of, 600–605
　characteristics, prevalence, and diagnosis, 602–605
　frontotemporal neurocognitive disorder, 611
　HIV infection, 618
　Huntington's disease, 619
　individual's activities, 620–621
　Lewy body dementia, 617
　Parkinson's disease, 617
　prevention of, 620
　prion disease, 619
　silent epidemic of concussion, 615–617
　substance-induced disorder, 618–619
　TBIs, 615
　treatment, 621–623
　vascular problems, 611
Neurodevelopmental disorders, 165
Neuroethics, 70
Neurofeedback, 201–202
Neurofibrillary tangles, 606
Neurological disorders, 82
Neurons, 9 (figure), 49, 51–54, 51 (figure)
　brain networks, 71–73, 72 (figure)
Neuropeptides, 53
Neuropsychological testing, 147–149
Neuropsychology, 97
Neuroscience, 647–649
　advantages and disadvantages, 67 (table)
　amygdala, 47, 47 (figure)
　brain anatomy, neurons and neurotransmitters, 49–56
　brain networks, 71–74
　diagnosis and treatment, 152–153
　EEG, 57–61
　evolution and psychopathology, 85–89
　fMRI, 63–66, 65 (figure)
　fusiform face area, 46 (figure)
　genetics and evolutionary perspective, 47–49
　genetics and psychopathology, 75–84
　MEG, 61, 62 (figure)
　neuroethics, 70
　perspective, 7
　PET, 62–63, 62 (figure)
　spatial and temporal resolution, 66, 68 (figure)
　techniques, 95, 149–150, 149 (figure)
Neuroticism, 556
Neurotransmitter dysregulation, 247
Neurotransmitters, 51–54, 54 (table), 532–533
NFL. See National Football League (NFL)
Nicotine, 485–486

NIMH. See National Institute of Mental Health (NIMH)
No Country for Old Men (movie), 564
Noninvasive techniques, 31, 49
Normalcy, 14
NSSHB. See National Survey of Sexual Health and Behavior (NSSHB)
Null hypothesis, 111–113

Obesity, 368
　adolescence, 373
　biological factors, 372
　BMI, 375, 377 (figure)
　body image and attitudes, 377–379
　calorie-rich substances, 372
　childhood, 371
　daily calorie intake, 375, 376 (figure)
　environmental factors, 372, 373
　fast foods, 371–372
　food choices, 371
　health problems, 377
　intake of food and drugs, 372–373, 373 (figure)
　prevalence, 374–377, 374 (figure)
　psychological factors, 372
　rates in United States, 375, 376 (figure)
　thrifty gene hypothesis, 371
Observational learning, 38
Obsessional thinking, 136
Obsessive-compulsive and related disorders (OCRD), 330–332
Obsessive-compulsive disorder (OCD), 32, 137, 328, 579–580
　behavioral data, 334
　body dysmorphic disorder, 332
　brain imaging techniques (fMRI), 333–334
　characteristics, prevalence, and significant aspects, 329–331
　cognitive dysfunction, 333
　compulsions, 328
　DSM-5-TR diagnostic criteria, 329 (table), 330–333
　excoriation (skin picking disorder), 331
　hoarding disorder, 331–332
　obsessions, 328
　and OCRD, 331–333
　treatment, 334–335
　trichotillomania (hair pulling disorder), 332
OCD. See Obsessive-compulsive disorder (OCD)
O'Connor v. Donaldson (1975), 642
OCRD. See Obsessive-compulsive and related disorders (OCRD)
ODD. See Oppositional defiant disorder (ODD)
Odd, eccentric personality disorders (Cluster A), 560
　paranoid personality disorder, 560
　schizoid personality disorder, 560–561
　schizotypal personality disorder, 561–562

OFC. See Orbitofrontal cortex (OFC)
Old Bedlam, 26
One-trial learning, 370
On the Origin of Species by Means of Natural Selection (Darwin), 24
Openness, 556
Operant conditioning, 38
Operational definition, 103
Opioids, 449, 453, 478–479, 479 (figure)
Opium receptors, 479
Oppositional defiant disorder (ODD), 181, 183–184
Orange Is the New Black (TV series), 432
Orbitofrontal cortex (OFC), 457

PADs. See Psychiatric advance directives (PADs)
Panic disorder/attack, 301, 326–327, 326 (table)
Parahippocampus, 570, 571 (figure)
Paranoid personality disorder, 547, 560
Paranoid subtype, 511
Paraphilia, 422
Paraphilic disorders, 422, 429
　causes and treatment approaches, 430–431
　in DSM-5-TR, 423, 423 (table)
　exhibitionistic disorder, 424
　fetishistic disorder, 425
　frotteuristic disorder, 424–425
　life span, 549, 549 (figure)
　pedophilic disorder, 426–427
　sexual masochism disorder, 427
　sexual sadism disorder, 428
　sexual surveys, 422
　traditional vs. nontraditional sexual activities, 423
　transvestic disorder, 428
　unspecified paraphilic disorder, 429
　voyeuristic disorder, 428–429
Parasympathetic division, 269
Parent–child interaction therapy (PCIT), 184
Parkinson's disease, 483, 617–618
Passive dendrites, 51
Pathological gambling, 487
Patient Self-Determination Act (PSDA) of 1991, 642
Pattern of addiction, 453, 453 (figure), 454 (table)
　craving, 453
　psychoactive substance, 453
Pattern thinking, 188
Pedophilic disorder, 426–427
Personality disorders, 87, 546
　Amy James case, borderline, 568–569
　anxious fearful personality disorders, 578–580
　borderline, 559
　categories and dimensions, 559
　clusters, 547, 548 (table)
　comorbidity of, 551, 551–553 (table)

dramatic emotional personality disorders, 562–578
DSM-5 and DSM-5-TR, 546, 547 (table), 585–586
environmental and genetic studies, 552
evolution and characteristics, 556, 556–557 (table)
global mental health, 550
healthy self, 554–555
maladaptive personality traits, 557, 558–559 (table)
odd, eccentric personality disorders, 560–562
personality traits, 553–554
prevalence, 548–549, 549 (figure)
treatment, 580–585
Personality tests, 142–144
Personality traits, 121, 553–554
    endophenotypes, 252
      maladaptive traits, 557, 558–559 (table)
      personality disorders, 553–554
      psychometric approach, 555
Person-centered therapy, 35
PET. *See* Positron emission tomography (PET)
PFC. *See* Prefrontal cortex (PFC)
Phenotype, 77
Phenylketonuria (PKU), 205
Philosophy, 15
Physical disorders, 3
Physical pain, 273
Pica, 369–370
Pick's disease, 611
Placebo effect, 108
Police power authority, 642
Polygenic score, 83
Population, 109
Positive correlation, 101
Positive interpersonal relationships, 554
Positive symptoms, 507
Positron emission tomography (PET), 62–63, 62 (figure), 411, 481
Post-traumatic stress disorder (PTSD), 64, 97, 265, 615. *See also* Stress and trauma
    appetitive aggression, 284
    brain areas, 290, 290 (figure)
    causes, characteristics, and prevalence, 283–284
    CBT, 295
    child soldiers in Africa, 285–286
    DID, 351
    dissociation, 342
    DSM-5-TR diagnostic criteria, 286, 286–289 (table), 291
    EMDR, 294–295
    exposure therapy for, 292, 294
    invisible wounds, 293–294
    NET and WET, 294
    overview, 281–283
    physiological aspects, 290–291
    seeking safety, 295
    sensory, cognitive, emotional, and physiological processes, 291, 292 (figure)
    treatment, 292–296
    type of stressor, 283 (table)
    Victoria English, case of, 289
Predictive validity, 141
Prefrontal cortex (PFC), 456, 457 (table), 520
Premature ejaculation, 419, 421
Prevalence, 119
PRIDE (praising, reflecting, imitating, describing, enthusiasm), 184
Private personality, 128
Privileged communication, 639
Probability, 112
Problem-solving skills training (PSST), 184
Problem-solving techniques, 104
Process-experiential therapy, 35
Prohibition, 447
Projective instruments, 144
Projective tests, 144–147, 148 (table)
Prolonged grief disorder, 277, 281
Proteins, 77
Prozac (fluoxetine), 227–228
PSST. *See* Problem-solving skills training (PSST)
Psychedelics, 476
Psychiatric advance directives (PADs), 642
Psychoactive substances, 453
Psychoanalysis, 34
Psychodynamic perspective, 33–34, 34 (figure)
Psychodynamic therapy, 234
Psychogenic disorders, 357
Psychological assessment, 135
Psychological disorders. *See also* Mental disorders; Psychopathology
    assessment models, 141–150
    initial assessment and mental status exam, 135–136
    neurology, 134
    structured interviews and assessment considerations, 136–141
Psychological evaluation, 157 (figure)
Psychological research, nonexperimental methods
    case study, 96–98
    correlational approach, 100–103
    naturalistic observation, 98–100
Psychological stress, 264–265, 270–271
Psychological treatment
    behavioral and cognitive behavioral perspectives, 36–40
    evidence-based medicine, 32
    existential-humanistic perspective, 34–36
    psychodynamic perspective, 33–34, 34 (figure)
Psychology as the Behaviorist Views It (Watson), 37
Psychometric formulations, 141
Psychoneuroimmunology, 271
Psychopathic personality. *See* Antisocial personality disorder
Psychopathology
    adolescence, 177 (figure)
    Ancient Greek and Roman influences, 15–16, 16 (figure)
    assessment validity, 141
    behavioral and experiential perspective, 7
    biopsychosocial approach, 9, 10 (figure)
    brain function, 19–25
    brain networks, 71
    components, 3–4, 4 (table)
    definition, 3–4
    diagnostic considerations, 150–153
    evolution and culture, 10–14
    evolutionary perspective, 7–8, 86–89
    genetics, 75–84
    levels of analysis, 8–9
    measurement issues, 139
    mental disorders, 26–30
    Middle Ages, 16, 17 (figure)
    modern science, 16–19
    neuroscience perspective, 7
    non-Western groups, 14
    psychological treatment, 32–40
    reliability, 140, 140 (figure)
    research, 3
    themes of evolution, 85–86
Psychopathy, 87, 564
    brain involvement, 566–567
    checklist, 564, 565 (table)
    Cleckley's 16 diagnostic criteria, 564, 565 (table)
    evolutionary perspectives, 565
    externalizing vulnerability, 565
    fearlessness, 565
Psychosis, 14, 46
Psychosocial factors, schizophrenia
    CBT approaches, 538
    components, 538
    mental health networks, 540–541
    meta-analyses, 538
    NAVIGATE program, 541
    stress role, 540
Psychosocial stressors, 137
Psychosomatic disorder, 354
Psychotic disorders, 503
Psychotropic medications, 31
PTSD. *See* Post-traumatic stress disorder (PTSD)
PubMed, 436
Purging, 384, 393

RAD. *See* Reactive attachment disorder (RAD)
RAISE. *See* Recovery After an Initial Schizophrenia Episode (RAISE)
Randomization, 109

Randomized controlled trial (RCT), 109–110, 114–116, 115 (table)
Raven's Progressive Matrices test, 188, 188 (figure)
RCT. *See* Randomized controlled trial (RCT)
RDoC. *See* Research domain criteria (RDoC)
Reactive attachment disorder (RAD), 181
Reactive obsessions, 328
Recovery After an Initial Schizophrenia Episode (RAISE), 535
Reinforcement, 38
Reliability, 140, 140 (figure)
Repetitive TMS (rTMS), 230
Replication, 123
Repression, 33
Research domain criteria (RDoC), 82, 153, 154–155, 517
Research hypothesis, 111, 113–114
Reserve, 622
Reward system, 152, 153 (figure)
Ribonucleic acid (RNA), 77
Right to privacy, 128
Right ventral prefrontal cortex (RVPFC), 574
Risk, 120
Risk taking, 178–180, 179 (figure)
Romania adoption study, 173–175, 173 (figure)
Roper v. Simmons (2005), 648
Rorschach inkblots, 144–146
Rorschach Performance Assessment System (R-PAS), 146
Rumination disorder, 370
RVPFC. *See* Right ventral prefrontal cortex (RVPFC)

SAD. *See* Social anxiety disorder (SAD)
Salience network, 72
Sample, 112
Savant syndrome, 193
Scatterplot, 100, 101–102 (figure)
Schizoid personality disorder, 560–561
Schizophrenia, 8, 13, 81, 86, 120, 178, 502, 505–506
  and brain function, 525–526, 526–527 (figure)
  and brain networks, 531–532, 533 (figure)
  and brain structure, 527–531
  circumstantiality and tangentiality, 504
  and cognitive processes, 533–534
  Elyn Saks description, day-to-day life, 507–509
  endophenotypes associated with, 523–524, 524 (table)
  evolutionary perspective, 517–519
  factor analysis, 524–525
  genetic factors in, 520–522, 521 (figure)
  historical perspective, 515–517, 515 (figure)
  James Stern case, 504
  mood symptoms, 504
  multilevel process, 510–511
  neurotransmitters, 532–533
  phases in, 506–507, 506 (figure)
  positive symptoms, 507, 510
  prevalence and course, 504–507, 506 (figure)
  psychotic disorders, 503, 503 (table)
  subtypes of, 511–514
  treatment, 535–541
Schizotypal personality disorder, 561–562
Schizotypal traits, 518
School-based programs, 5
School shootings, 184–185 (figure), 185–186
SCID. *See* Structured Clinical Interview for *DSM* Disorders (SCID)
SCID-D. *See* Structured Clinical Interview for *DSM-IV* Dissociative Disorders (SCID-D)
Science
  detective work, 94
  doubt, 95
  facts, 95
  falsification, 96
  hypothesis testing, 95
  logic, 94
  luck, 94
  observation, 95 (figure)
  stages, 96
Scientific experiment, 125–130. *See also* Ethics
Scientific knowledge, 95
Scientist–participant dialogue, 127–128
Secure attachment pattern, 171
Secure base, 169
Selective serotonin reuptake inhibitors (SSRIs), 31, 228, 419, 430
Self-direction, 554
Self-preservation, 86
Sensory/affector system, 21
Sensory process, 37 (figure)
Separation anxiety disorder, 320–321
Serotonin and norepinephrine reuptake inhibitors (SNRIs), 228
Sex therapy, 420–421
Sexual aberrations (Stekel), 423
Sexual activities
  of Americans, 404
  brain and, 411, 411 (figure)
  erectile disorder, 417–418
Sexual arousal, 408, 410, 411, 422, 423, 425–427
  cross-dressing, 428
  sadism, 428
  voyeuristic disorder, 429
Sexual Behavior in the Human Female (Kinsey), 403
Sexual Behavior in the Human Male (Kinsey), 403
Sexual desire
  arousal, 408
  bisexual, 410–411
  brain and sexual activity, 411, 411 (figure)
  gay men, 410–411
  heterosexual women, 411
  LGBTQ community, 408
  motivation, 408
  normal sexual functioning, 412–415, 412–415 (figure)
  psychophysiological measures, 410
  sexual orientation, 410
Sexual disorders, 404, 408, 420, 422
Sexual dysfunction disorders, 416, 416 (table)
  delayed ejaculation, 419
  DSM-5-TR, 416, 416 (table)
  early ejaculation, 419
  emotional connections, 416
  erectile disorder, 417–418
  female orgasmic disorder, 418
  female sexual interest/arousal, 419
  genito-pelvic pain/penetration, 419–420
  male hypoactive sexual desire, 419
  mental disorders, 416
  in older Americans, 417, 418 (table)
  psychological conditions, 417
  relationship, 417
  treatment approaches, 420–421
Sexuality
  cultures, clashing of, 409–410
  historical perspectives, 403–404
  sexual activities of Americans, studies, 404–408, 405–407 (table)
  WHO description, 402
Sexually violent predator (SVP)/sexually dangerous person (SDP) statutes, 644
Sexual masochism disorder, 427
Sexual orientation, 410
Sexual predator laws, 642–643
Sexual responses, 415, 415 (figure)
  excitement, 413
  female external sexual anatomy, 412, 413 (figure)
  female reproductive system, 412, 412 (figure)
  male reproductive system, 412, 412 (figure)
  men, genital changes in, 412, 413 (figure)
  muscular spasms, 415
  orgasm, 415
  phases, four, 412
  plateau stage, 415
  women, genital changes in, 412, 414 (figure)
Sexual sadism disorder, 428
Sexual selection, 24
The Shining (movie), 564
Signal processing techniques, 58–59
Signs, 25
The Silence of the Lambs (movie), 564
Single-nucleotide polymorphisms (SNPs), 82, 83 (figure)
Single-subject design, 117
Sleep disturbance, 88

Small-N design. *See* Single-subject design
Small world framework, 72
SNPs. *See* Single-nucleotide polymorphisms (SNPs)
Social anxiety, 12–14, 87
Social anxiety disorder (SAD), 301
    amygdala activity, 319, 320
    brain regions, 319
    CBT, 320, 321
    DSM-5-TR diagnostic criteria, 318, 318 (table)
    exposure therapy, 320
    psychopharmacological approaches, 320
    social skills training, 320
Social brain, 178
Social determinations, 22
Social–emotional behavior, 169
Social learning theory, 184
Social pain, 273
Social stress, 277
Social transmission, 11
Solitary confinement, 646–647
Somatic symptom disorder, 353, 354
    conversion disorder, 356–363
    culture, 353
    in *DSM-5-TR*, 353–354, 354 (table)
    factitious disorder, 363–364
    illness anxiety disorder, 354–356
    overview, 352–354
    somatic symptom disorder, 354
    treatment, 364–365
Somatoform disorders, 354
Specific learning disorder, 202
Specific phobias, 321–322
    brain areas, 324–325
    clinical features, 322, 323 (table), 324
    DSM-5-TR diagnostic criteria, 322, 322 (table)
    fMRI session, 325
    gradual exposure techniques, 325
    lifetime prevalence and standard error (SE), 322, 323 (table)
    observational learning, 324
Spike trains, 54, 55 (figure)
Spirits, 15
SQUID. *See* Superconducting quantum interference device (SQUID)
SSRIs. *See* Selective serotonin reuptake inhibitors (SSRIs)
Statistically significant, 122–123
Stigma, 5–6
Strange situation, 171
Stream of consciousness, 73
Stress and trauma. *See also* Post-traumatic stress disorder (PTSD)
    acute stress disorder, 277, 278–280, 279 (table)
    adjustment disorders, 277, 278
    allostasis, 274
    allostatic load, 274
    ANS, 268–269, 270 (figure)
    epigenetics, 271–273
    fight-or-flight response, males and females, 275–277
    GAS, 274
    HPA axis, 266–268, 267 (figure), 269 (figure)
    human brain, 275 (figure)
    immune system, 270–271
    mental illness, 265
    physiological mechanisms, 265–273
    prolonged grief disorder, 277, 281
    psychological stress, 264–265, 270–271
    social and physical pain, 273
    social stress, 277
Stress reduction strategies, 110
Stroop test, 305, 305 (figure)
Structural equation model, 83
Structured Clinical Interview for *DSM* Disorders (SCID), 137
Structured Clinical Interview for *DSM-IV* Dissociative Disorders (SCID-D), 349
Structured interviews
    cultural dimensions, 137–138
    definition, 136
    reliability and validity, psychopathology, 139–141
    SCID, 137
Studies in the Psychology of Sex (Ellis), 403
Substance Abuse and Mental Health Services Administration (SAMHSA), 447, 447 (figure), 449
Substance-induced neurocognitive disorder, 618–619
Substance-related disorders
    addiction, 449, 490
    cocaine, 449–450
    controlled drinking approaches, 496–497
    DSM-5-TR and *ICD-11*, 450–451
    medications, 497
    principles, 491–492
    psychosocial and psychopharmacological approaches, 490
    psychosocial therapies and addiction, 494
    12-step program, 494–495, 495 (figure)
Substance tolerance, 488
Subtypes of schizophrenia
    catatonic subtype, 513
    disorganized subtype, 511
    DSM-5 and *DSM-5-TR*, 514
    paranoid subtype, 511
Successful aging, 591
Suicidal ideation, 249
Suicide, 249
    college students, 253–254
    cultural and gender differences, 250–251, 251 (figure)
    endophenotypes, 252
    interpersonal-psychological theory (ITPS), 249
    long-term and short-term factors, 252–253
    mental illness, 249
    in military, 254–255
    prevention, 255–257
    protective and risk factors, 256 (figure)
    suicidal ideation, 249
    type of attempt, 251, 252 (table)
    underreporting and methods, 252
    U.S. suicide rates, 249, 250 (figure)
    warning signs, 255, 256 (figure)
Sulci, 20
Superconducting quantum interference device (SQUID), 61
Sympathetic division, 269
Symptom questionnaires, 142
Symptoms, 25
Synapses, 51, 52 (figure)
Syndrome, 25

Tangentiality, 504
Tarasoff decision, 638–639
TAT. *See* Thematic apperception test (TAT)
TBIs. *See* Traumatic brain injuries (TBIs)
TCAs. *See* Tricyclic antidepressants (TCAs)
Temporal resolution, 66
Tend-and-befriend response, 275–276
Testosterone, 276, 417
Test–retest reliability, 140
TFP. *See* Transference-focused psychotherapy (TFP)
THC (Δ9-tetrahydrocannabinol), 472
THD. *See* Thought dysfunction (THD)
Thematic apperception test (TAT), 144, 146–147
Themes of evolution, 85–86
Theory of mind, 176
Thought dysfunction (THD), 143
Three-dimensional reconstruction of rod, 99 (figure)
Thrifty gene hypothesis, 371
TMS. *See* Transcranial magnetic stimulation (TMS)
Tobacco, 485
Tourette's syndrome, 25
Transcranial magnetic stimulation (TMS), 31, 229–230
Transcription, 77
Transdiagnostic therapy, 39
Transference-focused psychotherapy (TFP), 584
Transgender, 428, 432–434
Transsexual, 432
Transvestic disorder, 428
Transvestism, 428
Trauma- and stressor-related disorders, 165
Traumatic brain injuries (TBIs), 615
Treatment-resistant depression, 228
Treatment, sexual dysfunction disorders
    medications, 421
    sex therapy, 420–421
TREM2 receptor, 609

Trichotillomania (hair pulling disorder), 332
Tricyclic antidepressants (TCAs), 31
t test, 113
12-step program, 494–495, 495 (figure)
Twin studies, 122
Type 2 diabetes, 9

UCLA Young Autism Project, 195
Unified treatment model/unified protocol, 39
Unipolar depression, 213, 216 (figure)
U.S. suicide rates, 249, 250 (figure). *See also* Suicide

Vagal nerve stimulation (VNS), 229
Vaginismus, 419
Validity, 104, 106–107, 141
Variation, 24

Vascular neurocognitive disorder, 611
Vasocongestion, 413
Ventral tegmental area (VTA), 455
Ventrolateral prefrontal cortex (VLPFC), 525
Visual system, 46
Visual thinking, 188
VLPFC. *See* Ventrolateral prefrontal cortex (VLPFC)
VNS. *See* Vagal nerve stimulation (VNS)
Volitional test, 630
Voluntary participation, 127
Voyeuristic disorder, 428–429

WAIS. *See* Wechsler Adult Intelligence Scale (WAIS)
WCST. *See* Wisconsin Card Sorting Test (WCST)
Wechsler Adult Intelligence Scale (WAIS), 147

Well-being therapy, 232 (table)
Wernicke's area, 23
WET. *See* Written exposure therapy (WET)
White matter, 20, 20 (figure), 66–67 (figure), 72
WHO. *See* World Health Organization (WHO)
Wisconsin Card Sorting Test (WCST), 148, 523
Withdrawal, 450
Word and fact thinking, 188
World Federation of Societies of Biological Psychiatry, 431
World Health Organization (WHO), 4, 150, 170, 402, 461, 549
Written exposure therapy (WET), 294

Z-score, 598